PHILIP'S RO...

2021
ESSENTIAL
BRITAIN & IRELAND

www.philips-maps.co.uk

First published in 2009 as *Complete Road Atlas Britain and Ireland*
by Philip's, a division of Octopus Publishing Group Ltd
www.octopusbooks.co.uk
Carmelite House, 50 Victoria Embankment
London EC4Y 0DZ
An Hachette UK Company
www.hachette.co.uk

Twelfth edition 2020
First impression 2020

ISBN 978-1-84907-522-0 spiral-bound
ISBN 978-1-84907-533-6 perfect-bound

Cartography by Philip's
Copyright © 2020 Philip's

This product includes mapping data licensed from Ordnance Survey®, with the permission of the Controller of Her Majesty's Stationery Office. © Crown copyright 2020. All rights reserved. Licence number 100011710.

The map of Ireland on pages XVI–XVII is based upon the Crown Copyright and is reproduced with the permission of Land & Property Services under delegated authority from the Controller of Her Majesty's Stationery Office, © Crown Copyright and database right 2020, PMLPA number 100503, and on Ordnance Survey Ireland by permission of the Government © Ordnance Survey Ireland / Government of Ireland Permit number 9220.

Information for National Parks, Areas of Outstanding Natural Beauty, National Trails and Country Parks in Wales supplied by the Countryside Council for Wales.

Information for National Parks, Areas of Outstanding Natural Beauty, National Trails and Country Parks in England supplied by Natural England. Data for Regional Parks, Long Distance Footpaths and Country Parks in Scotland provided by Scottish Natural Heritage.

Gaelic name forms used in the Western Isles provided by Comhairle nan Eilean.

Data for the National Nature Reserves in England provided by Natural England. Data for the National Nature Reserves in Wales provided by Countryside Council for Wales. Darparwyd data'n ymwneud â Gwarchodfeydd Natur Cenedlaethol Cymru gan Gyngor Cefn Gwlad Cymru.

Information on the location of National Nature Reserves in Scotland was provided by Scottish Natural Heritage.

Data for National Scenic Areas in Scotland provided by the Scottish Executive Office. Crown copyright material is reproduced with the permission of the Controller of HMSO and the Queen's Printer for Scotland. Licence number C02W0003960.

Printed in Malaysia

*Data from Nielsen Total Consumer Market 2016 weeks 1–52

II Key to map symbols

III Motorway service areas

IV Restricted motorway junctions

VI Route planning maps

XVI Road map of Ireland

XVIII Tourism and transport

XX Distances and journey times

1 Key to road map pages

2 Road maps of Britain

161 Urban approach maps

161 Bristol *approaches*	167 Leeds *approaches*
162 Birmingham *approaches*	168 London *approaches*
164 Cardiff *approaches*	172 Liverpool *approaches*
165 Edinburgh *approaches*	173 Manchester *approaches*
166 Glasgow *approaches*	174 Newcastle *approaches*

175 Town plans

175 Aberdeen, Ayr, Bath	190 Manchester, Maidstone, Merthyr Tydfil
176 Birmingham, Blackpool, Bournemouth	191 Middlesbrough, Milton Keynes, Newcastle, Newport
177 Bradford, Brighton, Bristol	192 Newquay, Northampton, Norwich, Nottingham
178 Bury St Edmunds, Cambridge, Canterbury, Cardiff	193 Oxford, Perth, Peterborough, Plymouth
179 Carlisle, Chelmsford, Cheltenham, Chester	194 Poole, Portsmouth, Preston, Reading
180 Chichester, Colchester, Coventry, Derby	195 St Andrews, Salisbury, Scarborough, Shrewsbury,
181 Dorchester, Dumfries, Dundee, Durham	196 Sheffield, Stoke-on-Trent (Hanley), Southampton
182 Edinburgh, Exeter, Gloucester	197 Southend, Stirling, Stratford-upon-Avon, Sunderland
183 Glasgow, Grimsby, Harrogate	198 Swansea, Swindon, Taunton, Telford
184 Hull, Inverness, Ipswich, Kendal	199 Torquay, Truro, Winchester, Windsor
185 King's Lynn, Lancaster, Leeds	200 Wolverhampton, Worcester, Wrexham, York
186 London	
188 Leicester, Lincoln, Liverpool	
189 Llandudno, Llanelli, Luton, Macclesfield	

201 Index to town plans

213 Index to road maps of Britain

Inside back cover: **County and unitary authority boundaries**

Road map symbols

Motorway, toll motorway
Motorway junction – full, restricted access
Motorway service area – full, restricted access
Motorway under construction

Primary route – dual, single carriageway
Service area, roundabout, multi-level junction
Numbered junction – full, restricted access
Primary route under construction
Narrow primary route
Primary destination **Derby**

A road – dual, single carriageway
A road under construction, narrow A road
B road – dual, single carriageway
B road under construction, narrow B road

Minor road – over 4 metres, under 4 metres wide
Minor road with restricted access

Distance in miles
Scenic route
Toll, steep gradient – arrow points downhill
Tunnel

National trail – England and Wales
Long distance footpath – Scotland

Railway with station
Level crossing, tunnel
Preserved railway with station

National boundary
County / unitary authority boundary

Car ferry, catamaran
Passenger ferry, catamaran
Hovercraft
Ferry destination CALAIS Ferry
Car ferry – river crossing
Principal airport, other airport

National park, Area of Outstanding Natural Beauty –
England and Wales National Scenic Area – Scotland
Forest park / regional park / national forest

Beach
Linear antiquity
Roman road
Hillfort, battlefield – with date 1066
Viewpoint, nature reserve, spot height – in metres 795
Golf course, youth hostel, sporting venue
Camp site, caravan site, camping and caravan site
Shopping village, park and ride P&R
Adjoining page number – road maps **29**

Approach map symbols

Motorway
Toll motorway
Motorway junction – full, restricted access
Service area
Under construction
Primary route – dual, single carriageway
Service area
Multi-level junction
roundabout
Under construction
A road – dual, single carriageway A195

B road – dual, single carriageway B1288
Minor road – dual, single carriageway
Ring road
Distance in miles 3
Congestion charge area
Railway with station COSELEY
Tramway with station LOXDALE
Underground or metro station

Town plan symbols

Motorway
Primary route – dual, single carriageway
A road – dual, single carriageway
B road – dual, single carriageway
Minor through road
One-way street
Pedestrian roads
Shopping streets
Railway with station
Tramway with station City Hall

Bus or railway station building
Shopping precinct or retail park
Park
Building of public interest
Theatre, cinema
Parking, shopmobility
Underground station Bank
Metro station West St
Hospital, Police station H
Post office PO

Tourist information

Abbey, cathedral or priory
Ancient monument
Aquarium
Art gallery
Bird collection or aviary
Castle
Church
Country park
England and Wales
Scotland

Farm park
Garden
Historic ship
House
House and garden
Motor racing circuit
Museum
Picnic area
Preserved railway

Race course
Roman antiquity
Safari park
Theme park
Tourist information
Zoo
Other place of interest

Road map scales

1 : 200 000 • 1cm = 2km • 1 inch = 3·15 miles

0 1 2 3 4 5 6 7 8 9 10 km
0 1 2 3 4 5 6 miles

Parts of Scotland

1 : 265 000 • 1 cm = 2.65 km • 1 inch = 4.18 miles

0 2 4 6 8 10 km
0 1 2 3 4 5 6 miles

Scottish Highlands and Islands

1 : 332 000 • 1 cm = 3.32km • 1 inch = 5.24 miles

0 2 4 6 8 10 12 km
0 1 2 3 4 5 6 7 8 miles

Orkney and Shetland Islands 1:400 000 • 1cm = 4 km • 1 inch = 6.31 miles

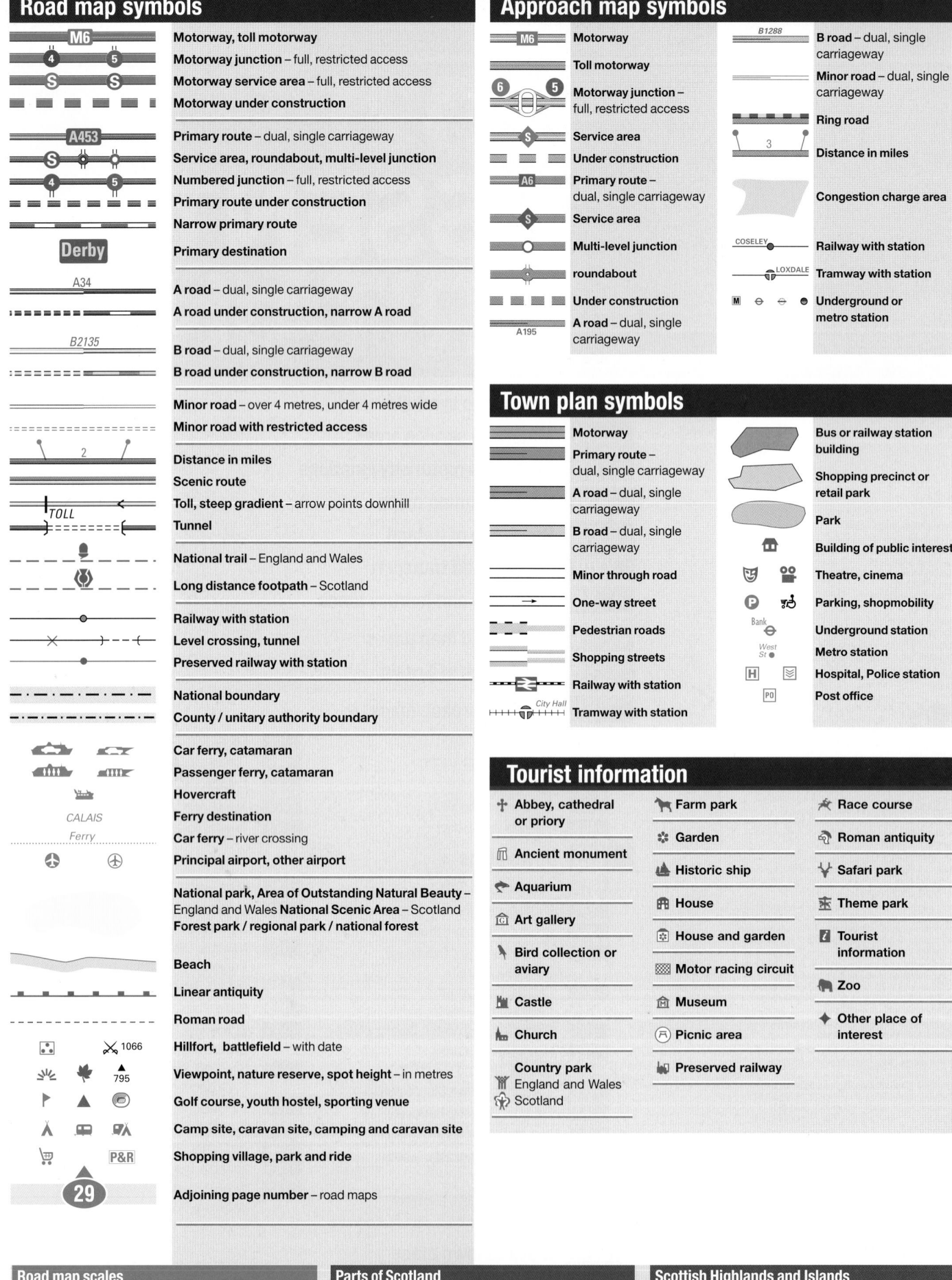

● Motorway service area

Restricted motorway junctions

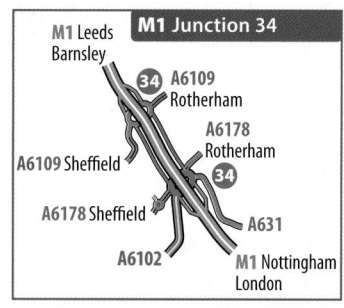

M1 Junction 34
(M1 Leeds, Barnsley; 34; A6109 Rotherham; A6178 Rotherham; 34; A6109 Sheffield; A6178 Sheffield; A631; A6102; M1 Nottingham London)

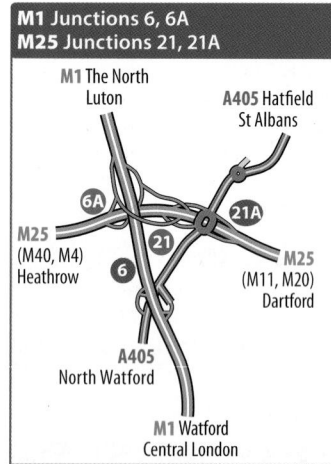

M1 Junctions 6, 6A
M25 Junctions 21, 21A
(M1 The North Luton; A405 Hatfield St Albans; 6A; 21A; M25 (M40, M4) Heathrow; 21; M25 (M11, M20) Dartford; 6; A405 North Watford; M1 Watford Central London)

M4 Junctions 25, 25A, 26
(A4042 Abergavenny Cwmbran; A4051 Cwmbran; 25A; 25; B4596 Caerleon; 26; A4042; A4051 Newport B4596; M4 Cardiff; M4 Chepstow London)

M5 Junction 11A
(A417 Gloucester; M5 Cheltenham (A40); 11A; M5 Bristol; B4641; A417 Cirencester)

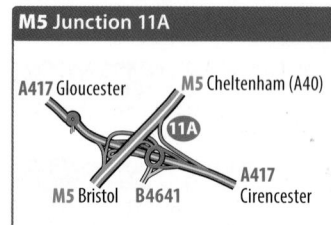

M8 Junctions 8, 9 · M73 Junctions 1, 2
M74 Junctions 2A, 3, 3A, 4
(M8 Glasgow; 9; M73 Stirling; 8; A89 Coatbridge; 2; A8 M8 Edinburgh; B7058; A74; B765; A74; M73; A74; M74 Glasgow; 2A; 3; M74; 3A; B7001; 1/4; A721; B758; B7071; M74 Carlisle; A763)

M1	Northbound	Southbound
2	No exit	No access
4	No exit	No access
6A	No exit. Access from M25 only	No access. Exit to M25 only
7	No exit. Access from A414 only	No access. Exit to A414 only
17	No access. Exit to M45 only	No exit. Access from M45 only
19	No exit to A14	No access from A14
21A	No access	No exit
23A		Exit to A42 only
24A	No exit	No access
35A	No access	No exit
43	No access. Exit to M621 only	No exit. Access from M621 only
48	No exit to A1(M) southbound	

M3	Eastbound	Westbound
8	No exit	No access
10	No access	No exit
13	No access to M27 eastbound	
14	No exit	No access

M4	Eastbound	Westbound
1	Exit to A4 eastbound only	Access from A4 westbound only
2	Access from A4 eastbound only	Access to A4 westbound only
21	No exit	No access
23	No access	No exit
25	No exit	No access
25A	No exit	No access
29	No exit	No access
38		No access
39	No exit or access	No exit
41	No access	No exit
41A	No exit	No access
42	Access from A483 only	Exit to A483 only

M5	Northbound	Southbound
10	No exit	No access
11A	No access from A417 eastbound	No exit to A417 westbound

M6	Northbound	Southbound
3A	No access.	No exit. Access from M6 eastbound only
4A	No exit. Access from M42 southbound only	No access. Exit to M42 only
5	No access	No exit
10A	No access. Exit to M54 only	No exit. Access from M54 only
11A	No exit. Access from M6 Toll only	No access. Exit to M6 Toll only
20	No exit to M56 eastbound	No access from M56 westbound
24	No exit	No access
25	No access	No exit
30	No exit. Access from M61 northbound only	No access. Exit to M61 southbound only
31A	No access	No exit
45	No access	No exit

M6 Toll	Northbound	Southbound
T1		No exit
T2	No exit, no access	No access
T5	No exit	No access
T7	No access	No exit
T8	No access	No exit

M8	Eastbound	Westbound
6	No exit	No access
6A	No access	No exit
7	No Access	No exit
7A	No exit. Access from A725 northbound only	No access. Exit to A725 southbound only
8	No exit to M73 northbound	No access from M73 southbound
9	No access	No exit
13	No exit southbound	Access from M73 southbound only
14	No access	No exit
16	No exit	No access
17	No exit	
18		No exit
19	No exit to A814 eastbound	No access from A814 westbound
20	No exit	No access
21	No access from M74	No exit
22	No exit. Access from M77 only	No access. Exit to M77 only
23	No exit	No access
25	Exit to A739 northbound only. Access from A739 southbound only	
25A	No exit	No access
28	No exit	No access
28A	No exit	No access
29A	No exit	No access

M9	Eastbound	Westbound
2	No access	No exit
3	No exit	No access
6	No access	No exit
8	No exit	No access

M11	Northbound	Southbound
4	No exit	No access
5	No access	No exit
8A	No access	No exit
9	No access	No exit
13	No access	No exit
14	No exit to A428 westbound	No exit. Access from A14 westbound only

M20	Eastbound	Westbound
2	No access	No exit
3	No exit. Access from M26 eastbound only	No access Exit to M26 westbound only
10A	No exit	No access
11A	No access	No exit

M23	Northbound	Southbound
7	No exit to A23 southbound	No access from A23 northbound
10A	No access	No access

M25	Clockwise	Anticlockwise
5	No exit to M26 eastbound	No access from M26 westbound
19	No access	No exit
21	No exit to M1 southbound. Access from M1 southbound only	No exit to M1 southbound. Access from M1 southbound only
31	No exit	No access

M27	Eastbound	Westbound
10	No exit	No access
12	No access	No exit

M40	Eastbound	Westbound
3	No exit	No access
7	No exit	No access
8	No exit	No access
13	No exit	No access
14	No access	No exit
16	No access	No exit

M42	Northbound	Southbound
1	No exit	No access
7	No access Exit to M6 northbound only	No exit. Access from M6 northbound only
7A	No access. Exit to M6 southbound only	No exit
8	No exit. Access from M6 southbound only	Exit to M6 northbound only. Access from M6 southbound only

M45	Eastbound	Westbound
M1 J17	Access to M1 southbound only	No access from M1 southbound
With A45	No access	No exit

M48	Eastbound	Westbound
M4 J21	No exit to M4 westbound	No access from M4 eastbound
M4 J23	No access from M4 westbound	No exit to M4 eastbound

M49	Southbound	Northbound
18A	No exit to M5 northbound	No access from M5 southbound

M53	Northbound	Southbound
11	Exit to M56 eastbound only. Access from M56 westbound only	Exit to M56 eastbnd only. Access from M56 westbound only

M56	Eastbound	Westbound
2	No exit	No access
3	No access	No exit
4	No exit	No access
7		No access
8	No exit or access	No exit
9	No access from M6 northbound	No access to M6 southbound
15	No exit to M53	No access from M53 northbound

M57	Northbound	Southbound
3	No exit	No access
5	No exit	No access

M58	Eastbound	Westbound
1	No exit	No access

M60	Clockwise	Anticlockwise
2	No exit	No access
3	No exit to A34 northbound	No exit to A34 northbound
4	No access from M56	No exit to M56
5	No exit to A5103 southbound	No exit to A5103 northbound
14	No exit	No access
16	No exit	No access
20	No access	No exit
22		No access
25	No access	
26		No exit or access
27	No exit	No access

M61	Northbound	Southbound
2	No access from A580 eastbound	No exit to A580 westbound
3	No access from A580 eastbound. No access from A666 southbound	No exit to A580 westbound
M6 J30	No exit to M6 southbound	No access from M6 northbound

M62	Eastbound	Westbound
23	No access	No exit

M65	Eastbound	Westbound
9	No access	No exit
11	No exit	No access

M66	Northbound	Southbound
1	No access	No exit

M67	Eastbound	Westbound
1A	No access	No exit
2	No exit	No access

M69	Northbound	Southbound
2	No exit	No access

M73	Northbound	Southbound
2	No access from M8 eastbound	No exit to M8 westbound

M74	Northbound	Southbound
3	No access	No exit
3A	No access	No access
7	No exit	No access
9	No exit or access	No access
10		No exit
11	No exit	No access
12	No access	No access

M77	Northbound	Southbound
4	No exit	No access
6	No exit	No access
7	No exit	
8	No access	No access

M80	Northbound	Southbound
4A	No access	No exit
6A	No access	No access
8	Exit to M876 northbound only. No access	Access from M876 southbound only. No exit

M90	Northbound	Southbound
1	Access from A90 northbound only	No access. Exit to A90 southbound only
2A	No access	No exit
7	No exit	No access
8	No access	No exit
10	No access from A912	No exit to A912

M180	Eastbound	Westbound
1	No access	No exit

M621	Eastbound	Westbound
2A	No exit	No access
4	No exit	
5	No exit	No access
6	No access	No exit

M876	Northbound	Southbound
2	No access	No exit

A1(M)	Northbound	Southbound
2	No access	No exit
3		No access
5	No exit	No exit, no access
14	No access	No access
40	No access	No access
43	No exit. Access from M1 only	No access. Exit to M1 only
57	No access	No exit
65	No access	No exit

A3(M)	Northbound	Southbound
1	No exit	No access
4	No access	No exit

A38(M) with Victoria Rd, (Park Circus) Birmingham	
Northbound	No exit
Southbound	No access

A48(M)	Northbound	Southbound
M4 Junc 29	Exit to M4 eastbound only	Access from M4 westbound only
29A	Access from A48 eastbound only	Exit to A48 westbound only

A57(M)	Eastbound	Westbound
With A5103	No access	No exit
With A34	No access	No exit

A58(M)	Southbound
With Park Lane and Westgate, Leeds	No access

A64(M)	Eastbound	Westbound
With A58 Clay Pit Lane, Leeds	No access from A58	No exit to A58

A74(M)	Northbound	Southbound
18	No access	No exit
22		No exit to A75

A194(M)	Northbound	Southbound
A1(M) J65 Gateshead Western Bypass	Access from A1(M) northbound only	Exit to A1(M) southbound only

M3 Junctions 13, 14 · M27 Junction 4

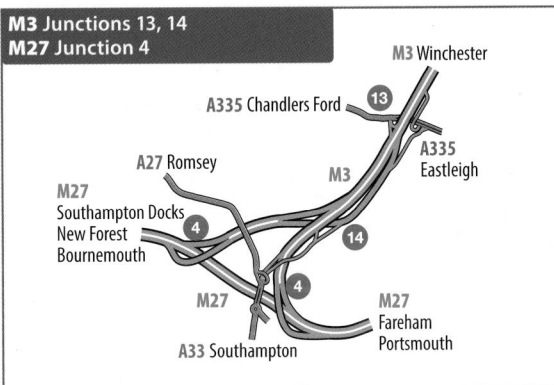

- M3 Winchester
- A335 Chandlers Ford — 13
- A27 Romsey
- M3
- A335 Eastleigh
- M27 Southampton Docks New Forest Bournemouth — 4
- 14
- M27 — 4
- M27 Fareham Portsmouth
- A33 Southampton

M6 Junctions 3A, 4A · M42 Junctions 7, 7A, 8, 9
M6 Toll Junctions T1, T2

- A446 Lichfield
- M6 Toll Lichfield
- A4091 Tamworth
- M42 Derby Burton upon Trent
- T2
- T1
- A4097 Kingsbury
- A4097 Sutton Coldfield — 9
- M42 — A446
- M6 Birmingham (N)
- 4A
- 8
- Coleshill
- M42
- M6
- 7A
- 3A
- 7
- 4
- A446 Coventry Warwick
- M42 Birmingham (S)
- M6 Coventry (N & E)

M6 Junction 20 · M56 Junction 9

- M6 Preston Liverpool
- A50 Warrington
- B5158 Lymm
- LYMM SERVICES
- M56 Manchester
- 20 — S
- A50 Knutsford Macclesfield
- 9
- M56 Runcorn Chester
- M6 Birmingham

M62 Junctions 32A, 33 · A1(M) Junctions 40, 41

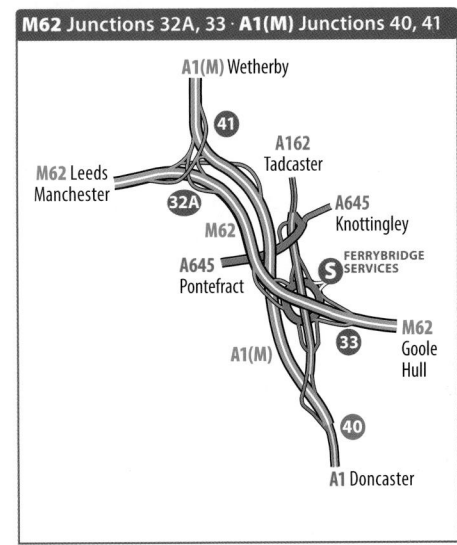

- A1(M) Wetherby
- 41
- A162 Tadcaster
- M62 Leeds Manchester
- 32A
- A645 Knottingley
- M62
- A645 Pontefract
- S FERRYBRIDGE SERVICES
- M62 Goole Hull — 33
- A1(M)
- 40
- A1 Doncaster

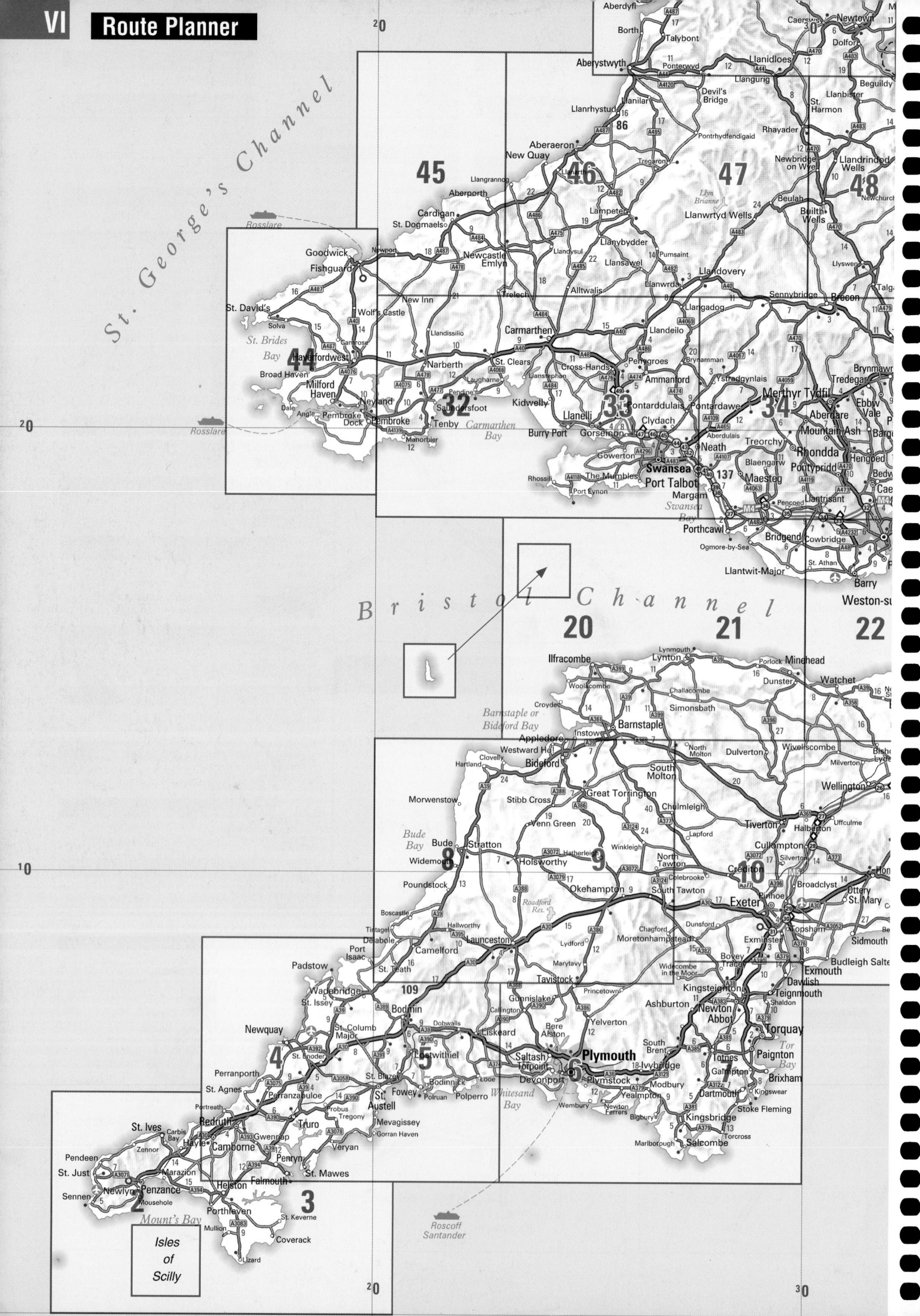

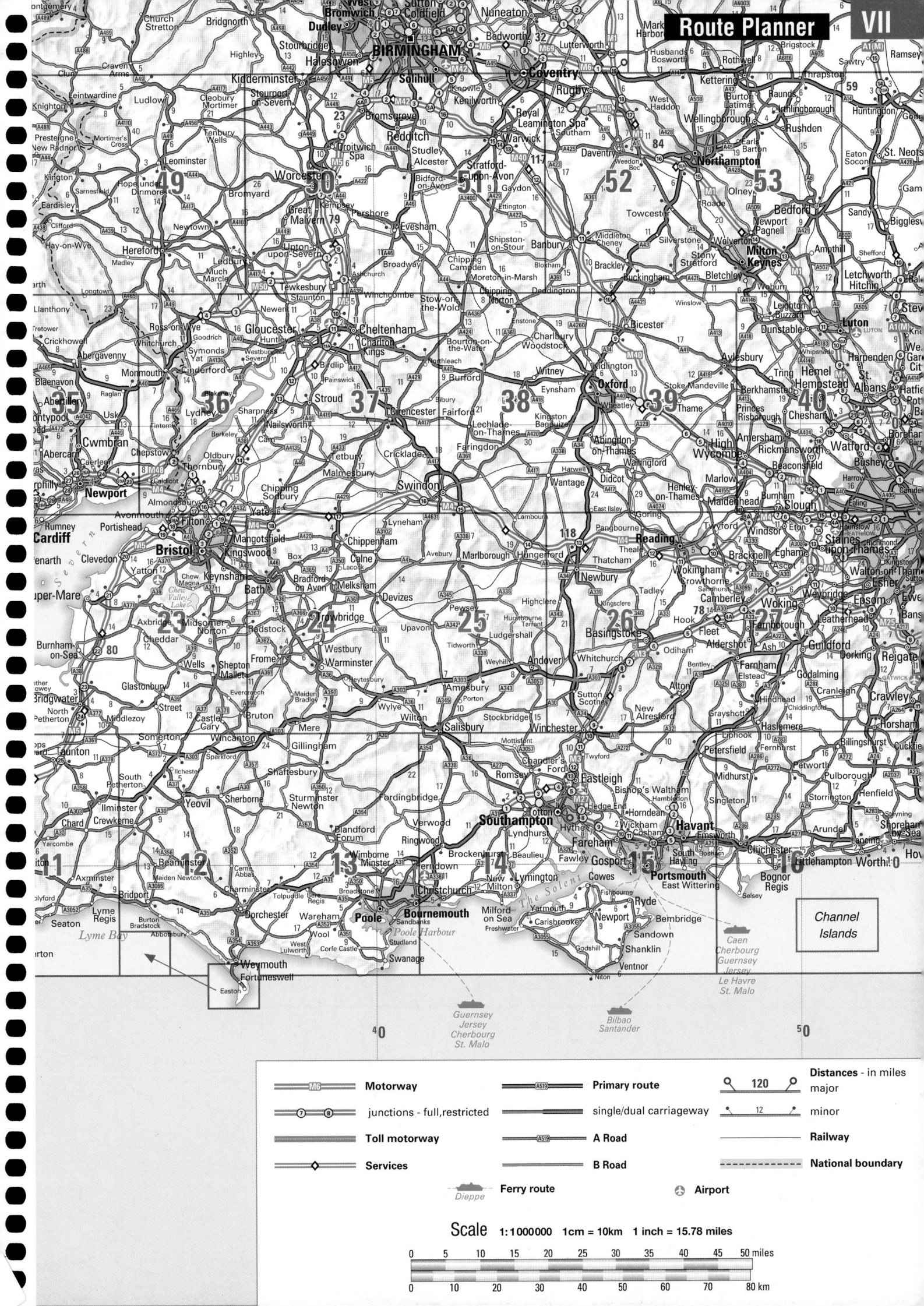

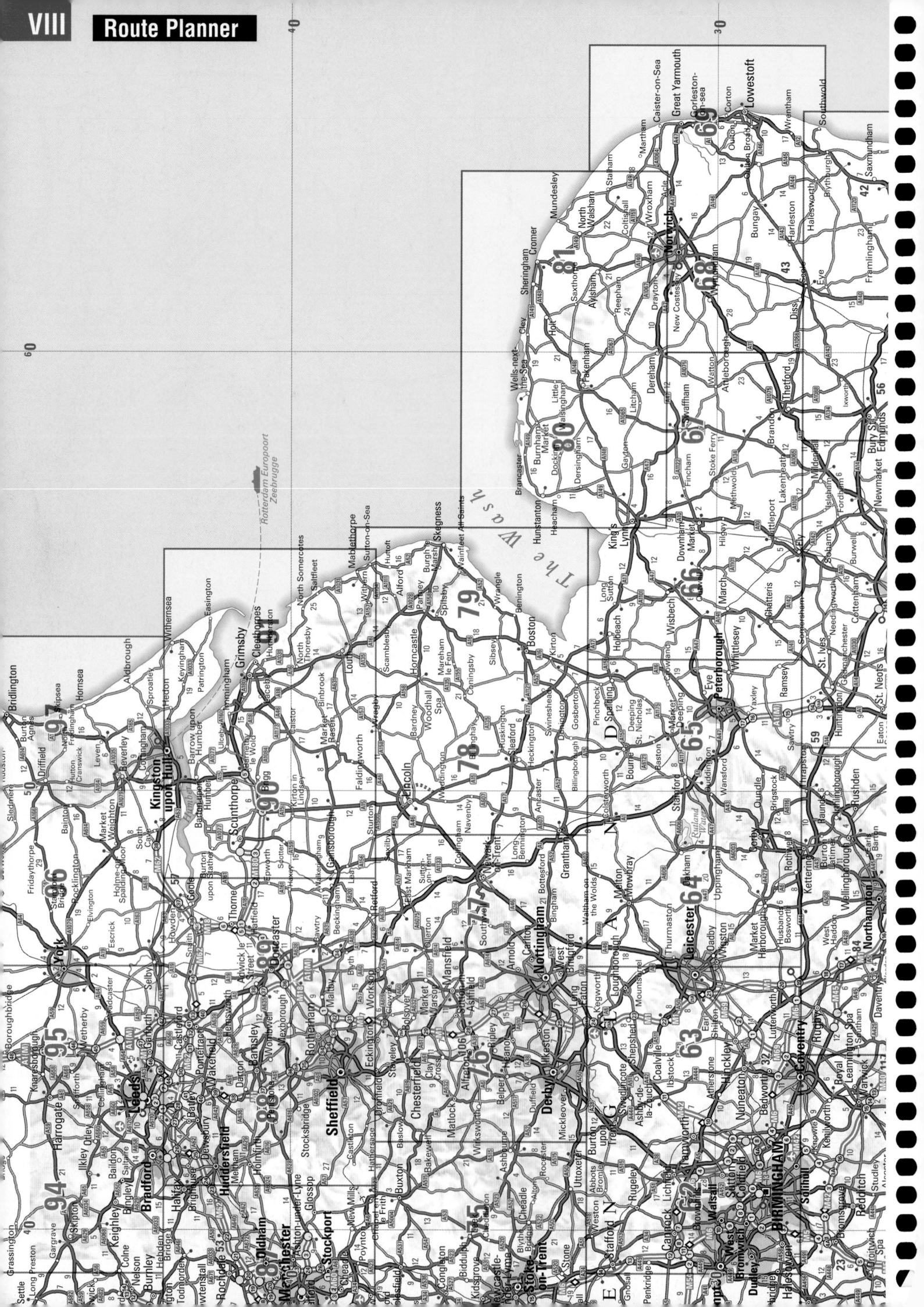

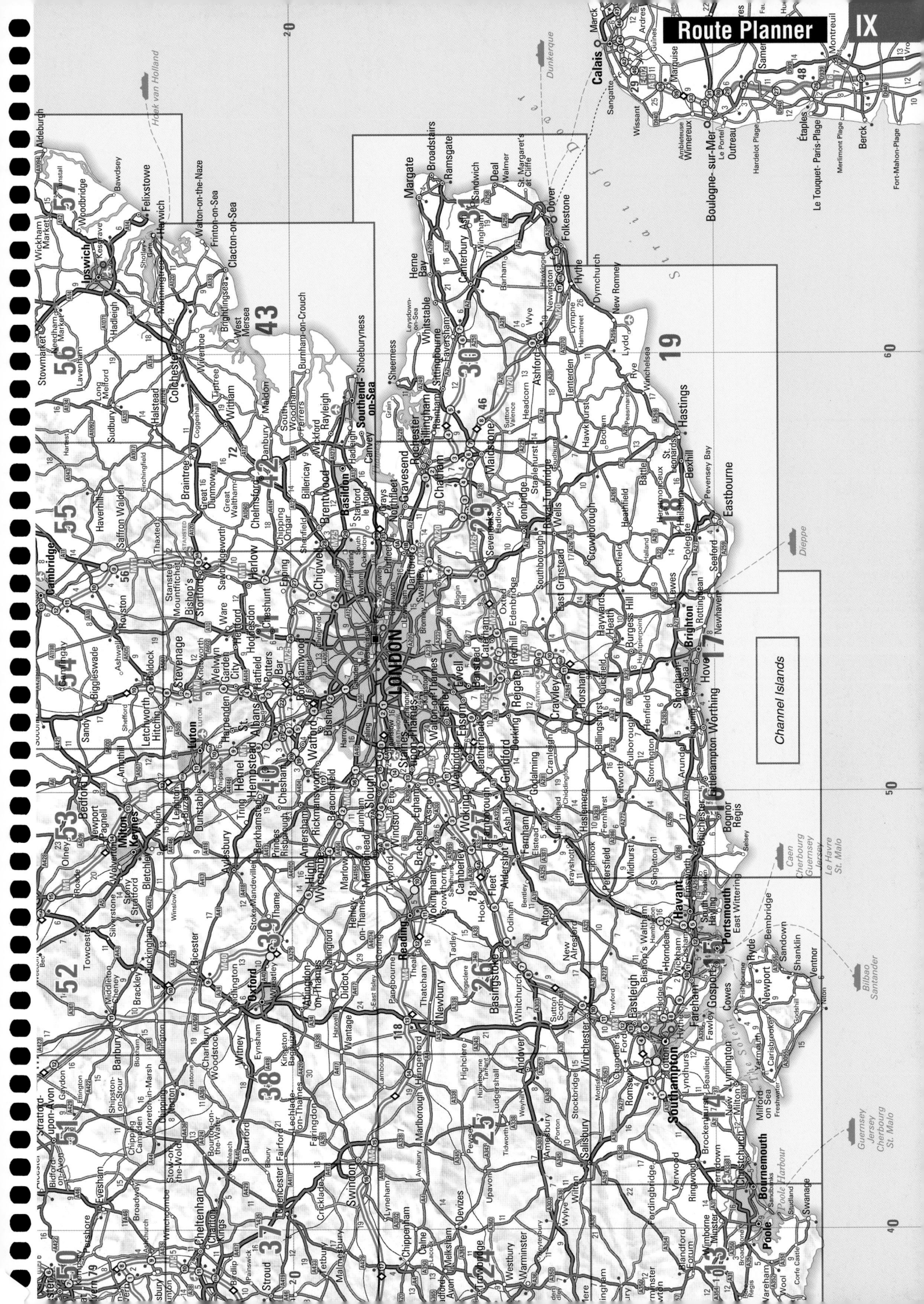

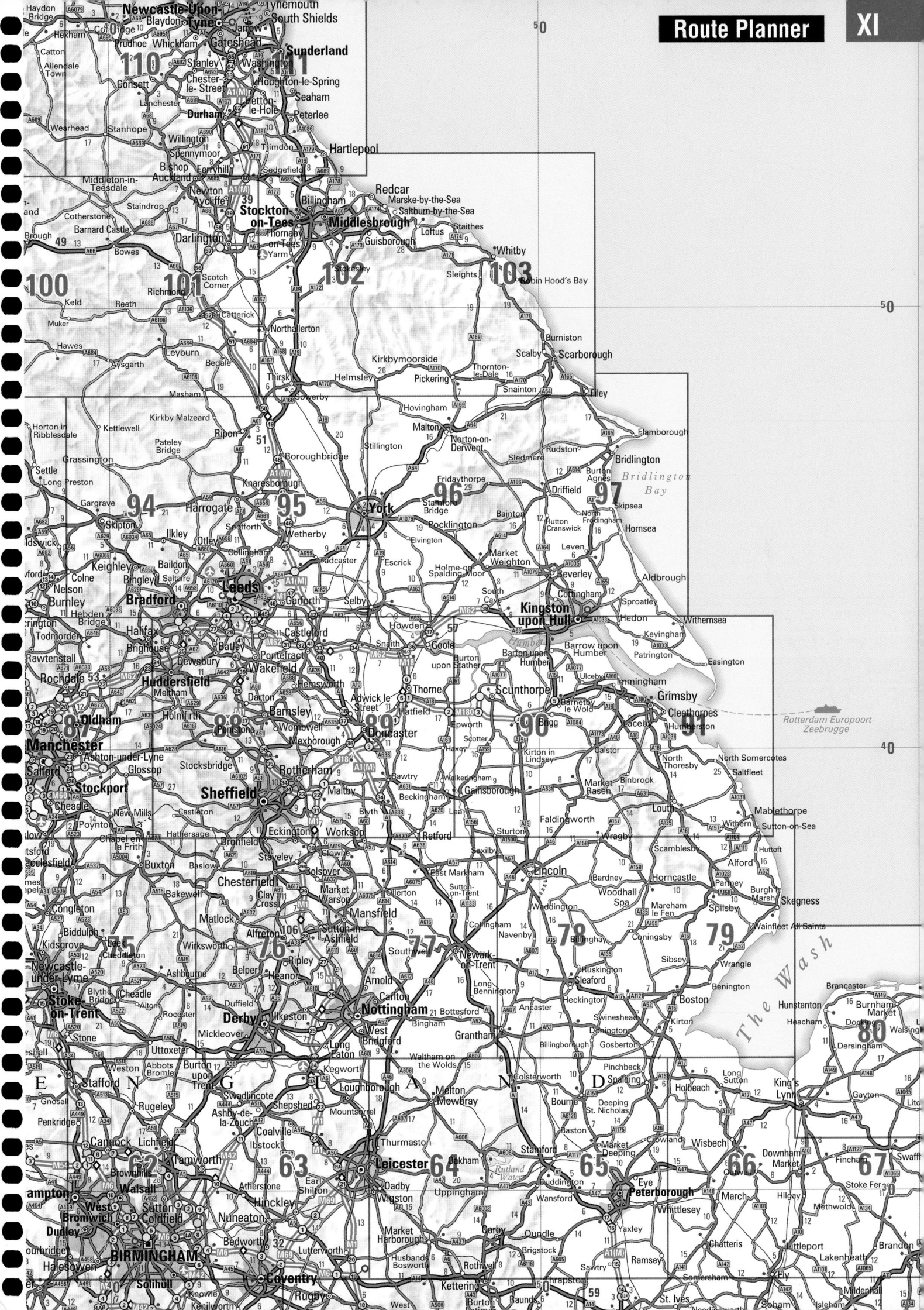

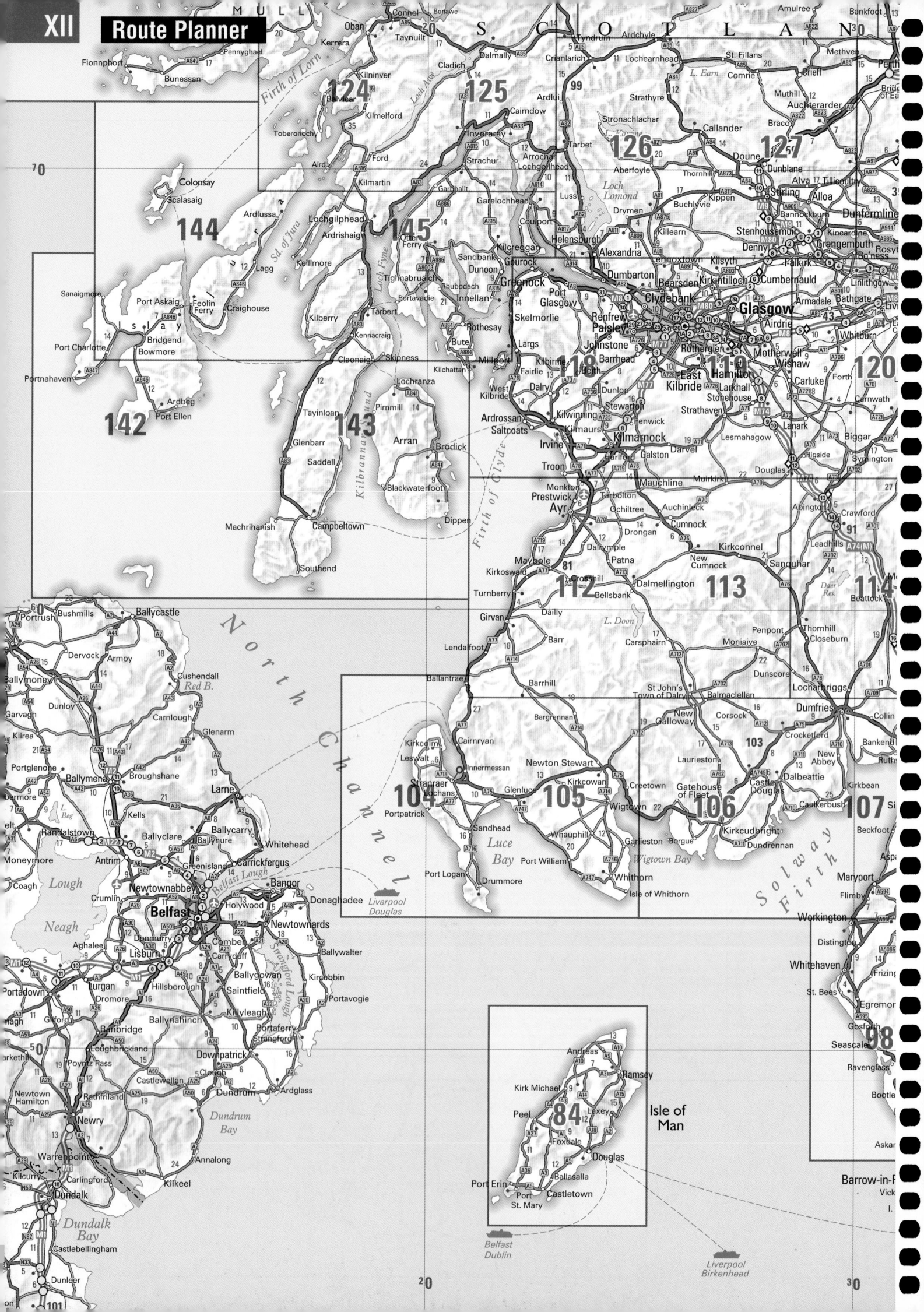

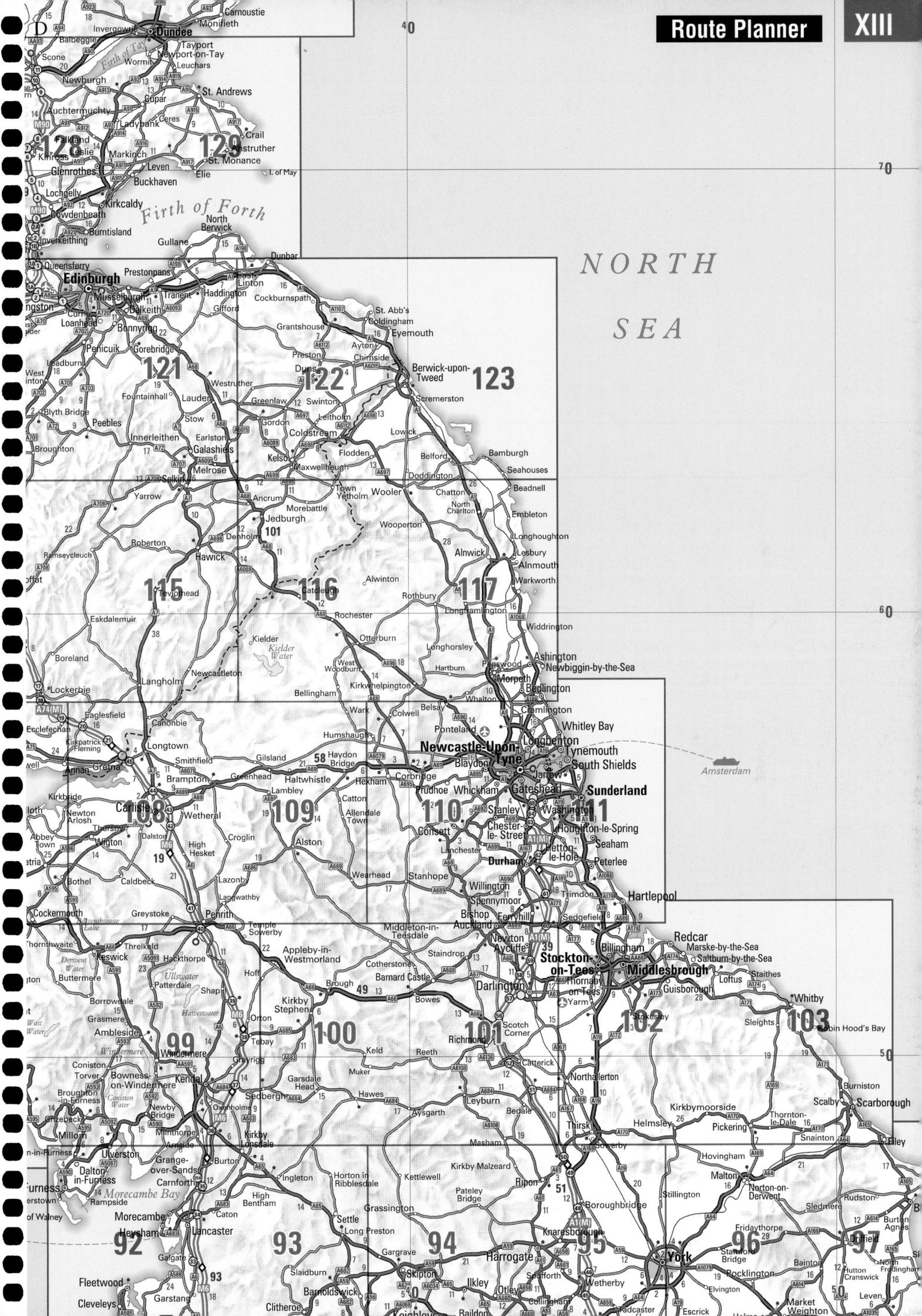

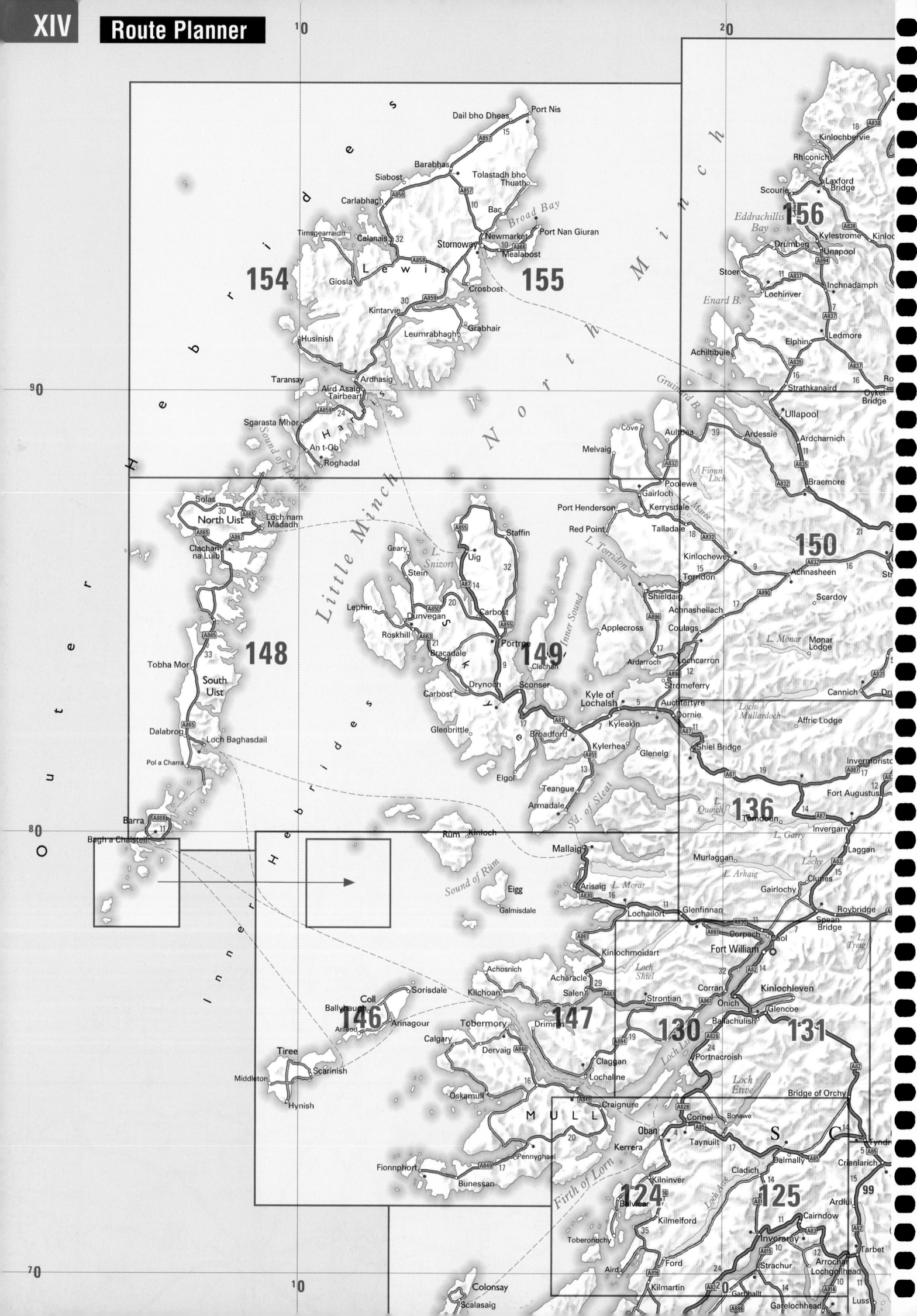

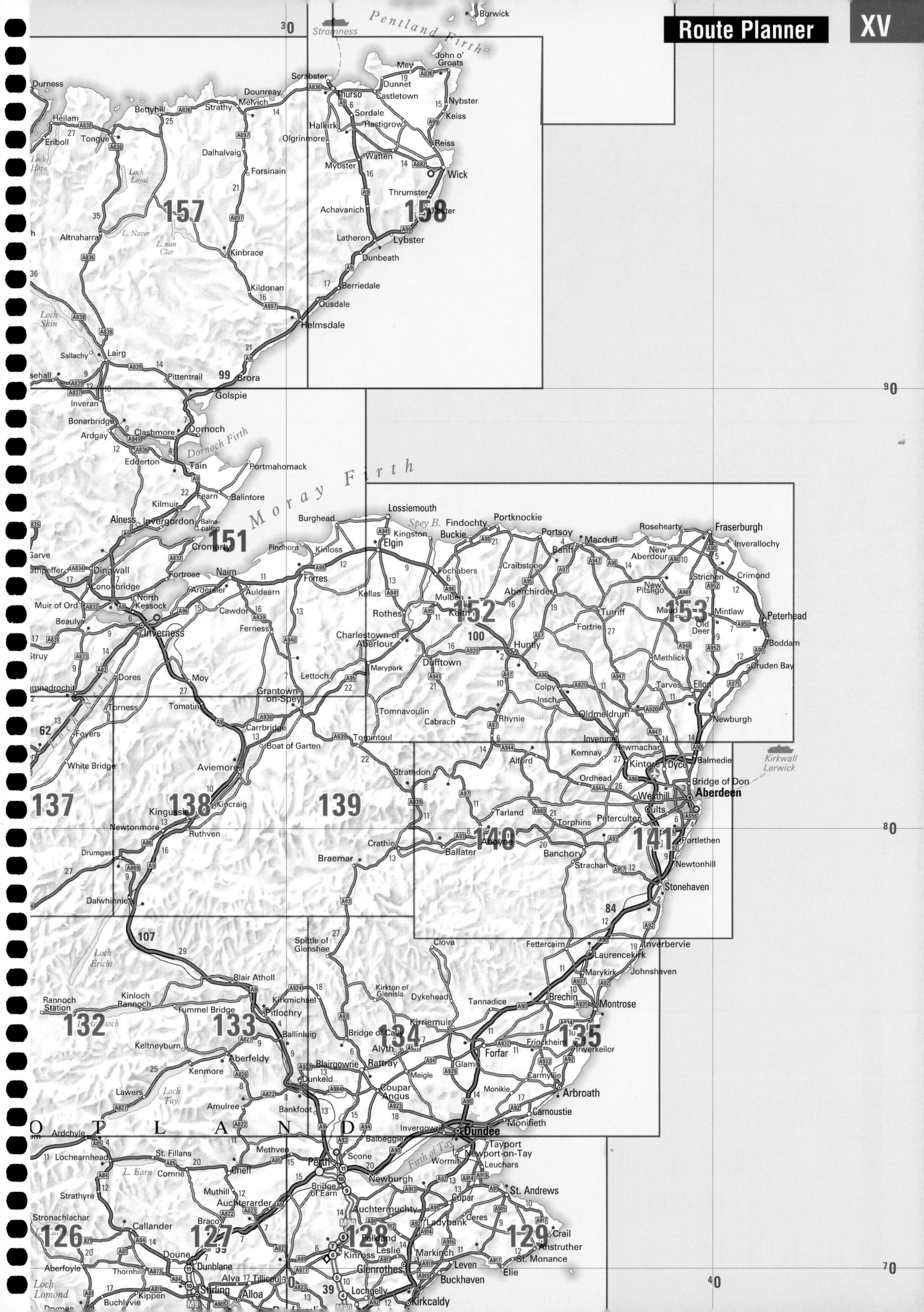

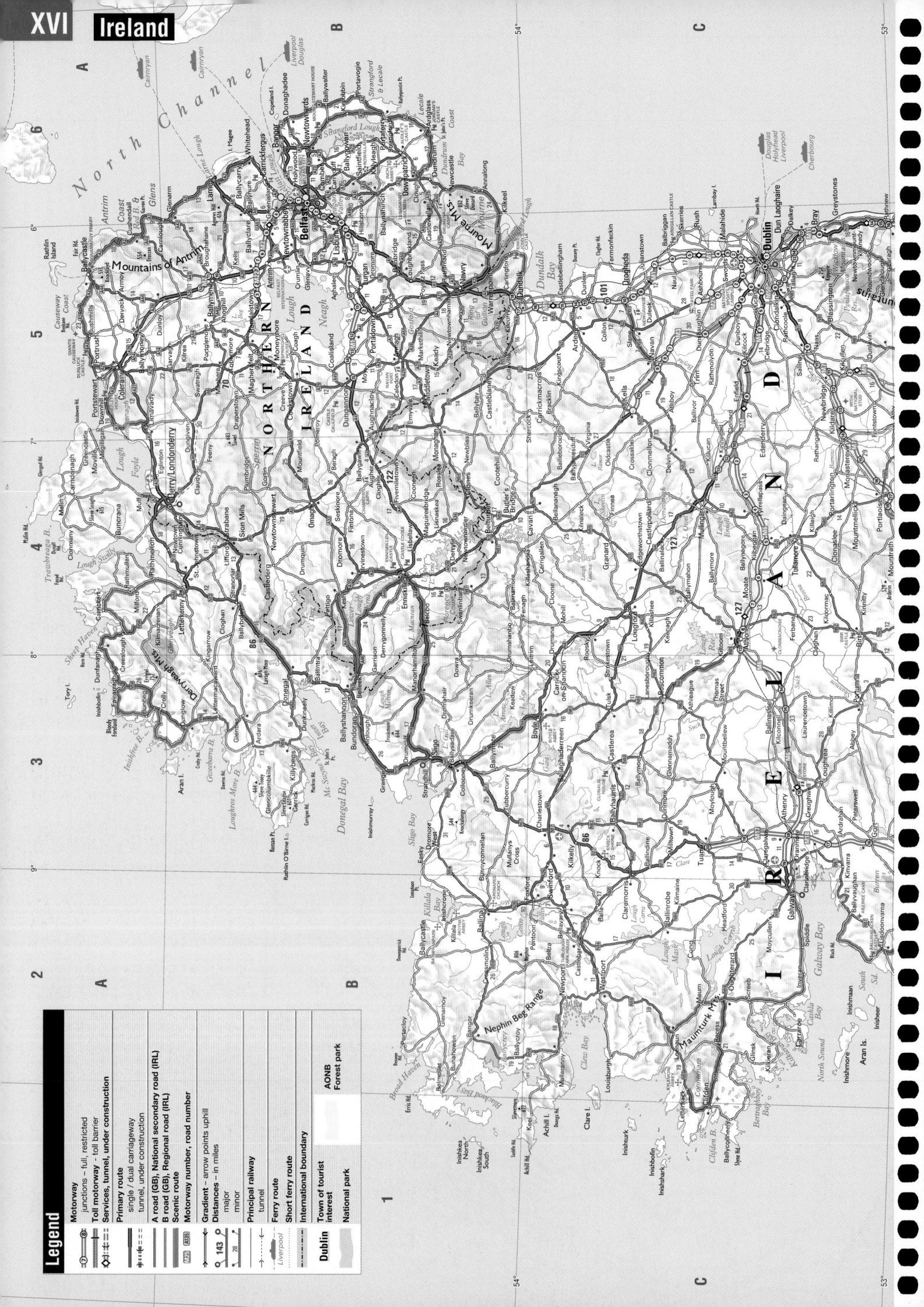

Legend

Motorway
junctions – full, restricted

Toll motorway – toll barrier

Services, tunnel, under construction

Primary route
single / dual carriageway
tunnel, under construction

A road (GB), National secondary road (IRL)

B road (GB), Regional road (IRL)

Scenic route

Motorway number, road number

Gradient – arrow points uphill

Distances – in miles
major
minor

Principal railway
tunnel

Ferry route

Short ferry route

International boundary

Dublin Town of tourist interest

National park

AONB

Forest park

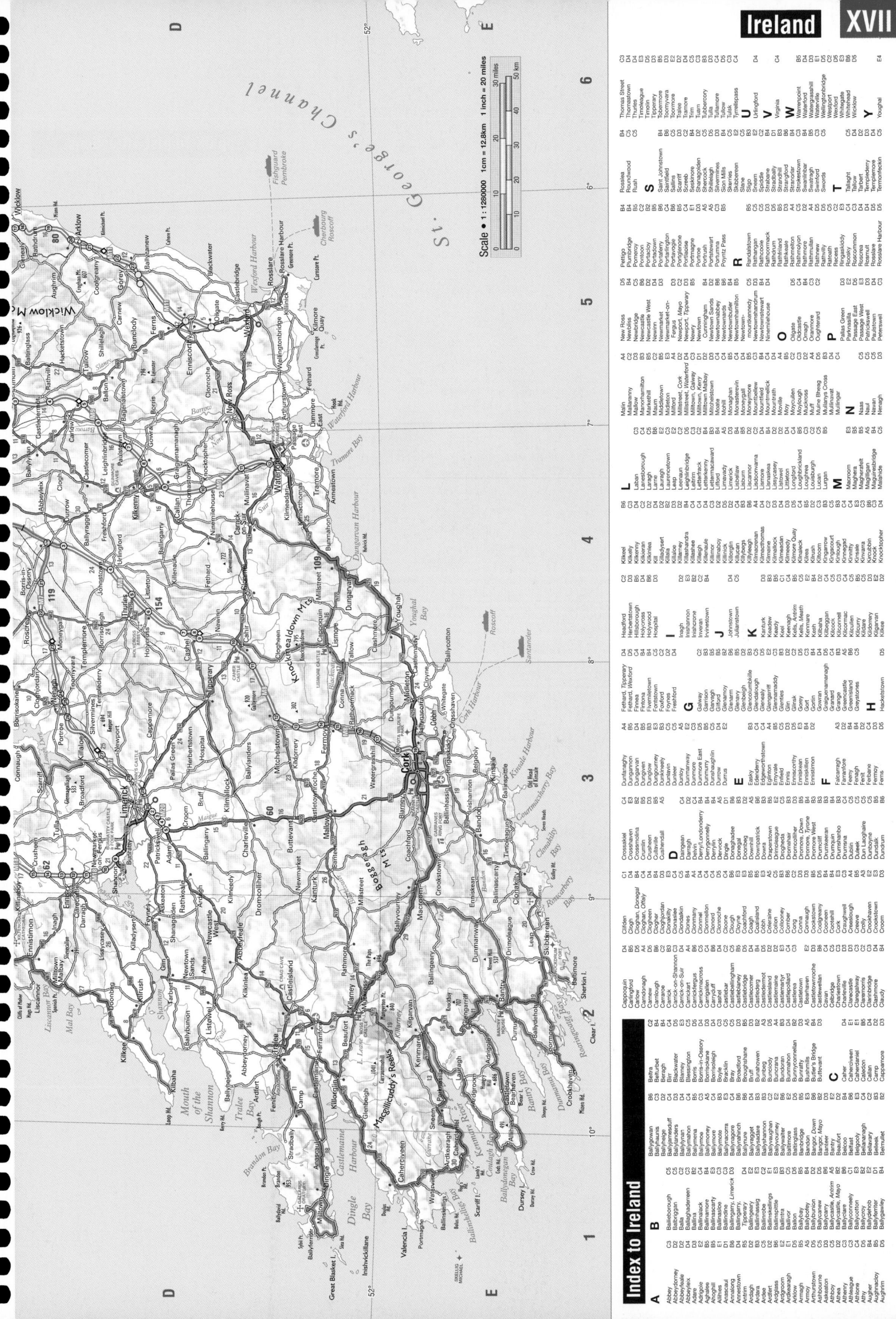

St. George's Channel

Wicklow Mts

Knockmealdown Mts

Scale · 1 : 1 280 000   1 cm = 12.8 km   1 inch = 20 miles

0   10   20   30 miles

0   10   20   30   40   50 km

Tourism

Tourism

	National Park
	Area of Outstanding Natural Beauty
	National Scenic Area
	Built-up area
	Long distance footpath
●	Town of tourist interest
◆	Other tourist attraction
○	Other town

Top Ireland Tourist Attractions

		Visitors in millions (2018)
1.	Guinness Storehouse, Dublin	1.7
2.	Cliffs of Moher Visitor Experience, Clare	1.6
3.	Dublin Zoo	1.2
4.	Book of Kells, Dublin	1.1
5.	National Gallery of Ireland, Dublin	0.8
6.	Glendalough Site, Wicklow	0.7
7.	Tayto Park, Dublin	0.7
8.	National Botanic Gardens, Dublin	0.7
9.	St Patrick's Cathedral, Dublin	0.6
10.	Kylemore Abbey & Gardens, Galway	0.6

Top UK Tourist Attractions

		Visitors in millions (2018)
1.	Tate Modern, London	5.9
2.	British Museum, London	5.8
3.	National Gallery, London	5.7
4.	Natural History Museum, London	5.2
5.	Southbank Centre, London	4.5
6.	Victoria & Albert Museum, London	4.0
7.	Science Museum, London	3.2
8.	Somerset House, London	3.1
9.	Tower of London	2.9
10.	Royal Museums, Greenwich	2.5
11.	National Museum of Scotland, Edinburgh	2.2
12.	Edinburgh Castle	2.1
13.	Chester Zoo	2.0
14.	Royal Botanic Gardens, Kew	1.9
15.	Royal Albert Hall, London	1.8
16.	Scottish National Gallery, Edinburgh	1.7
17.	St Paul's Cathedral, London	1.7
18.	Royal Academy, London	1.6
19.	National Portrait Gallery, London	1.6
20.	Stonehenge, Wiltshire	1.6

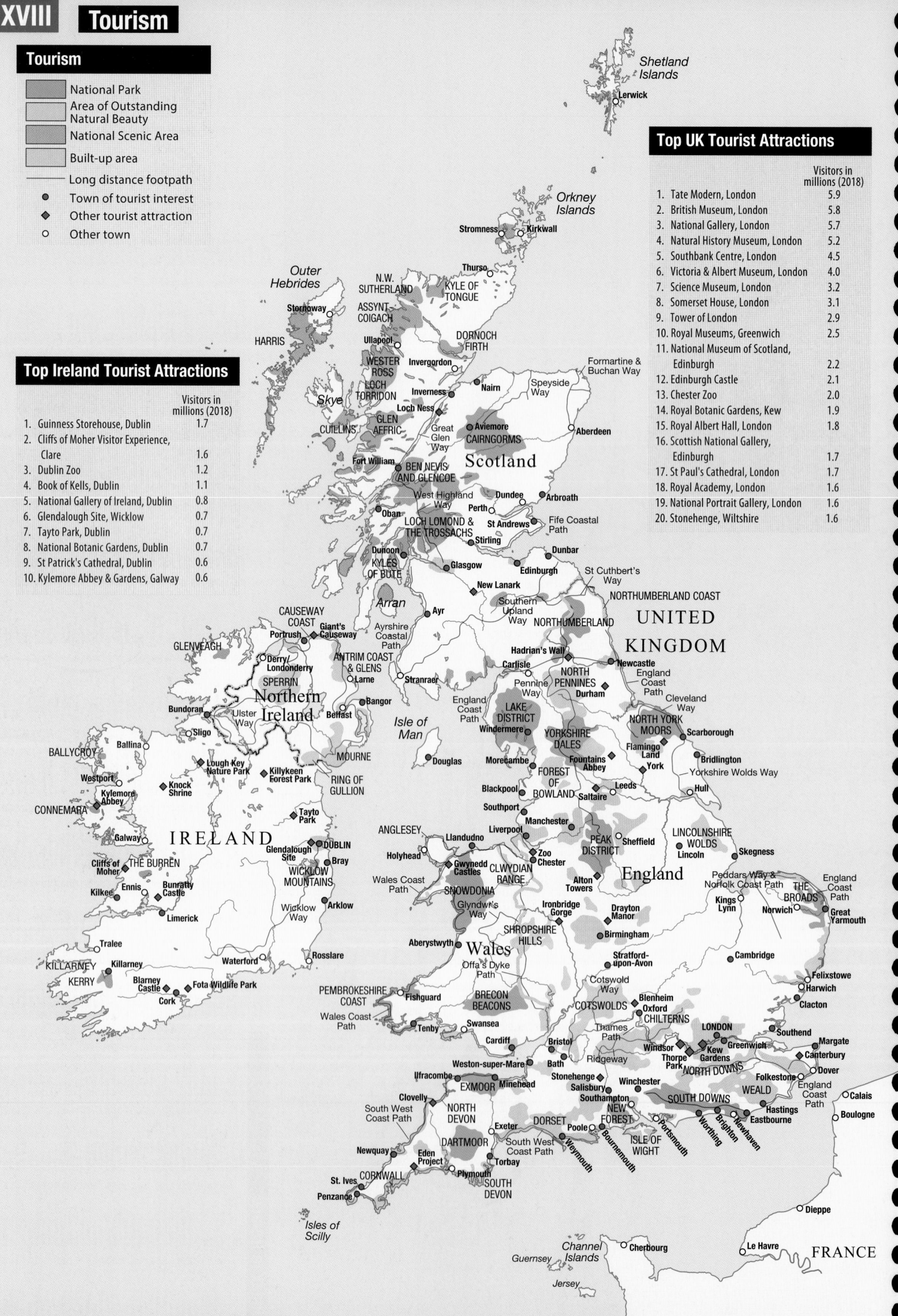

Transport

———	Motorway
———	Other important road
———	Main railway
———	Main ferry route
- - -	Channel Tunnel
✈	Main airport
⚓	Main ferry port
○	Other town

Top UK Ferry ports

		Passengers in thousands (2018)
1.	Dover	11,783
2.	Holyhead	1,914
3.	Portsmouth	1,848
4.	Hull	851
5.	Harwich	676
6.	Tyne	621
7.	Plymouth	433
8.	Newhaven	380
9.	Pembroke Dock	326
10.	Fishguard	295

Top UK Airports

		Passengers in millions (2018)
1.	London Heathrow	80.1
2.	London Gatwick	46.1
3.	Manchester	28.3
4.	London Stansted	28.0
5.	London Luton	16.8
6.	Edinburgh	14.3
7.	Birmingham	12.5
8.	Glasgow	9.7
9.	Bristol	8.7
10.	Belfast International	6.3
11.	Newcastle	5.3
12.	Liverpool John Lennon	5.0
13.	East Midlands	4.9
14.	London City	4.8
15.	Leeds Bradford	4.0
16.	Aberdeen	3.1
17.	George Best Belfast City	2.5
18.	Southampton	2.0
19.	Jersey	1.7
20.	Cardiff	1.6

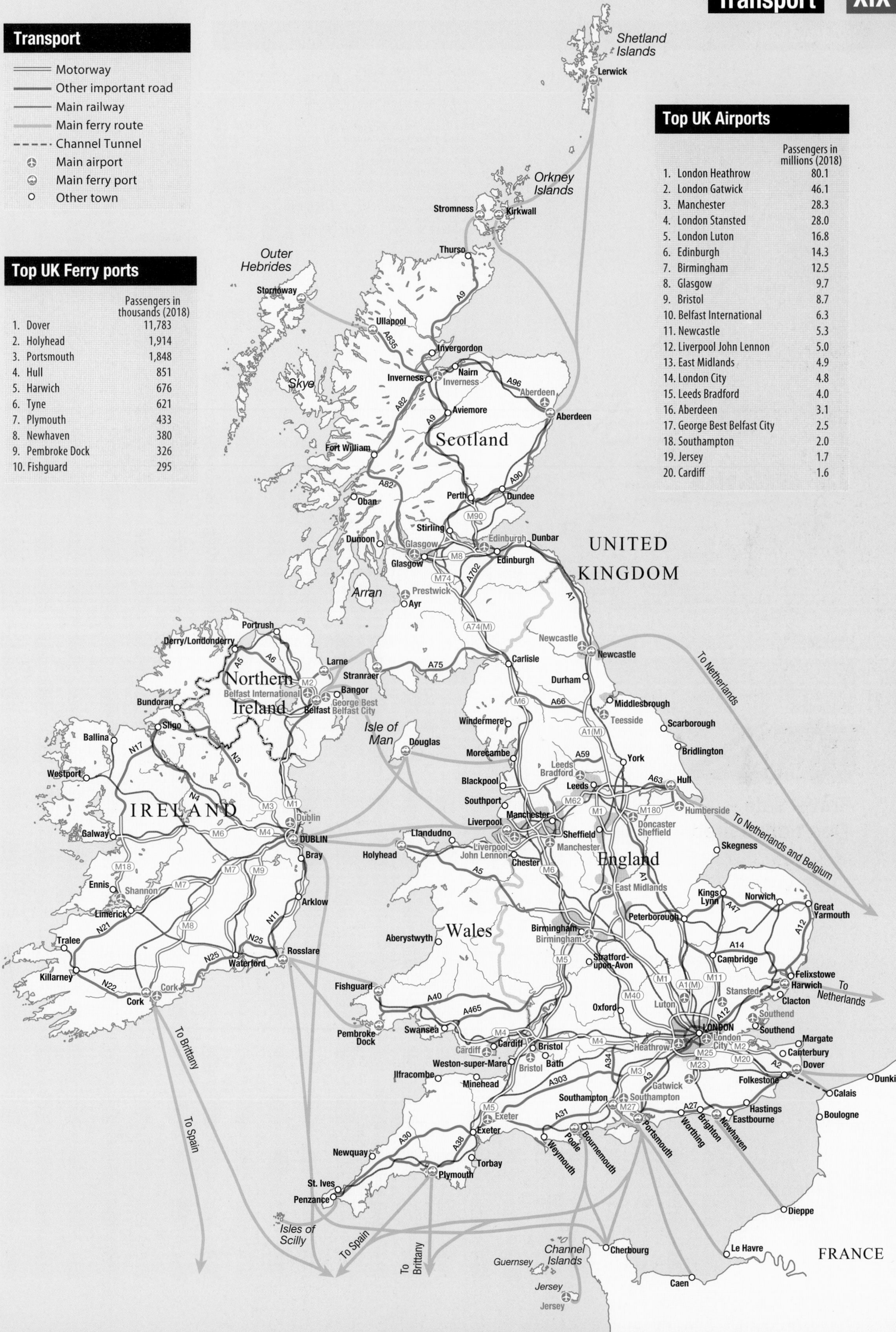

Distance table

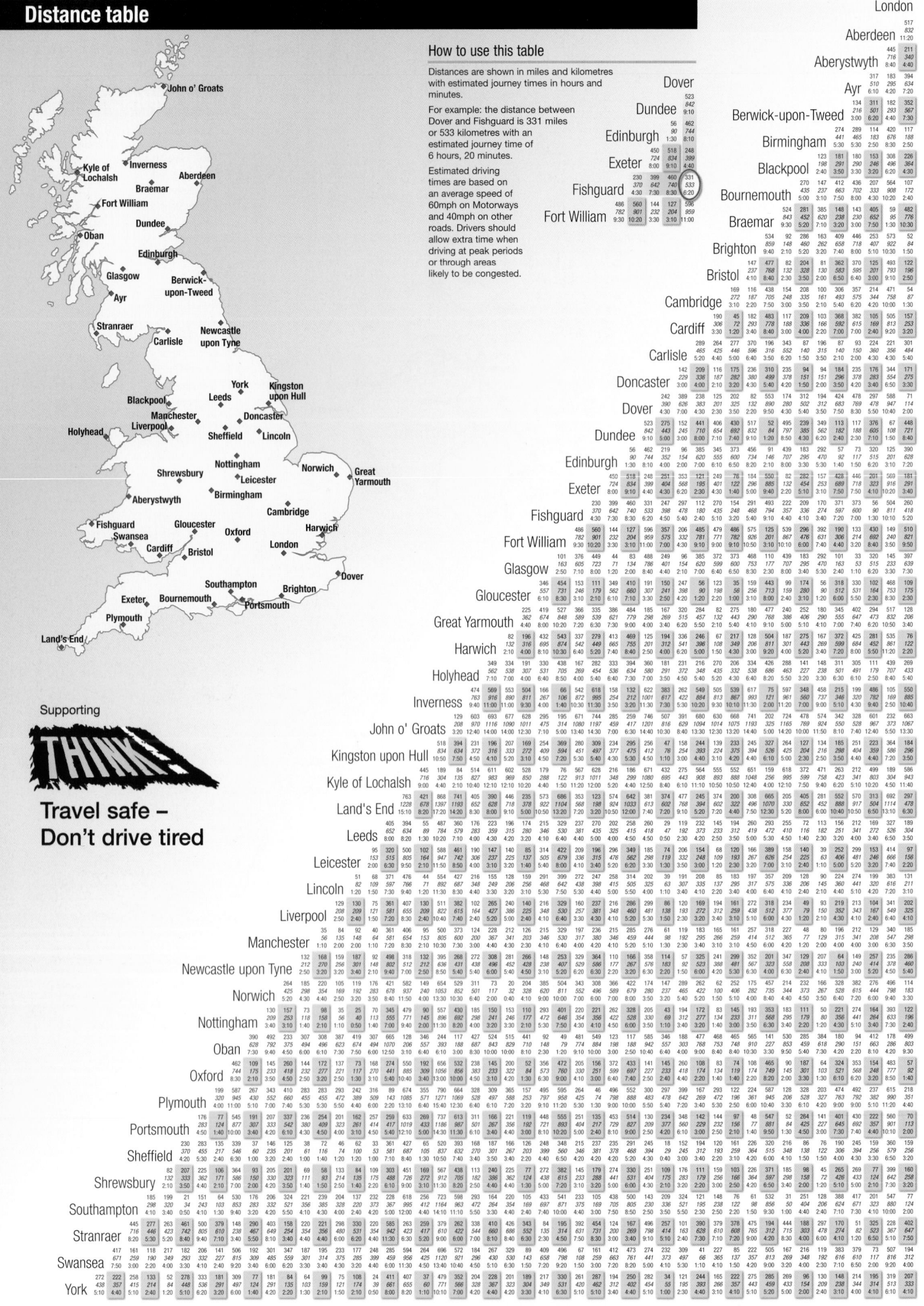

How to use this table

Distances are shown in miles and kilometres with estimated journey times in hours and minutes.

For example: the distance between Dover and Fishguard is 331 miles or 533 kilometres with an estimated journey time of 6 hours, 20 minutes.

Estimated driving times are based on an average speed of 60mph on Motorways and 40mph on other roads. Drivers should allow extra time when driving at peak periods or through areas likely to be congested.

Supporting

THINK!

Travel safe –
Don't drive tired

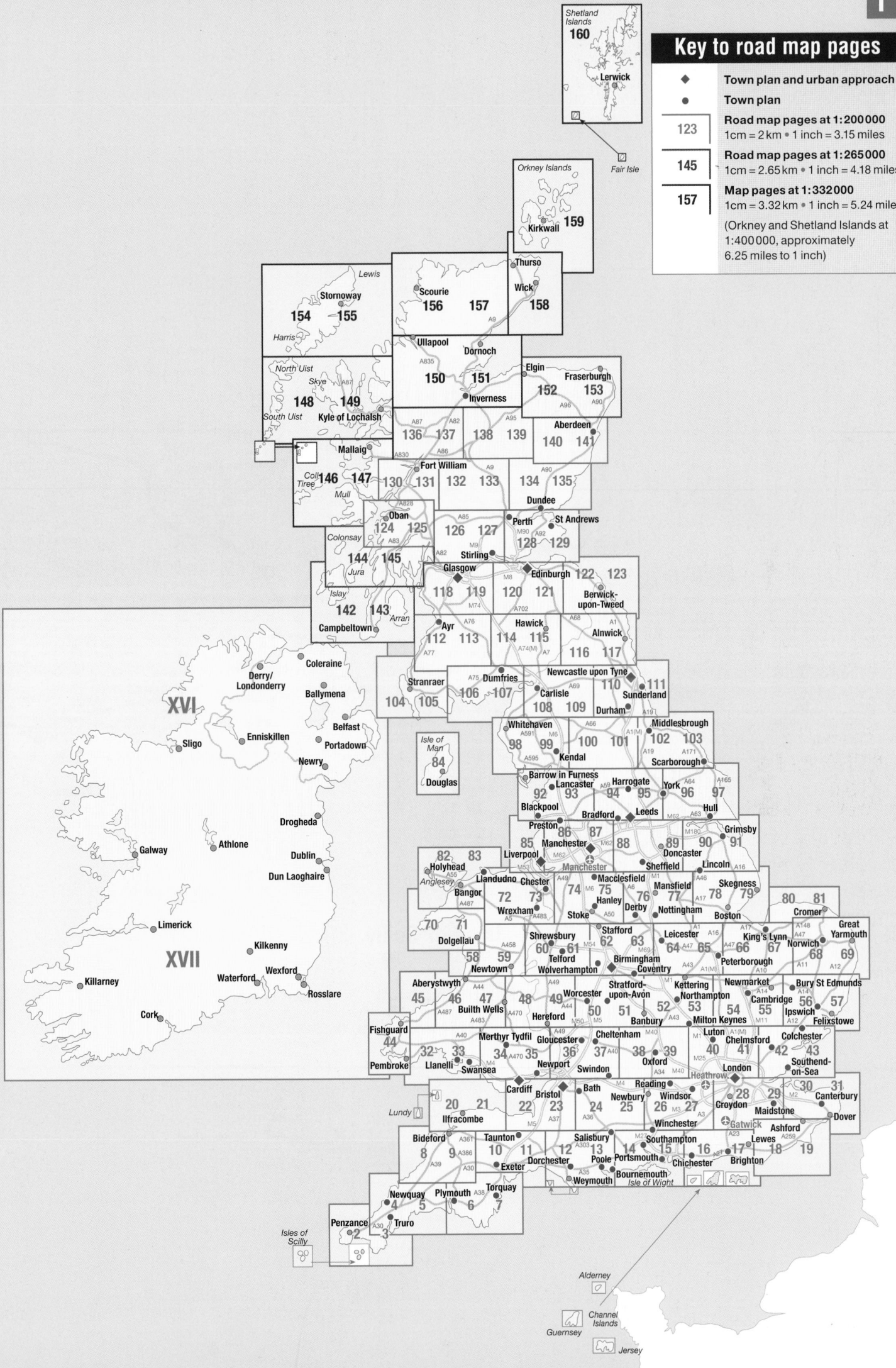

Key to road map pages

◆	Town plan and urban approach map
●	Town plan

123	**Road map pages at 1:200 000** 1cm = 2 km • 1 inch = 3.15 miles
145	**Road map pages at 1:265 000** 1cm = 2.65 km • 1 inch = 4.18 miles
157	**Map pages at 1:332 000** 1cm = 3.32 km • 1 inch = 5.24 miles (Orkney and Shetland Islands at 1:400 000, approximately 6.25 miles to 1 inch)

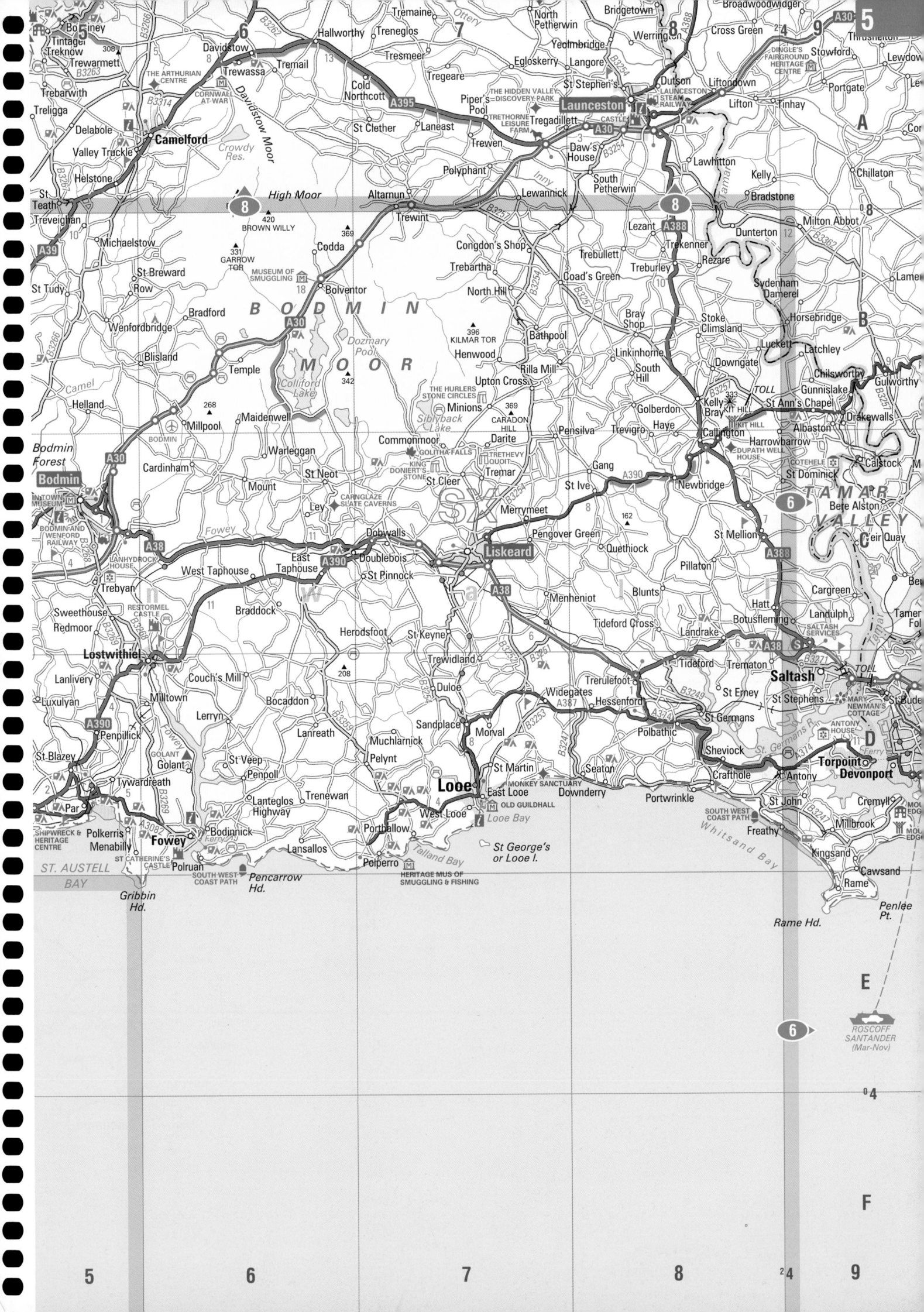

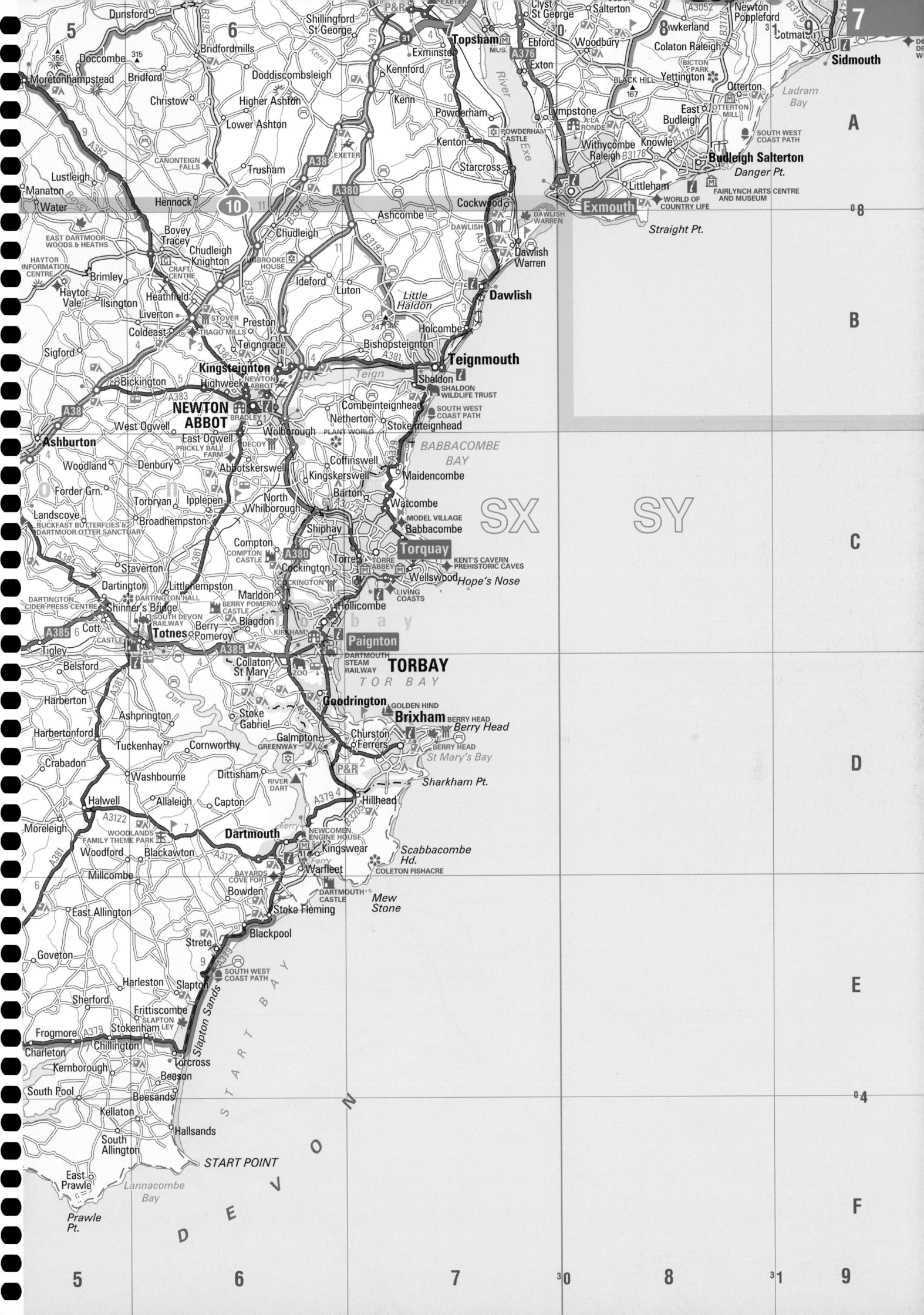

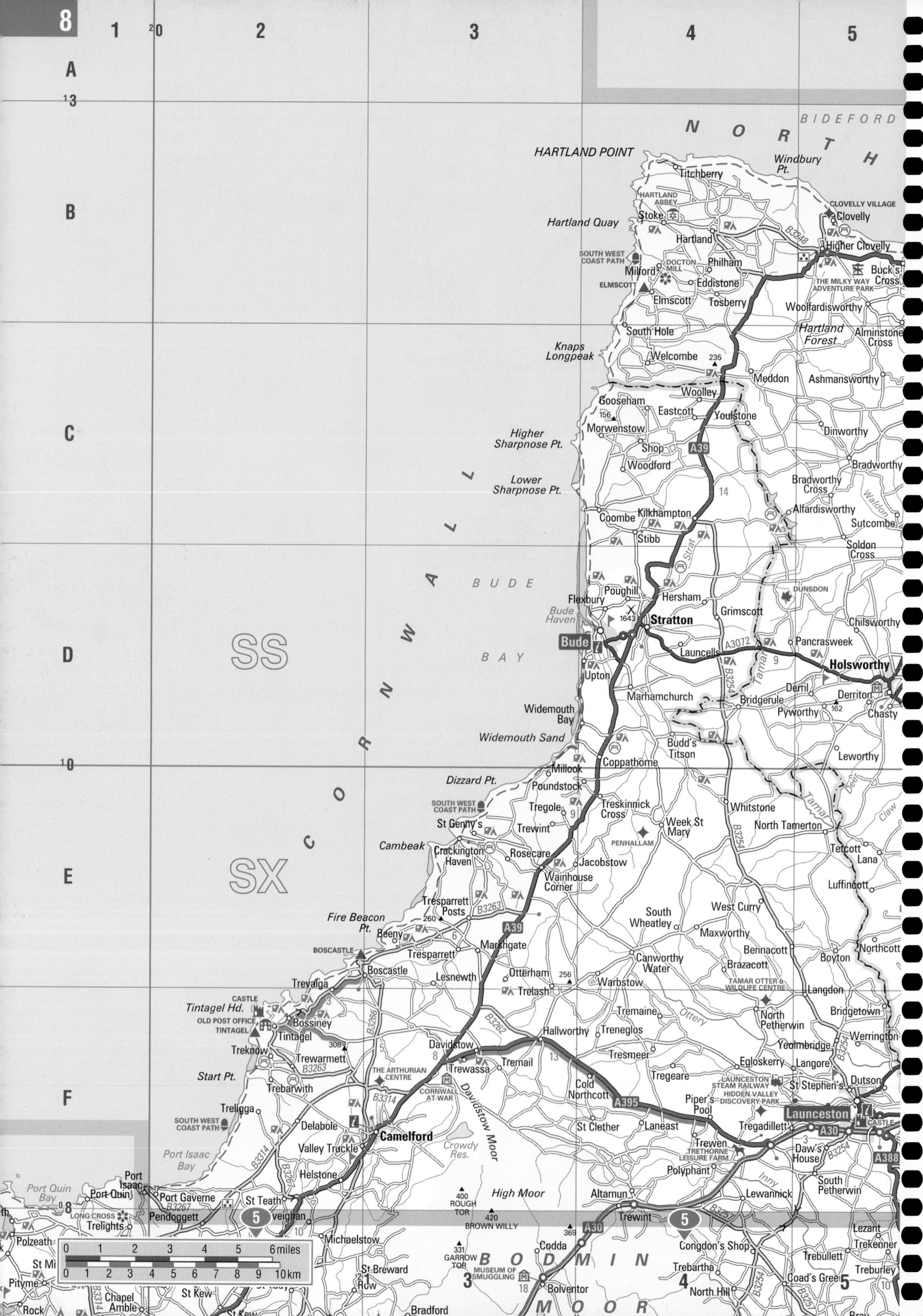

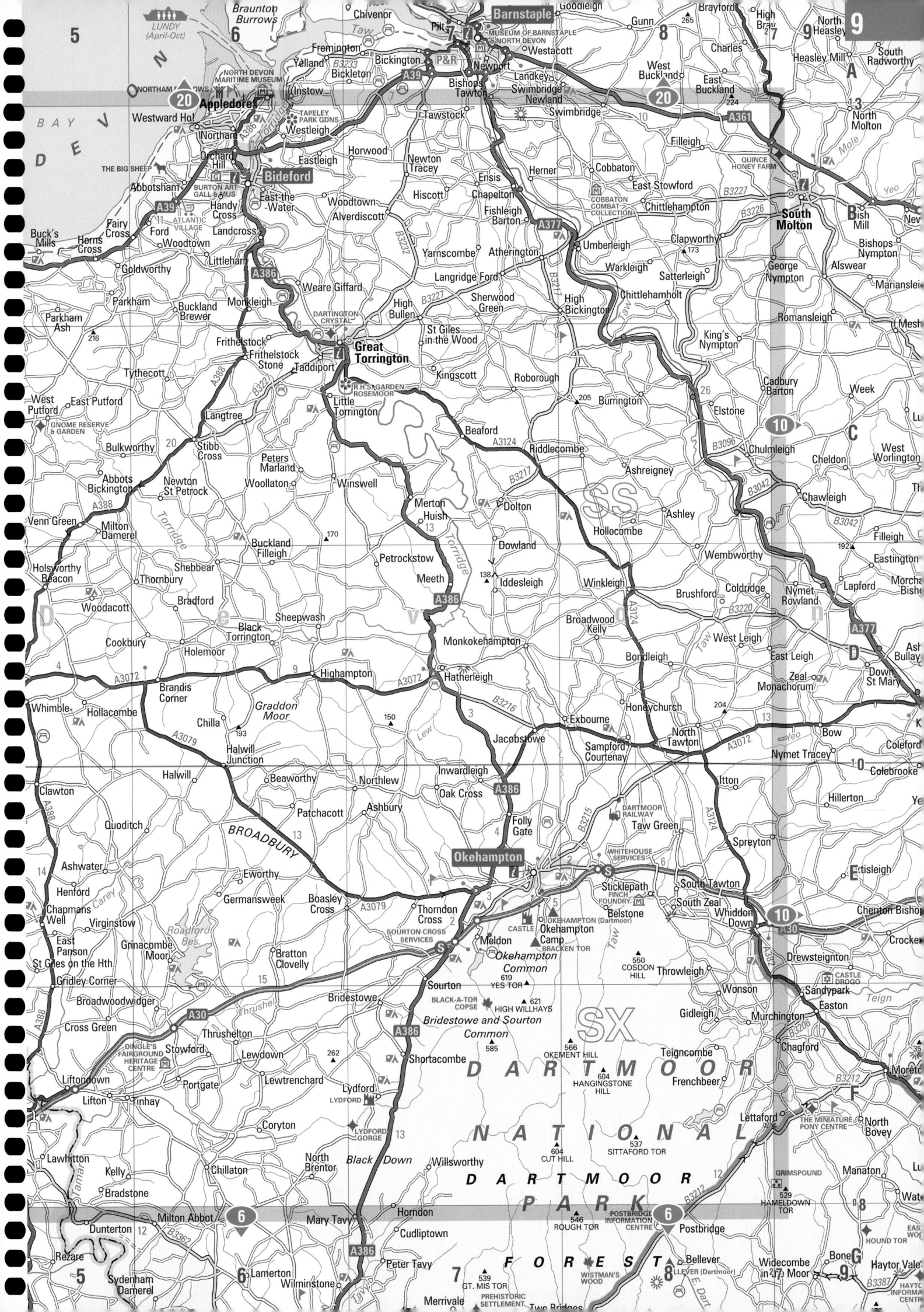

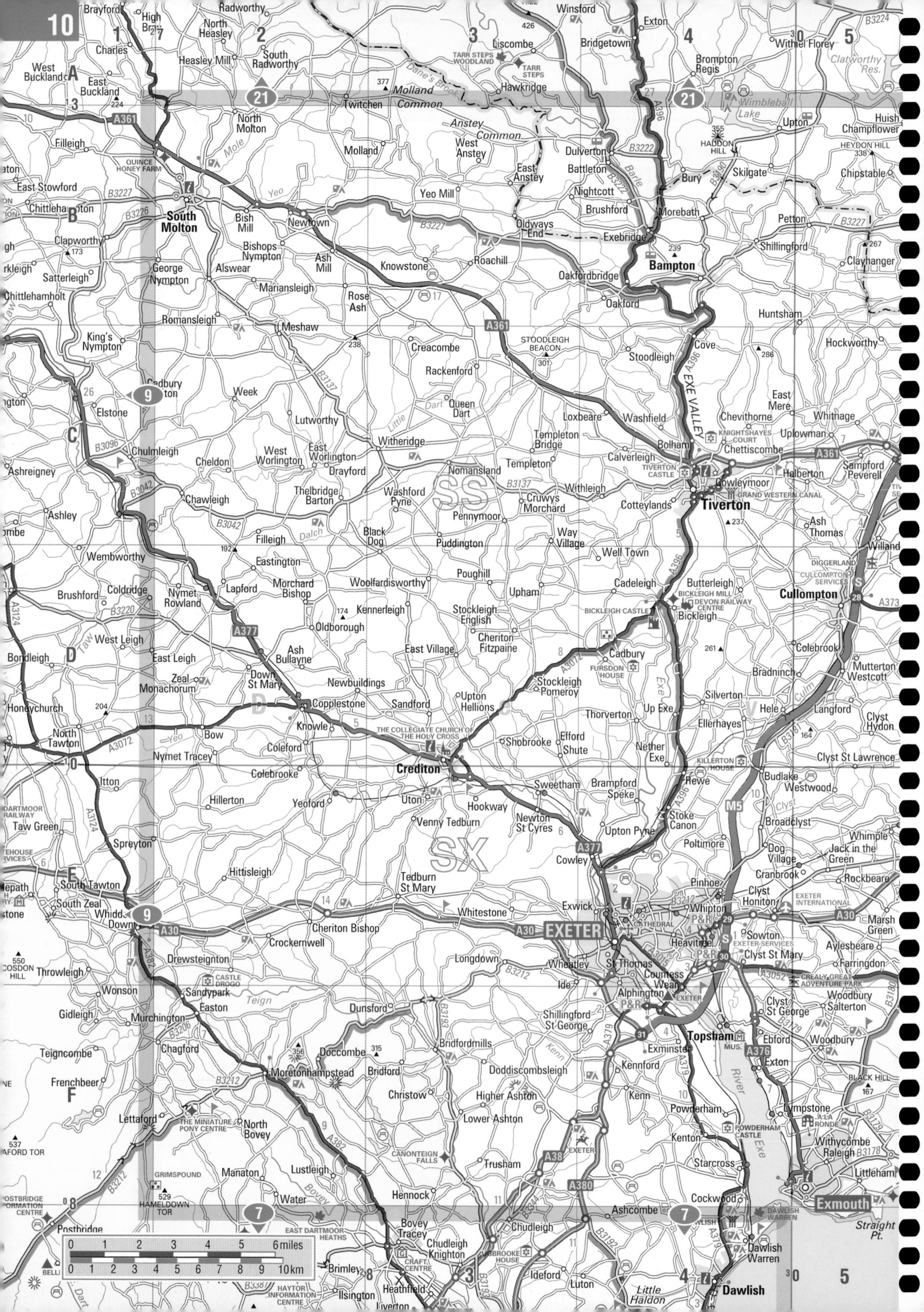

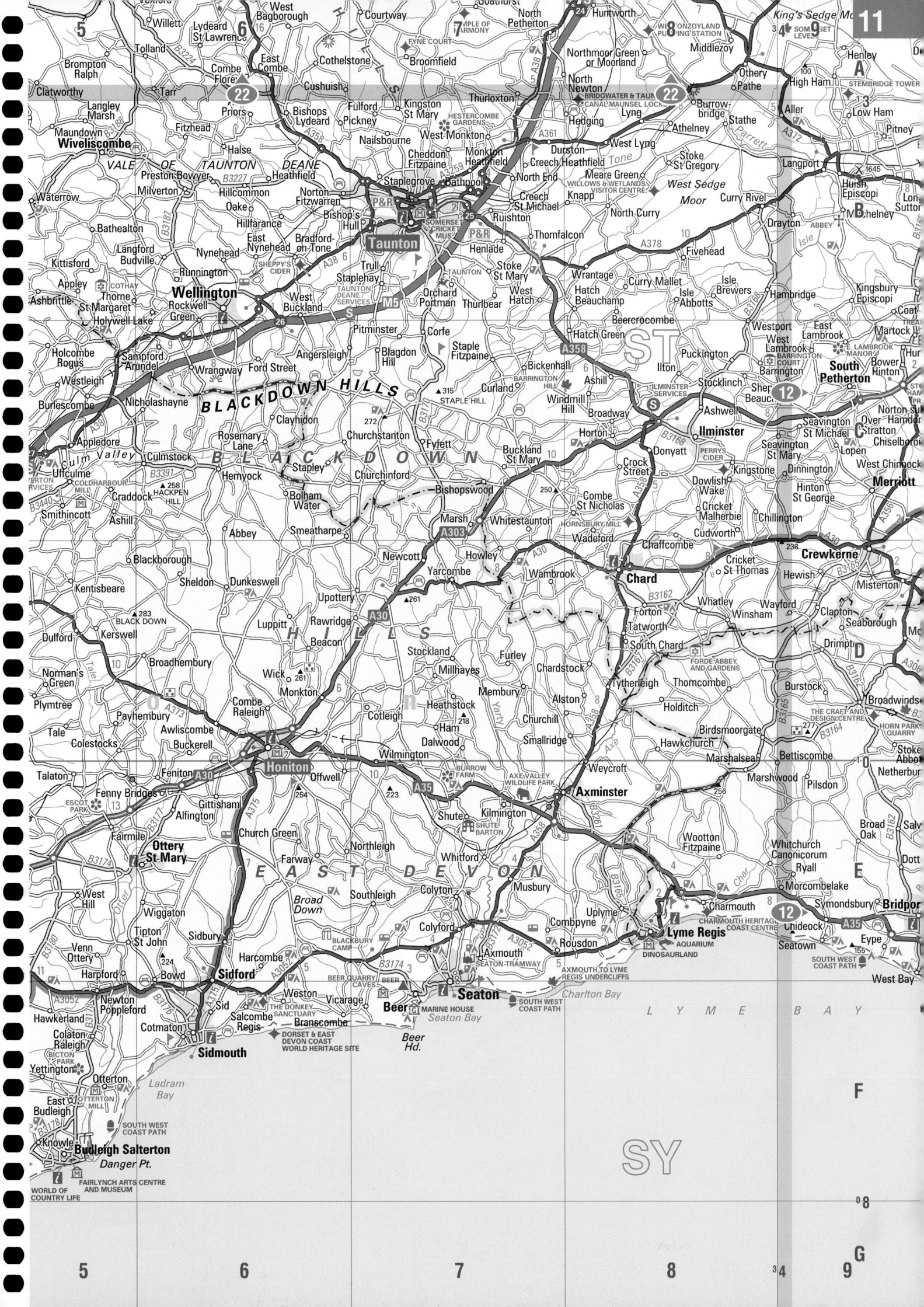

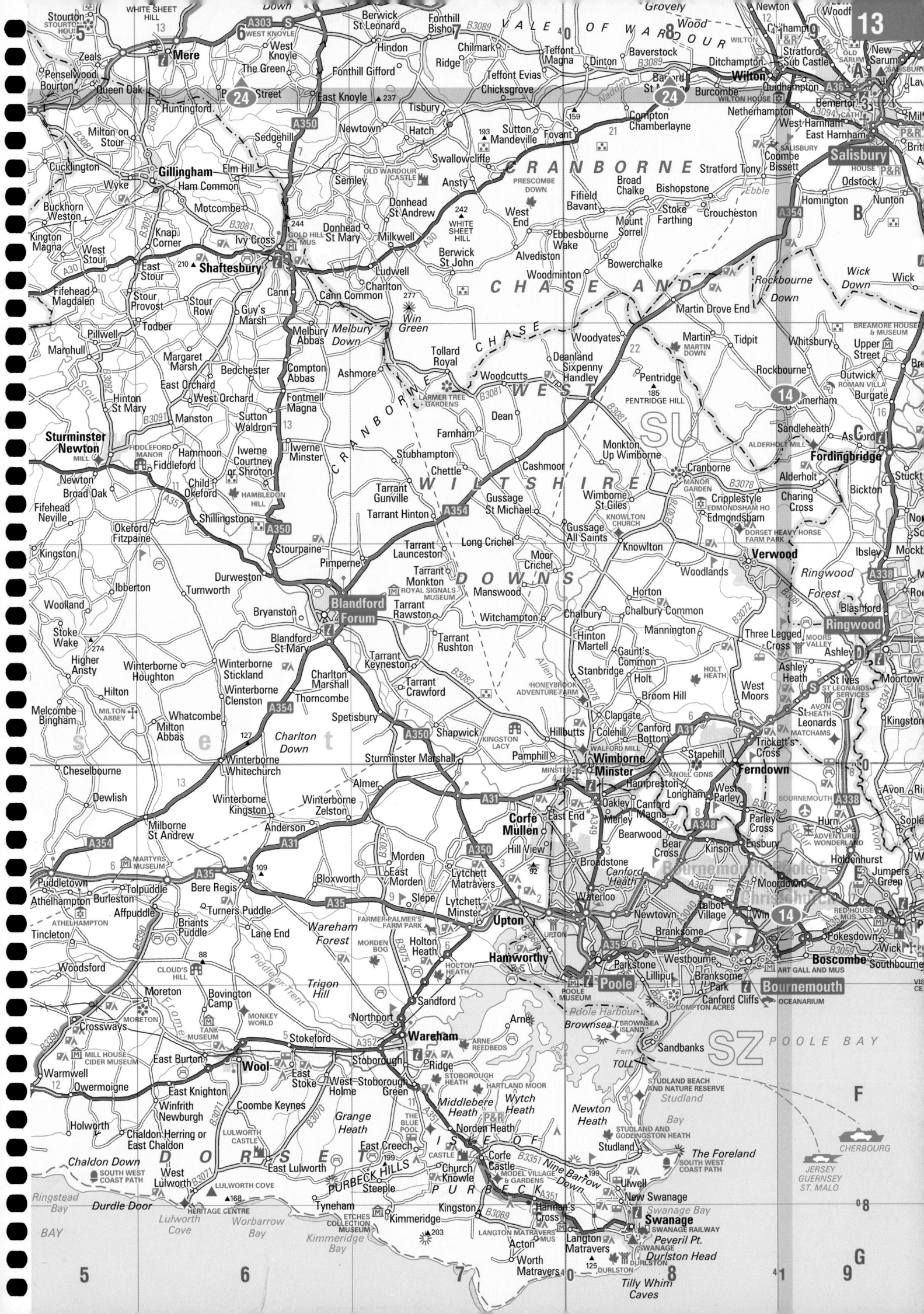

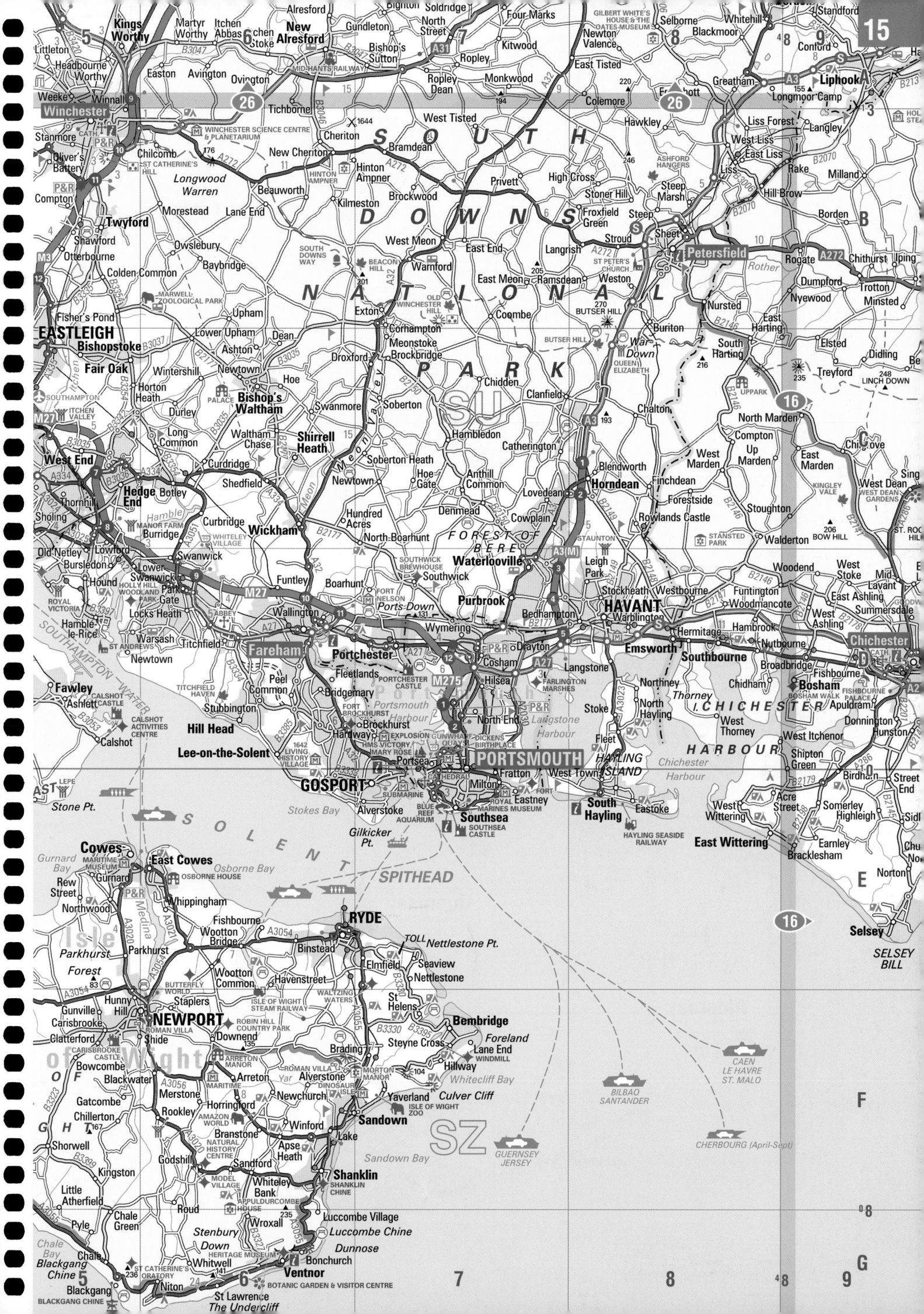

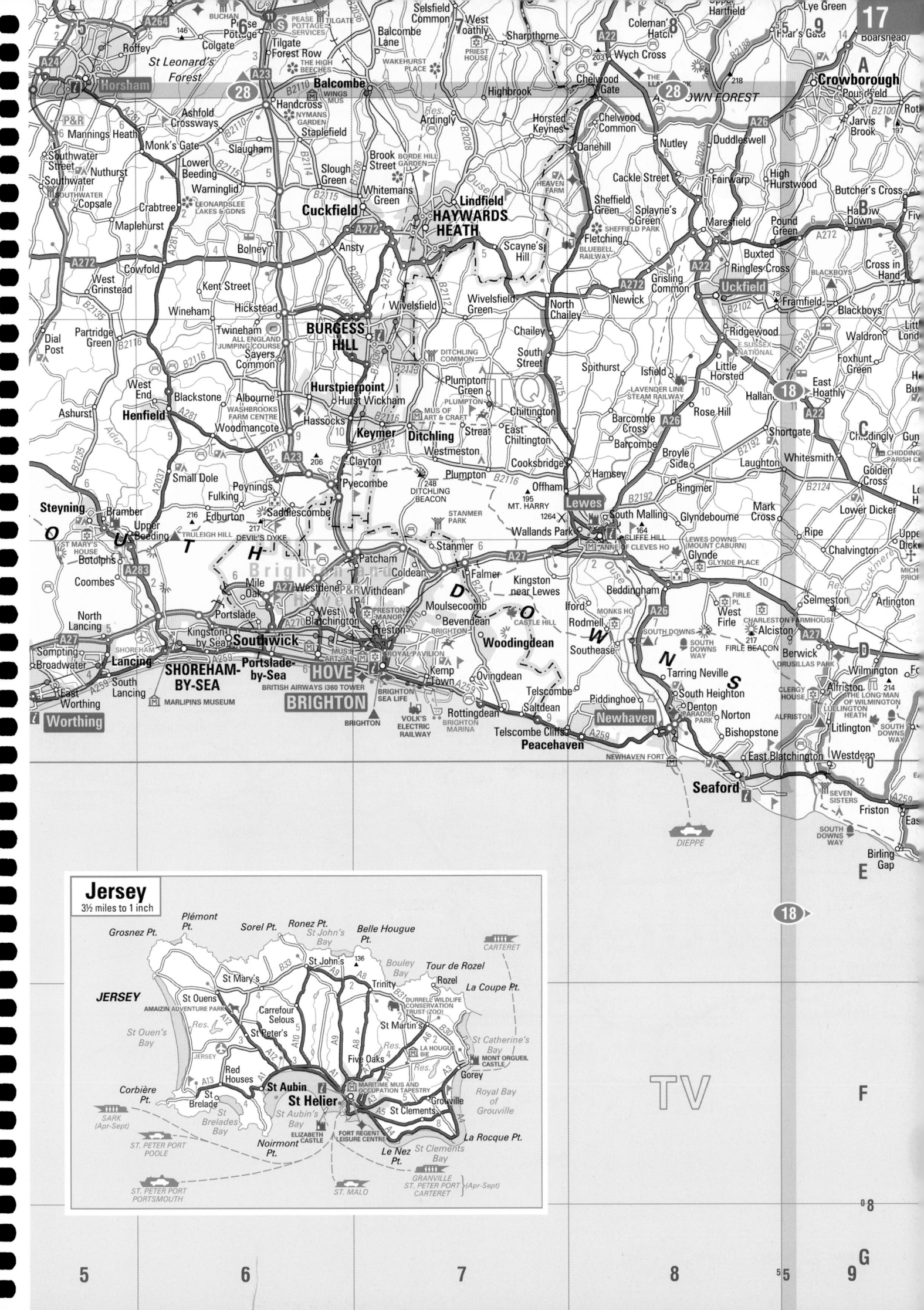

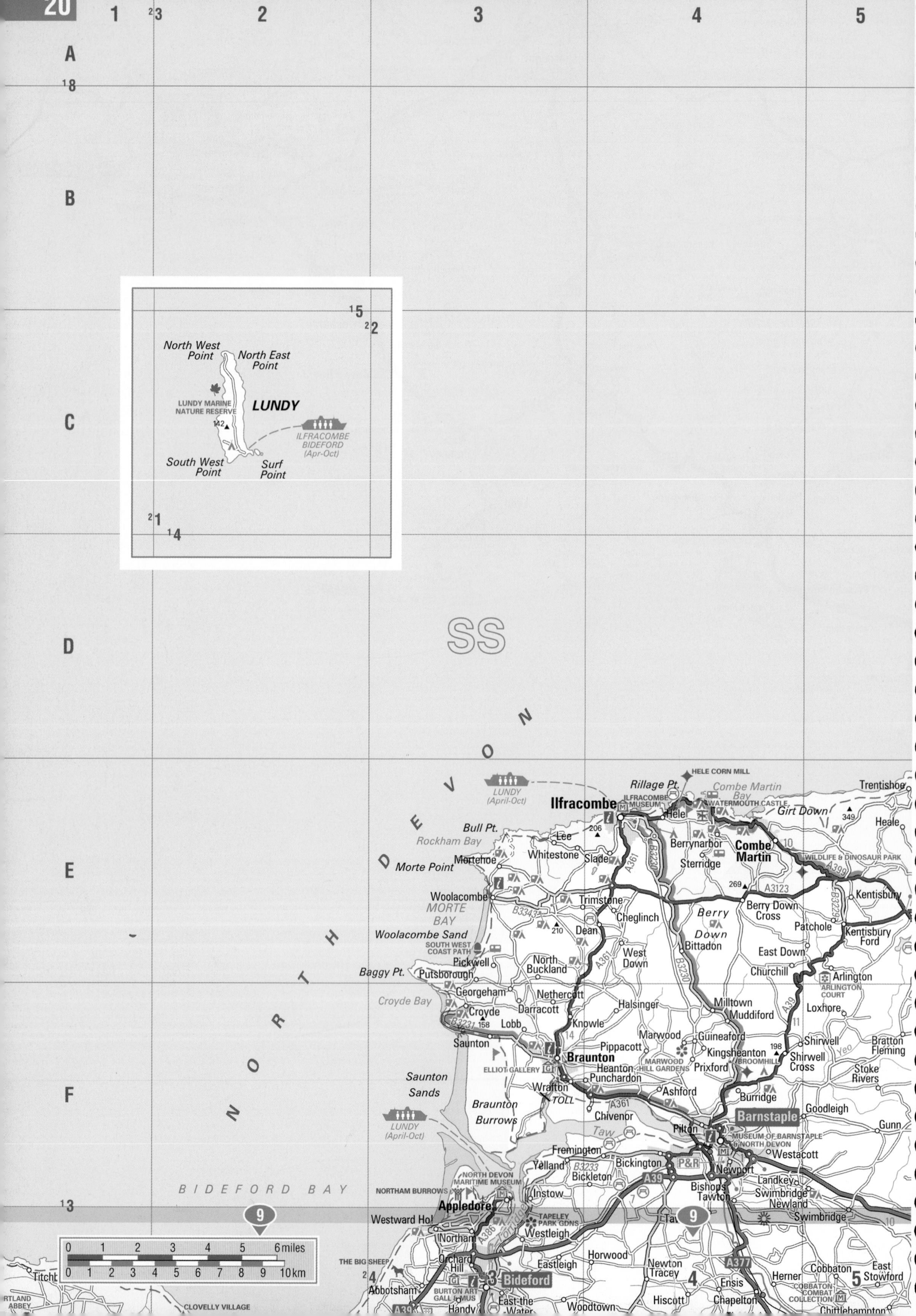

1   2   3   4   5

A

¹8

B

C

North West Point
North East Point

LUNDY MARINE NATURE RESERVE

LUNDY

¹5 ²2

142 ▲

ILFRACOMBE BIDEFORD (Apr-Oct)

South West Point
Surf Point

²1   ¹4

D

SS

NORTH DEVON

LUNDY (April-Oct)

Rillage Pt.   HELE CORN MILL   Combe Martin Bay   Trentishoe

Ilfracombe   ILFRACOMBE MUSEUM   WATERMOUTH CASTLE   Girt Down   349   Heale

Bull Pt.   206   Hele   Berrynarbor   Combe Martin   10   WILDLIFE & DINOSAUR PARK

Rockham Bay   Lee   Whitestone   Slade   A361   Sterridge   A399

E   Morte Point   Mortehoe   B3230   269   A3123   Berry Down Cross   Kentisbury

Woolacombe   Trimstone   Cheglinch   Berry Down   Patchole   Kentisbury Ford

MORTE BAY   B3343   210   Dean   West Down   Bittadon   East Down   B3229

Woolacombe Sand   SOUTH WEST COAST PATH   North Buckland   A36   Churchill   Arlington

Pickwell   B3230   ARLINGTON COURT

Baggy Pt.   Putsborough   Halsinger   Milltown   A39   Loxhore

Georgeham   Nethercott   Muddiford

Croyde Bay   Darracott   Knowle   Marwood   Guineaford   Shirwell   Bratton Fleming

B3231   158   Lobb   Pippacott   MARWOOD   Kingsheanton   198   Shirwell Cross   Stoke Rivers

Saunton   Braunton   BROOMHILL   HILL GARDENS   Prixford   Yeo

ELLIOT GALLERY   Heanton Punchardon   Ashford   Burridge   Goodleigh   Gunn

F   Saunton Sands   Wrafton   TOLL   A361   Chivenor   Pilton   Barnstaple   Westacott

Braunton Burrows   MUSEUM OF BARNSTAPLE & NORTH DEVON

LUNDY (April-Oct)   Taw   Fremington   P&R   Newport   Landkey

BIDEFORD BAY   NORTH DEVON MARITIME MUSEUM   Yelland   Bickleton   Bickington   A39   Bishops Tawton   Swimbridge Newland   Swimbridge

Instow   TAPELEY PARK GDNS   10

¹3   Appledore   Tawstock   9

9   Westward Ho!   Westleigh

Northam   Westlegh   A377

0 1 2 3 4 5 6miles   THE BIG SHEEP   Orchard Hill   Bideford   Eastleigh   Horwood   Newton Tracey   Herner   Cobbaton   East Stowford

0 1 2 3 4 5 6 7 8 9 10km   ²4   Abbotsham   BURTON ART GALL & MUS   East-the-   Woodtown   Hiscott   Chapelton   COBBATON COMBAT COLLECTION

Titchb   CLOVELLY VILLAGE   Handy   Water   Chittlehampton

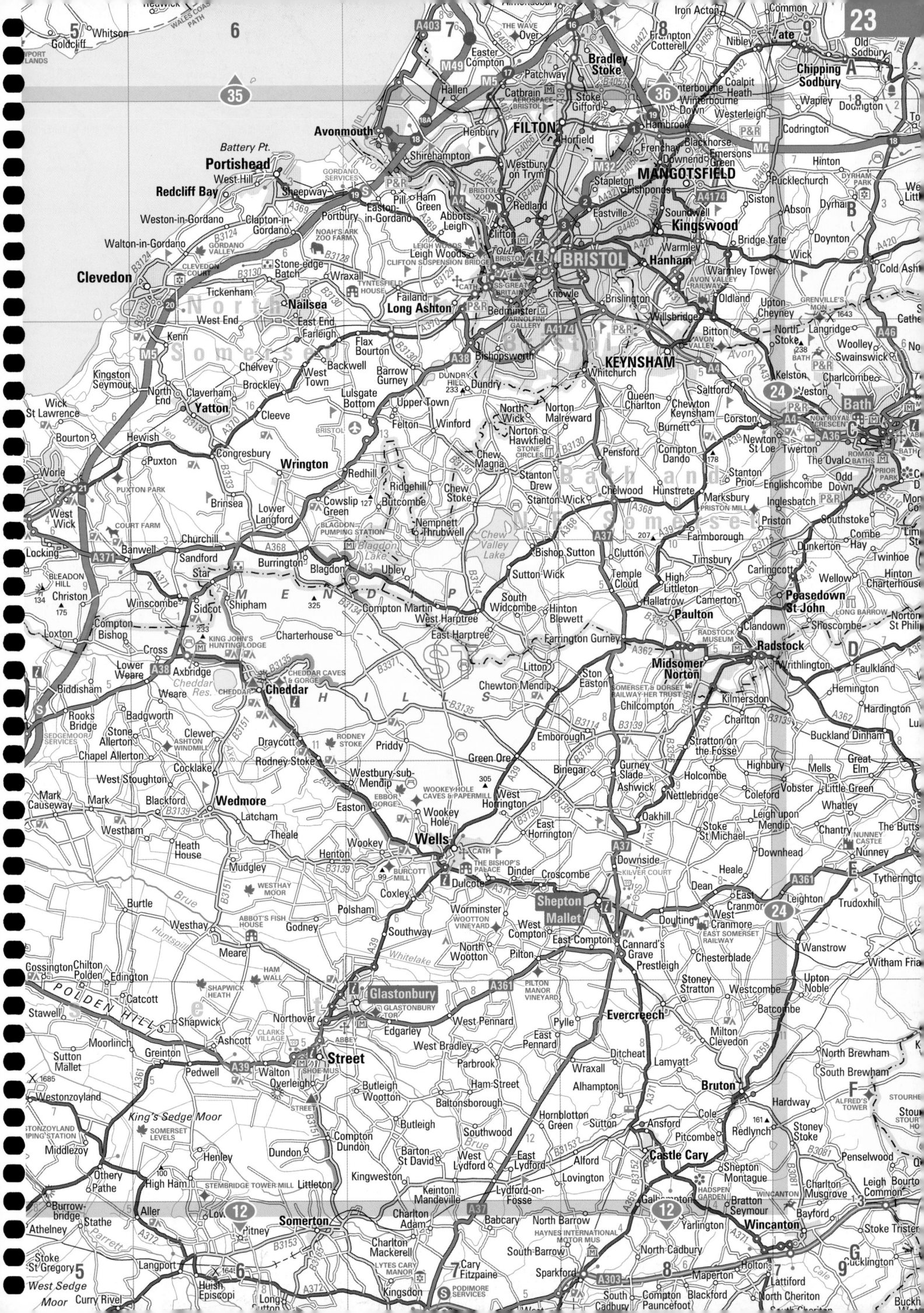

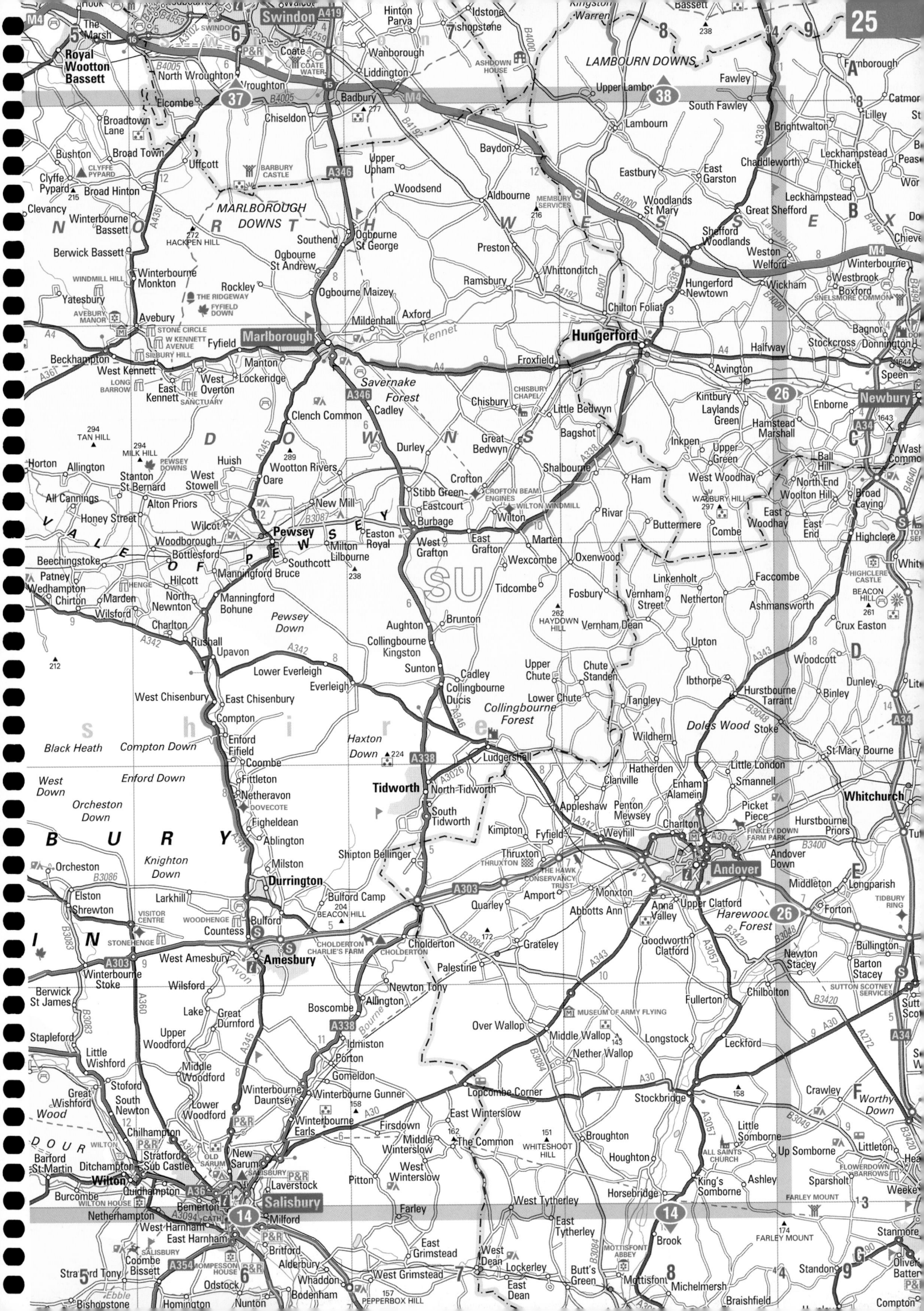

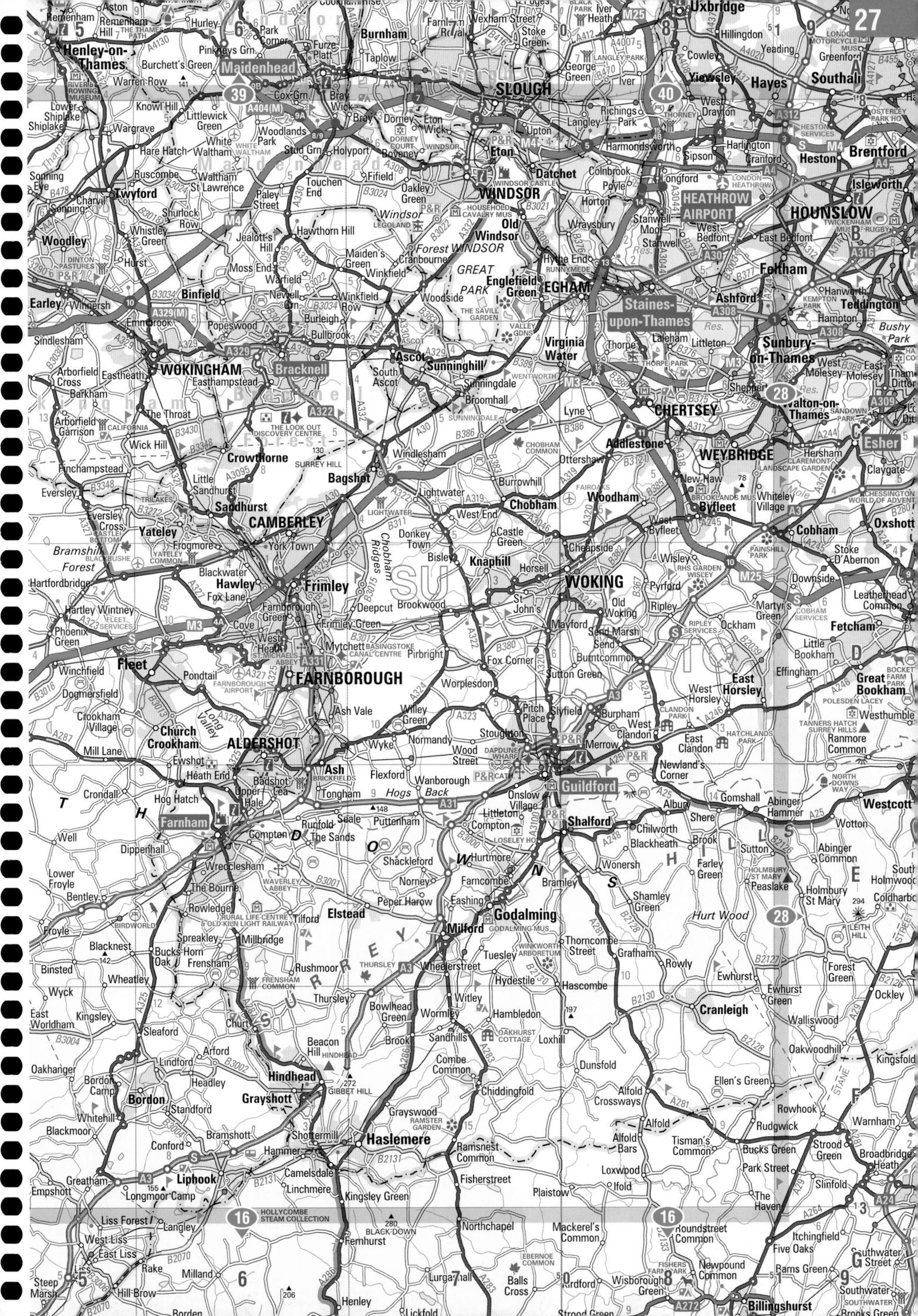

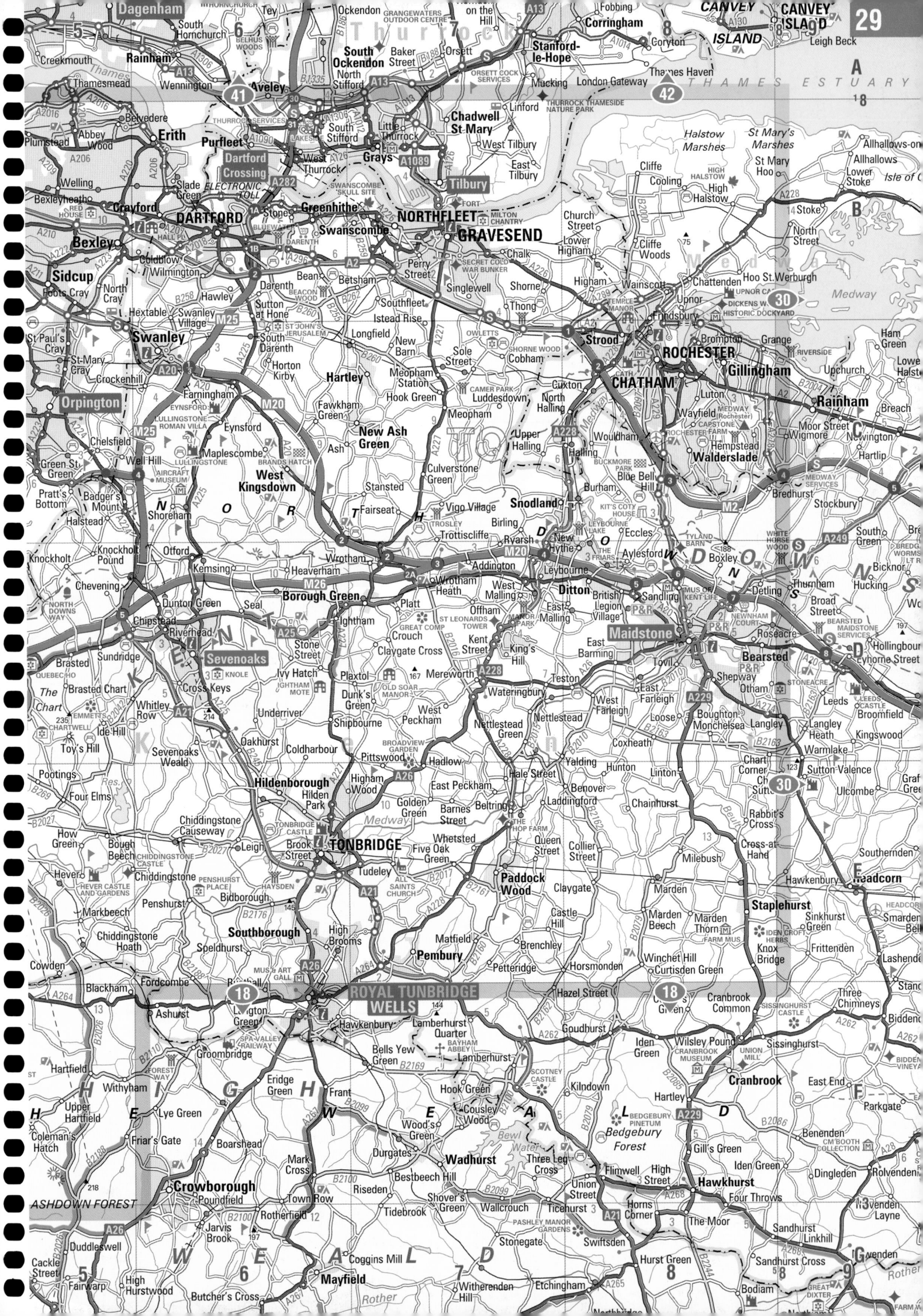

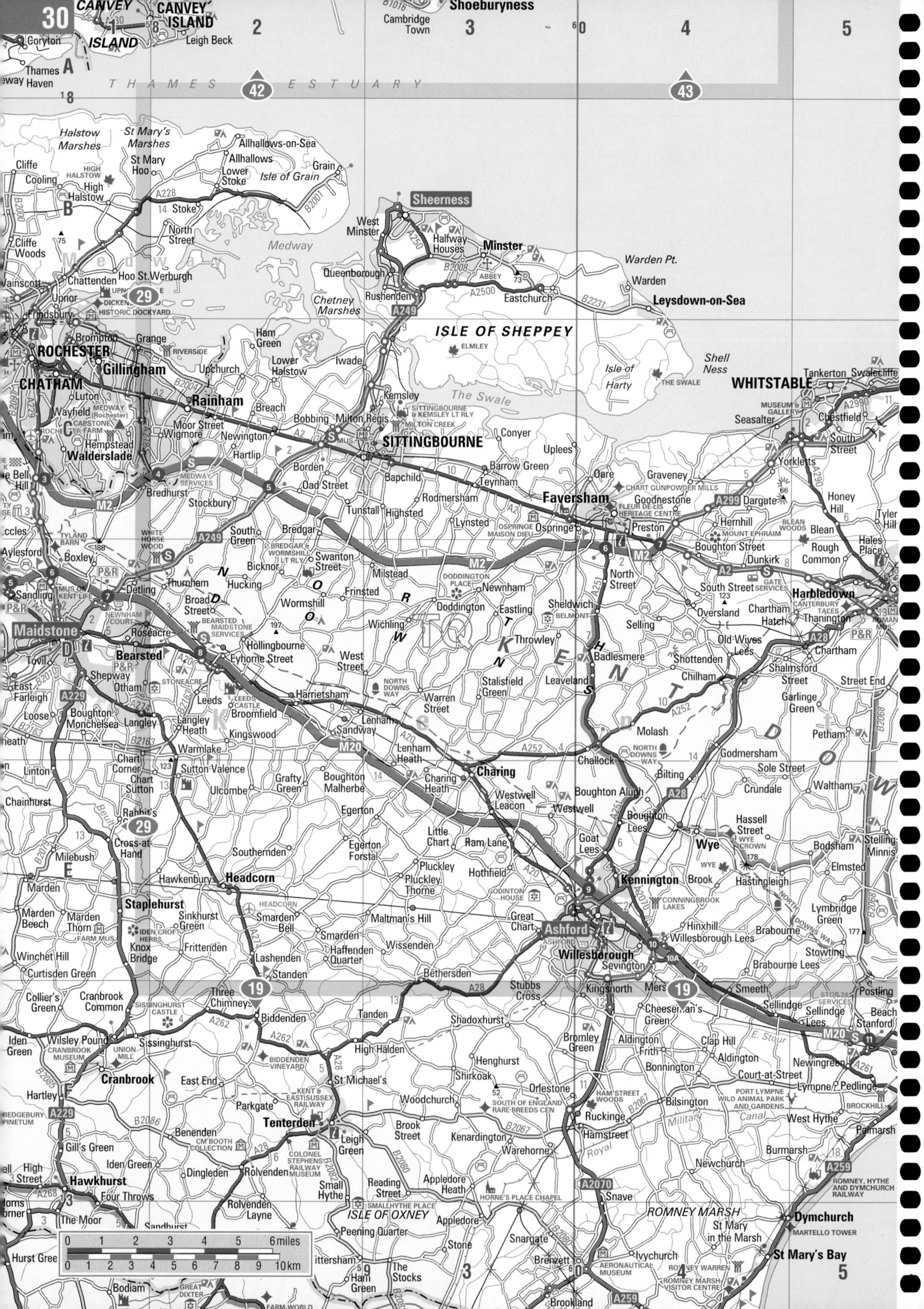

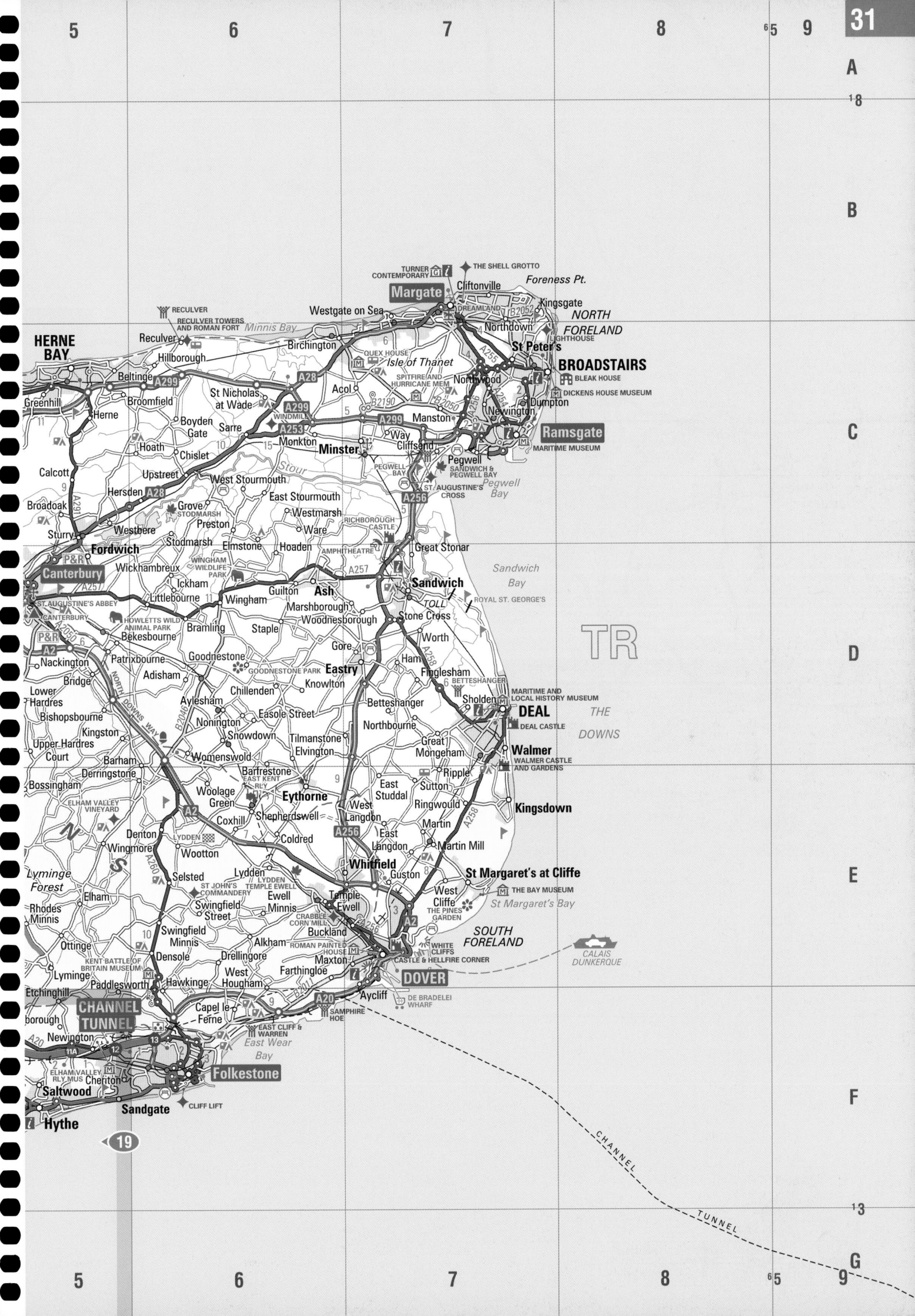

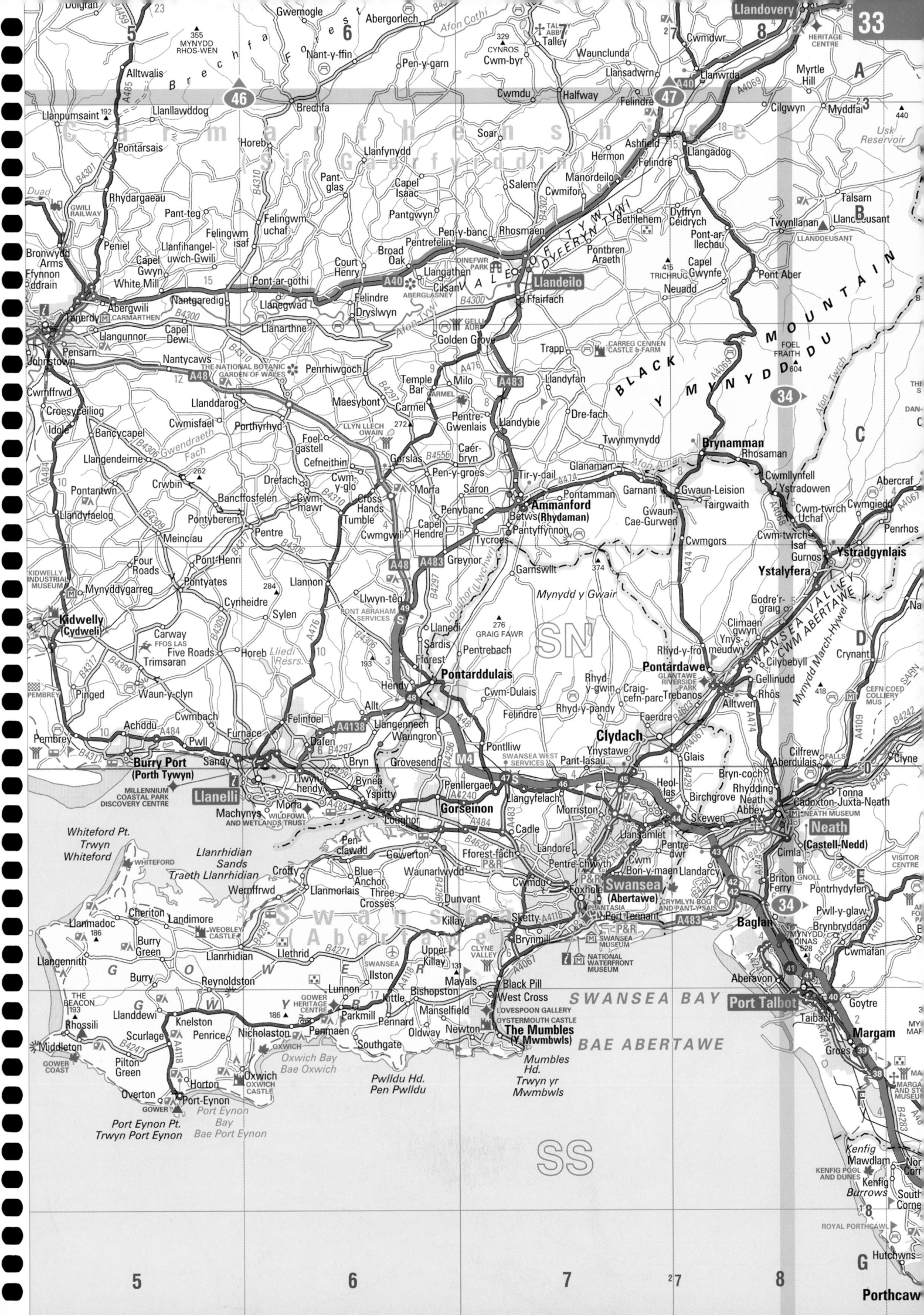

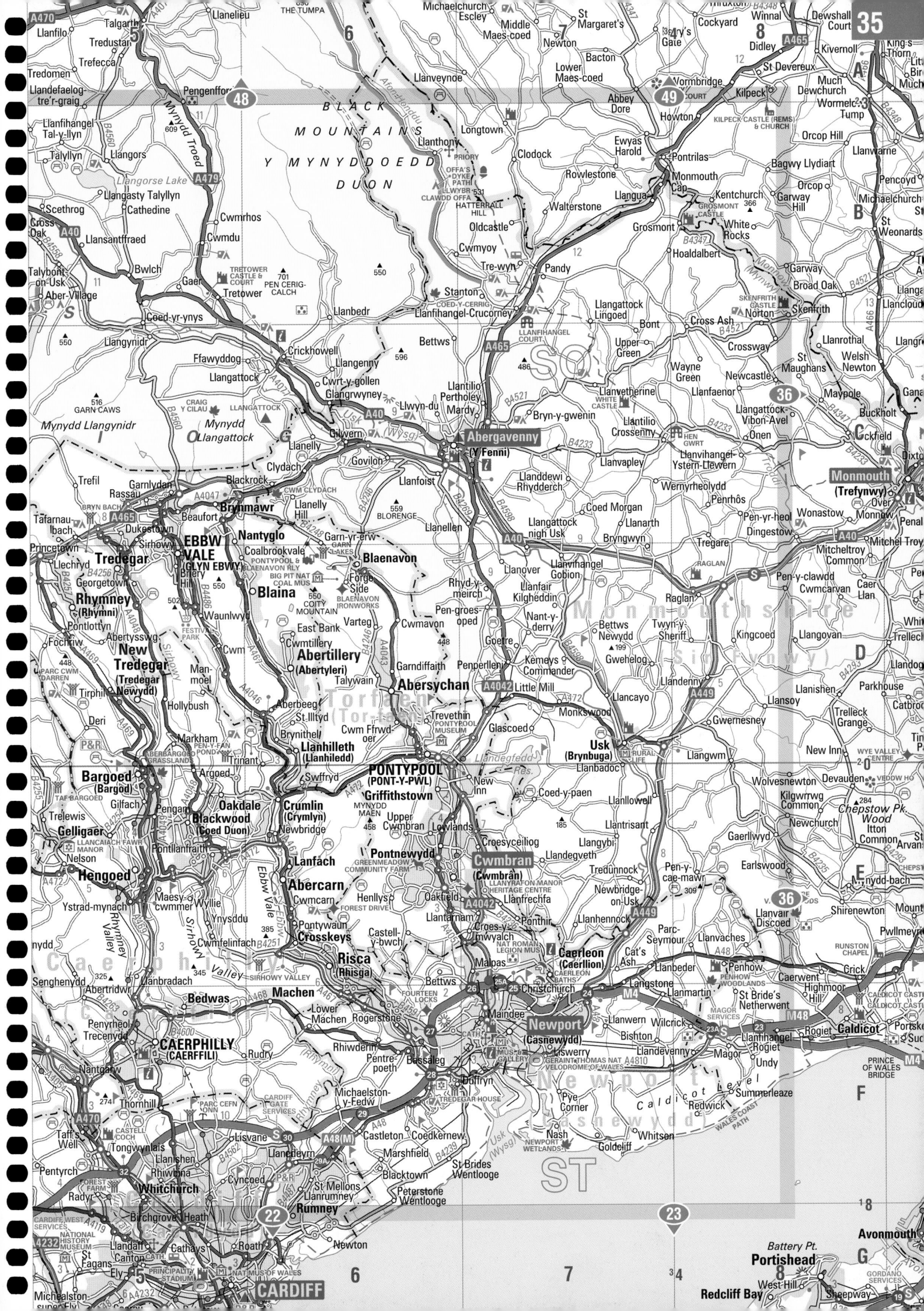

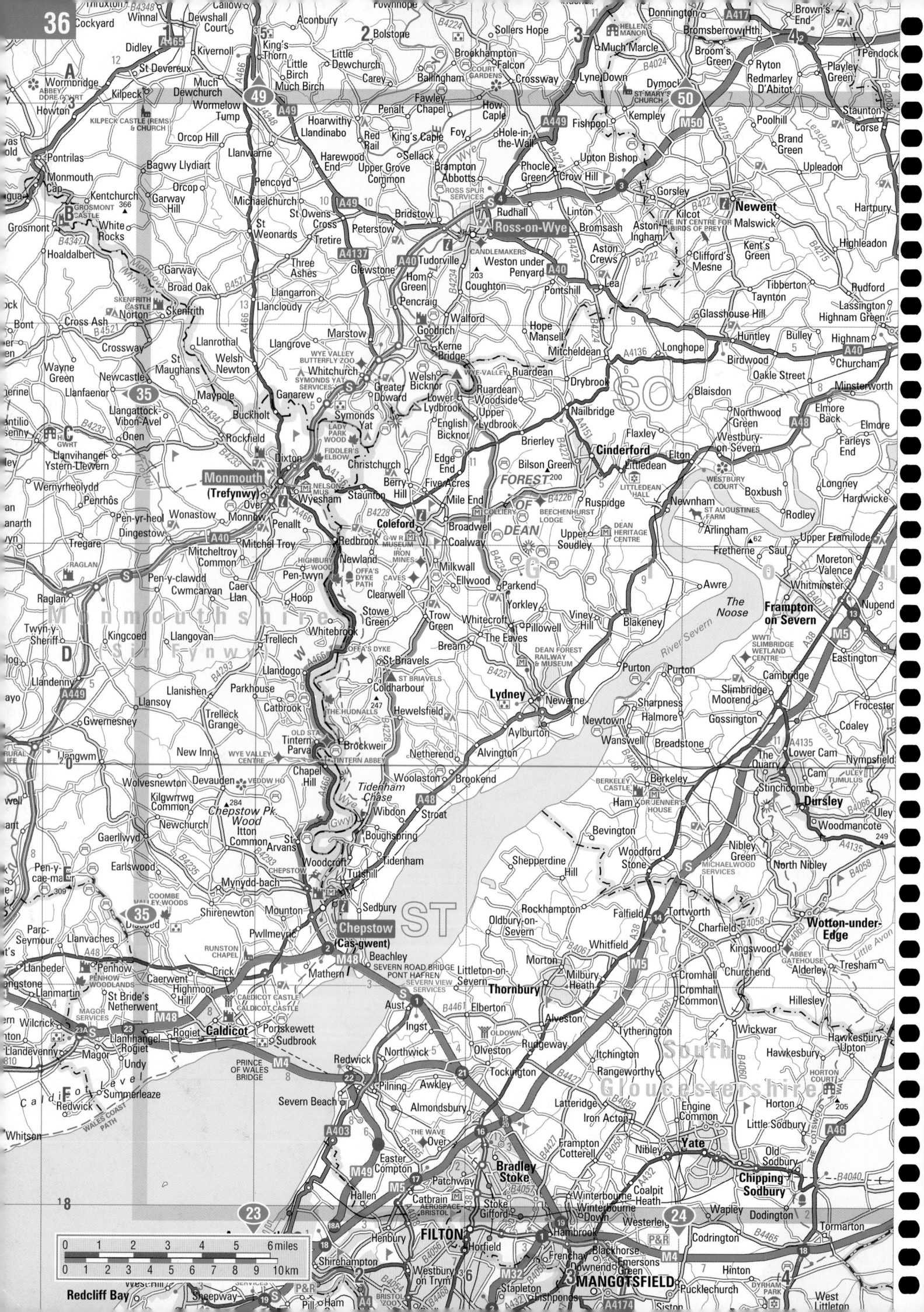

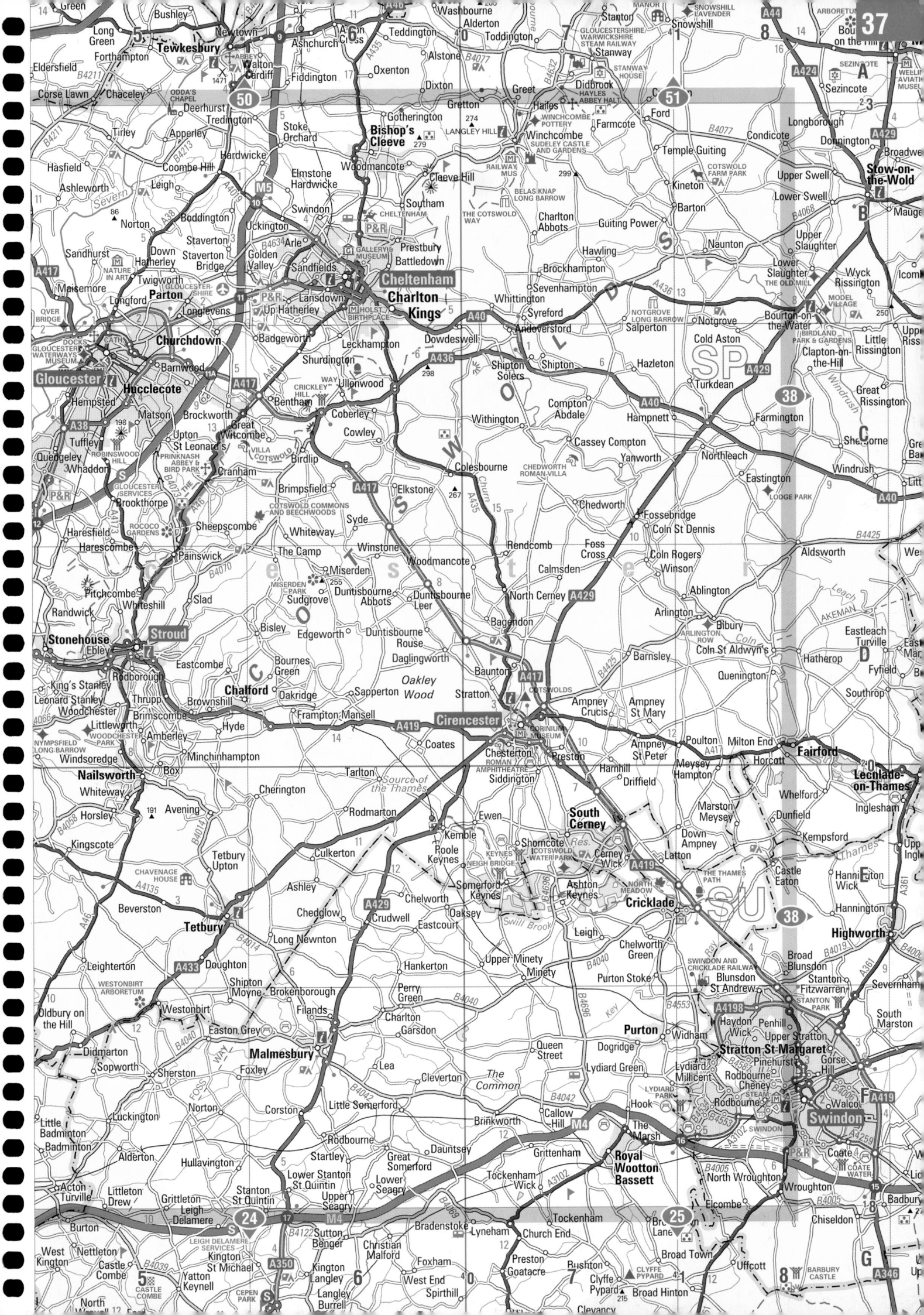

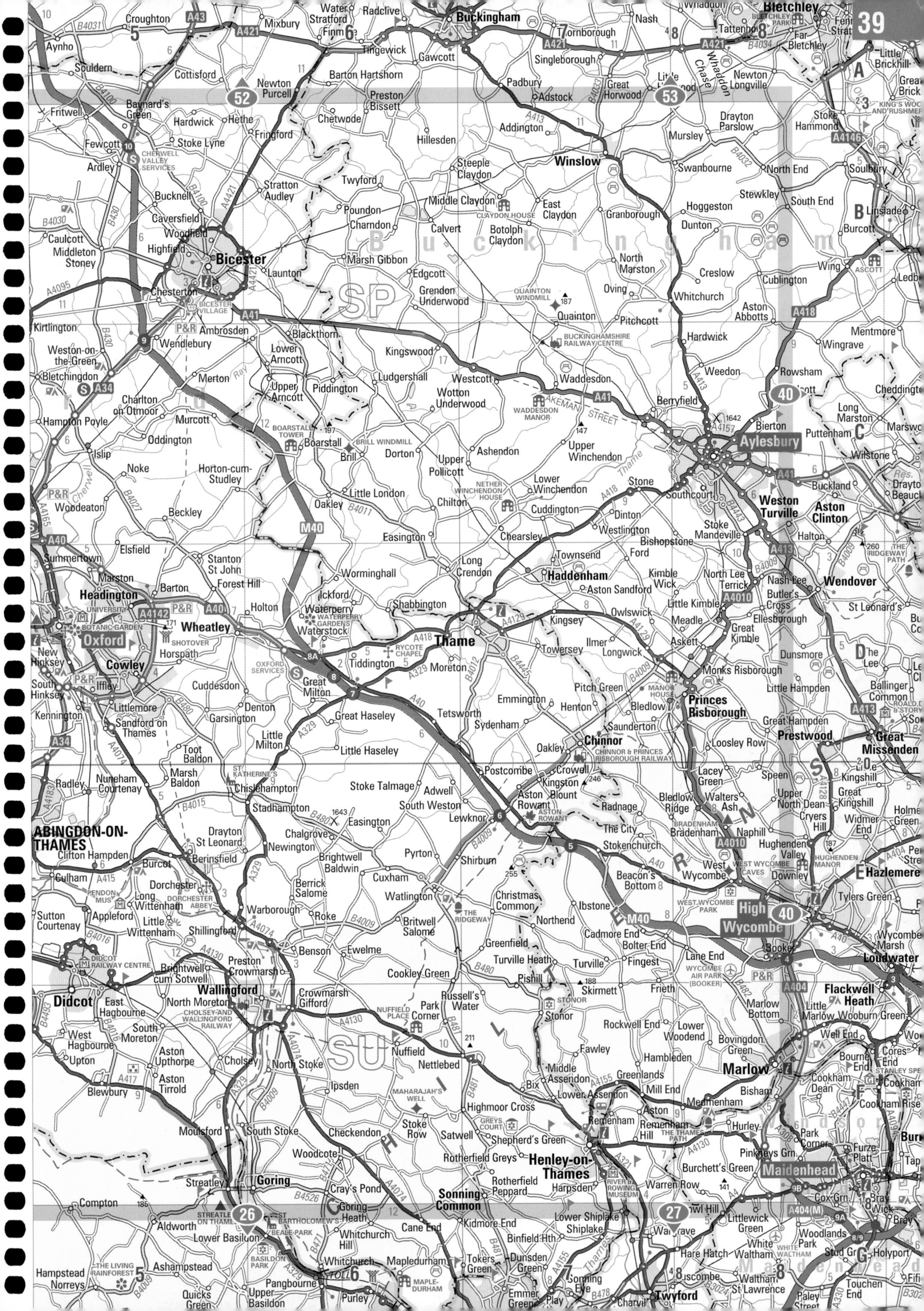

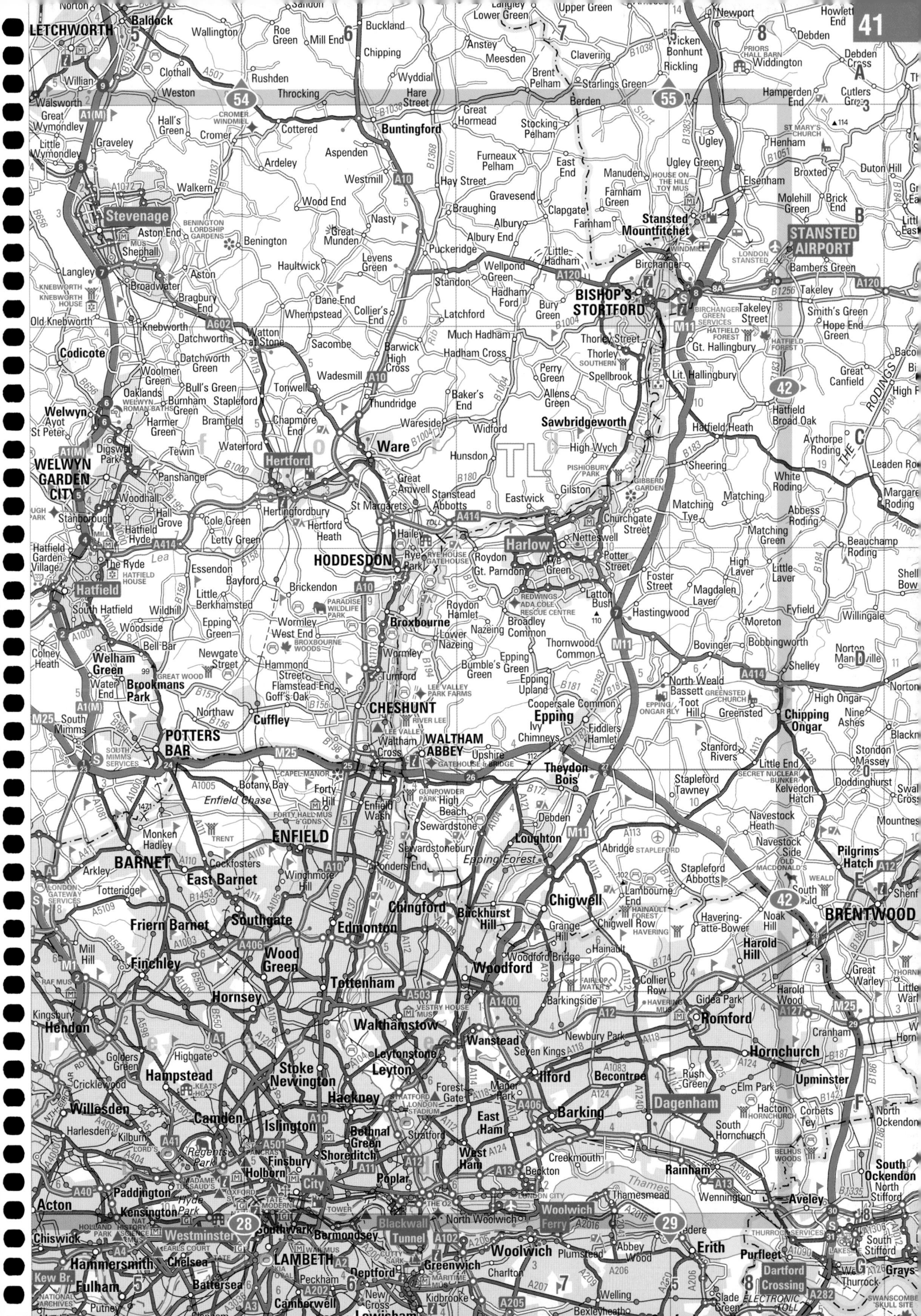

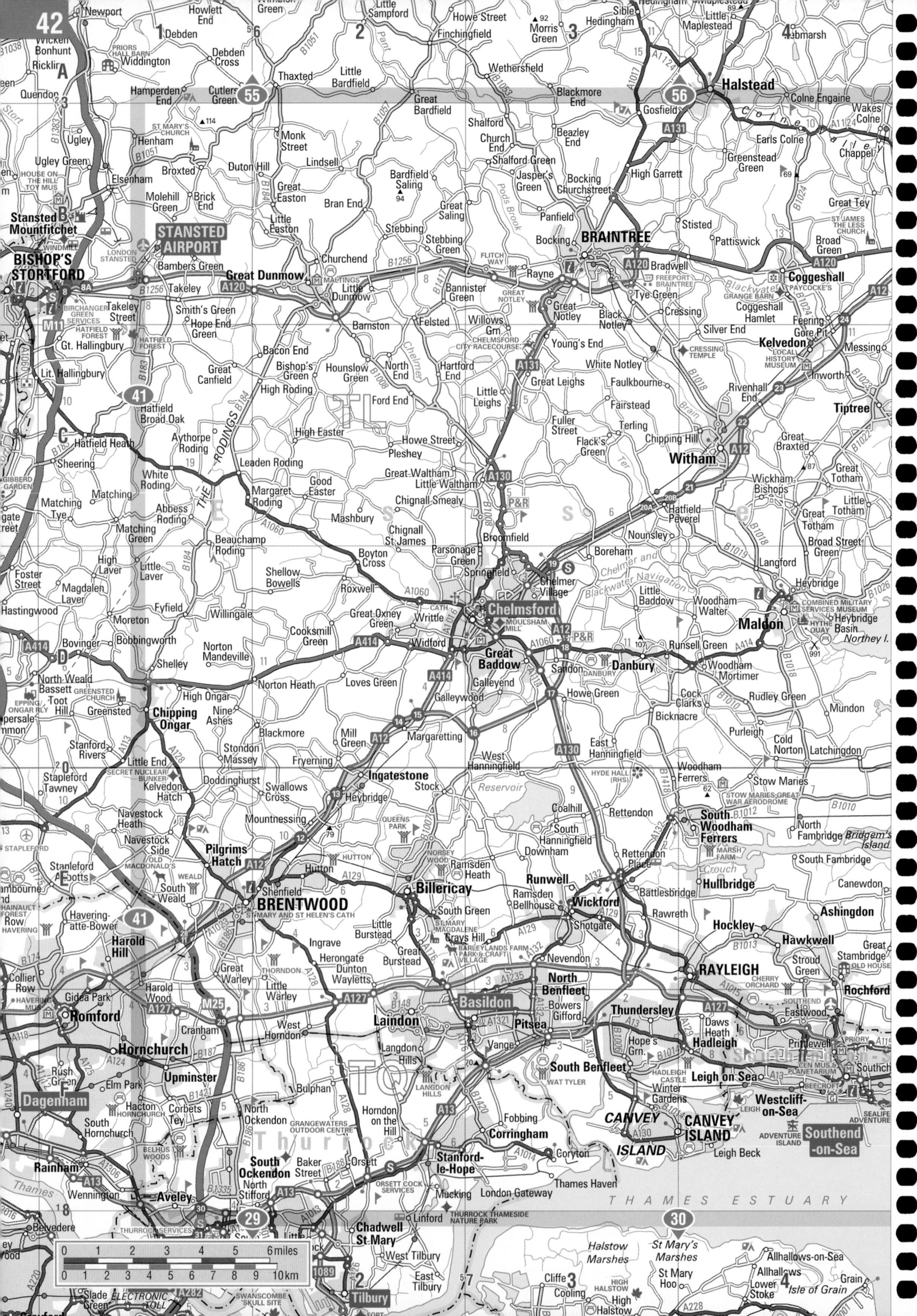

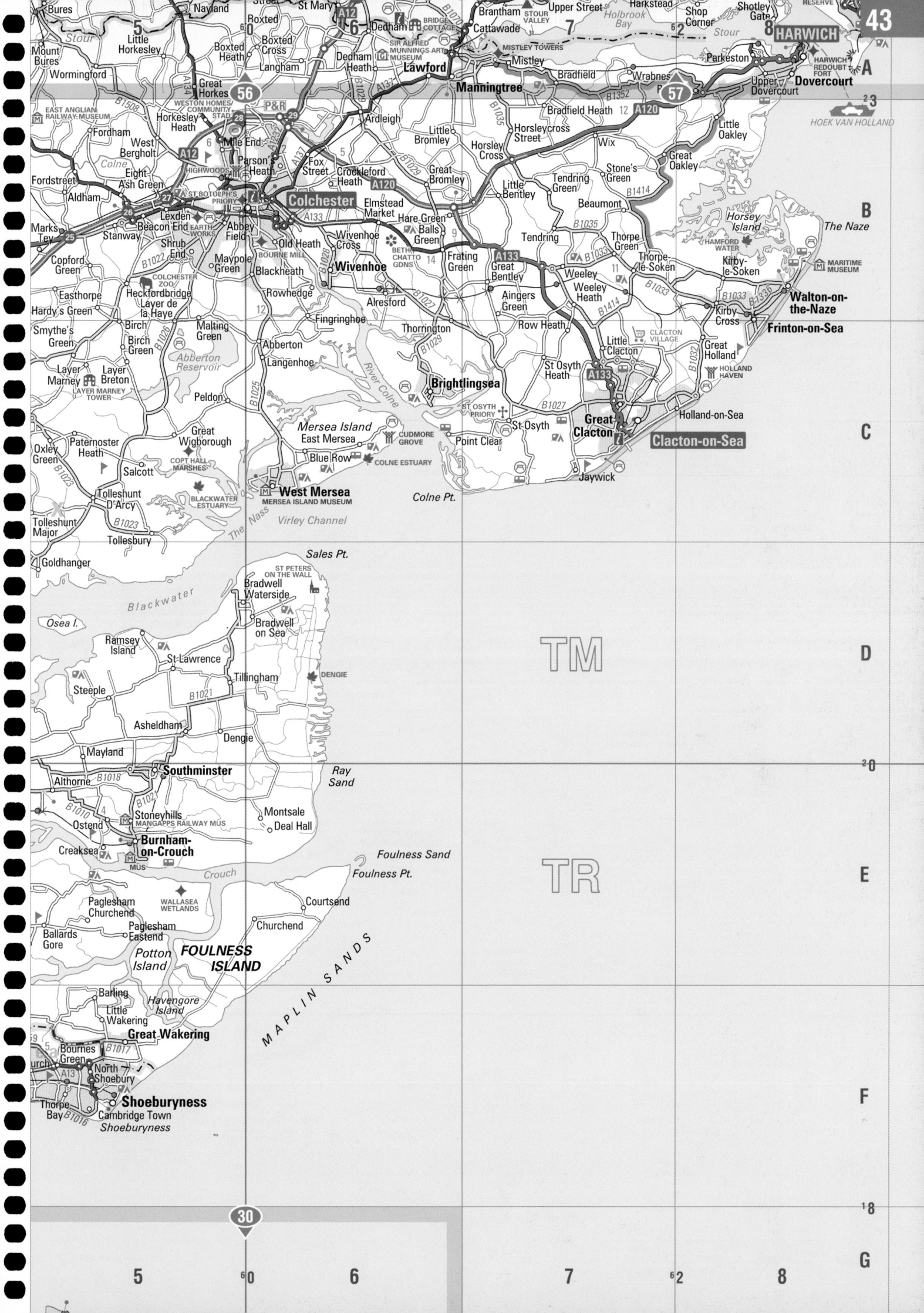

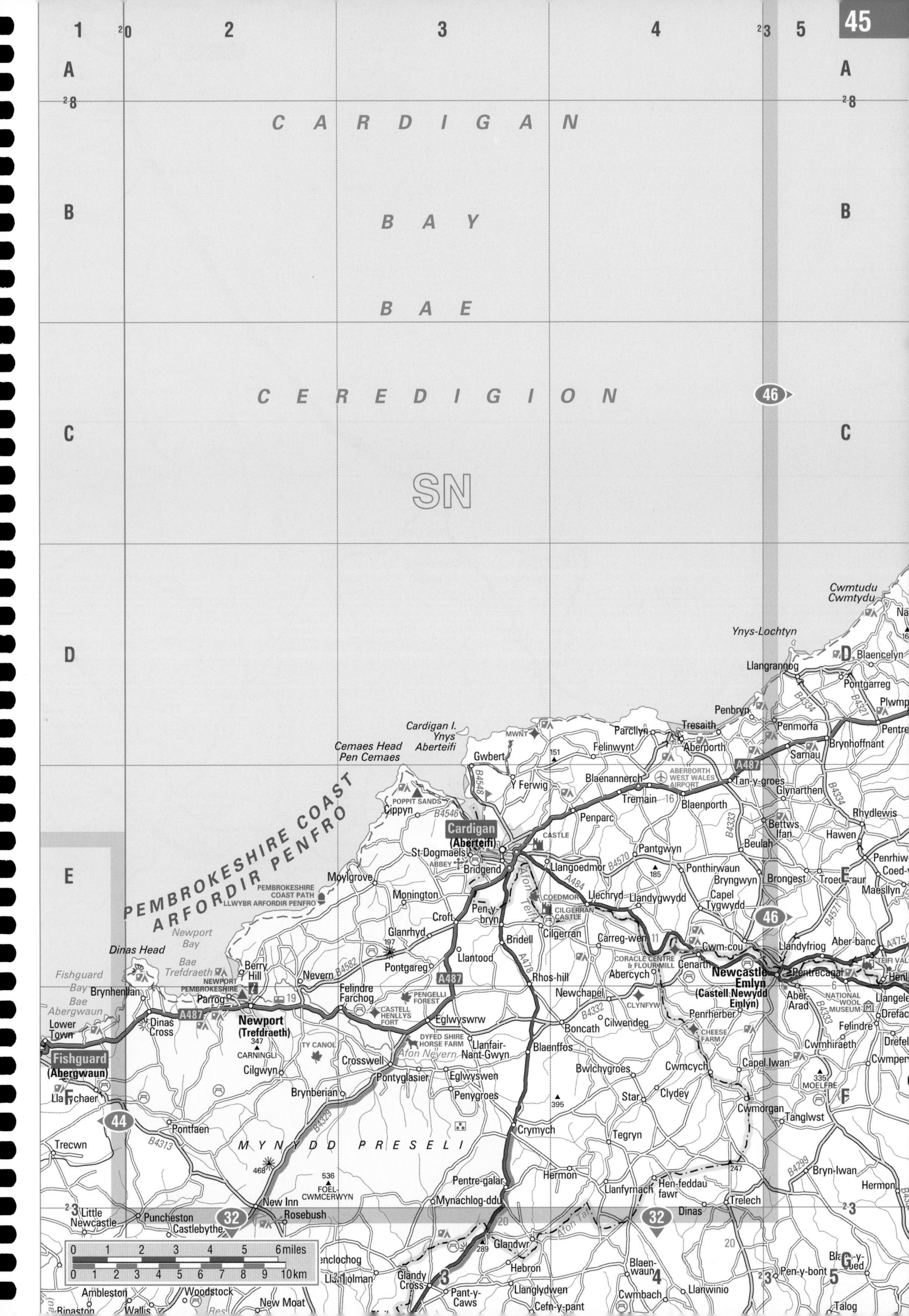

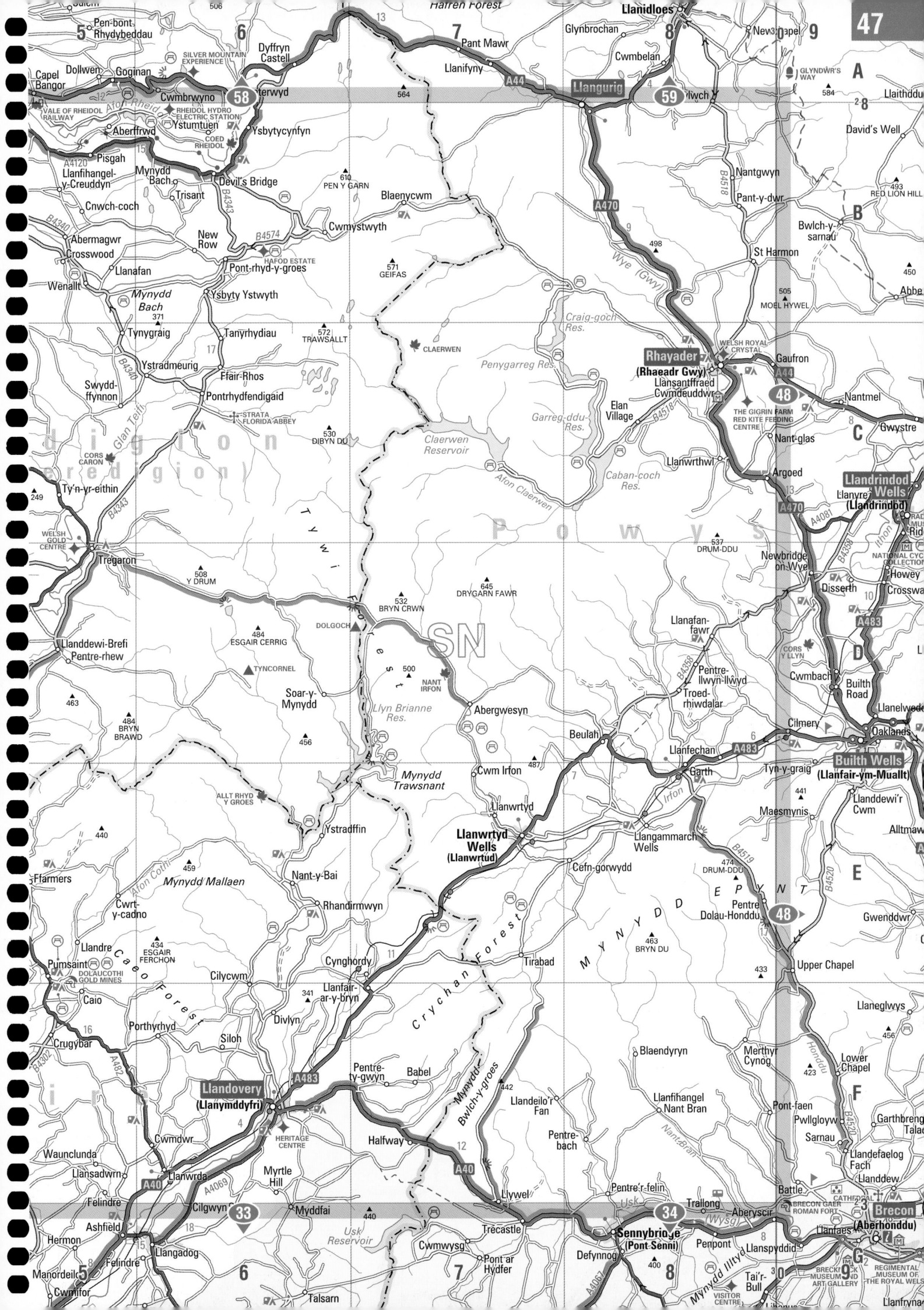

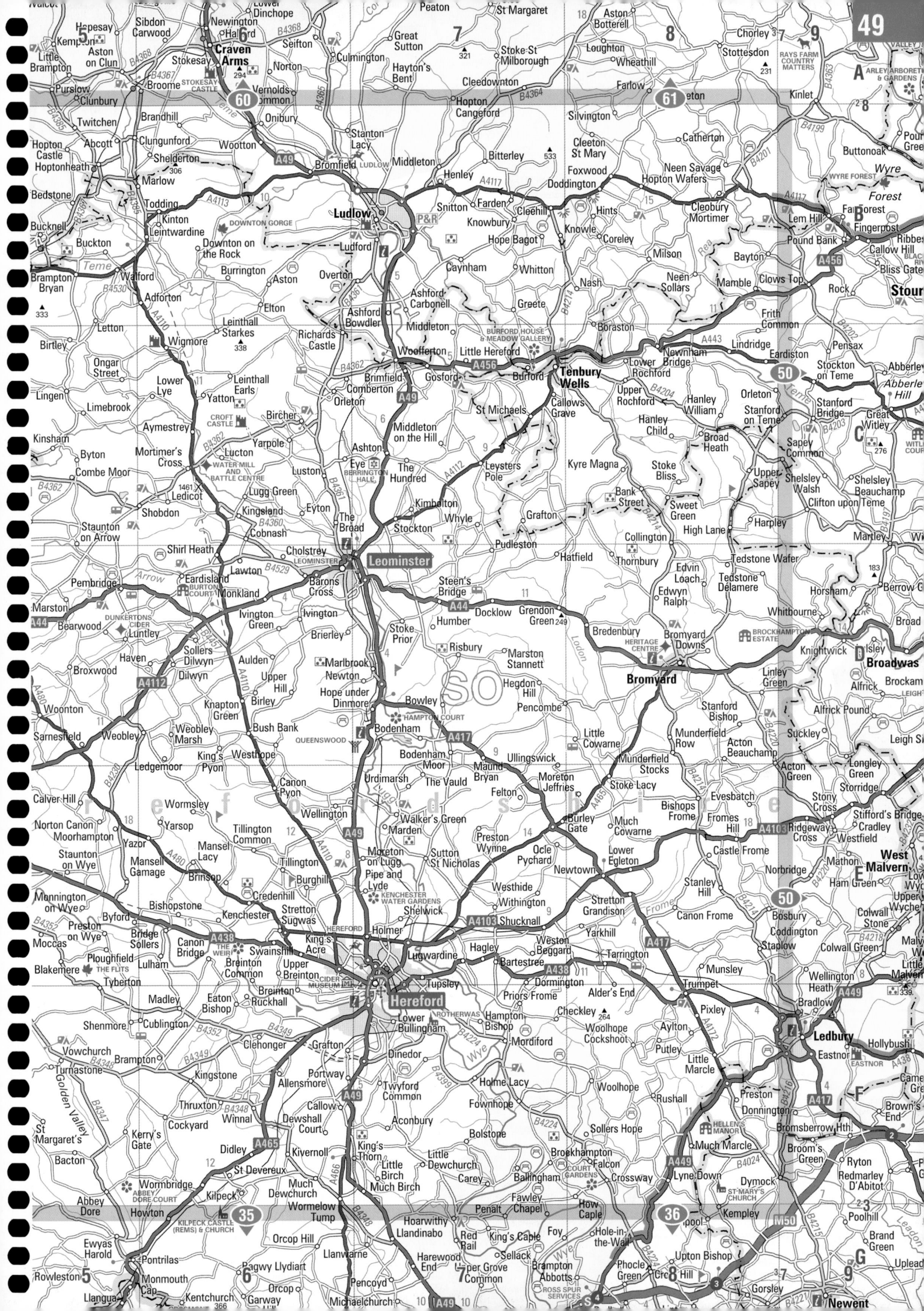

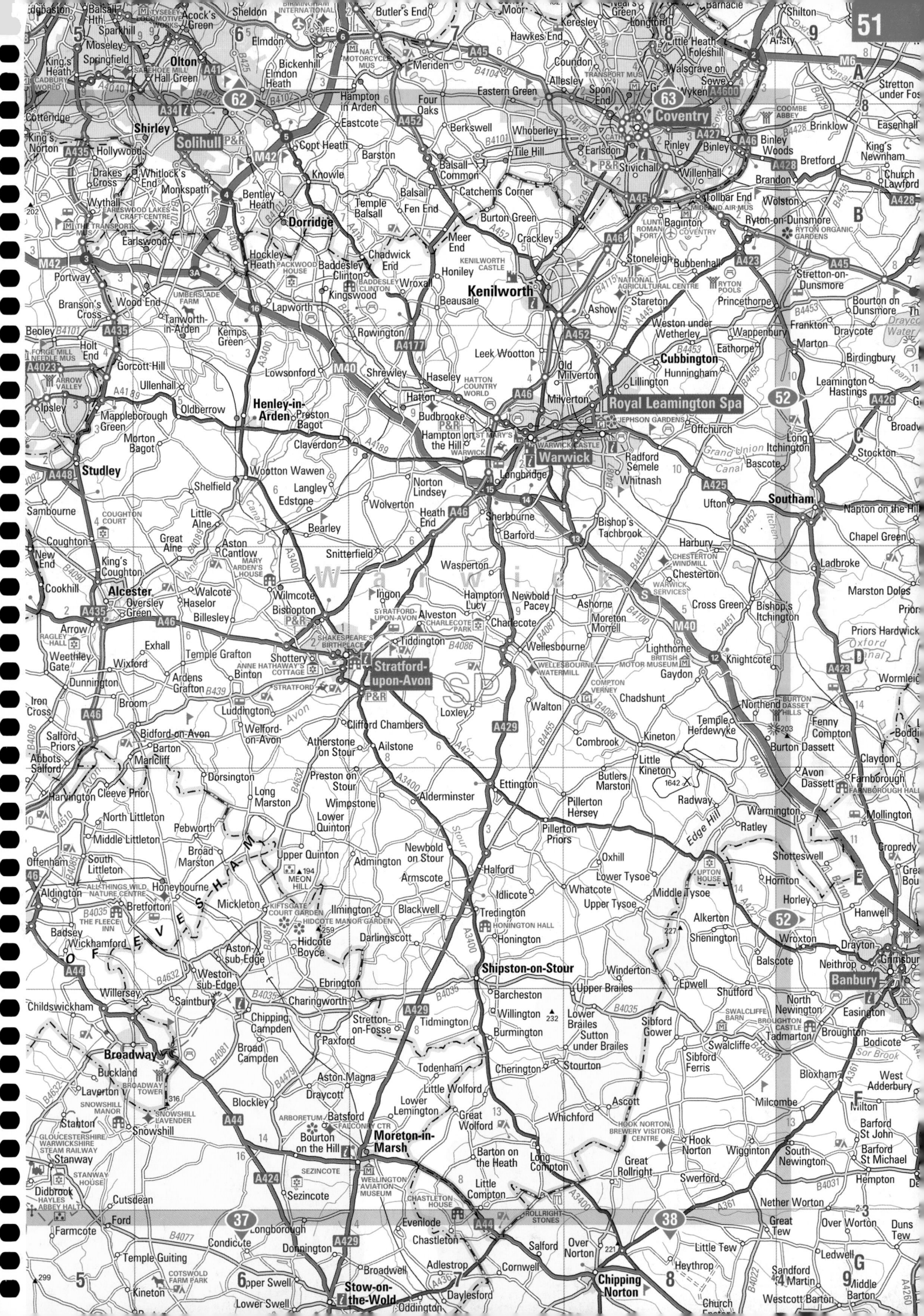

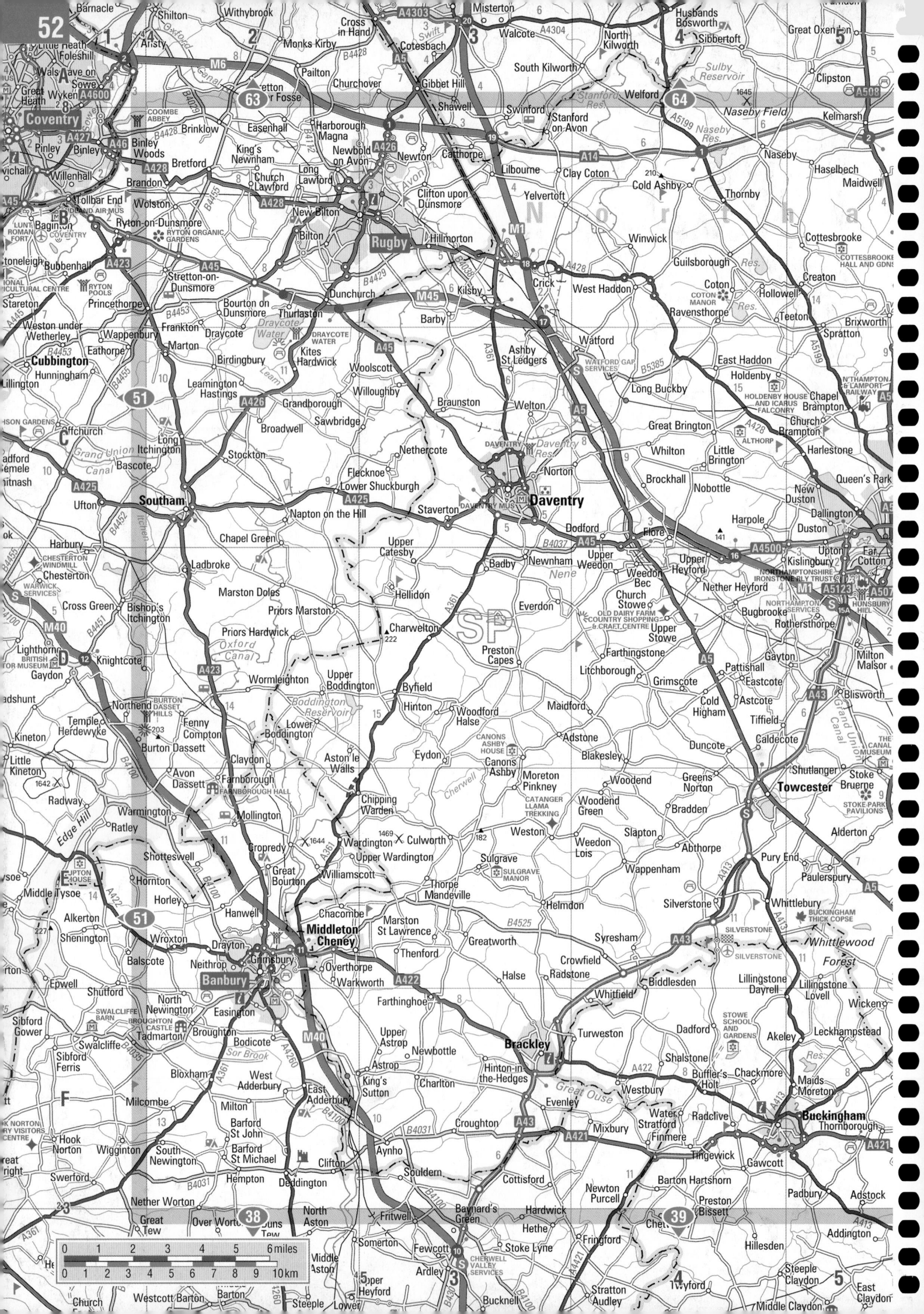

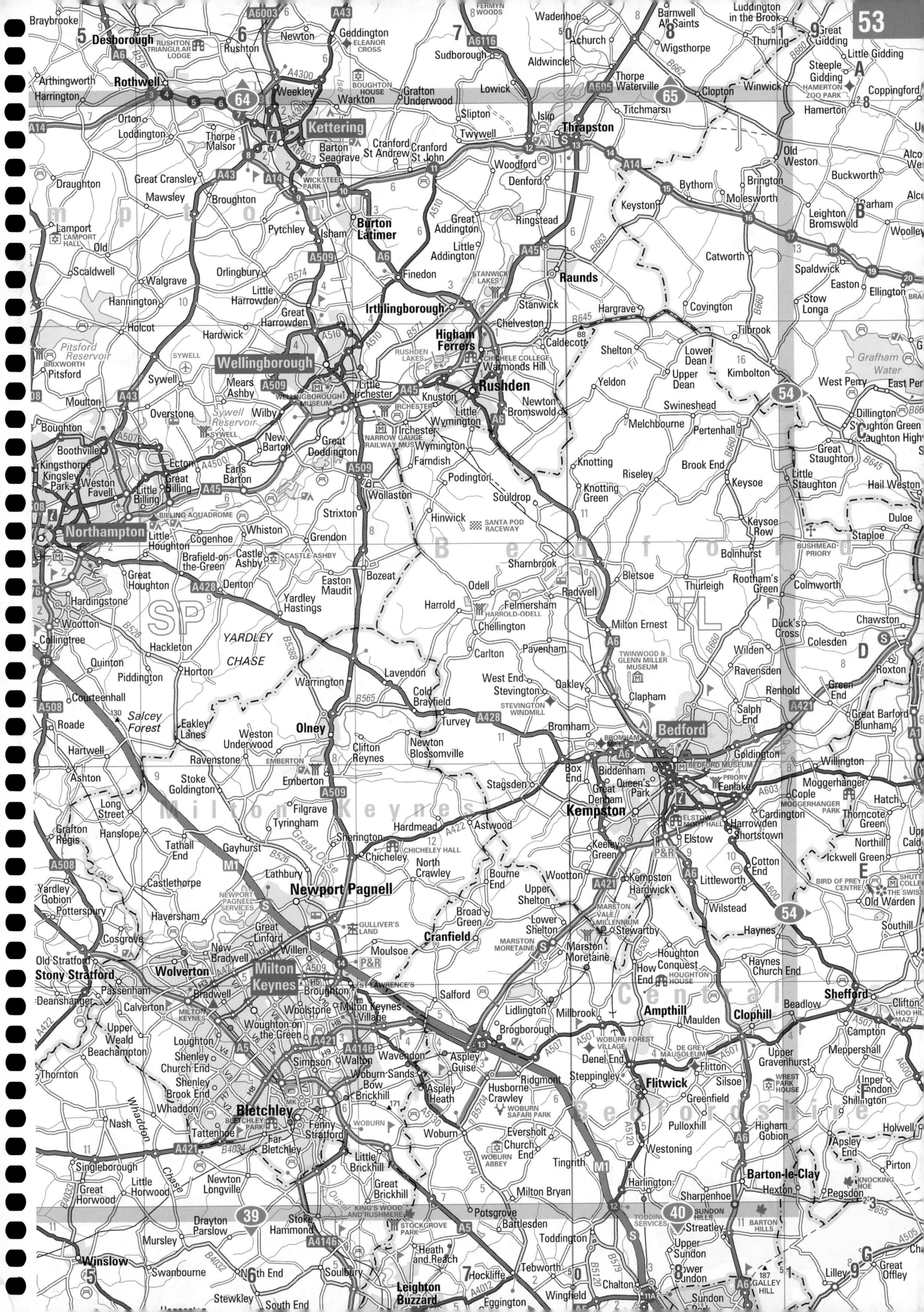

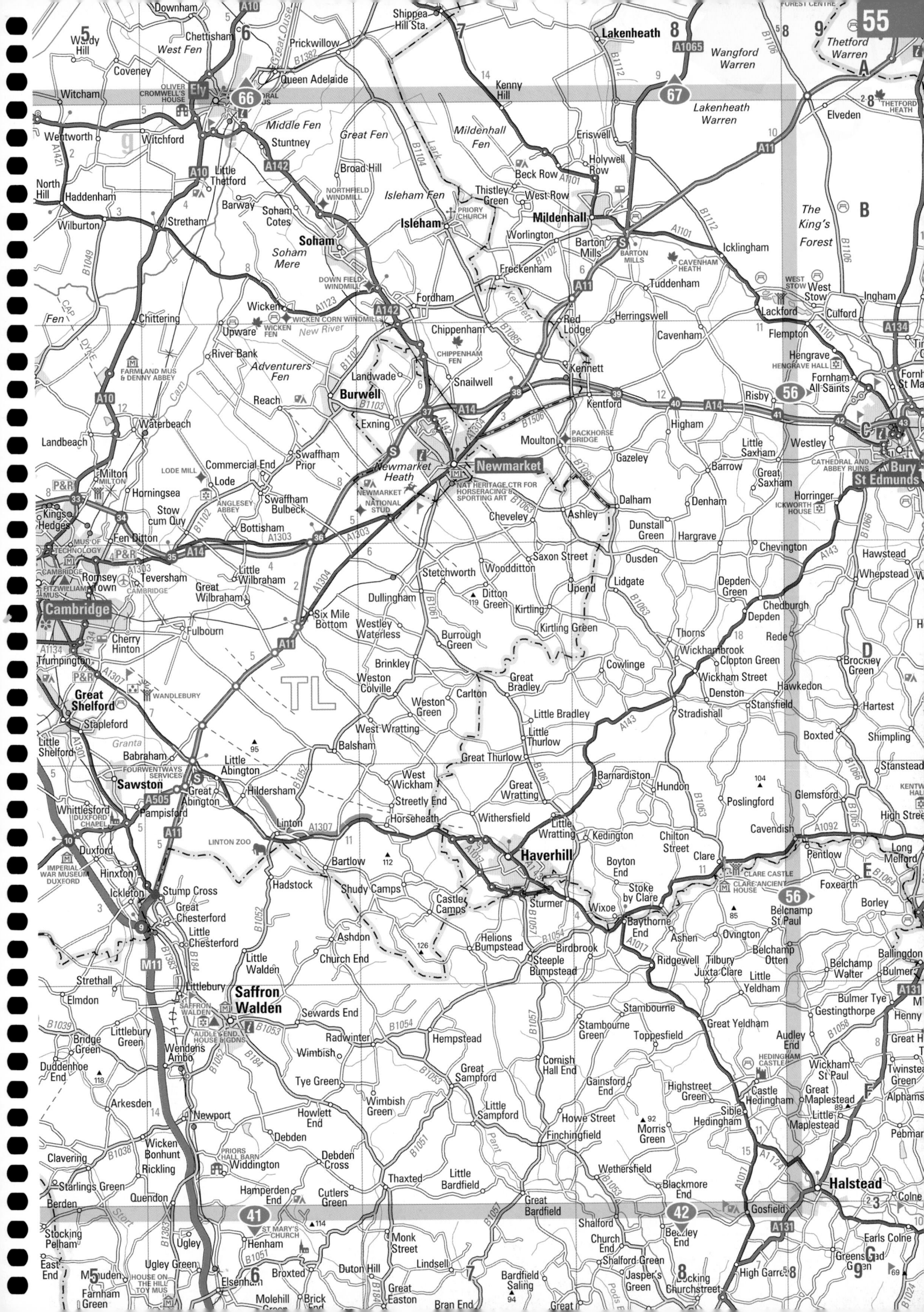

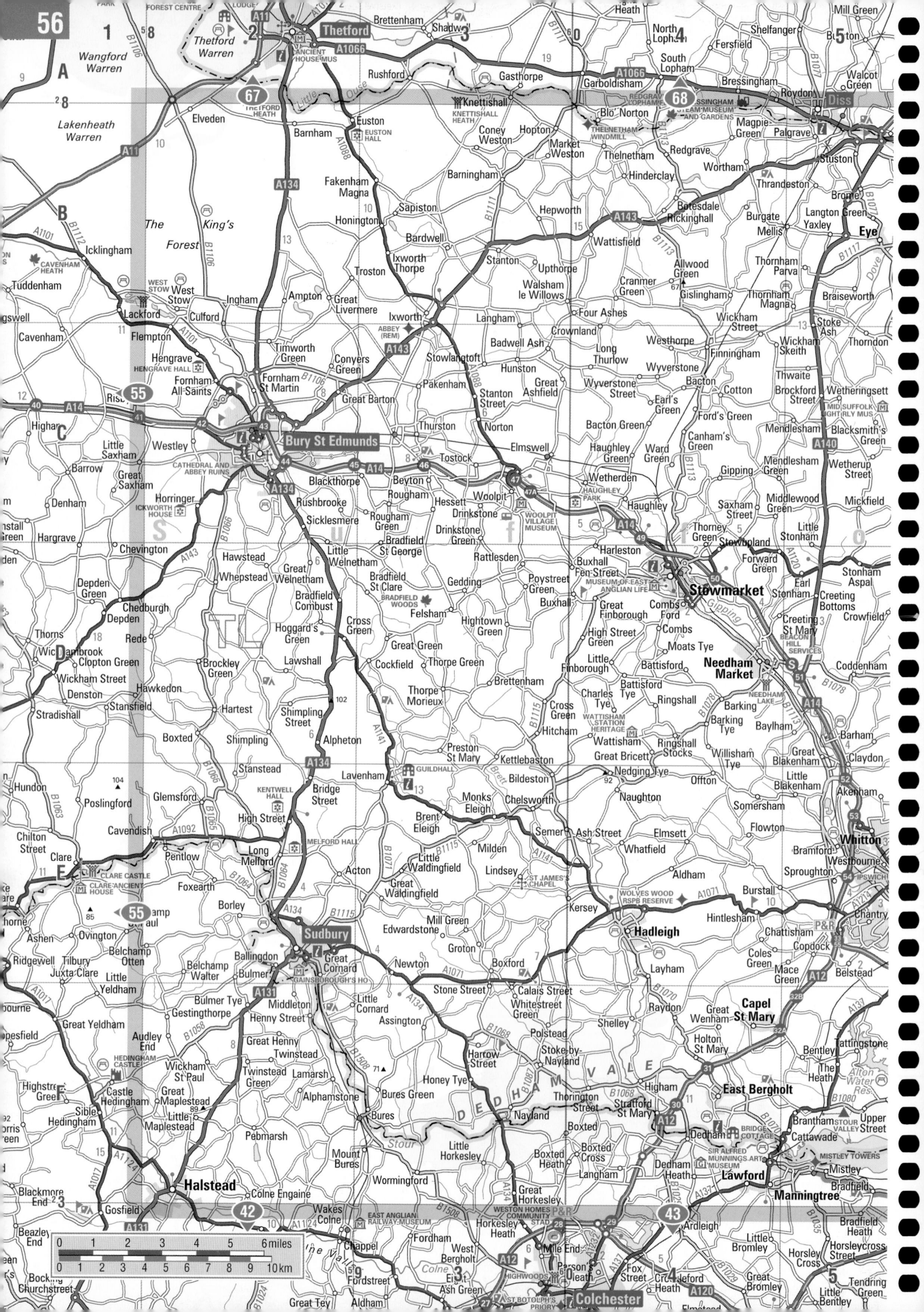

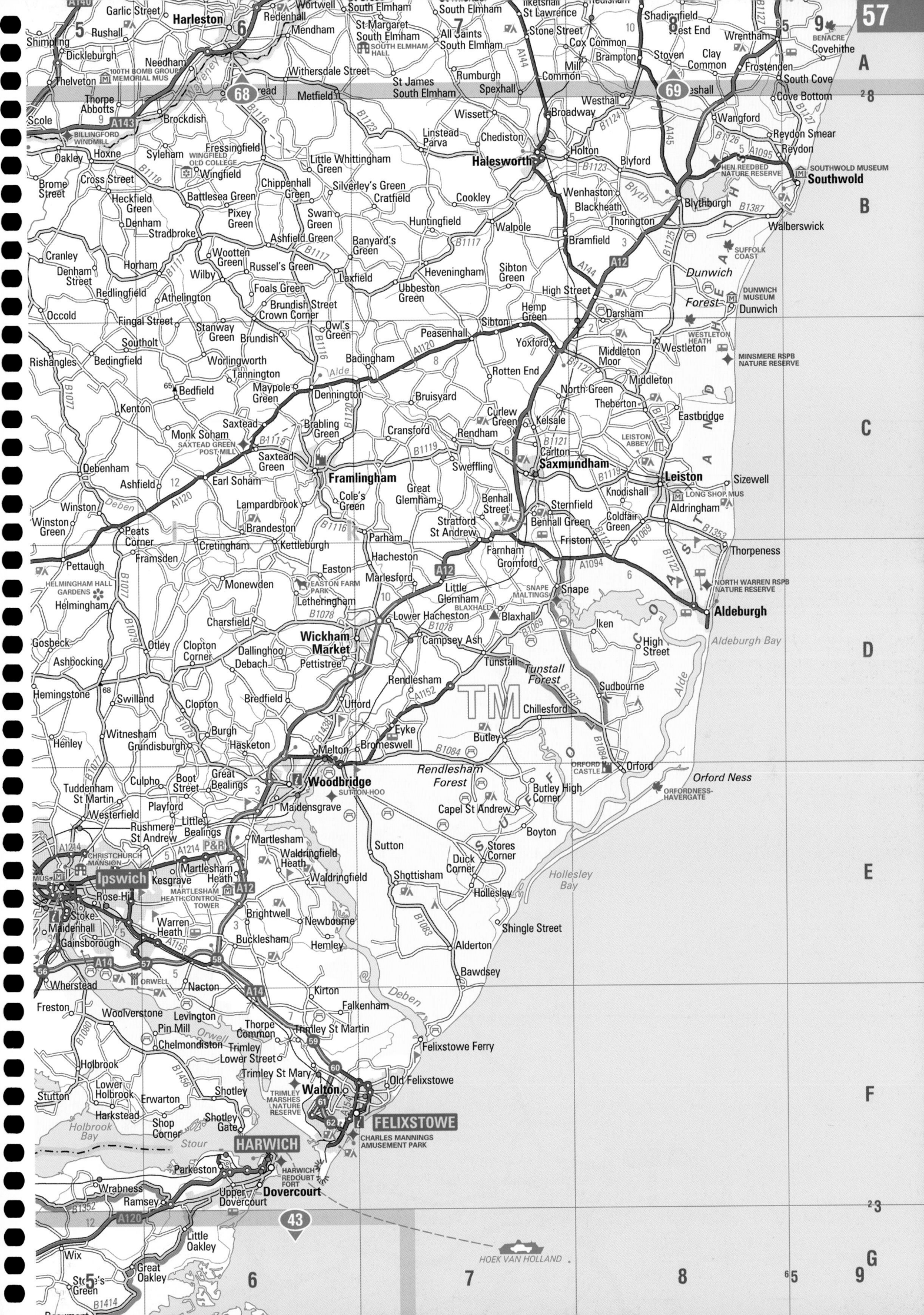

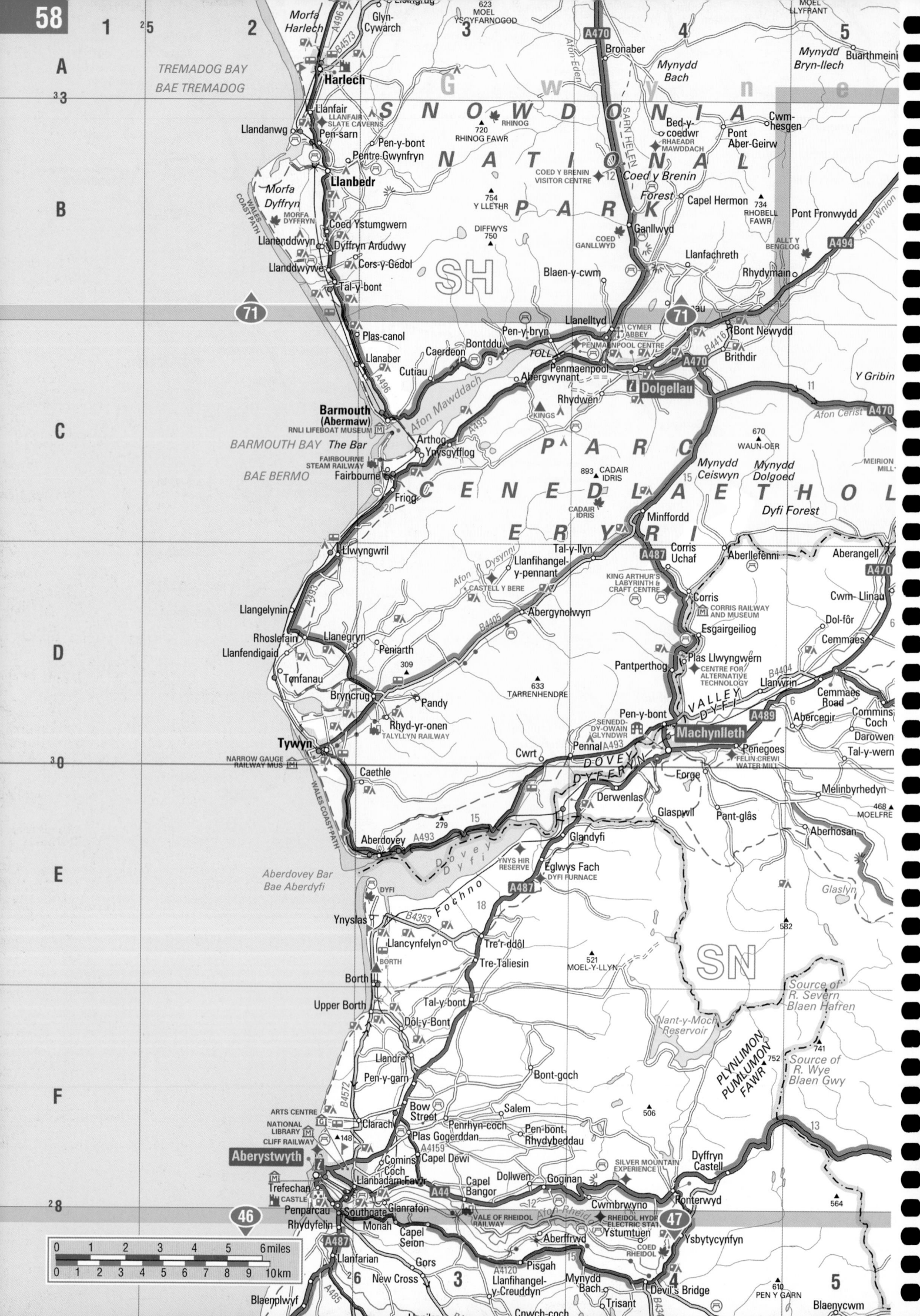

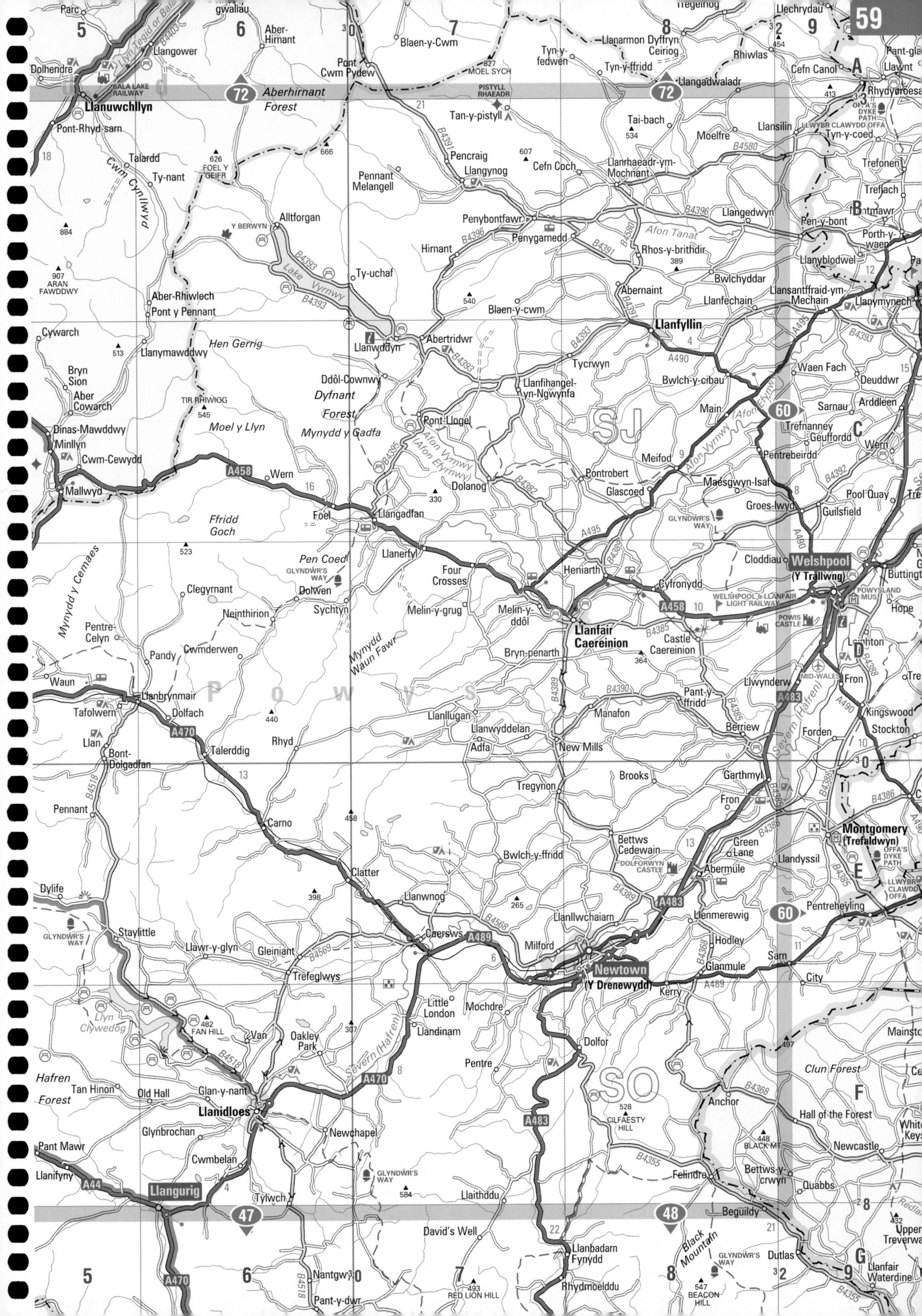

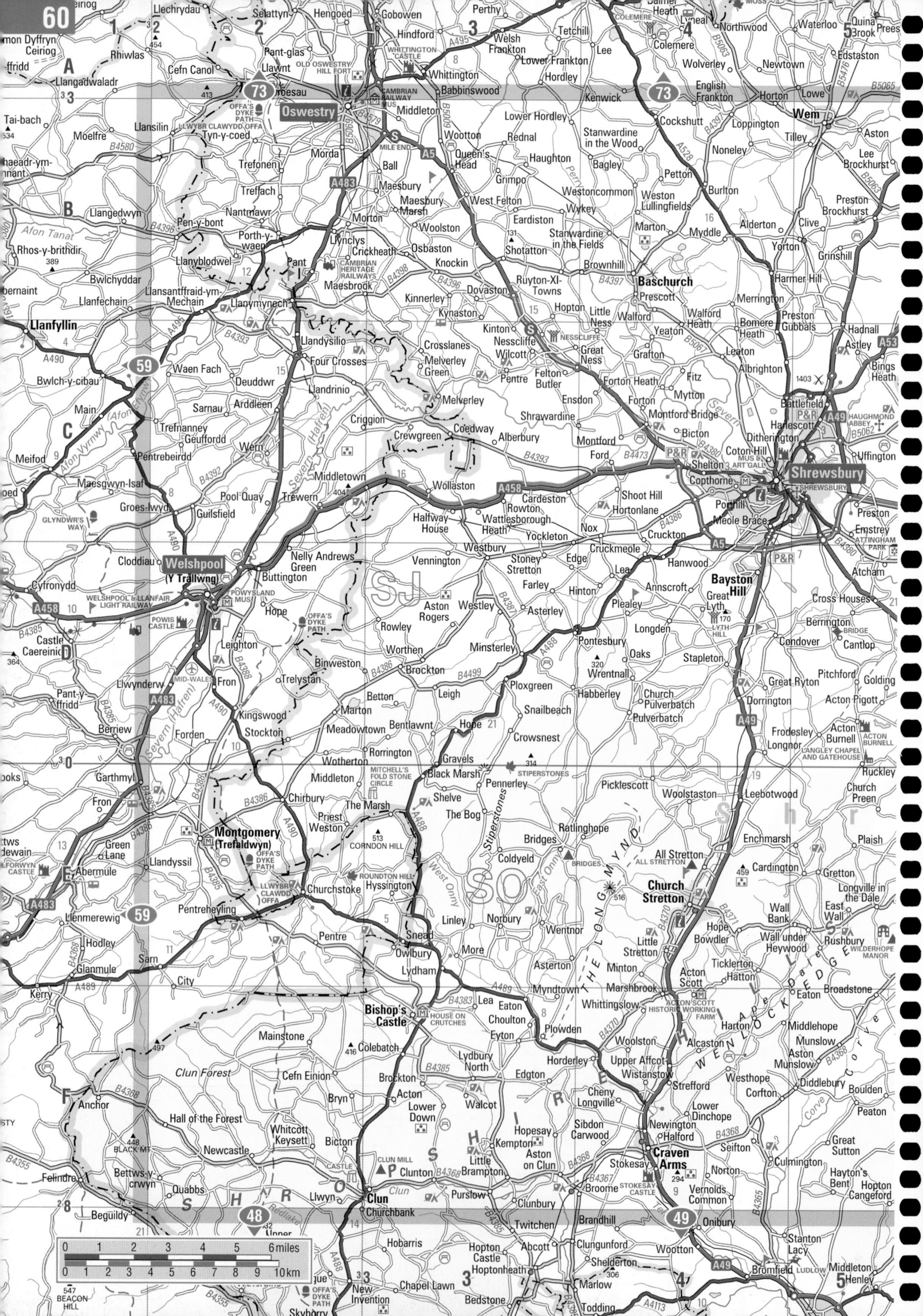

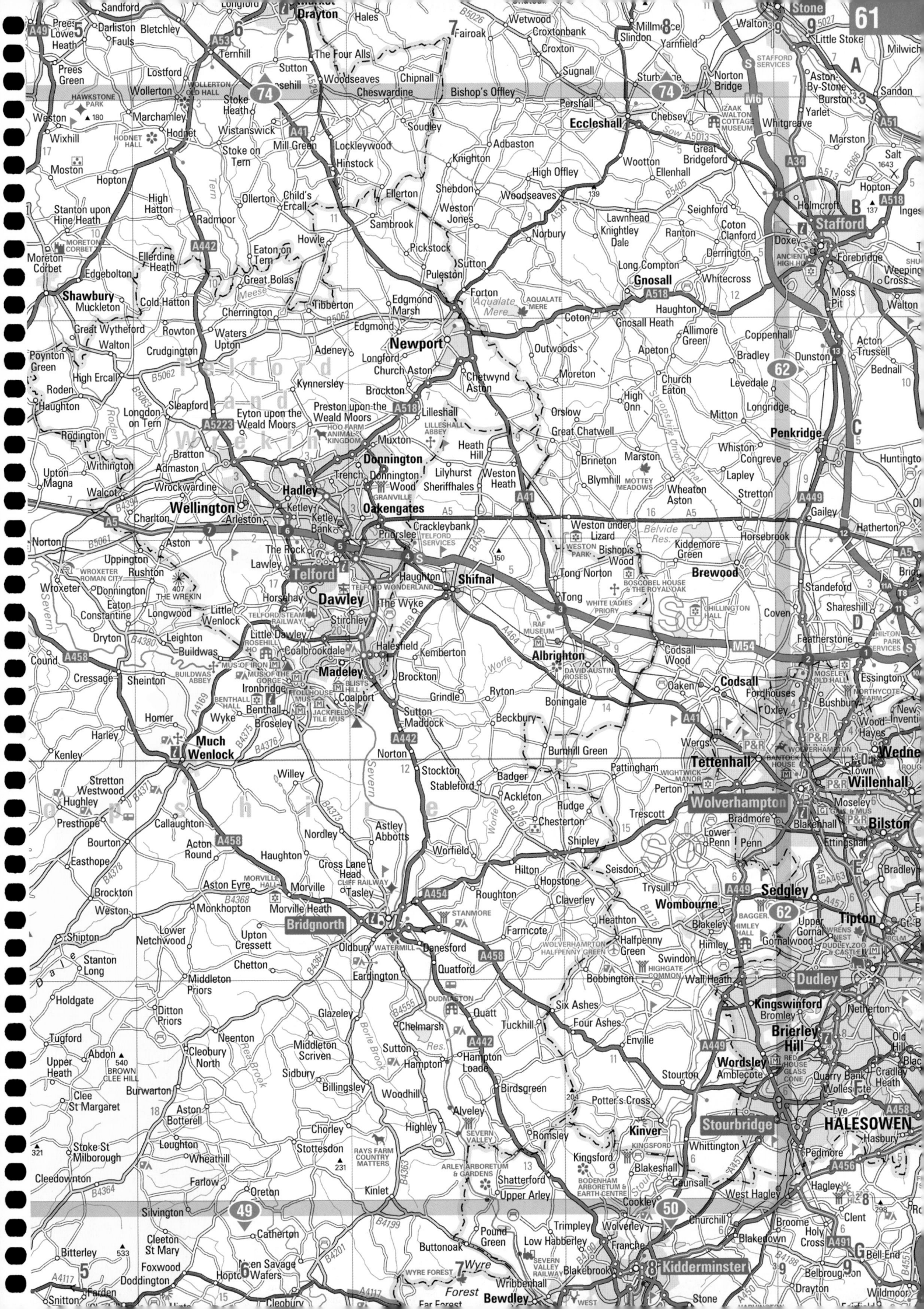

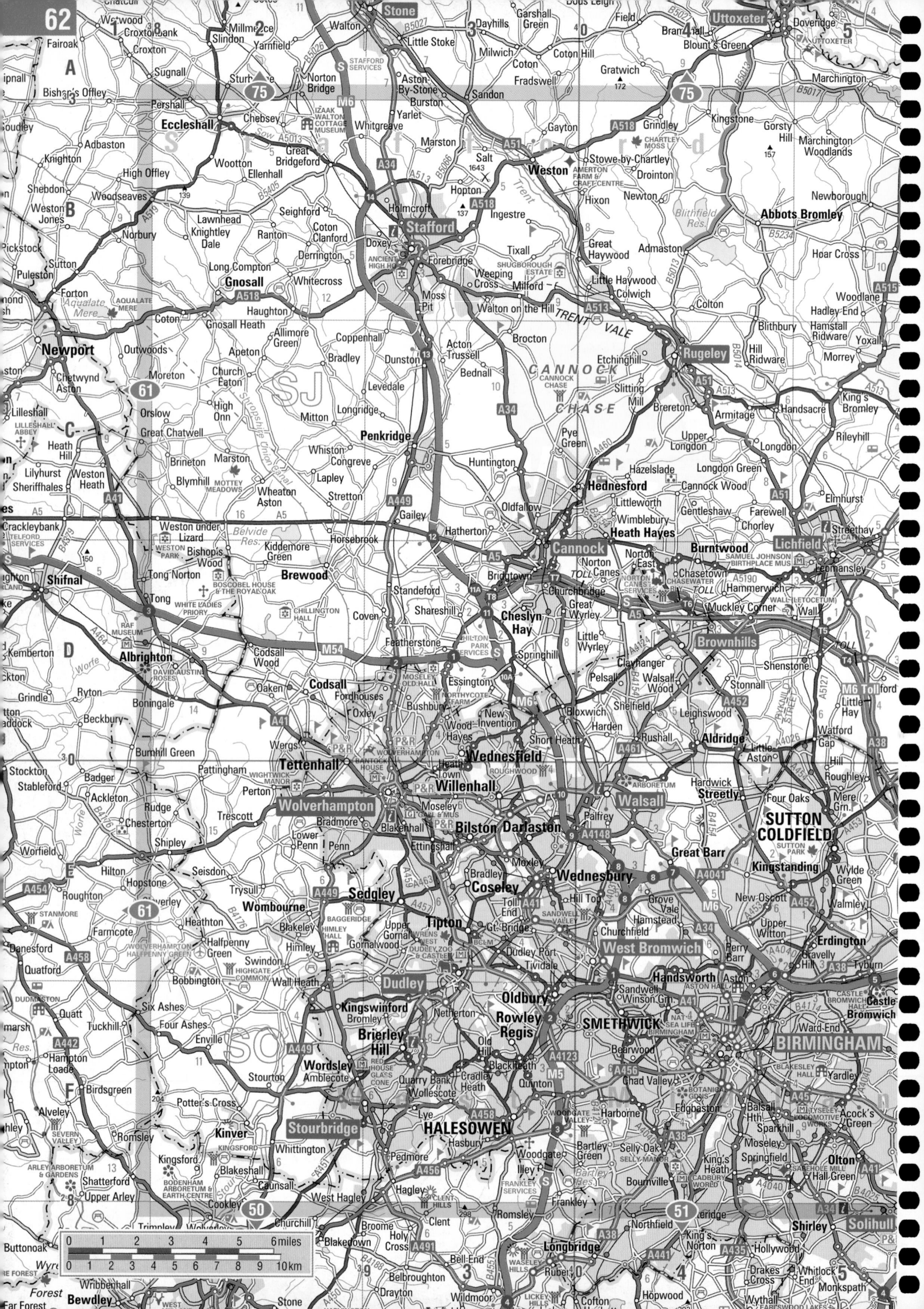

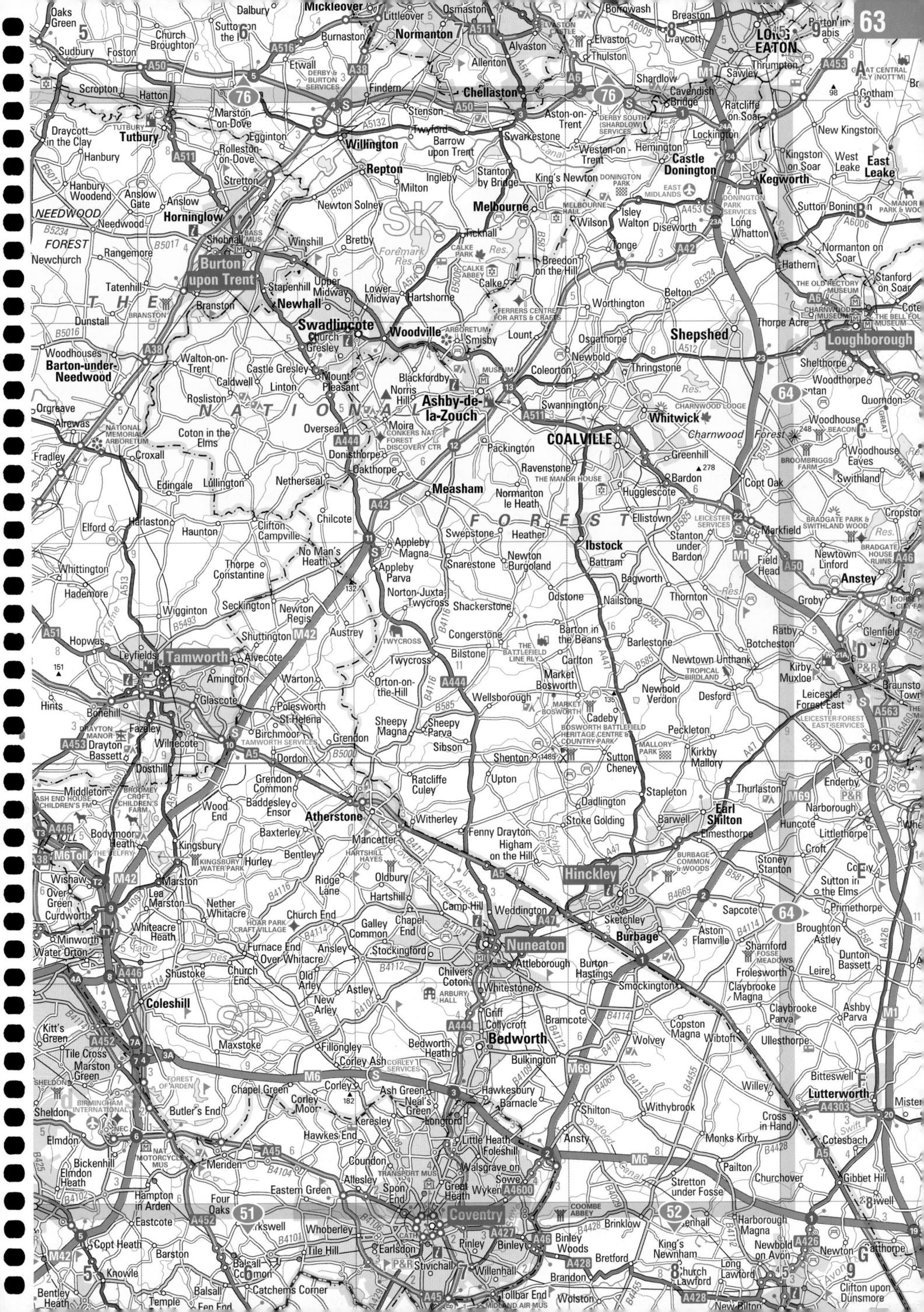

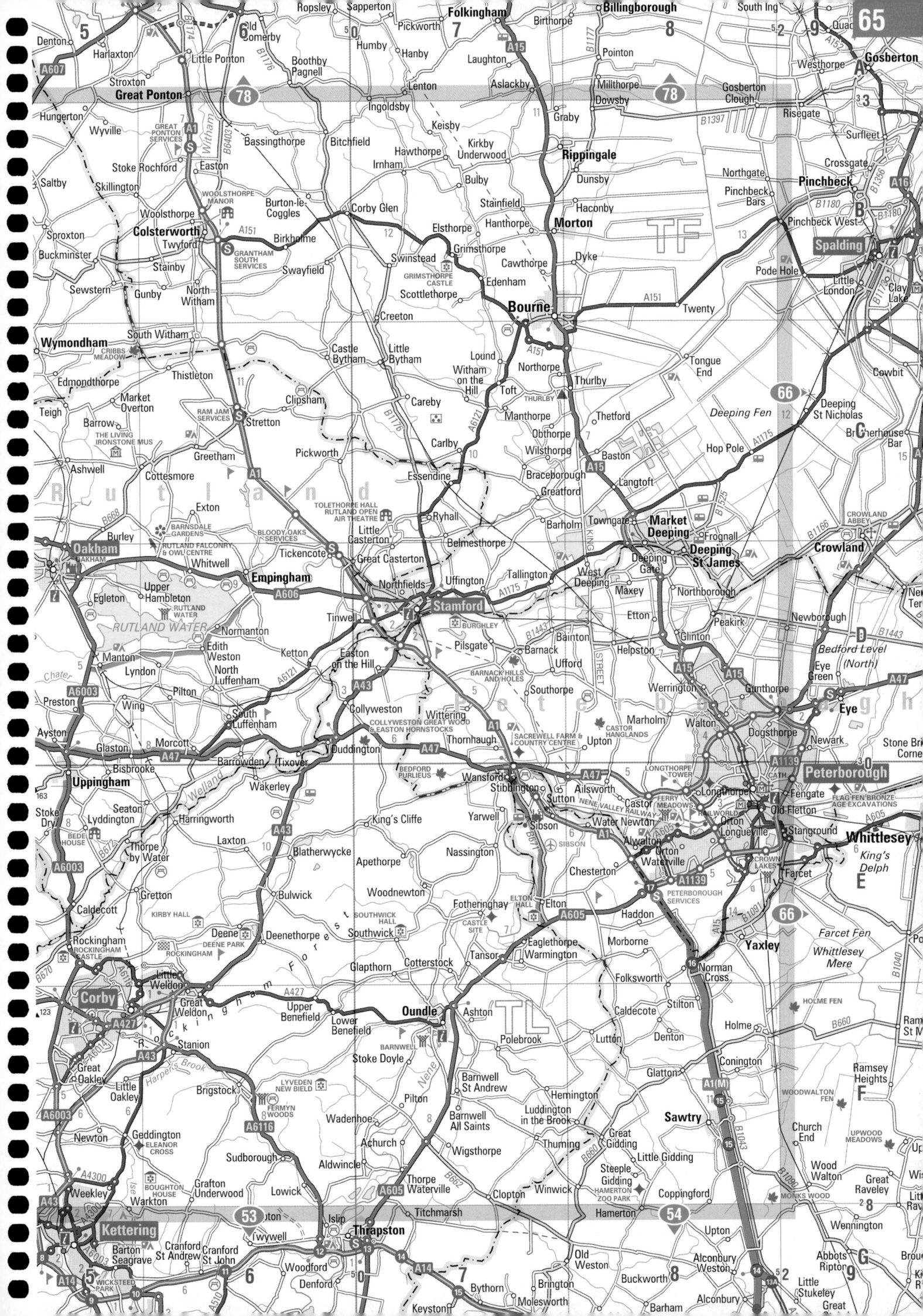

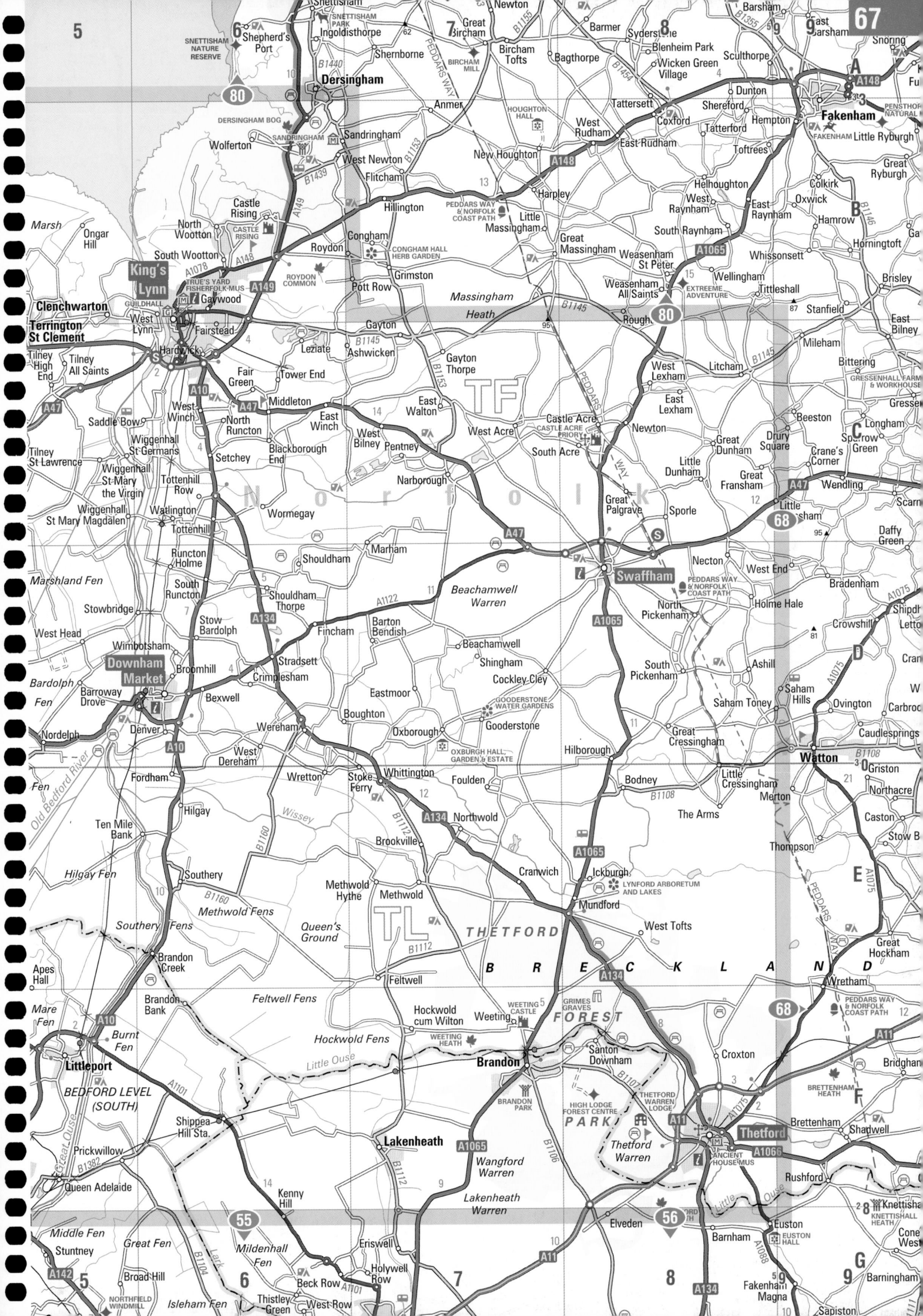

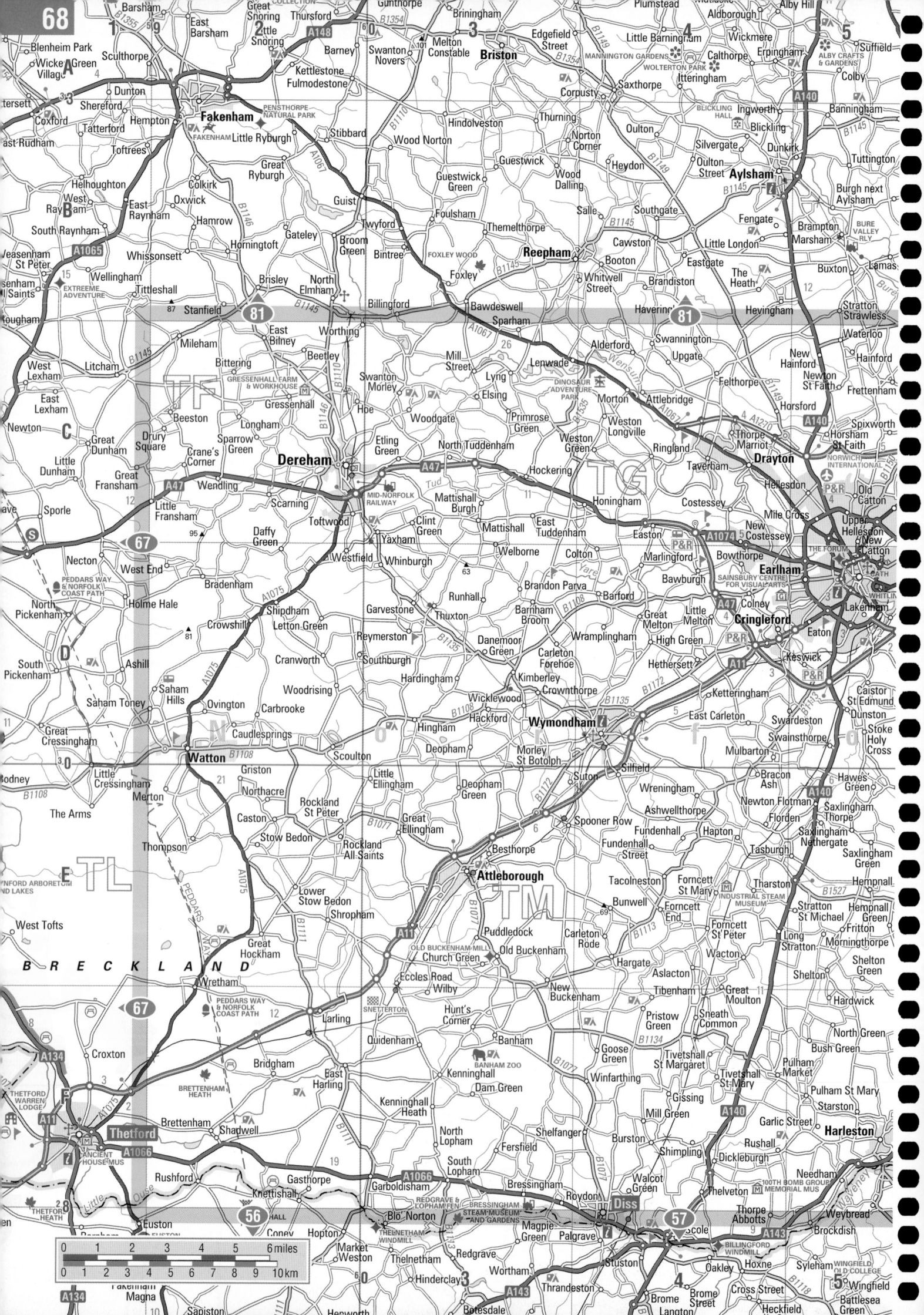

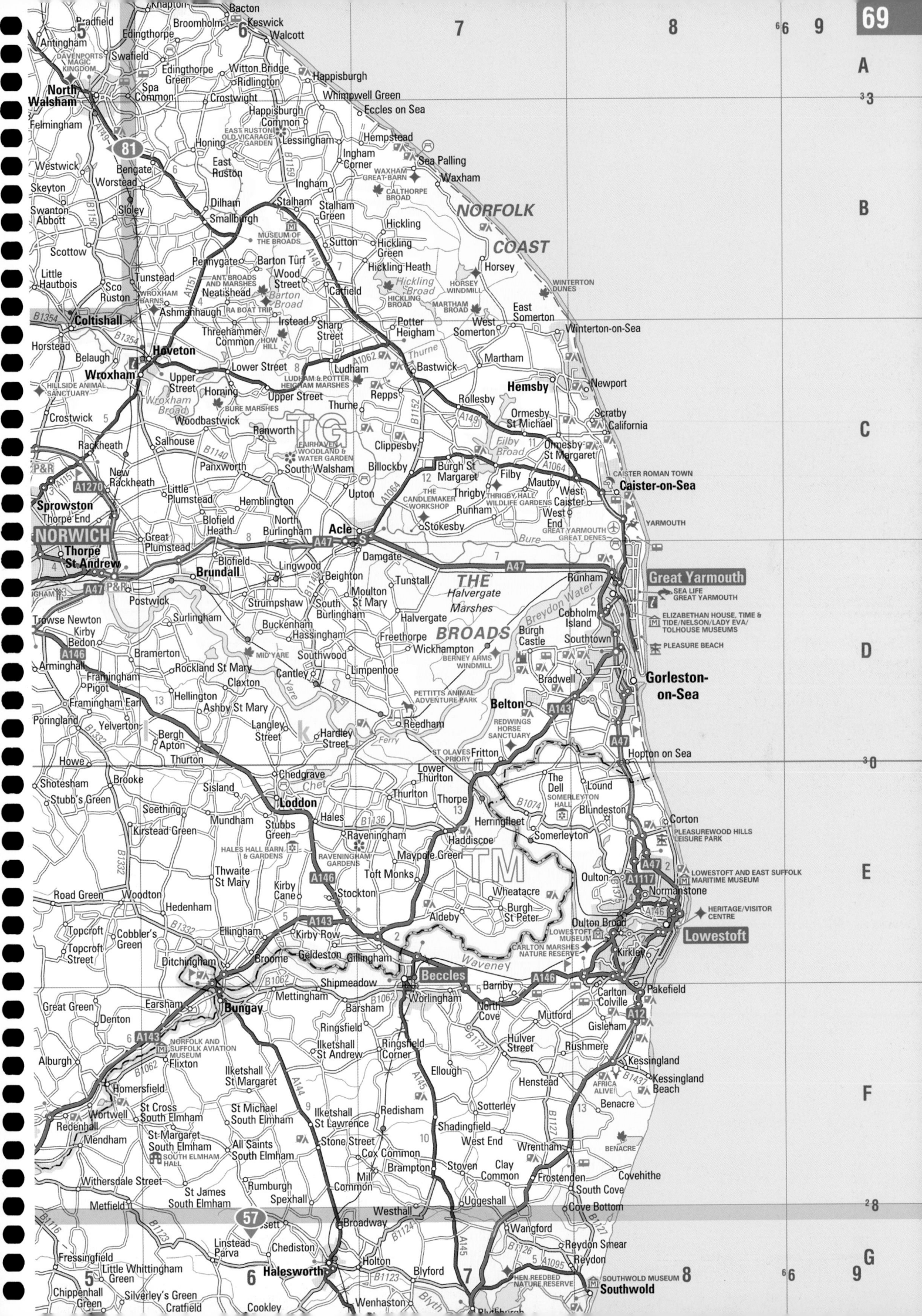

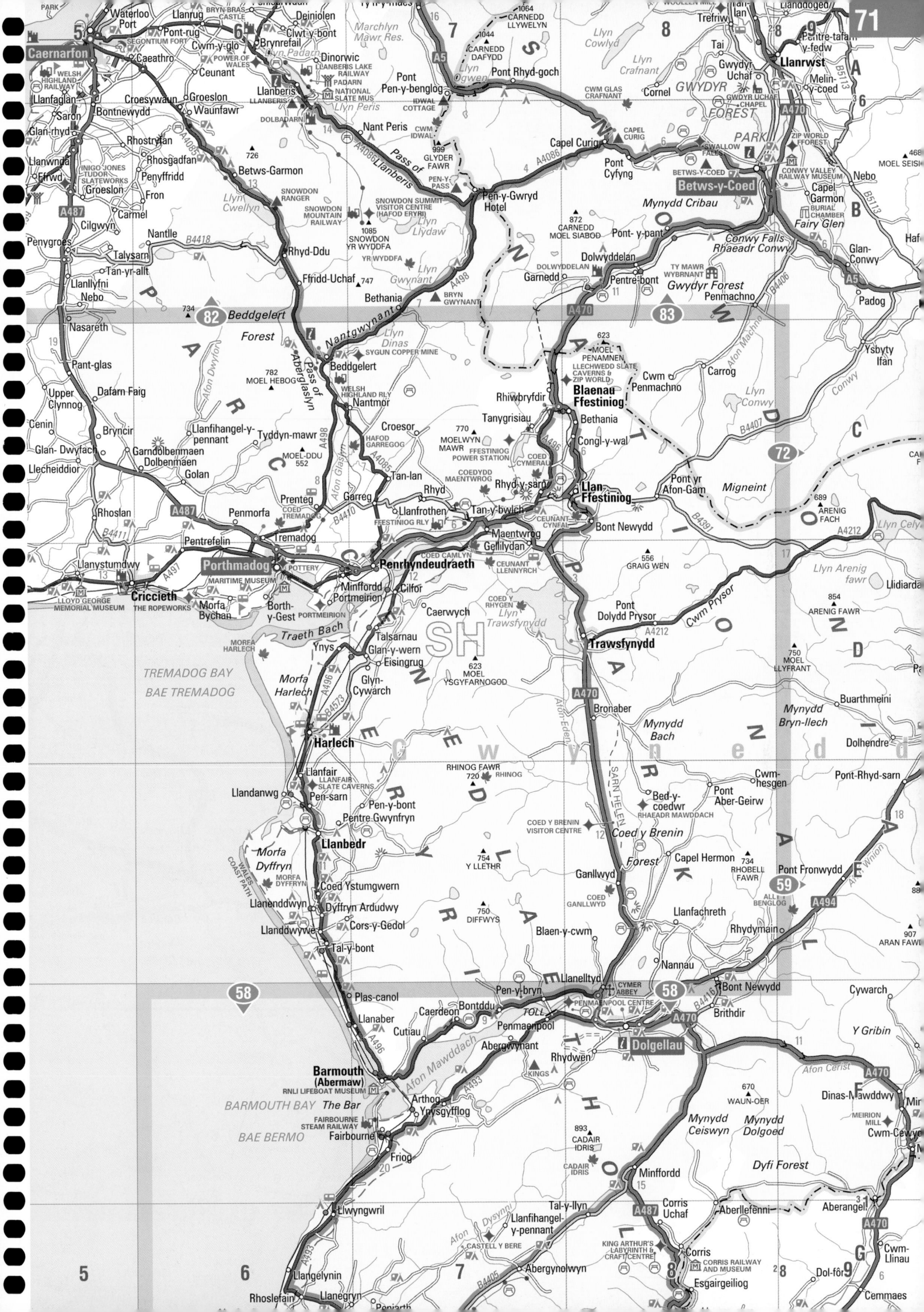

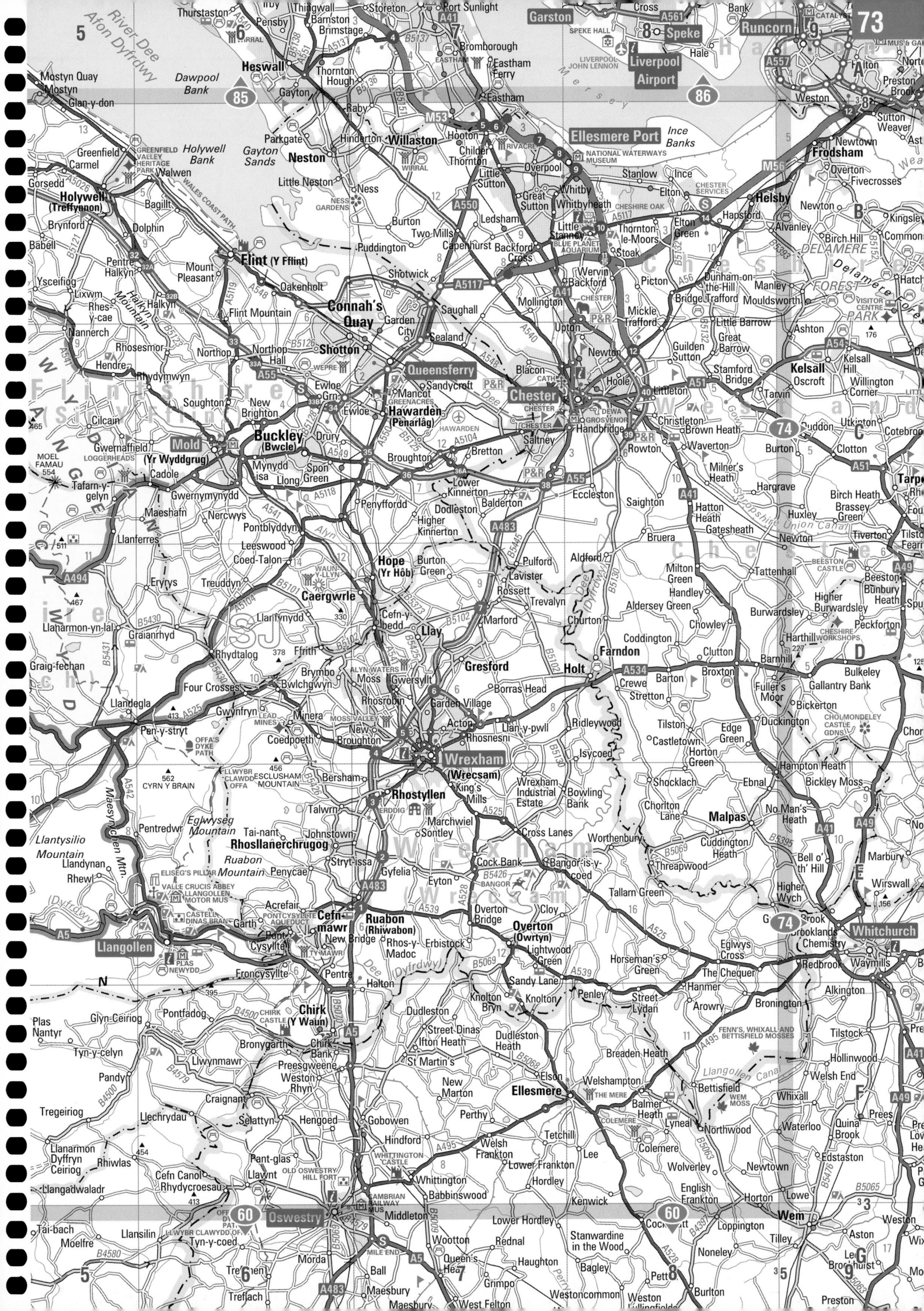

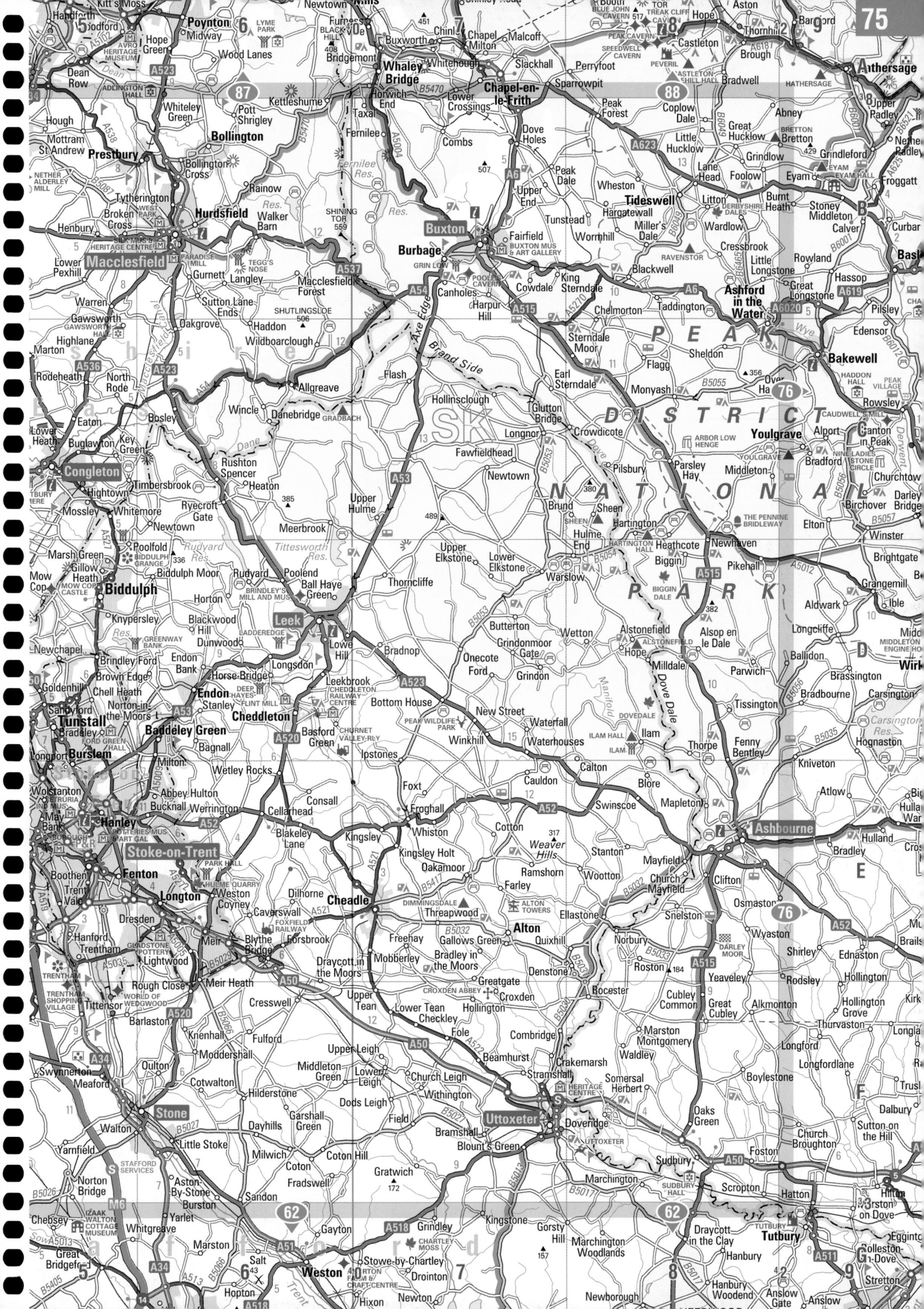

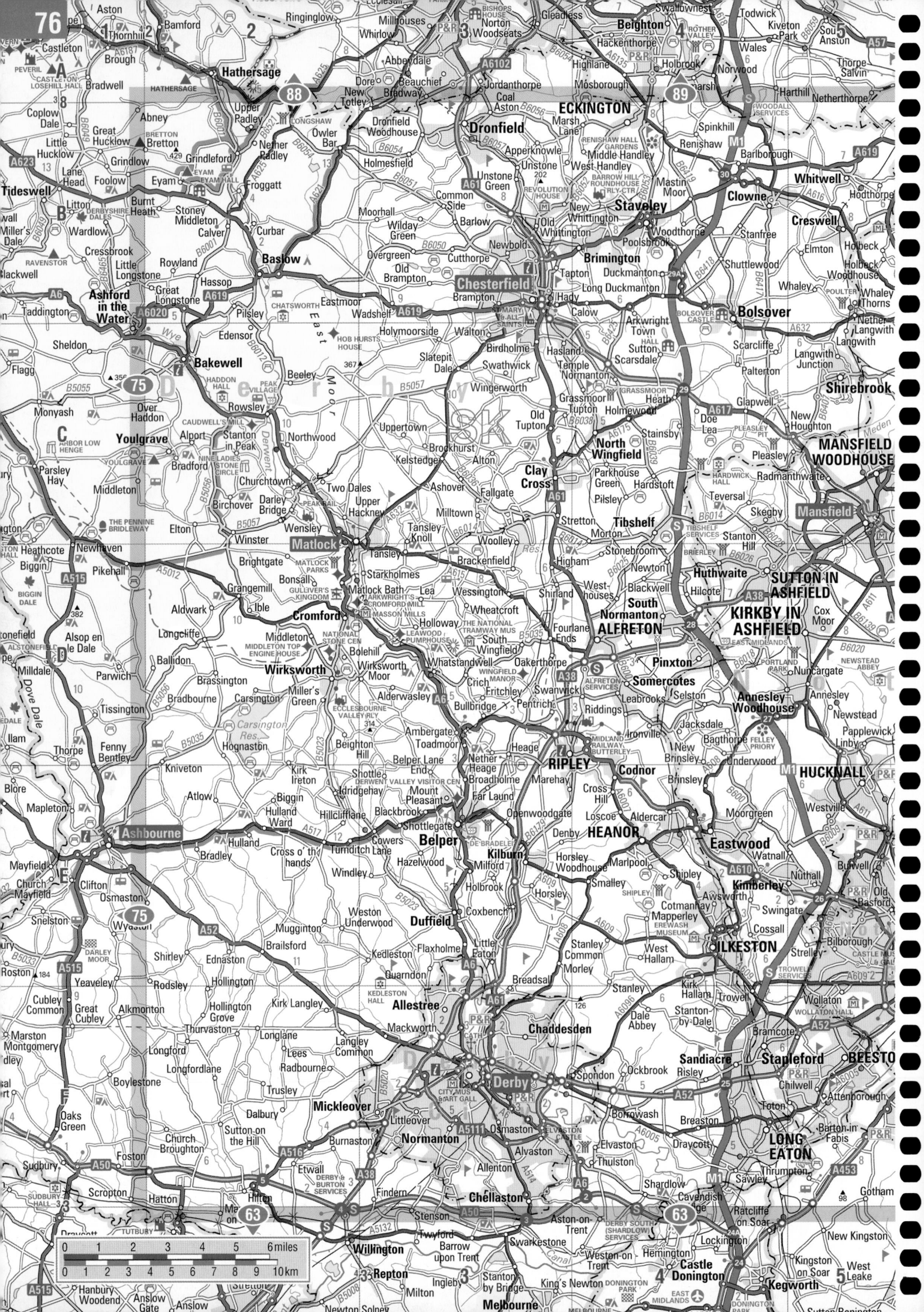

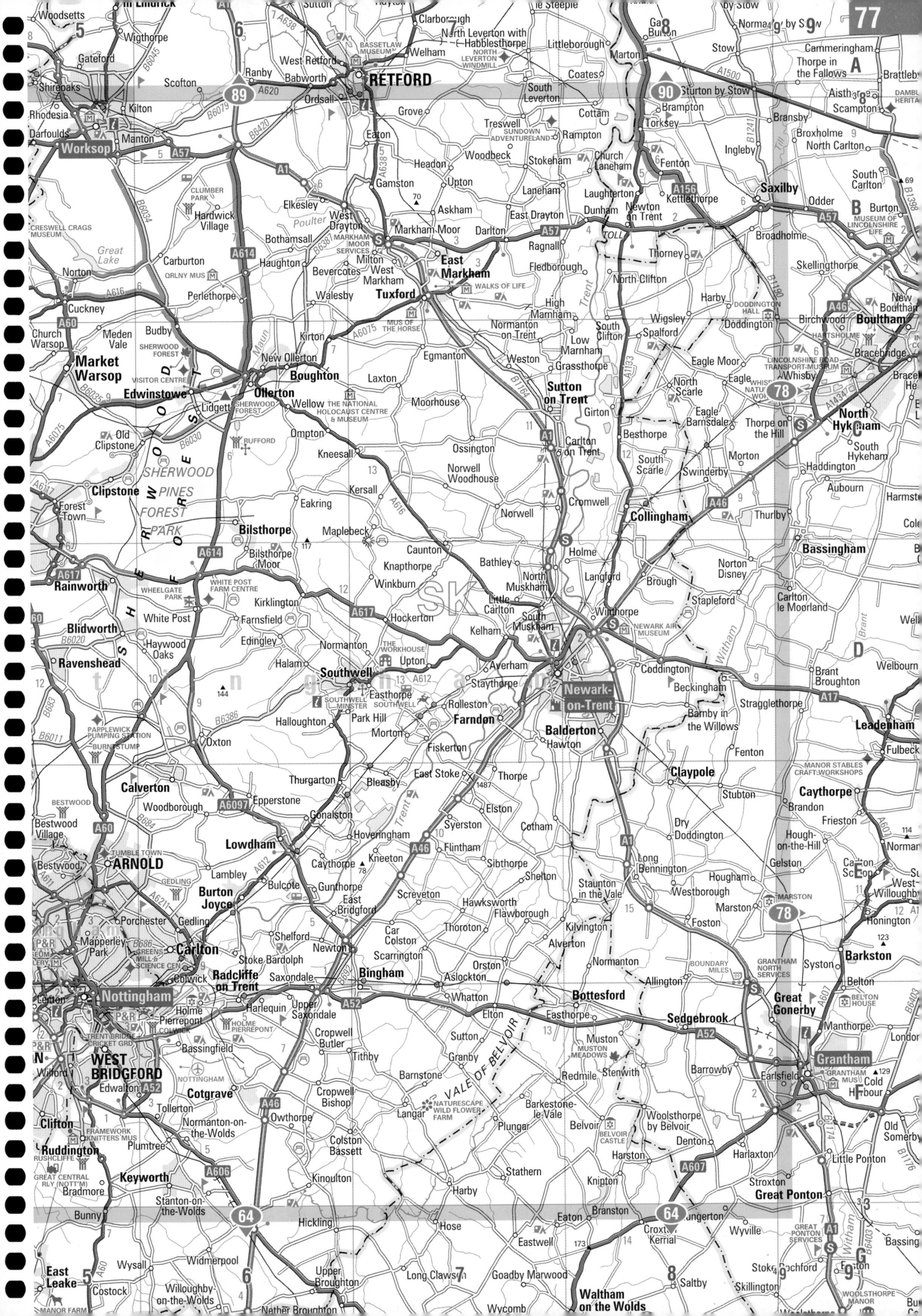

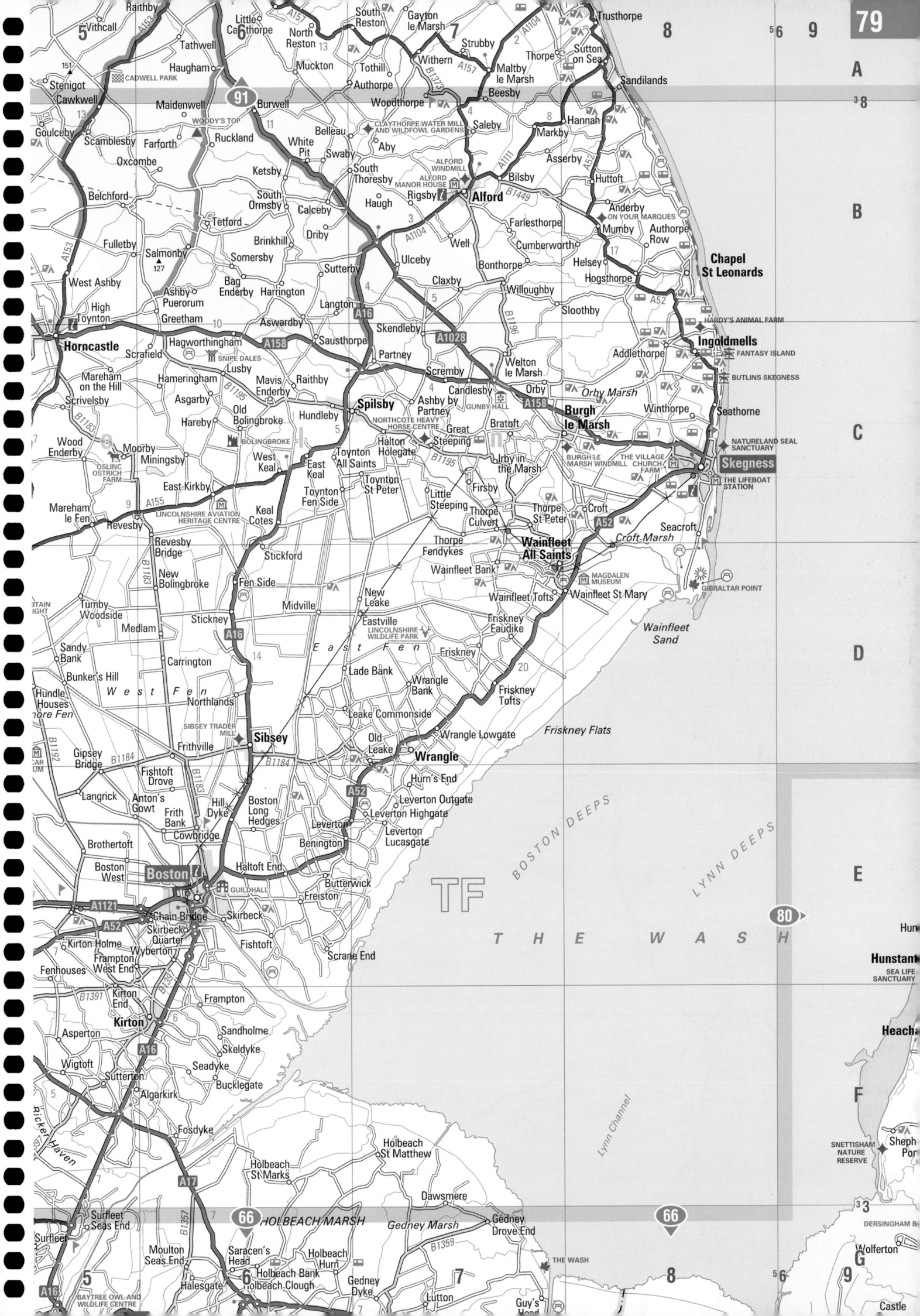

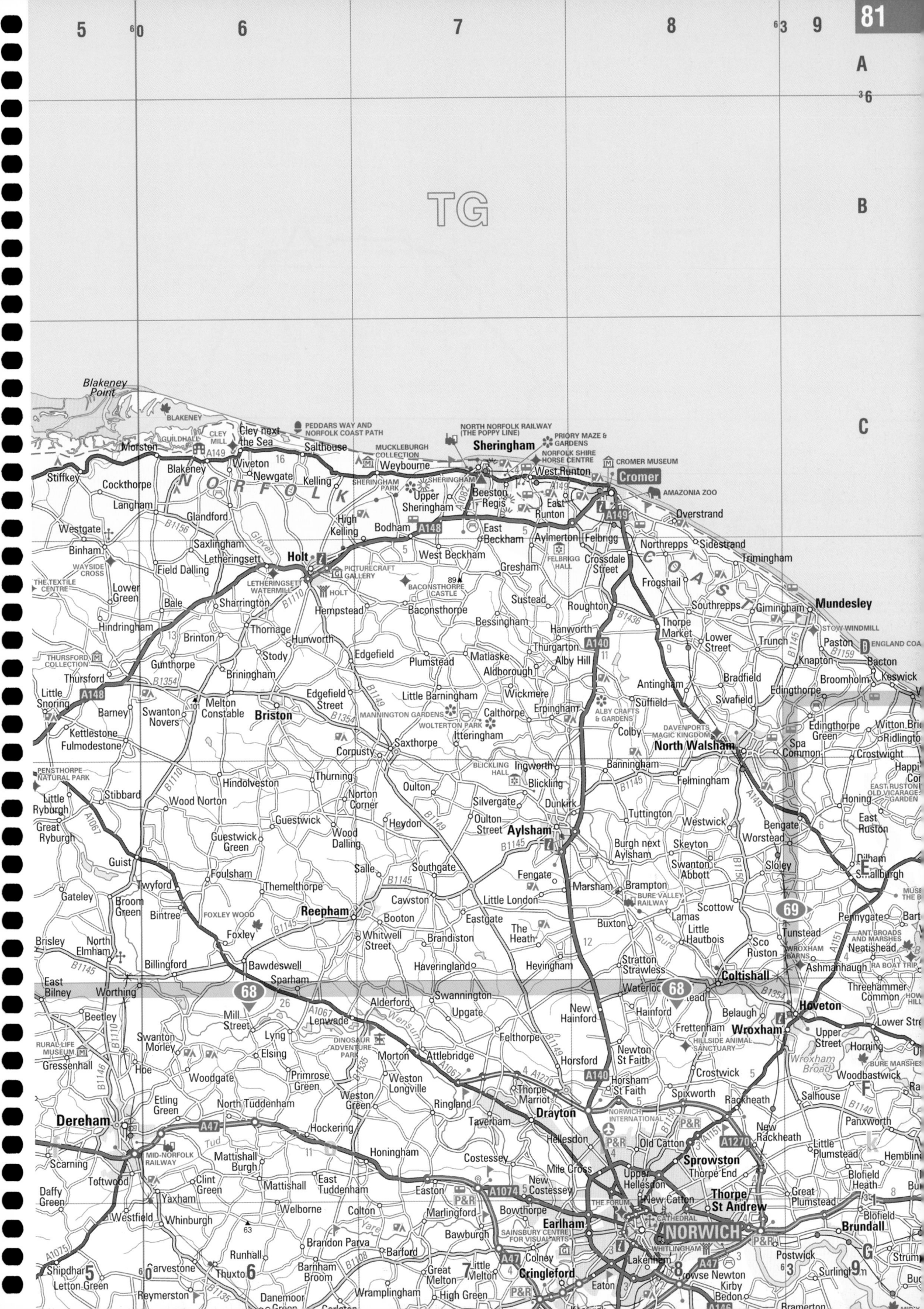

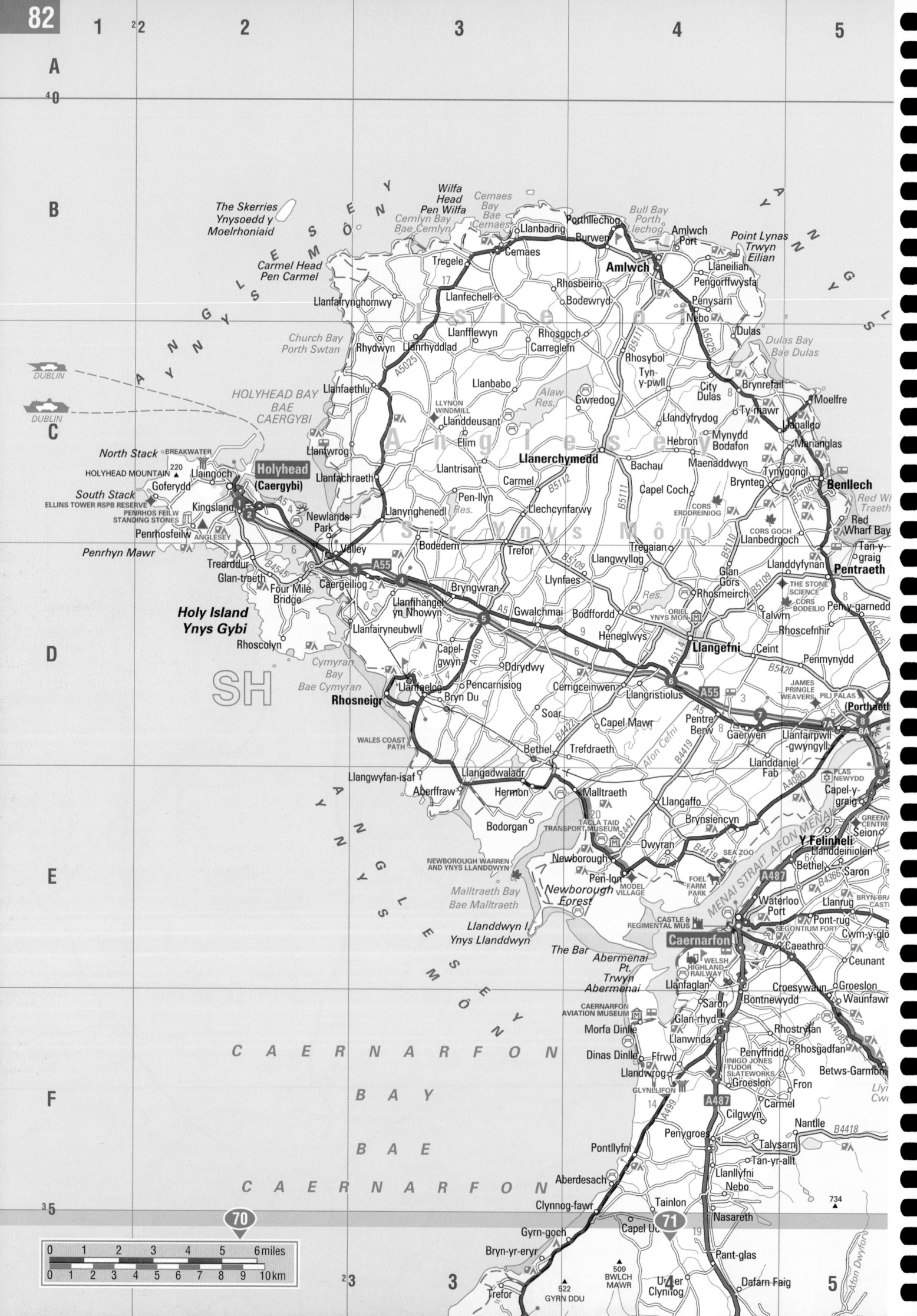

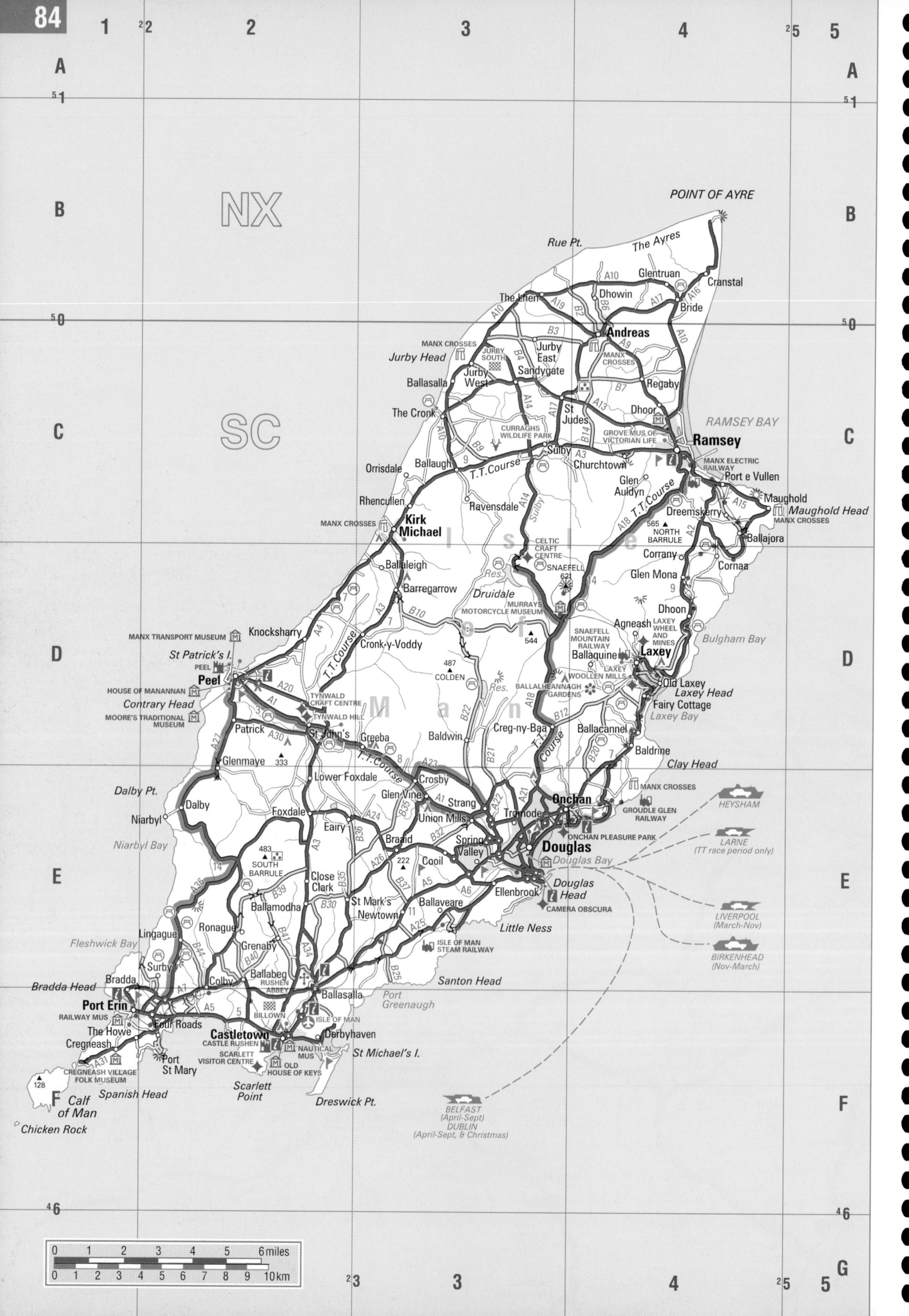

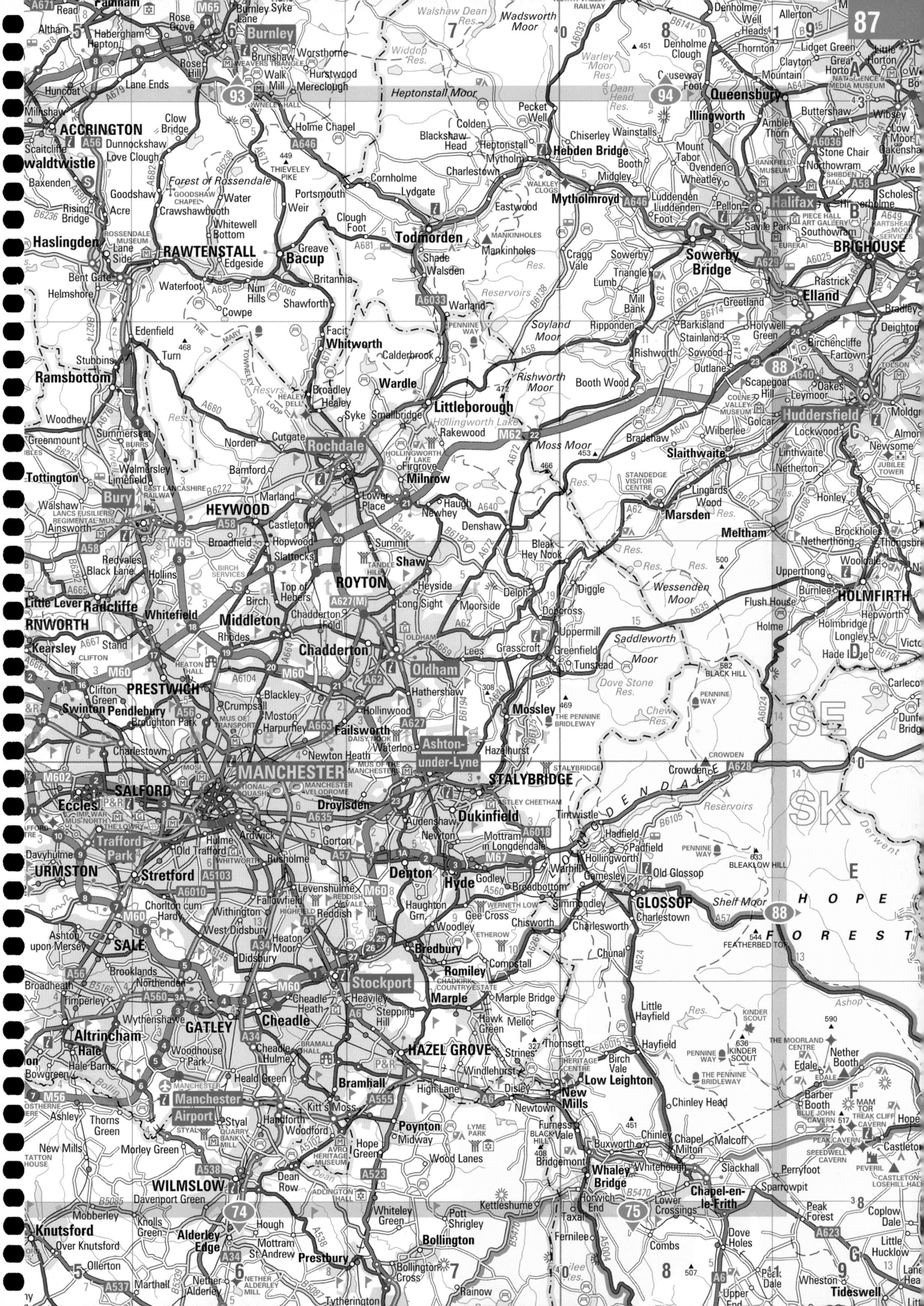

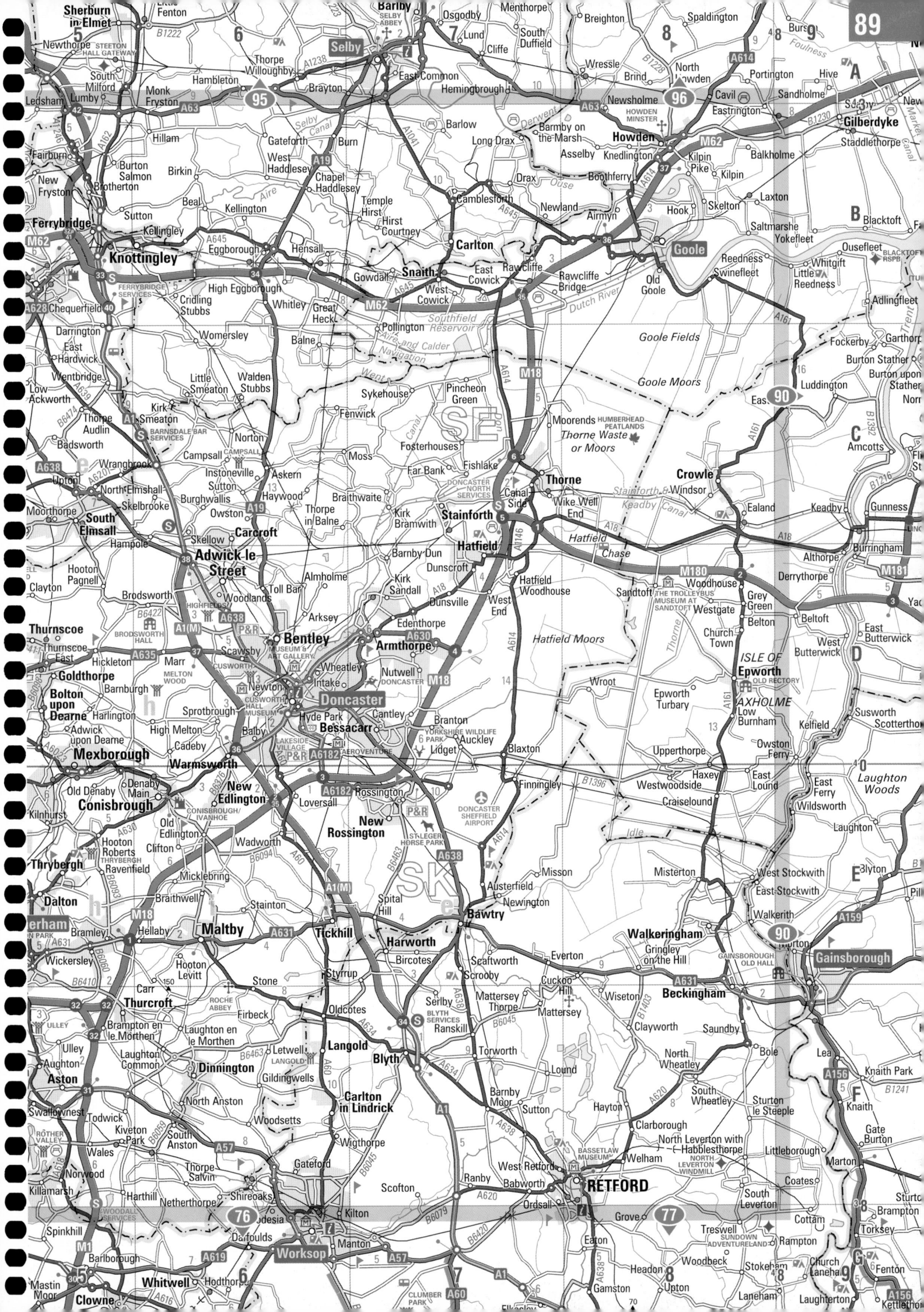

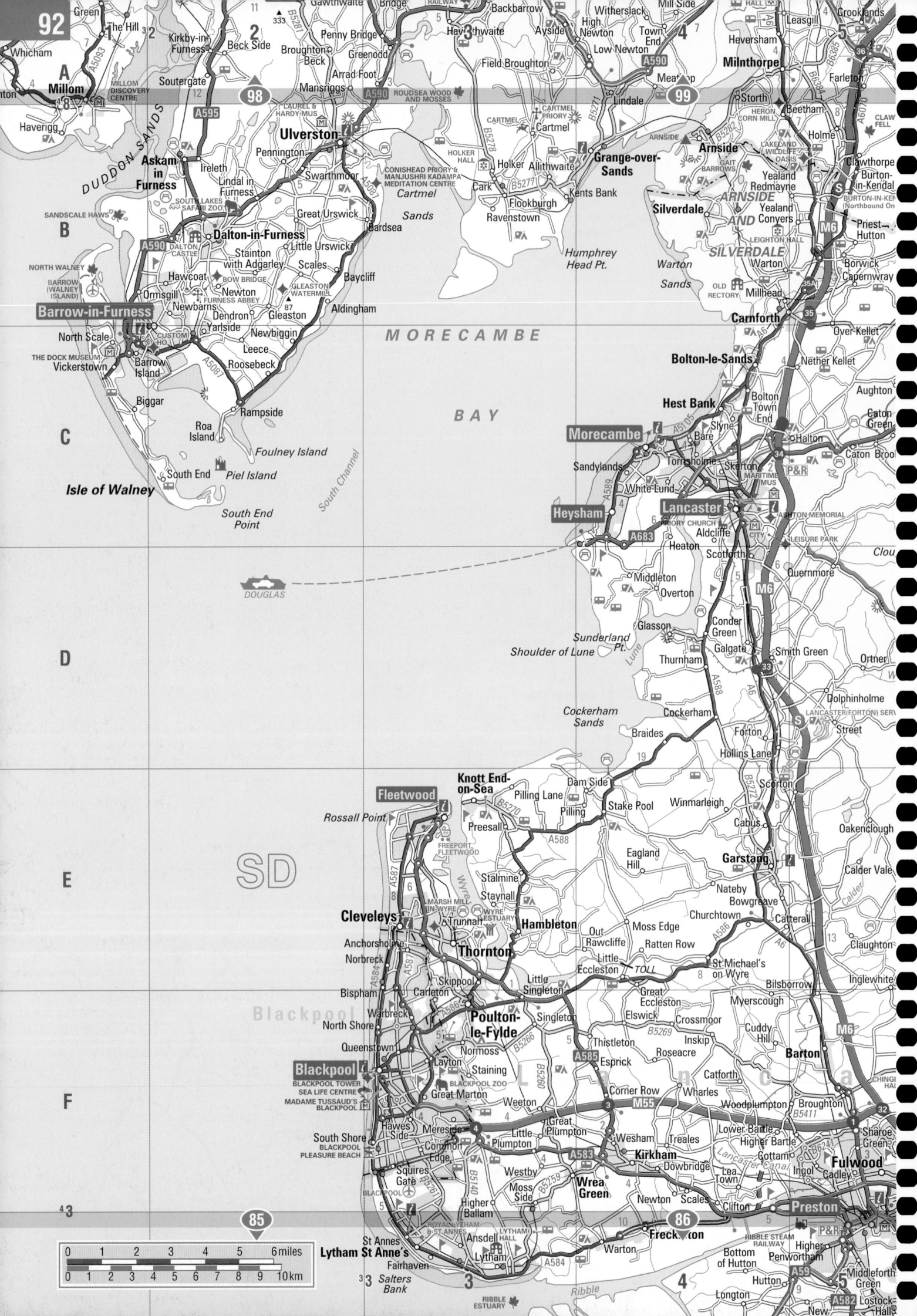

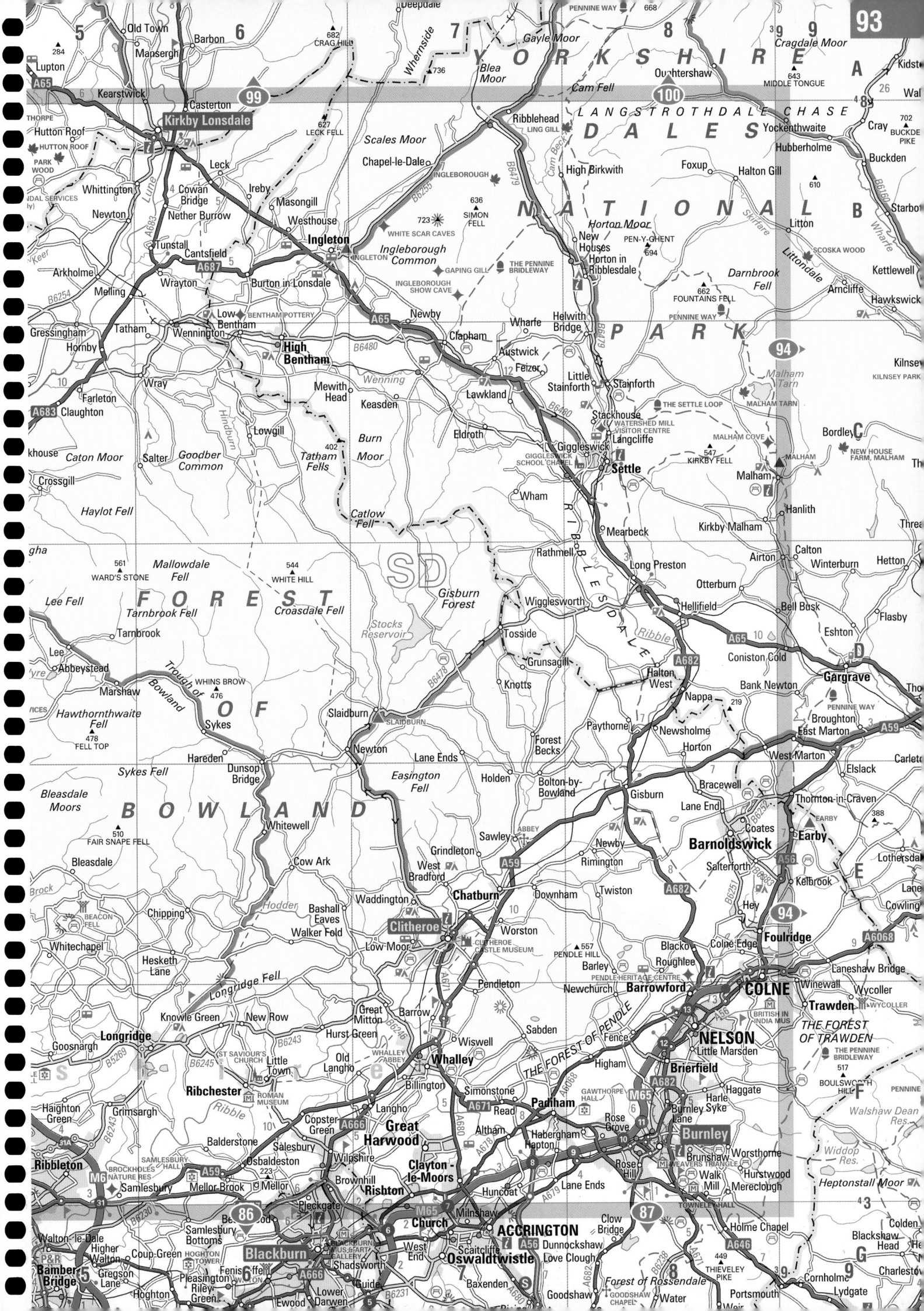

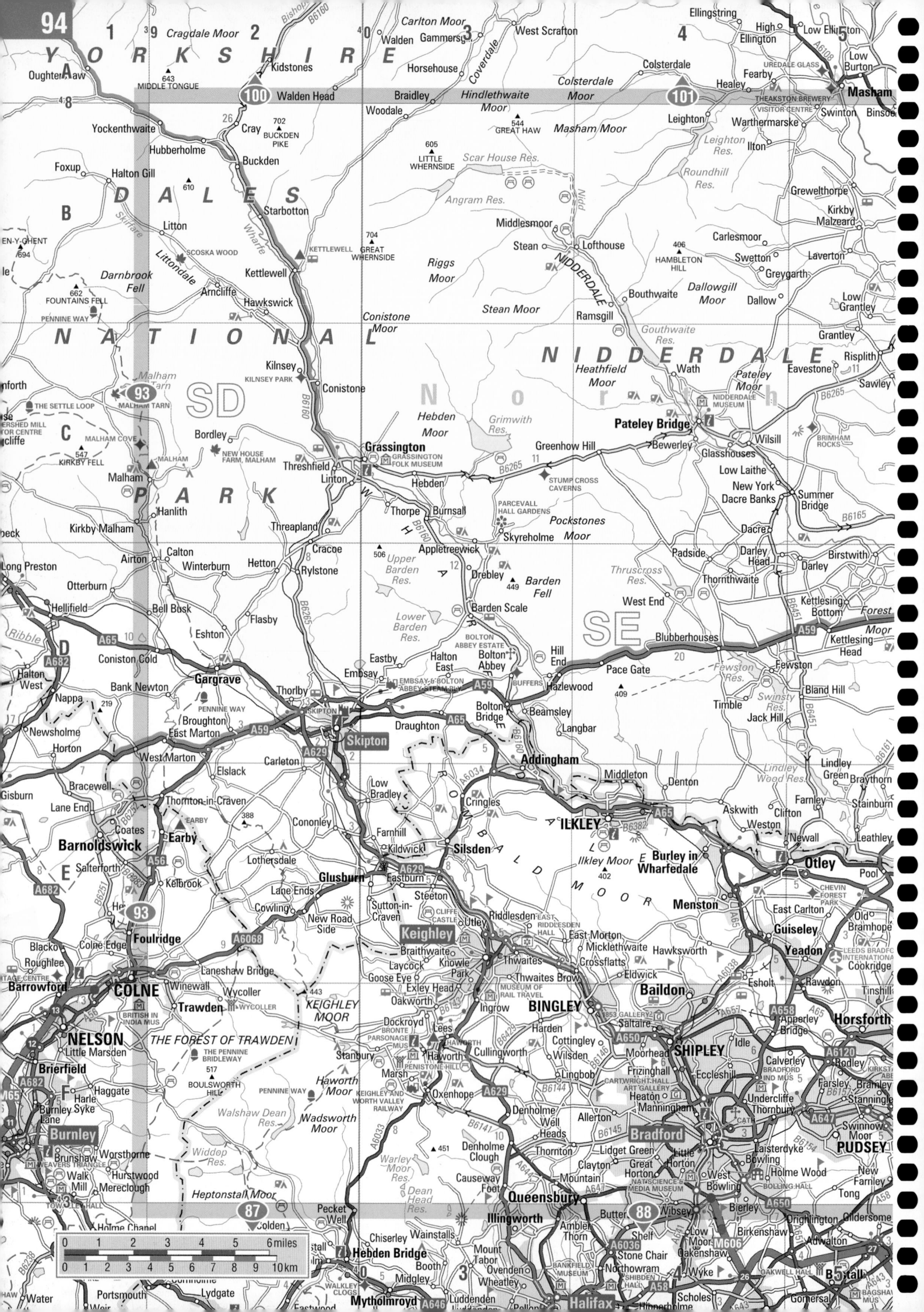

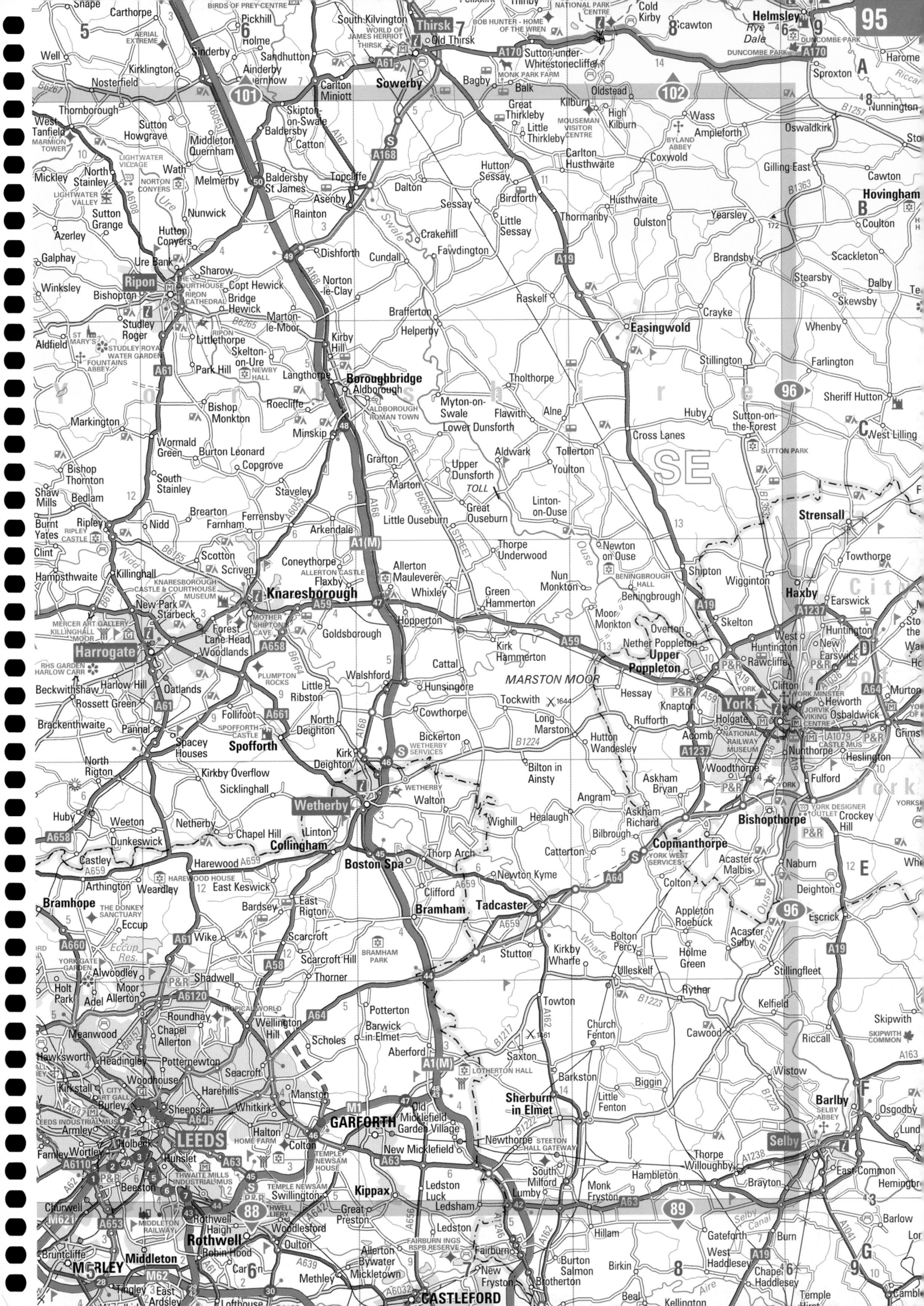

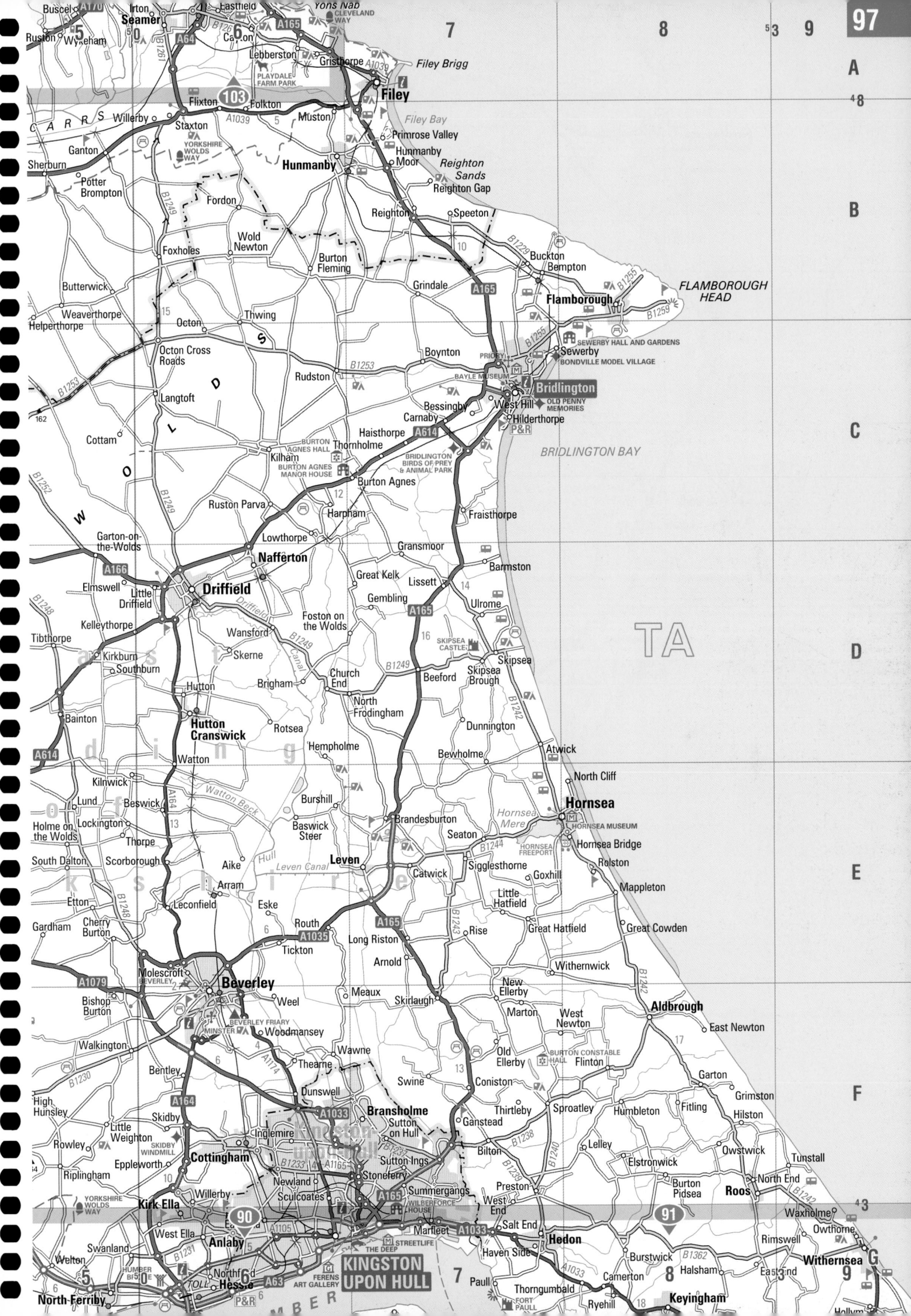

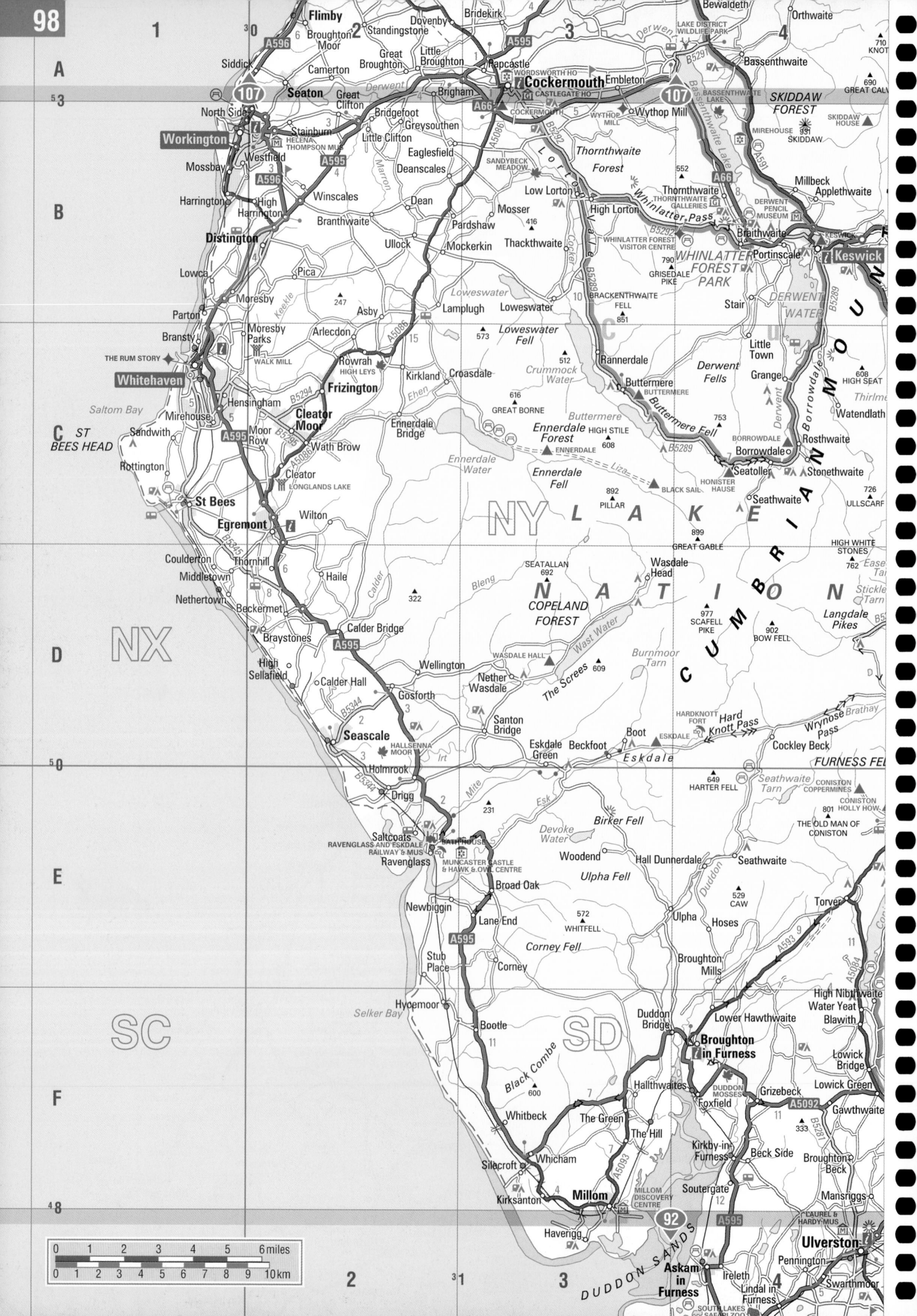

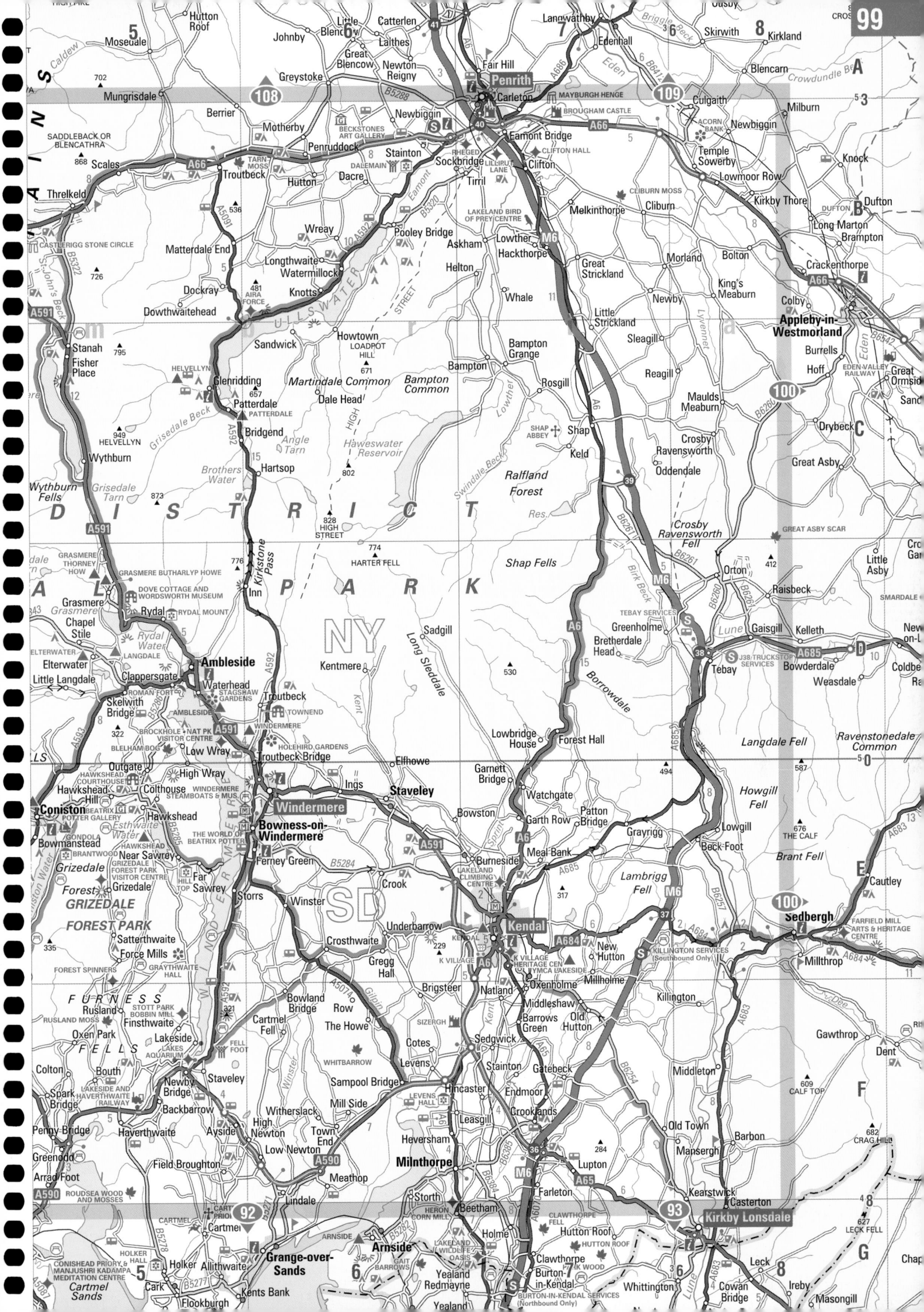

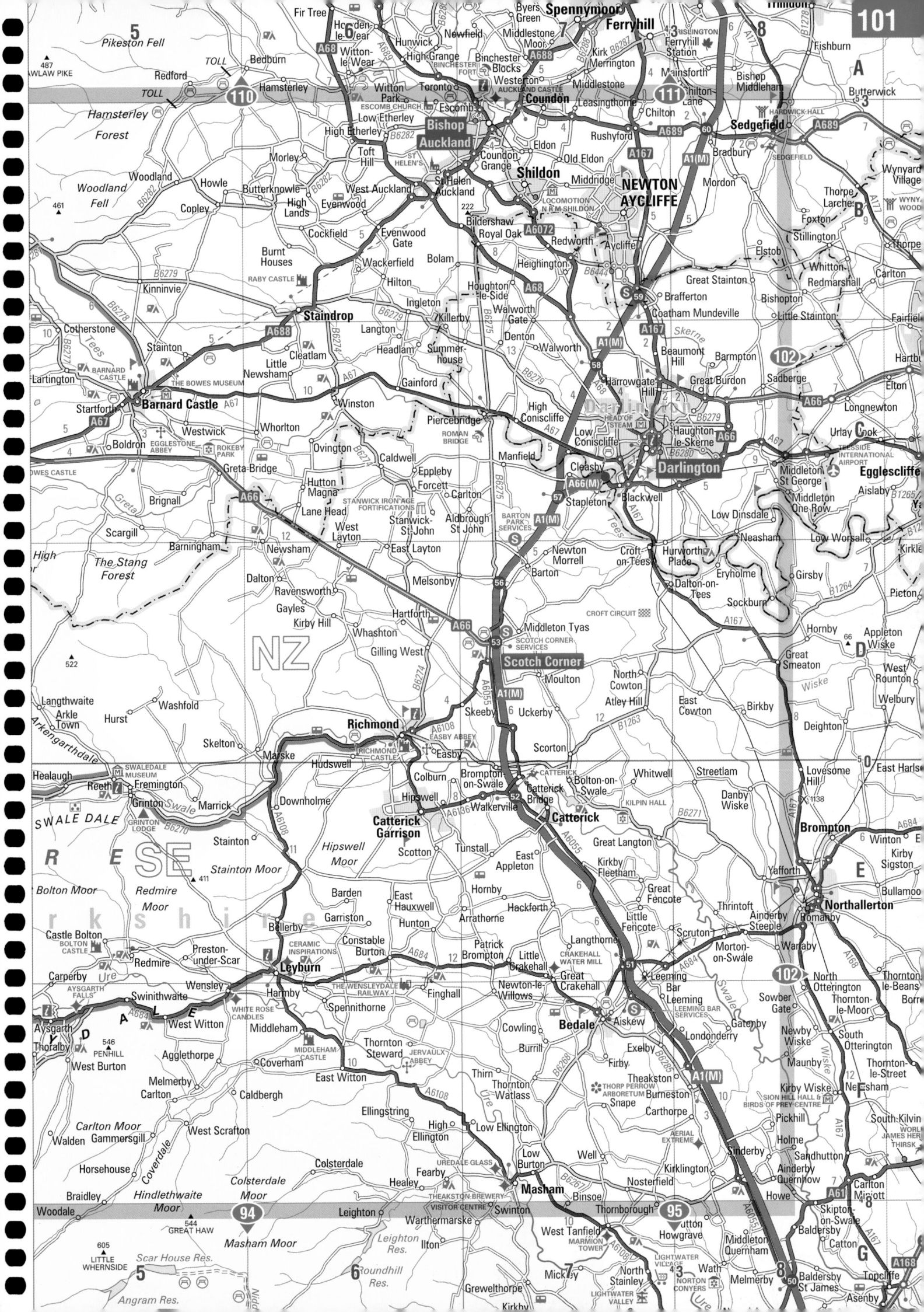

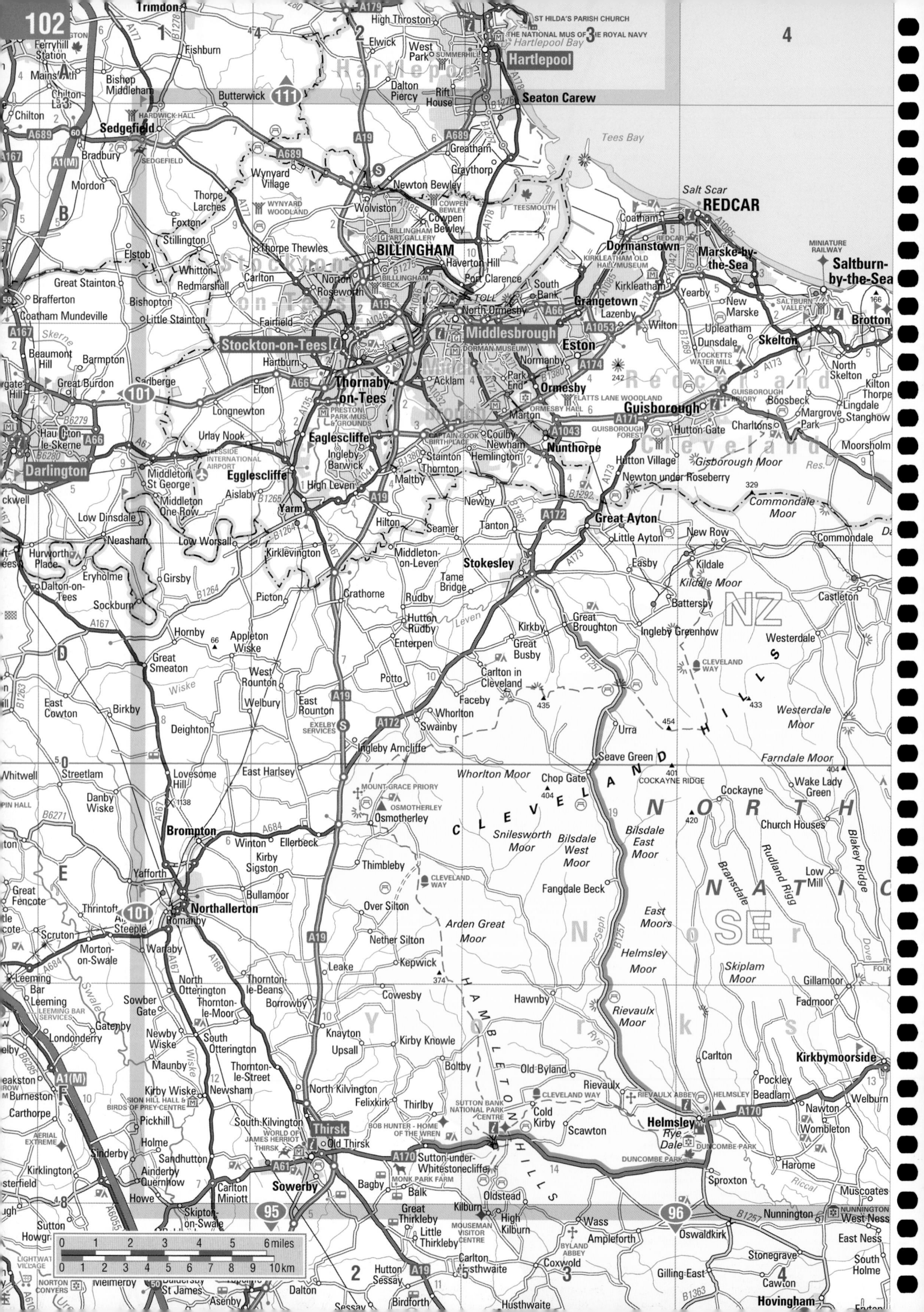

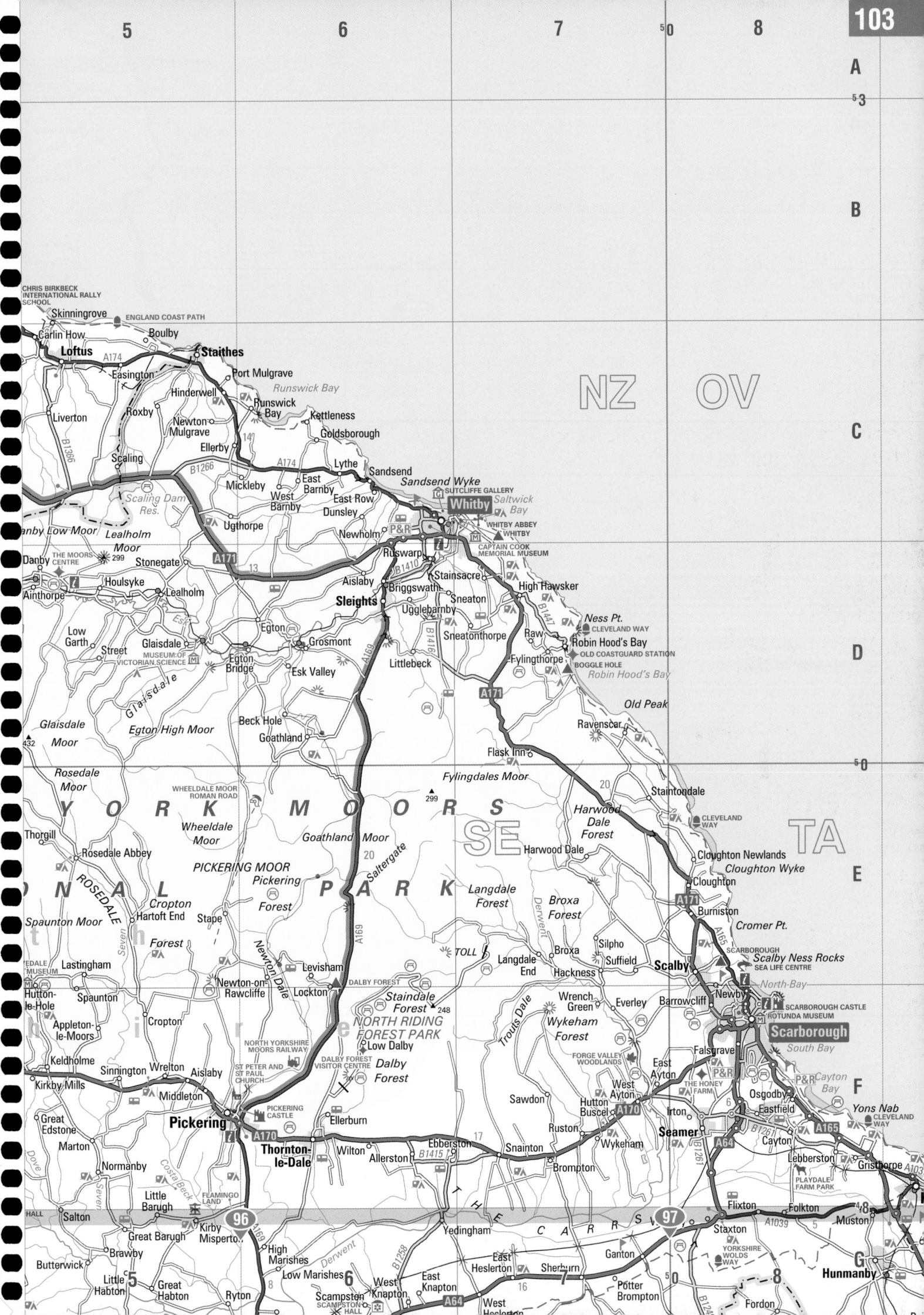

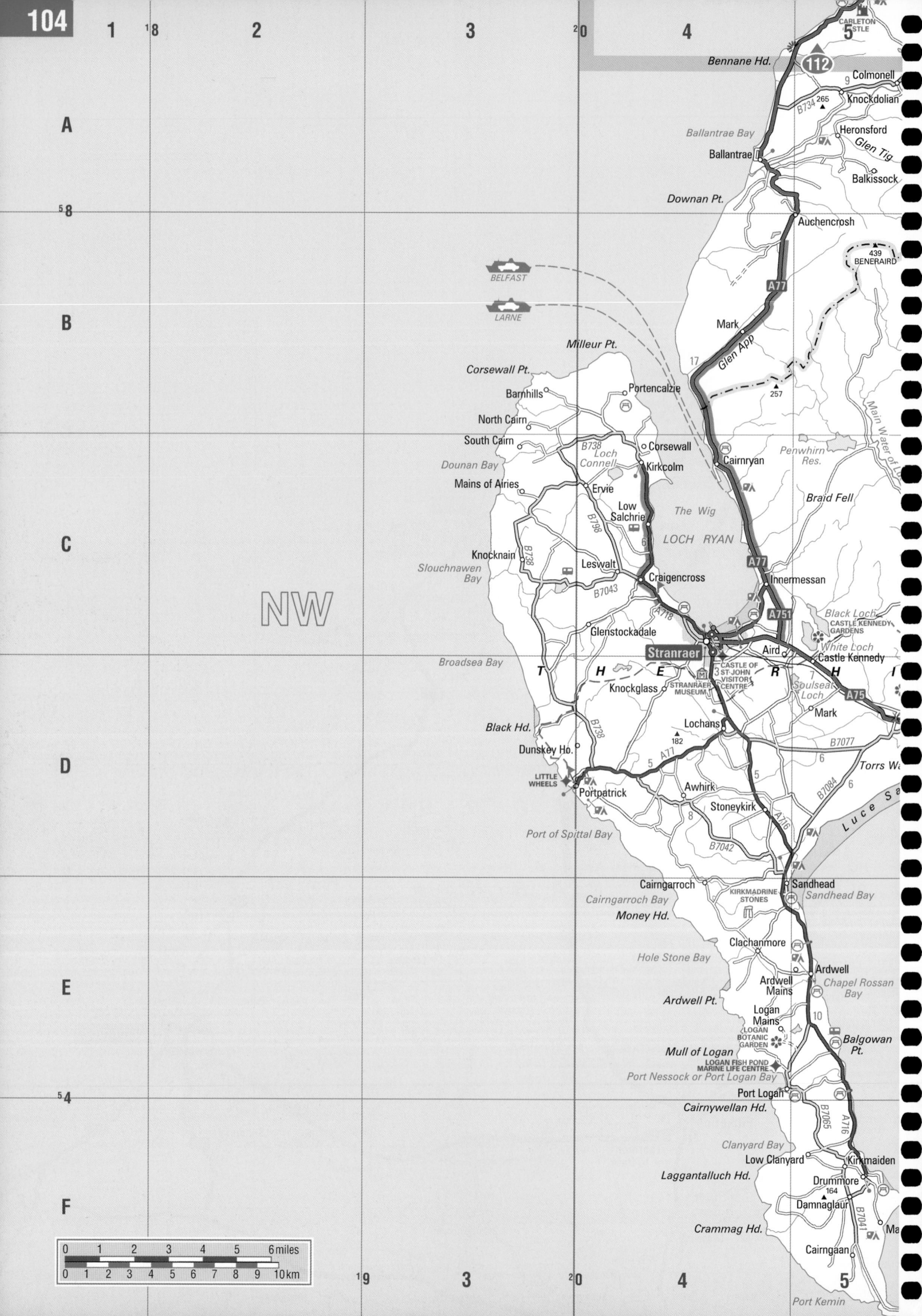

1 8 2 3 20 4 5

CARLETON
STLE
Bennane Hd. 112 9 Colmonell
B734 265 Knockdolian
Ballantrae Bay Heronsford
Ballantrae Glen Tig
Downan Pt. Balkissock

A Auchencrosh

439
BENERAIRD

BELFAST

LARNE A77 Mark

Milleur Pt. Glen App

B Corsewall Pt.
Barnhills Portencalzie 17 257
North Cairn

South Cairn Corsewall Cairnryan Penwhirn
Dounan Bay B738 Kirkcolm Res.
Loch
Connell Main Water of L

Mains of Airies Ervie Braid Fell
Low The Wig
Salchrie LOCH RYAN

C B798 Knocknain Leswalt A77 Innermessan
Slouchnawen B738 Craigencross Black Loch
Bay B7043 CASTLE KENNEDY
A751 GARDENS

A718 CASTLE KENNEDY
Glenstockadale White Loch

Broadsea Bay Stranraer Aird Castle Kennedy
T H E R Soulseat R H I
Knockglass CASTLE OF Loch A75
ST JOHN
STRANRAER VISITOR
MUSEUM CENTRE Mark
Black Hd. Lochans
182 B7077

D Dunskey Ho. 5 A77 5 Torrs W
LITTLE B738 B7084 6
WHEELS Awhirk A716
Portpatrick Stoneykirk Luce Sa
8
Port of Spittal Bay B7042

Cairngarroch Sandhead
KIRKMADRINE Sandhead Bay
Cairngarroch Bay STONES
Money Hd.

Clachanmore

Hole Stone Bay Ardwell

E Ardwell Chapel Rossan
Mains Bay
Ardwell Pt. Logan
Mains 10
LOGAN Balgowan
BOTANIC Pt.
Mull of Logan GARDEN
LOGAN FISH POND
MARINE LIFE CENTRE
Port Nessock or Port Logan Bay
Port Logan
5 4 Cairnywellan Hd. B7065 A716

Clanyard Bay
Low Clanyard Kirkmaiden
Laggantalluch Hd. Drummore
164

F Damnaglaur Ma
B7041
Crammag Hd.
Cairngaan

19 3 20 4 5

NW

0 1 2 3 4 5 6 miles
0 1 2 3 4 5 6 7 8 9 10km

Port Kemin

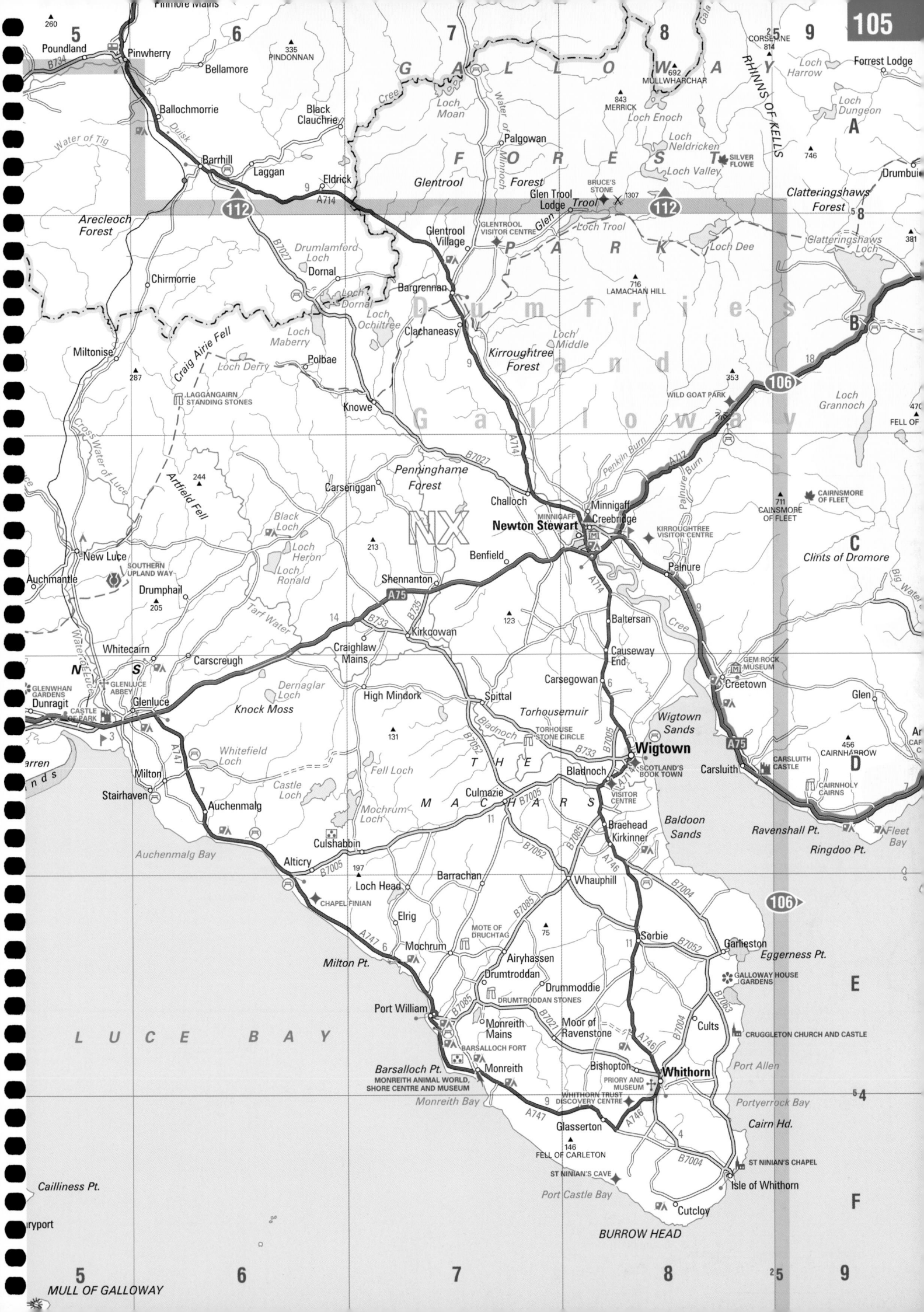

Finmore Mains
260
Poundland
B734
Pinwherry
Bellamore
PINDONNAN
335
GALLOWAY
CORSE LINE
814
25
Loch Harrow
Forrest Lodge
9

Ballochmorrie
Black Clauchrie
Cree
Loch Moan
F
O
R
E
S
T
MULLWHARCHAR
692
W
843
MERRICK
Loch Enoch
Loch Neldricken
SILVER FLOWE
Loch Dungeon
A

Water of Tig
Dusk
Barrhill
Laggan
Eldrick
9
Water of Minnoch
Palgowan
Loch Valley
746
Drumbui

4
Arecleoch Forest
A714
112
Glentrool Forest
BRUCE'S STONE
1307
Glen Trool Lodge
X
Trool
112
Loch Dee
Clatteringshaws Forest
381
8

B7027
Drumlamford Loch
Glentrool Village
Glentrool Visitor Centre
Glen
Loch Trool
P A R K
Glatteringshaws Loch
B

Chirmorrie
Dornal
Loch Dornal
Bargrennan
Dumfries
353
106
18
B

Miltonise
Craig Airie Fell
287
Loch Maberry
Polbae
Loch Ochiltree
Clachaneasy
Kirroughtree Forest
Loch Middle
WILD GOAT PARK
Loch Grannoch
470
FELL OF

LAGGANGAIRN STANDING STONES
Loch Derry
Knowe
9
and
A712
Penkiln Burn
Palnure Burn
CAIRNSMORE OF FLEET
Artfield Fell
244
Carseriggan
Penninghame Forest
B7027
Challoch
Minnigaff
Creebridge
711
CAIRNSMORE OF FLEET
Galloway

New Luce
Black Loch
213
Shennanton
A714
NX
Newton Stewart
MINNIGAFF
Clints of Dromore
C
Auchmantle
SOUTHERN UPLAND WAY
Loch Heron
Loch Ronald
Benfield
Benfield
A714
Big Water

Drumphail
205
A75
Kirkcowan
123
Baltersan
Cree
9
GEM ROCK MUSEUM
Glen
Ar CAP

Whitecairn
N S
Carscreugh
B733
14
B735
Craighlaw Mains
High Mindork
131
Spittal
Torhousemuir
Carsegowan
6
Causeway End
Creetown
456
CAIRNHARROW

GLENWHAN GARDENS
GLENLUCE ABBEY
Dernaglar Loch
TORHOUSE STONE CIRCLE
B733
Wigtown Sands
A75
CAIRNHOLY CAIRNS

Dunragit
CASTLE OF PARK
Glenluce
Whitefield Loch
Fell Loch
B7052
Bladnoch
B7005
Wigtown
Carsluith
CARSLUITH CASTLE
D

3
A147
Milton
Castle Loch
T H E
Culmazie
B7005
SCOTLAND'S BOOK TOWN
Baldoon Sands
Ravenshall Pt.
Fleet Bay

Stairhaven
7
Auchenmalg
Mochrum Loch
M A C H A R S
Braehead
Kirkinner
Ringdoo Pt.

Auchenmalg Bay
Culshabbin
Alticry
197
Barrachan
B7085
Whauphill
B7004
106

CHAPEL FINIAN
A747
Loch Head
Elrig
MOTE OF DRUCHTAG
75
Sorbie
B7052
Garlieston
Eggerness Pt.
E

Milton Pt.
6
Mochrum
Airyhassen
11
GALLOWAY HOUSE GARDENS
B7063

Drumtroddan
Drummoddie
DRUMTRODDAN STONES
Cults
CRUGGLETON CHURCH AND CASTLE

Port William
B7085
Monreith Mains
Moor of Ravenstone
A746
Bishopton
Whithorn
Port Allen

L U C E   B A Y
Barsalloch Fort
Monreith
PRIORY AND MUSEUM
Portyerrock Bay
5
4

Barsalloch Pt.
MONREITH ANIMAL WORLD, SHORE CENTRE AND MUSEUM
9
WHITHORN TRUST DISCOVERY CENTRE
A746
Cairn Hd.

Monreith Bay
Glasserton
A747
ST NINIAN'S CHAPEL

Caillness Pt.
FELL OF CARLETON
146
B7004
Isle of Whithorn

ST NINIAN'S CAVE
Cutcloy
F

ryport
Port Castle Bay
BURROW HEAD

5
6
7
8
25
9

MULL OF GALLOWAY

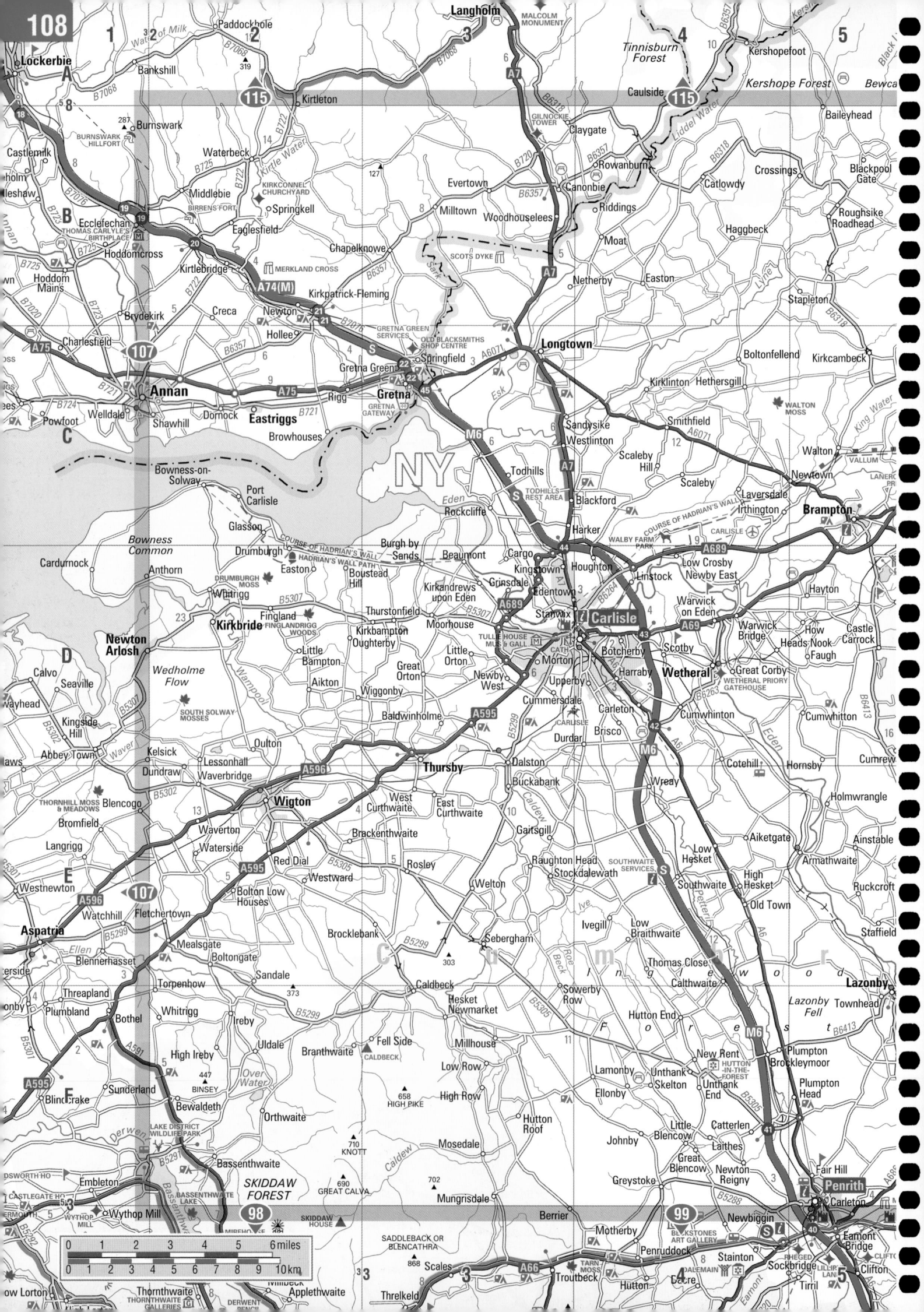

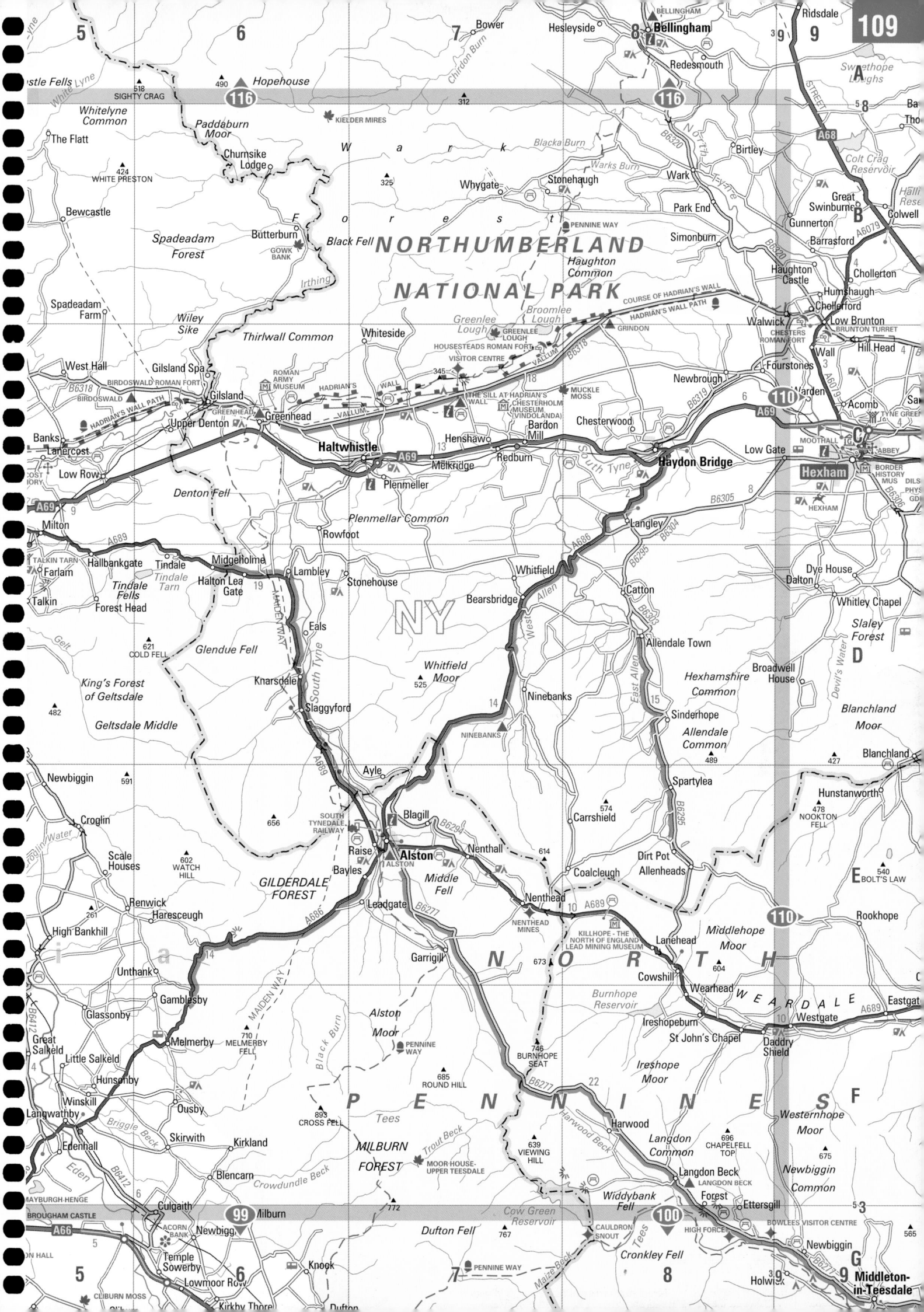

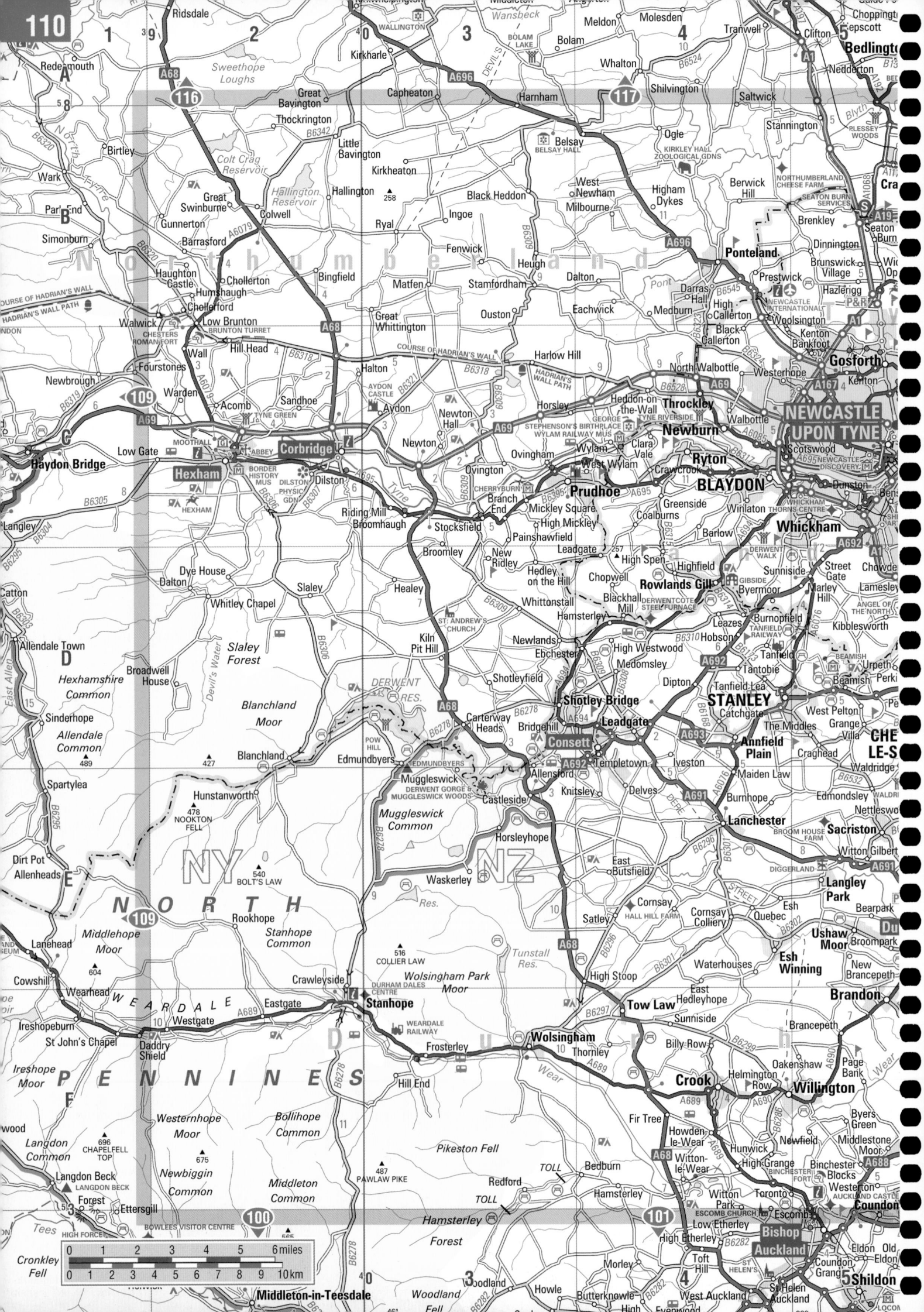

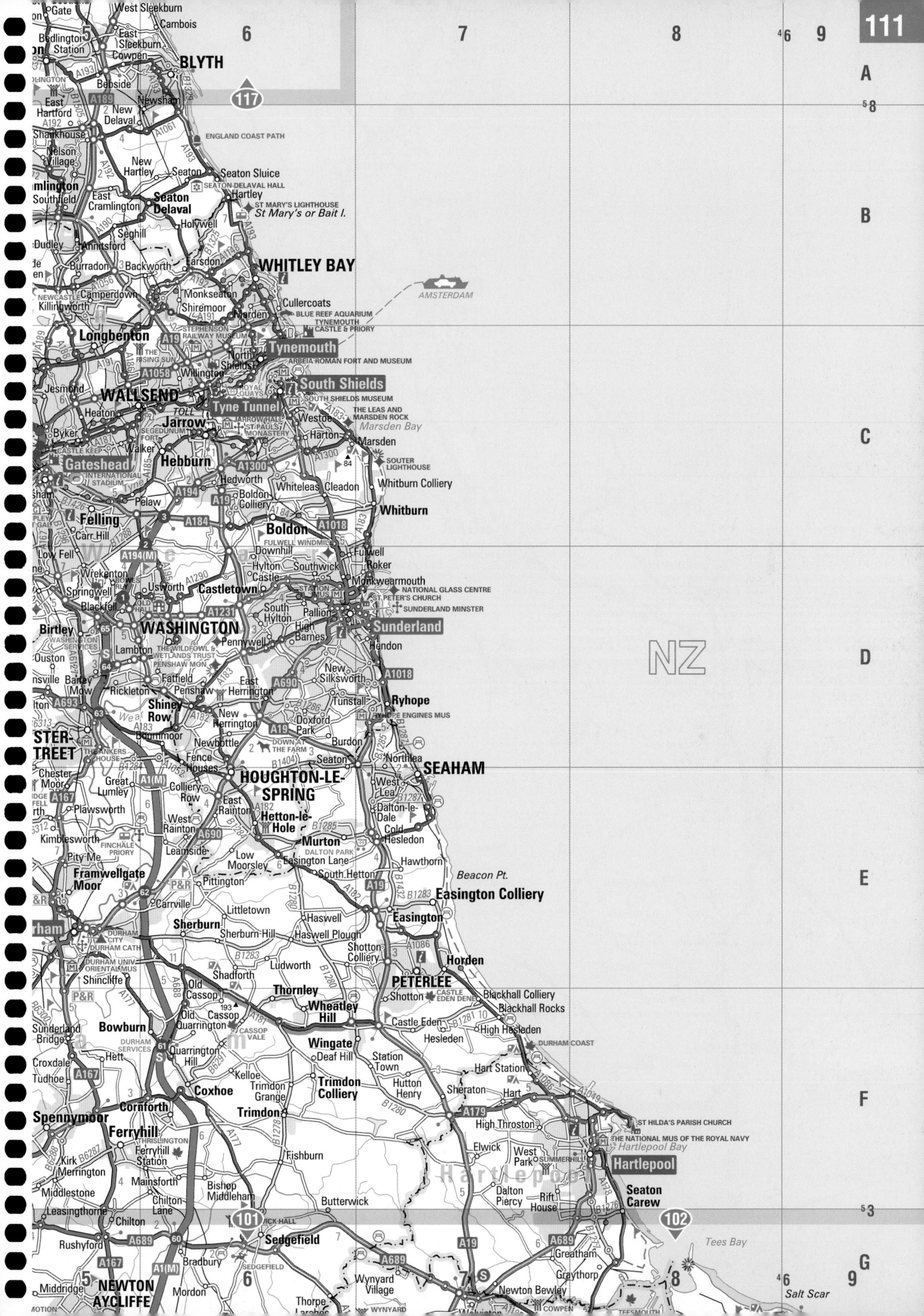

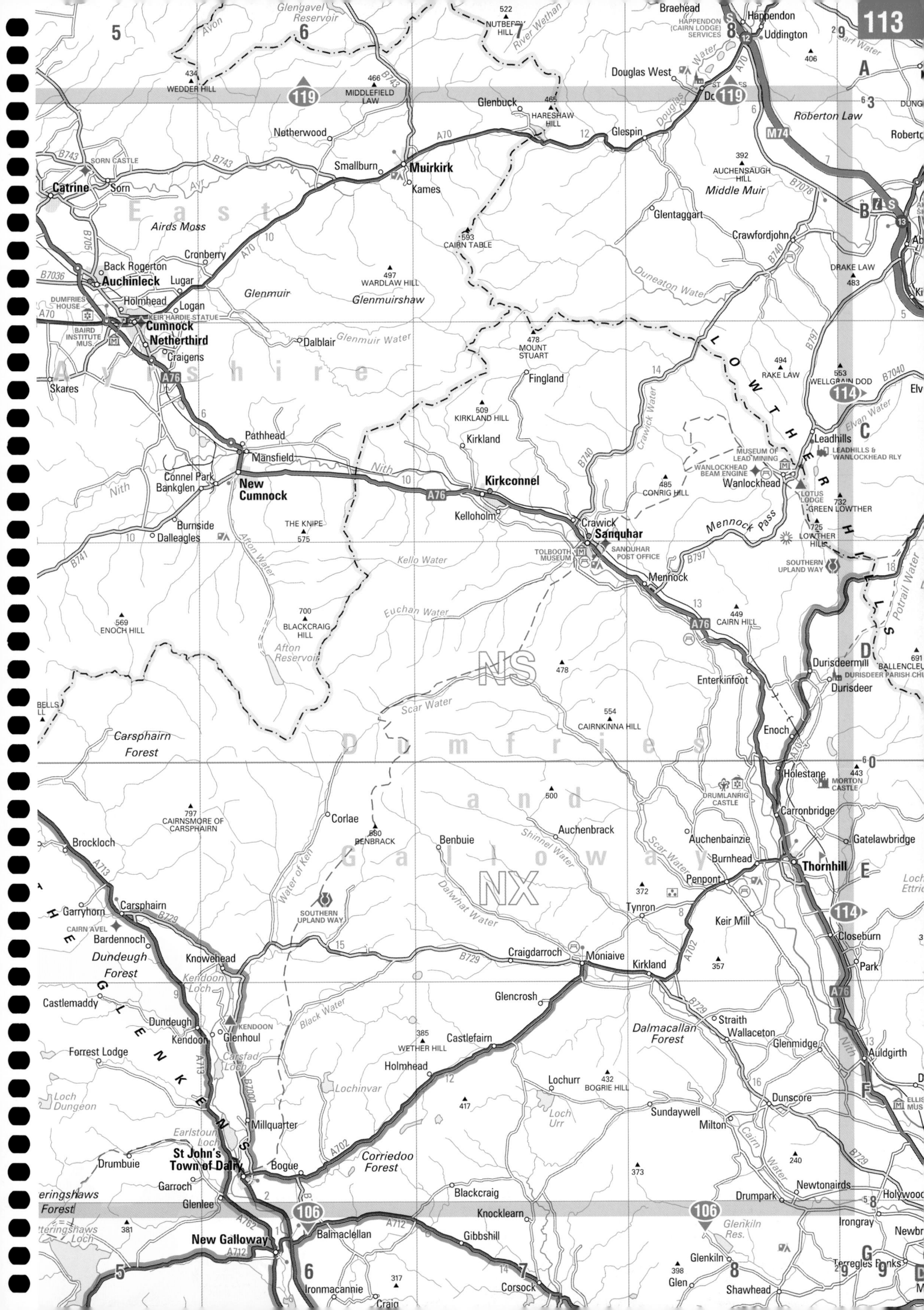

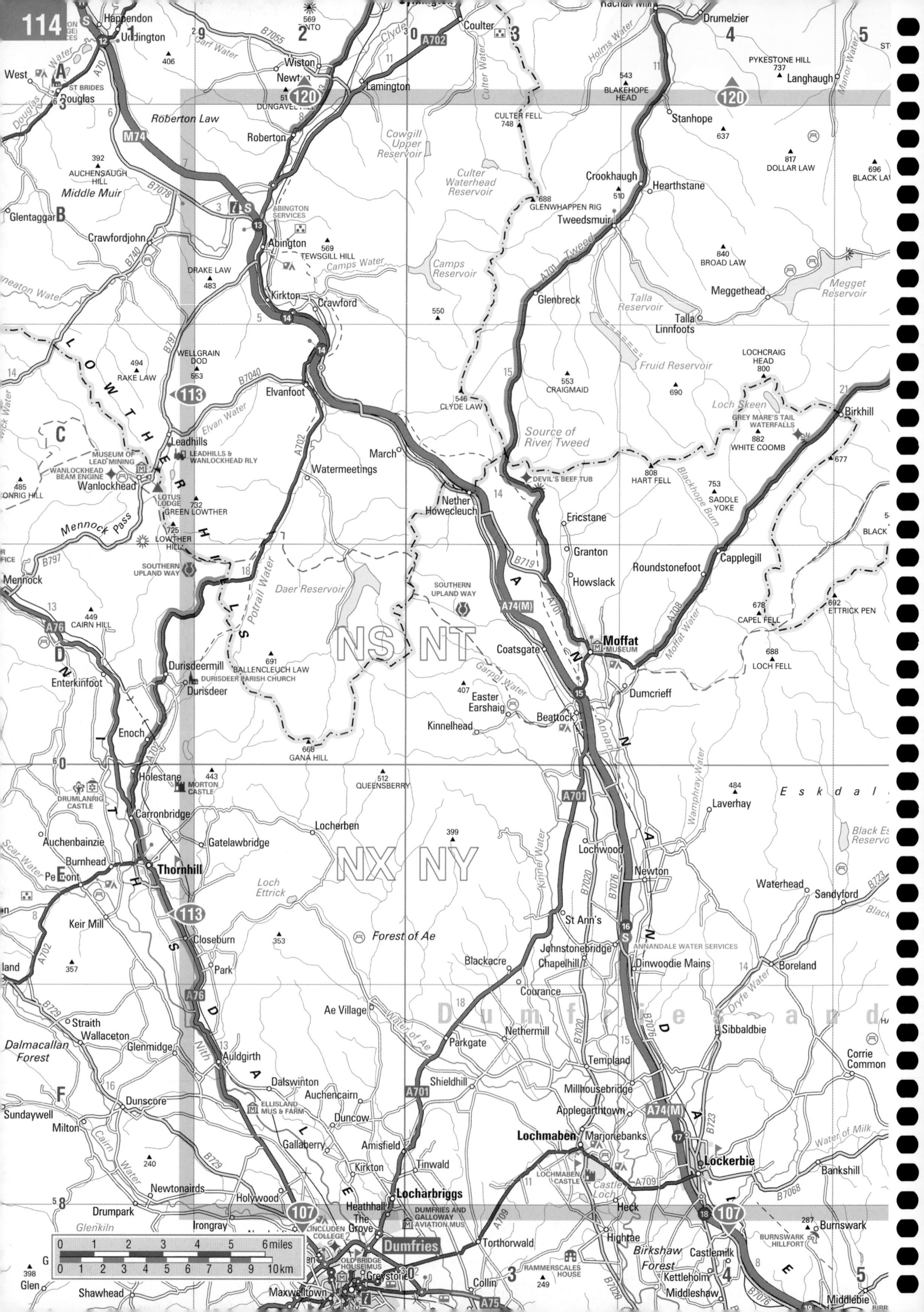

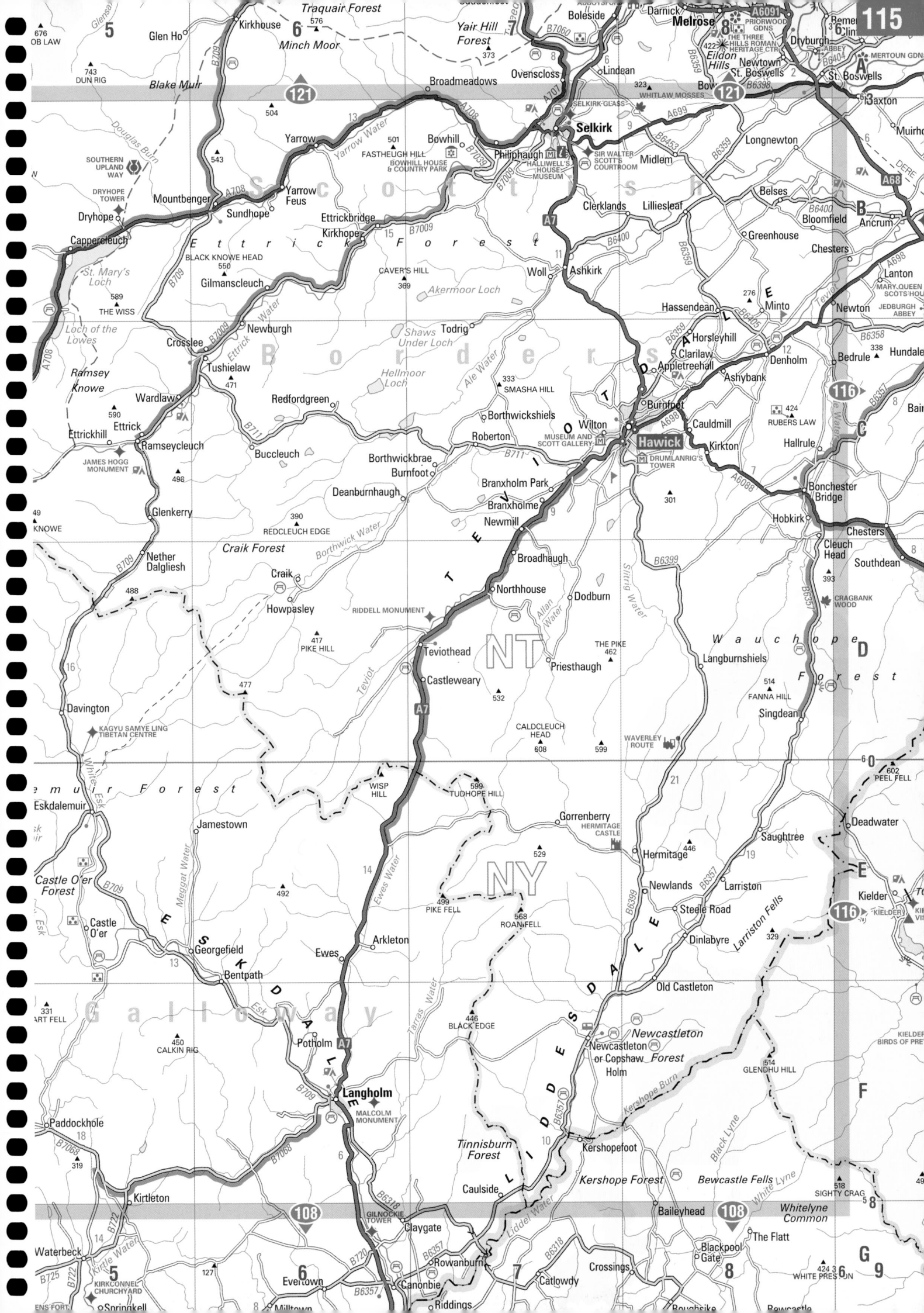

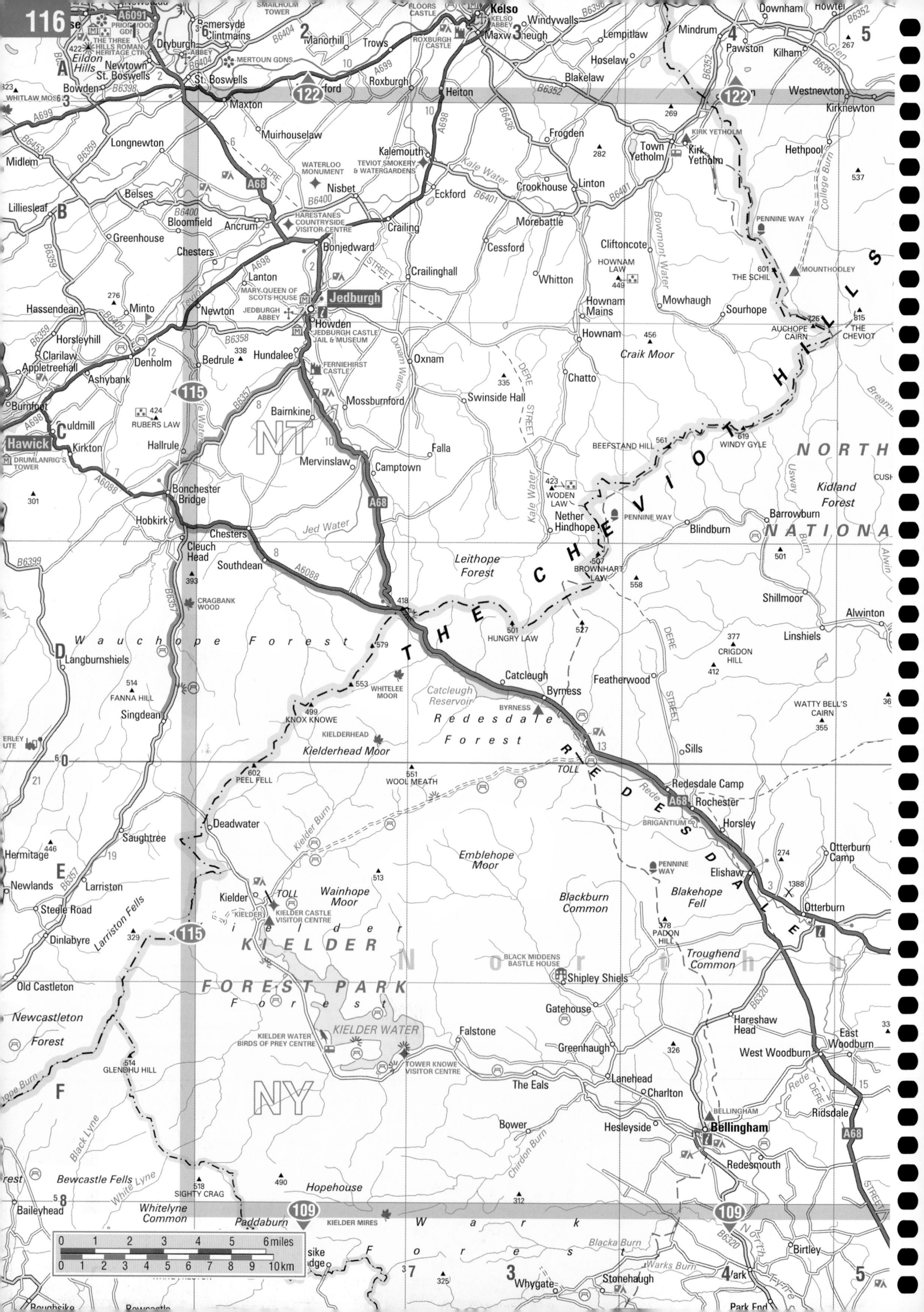

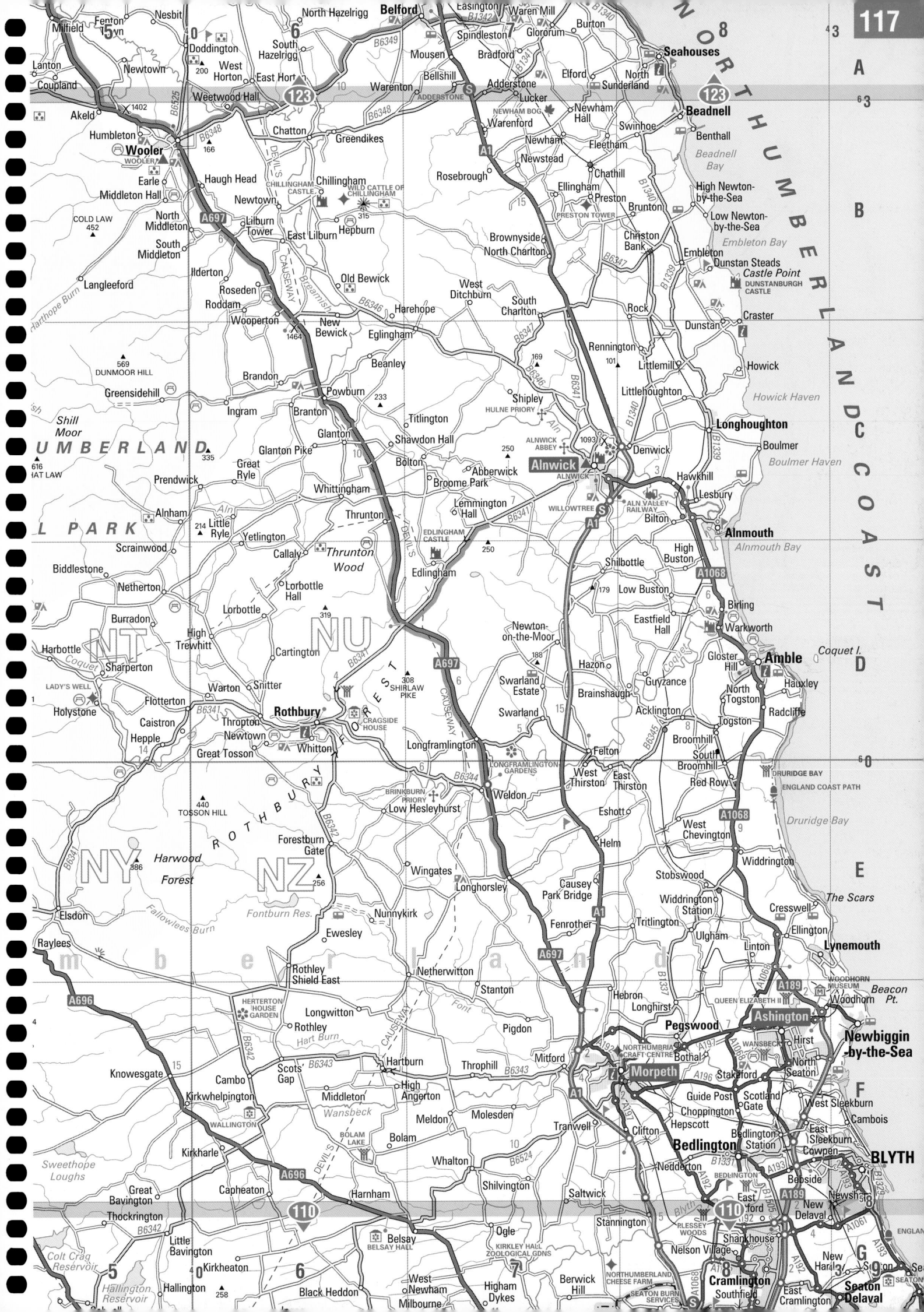

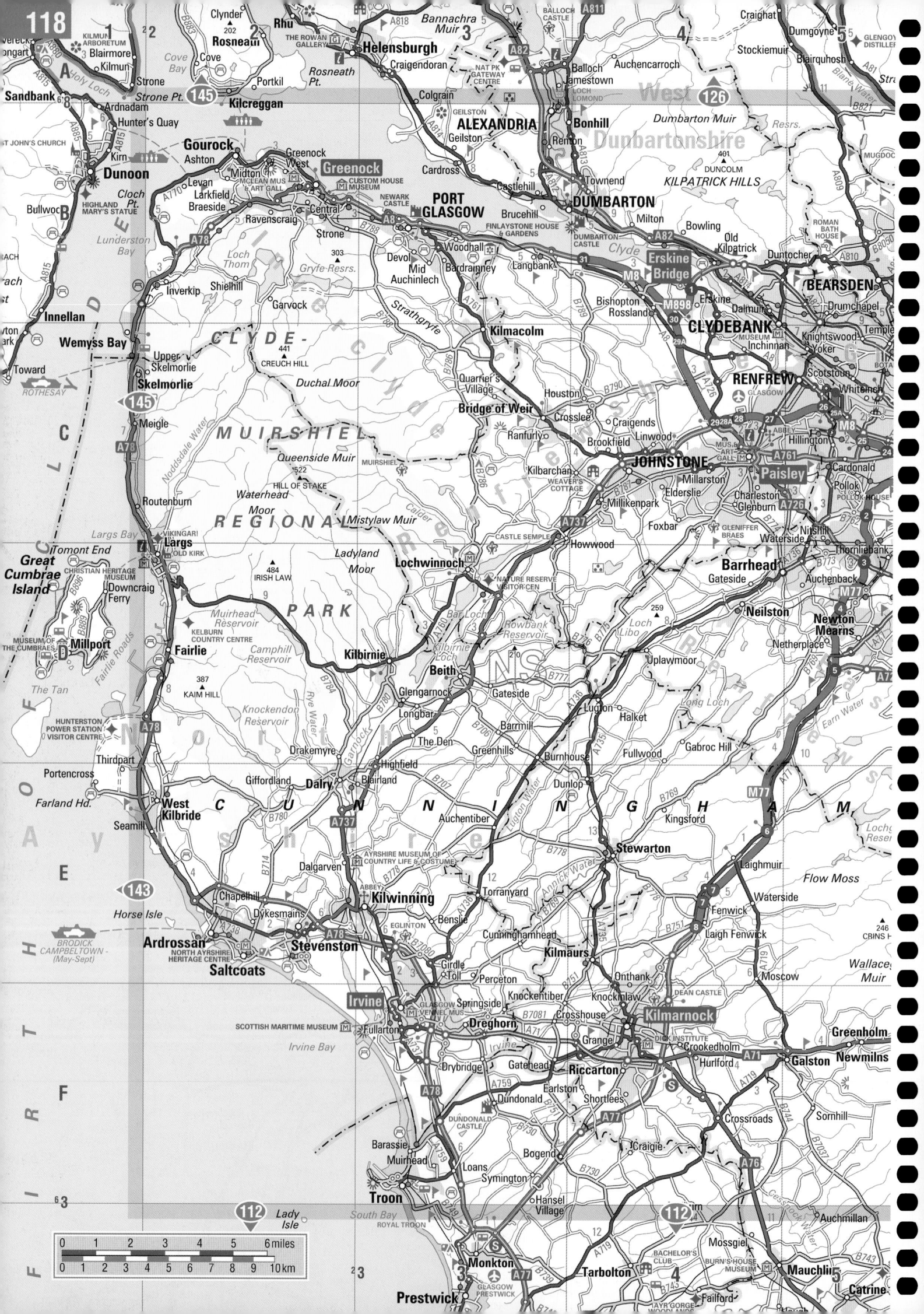

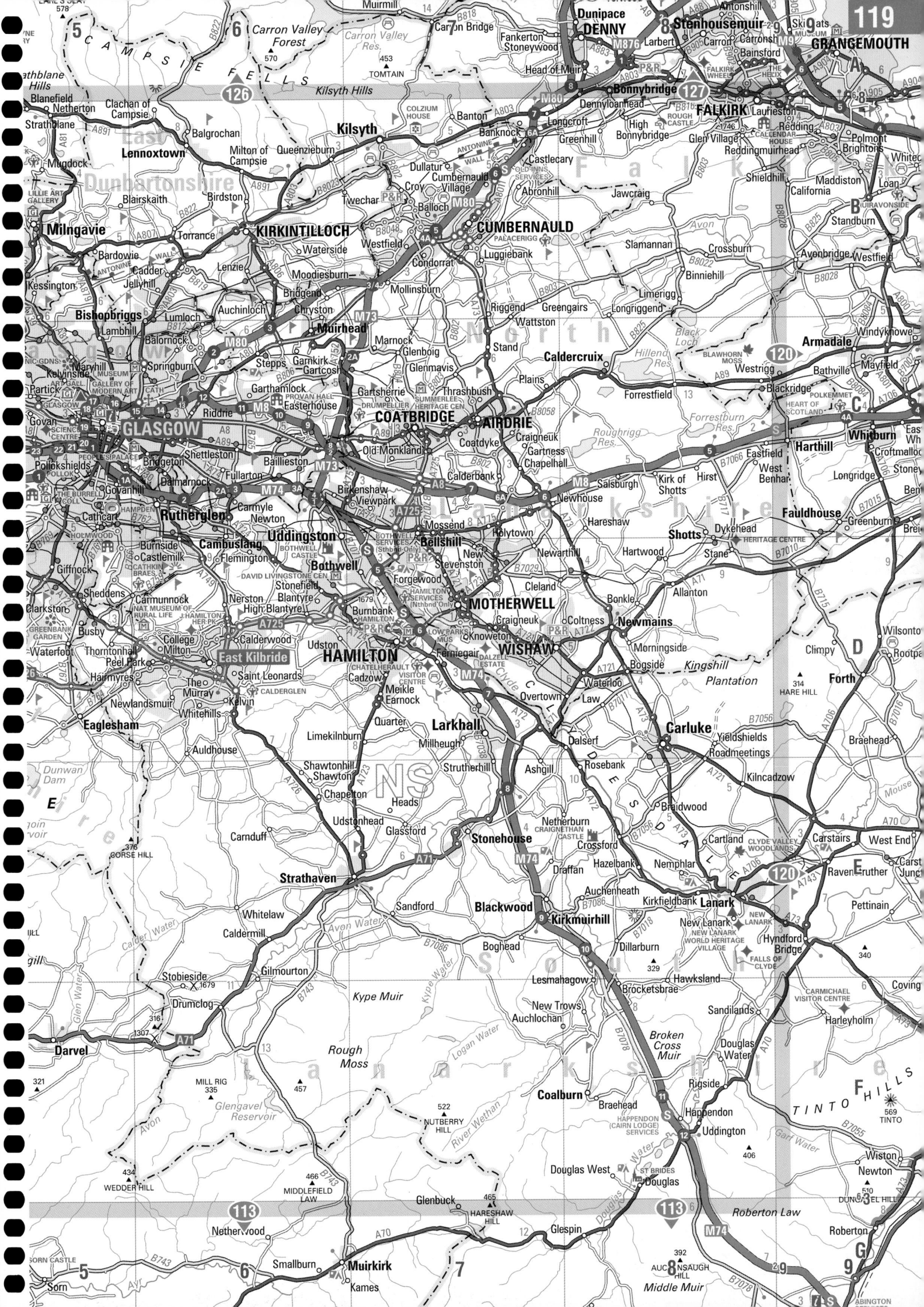

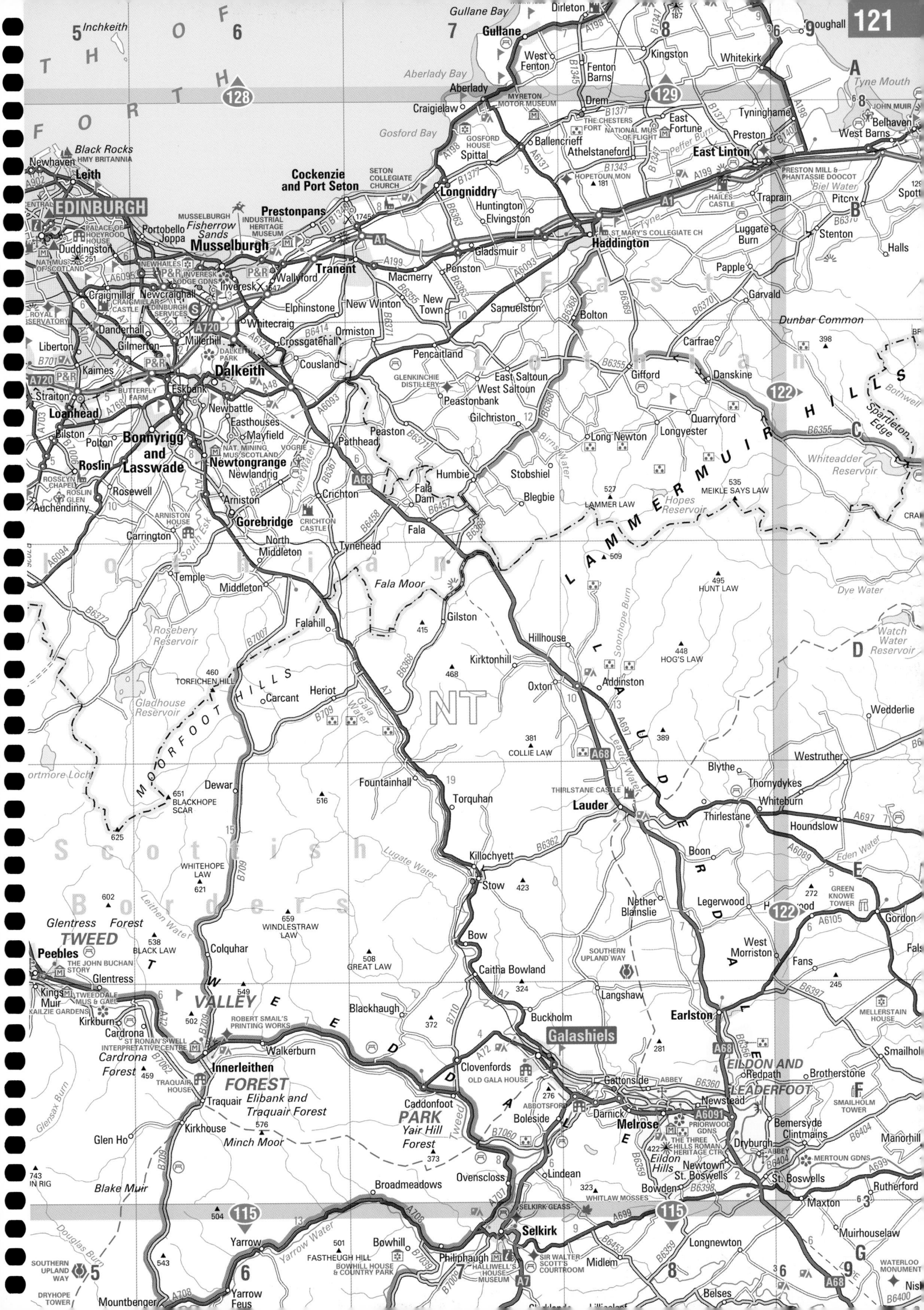

5   6   7   8   43   9

A

68

B

C

EYEMOUTH MUSEUM

Burnmouth

Lamberton Beach

Lamberton

NU

D

1333

Highfields

Berwick-upon-Tweed
BERWICK-UPON-TWEED
BARRACKS & MAIN GUARD
BERWICK

B6461

East Ord

Tweedmouth

Spittal

Tweed

Prior Park

Redshin Cove

A698

108

Murton

Thornton

Scremerston

West Allerdean

Cheswick

Shoresdean

B6354

Goswick

E

Ancroft

North Low

Haggerston

DEVIL'S CAUSEWAY

B6525

Berrington

South Low

Beal

Lindisfarne

Emmanuel Hd.

**Holy Island
(Lindisfarne)**

Bowsden

A1

Causeway
Holy
Island
Sands

Holy
Island

LINDISFARNE CASTLE

Castle Pt.

82

12

B6353

Fenham

HERITAGE
CENTRE

LINDISFARNE
PRIORY

Barmoor
Castle

Barmoor
Lane End

West
Kyloe

Fenwick

Guile
Pt.

HERSLAW
MILL

B6353

Lowick

Kyloe
Hills

East
Kyloe

Buckton

Farne
Islands

LADY WATERFORD HALL

157

Holburn

Detchant

Elwick

Ross

Budle
Bay

Staple Sound

FARNE ISLANDS

Kimmerston

Hetton
Steads

211

Middleton

Budle

BAMBURGH
CASTLE

Inner Sound

F

Fenton
Town

Nesbit

North Hazelrigg

Belford

Easington

Waren Mill

Bamburgh

B1340

63

Doddington

South
Hazelrigg

B6349

Spindlestone

Glororum

Burton

200

West
Horton

East Horton

10

Mousen

Bradford

B1340

Elford

North
Sunderland

Seahouses

Newtown

Warenton

Bellshill

Adderstone

Lucker

Akeld

1402

Weetwood Hall

ADDERSTONE

117

NEWHAM BOG

Newham
Hall

Beal

117

Humbleton

A697

B6625

B6348

Chatton

Greendikes

Warenford

Warenford

Newham

Swinhoe

Benthall

Beadnell
Bay

Wooler

WOOLER

166

DEVIL'S

A1

Newstead

Fleetham

B1340

5   4 0   6   7   8   43   9

Earle

Haugh Head

CHILLINGHAM
CASTLE

Chillingham

WILD CATTLE OF
CHILLINGHAM

Rosebrough

Chathill

G

Middleton Hall

Newtown

Ellingham

Preston

High Newton-
by-the-Sea

15

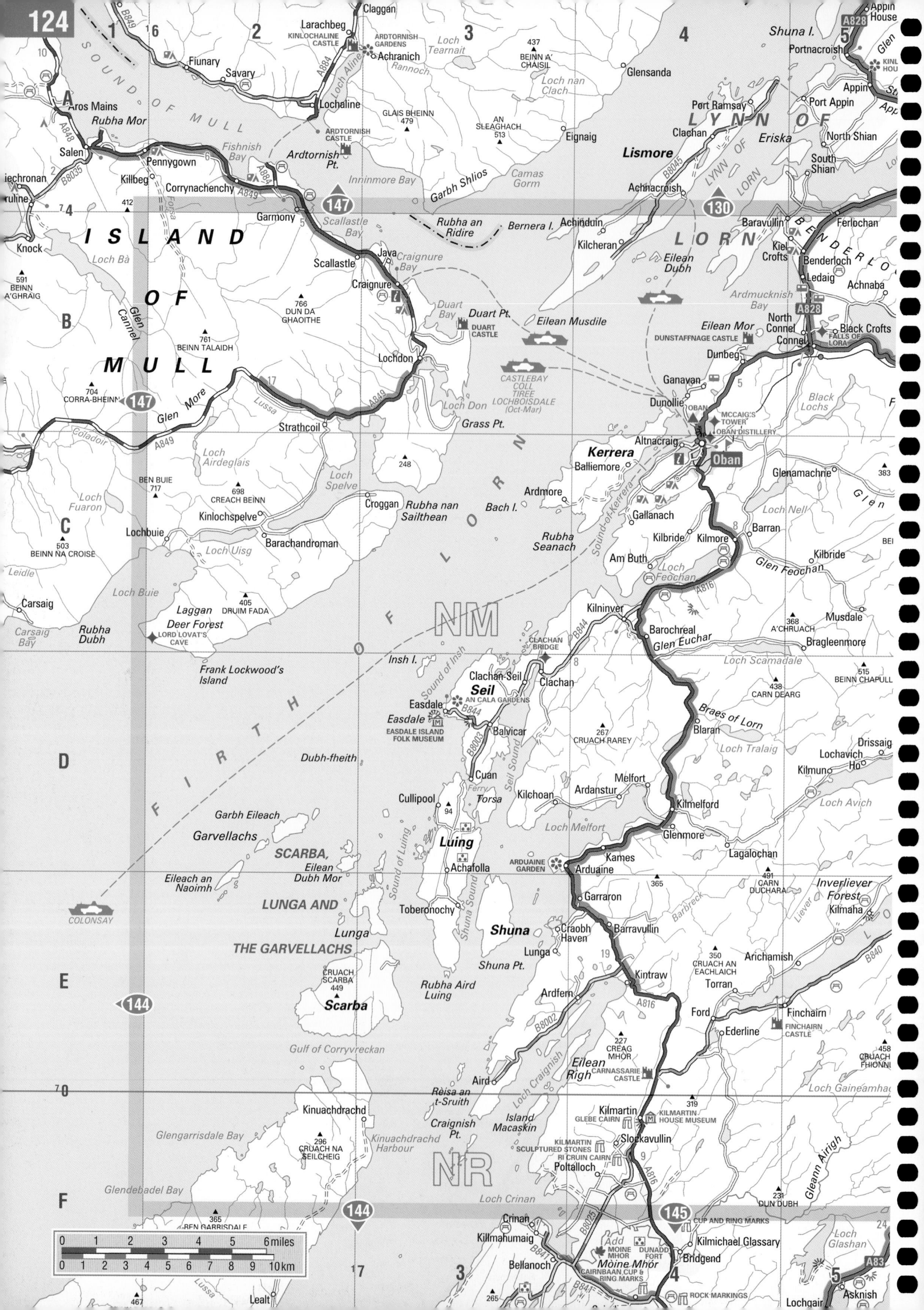

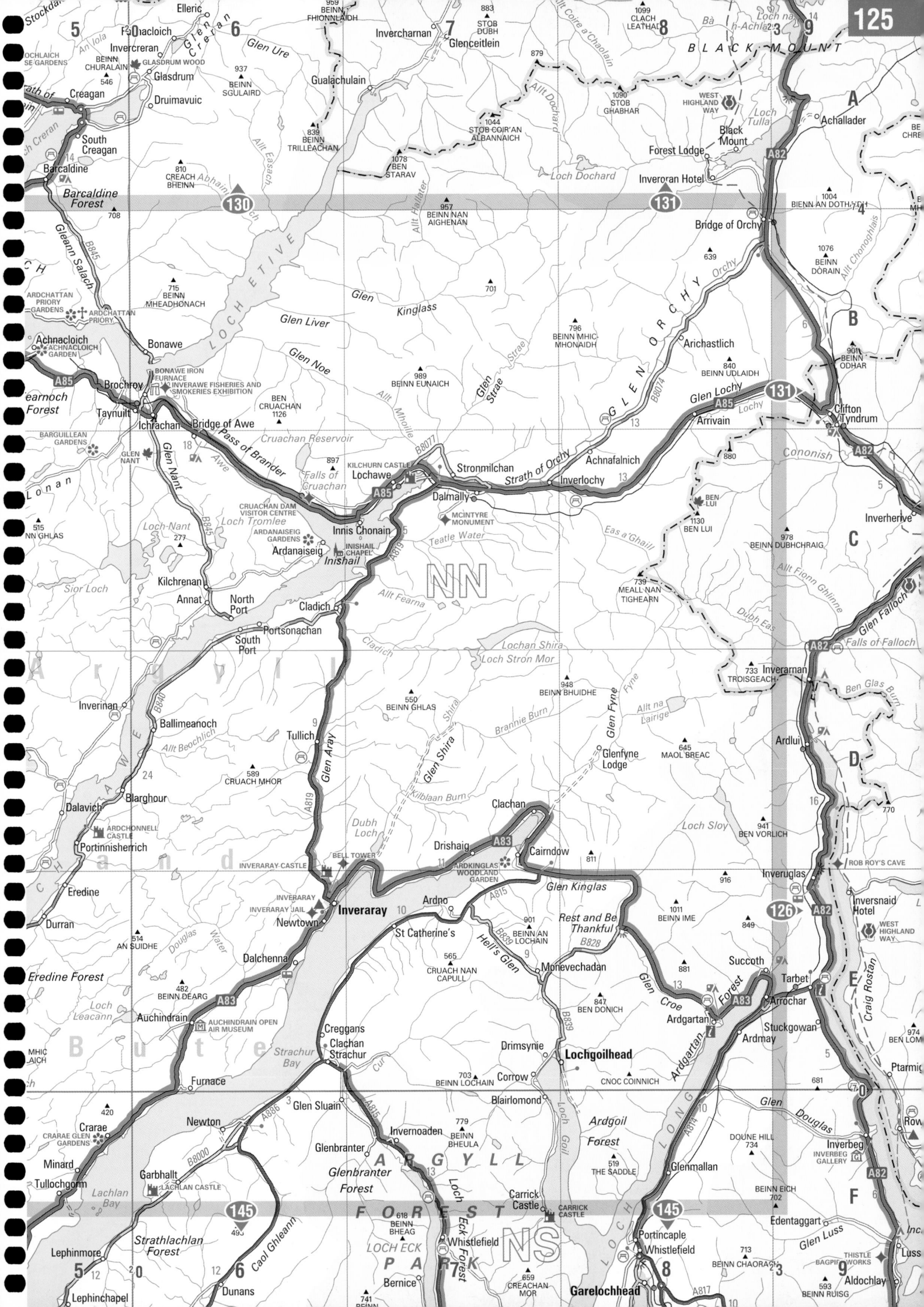

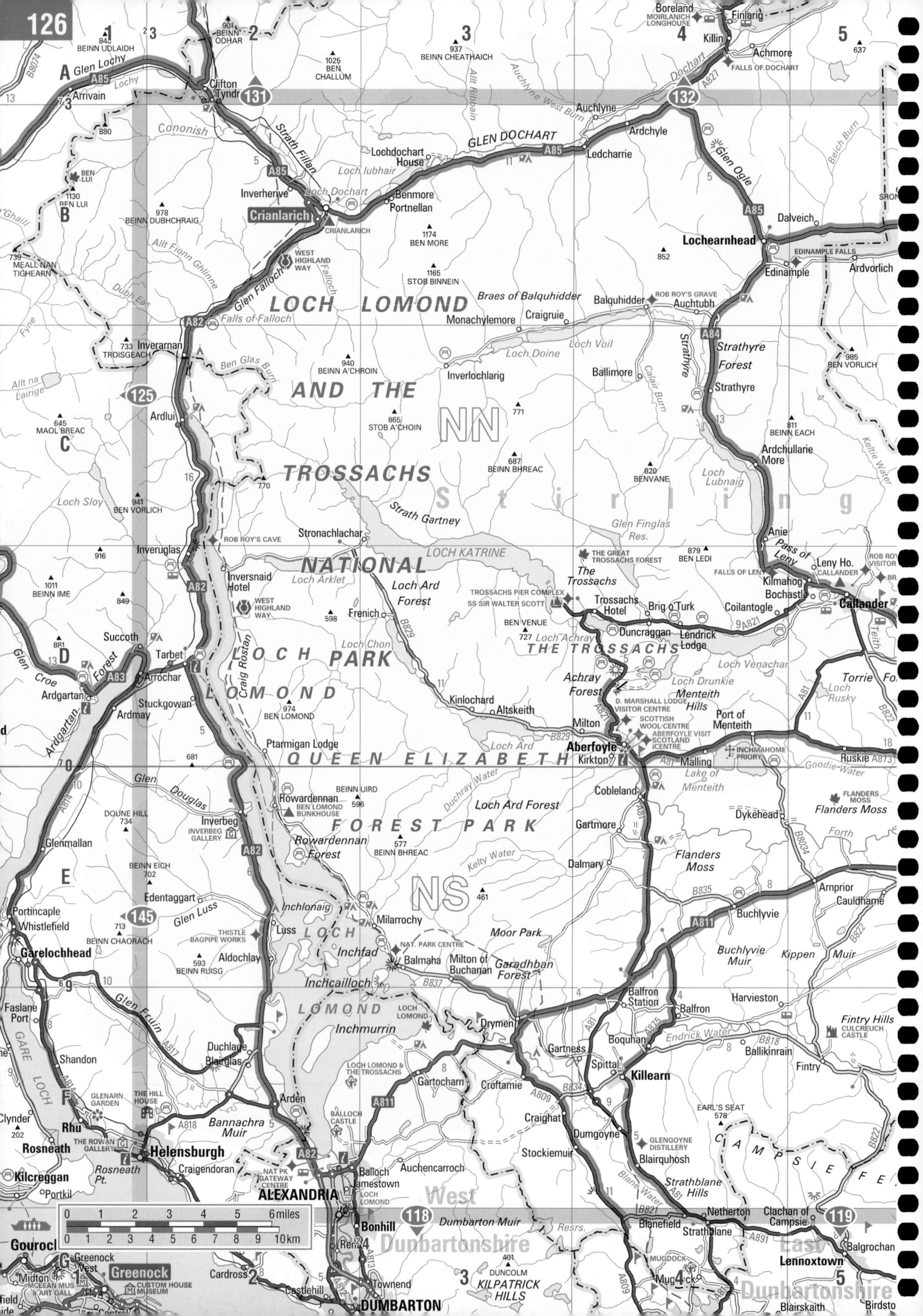

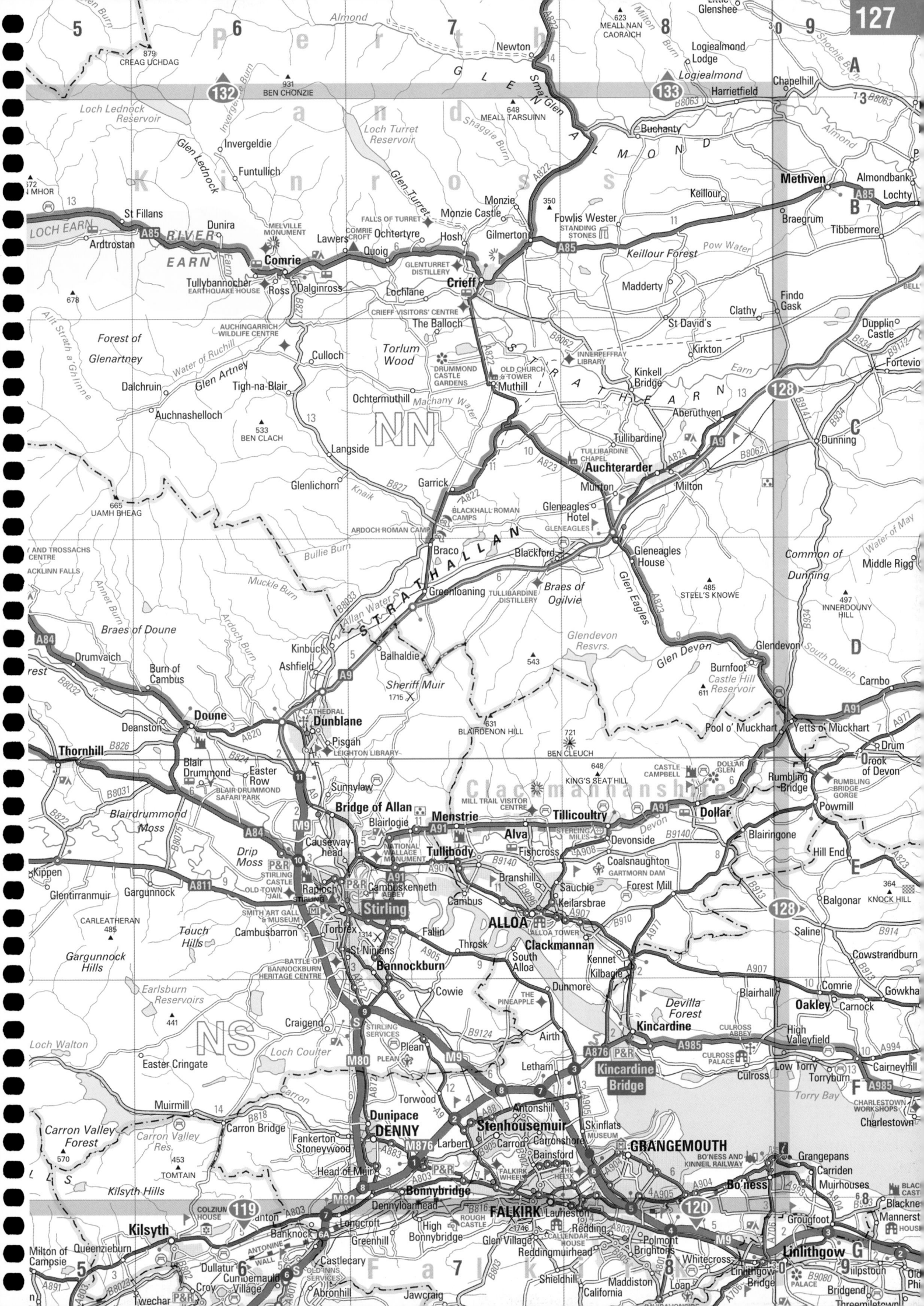

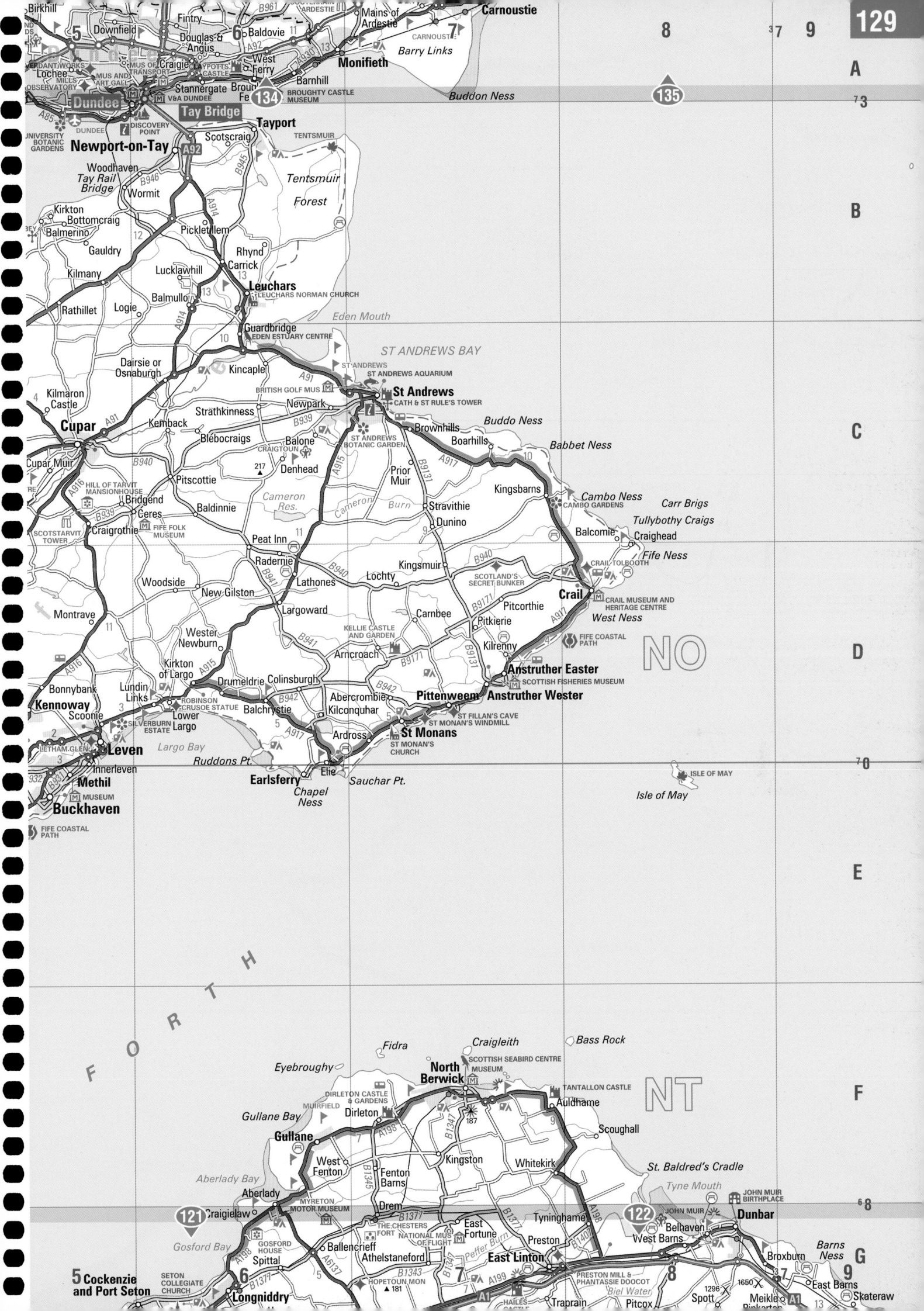

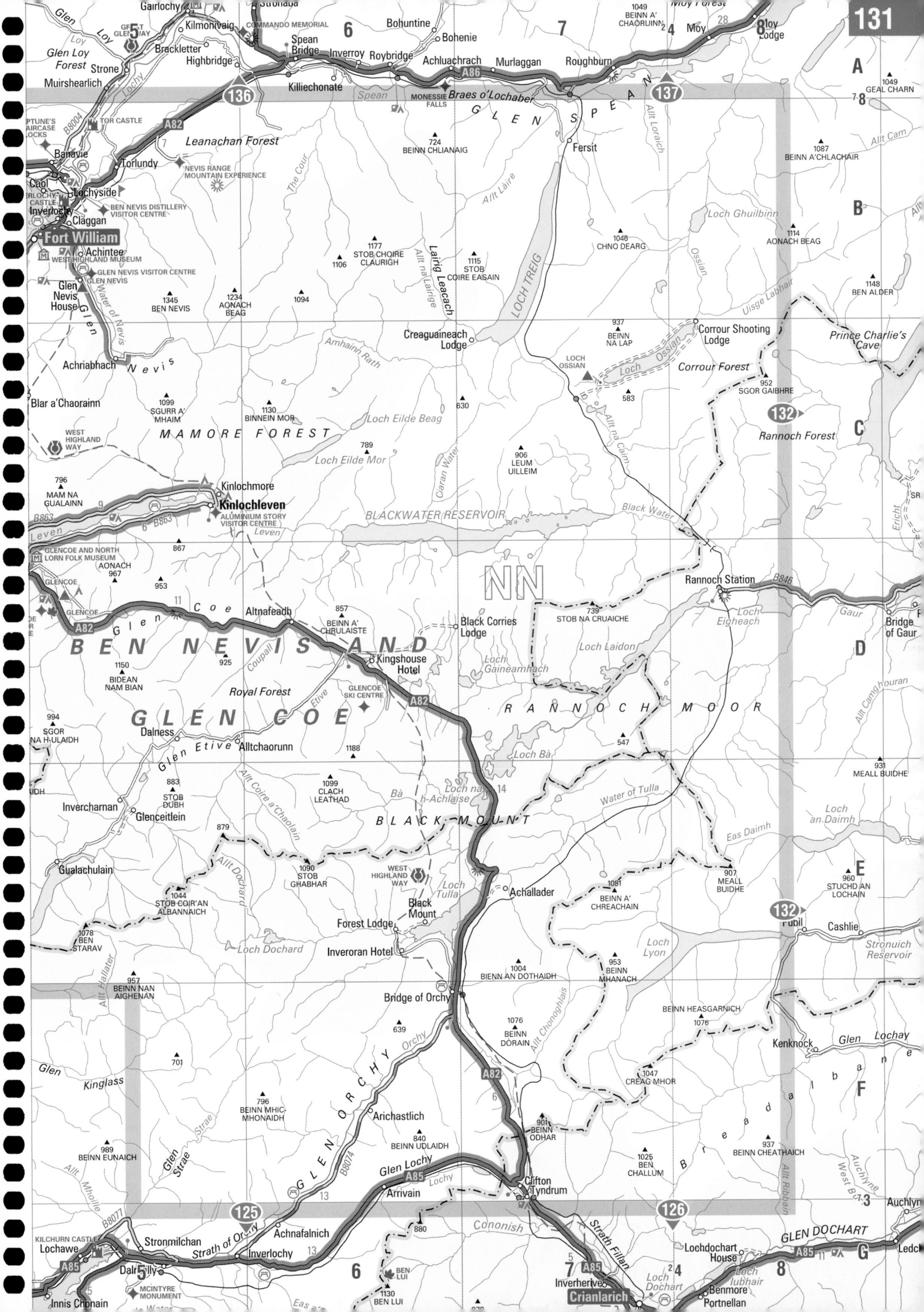

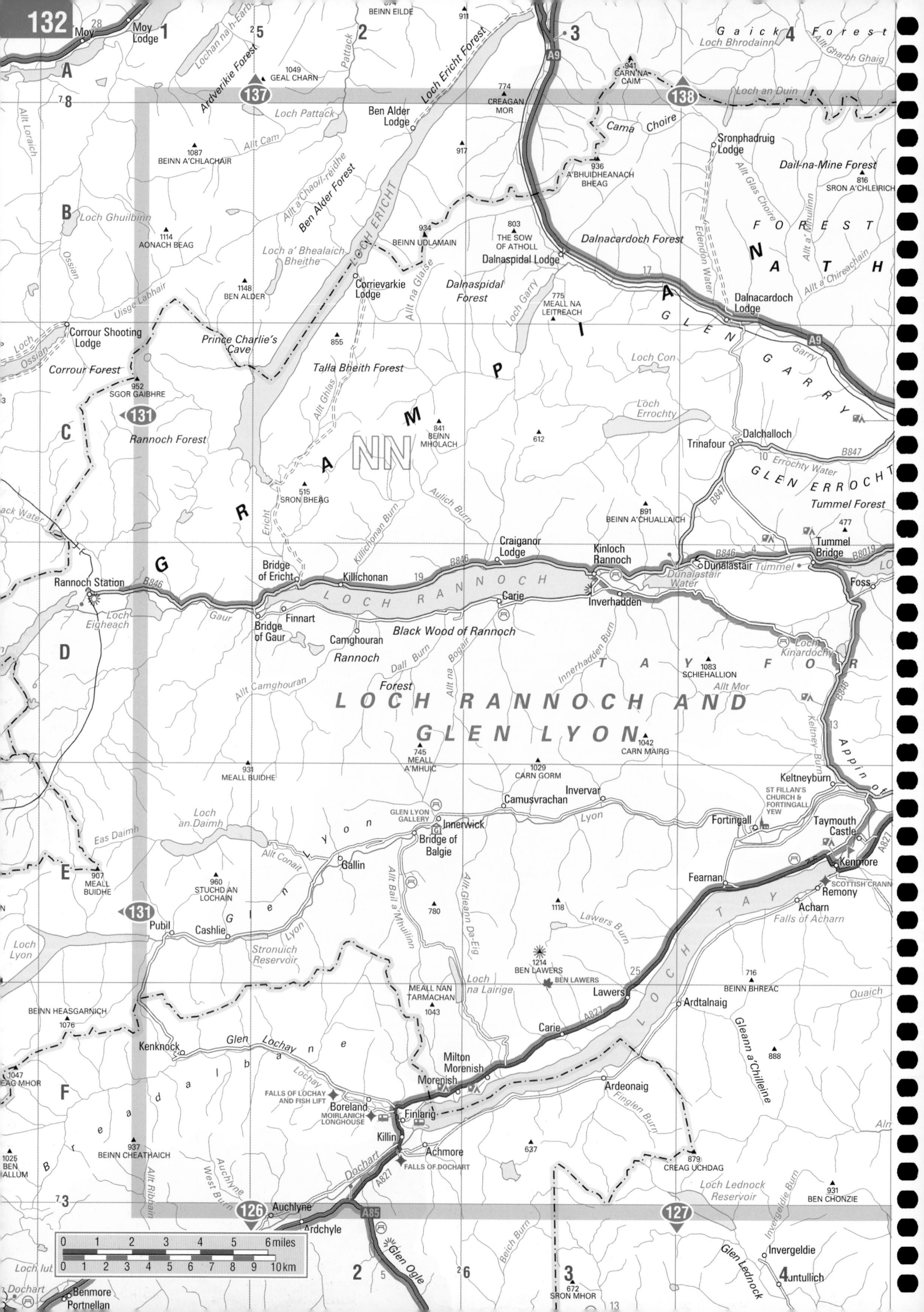

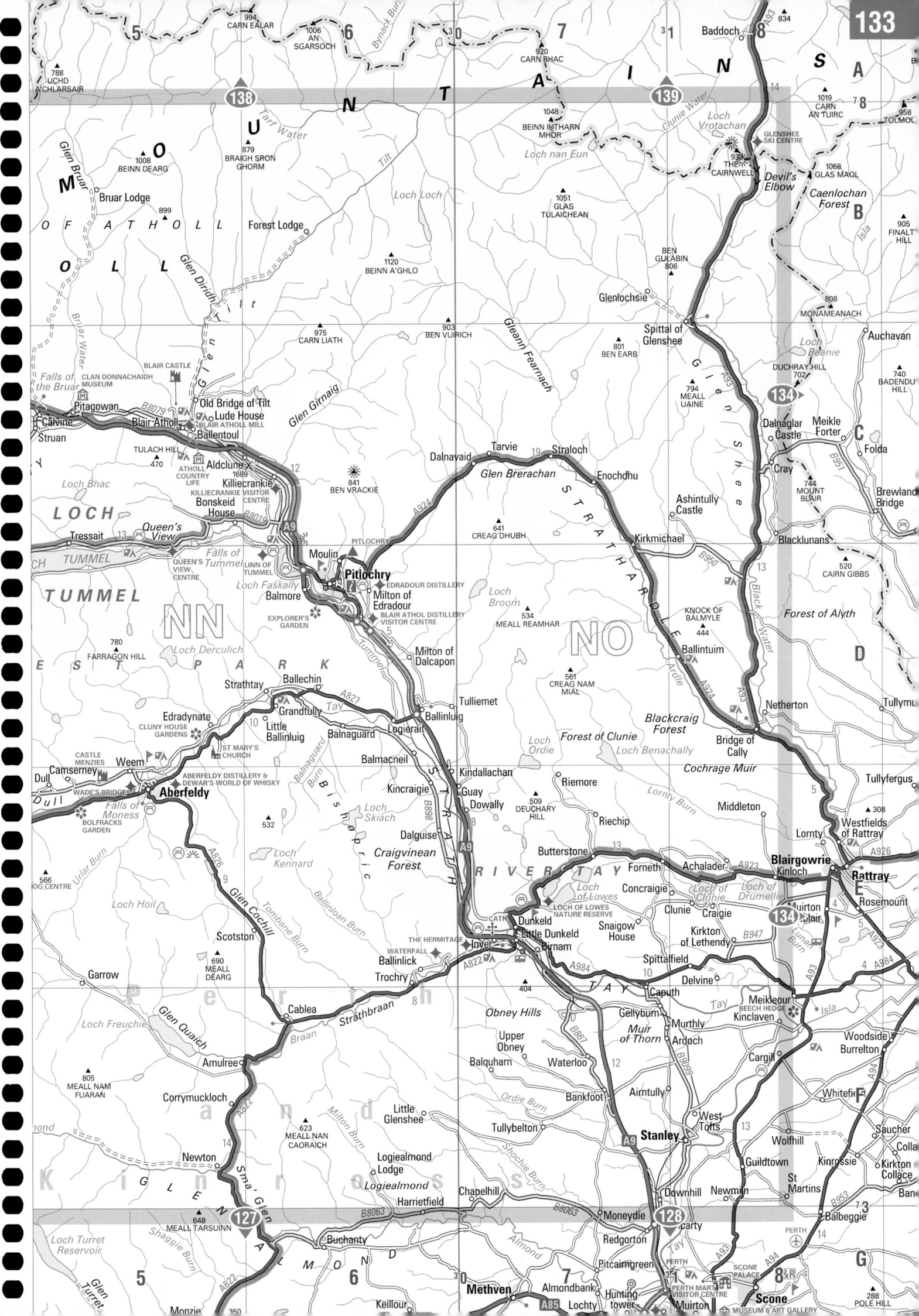

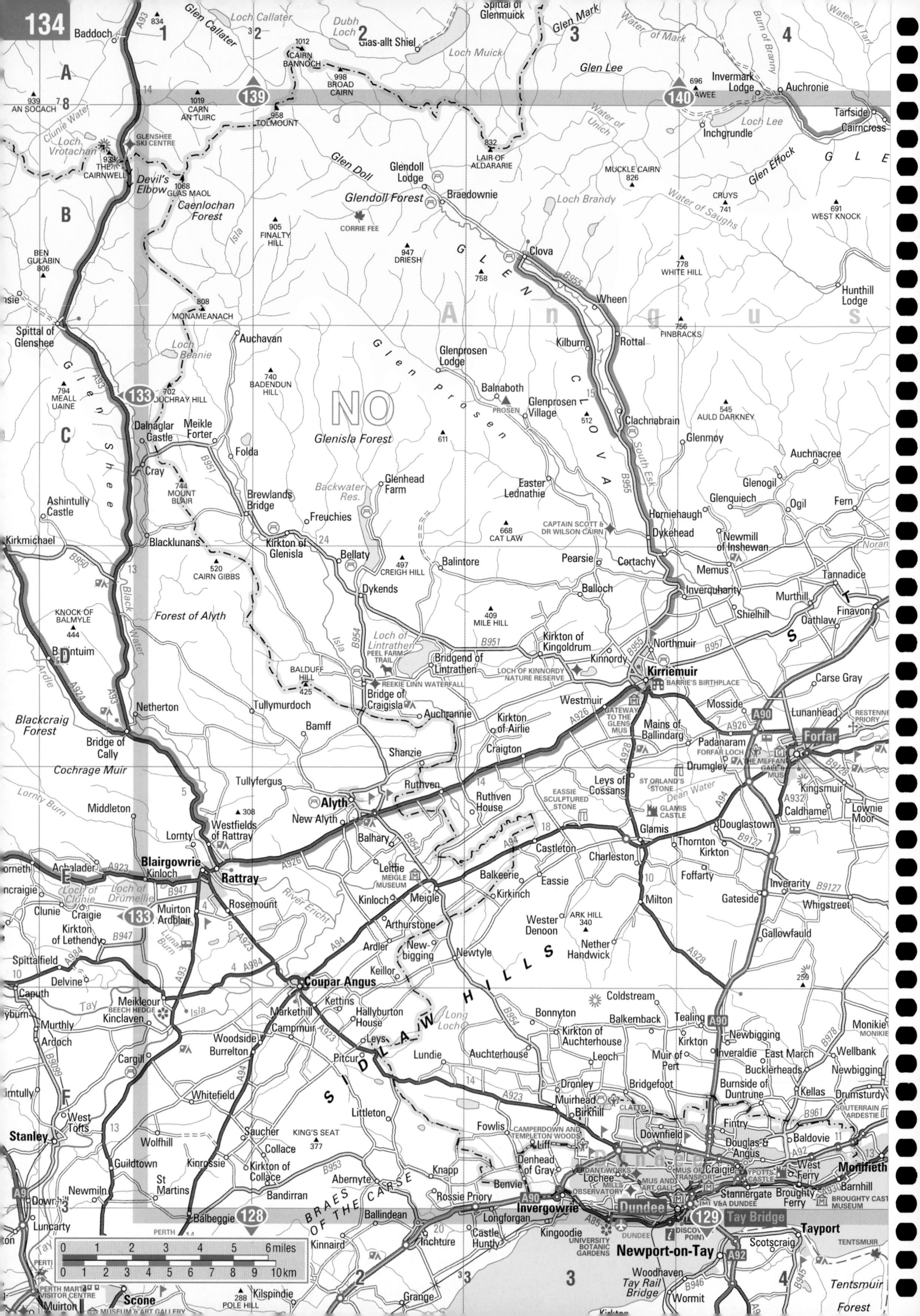

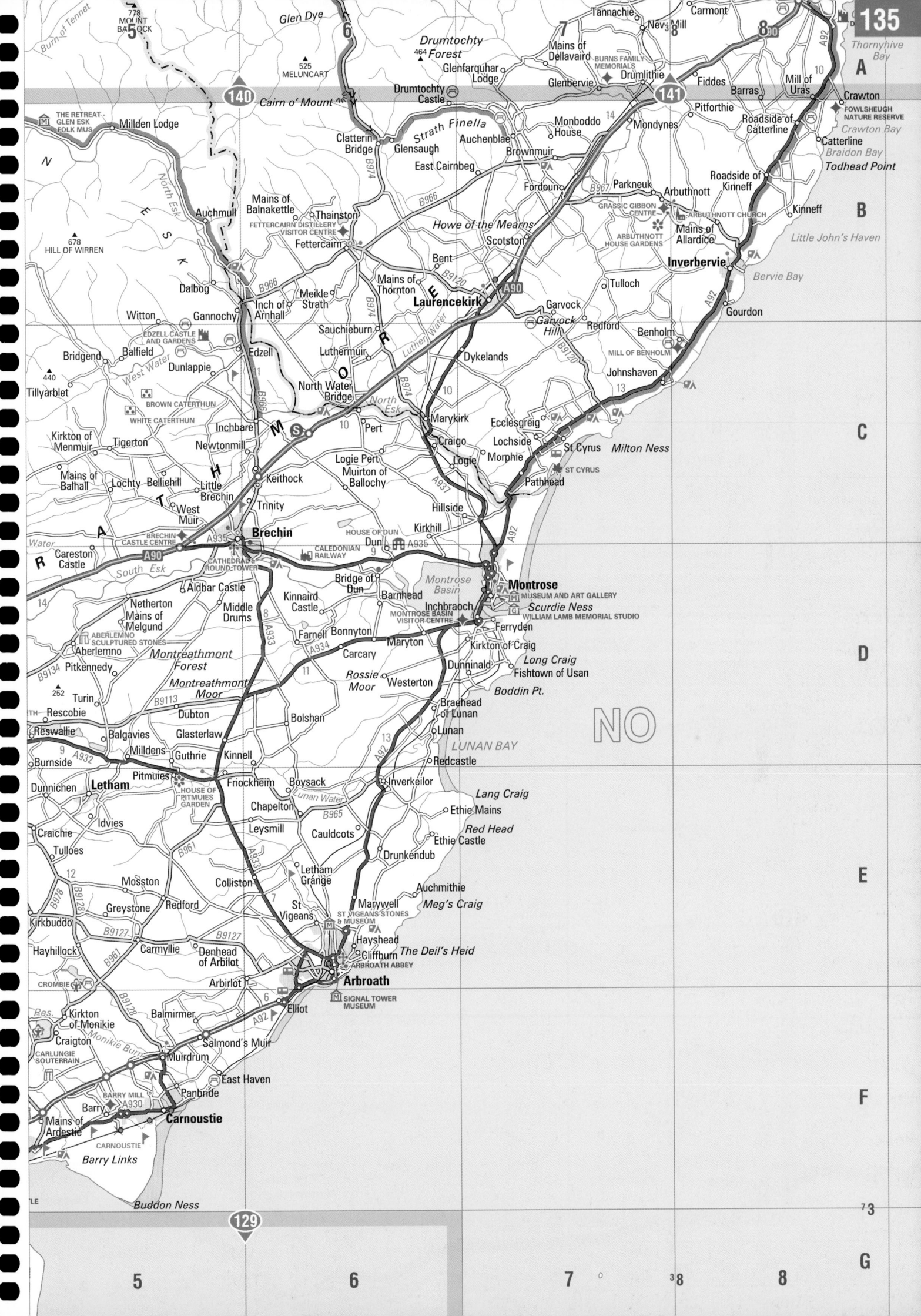

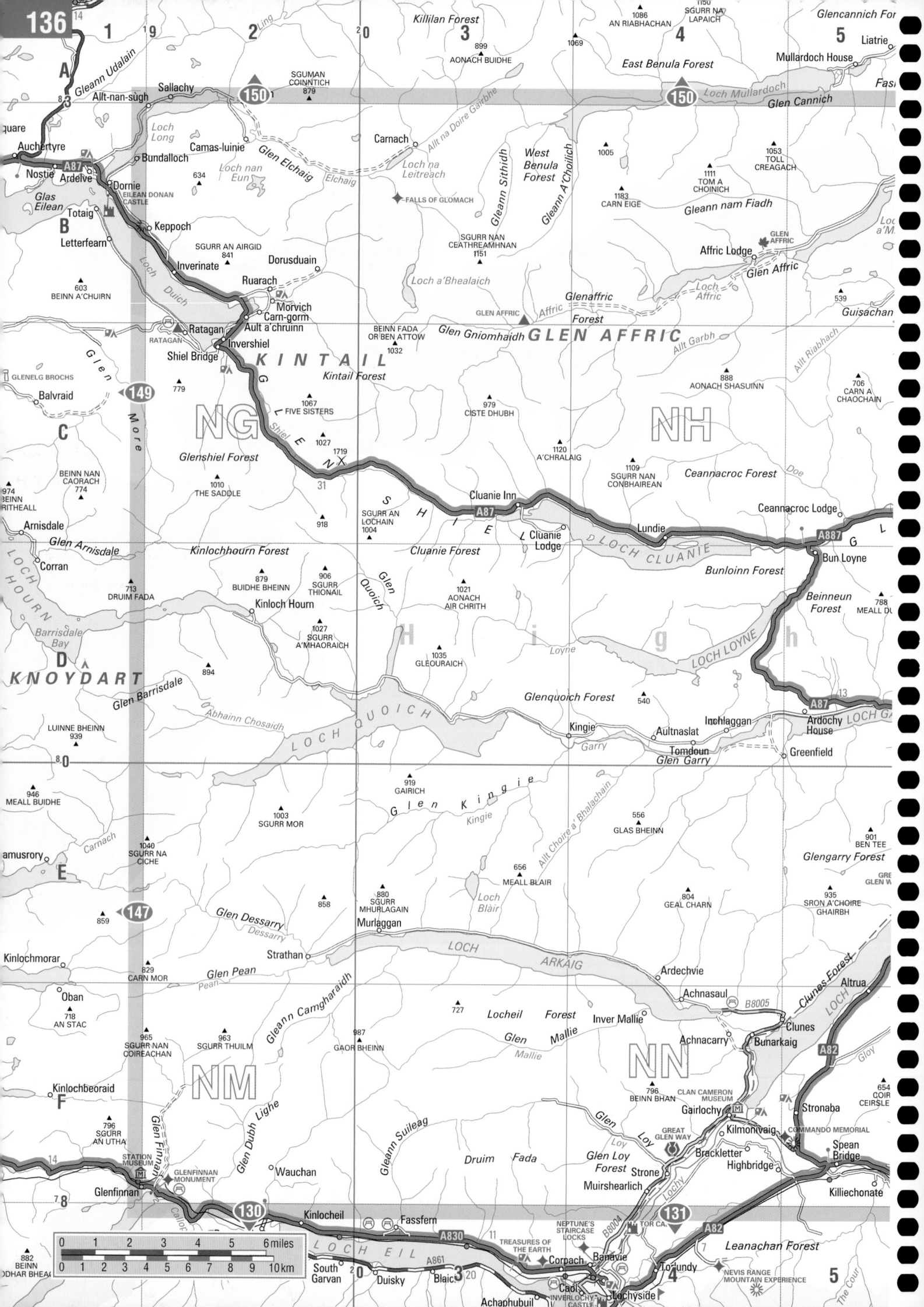

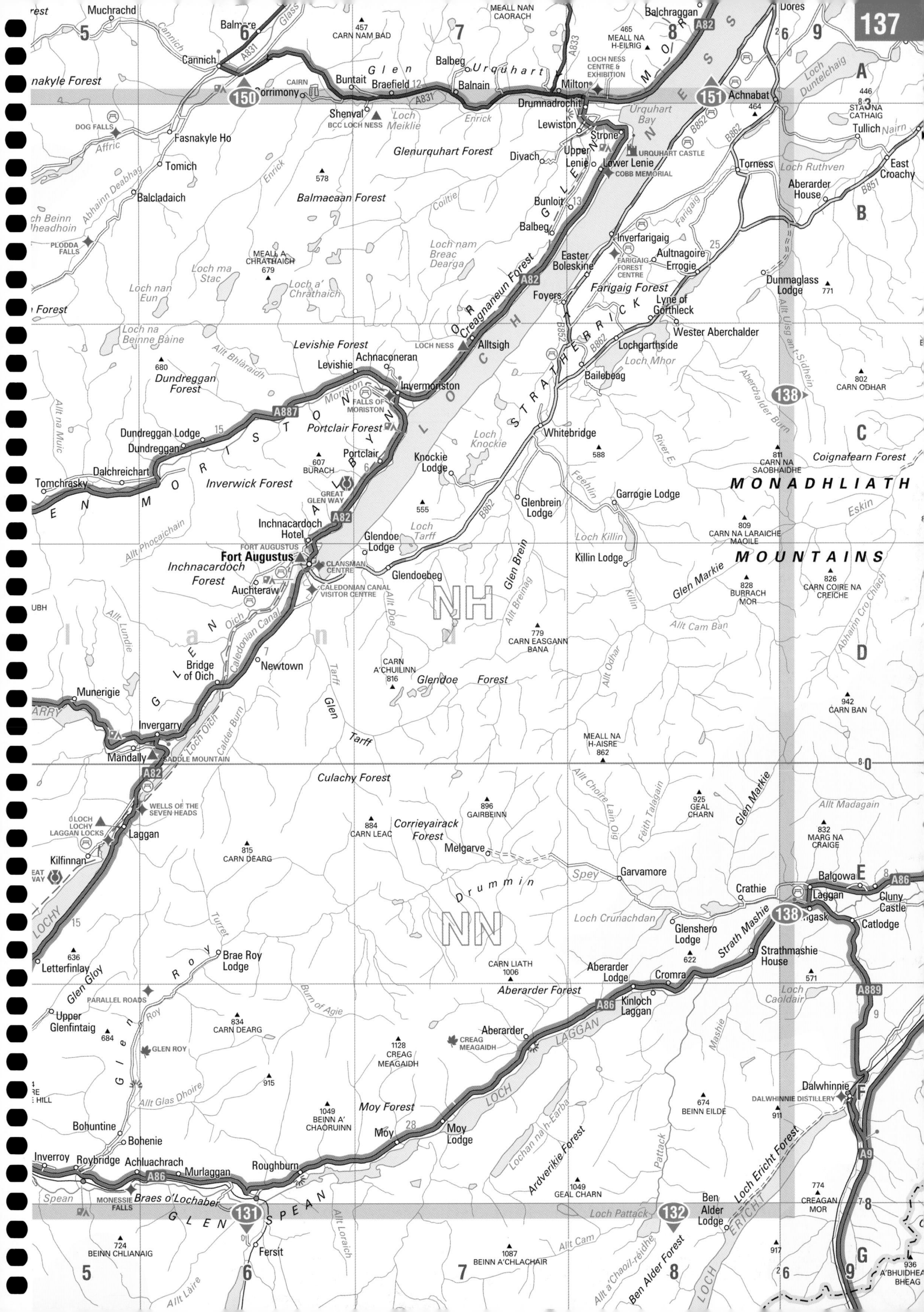

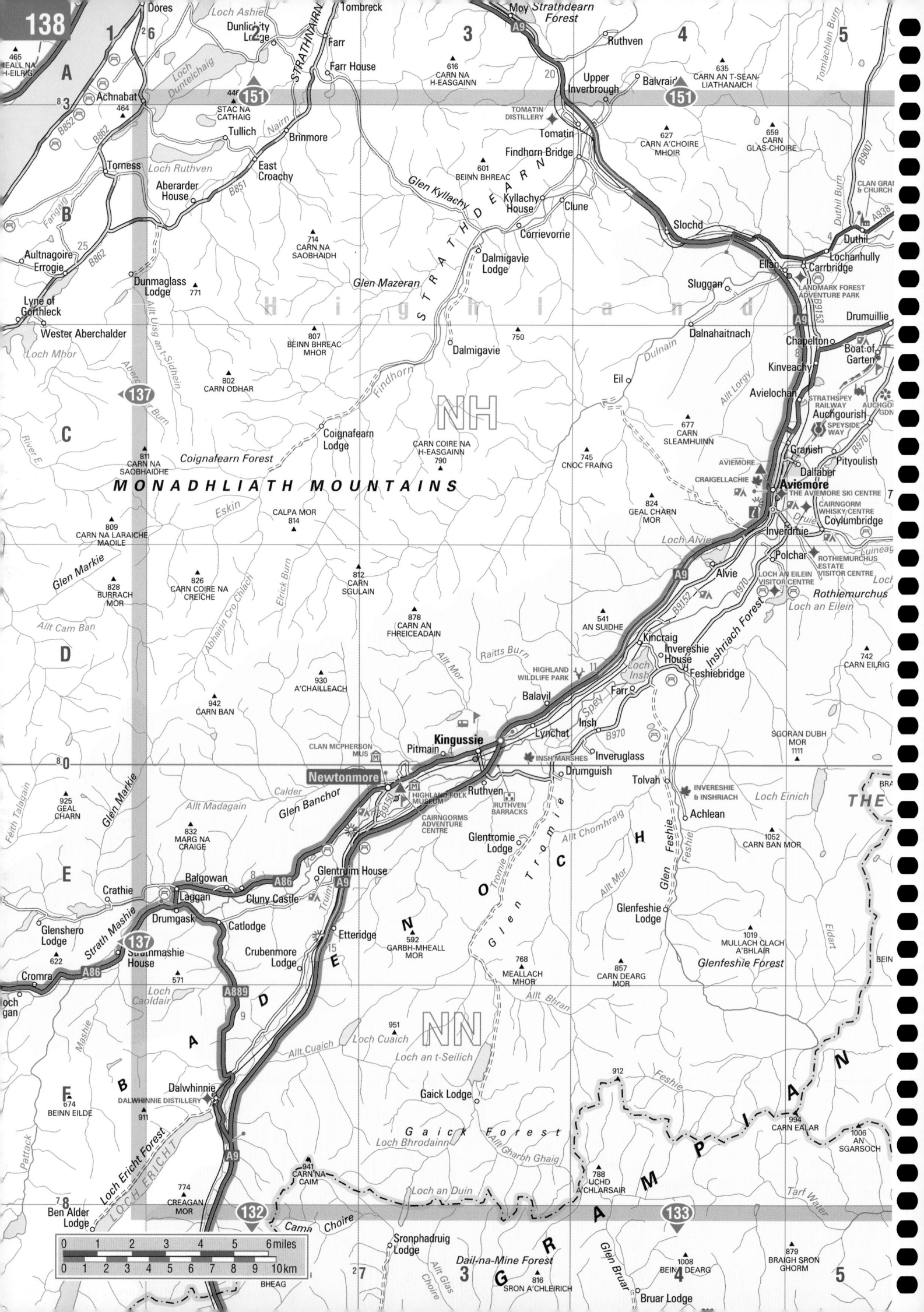

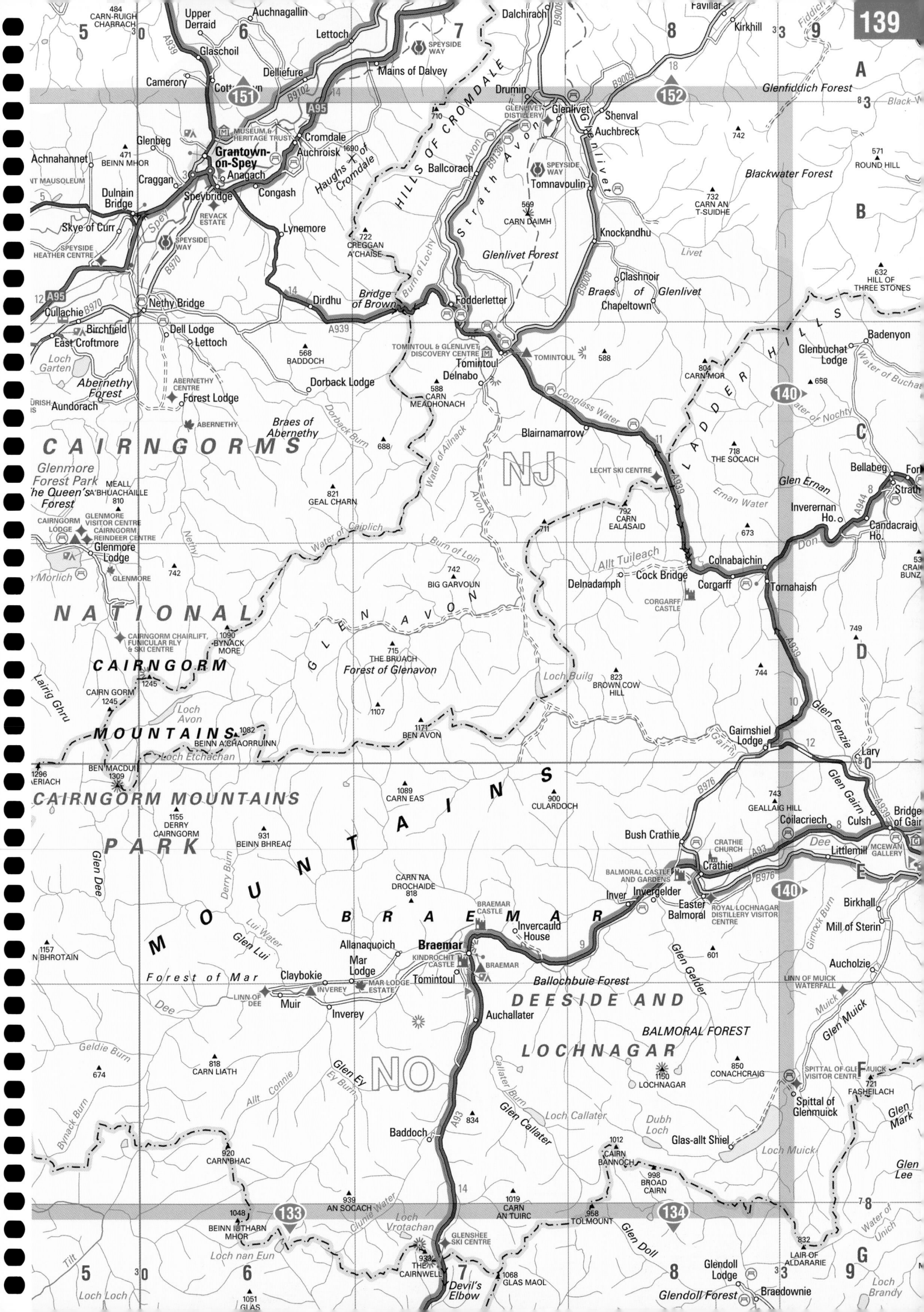

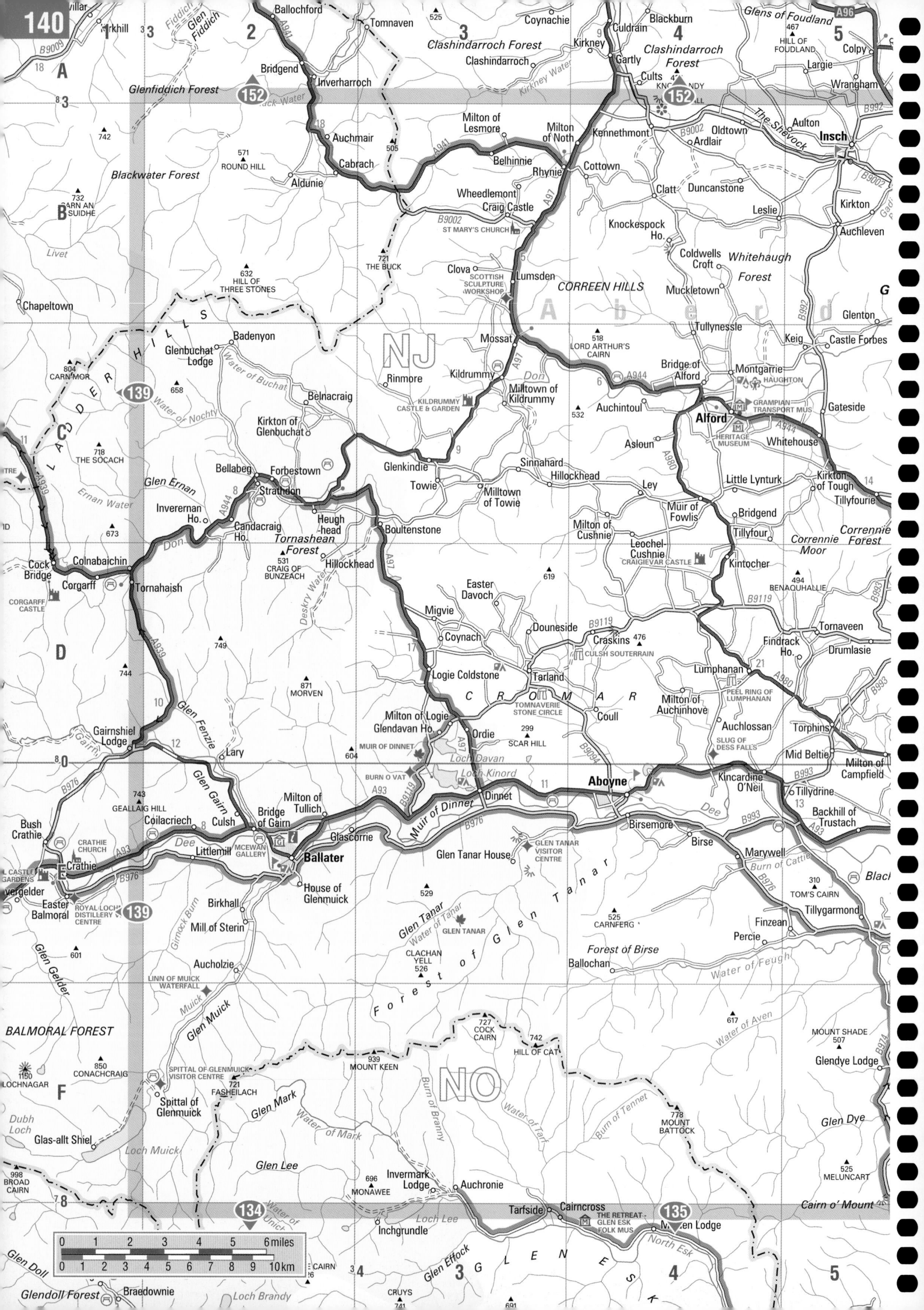

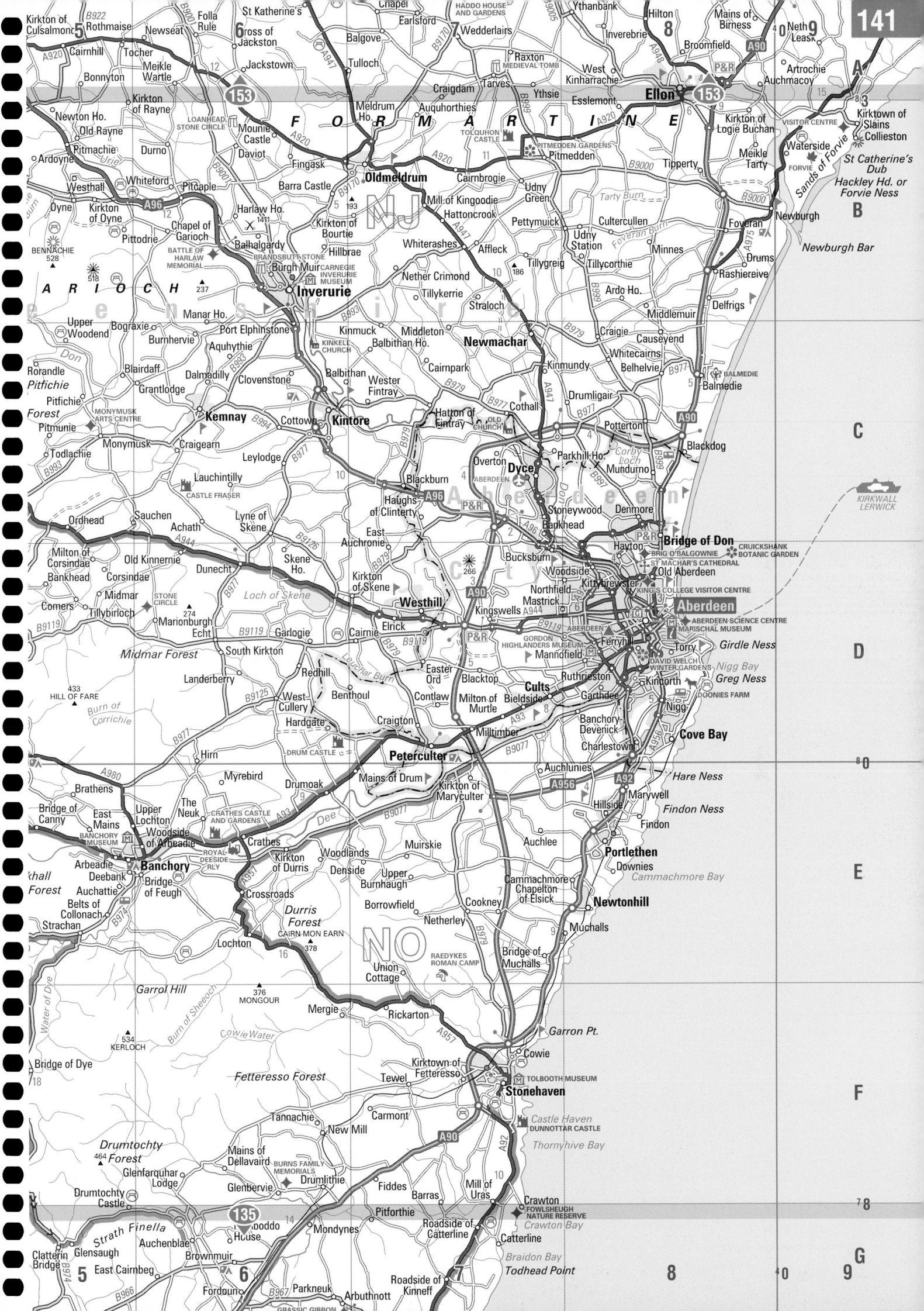

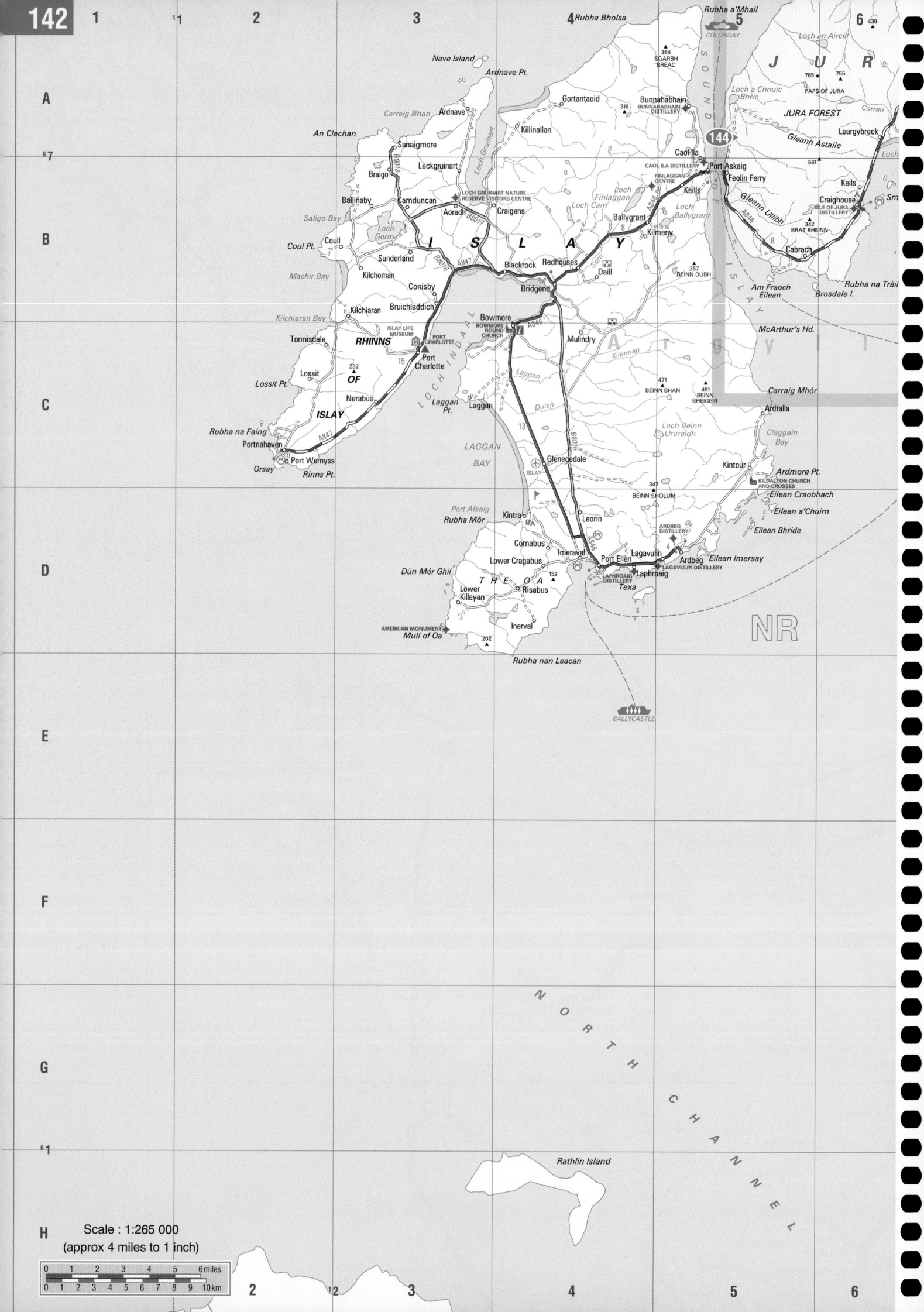

Scale : 1:265 000
(approx 4 miles to 1 inch)

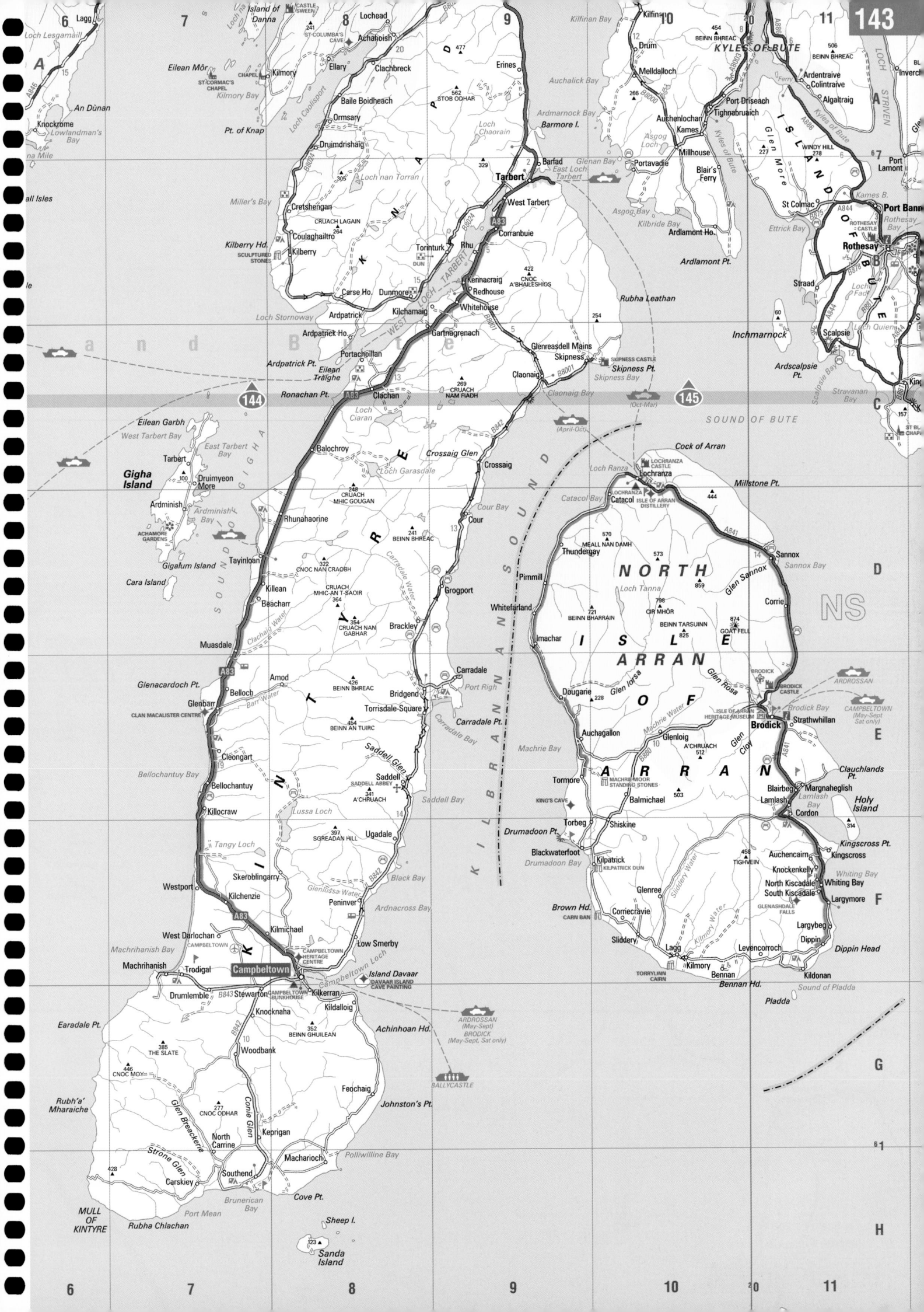

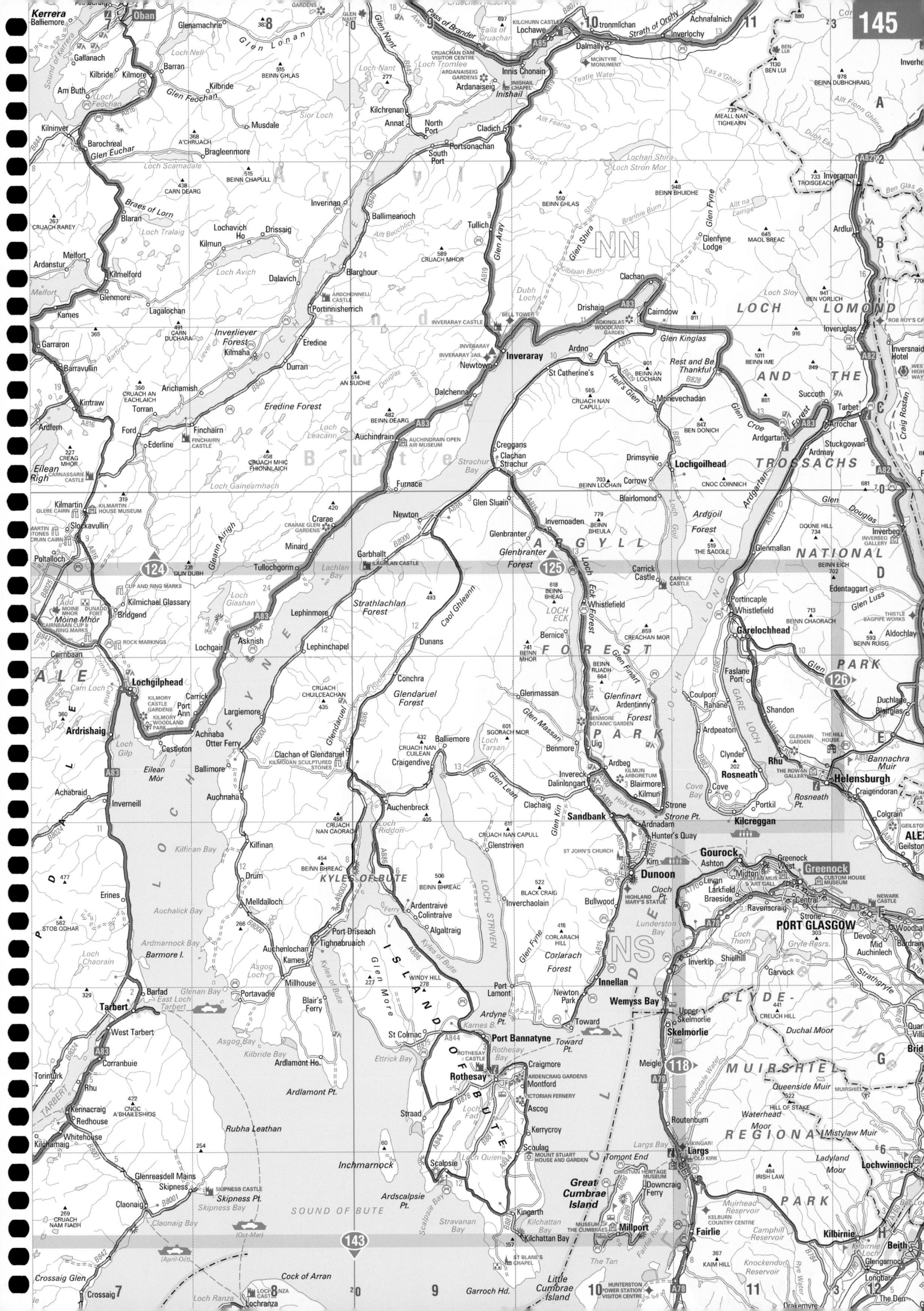

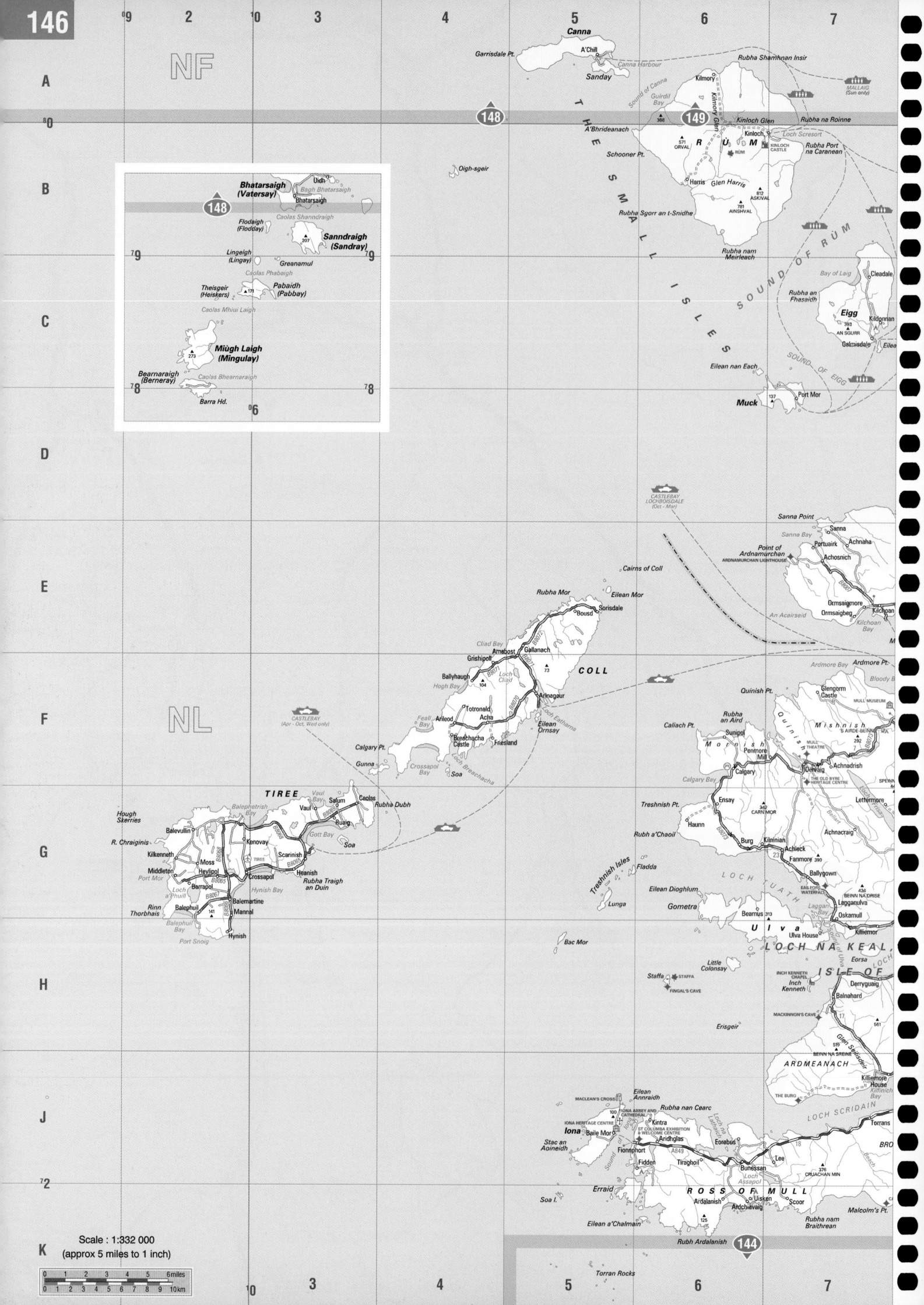

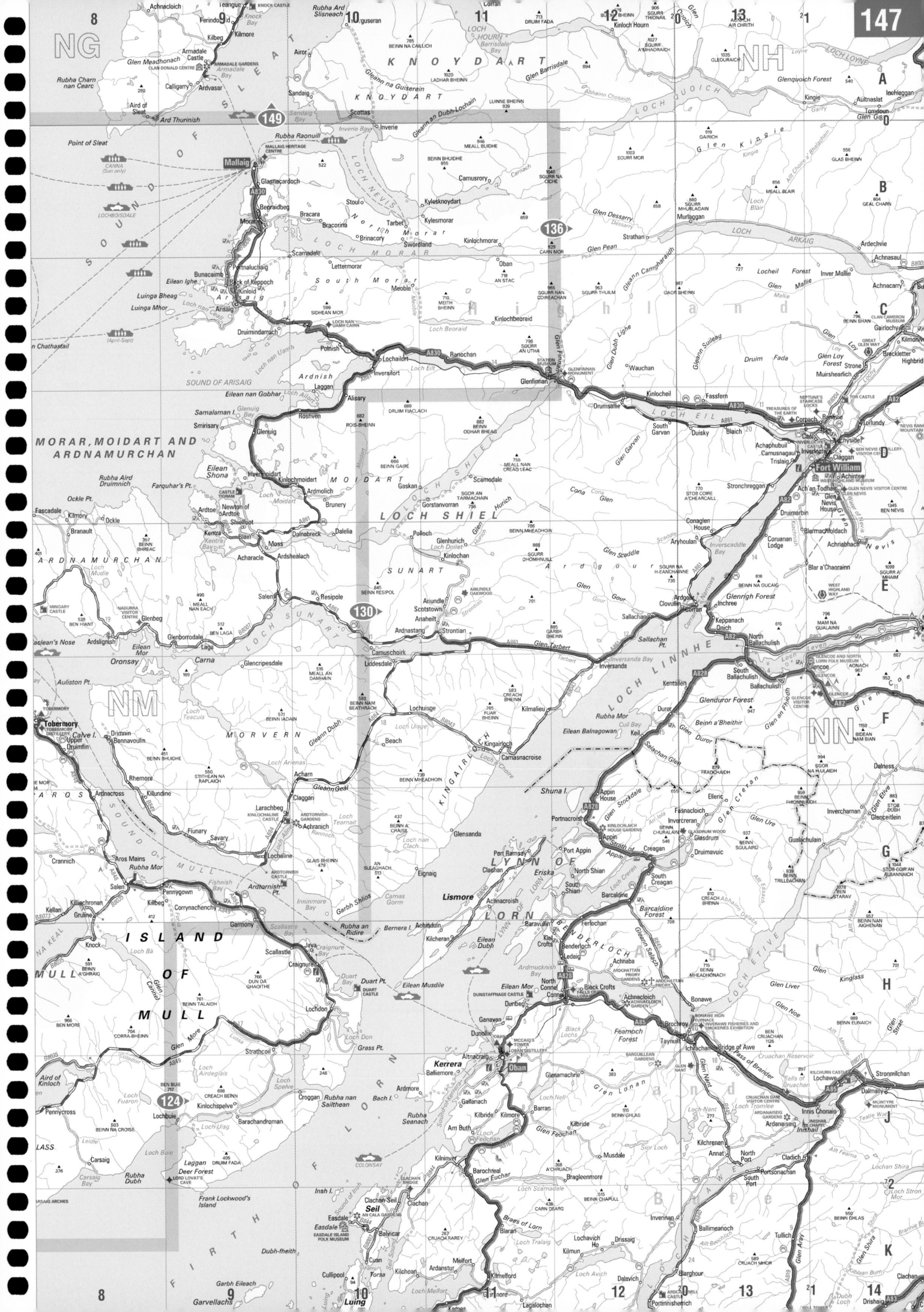

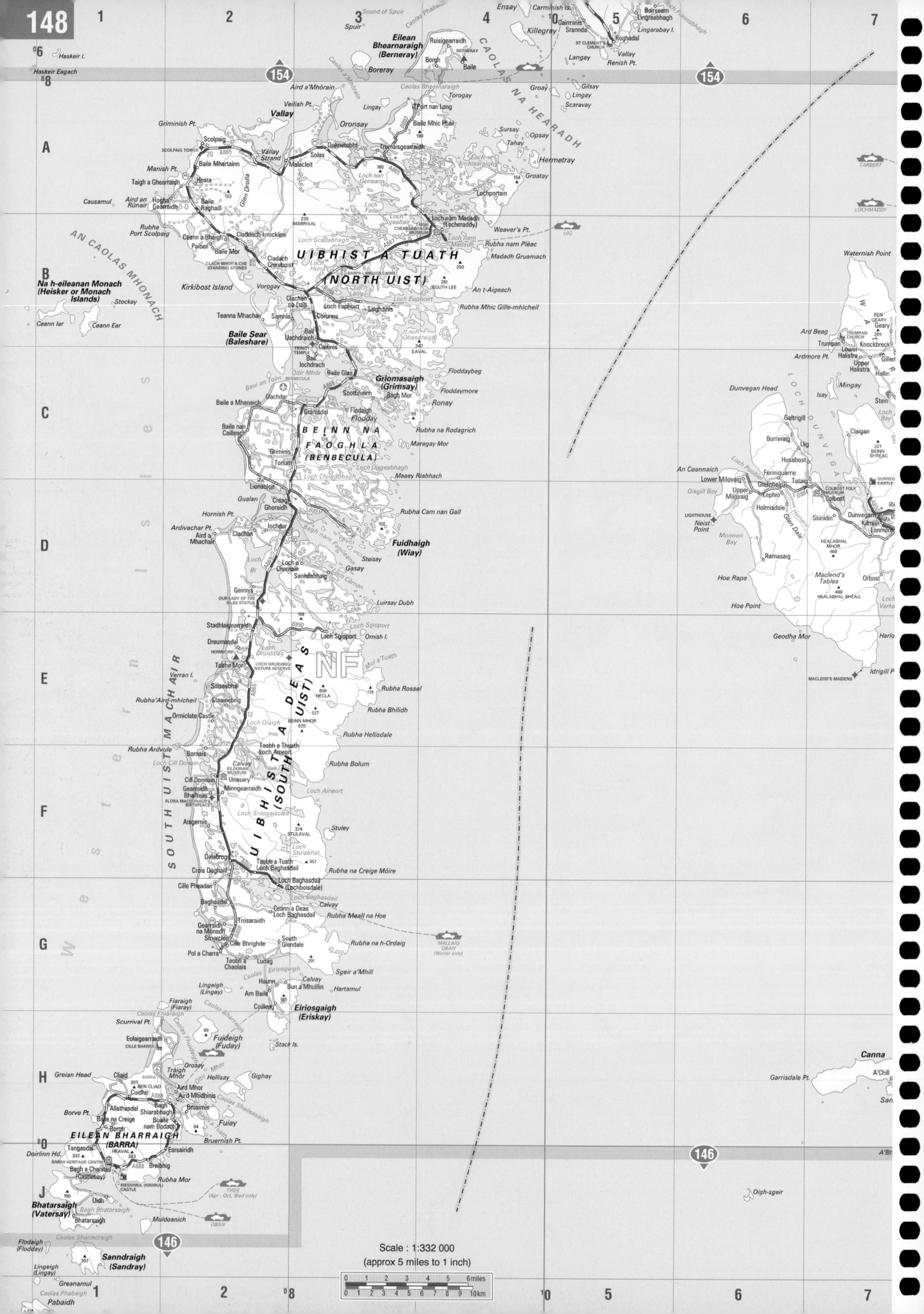

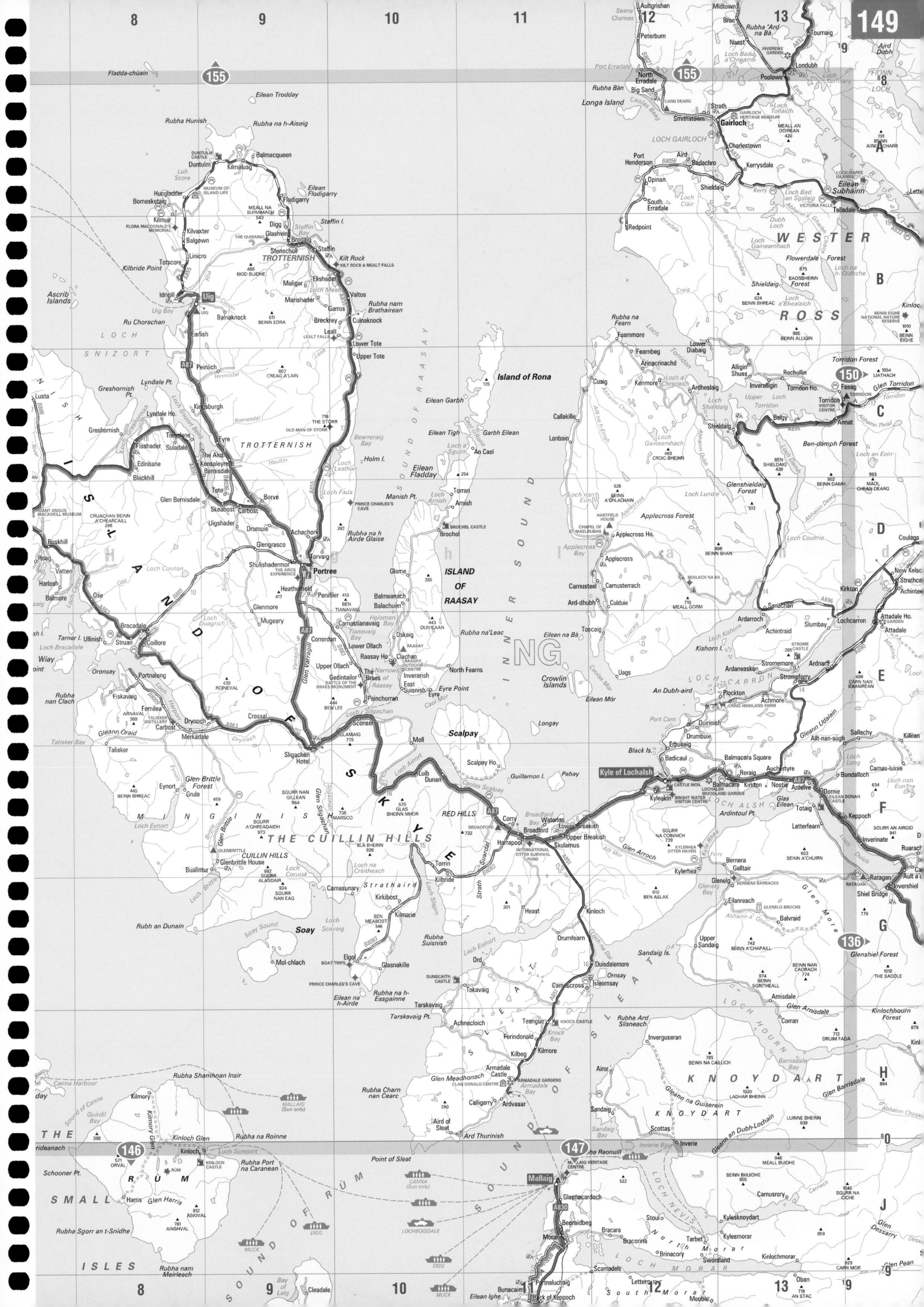

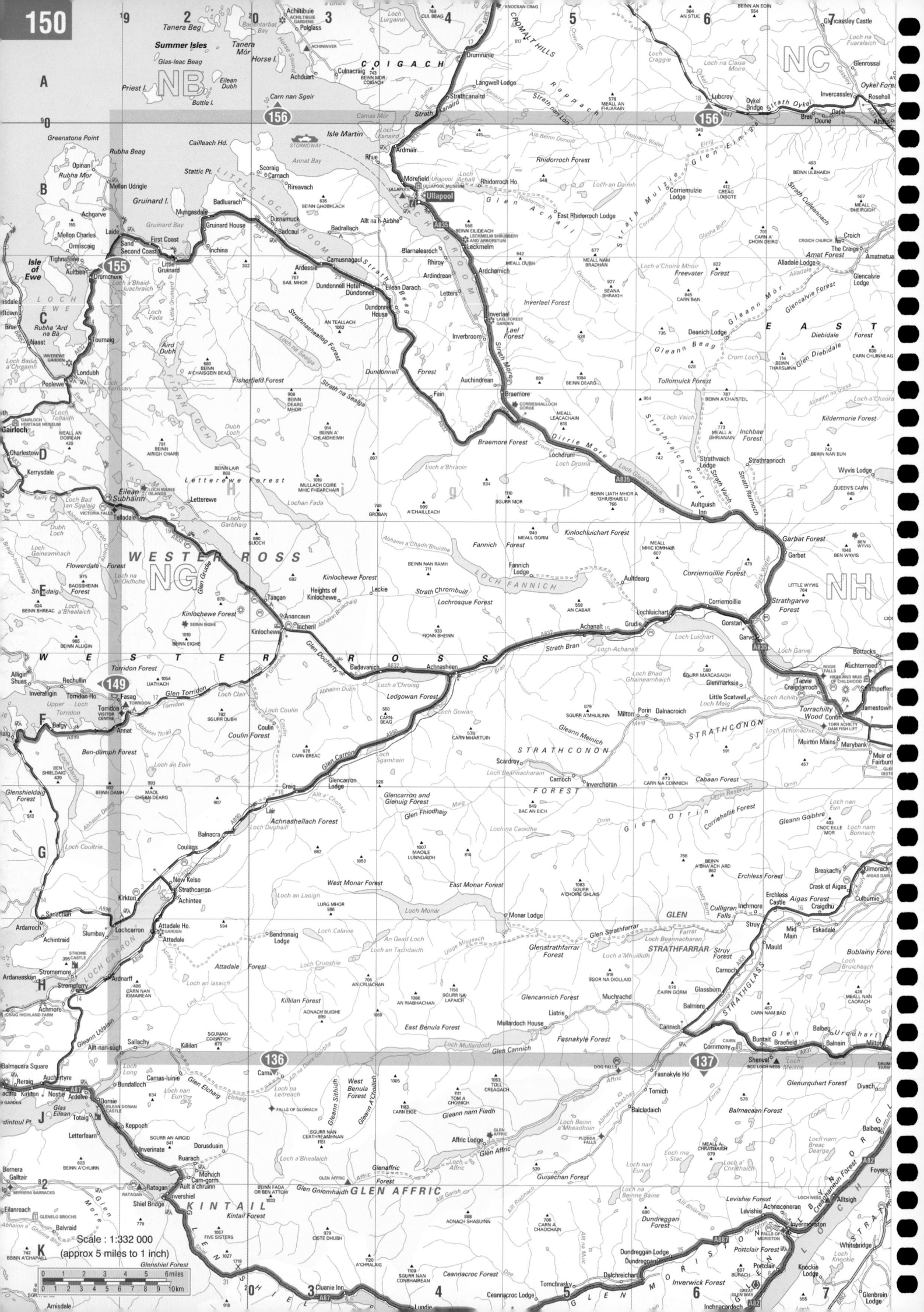

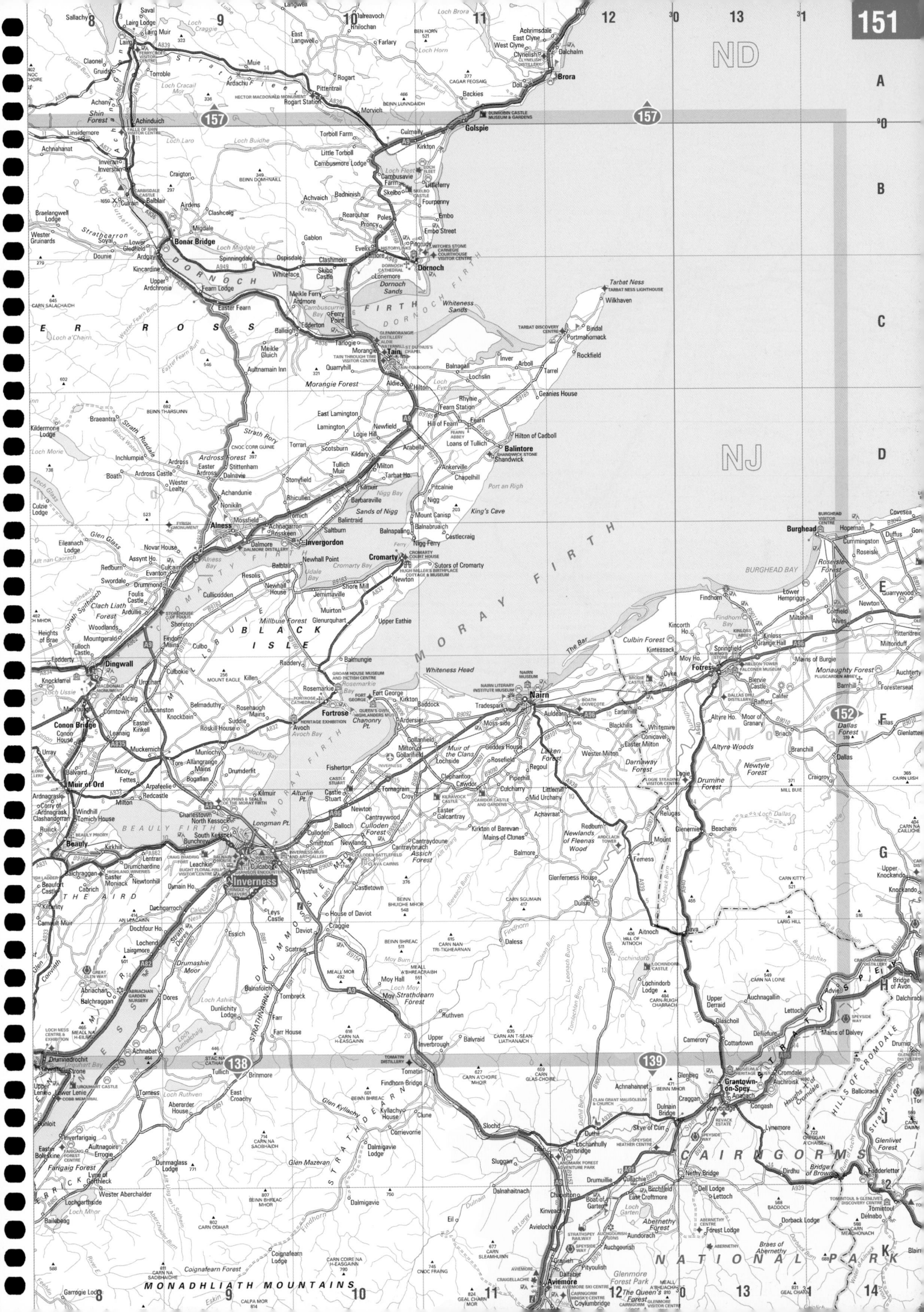

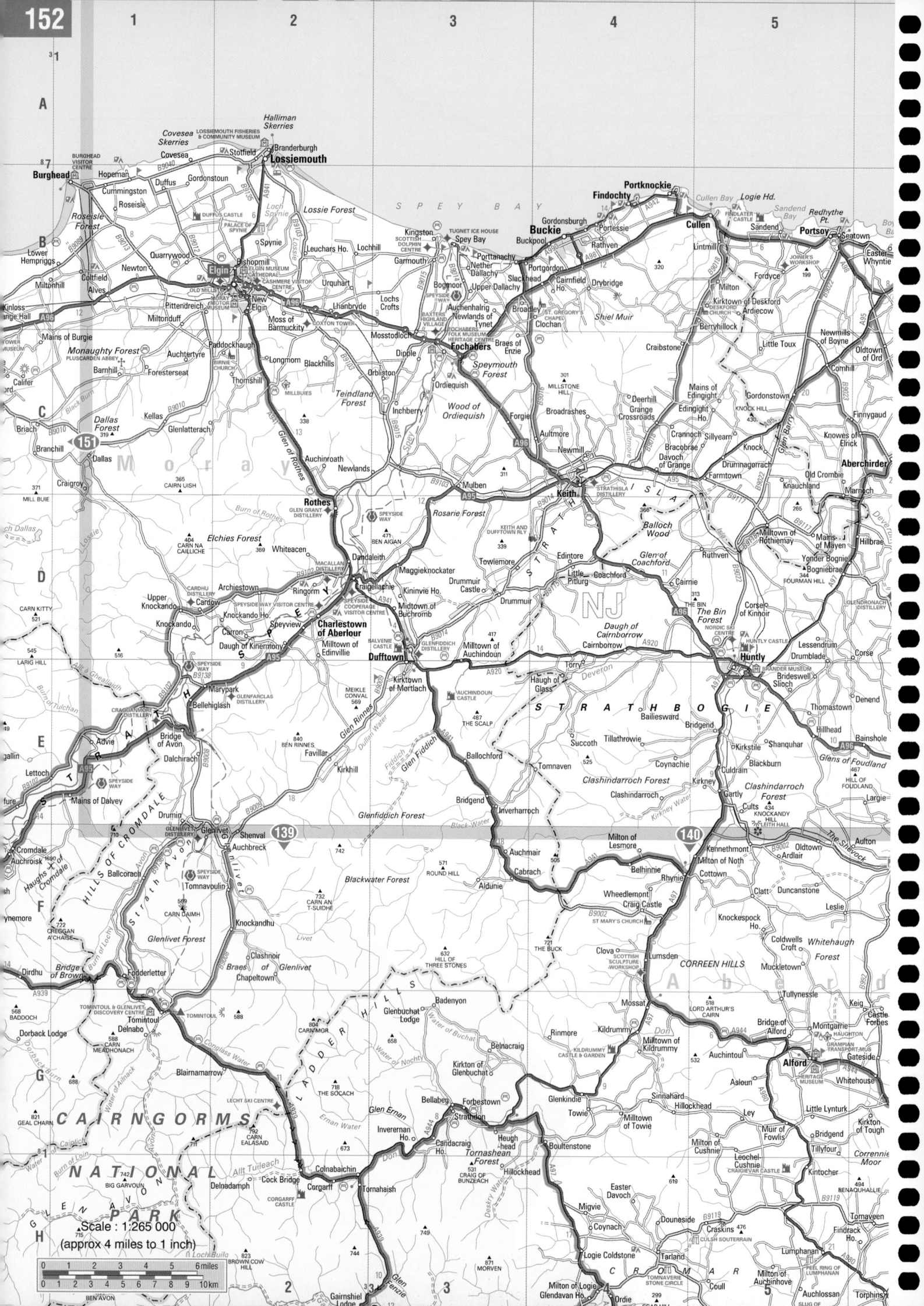

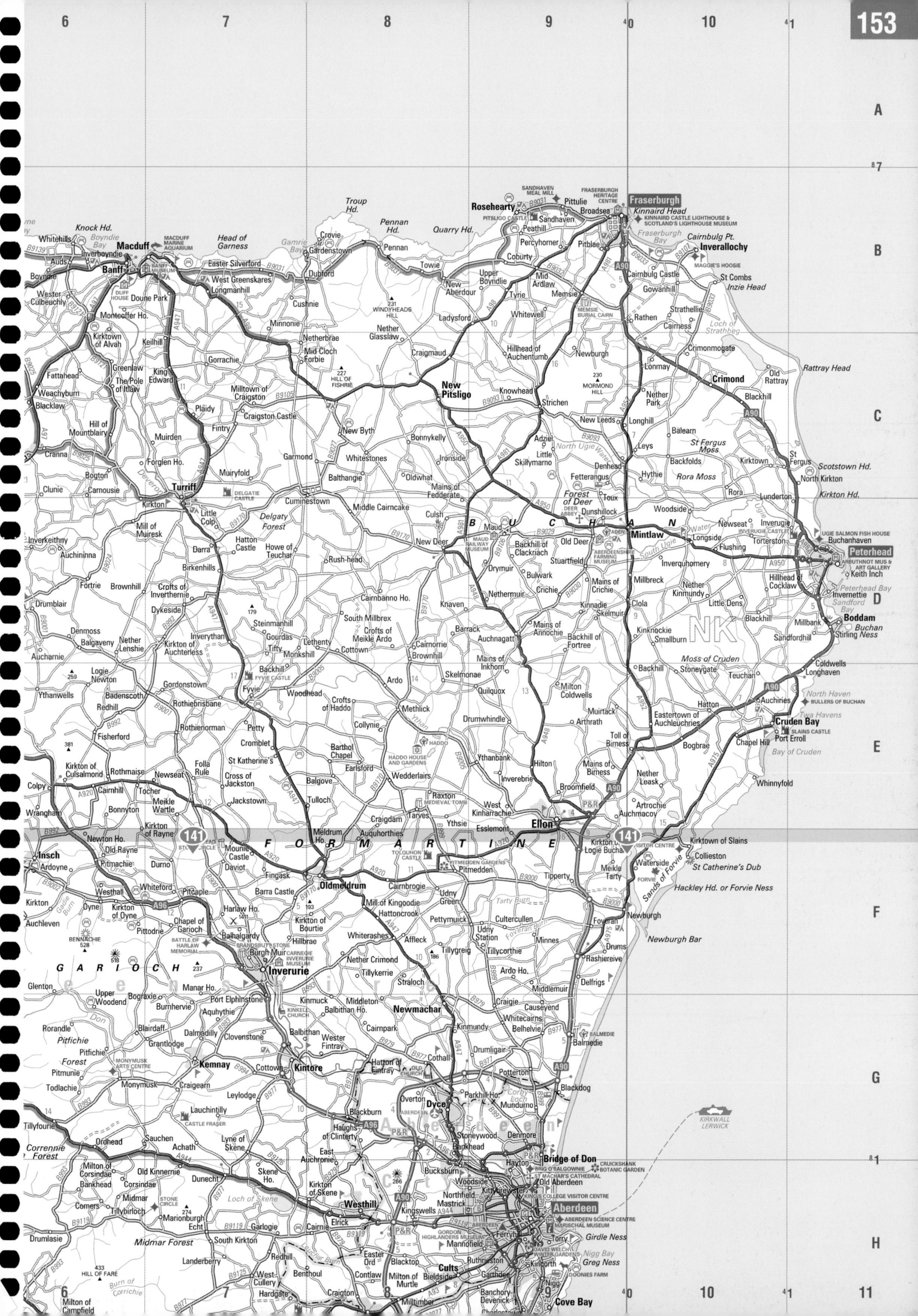

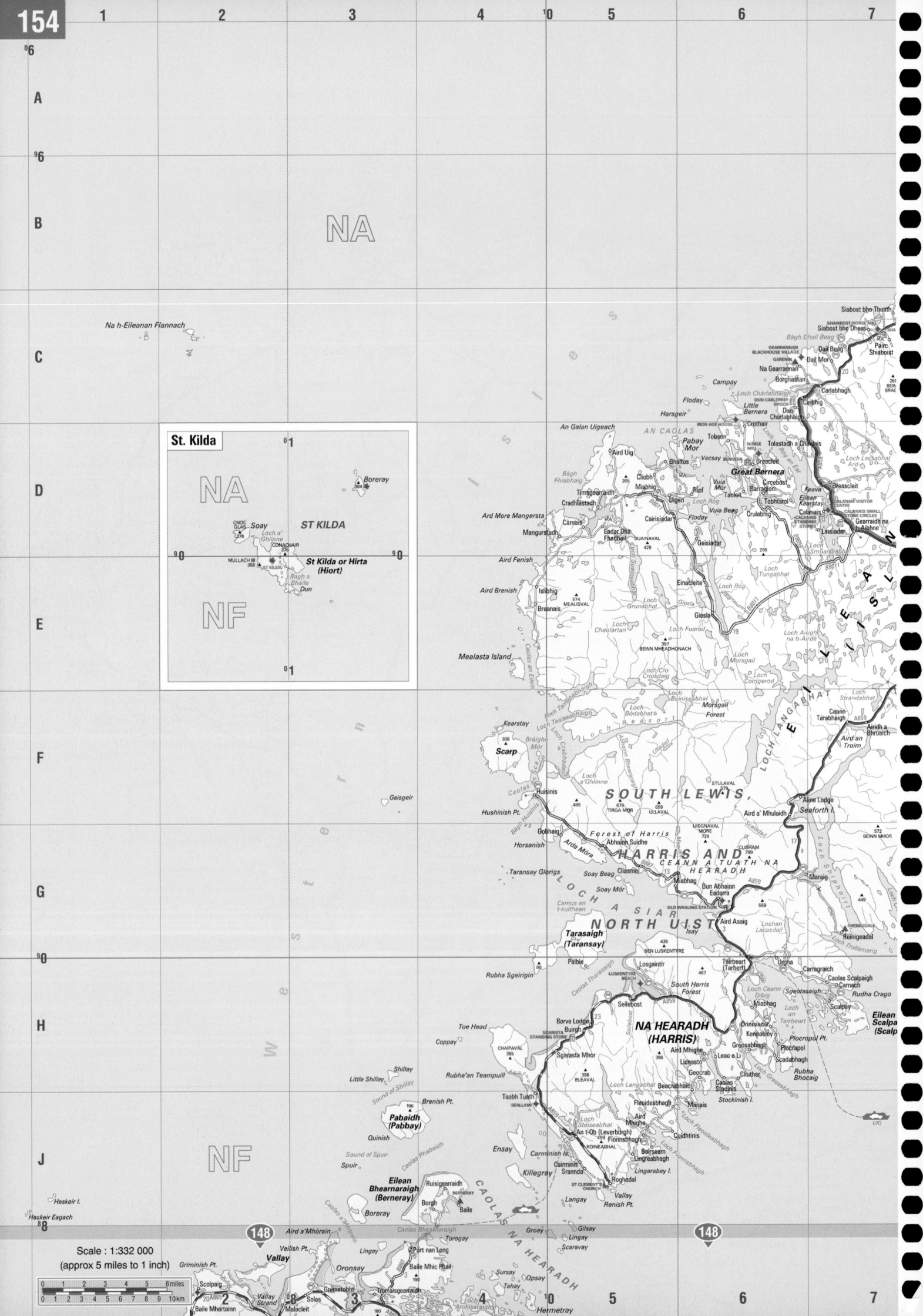

St. Kilda

NA

NF

ST KILDA

Boreray

Soay

CNOC GLAS

Loch a' Ghlinne

CONACHAIR

MULLACH BI

St Kilda or Hirta (Hiort)

Bagh a' Bhaile

Dun

NA

NF

Scale : 1:332 000
(approx 5 miles to 1 inch)

0   1   2   3   4   5   6 miles
0 1 2 3 4 5 6 7 8 9 10km

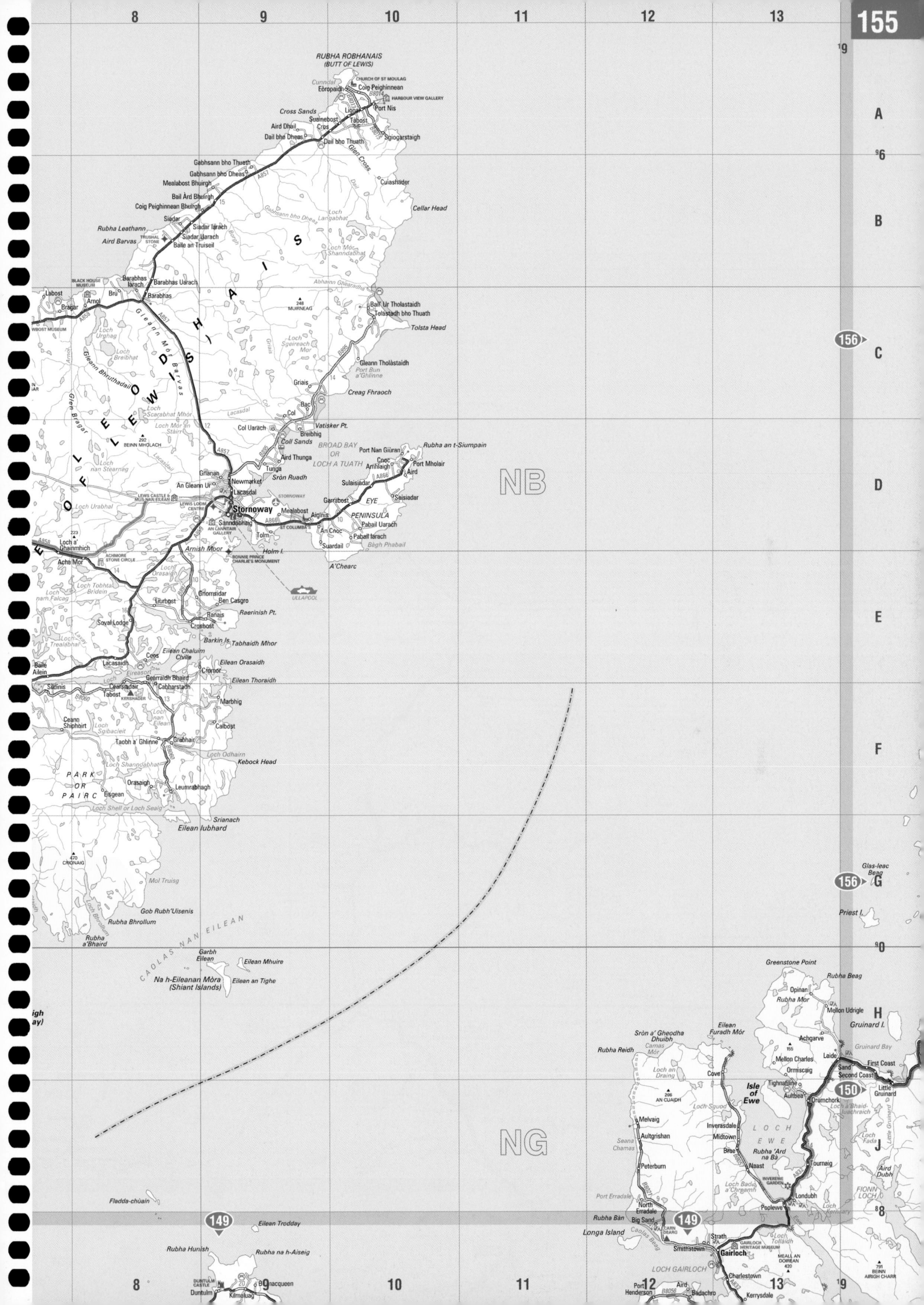

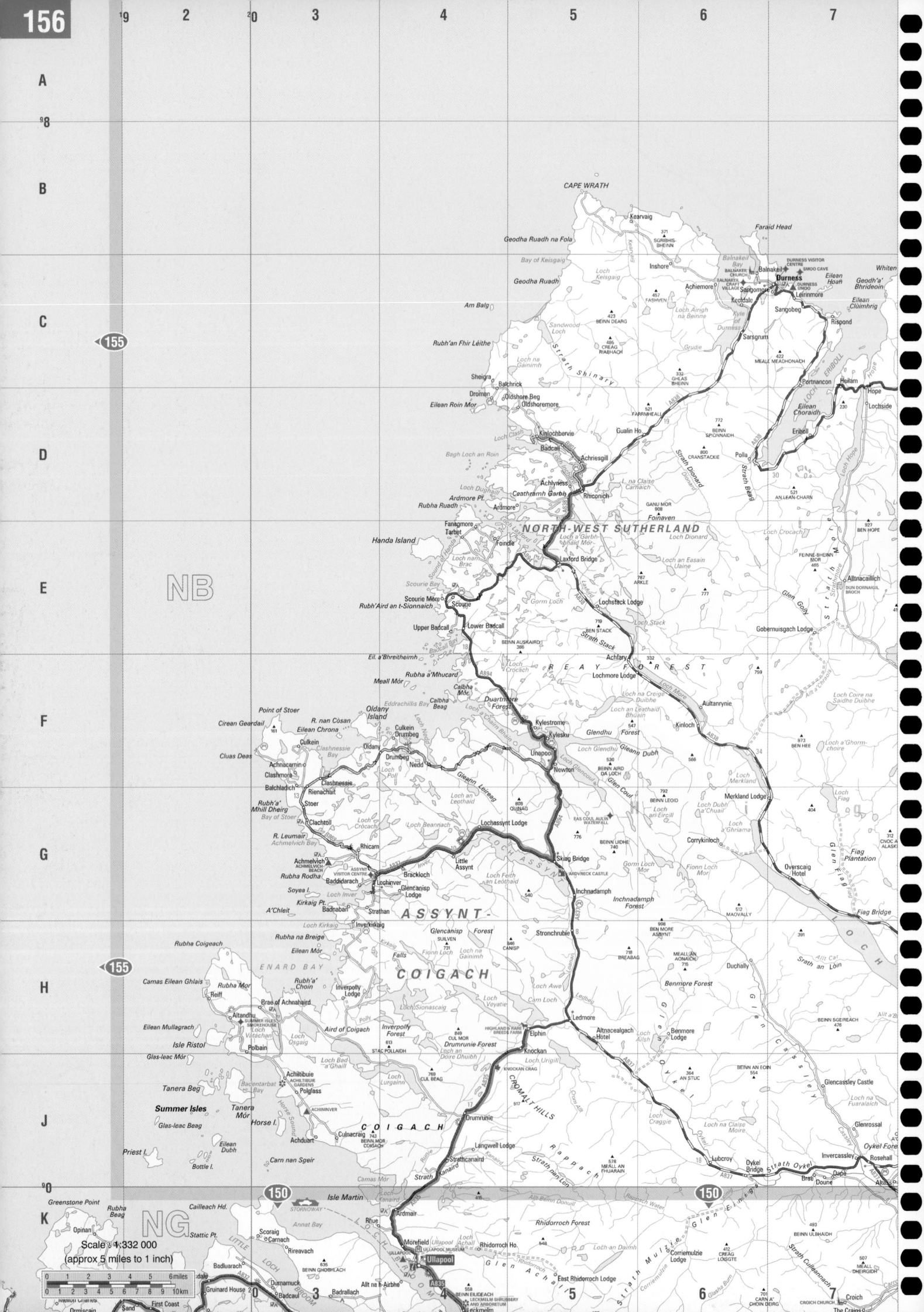

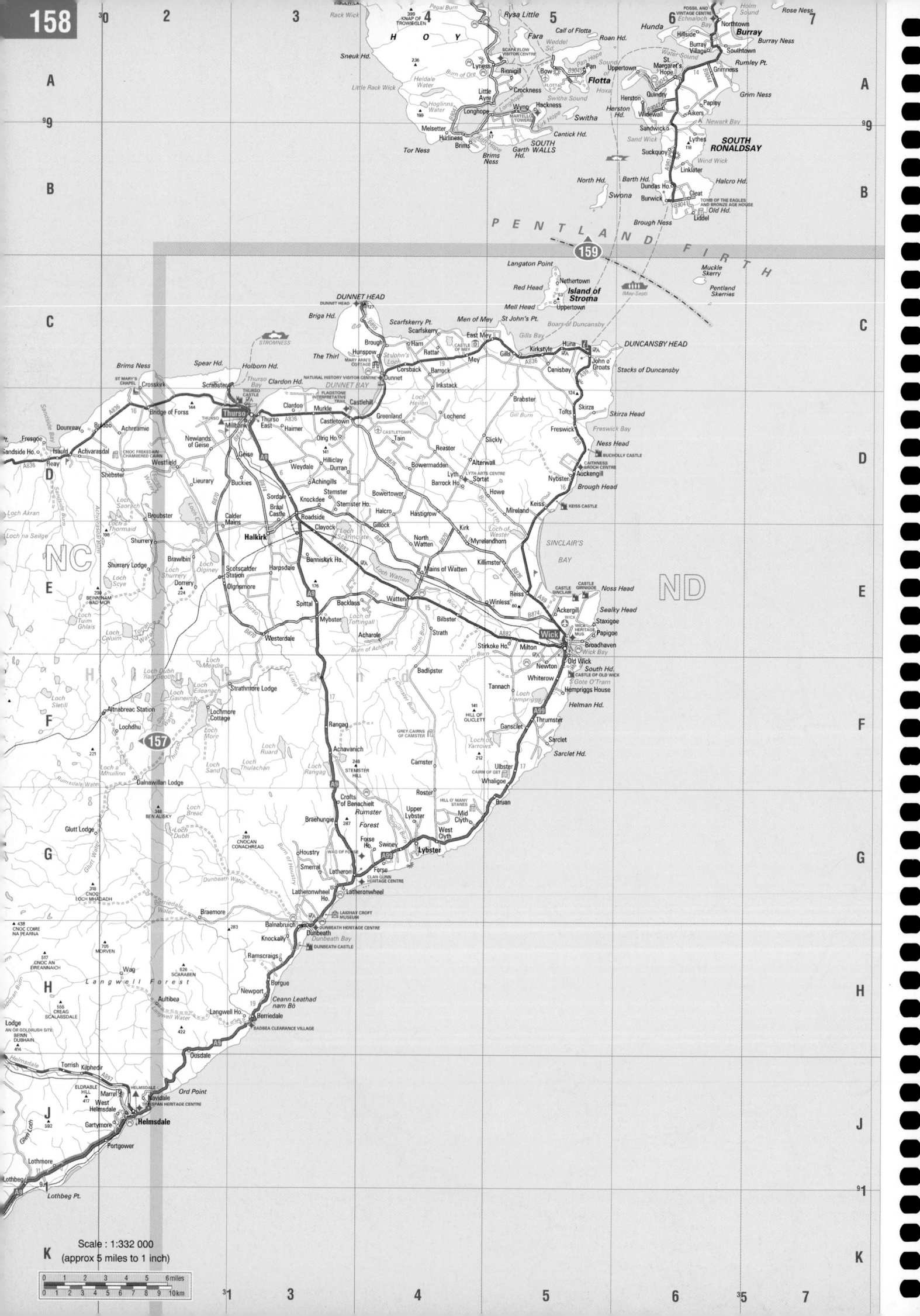

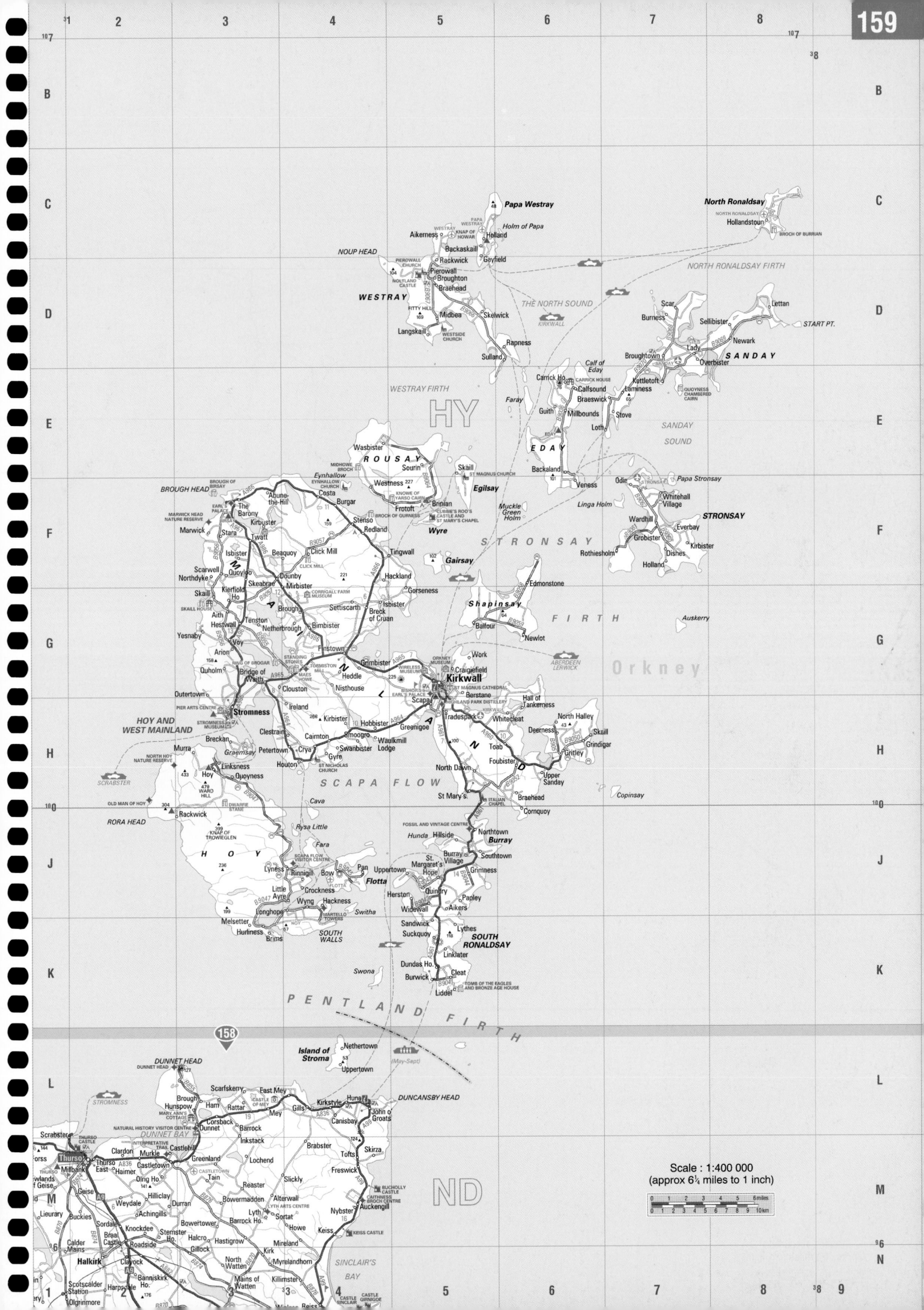

Scale : 1:400 000
(approx 6¼ miles to 1 inch)

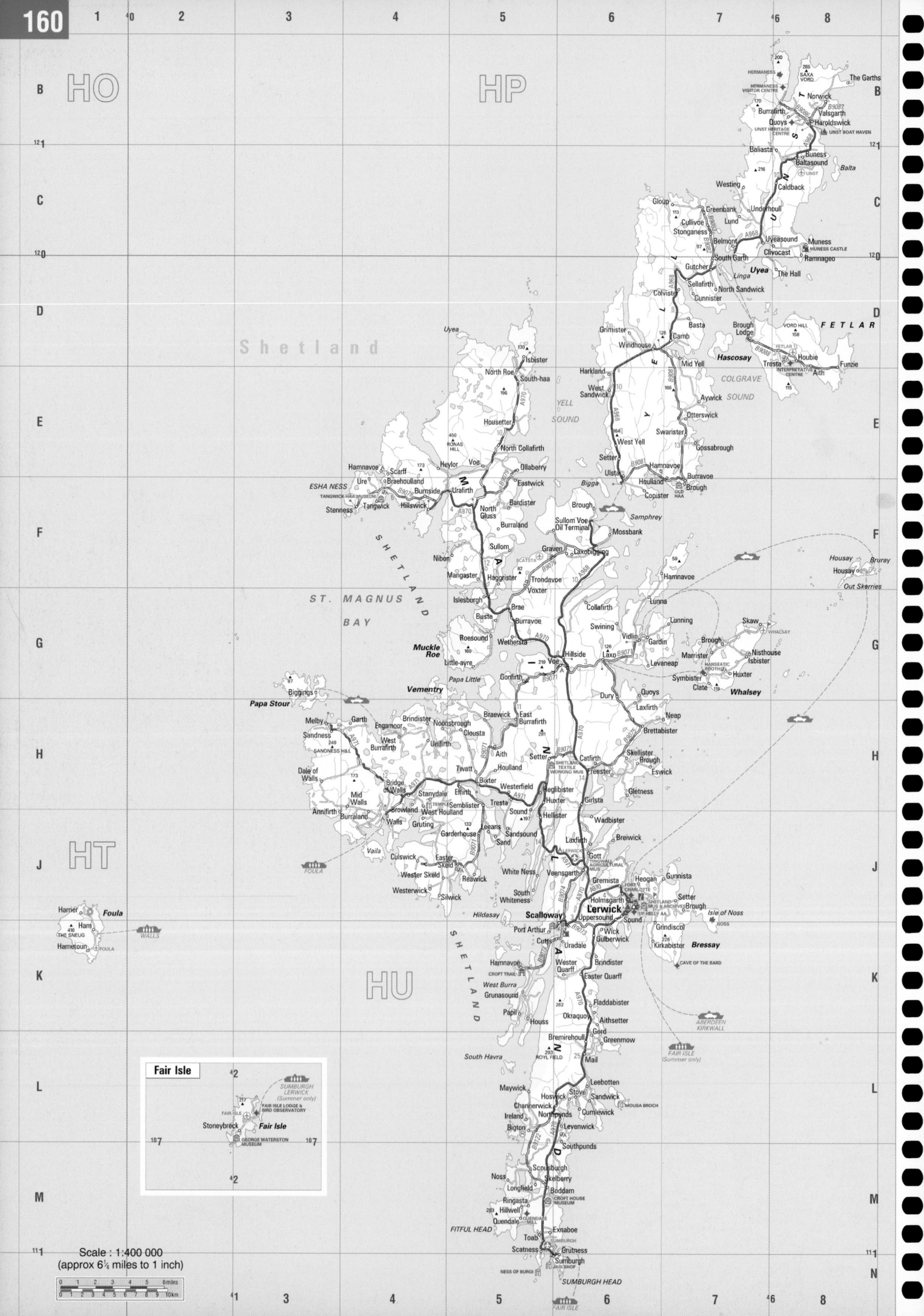

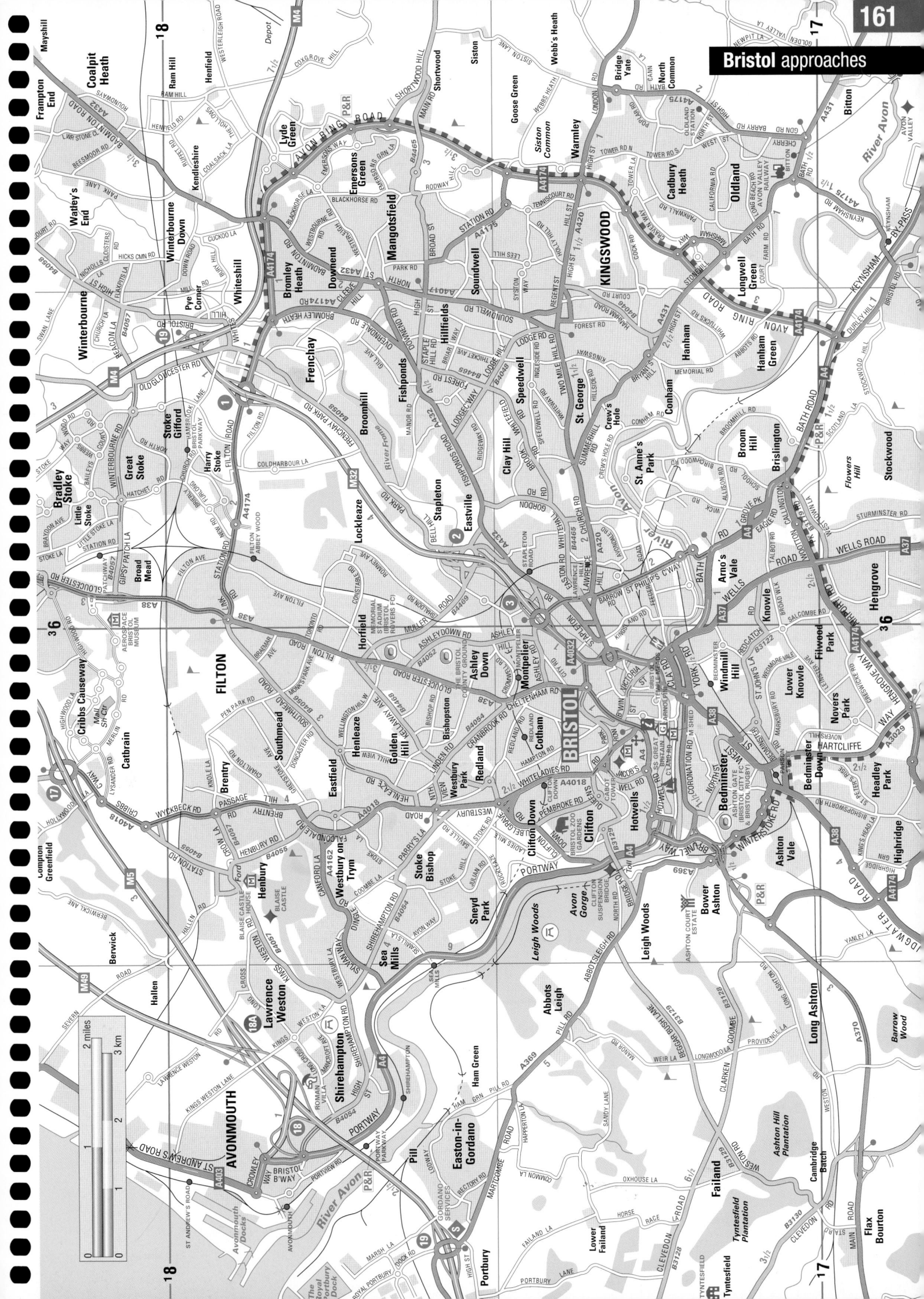

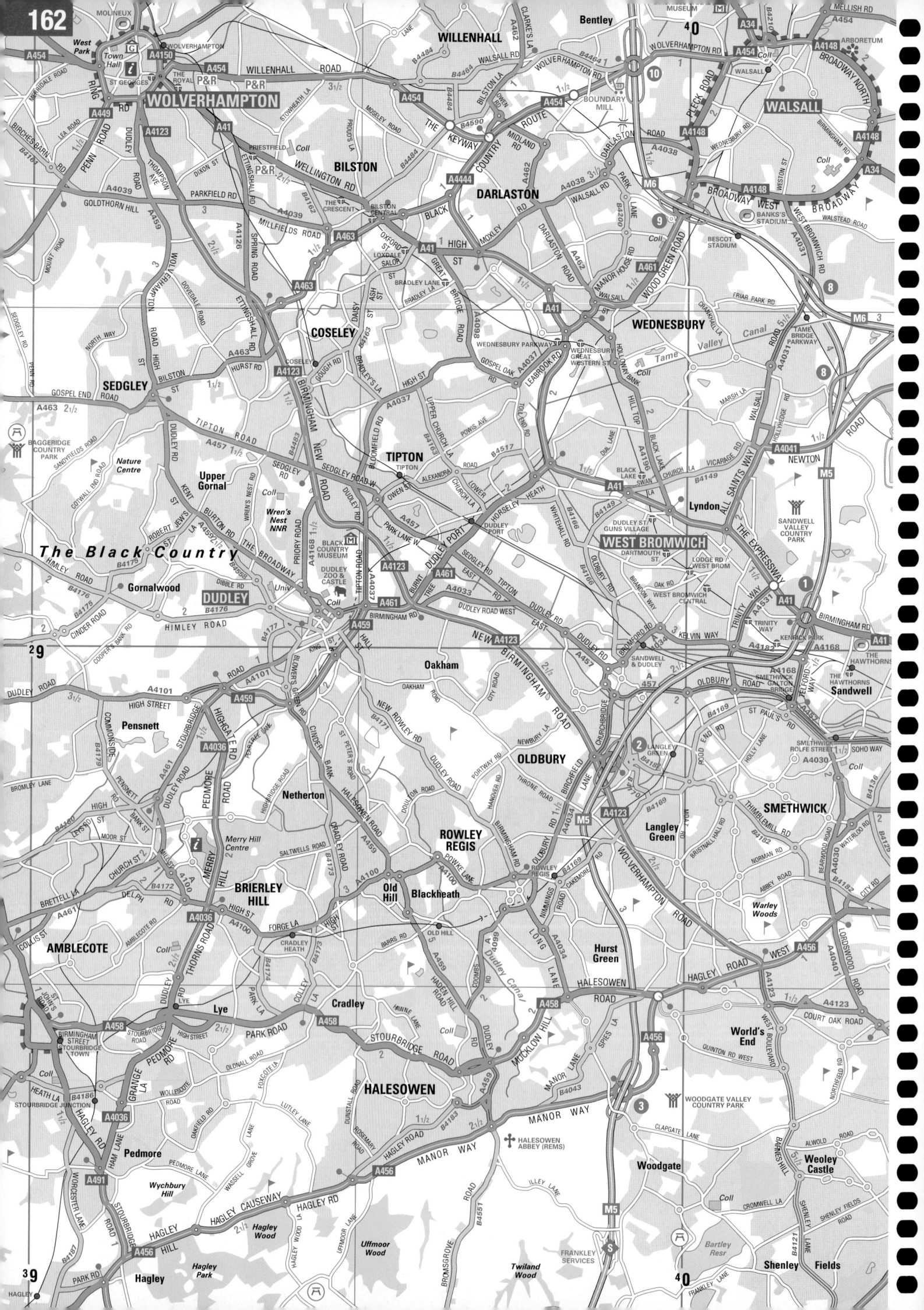

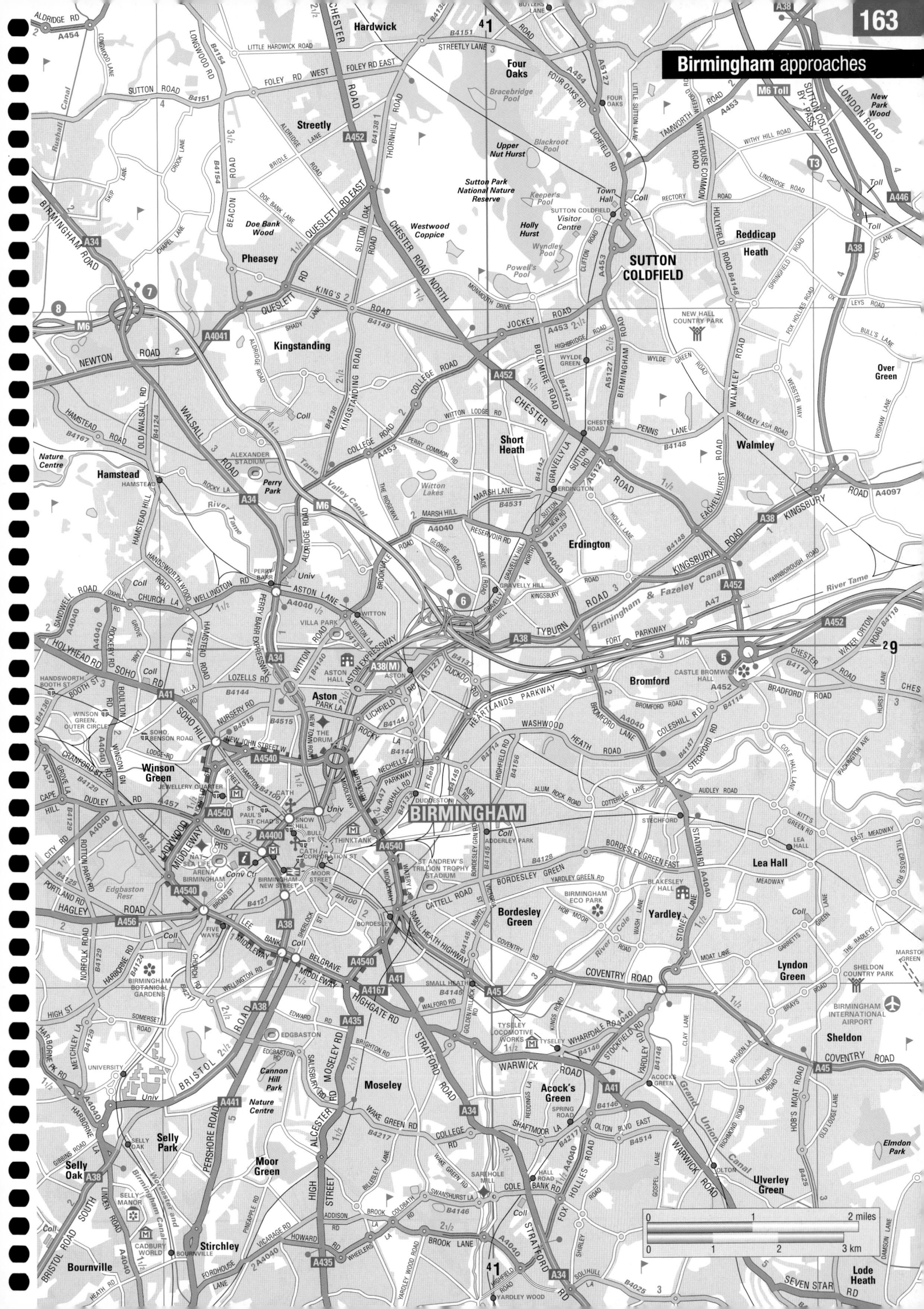

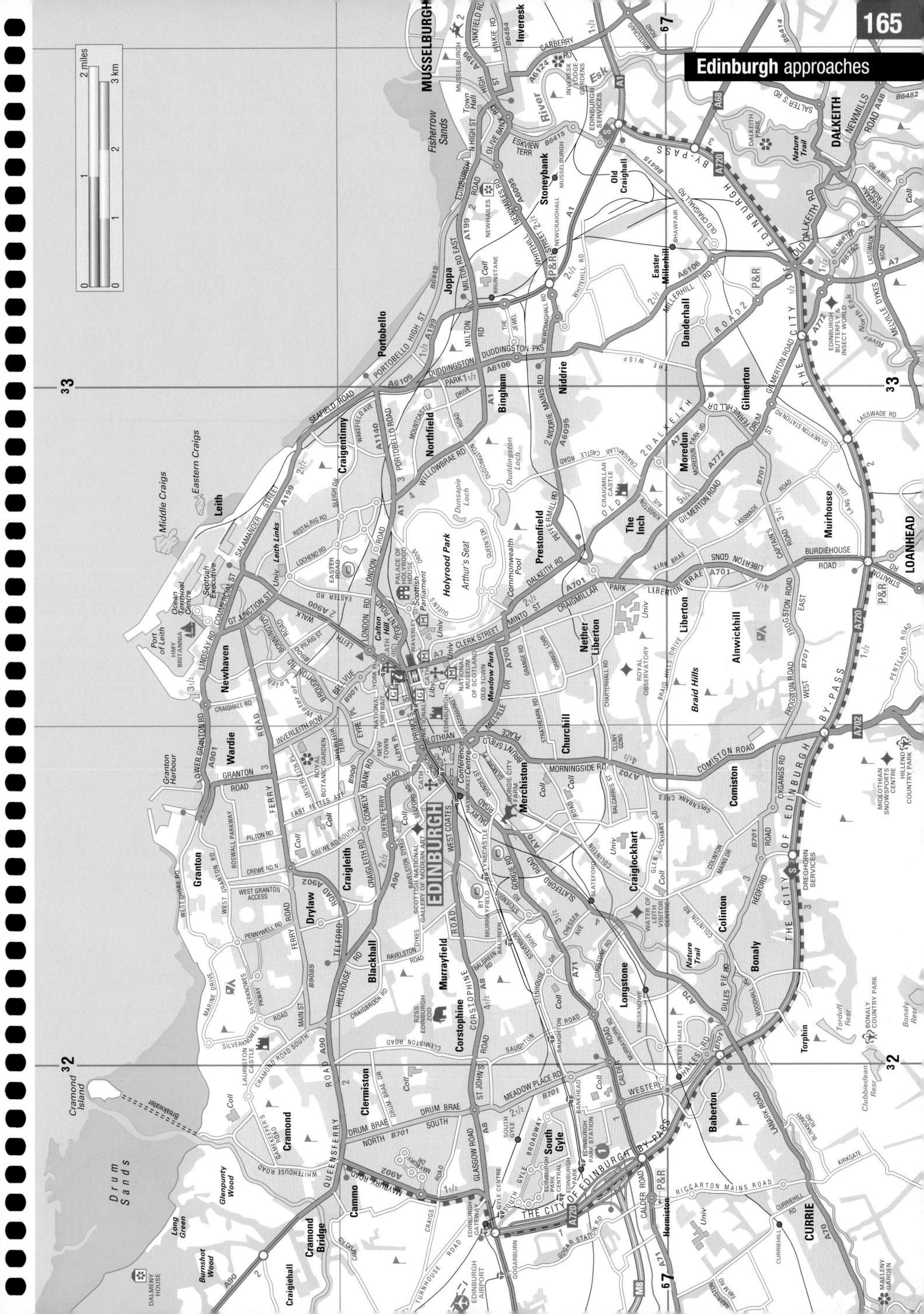

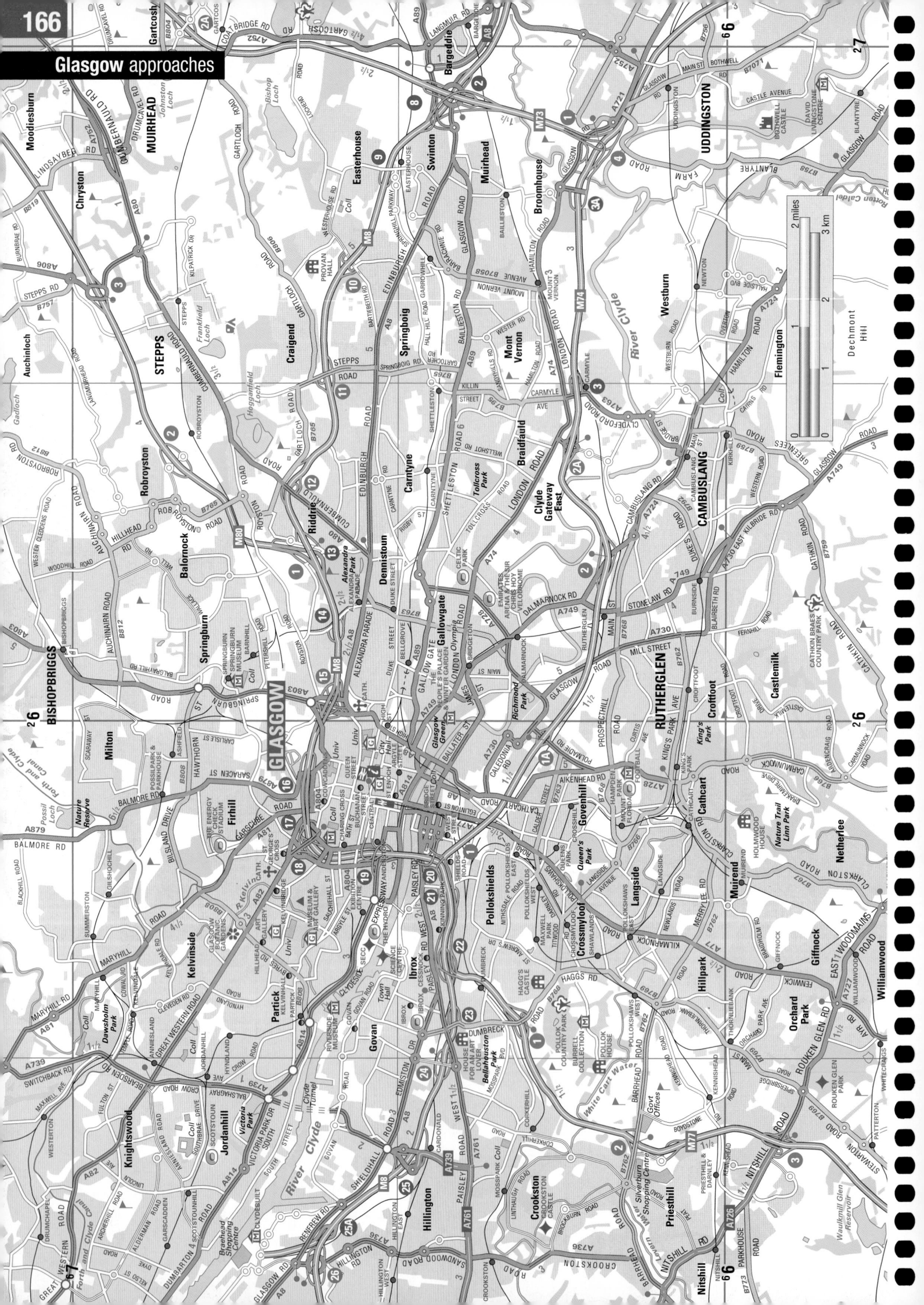

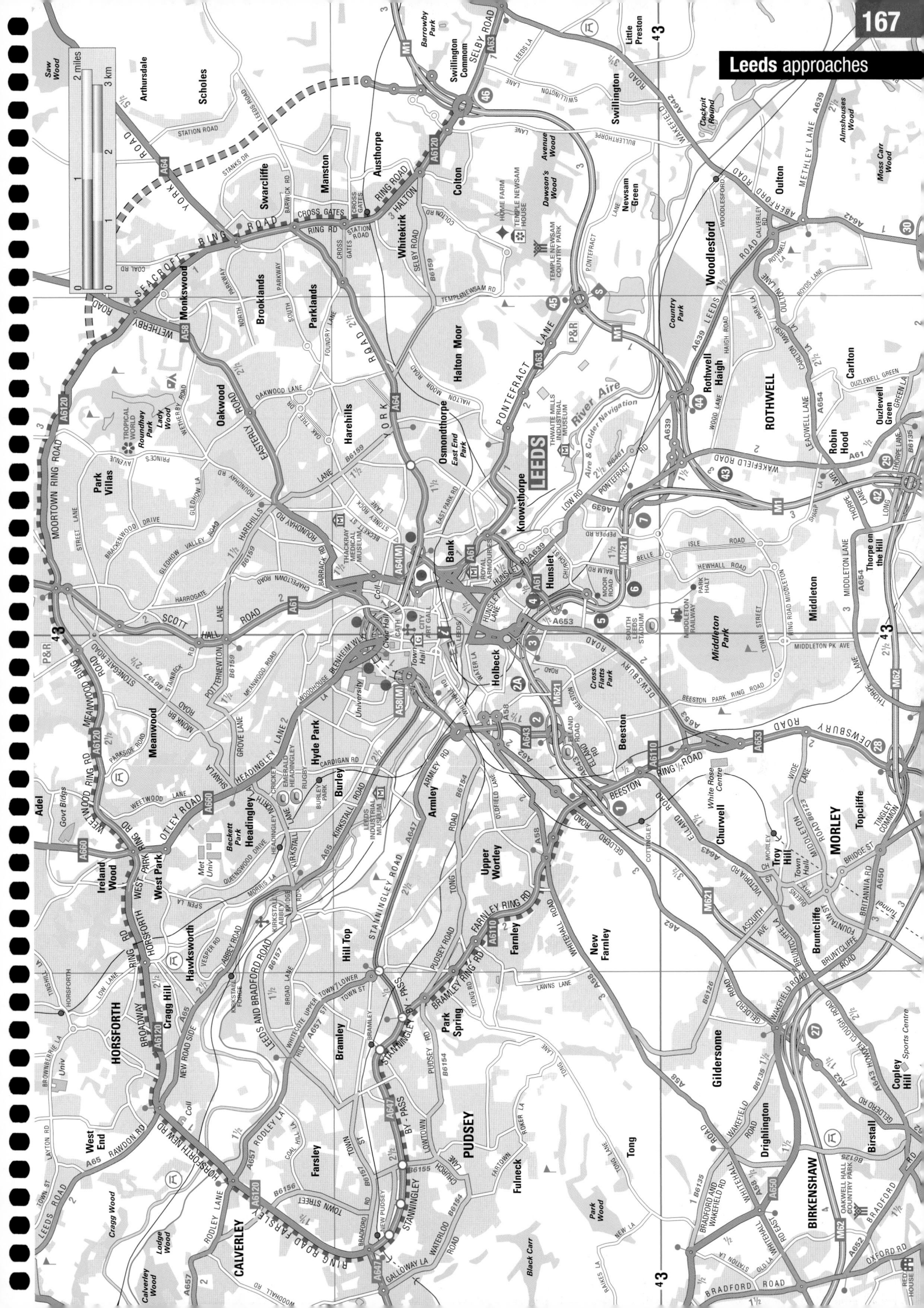

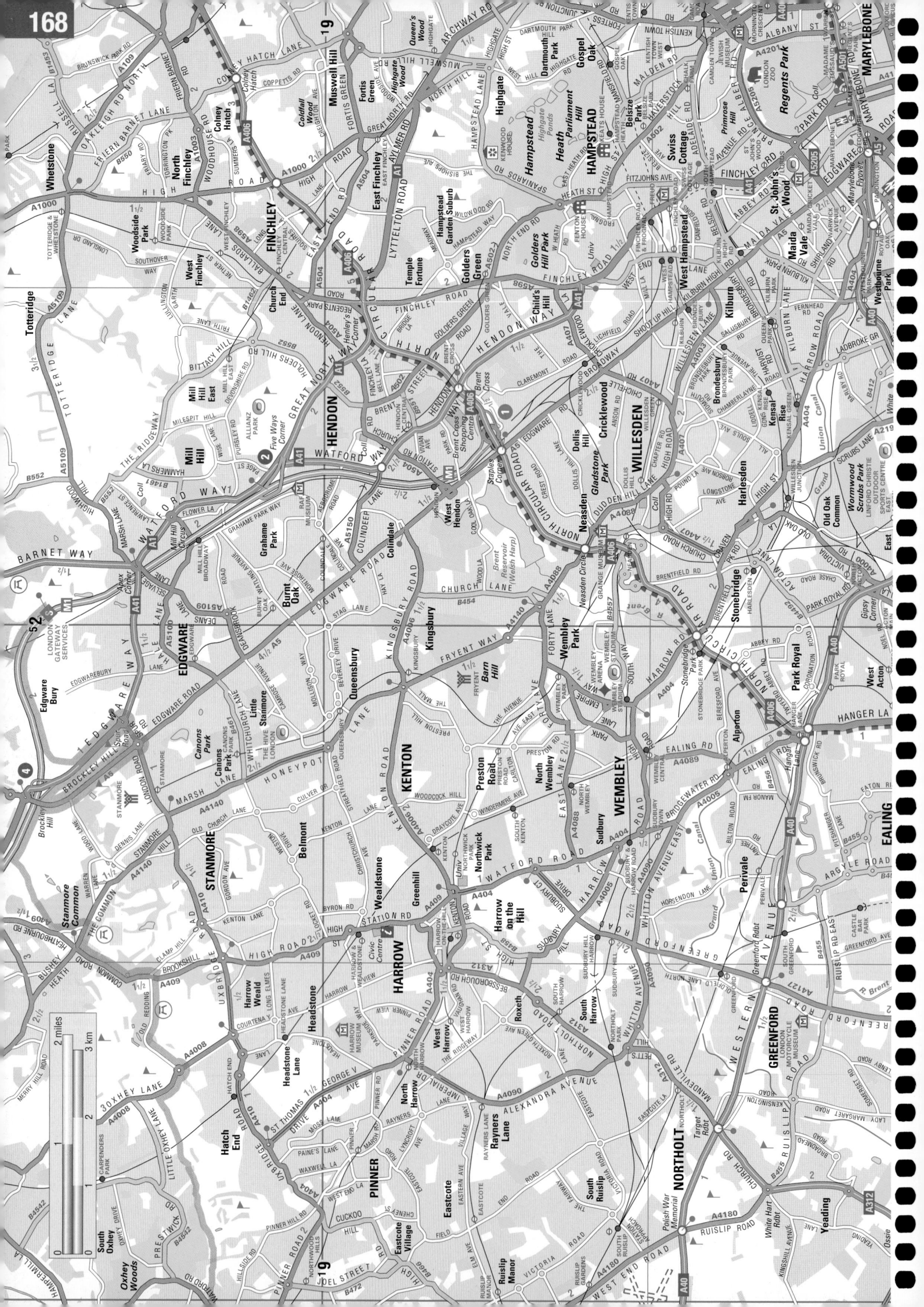

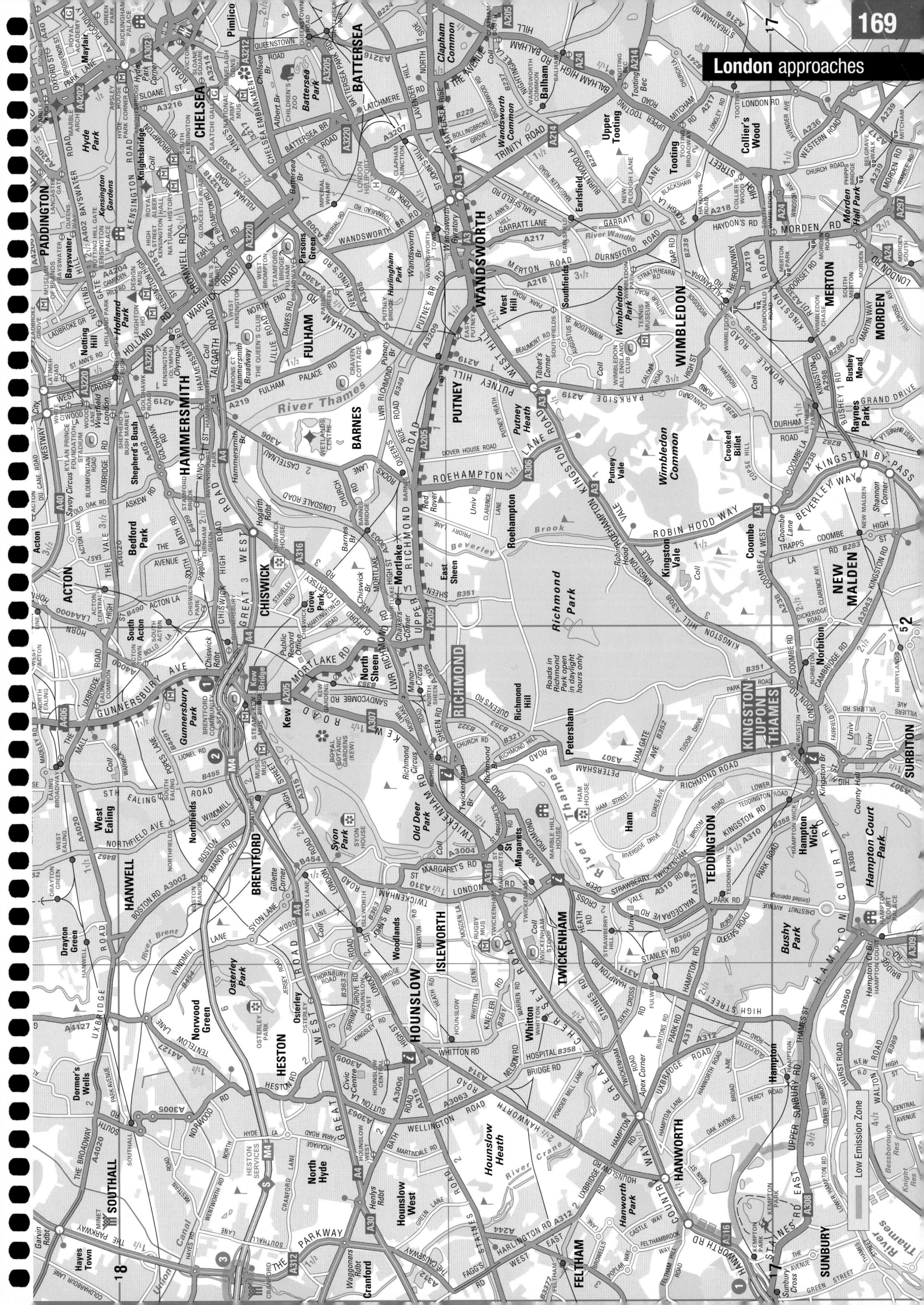

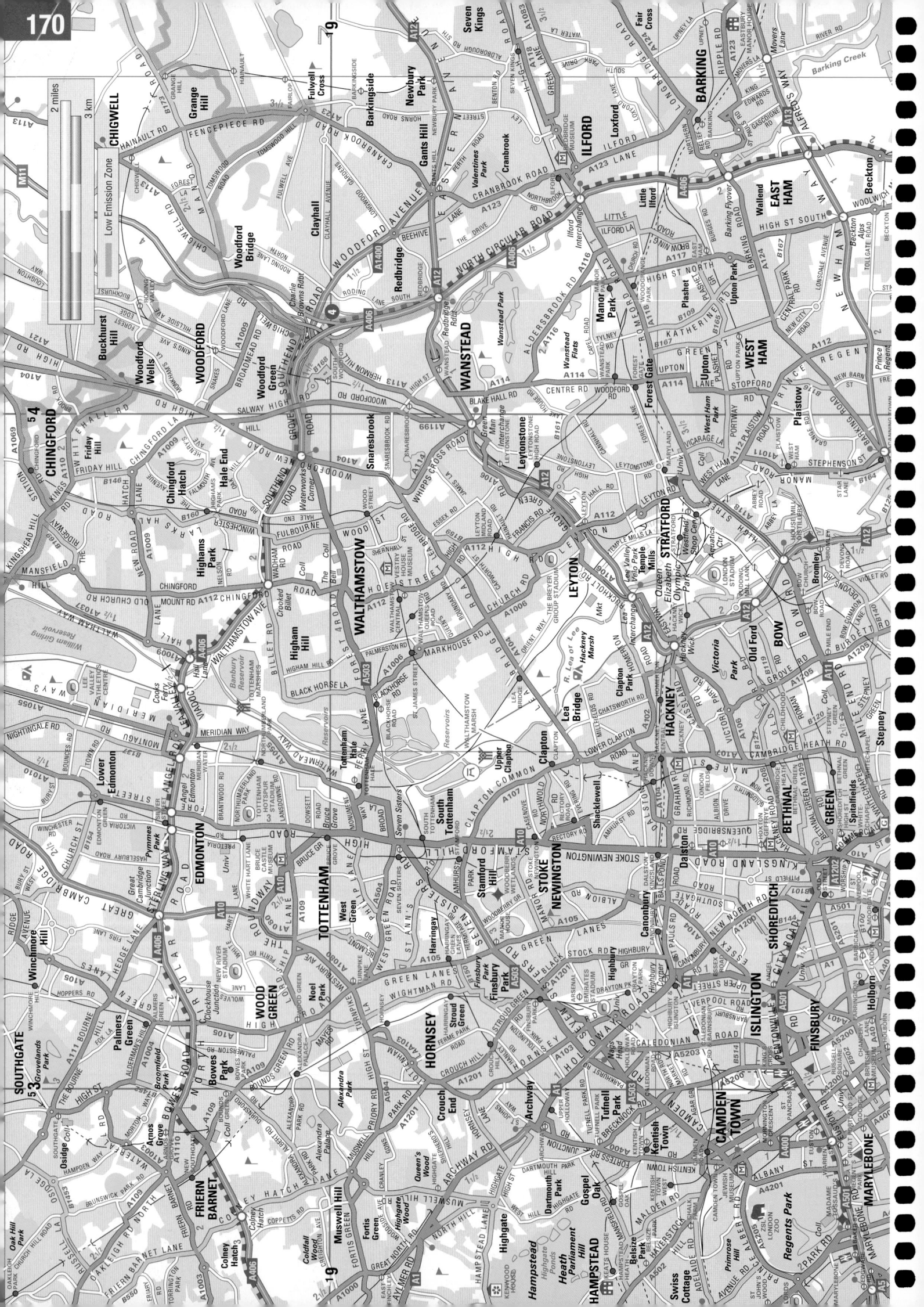

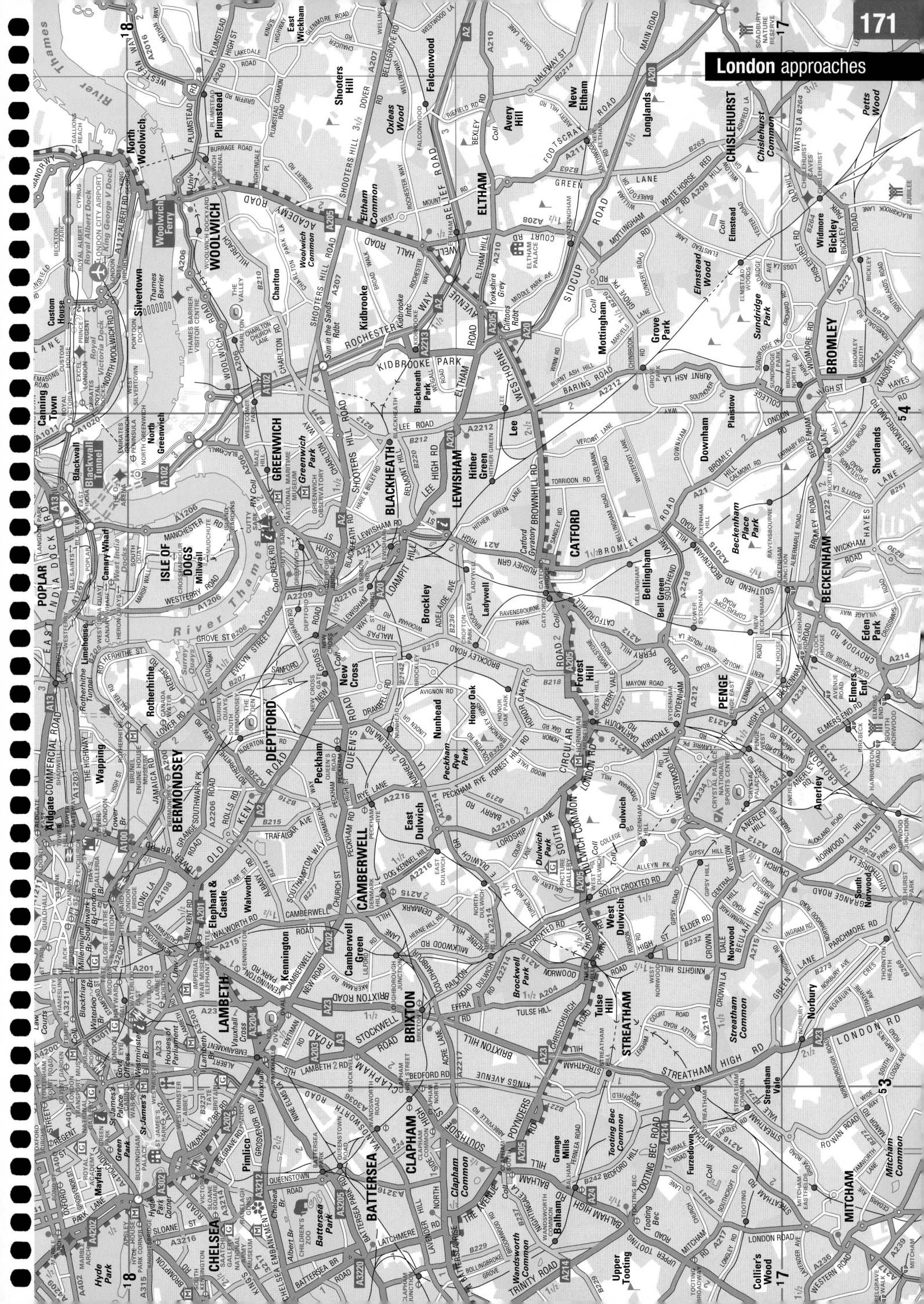

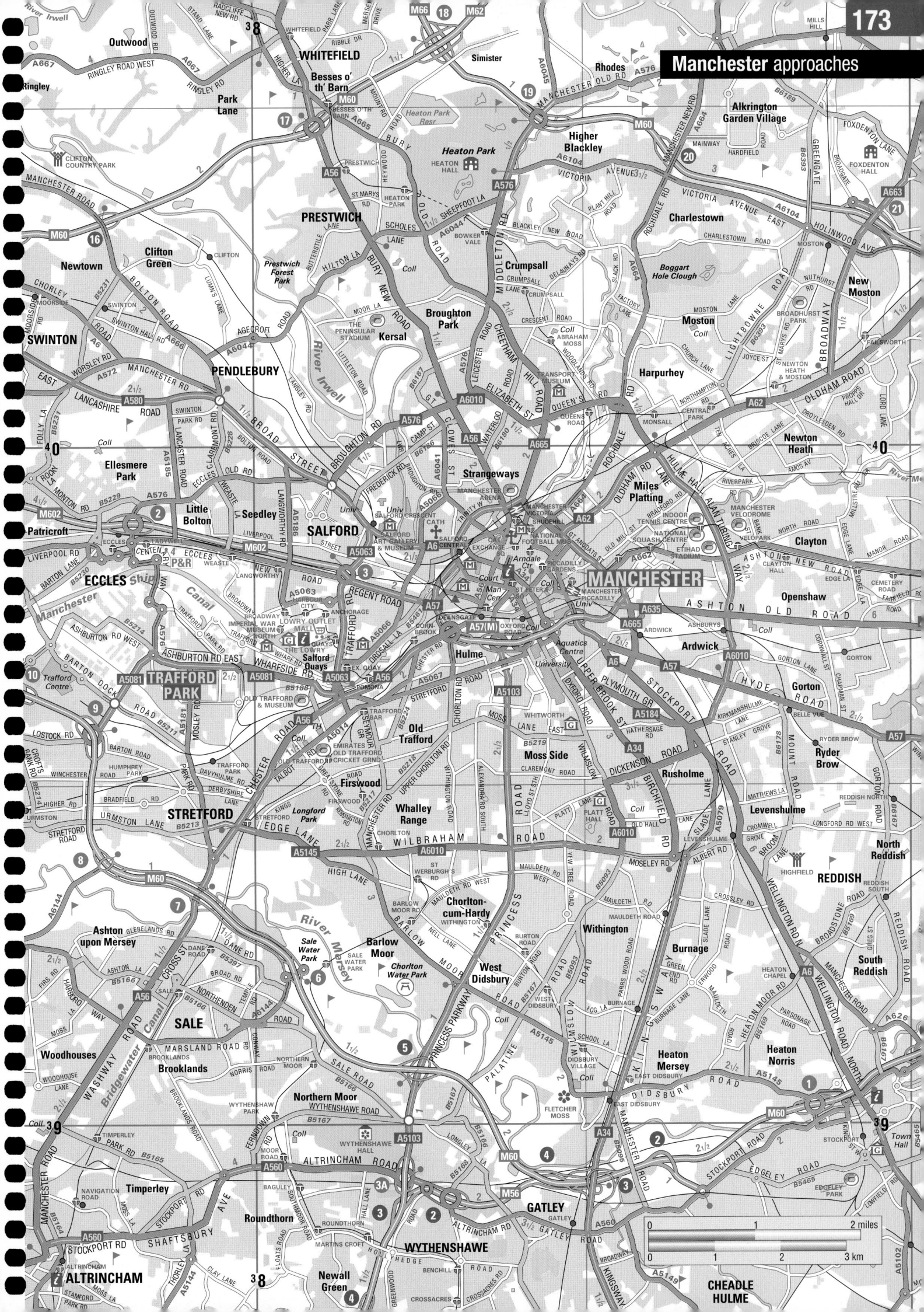

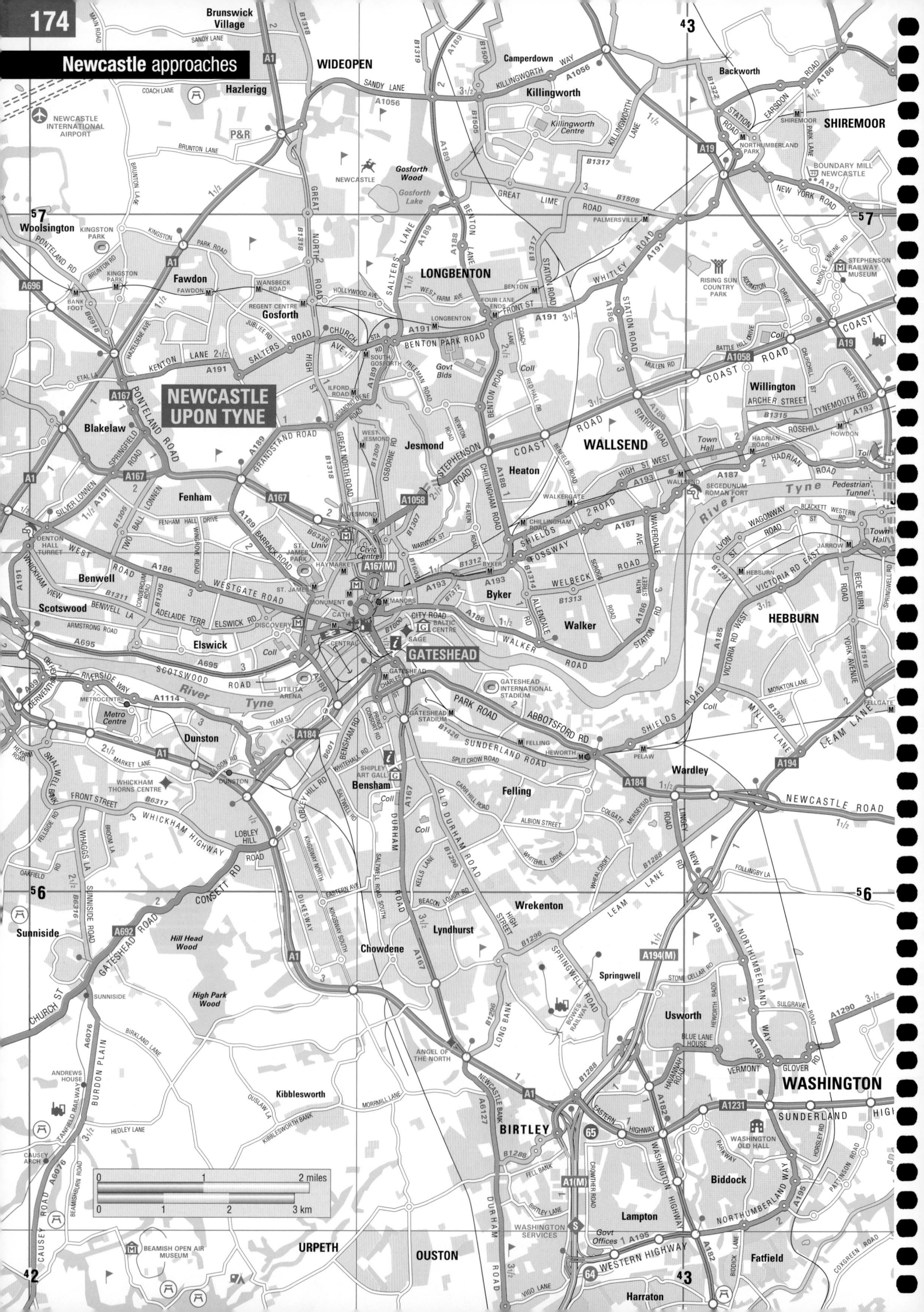

Town plan symbols

Motorway			
Primary route – dual, single carriageway			
A road – dual, single carriageway			
B road – dual, single carriageway			

Minor through road

One-way street

Pedestrian roads

Shopping streets

Railway with station

Tramway with station

Underground or Metro station

🅗 Hospital

🅟 Parking

Police

🅟🅞 Post Office

Shopmobility

▲ Youth hostel

Bus or railway station building

Shopping precinct or retail park

Park

Congestion charge zone

✝ Abbey or cathedral

Ancient monument

Aquarium

Art gallery

Bird collection or aviary

Building of interest

Castle

Church of interest

Cinema

Garden

Historic ship

House

House and garden

Museum

Preserved railway

Roman antiquity

Safari park

Theatre

ℹ Tourist information

Zoo

✦ Other place of interest

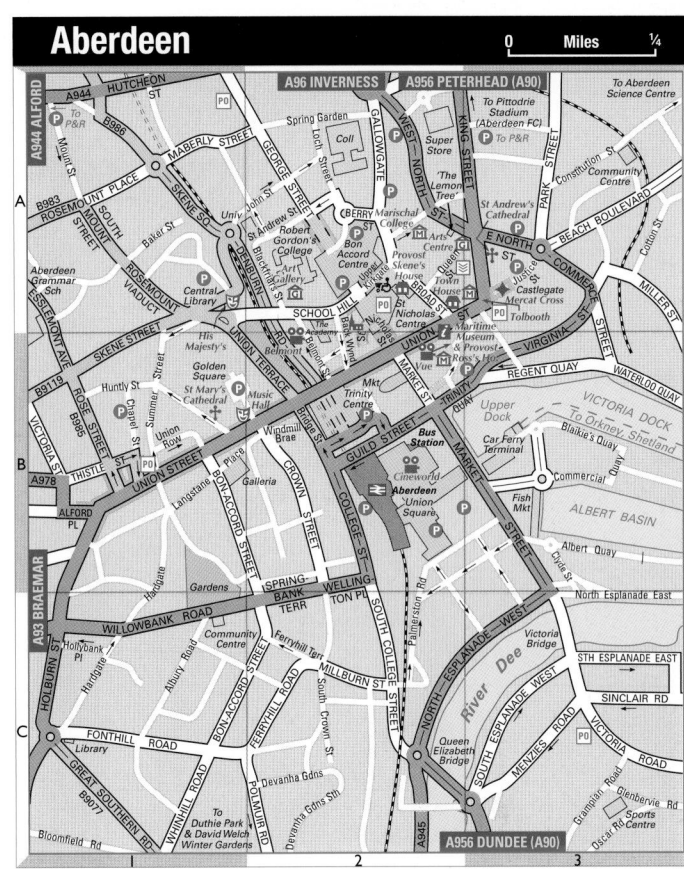

Aberdeen   0 ⎯ Miles ⎯ ¼

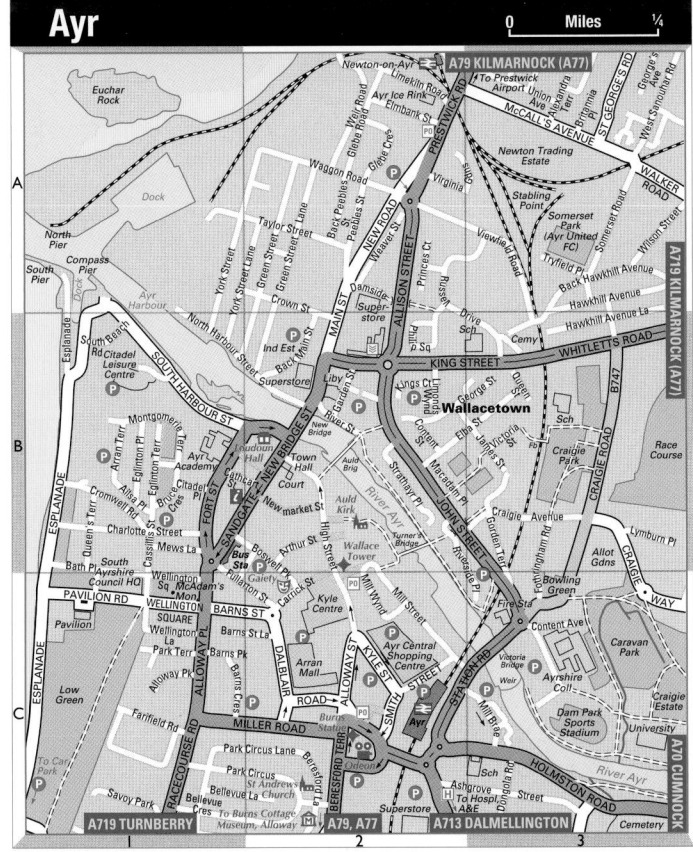

Ayr   0 ⎯ Miles ⎯ ¼

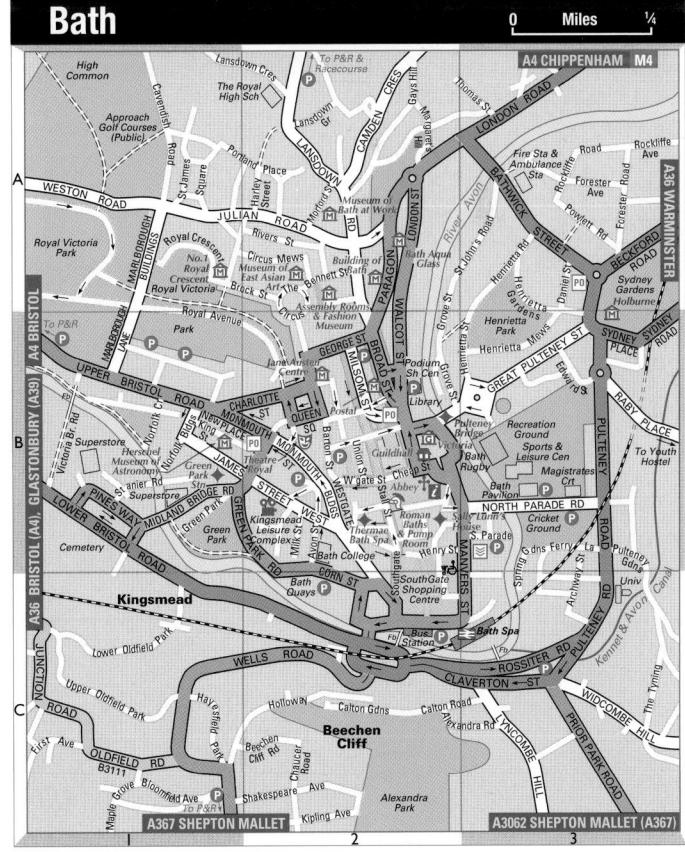

Bath   0 ⎯ Miles ⎯ ¼

Birmingham

0   Miles   ¼

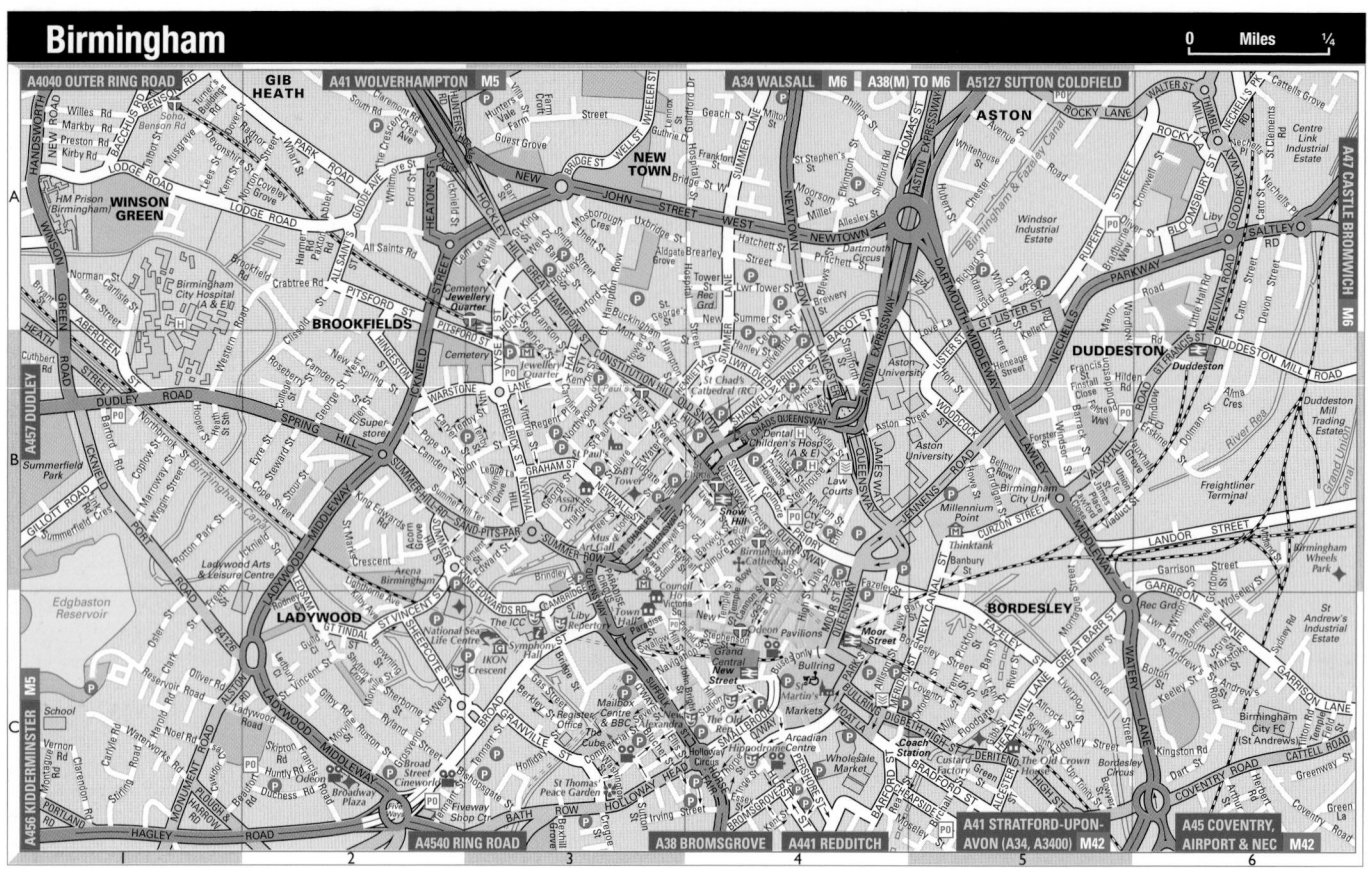

Blackpool

0   Miles   ¼

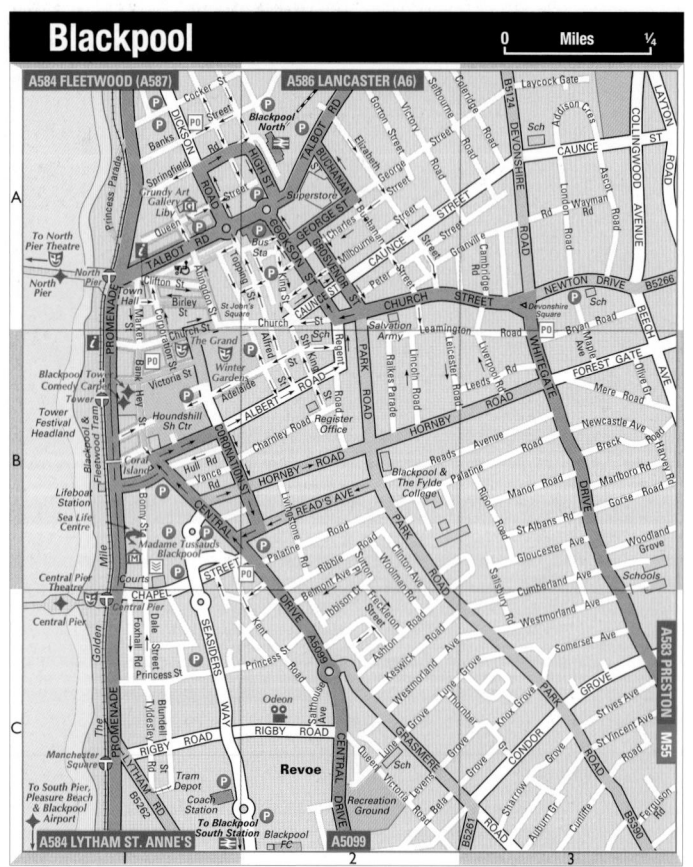

Bournemouth

0   Miles   ¼

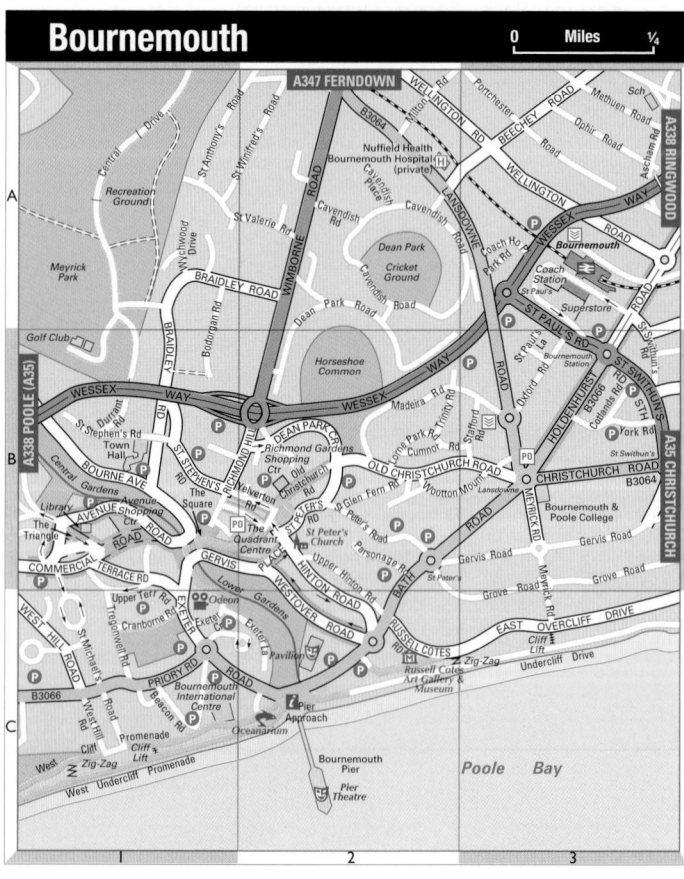

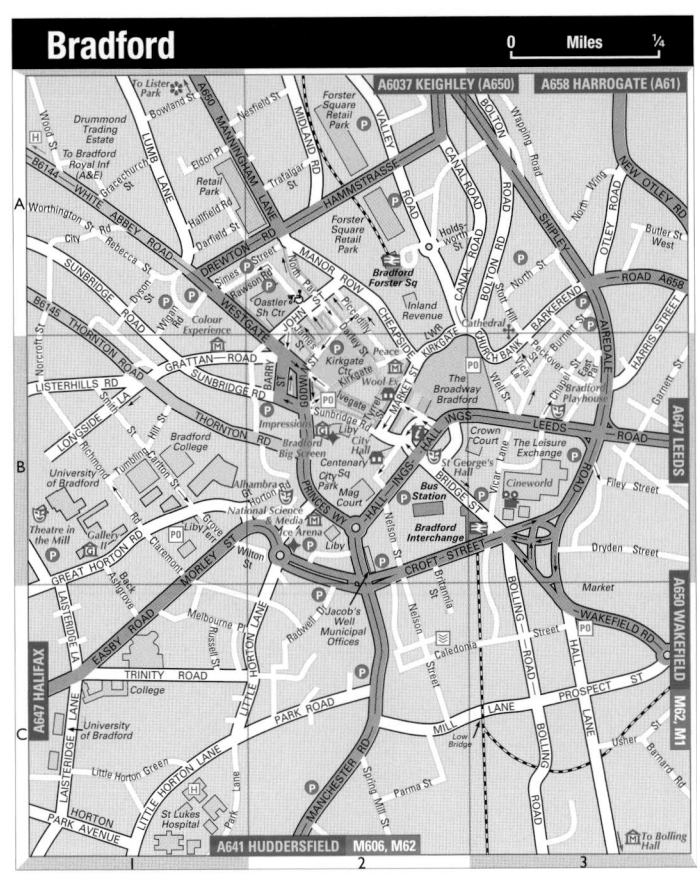

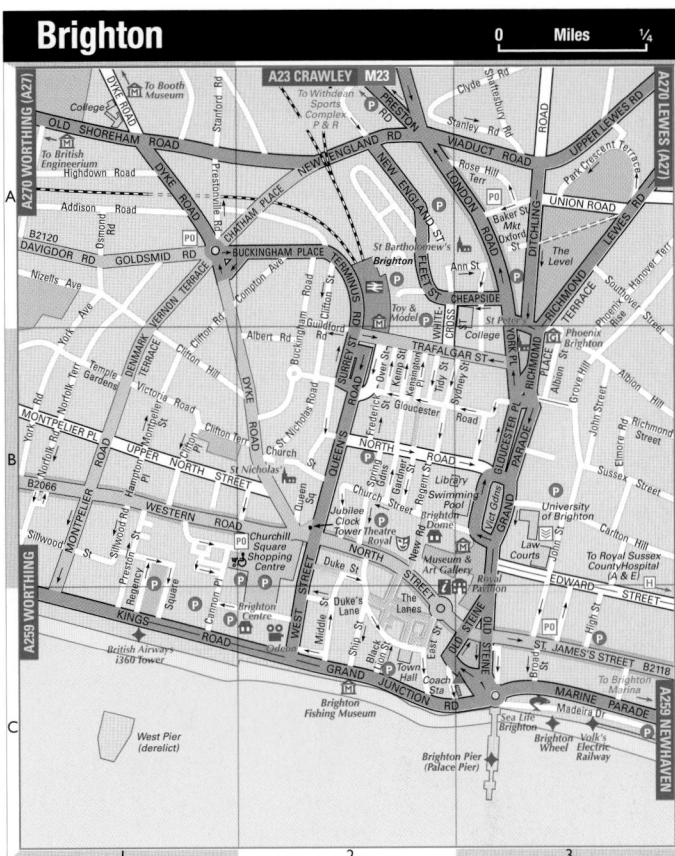

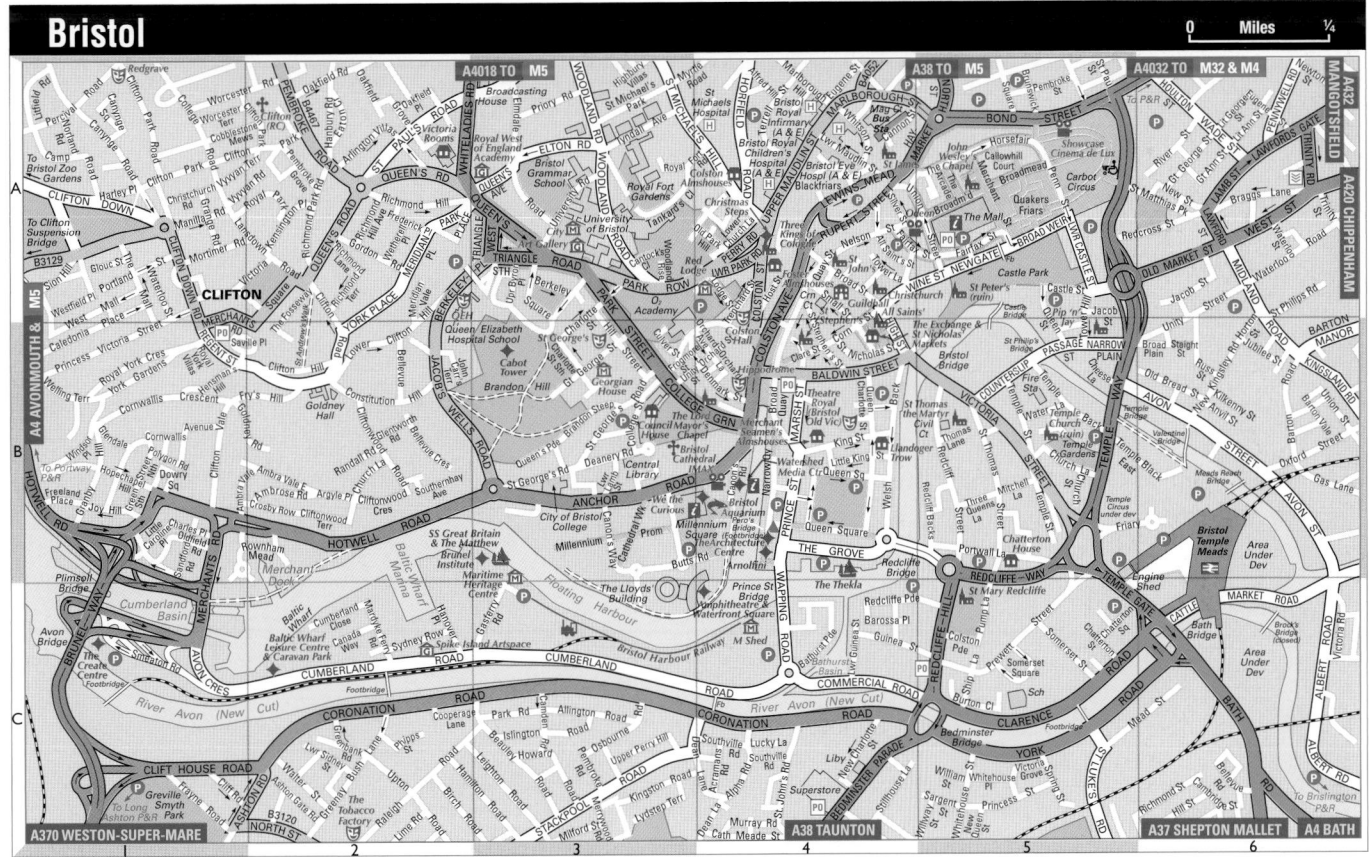

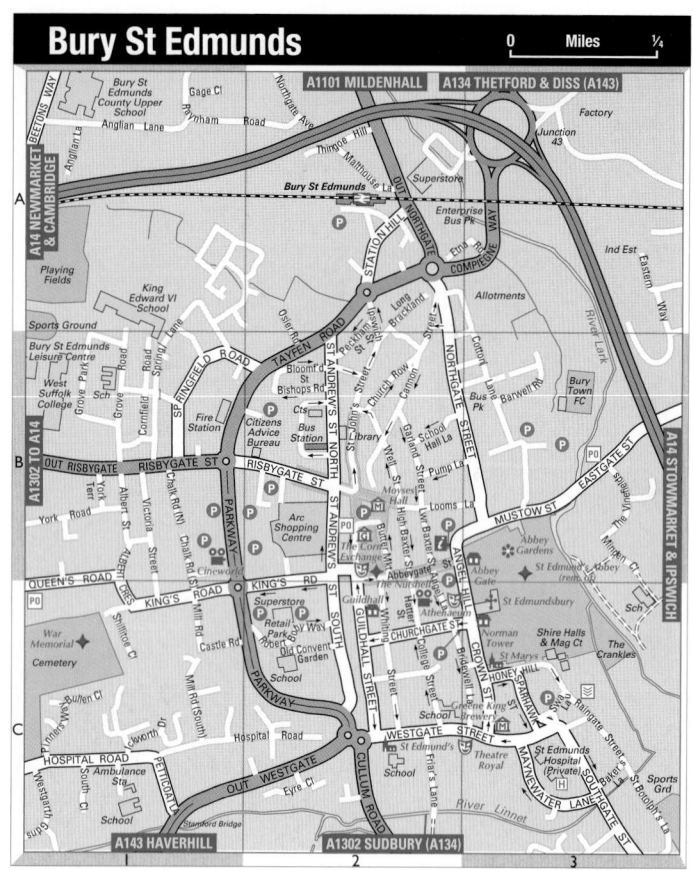

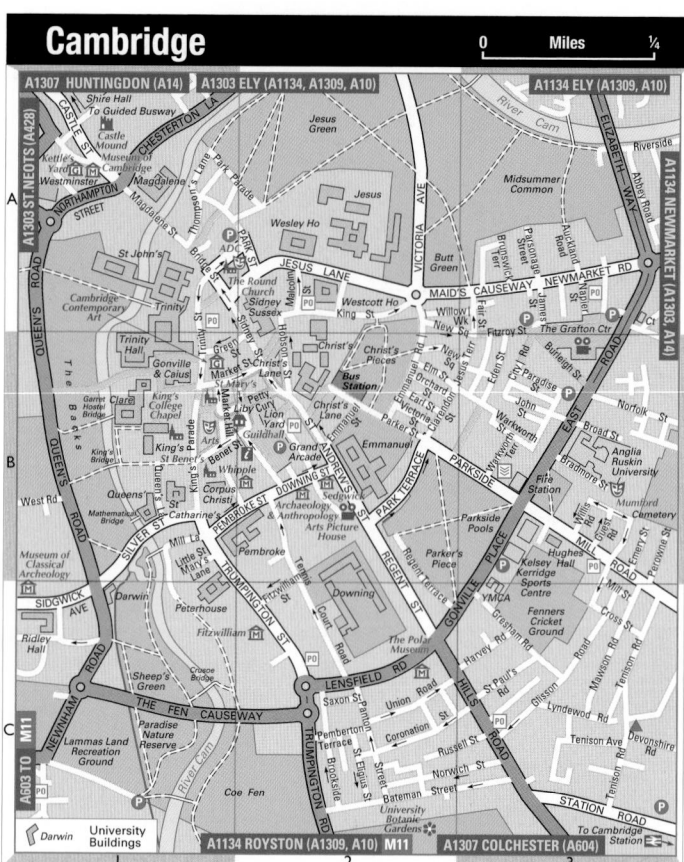

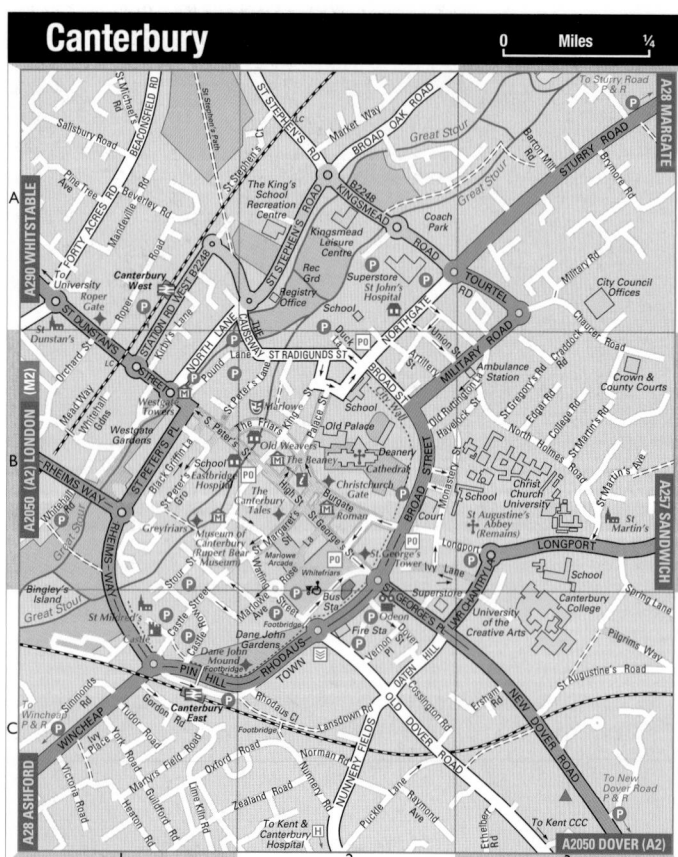

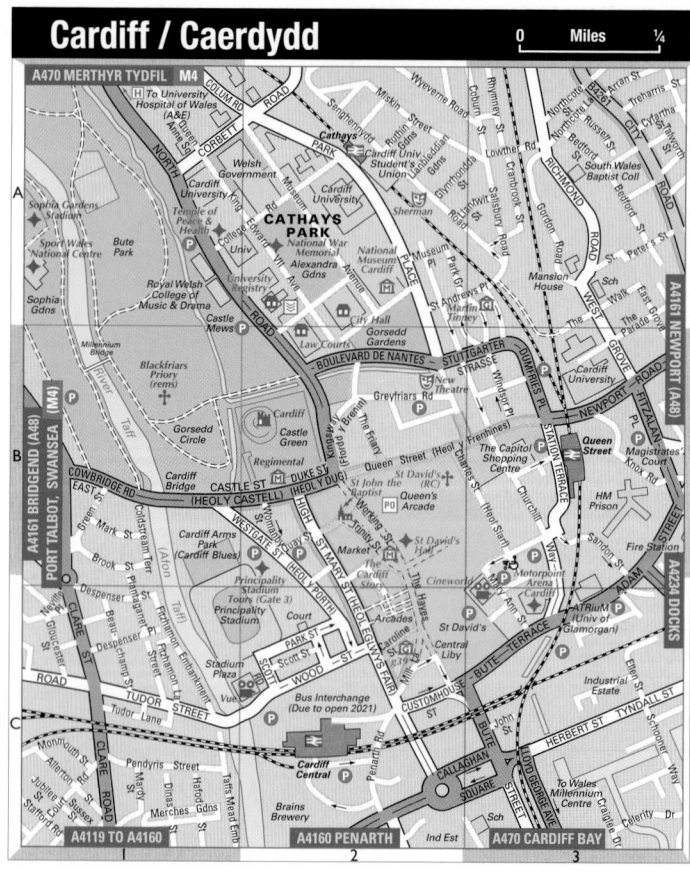

Carlisle

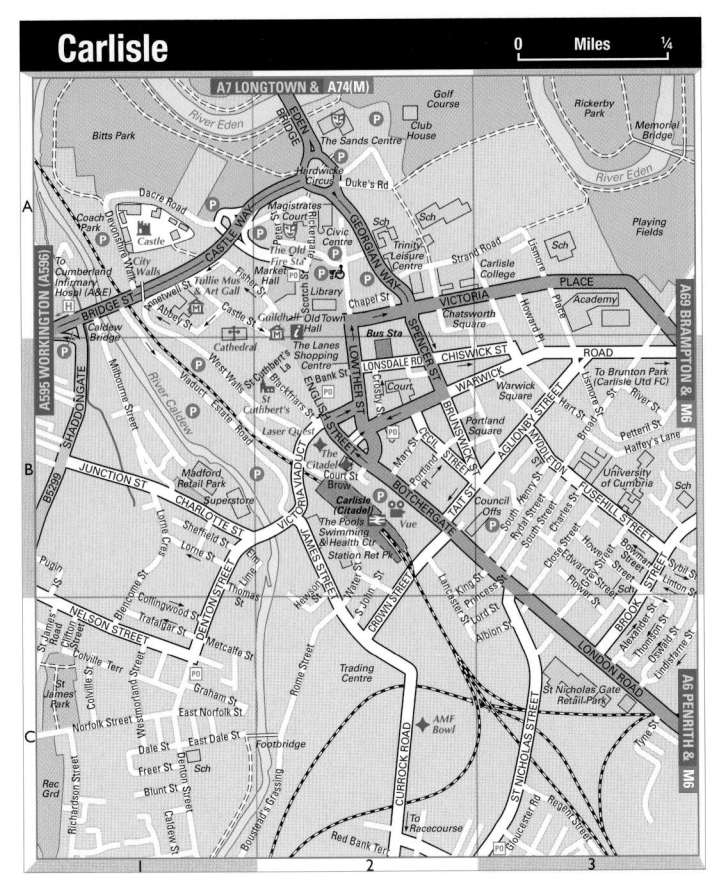

Chelmsford

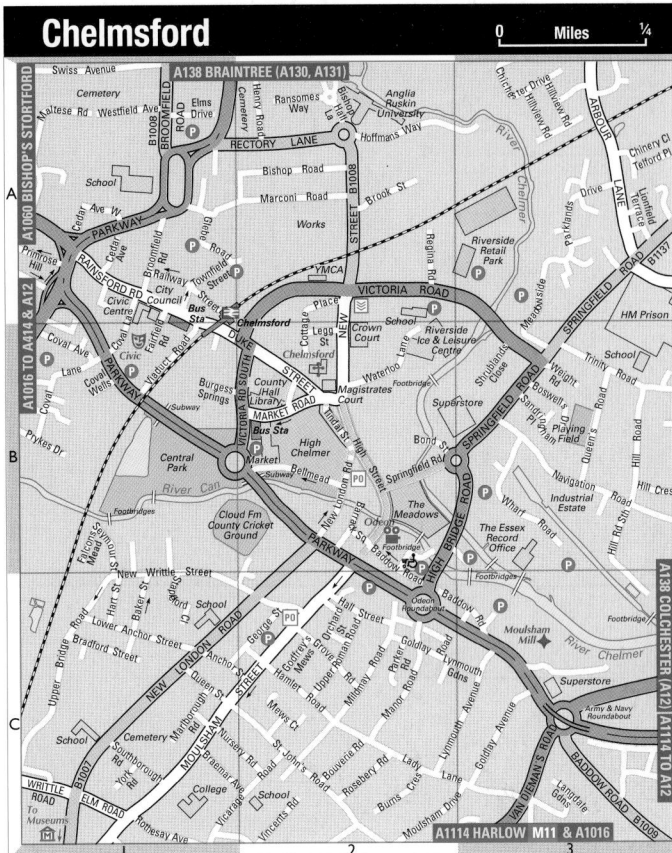

Cheltenham

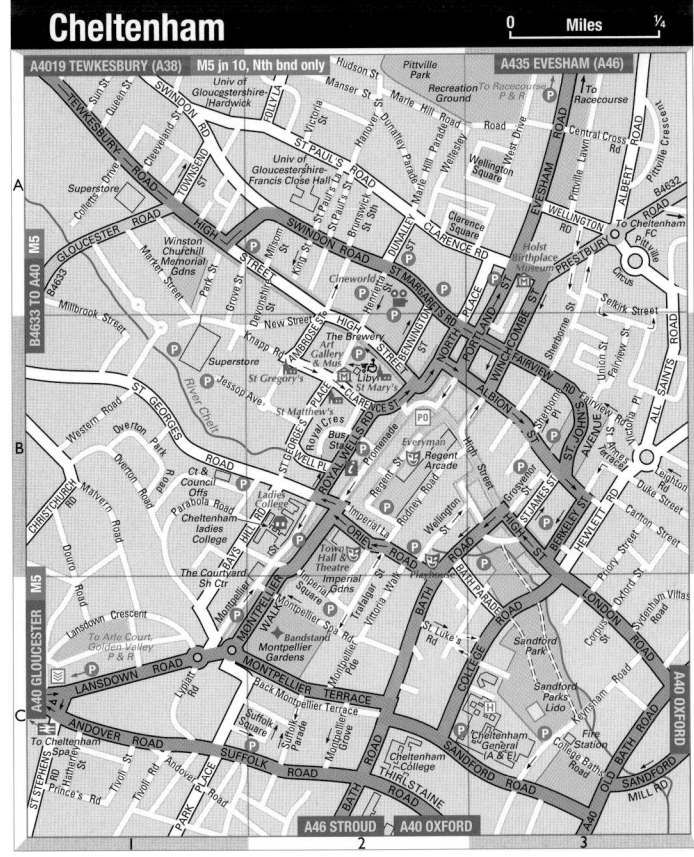

Chester

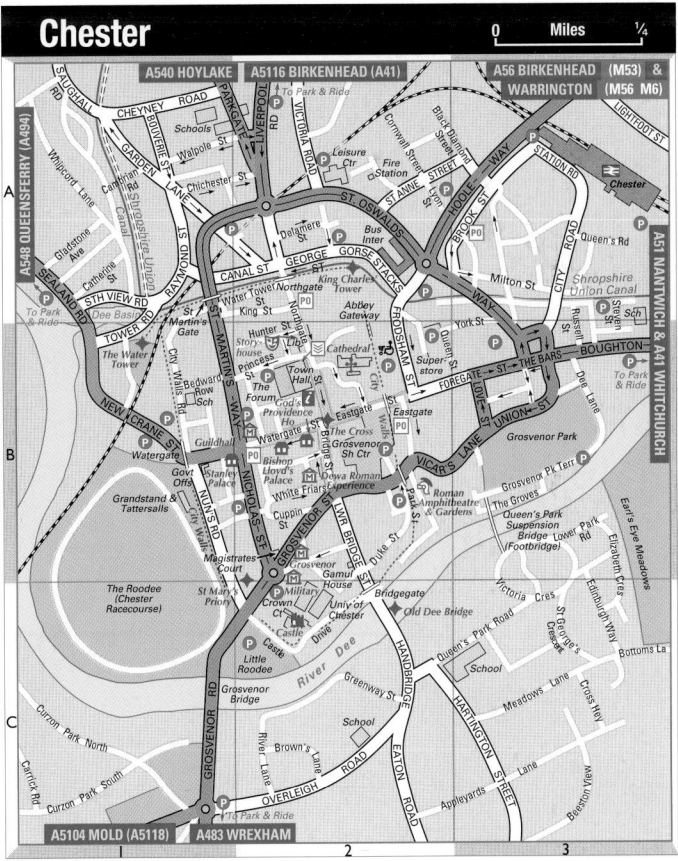

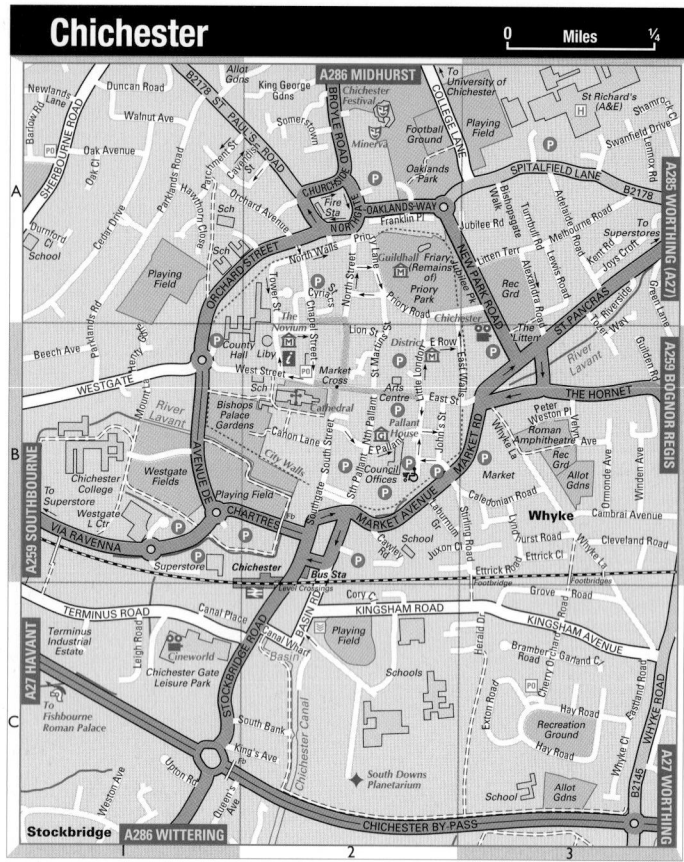

Chichester

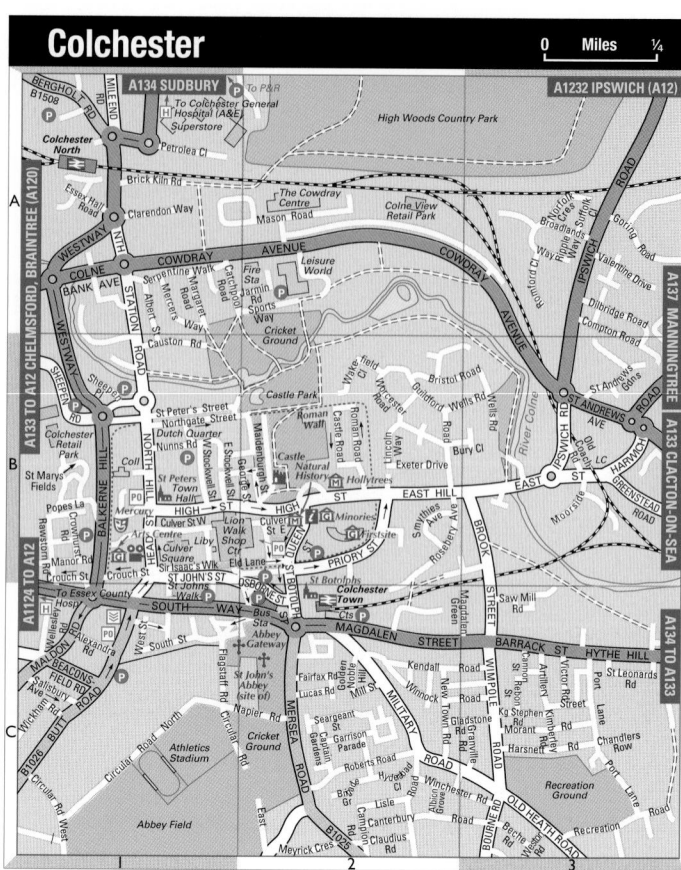

Colchester

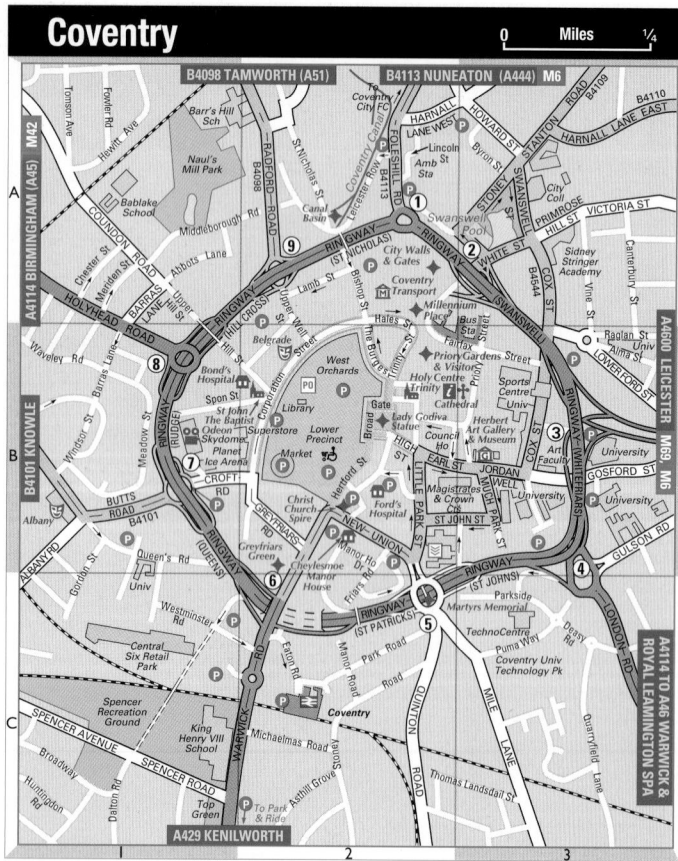

Coventry

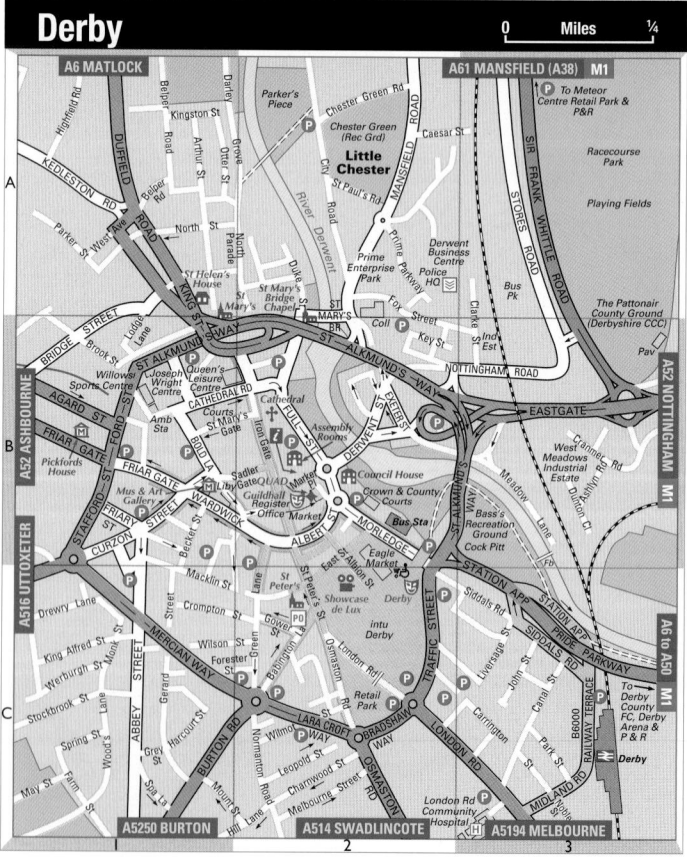

Derby

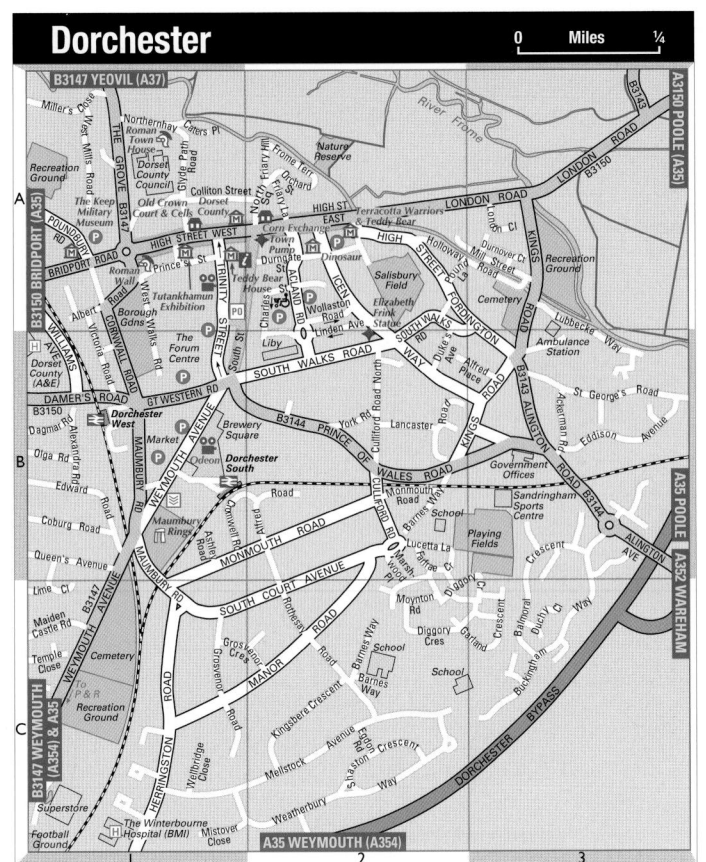

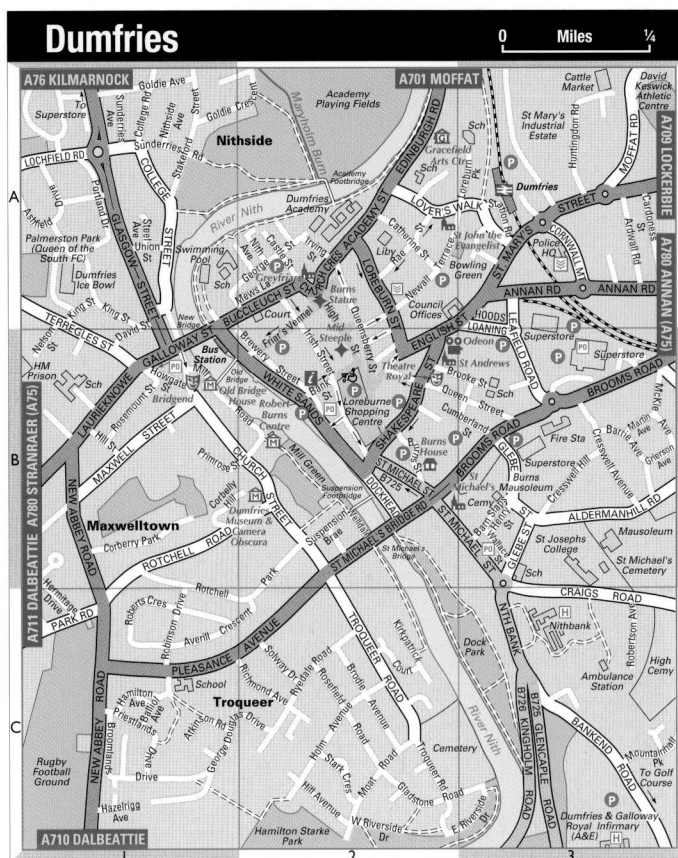

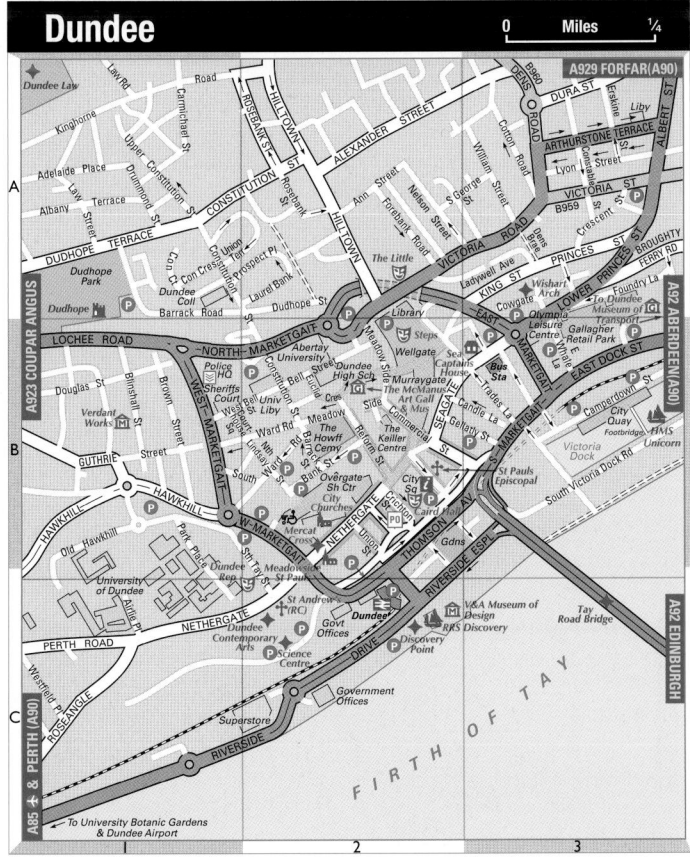

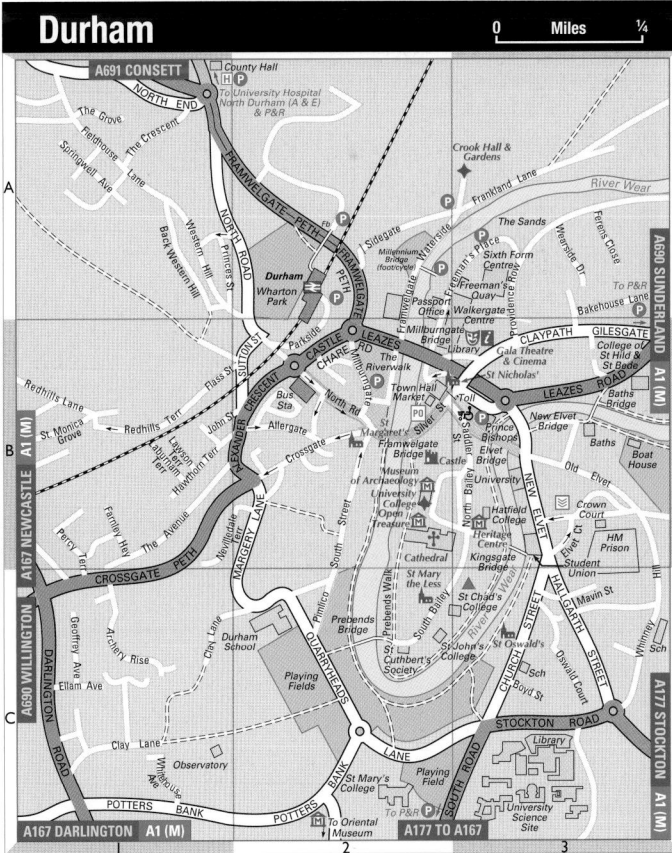

Edinburgh

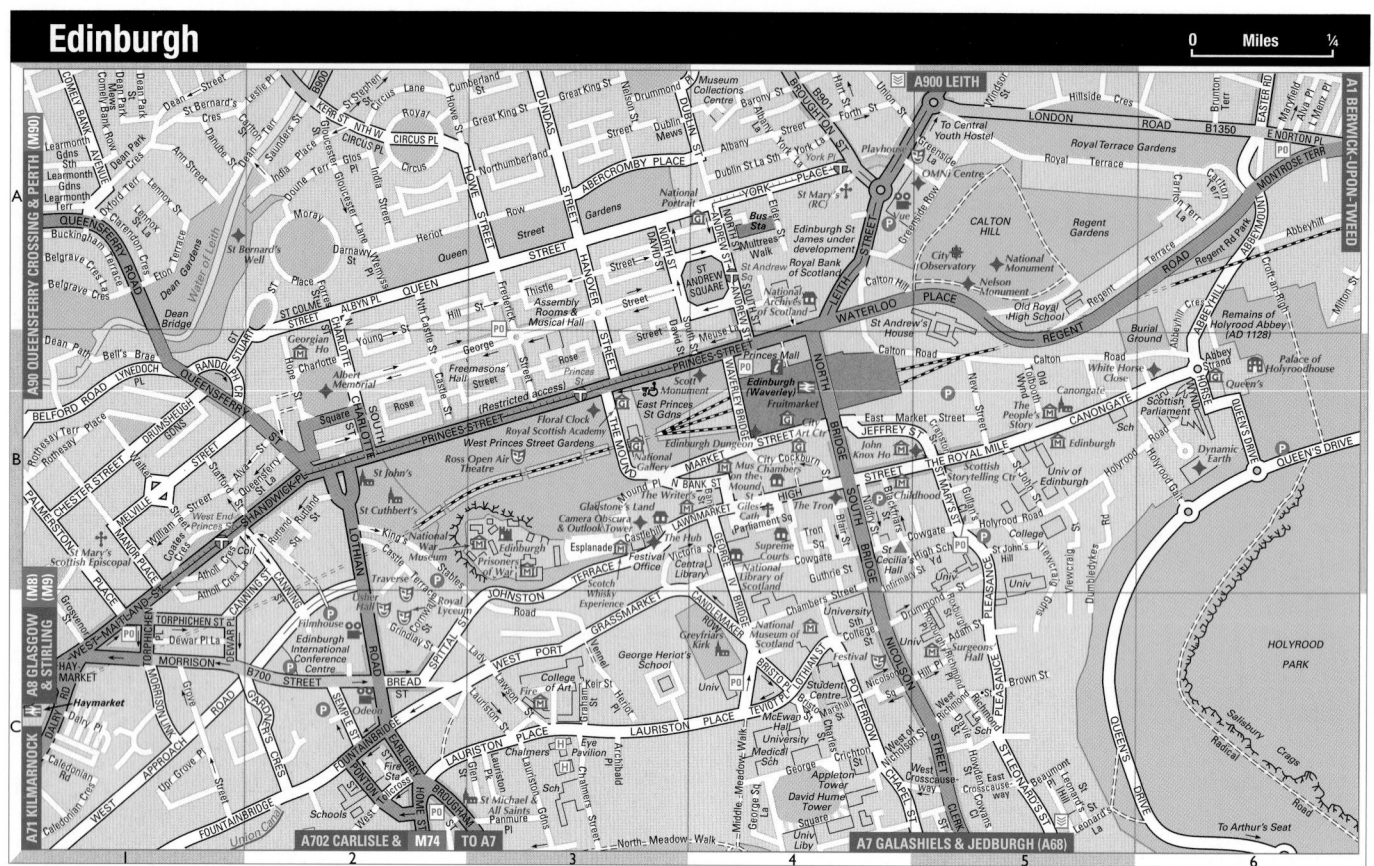

Exeter

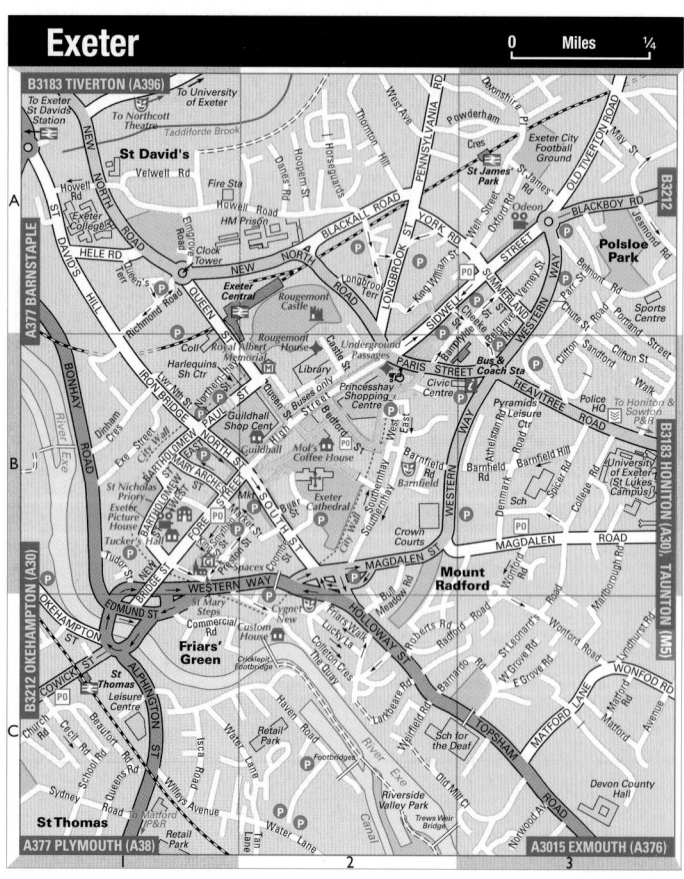

Gloucester

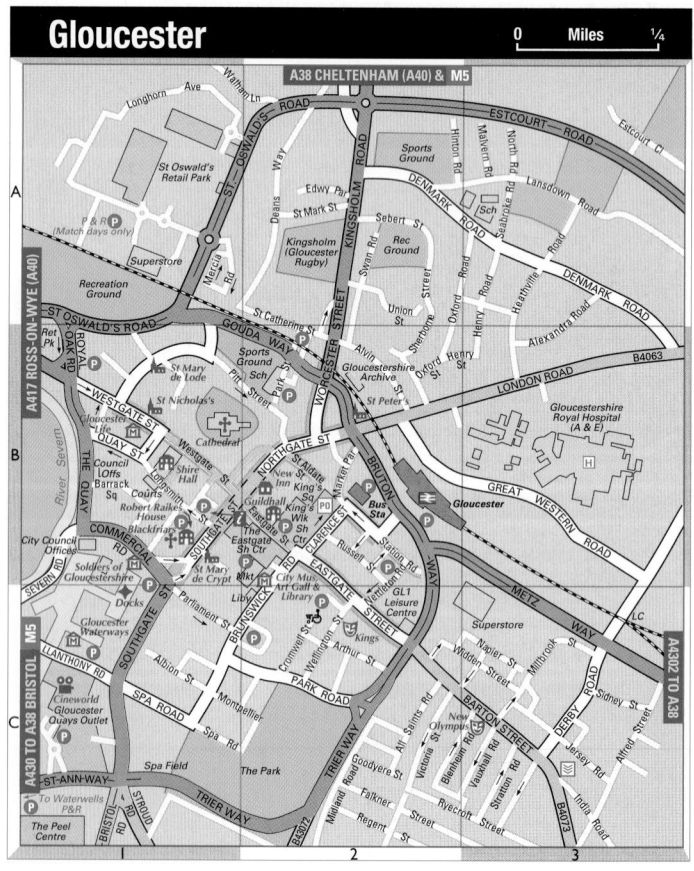

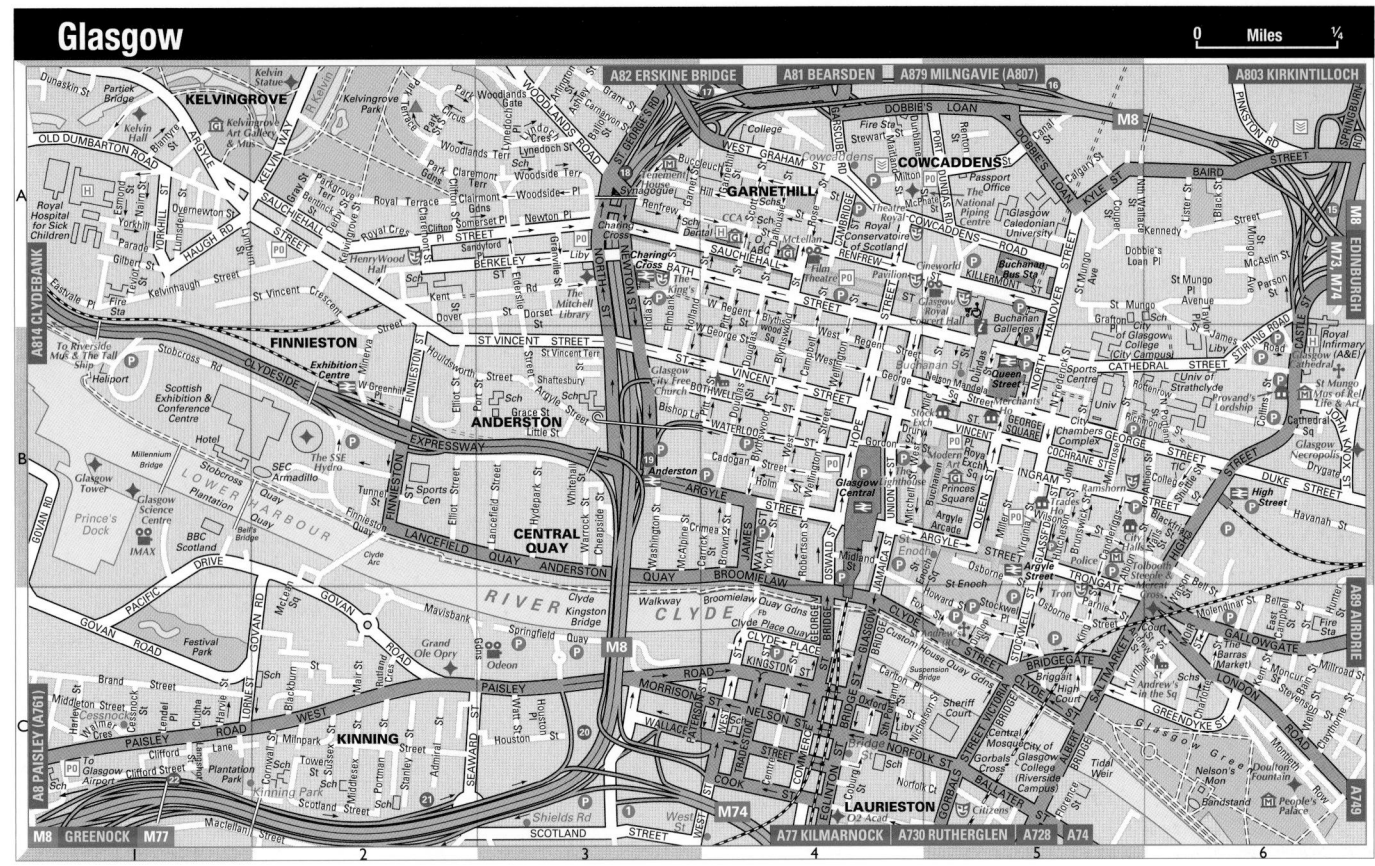

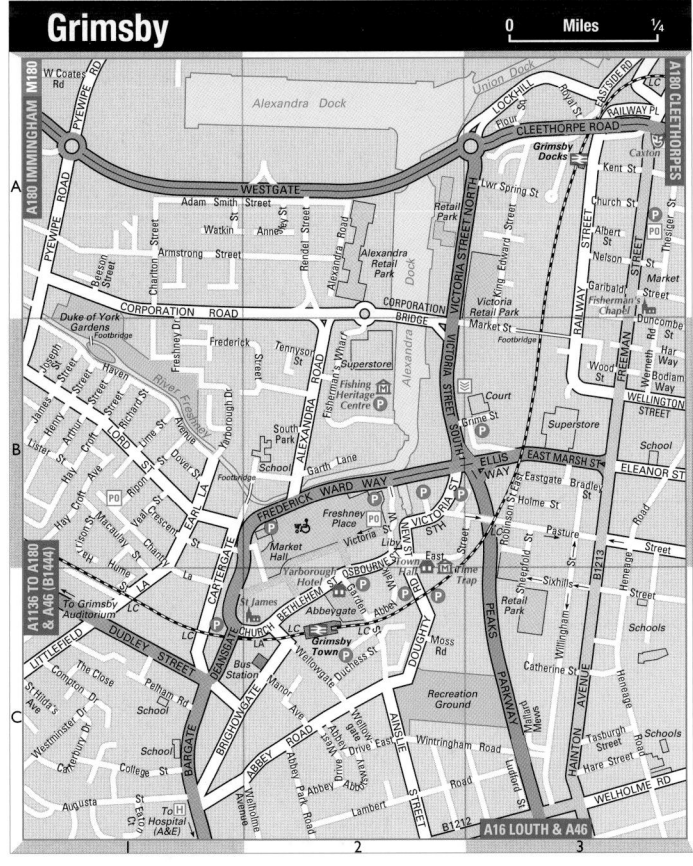

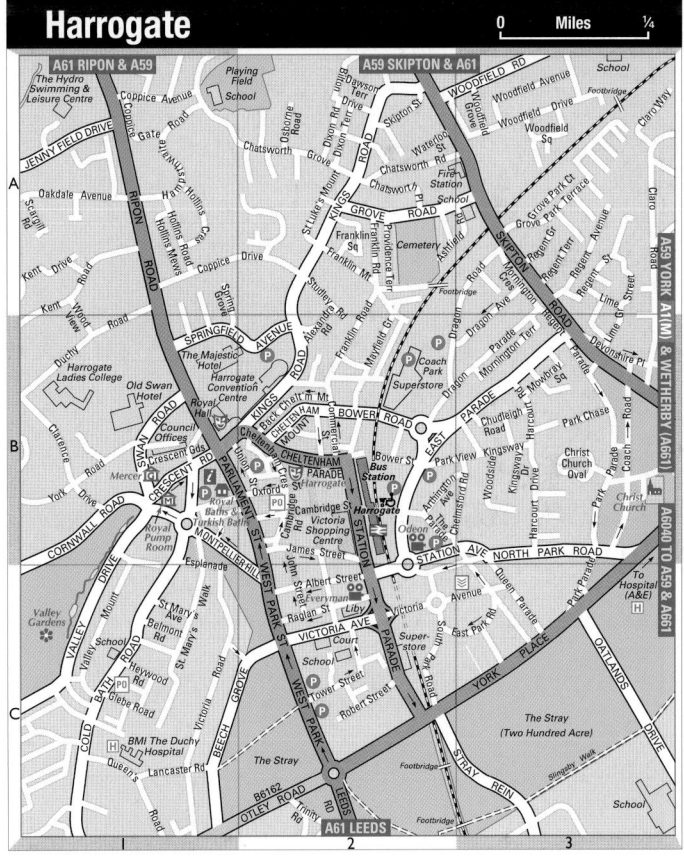

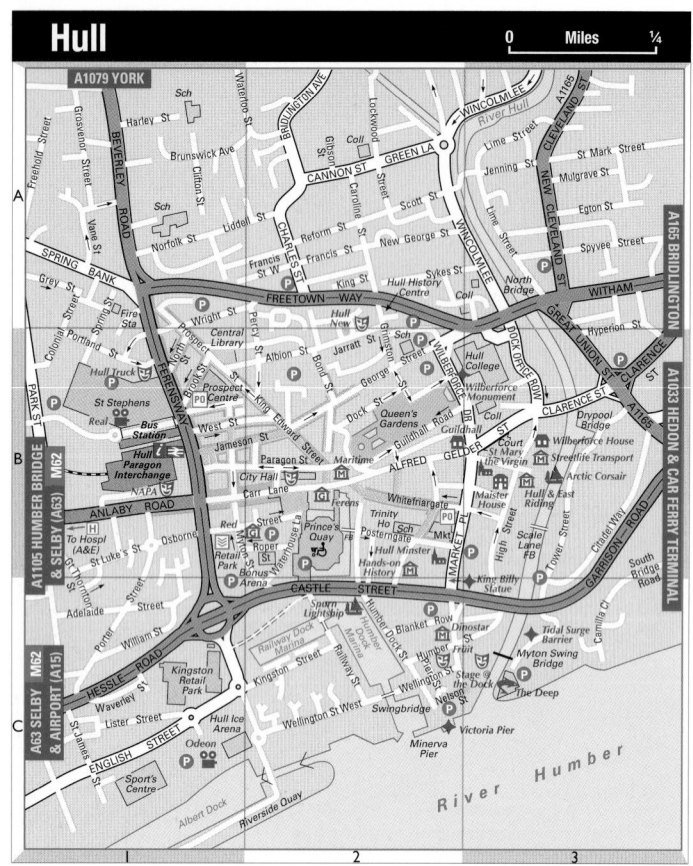

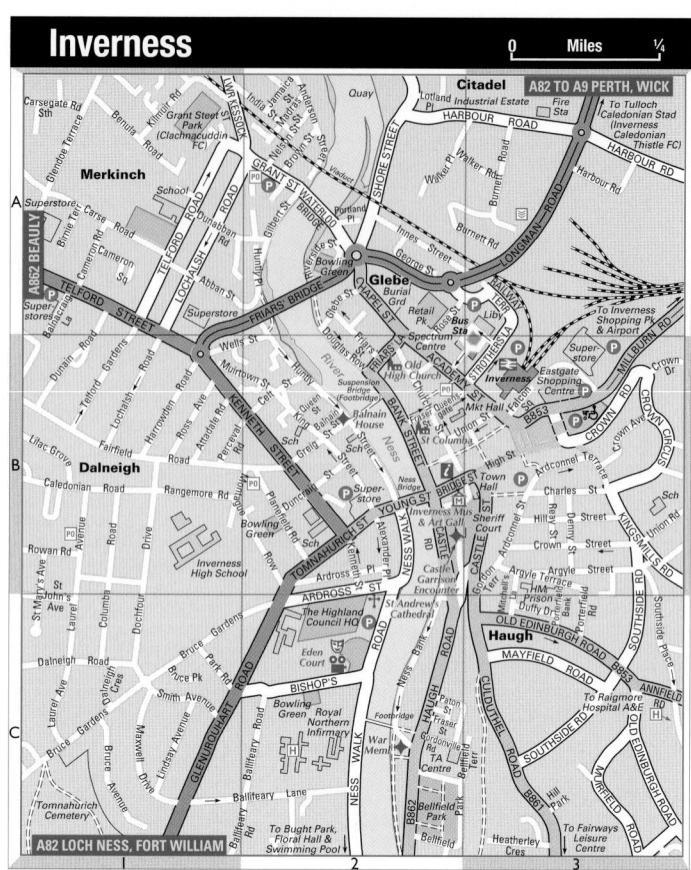

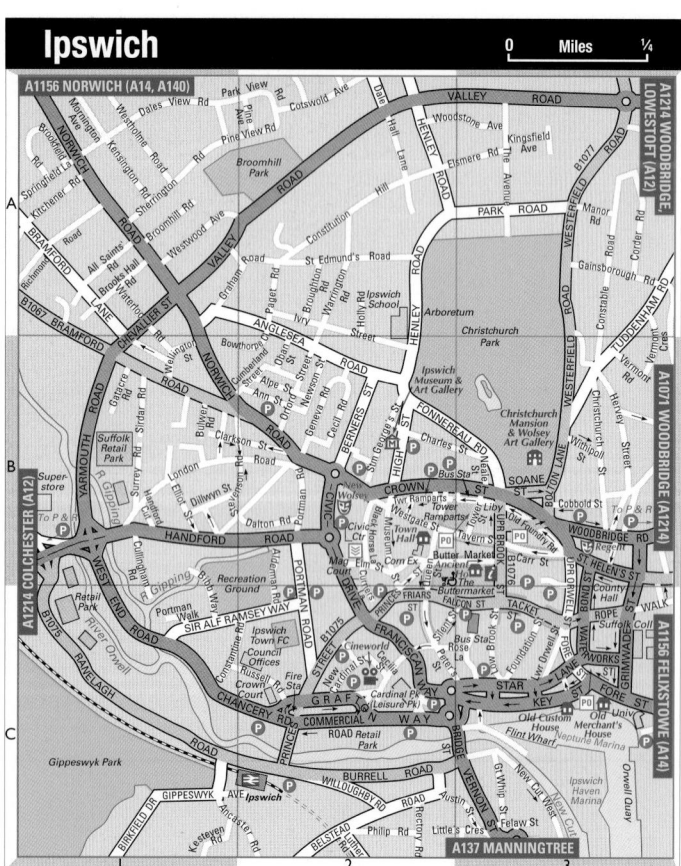

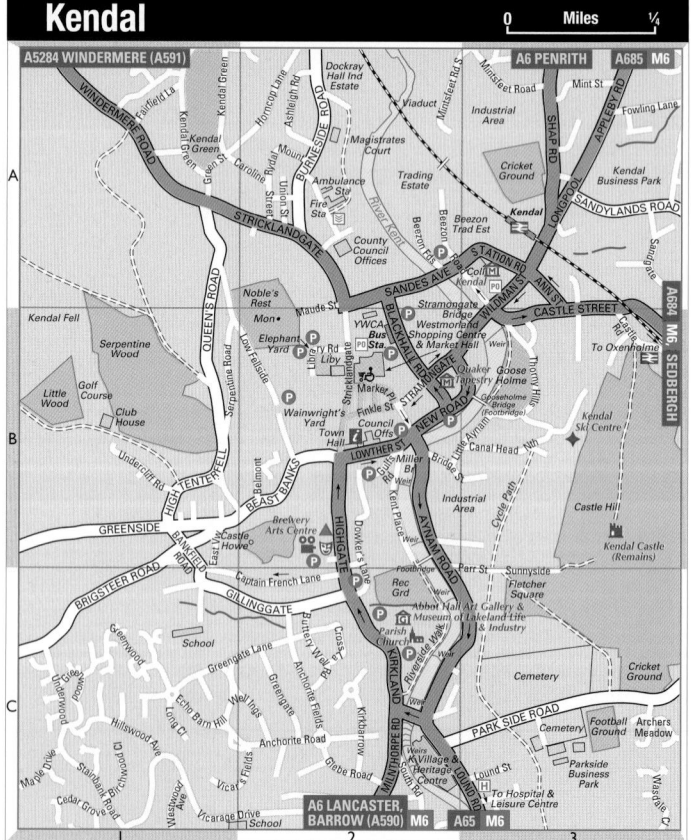

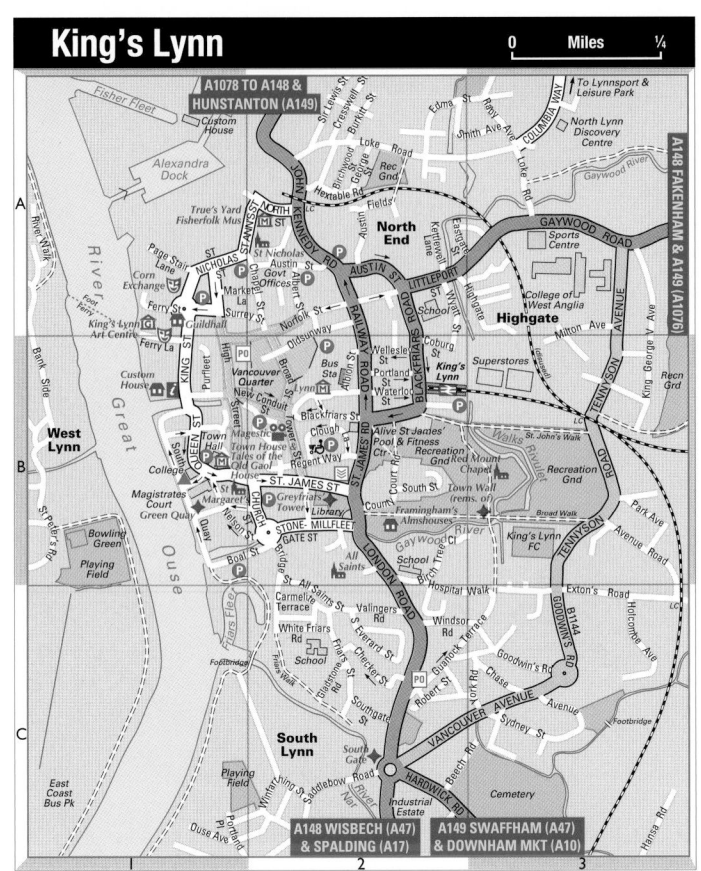

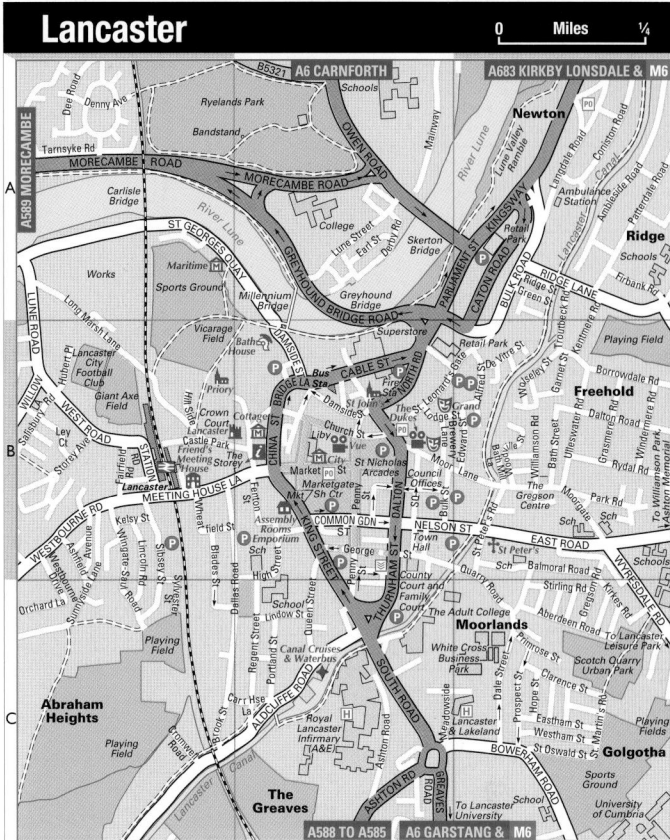

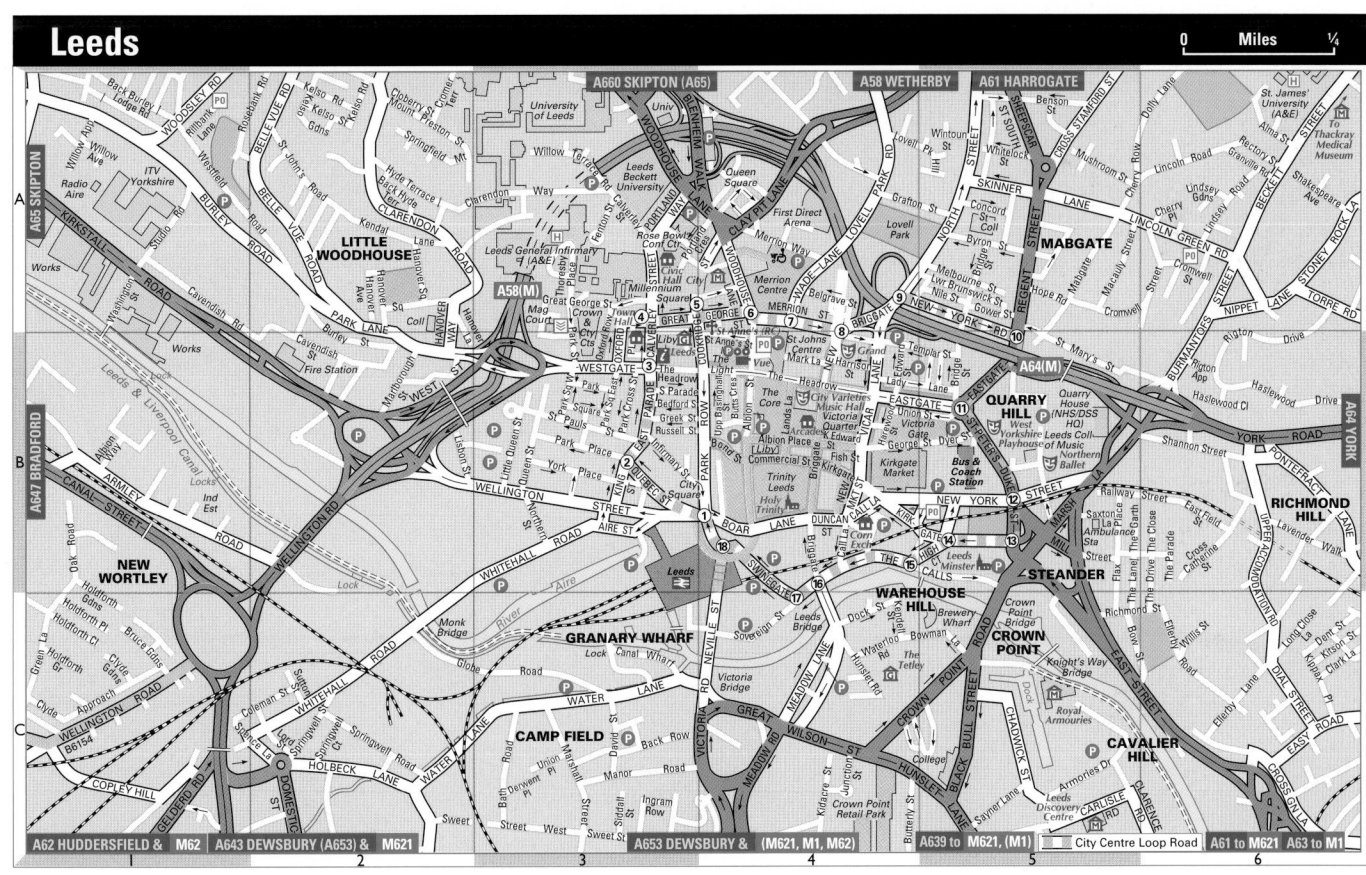

London Docklands

Congestion Charging Zone

0 Miles 1

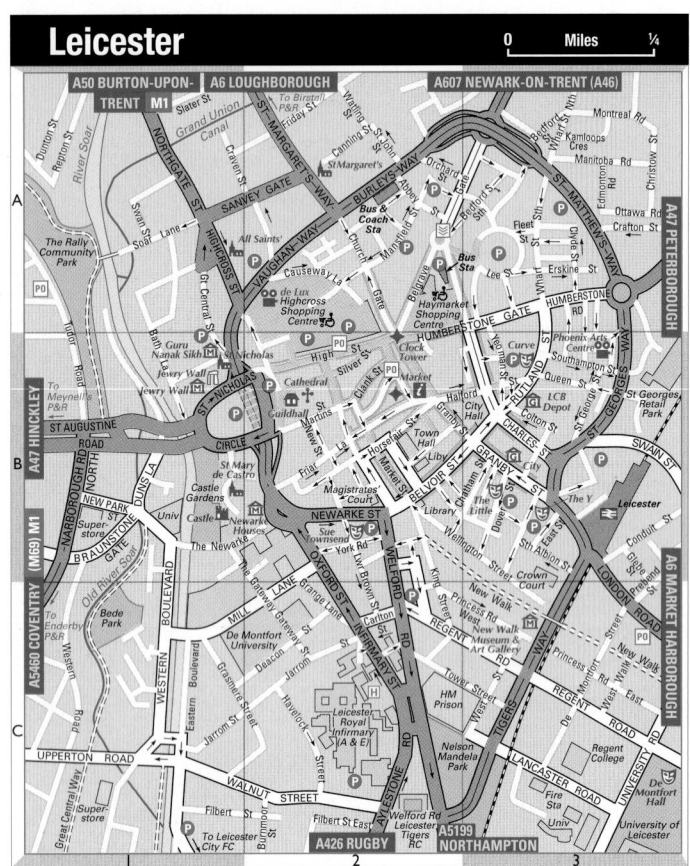

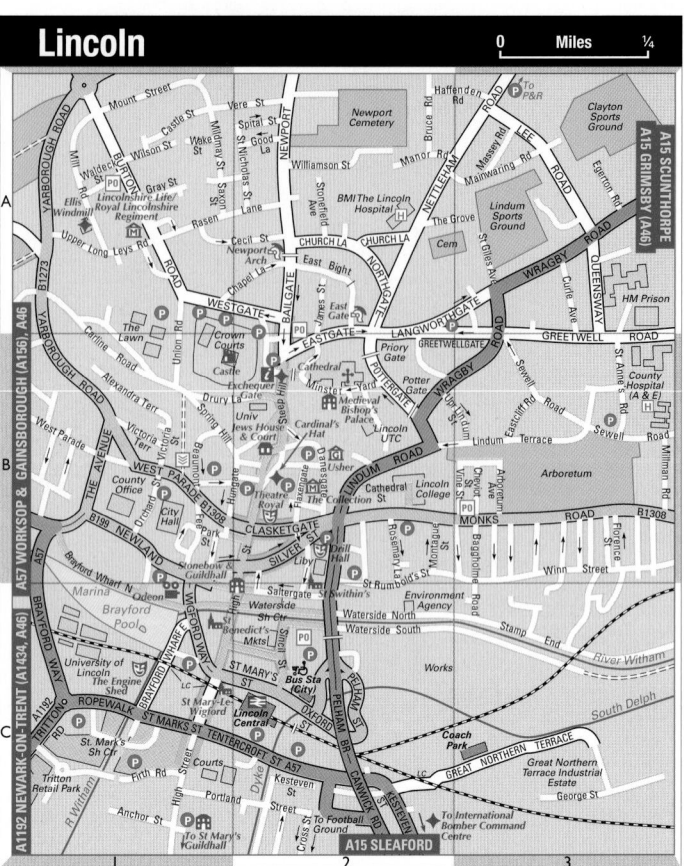

Llandudno

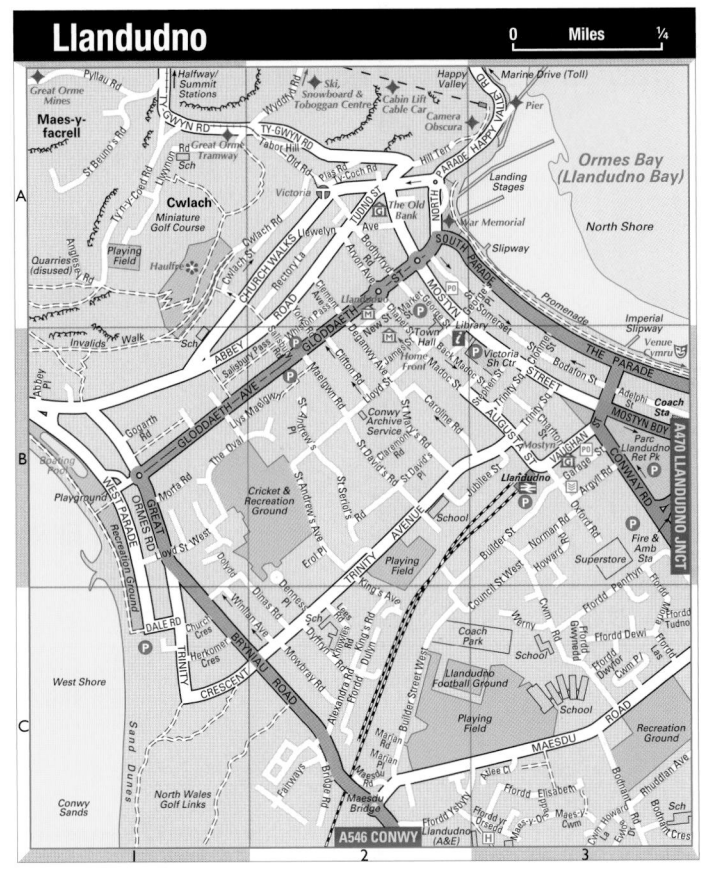

Llanelli

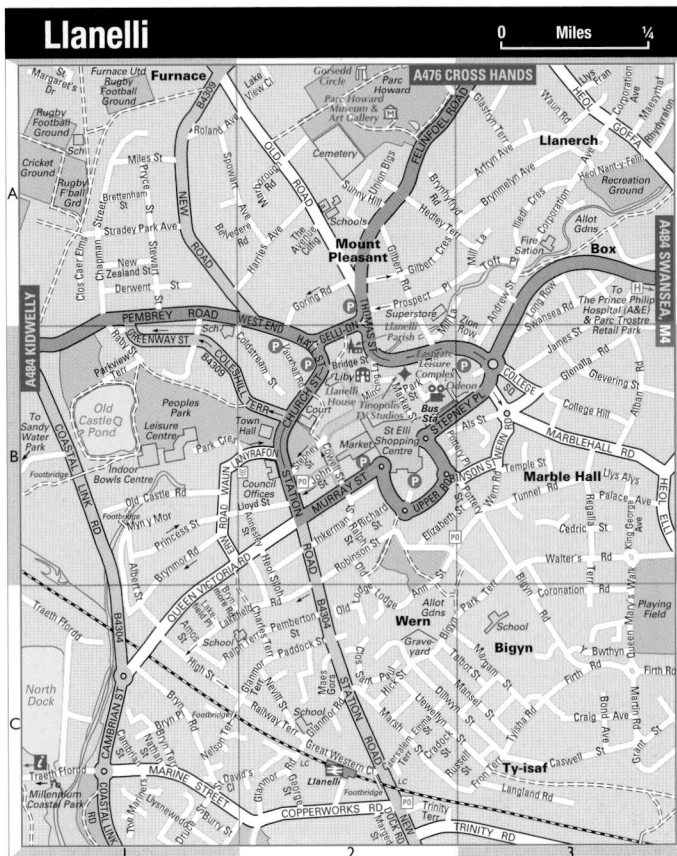

Luton

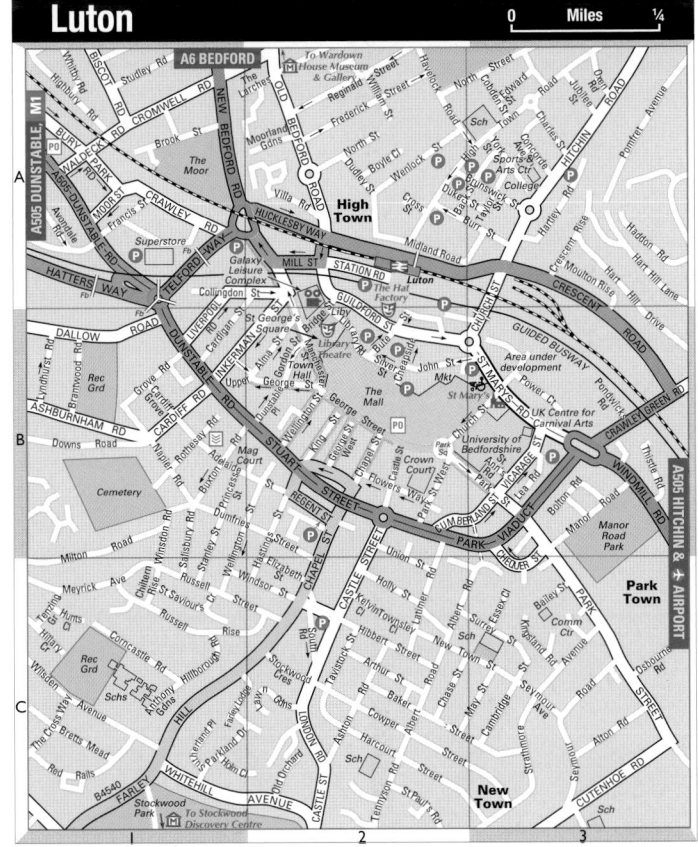

Macclesfield

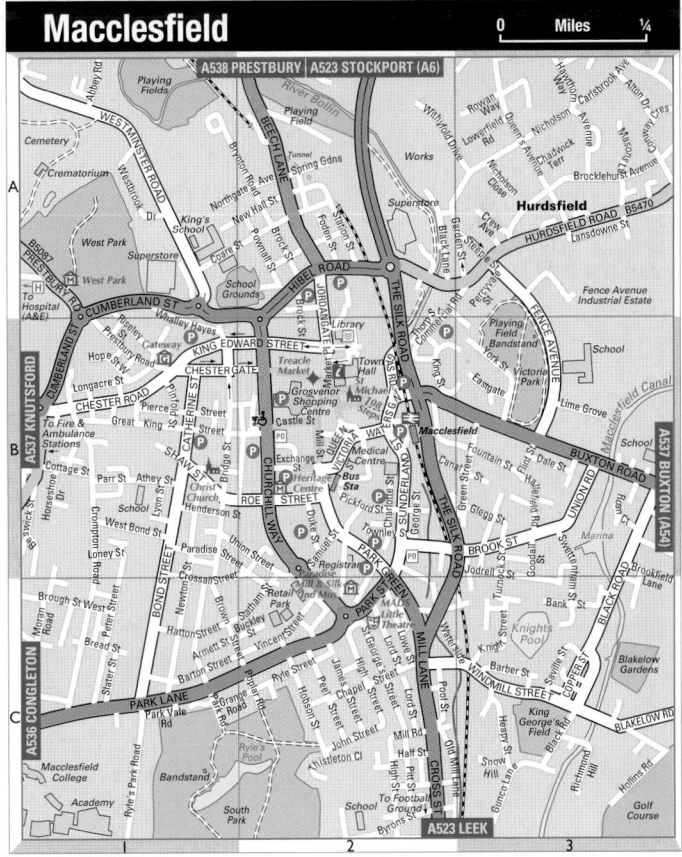

Manchester

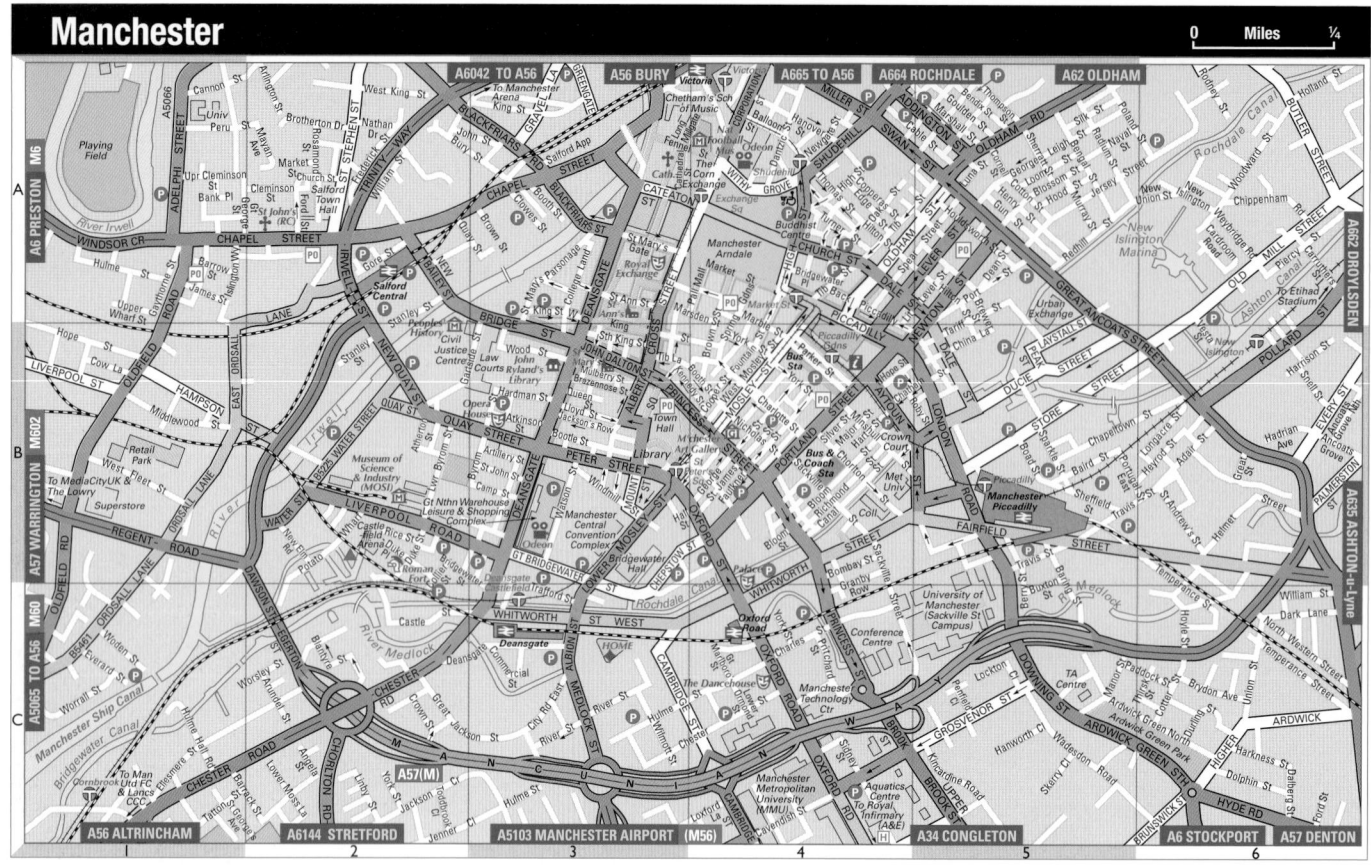

Maidstone

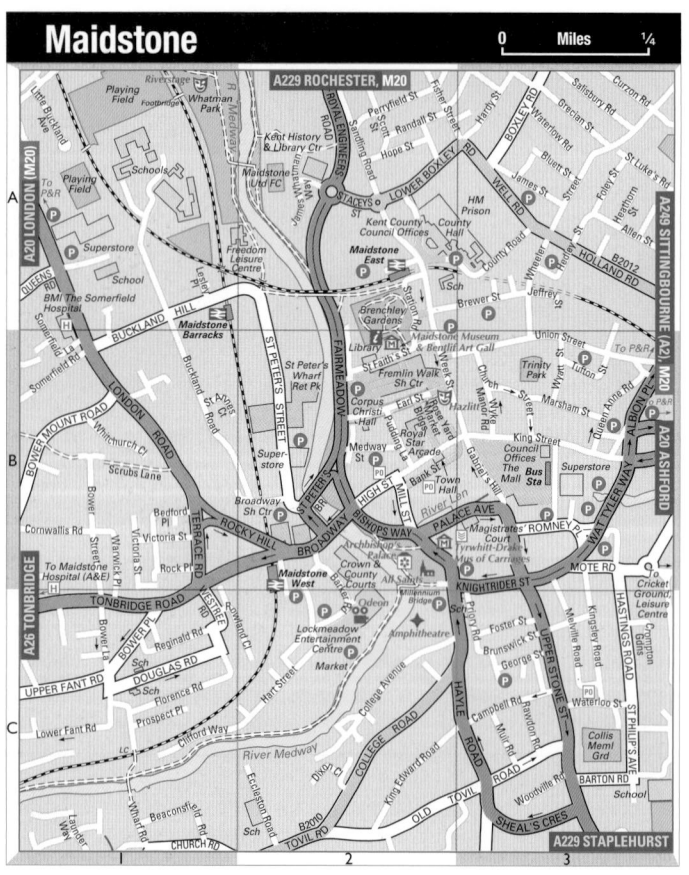

Merthyr Tydfil / Merthyr Tudful

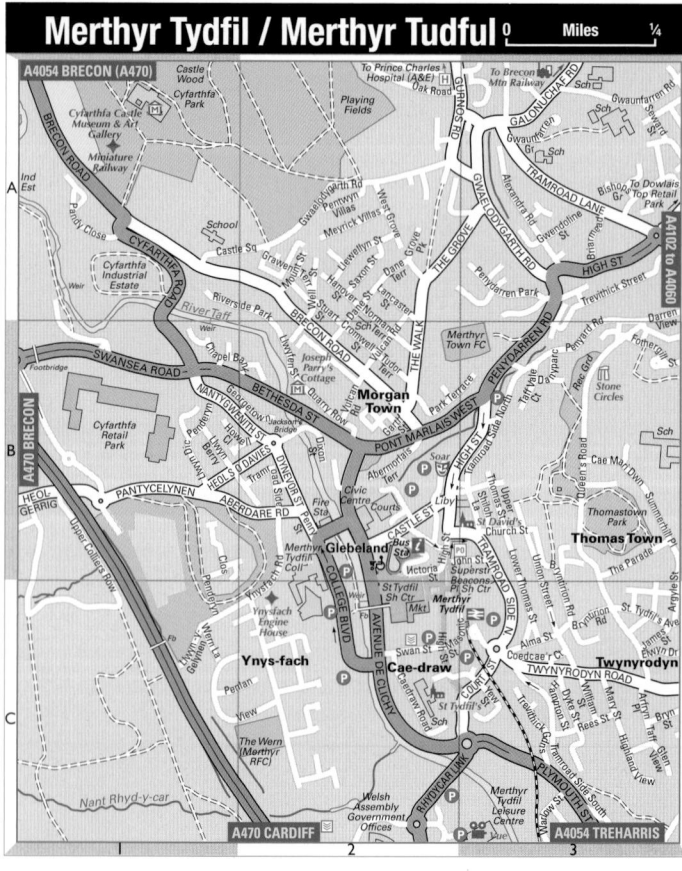

Middlesbrough

0   Miles   ¼

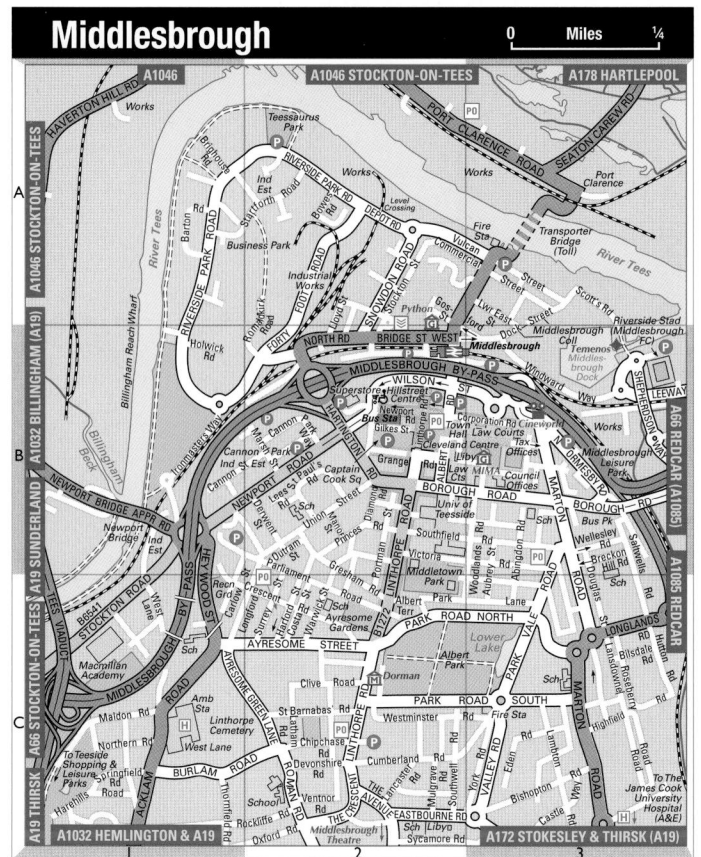

Milton Keynes

0   Miles   ¼

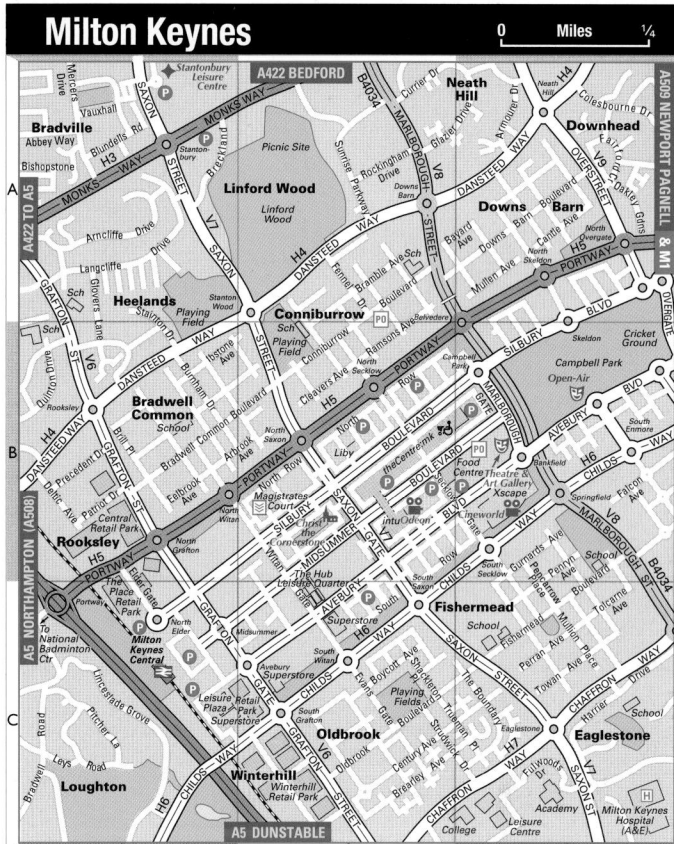

Newcastle upon Tyne

0   Miles   ¼

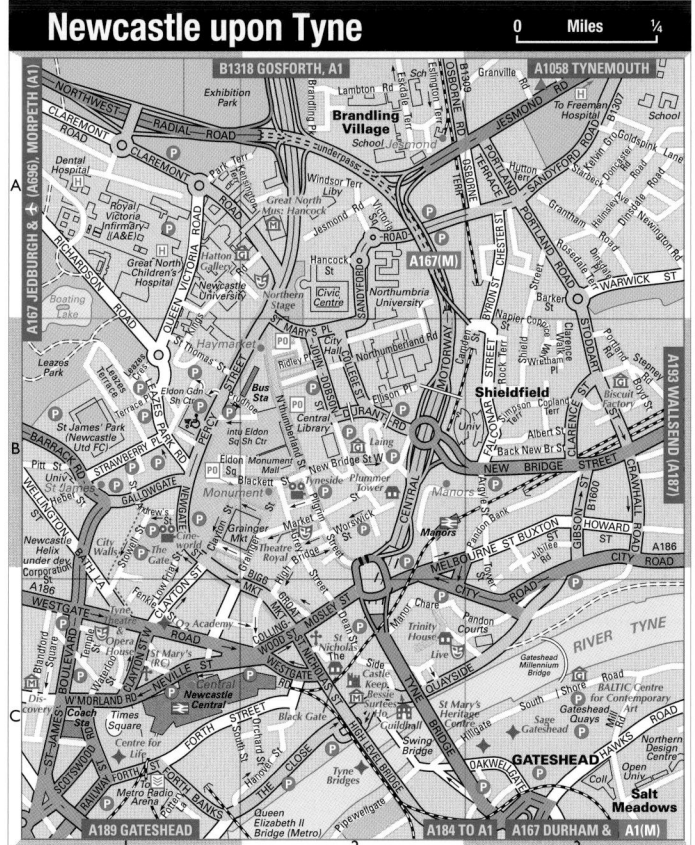

Newport / Casnewydd

0   Miles   ¼

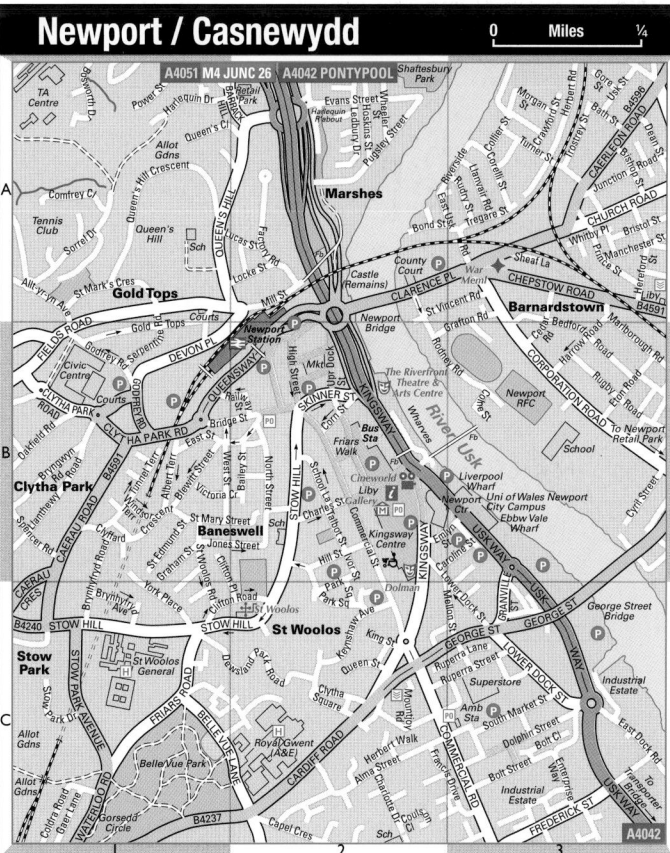

Newquay

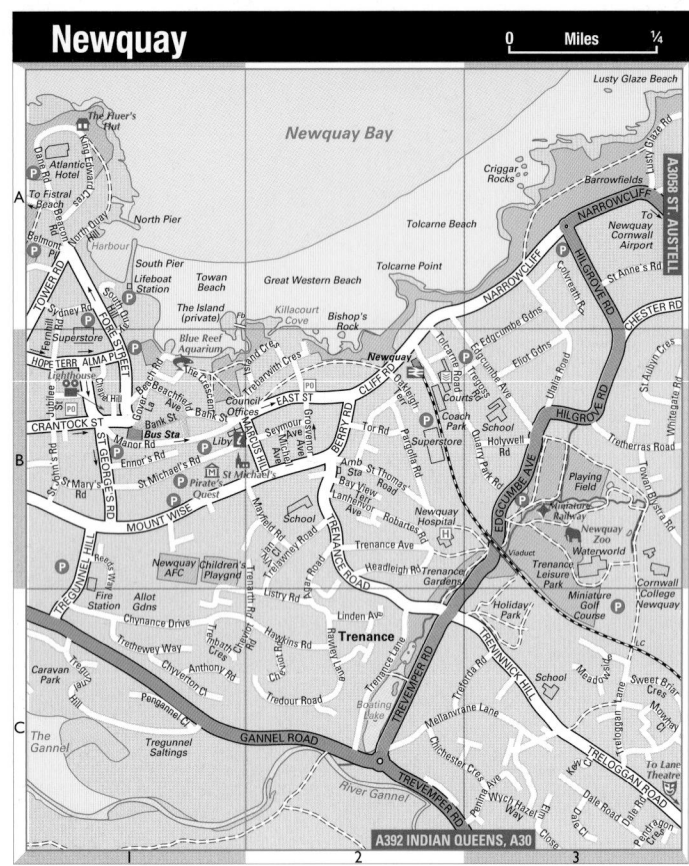

Northampton

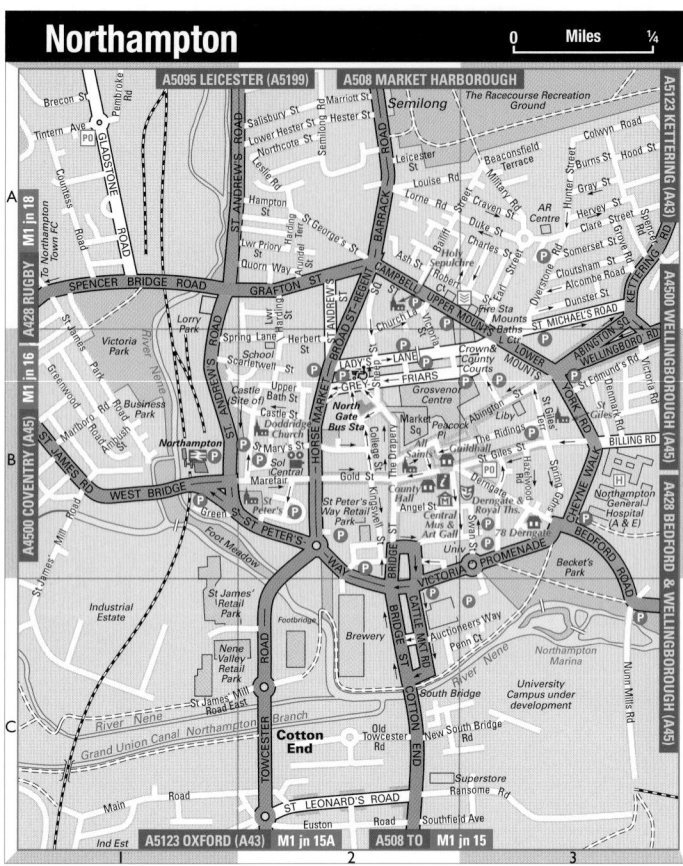

Norwich

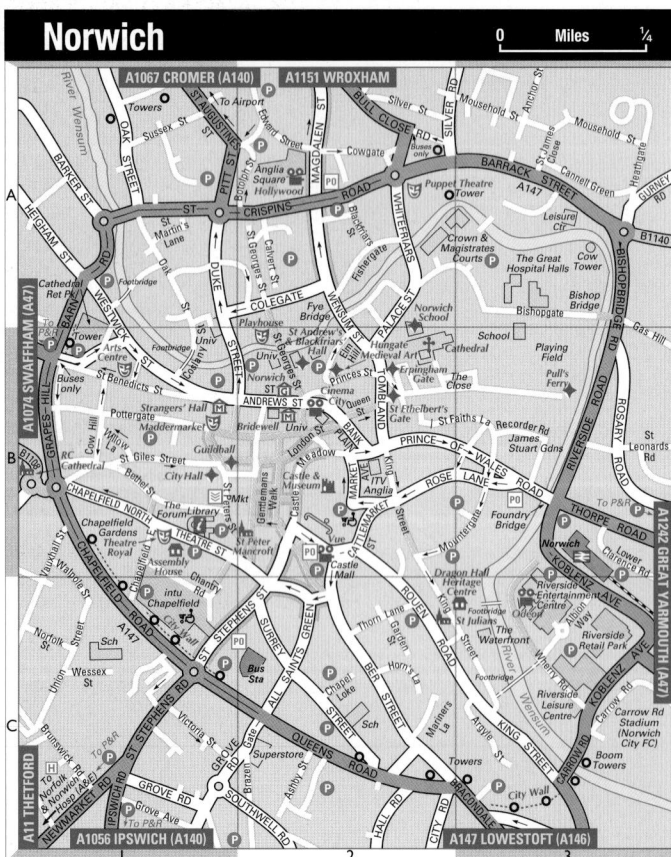

Nottingham

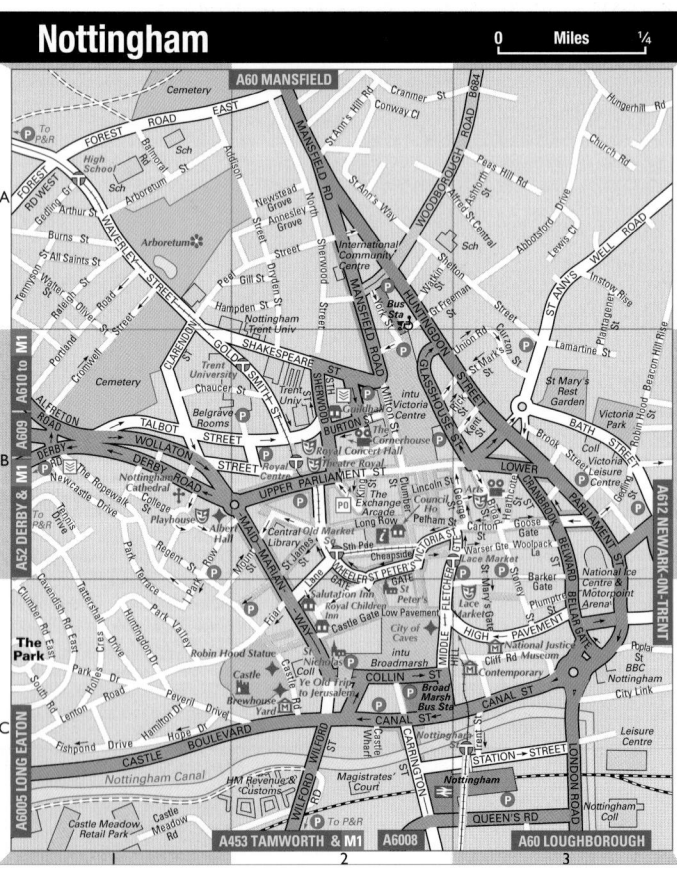

Oxford

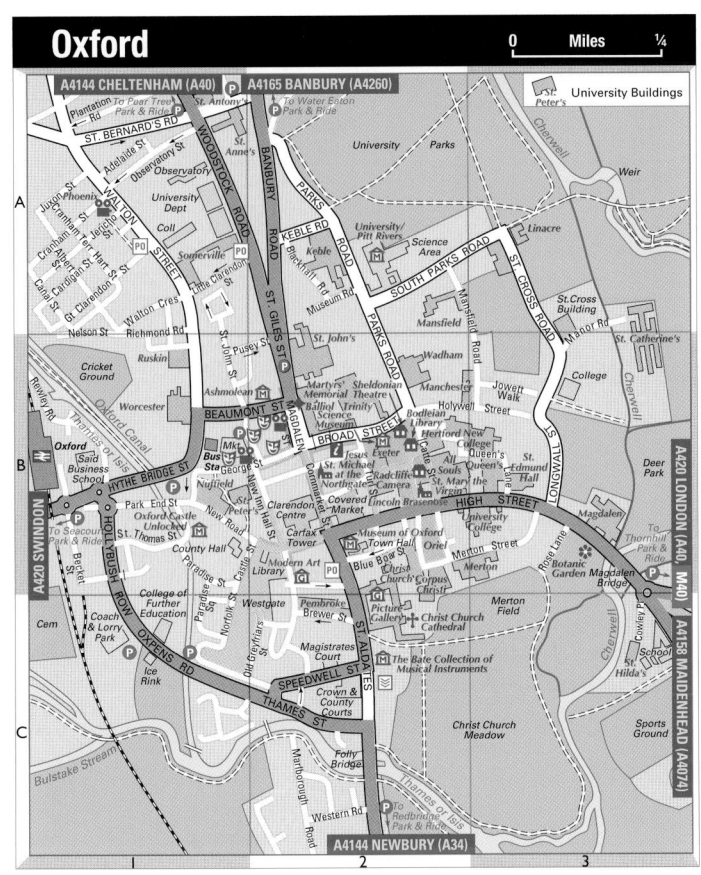

Perth

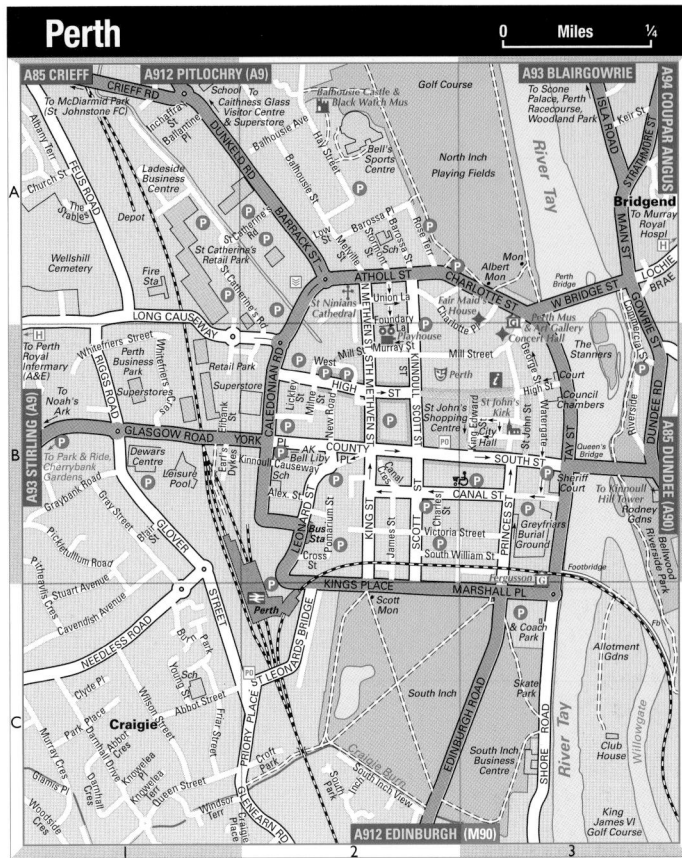

Peterborough

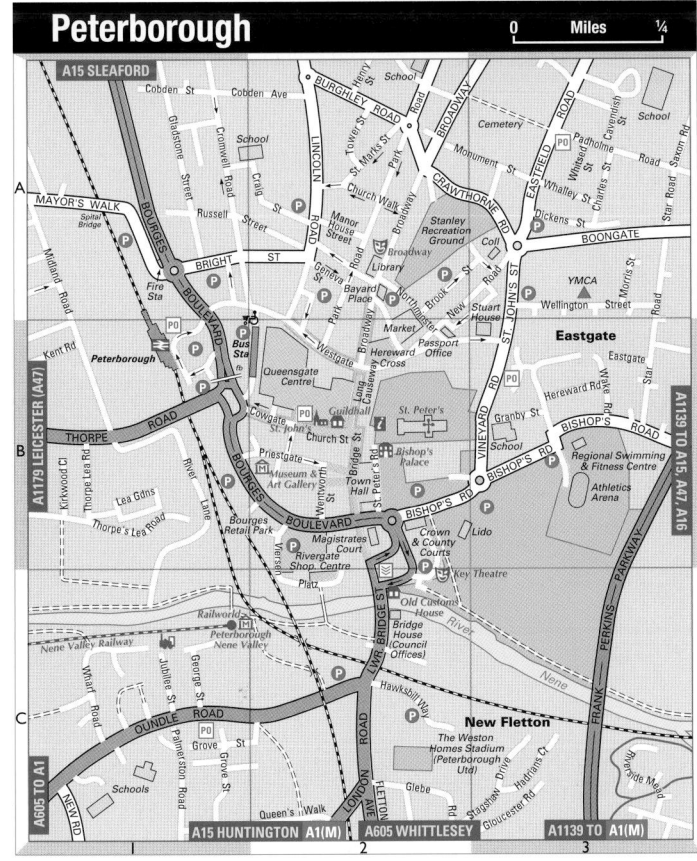

Plymouth

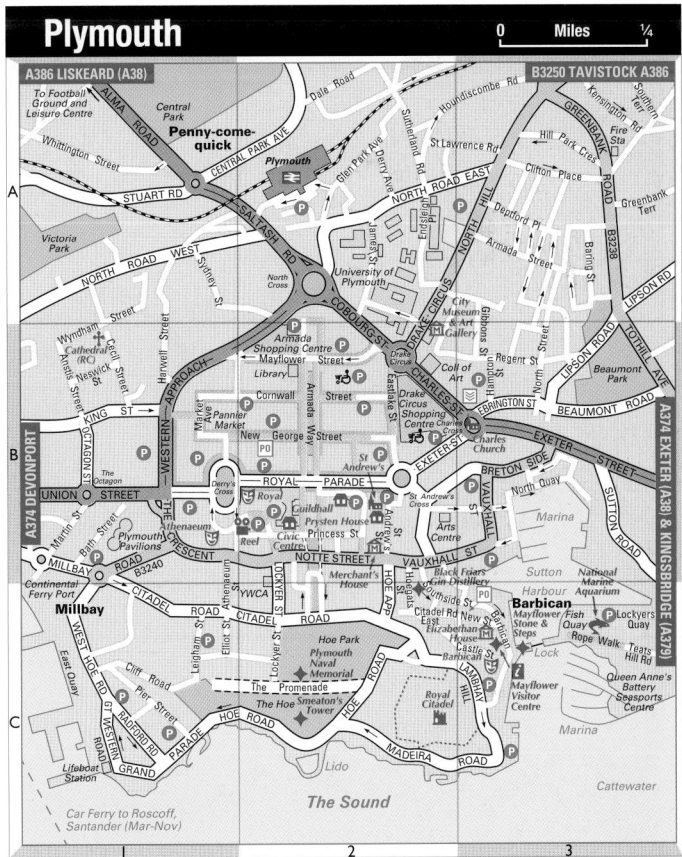

Poole

0   Miles   ¼

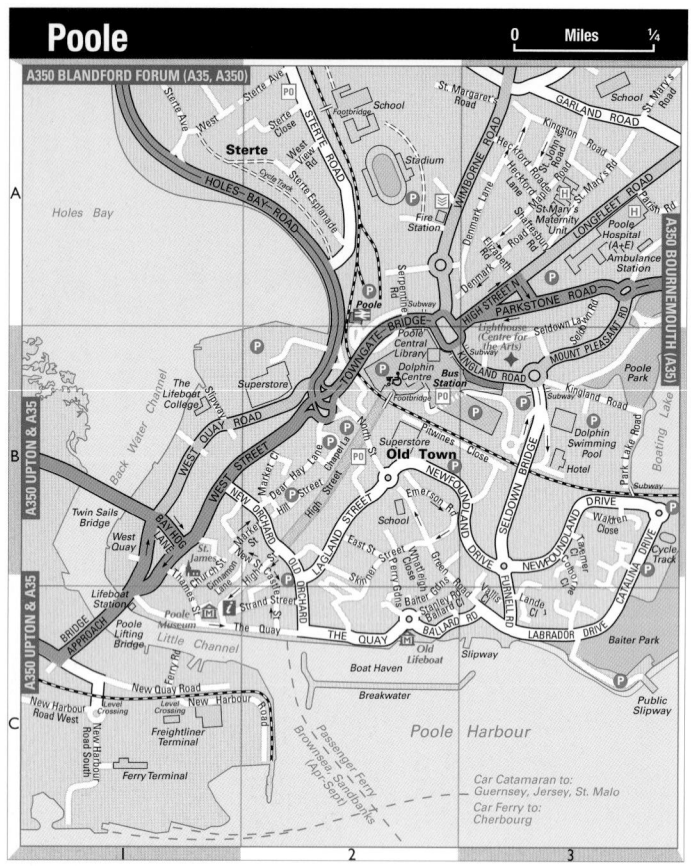

Portsmouth

0   Miles   ¼

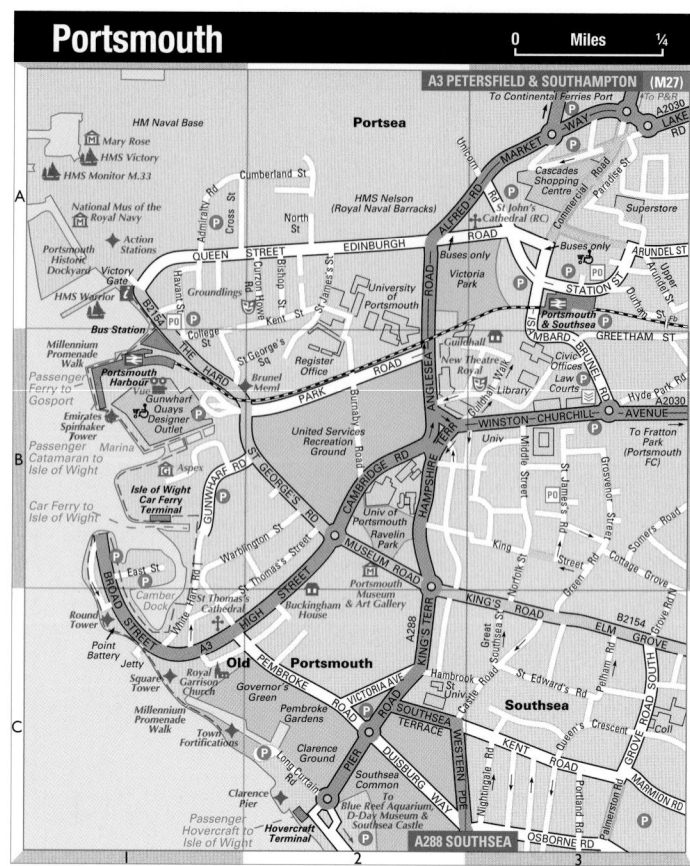

Preston

0   Miles   ¼

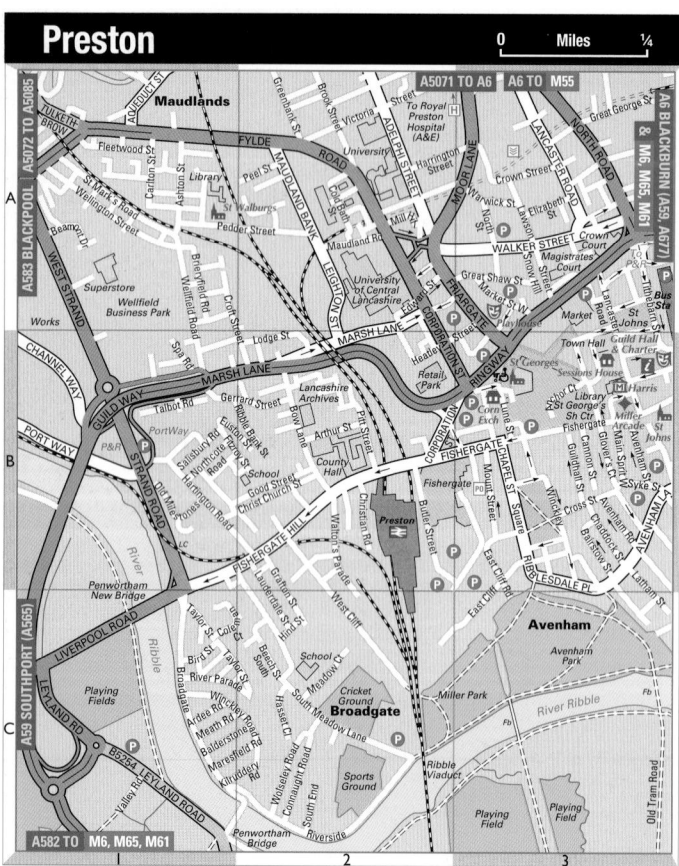

Reading

0   Miles   ¼

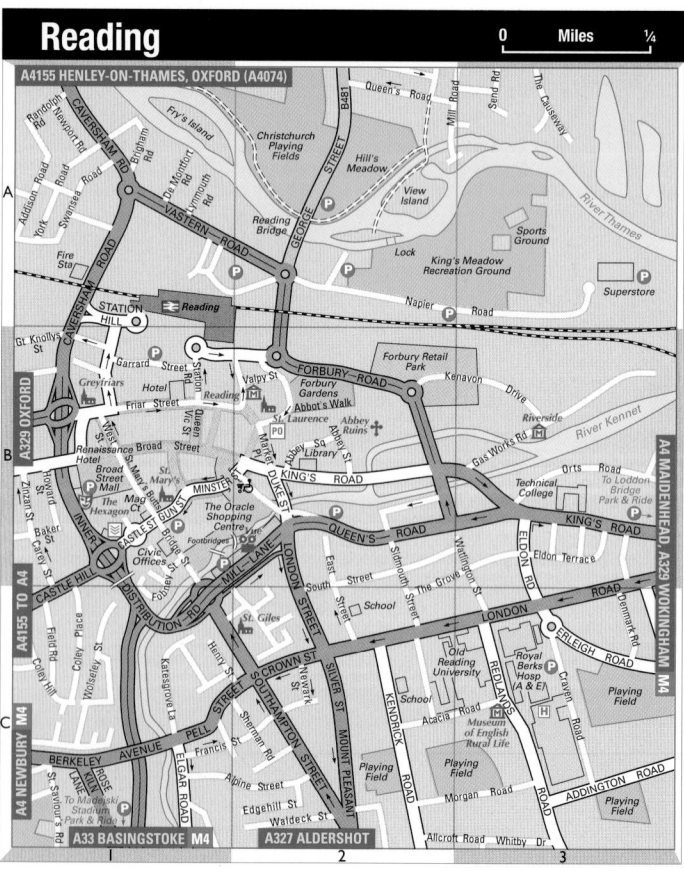

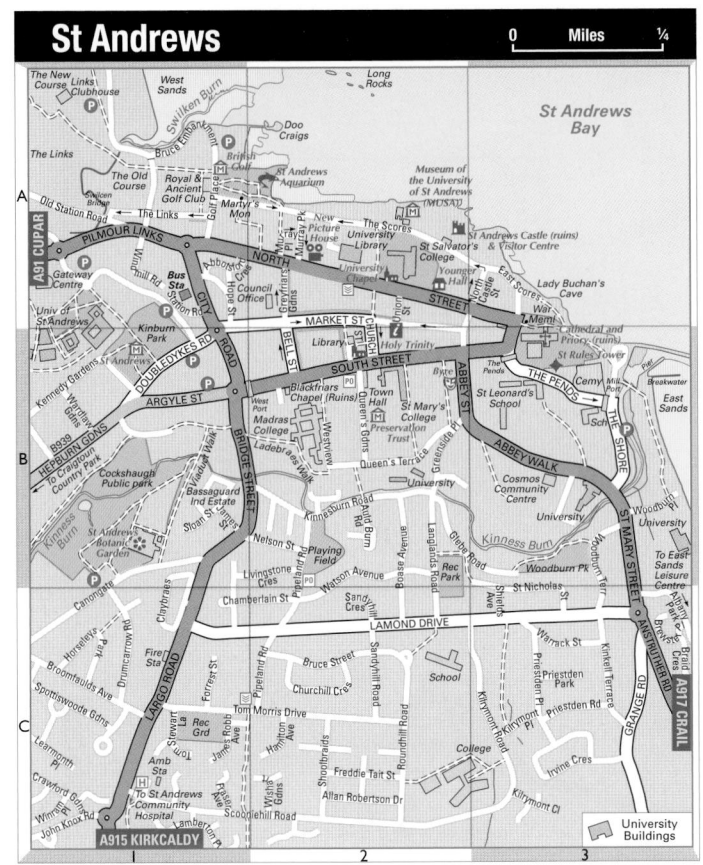

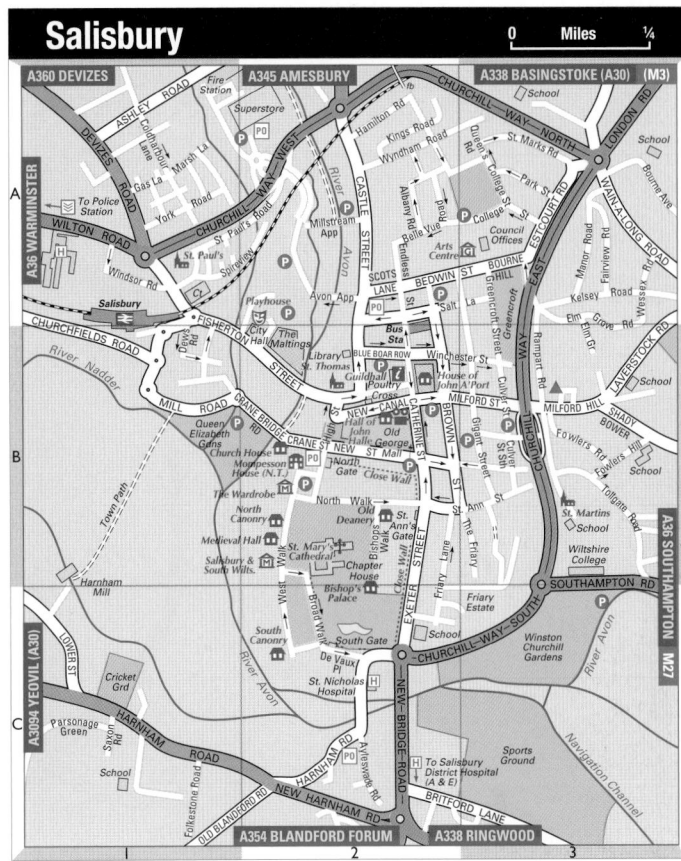

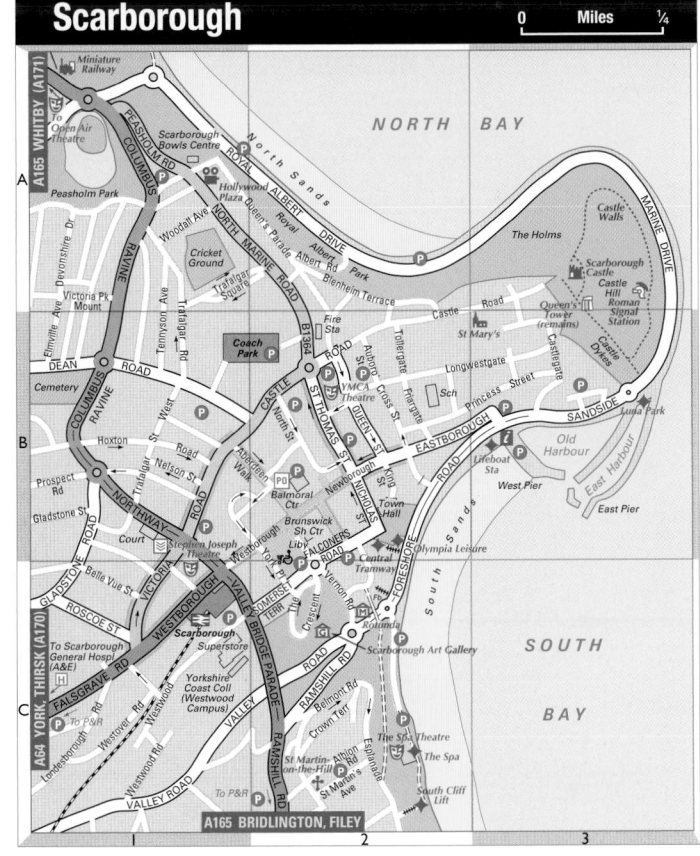

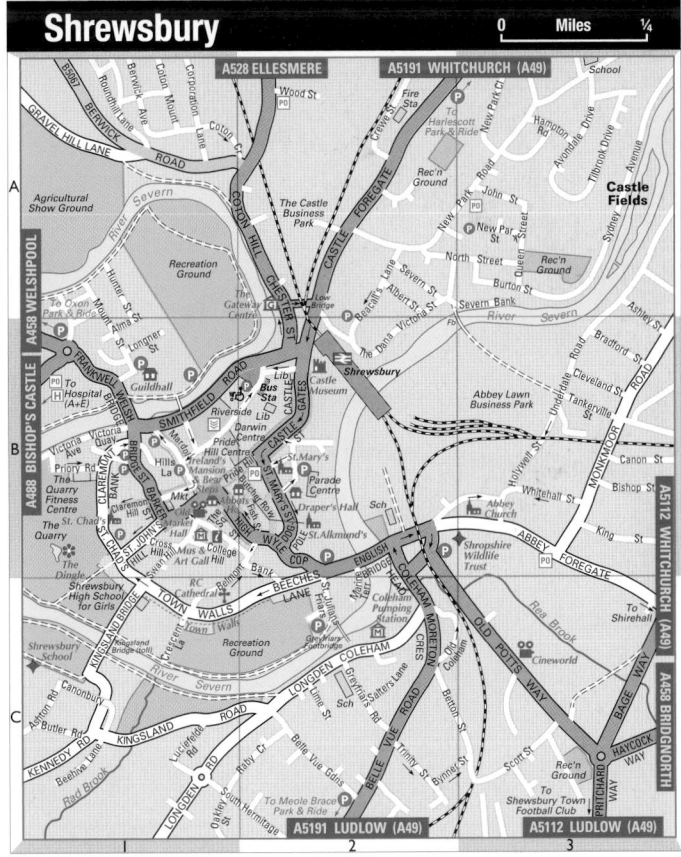

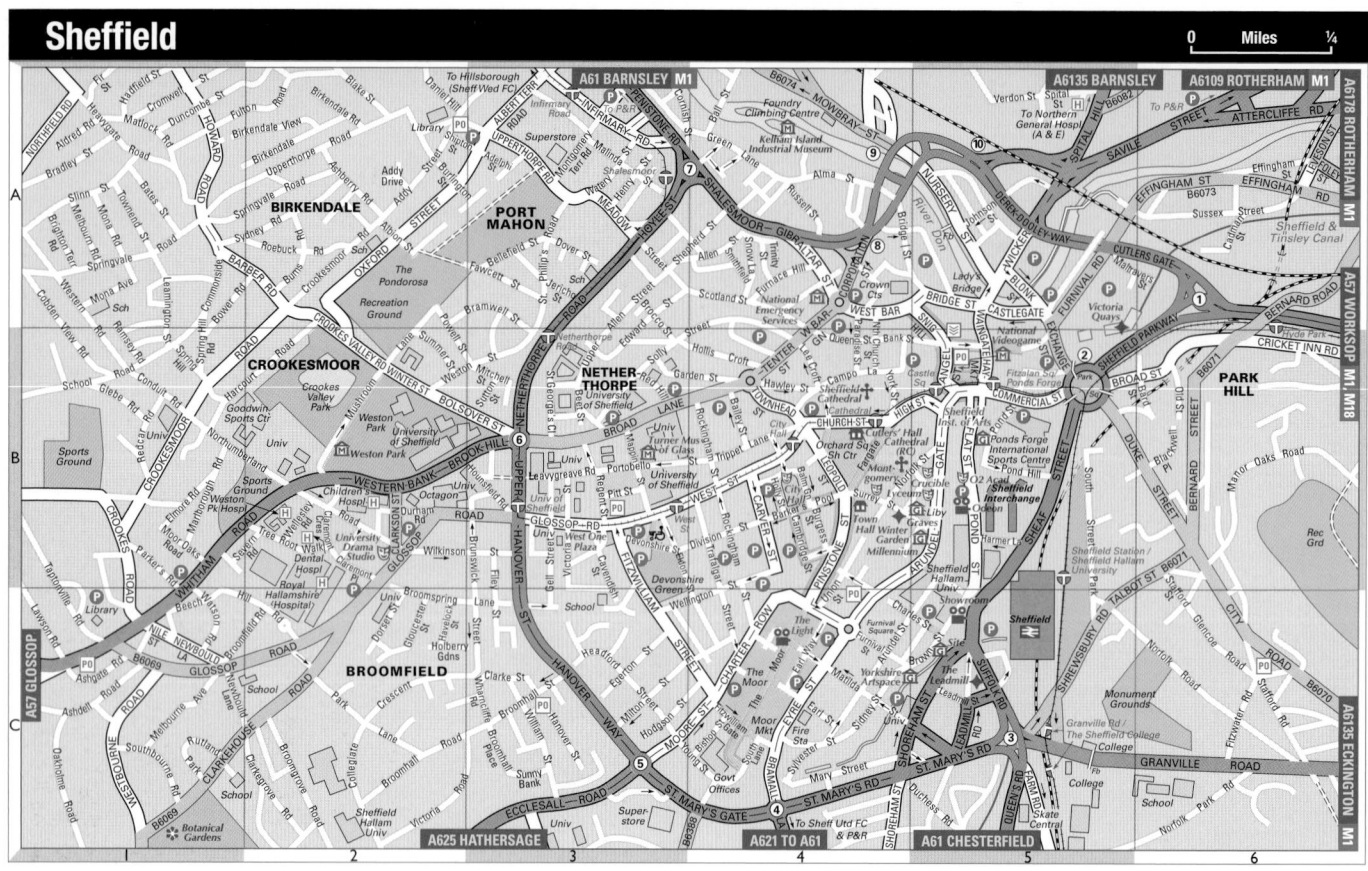

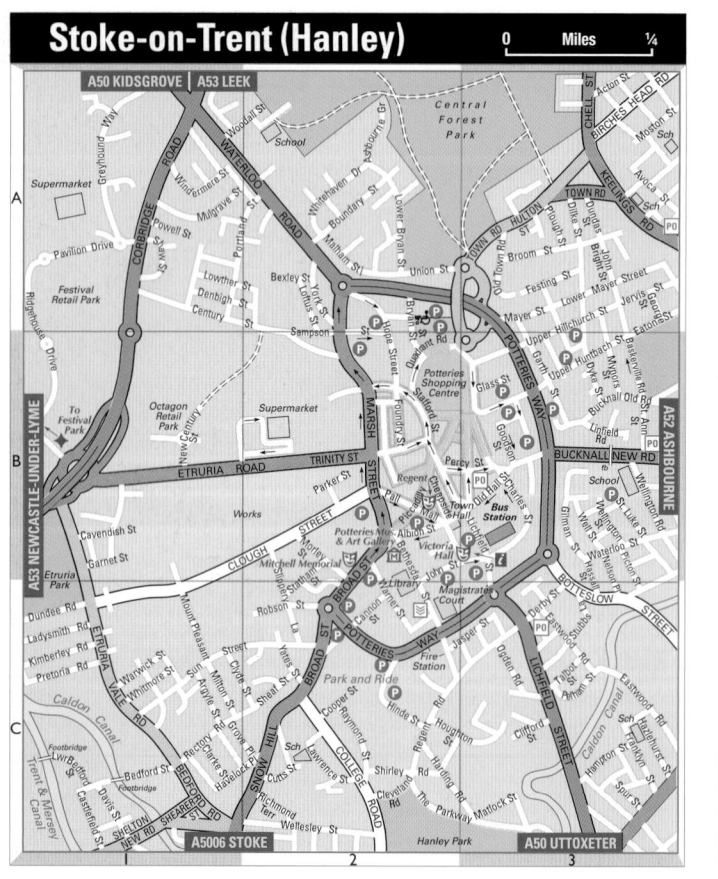

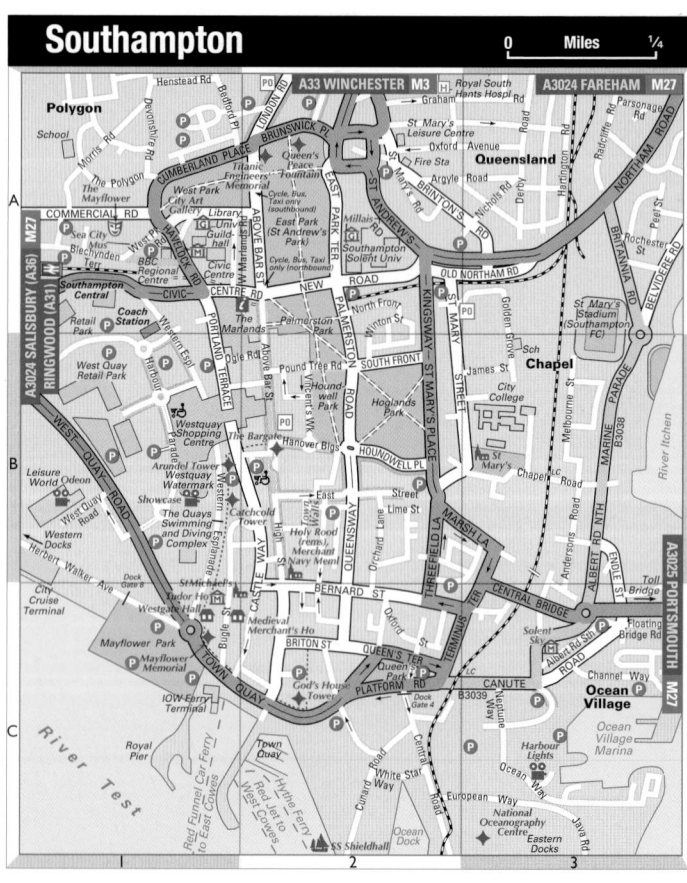

Southend-on-Sea

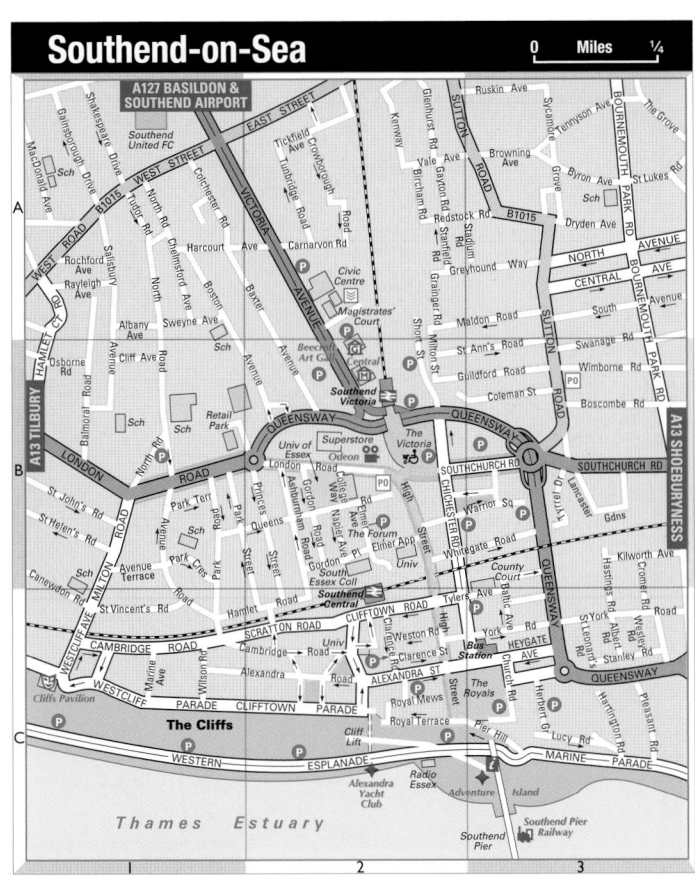

Stirling

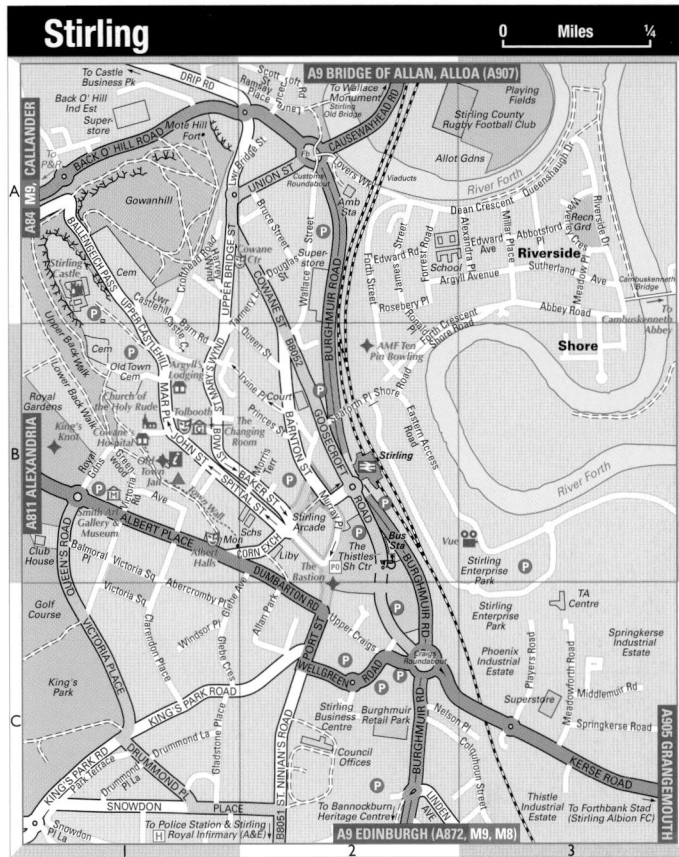

Stratford-upon-Avon

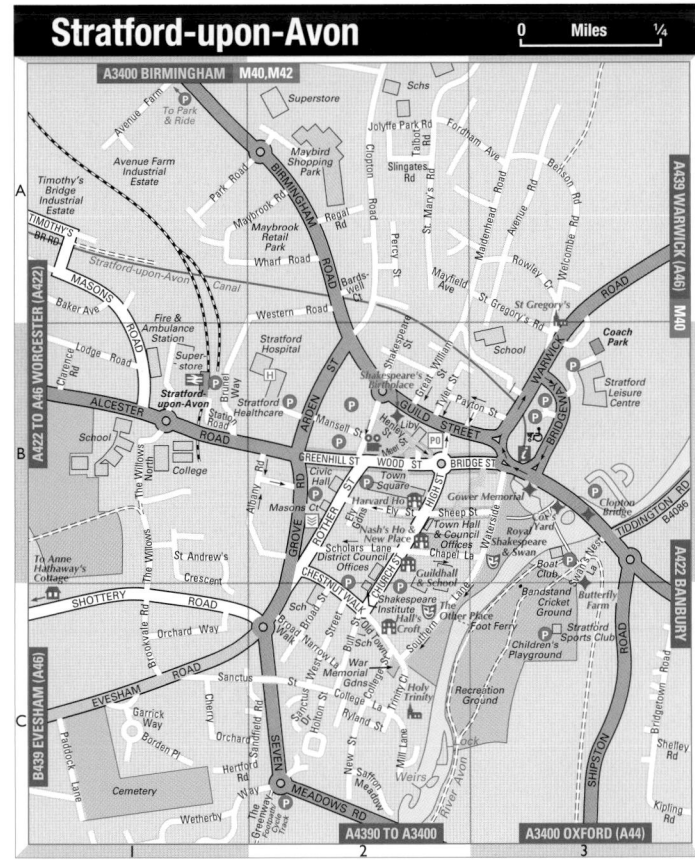

Sunderland

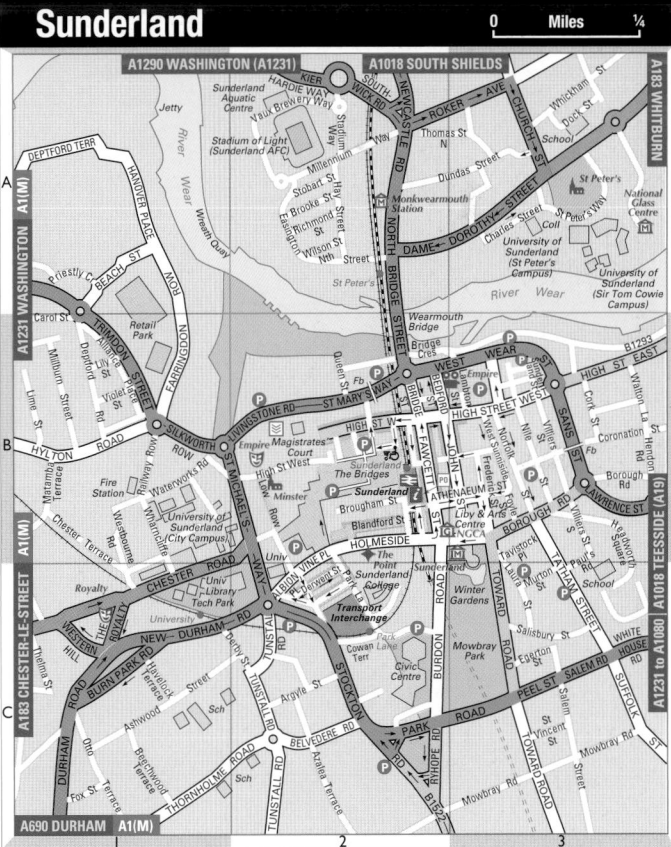

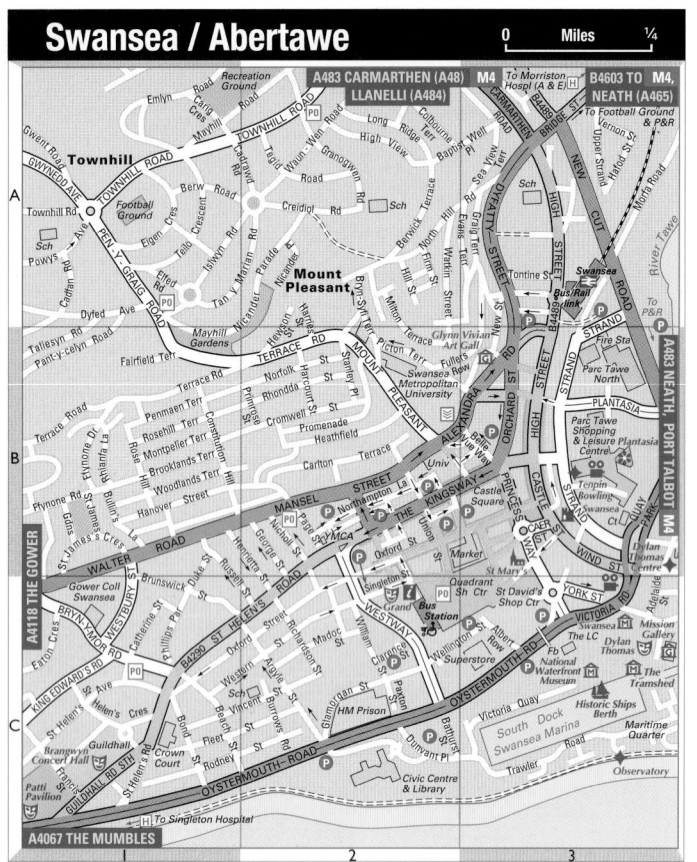

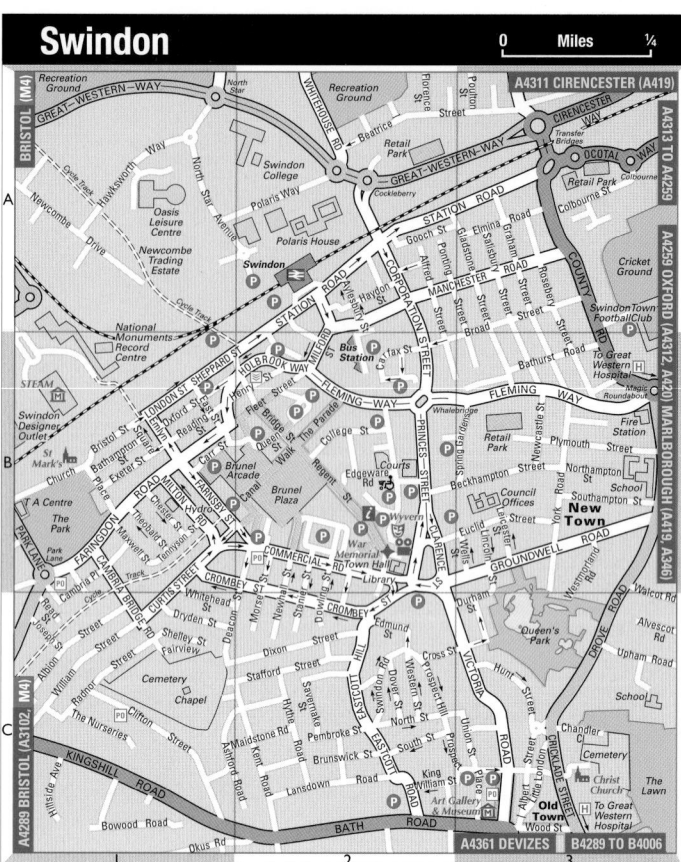

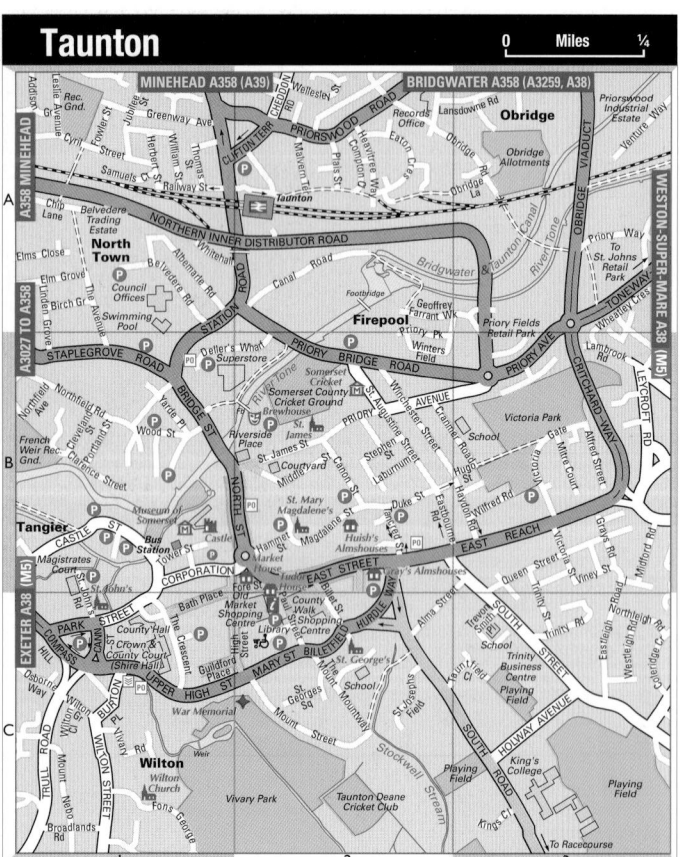

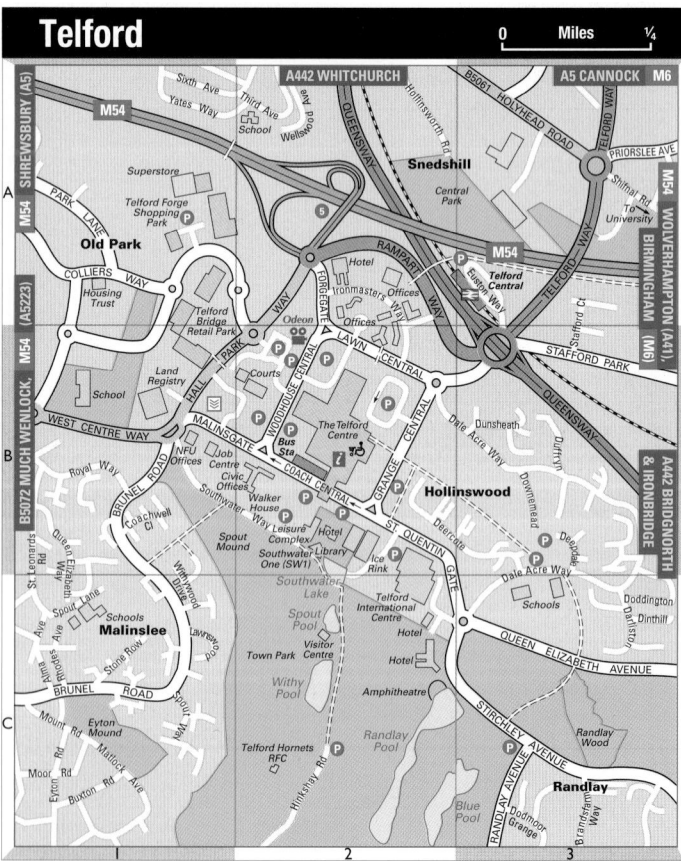

Torquay
0 Miles ¼

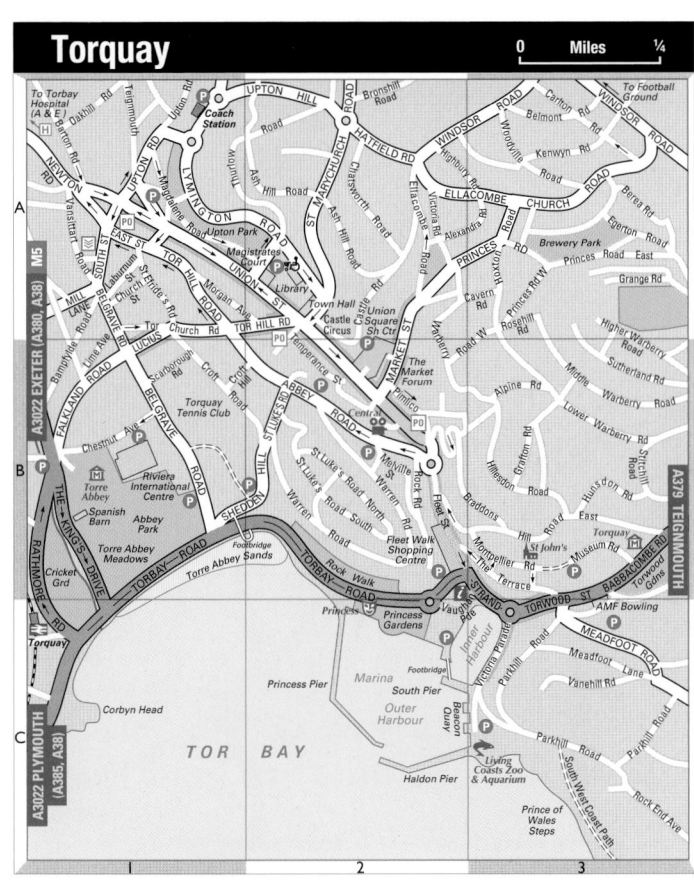

Truro
0 Miles ¼

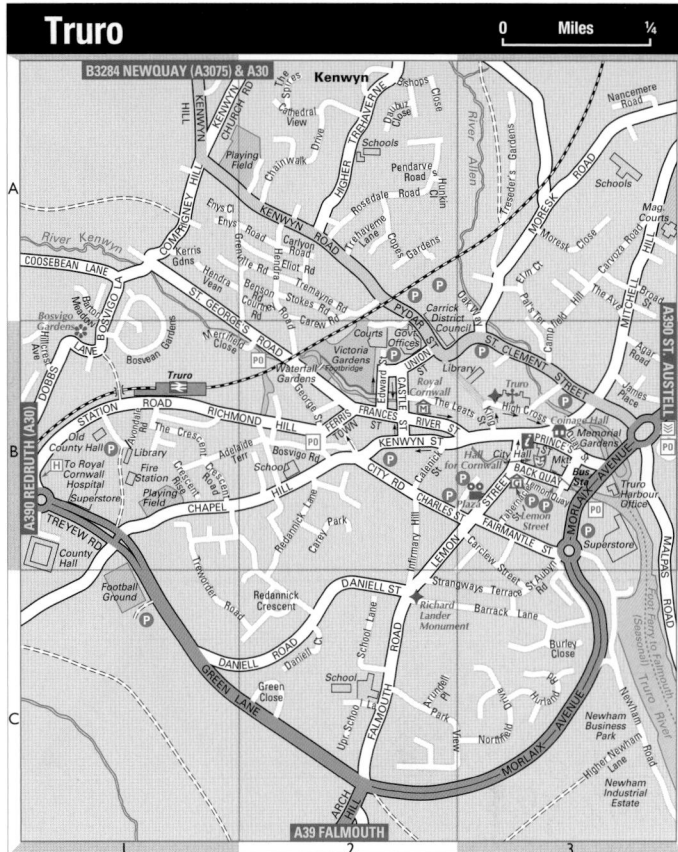

Winchester
0 Miles ¼

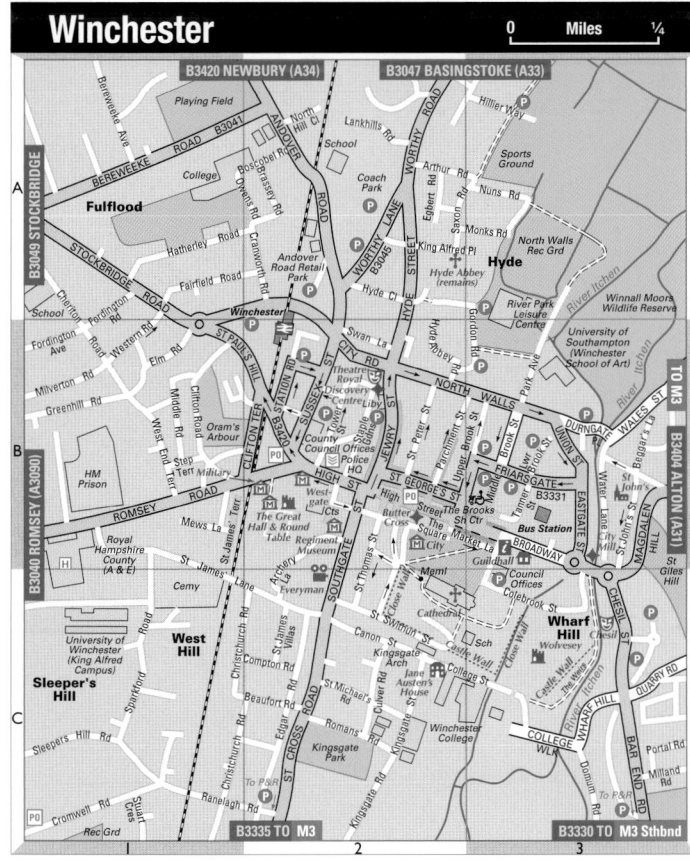

Windsor
0 Miles ¼

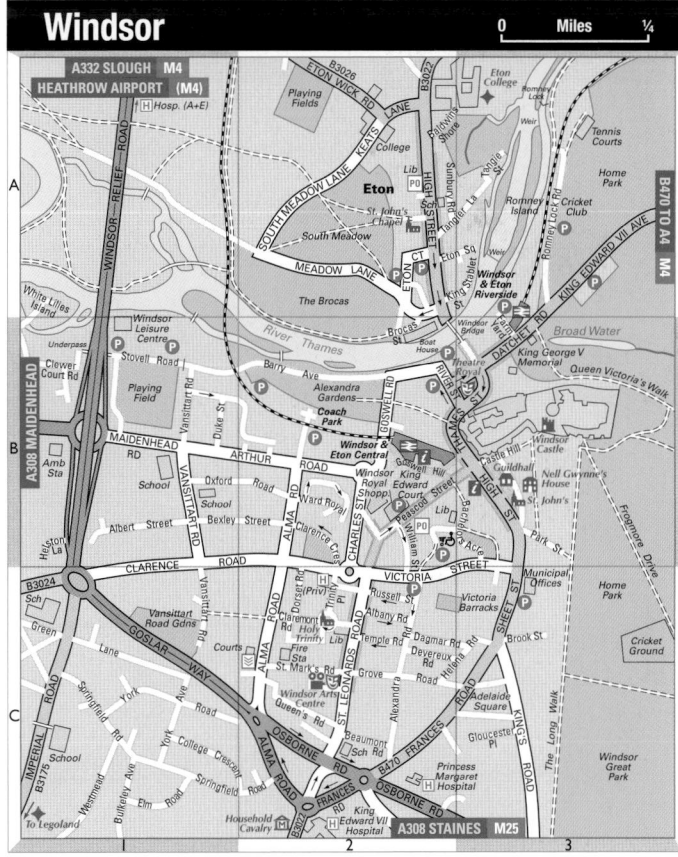

Wolverhampton

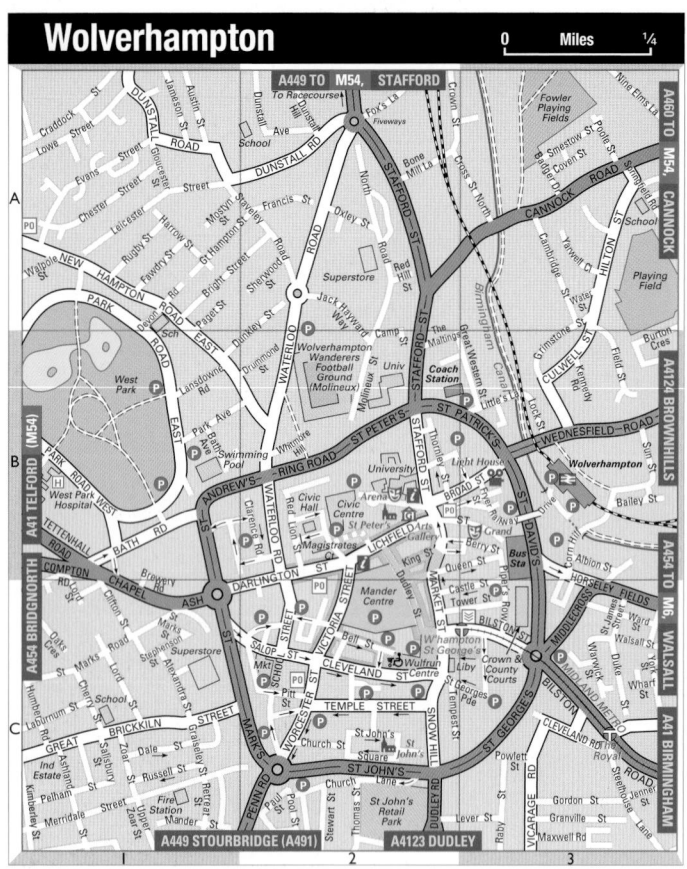

Worcester

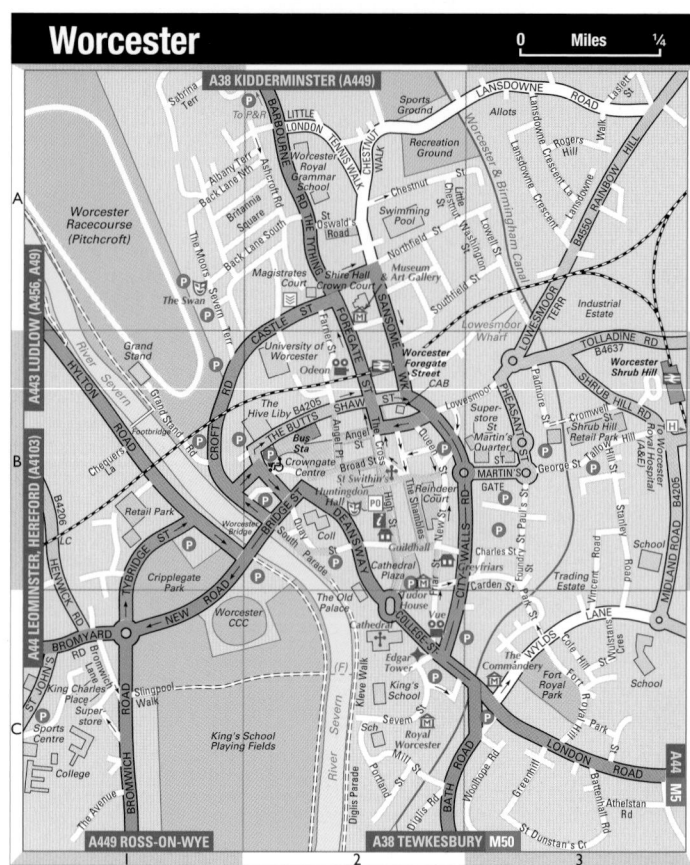

Wrexham / Wrecsam

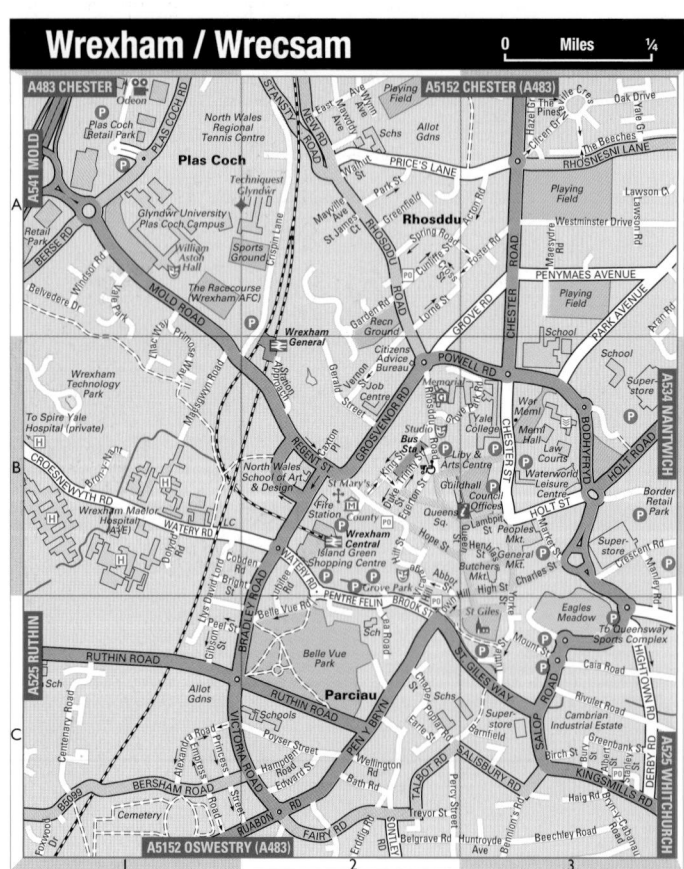

York

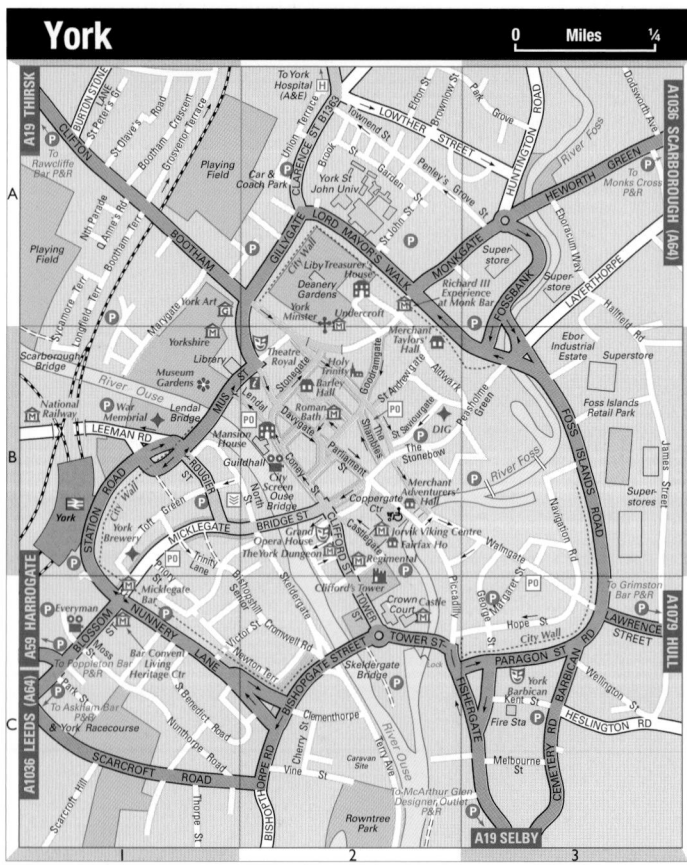

Town plan indexes

Aberdeen 175

Aberdeen B2
Aberdeen Grammar
  School A1
Academy,The B2
Albert Basin B3
Albert Quay B3
Albury Rd C1
Alford Place B1
Art Gallery ✦ A2
Arts Centre ✦ A2
Back Wynd B2
Baker St A1
Beach Blvd A3
Belmont St B2
Belmont St B2
Berry St A2
Blackfriars St B2
Blaikie's Quay B3
Bloomfield Rd C1
Bon Accord Ctr A2
Bon-Accord St B1/C1
Bridge St B2
Broad St B2
Bus Station B2
Car Ferry Terminal . . B3
Castlegate A3
Central Library ✦ . . . B1
Chapel St B1
Cineworld ✦ B1
Clyde St B3
College C2
College St B2
Commerce St B3
Commercial Quay . . . B3
Com Centre A3/C1
Constitution St A3
Cotton St A3
Crown St B2
Denburn Rd B2
Devanha Gdns C2
Devanha Gdns
  South C2
East North St A3
Esslemont Ave A1
Ferryhill Rd C2
Ferryhill Terr C2
Fish Market B3
Fonthill Rd C1
Galleria A2
Gallowgate A2
George St A2
Glenbervie Rd C3
Golden Sq B1
Grampian Rd C3
Great Southern Rd . . C1
Guild St B2
Hardgate B1/C1
His Majesty's
  Theatre ✦ A1
Holburn St C1
Hollybank Place C1
Huntly St B1
Hutcheon St A1
Information Ctr ✦ . . . B2
John St A2
Justice St A3
King St A3
Langstane Place B1
Lemon Tree,The A2
Library C1
Loch St A2
Maberly St A1
Mariachal Coll ✦ . . . A2
Maritime Museum &
  Provost Ross's
  House B2
Market B2
Market St B2/B3
Menzies St C1
Mercat Cross ✦ A3
Millburn St C2
Miller St A3
Mount St A1
Music Hall ✦ B1
North Esp East C3
North Esp West C2
Oscar Rd C3
Palmerston Rd C2
Park St A3
Police Station ✦ . . . A2
Polmuir Rd C2
Post Office
  ✉ A1/A2/A3/B1/C3
Provost Skene's
  House ✦ A2
Queen Elizabeth Br C2
Queen St A2
Regent Quay B3
Regent Road B3
Robert Gordon's
  College B1
Rose St B1
Rosemount Place . . . A1
Rosemount Viaduct A1
St Andrew St A2
St Andrew's Cath ✦ . A3
St Mary's Cath ✦ . . . A1
St Nicholas Centre . . A2
St Nicholas St A2
School Hill A2
Sinclair Rd C3
Skene Sq A1
Skene St B1
South College St . . . C2
South Crown St C2
South Esp East C3
South Esp West C3
South Mount St A1
Sports Centre C3
Spring Garden A2
Springbank Terr C1
Summer St B1
Superstore A2
Thistle St B1
Tolbooth ✦ B3
Town House ✦ A2
Trinity Centre B2
Union Row B1
Union Square B2
Union St B1/B2
University A2
Upper Dock B3
Upper Kirkgate A2
Victoria Bridge C3
Victoria Dock B3
Victoria Rd C3
Victoria St B1
Virginia St A3
Vue ✦ B1
Waterloo Quay A3
Wellington Place . . . B2
West North St A2
Whinhill Rd C1
Willowbank Rd C1
Windmill Brae B2

Ayr 175

Ailsa Place B1
Alexandra Terr A3
Allison St A2
Alloway Pk C1
Alloway Place C1
Alloway St C2
Arran Mall C2
Arran Terr A2
Arthur St B2
Ashgrove St C2
Auld Brig B2
Auld Kirk ✦ B2
Ayr Academy B1
Ayr Central
  Shopping Centre . . C2
Ayr Harbour A1
Ayr Ice Rink A2
Ayrshire Coll C2
Back Hawkhill Ave . . A3
Back Main St B2
Back Peebles St A2
Barns Cres C1
Barns Pk C1
Barns St C1
Barns Street La C1
Bath Place B1
Bellevue Cres C1
Bellevue La C1
Beresford La C2
Beresford Terr C2
Boswell Pk B2
Britannia Place A3
Bruce Cres A2
Burns Statue ✦ C2
Bus Sta B1
Carrick St B2
Cassillis St B1
Cathcart St B1
Charlotte St B1
Citadel Leisure Ctr . . B1
Citadel Place B1
Compass Pier A1
Content Ave B3
Content St B2
Craigie Ave B3
Craigie Rd B3
Craigie Way B3
Cromwell Rd B3
Crown St A2
Dalblair Rd C2
Dam Park Sports
  Stadium A3
Damside C2
Dongola Rd C2
Eglinton Place B1
Eglinton Terr B1
Elba St B2
Elmbank St A2
Esplanade C1
Euchar Rock A1
Farifield Rd A2
Fort St B2
Fothringham Rd C3
Fullarton St B1
Gaiety ✦ C2
Garden St B2
George St B2
George's Ave A3
Glebe Cres A2
Glebe Rd A2
Gorden Terr B3
Green St A2
Green Street La A2
Hawkhill Ave A3
Hawkhill
  Avenue Lane B3
High St B2
Holmston Rd C3
Information Ctr ✦ . . . C2
James St B3
John St B2
King St B1
Kings Ct B2
Kyle Centre C2
Kyle St C2
Library B2
Limekiln Rd A2
Limonds Wynd B2
Loudoun Hall ✦ B1
Lymburn Place A3
Macadam Place B1
Main St B2
Mcadam's
  Monument A1
Mccall's Ave C3
Mews La B1
Mill Brae C2
Mill St C2
Mill Wynd C2
Miller Rd C2
Montgomerie Terr . . B1
New Bridge B2
New Bridge St B2
New Rd A2
Newmarket St B2
Newton-on-Ayr
  Station ➤ A1
North Harbour St . . . B1
North Pier A1
Odeon ✦ C2
Park Circus C1
Park Circus La C1
Park Terr C1
Pavilion Rd A1
Peebles St A2
Philip Sq C2
Police Station ✦ . . . B2
Prestwick Rd A2
Princes St A2
Queen St B3
Queen's Terr B1
Racecourse Rd C1
River St B1
Riverside Place B1
Russell Dr A3
St Andrews
  Church B2
St George's Rd C3
Sandgate B1
Savoy Park C1
Smith St C2
Somerset Park
  (Ayr United FC) . . . A2
Somerset Rd A2
South Beach Rd C1
South Harbour St . . . B1
South Pier A1
Station Rd C2
Strathayr Place B2
Superstore A2/B2
Taylor St B2
Town Hall B2
Tryfield Place C1
Turner's Bridge B2
Union Ave A3
Victoria Bridge C3
Victoria St B3
Viewfield Rd A2
Virginia Gdns A2
Waggon Rd A2
Walker Rd A3
Wallace Tower ✦ . . . B2
Weaver St A2
Weir Rd A2
Wellington La C1
Wellington Sq C1
West Sanquhar Rd . . A3
Whitletts Rd B3
Wilson St B1
York St A1
York Street La B1

Bath 175

Alexandra Park C2
Alexandra Rd C2
Ambulance Station . . A3
Approach Golf
  Courses (Public) . . A1
Archway St C3
Assembly Rooms &
  Fashion Mus ✦ . . . B2
Avon St B2
Bath Abbey ✝ B2
Bath Aqua Glass ✦ . . B2
Bath College B2
Bath Rugby
  (The Rec) B3
Bath Spa
  Station ➤ C3
Bathwick St A3
Beckford Road A3
Beechen Cliff Rd . . . C2
Bennett St A2
Bloomfield Ave. C1
Broad Quay C2
Broad St B2
Brock St A1
Building of Bath
  Museum ✦ A2
Bus Station C2
Calton Gdns C2
Calton Rd C2
Camden Cres A2
Cavendish Rd A1
Cemetery B1
Charlotte St B1
Chaucer Rd C2
Cheap St B2
Circus Mews A2
Claverton St C2
Corn St C2
Cricket Ground B3
Daniel St A3
Edward St A3
Ferry La B3
First Ave C1
Fire Station B1
Forester Ave A3
Forester Rd A3
Gays Hill A2
George St B2
Great Pulteney St . . . B3
Green Park B1
Green Park Rd B1
Green Park
  Station ➤ B1
Grove St B2
Guildhall ✦ B2
Harley St A2
Hayesfield Park C1
Henrietta Gdns A3
Henrietta Mews A3
Henrietta Park A3
Henrietta Rd A3
Henrietta St A3
Henry St B2
Herschel Museum
  of Astronomy ✦ . . . B1
High Common A1
Holburne Mus ✦ . . . B3
Holloway C2
Information Ctr ✦ . . . B2
James St West . B1/B2
Jane Austen Ctr ✦ . . B2
Julian Rd A1
Junction Rd C1
Kingsmead Leisure
  Complex B1
Kipling Ave C1
Lansdown Cres. A1
Lansdown Grove . . . A2
Lansdown Rd A2
Library B2
London Rd A3
London St A2
Lower Bristol Rd . . . B1
Lower Oldfield
  Park C1
Lyncombe Hill C3
Magistrates' Court . . B2
Manvers St C2
Maple Grove C2
Margaret's Hill A2
Marlborough
  Bldgs A1
Marlborough La B1
Midland Bridge Rd . . B1
Milk St B2
Milsom St B2
Monmouth St B2
Morford St A2
Museum of Bath at
  Work ✦ A2
Museum of East
  Asian Art ✦ A2
New King St B1
No 1 Royal Cres ✦ . . A1
Norfolk Bldgs B1
Norfolk Cres B1
North Parade Rd . . . C3
Oldfield Rd C1
Paragon A2
Pines Way C1
Podium Shopping
  Centre B2
Police Station ✦ . . . B2
Portland Place A2
Post Office
  ✉ A3/B2/C2
Postal Museum ✦ . . . B2
Powlett Rd A3
Prior Park Rd C3
Pulteney Bridge ✦ . . B2
Pulteney Gdns C3
Pulteney Rd B3/C3
Queen Sq B2
Raby Place A3
Recreation Ground . . B3
Rivers St A2

Birmingham 176

Abbey St A2
Aberdeen St B1
Acorn Grove A1
Adams St A5
Adderley St C5
Albert St B4
Albion St A2
Alcester St C5
Aldgate Grove A3
All Saint's St A1
All Saints Rd A2
Allcock St C5
Allesley St A4
Allison St C4
Alma Cres B6
Alston Rd C1
Arcadian Centre C4
Arena
  Birmingham ✦ . . . C3
Arthur St C6
Assay Office A3
Aston Expressway . . A5
Aston St B4
Aston
  University . . . B4/B5
Avenue Rd A5
Bacchus Rd A1
Bagot St A4
Banbury St B5
Barford Rd B1
Barford St C4
Barn St C5
Barnwell Rd B5
Barr St A3
Barrack St B5
Barwick St B3
Bath Row C3
Beaufort Rd C1
Belmont Row B5
Benson Rd A1
Berkley St B3
Bexhill Grove C3
Birchall St C5
Birmingham City
  FC C6
Birmingham City
  Hospital (A&E) ✦ . . A1
Birmingham City
  Univ A3
Birmingham Wheels
  Park ✦ B6
Bishopsgate St C3
Blews St A4
Bloomsbury St B5
Blucher St C3
Bordesley St C5
Bowyer St C5
Bradburne Way A5
Bradford St C4
Branston St A3
Brearley St A4
Brewery St A4
Bridge St C3
Bridge St B6
Bridge St West A4
Brindley Dr B3
Broad St C2
Broad Street
  Cineworld ✦ C2
Broadway Plaza ✦ . . C2
Bromley St C5
Bromsgrove St C4
Brookfield Rd A2
Browning St C2
Bryant St A1
BT Tower ✦ B3
Buckingham St A3
Bull St ➤ B4
Bull St B4
Bullring C4
Cambridge St B3
Camden Dr B2
Camden St B2
Cannon St B4
Cardigan St B5
Carlisle St A1
Carlyle Rd B1
Caroline St A3
Carver St B2
Cato St A6
Cattell Rd C6
Cattells Grove A6
Cawdor Cres C1
Cecil St A4
Cemetery A2/B2
Cemetery La A2
Centenary Sq B3
Charlotte St B3
Cheapside C4
Chester St A5
Children's Hospital
  (A&E) ✦ B4
Church St B4
Claremont Rd A1
Clarendon Rd C1
Clark St C1
Clement St B3
Clissold St B2
Cliveland St B4
Coach Station C5
College St B2
Colmore Circus B4
Colmore Row B4
Commercial St C3
Constitution Hill B3
Convention Ctr,The . . C3
Cope St B2
Coplow St B1
Corporation St ➤ . . . C4
Council House ✦ . . . B3
County Court B4
Coveley Grove A2
Coventry Rd C6
Coventry St C5
Cox St B3
Crabtree Rd A2
Cregoe St C3
Crescent Ave A2
Crescent Theatre ✦ . C3
Crescent,The A2
Cromwell St A6
Cromwell St B5
Cube,The C3
Curzon St B5
Custard Factory ✦ . . C5
Cuthbert Rd B1
Dale End B4
Dart St C6
Dartmouth Circus . . A4
Dartmouth
  Middleway A5
Dental Hospital ✦ . . B4
Deritend C5
Devon St A6
Devonshire St A1
Digbeth High St C4
Dolman St B6
Dover St A1
Duchess Rd C2
Duddeston ➤ B6
Duddeston Manor
  Rd A5
Duddeston Mill Rd . . B6
Duddeston Mill
  Trading Estate . . . B6
Dudley Rd B1
Edmund St B3
Edward St B2
Elkington St A4
Ellen St A3
Ellis St C3
Erskine St B5
Essex St C4
Eyre St B1
Farm Croft A3
Farm St A3
Fazeley St B4/C5
Felstead Way B5
Finstall Cl B5
Five Ways C2
Fiveway Shopping
  Centre C2
Fleet St B3
Floodgate St C5
Ford St A2
Fore St C4
Forster St B5
Francis Rd C2
Francis St B5
Frankfort St A4
Frederick St B3
Freeth St C1
Freightliner
  Terminal B6
Garrison La C6
Garrison St B6
Gas St C3
Geach St A4
George St B3
George St West B2
Gibb St C5
Gilby Rd C2
Gillott Rd B1
Glover St C5
Goode Ave A2
Goodrick Way A5
Gordon St B6
Graham St B3
Grand Central C4
Granville St C3
Gray St C6
Great Barr St C5
Great Charles St
  Queensway B3
Great Francis St B6
Great Hampton
  Row A3
Great Hampton St . . A3
Great King St A3
Great Lister St A5
Great Tindal St C2
Green La C6
Green St C4
Greenway St C6
Grosvenor St West . . C2
Guest Grove A3
Guild Cl C2
Guildford Dr A4
Guthrie Cl A3
Hagley Rd C1
Hall St B3
Hampton St A3
Handsworth
  New Rd A1
Hanley St B4
Harford St A3
Harmer Rd A1
Harold Rd C1
Hatchett St A4
Heath Mill La C5
Heath St B1
Heath St South B1
Heaton St A2
Heneage St B5
Henrietta St B4
Herbert Rd C6
High St C4
Hilden Rd C6
Hill St C3/C4
Hindlow Cl B6
Hingeston St B2
Hippodrome
  Theatre ✦ C4
HM Prison A1
Hockley Circus A2

Blackpool 176

Abingdon St B1
Addison Cres A3
Adelaide St B1
Albert Rd B2
Alfred St B2
Ascot Rd A3
Ashton Rd C2
Auburn Grove B3
Bank Hey St B1
Banks St A1
Beech Ave B3
Bela Grove C2
Belmont Ave B2
Birley St A1
Blackpool &
  Fleetwood Tram ✦ . A1
Blackpool & the
  Fylde College B2
Blackpool FC C2
Blackpool North ➤ . . B2
Blackpool Tower ✦ . . B1
Blundell St C1
Bonny St B1
Breck Rd B3
Bryan Rd B3
Buchanan St A2
Bus Station C1
Cambridge Rd A3
Caunce St A2/A3
Central Dr B1/C2
Central Pier ✦ C1
Central Pier ➤ C1
Central Pier
  Theatre ✦ C1
Chapel St C1
Charles St A2
Charnley Rd B2
Church St A1/A2
Clinton Ave B2
Coach Station . . . A2/C1
Cocker St A1
Coleridge Rd A3
Collingwood Ave . . . A3
Comedy Carpet ✦ . . B1
Condor Grove C3
Cookson St A2
Coronation St B1
Corporation St A1
Courts A1
Cumberland Ave . . . B3
Cunliffe Rd A3
Dale St C1
Devonshire Rd A3
Devonshire Sq A3
Dickson Rd A1
Elizabeth St A2
Ferguson Rd C3
Forest Gate B3
Foxhall Rd C1
Freckleton St C2
George St A2
Gloucester Ave B3
Golden Mile,The . . . C1
Gorse Rd C3
Gorton St A2
Grand Theatre,
  The ✦ B1
Granville Rd A2
Grasmere Rd C2
Grosvenor St A2
Grundy
  Art Gallery ✦ A1
Harvey Rd A3
Hornby Rd B2
Houndshill
  Shopping Centre . . B1
Hull Rd B1
Ibbison Ct C2
Information Ctr ✦ . . . B1
Kent Rd C1
Keswick Rd C3
King St A1
Knox Grove C3
Laycock Gate A3
Layton Rd A3
Leamington Rd B2
Leeds Rd B3
Leicester Rd B2
Levens Grove C2
Library A1
Lifeboat Station B1
Lincoln Rd B2
Liverpool Rd B3
Livingstone Rd B2
London Rd B3
Lune Grove C2
Lytham Rd C1
Madame Tussaud's
  Blackpool ✦ B1
Manchester Sq ✦ . . . B1
Manor Rd B3
Maple Ave B3
Market St A1
Marlboro Rd B3
Mere Rd B3
Milbourne St A2
Newcastle Ave B3
Newton Dr A3
North Pier ✦ A1
North Pier ➤ A1
North Pier
  Theatre ✦ A1
Odeon ✦ A1
Olive Grove B3
Palatine Rd B2
Park Rd B2/C3
Peter St B2
Police Station ✦ . . . B1
Post Office
  ✉ A1/A2/B1/B2
Princess Parade A1
Princess St C1/C2
Promenade A1/C1
Queen St A1
Queen Victoria Rd . . B3
Raikes Pde B2
Reads Ave B2
Regent Rd B2
Register Office B3
Ribble Rd B2
Rigby Rd B1/C2
Ripon Rd B3
St Albans Rd B3
St Ives Ave C3
St John's Square . . . A1
St Vincent Ave C3
Salisbury Rd B3
Salthouse Ave C2
Salvation Army Ctr . . C2
Sands Way C1

Bournemouth 176

Ascham Rd A3
Avenue Rd B1
Ave Shopping Ctr . . . B1
Bath Rd C2
Beacon Rd C1
Beechey Rd A3
Bodorgan Rd B1
Bourne Ave B1
Bournemouth ➤ . . . A3
Bournemouth &
  Poole College A3
Bournemouth
  International Ctr . . . C1
Bournemouth Pier ✦ . C2
Bournemouth
  Station ⏺ B3
Braidley Rd A1
Cavendish Place . . . A2
Cavendish Rd A2
Central Drive A1
Central Gdns B1
Christchurch Rd B3
Cliff Lift C1/C3
Coach House Place . . A3
Coach Station A3
Commercial Rd B1
Cotlands Rd B3
Cranborne Rd C1
Cricket Ground A2
Cumnor Rd B2
Dean Park A2
Dean Park Cres A2
Dean Park Rd A2
Durrant Rd B1
East Overcliff Dr . . . C2
Exeter Cres C1
Exeter La C2
Exeter Rd C1
Gervis Place B1
Gervis Rd C2
Glen Fern Rd B2
Golf Club A3
Grove Rd C2
Hinton Rd B2
Holdenhurst Rd A3
Horseshoe Comm . . B2
Information Ctr ✦ . . . B2
Lansdowne ⏺ B3
Lansdowne Rd A2
Lorne Park Rd B2
Lower Gdns B1/C2
Madeira Rd A2
Methuen Rd A3
Meyrick Park A1
Meyrick Rd B3
Milton Rd A2
Nuffield Health
  Bournemouth Hosp
  (private) ✦ A2
Oceanarium ✦ C2
Odeon Cinema ✦ . . . B1
Old Christchurch
  Rd B2
Ophir Rd A3
Oxford Rd A3
Park Rd A3
Parsonage Rd B2
Pavilion ✦ C2
Pier Approach C2
Pier Theatre ✦ C2
Police Station ✦ . A3/B3
Portchester Rd A3
Post Office
  ✉ B1/B3
Priory Rd C1
Quadrant,The B1
Recreation Ground . . A1
Richmond Gardens
  Shopping Centre . . B1
Richmond Hill Rd . . . B1
Russell-Cotes Art
  Gallery & Mus ✦ . . C2
Russell Cotes Rd . . . C2
St Anthony's Rd A1
St Michael's Rd C1
St Paul's ⏺ A3
St Paul's La A3
St Paul's Rd A3
St Peter's ✦ B2
St Peter's Rd B2
St Stephen's Rd . . B1/B2
St Swithun's Rd . . B3/C3
St Swithun's Rd
  South B3
St Valerie Rd A1
St Winifred's Rd A2
Square,The B1
Stafford Rd B2
Terrace Rd B1
Town Hall B1
Tregonwell Rd C1
Triangle,The B1
Trinity Rd B2
Undercliff Drive C3
Upper Hinton Rd . . . B2
Upper Terr Rd C1
Wellington Rd . . . A2/A3
Wessex Way . B1/B2/B3
West Cliff Prom C1
West Hill Rd C1
West Undercliff
  Promenade C1

Bradford 177

Alhambra ✦ B1
Back Ashgrove A1
Barkerend Rd A3
Barnard Rd C2
Barry St B2
Bolling Rd C3
Bolton Rd A3
Bowland St A1
Bradford
  Big Screen ✦ B2
Bradford College . . . B1
Bradford
  Forster Sq ➤ A2
Bradford
  Interchange ➤ B3
Bradford
  Playhouse ✦ B3
Bridge St B2
Britannia St B2
Broadway Bradford,
  The. B2
Burnett St B3
Bus Station B3
Butler St West A3
Caledonia St C2
Canal Rd A2
Carlton St B1
Cathedral ✝ A3
Centenary Sq B2
Chapel St B3
Cheapside A2
Church Bank A3
Cineworld ✦ B2
City Hall ✦ B2
City Rd A1
Claremont C1
Colour
  Experience ✦ B5
Croft St C2
Crown Court B3
Darfield St A1
Darley St A2
Drewton Rd A1
Drummond Trading
  Estate A1
Dryden St B3
Dyson St A1
Easby Rd C1
East Parade B3
Eldon Place A1
Filey St B3
Forster Square
  Retail Park A2
Gallery II ✦ B1
Garnett St B3
Godwin St B2
Gracechurch St A1
Grattan Rd B1
Great Horton Rd B1/B2
Grove Terr B1
Hall Ings B2
Hall La C3
Hallfield Rd A1
Hammstrasse A2
Harris St B3
Holdsworth St A2
Ice Arena ✦ B2
Impressions ✦ B2
Information Ctr ✦ . . . B2
Ivegate B2
Jacob's Well C2
Municipal Offices. . . B2
James St A2
John St A2
Kirkgate B2
Kirkgate Centre B2
Laisteridge La C1
Leeds Rd B3
Leisure Exchange,
  The. B3
Library B1/B2
Listerhills Rd B1
Little Horton Green C1
Little Horton La C1
Longside La B1
Lumb La A1
Magistrates Court . . B2
Manchester Rd C2
Manningham La A1
Manor Row A2
Market B2
Market St B2
Melbourne Place . . . C1
Midland Rd A2
Mill La C2
Morley St B1
National Science and
  Media Museum ✦ . B2
Nelson St B2/C2
Nesfield St A2
New Otley Rd A3
Norcroft St B1
North Parade A2
North St A2
North Wing C3
Oastler Shopping
  Centre A2
Otley Rd A3
Park Ave C1
Park La C1
Park Rd C2
Parma St C2
Peace Museum ✦ . . B2
Peckover St B3
Piccadilly A2
Police Station ✦ . . . B3
Post Office
  ✉ B2/B3/C3
Princes Way B2
Prospect St C2
Radwell Drive C1
Rawson Rd A1
Rebecca St A1
Richmond Rd B1
Russell St C2
St George's Hall ✦ . . B2
St Lukes Hospital ✦ C1
Shipley Airedale
  Rd A3/B3
Shopmobility A2

Simes St A1
Smith St B1
Spring Mill St C2
Stott Hill A3
Sunbridge Rd A1/B1/B2
Theatre in the Mill 🎭 B1
Thornton Rd A1/B1
Trafalgar St A2
Trinity Rd C1
Tumbling Hill St B1
Tyrrel St B2
University of Bradford B1/C1
Usher St C3
Valley Rd A2
Vicar La B3
Wakefield Rd C3
Wapping Rd A3
Well St B3
Westgate A1
White Abbey Rd A1
Wigan Rd A1
Wilton St B1
Wood St A1
Wool Exchange ⌂ B2
Worthington St A1

Brighton 177

Addison Rd A1
Albert Rd B2
Albion Hill B3
Albion St B3
Ann St A3
Baker St A3
Black Lion St C2
Brighton ⇌ A2
Brighton Centre ⌂ C2
Brighton Fishing Museum 🏛 C2
Brighton Pier (Palace Pier) ✦ C3
Brighton Wheel ✦ C3
British Airways i360 Tower ✦ C1
Broad St C3
Buckingham Place A2
Buckingham Rd B2
Cannon Place C1
Carlton Hill B3
Chatham Place A1
Cheapside A3
Church St B2
Churchill Square Shopping Centre B2
Clifton Hill B1
Clifton Place B1
Clifton Rd B1
Clifton St A2
Clifton Terr B1
Clyde Rd A3
Coach Station C3
Compton Ave A2
Davigdor Rd A1
Denmark Terr B1
Ditchling Rd A3
Dome ⌂ B2
Duke St B2
Duke's La C2
Dyke Rd A1/B2
East St C2
Edward St B3
Elmore Rd B3
Fleet St A2
Frederick St B2
Gardner St B2
Gloucester Place B3
Gloucester Rd B2
Goldsmid Rd A1
Grand Junction Rd C2
Grand Parade B3
Grove Hill B3
Guildford St A2
Hampton Place B1
Hanover Terrace A3
High St C3
Highdown Rd A1
Information Ctr ℹ C2
John St B3
Jubilee Clock Tower B2
Kemp St B2
Kensington Place B2
Kings Rd C1
Lanes, The C2
Law Courts B3
Lewes Rd A3
Library B2
London Rd A3
Madeira Dr C3
Marine Pde C3
Middle St C2
Montpelier Place B1
Montpelier Rd B1
Montpelier St B1
Museum & Art Gallery 🏛 B3
New England Rd A2
New England St A2
New Rd B2
Nizells Ave A1
Norfolk Rd B1
Norfolk Terr B1
North Rd B2
North St B2
Odeon 🎥 C2
Old Shoreham Rd A1
Old Steine C3
Osmond Rd A1
Over St B2
Oxford St A3
Park Crescent Terr A3
Phoenix Brighton 🖼 B3
Phoenix Rise A3
Police Station 🛡 B3
Post Office ✉ A1/A3/C3
Preston Rd A2
Preston St B1
Prestonville Rd A1
Queen's Rd B2
Queen Sq B2
Regency Sq C1
Regent St B2
Richmomd Place B3
Richmond St B3
Richmond Terr A3
Rose Hill Terr A3
Royal Pavilion 🕌 B2
St Bartholomew's ⛪ A3
St James's St C3
St Nicholas Rd B2
St Nicholas' ⛪ B2
St Peter's ⛪ A3
Sea Life Brighton 🐟 C3
Shaftesbury Rd A3
Ship St C2
Sillwood Rd B1
Sillwood St B1
Southover St A3
Spring Gdns B2
Stanford Rd A1
Stanley Rd A3
Surrey St B2
Sussex St B3
Swimming Pool B3
Sydney St B3
Temple Gdns B1
Terminus Rd A2
Theatre Royal 🎭 B2
Tidy St B2
Town Hall C2
Toy & Model Mus 🏛 A2
Trafalgar St B2
Union Rd A3
Univ of Brighton B3
Upper Lewes Rd A3
Upper North St B1
Viaduct Rd A3
Victoria Gdns B3
Victoria Rd B1
Volk's Electric Railway ✦ C3
West Pier (derelict) C1
West St C2
Western Rd B1
Whitecross St B2
YHA ▲ C3
York Ave B1
York Place B3
York Rd B1

Bristol 177

Acramans Rd C4
Albert Rd C6
Alfred Hill A4
All Saint's St A4
All Saints' ⛪ B4
Allington Rd C3
Alpha Rd C4
Ambra Vale B1
Ambra Vale East B2
Ambrose Rd B2
Amphitheatre & Waterfront Sq ✦ C4
Anchor Rd B3
Anvil St B6
Arcade, The A5
Architecture Centre, The ✦ B4
Argyle Place B2
Arlington Villas A2
Arnolfini ✦ B4
Art Gallery 🖼 A3
Ashton Gate Rd C2
Ashton Rd C1
Avon Bridge C1
Avon Cres C1
Avon St B6
Baldwin St B4
Baltic Wharf C2
Baltic Wharf Leisure Centre & Caravan Park ✦ C2
Baltic Wharf Marina C2
Barossa Place C4
Barton Manor B6
Barton Rd B6
Barton Vale B6
Bath Rd C6
Bathurst Basin C4
Bathurst Parade C4
Beauley Rd C3
Bedminster Bridge C5
Bedminster Parade C4
Bellevue B2
Bellevue Cres B2
Bellevue Rd C6
Berkeley Place A2
Berkeley Sq A3
Birch Rd C2
Blackfriars A4
Bond St A5
Braggs La A6
Brandon Hill B3
Brandon Steep B3
Bristol Aquarium 🐟 B4
Bristol Bridge B5
Bristol Cath (CE) ✝ B3
Bristol Eye Hospital (A&E) A4
Bristol Grammar School A3
Bristol Harbour Railway 🚂 C3
Bristol Royal Children's Hosp Ⓗ A4
Bristol Royal Infirmary (A&E) Ⓗ A4
Bristol Temple Meads Station ⇌ B6
Broad Plain B6
Broad Quay B4
Broad St A4
Broad Weir A5
Broadcasting Ho A3
Broadmead A5
Brunel Institute ✦ B3
Brunel Way C1
Brunswick Sq A5
Burton Cl C5
Bus Station A4
Butts Rd B3
Cabot Circus A5
Cabot Tower ✦ B3
Caledonia Place B1
Callowhill Ct A5
Cambridge St C6
Camden Rd C3
Camp Rd A1
Canada Way C2
Cannon St A4
Canon's Way B3
Cantock's Cl A3
Canynge Rd A1
Canynge Sq A1
Castle Park A5
Castle St A5
Cathedral Walk B3
Catherine Meade St C4
Cattle Market Rd C6
Central Library B3
Charles Place B1
Charlotte St B3
Charlotte St South B3
Chatterton Ho ⌂ B5
Chatterton Sq C5
Chatterton St C5
Cheese La B5
Christchurch ⛪ A4
Christchurch Rd A1
Christmas Steps ✦ A4
Church La B2/B5
Church St B5
City Museum 🏛 A3
City of Bristol College B3
Civil and Family Justice Centre B5
Clare St B4
Clarence Rd C5
Cliff Rd C1
Clift House Rd C1
Clifton Cath (RC) ✝ A2
Clifton Down A1
Clifton Down Rd A1
Clifton Hill B2
Clifton Park A1/A2
Clifton Park Rd A1
Clifton Rd A2
Clifton Vale B1
Cliftonwood Cres B2
Cliftonwood Rd B2
Cliftonwood Terr B2
Cobblestone Mews A1
College Green B3
College Rd A1
College St B3
Colston Almshouses ⌂ A4
Colston Ave B4
Colston Hall 🎭 B4
Colston Parade C5
Colston St A4
Commercial Rd C4
Constitution Hill B2
Cooperage La C2
Corn St B4
Cornwallis Ave B1
Cornwallis Cres B1
Coronation Rd C2/C4
Council House ⌂ B3
Counterslip B5
Create Ctr, The ✦ C1
Crosby Row B2
Crown Court A4
Culver St B3
Cumberland Basin C1
Cumberland Cl C2
Cumberland Rd C2/C3
Dean La C4
Deanery Rd B3
Denmark St B4
Dowry Sq B1
Eaton Cres A2
Elmdale Rd A3
Elton Rd A3
Eugene St A4/A6
Exchange and St Nicholas' Mkts, The ⌂ B4
Fairfax St A4
Fire Station B5
Floating Harbour C3
Fosseway, The A2
Foster Almshouses ⌂ A4
Frayne Rd C1
Frederick Place A2
Freeland Place B1
Friary B5
Frogmore St B3
Fry's Hill B2
Gas La B6
Gasferry Rd C3
Georgian House 🏛 B3
Glendale B1
Glentworth Rd B2
Gloucester St A1
Goldney Hall B2
Goldney Rd B1
Gordon Rd A2
Granby Hill B1
Grange Rd A1
Great Ann St A6
Great George Rd B3
Great George St A6/B3
Green St North B1
Green St South B1
Greenay Bush La C2
Greenbank Rd C2
Greville Smyth Pk C1
Grove, The B4
Guildhall 🕌 A4
Guinea St C4
Hamilton Rd C3
Hanbury Rd A2
Hanover Place C2
Harley Place A1
Haymarket A5
Hensman's Hill B1
High St B4
Highbury Villas A3
Hill St B3
Hill St C6
Hippodrome 🎭 B4
Hopechapel Hill B1
Horfield Rd A4
Horsefair, The A5
Horton St B6
Host St A4
Hotwell Rd B1/B2
Houlton St A6
Howard Rd C3
IMAX Cinema 🎥 B4
Information Ctr ℹ B4
Islington Rd C3
Jacob St A5/A6
Jacob's Wells Rd B2
John Carr's Terr B2
John Wesley's Chapel ⛪ A5
Joy Hill B1
Jubilee St B6
Kensington Place A2
Kilkenny St B6
King St B4
Kingsland Rd B6
Kingston Rd C3
Lamb St A6
Lansdown Rd A2
Lawford St A6
Lawfords Gate A6
Leighton Rd C3
Lewins Mead A4
Lime Rd C2
Litfield Rd A1
Little Ann St A6
Little Caroline Place B1
Little George St A6
Little King St B4
Llandoger Trow ⌂ B4
Lloyds' Building, The C3
Lodge St A4
Lord Mayor's Chapel, The ⛪ B4
Lower Castle St A5
Lower Church La A4
Lower Clifton Hill B2
Lower Guinea St C4
Lower Lamb St B3
Lower Maudlin St A4
Lower Park Rd A4
Lower Sidney St C2
Lucky La C4
Lydstep Terr C3
M Shed 🏛 C4
Magistrates' Court A4
Mall (Galleries Shopping Ctr), The A5
Mall, The A1
Manilla Rd A1
Mardyke Ferry Rd C2
Maritime Heritage Centre 🏛 B3
Marlborough Hill A4
Marlborough St A4
Marsh St B4
Mead St C5
Merchant Dock B2
Merchant Seamen's Almshouses ⌂ B4
Merchant St A5
Merchants Rd A1
Merchants Rd C1
Meridian Place A2
Meridian Vale A2
Merrywood Rd C3
Midland Rd A6
Milford St C3
Millennium Prom B3
Millennium Sq B3
Mitchell La B5
Mortimer Rd A1
Murray Rd C4
Myrtle Rd A3
Narrow Plain B5
Narrow Quay B4
Nelson St A4
New Charlotte St C4
New Kingsley Rd B6
New Queen St C5
New St A6
Newgate A5
Newton St A6
Norland Rd A1
North St C2
O2 Academy B3
Oakfield Grove A2
Oakfield Place A2
Oakfield Rd A2
Old Bread St B6
Old Market St A6
Old Park Hill A4
Oldfield Rd B1
Orchard Ave B4
Orchard La B4
Orchard St B4
Osbourne Rd C3
Oxford St B6
Park Place A2
Park Rd C3
Park Row A3
Park St A3
Passage St B5
Pembroke Grove A2
Pembroke Rd A2
Pembroke Rd C3
Pembroke St A5
Penn St A5
Pennywell Rd A6
Percival Rd A1
Pero's Bridge B4
Perry Rd A4
Phipps St C2
Pip 'n' Jay ⛪ B5
Plimsoll Bridge B1
Police Sta 🛡 A6
Polygon Rd B1
Portland St A1
Portwall La B5
Post Office ✉ A1/A3/A5/B1/B4/C4/C5
Prewett St C5
Prince St B4
Prince St Bridge C4
Princess St C5
Princess Victoria St B1
Priory Rd A3
Pump La C5
QEH Theatre 🎭 A2
Quakers Friars A5
Quay St A4
Queen Charlotte St B4
Queen Elizabeth Hospital School B2
Queen Sq B4
Queen St A5
Queen's Ave A3
Queen's Parade B3
Queen's Rd A2/A3
Raleigh Rd C2
Randall Rd B2
Red Lodge 🏛 A4
Redcliffe Backs B5
Redcliffe Bridge B4
Redcliffe Hill C5
Redcliffe Parade C4
Redcliffe St B5
Redcliffe Way B5
Redcross St A6
Redgrave Theatre 🎭 A1
Regent St B1
Richmond Hill A2
Richmond Hill Ave A2
Richmond La A2
Richmond Park Rd A2
Richmond St C6
Richmond Terr A2
River St A6
Rownham Mead B2
Royal Fort Rd A3
Royal Park A2
Royal West of England Academy 🖼 A3
Royal York Cres B1
Royal York Villas B1
Rupert St A4
Russ St B6
St Andrew's Walk B2
St George's 🎭 B3
St George's Rd B3
St James ⛪ A4
St John's ⛪ A4
St John's Rd C4
St Luke's Rd C5
St Mary Redcliffe ⛪ C5
St Matthias Park A6
St Michael's Hill A3
St Michael's Hospital Ⓗ A4
St Michael's Park A3
St Nicholas St B4
St Paul St A5
St Paul's Rd A2
St Peter's (ruin) ⛪ A5
St Philip's Bridge B5
St Philips Rd A6
St Stephen's ⛪ B4
St Stephen's St B4
St Thomas St B5
St Thomas the Martyr ⛪ B5
Sandford Rd B1
Sargent St C5
Saville Place B1
Ship La C5
Shopmobility A5
Showcase Cinema de Lux 🎥 A5
Silver St A4
Sion Hill A1
Small St A4
Smeaton Rd C1
Somerset Sq C5
Somerset St C5
Southernhay Ave B2
Southville Rd C4
Spike Island Artspace 🖼 C2
Spring St C5
Superstore C4
SS Great Britain and the Matthew ⛴ B2
Stackpool Rd C3
Staight St B6
Stillhouse La C4
Sydney Row C2
Tankard's Cl A3
Temple Back B5
Temple Back East B5
Temple Bridge B5
Temple Church ⛪ B5
Temple Circus B5
Temple Gate C5
Temple St B5
Temple Way B5
Terrell St A4
Theatre Royal (Bristol Old Vic) 🎭 B4
Thekla ⛴ B4
Thomas La B5
Three Kings of Cologne ⛪ A4
Three Queens La B5
Tobacco Factory, The 🎭 C2
Tower Hill B5
Tower La A4
Trenchard St A4
Triangle South A3
Triangle West A3
Trinity Rd A6
Trinity St A6
Tyndall Ave A3
Union St A5
Union St B6
Unity St A6
Unity St B3
University of Bristol A3
University Rd A3
Upper Byron Place A3
Upper Maudlin St A4
Upper Perry Hill C3
Upton Rd C2
Valentine Bridge B6
Victoria Grove C5
Victoria Rd C6
Victoria Rooms ⌂ A2
Victoria Sq A2
Victoria St B5
Vyvyan Rd A1
Vyvyan Terr A1
Wade St A6
Walter St C2
Wapping Rd C4
Water La B5
Waterloo Rd A6
Waterloo St A1
Waterloo St A6
Watershed Media Centre ✦ B4
We the Curious ✦ B3
Welling Terr B1
Welsh Back B4
West Mall A1
West St A6
Westfield Place A1
Wetherell Place A2
Whitehouse Place C5
Whitehouse St C5
Whiteladies Rd A2
Whitson St A4
William St C5
Willway St C5
Windsor Place B1
Wine St A4
Woodland Rd A3
Woodland Rise A3
Worcester Rd A1
Worcester Terr A1
YHA ▲ B4
York Gdns B1
York Place A2
York Rd C5

Bury St Edmunds 178

Abbey Gardens ✿ B3
Abbey Gate ⌂ B3
Abbeygate St B2
Albert Cres B1
Albert St B1
Ambulance Sta C1
Angel Hill B2
Angel La B2
Anglian Lane A1
Arc Shopping Ctr B2
Athenaeum 🎭 C2
Baker's La C3
Barwell Rd B3
Beetons Way A1
Bishops Rd B2
Bloomfield St B2
Bridewell La C2
Bullen Cl C1
Bury St Edmunds ⇌ A2
Bury St Edmunds County Upper School A1
Bury St Edmunds Leisure Centre B1
Bury Town FC B3
Bus Station B2
Business Park B3
Butter Mkt B2
Cannon St B2
Castle Rd C1
Cemetery C1
Chalk Rd (N) B1
Chalk Rd (S) B1
Church Row B2
Churchgate St C2
Cineworld 🎥 B1
Citizens Advice Bureau B2
College St C2
Compiegne Way A3
Corn Exchange, The 🎭 B2
Cornfield Rd B1
Cotton Lane B3
Courts B2
Covent Garden C2
Crown St C3
Cullum Rd C2
Eastern Way A3
Eastgate St B3
Enterprise Bsns Pk A2
Etna Rd A2
Eyre Cl C2
Fire Station B1
Friar's Lane C2
Gage Cl A1
Garland St B2
Greene King Brewery 🏛 C3
Grove Park B1
Grove Rd B1
Guildhall ⌂ C2
Guildhall St C2
Hatter St C2
High Baxter St B2
Honey Hill C3
Hospital Rd C1/C2
Ickworth Dr C1
Industrial Estate A3
Information Ctr ℹ B2
Ipswich St A2
King Edward VI School A1
King's Rd C1/B2
Library B2
Long Brackland A2
Looms La B2
Lwr Baxter St B2
Malthouse La A2
Maynewater La C3
Mill Rd C1
Mill Rd (South) C1
Minden Close B3
Moyses Hall 🏛 B2
Mustow St B3
Norman Tower ⌂ C3
Northgate Ave A2
Northgate St B2
Nutshell, The 🎥 B2
Osier Rd A2
Out Northgate A2
Out Risbygate B1
Out Westgate C2
Parkway B1/C2
Peckham St B2
Petticoat La C1
Phoenix Day Hospital Ⓗ C1
Pinners Way C1
Police Station 🛡 C3
Post Office ✉ B2/B3
Pump La B2
Queen's Rd B1
Raingate St C3
Raynham Rd A1
Retail Park C2
Risbygate St B1/B2
Robert Boby Way C2
St Andrew's St North B2
St Andrew's St South B2
St Botolph's La C3
St Edmund's ⛪ C2
St Edmund's Abbey (Remains) ✦ B3
St Edmunds Hospital (private) Ⓗ C3
St Edmundsbury ✝ C3
St John's St B2
St Marys ⛪ C3
School Hall La B2
Shillitoe Cl C1
Shire Halls & Magistrates Ct C3
South Cl C1
Southgate St C3
Sparhawk St C3
Spring Lane B1
Springfield Rd B1
Station Hill A2
Swan La C3
Tayfen Rd B2
Theatre Royal 🎭 C3
Thingoe Hill A2
Victoria St B1
Vinefields, The B3
War Memorial ✦ C1
Well St B2
West Suffolk Coll B1
Westgarth Gdns C1
Westgate St C2
Whiting St C2
York Rd B1
York Terr B1

Cambridge 178

Abbey Rd A3
ADC 🎭 A2
Anglia Ruskin Univ B3
Archaeology & Anthropology 🏛 B2
Arts Picture Ho 🎥 B2
Arts Theatre 🎭 B1
Auckland Rd A3
Backs, The B1
Bateman St C2
Benet St B1
Bradmore St B3
Bridge St A1
Broad St B3
Brookside C2
Brunswick Terr A3
Burleigh St B3
Bus Station B2
Butt Green A2
Cambridge Contemporary Art Gallery 🖼 B1
Castle Mound 🏰 A1
Castle St A1
Cemetery B3
Chesterton La A1
Christ's (Coll) B2
Christ's Lane B2
Christ's Pieces B2
City Rd B3
Clare (Coll) B1
Clarendon St B2
Coe Fen C2
Coronation St C2
Corpus Christi (Coll) B1
Court A3
Cross St C3
Crusoe Bridge C1
Darwin (Coll) C1
Devonshire Rd C3
Downing (Coll) C2
Downing St B2
Earl St B2
East Rd B3
Eden St B3
Elizabeth Way A3
Elm St B2
Emery St B3
Emmanuel (Coll) B2
Emmanuel Rd B2
Emmanuel St B2
Fair St A3
Fen Causeway, The C1
Fenner's Cricket Gd C3
Fire Station B3
Fitzroy St A3
Fitzwilliam Mus 🏛 C2
Fitzwilliam St C2
Garrett Hostel Bridge B1
Glisson Rd C3
Gonville & Caius (Coll) B1
Gonville Place C2
Grafton Centre, The A3
Grand Arcade B2
Green St B1
Gresham Rd C3
Guest Rd B3
Guildhall ⌂ B2
Harvey Rd C3
Hills Rd C3
Hobson St B2
Hughes Hall (Coll) B3
Information Ctr ℹ B2
James St A3
Jesus (Coll) A2
Jesus Green A2
Jesus La A2
Jesus Terr B3
John St B3
Kelsey Kerridge Sports Centre B3
Kettle's Yard 🖼 A1
King's Bridge B1
King St A2
King's (Coll) B1
King's College Chapel ⛪ B1
King's Parade B1
Lammas Land Recreation Gd C1
Lensfield Rd C2
Library B2
Lion Yard B2
Little St Mary's La B1
Lyndewod Rd C3
Magdalene (Coll) A1
Magdalene St A1
Maid's Causeway A3
Malcolm St A2
Market Hill B1
Market St B1
Mathematical Bridge B1
Mawson Rd C3
Midsummer Comm A3
Mill La B1
Mill Rd B3
Mill St C3
Mumford 🎭 B3
Museum of Cambridge 🏛 A1
Museum of Classical Archeology 🏛 C1
Napier St A3
New Square A2
Newmarket Rd A3
Newnham Rd C1
Norfolk St B3
Northampton St A1
Norwich St C2
Orchard St B2
Panton St C2
Paradise Nature Reserve C1
Paradise St B3
Park Parade A1
Park St A2
Park Terr B2
Parker St B2
Parker's Piece B2
Parkside B3
Parkside Pools B3
Parsonage St A3
Pemberton Terr C2
Pembroke (Coll) B2
Pembroke St B1
Perowne St B3
Peterhouse (Coll) C1
Petty Cury B2
Polar Mus, The 🏛 C2
Police Station 🛡 B3
Post Office ✉ A1/A3/B2/B3/C1/C2/C3
Queen's La B1
Queen's Rd B1
Queens' (Coll) B1
Regent St B2
Regent Terr B2
Ridley Hall (Coll) C1
Riverside A3
Round Church, The ⛪ A1
Russell St C2
St Andrew's St B2
St Benet's ⛪ B1
St Catharine's (Coll) B1
St Eligius St C2
St John's (Coll) A1
St Mary's ⛪ B1
St Paul's Rd C3
Saxon St C2
Sedgwick Mus 🏛 B2
Sheep's Green C1
Shire Hall A1
Sidgwick Ave C1
Sidney St A2
Sidney Sussex (Coll) A2
Silver St B1
Station Rd C3
Tenison Ave C3
Tenison Rd C3
Tennis Court Rd B2
Thompson's La A1
Trinity (Coll) A1
Trinity Hall (Coll) B1
Trinity St B1
Trumpington Rd C2
Trumpington St B1
Union Rd C2
University Botanic Gardens ✿ C2
Victoria Ave A2
Victoria St B2
Warkworth St B3
Warkworth Terr B3
Wesley House (Coll) A2
West Rd B1
Westcott Ho (Coll) A2
Westminster (Coll) A1
Whipple 🏛 B2
Willis Rd B3
Willow Walk A2
YMCA C3

Canterbury 178

Artillery St B2
Barton Mill Rd A3
Beaconsfield Rd A1
Beaney, The 🏛 B2
Beverley Rd A1
Bingley's Island B1
Black Griffin La B1
Broad Oak Rd A2
Broad St B2
Brymore Rd A3
Burgate B2
Bus Station C2
Canterbury College C3
Canterbury East ⇌ C1
Canterbury Tales, The ✦ B2
Canterbury West ⇌ A1
Castle 🏰 C1
Castle Row C1
Castle St C1
Cathedral ✝ B2
Causeway, The A2
Chaucer Rd A3
Christ Church Univ B3
Christchurch Gate ✦ B2
City Council Offices A3
City Wall B2
Coach Park A2
College Rd B3
Cossington Rd C2
Court B2
Craddock Rd A3
Crown & County Courts B3
Dane John Gdns C2
Dane John Mound ✦ C1
Deanery B2
Dover St C2
Duck La B2
Eastbridge Hosp ⌂ B1
Edgar Rd B3
Ersham Rd C3
Ethelbert Rd C3
Fire Station C2
Forty Acres Rd A1
Friars, The B2
Gordon Rd C1
Greyfriars ✦ B1
Guildford Rd C1
Havelock St B2
Heaton Rd C1
High St B2
Information Ctr ℹ A2/B2
Ivy La B2
Ivy Place C1
King St B2
King's School B2/B3
King's School Rec Ctr, The A2
Kingsmead Leisure Centre A2
Kingsmead Rd A2
Kirby's La B1
Lansdown Rd C2
Lime Kiln Rd C1
Longport B3
Lower Chantry La C3
Mandeville Rd A1
Market Way A2
Marlowe Arcade B2
Marlowe Ave C2
Marlowe Theatre 🎭 B2
Martyrs Field Rd C1
Mead Way B1
Military Rd B2
Monastery St B2
Museum of Canterbury (Rupert Bear Museum) 🏛 B1
New Dover Rd C3
Norman Rd C2
North Holmes Rd B3
North La B1
Northgate A2
Nunnery Fields C2
Nunnery Rd C2
Oaten Hill C2
Odeon Cinema 🎥 C2
Old Dover Rd C2
Old Palace B2
Old Ruttington La B2
Old Weavers ⌂ B2
Orchard St B1
Oxford Rd C1
Palace St B2
Pilgrims Way C3
Pin Hill C1
Pine Tree Ave A1
Police Station 🛡 C2
Post Office ✉ B2
Pound La B1
Puckle La C2
Raymond Ave C2
Recreation Ground A2
Registry Office A2
Rheims Way B1
Rhodaus Cl C2
Rhodaus Town C2
Roman Museum 🏛 B2
Roper Gateway A1
Roper Rd A1
Rose La B2
Shopmobility B2
St Augustine's Abbey (remains) ✝ B3
St Augustine's Rd C3
St Dunstan's ⛪ A1
St Dunstan's St A1
St George's Place C2
St George's St B2
St George's Tower ✦ B2
St Gregory's Rd B3
St John's Hosp ⌂ A2
St Margaret's St B2
St Martin's ⛪ B3
St Martin's Ave B3
St Martin's Rd B3
St Michael's Rd A1
St Mildred's ⛪ C1
St Peter's Grove B1
St Peter's La B2
St Peter's Place B1
St Peter's St B1
St Radigunds St B2
St Stephen's Ct A1
St Stephen's Path A1
St Stephen's Rd A2
Salisbury Rd A1
Simmonds Rd C1
Spring La C3
Station Rd West B1
Stour St B1
Sturry Rd A3
Tourtel Rd A3
Tudor Rd C1
Union St B2
University for the Creative Arts C3
Vernon Place C2
Victoria Rd C1
Watling St B2
Westgate Gdns B1
Westgate Towers 🏛 B1
Whitefriars B2
Whitehall Gdns B1
Whitehall Rd B1
Wincheap C1
York Rd C1
Zealand Rd C2

Cardiff
Caerdydd 178

Adam St B3
Alexandra Gdns A2
Allerton St C1
Arran St A3
ATRiuM (Univ of Glamorgan) C3
Beauchamp St C1
Bedford St A3
Blackfriars Priory (rems) ✝ B1
Bvd De Nantes B2
Brains Brewery C2
Brook St B1
Bute Park A1
Bute St C2
Bute Terr C3
Callaghan Sq C2/C3
Capitol Shopping Centre, The B3
Cardiff Arms Park (Cardiff Blues) B1
Cardiff Bridge B1
Cardiff Castle 🏰 B2
Cardiff Central Station ⇌ C2
Cardiff Story, The 🏛 B2
Cardiff Univ A1/A2/B3
Cardiff University Student's Union A2
Caroline St C2
Castle Green B2
Castle Mews A1
Castle St (Heol y Castell) B1
Cathays Station ⇌ A2
Celerity Drive C3
Central Library C2
Charles St (Heol Siarl) B3
Churchill Way B3
City Hall ⌂ A2
City Rd A3
Clare Rd C1
Clare St C1
Coburn St A3
Coldstream Terr B1
College Rd A1
Colum Rd A1
Court C2
Court Rd C1
Craiglee Drive C3
Cranbrook St A3
Customhouse St C2
Cyfartha St A3
David's B2/C2
Despenser Place C1
Despenser St C1
Dinas St C1
Duke St (Heol y Dug) B2
Dumfries Place B3
East Grove A3
Ellen St C3
Fire Station B3
Fitzalan Place B3
Fitzhamon Emb C1
Fitzhamon La C1
Friary, The B2
g39 🖼 C2
Gloucester St C1
Glynrhondda St A2
Gordon Rd A3
Gorsedd Gdns B2
Green St B1
Greyfriars Rd B2
Hafod St C1
Hayes, The B2
Herbert St C3
High St B2
HM Prison B3
Industrial Estate C3
John St C3
Jubilee St C1
King Edward VII Ave A1
Kingsway (Ffordd y Brenin) B2
Knox Rd B3
Law Courts B2
Llanbleddian Gdns A2
Llantwit St A2
Lloyd George Ave C3
Lower Cathedral Rd B1
Lowther Rd A3
Magistrates Court B3
Mansion House A3
Mardy St C1
Mark St B1
Market B2
Mary Ann St C3
Merches Gdns C1
Mill La C2
Millennium Bridge B1
Miskin St A2
Monmouth St C1
Motorpoint Arena Cardiff ✦ C3
Museum Ave A2
Museum Place A2
National Museum Cardiff 🏛 A2
National War Memorial ✦ A2
Neville Place C1
New Theatre 🎭 B2
Newport Rd B3
Northcote La A3
Northcote St A3
Parade, The A3
Park Grove A4
Park Place A2
Park St C2
Penarth Rd C2
Pendyris St C1
Plantaganet St C1
Post Office B2
Principality Stadium C1
Principality Stadium Tours (Gate 3) ✦ B2
Quay St B2
Queen's Arcade B2
Queen Anne Sq A1
Queen St (Heol y Frenhines) B2
Queen St Station ⇌ B3
Regimental Museums 🏛 B2
Rhymney St A3
Richmond Rd A3
Royal Welsh Coll of Music and Drama A1
Russell St A3
Ruthin Gdns A2
St Andrews Place A2
St David's ✝ B2
St David's Hall ✦ B2
St John the Baptist ⛪ B2
St Mary St (Heol Eglwys Fair) B2
St Peter's St A3
Salisbury Rd A3
Sandon St B3
Schooner Way C3
Scott Rd C2
Scott St C2
Senghennydd Rd A2
Sherman Theatre 🎭 A2
Sophia Gardens A1
Sophia Gardens Stadium ✦ A1
South Wales Baptist College A3
Sport Wales National Ctr ✦ A1
Stafford Rd C1
Stadium Plaza C1
Station Terr B3
Stuttgarter Strasse B2
Sussex St C1
Taffs Mead Emb C1
Talworth St A3
Temple of Peace & Health ✦ A1
Treharris St A3
Trinity St B2
Tudor La C1
Tudor St C1
Tyndall St C3
Vue 🎥 C1
Walk, The A3
Welsh Government A1
West Grove A3
Westgate St (Heol y Porth) B2
Windsor Place B3
Womanby St B2
Wood St C2
Working St B2
Wyeverne Rd A2

Carlisle 179

Abbey St A1
Aglionby St B3
Albion St C3
Alexander St C3
AMF Bowl ✦ C2
Annetwell St A1
Bank St B2
Bitts Park A1
Blackfriars St B2
Blencome St C1
Blunt St C1
Botchergate B2
Boustead's Grassing C2
Bowman St B3
Bridge St A1
Broad St B3
Brook St C3
Brunswick St B2
Bus Station B2
Caldew Bridge A1
Caldew St C1
Carlisle (Citadel) Station ⇌ B2
Carlisle College A2
Castle 🏰 A1
Castle St A1
Castle Way A1
Cathedral ✝ A1
Cecil St B2
Chapel St A2
Charles St B3
Charlotte St B1
Chatsworth Sq A2
Chiswick St B2
Citadel, The ✦ B2
City Walls A1
Civic Centre A2
Clifton St C1
Close St B3
Collingwood St C1
Colville St C1
Colville Terr C1
Council Offices B3
Court B2
Court St Brow B2
Crosby St B2
Crown St C2

Chelmsford • Cheltenham • Chester • Chichester • Colchester • Coventry • Derby • Dorchester • Dumfries 203

Currock Rd C2
Dacre Rd A1
Dale St C1
Denton St C1
Devonshire Walk A1
Duke's Rd A2
East Dale St C1
East Norfolk St C1
Eden Bridge A2
Edward St B1
Elm St B1
English St B2
Fire Station A2
Fisher St A1
Flower St B3
Freer St C1
Fusehill St B3
Georgian Way A2
Gloucester Rd C3
Golf Course A2
Graham St C1
Grey St B3
Guildhall Mus A2
Halfey's La B3
Hardwicke Circus A2
Hart St B3
Hewson St C2
Howard Place A3
Howe St B3
Information Ctr A2
James St B2
Junction St B1
King St B2
Lancaster St B2
Lanes Shopping Centre, The B2
Laser Quest B2
Library A2
Lime St B1
Lindisfarne St C3
Linton St B3
Lismore Place A3
Lismore St B3
London Rd C3
Lonsdale Rd B2
Lord St C3
Lorne Cres B1
Lorne St B1
Lowther St B2
Madford Retail Pk B1
Magistrates' Ct A2
Market Hall A2
Mary St B2
Memorial Bridge A3
Metcalfe St C1
Milbourne St B1
Myddleton St B3
Nelson St C1
Norfolk St C1
Old Fire Sta, The A2
Old Town Hall A2
Oswald St C3
Peter St A2
Petteril St B3
Pools B2
Portland Place B2
Portland Sq B2
Post Office A2/B2/C1/C3
Princess St C2
Pugin St B1
Red Bank Terr C2
Regent St C3
Richardson St C1
Rickerby Park A3
Rickergate A2
River St B3
Rome St C2
Rydal St B3
St Cuthbert's B2
St Cuthbert's La B2
St James' Park C1
St James' Rd C1
St Nicholas Gate Retail Park C3
St Nicholas St C3
Sands Centre, The A2
Scotch St A2
Shaddongate B1
Sheffield St B1
Shopmobility A2
South Henry St B3
South John St C2
South St B3
Spencer St B2
Station Retail Park B2
Strand Rd A2
Superstore B1
Sybil St B3
Tait St B2
Thomas St B1
Thomson St C3
Trafalgar St C1
Trinity Leisure Ctr A2
Tullie Museum & Art Gallery A1
Tyne St C3
Univ of Cumbria B3
Viaduct Estate Rd B1
Victoria Place A2
Victoria Viaduct B2
Vue B2
Warwick Rd B2
Warwick Sq B3
Water St B2
West Walls B1
Westmorland St C1

Chelmsford 179

Anchor St C1
Anglia Ruskin Univ A2
Arbour La A3
Baddow Rd B2/C3
Baker St C1
Barrack Sq B2
Bellmead B2
Bishop Hall La A2
Bishop Rd A2
Bond St B2
Boswells Dr B3
Bouverie Rd C2
Bradford St C1
Braemar Ave C1
Brook St A2
Broomfield Rd A1
Burgess Springs B3
Burns Cres C2
Bus Station B1/B2
Cedar Ave A1
Cedar Ave West A1
Cemetery A1
Cemetery A2
Cemetery C1
Central Park B1
Chelmsford B2
Chelmsford A1
Chichester Dr A3
Chinery Cl A3
City Council A1
Civic Centre A1
Civic Theatre B1
Cloud Fm County Cricket Ground B2
College C1
Cottage Place A2
County Hall B2
Coval Ave B1
Coval La B1
Coval Wells B1
Crown Court B2
Duke St B2
Elm Rd C1
Elms Dr A1
Essex Record Office, The B3
Fairfield Rd B1
Falcons Mead B1
George St C2
Glebe Rd A1
Godfrey's Mews C2
Goldlay Ave C3
Goldlay Rd C2
Grove Rd C2
Hall St C2
Hamlet Rd C2
Hart St C1
Henry Rd A2
High Bridge Rd B2
High Chelmer Shopping Centre B2
High St B2
Hill Cres B3
Hill Rd B3
Hill Rd Sth B3
Hillview Rd A3
HM Prison A3
Hoffmans Way A2
Hospital A2
Lady La C2
Langdale Gdns C3
Legg St B2
Library B2
Lionfield Terr A3
Lower Anchor St C1
Lynmouth Ave C2
Lynmouth Gdns C3
Magistrates Court B2
Maltese Rd A1
Manor Rd C2
Marconi Rd A2
Market B2
Market Rd B2
Marlborough Rd C1
Meadows Shopping Centre, The B2
Meadowside A3
Mews Ct C2
Mildmay Rd C2
Moulsham Dr C2
Moulsham Mill C3
Moulsham St C1/C2
Navigation Rd B3
New London Rd B2/C1
New St A2/B2
New Writtle St C1
Nursery Rd C2
Orchard St C2
Odeon B2
Parker Rd C2
Parklands Dr A3
Parkway A1/B1/B2
Police Station A2
Post Office B2/C2
Primrose Hill A1
Prykes Dr B1
Queen St C1
Queen's Rd B3
Railway St A1
Rainsford Rd A1
Ransomes Way A2
Rectory La A2
Regina Rd A2
Riverside Ice & Leisure Centre B2
Riverside Retail Pk A3
Rosebery Rd C2
Rothesay Ave C1
St John's Rd C2
Sandringham Place B3
Seymour St B1
Shopmobility B2
Shrublands Cl B3
Southborough Rd C1
Springfield Rd A3/B2/B3
Stapleford Cl C1
Superstore B2/C3
Swiss Ave A1
Telford Place A3
Tindal St B2
Townfield St A1
Trinity Rd B3
University B1
Upper Bridge Rd C1
Upper Roman Rd C2
Van Dieman's Rd C3
Viaduct Rd B1
Vicarage Rd C1
Victoria Rd A2
Victoria Rd South B2
Vincents Rd C2
Waterloo La B2
Weight Rd B3
Westfield Ave A1
Wharf Rd B3
Writtle Rd C1
YMCA A2
York Rd C1

Cheltenham 179

Albert Rd A3
Albion St B3
All Saints Rd B3
Ambrose St B2
Andover Rd C1
Art Gallery & Museum B2
Back Montpellier Terrace C2
Bandstand C2
Bath Pde B2
Bath Rd C2
Bays Hill Rd C1
Bennington St B2
Berkeley St B3
Brewery, The A2
Brunswick St South A2
Bus Station B2
Carlton St B3
Central Cross Road A3
Cheltenham Coll C2
Cheltenham FC A3
Cheltenham General (A&E) C3
Cheltenham Ladies College B2
Christchurch Rd B1
Cineworld A2
Clarence Rd A2
Clarence Sq A2
Clarence St B2
Cleeveland St A1
College Baths Rd C3
College Rd C2
Colletts Dr A1
Corpus St C3
Council Office B1
Court B1
Devonshire St A2
Douro Rd B1
Duke St B3
Dunalley Parade A2
Dunalley St A2
Everyman B2
Evesham Rd A3
Fairview Rd B3
Fairview St A3
Fire Station C3
Folly La A2
Gloucester Rd A1
Grosvenor St B3
Grove St A1
Hanover St A2
Hatherley St C1
Henrietta St A2
Hewlett Rd B3
High St B2/B3
Holst Birthplace Museum A3
Hudson St A2
Imperial Gdns C2
Imperial La B2
Imperial Sq C2
Information Ctr B2
Keynsham Rd C3
King St A2
Knapp Rd B2
Ladies College B2
Lansdown Cres C1
Lansdown Rd C1
Leighton Rd B3
Library B2
London Rd C3
Lypiatt Rd C1
Malvern Rd B1
Manser St A2
Market St A1
Marle Hill Parade A2
Marle Hill Rd A2
Millbrook St A1
Milsom St A2
Montpellier Gdns C2
Montpellier Grove C2
Montpellier Pde C2
Montpellier Spa Rd C2
Montpellier St C1
Montpellier Terr C2
Montpellier Walk C2
New St B2
North Place B2
Old Bath Rd C3
Oriel Rd B2
Overton Park Rd B1
Overton Rd B1
Oxford St C3
Parabola Rd B1
Park Place C1
Park St A1
Pittville Circus A3
Pittville Crescent A3
Pittville Lawn A3
Pittville Park A2
Playhouse B2
Police Station C1
Portland St B3
Prestbury Rd A3
Prince's Rd C1
Priory St B3
Promenade B2
Queen St A1
Recreation Ground A2
Regent Arcade B2
Regent St B2
Rodney Rd B2
Royal Cres B2
Royal Wells Rd B2
St George's Place B2
St Georges Rd B1
St Gregory's B2
St James St B3
St John's Ave B3
St Luke's Rd C2
St Margarets Rd A2
St Mary's B2
St Matthew's B2
St Paul's La A2
St Paul's Rd A2
St Paul's St A2
St Stephen's Rd C1
Sandford Parks Lido C3
Sandford Mill Rd C3
Sandford Park C3
Sandford Rd C2
Selkirk St A3
Sherborne Place B3
Sherborne St B3
Shopmobility B2
Suffolk Parade C2
Suffolk Rd C1
Suffolk Sq C1
Sun St A1
Swindon Rd B2
Sydenham Villas Rd C3
Tewkesbury Rd A1
The Courtyard B1
Thirlstaine Rd C2
Tivoli Rd C1
Tivoli St C1
Town Hall & Theatre B2
Townsend St A1
Trafalgar St C2
Union St B3
Univ of Gloucestershire (Francis Close Hall) A2
University of Gloucestershire (Hardwick) A1
Victoria Place B3
Victoria St A2
Vittoria Walk C2
Wel Place B2
Wellesley Rd A2
Wellington Rd A3
Wellington Sq A3
Wellington St B2
West Drive A3
Western Rd B1
Winchcombe St B3
Winston Churchill Meml Gardens A1

Chester 179

Abbey Gateway A2
Appleyards La C3
Bars, The B3
Bedward Row B1
Beeston View C3
Bishop Lloyd's Palace B2
Black Diamond St A2
Bottoms La C3
Boughton B3
Bouverie St A1
Bus Interchange A2
Bridge St B2
Bridgegate C2
Brook St A3
Brown's La C2
Cambrian Rd A1
Canal St A2
Carrick Rd C1
Castle C2
Castle Dr C2
Cathedral B2
Catherine St A1
Chester A3
Cheyney Rd A1
Chichester St A1
City Rd A3
City Walls B1/B2
City Walls Rd B1
Cornwall St A2
Cross Hey C3
Cross, The B2
Crown Ct C2
Cuppin St B2
Curzon Park North C1
Curzon Park South C1
Dee Basin A1
Dee La B3
Delamere St A2
Dewa Roman Experience B2
Duke St B2
Eastgate B2
Eastgate St B2
Eaton Rd C2
Edinburgh Way C3
Elizabeth Cres B3
Fire Station A2
Foregate St B2
Forum, The B2
Frodsham St B2
Gamul House B2
Garden La A1
George St A2
Gladstone Ave A1
God's Providence House B2
Gorse Stacks A2
Greenway St C2
Grosvenor Bridge C1
Grosvenor Mus B2
Grosvenor Park B3
Grosvenor Park Terrace C1
Grosvenor Shopping Ctr B2
Grosvenor St B2
Groves Rd B3
Groves, The B3
Guildhall Mus B1
Handbridge C2
Hartington St C3
Hoole Way A2
Hunter St B2
Information Ctr B2
King Charles' Tower A2
King St A2
Leisure Centre A2
Library B2
Lightfoot St A3
Little Roodee C2
Liverpool Rd A2
Love St B3
Lower Bridge St B2
Lower Park Rd B3
Lyon St A2
Magistrates Court B2
Meadows La C3
Meadows, The B3
Military Museum C2
Milton St A3
New Crane St B1
Nicholas St B2
Northgate A2
Northgate St A2
Nun's Rd B1
Old Dee Bridge C2
Overleigh Rd C2
Park St B2
Police Station B2
Post Office A2/A3/B2
Princess St B2
Queen St B2
Queen's Park Rd C3
Queen's Rd A3
Race Course B1
Raymond St A1
River La C2
Roman Amphitheatre & Gardens B2
Roodee (Chester Racecourse), The B1
Russell St A3
St Anne St A2
St George's Cres C3
St Martin's Gate A1
St Martin's Way B1
St Mary's Priory B2
St Oswalds Way A2
Saughall Rd A1
Sealand Rd A1
South View Rd A1
Stanley Palace B1
Station Rd A3
Steven St A3
Storyhouse B2
Superstore B2
Tower Rd B1
Union St B3
Univ of Chester C2
Vicar's La B2
Victoria Cres C3
Victoria Rd A2
Walpole St A1
Water Tower St A1
Water Tower, The B1
Watergate B1
Watergate St B2
Whipcord La A1
White Friars B2
York St B3

Chichester 180

Adelaide Rd A3
Alexandra Rd A3
Arts Centre B2
Ave de Chartres B1/B2
Barlow Rd A1
Basin Rd C2
Beech Ave B1
Bishops Palace Gardens B2
Bishopsgate Walk A3
Bramber Rd C3
Broyle Rd A2
Bus Station B2
Caledonian Rd B3
Cambrai Ave B3
Canal Place C1
Canal Wharf C2
Canon La B2
Cathedral B2
Cavendish St A1
Cawley Rd B2
Cedar Dr A1
Chapel St A2
Cherry Orchard Rd C3
Chichester B2
Chichester By-Pass C2/C3
Chichester Coll B1
Chichester Cinema B3
Chichester Festival A2
Chichester Gate Leisure Pk C1
Churchside A2
Cineworld C1
City Walls B2
Cleveland Rd B3
College La A2
Cory Cl C2
Council Offices B2
County Hall B2
District B2
Duncan Rd A1
Durnford Close A1
East Pallant B2
East Row B2
East St B2
East Walls B3
Eastland Rd C3
Ettrick Cl B3
Ettrick Rd B3
Exton Rd C3
Fire Station A2
Football Ground A2
Franklin Place A2
Friary (Rems of) A2
Garland Close C3
Green La A3
Grove Rd C3
Guilden Rd B3
Guildhall A2
Hawthorn Close A1
Hay Rd C3
Henty Gdns B1
Herald Dr C3
Hornet, The B3
Information Ctr B2
John's St B2
Joys Croft A3
Jubilee Pk A3
Jubilee Rd A3
Juxon Cl B1
Kent Rd A3
King George Gdns A2
King's Ave C2
Kingsham Ave C3
Kingsham Rd C2
Laburnum Grove B2
Leigh Rd C1
Lennox Rd A3
Lewis Rd A3
Library B2
Lion St B2
Litten Terr A3
Litten, The A3
Little London B2
Lyndhurst Rd B3
Market B3
Market Ave B2
Market Cross B2
Market Rd B3
Melbourne Rd A3
Minerva B2
Mount La B1
New Park Rd A3
Newlands La A1
North Pallant B2
North St A2
North Walls A2
Northgate A2
Novium, The B2
Oak Ave A1
Oak Cl A1
Oaklands Park A2
Oaklands Way A2
Orchard Ave A1
Orchard St A1
Ormonde Ave B3
Pallant House B2
Parchment St A1
Parklands Rd A1/B1
Peter Weston Place B3
Police Station C2
Post Office A1/B2/C3
Priory La A2
Priory Park A2
Priory Rd A2
Queen's Ave C1
Riverside A3
Roman Amphitheatre B3
St Cyriacs A2
St Martins' St B2
St Pancras A3
St Paul's Rd A2
St Richard's Hospital (A&E) A3
Shamrock Cl A3
Sherbourne Rd A1
Somerstown A2
South Bank C2
South Downs Planetarium C2
South Pallant B2
South St B2
Southgate B2
Spitalfield La A3
Stirling Rd B3
Stockbridge Rd C1/C2
Swanfield Dr A3
Terminus Ind Est C1
Tower St A2
Tozer Way A3
Turnbull Rd A3
Upton Rd C1
Velyn Ave B3
Via Ravenna B1
Walnut Ave A1
West St B2
Westgate B1
Westgate Fields B1
Westgate Leisure Centre B1
Weston Ave C1
Whyke Cl C3
Whyke La B3
Whyke Rd C3
Winden Ave B3

Colchester 180

Abbey Gateway C2
Albert St A1
Albion Grove C2
Alexandra Rd C1
Artillery St C3
Arts Centre B1
Balkerne Hill B1
Barrack St C3
Beaconsfield Rd C1
Beche Rd C3
Bergholt Rd A1
Bourne Rd C3
Brick Kiln Rd A1
Brigade Grove C2
Bristol Rd B2
Broadlands Way A3
Brook St B3
Bury Cl B2
Bus Sta B2
Butt Rd C1
Campion Rd C2
Cannon St C3
Canterbury Rd C2
Captain Gardens C2
Castle B2
Castle Park B2
Castle Rd B2
Catchpool Rd A1
Causton Rd B1
Chandlers Row C3
Circular Rd East C2
Circular Rd North C1
Circular Rd West C1
Clarendon Way A1
Claudius Rd C2
Colchester A1
Colchester Camp Abbey Field C1
Colchester Retail Park B1
Colchester Town C2
Colne Bank Ave A1
Colne View Retail Park A2
Compton Rd A3
Cowdray Ave A1/A2
Cowdray Ctr, The A2
Crouch St B1
Crowhurst Rd B1
Culver Square Shopping Centre B1
Culver St East B2
Culver St West B1
Dilbridge Rd A3
East Hill B2
East St B3
East Stockwell St B1
Eld La B1
Essex Hall Rd A1
Exeter Dr B2
Fairfax Rd C2
Fire Station A2
Firstsite B2
Flagstaff Rd C1
Garrison Parade C2
George St B2
Gladstone Rd C2
Golden Noble Hill C2
Goring Rd A3
Granville Rd C3
Greenstead Rd B3
Guildford Rd B2
Harsnett Rd C3
Harwich Rd B3
Head St B1
High St B1/B2
High Woods Ctry Pk A2
Hollytrees B2
Hyderabad Cl C2
Hythe Hill C3
Information Ctr B2
Jarmin Rd A2
Kendall Rd C2
Kimberley Rd C3
King Stephen Rd C3
Leisure World A2
Library B1
Lincoln Way B2
Lion Walk Shopping Centre B1
Lisle Rd C2
Lucas Rd C2
Magdalen Green C3
Magdalen St C2
Maidenburgh St B2
Maldon Rd C1
Manor Rd B1
Margaret Rd A1
Mason Rd A2
Mercers Way A1
Mercury B1
Mersea Rd C2
Meyrick Cres C2
Mile End Rd A1
Military Rd C2
Mill St C2
Minories B2
Moorside B3
Morant Rd C3
Napier Rd C2
Natural History B2
New Town Rd C2
Norfolk Cres A3
North Hill B1
North Station Rd A1
Northgate St B1
Nunns Rd B1
Odeon B1
Old Coach Rd B3
Old Heath Rd C3
Osborne St B2
Petrolea Cl A1
Police Station C1
Popes La B1
Port La C3
Post Office B2/C1
Priory St B2
Queen St B2
Rawstorn Rd B1
Rebon St C3
Recreation Rd C3
Ripple Way A3
Roberts Rd C2
Roman Rd B2
Roman Wall B2
Romford Cl A3
Rosebery Ave B2
St Andrews Ave B3
St Andrews Gdns B3
St Botolph St B2
St Botolphs B2
St John's Abbey (site of) C2
St John's St B1
St Johns Walk Shopping Centre B1
St Leonards Rd C3
St Marys Fields B1
St Peter's St B1
St Peters B1
Salisbury Ave C1
Saw Mill Rd C3
Sergeant St C2
Serpentine Walk A1
Sheepen Place B1
Sheepen Rd B1
Sir Isaac's Walk B1
Smythies Ave B2
South St C1
South Way C1
Sports Way A2
Suffolk Cl A3
Superstore A1
Town Hall B1
Valentine Dr A3
Victor Rd C3
Wakefield Cl B2
Wellesley Rd C1
Wells Rd B2/B3
West St C1
West Stockwell St B1
Weston Rd C3
Westway A1
Wickham Rd C1
Wimpole Rd C3
Winchester Rd C2
Winnock Rd C2
Worcester Rd B2

Coventry 180

Abbots La A1
Albany B1
Albany Rd B1
Alma St B3
Ambulance Sta A2
Art Faculty B3
Asthill Grove C2
Bablake School A1
Barras La A1/B1
Barr's Hill School A1
Belgrade B2
Bishop St A2
Bond's Hospital B1
Broad Gate B2
Broadway C1
Burges, The B2
Bus Station A3
Butts Radial B1
Byron St A3
Canal Basin A2
Canterbury St A3
Cathedral B3
Central Six Retail Park C1
Chester St A1
Cheylesmore Manor House B2
Christ Church Spire B2
City Coll A3
City Walls & Gates A2
Corporation St B2
Council House B2
Coundon Rd A1
Coventry Sta C2
Coventry Transport Museum A2
Coventry University Technology Park C3
Cox St A3
Croft Rd B1
Dalton Rd C1
Deasy Rd C3
Earl St B2
Eaton Rd C2
Fairfax St B2
Foleshill Rd A2
Ford's Hospital B2
Fowler Rd A1
Friars Rd C2
Gordon St C1
Gosford St B3
Greyfriars Green B2
Greyfriars Rd B2
Gulson Rd B3
Hales St A2
Harnall Lane East A3
Harnall Lane West A2
Herbert Art Gallery & Museum B3
Hertford St B2
Hewitt Ave A1
High St B2
Hill St B1
Holy Trinity B2
Holyhead Rd A1
Howard St A3
Huntingdon Rd C1
Information Ctr B2
Jordan Well B3
King Henry VIII School C1
Lady Godiva Statue B2
Lamb St A2
Leicester Row A2
Library B2
Lincoln St A2
Little Park St B2
London Rd C3
Lower Ford St B3
Lower Precinct Shopping Centre B2
Magistrates & Crown Courts B2
Manor House Drive B2
Manor Rd C2
Market B2
Martyrs Meml C2
Meadow St B1
Meriden St A1
Michaelmas Rd C2
Middleborough Rd A1
Mile La C3
Millennium Place A2
Much Park St B3
Naul's Mill Park A1
New Union B2
Odeon B1
Park Rd C2
Parkside C3
Planet Ice Arena B1
Post Office B2
Primrose Hill St A3
Priory Gardens & Visitor Centre B2
Priory St B3
Puma Way C3
Quarryfield La C3
Queen's Rd B1
Quinton Rd C2
Radford Rd A2
Raglan St B3
Ringway (Hill Cross) A1
Ringway (Queens) B1
Ringway (Rudge) B1
Ringway (St Johns) B3
Ringway (St Nicholas) A2
Ringway (St Patricks) C2
Ringway (Swanswell) A2
Ringway (Whitefriars) B3
St John St B2
St John the Baptist B2
St Nicholas St A2
Sidney Stringer Academy A3
Skydome B1
Spencer Ave C1
Spencer Rec Gnd C1
Spencer Rd C1
Spon St B1
Sports Centre B3
Stoney Rd C2
Stoney Stanton Rd A3
Superstore B2
Swanswell Pool A3
Technocentre C3
Thomas Landsdail St C2
Tomson Ave A1
Top Green C1
Trinity St B2
University B3
Univ Sports Ctr B3
Upper Hill St A1
Upper Well St A2
Victoria St A3
Vine St A3
Warwick Rd C2
Waveley Rd B1
West Orchards Shopping Ctr B2
Westminster Rd C1
White St A3
Windsor St B1

Derby 180

Abbey St C1
Agard St B1
Albert St B2
Albion St B2
Ambulance Station B1
Arthur St A1
Ashlyn Rd B3
Assembly Rooms B2
Babington La C2
Becket St B1
Belper Rd A1
Bold La B1
Bradshaw Way C2
Bradshaw Way Retail Park C2
Bridge St B1
Brook St B1
Burton Rd C1
Bus Station B2
Business Park A3
Caesar St A2
Canal St C3
Carrington St C3
Cathedral B2
Cathedral Rd B1
Charnwood St C2
Chester Green Rd A2
City Rd A2
Clarke St A3
Cock Pitt B3
Council House B2
Courts B1
Cranmer Rd B3
Crompton St C1
Crown & County Courts B2
Curzon St B1
Darley Grove A1
Derby C3
Derby B2
Derwent Bsns Ctr A2
Derwent St B2
Drewry La C1
Duffield Rd A1
Duke St A2
Dunton Cl B3
Eagle Market C2
East St B2
Eastgate B3
Exeter St B2
Farm St C1
Ford St B1
Forester St C1
Fox St A2
Friar Gate B1
Friary St B1
Full St B2
Gerard St C1
Gower St C2
Green La C2
Grey St C1
Guildhall B2
Harcourt St C1
Highfield Rd A1
Hill La C2
Information Ctr B2
intu Derby C2
Iron Gate B2
John St C3
Joseph Wright Ctr B1
Kedleston Rd A1
Key St B2
King Alfred St C1
King St A1
Kingston St A1
Lara Croft Way C2
Leopold St C2
Library B1
Liversage St C3
Lodge La B1
London Rd C2
London Rd Com Hosp C2
Macklin St C1
Mansfield Rd A2
Market B2
Market Place B2
May St C1
Meadow La B3
Melbourne St C2
Mercian Way C1
Midland Rd C3
Monk St C1
Morledge B2
Mount St C1
Museum & Art Gallery B1
Noble St C3
North Parade A1
North St A1
Nottingham Rd B3
Osmaston Rd C2
Otter St A1
Park St C3
Parker St A1
Pickfords House B1
Police HQ A2
Police Station B2
Post Office A1/A2/B1/C2/C3
Pride Parkway C3
Prime Enterprise Park A2
Prime Parkway A2
QUAD B2
Queens Leisure Ctr B1
Racecourse Park A3
Railway Terr C3
Register Office B2
Sadler Gate B1
St Alkmund's Way B1/B2
St Helens House A1
St Mary's A1
St Mary's Bridge A2
St Mary's Bridge Chapel A2
St Mary's Gate B1
St Paul's Rd A2
St Peter's C2
St Peter's St C2
Showcase De Lux C2
Siddals Rd C3
Sir Frank Whittle Rd A3
Spa La C1
Spring St C1
Stafford St B1
Station Approach C3
Stockbrook St C1
Stores Rd A3
The Pattonair County Ground (Derbyshire CCC) B3
Traffic St C2
Wardwick B1
Werburgh St C1
West Ave A1
West Meadows Industrial Estate B3
Wharf Rd A2
Wilmot St C2
Wilson St C1
Wood's La C1

Dorchester 181

Ackerman Rd B3
Acland Rd A2
Albert Rd A1
Alexandra Rd B1
Alfred Place B3
Alfred Rd B2
Alington Ave B3
Alington Rd B3
Ambulance Station B3
Ashley Rd B1
Balmoral Cres C3
Barnes Way B2/C2
Borough Gdns A1
Brewery Sq B1
Bridport Rd A1
Buckingham Way C3
Caters Place A1
Cemetery A3/C1
Charles St A2
Coburg Rd B1
Colliton St A1
Cornwall Rd A1
Cromwell Rd B1
Culliford Rd B2
Culliford Rd North B2
Dagmar Rd B1
Damer's Rd B1
Diggory Cres C2
Dinosaur Mus A2
Dorchester Bypass C2
Dorchester South Station B1
Dorchester West Station B1
Dorset County (A&E) B1
Dorset County Council Offices A1
Dorset County Museum A1
Duchy Close C3
Duke's Ave B2
Durngate St A2
Durnover Court A3
Eddison Ave B3
Edward Rd B1
Egdon Rd C2
Elizabeth Frink Statue B2
Farfrae Cres B2
Forum Centre, The B1
Friary Hill A2
Friary Lane A2
Frome Terr A2
Garland Cres C3
Glyde Path Rd A1
Government Offices B3
Grosvenor Cres C1
Grosvenor Rd C1
Grove, The A1
Gt Western Rd B1
Herrington Rd C1
High St East A2
High St Fordington A2
High Street West A1
Holloway Rd A2
Icen Way A2
Keep Military Museum, The A1
Kings Rd A3/B3
Kingsbere Cres C2
Lancaster Rd B2
Library B1
Lime Cl C1
Linden Ave B2
London Cl A3
London Rd A2/A3
Lubbecke Way A3
Lucetta La B2
Maiden Castle Rd C1
Manor Rd C2
Market B1
Marshwood Place B2
Maumbury Rd B1
Maumbury Rings B1
Mellstock Ave C2
Mill St A3
Miller's Cl A1
Mistover Cl C1
Monmouth Rd B1/B2
Moynton Rd C2
Nature Reserve A2
North Sq A2
Northernhay A1
Odeon B1
Old Crown Court & Cells A1
Olga Rd B1
Orchard St A2
Police Station A1
Post Office A1
Pound Lane A2
Poundbury Rd A1
Prince of Wales Rd B2
Prince's St A1
Queen's Ave B1
Roman Town Ho A1
Roman Wall A1
Rothesay Rd C2
St George's Rd B3
Salisbury Field A2
Sandringham Sports Centre B3
Shaston Cres C2
Smokey Hole La B3
South Court Ave C1
South St B1
South Walks Rd B2
Superstore C3
Teddy Bear Ho A1
Temple Cl C1
Terracotta Warriors & Teddy Bear Mus A2
Town Hall A2
Town Pump A2
Trinity St A1
Tutankhamun Exhibition A1
Victoria Rd B1
Weatherbury Way C2
Wellbridge Cl C1
West Mills Rd A1
West Walks Rd A1
Weymouth Ave C1
Williams Ave B1
Winterbourne (BMI) C1
Wollaston Rd A2
York Rd B2

Dumfries 181

Academy St A2
Aldermanhill Rd B3
Ambulance Station C3
Annan Rd A3
Ardwall Rd A3
Ashfield Dr A1
Atkinson Rd C1
Averill Cres C1
Balliol Ave C1
Bank St B2
Bankend Rd C3
Barn Slaps B3
Barrie Ave B3
Beech Ave A1
Bowling Green A3
Brewery St B2
Bridgend Theatre B1
Brodie Ave C2
Brooke St B2
Broomlands Dr C1
Brooms Rd B3
Buccleuch St A2
Burns House B2
Burns Mausoleum B3
Burns St B2
Burns Statue A2
Bus Station B1
Cardoness St A3
Castle St A2
Catherine St A2
Cattle Market A3
Cemetery B3
Cemetery C2
Church Cres A2
Church St B2
College Rd A1
College St A1
Corbelly Hill B1
Corberry Park B1
Cornwall Mt A3
Council Offices A2
Court A2
Craigs Rd C3
Cresswell Ave B3
Cresswell Hill B3
Cumberland St B3
David Keswick Athletic Centre A3
David St B1
Dock Park C3
Dockhead B2
Dumfries A3
Dumfries Academy A2
Dumfries Ice Bowl A1
Dumfries Museum & Camera Obscura B2
Dumfries & Galloway Royal Infirmary (A&E) C3
East Riverside Dr C3
Edinburgh Rd A2
English St B2

Fire Station....B3
Friar's Vennel....A2
Galloway St....A1
George Douglas Dr....C1
George St....A2
Gladstone Rd....C2
Glasgow St....A1
Glebe St....A1
Glencaple Rd....C3
Goldie Ave....A1
Goldie Cres....A1
Golf Course....A1
Gracefield Arts Centre....A2
Greyfriars....B3
Grierson Ave....B3
Hamilton Ave....C1
Hamilton Starke Pk....C2
Hazelrigg Ave....C1
Henry St....C1
Hermitage Dr....C1
High Cemetery....A1
High St....A2
Hill Ave....B1
Hill St....B1
HM Prison....A2
Holm Ave....C2
Hoods Loaning....A1
Howgate St....B3
Huntingdon Rd....B1
Information Ctr....B2
Irish St....B3
Irving St....A3
King St....A1
Kingholm Rd....C3
Kirkpatrick Ct....C1
Laurieknowe....B1
Leafield Rd....A2
Library....A2
Lochfield Rd....A3
Loreburn Pk....A3
Loreburn St....A2
Loreburne Shopping Centre....A2
Lover's Walk....B3
Martin Ave....B3
Mausoleum....A1
Maxwell St....A3
McKie Ave....A3
Mews La....B2
Mid Steeple ✦....B2
Mill Green....B3
Mill Rd....B3
Moat Rd....C2
Moffat St....A3
Mountainhall Pk....C2
Nelson St....A3
New Abbey Rd....B1/C1
New Bridge....B1
Newall Terr....A2
Nith Ave....A2
Nith Bank....A3
Nithbank Hosp....C3
Nithside Ave....A1
Odeon....B2
Old Bridge....A2
Old Bridge Ho....A2
Palmerston Park (Queen of the South FC)....A1
Park Rd....C1
Pleasance Ave....C1
Police HQ....A2
Police Sta....A2/A3
Portland Dr....A1
Post Office....B1/B2/B3
Priestlands Dr....C1
Primrose St....A2
Queen St....B3
Queensberry St....A2
Rae St....A2
Richmond Ave....C2
Robert Burns Ctr....B2
Roberts Cres....C1
Robertson Ave....C1
Robinson Dr....C1
Rosefield Rd....C1
Rosemount St....B1
Rotchell Park....C1
Rotchell Rd....C1
Rugby Football Gd....C1
Ryedale Rd....C2
St Andrews
St John the Evangelist....A2
St Josephs College....B3
St Mary's Ind Est....A3
St Mary's St....A3
St Michael St....A3
St Michael's St....A3
St Michael's Bridge....B2
St Michael's Bridge Rd....B2
St Michael's Cemetery....B3
Shakespeare St....B2
Solway Dr....C2
Stakeford St....A1
Stark Cres....A1
Station Rd....A3
Steel Ave....A1
Sunderries Ave....A1
Sunderries Rd....A1
Superstore....B3
Suspension Brae....B2
Swimming Pool....A1
Terregles St....C1
Theatre Royal....B2
Troqueer Rd....B2
Union St....A1
Wallace St....A1
Welldale....B2
West Riverside Dr....B2
White Sands....B2

Dundee 181
Abertay University....B2
Adelaide Place....A1
Airlie Pl....C1
Albany Terr....A1
Albert St....A3
Alexander St....A3
Ann St....A2
Arthurstone Terr....A3
Bank St....B2
Barrack Rd....B2
Barrack St....B2
Bell St....B2
Blinshall St....B1
Broughty Ferry Rd....A3
Brown St....B1
Bus Station....B3
Caird Hall....B2
Camperdown St....B3
Candle La....B3

Carmichael St....A1
City Churches....B2
City Quay....B3
City Sq....B2
Commercial St....B2
Constable St....A3
Constitution Cres....A1
Constitution Ct....A1
Constitution Rd....A1/B2
Cotton Rd....A3
Courthouse Sq....B1
Cowgate....A3
Crescent St....A3
Crichton St....B2
Dens Brae....A3
Dens Rd....A3
Discovery Point ✦....C2
Douglas St....A3
Drummond St....A1
Dudhope Castle....A1
Dudhope St....A2
Dudhope Terr....A1
Dundee ⇌....C2
Dundee Contemporary Arts....C2
Dundee High School....B2
Dundee Law ✦....A1
Dundee Repertory....C2
Dunhope Park....A1
Dura St....A3
East Dock St....B3
East Marketgait....B3
East Whale La....B3
Erskine St....A3
Euclid Cres....B2
Forebank Rd....A2
Foundry La....A3
Gallagher Retail Pk....B3
Gellatly St....B3
Government Offices....C2
Guthrie St....B1
Hawkhill....C1
Hilltown....A2
HMS Unicorn ✦....B3
Howff Cemetery, The....B2
Information Ctr....B2
Keiller Shopping Centre....B2
Keiller Ctr,The....B2
King St....A3
Kinghorne Rd....A1
Ladywell Ave....A3
Laurel Bank....C1
Law Rd....A1
Law St....A2
Library....A2/A3
Library and Steps Theatre....A3
Little Theatre, The....A3
Lochee Rd....B1
Lower Princes St....A3
Lyon St....A3
McManus Art Gallery & Museum,The....B2
Meadow Side....B2
Meadowside St Pauls....B2
Mercat Cross ✦....B2
Murraygate....B2
Nelson St....A2
Nethergate....B2/C1
North Lindsay St....B2
North Marketgait....B2
Old Hawkhill....C1
Olympia Leisure Centre....B3
Overgate Shopping Centre....B2
Park Place....C1
Perth Rd....C1
Police Station....B2
Post Office....A1/B2
Princes St....A3
Prospect Place....A2
Reform St....B2
Riverside Dr....C1
Riverside Esplanade....C2
Roseangle....C1
Rosebank St....A2
RRS Discovery ✦....C2
St Andrew's....B3
St Pauls Episcopal....B2
Science Centre ✦....C2
Seagate....B3
Sheriffs Court....B2
Shopmobility....B2
South George St....B2
South Marketgait....B2
South Tay St....B1
South Victoria Dock Road....B3
South Ward Rd....B2
Tay Road Bridge ✦....C3
Thomson Ave....A1
Trades La....B3
Union St....B2
Union Terr....A2
University Library....C1
Univ of Dundee....C1
Upper Constitution St....A1
Verdant Works ✦....B1
V&A Museum of Design....C2
Victoria Dock....B3
Victoria Rd....B2
Victoria St....A3
Ward Rd....B2
Wellgate....B2
West Bell St....B1
West Marketgait....B1/B2
Westfield Pl....C1
William St....A3
Wishart Arch ✦....A3

Durham 181
Alexander Cres....A3
Allergate....B1
Archery Rise....C1
Avenue,The....B1
Back Western Hill....A1
Bakehouse La....B2
Baths....B2
Baths Bridge....B2
Boat House....B3
Bowling....B3
Boyd St....C3
Bus Station....B2
Castle....B2

Castle Chare....B2
Cathedral....B2
Church St....C3
Clay La....C1
Claypath....B2
College of St Hild & St Bede....B3
County Hall....A1
County Hospital....B1
Crescent,The....A1
Crook Hall & Gardens ✦....A2
Crossgate....B2
Crossgate Peth....C1
Crown Court....B1
Darlington St....C1
Durham ⇌....C2
Durham School....C2
Durham University Science Site....C2
Ellam Ave....C1
Elvet Bridge....B2
Elvet Court....B2
Farnley Hey....B1
Ferens Cl....A1
Fieldhouse La....A1
Flass St....A1
Framwelgate Bridge....B2
Framwelgate....A2
Framwelgate Peth....A2
Framwelgate Waterside....A2
Frankland La....A3
Freeman's La....A3
Freeman's Quay Leisure Centre....A3
Gala Theatre & Cinema....B3
Geoffrey Ave....C1
Gilesgate....B3
Grey College....C3
Grove,The....A1
Hallgarth St....C3
Hatfield College....B2
Hawthorn Terr....B1
Heritage Centre....B3
HM Prison....B3
Information Ctr....B3
John St....B1
Kingsgate Bridge....B2
Laburnum Terr....B1
Lawson Terr....B1
Leazes Rd....B2/B3
Library....B1
Library....C3
Margery La....B1
Market....B2
Mavin St....C3
Millburngate....B2
Millburngate Bridge....B2
Millennium Bridge (foot/cycle)....B2
Mountjoy Research Centre....C3
Museum of Archaeology....B2
Nevilledale Terr....B1
New Elvet....B2
New Elvet Bridge....B3
North Bailey....B3
North End....A1
North Rd....A1/B2
Observatory....C1
Old Elvet....B2
Open Treasure....B2
Oriental Mus....C2
Oswald Court....C1
Parkside....B2
Passport Office....B1
Percy Terr....B1
Pimlico....C2
Police Station....B2
Post Office....A1/B2
Potters Bank....C1/C2
Prebends Bridge....C2
Prebends Walk....C2
Prince Bishops Shopping Centre....B2
Princes St....A3
Providence Row....A3
Quarryheads La....C2
Redhills La....B1
Redhills Terr....B1
Riverwalk,The....B2
Saddler St....B2
St Chad's College....B3
St Cuthbert's Society....B2
St John's College....B3
St Margaret's....B2
St Mary the Less....C2
St Mary's College....C2
St Monica Grove....B1
St Nicholas'....B2
St Oswald's....C3
Sands,The....A3
Shopmobility....B2
Sidegate....B2
Silver St....B2
Sixth Form College....C1
South Bailey....C2
South Rd....C3
South St....B2
Springwell Ave....A1
Stockton Rd....C2
Student Union....B3
Sutton St....B1
Town Hall....B2
Univ Arts Block....C2
University Coll ✦....B2
Walkergate Centre....B2
Wearside Dr....A1
Western Hill....A1
Wharton Park....A2
Whinney Hill....C3
Whitehouse Ave....C1
YHA ▲....B2

Edinburgh 182
Abbey Strand....B6
Abbeyhill....A6
Abbeyhill Cres....A6
Abbeymount....A6
Abercromby Place....A3
Adam St....C4
Albany La....A4
Albany St....A4
Albert Memorial ✦....B2
Albyn Place....A2
Alva Place....A6
Alva St....B1
Ann St....A1
Appleton Tower....C4
Archibald Place....C3

Assembly Rooms & Musical Hall....A3
Atholl Cres....B1
Atholl Crescent La....C1
Bank St....B4
Barony St....A4
Beaumont Place....C5
Belford Rd....B1
Belgrave Cres....A1
Belgrave Cres La....A1
Bell's Brae....B1
Blackfriars St....B4
Blair St....B4
Bread St....C2
Bristo Place....C4
Bristo St....C4
Broughton St....A4
Brown St....C5
Brunton Terr....A6
Buckingham Terr....A1
Burial Ground....A6
Bus Station....A4
Caledonian Cres....C1
Caledonian Rd....C1
Calton Hill....A4
Calton Hill....A4
Calton Rd....B4
Camera Obscura & Outlook Tower ✦....B3
Candlemaker Row....C4
Canning St....C1
Canongate....B5
Canongate....A6
Carlton St....A1
Carlton Terr....A6
Carlton Terrace La....A6
Castle St....B2
Castle Terr....B2
Castlehill....B3
Central Library....B4
Chalmers St....C3
Chambers St....C4
Chapel St....C4
Charles St....C4
Charlotte Sq....B2
Chester St....B1
Circus La....A2
Circus Place....A2
City Art Centre ✦....B4
City Chambers....B4
City Observatory ✦....A5
Clarendon Crescent....A1
Clerk St....C5
Coates Cres....B1
Cockburn St....B4
College of Art....C3
Comely Bank Ave....A1
Comely Bank Row....A1
Cornwall St....C2
Cowans Cl....B5
Cowgate....B4
Cranston St....B5
Crichton St....C4
Croft-An-Righ....A6
Cumberland St....A2
Dalry Place....C1
Dalry Rd....C1
Danube St....A1
Darnaway St....A2
David Hume Tower....C5
Davie St....C5
Dean Bridge....A1
Dean Gdns....A1
Dean Park Cres....A1
Dean Park Mews....A1
Dean Path....A1
Dean St....A1
Dean Terr....A1
Dewar Place....C1
Dewar Place La....C1
Doune Terr....A2
Drummond Place....A3
Drummond St....C5
Drumsheugh Gdns....B1
Dublin Mews....A3
Dublin St....A4
Dublin St La South....A4
Dumbiedykes Rd....B5
Dundas St....A3
Dynamic Earth ✦....B6
Earl Grey St....C2
East Crosscauseway....C5
East Market St....B4
East Norton Place....A6
East Princes St Gdns....B3
Easter Rd....A6
Edinburgh (Waverley) ⇌....B4
Edinburgh Castle....B3
Edinburgh Dungeon ✦....B4
Edinburgh Int Conference Ctr....C2
Elder St....A4
Esplanade....B3
Eton Terr....A1
Eye Pavilion....C2
Festival Office
Festival Theatre Edinburgh....C4
Filmhouse....C2
Fire Station....C2
Floral Clock ✦....B3
Forres St....A2
Forth St....A4
Fountainbridge....C1
Frederick St....A3
Freemasons' Hall....B3
Fruitmarket ✦....B4
Gardner's Cres....C1
George Heriot's School....C3
George IV Bridge....B4
George Sq....C4
George Sq La....C4
George St....B2
Georgian House....B2
Gladstone's Land ✦....B3
Glen St....C3
Gloucester La....A2
Gloucester Place....A2
Gloucester St....A2
Graham St....C1
Grassmarket....C3
Great King St....A2
Great Stuart....B2
Greenside La....A5
Greenside Row....A5
Greyfriars Kirk ✦....C4
Grindlay St....C2

Grosvenor St....C1
Grove St....C1
Gullan's Cl....B5
Guthrie St....B4
Hanover St....A3
Hart St....A4
Haymarket....C1
Haymarket Sta ⇌....C1
Heriot Place....C3
Heriot Row....A2
High School Yard....B5
High St....B4
Hill Place....C5
Hill St....A2
Hillside Cres....A5
Holyrood Abbey, remains of (AD 1128)....A6
Holyrood Gait....B6
Holyrood Park....B6
Holyrood Rd....B5
Home St....C2
Hope St....B2
Horse Wynd....B6
Howden St....C5
Howe St....A2
Hub,The ✦....B3
India Place....A2
India St....A2
Infirmary St....B4
Information Ctr....B4
Jeffrey St....B4
John Knox Ho ✦....B4
Johnston Terr....C3
Keir St....C3
Kerr St....A1
King's Stables Rd....B2
Lady Lawson St....C3
Lauriston Gdns....C3
Lauriston Park....C3
Lauriston Place....C3
Lauriston St....C3
Lawnmarket....B3
Learmonth Gdns....A1
Learmonth Terr....A1
Leith St....A4
Lennox St....A1
Lennox St La....A1
Leslie Place....A1
London Rd....A5
Lothian Rd....B2
Lothian St....C4
Lower Menz Place....A6
Lynedoch Place....B1
Manor Place....B1
Market St....B4
Marshall St....C4
Maryfield....A6
McEwan Hall....C4
Medical School....C4
Melville St....B1
Meuse La....B3
Middle Mdw Walk....C4
Milton St....A6
Montrose Terr....A6
Moray Place....A2
Morrison Link....C1
Morrison St....C1
Mound Place....B3
Mound,The....B3
Multrees Walk....A4
Mus Collections Ctr....A4
Museum of Childhood....B5
Museum of Edinburgh....B5
Museum of Scotland....B4
Museum on the Mound....B4
National Archives of Scotland....A4
National Museum of Scotland....B4
National Gallery....B3
National Library of Scotland....B4
National Monument ✦....A5
National Portrait Gallery....A4
National War Museum....B3
Nelson Monument ✦....A5
Nelson St....A4
New St....B5
Nicolson Sq....C4
Nicolson St....C4
Niddry St....B4
North Bank St....B4
North Bridge....B4
North Castle St....A2
North Charlotte St....A2
North Meadow Walk....C4
North St Andrew St....A4
North St David St....A3
North West Circus Place....A2
Northumberland St....A3
Odeon....C4
Old Royal High School....A5
Old Tolbooth Wynd....B5
OMNi Centre ✦....A4
Oxford Terr....A1
Palace of Holyroodhouse....B6
Palmerston Place....B1
Panmure Place....C3
Parliament Sq....B4
People's Story, The ✦....B5
Playhouse Theatre ✦....A4
Pleasance....C5
Police Station....C2
Ponton St....C2
Post Office....A4/B5/C1/C2/C4
Potterrow....C4
Princes Mall....B4
Princes St....B3
Princes St ⇌....B3
Prisoners of War ✦....B3
Queen's Gallery ✦....B6
Queen St....A2
Queen Street Gdns....A3
Queen's Dr....B6/C6
Queensferry Rd....A1
Queensferry St....B1
Queensferry St La....B1
Radical Rd....C6
Randolph Cres....A1
Regent Gdns....A5
Regent Rd....A5
Regent Rd Park....A6

Regent Terr....A5
Richmond La....C5
Richmond Place....C5
Rose St....B2
Ross Open Air Theatre....B3
Rothesay Place....B1
Rothesay Terr....B1
Roxburgh Place....C5
Roxburgh St....C5
Royal Bank of Scotland....A4
Royal Circus....A2
Royal Lyceum ✦....C2
Royal Mile,The....B5
Royal Scottish Academy....B3
Royal Terr....A5
Royal Terrace Gdns....A5
Rutland Sq....B2
Rutland St....B2
St Andrew Sq....A4
St Andrew's House....A4
St Bernard's Cres....A1
St Bernard's Well ✦....A1
St Cecilia's Hall....B4
St Colme St....A2
St Cuthbert's ✦....B2
St Giles'....B4
St John St....B5
St John's ✦....B2
St John's Hill....B5
St Leonard's Hill....C5
St Leonard's La....C5
St Leonard's St....C5
St Mary's....A4
St Mary's Scottish Episcopal....B1
St Mary's St....B4
St Michael & All Saints....C3
St Stephen St....A2
Salisbury Crags....C6
Saunders St....A2
Scotch Whisky Experience ✦....B3
Scott Monument ✦....B4
Scottish Parliament....B6
Scottish Storytelling Centre ✦....B5
Semple St....C2
Shandwick Place....B1
South Bridge....B4
South Charlotte St....B2
South College St....C4
South Learmonth Gdns....A1
South St Andrew St....A4
South St David St....A3
Spittal St....C2
Stafford St....B1
Student Centre....C4
Surgeons' Hall....C5
Supreme Courts....B4
Teviot Place....C4
Thistle St....A3
Torphichen Place....C1
Torphichen St....C1
Traverse Theatre ✦....C2
Tron Sq....B4
Tron,The ✦....B4
Union St....A4
University....C4
University Library....C4
Univ of Edinburgh....B5
Upper Grove Place....C1
Usher Hall ✦....C2
Vennel....C3
Victoria St....B3
Viewcraig Gdns....B5
Viewcraig St....B5
Vue....A4
Walker St....B1
Waterloo Place....A4
Waverley Bridge....B4
Wemyss Place....A2
West Approach Rd....C1
West Crosscauseway....C5
West End Princess St ✦....B1
West Maitland St....B1
West of Nicholson St....C4
West Port....C3
West Princes Street Gardens....B3
West Richmond St....C4
West Tollcross....C2
White Horse Cl ✦....B6
William St....B1
Windsor St....A5
Writer's Museum, The ✦....B4
York La....A4
York Place....A4
York Place ⇌....A4
Young St....B2

Exeter 182
Alphington St....C1
Athelstan Rd....B3
Bampfylde St....B2
Barnardo Rd....C2
Barnfield Hill....B3
Barnfield Rd....B2/B3
Barnfield Theatre ✦....B2
Bartholomew St East....B1
Bartholomew St West....B1
Bear St....B2
Beaufort Rd....C1
Bedford St....B2
Belgrave Rd....A3
Belmont Rd....A3
Blackall Rd....A2
Blackboy Rd....A3
Bull Meadow Rd....C2
Bus & Coach Sta....B3
Castle St....B2
Cecil Rd....C1
Cheeke St....A3
Church Rd....C1
Chute St....A3
City Wall....B1/B2
Civic Centre....B2
Clifton Rd....B3
Clifton St....B3
Clock Tower....B1
College Rd....B3
Colleton Cres....C2

Commercial Rd....C1
Coombe St....C2
Cowick St....C1
Crown Courts....B1
Custom House....C2
Cygnet New Theatre ✦....B2
Danes' Rd....A2
Denmark Rd....B3
Devon County Hall....C3
Devonshire Place....A3
Dinham Cres....B1
East Grove Rd....C3
Edmund St....C1
Elmgrove Rd....A3
Exe St....B1
Exeter Cathedral....B2
Exeter Central Station ⇌....B2
Exeter City Football Ground....A3
Exeter College....B2
Exeter Picture House....B2
Fire Station....B1
Fore St....B1
Friars Walk....C2
Guildhall....B2
Guildhall Shopping Centre....B2
Harlequins Shopping Centre....B1
Haven Rd....C2
Heavitree Rd....B3
Hele Rd....A1
High St....B2
HM Prison....A2
Holloway St....C2
Hoopern St....A2
Horseguards....A2
Howell Rd....A1
Information Ctr....B2
Iron Bridge....B1
Isca Rd....C1
Jesmond Rd....A3
King St....B1
King William St....A2
Larkbeare Rd....C2
Leisure Centre....C1
Library....C1
Longbrook St....A2
Longbrook Terr....A2
Lower North St....B1
Lucky La....C2
Lyndhurst Rd....C3
Magdalen Rd....C3
Magdalen St....C2
Market....B2
Market St....B2
Marlborough Rd....C3
Mary Arches St....B1
Matford Ave....C2
Matford La....C3
Matford Rd....C3
May St....A3
Mol's Coffee House ✦....B2
New Bridge St....B1
New North Rd....A1/A2
North St....B1
Northernhay St....B1
Norwood Ave....C3
Odeon....B2
Okehampton St....C1
Old Mill Close....C2
Old Tiverton Rd....A3
Oxford Rd....A3
Paris St....B2
Parr St....A3
Paul St....B1
Pennsylvania Rd....A2
Police HQ....B1
Portland Street....A3
Post Office....A3/B2/B3/C1
Powderham Cres....A3
Preston St....B1
Princesshay Shopping Centre....B2
Pyramids Leisure Centre....C2
Quay,The....C2
Queen St....B1
Queen's Terr....A1
Queens Rd....C1
Radford Rd....C2
Richmond Rd....B1
Roberts Rd....C2
Rougemont Castle....B2
Rougemont Ho ✦....B2
Royal Albert Memorial Museum ✦....B2
St David's Hill....A1
St James' Pk Sta ⇌....A2
St James' Rd....A3
St Leonard's Rd....C3
St Mary Steps....C1
St Nicholas Priory....B1
St Thomas Sta ⇌....C1
Sandford Walk....A3
School for the Deaf....A2
School Rd....C1
Sidwell St....A2
Smythen St....B1
South St....B2
Southernhay East....B2
Southernhay West....B2
Spacex Gallery ✦....B2
Spicer Rd....B3
Sports Centre....A3
Summerland St....A3
Sydney Rd....C1
Tan La....C2
Thornton Hill....A2
Topsham Rd....C3
Tucker's Hall....B1
Tudor St....B1
Underground Passages ✦....B2
University of Exeter (St Luke's Campus)....B3
Velwell Rd....A1
Verney St....A3
Water La....C1/C2
Weirfield Rd....C2
Well St....A2
West Ave....A1
West Grove Rd....C3
Western Way....A3/B1/B2
Willeys Ave....C1
Wonford Rd....B3/C3
York Rd....A2

Glasgow 183
Admiral St....C2
Albert Bridge....C5
Albion St....B5
Anderston ⇌....B3
Anderston Quay....B3
Argyle Arcade....B5
Argyle St....A1/A2/B3/B4/B5
Argyle Street ⇌....B5
Arlington St....A3
Arts Centre....A3
Ashley St....A3
Bain St....C6
Baird St....A6
Baliol St....A3
Ballater St....C5
Barras (Mkt),The....C6
Bath St....B3
BBC Scotland....B1
Bell St....B5
Bell's Bridge....C1
Bentinck St....A2
Berkeley St....B2
Bishop La....B3
Black St....A6
Blackburn St....C2
Blackfriars St....B5
Blantyre St....A1
Blythswood Sq....B3
Blythswood St....B4
Bothwell St....B3
Brand St....C1
Breadalbane St....A2
Bridge St....C4
Bridgegate....C5
Briggait....C5
Broomielaw....B4
Broomielaw Quay Gdns....B4
Brown St....B4
Brunswick St....B5
Buccleuch St....A3
Buchanan Bus Sta....A5
Buchanan Galleries....A5
Buchanan St....B5
Buchanan St....B5
Cadogan St....B4
Caledonian Univ....A5
Calgary St....A5
Cambridge St....A4
Canal St....A5
Candleriggs....B5
Carlton Place....C4
Carnarvon St....A3
Carrick St....B4
Castle St....B6
Cathedral Sq....B6
Cathedral St....B5
Central Mosque....C5
Ctr for Contemporary Arts....A3
Centre St....C4
Cessnock....C1
Cessnock St....C1
Charing Cross ⇌....A3
Charlotte St....C5
Cheapside St....B3
Cineworld ✦....A4
Citizens' Theatre ✦....C5
City Chambers Complex....B5
City Halls....B5
City of Glasgow Coll (City Campus)....B6
City of Glasgow Coll (Riverside Campus)....C5
Clairmont Gdns....A2
Claremont St....A2
Claremont Terr....A2
Claythorne St....C6
Cleveland St....A3
Clifford La....C1
Clifford St....C1
Clifton Place....A2
Clifton St....A2
Clutha St....C1
Clyde Arc....C1
Clyde Place....C4
Clyde Place Quay....C4
Clyde St....B5
Clyde Walkway....C5
Clydeside Expressway....B1
Coburg St....C4
Cochrane St....B5
College St....B5
Collins St....B6
Commerce St....C4
Cook St....C4
Cornwall St....C1
Couper St....A5
Cowcaddens....A4
Cowcaddens Rd....A5
Crimea St....B4
Custom House Quay Gardens....C5
Dalhousie St....A4
Dental Hospital....A4
Derby St....A2
Dobbie's Loan....A4/A5
Dobbie's Loan Place....A5
Doulton Fountain ✦....C6
Dover St....A2
Drury St....B4
Drygate....B6
Duke St....B6
Dunaskin St....A1
Dunblane St....A4
Dundas St....B5
Dunlop St....B5
East Campbell St....C6
Eastvale Place....A1
Eglinton St....C4
Elderslie St....A2
Elliot St....B2
Elmbank St....A3
Esmond St....A1
Exhibition Ctr ⇌....B1
Festival Park....C1
Film Theatre ✦....A3
Finnieston Quay....B1
Finnieston St....B1
Fire Station....C6
Florence St....C5
Fox St....C5
Gallowgate....C6
Garnet St....A3
Garnethill St....A4
Garscube Rd....A4

George Sq....B5
George St....B5
George V Bridge....C4
Gilbert St....A1
Glasgow Bridge....C4
Glasgow Cath....B6
Glasgow Central ⇌....B4
Glasgow City Free Church....B5
Glasgow Green....C6
Glasgow Necropolis ✦....B6
Glasgow Royal Concert Hall....A5
Glasgow Science Centre ✦....B1
Glasgow Tower ✦....B1
Glassford St....B5
Glebe St....A6
Gorbals Cross....C5
Gordon St....B4
Govan Rd....B1/C1/C2
Grace St....B2
Grafton Place....A5
Grand Ole Opry ✦....C2
Granby La....A2
Granville St....A3
Gray St....A2
Greendyke St....C6
Grey Eagle St....B7
Harley St....A1
Harvie St....C1
Haugh Rd....A1
Havannah St....B6
Heliport....B1
Henry Wood Hall ✦....A2
High Court....C5
High St....B6
High St ⇌....B6
Hill St....A3
Holland St....A3
Holm St....B4
Hope St....A5
Houldsworth St....B2
Houston St....C2
Howard St....C5
Hunter St....C6
Hutcheson St....B5
Hydepark St....B3
Imax Cinema ✦....B1
India St....A3
Information Ctr....B5
Ingram St....B5
Jamaica St....B4
James Watt St....B4
John Knox St....B6
John St....B5
Kelvin Hall ✦....A1
Kelvin Statue ✦....A2
Kelvin Way....A2
Kelvingrove Art Gallery & Mus....A1
Kelvingrove Park....A2
Kelvingrove St....A2
Kelvinhaugh St....A1
Kennedy St....A6
Kent Rd....A2
Killermont St....A5
King St....B5
King's,The ✦....A3
Kingston Bridge....C3
Kingston St....C4
Kinning Park....C2
Kyle St....A5
Lancefield Quay....B2
Lancefield St....B2
Langshot St....C1
Lendel Place....C1
Lighthouse,The ✦....B4
Lister St....A6
Little St....B3
London Rd....C6
Lorne St....C1
Lower Harbour....B1
Lumsden St....A1
Lymburn St....A1
Lyndoch Cres....A2
Lyndoch Place....A3
Lyndoch St....A3
Maclellan St....C1
Mair St....C2
Maitland St....A4
Mansell St....C7
Mavisbank Gdns....C1
Mcalpine St....B3
Mcaslin St....A6
McLean Sq....C2
McLellan Gallery....A4
McPhater St....A4
Merchants' Ho....B5
Middlesex St....C2
Middleton St....C1
Midland St....B4
Miller St....B5
Millennium Bridge....B1
Millroad St....C6
Minpark St....C2
Milton St....A4
Minerva St....B2
Mitchell St West....B4
Mitchell Library ✦....A3
Modern Art Gall....B5
Molendinar St....C6
Moncur St....C6
Montieth Row....C6
Montrose St....B5
Morrison St....C3
Nairn St....A1
National Piping Centre,The ✦....A5
Nelson Mandela Sq....B5
Nelson's Monument ✦....C6
Newton Place....A2
Nicholson St....C4
Nile St....B5
Norfolk Court....C4
North Frederick St....B5
North Hanover St....B5
North Portland St....B6
North Wallace St....A5

Paisley Rd....C3
Paisley Rd West....C1
Park Circus....A2
Park Gdns....A2
Park St South....A2
Park Terr....A2
Parkgrove Terr....C5
Parnie St....C5
Parson St....A6
Partick Bridge....A1
Passport Office....B4
Pavilion Theatre ✦....A4
Pembroke St....A2
People's Palace....C6
Pinkston Rd....A6
Pitt St....A4/B4
Plantation Park....C1
Plantation Quay....C1
Police Mus....B5
Police Station....A4/A6
Port Dundas Rd....A5
Port St....A2
Portman St....C2
Prince's Dock....C1
Princes Sq....B5
Provand's Lordship....B6
Queen St....B5
Queen Street ⇌....B5
Ramshorn....B5
Renfrew St....A3/A4
Renton St....A5
Richmond St....B5
Robertson St....B4
Rose St....A4
Rottenrow....B5
Royal Concert Hall....A5
Royal Conservatoire of Scotland....A4
Royal Cres....A2
Royal Exchange Sq....B5
Royal Highland Fusiliers Mus....A3
West Glasgow Ambulatory Care....A1
Royal Infirmary....B6
Royal Terr....A2
Rutland Cres....C2
St Andrew's in the Square ✦....C6
St Andrew's (RC)....C5
St Andrew's St....C5
St Enoch....B5
St Enoch Shopping Centre....B5
St Enoch Sq....B5
St George's Rd....A3
St James Rd....B6
St Kent St....C6
St Mungo Ave....A5/A6
St Mungo Museum of Religious Life & Art ✦....B6
St Mungo Place....B6
St Vincent Cres....A2
St Vincent Place....B5
St Vincent St....B3/B4
St Vincent Terr....A2
Saltmarket....C5
Sandyford Place....A2
Sauchiehall St....A2/A4
School of Art....A4
SEC Armadillo....B1
Sclater St....B7
Scotland St....C2
Scott St....A4
Scottish Exhibition & Conference Ctr....B1
Seaward St....C2
Shaftesbury St....A2
Sheriff Court....C5
Shields Rd....C3
Shopmobility....B5
Shuttle St....B5
Somerset Place....A2
South Portland St....C4
Springburn Rd....A6
Springfield Quay....C3
SSE Hydro The ✦....B1
Stanley St....C2
Stevenson St....C6
Stewart St....A4
Stirling Rd....B6
Stobcross Quay....B1
Stobcross St....B1
Stock Exchange....B5
Stockwell Place....C5
Stockwell St....C5
Stow College....A4
Sussex St....C2
Synagogue....A2
Taylor Place....A6
Tenement House....A3
Teviot St....A1
Theatre Royal ✦....A4
Tolbooth Steeple & Mercat Cross ✦....C6
Tower St....C2
Trades House....B5
Tradeston St....C4
Transport Mus....A1
Tron ✦....C4
Trongate....C5
Tunnel St....B1
Turnbull St....C5
Union St....B4
Univ of Strathclyde....B6
Victoria Bridge....C5
Virginia St....B5
Wallace St....C3
Walls St....B5
Walmer Cres....C1
Warrock St....B3
Washington St....B3
Waterloo St....B4
Watson St....C5
Watt St....C2
Wellington St....B4
West Campbell St....B4
West George St....B4
West Graham St....A3
West Greenhill Place....B2
West Regent St....B4
West Regent St....B3
West Regent St....B4
West St....C3
Whitehall St....B3
Wilkes St....C7
Wilson St....B5
Woodlands Gate....A2
Woodlands Rd....A2
Woodlands Rd....A3
Woodside Place....A3
Woodside Terr....A3

Gloucester • Grimsby • Harrogate • Hull • Inverness • Ipswich • Kendal • King's Lynn • Lancaster 205

York St B4
Yorkhill Pde A1
Yorkhill St A1

Gloucester 182

Albion St C1
Alexandra Rd B3
Alfred St C3
All Saints Rd C2
Alvin St B2
Arthur St C2
Barrack Square B1
Barton St C2
Blackfriars † B1
Blenheim Rd C2
Bristol Rd C1
Brunswick Rd C2
Bruton Way B2
Bus Station B2
Cineworld C1
City Council Offices B1
City Mus, Art Gallery & Library B2
Clarence St B2
Commercial Rd B1
Council Offices B1
Courts B1
Cromwell St C2
Deans Way A2
Denmark Rd A3
Derby Rd C3
Docks ✦ C1
Eastgate St B2
Eastgate,The B1
Edwy Pde A2
Estcourt Cl A3
Estcourt Rd A3
Falkner St C2
GL1 Leisure Centre C2
Gloucester Cath † B1
Gloucester Life B1
Gloucester Quays Outlet C1
Gloucester Sta B2
Gloucester Waterways C1
Gloucestershire Archive B2
Gloucestershire Royal Hospital (A&E) B3
Goodyere St C2
Gouda Way A1
Great Western Rd B3
Guildhall B2
Heathville Rd A3
Henry Rd B3
Henry St B2
Hinton Rd A2
India Rd C3
Information Ctr B1
Jersey Rd C3
King's B2
King's Walk Shopping Centre B2
Kingsholm (Gloucester Rugby) A2
Kingsholm Rd A2
Lansdown Rd A3
Library C2
Llanthony Rd C1
London Rd B3
Longhorn Ave A1
Longsmith St B1
Malvern Rd A3
Market B2
Market Parade B2
Mercia Rd A1
Metz Way C3
Midland Rd C2
Millbrook St C3
Montpellier C1
Napier St C3
Nettleton Rd C2
New Inn B2
New Olympus C3
North Rd A3
Northgate St B2
Oxford Rd A2
Oxford St B2
Park & Ride Gloucester A1
Park Rd C2
Park St B2
Park,The C2
Parliament St C1
Peel Centre,The C1
Pitt St B1
Police Station C3
Post Office B2
Quay St B1
Quay,The B1
Recreation Gd A1/A2
Regent St C2
Robert Raikes Ho B1
Royal Oak Rd B1
Russell St B2
Ryecroft St C2
St Aldate St B2
St Ann Way C1
St Catherine St A2
St Mark St A2
St Mary de Crypt B1
St Mary de Lode B1
St Nicholas's B1
St Oswald's Rd A1
St Oswald's Retail Park A1
St Peter's B2
Seabroke Rd A3
Sebert St A2
Severn Rd C1
Sherborne St B2
Shire Hall B1
Sidney St C3
Soldiers of Gloucestershire B1
Southgate St B1/C1
Spa Field C1
Spa Rd C1
Sports Ground A2/B2
Station Rd B2
Stratton Rd C3
Stroud Rd C1
Superstore A1
Swan Rd A2
Trier Way C1/C2
Union St A2
Vauxhall Rd C3
Victoria St C2
Walham Lane A1
Wellington St C2
Westgate Retail Pk B1
Westgate St B1
Widden St C2
Worcester St B2

Grimsby 183

Abbey Drive East C2
Abbey Drive West C2
Abbey Park Rd C2
Abbey Rd C2
Abbey Walk C2
Abbeygate Shopping Centre C2
Abbotsway C2
Adam Smith St A1/A2
Ainslie St C2
Albert St A3
Alexandra Dock A2/B2
Alexandra Rd A2/B2
Alexandra Retail Pk A2
Annesley St A2
Armstrong St A1
Arthur St B1
Augusta St C1
Bargate C1
Beeson St A1
Bethlehem St C2
Bodiam Way B3
Bradley St B3
Brighowgate C1/C2
Bus Station C2
Canterbury Dr C1
Cartergate B1/C1
Catherine St C3
Caxton A3
Chantry La B1
Charlton St A1
Church La C2
Church St A3
Cleethorpe Rd A3
Close,The C1
College St C1
Compton Dr C1
Corporation Bridge A2
Corporation Rd A1
Court B3
Crescent St B1
Deansgate C1
Doughty Rd C2
Dover St B1
Duchess St C2
Dudley St C1
Duke of York Gardens B1
Duncombe St B3
Earl La B1
East Marsh St B3
East St B2
Eastgate B3
Eastside Rd A3
Eaton Ct C1
Eleanor St B3
Ellis Way B3
Fisherman's Chapel A3
Fisherman's Wharf B2
Fishing Heritage Centre B2
Flour Sq A3
Frederick St B1
Frederick Ward Way B2
Freeman St A3/B3
Freshney Dr B1
Freshney Place B2
Garden St C2
Garibaldi St A3
Garth La B2
Grime St B3
Grimsby Docks Station A3
Grimsby Town Station C2
Hainton Ave C3
Har Way B3
Hare St C3
Harrison St B1
Haven Ave B1
Hay Croft Ave B1
Hay Croft St B1
Heneage Rd B3/C3
Henry St B1
Holme St B3
Hume St C1
James St B1
Joseph St B1
Kent St A3
King Edward St A3
Lambert Rd C2
Library B2
Lime St B1
Lister St B1
Littlefield La C1
Lockhill A3
Lord St B1
Lower Spring St A3
Ludford St C3
Macaulay St B1
Mallard Mews C3
Manor Ave C2
Market A3
Market Hall B2
Market St B3
Moss Rd C2
Nelson St A3
New St B2
Osbourne St B2
Pasture St B3
Peaks Parkway C3
Pelham Rd C1
Police Station B3
Post Office B1/B2
Pyewipe Rd A1
Railway Place A3
Railway St A3
Recreation Ground C2
Rendel St A2
Retail Park A2/B3
Richard St B1
Ripon St B1
Robinson St East B3
Royal St A3
St Hilda's Ave C1
St James C2
Sheepfold St B3/C3
Shopmobility B2
Sixhills St C3
South Park B2
Superstore B3/B2
Tasburgh St C3
Tennyson St B2
Thesiger St A3
Time Trap C2
Town Hall B2
Veal St B1
Victoria Retail Park A3
Victoria St North A2
Victoria St South B2
Victoria St West B2
Watkin St A1
Welholme Ave C2
Welholme Rd C3
Wellington St B3
Wellowgate C2
Werneth Rd B3
West Coates Rd A1
Westgate A2
Westminster Dr C1
Willingham St C3
Wintringham Rd C2
Wood St B3
Yarborough Dr B1
Yarborough Hotel C2

Harrogate 183

Albert St C2
Alexandra Rd B2
Arthington Ave B2
Ashfield Rd A2
Back Cheltenham Mount B2
Beech Grove C1
Belmont Rd C1
Bilton Dr A2
BMI The Duchy Hospital C1
Bower Rd B2
Bower St B2
Bus Station B2
Cambridge Rd B2
Cambridge St B2
Cemetery A2
Chatsworth Grove A2
Chatsworth Place A2
Chatsworth Rd A2
Chelmsford Rd B3
Cheltenham Cres B2
Cheltenham Mt B2
Cheltenham Pde B2
Christ Church B3
Christ Church Oval B3
Chudleigh Rd B3
Clarence Dr B1
Claro Rd A3
Claro Way A3
Coach Park B2
Coach Rd B3
Cold Bath Rd C1
Commercial St B2
Coppice Ave A1
Coppice Dr A1
Coppice Gate A1
Cornwall Rd B1
Council Offices B1
Crescent Gdns B1
Crescent Rd B1
Dawson Terr A2
Devonshire Place B3
Dixon Rd A2
Dixon Terr A2
Dragon Ave B3
Dragon Parade B2
Dragon Rd B2
Duchy Rd B1
East Parade B2
East Park Rd C3
Esplanade B1
Everyman B2
Fire Station A2
Franklin Mount A2
Franklin Rd B2
Franklin Square A2
Glebe Rd C1
Grove Park Ct A3
Grove Park Terr A3
Grove Rd A2
Hampsthwaite Rd A1
Harcourt Dr B3
Harcourt Rd B3
Harrogate B2
Harrogate Convention Ctr B1
Harrogate Justice Ctr (Magistrates' and County Courts) C2
Harrogate Ladies College B1
Harrogate Theatre B2
Heywood Rd C1
Hollins Cres A1
Hollins Mews A1
Hollins Rd A1
Hydro Leisure Centre,The A1
Information Ctr B1
James St B2
Jenny Field Dr A1
John St B2
Kent Dr A1
Kent Rd A1
Kings Rd A2
Kingsway B3
Kingsway Dr B3
Lancaster Rd C1
Leeds Rd C2
Lime Grove B3
Lime St A3
Mayfield Grove B2
Mercer B1
Montpellier Hill B1
Mornington Cres A3
Mornington Terr B3
Mowbray Sq B3
North Park Rd B3
Oakdale Ave A1
Oatlands Dr C3
Odeon B2
Osborne Rd A2
Otley Rd C2
Oxford St B2
Parade,The B2
Park Chase B3
Park Parade B3
Park View B2
Parliament St B1
Police Station B3
Post Office B2/C1
Providence Terr A2
Queen Parade C3
Queen's Rd C1
Raglan St C2
Regent Ave A3
Regent Grove A3
Regent Parade A3
Regent St A3
Regent Terr A3
Ripon Rd A1
Robert St C2
Royal Baths & Turkish Baths B1
Royal Pump Room B1
St Luke's Mount A2
St Mary's Ave C1
St Mary's Walk C1
Scargill Rd A1
Skipton Rd A3
Skipton St A2
Slingsby Walk C3
South Park Rd C2
Spring Grove A1
Springfield Ave B1
Station Ave B2
Station Parade B2
Stray Rein C3
Stray,The C2/C3
Studley Rd A2
Superstore B2/C1
Swan Rd B1
Tower St C2
Trinity Rd C2
Union St B2
Valley Dr C1
Valley Gardens C1
Valley Mount C1
Victoria Ave C2
Victoria Rd C1
Victoria Shopping Centre B2
Waterloo St A2
West Park C2
West Park St C2
Wood View A1
Woodfield Ave A3
Woodfield Dr A3
Woodfield Grove A3
Woodfield Rd A3
Woodfield Square A3
Woodside B3
York Place C3
York Rd B1

Hull 184

Adelaide St C1
Albert Dock C1
Albion St B2
Alfred Gelder St B2
Anlaby Rd B1
Arctic Corsair ✦ B3
Beverley Rd A1
Blanket Row C2
Bond St B2
Bonus Arena B2
Bridlington Ave A2
Brook St B1
Brunswick Ave A1
Bus Station B1
Camilla Cl C3
Cannon St A2
Caroline St A2
Carr La B2
Castle St C2
Central Library B1
Charles St A2
Citadel Way B3
City Hall B2
City Hall Theatre B2
Clarence St B3
Cleveland St A3
Clifton St A1
Colonial St B1
Court B2
Deep,The C3
Dinostar C2
Dock Office Row B3
Dock St B2
Drypool Bridge B3
Egton St A3
English St C1
Ferens Gallery B2
Ferensway B1
Fire Sta A1
Francis St A2
Francis St West A2
Freehold St A1
Freetown Way A2
FrüitTheatre C2
Garrison Rd B3
George St B2
Gibson St A2
Great Thornton St B1
Great Union St A3
Green La A2
Grey St A1
Grimston St B2
Grosvenor St A1
Guildhall B2
Guildhall Rd B2
Hands-on History B2
Harley St A1
Hessle Rd C1
High St B3
Hull Minster B2
Hull Paragon Interchange Sta B1
Hull & East Riding Museum B3
Hull Ice Arena C1
Hull College B3
Hull History Centre A2
Hull New Theatre A2
Hull Truck Theatre B1
Humber Dock Marina C2
Humber Dock St C2
Humber St C2
Hyperion St A3
Information Ctr B1
Jameson St B1
Jarratt St B2
Jenning St A3
King Billy Statue ✦ C2
King Edward St B2
King St A2
Kingston Retail Pk C1
Kingston St C2
Liddell St A1
Lime St A3
Lister St C1
Lockwood St A2
Maister House B3
Maritime Mus B2
Market B2
Market Place B2
Minerva Pier C2
Mulgrave St A3
Myton Swing Bridge C3
Myton St B1
NAPA (Northern Acad of Performing Arts) B1
Nelson St C2
New Cleveland St A3
New George St A2
Norfolk St A1
North Bridge A3
North St B1
Odeon C1
Old Harbour C3
Osborne St B1
Paragon St B2
Park St B1
Percy St A2
Pier St C2
Police Station B1
Porter St C1
Portland St B1
Post Office B1/B2
Posterngate B2
Prince's Quay B2
Prospect Centre B1
Prospect St B1
Queen's Gdns B2
Railway Dock Marina C2
Railway St C2
Real B1
Red Gallery B1
Reform St A2
Retail Park B1
Riverside Quay C2
Roper St B2
St James St C1
St Luke's St B1
St Mark St A3
St Mary the Virgin B3
St Stephens Shopping Centre B1
Scale Lane Footbridge B3
Scott St A2
South Bridge Rd B3
Sport's Centre C1
Spring Bank A1
Spring St B1
Spurn Lightship C2
Spyvee St A3
Stage @ the Dock C3
Streetlife Transport Museum B3
Sykes St A2
Tidal Surge Barrier ✦ C3
Tower St B3
Trinity House B2
Vane St A1
Victoria Pier ✦ C2
Waterhouse La B2
Waterloo St A1
Waverley St C1
Wellington St C2
Wellington St West C2
West St B1
Whitefriargate B2
Wilberforce Dr B2
Wilberforce Ho B3
Wilberforce Monument ✦ B3
William St C1
Wincolmlee A3
Witham A3
Wright St A1

Inverness 184

Abban St A1
Academy St B2
Alexander Place B2
Anderson St A2
Annfield Rd C3
Ardconnel St B3
Ardconnel Terr B3
Ardross Place B2
Ardross St B2
Argyle St B3
Argyle Terr B3
Attadale Rd B1
Ballifeary La C2
Ballifeary Rd C1/C2
Balnacraig La A1
Balnain House ✦ B2
Balnain St B2
Bank St B2
Bellfield Park C2
Bellfield Terr C3
Benula Rd A1
Birnie Terr A1
Bishop's Rd C2
Bowling Green C2
Bridge St B2
Brown St A2
Bruce Ave C1
Bruce Gdns C1
Bruce Pk C1
Burial Ground A2
Burnett Rd A3
Bus Station B3
Caledonian Rd B1
Cameron Rd A1
Cameron Sq A1
Carse Rd A1
Carsegate Rd Sth A1
Castle Garrison Encounter ✦ B2
Castle Rd B2
Castle St B3
Celt St B2
Chapel St A2
Charles St B3
Church St B2
Columba Rd B1/C1
Crown Ave B3
Crown Circus B3
Crown Dr B3
Crown Rd B3
Crown St B3
Culduthel Rd C3
Dalneigh Cres C1
Dalneigh Rd C1
Denny St B3
Dochfour Dr B1/C1
Douglas Row B2
Duffy Dr C3
Dunabban Rd A1
Dunain Rd B1
Duncraig St B2
Eastgate Shopping Centre B3
Eden Court C2
Fairfield Rd B1
Falcon Sq B3
Fire Station A3
Fraser St B2
Fraser St C2
Friars' Bridge A2
Friars' La B2
Friars' St A2
George St A2
Gilbert St A2
Glebe St A2
Glendoe Terr A1
Glenurquhart Rd C1
Gordon Terr B3
Gordonville Rd C2
Grant St A2
Grant Street Park (Clachnacuddin FC) A1
Greig St B2
Harbour Rd A3
Harrowden Rd B1
Haugh Rd C2
Heatherley Cres C3
High St B3
Highland Council HQ,The C2
Hill Park C3
Hill St B3
HM Prison B3
Huntly Place A2
Huntly St B2
India St A2
Industrial Estate A3
Information Ctr B2
Innes St A2
Inverness B3
Inverness High School B1
Inverness Museum & Art Gallery B2
Jamaica St A2
Kenneth St B2
Kilmuir Rd A1
King St B2
Kingsmills Rd B3
Laurel Ave B1/C1
Library A3
Lilac Grove B1
Lindsay Ave C1
Lochalsh Rd A1/B1
Longman Rd A3
Lotland Place A2
Lower Kessock St A1
Madras St A2
Maxwell Dr C1
Mayfield Rd C3
Millburn Rd B3
Mitchell's La C3
Montague Row B2
Muirfield Rd C3
Muirtown St B1
Nelson St A2
Ness Bank C2
Ness Bridge B2
Ness Walk B2/C2
Old Edinburgh Rd C3
Old High Church B2
Park Rd C1
Paton St C2
Perceval Rd B1
Planefield Rd B2
Police Station A3
Porterfield Bank C3
Porterfield Rd C3
Portland Place A2
Post Office A2/B1/B2
Queen St B2
Queensgate B2
Railway Terr A3
Rangemore Rd B1
Reay St B3
Riverside St A2
Rose St A2
Ross Ave B1
Rowan Rd B1
Royal Northern Infirmary C2
St Andrew's Cathedral † C2
St Columba B2
St John's Ave C1
St Mary's Ave C1
Sheriff Court B3
Shore St A2
Smith Ave C1
Southside Place C3
Southside Rd C3
Spectrum Centre B2
Strothers La B3
Superstore A1/B2
TA Centre C2
Telford Gdns B1
Telford Rd A1
Telford St A1
Tomnahurich Cemetery C1
Tomnahurich St B2
Town Hall B3
Union Rd B3
Union St B3
Victorian Market B3
Walker Place A2
Walker Rd A3
War Memorial ✦ C2
Waterloo Bridge A2
Wells St B1
Young St B2

Ipswich 184

Alderman Rd B2
All Saints' Rd A1
Alpe St B2
Ancaster Rd C1
Ancient House B3
Anglesea Rd B2
Ann St B2
Arboretum A2
Austin St C2
Avenue,The A3
Belstead Rd C2
Berners St B2
Bibb Way B1
Birkfield Dr C1
Black Horse La B2
Bolton La B3
Bond St C3
Bowthorpe Cl B2
Bramford La A1
Bramford Rd A1
Bridge St C2
Brookfield Rd A1
Brooks Hall Rd A1
Broomhill Park A2
Broomhill Rd A1
Broughton Rd A2
Bulwer Rd B1
Burrell Rd C2
Bus Station B3
Butter Market B2
Buttermarket Shopping Ctr,The B3
Cardinal Park Leisure Park C2
Carr St B3
Cecil Rd B2
Cecilia St C2
Chancery Rd C2
Charles St B2
Chevallier St A1
Christchurch Mansion & Wolsey Art Gallery B3
Christchurch Park A3
Christchurch St B3
Cineworld C2
Civic Centre B2
Civic Dr B2
Clarkson St B1
Cobbold St B3
Commercial Rd C2
Constable Rd A3
Constantine Rd C1
Constitution Hill A2
Corder Rd A3
Corn Exchange B2
Cotswold Ave A2
Council Offices C2
County Hall B3
Crown Court C2
Crown St B2
Cullingham Rd B1
Cumberland St B2
Curriers La B2
Dale Hall La A2
Dales View Rd A1
Dalton Rd B2
Dillwyn St B1
Elliot St B1
Elm St B2
Elsmere Rd A3
Falcon St C2
Felaw St C3
Fire Station C2
Flint Wharf C3
Fonnereau Rd B2
Fore St C3
Foundation St C3
Franciscan Way C2
Friars St C2
Gainsborough Rd A3
Gatacre Rd B1
Geneva Rd B2
Gippeswyk Ave C1
Gippeswyk Park C1
Grafton Way C2
Graham Rd A1
Great Whip St C3
Grimwade St C3
Handford Cut B1
Handford Rd B1
Henley Rd A2
Hervey St B3
High St B2
Holly Rd A2
Information Ctr B3
Ipswich Haven Marina ✦ C3
Ipswich Museum & Art Gallery B2
Ipswich School A2
Ipswich Station C2
Ipswich Town FC (Portman Road) C2
Ivry St A2
Kensington Rd A1
Kesteven Rd C1
Key St C3
Kingsfield Ave A3
Kitchener Rd A1
Little's Cres C2
London Rd B1
Low Brook St C3
Lower Orwell St C3
Luther Rd C2
Magistrates Court B2
Manor Rd A3
Mornington Ave A1
Museum St B2
Neale St B3
New Cardinal St C2
New Cut East C3
New Cut West C3
New Wolsey B2
Newson St B2
Norwich Rd A1/B1
Oban St B2
Old Custom Ho C3
Old Foundry Rd B3
Old Merchant's House C3
Orford St B2
Paget Rd A2
Park Rd A3
Park View Rd A2
Peter's St C2
Philip Rd C2
Pine Ave A2
Pine View Rd A2
Police Station B2
Portman Rd B2
Portman Walk C1
Post Office B2
Princes St C2
Prospect St B1
Queen St B2
Ranelagh Rd C1
Recreation Ground B1
Rectory Rd C2
Regent Theatre B3
Retail Park C1
Retail Park C2
Richmond Rd A1
Rope Walk C3
Rose La C2
Russell Rd C2
St Edmund's Rd A2
St George's St B2
St Helen's St B3
Sherrington Rd A1
Shopmobility B2
Silent St C2
Sir Alf Ramsey Way C1
Sirdar Rd B1
Soane St B3
Springfield La A1
Star La C3
Stevenson Rd B1
Suffolk College C3
Suffolk Retail Park B1
Superstore B1
Surrey Rd B1
Tacket St C3
Tavern St B3
Tower Ramparts B2
Tower Ramparts Shopping Ctr B2
Tower St B3
Town Hall B2
Tuddenham Rd A3
University C3
Upper Brook St B3
Upper Orwell St B3
Valley Rd A2
Vermont Cres B3
Vermont Rd B3
Vernon St C3
Warrington Rd A2
Waterloo Rd A1
Waterworks St C3
Wellington St B1
West End Rd B1
Westerfield Rd A3
Westgate St B2
Westholme Rd A1
Westwood Ave A1
Willoughby Rd C2
Withipoll St B3
Woodbridge Rd B3
Woodstone Ave A3
Yarmouth Rd B1

Kendal 184

Abbot Hall Art Gallery & Mus of Lakeland Life & Industry C2
Ambulance Station A2
Anchorite Fields C2
Anchorite Rd C2
Ann St A3
Appleby Rd A3
Archers Meadow C3
Ashleigh Rd A2
Aynam Rd B2
Bankfield Rd B1
Beast Banks B2
Beezon Fields A2
Beezon Rd A2
Beezon Trad Est A3
Belmont B2
Birchwood Cl C1
Blackhall Rd B2
Brewery Arts Centre B2
Bridge St B2
Brigsteer Rd C1
Burneside Rd A2
Bus Station B2
Buttery Well Rd C2
Canal Head North B3
Captain French La C2
Caroline St A2
Castle Hill B3
Castle Howe B2
Castle Rd B3
Castle St A3/B3
Cedar Grove C1
Council Offices B2
County Council Offices A2
Cricket Ground A3
Cricket Ground C3
Cross La C2
Dockray Hall Industrial Estate A2
Dowker's La B2
East View B1
Echo Barn Hill C1
Elephant Yard B2
Fairfield La A1
Finkle St B2
Fire Station A2
Fletcher Square C3
Football Ground C3
Fowling La A3
Gillinggate C2
Glebe Rd C2
Golf Course B1
Goose Holme B3
Gooseholme Bridge B3
Green St A1
Greengate C2
Greengate La C1/C2
Greenside B1
Greenwood C1
Gulfs Rd B2
High Tenterfell B1
Highgate B2
Hillswood Ave C1
Horncop La A2
Information Ctr B2
Kendal A3
Kendal Bsns Park A3
Kendal Castle (Remains) B3
Kendal Fell B1
Kendal Green A1
Kendal Ski Ctr ✦ B3
Kendal Station A3
Kent Place B2
Kirkbarrow C2
Kirkland C2
Library B2
Library Rd B2
Little Aynam B3
Little Wood B1
Long Cl C1
Longpool A3
Lound Rd C3
Lound St C3
Low Fellside B2
Lowther St B2
Magistrates Court A2
Maple Dr C1
Market Place B2
Maude St B2
Miller Bridge B2
Milnthorpe Rd C2
Mint St A3
Mintsfeet Rd A3
Mintsfeet Rd South A2
New Rd B2
Noble's Rest B2
Parish Church C2
Park Side Rd C3
Parkside Bsns Park C3
Parr St B3
Police Station A2
Post Office A3/B2
Quaker Tapestry ✦ B2
Queen's Rd B1
Riverside Walk C2
Rydal Mount A2
Sandes Ave A2
Sandgate A3
Sandylands Rd A3
Serpentine Rd B1
Serpentine Wood B1
Shap Rd A3
South Rd C2
Stainbank Rd C1
Station Rd A3
Stramongate B2
Stramongate Bridge B2
Stricklandgate A2/B2
Sunnyside C3
Thorny Hills B3
Town Hall B2
Undercliff Rd B1
Underwood C1
Union St A2
Vicar's Fields C2
Vicarage Dr C1/C2
Wainwright's Yard B2
Wasdale Close C3
Well Ings C2
Westmorland Shopping Centre & Market Hall B2
Westwood Ave C1
Wildman St A3
Windermere Rd A1
YHA B2
YWCA B2

King's Lynn 185

Albert St A2
Albion St B2
Alive St James' Swimming Pool B2
All Saints B2
All Saints St B2
Austin Fields A2
Austin St A2
Avenue Rd B3
Bank Side B1
Beech Rd C2
Birch Tree Cl B2
Birchwood St A2
Blackfriars Rd B2
Blackfriars St B2
Boal St B1
Bridge St B2
Broad St B2
Broad Walk B3
Burkitt St A2
Bus Station A2
Carmelite Terr C2
Chapel St A2
Chase Ave C3
Checker St C2
Church St B2
Clough La B2
Coburg St B2
Coll of West Anglia A3
Columbia Way A3
Corn Exchange A1
County Court Rd B2
Cresswell St A2
Custom House A1
East Coast Bsns Pk C1
Eastgate St A2
Edma St A2
Exton's Rd C3
Ferry La B1
Ferry St A1
Framingham's Almshouses B2
Friars St C2
Friars Walk C2
Gaywood Rd A3
George St A2
Gladstone Rd C2
Goodwin's Rd C3
Green Quay ✦ B1
Greyfriars' Tower ✦ B2
Guanock Terr C2
Guildhall A1
Hansa Rd C3
Hardwick Rd C2
Hextable Rd A2
High St B1
Holcombe Ave C3
Hospital Walk C2
Information Ctr B1
John Kennedy Rd A2
Kettlewell Lane A2
King George V Ave B3
King St B1
King's Lynn Art Centre A1
King's Lynn FC B3
King's Lynn Sta B2
Library B2
Littleport St A2
Loke Rd A2
London Rd B2
Lynn Museum B2
Magistrates Court B1
Majestic B2
Market La A1
Millfleet B2
Milton Ave A3
Nar Valley Walk C2
Nelson St B1
New Conduit St B2
Norfolk St A2
North Lynn Discovery Centre ✦ A3
North St A2
Oldsunway B2
Ouse Ave C1
Page Stair Lane A1
Park Ave B3
Police Station B2
Portland Place C1
Portland St B2
Purfleet B1
Queen St B1
Raby Ave A3
Railway Rd A2
Red Mount Chapel B3
Regent Way B2
River Walk A1
Robert St C2
Saddlebow Rd C2
Shopmobility B2
St Ann's St A1
St James' Rd B2
St James St B2
St John's Walk B3
St Margaret's B1
St Nicholas A2
St Nicholas St A1
St Peter's Rd B1
Sir Lewis St A2
Smith Ave A3
South Everard St C2
South Gate ✦ C2
South Quay B1
South St B2
Southgate St C2
Stonegate St B2
Surrey St A1
Sydney St C3
Tennyson Ave B3
Tennyson Rd B3
Tower St B2
Town Hall B1
Town Ho & Tales of the Old Gaol Ho B1
Town Wall (Remains) ✦ B3
True's Yard Fisherfolk Museum A2
Valingers Rd C2
Vancouver Ave C2
Vancouver Quarter B2
Waterloo St B2
Wellesley St B2
White Friars Rd C2
Windsor Rd C2
Winfarthing St C2
Wyatt St A2
York Rd C3

Lancaster 185

Aberdeen Rd C3
Adult College,The C3
Aldcliffe Rd C2
Alfred St B3
Ambleside Rd A3
Ambulance Sta A3
Ashfield Ave B1
Ashton Rd C2
Assembly Rooms Emporium B2
Balmoral Rd B3
Bath House B2
Bath Mill La B3
Bath St B3
Blades St B1
Borrowdale Rd B3
Bowerham Rd C3
Brewery La B2
Bridge La B2
Brook St C1
Bulk Rd A3
Bulk St B2
Bus Station B2
Cable St B2
Canal Cruises & Waterbus ✦ C2
Carlisle Bridge A1
Carr House La C2
Castle B1
Castle Park B1
Caton Rd A3
China St B2
Church St B2
City Museum B2
Clarence St C3
Common Gdn St B2
Coniston Rd A3
Cottage Museum B2
Council Offices B2
County Court & Family Court B2
Cromwell Rd C1
Crown Court B1
Dale St C3
Dallas Rd B1/C1
Dalton Rd B3
Dalton Sq B2
Damside St B2
De Vitre St B3
Dee Rd A1
Denny Ave A1
Derby Rd A2
Dukes,The B2
Earl St A2
East Rd B3
Eastham St C3
Edward St B3
Fairfield Rd B1
Fenton St B2
Firbank Rd A3
Fire Station B2
Friend's Meeting House B1
Garnet St B3
George St B2
Giant Axe Field B1
Grand B2
Grasmere Rd B3
Greaves Rd C2
Green St A3
Gregson Ctr,The B3
Gregson Rd C3
Greyhound Bridge A2
Greyhound Bridge Rd A2
High St B2
Hill Side B1
Hope St C3
Hubert Place B1
Information Ctr B2
Kelsy St B1
Kentmere Rd B3
King St B2
Kingsway A3
Kirkes Rd C3
Lancaster & Lakeland C3
Lancaster City Football Club B1
Lancaster Sta B1
Langdale Rd A3
Ley Ct B1
Library B2
Lincoln Rd B1
Lindow St C2
Lodge St B2
Long Marsh La B1
Lune Rd A1
Lune St A2
Lune Valley Ramble A3
Mainway A2
Maritime Mus A1
Marketgate Shopping Centre B2
Market St B2
Meadowside C2
Meeting House La B1
Millennium Bridge A2
Moor La B2
Moorgate B3
Morecambe Rd A1/A2
Nelson St B2
North Rd B2
Orchard La C1
Owen Rd A2
Park Rd B3
Parliament St A3
Patterdale Rd A3
Penny St B2
Police Station B2
Portland St C2
Post Office B2
Primrose St C3
Priory B1
Prospect St C3
Quarry Rd B3
Queen St C2
Regent St C2
Ridge La A3
Ridge St A3
Royal Lancaster Infirmary (A&E) C2
Rydal Rd B3
Ryelands Park A1
St Georges Quay A1
St John's B2

206 Leeds • Leicester • Lincoln • Liverpool • Llandudno • Llanelli

St Leonard's Gate B2
St Martin's Rd C3
St Nicholas Arcades Shopping Centre B2
St Oswald St C3
St Peter's ✝ B3
St Peter's Rd B3
Salisbury Rd B1
Scotch Quarry Urban Park C3
Sibsey St B1
Skerton Bridge A2
South Rd C2
Station Rd B1
Stirling Rd C3
Storey Ave B1
Sunnyside La C1
Sylvester St B1
Tarnsyke Rd A1
Thurnham St C2
Town Hall B2
Troutbeck Rd B3
Ulleswater Rd B3
Univ of Cumbria C3
Vicarage Field B1
Vue B2
West Rd B1
Westbourne Dr C1
Westbourne Rd B1
Westham St C3
Wheatfield St B1
White Cross Business Park C2
Williamson Rd B3
Willow La B1
Windermere Rd B3
Wingate-Saul Rd B1
Wolseley St B3
Woodville St B3
Wyresdale Rd C3

Leeds 185

Aire St B3
Albion Place B4
Albion St B4
Albion Way B1
Alma St A6
Ambulance Sta B5
Arcades B4
Armley Rd B1
Armories Dr C5
Back Burley Lodge Rd A1
Back Hyde Terr A2
Back Row C3
Bath Rd C3
Beckett St A6
Bedford St B3
Belgrave St A4
Belle Vue Rd A2
Benson St A5
Black Bull St C5
Blenheim Walk A3
Boar La B4
Bond St B4
Bow St C5
Bowman La C4
Brewery ✦ C4
Brewery Wharf C5
Bridge St A5/B5
Briggate B4
Bruce Gdns C1
Burley Rd A1
Burley St B1
Burmantofts St B6
Bus & Coach Sta B5
Butterly St C4
Butts Cres B4
Byron St A5
Call La B4
Calls,The B5
Calverley St A3/B3
Canal St B1
Canal Wharf C3
Carlisle Rd C5
Cavendish Rd A1
Cavendish St A2
Chadwick St C5
Cherry Place A6
Cherry Row A5
City Museum A4
City Varieties Music Hall B4
City Sq B3
Civic Hall A3
Clarence Road C5
Clarendon Rd A2
Clarendon Way A3
Clark La C6
Clay Pit La A4
Cloberry St A2
Close,The B6
Clyde Approach C1
Clyde Gdns C1
Coleman St C2
Commercial St B4
Concord St A5
Cookridge St A4
Copley Hill C1
Core,The B4
Corn Exchange B4
Cromer Terr A2
Cromwell St A5
Cross Catherine St B6
Cross Green La C6
Cross Stamford St A5
Crown & County Courts A3
Crown Point Bridge C5
Crown Point Rd C4
Crown Point Retail Park C4
David St C3
Dent St C6
Derwent Place C3
Dial St C6
Dock St C4
Dolly La A6
Domestic St C2
Drive,The B6
Duke St B5
Duncan St B4
Dyer St B5
East Field St B6
East Pde B3
East St C5
Eastgate B5
Easy Rd C6
Edward St B4
Ellerby La C6
Ellerby Rd C6
Fenton St A3
Fire Station B2
First Direct Arena A4
Fish St B4
Flax Place B5
Garth,The B5
Gelderd Rd C1
George St B4
Globe Rd C2
Gower St A5
Grafton St A4
Grand Theatre B4
Granville Rd A6
Great George St A3
Great Wilson St C4
Greek St B3
Green La C1
Hanover Ave A2
Hanover La A2
Hanover Sq A2
Hanover Way A2
Harewood St B4
Harrison St B4
Haslewood Cl B6
Haslewood Drive B6
Headrow,The B3/B4
High Court B5
Holbeck La C2
Holdforth Cl C1
Holdforth Gdns B1
Holdforth Grove C1
Holdforth Place C1
Holy Trinity B4
Hope Rd A5
Hunslet La C4
Hunslet Rd C4
Hyde Terr A2
Infirmary St B3
Information Ctr B3
Ingram Row C3
ITV Yorkshire A1
Junction St C4
Kelso Gdns A2
Kelso Rd A2
Kelso St A2
Kendal La A2
Kendell St C4
Kidacre St C4
King Edward St B4
King St B3
Kippax Place C6
Kirkgate B4
Kirkgate Market B4
Kirkstall Rd A1
Kitson St C6
Knight's Way Bridge C5
Lady La B4
Lands La B3
Lane,The B5
Lavender Walk B6
Leeds Art Gallery B3
Leeds Beckett Univ A3
Leeds Bridge C4
Leeds Coll of Music B5
Leeds Discovery Centre C5
Leeds General Infirmary (A&E) A3
Leeds Minster B5
Leeds Station B3
Library B3/B4
Light,The B4
Lincoln Green Rd A6
Lincoln Rd A6
Lindsey Gdns A6
Lindsey Rd A6
Lisbon St B3
Little Queen St B3
Long Close La C6
Lord St C2
Lovell Park A4
Lovell Park Hill A4
Lovell Park Rd A4
Lower Brunswick St A5
Mabgate A5
Macauly St A5
Magistrates Court A3
Manor Rd C3
Mark La B4
Marlborough St B2
Marsh La B5
Marshall St C3
Meadow La C4
Meadow Rd C4
Melbourne St A5
Merrion Centre A4
Merrion St A4
Merrion Way A4
Mill St B5
Millennium Sq A3
Monk Bridge C2
Mount Preston St A2
Mushroom St A5
Neville St C4
New Briggate A4/B4
New Market St B4
New York Rd A5
New York St B5
Nile St A5
Nippet La A6
North St A4
Northern St B3
Oak Rd B1
Oxford Place B3
Oxford Row A3
Parade,The B6
Park Cross St B3
Park La A2
Park Place B3
Park Row B4
Park Sq B3
Park Sq East B3
Park Sq West B3
Park St B3
Police Station B5
Pontefract La B6
Portland Cres A3
Portland Way A3
Post Office B4/B5
Quarry House (NHS/DSS HQ) B5
Quebec St B3
Queen St B3
Radio Aire A1
Railway St B5
Rectory St A6
Regent St A5
Richmond St C5
Rigton Approach B6
Rigton Dr B6
Rillbank La A1
Rosebank Rd A1
Rose Bowl Conference Ctr A3
Royal Armouries C5
Russell St B3
St Anne's Cathedral (RC) ✝ A4
St Anne's St B4
St James' Hosp A6
St John's Rd A2
St Johns Centre B4
St Mary's St B5
St Pauls St B3
Saxton La B5
Sayner La C5
Shakespeare Ave A6
Shannon St B6
Sheepscar St South A5
Siddall St C3
Skinner La A5
South Pde B3
Sovereign St C4
Spence La C2
Springfield Mount A2
Springwell Ct C2
Springwell Rd C2
Springwell St C2
Stoney Rock La A6
Studio Rd A1
Sutton St C2
Sweet St C3
Sweet St West C3
Swinegate B4
Templar St B5
Tetley,The C4
Thoresby Place A3
Torre Rd A6
Town Hall A3
Trinity Leeds B4
Union Place C3
Union St B5
University of Leeds A3
Upper Accomodation Rd B6
Upper Basinghall St B4
Vicar La B4
Victoria Bridge C4
Victoria Gate B4
Victoria Quarter B4
Victoria Rd C4
Vue B4
Wade La A4
Washington St A1
Water La C3
Waterloo Rd C4
Wellington Rd B2/C1
Wellington St B3
West St B2
West Yorkshire Playhouse B5
Westfield Rd A1
Westgate B3
Whitehall Rd B3/C2
Whitelock St A5
Willis St C6
Willow Approach A1
Willow Ave A1
Willow Terrace Rd A3
Wintoun St A5
Woodhouse La A3/A4
Woodsley Rd A1
York Place B3
York Rd B6

Leicester 188

Abbey St A2
All Saints' A1
Aylestone Rd C2
Bath La A1
Bede Park C1
Bedford St A3
Bedford St South A3
Belgrave Gate A2
Belvoir St B2
Braunstone Gate B1
Burleys Way A2
Burnmoor St C2
Bus & Coach Sta A2
Canning St A2
Carlton St C2
Castle B1
Castle Gardens B1
Cathedral ✝ B2
Causeway La A2
Charles St B3
Chatham St B2
Christow St A3
Church Gate A2
City Gallery B3
City Hall B3
Clank St B2
Clock Tower ✦ B2
Clyde St A3
Colton St B3
Conduit St B3
Crafton St A3
Craven St A1
Crown Courts B3
Curve B3
De Lux B2
De Montfort Hall C3
De Montfort St C3
De Montfort Univ C1
Deacon St C2
Dover St B3
Duns La B1
Dunton St A1
East St B3
Eastern Boulevard C1
Edmonton Rd A3
Erskine St A3
Filbert St C1
Filbert St East C2
Fire Station C3
Fleet St A3
Friar La B2
Friday St A2
Gateway St C2
Gateway,The C2
Glebe St B3
Granby St B3
Grange La C2
Grasmere St C1
Great Central St A1
Guildhall B2
Guru Nanak Sikh Museum B1
Halford St B2
Havelock St C2
Haymarket Shopping Centre A2
High St A2
Highcross Shopping Centre A2
Highcross St A1
HM Prison C2
Horsefair St B2
Humberstone Gate B2
Humberstone Rd A3
Infirmary St C2
Information Ctr B2
Jarrom St C2
Jewry Wall B1
Kamloops Cres A3
King St B2
Lancaster Rd C3
LCB Depot B3
Lee St A3
Leicester Royal Infirmary (A&E) C2
Leicester Sta B3
Library B2
London Rd C3
Lower Brown St B2
Magistrates' Court B2
Manitoba Rd A3
Mansfield St A2
Market ✦ B2
Market St B2
Mill La C2
Montreal Rd A3
Narborough Rd North B1
Nelson Mandela Pk C2
New Park St B1
New St B2
New Walk C3
New Walk Museum & Art Gallery C3
Newarke Houses B2
Newarke St B2
Newarke,The B1
Northgate St A1
Orchard St A2
Ottawa Rd A3
Oxford St C2
Phoenix Arts Ctr B3
Police Station A3
Post Office A1/B2/C3
Prebend St C3
Princess Rd East C3
Princess Rd West C3
Queen St B3
Rally Community Park,The A2
Regent College C3
Regent Rd C2/C3
Repton St A1
Rutland St B3
St Augustine Rd B1
St Georges Retail Park B3
St George St B3
St Georges Way B3
St John St A2
St Margaret's A2
St Margaret's Way A2
St Martins B2
St Mary de Castro B1
St Matthew's Way A3
St Nicholas B1
St Nicholas Circle B1
Sanvey Gate A2
Silver St B2
Slater St A1
Soar La A1
South Albion St B3
Southampton St B3
Sue Townsend Theatre B2
Swain St B3
Swan St A1
Tigers Way C3
Tower St C3
Town Hall B2
Tudor Rd B1
Univ of Leicester C3
University Rd C3
Upper Brown St B2
Upperton Rd C1
Vaughan Way A2
Walnut St C2
Watling St A2
Welford Rd B2
Welford Rd Leicester Tigers RC C2
Wellington St B2
West St C3
West Walk C3
Western Boulevard C1
Western Rd C1
Wharf St North A3
Wharf St South A3
Y Theatre,The B3
Yeoman St B3
York Rd B2

Lincoln 188

Alexandra Terr B1
Anchor St C1
Arboretum B3
Arboretum Ave B3
Avenue,The B1
Baggholme Rd B3
Bailgate A2
Beaumont Fee B1
BMI The Lincoln Hospital A2
Brayford Way C1
Brayford Wharf East C1
Brayford Wharf North B1
Bruce Rd A2
Burton Rd A1
Bus Station (City) C2
Canwick Rd C2
Cardinal's Hat ✦ B2
Carline Rd B1
Castle B1
Castle St A1
Cathedral ✝ B2
Cathedral St B2
Cecil St A2
Chapel La A2
Cheviot St B3
Church La A2
City Hall B1
Clasketgate B2
Clayton Sports Gd A3
Coach Park C2
Collection,The B2
County Hospital (A&E) B3
County Office B1
Courts C1
Cross St C2
Crown Courts B1
Curle Ave A3
Danesgate B2
Drill Hall B2
Drury La B1
East Bight A2
East Gate A2
Eastcliff Rd B3
Eastgate B2
Egerton Rd A3
Ellis Windmill A1
Engine Shed, The C1
Environment Agency C2
Exchequer Gate ✦ B2
Firth Rd C1
Flaxengate B2
Florence St B3
George St C3
Good La A2
Gray St A1
Great Northern Terr C3
Great Northern Terr Ind Est C3
Greetwell Rd B3
Greetwellgate B3
Grove,The A3
Haffenden Rd A2
High St B2/C1
HM Prison A3
Hungate B2
James St A2
Jews House & Ct B2
Kesteven St C2
Langworthgate A2
Lawn,The B1
Lee Rd A3
Library B2
Lincoln Central Station C2
Lincoln College B2
Lincolnshire Life/ Royal Lincolnshire Regiment Mus A1
Lincoln University Tech Coll (UTC) B2
Lindum Rd B2
Lindum Sports Gd A3
Lindum Terr B3
Mainwaring Rd A3
Manor Rd A2
Market C2
Massey Rd A3
Medieval Bishop's Palace B2
Mildmay St A1
Mill Rd A1
Millman Rd B3
Minster Yard B2
Monks Rd B3
Montague St B2
Mount St A1
Nettleham Rd A2
Newland B1
Newport A2
Newport Arch A2
Newport Cemetery A2
Northgate A2
Odeon C1
Orchard St B1
Oxford St C2
Park St B1
Pelham Bridge C2
Pelham St C2
Police Station B1
Portland St C2
Post Office A1/B3/C2
Potter Gate B2
Priory Gate B2
Queensway A3
Rasen La A1
Ropewalk C1
Rosemary La B2
St Anne's Rd B3
St Benedict's C1
St Giles Ave A3
St Mark's Shopping Centre C1
St Marks St C1
St Mary-le-Wigford C1
St Mary's St C2
St Nicholas St A2
St Rumbold's St B2
St Swithin's B2
Saltergate C1
Saxon St A1
Sewell Rd B3
Silver St B2
Sincil St C2
Spital St A2
Spring Hill B1
Stamp End C3
Steep Hill B2
Stonebow & Guildhall C2
Stonefield Ave A2
Tentercroft St C1
Theatre Royal B2
Tritton Rd C1
Tritton Retail Park C1
Union Rd B1
Univ of Lincoln C1
Upper Lindum St B3
Upper Long Leys Rd A1
Usher B2
Vere St A2
Victoria St B1
Victoria Terr B1
Vine St B3
Wake St A1
Waldeck St A1
Waterside North C2
Waterside Shopping Centre C2
Waterside South C2
West Pde B1
Westgate A2
Wigford Way C1
Williamson St A2
Wilson St A1
Winn St B3
Wragby Rd A3
Yarborough Rd A1

Liverpool 188

Abercromby Sq C5
Addison St A3
Adelaide Rd B6
Ainsworth St B4
Albany Rd B6
Albert Edward Rd B6
Angela St C6
Anson St B4
Argyle St C3
Arrad St C4
Ashton St B5
Audley St A4
Back Leeds St A2
Basnett St B3
Bath St A1
Beacon,The ✦ B3
Beatles Story, The C2
Beckwith St C3
Bedford Close C5
Bedford St North C5
Bedford St South C5
Benson St C4
Berry St C4
Birkett St A4
Bixteth St B2
Blackburne Place C4
Bluecoat B3
Bold Place C4
Bold St C4
Bolton St B3
Bridport St B4
Bronte St B4
Brook St A1
Brownlow Hill B4/B5
Brownlow St B5
Brunswick Rd A5
Brunswick St B1
Bus Station C2
Butler Cres A6
Byrom St A3
Caledonia St C4
Cambridge St C5
Camden St A4
Canada Blvd B1
Canning Dock C2
Canterbury St A4
Cardwell St C6
Carver St A4
Cases St B3
Castle St B2
Catherine St C5
Cavern Club B3
Central Library A3
Chapel St B2
Charlotte St B3
Chatham Place C6
Chatham St C5
Cheapside B2
Chavasse Park C2
Chestnut St C5
Christian St A3
Church St B3
Clarence St B4
Clayton Square Shopping Centre B3
Coach Station A4
Cobden St A5
Cockspur St A2
College St C3
College St North A5
College St South A5
Colquitt St C4
Comus St A3
Concert St C3
Connaught Rd B6
Cook St B2
Copperas Hill B4
Cornwallis St C3
Covent Garden B2
Craven St A4
Cropper St B3
Crown St B5/C6
Cumberland St B2
Cunard Building B1
Dale St B2
Dansie St B4
Daulby St B5
Dawson St B3
Dental Hospital B5
Derby Sq B2
Drury La B2
Duckinfield St B4
Duke St C3
Earle St A2
East St A2
Eaton St A2
Echo Arena ✦ C2
Edgar St A3
Edge La B6
Edinburgh Rd A6
Edmund St B2
Elizabeth St B5
Elliot St B3
Empire Theatre B4
Empress Rd B6
Epstein Theatre B3
Epworth St A5
Erskine St A5
Everyman Theatre C5
Exchange St East B2
FACT C4
Falkland St A5
Falkner St C5/C6
Farnworth St A6
Fenwick St B2
Fielding St A6
Fire Sta A4
Fleet St C3
Fraser St A4
Freemasons Row A2
Gardner Row A3
Gascoyne St A2
George St B2
Gibraltar Road A1
Gilbert St C3
Gildart St A4
Gill St B4
Goree B2
Gower St C2
Gradwell St C3
Great Crosshall St A3
Great George St C4
Great Howard St A1
Great Newton St B4
Greek St B4
Green La B4
Greenside A5
Greetham St C3
Gregson St A5
Grenville St C3
Grinfield St C6
Grove St C5
Guelph St A6
Hackins Hey B2
Haigh St A4
Hall La B6
Hanover St B3
Harbord St C6
Hardman St C4
Harker St A4
Hart St B4
Hatton Garden A2
Hawke St B4
Helsby St B6
Henry St C3
Highfield St A2
Highgate St B6
Hilbre St B4
Hope Place C4
Hope St C4
Hope University A5
Houghton St B3
Hunter St A3
Hutchinson St A6
Information Centre B4/C2
Institute for the Performing Arts C4
International Slavery Mus C2
Irvine St B6
Irwell St B2
Islington A4
James St B2
James St Station B2
Jenkinson St A4
John Moores Univ A2/A3/A4/B4/C4
Johnson St A3
Jubilee Drive B6
Kempston St A4
Kensington A6
Kensington Gdns B6
Kensington St A6
Kent St C3
King Edward St A1
Kinglake St B6
Knight St C4
Lace St A3
Langsdale St A4
Law Courts C2
Leece St C4
Leeds St A2
Leopold Rd B6
Lime St B3
Lime St Station B4
Liver St C2
Liverpool Central Station B3
Liverpool Landing Stage B1
Liverpool Institute for Performing Arts (LIPA) C4
Liverpool ONE C2
Liverpool Wheel, The C2
London Rd A4/B4
Lord Nelson St B4
Lord St B2
Lovat St C6
Low Hill A5
Low Wood St A6
Lydia Ann St C3
Mansfield St A4
Marmaduke St B6
Marsden St A6
Martensen St B6
Marybone A3
Maryland St C4
Mason St B6
Mathew St B2
May St B4
Melville Place C6
Merseyside Maritime Museum C2
Metquarter B3
Metropolitan Cathedral (RC) ✝ B5
Midghall St A2
Molyneux Rd A6
Moor Place B4
Moorfields B2
Moorfields Sta B2
Moss St A5
Mount Pleasant B4/B5
Mount St C4
Mount Vernon B6
Mulberry St C5
Municipal Buildings B2
Mus of Liverpool C2
Myrtle St C5
Naylor St A2
Nelson St C4
New Islington A4
New Quay B1
Newington St C3
North John St B2
North St A3
North View B6
Norton St A4
O2 Academy B4
Oakes St B5
Odeon B2
Old Hall St A1
Old Leeds St A2
Oldham Place C4
Oldham St C4
Olive St C6
Open Eye Gallery C3
Oriel St A2
Ormond St B2
Orphan St C6
Overbury St C6
Overton St B6
Oxford St C5
Paisley St A1
Pall Mall A2
Paradise St C3
Park La C3
Parker St B3
Parr St C3
Peach St B5
Pembroke Place B4
Pembroke St B5
Philharmonic Hall C5
Phythian Park A6
Pickop St A2
Pilgrim St C4
Pitt St C3
Playhouse Theatre B3
Pleasant St B4
Police HQ C2
Police Sta A4/A6/B4
Pomona St B4
Port of Liverpool Building B2
Post Office A2/A4/A5/B2/B3/B4/C4
Pownall St C2
Prescot St A5
Preston St B3
Princes Dock A1
Princes Gdns A2
Princes Jetty A1
Princes Pde B1
Princes St B2
Pythian St A6
Queen Sq Bus Sta B3
Queensland St C6
Queensway Tunnel (Docks exit) B1
Queensway Tunnel (Entrance) B3
Radio City B2
Ranelagh St B3
Redcross St B2
Renfrew St B6
Renshaw St B4
Richmond Row A4
Richmond St B3
Rigby St A2
Roberts St A1
Rock St B4
Rodney St C4
Rokeby St A4
Romily St A6
Roscoe La C4
Roscoe St C4
Rose Hill A3
Royal Albert Dock C2
Royal Ct Theatre B3
Royal Liver Building B1
Royal Liverpool Hospital (A&E) B5
Royal Mail St B4
Rumford Place B2
Rumford St B2
Russell St B4
St Andrew St B4
St Anne St A4
St Georges Hall B3
St John's Centre B3
St John's Gdns B3
St John's La B3
St Joseph's Cres A4
St Minishull St B5
St Nicholas Place B1
St Paul's Sq A2
Salisbury St A4
Salthouse Dock C2
Salthouse Quay C2
Sandon St C5
Saxony Rd B6
Schomberg St A6
School La B2
Seel St C3
Seymour St B4
Shaw St A5
Shopmobility C2
Sidney Place C6
Sir Thomas St B3
Skelhorne St B4
Slater St C3
Smithdown La B6
Soho Sq A4
Soho St A4
South John St B2
Springfield A4
Stafford St A4
Standish St A3
Stanley St B2
Strand St C2
Strand,The B2
Suffolk St C3
Sydney Jones Liby C5
Tabley St C3
Tarleton St B3
Tate Liverpool Gallery C2
Teck St B6
Temple St B2
Titanic Memorial ✦ B1
Tithebarn St B2
Town Hall B2
Trowbridge St B4
Trueman St A3
Union St B2
Unity Theatre C4
University C5
Univ of Liverpool B5
Upper Baker St A6
Upper Duke St C4
Upper Frederick St C3
Vauxhall Rd A2
Vernon St B2
Victoria Gallery & Museum B5
Victoria St B2
Vine St C5
Wakefield St A4
Walker Art Gallery A3
Walker St A6
Wapping C2
Water St B1/B2
Waterloo Rd A1
Wavertree Rd B6
West Derby Rd A6
West Derby St B5
Western Approaches War Museum B2
Whitechapel B3
Whitley Gdns A5
William Brown St B3
William Henry St A4
Williamson Sq B3
Williamson St B3
Williamson's Tunnels Heritage Centre ✦ C6
Women's Hosp C6
Wood St B3
World Museum, Liverpool A3
York St C3

Llandudno 189

Abbey Place B1
Abbey Rd B1
Adelphi St B3
Alexandra Rd C2
Anglesey Rd A1
Argyll Rd B3
Arvon Ave A2
Atlee Cl C3
Augusta St B3
Back Madoc St B2
Bodafon St B3
Bodhyfryd Rd A2
Bodnant Cres C3
Bodnant Rd C3
Bridge Rd C2
Bryniau Rd C1
Builder St B3
Builder St West C2
Cabin Lift A2
Cable Car ✦ A2
Camera Obscura ✦ A3
Caroline Rd B2
Chapel St A2
Charlton St B3
Church Cres C1
Church Walks A2
Claremont Rd B2
Clement Ave A2
Clifton Rd B2
Clonmel St B3
Coach Station B3
Conway Rd B3
Conwy Archive Service B2
Council St West C3
Cricket and Rec Gd B2
Cwlach Rd A2
Cwlach St A1
Cwm Howard La C3
Cwm Place C3
Cwm Rd C3
Dale Rd C1
Deganwy Ave B2
Denness Place C2
Dinas Rd C2
Dolydd B1
Erol Place B2
Ewloe Dr C3
Fairways C2
Ffordd Dewi C3
Ffordd Dulyn C2
Ffordd Dwyfor C3
Ffordd Elisabeth C3
Ffordd Gwynedd C3
Ffordd Las C3
Ffordd Morfa C3
Ffordd Penrhyn C3
Ffordd Tudno C3
Ffordd yr Orsedd C3
Ffordd Ysbyty C2
Fire & Ambulance Station B3
Garage St B3
George St A2
Gloddaeth Ave B1
Gloddaeth St B2
Gogarth Rd B1
Great Orme Mines ✦ A1
Great Ormes Rd B1
Great Orme Tramway ✦ A2
Happy Valley A2
Happy Valley Rd A3
Haulfre Gardens A1
Herkomer Cres C1
Hill Terr A2
Home Front Mus B2
Hospice B1
Howard Rd B3
Information Ctr B2
Invalids' Walk B1
James St B2
Jubilee St B3
King's Ave C2
King's Rd C2
Knowles Rd C2
Lees Rd C2
Library B2
Llandudno A2
Llandudno (A&E) C2
Llandudno Sta B3
Llandudno Football Ground C2
Llewelyn Ave A2
Lloyd St B2
Lloyd St West B1
Llwynon Rd A1
Llys Maelgwn B1
Madoc St B2
Maelgwn Rd B2
Maes-y-Cwm C3
Maes-y-Orsedd C3
Maesdu Bridge C2
Maesdu Rd C2/C3
Marian Place C2
Marian Rd C2
Marine Drive (Toll) A3
Market St A2
Miniature Golf Course A1
Morfa Rd B1
Mostyn B3
Mostyn Broadway B3
Mostyn St B3
Mowbray Rd C2
New St A2
Norman Rd B3
North Parade A2
North Wales Golf Links C1
Old Bank,The A2
Old Rd A2
Oval,The B1
Oxford Rd B3
Parade,The B3
Parc Llandudno Retail Park B3
Pier ✦ A3
Plas Rd A2
Police Station B3
Post Office A2/B3
Promenade A3
Pyllau Rd A1
Rectory La A2
Rhuddlan Ave C3
St Andrew's Ave B2
St Andrew's Place B2
St Beuno's Rd A1
St David's Place B2
St David's Rd B2
St George's Place A3
St Mary's Rd B2
St Seriol's Rd B2
Salisbury Pass B1
Salisbury Rd B2
Somerset St B3
South Parade A2
Stephen St B3
Tabor Hill A2
Town Hall B2
Trinity Ave B1
Trinity Cres C1
Trinity Sq B3
Tudno St A2
Ty-Coch Rd A2
Ty-Gwyn Rd A1/A2
Ty'n-y-Coed Rd A1
Vaughan St B3
Victoria Shopping Centre B3
Victoria A2
War Memorial ✦ A2
Werny Wylan C3
West Parade B1
Whiston Pass A2
Winllan Ave C2
Wyddfyd Rd A2
York Rd A2

Llanelli 189

Alban Rd B3
Albert St B1
Als St B3
Amos St C1
Andrew St A3
Ann St C2
Annesley St B2
Arfryn Ave A3
Avenue Cilfig,The A2
Belvedere Rd A1
Bigyn Park Terr C3
Bigyn Rd C3
Bond Ave C3
Brettenham St A1
Bridge St B2
Bryn Place C1
Bryn Rd C1
Bryn Terr C1
Bryn-More Rd C1
Brynhyfryd Rd A2
Brynmelyn Ave A3
Brynmor Rd B1
Burry St C1
Bus Station B2
Caersalem Terr C2
Cambrian St C1
Caswell St C3
Cedric St B3
Cemetery A2
Chapman St A1
Charles Terr C2
Church St B2
Clos Caer Elms A1
Clos Sant Paul C2
Coastal Link Rd B1/C1
Coldstream St B2
Coleshill Terr B1
College Hill B3
College Sq B3
Copperworks Rd C2
Coronation Rd C3
Corporation Ave A3
Council Offices B2
Court B2
Cowell St B2
Cradock St C2
Craig Ave C3
Cricket Ground A1
Derwent St A1
Dillwyn St C2
Druce St C1
Eastgate Leisure Complex ✦ B2
Elizabeth St B2
Emma St C2
Erw Rd B1
Felinfoel Rd A2
Fire Station A3
Firth Rd C3
Fron Terr C3
Furnace United Rugby Football Ground A1
Gelli-On B2
George St C2
Gilbert Cres A2
Gilbert Rd A2
Glanmor Rd C2
Glanmor Terr C2
Glasfryn Terr A3
Glenalla Rd B3
Glevering St B3
Goring Rd A2
Gorsedd Circle A2
Grant St C3
Graveyard C2
Great Western Cl C2
Greenway St B1
Hall St B2
Harries Ave A2
Hedley Terr A2
Heol Elli B3
Heol Goffa A3
Heol Nant-y-Felin A3
Heol Siloh B2
Hick St C2
High St C1
Indoor Bowls Ctr B1
Inkerman St B2
Island Place B2
James St B3
John St B2
King George Ave B3
Lake View Cl A2
Lakefield Place C1
Lakefield Rd C1
Langland Rd C3
Leisure Centre B1
Library B2
Llanelli House B2
Llanelli Parish Church B2
Llanelli Station C2
Llewellyn St C2
Lliedi Cres A3
Lloyd St B2
Llys Alys B3
Llys Fran A3
Llysnewedd C1
Long Row A3
Maes Gors C2
Maesyrhaf A3
Mansel St C3
Marblehall Rd B3
Marborough Rd A2
Margam St C3
Marged St C2
Marine St C1
Mariners,The C1
Market B2
Market St B2
Marsh St C2
Martin Rd C3
Miles St A1
Mill La A3/B2
Mincing La B2
Murray St B2
Myn y Mor B1
Nathan St C1
Nelson Terr C1
Nevill St C2
New Dock Rd C2
New Rd A1
New Zealand St A1
Odeon B2
Old Lodge C2
Old Rd A2
Paddock St C2
Palace Ave B3
Parc Howard A2
Parc Howard Museum & Art Gallery A2
Park Cres B1
Park St B2
Parkview Terr B1
Pemberton St C2
Pembrey Rd A1
Peoples Park B1
Police Station B2
Post Office B2/C2
Pottery Place B3
Pottery St B3
Princess St B1
Prospect Place A2
Pryce St A1
Queen Mary's Walk C3
Queen Victoria Rd C1
Raby St B1
Railway Terr C2
Ralph St B2
Ralph Terr C1
Regalia Terr B3

Rhydyrafon A3
Richard St B2
Robinson St B2
Roland Ave A1
Russell St C3
St David's Cl C1
St Elli Shopping Ctr B2
St Margaret's Dr A1
Spowart Ave A1
Station Rd B2/C2
Stepney Place B2
Stepney St B2
Stewart St A1
Stradey Park Ave A1
Sunny Hill A2
Superstore A2
Swansea Rd A3
Talbot St C3
Temple St B3
Thomas St A2
Tinopolos TV Studios ✦ B2
Toft Place A3
Town Hall B2
Traeth Ffordd C1
Trinity Rd C3
Trinity Terr C2
Tunnel Rd B3
Tyisha Rd C3
Union Blgs A2
Upper Robinson St B2
Vauxhall Rd B2
Walter's Rd B3
Waun Lanyrafon B2
Waun Rd A3
Wern Rd B3
West End A2
Y Bwthyn C3
Zion Row B3

London 186

Abbey Orchard St E3
Abchurch La D6
Abingdon St E4
Achilles Way D2
Acton St B4
Addington St E4
Air St D3
Albany St B2
Albemarle St D3
Albert Embankment F4
Aldenham St A3
Aldersgate St C6
Alford St D2
Aldgate ⊖ C7
Aldgate High St C7
Aldwych C4
Allsop Place B1
Amwell St B5
Andrew Borde St C3
Angel ⊖ A5
Appold St C7
Argyle Sq B4
Argyle St B4
Argyll St C3
Arnold Circus B7
Artillery La C7
Artillery Row E3
Association of Photographers Gallery 🏛 B6
Baker St ⊖ B1
Baker St B1
Baldwin's Gdns C5
Baltic St B6
Bank ⊖ C6
Bank Museum 🏛 C6
Bank of England C6
Bankside D6
Bankside Gallery 🏛 D5
Banner St B6
Barbican ≥⊖ C6
Barbican Centre for Arts,The C6
Barbican Gallery 🏛 C6
Basil St E1
Bastwick St B6
Bateman's Row B7
Bath St B6
Bayley St C3
Baylis Rd E5
Beak St D3
Bedford Row C4
Bedford Sq C3
Bedford St D4
Bedford Way B3
Beech St C6
Belgrave Place E2
Belgrave Sq E2
Bell La C7
Belvedere Rd E4
Berkeley Sq D2
Berkeley St D2
Bernard St B4
Berners Place C3
Berners St C3
Berwick St C3
Bethnal Green Rd B7
Bevenden St B6
Bevis Marks C7
BFI (British Film Institute) 🎦 D4
BFI London IMAX Cinema 🎦 D5
Bidborough St B4
Binney St C2
Birdcage Walk E3
Bishopsgate C7
Blackfriars ≥⊖ D5
Blackfriars Bridge D5
Blackfriars Rd E5
Blandford St C1
Blomfield St C6
Bloomsbury St C3
Bloomsbury Way C4
Bolton St D2
Bond St ⊖ C2
Borough High St E6
Boswell St C4
Bow St C4
Bowling Green La B5
Brad St D5
Bressenden Place E3
Brewer St D3
Brick St D2
Bridge St E4
Britannia Walk B6
British Film Institute (BFI) 🎦 D4
British Library 🏛 B3
British Museum 🏛 C4
Britton St B5
Broad Sanctuary E3
Broadway E3
Brook Dr F5
Brook St D2
Brunswick Place B6
Brunswick Shopping Centre,The B4
Brunswick Sq B4
Brushfield St C7
Bruton St D2
Bryanston St C1
BT Centre C6
Buckingham Gate E3
Buckingham Pal 🏛 E3
Buckingham Pal Rd F2
Bunhill Row B6
Byward St D7
Cabinet War Rooms & Churchill Mus 🏛 E3
Cadogan La E2
Cadogan Place E1
Cadogan Sq F1
Caledonian Rd A4
Calshot St A4
Calthorpe St B4
Calvert Ave B7
Cambridge Circus C3
Camomile St C7
Cannon St D6
Cannon St ≥⊖ D6
Carey St C4
Carlisle La E4
Carlisle Place E3
Carlton House Terr D3
Carmelite St D5
Carnaby St C3
Carter La C5
Carthusian St C6
Cartwright Gdns B4
Castle Baynard St D5
Cavendish Place C2
Cavendish Sq C2
Caxton Hall E3
Caxton St E3
Central St B6
Chalton St B3
Chancery Lane ⊖ C5
Chapel St E2
Charing Cross ≥⊖ D4
Charing Cross Rd C3
Charles II St D3
Charles Dickens Museum 🏛 B4
Charles Sq B6
Charles St D2
Charlotte Rd B7
Charlotte St C3
Chart St B6
Charterhouse Sq C5
Charterhouse St C5
Cheapside C6
Chenies St C3
Chesham St E2
Chester Sq F2
Chesterfield Hill D2
Chiltern St C2
Chiswell St C6
City Garden Row A5
City Rd B6
City Thameslink ≥ C5
City University,The B5
Claremont Sq A5
Clarges St D2
Clerkenwell Cl B5
Clerkenwell Green B5
Clerkenwell Rd B5
Cleveland St C3
Clifford St D3
Clink Prison Mus 🏛 D6
Clock Museum 🏛 C6
Club Row B7
Cockspur St D3
Coleman St C6
Columbia Rd B7
Commercial St C7
Compton St B5
Conduit St D2
Constitution Hill E2
Copperfield St E5
Coptic St C4
Cornhill C6
Cornwall Rd D5
Coronet St B7
Courtauld Gallery 🏛 D4
Covent Garden ⊖ D4
Covent Garden ✦ D4
Cowcross St C5
Cowper St B6
Cranbourn St D3
Craven St D4
Crawford St C1
Creechurch La C7
Cremer St A7
Cromer St B4
Cumberland Gate D1
Cumberland Terr A2
Curtain Rd B7
Curzon St D2
Cut,The E5
D'arblay St C3
Davies St C2
Dean St C3
Deluxe Gallery 🏛 B7
Denmark St C3
Dering St C2
Devonshire St C2
Diana, Princess of Wales Meml Wlk E3
Dingley Rd B6
Dorset St C1
Doughty St B4
Dover St D2
Downing St E4
Druid St E7
Drummond St B3
Drury La C4
Drysdale St B7
Duchess St C2
Dufferin St B6
Duke of Wellington Place E2
Duke St C2
Duke St D3
Duke St Hill D6
Duke's Place C7
Duncannon St D4
East Rd B6
Eastcastle St C3
Eastcheap D7
Eastman Dental Hospital [H] B4
Eaton Place E2
Eaton Sq E2
Eccleston St E2
Edgware Rd C1
Eldon St C6
Embankment ⊖ D4
Endell St C4
Endsleigh Place B3
Euston ≥⊖ B3
Euston Rd B3
Euston Square ⊖ B3
Evelina Children's Hospital E4
Eversholt St A3
Exmouth Market B5
Fann St B6
Farringdon ≥⊖ C5
Farringdon Rd C5
Farringdon St C5
Featherstone St B6
Fenchurch St D7
Fenchurch St ≥ D7
Fetter La C5
Finsbury Circus C6
Finsbury Pavement C6
Finsbury Sq B6
Fitzalan St F5
Fitzmaurice Place D2
Fleet St C5
Floral St D4
Florence Nightingale Museum 🏛 E4
Folgate St C7
Foot Hospital [H] B3
Fore St C6
Foster La C6
Francis St F3
Frazier St E5
Freemason's Hall C4
Friday St C6
Gainsford St E7
Garden Row E5
Gee St B6
George St C1
Gerrard St D3
Giltspur St C5
Glasshouse St D3
Gloucester Place C1
Golden Hinde ⛴ D6
Golden La B6
Golden Sq D3
Goodge St ⊖ C3
Goodge St C3
Gordon Sq B3
Goswell Rd B5
Gough St B4
Goulston St C7
Gower St B3
Gracechurch St D6
Grafton Way B3
Gray's Inn Rd B4
Great College St E4
Great Cumberland Place C1
Great Eastern St B7
Great Guildford St D6
Great Marlborough St C3
Great Ormond St B4
Great Ormond St Children's Hosp [H] B4
Great Percy St B4
Great Peter St E3
Great Portland St ⊖ B2
Great Portland St C2
Great Queen St C4
Great Russell St C3
Great Scotland Yd D4
Great Smith St E3
Great Suffolk St D5
Great Titchfield St C3
Great Tower St D7
Great Windmill St D3
Greek St C3
Green Park ⊖ D3
Green St D2
Greencoat Place F3
Gresham St C6
Greville St B4/C5
Greycoat Hosp Sch E3
Greycoat Place E3
Grosvenor Cres E2
Grosvenor Gdns E2
Grosvenor Place E2
Grosvenor Sq D2
Grosvenor St D2
Guards Museum and Chapel 🏛 E3
Guildhall Art Gallery 🏛 C6
Guilford St B4
Guy's Hospital [H] D6
Haberdasher St B6
Hackney Rd B7
Half Moon St D2
Halkin St E2
Hall St B5
Hallam St C2
Hampstead Rd B3
Hanover Sq C2
Hans Cres E1
Hanway St C3
Hardwick St B5
Harley St C2
Harrison St B4
Hastings St B4
Hatfields D5
Hay's Galleria D7
Hay's Mews D2
Hayles St F5
Haymarket D3
Hayne St C5
Hayward Gallery 🏛 D4
Helmet Row B6
Herbrand St B4
Hercules Rd E4
Hertford St D2
High Holborn C4
Hill St D2
HMS Belfast ⛴ D7
Hobart Place E2
Holborn ⊖ C4
Holborn C5
Holborn Viaduct C5
Holland St D5
Holmes Mus 🏛 B1
Holywell La B7
Horse Guards' Rd D3
Houndsditch C7
Houses of Parliament 🏛 E4
Howland St C3
Hoxton Sq B7
Hoxton St B7
Hunter St B4
Hunterian Mus 🏛 C4
Hyde Park D1
Hyde Park Cnr ⊖ E2
Imperial War Museum 🏛 E5
Inner Circle B2
Inst of Archaeology (London Univ) B2
Ironmonger Row B6
James St C2
James St D4
Jermyn St D3
Jockey's Fields C4
John Carpenter St D5
John St B4
Judd St B4
Kennington Rd E5
King Charles St E4
King St D3
King St C6
King William St C6
King's Coll London D5
King's Cross ≥ A4
King's Cross Rd B4
King's Cross St Pancras ⊖ A4
King's Rd E2
Kingley St C3
Kingsland Rd B7
Kingsway C4
Kinnerton St E2
Knightsbridge ⊖ E1
Lamb St C7
Lamb's Conduit St C4
Lambeth Bridge F4
Lambeth High St F4
Lambeth North ⊖ E5
Lambeth Palace 🏛 E4
Lambeth Palace Rd E4
Lambeth Rd E5
Lambeth Walk F4
Lancaster Place D4
Langham Place C2
Leadenhall St C7
Leake St E4
Leather La C5
Leicester Sq ⊖ D3
Leicester St D3
Leonard St B6
Lever St B6
Lexington St D3
Lidlington Place A3
Lime St D7
Lincoln's Inn Fields C4
Lindsey St C5
Lisle St D3
Liverpool St C7
Liverpool St ≥⊖ C7
Lloyd Baker St B5
Lloyd Sq B5
Lombard St C6
London Aquarium 🐟 E4
London Bridge ≥⊖ D6
London Bridge Hospital [H] D6
London City Hall 🏛 D7
London Dungeon, The 🏛 E4
London Film Mus ✦ E4
London Guildhall University C6
London Rd E5
London Transport Museum 🏛 D4
London Wall C6
London Eye ✦ E4
Long Acre D4
Long La C5
Longford St B2
Lower Belgrave St E2
Lower Grosvenor Place E2
Lower Marsh E5
Lower Thames St D6
Lowndes St E2
Ludgate Circus C5
Ludgate Hill C5
Luxborough St C2
Lyall St E2
Macclesfield Rd B6
Madame Tussaud's ✦ B2
Maddox St D2
Malet St C3
Mall,The E3
Manchester Sq C2
Manchester St C2
Mandeville Place C2
Mansell St D7
Mansion House 🏛 C6
Mansion House ⊖ D6
Maple St C3
Marble Arch ⊖ C1
Marble Arch D1
Marchmont St B4
Margaret St C3
Margery St B5
Mark La D7
Marlborough Rd D3
Marshall St C3
Marsham St E3
Marylebone High St C2
Marylebone La C2
Marylebone Rd B2
Marylebone St C2
Mecklenburgh Sq B4
Middle Temple La C5
Middlesex St (Petticoat La) C7
Midland Rd A3
Migration Mus 🏛 F5
Minories C7
Monck St E3
Monmouth St C4
Montagu Place C1
Montagu Sq C1
Montagu St C4
Montague Place C3
Monument ⊖ D6
Monument St D6
Monument,The ✦ D6
Moor La C6
Moorfields C6
Moorfields Eye Hospital [H] B6
Moorgate C6
Moorgate ≥⊖ C6
Moreland St B5
Morley St E5
Mortimer St C3
Mount Pleasant B5
Mount St D2
Murray Grove A6
Museum of Garden History 🏛 E4
Mus of London 🏛 C6
Museum St C4
Myddelton Sq B5
Myddelton St B5
National Gallery 🏛 D3
National Hospital [H] B4
National Portrait Gallery 🏛 D3
Neal St C4
Nelson's Column ✦ D4
New Bond St C2/D2
New Bridge St C5
New Cavendish St C2
New Change C6
New Fetter La C5
New Inn Yard B7
New North Rd A6
New Oxford St C3
New Scotland Yard E3
New Sq C4
Newgate St C5
Newton St C4
Nile St B6
Noble St C6
Noel St C3
North Audley St D2
North Cres C3
North Row D2
Northampton Sq B5
Northington St B4
Northumberland Ave D4
Norton Folgate C7
Nottingham Place C2
Obstetric Hosp [H] B3
Old Bailey C5
Old Broad St C6
Old Compton St C3
Old County Hall E4
Old Gloucester St C4
Old King Edward St C6
Old Nichol St B7
Old Paradise St F4
Old Spitalfields Mkt C7
Old St B6
Old St ≥⊖ B6
Old Vic 🎭 E5
Open Air Theatre 🎭 B2
Operating Theatre Museum 🏛 D6
Orange St D3
Orchard St C2
Ossulston St A3
Outer Circle B1
Oxford Circus ⊖ C3
Oxford St C2/C3
Paddington St C2
Palace St E3
Pall Mall D3
Pall Mall East D3
Pancras Rd A4
Panton St D3
Paris Gdn D5
Park Cres B2
Park La D2
Park Rd B1
Park St D2
Park St D6
Parker St C4
Parliament Sq E4
Parliament St E4
Paternoster Sq C5
Paul St B6
Pear Tree St B5
Penton Rise B4
Penton St A5
Pentonville Rd A4/A5
Percival St B5
Petticoat La (Middlesex St) C7
Petty France E3
Phoenix Place B4
Phoenix Rd A3
Photo Gallery 🏛 D3
Piccadilly D2
Piccadilly Circus ⊖ D3
Pitfield St B7
Pollock's Toy Museum 🏛 C3
Polygon Rd A3
Pont St E1
Portland Place C2
Portman Mews C2
Portman Sq C2
Portman St C1
Portugal St C4
Postal Museum, The 🏛 B4
Poultry C6
Primrose St C7
Princes St C6
Procter St C4
Provost St B6
Quaker St B7
Queen Anne St C2
Queen Elizabeth Hall 🎭 D4
Queen Sq B4
Queen St D6
Queen Street Place D6
Queen Victoria St D5
Queens Gallery 🏛 E3
Radnor St B6
Rathbone Place C3
Rawstorne St B5
Red Lion Sq C4
Red Lion St C4
Redchurch St B7
Redcross Way D6
Regency St F3
Regent Sq B4
Regent St C3
Regent's Park B2
Richmond Terr E4
Ridgmount St C3
Rivington St B7
Robert St B2
Rochester Row F3
Ropemaker St C6
Rosebery Ave B5
Roupell St D5
Royal Academy of Arts 🏛 D3
Royal Academy of Dramatic Art B3
Royal Acad of Music B2
Royal Artillery Memorial ✦ E2
Royal College of Nursing C2
Royal College of Surgeons C4
Royal Festival Hall 🎭 D4
Royal London Hospital for Integrated Medicine C4
Royal National Theatre 🎭 D5
Royal National Throat, Nose and Ear Hospital [H] B4
Royal Opera Ho 🎭 D4
Russell Sq B3
Russell Square ⊖ B4
Sackville St D3
Sadlers Wells 🎭 B5
Saffron Hill C5
St Alban's St D3
St Andrew St C5
St Bartholomew's Hospital [H] C5
St Botolph St C7
St Bride St C5
St George's Circus E5
St George's Rd E5
St Giles High St C3
St James's Pal 🏛 D3
St James's Park ⊖ E3
St James's St D3
St John St B5
St Margaret St E4
St Mark's Hosp [H] B5
St Martin's La D4
St Martin's Le Grand C6
St Mary Axe C7
St Pancras Int ≥ A4
St Paul's ⊖ C6
St Paul's Cath ✝ C6
St Paul's Churchyard C5
St Peter's Hosp [H] C4
St Thomas St D6
St Thomas' Hosp [H] E4
Savile Row D3
Savoy Place D4
Savoy St D4
School of Hygiene & Tropical Medicine C3
Scrutton St B7
Sekforde St B5
Serpentine Rd D1
Seven Dials C4
Seward St B5
Seymour St C1
Shad Thames D7
Shaftesbury Ave D3
Shakespeare's Globe Theatre 🎭 D6
Shepherd Market D2
Sherwood St D3
Shoe La C5
Shoreditch High St B7
Shoreditch High St ⊖ B7
Shorts Gdns C4
Sidmouth St B4
Silk St C6
Sir John Soane's Museum 🏛 C4
Skinner St B5
Sloane St E1
Snow Hill C5
Soho Sq C3
Somerset House 🏛 D4
South Audley St D2
South Carriage Dr E1
South Molton St C2
South Place C6
South St D2
Southampton Row C4
Southampton St D4
Southwark ⊖ D5
Southwark Bridge D6
Southwark Bridge Rd D6
Southwark Cath ✝ D6
Southwark St D6
Speakers' Corner D1
Spencer St B5
Spital Sq C7
Stamford St D5
Stanhope St B3
Stephenson Way B3
Stock Exchange C5
Stoney St D6
Strand C5
Stratton St D2
Sumner St D5
Sutton's Way B6
Swanfield St B7
Swinton St B4
Tabernacle St B6
Tate Modern 🏛 D6
Tavistock Place B4
Tavistock Sq B3
Tea & Coffee Museum 🏛 D6
Temple ⊖ D5
Temple Ave D5
Temple Place D4
Terminus Place E2
Thayer St C2
Theobald's Rd C4
Thorney St F4
Threadneedle St C6
Throgmorton St C6
Tonbridge St B4
Tooley St D7
Torrington Place B3
Tothill St E3
Tottenham Ct Rd B3
Tottenham Ct Rd ⊖ C3
Tottenham St C3
Tower Bridge ✦ D7
Tower Bridge App D7
Tower Bridge Rd E7
Tower Hill D7
Tower Hill ⊖ D7
Tower of London, The 🏰 D7
Toynbee St C7
Trafalgar Square D3
Trinity Sq D7
Trocadero Centre D3
Tudor St D5
Turnmill St C5
Ufford St E5
Union St D5
Univ Coll Hosp [H] B3
Univ of London C3
University of Westminster C2
University St B3
Upper Belgrave St E2
Upper Berkeley St C1
Upper Brook St D2
Upper Grosvenor St D2
Upper Ground D5
Upper Montague St C1
Upper St Martin's La D4
Upper Thames St D6
Upper Wimpole St C2
Upper Woburn Place B3
Vere St C2
Vernon Place C4
Vestry St B6
Victoria ≥⊖ E2
Victoria Emb D4
Victoria Place Shopping Centre F2
Victoria St E3
Villiers St D4
Vincent Sq F3
Vinopolis City of Wine 🏛 D6
Virginia Rd B7
Wakley St B5
Walbrook C6
Wallace Collection 🏛 C2
Wardour St C3/D3
Warner St B5
Warren St ⊖ B3
Warren St B3
Waterloo ≥⊖ E5
Waterloo Bridge D4
Waterloo East ≥ D5
Waterloo Rd E5
Watling St C6
Webber St E5
Welbeck St C2
Wellington Arch ✦ E2
Wellington Mus 🏛 E2
Wells St C3
Wenlock St A6
Wentworth St C7
West Smithfield C5
West Sq E5
Westminster ⊖ E4
Westminster Abbey ✝ E4
Westminster Bridge E4
Westminster Bridge Rd E5
Westminster Cathedral (RC) ✝ E3
Westminster City Hall E3
Westminster Hall 🏛 E4
Weymouth St C2
Wharf Rd A6
Wharton St B4
Whitcomb St D3
White Cube 🏛 B7
White Lion Hill D5
White Lion St A5
Whitecross St B6
Whitefriars St C5
Whitehall D4
Whitehall Place D4
Wigmore Hall C2
Wigmore St C2
William IV St D4
Wilmington Sq B5
Wilson St C6
Wilton Cres E2
Wimpole St C2
Windmill Walk D5
Woburn Place B4
Woburn Sq B3
Women's Hosp [H] C3
Wood St C6
Woodbridge St B5
Wootton St D5
Wormwood St C7
Worship St B6
Wren St B4
Wynyatt St B5
York Rd E4
York St C1
York Terrace East B2
York Terrace West B2
York Way A4

Luton 189

Adelaide St B1
Albert Rd C2
Alma St B2
Alton Rd C3
Anthony Gdns C1
Arthur St C2
Ashburnham Rd B1
Ashton Rd C2
Avondale Rd A1
Back St A2
Bailey St C3
Baker St C2
Biscot Rd A1
Bolton Rd B3
Boyle Cl A2
Brantwood Rd B1
Bretts Mead C1
Bridge St B2
Brook St A1
Brunswick St A3
Burr St A3
Bury Park Rd A1
Bute St B2
Buxton Rd B2
Cambridge St C3
Cardiff Grove B1
Cardiff Rd B1
Cardigan St A2
Castle St B2/C2
Chapel St C2
Charles St A3
Chase St C2
Cheapside B2
Chequer St C3
Chiltern Rise C1
Church St B2/B3
Cinema 🎦 A2
Cobden St A3
College A3
Collingdon St A1
Community Centre C3
Concorde Ave A3
Corncastle Rd C1
Cowper St C2
Crawley Green Rd B3
Crawley Rd A1
Crescent Rd A3
Crescent Rise A3
Cromwell Rd A1
Cross St A2
Cross Way,The C1
Crown Court B2
Cumberland St B2
Cutenhoe Rd C3
Dallow Rd B1
Downs Rd B1
Dudley St A2
Duke St A2
Dumfries St B1
Dunstable Place B2
Dunstable Rd A1/B1
Edward St A3
Elizabeth St C2
Essex Cl C3
Farley Hill C1
Farley Lodge C1
Flowers Way B2
Francis St A1
Frederick St A2
Galaxy Leisure Complex A2
George St B2
George St West B2
Gordon St B2
Grove Rd B1
Guildford St A2
Haddon Rd A3
Harcourt St C2
Hart Hill Drive A3
Hart Hill Lane A3
Hartley Rd A3
Hastings St B2
Hat Factory,The 🎭 B2
Hatters Way A1
Havelock Rd A2
Hibbert St C2
High Town Rd A3
Highbury Rd A1
Hightown Community Sports & Arts Ctr A3
Hillary Cres C1
Hillborough Rd C1
Hitchin Rd A3
Holly St C2
Holm C1
Hucklesby Way A2
Hunts Cl C1
Inkerman St A2
John St B2
Jubilee St A3
Kelvin Cl C2
King St B2
Kingsland Rd C3
Larches,The A2
Latimer Rd C2
Lawn Gdns C2
Lea Rd B3
Library B2
Library Rd B2
Library Theatre 🎭 B2
Liverpool Rd B1
London Rd C2
Luton Station ≥ A2
Lyndhurst Rd B1
Magistrates Court B2
Mall,The B2
Manchester St B2
Manor Rd B3
Manor Road Park B3
May St C3
Meyrick Ave C1
Midland Rd A2
Mill St A2
Milton Rd B1
Moor St A1
Moor,The A1
Moorland Gdns A2
Moulton Rise A3
Napier Rd B1
New Bedford Rd A1
New Town St C2
North St A3
Old Bedford Rd A2
Old Orchard C2
Osbourne Rd C3
Oxen Rd A3
Park Sq B2
Park St B3/C3
Park St West B2
Park Viaduct B3
Parkland Drive C1
Police Station ☒ B2
Pomfret Ave A3
Pondwicks Rd B3
Post Office ✉ A1/B2
Power Court B3
Princess St B1
Red Rails C1
Regent St B2
Reginald St A2
Rothesay Rd B1
Russell Rise C1
Russell St C1
St Ann's Rd B3
St George's Square B2
St Mary's ⛪ B3
St Marys Rd B3
St Paul's Rd C2
St Saviour's Cres C1
Salisbury Rd B1
Seymour Ave C3
Seymour Rd C3
Silver St B2
South Rd C2
Stanley St B1
Station Rd A2
Stockwood Cres C2
Stockwood Park C1
Strathmore Ave C2
Stuart St B2
Studley Rd A1
Surrey St C3
Sutherland Place C1
Tavistock St C2
Taylor St A3
Telford Way A1
Tennyson Rd C2
Tenzing Grove C1
Thistle Rd B3
Town Hall B2
Townsley Cl C2
UK Centre for Carnival Arts ✦ B3
Union St B2
University of Bedfordshire B3
Upper George St B2
Vicarage St B3
Villa Rd A2
Waldeck Rd A1
Wardown House Mus & Gallery 🏛 A2
Wellington St B1/B2
Wenlock St A2
Whitby Rd A1
Whitehill Ave C1
William St A2
Wilsden Ave C1
Windmill Rd B3
Windsor St C2
Winsdon Rd B1
York St A3

Macclesfield 189

108 Steps B2
Abbey Rd A1
Alton Dr A3
Armett St C1
Athey St B1
Bank St C3
Barber St C3
Barton St C1
Beech La A2
Beswick St B1
Black La A2
Black Rd C3
Blakelow Gardens C3
Blakelow Rd C3
Bond St B1/C1
Bread St C1
Bridge St B1
Brock St A2
Brocklehurst Ave A3
Brook St B3
Brookfield La B3
Brough St West C1
Brown St C1
Brynton Rd A2
Buckley St C2
Bus Station B2
Buxton Rd B3
Byrons St C2
Canal St B3
Carlsbrook Ave A3
Castle St B2
Catherine St B1
Cemetery A1
Chadwick Terr A3
Chapel St C2
Charlotte St B2
Chester Rd B1
Chestergate B1
Christ Church ⛪ B1
Churchill Way B2
Coare St A1
Commercial Rd B2
Conway Cres A3
Copper St C3
Cottage St B1
Crematorium A1
Crew Ave A3
Crompton Rd B1/C1
Cross St C2
Crossall St C1
Cumberland St A1/B1
Dale St B3
Duke St B2
Eastgate B3
Exchange St B2
Fence Ave B3
Fence Ave Ind Est A3
Flint St B3
Foden St A2
Fountain St B3
Garden St A3
Gas Rd B2
Gateway Gallery ✦ B1
George St B2
Glegg St B3
Golf Course C3
Goodall St B3
Grange Rd C1
Great King St B1
Green St B3
Grosvenor Shopping Centre B2
Gunco La C3
Half St C2
Hallefield Rd B3
Hatton St C1
Hawthorn Way A3
Heapy St C3
Henderson St B1
Heritage Centre 🏛 B2
Hibel Rd A2
High St C2
Hobson St C2
Hollins Rd C3
Hope St West C1
Horseshoe Dr B1
Hurdsfield Rd A3
Information Ctr ℹ B2
James St C2
Jodrell St B3
John St C2
Jordangate B2
King Edward St B2
King George's Field C3
King St B2
King's School A1
Knight Pool C3
Knight St C3
Lansdowne St A3
Library B2
Lime Grove B3
Loney St B1
Longacre St B1
Lord St C2
Lowe St C2
Lowerfield Rd A3
Lyon St B1
Macclesfield Coll C1
Macclesfield Sta ≥ B2
MADS Little Theatre 🎭 C2
Marina B3
Market B2
Market Place B2
Masons La A3
Mill La C2
Mill Rd C2
Mill St B2
Moran Rd C1
New Hall St A2
Newton St C1
Nicholson Ave A3
Nicholson Cl A3
Northgate Ave A2
Old Mill La C2
Paradise Mill 🏛 C2
Paradise St B1
Park Green B2
Park La C1
Park Rd C1
Park St C2
Park Vale Rd C1
Parr St B1
Peel St C2
Percyvale St A3
Peter St C1
Pickford St B2
Pierce St B1
Pinfold St B1
Pitt St C2
Police Station ☒ B2
Pool St C2
Poplar Rd C2
Post Office ✉ B2
Pownall St A2
Prestbury Rd A1/B1
Queen Victoria St B2
Queen's Ave A3
Registrar B2
Retail Park C2
Richmond Hill C3
Riseley St B1
Roan Ct B3
Roe St B2
Rowan Way A3
Ryle St C2
Ryle's Park Rd C1
St George's St C2
St Michael's ⛪ B2
Samuel St B2
Saville St C3
Shaw St B1
Silk Rd,The A2/B2
Slater St C1
Snow Hill C3
South Park C1
Spring Gdns A2
Statham St C2
Station St A2
Steeple St A3
Sunderland St B2
Superstore A1/A2/C2
Swettenham St B3
Thistleton Cl C2
Thorp St B2
Town Hall B2
Townley St B2
Treacle Market ✦ B2
Turnock St C3
Union Rd B3
Union St B2
Victoria Park B3
Vincent St C2
Waters Green B2
Waterside C2
West Bond St B1
West Park A1
West Park Mus 🏛 A1
Westbrook Dr A1
Westminster Rd A1
Whalley Hayes B1
Windmill St C3
Withyford Dr A2
York St B3

Maidstone 190

Albion Place B3
All Saints ⛪ B2
Allen St A3
Amphitheatre ✦ C2
Archbishop's Palace 🏛 B2
Bank St B2
Barker Rd C2
Barton Rd C3
Beaconsfield Rd C1
Bedford Place B1
Bishops Way B2
Bluett St A3
BMI The Somerfield Hospital [H] A1
Bower La C1
Bower Mount Rd B1
Bower Place C1
Bower St B1
Boxley Rd A3
Brenchley Gardens A2
Brewer St A3
Broadway B2
Broadway Shopping Centre B2
Brunswick St C3
Buckland Hill A1
Buckland Rd B1
Bus Station B3
Campbell Rd C3
Church Rd C1
Church St B3
Cinema 🎦 C2
Clifford Way C1/C2
College Ave C2
College Rd C2
Collis Meml Gdn C3
Cornwallis Rd B1
Corpus Christi Hall B2
Council Offices B3
County Hall A2
County Rd A3
Crompton Gdns C3
Crown & County Courts B2
Curzon Rd A3
Dixon Cl C2
Douglas Rd C1
Earl St B2
Eccleston Rd C2
Fairmeadow B2
Fisher St A2
Florence Rd C1
Foley St A3
Foster St C3
Freedom Leisure Centre A1/A2
Fremlin Walk Shopping Centre B2
Gabriel's Hill B3
George St C3
Grecian St A3
Hardy St A3
Hart St C2
Hastings Rd C3
Hayle Rd C3
Hazlitt 🎭 B2
Heathorn St A3
Hedley St A3
High St B2
HM Prison A3
Holland Rd A3
Hope St A2
Information Ctr ℹ B2
James St A3
James Whatman Way A2
Jeffrey St A3
Kent County Council Offices A2
Kent History & Library Centre A2
King Edward Rd C2
King St B3
Kingsley Rd C3
Knightrider St B3
Launder Way C1
Lesley Place A1
Library B2
Little Buckland Ave A1
Lockmeadow Leisure Complex C2
London Rd B1
Lower Boxley Rd A2
Lower Fant Rd C1
Magistrates Court B3
Maidstone Barracks Station ≥ A1
Maidstone East Station ≥ A2
Maidstone Museum & Bentlif Art Gall 🏛 B2
Maidstone Utd FC A2
Maidstone West Station ≥ B2
Mall,The B3
Market C2
Market Buildings B2

208 Manchester • Merthyr Tydfil • Middlesbrough • Milton Keynes • Newcastle • Newport • Newquay

Marsham St B3
Medway St B2
Melville Rd C3
Mill St B2
Millennium Bridge C2
Mote Rd B3
Muir Rd C3
Old Tovil Rd C2
Palace Ave B3
Perryfield St A2
Police Station B3
Post Office B2/C3
Priory Rd C3
Prospect Place C1
Pudding La B2
Queen Anne Rd B3
Queens Rd A1
Randall St A2
Rawdon Rd C3
Reginald Rd C1
Riverstage A1
Rock Place B1
Rocky Hill B1
Romney Place B3
Rose Yard B2
Rowland Cl C1
Royal Engineers' Rd A2
Royal Star Arcade B2
St Annes Ct B1
St Faith's St B2
St Luke's Rd A3
St Peter St B2
St Peter's Bridge B2
St Peter's Wharf Retail Park B2
St Philip's Ave C3
Salisbury Rd A3
Sandling Rd A2
Scott St A2
Scrubs La B1
Sheal's Cres C3
Somerfield La B1
Somerfield Rd B1
Staceys St A2
Station Rd A2
Superstore A1/B2/B3
Terrace Rd B1
Tonbridge Rd C1
Tovil Rd C2
Town Hall B2
Trinity Park B3
Tufton St B3
Tyrwhitt-Drake Mus of Carriages B2
Union St B3
Upper Fant Rd C1
Upper Stone St C3
Victoria St B1
Warwick Place B1
Wat Tyler Way B3
Waterloo St C3
Waterlow Rd A3
Week St B2
Well Rd A3
Westree Rd C1
Wharf Rd C1
Whatman Park A1
Wheeler St A3
Whitchurch Close B1
Woodville Rd C3
Wyatt St B3
Wyke Manor Rd B3

Manchester 190

Adair St B6
Addington St A5
Adelphi St A1
Albert Sq B3
Albion St C3
Ancoats Grove B6
Ancoats Grove North B6
Angela St C2
Aquatics Centre C4
Ardwick Green North C5
Ardwick Green Pk C5
Ardwick Green South C5
Arlington St A2
Artillery St B3
Arundel St C2
Atherton St B2
Atkinson St B3
Aytoun St B4
Back Piccadilly A4
Baird St B5
Balloon St A4
Bank Place A1
Baring St B5
Barrack St C1
Barrow St A1
Bendix St A5
Bengal St A5
Berry St C5
Blackfriars Rd A3
Blackfriars St A3
Blantyre St C2
Bloom St B4
Blossom St A5
Boad St B5
Bombay St B4
Booth St A3
Booth St B4
Bootle St B3
Brazennose St B3
Brewer St A5
Bridge St A3
Bridgewater Hall B3
Bridgewater Place A4
Bridgewater St B2
Brook St C4
Brotherton Dr A2
Brown St A3
Brown St B4
Brunswick St C6
Brydon Ave C6
Buddhist Centre A4
Bury St A2
Bus & Coach Sta B4
Bus Station B4
Butler St A6
Buxton St C5
Byrom St B3
Cable St A5
Cambridge St C3/C4
Camp St B3
Canal St B4
Cannon St A1
Cardroom Rd A6
Carruthers St A6
Castle St C2
Castlefield Arena B2
Cateaton St A3
Cathedral † A3
Cathedral St A3
Cavendish St C4
Chapel St A1/A3
Chapeltown St B5
Charles St C4
Charlotte St B4
Chatham St B4
Chepstow St B3
Chester Rd C1/C2
Chester St C4
Chetham's Sch of Music A3
China La B5
Chippenham Rd A6
Chorlton Rd C2
Chorlton St B4
Church St A2
Church St A4
City Park A4
City Rd East C3
Civil Justice Ctr B2
Cleminson St A2
Clowes St A3
College Land A3
Collier St B2
Commercial St C3
Conference Centre C4
Cooper St B4
Copperas St A4
Corn Exchange, The A4
Cornbrook C1
Cornell St A5
Corporation St A4
Cotter St C6
Cotton St A5
Cow La B1
Cross St B3
Crown Court B4
Crown St C2
Dalberg St C6
Dale St A4/B5
Dancehouse, The C4
Dantzic St A4
Dark La C6
Dawson St C2
Dean St A5
Deansgate A3/B3/C2
Deansgate Castlefield C3
Deansgate Sta C3
Dolphin St C6
Downing St C5
Ducie St B5
Duke Place B2
Duke St B2
Durling St C6
East Ordsall La A2/B1
Edge St A4
Egerton St C2
Ellesmere St C1
Everard St C1
Every St B6
Exchange Sq A4
Fairfield St B5
Faulkner St B4
Fennel St A3
Ford St A2
Ford St C6
Fountain St B4
Frederick St A2
Gartside St B2
Gaythorne St A1
George Leigh St A5
George St B4
Gore St A2
Goulden St A5
Granby Row B4
Gravel La A3
Great St B6
Great Ancoats St A5
Great Bridgewater St B3
Great George St A1
Great Jackson St C2
Great Marlborough St C4
Great Northern Warehouse Leisure & Shopping Complex B3
Greengate A3
Grosvenor St C5
Gun St A5
Hadrian Ave B6
Hall St B3
Hampson St B1
Hanover St A4
Hanworth Cl C5
Hardman St B3
Harkness St C6
Harrison St B6
Hart St B4
Helmet St B6
Henry St A5
Heyrod St B6
High St A4
Higher Ardwick C6
Hilton St A4/A5
Holland St A6
HOME ✦ C3
Hood St A5
Hope St B1
Hope St B4
Houldsworth St A5
Hoyle St C6
Hulme Hall Rd C1
Hulme St A1
Hulme St C3
Hyde Rd C6
Islington Way A1
Information Ctr B4
Irwell St A2
Jackson Cres C2
Jackson's Row B3
James St A1
Jenner Cl C2
Jersey St A5
John Dalton St B3
John Ryland's Library B3
John St A2
Kennedy St B3
Kincardine Rd C5
King St A3
King St West A3
Law Courts B3
Laystall St B5
Lever St A5
Library B3
Linby St C2
Little Lever St A4
Liverpool Rd B2
Liverpool St B1
Lloyd St B3
Lockton Cl C5
London Rd B5
Long Millgate A3
Longacre St B6
Loom St A5
Lower Byrom St B2
Lower Mosley St B3
Lower Moss La C2
Lower Ormond St C4
Loxford La C4
Luna St A5
Major St B4
Manchester Arndale A4
Manchester Art Gallery B4
Manchester Central Convention Complex B3
Manchester Metropolitan Univ (MMU) B4/C4
Manchester Piccadilly Station B5
Manchester Technology Ctr C4
Mancunian Way C3
Manor St C5
Marble St A4
Market St A2
Market St A4
Market St A4
Marsden St A3
Marshall St A5
Mayan Ave A2
Medlock St C3
Middlewood St B1
Miller St A4
Minshull St B4
Mosley St A4
Mount St B3
Mulberry St B3
Murray St A5
Museum of Science & Industry (MOSI) B2
Nathan Dr A2
National Football Museum A4
Naval St A5
New Bailey St A2
New Elm Rd B2
New Islington A6
New Islington Sta B6
New Quay St B2
New Union St A6
Newgate St A4
Newton St A5
Nicholas St B4
North Western St C6
Oak St A4
Odeon A4/B3
Old Mill St A6
Oldfield Rd A1/C1
Oldham Rd A5
Oldham St A4
Opera House B3
Ordsall La C1
Oxford Rd C4
Oxford Rd C4
Oxford St B4
Paddock St C6
Palace Theatre B4
Pall Mall A3
Palmerston St B6
Parker St B4
Peak St B5
Penfield Cl C5
Peoples' History Museum B2
Peru St A1
Peter St B3
Piccadilly A4
Piccadilly B5
Piccadilly Gdns B4
Piercy St A6
Poland St A5
Police Sta B3/B5
Pollard St B6
Port St A5
Portland St B4
Portugal St East B5
Post Office A1/A2/A4/A5/B3/B4
Potato Wharf B2
Princess St B3/C4
Pritchard St C4
Quay St A2
Quay St B2
Queen St B3
Radium St A5
Redhill St A5
Regent Rd B1
Retail Park A5
Rice St B2
Richmond St B4
River St C3
Roby St B5
Rodney St A6
Roman Fort B2
Rosamond St A2
Royal Exchange A3
Sackville St B4
St Andrew's St B6
St Ann St A3
St Ann's A3
St George's Ave C1
St James St B4
St John St B3
St John's Cathedral (RC) † A2
St Mary's B3
St Mary's Gate A3
St Mary's Parsonage A3
St Peter's Sq B3
St Stephen St A2
Salford Approach A3
Salford Central A2
Sheffield St B5
Sherratt St A5
Shopmobility A4
Shudehill A4
Shudehill A4
Sidney St C4
Silk St A5
Silver St B4
Skerry Cl C5
Snell St B6
South King St B3
Sparkle St B5
Spear St A4
Spring Gardens A4
Stanley St A2/B2
Store St B5
Superstore B1
Swan St A4
Tariff St B5
Tatton St C1
Temperance St B6/C6
Thirsk St C6
Thomas St A4
Thompson St A5
Tib La B3
Tib St A4
Town Hall (Manchester) B3
Town Hall (Salford) A2
Trafford St C3
Travis St B5
Trinity Way A2
Turner St A4
Union St C6
Univ of Manchester (Sackville St Campus) C5
Univ of Salford A1
Upper Brook St C5
Upper Cleminson St A1
Upper Wharf St A1
Urban Exchange A5
Vesta St B6
Victoria A4
Victoria Station A4
Wadesdon Rd C5
Water St B2
Watson St B3
West Fleet St B1
West King St A2
West Mosley St B4
Weybridge Rd A6
Whitworth St B4
Whitworth St West C3
William St A2
William St C6
Wilmott St C3
Windmill St B3
Windsor Cres A1
Withy Grove A4
Woden St C1
Wood St B3
Woodward St A6
Worrall St C1
Worsley St C2
York St B4
York St C2
York St C4

Merthyr Tydfil
Merthyr Tudful 190

Aberdare Rd B2
Abermorlais Terr B2
Alexandra Rd A3
Alma St C3
Arfryn Place C3
Argyle St C3
Avenue De Clichy C2
Beacons Place Shopping Centre C2
Bethesda St B2
Bishops Grove A3
Brecon Rd A1/B2
Briarmead A3
Bryn St C3
Bryntirion Rd B3/C3
Bus Station B2
Cae Mari Dwn B3
Caedraw Rd C2
Castle Sq A1
Castle St B2
Chapel C2
Chapel Bank B1
Church St B3
Civic Centre B2
Clos Penderyn B1
Coedcae'r Ct C3
College Blvd C2
County and Crown Courts B2
Court St C3
Cromwell St B2
Cyfarthfa Castle, Mus and Art Gallery A1
Cyfarthfa Ind Est A1
Cyfarthfa Park A1
Cyfarthfa Retail Pk B1
Cyfarthfa Rd A1
Dane St A2
Dane Terr A2
Danyparc B3
Darren View A3
Dixon St B2
Dyke St C3
Dynevor St B2
Elwyn Dr C3
Fire Station B2
Fothergill St B3
Galonuchaf Rd A3
Garth St B2
Georgetown B2
Grawen Terr A2
Grove Pk A2
Grove, The A2
Gurnos Rd A2
Gwaelodygarth Rd A2/A3
Gwaunfarren Grove A3
Gwaunfarren Rd A3
Gwendoline St A3
Hampton St C3
Hanover St A2
Heol S O Davies B1
Heol-Gerrig B1
High St A3/B2/B3/C2
Highland View C3
Howell Cl B1
Information Ctr B2
Jackson's Bridge B2
James St C3
John St B3
Joseph Parry's Cottage B2
Lancaster St A2
Library B2
Llewellyn St A2
Llwyfen St B2
Llwyn Berry B1
Llwyn Dic Penderyn B1
Llwyn-y-Gelynen C1
Lower Thomas St B3
Market C2
Mary St C3
Masonic St C2
Merthyr Tydfil Coll B2
Merthyr Town FC B3
Merthyr Tydfil Leisure Centre C3
Merthyr Tydfil Station C3
Meyrick Villas A2
Miniature Railway ✦ A1
Mount St A2
Nantygwenith St B1
Norman Terr B2
Oak Rd A2
Old Cemetery B3
Pandy Cl A1
Pantycelynen B1
Parade, The B3
Park Terr B2
Penlan View C2
Penry St B2
Pentwyn Villas A2
Penyard Rd B3
Penydarren Park A3
Penydarren Rd B3
Plymouth St C3
Police Station C2
Pont Marlais West B2
Post Office B2
Quarry Row B2
Queen's Rd B3
Rees St C3
Rhydycar Link C2
Riverside Park A1
St David's B3
St Tydfil's C2
St Tydfil's Ave C3
St Tydfil's Square Shopping Centre C2
Saxon St A2
School of Nursing A2
Seward St A3
Shiloh La B3
Stone Circles B3
Stuart St A2
Summerhill Place B3
Superstore B3
Swan St C2
Swansea Rd B1
Taff Glen View C3
Taff Vale Ct B3
Theatre Soar B2
Thomastown Park B3
Tramroad La A3
Tramroad Side B2
Tramroad Side North B3
Tramroad Side South C3
Trevithick Gdns C3
Trevithick St A3
Tudor Terr B2
Twynyrodyn Rd C3
Union St B3
Upper Colliers Row B1
Upper Thomas St B3
Victoria St B2
Vue C3
Vulcan Rd B2
Walk, The B2
Warlow St C3
Well St A2
Welsh Assembly Government Offices C2
Wern La C1
Wern, The (Merthyr RFC) C2
West Grove A2
William St C3
Yew St C3
Ynysfach Engine House ✦ C2
Ynysfach Rd C2

Middlesbrough 191

Abingdon Rd C3
Acklam Rd C1
Albert Park C2
Albert Rd B2
Albert Terr C2
Ambulance Station C1
Aubrey St C3
Avenue, The C2
Ayresome Gdns C2
Ayresome Green La C1
Ayresome St C2
Barton Rd A1
Bilsdale Rd C3
Bishopton Rd C3
Borough Rd B2/B3
Bowes Rd A2
Breckon Hill Rd B3
Bridge St West B2
Brighouse Rd A1
Burlam Rd C1
Bus Station B2
Cannon Park B1
Cannon Park Way B2
Cannon St B1
Captain Cook Sq B2
Carlow St C1
Castle Way C3
Chipchase Rd C2
Cineworld B3
Cleveland Centre B2
Clive Rd C2
Commercial St A2
Corporation Rd B2
Costa St C2
Council Offices B3
Crescent Rd C2
Crescent, The C2
Cumberland Rd C2
Depot Rd A2
Derwent St B2
Devonshire Rd C2
Diamond Rd B2
Dock St B3
Dorman Mus C2
Douglas St B3
Eastbourne Rd C2
Eden Rd C3
Fire Sta A3
Forty Foot Rd A2
Gilkes St B2
Gosford St A2
Grange Rd B2
Gresham Rd B2
Harehills Rd C1
Harford St C2
Hartington Rd B2
Haverton Hill Rd A1
Hey Wood St B1
Highfield Rd C3
Hillstreet Centre B2
Holwick Rd B1
Hutton Rd C3
Ironmasters Way B1
Lambton Rd C3
Lancaster Rd C2
Lansdowne Rd C3
Latham Rd C2
Law Courts B2/B3
Lees Rd B2
Leeway B3
Library B2/C2
Linthorpe Cemetery C1
Linthorpe Rd B2
Lloyd St B2
Longford St C2
Longlands Rd C3
Lower East St A3
Lower Lake C3
Macmillan Acad C1
Maldon Rd C1
Manor St B2
Marsh St B2
Marton Rd B3
Middlesbrough By-Pass B2/C1
Middlesbrough Coll B3
Middlesbrough Dock B3
Middlesbrough Leisure Park B3
Middlesbrough Station B2
Middletown Park C2
MIMA B3
Mulgrave Rd C2
Newport Bridge B1
Newport Bridge Approach Rd B1
Newport Rd B2
North Ormesby Rd B3
North Rd B2
Northern Rd C1
Outram St B2
Oxford Rd C2
Park La C2
Park Rd North C2
Park Rd South C2
Park Vale Rd C3
Parliament Rd B1
Police Station A2
Port Clarence Rd A3
Portman St B2
Post Office B3/C1/C2
Princes Rd B2
Python A2
Riverside Park Rd A1
Riverside Stadium (Middlesbrough FC) B3
Rockliffe Rd C2
Romaldkirk Rd B1
Roman Rd C2
Roseberry Rd C3
St Barnabas' Rd C2
St Paul's Rd B2
Saltwells Rd B3
Scott's Rd A3
Seaton Carew Rd A3
Shepherdson Way B3
Shopmobility B2
Snowdon Rd A2
South West Ironmasters Park B1
Southfield Rd B2
Southwell Rd C2
Springfield Rd C1
Startforth Rd A2
Stockton Rd C1
Stockton St A2
Superstore B2
Surrey St C2
Sycamore Rd C2
Tax Offices B3
Tees Viaduct C1
Teessaurus Park A2
Teesside Tertiary College C3
Temenos ✦ B3
Thornfield Rd C1
Town Hall B2
Transporter Bridge (Toll) A3
Union St B2
Univ of Teesside B2
Upper Lake C2
Valley Rd C3
Ventnor Rd C2
Victoria Rd B2
Vulcan St A2
Warwick St C2
Wellesley Rd B3
West La C1
West Lane Hosp C1
Westminster Rd C2
Wilson St B2
Windward Way B3
Woodlands Rd B2
York Rd C3

Milton Keynes 191

Abbey Way A1
Arbrook Ave B1
Armourer Dr A3
Arncliffe Dr A1
Avebury C2
Avebury Blvd C2
Bankfield B3
Bayard Ave A2
Belvedere A2
Bishopstone A1
Blundells Rd A1
Boundary, The C3
Boycott Ave C2
Bradwell Common Blvd B1
Bradwell Rd C1
Bramble Ave A2
Brearley Ave C2
Breckland A1
Brill Place B1
Burnham Dr B1
Campbell Park B3
Cantle Ave A3
Central Retail Park C1
Century Ave C2
Chaffron Way C3
Childs Way C1
Christ the Cornerstone B2
Cineworld B2
Civic Offices B2
Cleavers Ave B2
Colesbourne Dr A3
Conniburrow Blvd B2
Currier Dr A2
Dansteed Way A2/A3/B1
Deltic Ave B1
Downs Barn A2
Downs Barn Blvd A3
Eaglestone C3
Eelbrook Ave B1
Elder Gate B1
Evans Gate C2
Fairford Cres A3
Falcon Ave B3
Fennel Dr A2
Fishermead Blvd C3
Food Centre B3
Fulwoods Dr C3
Glazier Dr A2
Glovers La A1
Grafton Gate C1
Grafton St A1/C2
Gurnards Ave B3
Harrier Dr C3
The Hub Leisure Quarter B2/C2
Ibstone Ave B1
intu Milton Keynes B2
Langcliffe Dr A1
Leisure Centre C3
Leisure Plaza C1
Leys Rd C1
Library B2
Linceslade Grove C1
Linford Wood A2
Magistrates Court B2
Marlborough Gate B3
Marlborough St A2/B3
Mercers Dr A1
Midsummer C2
Midsummer Blvd B2
Milton Keynes Central C1
Milton Keynes Hospital (A&E) C3
Monks Way A1
Mullen Ave A3
Mullion Place C3
Neath Hill A3
North Elder C1
North Grafton B1
North Overgate A3
North Row B2
North Saxon B2
North Secklow B2
North Skeldon A3
North Witan B1
Oakley Gdns A3
Odeon B2
Oldbrook Blvd C2
Open-Air Theatre B3
Overgate A3
Overstreet A3
Patriot Dr B1
Pencarrow Place B3
Penryn Ave B3
Perran Ave C3
Pitcher La C1
Place Retail Pk, The C1
Police Station B2
Portway B2
Post Office A2/B2/B3
Precedent Dr B1
Quinton Dr B1
Ramsons Ave B2
Retail Park C2
Rockingham Dr A2
Rooksley B1
Saxon Gate B2
Saxon St A1/C3
Secklow Gate B2
Shackleton Place C2
Shopmobility B2
Silbury Blvd B2
Skeldon A3
South Enmore B3
South Grafton C2
South Row C2
South Saxon C2
South Secklow B3
South Witan C2
Springfield B3
Stainton Dr A1/B1
Stanton Wood A1
Stantonbury A1
Stantonbury Leisure Centre ✦ A1
Strudwick Dr C2
Sunrise Parkway A2
Superstore C1/C2
Theatre & Art Gallery B3
theCentre:mk B2
Tolcarne Ave C3
Towan Ave C3
Trueman Place C2
Vauxhall A1
Winterhill Retail Pk C2
Witan Gate B2
Xscape B3

Newcastle upon Tyne 191

Albert St B3
Argyle St B3
Back New Bridge St B3
BALTIC Centre for Contemporary Art C3
Barker St A3
Barrack Rd B1
Bath La B1
Bessie Surtees House ✦ C2
Bigg Market C2
Biscuit Factory B3
Black Gate C2
Blackett St B2
Blandford Sq C1
Boating Lake A1
Boyd St B3
Brandling Park A2
Bus Station B2
Buxton St B3
Byron St A3
Camden St B2
Castle Keep C2
Central C1
Central Library B2
Central Motorway B2
Chester St A3
Cineworld B1
City Hall B2
City Rd B3/C3
City Walls ✦ C1
Civic Centre A2
Claremont Rd A1
Clarence St B3
Clarence Walk B3
Clayton St C1/B1
Clayton St West C1
Close, The C2
Coach Station C1
College St B2
Collingwood St C2
Copland Terr B3
Coppice Way B3
Corporation St B1
Courts C3
Crawhall Rd B3
Dean St C2
Dental Hospital A1
Dinsdale Place A3
Dinsdale Rd A3
Discovery C1
Doncaster Rd A3
Durant Rd B2
Eldon Sq B1
Ellison Place B2
Eskdale Terr A2
Eslington Terr A2
Exhibition Park A1
Falconar St B3
Fenkle St C1
Forth Banks C1
Forth St C1
Gallowgate B1
Gate, The ✦ B1
Gateshead Millennium Bridge C3
Gateshead Quays C3
Gibson St B3
Goldspink La A3
Grainger Market B2
Grainger St B2
Grantham Rd A3
Granville Rd A3
Great North Children's Hospital A1
Great North Mus:Hancock A2
Grey St B2
Groat Market C2
Guildhall C2
Hancock St A2
Hanover St C2
Hatton Gallery A1
Hawks Rd C3
Haymarket B2
Heber St B1
Helmsley Rd A3
High Bridge B2
High Level Bridge C2
Hillgate C3
Howard St B3
Hutton Terr A3
intu Eldon Sq Shopping Centre B2
Jesmond A2
Jesmond Rd A2/A3
John Dobson St B2
Jubilee Rd B3
Kelvin Grove A3
Kensington Terr A2
Laing Gallery B2
Lambton Rd A2
Leazes Cres B1
Leazes La B1
Leazes Park B1
Leazes Park Rd B1
Leazes Terr B1
Library A2
Live C2
Low Friar St C1
Manor Chare C2
Manors B2
Manors Station B2
Market St B2
Melbourne St B2
Mill Rd C3
Monument B2
Monument Mall Shopping Centre B2
Morpeth St A2
Mosley St C2
Napier St A3
New Bridge St West B2/B3
Newcastle Central Station C1
Newcastle Univ A1
Newgate St B1
Newington Rd A3
Northern Design Centre C3
Northern Stage Theatre A2
Northumberland Rd B2
Northumberland St B2
Northumbria Univ A2
Northwest Radial Rd A1
O2 Academy ✦ C1
Oakwellgate C3
Open Univ C3
Orchard St C2
Osborne Rd A2
Osborne Terr A3
Pandon C3
Pandon Bank B3
Park Terr A1
Percy St B1
Pilgrim St B2
Pipewellgate C2
Pitt St B1
Plummer Tower A2
Police Station C1
Portland Rd A3/B3
Portland Terr A3
Post Office B1/B2
Pottery La C1
Prudhoe Place B1
Prudhoe St B1
Quayside C2
Queen Elizabeth II Bridge C2
Queen Victoria Rd A1
Richardson Rd A1
Ridley Place B2
Rock Terr B3
Rosedale Terr A3
Royal Victoria Infirmary A1
Sage Gateshead ✦ C3
St Andrew's St B1
St James B1
St James' Blvd C1
St James' Park (Newcastle Utd FC) B1
St Mary's Heritage Centre ✦ C3
St Mary's (RC) † C1
St Mary's Place B2
St Nicholas † C2
St Nicholas St C2
St Thomas' St B1
Sandyford Rd A2/A3
Shield St B3
Shieldfield B3
Shopmobility B1
Side, The C2
Simpson Terrace B3
South Shore Rd C3
South St C1
Starbeck Ave A3
Stepney Rd B3
Stoddart St B3
Stowell St B1
Strawberry Place B1
Swing Bridge C2
Temple St C1
Terrace Place B1
Theatre Royal B2
Times Sq C1
Tower St B3
Trinity House C2
Tyne Bridge C2
Tyne Bridges ✦ C2
Tyne Theatre & Opera House C1
Tyneside B2
Victoria Sq A2
Warwick St A3
Waterloo St C1
Wellington St B1
Westgate Rd C1/C2
Windsor Terr A2
Worswick St B2
Wretham Place B3

Newport
Casnewydd 191

Albert Terr B1
Allt-yr-Yn Ave A1
Alma St C2
Ambulance Sta C3
Bailey St B2
Barrack Hill A2
Bath St A3
Bedford Rd B3
Belle Vue La C1
Belle Vue Park C1
Bishop St A3
Blewitt St B1
Bolt Cl C3
Bolt St C3
Bond St A2
Bosworth Dr A1
Bridge St B1
Bristol St A3
Bryngwyn Rd B1
Brynhyfryd Ave C1
Brynhyfryd Rd C1
Bus Station B2
Caerau Cres C1
Caerau Rd B1
Caerleon Rd A3
Capel Cres C2
Cardiff Rd C2
Caroline St B3
Castle (Remains) A2
Cedar Rd B3
Charles St B2
Charlotte Dr C2
Chepstow Rd A3
Church Rd A3
Cineworld B2
Civic Centre B1
Clarence Place A2
Clifton Place B1
Clifton Rd C1
Clyffard Cres B1
Clytha Park Rd B1
Clytha Sq C2
Coldra Rd C1
Collier St A3
Colne St B3
Comfrey Cl A1
Commercial Rd C3
Commercial St B2
Corelli St A3
Corn St B2
Corporation Rd B3
Coulson Cl C2
County Court A2
Courts A1
Courts B1
Crawford St A3
Cyril St B3
Dean St A3
Devon Place B1
Dewsland Park Rd C2
Dolman B2
Dolphin St C3
East Dock Rd C3
East St B1
East Usk Rd A3
Ebbw Vale Wharf B3
Emlyn St B2
Enterprise Way C3
Eton Rd B3
Evans St A2
Factory Rd A2
Fields Rd B1
Francis Dr C2
Frederick St C3
Friars Rd C1
Friars Walk B2
Gaer La C1
George St C3
George St Bridge C3
Godfrey Rd B1
Gold Tops B1
Gore St A3
Gorsedd Circle C1
Grafton Rd A3
Graham St B1
Granville St C3
Harlequin Dr A1
Harrow Rd B3
Herbert Rd A3
Herbert Walk C2
Hereford St A3
High St B2
Hill St B2
Hoskins St A2
Information Ctr B2
Ivor St B2
Jones St B1
Junction Rd A3
Keynshaw Ave C2
King St C2
Kingsway B2
Kingsway Centre B2
Ledbury Dr A2
Library A3
Library, Museum & Art Gallery B2
Liverpool Wharf B3
Llanthewy Rd B1
Llanvair Rd A3
Locke St A2
Lower Dock St C3
Lucas St A2
Manchester St A3
Market B2
Marlborough Rd B3
Mellon St C3
Mill St A2
Morgan St A3
Mountjoy Rd C2
Newport Bridge A2
Newport Ctr B2
Newport RFC B3
Newport Sta B2
North St B2
Oakfield Rd B1
Park Sq C2
Police Sta A3/C2
Post Office B2/C3
Power St A1
Prince St A3
Pugsley St A2
Queen St C2
Queen's Cl A1
Queen's Hill A1
Queen's Hill Cres A1
Queensway B2
Railway St B2
Riverfront Theatre & Arts Centre, The B2
Riverside A3
Rodney Rd B2
Royal Gwent (A&E) C2
Rudry St A3
Rugby Rd B3
Ruperra La C3
Ruperra St C3
St Edmund St B1
St Mark's Cres A1
St Mary St B1
St Vincent Rd A3
St Woolos † C2
St Woolos General (no A&E) C1
St Woolos Rd B1
School La B2
Serpentine Rd B1
Shaftesbury Park A2
Sheaf La A3
Skinner St B2
Sorrel Dr A1
South Market St C3
Spencer Rd B1
Stow Hill B2/C1/C2
Stow Park Ave C1
Stow Park Dr C1
TA Centre A1
Talbot St B2
Tennis Club A1
Tregare St A3
Trostrey St A3
Tunnel Terr B1
Turner St A3
Univ of Wales Newport City Campus B3
Upper Dock St B2
Usk St A3
Usk Way B3/C3
Victoria Cres B1
War Memorial A3
Waterloo Rd C1
West St B1
Wharves B2
Wheeler St A2
Whitby Place A3
Windsor Terr B1
York Place C1

Newquay 192

Agar Rd B2
Alma Place B1
Ambulance Station B2
Anthony Rd C1
Atlantic Hotel A1
Bank St B1
Barrowfields A3
Bay View Terr B2
Beach Rd B1
Beachfield Ave B1
Beacon Rd A1
Belmont Place A1
Berry Rd B2
Blue Reef Aquarium B1
Boating Lake C2
Bus Station B1
Chapel Hill B1
Chester Rd A3
Cheviot Rd C1/C2
Chichester Cres C2
Chynance Dr C1
Chyverton Cl C1
Cliff Rd B2
Coach Park B2
Colvreath Rd A3
Cornwall College Newquay B3
Council Ofices B1
Crantock St B1
Crescent, The B1
Criggar Rocks A3
Dale Cl C3
Dale Rd C3
Dane Rd A1
East St B2
Edgcumbe Ave B3
Edgcumbe Gdns B3
Eliot Gdns B3
Elm Cl C3
Ennor's Rd B1
Fernhill Rd B1
Fire Station B1
Fore St B1
Gannel Rd C2
Golf Driving Range B3
Gover La B1
Great Western Beach A2
Grosvenor Ave B2
Harbour A1
Hawkins Rd C2
Headleigh Rd B2
Hilgrove Rd A3/B3
Holywell Rd B3
Hope Terr B1
Huer's Hut, The A1
Information Ctr B1
Island Cres B2
Jubilee St B1
Kew Close C3
Killacourt Cove A2
King Edward Cres A1
Lanhenvor Ave B2
Library B1
Lifeboat Station A1
Lighthouse B1
Linden Ave C2
Listry Rd C2
Lusty Glaze Beach A3
Lusty Glaze Rd A3
Manor Rd B1
Marcus Hill B2
Mayfield Rd B2
Meadowside C3
Mellanvrane La C2

Michell Ave B2
Miniature Golf
Course C3
Miniature Railway
✦ B3
Mount Wise B1
Mowhay Cl C3
Narrowcliff A3
Newquay ⇌ B2
Newquay Hosp H . . B1
Newquay Town
Football Ground ✦ . A2
Newquay Zoo ✦ . . . A2
North Pier A1
North Quay Hill . . . B2
Oakleigh Terr B2
Pargolla Rd C3
Pendragon Cres . . . C3
Pengannel Cl C1
Penina Ave B3
Pirate's Quest ✦ . . B1
Police Station &
Courts ◨ A2
Post Office ⊠ . . . B1/B2
Quarry Park Rd B3
Rawley La C1
Reeds Way C3
Robartes Rd A3
St Anne's Rd A3
St Aubyn Cres B3
St George's Rd A1
St John's Rd A2
St Mary's Rd A1
St Michael's ⚓ . . . A1
St Michael's Rd . . . A1
St Thomas' Rd A3
Seymour Ave B1
South Pier A1
South Quay Hill . . . A1
Superstore B3
Sweet Briar Cres . . C3
Sydney Rd A2
Tolcarne Beach . . . A2
Tolcarne Point A2
Tolcarne Rd A2
Tor Rd B2
Towan Beach A1
Towan Blystra Rd . . B3
Tower Rd A1
Trebarwith Cres . . . A2
Tredour Rd C2
Treforda Rd C3
Tregoss Rd B3
Tregunnel Hill . . B1/C1
Tregunnel Saltings . C1
Trelawney Rd A2
Treloggan La C3
Treloggan Rd C3
Trembath Cres C1
Trenance Ave B2
Trenance Gardens . B2
Trenance La C2
Trenance Leisure
Park B3
Trenance Rd B2
Trenarth Rd B2
Treninnick Hill C3
Tretherras Rd B3
Trethewey Way C1
Trevemper Rd C1
Ulalia Rd B3
Vivian Cl B2
Waterworld B3
Whitegate Rd B3
Wych Hazel Way . . C3

Northampton 192

78 Derngate ⌂ . . . B3
Abington Sq A3
Abington St A3
Alcombe St A3
All Saints' ⛪ B1
Ambush St B1
Angel St B2
AR Centre A3
Arundel St A2
Ash St A2
Auctioneers Way . . C2
Bailiff St A2
Barrack Rd A2
Beaconsfield Terr . . A3
Becket's Park C3
Bedford Rd B3
Billing Rd B3
Brecon St A1
Brewery B2
Bridge St B2
Broad St B2
Burns St A3
Bus Station B2
Campbell St A2
Castle (Site of) . . . B2
Castle St B2
Cattle Market Rd . . B1
Central Museum &
Art Gallery ⌂ A2
Charles St A3
Cheyne Walk B3
Church La A2
Clare St A3
Cloutsham St A3
College St B2
Colwyn Rd A3
Cotton End C2
Countess Rd A1
County Hall ⌂ . . . B2
Court A2
Craven St A3
Crown & County
Courts A2
Denmark Rd B3
Derngate B2
Derngate & Royal
Theatres ⛫ B2
Doddridge Church
⛪ B1
Drapery, The B2
Duke St A2
Dunster St A3
Earl St A3
Euston Rd C2
Fire Station A2
Foot Meadow B2
Gladstone Rd A1
Gold St B2
Grafton St A2
Gray St A3
Green St B1
Greenwood Rd B1
Greyfriars B2
Grosvenor Centre . B2
Grove Rd A3
Guildhall ⌂ B2
Hampton St A3
Harding Terr A2
Hazelwood Rd B3

Herbert St B2
Hervey St A3
Hester St A2
Holy Sepulchre ⛪ . A2
Hood St A3
Horse Market B2
Hunter St A3
Information Ctr ⓘ . B2
Kettering Rd A3
Kingswell St B2
Lady's La A2
Leicester St A2
Leslie Rd A1
Library B3
Lorne Rd A2
Lorry Park A1
Louise Rd A1
Lower Harding St . . A1
Lower Hester St . . . A1
Lower Mounts B3
Lower Priory St . . . A1
Main Rd C1
Marefair B2
Market Sq B2
Marlboro Rd A1
Marriott St A1
Military Rd A3
Mounts Baths
Leisure Centre A3
Nene Valley
Retail Park C1
New South Bridge
Rd C2
Northampton General
Hospital (A&E) H . B3
Northampton
Marina B3
Northampton Sta ⇌ B1
Northcote St A2
Nunn Mills Rd C3
Old Towcester Rd . . C1
Overstone Rd A3
Peacock Place B2
Pembroke Rd A1
Penn Court C2
Police Station ◨ . . B3
Post Office ⊠ . . A1/B3
Quorn Way A1
Ransome Rd C3
Regent Sq A2
Ridings, The A2
Robert St A2
St Andrew's St B1
St Andrew's St A1
St Edmund's Rd . . . B3
St George's St B2
St Giles ⛪ B2
St Giles St B3
St Giles' Terr B3
St James Park Rd . . B1
St James Rd B1
St James Retail Pk . C1
St James' Mill Rd . . C1
St James' Mill Rd
East C1
St Leonard's Rd . . . C2
St Mary's St B2
St Michael's Rd . . . A3
St Peter's ⛪ B1
St Peter's Way
Shopping Precinct B2
St Peter's Way B1
Salisbury Rd A1
Scarletwell St B2
Semilong Rd A2
Sheep St B2
Sol Central
(Leisure Centre) . . . B2
Somerset St A3
South Bridge C2
Southfield Ave C2
Spencer Bridge Rd . A1
Spencer Rd A3
Spring Gdns B3
Spring La B1
Superstore A1
Swan St A3
Tintern Ave A1
Towcester Rd C2
Upper Bath St B2
Upper Mounts A2
Victoria Park A1
Victoria Prom B2
Victoria Rd B3
Victoria St A2
Wellingborough Rd B3
West Bridge C2
York Rd B3

Norwich 192

Albion Way C2
All Saints Green . . . C2
Anchor St A3
Anglia Sq A2
Argyle St C3
Arts Centre ⛫ B2
Ashby St C2
Assembly House ⛫ . B1
Bank Plain B2
Barker St A1
Barn Rd B1
Barrack St A3
Ber St C2
Bishop Bridge A3
Bishopbridge Rd . . A3
Bishopgate A2
Blackfriars St A2
Botolph St A2
Bracondale C3
Brazen Gate C2
Bridewell ⌂ B2
Brunswick Rd C1
Bull Close Rd A2
Bus Station C1
Calvert St A2
Cannell Green A3
Carrow Rd C3
Castle & Mus ⌂ ⌂ . B2
Castle Mall B2
Castle Meadow . . . B2
Cathedral † B2
Cathedral St B3
Cattlemarket St . . . B2
Chantry Rd B1
Chapel Loke C2
Chapelfield East . . . B1
Chapelfield Gdns . . B1
Chapelfield North . B1
Chapelfield Rd C1
Cinema City ⛫ . . . B2
City Hall ✦ B1
City Rd C3
City Wall C1/C3
Close, The B2/B3
Colegate A2

Coslany St B1
Cow Hill B1
Cow Tower A3
Cowgate A2
Crown & Magistrates'
Courts B1
Dragon Hall Heritage
Centre ⌂ C3
Duke St A1
Edward St A2
Elm Hill B2
Erpingham Gate ✦ . B2
Fishergate A2
Forum, The B1
Foundry Bridge . . . B3
Fye Bridge A2
Garden St C2
Gas Hill A3
Gentlemans Walk . . B1
Grapes Hill B1
Great Hospital Halls,
The A3
Grove Ave C1
Grove Rd C1
Guildhall ✦ B1
Gurney Rd A3
Hall Rd C2
Heathgate A3
Heigham St A1
Hollywood ⛫ A2
Horn's La C2
Hungate Medieval
Art ✦ A2
Information Ctr ⓘ . B2
intu Chapelfield . . . C1
Ipswich Rd C1
ITV Anglia A3
James Stuart Gdns . B3
King St B3
King St C3
Koblenz Ave C3
Leisure Centre A3
Library B1
London St B2
Lower Clarence Rd . B3
Maddermarket ⛫ . B1
Magdalen St A2
Mariners La C2
Market B1
Market Ave B2
Mountergate B2
Mousehold St A3
Newmarket Rd C1
Norfolk St C1
Norwich City FC . . . C3
Norwich Gallery ⌂ . B2
Norwich School ✦ . B2
Norwich Station ⇌ . B3
Oak St A1
Odeon ⛫ B1
Palace St A2
Pitt St A1
Playhouse ⛫ B2
Police Station B1
Post Office ⊠
. . . . A2/B2/B3/C1
Pottergate B1
Prince of Wales Rd . B2
Princes St B2
Pull's Ferry ✦ B3
Puppet Theatre ⛫ . A2
Queen St B2
Queens Rd C2
RC Cathedral † B1
Recorder Rd B3
Riverside
Entertainment Ctr . C3
Riverside Leisure
Centre C3
Riverside Rd B3
Riverside Retail Pk . C3
Rosary Rd B3
Rose La B2
Rouen Rd B2
St Andrews St B2
St Augustines St . . A1
St Benedicts St . . . B1
St Ethelbert's
Gate ✦ B2
St Faiths La B3
St Georges St A2
St Giles St B1
St James Cl A3
St Julians St C2
St Leonards Rd . . . A3
St Martin's La A1
St Peter
Mancroft ⛪ B2
St Peters St B1
St Stephens Rd . . . C1
St Stephens St C1
Shopmobility C1
Silver Rd A2
Silver St A2
Southwell Rd C2
St. Andrew's &
Blackfriars' Hall ✦ . B2
Strangers' Hall ⌂ . B1
Superstore C2
Surrey St C2
Sussex St A1
Theatre Royal ⛫ . . B1
Theatre St B1
Thorn La C2
Thorpe Rd B3
Tombland B2
Union St C1
Vauxhall St B1
Victoria St C1
Vue ⛫ B2
Walpole St B1
Waterfront, The . . . C3
Wensum St A2
Wessex St C1
Westwick St B1
Wherry Rd C3
Whitefriars A2
Willow La B1

Nottingham 192

Abbotsford Dr A3
Addison St A1
Albert Hall ⛫ B1
Alfred St Central . . A3
Alfreton Rd B1
All Saints St A1
Annesley Grove . . . A1
Arboretum ❀ A1
Arboretum St A1
Arthur St A1
Arts Theatre ⛫ . . . B3
Ashforth St A2
Balmoral Rd A1
Barker Gate B3
Bath St B3
BBC Nottingham . . C3

Beacon Hill Rise . . B3
Belgrave Rooms . . . B1
Bellar Gate B3
Belward St B3
Brewhouse Yard ⌂ . C1
Broad Marsh Bus
Station C2
Broad St B2
Brook St B3
Burns St A1
Burton St B2
Bus Station A2
Canal St C2
Carlton St B3
Carrington St C2
Castle ⌂ C1
Castle Blvd C1
Castle Gate C2
Castle Meadow Rd . C1
Castle Meadow
Retail Park C1
Castle Rd C1
Castle Wharf C2
Cavendish Rd East . A1
Cemetery A1/B1
Chaucer St A2
Cheapside B2
Church Rd A3
City Link C3
City of Caves ✦ . . . C2
Clarendon St B1
Cliff Rd C2
Clumber Rd East . . A1
Clumber St B2
College St B1
Collin St C2
Contemporary ⌂ . . C2
Conway Cl A2
Cornerhouse,
The ⛫ B2
Council House ⌂ . . B2
Cranbrook St B3
Cranmer St A2
Cromwell St B1
Curzon St B3
Derby Rd B1
Dryden St A2
Exchange Ctr, The . B2
Fishpond Dr C1
Fletcher Gate B3
Forest East Rd A1
Forest West Rd . . . A1
Friar La C2
Gedling Grove A1
Gedling St B3
George St B2
Gill St A2
Glasshouse St B2
Goldsmith St B2
Goose Gate B3
Great Freeman St . . A2
Guildhall ⌂ B2
Hamilton Dr C1
Hampden St A1
Heathcote St B3
High Pavement C3
High School ⌂ A1
HM Revenue &
Customs C2
Holles Cres C1
Hope Dr C1
Hungerhill Rd A3
Huntingdon Dr C1
Huntingdon St A2
Instow Rise A3
Int Com Ctr A2
intu Broadmarsh . . C2
intu Victoria Centre B2
Kent St B3
King St B2
Lace Market ⇌ . . . B3
Lace Mkt Theatre ⛫ C3
Lamartine St B3
Lenton Rd C1
Lewis Cl A3
Lincoln St B2
London Rd C3
Long Row B2
Low Pavement C2
Lower Parliament
St A3
Magistrates' Court . C2
Maid Marian Way . . B2
Mansfield Rd . . . A2/B2
Middle Hill C2
Milton St A2
Mount St B2
National Ice Centre &
Motorpoint Arena . C3
National Justice
Museum ⌂ C3
Newcastle Dr B1
Newstead Grove . . A2
North Sherwood St A2
Nottingham Arena . C3
Nottingham Cath † B2
Nottingham Coll. . . C2
Nottingham
Station ⇌ ⇌ C2
Nottingham Trent
University A2/B2
Old Mkt Square ⇌ . B2
Oliver St A1
Park Dr C1
Park Row B1
Park Terr C1
Park Valley C1
Park, The C1
Peas Hill Rd A3
Peel St A1
Pelham St B3
Peveril Dr C1
Plantagenet St A3
Playhouse
Theatre ⛫ B1
Plumptre St C3
Poplar St C3
Portland Rd C1
Post Office ⊠ B1
Queen's Rd C2
Raleigh St A1
Regent St B1
Rick St B3
Robin Hood St B3
Robin Hood
Statue ✦ C1
Ropewalk, The B1
Royal Centre ⇌ . . . B2
Royal Children Inn
⌂ C1
Royal Concert
Hall ⛫ B2
St Ann's Hill Rd . . . A1
St Ann's Way A3

St Ann's Well Rd . . A3
St James' St B2
St Mark's St A3
St Mary's Rest Gdn . B3
St Mary's Gate B3
St Nicholas ⛪ C2
St Peter's ⛪ B2
St Peter's Gate B2
Salutation Inn ⌂ . . C2
Shakespeare St . . . B2
Shelton St A2
Shopmobility B2
South Parade B2
South Rd C1
South Sherwood St B2
Station Street ⇌ . . C2
Stoney St B3
Talbot St B1
Tattershall Dr C1
Tennis Dr C1
Tennyson St A1
Theatre Royal ⛫ . . B2
Trent St C3
Trent University ⇌ . A1
Union Rd B3
Upper Parliament
St B1
Victoria Leisure
Centre B3
Victoria Park B3
Victoria St B2
Walter St A1
Warser Gate B3
Watkin St A2
Waverley St A1
Wheeler Gate B2
Wilford Rd C2
Wilford St C2
Wollaton St B1
Woodborough Rd . . A3
Woolpack La B3
Ye Old Trip to
Jerusalem ✦ C1
York St A2

Oxford 193

Adelaide St A1
Albert St A1
All Souls (Coll) B2
Ashmolean Mus ⌂ . B1
Balliol (Coll) B2
Banbury Rd A2
Bate Collection of
Musical
Instruments ⌂ . . . C2
Beaumont St B1
Becket St B1
Blackhall Rd A2
Blue Boar St B2
Bodleian Library ⌂ . B2
Botanic Garden ❀ . B2
Brasenose (Coll) . . B2
Brewer St C2
Broad St B2
Burton-Taylor
Theatre ⛫ B2
Bus Station B1
Canal St A1
Cardigan St A1
Carfax Tower B2
Castle ⌂ B1
Castle St B1
Catte St B2
Cemetery C1
Christ Church (Coll) B2
Christ Church
Cathedral † C2
Christ Church
Meadow C2
Clarendon Centre . B2
Coach & Lorry Park C1
College B1
Coll of Further Ed. . C1
Cornmarket St B2
Corpus Christi
(Coll) B2
County Hall B1
Covered Market . . . B2
Cowley Place C3
Cranham St A1
Cranham Terr A1
Cricket Ground B1
Crown & County
Courts C2
Deer Park B2
Exeter (Coll) B2
Folly Bridge C2
George St B1
Great Clarendon St A1
Hart St A1
Hertford (Coll) B2
High St B2
Hollybush Row B1
Holywell St B2
Hythe Bridge St . . . B1
Ice Rink B1
Information Ctr ⓘ . B2
Jericho St A1
Jesus (Coll) B2
Jowett Walk B2
Juxon St A1
Keble (Coll) A2
Keble Rd A2
Library B2
Linacre (Coll) A3
Lincoln (Coll) B2
Little Clarendon St. B1
Longwall St B3
Magdalen (Coll) . . . B3
Magdalen Bridge . . B3
Magdalen St B2
Magistrate's Court. . C2
Manchester (Coll) . B2
Manor Rd B3
Mansfield (Coll) . . . A3
Market B2
Marlborough Rd . . . C2
Merton (Coll) B2
Merton Field B2
Merton St B2
Museum of
Modern Art ⌂ B2
Mus of Oxford ⌂ . . B2
Museum Rd A2
New College (Coll) . B3
New Inn Hall St . . . B2
New Rd B1
New Theatre ⛫ . . . B2
Norfolk St C1
Nuffield (Coll) B1
Observatory A1
Observatory St A1
Odeon ⛫ B1/B2
Old Fire Station . . . B1

Old Greyfriars St . . C2
Oriel (Coll) B2
Oxford Station ⇌ . . B1
Oxford University
Research Centres . . A1
Oxpens Rd C1
Paradise Sq C1
Paradise St B1
Park End St B1
Parks Rd A2/B2
Pembroke (Coll) . . . C2
Phoenix ⛫ A1
Picture Gallery ⌂ . . B2
Plantation Rd A1
Playhouse ⛫ B2
Police Station ◨ . . C2
Post Office ⊠ . A1/B2
Pusey St B2
Queen's (Coll) B2
Queen's La B3
Radcliffe
Camera ⌂ B2
Rewley Rd B1
Richmond Rd A1
Rose La B3
Ruskin (Coll) B1
Said Bsns School . . A2
St Aldates C2
St Anne's (Coll) . . . A1
St Antony's (Coll) . . A1
St Bernard's Rd . . . A1
St Catherine's
(Coll) B3
St Cross Building . . A3
St Cross Rd A3
St Edmund Hall
(Coll) B3
St Giles St A2
St Hilda's (Coll) . . . C3
St John St B2
St John's (Coll) . . . B2
St Mary the Virgin B2
St Michael at the
Northgate ✦ B2
St Peter's (Coll) . . . B1
Science Area A2
Science Museum ⌂ B2
Sheldonian
Theatre ⛫ B2
Somerville (Coll) . . A1
South Parks Rd . . . A2
Speedwell St C2
Thames St C1
Town Hall B2
Trinity (Coll) B2
Turl St B2
Univ Coll (Coll) . . . B2
St Ninians Cath † . . A2
Scott Monument . . C1
Scott St B2
Sheriff Court A2
Shore Rd C3
Skate Park C2
South Inch C2
South Inch Bsns Ctr C2
South Inch View . . . C2
South Methven St . C1
South St B2
South William St . . B2
Stables, The A1
Stanners, The A3
Stormont St A2
Strathmore St A1
Stuart Ave C1
Superstore B1/B2
Tay St B3
Union La A2
Victoria St B2
Watergate B3
Wellshill Cemetery A1
West Bridge St A3
West Mill St B2
Whitefriers Cres. . . B1
Whitefriers St B1
Wilson St C1
Windsor Terr C1
Woodside Cres . . . C1
York Place B2
Young St C1

Univ Mus &
Pitt Rivers Mus ⌂ . A2
University Parks . . . A2
Wadham (Coll) B2
Walton Cres A1
Walton St A1
Western Rd C2
Westgate C2
Woodstock Rd A1
Worcester (Coll) . . B1

Perth 193

AK Bell Library B2
Abbot Cres C1
Abbot St C1
Albany Terr A1
Albert Monument . . A3
Alexandra St B2
Atholl St A2
Balhousie Ave A2
Balhousie Castle &
Museum ⌂ A2
Balhousie St A2
Ballantine Place . . . A1
Barossa Place A2
Barossa St A2
Barrack St A2
Bell's Sports Ctr . . . A2
Bellwood B3
Blair St B1
Burn Park C1
Bus Station B2
Caledonian Rd B1
Canal Cres C2
Canal St C2
Cavendish Ave C1
Charles St B2
Charlotte Place A2
Charlotte St A2
Church St A1
City Hall B2
Club House A3
Clyde Place C1
Coach Park A2
Commercial St B2
Concert Hall ⛫ . . . B2
Council Chambers . B2
Council Place B1
Court B2
Craigie Place C1
Crieff Rd A1
Croft Park C2
Cross St A2
Darnhall Cres C1
Darnhall Dr C1
Dewars Centre A1
Dundee Rd B3
Dunkeld Rd A1
Earl's Dykes B1
Edinburgh Rd C2
Elibank St C1
Fair Maid's Ho ✦ . . A2
Ferguson ✦ C3
Feus Rd A1
Fire Station B2
Foundary La A2
Friar St C1
Glamis Place C1
Glasgow Rd B1
Glenearn Rd C2
Glover St B1/C1
Golf Course A3
Gowrie St A3
Gray St B1
Graybank Rd B1
Greyfriars Burial
Grnd. A3
Hay St A2
High St B2/B3
Inchaffray St A1
Ind/Retail Park B1
Information Ctr ⓘ . B2
Isla Rd A3
James St B3
Keir St B1

Peterborough 193

Athletics Arena . . . A3
Bishop's Palace ⌂ . B2
Bishop's Rd B2/B3
Bishop's Rd B3
Boongate A3
Bourges Boulevard A1
Bourges Retail
Park B1/B2
Bridge House
(Council Offices) . . C2
Bright St A1
Broadway A2
Broadway ⛫ A2
Brook St A2
Burghley Rd A2
Bus Station A2
Cavendish St A3
Charles St A3
Church St B2
Church Walk A2
Cobden Ave A1
Cobden St A1
Cowgate B2
Craig St A1
Crawthorne Rd A2
Cromwell Rd A1
Dickens St A2
Eastfield Rd A3
Eastgate A3
Embankment Rd . . . B2
Exchange St B2
Fire Station B2
Fish Quay B3
Fitzwilliam St A2
Frank Perkins
Parkway C3
Geneva St A2
George St C1
Gladstone St A1
Glebe Rd C2
Gloucester Rd B3
Granby St A3
Grove St C1
Guildhall ⌂ B2
Hampton St B1
Harvest La B3
Hawksbill Way C1
Henry St A1
Hereward Cross
(shopping) B2
Hereward Rd B3
Information Ctr ⓘ . B2
Information Ctr ⓘ . B2
Jubilee St C1
Kent Rd A3
Key Theatre ⛫ . . . C2
Kirkwood Cl A1
Lea Gdns B1

Plymouth 193

Alma Rd A1
Anstis St A1
Armada Shopping
Ctr A2
Armada St A2
Armada Way B2
Arts Centre B2
Athenaeum ⛫ C1
Athenaeum St C1
Barbican C3
Barbican ⛫ C3
Baring St A3
Bath St C1
Bay Hog La C2
Beaumont Park A3
Beaumont Rd A3
Black Friars Gin
Distillery ✦ C3
Breton Side B3
Castle St C3
Cathedral (RC) † . . . A1
Cecil St A1
Central Park A1
Central Park Ave . . A1
Charles Church ⌂ . B3
Charles Cross ◑ . . B3
Charles St B2
Citadel Rd C1
Citadel Rd East . . . C2
City Museum &
Art Gallery ⌂ A2
Civic Centre ⌂ . . . B2
Cliff Rd C1
Clifton Place A3
Cobourg St A2
College of Art B2
Continental Ferry
Port A1
Cornwall St B2
Crescent, The B1
Dale Rd A1
Deptford Place A3
Derry Ave A2
Derry's Cross ◑ . . B2
Drake Circus B2
Drake Circus
Shopping Centre . . B2
Eastlake St B2
Ebrington St B3
Elizabethan Ho . . . C3
Elliot St C2
Endsleigh Place . . . A2
Exeter St B3
Fire Station A2
Fish Quay C3
Gibbons St A3
Glen Park Ave A2
Grand Parade C1
Great Western Rd . C1
Greenbank Rd A3
Greenbank Terr . . . A3
Guildhall ⌂ B2
Hampton St B3
Harwell St B1
Hill Park Cres A3
Hoe Approach C2
Hoe Rd C2
Hoe, The C2
Hoegate St C3
Houndiscombe Rd . A2
Information Ctr ⓘ . C3
Information Ctr ⓘ . A2
James St A2
Kensington Rd A3
King St B1
Lambhay Hill C3

Poole 194

Ambulance Station A3
Baiater Gdns C2
Baiter Park C3
Ballard Cl C2
Ballard Rd C2
Bridge Approach . . A1
Bus Station B2
Castle St A2
Catalina Dr C3
Chapel La A2
Church St B1
Cinnamon La A1
Colborne Cl B3
Dear Hay La B2
Denmark La A3
Denmark Rd A3
Dolphin Ctr B2
East St B2
Elizabeth Rd A3
Emerson Rd B2
Ferry Rd C1
Ferry Terminal A2
Fire Station A3
Freightliner
Terminal C2
Furnell Rd B3
Garland Rd A3
Green Rd B2
Heckford La A3
Heckford Rd A3
High St B2
High St North A3
Hill St B2
Holes Bay Rd A1
Hospital (A&E) H . . A3
Information Ctr ⓘ . C1
Kingland Rd B3
Kingston Rd A3
Labrador Dr C3
Lagland St B2
Lander Cl B3
Lifeboat Coll, The . . A2
Lighthouse, Poole Ctr
for the Arts ⛫ B2
Longfleet Rd A3
Maple Rd A3
Market Cl B2
Market St B2
Mount Pleasant Rd B3
New Harbour Rd . . . C1
New Harbour Rd
South C1
New Harbour Rd
West. C1
New Orchard B1
New Quay Rd B1
New St B2
Newfoundland Dr . . B2
Old Lifeboat ⌂ . . . A2
Old Orchard B2
Parish Rd A3
Park Lake Rd B3
Parkstone Rd A3
Perry Gdns B2

Pitwines Cl B2
Police Station ◨ . . A2
Poole Central Liby . B2
Poole Lifting
Bridge C1
Poole Park C3
Poole Station ⇌ . . . A2
Poole Museum ⌂ . . B1
Post Office ⊠ . . A2/B2
Quay, The C1
St John's Rd A3
St Margaret's Rd . . A3
St Mary's
Maternity Unit A3
St Mary's Rd A3
Seldown Bridge . . . B3
Seldown La B3
Seldown Rd B3
Serpentine Rd A2
Shaftesbury Rd . . . A3
Skinner St B2
Slipway C1
Stanley Rd B2
Sterte Ave A2
Sterte Ave West . . . A1
Sterte Cl A2
Sterte Esplanade . . A1
Sterte Rd A2
Strand St C2
Swimming Pool . . . B3
Taverner Cl B3
Thames St C1
Towngate Bridge . . B2
Twin Sails Bridge . . B1
Vallis Cl C1
Walden Rd A1
West Quay B1
West Quay Rd B1
West St C1
West View Rd A3
Whatleigh Cl B2
Wimborne Rd A3

Portsmouth 194

Action Stations ✦ . C1
Admiralty Rd A1
Alfred Rd A2
Anglesea Rd B2
Arundel St B3
Aspex ⌂ C2
Bishop St A1
Broad St C1
Buckingham Ho ⌂ . C2
Burnaby Rd B2
Bus Station B2
Camber Dock C1
Cambridge Rd B2
Car Ferry to Isle of
Wight. C1
Cascades Shopping
Centre A3
Castle Rd C2
Civic Offices A3
Clarence Pier C2
College St A1
Commercial Rd . . . A3
Cottage Grove B3
Cross St. A1
Cumberland St A1
Duisburg Way C2
Durham St B3
East St B1
Edinburgh Rd A2
Elm Grove C3
Emirates Spinnaker
Tower ✦ B1
Governor's Grn. . . . C1
Great Southsea St . C3
Green Rd B3
Greetham St B3
Grosvenor St B3
Groundlings ⛫ . . . A1
Grove Rd North . . . B3
Grove Rd South . . . C3
Guildhall ⌂ B3
Guildhall Walk B3
Gunwharf Quays
Designer Outlet . . . B1
Gunwharf Rd B1
Hambrook St C2
Hampshire Terrace B3
Hanover St A1
Hard, The B1
High St C2
HM Naval Base A1
HMS Nelson (Royal
Naval Barracks) . . . A2
HMS Monitor M.33 B1
HMS Victory ⚓ . . . A1
HMS Warrior ⚓ . . A1
Hovercraft
Terminal C2
Hyde Park Rd B3
Information Ctr
ⓘ A1/B3
Isambard Brunel Rd B3
Isle of Wight Car
Ferry Terminal B1
Kent Rd C3
Kent St A1
King St B3
King's Rd C3
King's Terr C3
Lake Rd A3
Law Courts B3
Library B3
Long Curtain Rd . . . C2
Marina B1
Market Way A3
Marmion Rd C3
Mary Rose ⌂ A1
Middle St B3
Millennium Prom
Walk. B1/C1
Museum Rd C2
National Museum of
the Royal Navy ⌂ . A1
Naval Rec Gd C1
Nightingale Rd C3
Norfolk St B3
North St A2
Osborne Rd C3
Paradise St A3
Park Rd A3
Passenger Catamaran
to Isle of Wight . . . B1
Passenger Ferry to
Gosport B1
Pelham Rd C3
Pembroke Gdns . . . C2
Pier Rd C2
Point Battery C1
Police Station ◨ . . B3
Portsmouth &
Southsea Sta ⇌ . . A3

Portsmouth Harbour Station ⇌ B1
Portsmouth Historic Dockyard 🏛 A1
Portsmouth Museum & Art Gallery 🏛 B2
Post Office 📮 A1/A3/B3
Queen St A1
Queen's Cres C3
Ravelin Park B2
Register Office B2
Round Tower ✦ C1
Royal Garrison Church ⛪ C1
St Edward's Rd C3
St George's Rd B2
St George's Sq B1
St George's Way B2
St James's Rd B3
St James's St A2
St John's Cathedral (RC) ✝ A3
St Thomas's Cath ✝ C1
St Thomas's St B2
Shopmobility A3/B1
Somers Rd B3
Southsea Common C2
Southsea Terr C2
Square Tower ✦ C1
Station St A3
Town Fortifications ✦ C1
Unicorn Rd A2
United Services Recreation Ground B2
University of Portsmouth A2/B2
Univ of Portsmouth B3
Upper Arundel St A3
Victoria Ave C2
Victoria Park A2
Victory Gate A1
Vue 🎥 B1
Warblington St B1
Western Pde C2
White Hart Rd C1
Winston Churchill Ave B3

Preston 194

Adelphi St A2
Anchor Ct B3
Aqueduct St A1
Ardee Rd C1
Arthur St B2
Ashton St A1
Avenham La B3
Avenham Park C3
Avenham Rd B3
Avenham St B3
Bairstow St B3
Balderstone Rd C1
Beamont Dr A1
Beech St South C2
Bird St C1
Bow La B2
Brieryfield Rd A1
Broadgate C1
Brook St A2
Bus Station A3
Butler St B2
Cannon St B3
Carlton St A1
Chaddock St B3
Channel Way B1
Chapel St B3
Christ Church St B2
Christian Rd B2
Cold Bath St A2
Coleman Ct C1
Connaught Rd C2
Corn Exchange 🏠 B3
Corporation St A2/B2
County Hall B2
Cricket Ground C2
Croft St A1
Cross St B3
Crown Court A3
Crown St A3
East Cliff C3
East Cliff Rd B3
Edward St A2
Elizabeth St A3
Euston St B1
Fishergate B2/B3
Fishergate Hill B2
Fishergate Shopping Centre B2
Fitzroy St B1
Fleetwood St A1
Friargate A3
Fylde Rd A1/A2
Gerrard St B2
Glover's Ct B3
Good St B2
Grafton St B2
Great George St A3
Great Shaw St A3
Greenbank St A2
Guild Way B1
Guild Hall & Charter 🎭 B3
Guildhall St B3
Harrington St A2
Harris Museum 🏛 B3
Hartington Rd B1
Hasset Cl C2
Heatley St B2
Hind St C2
Information Ctr ℹ B3
Kilruddery Rd C1
Lancashire Archives B2
Lancaster Rd A3/B3
Latham St B3
Lauderdale St C2
Lawson St A3
Leighton St A2
Leyland Rd C1
Library A1
Library B3
Liverpool Rd C1
Lodge St B2
Lune St B3
Magistrate's Court A3
Main Sprit West B3
Maresfield Rd C1
Market St West A3
Marsh La B1/B2
Maudland Bank A2
Maudland Rd A2
Meadow Ct C2
Meath Rd C1
Mill Hill A2
Miller Arcade ✦ B3
Miller Park C3
Moor La A3
Mount St B3
North Rd A3
North St A3
Northcote Rd B1
Old Milestones B1
Old Tram Rd C3
Pedder St A1/A2
Peel St A2
Penwortham Bridge C2
Penwortham New Bridge C1
Pitt St B2
Playhouse 🎭 A3
Police Station 🚓 A3
Port Way B1
Post Office 📮 B3
Preston Station ⇌ B2
Retail Park B2
Ribble Bank St B2
Ribble Viaduct C2
Ribblesdale Place B3
Ringway B3
River Parade C1
Riverside C2
St George's Shopping Centre B3
St Georges ⛪ B3
St Johns ⛪ B3
St Johns Shopping Centre A3
St Mark's Rd A1
St Walburges ⛪ A1
Salisbury Rd B1
Sessions House 🏠 B3
Snow Hill A3
South End C2
South Meadow La C2
Spa Rd B1
Sports Ground C2
Strand Rd B1
Syke St B3
Talbot Rd B1
Taylor St C1
Tithebarn St A3
Town Hall B3
Tulketh Brow A1
University of Central Lancashire A2
Valley Rd C1
Victoria St A2
Walker St A3
Walton's Parade B2
Warwick St A3
Wellfield Bsns Park A1
Wellfield Rd A1
Wellington St A1
West Cliff C2
West Strand A1
Winckley Rd C1
Winckley Square B3
Wolseley Rd C2

Reading 194

Abbey Ruins ✝ B2
Abbey Sq B2
Abbey St B2
Abbot's Walk B2
Acacia Rd C2
Addington Rd C3
Addison Rd A1
Allcroft Rd C3
Alpine St C2
Baker St B1
Berkeley Ave C1
Bridge St B1
Brigham Rd A1
Broad St B1
Broad Street Mall B1
Carey St B1
Castle Hill C1
Castle St B1
Causeway, The A3
Caversham Rd A1
Christchurch Playing Fields A2
Civic Offices B1
Coley Hill C1
Coley Place C1
Craven Rd C3
Crown St C2
De Montfort Rd A1
Denmark Rd C3
Duke St B2
East St B2
Edgehill St C2
Eldon Rd B3
Eldon Terr B3
Elgar Rd C1
Erleigh Rd C3
Field Rd C1
Fire Station A1
Fobney St B1
Forbury Gdns B2
Forbury Rd B2
Forbury Retail Park B2
Francis St C1
Friar St B1
Garrard St B1
Gas Works Rd B3
George St A2
Great Knollys St B1
Greyfriars ⛪ B1
Grove, The B2
Gun St B1
Henry St C1
Hexagon Theatre, The 🎭 B1
Hill's Meadow A2
Howard St B1
Inner Distribution Rd B1
Katesgrove La C1
Kenavon Dr B2
Kendrick Rd C2
King's Meadow Recreation Gd A2
King's Rd B2
Library B2
London Rd C3
London St B2
Lynmouth Rd A1
Magistrate's Court B1
Market Place B2
Mill La B2
Mill Rd A2
Minster St B1
Morgan Rd C3
Mount Pleasant C2
Museum of English Rural Life 🏛 C3
Napier Rd A2
Newark St C2
Newport Rd A1
Old Reading Univ C3
Oracle Shopping Centre, The B1
Orts Rd B3
Pell St C1
Police Station 🚓 B1
Post Office 📮 B2
Queen Victoria St B1
Queen's Rd A2
Queen's Rd B2
Randolph Rd A1
Reading Bridge A2
Reading Station ⇌ A1
Redlands Rd C3
Renaissance Hotel B1
Riverside Mus 🏛 B3
Rose Kiln La C1
Royal Berks Hospital (A&E) 🏥 C3
St Giles ⛪ C2
St Laurence ⛪ B2
St Mary's ⛪ B1
St Mary's Butts B1
St Saviour's Rd C1
Send Rd A3
Sherman Rd C2
Sidmouth St B2
Silver St C2
South St B2
Southampton St C2
Station Hill A1
Station Rd B1
Superstore A3
Swansea Rd A1
Technical College B3
Valpy St B2
Vastern Rd A1
Vue 🎥 B2
Waldeck St C2
Watlington St B3
West St B1
Whitby Dr C3
Wolseley St C1
York Rd A1
Zinzan St B1

St Andrews 195

Abbey St B2
Abbey Walk B3
Abbotsford Cres A1
Albany Pk C3
Allan Robertson Dr C2
Ambulance Station C1
Anstruther Rd C3
Argyle St B1
Auld Burn Rd B2
Bassaguard Ind Est B1
Bell St B2
Blackfriars Chapel (Ruins) B2
Boase Ave B2
Braid Cres C3
Brewster Place C3
Bridge St B1
British Golf Mus 🏛 A1
Broomfaulds Ave C1
Bruce Embankment A1
Bruce St C2
Bus Station A1
Byre Theatre 🎭 B2
Canongate C1
Cathedral and Priory (Ruins) ✝ B3
Cemetery B3
Chamberlain St C1
Church St B2
Churchill Cres C2
City Rd A1
Claybraes C1
Cockshaugh Public Park B1
Cosmos Com Ctr B3
Council Office A2
Crawford Gdns C1
Doubledykes Rd B1
Drumcarrow Rd C1
East Sands B3
East Scores A3
Fire Station C1
Forrest St C1
Fraser Ave C1
Freddie Tait St C2
Gateway Centre A1
Glebe Rd B2
Golf Place A1
Grange Rd C3
Greenside Place B2
Greyfriars Gdns A2
Hamilton Ave C2
Hepburn Gdns B1
Holy Trinity ⛪ B2
Horseleys Park C1
Information Ctr ℹ B2
Irvine Cres C3
James Robb Ave C1
James St B1
John Knox Rd C1
Kennedy Gdns B1
Kilrymont Close C3
Kilrymont Place C3
Kilrymont Rd C3
Kinburn Park B1
Kinkell Terr C3
Kinnesburn Rd B2
Ladebraes Walk B2
Lady Buchan's Cave A3
Lamberton Place C1
Lamond Dr C2
Langlands Rd B2
Largo Rd C1
Learmonth Place C1
Library B2
Links Clubhouse A1
Links, The A1
Livingstone Cres B2
Long Rocks A2
Madras College B2
Market St A2
Martyr's Monument A1
Murray Pk A2
Murray Place A2
Mus of the Univ of St Andrews (MUSA) ✦ A2
Nelson St B2
New Course, The A1
New Picture Ho 🎥 A2
North Castle St A3
North St A2
Old Course, The A1
Old Station Rd A1
Pends, The B3
Pilmour Links A1
Pipeland Rd B2/C2
Police Sta 🚓 A2/C1
Post Office 📮 B2
Preservation Trust 🏛 B2
Priestden Pk C3
Priestden Place C3
Priestden Rd C3
Queen's Gdns B2
Queen's Terr B2
Roundhill Rd C2
Royal & Ancient Golf Club A1
St Andrews 🏛 B1
St Andrews Aquarium 🐟 A2
St Andrews Botanic Garden ✿ B1
St Andrews Castle (Ruins) & Visitor Centre 🏰 A2
St Leonard's Sch B3
St Mary St B3
St Mary's College B2
St Nicholas St C3
St Rules Tower ✦ B3
St Salvator's Coll A2
Sandyhill Cres C2
Sandyhill Rd C2
Scooniehill Rd C2
Scores, The A2
Shields Ave C3
Shoolbraids C2
Shore, The B3
Sloan St B1
South St B2
Spottiswoode Gdns C1
Station Rd A1
Swilcen Bridge A1
Tom Morris Dr C2
Tom Stewart La C1
Town Hall B2
Union St A2
Univ Chapel ⛪ A2
University Library A2
Univ of St Andrews A1
Viaduct Walk B1
War Memorial A3
Wardlaw Gdns B1
Warrack St C3
Watson Ave B2
West Port B2
West Sands A1
Westview B2
Windmill Rd A1
Winram Place C1
Wishart Gdns C2
Woodburn Pk B3
Woodburn Place B3
Woodburn Terr B3
Younger Hall 🏠 A2

Salisbury 195

Albany Rd A2
Arts Centre 🖼 A3
Ashley Rd A1
Avon Approach A2
Ayleswade Rd C2
Bedwin St A2
Belle Vue A2
Bishop's Palace 🏠 C2
Bishops Walk B2
Blue Boar Row B2
Bourne Ave A3
Bourne Hill A3
Britford La C2
Broad Walk C2
Brown St B2
Bus Station B2
Castle St A2
Catherine St B2
Chapter House B2
Church House 🏠 B2
Churchfields Rd B1
Churchill Way East B3
Churchill Way North A3
Churchill Way South C2
Churchill Way West A1
City Hall B2
Close Wall B2
Coldharbour La A1
College St A3
Council Offices A3
Court A1
Crane Bridge Rd B2
Crane St B2
Cricket Ground C1
Culver St South B3
De Vaux Place C2
Devizes Rd A1
Dews Rd B1
Elm Grove B3
Elm Grove Rd A3
Endless St A2
Estcourt Rd A3
Exeter St C2
Fairview Rd A3
Fire Station A1
Fisherton St A1
Folkestone Rd C1
Fowlers Hill B3
Fowlers Rd B3
Friary Estate C3
Friary La B2
Friary, The B3
Gas La A1
Gigant St B3
Greencroft B3
Greencroft St A3
Guildhall 🏠 B2
Hall of John Halle 🏠 B2
Hamilton Rd A2
Harnham Mill B1
Harnham Rd C1/C2
High St B2
Hospital 🏥 A1
House of John A'Port 🏠 B2
Information Ctr ℹ B2
Kelsey Rd A3
King's Rd A2
Laverstock Rd B3
Library B2
London Rd A3
Lower St C1
Maltings, The B2
Manor Rd A3
Marsh La A1
Medieval Hall 🏠 B2
Milford Hill B3
Milford St B3
Mill Rd B1
Millstream Approach A2
Mompesson House (NT) 🏛 B2
New Bridge Rd C2
New Canal B2
New Harnham Rd C2
New St B2
North Canonry 🏠 B2
North Gate B2
North Walk B2
Old Blandford Rd C1
Old Deanery 🏠 B2
Old George Hall B2
Park St A3
Parsonage Green C1
Playhouse Theatre 🎭 A2
Post Office 📮 A2/B2/C2
Poultry Cross B2
Queen Elizabeth Gardens B1
Queen's Rd A3
Rampart Rd B3
St Ann St B2
St Ann's Gate B2
St Marks Rd A3
St Martins ⛪ B3
St Mary's Cath ✝ B2
St Nicholas Hosp 🏥 C2
St Paul's ⛪ A1
St Paul's Rd A1
St Thomas ⛪ B2
Salisbury & South Wiltshire Mus 🏛 B2
Salisbury Station ⇌ A1
Salt La A3
Saxon Rd C1
Scots La A2
Shady Bower B3
South Canonry 🏠 C2
South Gate C2
Southampton Rd B2
Spire View A1
Sports Ground C3
Tollgate Rd B3
Town Path B1
Wain-a-Long Rd A3
Wardrobe, The 🏛 B2
Wessex Rd A3
West Walk C2
Wilton Rd A1
Wiltshire College B3
Winchester St B3
Windsor Rd A1
Winston Churchill Gdns C3
Wyndham Rd A2
YHA ▲ B3
York Rd A1

Scarborough 195

Aberdeen Walk B2
Albert Rd A2
Albion Rd C2
Auborough St B2
Balmoral Ctr B2
Belle Vue St C1
Belmont Rd C2
Blenheim Terrace A2
Brunswick Shopping Centre B2
Castle Dykes B3
Castle Hill A3
Castle Rd B2
Castle Walls A3
Castlegate B3
Cemetery B1
Central Tramway ✦ B2
Coach Park B1
Columbus Ravine A1
Court B1
Crescent, The C2
Cricket Ground A1
Cross St B2
Crown Terrace C2
Dean Rd B1
Devonshire Dr A1
East Harbour B3
East Pier B3
Eastborough B2
Elmville Ave B1
Esplanade C2
Falconers Rd B2
Falsgrave Rd C1
Fire Station B2
Foreshore Rd B2
Friargate B2
Gladstone Rd B1
Gladstone St B1
Hollywood Plaza 🎥 A1
Holms, The A3
Hoxton Rd B1
King St B2
Library B2
Lifeboat Station ✦ B3
Londesborough Rd C1
Longwestgate B3
Marine Dr A3
Luna Park B3
Miniature Railway 🚂 A1
Nelson St B1
Newborough B2
Nicolas St B2
North Marine Rd A1
North St B2
Northway B1
Old Harbour B3
Olympia Leisure ✦ B2
Peasholm Park A1
Peasholm Rd A1
Police Station 🚓 B1
Post Office 📮 B2
Princess St B3
Prospect Rd B1
Queen St B2
Queen's Parade A2
Queen's Tower (Remains) 🏛 A3
Ramshill Rd C2
Roman Signal Station ✦ A3
Roscoe St C1
Rotunda Mus 🏛 C2
Royal Albert Dr A2
Royal Albert Park A2
St Martin-on-the-Hill ⛪ C2
St Martin's Ave C2
St Mary's ⛪ B3
St Thomas St B2
Sandside B3
Scarborough ⇌ C1
Scarborough Art Gallery 🖼 C2
Scarborough Bowls Centre A1
Scarborough Castle 🏰 A3
Shopmobility C2
Somerset Terr C2
South Cliff Lift ✦ C2
Spa Theatre, The 🎭 C2
Spa, The ✦ C2
Stephen Joseph Theatre 🎭 C1
Tennyson Ave B1
Tollergate B2
Town Hall B2
Trafalgar Rd B1
Trafalgar Square A1
Trafalgar St West B1
Valley Bridge Par C2
Valley Rd C1
Vernon Rd C2
Victoria Park Mount A1
Victoria Rd B1
West Pier B3
Westborough C1
Westover Rd C1
Westwood C1
Woodall Ave A1
YMCA Theatre 🎭 B2
York Place B2
Yorkshire Coast College (Westwood Campus) C1

Sheffield 196

Addy Dr A2
Addy St A2
Adelphi St A3
Albert Terrace Rd A3
Albion St A2
Aldred Rd A1
Allen St A4
Alma St A4
Angel St B5
Arundel Gate B5
Arundel St C4
Ashberry Rd A2
Ashdell Rd C1
Ashgate Rd C1
Athletics Centre B2
Attercliffe Rd A6
Bailey St B4
Ball St A4
Balm Green B4
Bank St B4
Barber Rd A2
Bard St B5
Barker's Pool B4
Bates St A1
Beech Hill Rd C1
Beet St B3
Bellefield St A3
Bernard Rd A6
Bernard St B6
Birkendale A2
Birkendale Rd A2
Birkendale View A1
Bishop St C4
Blackwell Place B6
Blake St A2
Blonk St A5
Bolsover St B2
Botanical Gdns ✿ C1
Bower Rd A1
Bradley St A1
Bramall La C4
Bramwell St A3
Bridge St A4/A5
Brighton Terr Rd A1
Broad La B3
Broad St B6
Brocco St A3
Brook Hill B3
Broomfield Rd C1
Broomgrove Rd C2
Broomhall Place C3
Broomhall Rd C2
Broomhall St C3
Broomspring La C2
Brown St C5
Brunswick St B3
Burgess St B4
Burlington St A2
Burns Rd A2
Cadman St A6
Cambridge St B4
Campo La B4
Carver St B4
Castle Square 🚊 B5
Castlegate A5
Cathedral 🚊 B4
Cathedral (RC) ✝ B4
Cavendish St B3
Charles St C4
Charter Row C4
Children's Hosp 🏥 B2
Church St B4
City Hall 🎭 B4
City Hall 🚊 B4
City Rd C6
Claremont Cres B2
Claremont Place B2
Clarke St C3
Clarkegrove Rd C2
Clarkehouse Rd C1
Clarkson St B2
Cobden View Rd A1
Collegiate Cres C2
Commercial St B5
Commonside A1
Conduit Rd B1
Cornish St A3
Corporation St A4
Cricket Inn Rd B6
Cromwell St A1
Crookes Rd B1
Crookes Valley Park B2
Crookes Valley Rd B2
Crookesmoor Rd A2
Crown Court A4
Crucible Theatre 🎭 B5
Cutlers' Hall 🏠 B4
Cutlers Gate A6
Daniel Hill A2
Dental Hospital 🏥 B2
Derek Dooley Way A5
Devonshire Green B3
Devonshire St B3
Division St B4
Dorset St C2
Dover St A3
Duchess Rd C5
Duke St B5
Duncombe St A1
Durham Rd B2
Earl St C4
Earl Way C4
Ecclesall Rd C3
Edward St B3
Effingham Rd A6
Effingham St A6
Egerton St C3
Eldon St B3
Elmore Rd B1
Exchange St B5
Eyre St C4
Fargate B4
Farm Rd C5
Fawcett St A3
Filey St B3
Fir St A1
Fire Station C4
Fitzalan Sq/Ponds Forge 🚊 B5
Fitzwater Rd C6
Fitzwilliam Gate C4
Fitzwilliam St B3
Flat St B5
Foley St A6
Foundry Climbing Centre A4
Fulton Rd A1
Furnace Hill A4
Furnival Rd A5
Furnival Sq C4
Furnival St C4
Garden St B3
Gell St B3
Gibraltar St A4
Glebe Rd B1
Glencoe Rd C6
Glossop Rd B2/B3/C1
Gloucester St C2
Government Offices C4
Granville Rd C6
Granville Rd / The Sheffield Coll 🚊 C5
Graves Gallery 🖼 B5
Green La A4
Hadfield St A1
Hanover St C3
Hanover Way C3
Harcourt Rd B1
Harmer La B5
Havelock St C2
Hawley St B4
Haymarket B5
Headford St C3
Heavygate Rd A1
Henry St A3
High St B4
Hodgson St C3
Holberry Gdns C2
Hollis Croft B4
Holly St B4
Hounsfield Rd B3
Howard Rd A1
Hoyle St A3
Hyde Park 🚊 A6
Infirmary Rd A3
Infirmary Rd 🚊 A3
Jericho St A3
Johnson St A5
Kelham Island Industrial Mus 🏛 A4
Lawson Rd C1
Leadmill Rd C5
Leadmill St C5
Leadmill, The ✦ C5
Leamington St A1
Leavygreave Rd B3
Lee Croft B4
Leopold St B4
Leveson St A6
Library A2/B5/C1
Light, The 🎥 C4
Lyceum Theatre 🎭 B5
Malinda St A3
Maltravers St A5
Manor Oaks Rd B6
Mappin St B3
Marlborough Rd B1
Mary St C4
Matilda St C4
Matlock Rd A1
Meadow St A3
Melbourn Rd A1
Melbourne Ave C1
Millennium Galleries 🖼 B5
Milton St C3
Mitchell St B3
Mona Ave A1
Mona Rd A1
Montgomery Terrace Rd A3
Montgomery Theatre 🎭 B4
Monument Grounds C6
Moor Oaks Rd B1
Moor, The C4
Moor, The C4
Moor Market C4
Moore St C3
Mowbray St A4
Mushroom La B2
National Emergency Service 🏛 A4
National Videogame 🏛 B5
Netherthorpe Rd B3
Netherthorpe Rd 🚊 B3
Newbould La C1
Nile St C1
Norfolk Park Rd C6
Norfolk Rd C6
Norfolk St B4
North Church St B4
Northfield Rd A1
Northumberland Rd B1
Nursery St A5
O2 Academy 🎭 B5
Oakholme Rd C1
Octagon B2
Odeon 🎥 B5
Old St B6
Orchard Square B4
Orchard Square Shopping Ctr B4
Oxford St A2
Paradise St B4
Park La C2
Park Sq B5
Parker's Rd B1
Pearson Building (Univ) C2
Penistone Rd A3
Pinstone St B4
Pitt St B3
Police Station 🚓 B5
Pond Hill B5
Pondorosa, The A2
Pond St B5
Ponds Forge Int Sports Ctr B5
Portobello St B3
Post Office 📮 A2/B3/B5/C1/C3/C4/C6
Powell St A2
Queen St B4
Queen's Rd C5
Ramsey Rd B1
Red Hill B3
Redcar Rd B1
Regent St B3
Rockingham St B4
Roebuck Rd A2
Royal Hallamshire Hospital 🏥 C2
Russell St A4
Rutland Park C1
St George's Cl B3
St Mary's Gate C3
St Mary's Rd C4/C5
St Philip's Rd A3
Savile St A5
School Rd B1
Scotland St A4
Severn Rd B1
Shalesmoor A4
Shalesmoor 🚊 A3
Sheaf St B5
Sheffield Cath ✝ B4
Sheffield Hallam University B5
Sheffield Ice Sports Centre – Skate Central C5
Sheffield Institute of Arts 🖼 B5
Sheffield Interchange B5
Sheffield Parkway A6
Sheffield Station ⇌ C5
Sheffield Station/Sheffield Hallam University 🚊 B5
Sheffield University B2
Shepherd St A3
Shipton St A2
Shopmobility B3
Shoreham St C4
Showroom 🎥 C5
Shrewsbury Rd C5
Sidney St C4
Site Gallery 🖼 C5
Slinn St A1
Smithfield A4
Snig Hill A5
Snow La A4
Solly St B3
South La C4
South Street Park B5
Southbourne Rd C1
Spital Hill A5
Spital St A5
Spring Hill B1
Spring Hill Rd B1
Springvale Rd A1
Stafford Rd C6
Stafford St B6
Suffolk Rd C5
Summer St B2
Sunny Bank C3
Superstore A3/C3
Surrey St B4
Sussex St A6
Sutton St B3
Sydney Rd A2
Sylvester St C4
Talbot St B5
Taptonville Rd B1
Tenter St B4
Town Hall 🏠 B4
Townend St A1
Townhead St B4
Trafalgar St B4
Tree Root Walk B2
Trinity St A4
Trippet La B4
Turner Museum of Glass 🏛 B3
Union St B4
University Drama Studio 🎭 B2
Univ of Sheffield 🚊 B3
Upper Allen St A3
Upper Hanover St B3
Upperthorpe Rd A2/A3
Verdon St A5
Victoria Rd C2
Victoria St B3
Waingate B5
Watery St A3
Watson Rd C1
Wellesley Rd B2
Wellington St C3
West Bar A4
West Bar Green A4
West One Plaza B3
West St B3
West St 🚊 B3
Westbourne Rd C1
Western Bank B2
Western Rd A1
Weston Park B2
Weston Park Hospital 🏥 B2
Weston Park Museum 🏛 B2
Weston St B2
Wharncliffe Rd C3
Whitham Rd B1
Wicker A5
Wilkinson St B2
William St C3
Winter Garden ✦ B4
Winter St B2
York St B4
Yorkshire Artspace C5
Young St C4

Shrewsbury 195

Abbey Church ⛪ B3
Abbey Foregate B3
Abbey Lawn Business Park B3
Abbots House 🏠 B2
Agricultural Show Ground A1
Albert St A2
Alma St B1
Ashley St A3
Ashton Rd C1
Avondale Dr A3
Bage Way C3
Barker St B1
Beacall's La A2
Beeches La C2
Beehive La C1
Belle Vue Gdns C2
Belle Vue Rd C2
Belmont Bank C1
Berwick Ave A1
Berwick Rd A1
Betton St C2
Bishop St B3
Bradford St B3
Bridge St B1
Burton St A3
Bus Station B2
Butcher Row B2
Butler Rd C1
Bynner St C2
Canon St B3
Canonbury C1
Castle Business Park, The A2
Castle Foregate A2
Castle Gates B2
Castle Museum 🏰 B2
Castle St B2
Cathedral (RC) ✝ C1
Chester St A2
Cineworld 🎥 C3
Claremont Bank B1
Claremont Hill B1
Cleveland St B3
Coleham Head B2
Coleham Pumping Station 🏛 C2
College Hill B1
Corporation La A1
Coton Cres A1
Coton Hill A2
Coton Mount A1
Crescent La C1
Crewe St A2
Cross Hill B1
Dana, The B2
Darwin Centre B2
Dingle, The ✿ B1
Dogpole B2
Draper's Hall 🏠 B2
English Bridge B2
Fish St B2
Frankwell B1
Gateway Centre, The 🖼 A2
Gravel Hill La A1
Greyfriars Rd C2
Guildhall 🏠 B1
Hampton Rd A3
Haycock Way C3
High St B1
Hills La B1
Holywell St B3
Hunter St A1
Information Ctr ℹ B1
Ireland's Mansion & Bear Steps 🏠 B1
John St A3
Kennedy Rd C1
King St B3
Kingsland Bridge C1
Kingsland Bridge (toll) C1
Kingsland Rd C1
Library B2
Lime St C2
Longden Coleham C2
Longden Rd C1
Longner St B1
Luciefelde Rd C1
Mardol B1
Marine Terr C2
Market B1
Monkmoor Rd B3
Moreton Cres C2
Mount St A1
New Park Cl A3
New Park Rd A2
New Park St A3
North St A2
Oakley St C1
Old Coleham C2
Old Market Hall 🎥 B1
Old Potts Way C3
Parade Centre B2
Police Station 🚓 B1
Post Office 📮 A2/B1/B2/B3
Pride Hill B1
Pride Hill Centre B1
Priory Rd B1
Pritchard Way C3
Quarry, The B1
Queen St A3
Raby Cres C2
Rad Brook C1
Rea Brook C3
Riverside B1
Roundhill La A1
St Alkmund's ⛪ B2
St Chad's ⛪ B1
St Chad's Terr B1
St John's Hill B1
St Julians Friars C2
St Mary's ⛪ B2
St Mary's St B2
Salters La C2
Scott St C3
Severn Bank A3
Severn St A2
Shrewsbury ⇌ B2
Shrewsbury High School for Girls C1
Shrewsbury Mus & Art Gallery 🏛 B1
Shrewsbury School ✦ C1
Shropshire Wildlife Trust ✦ B3
Smithfield Rd B1
South Hermitage C1
Square, The B1
Swan Hill B1
Sydney Ave A3
Tankerville St B3
Tilbrook Dr A3
Town Walls C1
Trinity St C2
Underdale Rd B3
Victoria Ave B1
Victoria Quay B1
Victoria St B2
Welsh Bridge B1
Whitehall St B3
Wood St A2
Wyle Cop B2

Southampton 196

Above Bar St A2
Albert Rd North B3
Albert Rd South C3
Andersons Rd B3
Argyle Rd A2
Arundel Tower ✦ B1
Bargate, The ✦ B2
BBC Regional Ctr A1
Bedford Place A1
Belvidere Rd A3
Bernard St C2
Blechynden Terr A1
Brinton's Rd A2
Britannia Rd A3
Briton St C2
Brunswick Place A2
Bugle St C1
Canute Rd C3
Castle Way C2
Catchcold Tower ✦ B1
Central Bridge C3
Central Rd C2
Channel Way C3
Chapel Rd B3
City Art Gallery 🖼 A1
City College B3
City Cruise Terminal C1
Civic Centre A1
Civic Centre Rd A1
Coach Station B1
Commercial Rd A1
Cumberland Place A1
Cunard Rd C2
Derby Rd A3
Devonshire Rd A1
Dock Gate 4 C2
Dock Gate 8 B1
East Park (Andrew's Park) A2
East Park Terr A2
East St B2
Endle St B3
European Way C2
Fire Station A2
Floating Bridge Rd C3
God's Ho Tower ✦ C2
Golden Grove A3
Graham Rd A2
Guildhall A1
Hanover Buildings B2
Harbour Lights 🎥 C3
Harbour Pde B1
Hartington Rd A3
Havelock Rd A1
Henstead Rd A1
Herbert Walker Ave B1
High St B2
Hoglands Park B2
Holy Rood (Rems), Merchant Navy Memorial ⛪ B2
Houndwell Park B2
Houndwell Place B2
Hythe Ferry C2
Information Ctr ℹ A1
Isle of Wight Ferry Terminal C1
James St B3
Kingsway A2
Leisure World B1
Library A1
Lime St B2
London Rd A2
Marine Pde B3
Marlands Shopping Centre, The A1
Marsh La B2
Mayflower Meml ✦ C1
Mayflower Park C1
Mayflower Theatre, The 🎭 A1
Medieval Merchant's House 🏠 C1
Melbourne St B3
Millais 🖼 A2
Morris Rd A1
National Oceanography Centre ✦ C3
Neptune Way C3
New Rd A2
Nichols Rd A3
North Front A2
Northam Rd A3
Ocean Dock C2
Ocean Village Marina C3
Ocean Way C3
Odeon 🎥 B1
Ogle Rd B1
Old Northam Rd A2
Orchard La B2
Oxford Ave A2
Oxford St C2
Palmerston Park A2
Palmerston Rd A2
Parsonage Rd A3
Peel St A3
Platform Rd C2
Polygon, The A1
Portland Terr B1
Post Office 📮 A2/A3/B2
Pound Tree Rd B2
Quays Swimming & Diving Complex, The B1
Queen's Park C2
Queen's Peace Fountain ✦ A2
Queen's Terr C2
Queensway B2
Radcliffe Rd A3
Rochester St A3
Royal Pier C1
Royal South Hants Hospital 🏥 A2
St Andrew's Rd A2
St Mary's ⛪ B3
St Mary St A2
St Mary's Leisure Centre A2
St Mary's Place B2
St Mary's Rd A2
St Mary's Stadium (Southampton FC) A3
St Michael's ⛪ C1
Sea City Mus 🏛 A1
Showcase Cinema de Lux 🎥 B1
Solent Sky 🏛 C3
South Front B2
Southampton Central Station ⇌ A1

Southampton Solent University A2
SS Shieldhall C2
Terminus Terr C2
Threefield La B2
Titanic Engineers' Memorial A2
Town Quay C1
Town Walls B2
Tudor House C1
Vincent's Walk B2
Westgate Hall C1
West Marlands Rd A1
West Park A1
West Park Rd A1
West Quay Rd B1
West Quay Retail Pk B1
Western Esplanade B1
Westquay Shopping Centre B1
Westquay Watermark B1
White Star Way C2
Winton St A2

Southend-on-Sea 197

Adventure Island C3
Albany Ave A1
Albert Rd C3
Alexandra Rd C2
Alexandra St C2
Alexandra Yacht Club C2
Ashburnham Rd B2
Ave Rd B1
Avenue Terr B1
Balmoral Rd B1
Baltic Ave B3
Baxter Ave A2/B2
Beecroft Art Gallery B2
Bircham Rd A2
Boscombe Rd B3
Boston Ave A1/B2
Bournemouth Park Rd A3
Browning Ave A3
Bus Station C3
Byron Ave A3
Cambridge Rd C1/C2
Canewdon Rd B1
Carnarvon Rd A2
Central Ave A3
Central Museum B2
Chelmsford Ave A1
Chichester Rd B2
Church Rd C3
Civic Centre A2
Clarence Rd C2
Clarence St C2
Cliff Ave B1
Cliffs Pavilion C1
Clifftown Parade C2
Clifftown Rd C2
Colchester Rd A1
Coleman St B3
College Way B2
County Court B3
Cromer Rd B3
Crowborough Rd A2
Dryden Ave A3
East St A2
Elmer App B2
Elmer Ave B2
Forum, The B2
Gainsborough Dr A1
Gayton Rd A2
Glenhurst Rd A2
Gordon Place B2
Gordon Rd B2
Grainger Rd A2
Greyhound Way A3
Grove, The A3
Guildford Rd B3
Hamlet Ct Rd B1
Hamlet Rd C1
Harcourt Ave A1
Hartington Rd C3
Hastings Rd B3
Herbert Grove C3
Heygate Ave C3
High St B2/C2
Information Ctr C3
Kenway A2
Kilworth Ave B3
Lancaster Gdns B3
London Rd B1
Lucy Rd C3
MacDonald Ave A1
Magistrates' Court A2
Maldon Rd A2
Marine Ave C1
Marine Parade C3
Marine Rd C1
Milton Rd B1
Milton St B2
Napier Ave B2
North Ave A3
North Rd A1/B1
Odeon B2
Osborne Rd B1
Park Cres B1
Park Rd B1
Park St B1
Park Terr B1
Pier Hill C3
Pleasant Rd C3
Police Station A2
Post Office B2/B3
Princes St B2
Queens Rd B2
Queensway B2/B3/C3
Radio Essex C2
Rayleigh Ave A1
Redstock Rd A2
Rochford Ave A1
Royal Mews C2
Royal Terr C2
Royals Shopping Centre, The C3
Ruskin Ave A3
St Ann's Rd B3
St Helen's Rd B1
St John's Rd B1
St Leonard's Rd C3
St Lukes Rd A3
St Vincent's Rd C1
Salisbury Ave A1/B1
Scratton Rd C2
Shakespeare Dr A1
Shopmobility B2
Short St A2
South Ave A3
Southchurch Rd B3
Southend Central B2
Southend Pier Railway C3
Southend United FC A1
Southend Victoria B2
Stanfield Rd A2
Stanley Rd C3
Sutton Rd A3/B3
Swanage Rd B3
Sweyne Ave A1
Sycamore Grove A3
Tennyson Ave A3
Tickfield Ave A2
Tudor Rd A1
Tunbridge Rd A2
Tylers Ave B3
Tyrrel Dr B3
Univ of Essex B2/C2
Vale Ave A2
Victoria Ave A2
Victoria Shopping Centre, The B2
Warrior Sq B3
Wesley Rd C3
West Rd A1
West St A1
Westcliff Ave C1
Westcliff Parade C1
Western Esplanade C1
Weston Rd C2
Whitegate Rd B3
Wilson Rd C1
Wimborne Rd B3
York Rd C3

Stirling 197

Abbey Rd A3
Abbotsford Place A3
Abercromby Place C1
Albert Halls B1
Albert Place B1
Alexandra Place A3
Allan Park C2
Ambulance Station A2
AMF Ten Pin Bowling B2
Argyll Ave A3
Argyll's Lodging B1
Back O' Hill Ind Est A1
Back O' Hill Rd A1
Baker St B2
Ballengeich Pass A1
Balmoral Place B1
Barn Rd B1
Barnton St B2
Bastion, The C2
Bow St B1
Bruce St A2
Burghmuir Retail Park C2
Burghmuir Rd A2/B2/C2
Bus Station B2
Cambuskenneth Bridge A3
Castle Ct B1
Causewayhead Rd A2
Cemetery A1
Changing Room, The B1
Church of the Holy Rude B1
Clarendon Place C1
Club House B1
Colquhoun St C3
Corn Exchange B2
Council Offices C2
Court B2
Cowane Ctr A2
Cowane St A2
Cowane's Hosp B1
Crofthead Rd A1
Dean Cres A3
Douglas St A2
Drip Rd A1
Drummond La C1
Drummond Place C1
Drummond Pl La C1
Dumbarton Rd C2
Eastern Access Rd B2
Edward Ave A3
Edward Rd A2
Forrest Rd A2
Fort A1
Forth Cres B2
Forth St A2
Gladstone Place C1
Glebe Ave C1
Glebe Cres C1
Golf Course C1
Goosecroft Rd B2
Gowanhill A1
Greenwood Ave B1
Harvey Wynd A1
Information Ctr B1
Irvine Place B2
James St A2
John St B1
Kerse Rd C3
King's Knot B1
King's Park C1
King's Park Rd C1
Laurencecroft Rd A2
Leisure Pool B2
Library B2
Linden Ave C2
Lovers Wk A2
Lower Back Walk B1
Lower Bridge St A2
Lower Castlehill A1
Mar Place B1
Meadow Place A3
Meadowforth Rd C3
Middlemuir Rd C3
Millar Place A3
Morris Terr B2
Mote Hill A1
Murray Place B2
Nelson Place C2
Old Town Cemetery B1
Old Town Jail B1
Park Terr C1
Phoenix Ind Est C3
Players Rd C3
Port St C2
Post Office B2
Princes St B2
Queen St B2
Queen's Rd B1
Queenshaugh Dr A3
Ramsay Place A2
Riverside Dr A3
Ronald Place A1
Rosebery Place A2
Royal Gardens B1
Royal Gdns B1
St Mary's Wynd B1
St Ninian's Rd C2
Scott St A2
Seaforth Place B2
Shore Rd B2
Smith Art Gallery & Museum B1
Snowdon Place C1
Snowdon Place La C1
Spittal St B2
Springkerse Ind Est C3
Springkerse Rd C3
Stirling Arcade B2
Stirling Bsns Centre C2
Stirling Castle A1
Stirling County Rugby Football Club A3
Stirling Enterprise Park B3
Stirling Old Bridge A2
Stirling Station B2
Superstore A1/A2
Sutherland Ave A3
TA Centre C3
Tannery La A2
Thistle Ind Est C3
Thistles Shopping Centre, The B2
Tolbooth B1
Town Wall B1
Union St A2
Upper Back Walk B1
Upper Bridge St A1
Upper Castlehill B1
Upper Craigs C2
Victoria Place C1
Victoria Rd B1
Victoria Sq B1/C1
Vue f
Wallace St A2
Waverley Cres A3
Wellgreen Rd C2
Windsor Place C1
YHA B1

Stoke-on-Trent (Hanley) 196

Acton St A3
Albion St B2
Argyle St C1
Ashbourne Grove A2
Avoca St A3
Baskerville Rd B3
Bedford Rd C1
Bedford St C1
Bethesda St B2
Bexley St A2
Birches Head Rd A3
Botteslow St C3
Boundary St A2
Broad St C2
Broom St A3
Bryan St A2
Bucknall New Rd B3
Bucknall Old Rd B3
Bus Station B3
Cannon St C2
Castlefield St C1
Cavendish St B1
Central Forest Pk A2
Charles St B3
Cheapside B2
Chell St A3
Clarke St C1
Cleveland Rd C2
Clifford St C3
Clough St B2
Clyde St C1
College Rd C2
Cooper St C2
Corbridge Rd A1
Cutts St C2
Davis St C1
Denbigh St A1
Derby St C3
Dilke St A3
Dundas St A3
Dundee Rd C1
Dyke St B3
Eastwood Rd C3
Eaton St A3
Etruria Park B1
Etruria Rd B1
Etruria Vale Rd C1
Festing St A3
Festival Retail Park A1
Fire Station C2
Foundry St B2
Franklyn St C3
Garnet St B1
Garth St B3
George St A3
Gilman St B3
Glass St B3
Goodson St B3
Greyhound Way A1
Grove Place C1
Hampton St C3
Hanley Park C2
Hanley Park C2
Harding Rd C2
Hassall St B3
Havelock Place C1
Hazlehurst St C3
Hinde St C2
Hope St B2
Houghton St C2
Hulton St A3
Information Ctr B3
Jasper St C2
Jervis St A3
John Bright St A3
John St B2
Keelings Rd A3
Kimberley Rd C1
Ladysmith Rd C1
Lawrence St C2
Leek Rd C3
Library C2
Lichfield St C3
Linfield Rd B3
Loftus St A2
Lower Bedford St C1
Lower Bryan St A2
Lower Mayer St A3
Lowther St A1
Magistrates Court C2
Malham St A2
Marsh St B2
Matlock St C3
Mayer St A3
Milton St C1
Mitchell Memorial Theatre B2
Morley St B2
Moston St A3
Mount Pleasant C1
Mulgrave St A1
Mynors St B3
Nelson Place B3
New Century St B1
Octagon Retail Park B1
Ogden Rd C3
Old Hall St B3
Old Town Rd A3
Pall Mall B2
Palmerston St C3
Park and Ride C2
Parker St B2
Parkway, The C2
Pavilion Dr A1
Pelham St C3
Percy St B2
Piccadilly B2
Picton St B3
Plough St A3
Police Station C2
Portland St A1
Post Office A3/B3/C3
Potteries Museum & Art Gallery B2
Potteries Shopping Centre B2
Potteries Way C2
Powell St A1
Pretoria Rd C1
Quadrant Rd B2
Ranelagh St C2
Raymond St C2
Rectory Rd C1
Regent Rd C2
Regent Theatre B2
Richmond Terr C2
Ridgehouse Dr A1
Robson St C2
St Ann St B3
St Luke St B3
Sampson St B2
Shaw St A1
Sheaf St C2
Shearer St C1
Shelton New Rd C1
Shirley Rd C2
Slippery La B2
Snow Hill C2
Spur St C3
Stafford St B2
Statham St B2
Stubbs La C3
Sun St C1
Supermarket A1/B2
Talbot St C3
Town Hall B2
Town Rd A3
Trinity St B2
Union St A2
Upper Hillchurch St A3
Upper Huntbach St B3
Victoria Hall Theatre B3
Warner St C2
Warwick St C1
Waterloo Rd A1
Waterloo St B3
Well St B3
Wellesley St C2
Wellington Rd B3
Wellington St B3
Whitehaven Dr A2
Whitmore St C1
Windermere St A1
Woodall St A1
Yates St C2
York St A2

Stratford-upon-Avon 197

Albany Rd B1
Alcester Rd B1
Ambulance Station B1
Arden St B2
Avenue Farm A1
Ave Farm Ind Est A1
Avenue Rd A3
Baker Ave A1
Bandstand C3
Benson Rd A3
Birmingham Rd A2
Boat Club B3
Borden Place C1
Bridge St B2
Bridgetown Rd C3
Bridgeway B3
Broad St C2
Broad Walk C2
Brookvale Rd C1
Brunel Way B1
Bull St C2
Butterfly Farm C3
Cemetery C1
Chapel La B2
Cherry Orchard C1
Chestnut Walk B2
Children's Playground C3
Church St C2
Civic Hall B2
Clarence Rd B1
Clopton Bridge B3
Clopton Rd A2
College B1
College La C2
College St C2
Com Sports Centre B1
Council Offices (District) B2
Courtyard, The C2
Cox's Yard B3
Cricket Ground C3
Ely Gdns B2
Ely St B2
Evesham Rd C1
Fire Station B1
Foot Ferry C3
Fordham Ave A2
Garrick Way C1
Gower Memorial B3
Great William St B2
Greenhill St B2
Greenway, The C2
Grove Rd B2
Guild St B2
Guildhall & School B2
Hall's Croft C2
Harvard House B2
Henley St B2
Hertford Rd C1
High St B2
Holton St C2
Holy Trinity C2
Information Ctr B3
Jolyffe Park Rd A2
Kipling Rd C3
Library B2
Lodge Rd B1
Maidenhead Rd A3
Mansell St B2
Masons Court B2
Masons Rd A1
Maybird Shopping Park A2
Maybrook Retail Park A2
Maybrook Rd A1
Mayfield Ave A2
Meer St B2
Mill La C2
Moat House Hotel B3
Narrow La C2
Nash's House & New Place B2
New St C2
Old Town C2
Orchard Way C1
Other Place, The C2
Paddock La C1
Park Rd A1
Payton St B2
Percy St A2
Police Station B2
Post Office B2
Recreation Ground C2
Regal Road A2
Rother St B2
Rowley Cres A3
Royal Shakespeare Theatre B3
Ryland St C2
Saffron Meadow C2
St Andrew's Cres B1
St Gregory's A3
St Gregory's Rd A3
St Mary's Rd A2
Sanctus Dr C2
Sanctus St C1
Sandfield Rd C2
Scholars La B2
Seven Meadows Rd C2
Shakespeare Inst C2
Shakespeare St B2
Shakespeare's Birthplace B2
Sheep St B2
Shelley Rd C3
Shipston Rd C3
Shottery Rd C1
Slingates Rd A2
Southern La C2
Station Rd B1
Stratford Healthcare B2
Stratford Hosp B2
Stratford Leisure Centre B3
Stratford Sports Club B1
Stratford-upon-Avon Station B1
Swan Theatre B3
Swan's Nest La B3
Talbot Rd A2
Tiddington Rd B3
Timothy's Bridge Industrial Estate A1
Timothy's Bridge Rd A1
Town Hall & Council Offices B2
Town Sq B2
Trinity Cl C2
Tyler St B2
War Memorial Gdns B3
Warwick Rd B3
Waterside B3
Welcombe Rd A3
West St C2
Western Rd A2
Wharf Rd A2
Willows North, The B1
Willows, The B1
Wood St B2

Sunderland 197

Albion Place C2
Alliance Place B1
Argyle St C2
Ashwood St C1
Athenaeum St B2
Azalea Terr C2
Beach St A1
Bedford St B2
Beechwood Terr C1
Belvedere Rd C2
Blandford St B2
Borough Rd B3
Bridge Cres B2
Bridge St B2
Bridges, The B2
Brooke St A2
Brougham St B2
Burdon Rd C2
Burn Park C1
Burn Park Rd C1
Burn Park Tech Park C1
Carol St B1
Charles St A3
Chester Rd C1
Chester Terr B1
Church St A3
Civic Centre C2
Cork St B3
Coronation St B3
Cowan Terr C2
Dame Dorothy St A2
Deptford Rd B1
Deptford Terr A1
Derby St C2
Derwent St C2
Dock St A3
Dundas St A2
Durham Rd C1
Easington St A2
Egerton St C3
Empire B3
Empire Theatre B2
Farringdon Row B1
Fawcett St B2
Fire Station B1
Fox St C1
Foyle St B3
Frederick St B3
Hanover Place A1
Havelock Terr C1
Hay St A2
Headworth Sq B3
Hendon Rd B3
High St East B3
High St West B2/B3
Holmeside B2
Hylton Rd B1
Information Ctr B2
John St B3
Kier Hardie Way A2
Lambton St B3
Laura St C3
Lawrence St B3
Library & Arts Ctr B3
Lily St B1
Lime St B1
Livingstone Rd B2
Low Row B2
Magistrates' Court B2
Matamba Terr B1
Millburn St B1
Millennium Way A2
Minster B2
Monkwearmouth Sta Mus A2
Mowbray Park C3
Mowbray Rd C3
Murton St C3
National Glass Centre A3
New Durham Rd C1
Newcastle Rd A2
Nile St B3
Norfolk St B3
North Bridge St A2
Northern Gallery for Contemporary Art B3
Otto Terr C1
Park La C2
Park Lane C2
Park Rd C2
Paul's Rd B3
Peel St C3
Point, The B2
Police Station B2
Priestly Cres A1
Queen St B2
Railway Row B1
Retail Park B1
Richmond St A2
Roker Ave A2
Royalty Theatre C1
Royalty, The C1
Ryhope Rd C2
St Mary's Way B2
St Michael's Way B2
St Peter's A3
St Peter's A2
St Peter's Way A3
St Vincent St C3
Salem Rd C3
Salem St C3
Salisbury St C3
Sans St B3
Shopmobility B2
Silkworth Row B1
Southwick Rd A2
Stadium of Light (Sunderland AFC) A2
Stadium Way A2
Stobart St A2
Stockton Rd C2
Suffolk St C3
Sunderland B2
Sunderland Aquatic Centre A2
Sunderland College C2
Sunderland Mus B3
Sunderland St B3
Sunderland Sta B2
Tatham St C3
Tavistock Place B3
Thelma St C1
Thomas St North A2
Thornholme Rd C1
Toward Rd C3
Transport Interchange C2
Trimdon St Way B1
Tunstall Rd C2
University C1
University Library C1
Univ of Sunderland (City Campus) B1
Univ of Sunderland (St Peter's Campus) A3
University of Sunderland (Sir Tom Cowie Campus) A3
Vaux Brewery Way A2
Villiers St B3
Villiers St South B3
Vine Place C2
Violet St B1
Walton La B3
Waterworks Rd B1
Wearmouth Bridge B2
West Sunniside B3
West Wear St B3
Westbourne Rd B1
Western Hill C1
Wharncliffe B1
Whickham St A3
White House Rd C3
Wilson St North A2
Winter Gdns C3
Wreath Quay A1

Swansea
Abertawe 198

Adelaide St C3
Albert Row C3
Alexandra Rd B3
Argyle St C1
Baptist Well Place A2
Beach St C1
Belle Vue Way B3
Berw Rd A1
Berwick Terr A2
Bond St C1
Brangwyn Concert Hall C1
Bridge St A3
Brooklands Terr B1
Brunswick St C1
Bryn-Syfi Terr A2
Bryn-y-Mor Rd C1
Bullins La B1
Burrows Rd C1
Bus Station C2
Bus/Rail link A3
Cadfan Rd A1
Cadrawd Rd A1
Caer St B3
Carig Cres A1
Carlton Terr B2
Carmarthen Rd A3
Castle Square B3
Castle St B3
Catherine St C1
Cinema C3
Civic Ctr & Library C2
Clarence St C2
Colbourne Terr A2
Constitution Hill B1
Court B3
Creidiol Rd A2
Cromwell St B2
Crown Courts C1
Duke St B1
Dunvant Place C2
Dyfatty Park A3
Dyfatty St A3
Dyfed Ave A1
Dylan Thomas Ctr B3
Dylan Thomas Theatre C3
Eaton Cres C1
Eigen Cres A1
Elfed Rd A1
Emlyn Rd A1
Evans Terr A3
Fairfield Terr B1
Ffynone Dr B1
Ffynone Rd B1
Fire Station B3
Firm St A2
Fleet St C1
Francis St C1
Fullers Row B2
George St B2
Glamorgan St C2
Glynn Vivian Art Gallery B3
Gower Coll Swansea C1
Graig Terr A3
Grand Theatre C2
Granogwen Rd A2
Guildhall C1
Guildhall Rd South C1
Gwent Rd A1
Gwynedd Ave A1
Hafod St A3
Hanover St B1
Harcourt St B2
Harries St A2
Heathfield B2
Henrietta St B1
Hewson St B2
High St A3/B3
High View A2
Hill St A2
Historic Ships Berth C3
HM Prison C2
Information Ctr C2
Islwyn Rd A1
King Edward's Rd C1
Kingsway, The B2
LC, The C3
Long Ridge A2
Madoc St C2
Mansel St B2
Maritime Quarter C3
Market B3
Mayhill Gdns B1
Mayhill Rd A1
Milton Terr A2
Mission Gallery C3
Montpelier Terr B1
Morfa Rd A3
Mount Pleasant B2
National Waterfront Museum C3
New Cut Rd A3
New St A3
Nicander Parade A2
Nicander Place A2
Nicholl St B2
Norfolk St B2
North Hill Rd A2
Northampton La B2
Observatory C3
Orchard St B3
Oxford St B2
Oystermouth Rd C1
Page St B2
Pant-y-Celyn Rd B1
Parc Tawe North B3
Parc Tawe Shopping & Leisure Centre B3
Patti Pavilion C1
Paxton St C2
Pen-y-Graig Rd A1
Penmaen Terr B1
Phillips Parade C1
Picton Terr B2
Plantasia B3
Plantasia B3
Police Station B2
Post Office A1/A2/C1/C2
Powys Ave A1
Primrose St B2
Princess Way B3
Promenade B2
Pryder Gdns A1
Quadrant Shopping Centre C2
Quay Park B3
Rhianfa La B1
Rhondda St B2
Richardson St C2
Rodney St C1
Rose Hill B1
Rosehill Terr B1
Russell St B1
St David's Shopping Centre C3
St Helen's Ave C1
St Helen's Cres C1
St Helen's Rd C1
St James Gdns B1
St James's Cres B1
St Mary's B3
Sea View Terr A3
Singleton St C2
South Dock C3
Stanley Place B2
Strand B3
Swansea Castle B3
Swansea Metropolitan University B2
Swansea Mus C3
Swansea Station A3
Taliesyn Rd B1
Tan y Marian Rd A1
Tegid Rd A2
Teilo Cres A1
Tenpin Bowling B3
Terrace Rd B1/B2
Tontine St A3
Townhill Rd A1
Tramshed, The C3
Trawler Rd C3
Union St B2
Upper Strand A3
Vernon St A3
Victoria Quay C3
Victoria Rd B3
Vincent St C1
Walter Rd B1
Watkin St A2
Waun-Wen Rd A2
Wellington St C2
Westbury St C1
Western St C1
Westway C2
William St C2
Wind St B3
Woodlands Terrace B1
YMCA B2
York St C3

Swindon 198

Albert St C3
Albion St C1
Alfred St A2
Alvescot Rd C3
Art Gallery & Museum C3
Ashford Rd C1
Aylesbury St A2
Bath Rd C2
Bathampton St B1
Bathurst Rd B3
Beatrice St A2
Beckhampton St B3
Bowood Rd C1
Bristol St B1
Broad St A3
Brunel Arcade B2
Brunel Plaza B2
Brunswick St C2
Bus Station B2
Cambria Bridge Rd B1
Cambria Place B1
Canal Walk B2
Carfax St B2
Carr St B1
Cemetery C1/C3
Chandler Cl C3
Chapel C1
Chester St B1
Christ Church C3
Church Place B1
Cirencester Way A3
Clarence St B2
Clifton St C1
Cockleberry A2
Colbourne A3
Colbourne St A3
College St B2
Commercial Rd B2
Corporation St A2
Council Offices B3
County Rd A3
Courts B2
Cricket Ground A3
Cricklade Street C3
Crombey St B1/C2
Cross St C2
Curtis St B1
Deacon St C1
Designer Outlet (Great Western) B1
Dixon St C2
Dover St C2
Dowling St C2
Drove Rd C3
Dryden St C1
Durham St C3
East St B1
Eastcott Hill C2
Eastcott Rd C2
Edgeware Rd B2
Edmund St C2
Elmina Rd A3
Emlyn Square B1
Euclid St B3
Exeter St B1
Fairview C1
Faringdon Rd B1
Farnsby St B1
Fire Station B3
Fleet St B2
Fleming Way B2/B3
Florence St A2
Gladstone St A3
Gooch St A2
Graham St A3
Great Western Way A1/A2
Groundwell Rd B3
Hawksworth Way A1
Haydon St A2
Henry St B2
Hillside Ave C1
Holbrook Way B2
Hunt St C3
Hydro B1
Hythe Rd C2
Information Ctr B2
Joseph St C1
Kent Rd C2
King William St C2
Kingshill Rd C1
Lansdown Rd C2
Lawn, The C3
Leicester St B3
Library B2
Lincoln St B3
Little London C3
London St B1
Magic B3
Maidstone Rd C2
Manchester Rd A3
Maxwell St B1
Milford St B2
Milton Rd B1
Morse St C2
National Monuments Record Centre B1
Newcastle St B3
Newcombe Drive A1
Newcombe Trading Estate A1
Newhall St C2
North St C2
North Star A1
North Star Ave A1
Northampton St B3
Nurseries, The C1
Oasis Leisure Ctr A1
Ocotal Way A3
Okus Rd C1
Old Town C3
Oxford St B1
Parade, The B2
Park Lane B1
Park Lane B1
Park, The B1
Pembroke St C2
Plymouth St B3
Polaris House A2
Polaris Way A2
Police Station B2
Ponting St A2
Post Office B1/B2/C1/C3
Poulton St A3
Princes St B2
Prospect Hill C2
Prospect Place C2
Queen St B2
Queen's Park C3
Radnor St C1
Read St C1
Reading St B1
Regent St B2
Retail Park A2/A3/B3
Rosebery St A3
St Mark's B1
Salisbury St A3
Savernake St C2
Shelley St C1
Sheppard St B1
South St C2
Southampton St B3
Spring Gardens B3
Stafford Street C2
Stanier St C2
Station Road A2
STEAM B1
Swindon College A2
Swindon Rd C2
Swindon Station A2
Swindon Town Football Club A3
T A Centre B1
Tennyson St B1
Theobald St B1
Town Hall B2
Transfer Bridges A3
Union St C2
Upham Rd C3
Victoria Rd C3
Walcot Rd B3
War Memorial B2
Wells St B3
Western St C2
Westmorland Rd B3
Whalebridge B2
Whitehead St C1
Whitehouse Rd A2
William St C1
Wood St C3
Wyvern Theatre & Arts Centre B2
York Rd B3

Taunton 198

Addison Grove A1
Albemarle Rd A1
Alfred St B3
Alma St C2
Avenue, The A1
Bath Place C1
Belvedere Rd A1
Billet St B2
Billetfield C2
Birch Grove A1
Brewhouse Theatre B2
Bridge St B1
Bridgwater & Taunton Canal A2
Broadlands Rd C1
Burton Place C1
Bus Station B1
Canal Rd A2
Cann St C1
Canon St B2
Castle B1
Castle St B1
Cheddon Rd A2
Chip Lane A1
Clarence St B1
Cleveland St B1
Clifton Terr A2
Coleridge Cres C3
Compass Hill C1
Compton Cl A2
Corporation St B1
Council Offices A1
County Walk Shopping Centre C2
Courtyard B2
Cranmer Rd B2
Crescent, The C1
Critchard Way B3
Cyril St A1
Deller's Wharf B1
Duke St B2
East Reach B3
East St B3
Eastbourne Rd B2
Eastleigh Rd C3
Eaton Cres A2
Elm Grove A1
Elms Cl A1
Fons George C1
Fore St B2
Fowler St A1
French Weir Recreation Grd B1
Geoffrey Farrant Walk A2
Gray's Almshouses B2
Grays Rd B3
Greenway Ave A1
Guildford Place C1
Hammet St B2
Haydon Rd B3
Heavitree Way A2
Herbert St A1
High St C2
Holway Ave C3
Hugo St B3
Huish's Almshouses B2
Hurdle Way C2
Information Ctr C2
Jubilee St A1
King's College C3
Kings Cl C3
Laburnum St B2
Lambrook Rd B3
Lansdowne Rd A3
Leslie Ave A1
Leycroft Rd B3
Library C2
Linden Grove A1
Magdalene St B2
Magistrates Court B1
Malvern Terr A2
Market House B2
Mary St C2
Middle St B2
Midford Rd B3
Mitre Court B3
Mount Nebo C1
Mount St C2
Mount, The C2
Mountway C2
Mus of Somerset B1
North St B2
Northern Inner Distributor Rd A1
Northfield Ave B1
Northfield Rd B1
Northleigh Rd C3
Obridge Allotments A3
Obridge Lane A3
Obridge Rd A3
Obridge Viaduct A3
Old Market Shopping Centre C2
Osborne Way C1
Park St C1
Paul St C2
Plais St A2
Playing Field C3
Police Station C1
Portland St B1
Post Office B1/B2/C1
Priorswood Ind Est A3
Priorswood Rd A2
Priory Ave B2
Priory Bridge Rd B2
Priory Fields Retail Park A3
Priory Park A2
Priory Way A3
Queen St B3
Railway St A1
Records Office A2
Recreation Grd A1
Riverside Place B2
St Augustine St B2
St George's C2
St Georges Sq C2
St James B2
St James St B2
St John's C1
St John's Rd B1
St Josephs Field C2
St Mary Magdalene's B2
Samuels Ct A1
Shire Hall & Law Courts C1
Somerset County Cricket Ground B2
Somerset County Hall C1
Somerset Cricket B2
South Rd C3
South St C3
Staplegrove Rd B1
Station Rd A1
Stephen St B2
Swimming Pool A1
Tancred St B2
Tauntfield Cl C3
Taunton Dean Cricket Club C2
Taunton Station A2
Thomas St A1
Toneway A3
Tower St B1
Trevor Smith Place C3
Trinity Bsns Centre C3
Trinity Rd C3
Trinity St B3
Trull Rd C1
Tudor House B2
Upper High St C1
Venture Way A3
Victoria Gate B3
Victoria Park B3
Victoria St B3
Viney St B3
Vivary Park C2
Vivary Rd C1
War Memorial C1
Wellesley St A2
Wheatley Cres A3
Whitehall A1
Wilfred Rd B3
William St A1
Wilton Church C1
Wilton Cl C1
Wilton Grove C1
Wilton St C1
Winchester St B2
Winters Field B2
Wood St B1
Yarde Place B1

Telford 198

Alma Ave C1
Amphitheatre C2
Bowling Alley B2
Brandsfarm Way C3
Brunel Rd B1
Bus Station B2
Buxton Rd C1
Central Park A2
Civic Offices B2
Coach Central B2
Coachwell Cl B1
Colliers Way A1
Courts B2
Dale Acre Way B3
Darliston C3
Deepdale B3
Deercote B2
Dinthill C3
Doddington C3
Dodmoor Grange C3
Downemead B3
Duffryn B3
Dunsheath B3
Euston Way A3
Eyton Mound C1
Eyton Rd C1
Forgegate A2
Grange Central B2
Hall Park Way B1
Hinkshay Rd C2
Hollinsworth Rd A2

Holyhead Rd A3
Housing Trust A1
Ice Rink A1
Information Ctr [i] .. B2
Ironmasters Way .. A2
Job Centre A1
Land Registry B1
Lawn Central C1
Lawnswood C1
Library B1
Malinsgate B1
Matlock Ave C1
Moor Rd C1
Mount Rd C1
NFU Offices B1
Odeon B1
Park Lane A1
Police Station [§] .. A1
Priorslee Ave A3
Queen Elizabeth Ave. C3
Queen Elizabeth Way A1
Queensway ... A2/B3
Rampart Way A2
Randlay Ave C2
Randlay Wood C2
Rhodes Ave C1
Royal Way B1
St Leonards Rd ... B1
St Quentin Gate .. B2
Shifnal Rd C1
Sixth Ave C1
Southwater One (SW1) B2
Southwater Way .. C1
Spout Lane C1
Spout Mound C1
Spout Way C1
Stafford Court ... B3
Stafford Park B3
Stirchley Ave C1
Stone Row C1
Telford Bridge Retail Park A1
Telford Central Station [≠] A2
Telford Centre,The . C1
Telford Forge Shopping Park A1
Telford Hornets RFC C2
Telford Int Ctr ... C2
Telford Way A2
Third Ave C2
Town Park C2
Town Pk Visitor Ctr. B2
Walker House B2
Wellswood Ave ... A2
West Centre Way .. A1
Withywood Drive .. C1
Woodhouse Central B2
Yates Way A1

Torquay 199
Abbey Rd B2
Alexandra Rd A3
Alpine Rd A3
AMF Bowling C3
Ash Hill Rd B3
Babbacombe Rd... B3
Bampfylde Rd.... B1
Barton Rd A1
Beacon Quay C2
Belgrave Rd A1/B1
Belmont Rd A3
Berea Rd A3
Braddons Hill Rd East A3
Brewery Park A3
Bronshill Rd A2
Carlton Rd A3
Castle Circus ... A2
Castle Rd A2
Cavern Rd A3
Central B2
Chatsworth Rd ... A2
Chestnut Ave ... A2
Church St A1
Coach Station ... C1
Corbyn Head.... C1
Croft Hill B1
Croft Rd B1
East St. B1
Egerton Rd A3
Ellacombe Church Rd A3
Ellacombe Rd.... B1
Falkland Rd B1
Fleet St B2
Fleet Walk Shopping Centre B2
Grafton Rd A3
Grange Rd A3
Haldon Pier C2
Hatfield Rd A2
Highbury Rd A2
Higher Warberry Rd A3
Hillesdon Rd A2
Hoxton Rd A3
Hunsdon Rd A3
Information Ctr [i] .. B2
Inner Harbour ... C2
Kenwyn Rd A2
King's Drive,The .. B1
Laburnum St..... A1
Law Courts A2
Library A2
Lime Ave A2
Living Coasts ... C2
Lower Warberry Rd A3
Lucius St. A1
Lymington Rd ... A1
Magdalene Rd ... A1
Marina C2
Market Forum,The. B2
Market St B2
Meadfoot Lane ... C3
Meadfoot Rd C3
Melville St B2
Middle Warberry Rd B3
Mill Lane A1
Montpellier Rd... B3
Morgan Ave A1
Museum Rd B3

Newton Rd A1
Oakhill Rd A1
Outer Harbour ... C2
Parkhill Rd C3
Pimlico B2
Police Station [§] .. A1
Post Office [PO] ... A1
Prince of Wales Steps C3
Princes Rd A3
Princes Rd East .. A3
Princes Rd West .. A3
Princess Gdns ... C2
Princess Pier ... C2
Princess Theatre [§] C2
Rathmore Rd ... B1
Recreation Grd... B1
Riviera Int Ctr ... C2
Rock End Ave ... C3
Rock Rd B2
Rock Walk B2
Rosehill Rd A3
St Efride's Rd ... A1
St John's B2
St Luke's Rd B2
St Luke's Rd North. B2
St Luke's Rd South. B2
St Marychurch Rd . A1
Scarborough Rd.. B1
Shedden Hill.... B2
South Pier C2
South St B1
Spanish Barn ... B1
Stitchill Rd B3
Strand B2
Sutherland Rd... A1
Teignmouth Rd... A1
Temperance St... B2
Terrace,The A2
Thurlow Rd A1
Tor Bay C2
Tor Church Rd ... A1
Tor Hill Rd A1
Torbay Rd C2
Torquay Mus [m] .. B3
Torquay Station [≠] C1
Torquay Tennis Club B1
Torre Abbey Meadows B1
Torre Abbey Sands. B1
Torwood Gdns ... C3
Torwood St. C3
Town Hall A2
Union Square Shopping Centre A2
Union St A1
Upton Hill A1
Upton Park A1
Upton Rd. A1
Vanehill Rd C3
Vansittart Rd ... A1
Vaughan Parade.. C2
Victoria Parade .. C2
Victoria Rd A2
Warberry Rd West . A3
Warren Rd. B2
Windsor Rd A2/A3
Woodville Rd A3

Truro 199
Adelaide Ter B1
Agar Rd C2
Arch Hill C2
Arundell Place ... B1
Avenue,The A3
Back Quay. B3
Barrack La C2
Barton Meadow .. A1
Benson Rd C2
Bishops Cl. B2
Bosvean Gardens. B1
Bosvigo Gardens [m] B1
Bosvigo La A1
Bosvigo Rd B2
Broad St B3
Burley Cl C3
Bus Station B3
Calenick St B2
Campfield Hill ... B3
Carclew St B3
Carew Rd A2
Carey Park B2
Carlyon Rd A2
Carvoza Rd A2
Castle St B2
Cathedral View... A3
Chainwalk Dr A2
Chapel Hill B1
Charles St. B2
City Hall B3
City Rd. B2
Coinage Hall [§] .. B3
Comprigney Hill.. A1
Coosebean La.... A1
Copes Gdns B1
County Hall. B1
Courtney Rd B1
Crescent Rd C1
Crescent Rise ... B1
Crescent,The B1
Daniell Court ... C2
Daniell Rd C2
Daniell St C2
Daubuz Close ... A1
Dobbs La. B1
Edward St. B2
Eliot Rd B2
Elm Court A3
Enys Cl A1
Enys Rd A1
Fairmantle St ... B3
Falmouth Rd ... C2
Ferris Town B2
Fire Station. B1
Frances St. B2
George St. B2
Green Close C2
Green La. C1
Grenville Rd C2
Hall For Cornwall [§] B3
Hendra Rd A2

Hendra Vean A1
High Cross B3
Higher Newham La A3
Higher Trehaverne. A2
Hillcrest Ave B1
Hospital [H] B2
Hunkin Cl A2
Hurland Rd C3
James Place. B3
Kenwyn Church Rd A1
Kenwyn Hill A1
Kenwyn Rd A2
Kerris Gdns A2
King St B2
Leats,The B2
Lemon Quay B3
Lemon St Gallery [§] C2
Library B1/B3
Malpas Rd C3
Magistrates Court . B3
Market B3
Memorial Gdns .. B2
Merrifield Close... B1
Mitchell Hill B3
Moresk Cl A2
Moresk Rd A2
Morlaix Ave..... C2
Nancemere Rd ... A3
Newham Bsns Park C3
Newham Ind Est .. C3
Newham Rd C3
Northfield Dr ... C1
Oak Way A3
Pal's Terr. A1
Park View C2
Pendarves Rd ... C2
Plaza Cinema [§] .. B3
Police Station [§] .. B3
Post Office [PO] .. B2/B3
Prince's St C2
Pydar St B2
Quay St B3
Redannick Cres .. C2
Redannick La C2
Richard Lander Monument [♦] A1
Richmond Hill ... B1
River St B2
Rosedale Rd A2
Royal Cornwall Museum [m] B2
St Aubyn Rd C3
St Clement St ... B3
St George's Rd .. A1
School La C2
Spires,The A3
Station Rd B3
Stokes Rd A3
Strangways Terr .. C2
Tabernacle St ... B3
Trehaverne La ... A1
Tremayne Rd ... A1
Treseder's Gdns .. A1
Treworder Rd ... C1
Treyew Rd C1
Truro Cathedral [†] B2
Truro Harbour Office B3
Truro Station [≠] .. B3
Union St B3
Upper School La .. C1
Victoria Gdns ... B1
Waterfall Gdns... C1

Winchester 199
Andover Rd A1
Andover Road Retail Park A1
Archery La C2
Arthur Rd A2
Bar End Rd C3
Beaufort Rd C2
Beggar's La B2
Bereweeke Ave.. A1
Bereweeke Rd ... A1
Boscobel Rd A2
Brassey Rd A1
Broadway B3
Brooks Shopping Centre,The B3
Bus Station B3
Butter Cross [§] .. B2
Canon St. C2
Castle Wall .. C2/C3
Cathedral [†] C2
Cheriton Rd A1
Chesil St C3
Chesil Theatre [§] .. C3
Christchurch Rd... C1
City Hall [♦] C2
City Museum [m] . C2
City Rd. B2
Clifton Rd. B2
Clifton Terr B2
Close Wall C2/C3
Coach Park B2
Colebrook St ... C2
College St. C2
College Walk ... C2
Compton Rd ... C1
Council Offices ... B2
County Council Offices B2
Cranworth Rd ... A2
Cromwell Rd C1
Culver Rd C2
Domum Rd C3
Durngate Place ... B3
Eastgate St B3
East Hill. C3
Edgar Rd C2
Egbert Rd A2
Elm Rd. B1
Everyman [§] B2
Fairfield Rd A1
Fire Station. B1
Fordington Ave... B1
Fordington Rd ... B1
Friarsgate. B3
Gordon Rd B3
Great Hall & Round Table,The [♦] B2
Greenhill Rd B1

Guildhall [§] B3
Hatherley Rd ... A1
High St B2
Hillier Way A3
HM Prison. B1
Hyde Abbey (Remains) [†] A2
Hyde Abbey Rd .. B2
Hyde Cl A2
Hyde St A2
Jane Austen's House [m] C2
Jewry St B2
King Alfred Place.. A2
Kingsgate Arch .. C2
Kingsgate Park .. C3
Kingsgate Rd ... C2
Kingsgate St C2
Lankhills Rd A2
Law Courts B2
Library B2
Lower Brook St... B3
Magdalen Hill... B3
Market La B2
Mews La B1
Middle Brook St .. B3
Middle Rd. B1
Military Museums [m] C2
Milland Rd C3
Milverton Rd B1
Monks Rd A3
North Hill Cl A2
North Walls. B2
North Walls Rec Ground A3
Nuns Rd A3
Oram's Arbour ... B1
Owens Rd A2
Parchment St ... B2
Park & Ride. C3
Park Ave B1
Playing Field ... A1
Police HQ [§] C2
Portal Rd. C3
Post Office [PO] .. B2/C1
Ranelagh Rd.... C1
Regiment Mus [m] . B2
River Pk Leisure Ctr B3
Romans' Rd C3
Romsey Rd B1
Royal Hampshire County Hospital (A&E) [H] B1
St Cross Rd C2
St George's St ... B2
St Giles Hill C3
St James Villas .. C2
St James' La C2
St James'Terr. ... C2
St John's St B3
St John's St B3
St Michael's Rd .. C2
St Paul's Hill B1
St Peter St. B2
St Swithun St ... C2
StThomas St C2
Saxon Rd A2
School of Art ... B3
Sleepers Hill Rd .. C1
Southgate St ... C2
Sparkford Rd ... C1
Square,The. B2
Staple Gdns B2
Station Rd B2
Step Terr. B1
Stockbridge Rd .. A1
Stuart Cres C1
Sussex St B2
Swan Lane B2
Tanner St B3
Theatre Royal [§] .. B2
Tower St B2
Union St B3
Univ of Southampton (Winchester School of Art) C1
University of Winchester (King Alfred Campus) C1
Upper Brook St .. B3
Wales St B3
Water Lane B3
Weirs,The C3
West End Terr ... B3
Western Rd B1
Wharf Hill. C3
Winchester Sta [≠] A2
Winnall Moors Wildlife Reserve A3
Wolvesey Castle [♦] C3
Worthy Lane A2
Worthy Rd. A2

Windsor 199
Adelaide Sq C3
Albany Rd C3
Albert St B3
Alexandra Gdns .. C2
Alexandra Rd ... C2
Alma Rd B1
Ambulance Station B2
Arthur Rd A2
Bachelors Acre... B2
Barry Ave C2
Beaumont Rd ... C2
Bexley St. B1
Boat House A3
Brocas St A2
Brocas,The..... A2
Brook St A2
Bulkeley Ave.... C1
Castle Hill B2
Charles St. B3
Claremont Rd ... C2
Clarence Cres... C2
Clarence Rd C2
Clewer Court Rd... C1
Coach Park C2
College Cres.... C1
Cricket Club A3
Cricket Ground... C3

Dagmar Rd C2
Datchet Rd B3
Devereux Rd C2
Dorset Rd C2
Duke St C1
Elm Rd. C1
Eton College [♦] .. A3
Eton Court A3
Eton Square A3
Eton Wick Rd ... A2
Farm Yard A3
Fire Station. C2
Frances Rd C2
Frogmore Dr.... C2
Gloucester Place .. C1
Goslar Way..... C1
Goswell Hill B2
Goswell Rd B2
Green La C1
Grove Rd C2
Helena Rd C2
Helston La. B1
High St A2/B3
Holy Trinity [♣] ... A2
Home Park,The A3/C3
Hosp (Private) [H] .. C1
Household Cavalry [m] C1
Imperial Rd. C1
Information Ctr [i] B2/B3
Keats La C2
King Edward Ct .. B2
King Edward VII Ave B2
King Edward VII Hospital [H] B1
King George V Memorial B2
King Stable St... A2
King's Rd C2
Library C2
Long Walk,The ... C3
Maidenhead Rd .. B1
Meadow La C2
Municipal Offices . C3
Nell Gwynne's House [♦] B2
Osborne Rd C2
Oxford Rd B1
Park St C2
Peascod St B2
Police Station [§] .. B2
Post Office [PO] .. A2
Princess Margaret Hospital [H] A2
Queen Victoria's Walk B3
Queen's Rd C2
River St B2
Romney Island ... A3
Romney Lock ... A3
Romney Lock Rd .. A3
Russell St C2
St John's B2
St John's Chapel [♣] A2
St Leonards Rd .. C2
St Mark's Rd ... C2
Sheet St C2
South Meadow .. A2
South Meadow La . A2
Springfield Rd ... C1
Stovell Rd. B1
Sunbury Rd A2
Tangier La. A2
Tangier St A2
Temple Rd. C2
Thames St. B3
Theatre Royal [§] .. B2
Trinity Place C1
Vansittart Rd ... C1
Vansittart Rd Gdns . C1
Victoria Barracks .. C2
Victoria St. C2
Ward Royal B1
Westmead C1
White Lilies Island .. B1
William St. B2
Windsor & Eton Central [≠] B2
Windsor & Eton Riverside [≠] A3
Windsor Arts Centre [§] C2
Windsor Bridge .. A3
Windsor Castle [♦] B3
Windsor Great Pk . C3
Windsor Leisure Ctr B1
Windsor Relief Rd .. A1
Windsor Royal Shopping B2
York Ave C1
York Rd C1

Wolverhampton 200
Albion St. B3
Alexandra St. ... C1
Arena [§] B2
Arts Gallery [m] .. B2
Ashland St C1
Austin St. A3
Badger Dr. A3
Bailey St. A3
Bath Ave B1
Bath Rd. C2
Bell St. B2
Berry St. B3
Bilston Rd C3
Bilston St B3
Birmingham Canal. A3
Bone Mill La A2
Brewery Rd A1
Bright St. A2
Burton Cres A3
Bus Station B3
Cambridge St ... A3
Cannock Rd A3
Castle St B2
Chapel Ash C1
Cherry St. C1
Chester St A1
Church La C1
Church St C2

Civic Centre B2
Civic Hall. B2
Clarence Rd A2
Cleveland St ... C2
Clifton St. C1
Coach Station... B3
Compton Rd ... B1
Corn Hill. B3
Coven St A1
Craddock St ... A1
Cross St North .. A1
Crown & County Courts C3
Crown St C2
Culwell St A3
Dale St. C1
Darlington St ... B1
Devon Rd A1
Drummond St... B2
Dudley Rd C2
Dudley St. B2
Duke St C3
Dunkley St A2
Dunstall Ave A2
Dunstall Hill A2
Dunstall Rd. ... A1/A2
Evans St A1
Fawdry St A1
Field St. C3
Fire Station. C1
Fiveways A3
Fowler Playing Fields A3
Fox's La. A2
Francis St A2
Fryer St. B3
Gloucester St ... A1
Gordon St. C3
Graiseley St C1
Grand [§] C2
Granville St. ... C3
Great Brickkiln St. . C1
Great Hampton St . A1
Great Western St .. A2
Grimstone St ... B3
Harrow St A1
Hilton St A3
Hive Liby The .. B2
Horseley Fields .. C3
Humber Rd C1
Jack Hayward Way. A2
Jameson St A1
Jenner St C3
Kennedy Rd C3
Kimberley St ... C1
King St B2
Laburnum St... A3
Lansdowne Rd .. A1
Leicester St A2
Lever St. C3
Library C3
Lichfield St B3
Light House [§] .. B3
Little's La B3
Lock St A3
Lord St C1
Lowe St. A3
Maltings,The ... A1
Mander Centre... B2
Mander St. C1
Market B3
Market St B3
Maxwell Rd C3
Merridale St ... C1
Middlecross ... A2
Molineux St A2
Mostyn St A1
New Hampton Rd East A1
Nine Elms La ... A3
North Rd A2
Oaks Cres C1
Oxley St. A2
Paget St A1
Park Ave A1
Park Road East .. A1
Park Road West .. B1
Paul St. C2
Pelham St C1
Penn Rd C2
Piper's Row B3
Pitt St C2
Police Station [§] .. B3
Pool St C2
Poole St A1
Post Office [PO] .. A1/B2/B2/C2
Powlett St C3
Queen St B3
Raby St C2
Railway Dr. B3
Red Hill St A2
Red Lion St B2
Retreat St C1
Ring Rd. B2
Royal,The [§] C3
Rugby St A2
Russell St C1
St Andrew's A1
St David's B3
St George's ... C2
St George's Parade B2
St James St. C3
St John's C2
St John's Retail Pk. . C3
St John's Square .. C2
St Mark's. C1
St Mark's Rd ... C1
St Marks St. ... C1
St Patrick's. B2
St Peter's. B2
Salisbury St ... C1
Salop St C2
School St C2
Sherwood St ... A2
Smestow St ... A3
Snow Hill C3
Springfield Rd ... A3
Stafford St ... A2/B2
Staveley Rd. A1
Steelhouse La ... C3
Stephenson St ... C1
Stewart St C1
Sun St B3

Tempest St C2
Temple St C2
Tettenhall Rd ... B1
Thomas St. C2
Thornley St B2
Tower St A2
University C1
Upper Zoar St ... C1
Vicarage Rd ... C3
Victoria St. B2
Walpole St A1
Walsall St C3
Ward St C1
Warwick St C3
Water St A1
Waterloo Rd B2
Wednesfield Rd .. B3
West Park (not A&E) [H] B1
West Park Swimming Pool B1
Wharf St C3
Whitmore Hill... B2
Wolverhampton [≠] B3
Wolverhampton St George's [♣] B2
Wolverhampton Wanderers Football Gnd (Molineux) B2
Worcester St ... C2
Wulfrun Centre .. C2
Yarwell Cl A3
York St C2
Zoar St C1

Worcester 200
Albany Terr A1
Angel Place B2
Angel St B2
Ashcroft Rd.... A2
Athelstan Rd ... C3
Avenue,The A1
Back Lane North .. A1
Back Lane South .. A1
Barbourne Rd .. A1
Bath Rd C2
Battenhall Rd ... C3
Bridge St. B2
Britannia Sq. ... A1
Broad St. B2
Bromwich La ... C1
Bromwich Rd ... C1
Bromyard Rd ... C1
Bus Station B2
Butts,The B2
Carden St C3
Castle St A2
Cathedral [†] C2
Cathedral Plaza .. B2
Charles St. B3
Chequers La ... A3
Chestnut St. ... A2
Chestnut Walk .. A2
Citizens' Advice Bureau B2
City Walls Rd. ... B2
Cole Hill C3
College St. C2
Commandery, The [♦] C2
Cripplegate Park . C1
Croft Rd. B1
Cromwell St ... B3
Cross,The B2
Crowngate Ctr .. B2
Deansway B2
Diglis Pde. C2
Diglis Rd C2
Edgar Tower [♦] .. C2
Farrier St. B2
Foregate St ... B2
Fort Royal Hill .. C3
Fort Royal Park .. C3
Foundry St B3
Friar St B2
George St. B3
Grand Stand Rd .. B1
Greenhill. C3
Greyfriars [m] ... B2
Guildhall [♦] B2
Henwick Rd ... B1
High St B2
Hill St C3
Hive,The B2
Huntingdon Hall [§] B2
Hylton Rd. B1
Information Ctr [i] B2
King Charles Place Shopping Centre C1
King's School. ... C2
King's School Playing Field C2
Kleve Walk C2
Lansdowne Cres. . A3
Lansdowne Rd .. A3
Lansdowne Walk . A3
Laslett St. A2
Little Chestnut St. . A2
Little London ... B2
London Rd C3
Lowell St. A2
Lowesmoor B2
Lowesmoor Terr. .. B2
Lowesmoor Wharf. B2
Magistrates Court . B2
Midland Rd C3
Mill St C1
Moors Severn Terr,The A1
Museum & Art Gallery [m] A2
Museum of Royal Worcester [m] C2
New Rd. B1
New St. B2
Northfield St ... A2
Odeon [§] B2
Old Palace The [♦] . C2
Padmore St. ... B3
Park St C2
Pheasant St ... B3
Pitchcroft Racecourse A1
Portland St. ... C2

Post Office [PO] ... B2
Quay St B2
Queen St B2
Rainbow Hill ... A2
Recreation Ground A2
Reindeer Court .. B2
Rogers Hill A3
Sabrina Terr. ... A1
St Dunstan's Cres. . C3
St John's B1
St Martin's Gate .. B3
St Martin's Quarter B3
St Oswald's Rd .. A2
St Paul's St B3
St Swithin's Church B2
St Wulstans Cres .. C3
Sansome Walk .. A2
Severn St C2
Shambles,The ... B2
Shaw St B2
Shire Hall Crown Ct C2
Shrub Hill Rd ... B3
Shrub Hill Retail Pk B3
Slingpool Walk... C1
South Parade ... B2
Southfield St ... A2
Sports Centre... A3
Stanley Rd C3
Swan,The [§] A1
Swimming Pool .. A2
Tallow Hill. B3
Tennis Walk ... A2
Tolladine Rd ... B3
Tudor House [m] .. B2
Tybridge St B1
Tything,The A2
Univ of Worcester . B1
Vincent Rd A3
Vue [§] B2
Washington St .. A3
Woolhope Rd ... C3
Worcester Bridge . B2
Worcester County Cricket Club A1
Worcester Foregate Street [≠] B2
Worcester Shrub Hill [≠] B3
Worcester Royal Grammar School A1
Wylds La. C3

Wrexham 200
Wrecsam
Abbot St B2
Acton Rd A3
Albert St B3
Alexandra Rd ... C1
Aran Rd. C3
Barnfield A3
Bath Rd. C2
Beeches,The ... A3
Beechley Rd C2
Belgrave Rd C2
Belle Vue Park ... C2
Belle Vue Rd ... C2
Belvedere Dr A1
Bennion's Rd ... C3
Berse Rd A1
Bersham Rd ... C1
Birch St C2
Bodhyfryd. B3
Border Retail Park. B3
Bradley Rd C2
Bright St B1
Bron-y-Nant A1
Brook St C2
Bryn-y-Cabanau Rd C3
Bury St C3
Bus Station B2
Butchers Market . B2
Caia Rd C3
Cambrian Ind Est .. C3
Caxton Place ... C1
Cemetery C1
Centenary Rd ... C1
Chapel St C2
Charles St. B2
Chester Rd A3
Chester St. B3
Cilcen Grove. ... A3
Citizens Advice Bureau B2
Cobden Rd B1
Council Offices... B3
County [§] B2
Crescent Rd C3
Crispin La A2
Croesnewyth Rd.. B1
Cross St. A3
Cunliffe St. A3
Derby Rd. C3
Dolydd Rd B1
Duke St B2
Eagles Meadow .. C3
Earle St. C3
East Ave C3
Edward St. C2
Egerton St. B2
Empress Rd ... C1
Erddig Rd C2
Fairy Rd. C2
Fire Station. B2
Foster Rd A2
Foxwood Dr C1
Garden Rd. B2
General Market .. B3
Gerald St. B2
Gibson St C1
Glyndŵr University Plas Coch Campus A1
Greenbank St ... C3
Greenfield A2
Grosvenor Rd ... B2
Grove Park [§] ... B3
Grove Rd. B3
Guildhall B2
Haig Rd. C3
Hampden Rd ... C3
Hazel Grove A3
Henblas St B2
High St B2
Hightown Rd ... C2

Hill St B2
Holt Rd B3
Holt St. B3
Hope St. B2
Huntroyde Ave .. C3
Information Ctr [i] B3
Island Green Shopping Centre B2
Job Centre B2
Jubilee Rd B2
King St B2
Kingsmills Rd ... C3
Lambpit St B3
Law Courts B2
Lawson Cl B3
Lawson Rd A3
Lea Rd. C2
Library & Arts Ctr. . B2
Lilac Way B3
Llys David Lord. .. B1
Lorne St C2
Maesgwyn Rd... B1
Maesydre Rd ... A3
Manley Rd. C3
Market St B2
Mawdsley Ave .. A3
Mayville Ave ... A3
Meml Gallery [m] . B2
Memorial Hall .. B2
Mold Rd A1
Mount St. C2
Neville Cres A3
New Rd. A3
North Wales Regional Tennis Centre A3
North Wales School of Art & Design A3
Oak Dr. A3
Park Ave A3
Park St C2
Peel St. C1
Pen y Bryn. C1
Pentre Felin C2
Penymaes Ave .. A3
Peoples Market .. B3
Percy St. C1
Pines,The A3
Plas Coch Rd ... A1
Plas Coch Retail Pk A1
Police Station [§] .. B3
Poplar Rd C2
Post Office [PO] .. A2/B2/C2/C3
Powell St. A2
Poyser St. C2
Price's La A2
Primrose Way ... B1
Princess St C1
Queen St. B3
Queens Sq B2
Regent St B2
Rhosddu Rd .. A2/B2
Rhosnesni La ... A3
Rivulet Rd C2
Ruabon Rd C2
Ruthin Rd C1/C2
St Giles [♣] B3
St Giles Way ... C3
St James Ct. ... A3
St Mary's [†] ... B2
Salisbury Rd ... C3
Salop Rd C3
Sontley Rd C2
Spring Rd A2
Stanley St C2
Stansty Rd A2
Station Approach.. B3
Studio [§] B2
Talbot Rd. C2
Techniquest Glyndŵr [♦] A1
Town Hill. C1
Trevor St. C2
Trinity St. B2
Tuttle St C2
Vale Park A1
Vernon St B2
Vicarage Hill. ... C2
Victoria Rd C2
Walnut St B2
War Memorial ... B3
Waterworld Leisure Centre [♣] C3
Watery Rd . B1/B2
Wellington Rd ... C2
Westminster Dr .. A3
William Aston Hall [♣] A1
Windsor Rd. ... C2
Wrecsam B2
Wrexham AFC ... C1
Wrexham Central [≠] B2
Wrexham General [≠] B1
Wrexham Maelor Hospital (A&E) [H] A1
Wrexham Technology Park B1
Wynn Ave A2
Yale College A3
Yale Grove. A3
Yorke St. C2

York 200
Aldwark B2
Barbican Rd C3
Bar Convent Living Heritage Ctr [♦] C1
Barley Hall [♦] .. B2
Bishopgate St. .. C1
Bishophill Senior . C2
Bishopthorpe Rd . C2
Blossom St C1
Bootham A1
Bootham Cres .. A1
Bootham Terr. .. A1
Bridge St. B2
Brook St A2
Brownlow St. ... A2
Burton Stone La . A1
Castle Museum [m] C2
Castlegate B2
Cemetery Rd. ... C3
Cherry St. C2

City Screen [§] ... B2
City Wall .. A2/B1/C3
Clarence St. ... A2
Clementhorpe ... C2
Clifford St B2
Clifford's Tower [♦] B2
Clifton A1
Coach park C1
Coney St B2
Coppergate Ctr .. B2
Cromwell Rd. ... C2
Crown Court C2
Davygate. B2
Deanery Gdns... A2
DIG [♦] B2
Dodsworth Ave.. A3
Eboracum Way .. A3
Ebor Industrial Est. C3
Eldon St A3
Everyman [§] C1
Fairfax House [♦] . C2
Fire Station. C1
Fishergate C2
Foss Islands Rd .. B3
Foss Islands Retail Park B3
Fossbank A3
Garden St A2
George St C2
Gillygate. A2
Goodramgate. .. B2
Grand Opera Ho [§] B2
Grosvenor Terr... A1
Guildhall. B2
Hallfield Rd B3
Heslington Rd ... C3
Heworth Green. .. A3
Holy Trinity [♣] .. B2
Hope St. C2
Huntington Rd .. A3
Information Ctr [i] B2
James St. B3
Jorvik Viking Ctr [♦] B2
Kent St C3
Lawrence St C3
Layerthorpe ... A3
Leeman Rd B1
Lendal B2
Lendal Bridge. .. B1
Library A2/B1
Longfield Terrace.. A1
Lord Mayor's Walk . A2
Lowther St A2
Mansion House [♣] B2
Margaret St C3
Marygate A1
Melbourne St ... C3
Merchant Adventurers' Hall [♣] B2
Merchant Taylors' Hall [♣] B2
Micklegate B1
Micklegate Bar [m] . C1
Monkgate A2
Moss St. C1
Museum Gdns [❀] . B1
Museum St B1
National Railway Museum [m] B1
Navigation Rd. .. B3
Newton Terr C1
North Pde A1
North St. B1
Nunnery La C1
Nunthorpe Rd .. C1
Ouse Bridge ... B2
Paragon St C3
Park Grove A3
Park St C1
Parliament St... B2
Peasholme Green . B3
Penley's Grove St. . A2
Piccadilly B2
Police Station [§] .. C1
Post Office [PO] .. B1/B2/C3
Priory St. C1
Queen Anne's Rd . A1
Regimental Mus [m] at Monk Bar [m] A2
Roman Bath [m] .. B2
Rowntree Park .. C2
St Andrewgate .. B2
St Benedict Rd .. C1
St John St. A2
St Olave's Rd ... A1
St Peter's Grove .. A1
St Saviourgate .. B2
Scarcroft Hill ... C1
Scarcroft Rd C1
Shambles,The ... B2
Shopmobility ... B2
Skeldergate C2
Skeldergate Bridge C2
Station Rd. B1
Stonebow,The ... B2
Stonegate B2
Superstore A3
Sycamore Terr .. A1
Terry Ave. C2
Theatre Royal [§] .. B2
Thorpe St C1
Toft Green. B1
Tower St C2
Townend St. ... A2
Treasurer's Ho [♣] . A2
Trinity La. B1
Undercroft Mus [m] B2
Union Terr. A2
Victor St. C2
Vine St. C2
Walmgate C3
War Memorial [♦] . C2
Wellington St ... C3
York Art Gallery [m] A1
York Barbican [§] . C3
York Brewery The [m] C1
York Dungeon,The [m] B2
York Minster [†] .. A2
York St John Uni. . A2
York Station [≠] ... B1

Abbreviations used in the index

Aberdeen	Aberdeen City
Aberds	Aberdeenshire
Ald	Alderney
Anglesey	Isle of Anglesey
Angus	Angus
Argyll	Argyll and Bute
Bath	Bath and North East Somerset
Bedford	Bedford
Bl Gwent	Blaenau Gwent
Blackburn	Blackburn with Darwen
Blackpool	Blackpool
BCP	Bournemouth, Christchurch and Poole
Borders	Scottish Borders
Brack	Bracknell
Bridgend	Bridgend
Brighton	City of Brighton and Hove
Bristol	City and County of Bristol
Bucks	Buckinghamshire
C Beds	Central Bedfordshire
Caerph	Caerphilly
Cambs	Cambridgeshire
Cardiff	Cardiff
Carms	Carmarthenshire
Ceredig	Ceredigion
Ches E	Cheshire East
Ches W	Cheshire West and Chester
Clack	Clackmannanshire
Conwy	Conwy
Corn	Cornwall
Cumb	Cumbria
Darl	Darlington
Denb	Denbighshire
Derby	City of Derby
Derbys	Derbyshire
Devon	Devon
Dorset	Dorset
Dumfries	Dumfries and Galloway
Dundee	Dundee City
Durham	Durham
E Ayrs	East Ayrshire
E Dunb	East Dunbartonshire
E Loth	East Lothian
E Renf	East Renfrewshire
E Sus	East Sussex
E Yorks	East Riding of Yorkshire
Edin	City of Edinburgh
Essex	Essex
Falk	Falkirk
Fife	Fife
Flint	Flintshire
Glasgow	City of Glasgow
Glos	Gloucestershire
Gtr Man	Greater Manchester
Guern	Guernsey
Gwyn	Gwynedd
Halton	Halton
Hants	Hampshire
Hereford	Herefordshire
Herts	Hertfordshire
Highld	Highland
Hrtlpl	Hartlepool
Hull	Hull
IoM	Isle of Man
IoW	Isle of Wight
Invclyd	Inverclyde
Jersey	Jersey
Kent	Kent
Lancs	Lancashire
Leicester	City of Leicester
Leics	Leicestershire
Lincs	Lincolnshire
London	Greater London
Luton	Luton
M Keynes	Milton Keynes
M Tydf	Merthyr Tydfil
Mbro	Middlesbrough
Medway	Medway
Mers	Merseyside
Midloth	Midlothian
Mon	Monmouthshire
Moray	Moray
N Ayrs	North Ayrshire
N Lincs	North Lincolnshire
N Lanark	North Lanarkshire
N Som	North Somerset
N Yorks	North Yorkshire
NE Lincs	North East Lincolnshire
Neath	Neath Port Talbot
Newport	City and County of Newport
Norf	Norfolk
Northants	Northamptonshire
Northumb	Northumberland
Nottingham	City of Nottingham
Notts	Nottinghamshire
Orkney	Orkney
Oxon	Oxfordshire
Pboro	Peterborough
Pembs	Pembrokeshire
Perth	Perth and Kinross
Plym	Plymouth
Powys	Powys
Ptsmth	Portsmouth
Reading	Reading
Redcar	Redcar and Cleveland
Renfs	Renfrewshire
Rhondda	Rhondda Cynon Taff
Rutland	Rutland
S Ayrs	South Ayrshire
S Glos	South Gloucestershire
S Lanark	South Lanarkshire
S Yorks	South Yorkshire
Scilly	Scilly
Shetland	Shetland
Shrops	Shropshire
Slough	Slough
Som	Somerset
Soton	Southampton
Staffs	Staffordshire
Southend	Southend-on-Sea
Stirling	Stirling
Stockton	Stockton-on-Tees
Stoke	Stoke-on-Trent
Suff	Suffolk
Sur	Surrey
Swansea	Swansea
Swindon	Swindon
T&W	Tyne and Wear
Telford	Telford and Wrekin
Thurrock	Thurrock
Torbay	Torbay
Torf	Torfaen
V Glam	The Vale of Glamorgan
W Berks	West Berkshire
W Dunb	West Dunbartonshire
W Isles	Western Isles
W Loth	West Lothian
W Mid	West Midlands
W Sus	West Sussex
W Yorks	West Yorkshire
Warks	Warwickshire
Warr	Warrington
Wilts	Wiltshire
Windsor	Windsor and Maidenhead
Wokingham	Wokingham
Worcs	Worcestershire
Wrex	Wrexham
York	City of York

How to use the index

Example

Trudoxhill Som **24** E2

- grid square
- page number
- county or unitary authority

A

Abbas Combe 12 B5
Abberley 50 C2
Abberton Essex 43 C6
Worcs 50 D4
Abberwick 117 C7
Abbess Roding 42 C1
Abbey 11 C6
Abbey-cwm-hir 48 B2
Abbeydale 88 F4
Abbey Dore 49 F5
Abbey Field 43 B5
Abbey Hulton 75 E6
Abbey St Bathans 122 C3
Abbeystead 93 D5
Abbey Town 107 D8
Abbey Village 86 B4
Abbey Wood 29 B5
Abbots Bickington 9 C5
Abbots Bromley 62 B4
Abbotsbury 12 F3
Abbotsham 9 B6
Abbotskerswell 7 C6
Abbots Langley 40 D3
Abbots Leigh 23 B7
Abbotsley 54 D3
Abbots Morton 50 D5
Abbots Ripton 54 B3
Abbots Salford 51 D5
Abbotswood 14 B4
Abbotts Ann 25 E8
Abcott 49 B5
Abdon 61 F5
Aber 46 E3
Aberaeron 46 C3
Aberaman 34 D4
Aberangell 58 C5
Aber-Arad 46 F2
Aberarder 137 F7
Aberarder House 138 B2
Aberarder Lodge 137 F8
Aberargie 128 C3
Aberarth 46 C3
Aberavon 33 E8
Aber-banc 46 E2
Aberbeeg 35 D6
Abercanaid 34 D4
Abercarn 35 E6
Abercastle 44 B3
Abercegir 58 D5
Aberchirder 152 C6
Aber Cowarch 59 C5
Abercraf 34 C2
Abercrombie 129 D7
Abercych 45 E4
Abercynafon 34 C4
Abercynon 34 E4
Aberdalgie 128 B2
Aberdâr
=Aberdare 34 D3
Aberdare
=Aberdâr 34 D3
Aberdaron 70 E2
Aberdaugleddau
=Milford Haven 44 E4
Aberdeen 141 D8
Aberdesach 82 F4
Aberdour 128 F3
Aberdovey 58 E3
Aberdulais 34 D1
Aberedw 48 E2
Abereiddy 44 B2
Abererch 70 D4
Aberfan 34 D4
Aberfeldy 133 E5
Aberffraw 82 E3
Aberffrwd 47 B5
Aberford 95 F7
Aberfoyle 126 D4
Abergavenny
=Y Fenni 35 C6
Abergele 72 B3
Aber-Giâr 46 E4
Abergorlech 46 F4
Abergwaun
=Fishguard 44 B4
Abergwesyn 47 D7
Abergwili 33 B5
Abergwynant 58 C3
Aber-gwynfi 34 E2
Abergwyngregyn 83 D6
Abergynolwyn 58 D3
Aber-Hirnant 72 F3
Aberhonddu
=Brecon 34 B4
Aberhosan 58 E5
Aberkenfig 34 F2
Aberlady 129 F6
Aberlemno 135 D5
Aberllefenni 58 D4
Abermagwr 47 B5
Abermaw
=Barmouth 58 C3
Abermeurig 46 D4
Abermule 59 E8
Abernaint 59 B8
Abernant 32 B4
Aber-nant 34 D4
Abernethy 128 C3
Abernyte 134 F2
Aberpennar
=Mountain Ash 34 E4
Aberporth 45 D4
Aber-Rhiwlech 59 B6
Abersoch 70 E4
Abersychan 35 D6
Abertawe
=Swansea 33 E7
Aberteifi
=Cardigan 45 E3
Aberthin 22 B2
Abertillery
=Abertyleri 35 D6
Abertridwr Caerph 35 F5
Powys 59 C7
Abertyleri
=Abertillery 35 D6
Abertysswg 35 D5
Aberuthven 127 C8
Aber-Village 35 B5
Aberyscir 34 B3
Aberystwyth 58 F2
Abhainn Suidhe 154 G5
Abingdon-on-Thames 38 E4
Abinger Common 28 E2
Abinger Hammer 27 E8
Abington 114 B2
Abington Pigotts 54 E4
Ab Kettleby 64 B4
Ab Lench 50 D5
Ablington Glos 37 D8
Wilts 25 E6
Abney 75 B8
Aboyne 140 E4
Abram 86 D4
Abriachan 151 H8
Abridge 41 E7
Abronhill 119 B7
Abson 24 B2
Abthorpe 52 E4
Abune-the-Hill 159 F3
Aby 79 B7
Acaster Malbis 95 E8
Acaster Selby 95 E8
Accrington 87 B5
Acha 146 F4
Achabraid 145 E7
Achachork 149 D9
Achafolla 124 D3
Achagary 157 D10
Achahoish 144 F6
Achalader 133 E8
Achallader 131 E7
Acha Mor 155 E8
Achanalt 150 E5
Achanamara 144 E6
Achandunie 151 D9
Ach'an Todhair 130 B4
Achany 157 J8
Achaphubuil 130 B4
Acharacle 147 E9
Acharn Highld 147 F10
Perth 132 E4
Acharole 158 E4
Achath 141 C6
Achavanich 158 F3
Achavraat 151 G12
Achddu 33 D5
Achduart 156 J3
Achentoul 157 F11
Achfary 156 F5
Achgarve 155 H13
Achiemore Highld 156 C6
Highld 157 D11
A'Chill 148 H7
Achiltibuie 156 J3
Achina 157 C10
Achinduich 157 J8
Achinduin 124 B4
Achingills 158 D3
Achintee Highld 131 B5
Highld 150 G2
Achintraid 149 E13
Achlean 138 E4
Achleck 146 G7
Achluachrach 137 F5
Achlyness 156 D5
Achmelvich 156 G3
Achmore Highld 149 E13
Stirling 132 F2
Achnaba Argyll 124 B5
Argyll 145 E8
Achnabat 151 H8
Achnacarnin 156 F3
Achnacarry 136 F4
Achnacloich Argyll 125 B5
Highld 149 H10
Achnaconeran 137 C7
Achnacraig 146 G7
Achnacroish 130 E2
Achnadrish 146 F7
Achnafalnich 125 C8
Achnagarron 151 E9
Achnaha 146 E7
Achnahanat 151 B8
Achnahannet 139 B5
Achnairn 157 H8
Achnaluachrach 157 J9
Achnasaul 136 F4
Achnasheen 150 F4
Achosnich 146 E7
Achranich 147 G10
Achreamie 157 C13
Achriabhach 131 C5
Achriesgill 156 D5
Achrimsdale 157 J12
Achtoty 157 C9
Achurch 65 F7
Achuvoldrach 157 D8
Achvaich 151 B10
Achvarasdal 157 C12
Ackergill 158 E5
Acklam Mbro 102 C2
N Yorks 96 C3
Ackleton 61 E7
Acklington 117 D8
Ackton 88 B5
Ackworth Moor Top 88 C5
Acle 69 C7
Acock's Green 62 F5
Acol 31 C7
Acomb Northumb 110 C2
York 95 D8
Aconbury 49 F7
Acre 87 B5
Acrefair 73 E6
Acre Street 15 E8
Acton Ches E 74 D3
Dorset 13 G7
London 41 F5
Shrops 60 F3
Suff 56 E2
Wrex 73 D7
Acton Beauchamp 49 D8
Acton Bridge 74 B2
Acton Burnell 60 D5
Acton Green 49 D8
Acton Pigott 60 D5
Acton Round 61 E6
Acton Scott 60 F4
Acton Trussell 62 C3
Acton Turville 37 F5
Adbaston 61 B7
Adber 12 B3
Adderley 74 E3
Adderstone 123 F7
Addiewell 120 C2
Addingham 94 E3
Addington Bucks 39 B7
Kent 29 D7
London 28 C4
Addinston 121 D8
Addiscombe 28 C4
Addlestone 27 C8
Addlethorpe 79 C8
Adel 95 F5
Adeney 61 C7
Adfa 59 D7
Adforton 49 B6
Adisham 31 D6
Adlestrop 38 B2
Adlingfleet 90 B2
Adlington 86 C4
Admaston Staffs 62 B4
Telford 61 C6
Admington 51 E7
Adstock 52 F5
Adstone 52 D3
Adversane 16 B4
Advie 152 E1
Adwalton 88 B3
Adwell 39 E6
Adwick le Street 89 D6
Adwick upon Dearne 89 D5
Adziel 153 C9
Ae Village 114 F2
Affleck 141 B7
Affpuddle 13 E6
Affric Lodge 136 B4
Afon-wen 72 B5
Afton 14 F4
Agglethorpe 101 F5
Agneash 84 D4
Aigburth 85 F4
Aiginis 155 D9
Aike 97 E6
Aikerness 159 C5
Aikers 159 J5
Aiketgate 108 E4
Aikton 108 D2
Ailey 48 E5
Ailstone 51 D7
Ailsworth 65 E8
Ainderby Quernhow 102 F1
Ainderby Steeple 101 E8
Aingers Green 43 B7
Ainsdale 85 C4
Ainsdale-on-Sea 85 C4
Ainstable 108 E5
Ainsworth 87 C5
Ainthorpe 103 D5
Aintree 85 E4
Aird Argyll 124 E3
Dumfries 104 C4
Highld 149 A12
W Isles 155 D10
Aird a Mhachair 148 D2
Aird a' Mhulaidh 154 F6
Aird Asaig 154 G6
Aird Dhail 155 A9
Airdens 151 B9
Aird Mhidhinis 148 H2
Aird Mhighe
W Isles 154 H6
W Isles 154 J5
Aird Mhor 148 H2
Aird of Sleat 149 H10
Airdrie 119 C7
Aird Thunga 155 D9
Airdtorrisdale 157 C9
Aird Uig 154 D5
Airidh a Bhruaich 154 F7
Airieland 106 D4
Airmyn 89 B8
Airntully 133 F7
Airor 149 H12
Airth 127 F7
Airton 94 D2
Airyhassen 105 E7
Aisby Lincs 78 F3
Lincs 90 E2
Aisgernis 148 F2
Aiskew 101 F7
Aislaby N Yorks 103 D6
N Yorks 103 F5
Stockton 102 C2
Aisthorpe 78 A2
Aith Orkney 159 G3
Shetland 160 D8
Shetland 160 H5
Aithsetter 160 K6
Aitkenhead 112 D3
Aitnoch 151 H12
Akeld 117 B5
Akeley 52 F5
Akenham 56 E5
Albaston 6 B2
Alberbury 60 C3
Albourne 17 C6
Albrighton Shrops 60 C4
Shrops 62 D2
Alburgh 69 F5
Albury Herts 41 B7
Sur 27 E8
Albury End 41 B7
Alby Hill 81 D7
Alcaig 151 F8
Alcaston 60 F4
Alcester 51 D5
Alciston 18 E2
Alcombe Som 21 E8
Wilts 24 C3
Alconbury 54 B2
Alconbury Weston 54 B2
Aldbar Castle 135 D5
Aldborough Norf 81 D7
N Yorks 95 C7
Aldbourne 25 B7
Aldbrough 97 F8
Aldbrough St John 101 C7
Aldbury 40 C2
Aldcliffe 92 C4
Aldclune 133 C6
Aldeburgh 57 D8
Aldeby 69 E7
Aldenham 40 E4
Alderbury 14 B2
Aldercar 76 E4
Alderford 68 C4
Alderholt 14 C2
Alderley 36 E4
Alderley Edge 74 B5
Aldermaston 26 C3
Aldermaston Wharf 26 C4
Alderminster 51 E7
Alder's End 49 E8
Aldersey Green 73 D8
Aldershot 27 D6
Alderton Glos 50 F5
Northants 52 E5
Shrops 60 B4
Suff 57 E7
Wilts 37 F5
Alderwasley 76 D3
Aldfield 95 C5
Aldford 73 D8
Aldham Essex 43 B5
Suff 56 E4
Aldie 151 C10
Aldingbourne 16 D3
Aldingham 92 B2
Aldington Kent 19 B7
Worcs 51 E5
Aldington Frith 19 B7
Aldochlay 126 E2
Aldreth 54 B5
Aldridge 62 D4
Aldringham 57 C8
Aldsworth 38 C1
Aldunie 140 B2
Aldwark Derbys 76 D2
N Yorks 95 C7
Aldwick 16 E3
Aldwincle 65 F7
Aldworth 26 B3
Alexandria 118 B3
Alfardisworthy 8 C4
Alfington 11 E6
Alfold 27 F8
Alfold Bars 27 F8
Alfold Crossways 27 F8
Alford Aberds 140 C4
Lincs 79 B7
Som 23 F8
Alfreton 76 D4
Alfrick 50 D2
Alfrick Pound 50 D2
Alfriston 18 E2
Algaltraig 145 F9
Algarkirk 79 F5
Alhampton 23 F8
Aline Lodge 154 F6
Alisary 147 D10
Alkborough 90 B2
Alkerton 51 E8
Alkham 31 E6
Alkington 74 F2
Alkmonton 75 F8
Alladale Lodge 150 C7
Allaleigh 7 D6
Allanaquoich 139 E7
Allangrange Mains 151 F9
Allanton Borders 122 D4
N Lanark 119 D8
Allathasdal 148 H1
All Cannings 25 C5
Allendale Town 109 D8
Allenheads 109 E8
Allensford 110 D3
Allens Green 41 C7
Allensmore 49 F6
Allenton 76 F3
Aller 12 B2
Allerby 107 F7
Allerford 21 E8
Allerston 103 F6
Allerthorpe 96 E3
Allerton Mers 86 F2
W Yorks 94 F4
Allerton Bywater 88 B5
Allerton Mauleverer 95 D7
Allesley 63 F7
Allestree 76 F3
Allet 3 B6
Allexton 64 D5
Allgreave 75 C6
Allhallows 30 B2
Allhallows-on-Sea 30 B2
Alligin Shuas 149 C13
Allimore Green 62 C2
Allington Lincs 77 E8
Wilts 25 C5
Wilts 25 F7

Allithwaite 92 B3
Alloa 127 E7
Allonby 107 E7
Alloway 112 C3
All Saints South Elmham 69 F6
All Stretton 60 E4
Allt 33 D6
Alltchaorunn 131 D5
Alltforgan 59 B6
Alltmawr 48 E2
Alltnacaillich 156 E7
Allt na h-Airbhe 150 B4
Allt-nan-sùgh 136 B2
Alltsigh 137 C7
Alltwalis 46 F3
Alltwen 33 D8
Alltyblaca 46 E4
Allwood Green 56 B4
Almeley 48 D5
Almer 13 E7
Almholme 89 D6
Almington 74 F4
Alminstone Cross 8 B5
Almondbank 128 B2
Almondbury 88 C2
Almondsbury 36 F3
Alne 95 C7
Alness 151 E9
Alnham 117 C5
Alnmouth 117 C8
Alnwick 117 C7
Alperton 40 F4
Alphamstone 56 F2
Alpheton 56 D2
Alphington 10 E4
Alport 76 C2
Alpraham 74 D2
Alresford 43 B6
Alrewas 63 C5
Alsager 74 D4
Alsagers Bank 74 E5
Alsop en le Dale 75 D8
Alston Cumb 109 E7
Devon 11 D8
Alstone 50 F4
Alstonefield 75 D8
Alswear 10 B2
Altandhu 156 H2
Altanduin 157 G11
Altarnun 8 F4
Altass 156 J7
Alterwall 158 D4
Altham 93 F7
Althorne 43 E5
Althorpe 90 D2
Alticry 105 D6
Altnabreac Station 157 E13

Altnacealgach Hotel....156 H5
Altnacraig....124 C4
Altnafeadh....131 D6
Altnaharra....157 F8
Altofts....88 B4
Alton Derbys....76 C3
Alton Hants....26 F5
Alton Staffs....75 E7
Alton Pancras....12 D5
Alton Priors....25 C6
Altrincham....87 F5
Altrua....136 F5
Altskeith....126 D3
Altyre House....151 F13
Alva....127 E7
Alvanley....73 B8
Alvaston....76 F3
Alvechurch....50 B5
Alvecote....63 D6
Alvediston....13 B7
Alveley....61 F7
Alverdiscott....9 B7
Alverstoke....15 E7
Alverstone....15 F6
Alverton....77 E7
Alves....152 B1
Alvescot....38 D2
Alveston S Glos....36 F3
Alveston Warks....51 D7
Alvie....138 D4
Alvingham....91 E7
Alvington....36 D3
Alwalton....65 E8
Alweston....12 C4
Alwinton....116 D5
Alwoodley....95 E5
Alyth....134 E2
Amatnatua....150 B7
Am Baile....148 G2
Ambergate....76 D3
Amber Hill....78 E5
Amberley Glos....37 D5
Amberley W Sus....16 C4
Amble....117 D8
Amblecote....62 F2
Ambler Thorn....87 B8
Ambleside....99 D5
Ambleston....44 C5
Am Buth....124 C4
Amcotts....90 C2
Amersham....40 E2
Amesbury....25 E6
Amington....63 D6
Amisfield....114 F2
Amlwch....82 B4
Amlwch Port....82 B4
Ammanford =Rhydaman....33 C7
Amod....143 E8
Amotherby....96 B3
Ampfield....14 B5
Ampleforth....95 B8
Ampney Crucis....37 D7
Ampney St Mary....37 D7
Ampney St Peter....37 D7
Amport....25 E7
Ampthill....53 F8
Ampton....56 B2
Amroth....32 D2
Amulree....133 F5
Anagach....139 B6
Anaheilt....130 C2
Anancaun....150 E3
An Caol....149 C11
Ancaster....78 E2
Anchor....59 F8
Anchorsholme....92 E3
An Cnoc....155 D9
Ancroft....123 E5
Ancrum....116 B2
Anderby....79 B8
Anderson....13 E6
Anderton....74 B3
Andover....25 E8
Andover Down....25 E8
Andoversford....37 C7
Andreas....84 C4
Anfield....85 E4
Angersleigh....11 C6
Angle....44 E3
An Gleann Ur....155 D9
Angmering....16 D4
Angram N Yorks....95 E8
Angram N Yorks....100 E3
Anie....126 C4
Ankerville....151 D11
Anlaby....90 B4
Anmer....80 E3
Annan....107 C8
Annat Argyll....125 C6
Annat Highld....149 C13
Anna Valley....25 E8
Annbank....112 B4
Annesley....76 D5
Annesley Woodhouse....76 D4
Annfield Plain....110 D4
Anniffrith....160 J3
Annitsford....111 B5
Annscroft....60 D4
Ansdell....85 B4
Ansford....23 F8
Ansley....63 E6
Anslow....63 B5
Anslow Gate....63 B5
Anstey Herts....54 F5
Anstey Leics....64 D2
Anstruther Easter....129 D7
Anstruther Wester....129 D7
Ansty Hants....26 E5
Ansty Warks....63 F7
Ansty Wilts....13 B7
Ansty W Sus....17 B6
Anthill Common....15 C7
Anthorn....107 D8
Antingham....81 D8
An t-Ob =Leverburgh....154 J5
Anton's Gowt....79 E5
Antonshill....127 F7
Antony....5 D8
Anwick....78 D4

Anwoth....106 D2
Aoradh....142 B3
Apes Hall....67 E5
Apethorpe....65 E7
Apeton....62 C2
Apley....78 B4
Apperknowle....76 B3
Apperley....37 B5
Apperley Bridge....94 F4
Appersett....100 E3
Appin....130 E3
Appin House....130 E3
Appleby....90 C3
Appleby-in-Westmorland....100 B1
Appleby Magna....63 D7
Appleby Parva....63 D7
Applecross....149 D12
Applecross House....149 D12
Appledore Devon....11 C5
Appledore Devon....20 F3
Appledore Kent....19 C6
Appledore Heath....19 B6
Appleford....39 E5
Applegarthtown....114 F4
Appleshaw....25 E8
Applethwaite....98 B4
Appleton Halton....86 F3
Appleton Oxon....38 D4
Appleton-le-Moors....103 F5
Appleton-le-Street....96 B3
Appleton Roebuck....95 E8
Appleton Thorn....86 F4
Appleton Wiske....102 D1
Appletreehall....115 C8
Appletreewick....94 C3
Appley....11 B5
Appley Bridge....86 D3
Apse Heath....15 F6
Apsley End....54 F2
Apuldram....16 D2
Aquhythie....141 C6
Arabella....151 D11
Arbeadie....141 E5
Arberth =Narberth....32 C2
Arbirlot....135 E6
Arboll....151 C11
Arborfield....27 C5
Arborfield Cross....27 C5
Arborfield Garrison....27 C5
Arbourthorne....88 F4
Arbroath....135 E6
Arbuthnott....135 B7
Archiestown....152 D2
Arclid....74 C4
Ardachu....157 J9
Ardalanish....146 K6
Ardanaiseig....125 C6
Ardaneaskan....149 E13
Ardanstur....124 D4
Ardargie House Hotel....128 C2
Ardarroch....149 E13
Ardbeg Argyll....142 D5
Ardbeg Argyll....145 E10
Ardcharnich....150 C4
Ardchiavaig....146 K6
Ardchullarie More....126 C4
Ardchyle....126 B4
Ard-dhubh....149 D12
Arddleen....60 C2
Ardechvie....136 E4
Ardeley....41 B6
Ardelve....149 F13
Arden....126 F2
Ardens Grafton....51 D6
Ardentinny....145 E10
Ardentraive....145 F9
Ardeonaig....132 F3
Ardersier....151 F10
Ardessie....150 C3
Ardfern....124 E4
Ardgartan....125 E8
Ardgay....151 B8
Ardgour....130 C4
Ardheslaig....149 C12
Ardiecow....152 B5
Ardindrean....150 C4
Ardingly....17 B7
Ardington....38 F4
Ardlair....140 B4
Ardlamont House....145 G8
Ardleigh....43 B6
Ardler....134 E2
Ardley....39 B5
Ardlui....126 C2
Ardlussa....144 E5
Ardmair....150 B4
Ardmay....125 E8
Ardminish....143 D7
Ardmolich....147 D10
Ardmore Argyll....124 C3
Ardmore Highld....151 C10
Ardmore Highld....156 D5
Ardnacross....147 G8
Ardnadam....145 F10
Ardnagrask....151 G8
Ardnarff....149 E13
Ardnastang....130 C2
Ardnave....142 A3
Ardno....125 E7
Ardo....153 E8
Ardoch....133 F7
Ardochy House....136 D5
Ardo House....141 B8
Ardoyne....141 B5
Ardpatrick....144 G6
Ardpatrick House....144 H6
Ardpeaton....145 E11
Ardrishaig....145 E7
Ardross Fife....129 D7
Ardross Highld....151 D9
Ardrossan....118 E2
Ardross Castle....151 D9
Ardshealach....147 E9
Ardsley....88 D4
Ardslignish....147 E8
Ardtalla....142 C5
Ardtalnaig....132 F4
Ardtoe....147 D9
Arduaine....124 D3
Ardullie....151 E8

Ardvasar....149 H11
Ardvorlich....126 B5
Ardwell....104 E5
Ardwell Mains....104 E5
Ardwick....87 E6
Areley Kings....50 B3
Arford....27 F6
Argoed Caerph....35 E5
Argoed Powys....47 C8
Arichamish....124 E5
Arichastlich....125 B8
Aridhglas....146 J6
Arileod....146 F4
Arinacrinachd....149 C12
Arinagour....146 F5
Arion....159 G3
Arisaig....147 C9
Ariundle....130 C2
Arkendale....95 C6
Arkesden....55 F5
Arkholme....93 B5
Arkleton....115 E6
Arkle Town....101 D5
Arkley....41 E5
Arksey....89 D6
Arkwright Town....76 B4
Arle....37 B6
Arlecdon....98 C2
Arlesey....54 F2
Arleston....61 C6
Arley....86 F4
Arlingham....36 C4
Arlington Devon....20 E5
Arlington E Sus....18 E2
Arlington Glos....37 D8
Armadale Highld....157 C10
Armadale W Loth....120 C2
Armadale Castle....149 H11
Armathwaite....108 E5
Arminghall....69 D5
Armitage....62 C4
Armley....95 F5
Armscote....51 E7
Armthorpe....89 D7
Arnabost....146 F5
Arncliffe....94 B2
Arncroach....129 D7
Arne....13 F7
Arnesby....64 E3
Arngask....128 C3
Arnisdale....149 G13
Arnish....149 D10
Arniston Engine....121 C6
Arnol....155 C8
Arnold E Yorks....97 E7
Arnold Notts....77 E5
Arnprior....126 E5
Arnside....92 B4
Aros Mains....147 G8
Arowry....73 F8
Arpafeelie....151 F9
Arrad Foot....99 F5
Arram....97 E6
Arrathorne....101 E7
Arreton....15 F6
Arrington....54 D4
Arrivain....125 B8
Arrochar....125 E8
Arrow....51 D5
Arthington....95 E5
Arthingworth....64 F4
Arthog....58 C3
Arthrath....153 E9
Arthurstone....134 E2
Artrochie....153 E10
Arundel....16 D4
Aryhoulan....130 C4
Asby....98 B2
Ascog....145 G10
Ascot....27 C7
Ascott....51 F8
Ascott-under-Wychwood....38 C3
Asenby....95 B6
Asfordby....64 C4
Asfordby Hill....64 C4
Asgarby Lincs....78 E5
Asgarby Lincs....79 C6
Ash Kent....29 C6
Ash Kent....31 D6
Ash Som....12 B2
Ash Sur....27 D6
Ashampstead....26 B3
Ashbocking....57 D5
Ashbourne....75 E8
Ashbrittle....11 B5
Ashburton....7 C5
Ashbury Devon....9 E7
Ashbury Oxon....38 F2
Ashby....90 D3
Ashby by Partney....79 C7
Ashby cum Fenby....91 D6
Ashby de la Launde....78 D3
Ashby-de-la-Zouch....63 C7
Ashby Folville....64 C4
Ashby Magna....64 E2
Ashby Parva....64 F2
Ashby Puerorum....79 B6
Ashby St Ledgers....52 C3
Ashby St Mary....69 D6
Ashchurch....50 F4
Ashcombe....7 B7
Ashcott....23 F6
Ashdon....55 E6
Ashe....26 E3
Asheldham....43 D5
Ashen....55 E8
Ashendon....39 C7
Ashfield Carms....33 B7
Ashfield Stirling....127 D6
Ashfield Suff....57 C6
Ashfield Green....57 B6
Ashfold Crossways....17 B6
Ashford Devon....20 F4
Ashford Hants....14 C2
Ashford Kent....30 E4
Ashford Sur....27 B8
Ashford Bowdler....49 B7
Ashford Carbonel....49 B7
Ashford Hill....26 C3
Ashford in the Water....75 C8
Ashgill....119 E7
Ash Green....63 F7
Ashill Devon....11 C5

Ashill continued
Ashill Norf....67 D8
Ashill Som....11 C8
Ashingdon....42 E4
Ashington Northumb....117 F8
Ashington Som....12 B3
Ashington W Sus....16 C5
Ashintully Castle....133 C8
Ashkirk....115 B7
Ashlett....15 D5
Ashleworth....37 B5
Ashley Cambs....55 C7
Ashley Ches E....87 F5
Ashley Devon....9 C8
Ashley Dorset....14 D2
Ashley Glos....37 E6
Ashley Hants....14 E3
Ashley Hants....25 F8
Ashley Northants....64 E4
Ashley Staffs....74 F4
Ashley Green....40 D2
Ashley Heath Dorset....14 D2
Ashley Heath Staffs....74 F4
Ash Magna....74 F2
Ashmanhaugh....69 B6
Ashmansworth....26 D2
Ashmansworthy....8 C5
Ash Mill....10 B2
Ashmore....13 C7
Ashorne....51 D8
Ashover....76 C3
Ashow....51 B8
Ashprington....7 D6
Ash Priors....11 B6
Ashreigney....9 C8
Ash Street....56 E4
Ashtead....28 D2
Ashton Ches W....74 C2
Ashton Corn....2 D5
Ashton Hants....15 C6
Ashton Hereford....49 C7
Ashton Invclyd....118 B2
Ashton Northants....53 E5
Ashton Northants....65 F7
Ashton Common....24 D3
Ashton-in-Makerfield....86 E3
Ashton Keynes....37 E7
Ashton under Hill....50 F4
Ashton-under-Lyne....87 E7
Ashton upon Mersey....87 E5
Ashurst Hants....14 C4
Ashurst Kent....18 B2
Ashurst W Sus....17 C5
Ashurstwood....28 F5
Ash Vale....27 D6
Ashwater....9 E5
Ashwell Herts....54 F3
Ashwell Rutland....65 C5
Ashwell Som....11 C8
Ashwellthorpe....68 E4
Ashwick....23 E8
Ashwicken....67 C7
Ashybank....115 C8
Askam in Furness....92 B2
Askern....89 C6
Askerswell....12 E3
Askett....39 D8
Askham Cumb....99 B7
Askham Notts....77 B7
Askham Bryan....95 E8
Askham Richard....95 E8
Asknish....145 D8
Askrigg....100 E4
Askwith....94 E4
Aslackby....78 F3
Aslacton....68 E4
Aslockton....77 F7
Asloun....140 C4
Aspatria....107 E8
Aspenden....41 B6
Asperton....79 F5
Aspley Guise....53 F7
Aspley Heath....53 F7
Aspull....86 D4
Asselby....89 B8
Asserby....79 B7
Assington....56 F3
Assynt House....151 E8
Astbury....74 C5
Astcote....52 D4
Asterley....60 D3
Asterton....60 E3
Asthall....38 C2
Asthall Leigh....38 C3
Astley Shrops....60 C5
Astley Warks....63 F7
Astley Worcs....50 C2
Astley Abbotts....61 E7
Astley Bridge....86 C5
Astley Cross....50 C3
Astley Green....86 E5
Aston Ches E....74 E3
Aston Ches W....74 B2
Aston Derbys....88 F2
Aston Hereford....49 B6
Aston Herts....41 B5
Aston Oxon....38 D3
Aston Shrops....60 B5
Aston Staffs....74 E4
Aston S Yorks....89 F5
Aston Wilts....25 D7
Aston Abbotts....39 B8
Aston Botterell....61 F6
Aston-by-Stone....75 F6
Aston Cantlow....51 D6
Aston Clinton....40 C1
Aston Crews....36 B3
Aston Cross....50 F4
Aston End....41 B5
Aston Eyre....61 E6
Aston Fields....50 C4
Aston Flamville....63 E8
Aston Ingham....36 B3
Aston juxta Mondrum....74 D3
Aston le Walls....52 D2
Aston Magna....51 F6
Aston Munslow....60 F5
Aston on Clun....60 F3
Aston-on-Trent....63 B8
Aston Rogers....60 D3

Aston Rowant....39 E7
Aston Sandford....39 D7
Aston Somerville....50 F5
Aston Subedge....51 E6
Aston Tirrold....39 F5
Aston Upthorpe....39 F5
Astrop....52 F3
Astwick....54 F3
Astwood M Keynes....53 E7
Astwood Worcs....50 D3
Astwood Bank....50 C5
Aswarby....78 F3
Aswardby....79 B6
Atcham....60 D5
Atch Lench....50 D5
Athelhampton....13 E5
Athelington....57 B6
Athelney....11 B8
Athelstaneford....121 B8
Atherington....9 B7
Atherstone....63 E7
Atherstone on Stour....51 D7
Atherton....86 D4
Atley Hill....101 D7
Atlow....76 E2
Attadale....150 H2
Attadale House....150 H2
Attenborough....76 F5
Atterby....90 E3
Attercliffe....88 F4
Atterton....63 E7
Attleborough Norf....68 E3
Attleborough Warks....63 E7
Attlebridge....68 C4
Atwick....97 D7
Atworth....24 C3
Aubourn....78 C2
Auchagallon....143 E9
Auchallater....139 F7
Aucharnie....153 D6
Auchattie....141 E5
Auchavan....134 C1
Auchbreck....139 B8
Auchenback....118 D5
Auchenbainzie....113 E8
Auchenblae....135 B7
Auchenbrack....113 E7
Auchenbreck....145 E9
Auchencairn Dumfries....106 D4
Auchencairn Dumfries....114 F2
Auchencairn N Ayrs....143 F11
Auchencrosh....104 B5
Auchencrow....122 C4
Auchendinny....121 C5
Auchengray....120 D2
Auchenhalrig....152 B3
Auchenheath....119 E8
Auchenlochan....145 F8
Auchenmalg....105 D6
Auchensoul....112 E2
Auchentiber....118 E3
Auchertyre....149 F13
Auchgourish....138 C5
Auchincarroch....126 F3
Auchindrain....125 E6
Auchindrean....150 C4
Auchininna....153 D6
Auchinleck....113 B5
Auchinloch....119 B6
Auchinroath....152 C2
Auchintoul....140 C4
Auchiries....153 E10
Auchlee....141 E7
Auchleven....140 B5
Auchlochan....119 F8
Auchlossan....140 D4
Auchlunies....141 E7
Auchlyne....126 B4
Auchmacoy....153 E9
Auchmair....140 B2
Auchmantle....105 C5
Auchmillan....112 B5
Auchmithie....135 E6
Auchmuirbridge....128 D4
Auchmull....135 B5
Auchnacree....134 C4
Auchnagallin....151 H13
Auchnagatt....153 D9
Auchnaha....145 E8
Auchnashelloch....127 C6
Aucholzie....140 E2
Auchrannie....134 D2
Auchroisk....139 B6
Auchronie....140 F3
Auchterarder....127 C8
Auchteraw....137 D6
Auchterderran....128 E4
Auchterhouse....134 F3
Auchtermuchty....128 C4
Auchterneed....150 F7
Auchtertool....128 E4
Auchtertyre....152 C1
Auchtubh....126 B4
Auckengill....158 D5
Auckley....89 D7
Audenshaw....87 E7
Audlem....74 E3
Audley....74 D4
Audley End....56 F2
Auds....153 B6
Aughton E Yorks....96 F3
Aughton Lancs....85 D4
Aughton Lancs....93 C5
Aughton S Yorks....89 F5
Aughton Wilts....25 D7
Aughton Park....86 D2
Auldearn....151 F12
Aulden....49 D6
Auldgirth....114 F2
Auldhame....129 F7
Auldhouse....119 D6
Ault a'chruinn....136 B2
Aultanrynie....156 F6
Aultbea....155 J13
Aultdearg....150 E5
Aultgrishan....155 J12
Aultguish Inn....150 D6
Aultibea....157 G13
Aultiphurst....157 C11
Aultmore....152 C4
Aultnagoire....137 B8
Aultnamain Inn....151 C9
Aultnaslat....136 D4
Aulton....140 B5
Aundorach....139 C5
Aunsby....78 F3
Aust....36 F2

Austendike....66 B2
Austerfield....89 E7
Austrey....63 D6
Austwick....93 C7
Authorpe....91 F8
Authorpe Row....79 B8
Avebury....25 C6
Aveley....42 F1
Avening....37 E5
Averham....77 D7
Aveton Gifford....6 E4
Avielochan....138 C5
Aviemore....138 C4
Avington Hants....26 F3
Avington W Berks....25 C8
Avoch....151 F10
Avon....14 E2
Avonbridge....120 B2
Avon Dassett....52 E2
Avonmouth....23 B7
Avonwick....6 D5
Awbridge....14 B4
Awhirk....104 D4
Awkley....36 F2
Awliscombe....11 D6
Awre....36 D4
Awsworth....76 E4
Axbridge....23 D6
Axford Hants....26 E4
Axford Wilts....25 B7
Axminster....11 E7
Axmouth....11 E7
Axton....85 F2
Aycliff....31 E7
Aycliffe....101 B7
Aydon....110 C3
Aylburton....36 D3
Ayle....109 E7
Aylesbeare....10 E5
Aylesbury....39 C8
Aylesby....91 D6
Aylesford....29 D8
Aylesham....31 D6
Aylestone....64 D2
Aylmerton....81 D7
Aylsham....81 E7
Aylton....49 F8
Aymestrey....49 C6
Aynho....52 F3
Ayot St Lawrence....40 C4
Ayot St Peter....41 C5
Ayr....112 B3
Aysgarth....101 F5
Ayside....99 F5
Ayston....65 D5
Aythorpe Roding....42 C1
Ayton....122 C5
Aywick....160 E7
Azerley....95 B5

B

Babbacombe....7 C7
Babbinswood....73 F7
Babcary....12 B3
Babel....47 F7
Babell....73 B5
Babraham....55 D6
Babworth....89 F7
Bac....155 C9
Bachau....82 C4
Backaland....159 E6
Backaskaill....159 C5
Backbarrow....99 F5
Backe....32 C3
Backfolds....153 C10
Backford Ches W....73 C7
Backford Cross....73 B7
Backhill Aberds....153 E7
Backhill Aberds....153 E8
Backhill of Clackriach....153 D9
Backhill of Fortree....153 D9
Backhill of Trustach....140 E5
Backies....157 J11
Backlass....158 E4
Back of Keppoch....147 C9
Back Rogerton....113 B5
Backwell....23 C6
Backworth....111 B6
Bacon End....42 C2
Baconsthorpe....81 D7
Bacton Hereford....49 F5
Bacton Norf....81 D9
Bacton Suff....56 C4
Bacton Green....56 C4
Bacup....87 B6
Badachro....149 A12
Badanloch Lodge....157 F10
Badavanich....150 F4
Badbury....38 F1
Badby....52 D3
Badcall....156 D5
Badcaul....150 B3
Baddeley Green....75 D6
Baddesley Clinton....51 B7
Baddesley Ensor....63 E6
Baddidarach....156 G3
Baddoch....139 F7
Baddock....151 F10
Badenscoth....153 E7
Badenyon....140 C2
Badger....61 E7
Badger's Mount....29 C5
Badgeworth....37 C6
Badgworth....23 D5
Badicaul....149 F12
Badingham....57 C7
Badlesmere....30 D4
Badlipster....158 F4
Badluarach....150 B2
Badminton....37 F5
Badnaban....156 G3
Badninish....151 B10
Badrallach....150 B3
Badsey....51 E5
Badshot Lea....27 E6
Badsworth....89 C5
Badwell Ash....56 C3
Bae Colwyn =Colwyn Bay....83 D8
Bagby....102 F2
Bag Enderby....79 B6
Bagendon....37 D7

Bagh a Chaisteil =Castlebay....148 J1
Baghasdal....148 G2
Bagh Mor....148 D3
Bagh Shiarabhagh....148 H2
Bagillt....73 B6
Baginton....51 B8
Baglan....33 E8
Bagley....60 B4
Bagnall....75 D6
Bagnor....26 C2
Bagshot Sur....27 C7
Bagshot Wilts....25 C8
Bagthorpe Norf....80 D3
Bagthorpe Notts....76 D4
Bagworth....63 D8
Bagwy Llydiart....35 B8
Baildon....94 F4
Baile....154 J4
Baile Ailein....155 E7
Baile a Mhanaich....148 D2
Baile an Truiseil....155 B8
Bailebeag....137 C8
Baile Boidheach....144 F6
Baile Glas....148 D3
Baile Mhartainn....148 A2
Baile Mhic Phail....148 A3
Baile Mor Argyll....146 J5
Baile Mor W Isles....148 B2
Baile na Creige....148 H1
Baile nan Cailleach....148 C2
Baile Raghaill....148 A2
Bailey....108 B5
Baileyward....152 E4
Baillieston....119 C6
Bail'lochdrach....148 C3
Bail Uachdraich....148 A3
Bail'Ur Tholastaidh....155 C10
Bainbridge....100 E4
Bainsford....127 F7
Bainshole....152 E6
Bainton E Yorks....97 D5
Bainton Pboro....65 D7
Bairnkine....116 C2
Baker's End....41 C6
Baker Street....42 F2
Bakewell....76 C2
Bala =Y Bala....72 F3
Balachuish....149 D10
Balavil....138 D3
Balbeg Highld....137 B7
Balbeg Highld....150 H7
Balbeggie....128 B3
Balbithan....141 C6
Balbithan House....141 C7
Balblair Highld....151 B9
Balblair Highld....151 E10
Balby....89 D6
Balchladich....156 F3
Balchraggan Highld....151 G8
Balchraggan Highld....151 H8
Balchrick....156 D4
Balchrystie....129 D6
Balcladaich....137 B5
Balcombe....28 F4
Balcombe Lane....28 F4
Balcomie....129 C8
Balcurvie....128 D5
Baldersby....95 B6
Baldersby St James....95 B6
Balderstone....93 F6
Balderton Ches W....73 C7
Balderton Notts....77 D8
Baldhu....3 B6
Baldinnie....129 C6
Baldock....54 F3
Baldovie....134 F4
Baldrine....84 D4
Baldslow....18 D4
Baldwin....84 D3
Baldwinholme....108 D3
Baldwin's Gate....74 E4
Bale....81 D6
Balearn....153 C10
Balemartine....146 G2
Balephuil....146 G2
Balerno....120 C4
Balevullin....146 G2
Balfield....135 C5
Balfour....159 G5
Balfron....126 F4
Balfron Station....126 F4
Balgaveny....153 D6
Balgavies....135 D5
Balgonar....128 E2
Balgove....153 E8
Balgowan....138 E2
Balgown....149 B8
Balgrochan....119 B6
Balgy....149 C13
Balhaldie....127 D7
Balhalgardy....141 B6
Balham....28 B3
Balhary....134 E2
Baliasta....160 C8
Baligill....157 C11
Balintore Angus....134 D2
Balintore Highld....151 D11
Balintraid....151 D10
Balk....102 F2
Balkeerie....134 E3
Balkemback....134 F3
Balkholme....89 B8
Balkissock....104 A5
Ball....60 B3
Ballabeg....84 E2
Ballacannel....84 D4
Ballachulish....130 D4
Ballajora....84 C4
Ballaleigh....84 D3
Ballamodha....84 E2
Ballantrae....104 A4
Ballaquine....84 D4
Ballards Gore....43 E5
Ballasalla IoM....84 C3
Ballasalla IoM....84 E2
Ballater....140 E2
Ballaugh....84 C3
Ballaveare....84 E3
Ballcorach....139 B7
Ballechin....133 D6
Balleigh....151 C10
Ballencrieff....121 B7

Ballentoul....133 C5
Ball Haye Green....75 D6
Ball Hill....26 C2
Ballidon....76 D2
Balliekine....143 E9
Balliemeanoch....125 D6
Balliemore Argyll....124 C4
Balliemore Argyll....145 E9
Ballikinrain....126 F4
Ballimeanoch....125 D6
Ballimore Argyll....145 E8
Ballimore Stirling....126 C4
Ballinaby....142 B3
Ballindean....128 B4
Ballingdon....56 E2
Ballinger Common....40 D2
Ballingham....49 F7
Ballingry....128 E3
Ballinlick....133 E6
Ballinluig....133 D6
Ballintuim....133 D8
Balloch Angus....134 D3
Balloch Highld....151 G10
Balloch N Lanark....119 B7
Balloch W Dunb....126 F2
Ballochan....140 E4
Ballochford....152 E3
Ballochmorrie....112 F2
Ballochmyle....112 B5
Ballochroy....143 D6
Balls Cross....16 B3
Balls Green....43 B6
Ballygown....146 G2
Ballygrant....142 B4
Ballyhaugh....146 F4
Balmacara....149 F13
Balmacara Square....149 F13
Balmaclellan....106 B3
Balmacneil....133 D6
Balmacqueen....149 A9
Balmae....106 E3
Balmaha....126 E3
Balmalcolm....128 D5
Balmeanach....149 D10
Balmedie....141 C8
Balmer Heath....73 F8
Balmerino....129 B5
Balmerlawn....14 D4
Balmichael....143 E10
Balmirmer....135 F5
Balmore Highld....149 D7
Balmore Highld....150 H6
Balmore Highld....151 G11
Balmore Perth....133 D6
Balmule....128 E4
Balmullo....129 B6
Balmungie....151 F10
Balnaboth....134 C3
Balnabruaich....151 E10
Balnabruich....158 H3
Balnacoil....157 H11
Balnacra....150 G2
Balnafoich....151 H9
Balnagall....151 C11
Balnaguard....133 D6
Balnahard Argyll....144 D3
Balnahard Argyll....146 H7
Balnain....150 H7
Balnakeil....156 C6
Balnaknock....149 B9
Balnapaling....151 E10
Balne....89 C6
Balochroy....143 C8
Balone....129 C6
Balornock....119 C6
Balquharn....133 F7
Balquhidder....126 B4
Balsall....51 B7
Balsall Common....51 B7
Balsall Heath....62 F4
Balscott....51 E8
Balsham....55 D6
Baltasound....160 C8
Balterley....74 D4
Baltersan....105 C8
Balthangie....153 C8
Baltonsborough....23 F7
Balvaird....151 F8
Balvicar....124 D3
Balvraid Highld....149 G13
Balvraid Highld....151 H11
Bamber Bridge....86 B3
Bambers Green....42 B1
Bamburgh....123 F7
Bamff....134 D2
Bamford Derbys....88 F3
Bamford Gtr Man....87 C6
Bampton Cumb....99 C7
Bampton Devon....10 B4
Bampton Oxon....38 D3
Bampton Grange....99 C7
Banavie....131 B5
Banbury....52 E2
Bancffosfelen....33 C5
Banchory....141 E5
Banchory-Devenick....141 D8
Bancycapel....33 C5
Bancyfelin....32 C4
Bancyffordd....46 F3
Bandirran....134 F2
Banff....153 B6
Bangor....83 D5
Bangor-is-y-coed =Bangor-on-Dee....73 E7
Bangor-on-Dee =Bangor-is-y-coed....73 E7
Banham....68 F3
Bank....14 D3
Bankend....107 C7
Bankfoot....133 F7
Bankglen....113 C6
Bankhead Aberdeen....141 D7
Bankhead Aberds....141 D5
Banknock....119 B7
Banks Cumb....109 C5
Banks Lancs....85 B4
Bankshill....114 F4
Bank Street....49 C8
Banningham....81 E8
Banniskirk House....158 E3
Bannister Green....42 B2
Bannockburn....127 E7
Banstead....28 D3
Bantham....6 E4
Banton....119 B7
Banwell....23 D5
Banyard's Green....57 B6

Bapchild....30 C3
Barabbas....155 C8
Barabhas Iarach....155 C8
Barabhas Uarach....155 B8
Barachandroman....124 C2
Barassie....118 F3
Baravullin....124 E4
Barber Booth....88 F2
Barbieston....112 C4
Barbon....99 F8
Barbridge....74 D3
Barbrook....21 E6
Barby....52 B3
Barcaldine....130 E3
Barcheston....51 F7
Barcombe....17 C8
Barcombe Cross....17 C8
Barden....101 E6
Barden Scale....94 D3
Bardfield Saling....42 B2
Bardister....160 F5
Bardney....78 C4
Bardon....63 C8
Bardon Mill....109 C7
Bardowie....119 B5
Bardrainney....118 B3
Bardsea....92 B3
Bardsey....95 E6
Bardwell....56 B3
Bare....92 C4
Barfad....145 G7
Barford Norf....68 D4
Barford Warks....51 C7
Barford St John....52 F2
Barford St Martin....25 F5
Barford St Michael....52 F2
Barfrestone....31 D6
Bargod =Bargoed....35 E5
Bargoed =Bargod....35 E5
Bargrennan....105 B7
Barham Cambs....54 B2
Barham Kent....31 D6
Barham Suff....56 D5
Barharrow....106 D3
Barhill....106 C5
Bar Hill....54 C4
Barholm....65 C7
Barkby....64 D3
Barkestone-le-Vale....77 F7
Barkham....27 C5
Barking London....41 F7
Barking Suff....56 D4
Barkingside....41 F7
Barking Tye....56 D4
Barkisland....87 C8
Barkston Lincs....78 E2
Barkston N Yorks....95 F7
Barkway....54 F4
Barlaston....75 F5
Barlavington....16 C3
Barlborough....76 B4
Barlby....96 F2
Barlestone....63 D8
Barley Herts....54 F4
Barley Lancs....93 E8
Barley Mow....111 D5
Barleythorpe....64 D5
Barling....43 F5
Barlow Derbys....76 B3
Barlow N Yorks....89 B7
Barlow T&W....110 C4
Barmby Moor....96 E3
Barmby on the Marsh....89 B7
Barmer....80 D4
Barmoor Castle....123 F5
Barmoor Lane End....123 F6
Barmouth =Abermaw....58 C3
Barmpton....101 C8
Barmston....97 D7
Barnack....65 D7
Barnacle....63 F7
Barnard Castle....101 C5
Barnard Gate....38 C4
Barnardiston....55 E8
Barnburgh....89 D5
Barnby....69 F7
Barnby Dun....89 D7
Barnby in the Willows....77 D8
Barnby Moor....89 F7
Barnes Street....29 E7
Barnet....41 E5
Barnetby le Wold....90 D4
Barney....81 D5
Barnham Suff....56 B2
Barnham W Sus....16 D3
Barnham Broom....68 D3
Barnhead....135 D6
Barnhill Ches W....73 D8
Barnhill Dundee....134 F4
Barnhill Moray....152 C1
Barnhills....104 B3
Barningham Durham....101 C5
Barningham Suff....56 B3
Barnoldby le Beck....91 D6
Barnoldswick....93 E8
Barns Green....16 B5
Barnsley Glos....37 D7
Barnsley S Yorks....88 D4
Barnstaple....20 F4
Barnston Essex....42 C2
Barnston Mers....85 F3
Barnstone....77 F7
Barnt Green....50 B5
Barnton Ches W....74 B3
Barnton Edin....120 B4
Barnwell All Saints....65 F7
Barnwell St Andrew....65 F7
Barnwood....37 C5
Barochreal....124 C4
Barons Cross....49 D6
Barr....112 E2
Barra Castle....141 B6
Barrachan....105 E7
Barrack....153 D8
Barraglom....154 D6
Barrahormid....144 E6
Barran....124 C4
Barrapol....146 G2
Barras Aberds....141 F7

Barras continued
Cumb. 100 C3
Barrasford 110 B2
Barravullin 124 E4
Barregarrow 84 D3
Barrhead 118 D4
Barrhill 112 F2
Barrington Cambs . . . 54 E4
Som 11 C8
Barripper 2 C5
Barrmill 118 D3
Barrock 158 C4
Barrock House 158 C4
Barrow Lancs 93 F7
Rutland 65 C5
Suff 55 C8
Barroway Drove 67 D5
Barrowburn 116 C4
Barrowby 77 F8
Barrowcliff 103 F8
Barrowden 65 D6
Barrowford 93 F8
Barrow Green 30 C3
Barrow Gurney 23 C7
Barrow Haven 90 B4
Barrow-in-Furness 92 C2
Barrow Island 92 C1
Barrow Nook 86 D2
Barrows Green
Ches E 74 D3
Cumb 99 F7
Barrow's Green 86 F3
Barrow Street 24 F3
Barrow upon Humber 90 B4
Barrow upon Soar . 64 C2
Barrow upon Trent 63 B7
Barry 135 F5
Barry = Y Barri 22 C3
Barry Island 22 C3
Barsby 64 C3
Barsham 69 F6
Barston 51 B7
Bartestree 49 E7
Barthol Chapel 153 E8
Barthomley 74 D4
Bartley 14 C4
Bartley Green 62 F4
Bartlow 55 E6
Barton Cambs 54 D5
Ches W. 73 D8
Glos. 37 B8
Lancs 85 D4
Lancs 92 F5
N Yorks 101 D7
Oxon 39 D5
Torbay 7 C7
Warks 51 D6
Barton Bendish 67 D7
Barton Hartshorn . 52 F4
Barton in Fabis 76 F5
Barton in the Beans 63 D7
Barton-le-Clay 53 F8
Barton-le-Street . 96 B3
Barton-le-Willows 96 C1
Barton Mills 55 B8
Barton on Sea 14 E3
Barton on the Heath 51 F7
Barton St David 23 F7
Barton Seagrave 53 B6
Barton Stacey 26 E2
Barton Turf 69 B6
Barton-under-Needwood 63 C5
Barton-upon-Humber 90 B4
Barton Waterside . 90 B4
Barugh 88 D4
Barway 55 B6
Barwell 63 E8
Barwick Herts. 41 C6
Som 12 C3
Barwick in Elmet . 95 F6
Baschurch 60 B4
Bascote 52 C2
Basford Green 75 D6
Bashall Eaves 93 E6
Bashley 14 E3
Basildon 42 F3
Basingstoke 26 D4
Baslow 76 B2
Bason Bridge 22 E5
Bassaleg 35 F6
Bassenthwaite 108 F2
Bassett 14 C5
Bassingbourn 54 E4
Bassingfield 77 F6
Bassingham 78 C2
Bassingthorpe 65 B6
Basta 160 D7
Baston 65 C8
Bastwick 69 C7
Baswick Steer 97 E6
Batchworth Heath . 40 E3
Batcombe Dorset 12 D4
Som 23 F8
Bate Heath 74 B3
Batford 40 C4
Bath 24 C2
Bathampton 24 C2
Bathealton 11 B5
Batheaston 24 C2
Bathford 24 C2
Bathgate 120 C2
Bathley 77 D7
Bathpool Corn 5 B8
Som 11 B7
Bathville 120 C2
Batley 88 B3
Batsford 51 F6
Battersby 102 D3
Battersea 28 B3
Battisborough Cross 6 E3
Battisford 56 D4
Battisford Tye 56 D4
Battle E Sus 18 D4
Powys 48 F2
Battledown 37 B6
Battlefield 60 C5
Battlesbridge 42 E3
Battlesden 40 B2
Battlesea Green 57 B6
Battleton 10 B4
Battram 63 D8
Battramsley 14 E4

Baughton 50 E3
Baughurst 26 D3
Baulking 38 E3
Baumber 78 B5
Baunton 37 D7
Baverstock 24 F5
Bawburgh 68 D4
Bawdeswell 81 E6
Bawdrip 22 F5
Bawdsey 57 E7
Bawtry 89 E7
Baxenden 87 B5
Baxterley 63 E6
Baybridge 15 B6
Baycliff 92 B2
Baydon 25 B7
Bayford Herts 41 D6
Som 12 B5
Bayles 109 E7
Baylham 56 D5
Baynard's Green 39 B5
Bayston Hill 60 D4
Baythorn End 55 F8
Bayton 49 B8
Beach 130 D1
Beachampton 53 F5
Beachamwell 67 D7
Beachans 151 G13
Beacharr 143 D7
Beachborough 19 B8
Beachley 36 E2
Beacon 11 D6
Beacon End 43 B5
Beacon Hill 27 F6
Beacon's Bottom . 39 E7
Beaconsfield 40 F2
Beacrabhaic 154 H6
Beadlam 102 F4
Beadlow 54 F2
Beadnell 117 B8
Beaford 9 C7
Beal Northumb. 123 E6
N Yorks 89 B6
Beamhurst 75 F7
Beaminster 12 D2
Beamish 110 D5
Beamsley 94 D3
Bean 29 B6
Beanacre 24 C4
Beanley 117 C6
Beaquoy 159 F4
Bear Cross 13 E8
Beardwood 86 B4
Beare Green 28 E2
Bearley 51 C6
Bearnus 146 G6
Bearpark 110 E5
Bearsbridge 109 D7
Bearsden 118 B5
Bearsted 29 D8
Bearstone 74 F4
Bearwood BCP 13 E8
Hereford 49 D5
W Mid 62 F4
Beattock 114 D3
Beauchamp Roding 42 C1
Beauchief 88 F4
Beaufort 35 C5
Beaufort Castle 151 G8
Beaulieu 14 D4
Beauly 151 G8
Beaumaris 83 D6
Beaumont Cumb 108 D3
Essex 43 B7
Beaumont Hill 101 C7
Beausale 51 B7
Beauworth 15 B6
Beaworthy 9 E6
Beazley End 42 B3
Bebington 85 F4
Bebside 117 F8
Beccles 69 E7
Becconsall 86 B2
Beckbury 61 D7
Beckenham 28 C4
Beckermet 98 D2
Beckfoot Cumb. 98 D3
Cumb. 107 E7
Beck Foot 99 E8
Beckford 50 F4
Beckhampton 25 C5
Beck Hole 103 D6
Beckingham Lincs 77 D8
Notts 89 F8
Beckington 24 D3
Beckley E Sus 19 C5
Hants. 14 E3
Oxon 39 C5
Beck Row 55 B7
Beck Side 98 F4
Beckton 41 F7
Beckwithshaw 95 D5
Becontree 41 F7
Bedale 101 F7
Bedburn 110 F4
Bedchester 13 C6
Beddau 34 F4
Beddgelert 71 C6
Beddingham 17 D8
Beddington 28 C4
Bedfield 57 C6
Bedford 53 D8
Bedham 16 B4
Bedhampton 15 D8
Bedingfield 57 C5
Bedlam 95 C5
Bedlington 117 F8
Bedlington Station 117 F8
Bedlinog 34 D4
Bedminster 23 B7
Bedmond 40 D3
Bednall 62 C3
Bedrule 116 C2
Bedstone 49 B5
Bedwas 35 F5
Bedworth 63 F7
Bedworth Heath 63 F7
Bed-y-coedwr 71 E8
Beeby 64 D3
Beech Hants 26 F4
Staffs. 75 F5
Beech Hill Gtr Man. 86 D3
W Berks. 26 C4
Beechingstoke 25 D5
Beedon 26 B2
Beeford 97 D7
Beeley 76 C2

Beelsby 91 D6
Beenham 26 C3
Beeny 8 E3
Beer 11 F7
Beercrocombe 11 B8
Beer Hackett 12 C3
Beesands 7 E6
Beesby 91 F8
Beeson 7 E6
Beeston C Beds. 54 E2
Ches W. 74 D2
Norf 68 C2
Notts 76 F5
W Yorks 95 F5
Beeston Regis. 81 C7
Beeswing 107 C5
Beetham 92 B4
Beetley 68 C2
Begbroke 38 C4
Beggar's Bush 48 C4
Beguildy 48 B3
Beighton Norf. 69 D6
S Yorks 88 F5
Beighton Hill 76 D2
Beith 118 D3
Bekesbourne 31 D5
Belaugh 69 C5
Belbroughton 50 B4
Belchamp Otten 56 E2
Belchamp St Paul . 55 E8
Belchamp Walter . 56 E2
Belchford 79 B5
Belelford 123 F7
Belfield 87 C7
Belford 123 F7
Belhaven 122 B2
Belhelvie 141 C8
Belhinnie 140 B3
Bellabeg 140 C2
Bellamore 112 F2
Bellanoch 144 D6
Bellaty 134 D2
Bell Bar 41 D5
Bell Busk 94 D2
Belleau 79 B7
Bellehiglash 152 E1
Bell End 50 B4
Bellerby 101 E6
Bellever 6 B4
Belliehill 135 C5
Bellingdon 40 D2
Bellingham 116 F4
Belloch 143 E7
Bellochantuy 143 E7
Bell o'th'Hill 74 E2
Bellsbank 112 D4
Bellshill N Lanark 119 C7
Northumb 123 F7
Bellspool 120 F4
Bellsquarry 120 C3
Bells Yew Green 18 B3
Belmaduthy 151 F9
Belmesthorpe 65 C7
Belmont Blackburn. 86 C4
London. 28 C3
S Ayrs. 112 B3
Shetland 160 C7
Belnacraig 140 C2
Belowda 4 C4
Belper 76 E3
Belper Lane End. 76 E3
Belsay 110 B4
Belses 115 B8
Belsford 7 D5
Belstead 56 E5
Belston 112 B3
Belstone 9 E8
Belthorn 86 B5
Beltinge 31 C5
Beltoft 90 D2
Belton Leics. 63 B8
Lincs 78 F2
N Lincs 89 D8
Norf. 69 D7
Belton in Rutland. . 64 D5
Beltring 29 E7
Belts of Collonach 141 E5
Belvedere. 29 B5
Belvoir 77 F8
Bembridge 15 F7
Bemersyde 121 F8
Bemerton 25 F6
Bempton 97 B7
Ben Alder Lodge . 132 B2
Ben Armine Lodge 157 H10
Benbuie 113 E7
Ben Casgro 155 E9
Benderloch 124 B5
Bendronaig Lodge 150 H3
Benenden 18 B5
Benfield 105 C7
Bengate 69 B6
Bengeworth 50 E5
Benhall Green. 57 C7
Benhall Street. 57 C7
Benholm 135 C8
Beningbrough 95 D8
Benington Herts 41 B5
Lincs 79 E6
Benllech 82 C5
Benmore Argyll. 145 E10
Stirling. 126 B3
Benmore Lodge . 156 H6
Bennacott 8 E4
Bennan 143 F10
Benniworth 91 F6
Benover 29 E8
Bensham 110 C5
Benslie 118 E3
Benson 39 E6
Bent 135 B6
Bent Gate 87 B5
Benthall Northumb. 117 B8
Shrops. 61 D6
Bentham 37 C6
Benthoul 141 D7
Bentlawnt 60 D3
Bentley E Yorks 97 F6
Hants. 27 E5
Suff 56 F5
S Yorks 89 D6
Warks 63 E6
Bentley Heath 51 B6
Benton 21 F6
Bentpath 115 E6

Bents 120 C2
Bentworth 26 E4
Benvie 134 F3
Benwick 66 E3
Beoley 51 C5
Beoraidbeg 147 B9
Bepton 16 C2
Berden 41 B7
Bere Alston 6 C2
Bere Ferrers 6 C2
Berepper 3 D5
Bere Regis 13 E6
Bergh Apton 69 D6
Berinsfield 39 E5
Berkeley 36 E3
Berkhamsted 40 D2
Berkley 24 E3
Berkswell 51 B7
Bermondsey 28 B4
Bernera 149 F13
Bernice. 145 D10
Bernisdale 149 C9
Berrick Salome 39 E6
Berriedale 158 H3
Berrier 99 B5
Berriew 59 D8
Berrington Northumb 123 E6
Shrops. 60 D5
Berrow 22 D5
Berrow Green 50 D2
Berry Down Cross . 20 E4
Berryfield 39 C7
Berry Hill Glos. 36 C2
Pembs. 45 E2
Berryhillock. 152 B5
Berrynarbor 20 E4
Berry Pomeroy 7 C6
Bersham 73 E7
Berstane 159 G5
Berwick 18 E2
Berwick Bassett 25 B5
Berwick Hill 110 B4
Berwick St James . 25 F5
Berwick St John 13 B7
Berwick St Leonard 24 F4
Berwick-upon-Tweed 123 D5
Bescar 85 C4
Besford 50 E4
Bessacarr 89 D7
Bessels Leigh 38 D4
Bessingby 97 C7
Bessingham 81 D7
Besthorpe Norf 68 E3
Notts 77 C8
Bestwood 77 E5
Bestwood Village . 77 E5
Beswick 97 E6
Betchworth 28 E3
Bethania Ceredig. 46 C4
Gwyn. 71 C8
Gwyn. 83 F6
Bethel Anglesey 82 D3
Gwyn. 72 F3
Gwyn. 82 E5
Bethersden 30 E3
Bethesda Gwyn 83 E6
Pembs. 32 C1
Bethlehem 33 B7
Bethnal Green. 41 F6
Betley 74 E4
Betsham 29 B7
Betteshanger 31 D7
Bettiscombe 11 E8
Bettisfield 73 F8
Betton Shrops. 60 D3
Shrops. 74 F3
Bettws Bridgend 34 F3
Mon 35 C6
Newport 35 E6
Bettws Cedewain. . 59 E8
Bettws Gwerfil Goch 72 E4
Bettws Ifan 46 E2
Bettws Newydd 35 D7
Bettws-y-crwyn. 60 F2
Bettyhill 157 C10
Betws 33 C7
Betws Bledrws 46 D4
Betws-Garmon 82 F5
Betws-y-Coed 83 F7
Betws-yn-Rhos 72 B3
Beulah Ceredig. 45 E4
Powys 47 D8
Bevendean 17 D7
Bevercotes 77 B6
Beverley 97 F6
Beverston 37 E5
Bevington 36 E3
Bewaldeth 108 F2
Bewcastle 109 B5
Bewdley 50 B2
Bewerley 94 C4
Bewholme 97 D7
Bexhill 18 E4
Bexley 29 B5
Bexleyheath 29 B5
Bexwell 67 D6
Beyton 56 C3
Bhaltos. 154 D5
Bhatarsaigh 148 J1
Bibury 37 D8
Bicester 39 B5
Bickenhall 11 C7
Bickenhill 63 F5
Bicker 78 F5
Bickershaw 86 D4
Bickerstaffe 86 D2
Bickerton Ches E 74 D2
N Yorks 95 D7
Bickington Devon 7 B5
Devon 20 F4
Bickleigh Devon 6 C3
Devon 10 D4
Bickleton 20 F4
Bickley 28 C5
Bickley Moss 74 E2
Bicknacre 42 D3
Bicknoller 22 F3
Bicknor 30 D2
Bickton 14 C2
Bicton Shrops 60 C4
Shrops. 60 F2
Bidborough 29 E6
Bidden 26 E5
Biddenden 19 B5
Biddenham 53 E8

Biddestone 24 B3
Biddisham 23 D5
Biddlesden 52 E4
Biddlestone 117 D5
Biddulph 75 D5
Biddulph Moor 75 D6
Bideford 9 B6
Bidford-on-Avon . 51 D6
Bidston 85 E3
Bielby 96 E3
Bieldside 141 D7
Bierley IoW 15 G6
W Yorks 94 F4
Bierton 39 C8
Big Sand 149 A12
Bigbury 6 E4
Bigbury on Sea 6 E4
Bigby 90 D4
Biggar Cumb. 92 C1
S Lanark 120 F3
Biggin Derbys 75 D8
Derbys. 76 E2
N Yorks. 95 F8
Biggings 160 G3
Biggin Hill 28 D5
Biggleswade 54 E2
Bighouse 157 C11
Bighton 26 F4
Bignor 16 C3
Bigton 160 L5
Bilberry 4 C5
Bilborough 76 E5
Bilbrook 22 E2
Bilbrough 95 E8
Bilbster 158 E4
Bildershaw. 101 B7
Bildeston 56 E3
Billesdon 64 D4
Billesley 51 D6
Billingborough 78 F4
Billinge 86 D3
Billingford 81 E6
Billingham 102 B2
Billinghay 78 D4
Billingshurst 16 B4
Billingsley 61 F7
Billington C Beds 40 B2
Lancs. 93 F7
Billockby 69 C7
Billy Row 110 F4
Bilsborrow 92 F5
Bilsby 79 B7
Bilsham 16 D3
Bilsington 19 B7
Bilson Green 36 C3
Bilsthorpe 77 C6
Bilsthorpe Moor 77 C6
Bilston Midloth 121 C5
W Mid 62 E3
Bilstone 63 D7
Bilting 30 E4
Bilton E Yorks 97 F7
Northumb 117 C8
N Yorks 95 D6
Warks 52 B2
Bilton in Ainsty 95 E7
Bimbister 159 G4
Binbrook 91 E6
Binchester Blocks. 110 F5
Bincombe 12 F4
Bindal 151 C12
Binegar 23 E8
Bines Green 17 C5
Binfield 27 B6
Binfield Heath. 26 B5
Bingfield. 110 B2
Bingham 77 F7
Bingley 94 F4
Bings Heath 60 C5
Binham 81 D5
Binley Hants. 26 D2
W Mid 51 B8
Binley Woods 51 B8
Binniehill 119 B8
Binsoe 94 B5
Binstead 15 E6
Binsted 27 E5
Binton 51 D6
Binweston 60 D3
Birch Essex 43 C5
Gtr Man. 87 D6
Bircham Newton . 80 D3
Bircham Tofts 80 D3
Birchanger. 41 B8
Bircher 49 C6
Birch Green 43 C5
Birchgrove Cardiff. 22 B3
Swansea 33 E8
Birch Heath 74 C2
Birch Hill 74 B2
Birchington 31 C6
Birchmoor 63 D6
Birchover 76 C2
Birch Vale 87 F8
Birchwood Lincs 78 C2
Warr 86 E4
Bircotes 89 E7
Birdbrook 55 E8
Birdforth 95 B7
Birdham 16 E2
Birdholme 76 C3
Birdingbury 52 C2
Birdlip 37 C6
Birdsall 96 C4
Birds Edge 88 D3
Birdsgreen 61 F7
Birdsmoor Gate . 11 D8
Birdston 119 B6
Birdwell 88 D4
Birdwood 36 C4
Birgham 122 F3
Birkby 101 D8
Birkdale 85 C4
Birkenhead 85 F4
Birkenhills. 153 D7
Birkenshaw N Lanark 119 C6
W Yorks. 88 B3
Birkhall 140 E2
Birkhill Angus 134 F3
Borders 114 C5
Birkin 89 B6
Birley 49 D6
Birling Kent. 29 C7
Northumb 117 D8

Birling Gap. 18 F2
Birlingham. 50 E4
Birmingham 62 F4
Birnam 133 E7
Birse 140 E4
Birsemore 140 E4
Birstall Leics. 64 D2
W Yorks. 88 B3
Birstwith 94 D5
Birthorpe 78 F4
Birtley Hereford 49 C5
Northumb 109 B8
T&W 111 D5
Birts Street 50 F2
Bisbrooke. 65 E5
Biscathorpe 91 F6
Biscot 40 B3
Bisham 39 F8
Bishampton. 50 D4
Bish Mill 10 B2
Bishop Auckland . 101 B6
Bishopbridge 90 E4
Bishopbriggs. 119 C6
Bishop Burton. 97 F5
Bishop Middleham 111 F6
Bishopmill 152 B2
Bishop Monkton 95 C6
Bishop Norton 90 E3
Bishopsbourne. 31 D5
Bishops Cannings . 24 C5
Bishop's Castle. 60 F3
Bishop's Caundle . 12 C4
Bishop's Cleeve 37 B6
Bishops Frome 49 E8
Bishop's Green 42 C2
Bishop's Hull 11 B7
Bishop's Itchington 51 D8
Bishops Lydeard . 11 B6
Bishops Nympton . 10 B2
Bishop's Offley 61 B7
Bishop's Stortford . 41 B7
Bishop's Sutton 26 F4
Bishop's Tachbrook 51 C8
Bishops Tawton 20 F4
Bishopsteignton . 7 B7
Bishopstoke. 15 C5
Bishopston 33 F6
Bishopstone Bucks . 39 C8
E Sus 17 D8
Hereford 49 E6
Swindon. 38 F2
Wilts 13 B8
Bishopstrow 24 E3
Bishop Sutton 23 D7
Bishop's Waltham . 15 C6
Bishopswood 11 C7
Bishop's Wood 62 D2
Bishopsworth 23 C7
Bishop Thornton . 95 C5
Bishopthorpe 95 E8
Bishopton Darl. 102 B1
Dumfries. 105 E8
N Yorks. 95 B6
Renfs. 118 B4
Warks 51 D6
Bishop Wilton. 96 D3
Bishton 35 F7
Bisley Glos. 37 D6
Sur. 27 D7
Bispham 92 E3
Bispham Green. 86 C2
Bissoe 3 B6
Bisterne Close 14 D3
Bitchfield 65 B6
Bittadon 20 E4
Bittaford 6 D4
Bittering 68 C2
Bitterley 49 B7
Bitterne 15 C5
Bitteswell 64 F2
Bitton 23 C8
Bix. 39 F7
Bixter. 160 H5
Blaby 64 E2
Blackacre 114 E3
Blackadder West . 122 D4
Blackawton 7 D6
Blackborough 11 D5
Blackborough End. 67 C6
Black Bourton. 38 D2
Blackboys. 18 C2
Blackbrook Derbys . 76 E3
Mers 86 E3
Staffs. 74 F4
Blackburn Aberds . 141 C7
Aberds. 152 E5
Blackburn. 86 B4
W Loth 120 C2
Black Callerton . 110 C4
Black Clauchrie . 112 F2
Black Corries Lodge 131 D6
Blackcraig 113 F7
Black Crofts 124 B5
Blackden Heath . 74 B4
Blackdog 141 C8
Black Dog 10 D3
Blackfell 111 D5
Blackford Cumb. . 108 C3
Perth 127 D7
Som 12 B4
Som 23 E6
Blackfordby. 63 C7
Blackgang 15 G5
Blackhall Colliery 111 F7
Blackhall Mill 110 D4
Blackhall Rocks. . 111 F7
Blackham 29 F5
Blackheath Essex . 43 B6
Suff 57 B8
Sur. 27 E8
W Mid 62 F3
Blackhill Aberds. . 153 C10
Aberds. 153 D10
Highld 149 C8
Blackhills Highld . 151 F12
Moray 152 C2
Blackhorse 23 B8
Blackland 24 C5
Black Lane 87 D5
Blacklaw 153 C6
Blackley 87 D6
Blacklunans 134 C1

Black Marsh 60 D3
Blackmill 34 F3
Blackmoor 27 F5
Blackmoor Gate. . 21 E5
Blackmore 42 D2
Blackmore End Essex 55 F8
Herts. 40 C4
Black Mount 131 E6
Blackness 120 B3
Blacknest 27 E5
Black Notley 42 B3
Blacko 93 E8
Black Pill 33 E7
Blackpool Blackpool 92 F3
Devon 7 E6
Pembs. 32 C1
Blackpool Gate 108 B5
Blackridge 119 C8
Blackrock Argyll. 142 B4
Mon 35 C6
Blackrod. 86 C4
Blackshaw 107 C7
Blackshaw Head. . 87 B7
Blacksmith's Green 56 C5
Blackstone. 17 C6
Black Tar 44 E4
Blackthorn. 39 C6
Blackthorpe. 56 C3
Blacktoft. 90 B2
Blacktop 141 D7
Black Torrington . 9 D6
Blacktown 35 F6
Blackwall Tunnel . 41 F6
Blackwater Corn. 3 B6
Hants. 27 D6
IoW 15 F6
Blackwaterfoot. 143 F9
Blackwell Darl 101 C7
Derbys. 75 B8
Derbys. 76 D4
Warks 51 E7
Worcs 50 B4
W Sus 28 F4
Blackwood 119 E7
Blackwood = Coed Duon. 35 E5
Blackwood Hill 75 D6
Blacon 73 C7
Bladnoch 105 D8
Bladon. 38 C4
Blaename 45 E4
Blaenau Ffestiniog . 71 C8
Blaenavon 35 D6
Blaencelyn 46 D2
Blaendyryn 47 F8
Blaenffos 45 F3
Blaengarw 34 E3
Blaengwrach 34 D2
Blaen-gwynfi 34 E2
Blaenpennal 46 C5
Blaenplwyf 46 B4
Blaenporth 45 E4
Blaenrhondda 34 D3
Blaen-waun 32 B3
Blaen-y-coed 32 B4
Blaenycwm 47 B7
Blaen-y-Cwm Denb 72 F4
Gwyn. 71 E8
Powys 59 B7
Blagdon N Som 23 D7
Torbay 7 C6
Blagdon Hill. 11 C7
Blagill 109 E7
Blaguegate 86 D2
Blaich 130 B4
Blain 147 E9
Blaina 35 D6
Blair Atholl. 133 C5
Blairbeg 143 E11
Blairdaff 141 C5
Blair Drummond . 127 E6
Blairglas 126 F2
Blairgowrie 134 E1
Blairhall 128 F2
Blairingone 127 E8
Blairland 118 E3
Blairlogie 127 E7
Blairlomond 125 F7
Blairmore 145 E10
Blairnamarrow 139 C8
Blairquhosh 126 F4
Blair's Ferry 145 G8
Blairskaith 119 B5
Blaisdon 36 C4
Blakebrook 50 B3
Blakedown 50 B3
Blakelaw 122 F3
Blakeley 62 E2
Blakeley Lane 75 E6
Blakemere 49 E5
Blakeney Glos. 36 D3
Norf. 81 C6
Blakenhall Ches E . 74 E4
W Mid 62 E3
Blakeshall 62 F2
Blakesley 52 D4
Blanchland 110 D2
Blandford Forum . 13 D6
Blandford St Mary . 13 D6
Bland Hill 94 D5
Blanefield 119 B5
Blankney. 78 C3
Blantyre 119 D6
Blar a'Chaorainn . 131 C5
Blaran 124 D4
Blarghour 125 D5
Blarmachfoldach . 130 C4
Blarnalearoch. 150 B4
Blashford 14 D2
Blaston 64 E5
Blatherwycke 65 E6
Blawith 98 F4
Blaxhall 57 D7
Blaxton 89 D7
Blaydon 110 C4
Bleadon 22 D5
Bleak Hey Nook . 87 D8
Blean 30 C5
Bleasby Lincs 90 F5
Notts 77 E7
Bleasdale 93 E6
Bleatarn 100 C2
Blebocraigs 129 C6
Bleddfa 48 C4
Bledington 38 B2
Bledlow 39 D7
Bledlow Ridge 39 E7

Blegbie 121 C7
Blencarn 109 F6
Blencogo 107 E8
Blendworth 15 C8
Blenheim Park 80 D4
Blennerhasset 107 E8
Blervie Castle 151 F13
Bletchingdon 39 C5
Bletchingley 28 D4
Bletchley M Keynes . 53 F6
Shrops. 74 F3
Bletherston 32 B1
Bletsoe 53 D8
Blewbury 39 F5
Blickling 81 E7
Blidworth 77 D5
Blindburn. 116 C4
Blindcrake 107 F8
Blindley Heath. 28 E4
Blisland 5 B6
Bliss Gate 50 B2
Blisworth 52 D5
Blithbury 62 B4
Blitterlees 107 D8
Blockley 51 F6
Blofield 69 D6
Blofield Heath. 69 C6
Blo' Norton 56 B4
Bloomfield 115 B8
Blore 75 E8
Blount's Green 75 F7
Blowick 85 C4
Bloxham 52 F2
Bloxholm 78 D3
Bloxwich. 62 D3
Bloxworth. 13 E6
Blubberhouses 94 D4
Blue Anchor Som. . 22 E2
Swansea 33 E6
Blue Row 43 C6
Blundeston 69 E8
Blunham 54 D2
Blunsdon St Andrew 37 F8
Bluntington 50 B3
Bluntisham 54 B4
Blunts. 5 C8
Blyborough 90 E3
Blyford 57 B8
Blymhill 62 C2
Blyth Northumb. 117 F9
Notts 89 F7
Blyth Bridge 120 E4
Blythburgh 57 B8
Blythe 121 E8
Blythe Bridge 75 E6
Blyton 90 E2
Boarhills 129 C7
Boarhunt 15 D7
Boars Head 86 D3
Boars Hill 38 D4
Boarstall 39 C6
Boasley Cross 9 E6
Boath 151 D8
Boat of Garten 138 C5
Bobbing 30 C2
Bobbington 62 E2
Bobbingworth. 41 D8
Bocaddon. 5 D6
Bochastle 126 D5
Bocking 42 B3
Bocking Churchstreet . 42 B3
Boddam Aberds 153 D11
Shetland 160 M5
Boddington 37 B5
Bodedern 82 C3
Bodelwyddan 72 B4
Bodenham Hereford 49 D7
Wilts 14 B2
Bodenham Moor . 49 D7
Bodermid 70 E2
Bodewryd 82 B3
Bodfari 72 B4
Bodffordd 82 D4
Bodham 81 C7
Bodiam 18 C4
Bodicote 52 F2
Bodieve. 4 B4
Bodinnick 5 D6
Bodle Street Green 18 D3
Bodmin 5 C5
Bodney 67 E8
Bodorgan 82 E3
Bodsham 30 E5
Boduan 70 D4
Bodymoor Heath . 63 E5
Bogallan 151 F9
Bogbrae 153 E10
Bogend Borders . 122 E3
S Ayrs. 118 F3
Boghall 120 C2
Boghead 119 E7
Bogmoor 152 B3
Bognie 153 D6
Bognor Regis 16 E3
Bograxie. 141 C6
Bogside 119 D8
Bogton 153 C6
Bogue 113 F6
Bohenie 137 F5
Bohortha 3 C7
Bohuntine 137 F5
Boirseam 154 J5
Bojewyan 2 C2
Bolam Durham 101 B6
Northumb 117 F6
Bolberry 6 F4
Bold Heath 86 F3
Boldon 111 C6
Boldon Colliery 111 C6
Boldre 14 E4
Boldron 101 C5
Bole 89 F7
Bolehill 76 D2
Boleside. 121 F7
Bolham 10 C4
Bolham Water. 11 C6
Bolingey 4 D2
Bollington 75 B6
Bollington Cross . 75 B6
Bolney 17 B6
Bolnhurst 53 D8
Bolshan 135 D6
Bolsover 76 B4

Bolsterstone 88 E3
Bolstone 49 F7
Boltby 102 F2
Bolter End 39 E7
Bolton Cumb 99 B8
E Loth. 121 B8
E Yorks. 96 D3
Gtr Man 86 D5
Northumb 117 C7
Bolton Abbey. 94 D3
Bolton Bridge 94 D3
Bolton-by-Bowland 93 E7
Boltonfellend 108 C4
Boltongate. 108 E2
Bolton-le-Sands . 92 C4
Bolton Low Houses 108 E2
Bolton-on-Swale 101 E7
Bolton Percy 95 E8
Bolton Town End . 92 C4
Bolton upon Dearne 89 D5
Bolventor 5 B6
Bomere Heath. 60 C4
Bonar Bridge. 151 B9
Bonawe 125 B6
Bonby 90 C4
Boncath 45 F4
Bonchester Bridge. 115 C8
Bonchurch 15 G6
Bondleigh 9 D8
Bonehill Devon. 6 B5
Staffs. 63 D5
Bo'ness 127 F8
Bonhill. 118 B3
Boningale 62 D2
Bonjedward. 116 B2
Bonkle. 119 D8
Bonnavoulin 147 F8
Bonnington Edin . 120 C4
Kent. 19 B7
Bonnybank. 129 D5
Bonnybridge 127 F7
Bonnykelly 153 C8
Bonnyrigg and Lasswade. 121 C6
Bonnyton Aberds . 153 E6
Angus 134 F3
Angus 135 D6
Bonsall 76 D2
Bonskeid House . 133 C5
Bont. 35 C7
Bontddu 58 C3
Bont-Dolgadfan. . 59 D5
Bont-goch 58 F3
Bonthorpe 79 B7
Bontnewydd Ceredig. 46 C5
Gwyn. 82 F4
Bont-newydd 72 B4
Bont Newydd Gwyn. 71 C8
Gwyn. 71 E8
Bontuchel 72 D4
Bonvilston 22 B2
Bon-y-maen 33 E7
Booker. 39 E8
Boon 121 E8
Boosbeck 102 C4
Boot 98 D3
Booth. 87 B8
Boothby Graffoe. . 78 D2
Boothby Pagnell. . 78 F2
Boothen 75 E5
Boothferry 89 B8
Boothville 53 C5
Booth Wood 87 C8
Bootle Cumb 98 F3
Mers 85 E4
Booton 81 E7
Boot Street 57 E6
Boquhan 126 F4
Boraston 49 B8
Borden Kent 30 C2
W Sus 16 B2
Bordley 94 C2
Bordon 27 F6
Boreham Essex 42 D3
Wilts 24 E3
Boreham Street 18 D3
Borehamwood 40 E4
Boreland Dumfries. 114 E4
Stirling. 132 F2
Borgh W Isles 148 H1
W Isles 154 J4
Borghastan 154 C7
Borgie 157 D9
Borgue Dumfries. . 106 E3
Highld 158 H3
Borley 56 E2
Bornais. 148 F2
Bornesketaig. 149 A8
Borness 106 E3
Boroughbridge. 95 C6
Borough Green 29 D7
Borras Head 73 D7
Borreraig 148 C6
Borrobol Lodge .157 G11
Borrowash 76 F4
Borrowby 102 F2
Borrowdale 98 C4
Borrowfield 141 E7
Borth 58 E3
Borthwickshiels 115 C7
Borth-y-Gest 71 D6
Borve 149 D9
Borve Lodge 154 H5
Borwick 92 B5
Bosavern 2 C2
Bosbury 49 E8
Boscastle 8 E3
Boscombe BCP 14 E2
Wilts 25 F7
Boscoppa 4 D5
Bosham 16 D2
Bosherston 44 F4
Boskenna 2 D3
Bosley 75 C6
Bossall 96 C3
Bossiney 8 F2
Bossingham 31 E5
Bossington 21 E7
Bostock Green 74 C3

Boston . . . 79 E6
Boston Long
Hedges . . . 79 E6
Boston Spa . . . 95 E7
Boston West . . . 79 E5
Boswinger . . . 3 B8
Botallack . . . 2 C2
Botany Bay . . . 41 E5
Botcherby . . . 108 D4
Botcheston . . . 63 D8
Botesdale . . . 56 B4
Bothal . . . 117 F8
Bothamsall . . . 77 B6
Bothel . . . 107 F8
Bothenhampton . . 12 E2
Bothwell . . . 119 D7
Botley Bucks . . 40 D2
Hants . . . 15 C6
Oxon . . . 38 D4
Botolph Claydon . 39 B7
Botolphs . . . 17 D5
Bottacks . . . 150 E7
Bottesford Leics . 77 F8
N Lincs . . . 90 D2
Bottisham . . . 55 C6
Bottlesford . . . 25 D6
Bottom Boat . . . 88 B4
Bottomcraig . . . 129 B5
Bottom House . . 75 D7
Bottom of Hutton . 86 B2
Bottom o'th'Moor . 86 C4
Botusfleming . . 6 C2
Botwnnog . . . 70 D3
Bough Beech . . 29 E5
Boughrood . . . 48 F3
Boughspring . . 36 E2
Boughton Norf . 67 D6
Northants . . . 53 C5
Notts . . . 77 C6
Boughton Aluph . 30 E4
Boughton Lees . 30 E4
Boughton
Malherbe . . . 30 E2
Boughton
Monchelsea . . 29 D8
Boughton Street . 30 D4
Boulby . . . 103 C5
Boulden . . . 60 F5
Boulmer . . . 117 C8
Boulston . . . 44 D4
Boultenstone . . 140 C3
Boultham . . . 78 C2
Bourn . . . 54 D4
Bourne . . . 65 B7
Bourne End Bucks . 40 F1
C Beds . . . 53 E7
Herts . . . 40 D3
Bournemouth . . 13 E8
Bournes Green
Glos . . . 37 D6
Southend . . . 43 F5
Bournheath . . . 50 B4
Bournmoor . . . 111 D6
Bournville . . . 62 F4
Bourton Dorset . 24 F2
N Som . . . 23 C5
Oxon . . . 38 F2
Shrops . . . 61 E5
Bourton on
Dunsmore . . . 52 B2
Bourton on the
Hill . . . 51 F6
Bourton-on-the-
Water . . . 38 B1
Bousd . . . 146 E5
Bousta Hill . . . 108 D2
Bouth . . . 99 F5
Bouthwaite . . . 94 B4
Boveney . . . 27 B7
Boverton . . . 21 C8
Bovey Tracey . . 7 B6
Bovingdon . . . 40 D3
Bovingdon Green
Bucks . . . 39 F8
Herts . . . 40 D3
Bovinger . . . 41 D8
Bovington Camp . 13 F6
Bow Borders . . 121 E7
Devon . . . 10 D2
Orkney . . . 159 J4
Bowbank . . . 100 B4
Bow Brickhill . . 53 F7
Bowburn . . . 111 F6
Bowcombe . . . 15 F5
Bowd . . . 11 E6
Bowden Borders . 121 F8
Devon . . . 7 E6
Bowden Hill . . . 24 C4
Bowderdale . . . 100 D1
Bowdon . . . 87 F5
Bower . . . 116 F3
Bowerchalke . . 13 B8
Bowerhill . . . 24 C4
Bower Hinton . . 12 C2
Bowermadden . 158 D4
Bowers Gifford . 42 F3
Bowershall . . . 128 E2
Bowertower . . . 158 D4
Bowes . . . 100 C4
Bowgreave . . . 92 E4
Bowgreen . . . 87 F5
Bowhill . . . 115 B7
Bowhouse . . . 107 C7
Bowland Bridge . 99 F6
Bowley . . . 49 D7
Bowlhead Green . 27 F7
Bowling W Dunb . 118 B4
W Yorks . . . 94 F4
Bowling Bank . . 73 E7
Bowling Green . . 50 D3
Bowmanstead . . 99 E5
Bowmore . . . 142 C4
Bowness-on-
Solway . . . 108 C2
Bowness-on-
Windermere . . 99 E6
Bow of Fife . . . 128 C5
Bowsden . . . 123 E5
Bowside Lodge . 157 C11
Bowston . . . 99 E6
Bow Street . . . 58 F3
Bowthorpe . . . 68 D4
Box Glos . . . 37 D5
Wilts . . . 24 C3
Boxbush . . . 36 C4
Box End . . . 53 E8

Boxford Suff . . . 56 E3
W Berks . . . 26 B2
Boxgrove . . . 16 D3
Boxley . . . 29 D8
Boxmoor . . . 40 D3
Boxted Essex . . 56 F4
Suff . . . 56 D2
Boxted Cross . . 56 F4
Boxted Heath . . 56 F4
Boxworth . . . 54 C4
Boxworth End . . 54 C4
Boyden Gate . . 31 C6
Boylestone . . . 75 F8
Boyndie . . . 153 B6
Boynton . . . 97 C7
Boysack . . . 135 E6
Boyton Corn . . 8 E5
Suff . . . 57 E7
Wilts . . . 24 F4
Boyton Cross . . 42 D2
Boyton End . . . 55 E8
Bozeat . . . 53 D7
Braaid . . . 84 E3
Braal Castle . . . 158 D3
Brabling Green . . 57 C6
Brabourne . . . 30 E4
Brabourne Lees . 30 E4
Brabster . . . 158 D5
Bracadale . . . 149 E8
Braceborough . . 65 C7
Bracebridge . . . 78 C2
Bracebridge Heath 78 C2
Bracebridge Low
Fields . . . 78 C2
Braceby . . . 78 F3
Bracewell . . . 93 E8
Brackenfield . . . 76 D3
Brackenthwaite
Cumb . . . 108 E2
N Yorks . . . 95 D5
Bracklesham . . 16 E2
Brackletter . . . 136 F4
Brackley Argyll . 143 D8
Northants . . . 52 F3
Brackloch . . . 156 G4
Bracknell . . . 27 C6
Braco . . . 127 D7
Bracobrae . . . 152 C5
Bracon Ash . . . 68 E4
Bracorina . . . 147 B10
Bradbourne . . . 76 D2
Bradbury . . . 101 B8
Bradda . . . 84 F1
Bradden . . . 52 E4
Braddock . . . 5 C6
Bradeley . . . 75 D5
Bradenham Bucks . 39 E8
Norf . . . 68 D2
Bradenstoke . . . 24 B5
Bradfield Essex . 56 F5
Norf . . . 81 D8
W Berks . . . 26 B4
Bradfield Combust 56 D2
Bradfield Green . 74 D3
Bradfield Heath . 43 B7
Bradfield St Clare . 56 D3
Bradfield
St George . . . 56 C3
Bradford Corn . . 5 B6
Derbys . . . 76 C2
Devon . . . 9 D6
Northumb . . . 123 F7
W Yorks . . . 94 F4
Bradford Abbas . 12 C3
Bradford-on-Avon 24 C3
Bradford-on-Tone 11 B6
Bradford Peverell . 12 E4
Brading . . . 15 F7
Bradley Derbys . 76 E2
Hants . . . 26 E4
NE Lincs . . . 91 D6
Staffs . . . 62 C2
W Mid . . . 62 E3
W Yorks . . . 88 B2
Bradley Green . . 50 C4
Bradley in the
Moors . . . 75 E7
Bradley Stoke . . 36 F3
Bradlow . . . 50 F2
Bradmore Notts . 77 F5
W Mid . . . 62 E2
Bradninch . . . 10 D5
Bradnop . . . 75 D7
Bradpole . . . 12 E2
Bradshaw Gtr Man . 86 C5
W Yorks . . . 87 C8
Bradstone . . . 9 F5
Bradwall Green . 74 C4
Bradway . . . 88 F4
Bradwell Derbys . 88 F2
Essex . . . 42 B4
M Keynes . . . 53 F6
Norf . . . 69 D8
Staffs . . . 74 E5
Bradwell Grove . 38 D2
Bradwell on Sea . 43 D6
Bradwell
Waterside . . . 43 D5
Bradworthy . . . 8 C5
Bradworthy Cross . 8 C5
Brae Dumfries . 107 B5
Highld . . . 155 J13
Highld . . . 156 J7
Shetland . . . 160 G5
Braeantra . . . 151 D8
Braedownie . . . 134 B2
Braefield . . . 150 H7
Braegrum . . . 128 B2
Braehead
Dumfries . . . 105 D8
Orkney . . . 159 D5
Orkney . . . 159 H6
S Lanark . . . 119 F8
S Lanark . . . 120 D2
Braehead of
Lunan . . . 135 D6
Braehoulland . . 160 F4
Braehungie . . . 158 G3
Braelangwell
Lodge . . . 151 B8
Braemar . . . 139 E7
Braemore Highld . 150 D4
Highld . . . 158 G2
Brae of
Achnahaird . . 156 H3
Brae Roy Lodge . 137 E6
Braeside . . . 118 B2

Braes of Enzie . . 152 C3
Braeswick . . . 159 E7
Braewick . . . 160 H5
Brafferton Darl . 101 B7
N Yorks . . . 95 B7
Brafield-on-the-
Green . . . 53 D6
Bragar . . . 155 C7
Bragbury End . . 41 B5
Bragleenmore . . 124 C5
Braichmelyn . . . 83 E6
Braid . . . 120 C5
Braides . . . 92 D4
Braidley . . . 101 F5
Braidwood . . . 119 E8
Braigo . . . 142 B3
Brailsford . . . 76 E2
Braintree . . . 42 B3
Braiseworth . . . 56 B5
Braishfield . . . 14 B4
Braithwaite Cumb . 98 B4
S Yorks . . . 89 C7
W Yorks . . . 94 E3
Braithwell . . . 89 E6
Bramber . . . 17 C5
Bramcote Notts . 76 F5
Warks . . . 63 F8
Bramdean . . . 15 B7
Bramerton . . . 69 D5
Bramfield Herts . 41 C5
Suff . . . 57 B7
Bramford . . . 56 E5
Bramhall . . . 87 F6
Bramham . . . 95 E7
Bramhope . . . 95 E5
Bramley Hants . 26 D4
Surr . . . 27 E8
S Yorks . . . 89 E5
W Yorks . . . 94 F5
Bramling . . . 31 D6
Brampford Speke . 10 E4
Brampton Cambs . 54 B3
Cumb . . . 100 B1
Cumb . . . 108 C5
Derbys . . . 76 B3
Hereford . . . 49 F6
Lincs . . . 77 B8
Norf . . . 81 E8
Suff . . . 69 F7
S Yorks . . . 88 D5
Brampton Abbotts 36 B3
Brampton Ash . . 64 F4
Brampton Bryan . 49 B5
Brampton en le
Morthen . . . 89 F5
Bramshall . . . 75 F7
Bramshaw . . . 14 C3
Bramshill . . . 26 C5
Bramshott . . . 27 F6
Branault . . . 147 E8
Brancaster . . . 80 C3
Brancaster Staithe 80 C3
Brancepeth . . . 110 F5
Branch End . . . 110 C3
Branchill . . . 151 F13
Branderburgh . . 152 A2
Brandesburton . . 97 E7
Brandeston . . . 57 C6
Brand Green . . . 36 B4
Brandhill . . . 49 B6
Brandis Corner . . 9 D6
Brandiston . . . 81 E7
Brandon Durham . 110 F5
Lincs . . . 78 E2
Northumb . . . 117 C6
Suff . . . 67 F7
Warks . . . 52 B2
Brandon Bank . . 67 F6
Brandon Creek . . 67 E6
Brandon Parva . . 68 D3
Brandsby . . . 95 B8
Brandy Wharf . . 90 E4
Brane . . . 2 D3
Bran End . . . 42 B2
Branksome . . . 13 E8
Branksome Park . 13 E8
Bransby . . . 77 B8
Branscombe . . . 11 F6
Bransford . . . 50 D2
Bransgore . . . 14 E2
Branshill . . . 127 E7
Bransholme . . . 97 F7
Branson's Cross . 51 B5
Branston Leics . 64 B5
Lincs . . . 78 C3
Staffs . . . 63 B6
Branston Booths . 78 C3
Branstone . . . 15 F6
Bransty . . . 98 C1
Brant Broughton . 78 D2
Brantham . . . 56 F5
Branthwaite Cumb . 98 B2
Cumb . . . 108 F2
Brantingham . . . 90 B3
Branton Northumb . 117 C6
S Yorks . . . 89 D7
Branxholme . . . 115 C7
Branxholm Park . 115 C7
Branxton . . . 122 F4
Brassey Green . . 74 C2
Brassington . . . 76 D2
Brasted . . . 29 D5
Brasted Chart . . 29 D5
Brathens . . . 141 E5
Bratoft . . . 79 C7
Brattleby . . . 90 F7
Bratton Telford . 61 C6
Wilts . . . 24 D4
Bratton Clovelly . 9 E6
Bratton Fleming . 20 F5
Bratton Seymour . 12 B4
Braughing . . . 41 B6
Braunston . . . 52 C3
Braunstone Town . 64 D2
Braunston-in-
Rutland . . . 64 D5
Braunton . . . 20 F3
Brawby . . . 96 B3
Brawl . . . 157 C11
Brawlbin . . . 158 E2
Bray . . . 27 B7
Braybrooke . . . 64 F4
Braye Ald . . . 16
Brayford . . . 21 F5
Bray Shop . . . 5 B8
Braystones . . . 98 D2
Braythorn . . . 94 E5
Brayton . . . 95 F9

Bray Wick . . . 27 B6
Brazacott . . . 8 E4
Breach . . . 30 C2
Breachacha
Castle . . . 146 F4
Breachwood
Green . . . 40 B4
Breacleit . . . 154 D6
Breaden Heath . 73 F8
Breadsall . . . 76 F3
Breadstone . . . 36 D4
Breage . . . 2 D5
Breakachy . . . 150 G7
Bream . . . 36 D3
Breamore . . . 14 C2
Brean . . . 22 D4
Breanais . . . 154 E4
Brearton . . . 95 C6
Breascleit . . . 154 D7
Breaston . . . 76 F4
Brechfa . . . 46 F4
Brechin . . . 135 C5
Breckan . . . 159 H3
Breck of Cruan . 159 G4
Breckrey . . . 149 B10
Brecon
= Aberhonddu . . 34 B4
Bredbury . . . 87 E7
Brede . . . 18 D5
Bredenbury . . . 49 D8
Bredfield . . . 57 D6
Bredgar . . . 30 C2
Bredhurst . . . 29 C8
Bredicot . . . 50 D4
Bredon . . . 50 F4
Bredon's Norton . 50 F4
Bredwardine . . . 48 E5
Breedon on the
Hill . . . 63 B8
Breibhig W Isles . 148 J1
W Isles . . . 155 D9
Breich . . . 120 C2
Breightmet . . . 86 D5
Breighton . . . 96 F3
Breinton . . . 49 F6
Breinton Common . 49 E6
Breiwick . . . 160 J6
Bremhill . . . 24 B4
Bremirehoull . . . 160 L6
Brenchley . . . 29 E7
Brendon . . . 21 E6
Brenkley . . . 110 B5
Brent Eleigh . . . 56 E3
Brentford . . . 28 B2
Brentingby . . . 64 C4
Brent Knoll . . . 22 D5
Brent Pelham . . 54 F5
Brentwood . . . 42 E1
Brenzett . . . 19 C7
Brereton . . . 62 C4
Brereton Green . . 74 C4
Brereton Heath . 74 C5
Bressingham . . . 68 F3
Bretby . . . 63 B6
Bretford . . . 52 B2
Bretforton . . . 51 E5
Bretherdale Head . 99 D7
Bretherton . . . 86 B2
Brettabister . . . 160 H6
Brettenham Norf . 68 F2
Suff . . . 56 D3
Bretton Derbys . 76 B2
Flint . . . 73 C7
Brewer Street . . 28 D4
Brewlands
Bridge . . . 134 C1
Brewood . . . 62 D2
Briach . . . 151 F13
Briants Puddle . . 13 E6
Brick End . . . 42 B1
Bricket Wood . . 40 D4
Brickhampton . . 50 E4
Bride . . . 84 B4
Bridekirk . . . 107 F8
Bridell . . . 45 E3
Bridestowe . . . 9 F7
Brideswell . . . 152 E5
Bridford . . . 10 F3
Bridfordmills . . . 10 F3
Bridge . . . 31 D5
Bridge End . . . 78 F4
Bridgefoot Angus . 134 F3
Cumb . . . 98 B2
Bridge Green . . 55 F5
Bridgehampton . 12 B3
Bridge Hewick . . 95 B6
Bridgehill . . . 110 D3
Bridgemary . . . 15 D6
Bridgemont . . . 87 F8
Bridgend Aberds . 140 C4
Aberds . . . 152 E5
Angus . . . 135 C5
Argyll . . . 142 B4
Argyll . . . 143 B8
Argyll . . . 145 D7
Cumb . . . 99 C5
Fife . . . 129 C5
Moray . . . 152 E3
N Lanark . . . 119 B6
Pembs . . . 45 E3
W Loth . . . 120 B3
Bridgend = Pen-y-Bont
ar Ogwr . . . 21 B8
Bridgend of
Lintrathen . . . 134 D2
Bridge of Alford . 140 C4
Bridge of Allan . 127 E6
Bridge of Avon . 152 E1
Bridge of Awe . . 125 C6
Bridge of Balgie . 132 E2
Bridge of Cally . 133 D8
Bridge of Canny . 141 E5
Bridge of
Craigisla . . . 134 D2
Bridge of Dee . . 106 D4
Bridge of Don . . 141 C8
Bridge of Dun . . 135 D6
Bridge of Dye . . 141 F5
Bridge of Earn . . 128 C3
Bridge of Ericht . 132 D2
Bridge of Feugh . 141 E6
Bridge of Forss . 157 C13
Bridge of Gairn . 140 E2
Bridge of Gaur . . 132 D2
Bridge of
Muchalls . . . 141 E7
Bridge of Oich . . 137 D6
Bridge of Orchy . 125 B8

Bridge of Waith . 159 G3
Bridge of Walls . 160 H4
Bridge of Weir . . 118 C3
Bridgerule . . . 8 D4
Bridges . . . 60 E3
Bridge Sollers . . 49 E6
Bridge Street . . 56 E2
Bridgeton . . . 119 C6
Bridgetown Corn . 8 F5
Som . . . 21 F8
Bridge Trafford . 73 B8
Bridge Yate . . . 23 B8
Bridgham . . . 68 F2
Bridgnorth . . . 61 E7
Bridgtown . . . 62 D3
Bridgwater . . . 22 F5
Bridlington . . . 97 C7
Bridport . . . 12 E2
Bridstow . . . 36 B2
Brierfield . . . 93 F8
Brierley Glos . . . 36 C3
Hereford . . . 49 D6
S Yorks . . . 88 C5
Brierley Hill . . . 62 F3
Briery Hill . . . 35 D5
Brigg . . . 90 D4
Briggswath . . . 103 D6
Brigham Cumb . 107 F7
E Yorks . . . 97 D6
Brighouse . . . 88 B2
Brighstone . . . 14 F5
Brightgate . . . 76 D2
Brighthampton . . 38 D3
Brightling . . . 18 C3
Brightlingsea . . 43 C6
Brighton Brighton . 17 D7
Corn . . . 4 D4
Brighton Hill . . . 26 E4
Brightons . . . 120 B2
Brightwalton . . . 26 B2
Brightwell . . . 57 E6
Brightwell
Baldwin . . . 39 E6
Brightwell cum
Sotwell . . . 39 E5
Brignall . . . 101 C5
Brig o'Turk . . . 126 D4
Brigsley . . . 91 D6
Brigsteer . . . 99 F6
Brigstock . . . 65 F6
Brill . . . 39 C6
Brilley . . . 48 E4
Brimaston . . . 44 C4
Brimfield . . . 49 C7
Brimington . . . 76 B4
Brimley . . . 7 B5
Brimpsfield . . . 37 C6
Brimpton . . . 26 C3
Brims . . . 159 K3
Brimscombe . . . 37 D5
Brimstage . . . 85 F4
Brinacory . . . 147 B10
Brind . . . 96 F3
Brindister
Shetland . . . 160 H4
Shetland . . . 160 K6
Brindle . . . 86 B4
Brindley Ford . . 75 D5
Brineton . . . 62 C2
Bringhurst . . . 64 E5
Brington . . . 53 B8
Brinian . . . 159 F5
Briningham . . . 81 D6
Brinkhill . . . 79 B6
Brinkley . . . 55 D7
Brinklow . . . 52 B2
Brinkworth . . . 37 F7
Brinmore . . . 138 B2
Brinscall . . . 86 B4
Brinsea . . . 23 C6
Brinsley . . . 76 E4
Brinsworth . . . 88 F5
Brinton . . . 81 D6
Brisco . . . 108 D4
Brisley . . . 81 E5
Brislington . . . 23 B8
Bristol . . . 23 B7
Briston . . . 81 D6
Britannia . . . 87 B6
Britford . . . 14 B2
Brithdir . . . 58 C4
British Legion
Village . . . 29 D8
Briton Ferry . . . 33 E8
Britwell Salome . 39 E6
Brixham . . . 7 D7
Brixton Devon . . 6 D3
London . . . 28 B4
Brixton Deverill . 24 F3
Brixworth . . . 52 B5
Brize Norton . . . 38 D3
Broad Blunsdon . 38 E1
Broadbottom . . . 87 E7
Broadbridge . . . 16 D2
Broadbridge Heath 28 F2
Broad Campden . 51 F6
Broad Chalke . . 13 B8
Broadclyst . . . 10 E4
Broadfield Gtr Man . 87 C6
Lancs . . . 86 B3
Pembs . . . 45 E3
Broadford . . . 149 F11
Broadford Bridge . 16 B4
Broad Green
C Beds . . . 53 E7
Essex . . . 42 B4
Sur . . . 27 D8
Worcs . . . 50 D2
Broadhaugh . . . 115 D7
Broadhaven . . . 158 E5
Broadheath . . . 87 F5
Broad Heath . . . 49 C8
Broadhembury . . 11 D6
Broadhempston . 7 C6
Broad Hill . . . 55 B6
Broad Hinton . . 25 B6
Broadholme Derbys 76 E3
Lincs . . . 77 B8
Broadland Row . 18 D5
Broadlay . . . 32 D4
Broad Laying . . 26 C2
Broadley Lancs . 87 C6
Moray . . . 152 B3
Broadley
Common . . . 41 D7
Broad Marston . . 51 E6
Broadmayne . . . 12 F5
Broadmeadows . 121 F7

Broadmere . . . 26 E4
Broadmoor . . . 32 D1
Broadoak . . . 31 C5
Broad Oak Carms . 33 B6
Cumb . . . 98 E3
Dorset . . . 12 E2
Dorset . . . 13 C5
E Sus . . . 18 C3
E Sus . . . 18 D5
Hereford . . . 36 B1
Mers . . . 86 E3
Broadrashes . . . 152 C4
Broadsea . . . 153 B9
Broadstairs . . . 31 C7
Broadstone BCP . 13 E8
Shrops . . . 60 F5
Broad Street . . . 30 D2
Broad Street
Green . . . 42 D4
Broad Town . . . 25 B5
Broadtown Lane . 25 B5
Broadwas . . . 50 D2
Broadwater Herts . 41 B5
W Sus . . . 17 D5
Broadway Carms . 32 D3
Pembs . . . 44 D3
Som . . . 11 C8
Suff . . . 57 B7
Worcs . . . 51 F5
Broadwell Glos . 36 C2
Glos . . . 38 B2
Oxon . . . 38 D2
Warks . . . 52 C2
Broadwell House . 110 D2
Broadwey . . . 12 F4
Broadwindsor . . 12 D2
Broadwood Kelly . 9 D8
Broadwoodwidger . 9 F6
Brobury . . . 48 E5
Brochel . . . 149 D10
Brochloch . . . 113 E5
Brochroy . . . 125 B6
Brockamin . . . 50 D2
Brockbridge . . . 15 C7
Brockdam . . . 117 B7
Brockdish . . . 57 B6
Brockenhurst . . 14 D4
Brocketsbrae . . 119 F8
Brockford Street . 56 C5
Brockhall . . . 52 C4
Brockham . . . 28 E2
Brockhampton
Glos . . . 37 B7
Hereford . . . 49 F7
Brockholes . . . 88 C2
Brockhurst Derbys 76 C3
Hants . . . 15 D7
Brocklebank . . . 108 E3
Brocklesby . . . 90 C5
Brockley . . . 23 C6
Brockley Green . . 56 D2
Brockleymoor . . 108 F4
Brockton Shrops . 60 D3
Shrops . . . 60 F3
Shrops . . . 61 D7
Shrops . . . 61 E5
Shrops . . . 61 E7
Telford . . . 61 C7
Brockweir . . . 36 D2
Brockwood . . . 15 B7
Brockworth . . . 37 C5
Brocton . . . 62 C3
Brodick . . . 143 E11
Brodsworth . . . 89 D6
Brogaig . . . 149 B9
Brogborough . . 53 F7
Brokenborough . 37 F6
Broken Cross
Ches E . . . 75 B5
Ches W . . . 74 B3
Bromborough . . 85 F4
Brome . . . 56 B5
Brome Street . . . 57 B5
Bromeswell . . . 57 D7
Bromfield Cumb . 107 E8
Shrops . . . 49 B6
Bromham Bedford . 53 D8
Wilts . . . 24 C4
Bromley London . 28 C5
W Mid . . . 62 F3
Bromley Common . 28 C5
Bromley Green . . 19 B6
Brompton Medway . 29 C8
N Yorks . . . 102 E1
N Yorks . . . 103 F7
Brompton-on-
Swale . . . 101 E7
Brompton Ralph . 22 F2
Brompton Regis . 21 F8
Bromsash . . . 36 B3
Bromsberrow
Heath . . . 50 F2
Bromsgrove . . . 50 B4
Bromyard . . . 49 D8
Bromyard Downs . 49 D8
Bronaber . . . 71 D8
Brongest . . . 46 E2
Bronington . . . 73 F8
Bronllys . . . 48 F3
Bronnant . . . 46 C5
Bronwydd Arms . 33 B5
Bronydd . . . 48 E4
Bronygarth . . . 73 F6
Brook Carms . . 32 D3
Hants . . . 14 B4
Hants . . . 14 C3
IoW . . . 14 F4
Kent . . . 30 E4
Sur . . . 27 E8
Sur . . . 27 F7
Brooke Norf . . . 69 E5
Rutland . . . 64 D5
Brookenby . . . 91 E6
Brookend . . . 36 E2
Brook End . . . 53 C8
Brookfield . . . 118 C4
Brook Hill . . . 14 C3
Brookhouse . . . 92 C5
Brookhouse Green 74 C5
Brookland . . . 19 C6
Brooklands
Dumfries . . . 106 B5
Gtr Man . . . 87 E5
Shrops . . . 74 E2
Brookmans Park . 41 D5
Brooks . . . 59 E8
Brooks Green . . 16 B5
Brook Street Kent . 19 B6
Kent . . . 29 E6
W Sus . . . 17 B7

Brookthorpe . . . 37 C5
Brookville . . . 67 E7
Brookwood . . . 27 D7
Broom C Beds . . 54 E2
S Yorks . . . 88 E5
Warks . . . 51 D5
Worcs . . . 50 B4
Broome Norf . . 69 E6
Shrops . . . 60 F4
Broomedge . . . 86 F5
Broome Park . . 117 C7
Broomer's Corner . 16 B5
Broomfield Aberds 153 E9
Essex . . . 42 C3
Kent . . . 30 D2
Kent . . . 31 C5
Som . . . 22 F4
Broomfleet . . . 90 B2
Broom Green . . 81 E5
Broomhall Ches E . 74 E3
Windsor . . . 27 C7
Broomhaugh . . . 110 C3
Broomhill Norf . 67 D6
Northumb . . . 117 D8
S Yorks . . . 88 D5
Broom Hill . . . 13 D8
Broomholm . . . 81 D9
Broomley . . . 110 C3
Broompark . . . 110 E5
Broom's Green . . 50 F2
Broomy Lodge . . 14 C3
Brora . . . 157 J12
Broseley . . . 61 D6
Brotherhouse Bar . 66 C2
Brotherstone . . 122 F2
Brothertoft . . . 79 E5
Brotherton . . . 89 B5
Brotton . . . 102 C4
Broubster . . . 157 C13
Brough Cumb . 100 C2
Derbys . . . 88 F2
E Yorks . . . 90 B3
Highld . . . 158 C4
Notts . . . 77 D8
Orkney . . . 159 G4
Shetland . . . 160 F6
Shetland . . . 160 G7
Shetland . . . 160 H6
Shetland . . . 160 J7
Brough Lodge . . 160 D7
Brough Sowerby . 100 C2
Broughall . . . 74 E2
Broughton
Borders . . . 120 F4
Cambs . . . 54 B3
Flint . . . 73 C7
Hants . . . 25 F8
Lancs . . . 92 F5
M Keynes . . . 53 E6
N Lincs . . . 90 D3
Northants . . . 53 B6
N Yorks . . . 94 D2
N Yorks . . . 96 B3
Orkney . . . 159 D5
Oxon . . . 52 F2
V Glam . . . 21 B8
Broughton Astley . 64 E2
Broughton Beck . 98 F4
Broughton
Common . . . 24 C3
Broughton Gifford 24 C3
Broughton
Hackett . . . 50 D4
Broughton in
Furness . . . 98 F4
Broughton Mills . 98 E4
Broughton Moor . 107 F7
Broughton Park . 87 D6
Broughton Poggs . 38 D2
Broughtown . . . 159 D7
Broughty Ferry . 134 F4
Browhouses . . . 108 C2
Browland . . . 160 H4
Brown Candover . 26 F3
Brown Edge Lancs . 85 C4
Staffs . . . 75 D6
Brown Heath . . 73 C8
Brownhill Aberds . 153 D8
Aberds . . . 153 D8
Blackburn . . . 93 F6
Shrops . . . 60 B4
Brownhills Fife . 129 C7
W Mid . . . 62 D4
Brownlow . . . 74 C5
Brownlow Heath . 74 C5
Brownmuir . . . 135 B7
Brown's End . . . 50 F2
Brownshill . . . 37 D5
Brownston . . . 6 D4
Brownyside . . . 117 B7
Broxa . . . 103 E7
Broxbourne . . . 41 D6
Broxburn E Loth . 122 B2
W Loth . . . 120 B3
Broxholme . . . 78 B2
Broxted . . . 42 B1
Broxton . . . 73 D8
Broxwood . . . 49 D5
Broyle Side . . . 17 C8
Brù . . . 155 C8
Bruairnis . . . 148 H2
Bruan . . . 158 G5
Bruar Lodge . . . 133 B5
Brucehill . . . 118 B3
Bruera . . . 73 C8
Bruern Abbey . . 38 B2
Bruichladdich . . 142 B3
Bruisyard . . . 57 C7
Brumby . . . 90 D2
Brund . . . 75 C8
Brundall . . . 69 D6
Brundish Street . 57 B6
Brundish . . . 57 C6
Brunery . . . 147 D10
Brunshaw . . . 93 F8
Brunswick
Village . . . 110 B5
Bruntcliffe . . . 88 B3
Bruntingthorpe . . 64 E3
Brunton Fife . . 128 B5
Northumb . . . 117 B8
Wilts . . . 25 D7
Brushford Devon . 10 A4
Som . . . 10 B4
Bruton . . . 23 F8
Bryanston . . . 13 D6
Bryant's Gill . . . 99 D6
Brydekirk . . . 107 B8
Bryher . . . 2 E3

Brymbo . . . 73 D6
Brympton . . . 12 C3
Bryn Carms . . 33 D6
Gtr Man . . . 86 D3
Neath . . . 34 E2
Shrops . . . 60 F2
Brynamman . . . 33 C8
Brynberian . . . 45 F3
Brynbryddan . . 34 E1
Brynbuga = Usk. . 35 D7
Bryncae . . . 34 F3
Bryncethin . . . 34 F3
Bryncir . . . 71 C5
Bryn-coch . . . 33 E8
Bryncroes . . . 70 D3
Bryncrug . . . 58 D3
Bryn Du . . . 82 D3
Bryneglwys . . . 72 E5
Brynford . . . 73 B5
Bryn Gates . . . 86 D3
Bryn Glas . . . 83 E8
Bryn Golau . . . 34 F3
Bryngwran . . . 82 D3
Bryngwyn Ceredig . 45 E4
Mon . . . 35 D7
Powys . . . 48 E3
Brynhenllan . . . 45 F2
Brynhoffnant . . 46 D2
Brynithel . . . 35 D6
Bryn-Iwan . . . 46 F2
Brynmawr . . . 35 C5
Bryn-mawr . . . 70 D3
Brynmenyn . . . 34 F3
Brynmill . . . 33 E7
Bryn-nantllech . . 72 C3
Bryn-penarth . . 59 D8
Brynrefail Anglesey . 82 C4
Gwyn . . . 83 E5
Bryn Rhyd-yr-
Arian . . . 72 C3
Brynsadler . . . 34 F4
Bryn Saith
Marchog . . . 72 D4
Brynsiencyn . . . 82 E4
Bryn Sion . . . 59 C5
Brynteg Anglesey . 82 C4
Ceredig . . . 46 E3
Bryn-y-gwenin . . 35 C7
Bryn-y-maen . . 83 D8
Bryn-yr-eryr . . . 70 C4
Buaile nam
Bodach . . . 148 H2
Bualintur . . . 149 F9
Buarthmeini . . . 72 F2
Bubbenhall . . . 51 B8
Bubwith . . . 96 F3
Buccleuch . . . 115 C6
Buchanhaven . . 153 D11
Buchanty . . . 127 B8
Buchlyvie . . . 126 E4
Buckabank . . . 108 E3
Buckden Cambs . 54 C2
N Yorks . . . 94 B2
Buckenham . . . 69 D6
Buckerell . . . 11 D6
Buckfast . . . 6 C5
Buckfastleigh . . 6 C5
Buckhaven . . . 129 E5
Buckholm . . . 121 F7
Buckholt . . . 36 C2
Buckhorn Weston . 13 B5
Buckhurst Hill . . 41 E7
Buckie . . . 152 B4
Buckies . . . 158 D3
Buckingham . . . 52 F4
Buckland Bucks . 40 C1
Devon . . . 6 E4
Glos . . . 51 F5
Hants . . . 14 E4
Herts . . . 54 F4
Kent . . . 31 E7
Oxon . . . 38 E3
Sur . . . 28 D3
Buckland Brewer . 9 B6
Buckland
Common . . . 40 D2
Buckland Dinham . 24 D2
Buckland Filleigh . 9 D6
Buckland in the
Moor . . . 6 B5
Buckland
Monachorum . . 6 C2
Buckland Newton . 12 D4
Buckland St Mary . 11 C7
Bucklebury . . . 26 B3
Bucklegate . . . 79 F6
Bucklerheads . . 134 F4
Bucklers Hard . . 14 E5
Bucklesham . . . 57 E6
Buckley = Bwcle . 73 C6
Bucklow Hill . . . 86 F5
Buckminster . . . 65 B5
Bucknall Lincs . 78 C4
Stoke . . . 75 E6
Bucknell Oxon . 39 B5
Shrops . . . 49 B5
Buckpool . . . 152 B4
Bucksburn . . . 141 D7
Buck's Cross . . . 8 B5
Bucks Green . . . 27 F8
Buckshaw Village . 86 B3
Bucks Horn Oak . 27 E6
Buckskin . . . 26 D4
Buck's Mills . . . 9 B5
Buckton E Yorks . 97 B7
Hereford . . . 49 B5
Northumb . . . 123 F6
Buckworth . . . 54 B2
Budbrooke . . . 51 C7
Buddby . . . 77 C6
Budleigh Salterton 11 F5
Budock Water . . 3 C6
Buerton . . . 74 E3
Buffer's Holt . . . 52 F4
Bugbrooke . . . 52 D4
Buglawton . . . 75 C5
Bugle . . . 4 D5
Bugley . . . 24 E3
Bugthorpe . . . 96 D3
Buildwas . . . 61 D6
Builth Road . . . 48 D2
Builth Wells =
Llanfair-ym-Muallt. 48 D2
Buirgh . . . 154 H5

Bulby . . . 65 B7
Bulcote . . . 77 E6
Buldoo . . . 157 C12
Bulford . . . 25 E6
Bulford Camp . . 25 E6
Bulkeley . . . 74 D2
Bulkington Warks . 63 F7
Wilts . . . 24 D4
Bulkworthy . . . 9 C5
Bullamoor . . . 102 E1
Bullbridge . . . 76 D3
Bullbrook . . . 27 C6
Bulley . . . 36 C4
Bullgill . . . 107 F7
Bull Hill . . . 14 E4
Bullington Hants . 26 E2
Lincs . . . 78 B3
Bull's Green . . . 41 C5
Bullwood . . . 145 F10
Bulmer Essex . . 56 E2
N Yorks . . . 96 C2
Bulmer Tye . . . 56 F2
Bulphan . . . 42 F2
Bulverhythe . . . 18 E4
Bulwark . . . 153 D9
Bulwell . . . 76 E5
Bulwick . . . 65 E6
Bumble's Green . 41 D7
Bun Abhainn
Eadarra . . . 154 G6
Bunacaimb . . . 147 C9
Bun a'Mhuilinn . 148 G2
Bunarkaig . . . 136 F4
Bunbury . . . 74 D2
Bunbury Heath . 74 D2
Bunchrew . . . 151 G9
Bundalloch . . . 149 F13
Buness . . . 160 C8
Bunessan . . . 146 J6
Bungay . . . 69 F6
Bunkers Hill . . . 38 C4
Bunker's Hill Lincs . 78 D5
Lincs . . . 79 D5
Bunloit . . . 137 B8
Bun Loyne . . . 136 D5
Bunnahabhain . 142 A5
Bunny . . . 64 B2
Buntait . . . 150 H6
Buntingford . . . 41 B6
Bunwell . . . 68 E4
Burbage Derbys . 75 B7
Leics . . . 63 E8
Wilts . . . 25 C7
Burchett's Green . 39 F8
Burcombe . . . 25 F5
Burcot . . . 39 E5
Burcott . . . 40 B1
Burdon . . . 111 D6
Bures . . . 56 F3
Bures Green . . . 56 F3
Burford Ches E . 74 D3
Oxon . . . 38 C2
Shrops . . . 49 C7
Burg . . . 146 G6
Burgar . . . 159 F4
Burgate Hants . 14 C2
Suff . . . 56 B4
Burgess Hill . . . 17 C7
Burgh . . . 57 D6
Burgh by Sands . 108 D3
Burgh Castle . . 69 D7
Burghclere . . . 26 C2
Burghead . . . 151 E14
Burghfield . . . 26 C4
Burghfield
Common . . . 26 C4
Burghfield Hill . . 26 C4
Burgh Heath . . 28 D3
Burghill . . . 49 E6
Burgh le Marsh . 79 C8
Burgh Muir . . . 141 B6
Burgh next
Aylsham . . . 81 E8
Burgh on Bain . 91 F6
Burgh St Margaret . 69 C7
Burgh St Peter . 69 E7
Burghwallis . . . 89 C6
Burham . . . 29 C8
Buriton . . . 15 B8
Burland . . . 74 D3
Burlawn . . . 4 B4
Burleigh . . . 27 C6
Burlescombe . . 11 C5
Burleston . . . 13 E5
Burley Hants . . 14 D3
Rutland . . . 65 C5
W Yorks . . . 95 F5
Burleydam . . . 74 E3
Burley Gate . . . 49 E7
Burley in
Wharfedale . . 94 E4
Burley Lodge . . 14 D3
Burley Street . . 14 D3
Burlingjobb . . . 48 D4
Burlow . . . 18 D2
Burlton . . . 60 B4
Burmarsh . . . 19 B7
Burmington . . . 51 F7
Burn . . . 89 B6
Burnaston . . . 76 F2
Burnbank . . . 119 D7
Burnby . . . 96 E4
Burncross . . . 88 E4
Burneside . . . 99 E7
Burness . . . 159 D7
Burneston . . . 101 F8
Burnett . . . 23 C8
Burnfoot Borders . 115 C7
Borders . . . 115 C8
E Ayrs . . . 112 D4
Perth . . . 127 D8
Burnham Bucks . 40 F2
N Lincs . . . 90 C4
Burnham
Deepdale . . . 80 C4
Burnham Green . 41 C5
Burnham Market . 80 C4
Burnham Norton . 80 C4
Burnham-on-
Crouch . . . 43 E5
Burnham-on-Sea . 22 E5
Burnham Overy
Staithe . . . 80 C4
Burnham Overy
Town . . . 80 C4
Burnham Thorpe . 80 C4
Burnhead
Dumfries . . . 113 E8
S Ayrs . . . 112 D2

Burnhervie......141 C6
Burnhill Green......61 D7
Burnhope......110 E4
Burnhouse......118 D3
Burniston......103 E8
Burnlee......88 D2
Burnley......93 F8
Burnley Lane......93 F8
Burnmouth......123 C5
Burn of Cambus......127 D6
Burnopfield......110 D4
Burnsall......94 C3
Burnside Angus......135 D5
  E Ayrs......113 C5
  Fife......128 D3
  Shetland......160 F4
  S Lanark......119 D3
  W Loth......120 B3
Burnside of
  Duntrune......134 F4
Burnswark......107 B8
Burntcommon......27 D8
Burnt Heath......76 B2
Burnthouse......3 C6
Burnt Houses......101 B6
Burntisland......128 F4
Burnton......112 D4
Burntwood......62 D4
Burnt Yates......95 C5
Burnwynd......120 C4
Burpham Sur......27 D8
  W Sus......16 D4
Burradon
  Northumb......117 D5
  T&W......111 B5
Burrafirth......160 B8
Burraland Shetland 160 F5
  Shetland......160 J4
Burras......3 C5
Burravoe Shetland 160 F7
  Shetland......160 G5
Burray Village......159 J5
Burrells......100 C1
Burrelton......134 F2
Burridge Devon......20 F4
  Hants......15 C6
Burrill......101 F7
Burringham......90 D2
Burrington Devon......9 C8
  Hereford......49 B6
  N Som......23 D6
Burrough Green......55 D7
Burrough on the
  Hill......64 C4
Burrow-bridge......11 B8
Burrowhill......27 C7
Burry......33 E5
Burry Green......33 E5
Burry Port
  =PorthTywyn......33 D5
Burscough......86 C2
Burscough Bridge......86 C2
Bursea......96 F4
Burshill......97 E6
Bursledon......15 D5
Burslem......75 E5
Burstall......56 E4
Burston Norf......68 F4
  Staffs......75 F6
Burstow......28 E4
Burstwick......91 B6
Burtersett......100 F3
Burtle......23 E5
Burton BCP......14 E2
  Ches W......73 B7
  Ches W......74 C2
  Lincs......78 B2
  Northumb......123 F7
  Pembs......44 E4
  Som......22 E3
  Wilts......24 B3
Burton Agnes......97 C7
Burton Bradstock......12 F2
Burton Dassett......51 D8
Burton Fleming......97 B6
Burton Green
  W Mid......51 B7
  Wrex......73 D7
Burton Hastings......63 E8
Burton-in-Kendal......92 B5
Burton in Lonsdale 93 B6
Burton Joyce......77 E6
Burton Latimer......53 B7
Burton Lazars......64 C4
Burton-le-Coggles 65 B6
Burton Leonard......95 C6
Burton on the
  Wolds......64 B2
Burton Overy......64 E3
Burton
  Pedwardine......78 E4
Burton Pidsea......97 F8
Burton Salmon......89 B5
Burton Stather......90 C2
Burton upon
  Stather......90 C2
Burton upon Trent..63 B6
Burtonwood......86 E3
Burwardsley......74 D2
Burwarton......61 F6
Burwash......18 C3
Burwash Common......18 C3
Burwash Weald......18 C3
Burwell Cambs......55 C6
  Lincs......79 B6
Burwen......82 B4
Burwick......159 K5
Bury Cambs......66 F2
  Gtr Man......87 C6
  Som......10 B4
  W Sus......16 C4
Bury Green......41 B7
Bury St Edmunds......56 C2
Burythorpe......96 C3
Busby......119 D5
Buscot......38 E2
Bush Bank......49 D6
Bushbury......62 D3
Bushby......64 D3
Bush Crathie......139 E8
Bushey......40 E4
Bushey Heath......40 E4
Bush Green......68 F5
Bushley......50 F3
Bushton......25 B5
Buslingthorpe......90 F4
Busta......160 G5
Butcher's Cross......18 C2

Butcombe......23 C7
Butetown......22 B3
Butleigh......23 F7
Butleigh Wootton......23 F7
Butler's Cross......39 D8
Butler's End......63 F6
Butlers Marston......51 E8
Butley......57 D7
Butley High
  Corner......57 E7
Butterburn......109 B6
Buttercrambe......96 C3
Butterknowle......101 B6
Butterleigh......10 D4
Buttermere Cumb......98 C3
  Wilts......25 C8
Buttershaw......88 B2
Butterstone......133 E7
Butterton......75 D7
Butterwick
  Durham......102 B1
  Lincs......79 E6
  N Yorks......96 B3
  N Yorks......97 B5
Butt Green......74 D3
Buttington......60 D2
Buttonoak......50 B2
Buttsash......14 D5
Butt's Green......14 B4
Buxhall......56 D4
Buxhall Fen Street......56 D4
Buxley......122 D4
Buxted......18 B8
Buxton Derbys......75 B7
  Norf......81 E8
Buxworth......87 F8
Bwcle =Buckley......73 C6
Bwlch......35 B5
Bwlchgwyn......73 D6
Bwlch-Llan......46 D4
Bwlchnewydd......32 B4
Bwlchtocyn......70 E4
Bwlch-y-cibau......59 C8
Bwlchyddar......59 B8
Bwlch-y-fadfa......46 E3
Bwlch-y-ffridd......59 E7
Bwlchgroes......45 F4
Bwlch-y-sarnau......48 B2
Byermoor......110 D4
Byers Green......110 F5
Byfield......52 D3
Byfleet......27 C8
Byford......49 E5
Bygrave......54 F3
Byker......111 C5
Bylchau......72 C3
Byley......74 C4
Bynea......33 E6
Byrness......116 D3
Bython......53 B8
Byton......49 C5
Byworth......16 B3

C

Cabharstadh......155 E8
Cablea......133 F6
Cabourne......90 D5
Cabrach Argyll......144 G3
  Moray......140 B2
Cabrich......151 G8
Cabus......92 E4
Cackle Street......17 B8
Cadbury......10 D4
Cadbury Barton......9 C8
Cadder......119 B6
Caddington......40 C3
Caddonfoot......121 F7
Cadeby Leics......63 D8
  S Yorks......89 D6
Cadeleigh......10 D4
Cade Street......18 C3
Cadgwith......3 E6
Cadham......128 D4
Cadishead......86 E5
Cadle......33 E7
Cadley Lancs......92 F5
  Wilts......25 C7
  Wilts......25 D7
Cadmore End......39 E7
Cadnam......14 C3
Cadney......90 D4
Cadole......73 C6
Cadoxton......22 C3
Cadoxton-Juxta-
  Neath......34 E1
Cadshaw......86 C5
Cadzow......119 D7
Caeathro......82 E4
Caehopkin......34 C2
Caenby......90 F4
Caenby Corner......90 F3
Caerau Bridgend......34 E2
  Cardiff......22 B3
Caér-bryn......33 C6
Caerdeon......58 C3
Caerdydd =Cardiff 22 B3
Caerfarchell......44 C2
Caerffili
  =Caerphilly......35 F5
Caerfyrddin
  =Carmarthen......33 B5
Caergeiliog......82 D3
Caergwrle......73 D7
Caergybi
  =Holyhead......82 C2
Caerleon......35 E7
Caer Llan......36 D1
Caerllion
  =Caerleon......35 E7
Caernarfon......82 E4
Caerphilly
  =Caerffili......35 F5
Caersws......59 E7
Caerwedros......46 D2
Caerwent......36 E1
Caerwych......71 D7
Caerwys......72 B5
Caethle......58 E3
Caim......37 C6
Caio......47 F5
Cairinis......148 B3
Cairisiadar......154 D5
Cairminis......154 J5
Cairnbaan......145 D7
Cairnbanno
  House......153 D8

Cairnborrow......152 D4
Cairnbrogie......141 B7
Cairnbulg Castle 153 B10
Cairncross Angus......134 B4
  Borders......122 C4
Cairndow......125 D7
Cairness......153 B10
Cairnfield House......152 B4
Cairngaan......104 F5
Cairngarroch......104 E4
Cairnhill......153 E6
Cairnie Aberds......141 D7
  Aberds......152 D4
Cairnorrie......153 D8
Cairnpark......141 C7
Cairnryan......104 C4
Cairnton......159 H4
Caister-on-Sea......90 D5
Caistor......90 D5
Caistor St Edmund......79 C7
Caistron......117 D5
Caitha Bowland......121 E7
Calais Street......56 F3
Calanais......154 D7
Calbost......155 F9
Calbourne......14 F5
Calceby......79 B6
Calcot Row......26 B4
Calcott......31 C5
Caldback......160 C8
Caldbeck......108 F3
Caldbergh......101 F5
Caldecote Cambs......54 D4
  Cambs......65 F8
  Herts......54 F3
  Northants......52 D4
Caldecott Northants 53 C7
  Oxon......38 E4
  Rutland......65 E5
Calderbank......119 C7
Calder Bridge......98 D2
Calderbrook......87 C7
Caldercruix......119 C8
Calder Hall......98 D2
Calder Mains......158 E2
Caldermill......119 E6
Calder Vale......92 E5
Calderwood......119 D6
Caldhame......134 E4
Caldicot......36 F1
Caldwell Derbys......63 C6
  N Yorks......101 C6
Caldy......85 F3
Caledrhydiau......46 D3
Calfsound......159 E6
Calgary......146 F6
Califer......151 F13
California Falk......120 B2
  Norf......69 C8
Calke......63 B7
Callakille......149 C11
Callaly......117 D6
Callander......126 D5
Callaughton......61 E6
Callestick......4 D2
Calligarry......149 H11
Callington......5 C8
Callow......49 F6
Callow End......50 E3
Callow Hill Wilts......37 B7
  Worcs......50 B2
Callows Grave......49 C7
Calmore......14 C4
Calmsden......37 D7
Calne......24 B5
Calow......76 B4
Calshot......15 D5
Calstock......6 C2
Calstone
  Wellington......24 C5
Calthorpe......81 D7
Calthwaite......108 E4
Calton N Yorks......94 D2
  Staffs......75 D8
Calveley......74 D2
Calver......76 B2
Calverhall......74 F3
Calver Hill......49 E5
Calverleigh......10 C4
Calverley......94 F5
Calvert......39 B6
Calverton M Keynes......53 F5
  Notts......77 E6
Calvine......133 C5
Calvo......107 D8
Cam......36 E4
Camas-luinie......149 F13
Camasnacroise......130 D2
Camastianavaig......149 E10
Camault Muir......151 G8
Camb......160 D7
Camber......19 D6
Camberley......27 C6
Camberwell......28 B4
Camblesforth......89 B7
Cambo......117 F6
Cambois......117 F9
Camborne......3 B5
Cambourne......55 D5
Cambridge Cambs......55 D5
  Glos......36 D4
Cambridge Town......43 F5
Cambus......127 E7
Cambusavie
  Farm......151 B10
Cambusbarron......127 E6
Cambuskenneth......127 E7
Cambuslang......119 C6
Cambusmore
  Lodge......151 B10
Camden......41 F5
Camelford......8 F3
Camelsdale......27 F6
Camerory......151 H13
Camer's Green......50 F2
Camerton Bath......24 D2
  Cumb......107 F7
  E Yorks......91 B6
Camghouran......132 D2
Cammachmore......141 E8
Cammeringham......90 F3
Camore......151 B10
Campbeltown......143 F8
Camperdown......111 B5
Camp Hill......63 E7
Campmuir......134 F2
Campsall......89 C6

Campsey Ash......57 D7
Campton......54 F2
Camptown......116 C2
Camrose......44 C4
Camserney......133 E5
Camster......158 F4
Camuschoirk......130 C1
Camuscross......149 G11
Camusnagaul
  Highld......130 B4
  Highld......150 C3
Camusrory......147 B11
Camusteel......149 D12
Camusterrach......149 D12
Camusvrachan......132 E3
Canada......14 C3
Canadia......18 D4
Canal Side......89 C7
Candacraig
  House......140 C2
Candlesby......79 C7
Candy Mill......120 E3
Cane End......26 B4
Canewdon......42 E4
Canford Bottom......13 D8
Canford Cliffs......13 F8
Canford Magna......13 E8
Canham's Green......56 C4
Canholes......75 B7
Canisbay......158 C5
Cann......13 B6
Cann Common......13 B6
Cannich......150 H6
Cannington......22 F4
Cannock......62 D3
Cannock Wood......62 C4
Canonbie......108 B3
Canon Bridge......49 E6
Canon Frome......49 E8
Canon Pyon......49 E6
Canons Ashby......52 D3
Canonstown......2 C4
Canterbury......30 D5
Cantley Norf......69 D6
  S Yorks......89 D7
Cantlop......60 D5
Canton......22 B3
Cantraybruich......151 G10
Cantraydoune......151 G10
Cantraywood......151 G10
Cantsfield......93 B6
Canvey Island......42 F3
Canwick......78 C2
Canworthy Water......8 E4
Caol......131 B5
Caolas......146 G3
Caolas Scalpaigh......154 H7
Caolas Stocinis......154 H6
Caol Ila......142 A5
Capel......28 E2
Capel Bangor......58 F3
Capel Betws
  Lleucu......46 D5
Capel Carmel......70 E2
Capel Coch......82 C4
Capel Curig......83 F7
Capel Cynon......46 E2
Capel Dewi Carms......3 B8
  Ceredig......46 E3
  Ceredig......58 F3
Capel Garmon......83 F8
Capel-gwyn......82 D3
Capel Gwyn......33 B5
Capel Gwynfe......33 B8
Capel Hendre......33 C6
Capel Hermon......71 E8
Capel Isaac......33 B6
Capel Iwan......45 F4
Capel le Ferne......31 F6
Capel Llanilltern......22 B2
Capel Mawr......82 D4
Capel St Andrew......57 E7
Capel St Mary......56 F4
Capel Seion......46 B5
Capel Tygwydd......45 E4
Capel Uchaf......70 C5
Capelulo......83 D7
Capel-y-graig......82 E5
Capenhurst......73 B7
Capernwray......92 B5
Capheaton......117 F6
Cappercleuch......115 B5
Capplegill......114 D4
Capton......7 D6
Caputh......133 F7
Carbis Bay......2 C4
Carbost Highld......149 D9
  Highld......149 E8
Carbrook......88 F4
Carbrooke......68 D2
Carburton......77 B6
Carcant......121 D6
Carcary......135 D6
Carclaze......4 D5
Carcroft......89 C6
Cardenden......128 E4
Cardeston......60 C3
Cardiff =Caerdydd 22 B3
Cardigan =Aberteifi 45 E3
Cardington Bedford......53 E8
  Shrops......60 E5
Cardinham......5 C6
Cardonald......118 C5
Cardow......152 D1
Cardrona......121 F6
Cardross......118 B3
Cardurnock......107 D8
Careby......65 C7
Careston Castle......135 D5
Carew......32 D1
Carew Cheriton......32 D1
Carew Newton......32 D1
Carey......49 F7
Carfrae......121 C8
Cargenbridge......107 B6
Cargill......134 F1
Cargo......108 D3
Cargreen......6 C2
Carham......122 F4
Carhampton......22 E2
Carharrack......3 C6
Carie Perth......132 D3
  Perth......132 F3
Carines......4 D2
Carisbrooke......15 F5
Carlabhagh......154 C7

Carland Cross......4 D3
Carlby......65 C7
Carlecotes......88 D2
Carlesmoor......94 B4
Carleton Cumb......99 B7
  Cumb......108 D4
  Lancs......92 F3
  N Yorks......94 E2
Carleton Forehoe......68 D3
Carleton Rode......68 E4
Carlingcott......23 D8
Carlin How......103 C5
Carlisle......108 D4
Carlops......120 D4
Carlton Bedford......53 D7
  Cambs......55 D7
  Leics......63 D7
  Notts......77 E6
  N Yorks......89 B7
  N Yorks......101 C6
  N Yorks......101 F5
  N Yorks......102 F4
  Stockton......102 B1
  Suff......57 C7
  S Yorks......88 C4
  W Yorks......88 B4
Carlton Colville......69 E8
Carlton Curlieu......64 E3
Carlton
  Husthwaite......95 B7
Carlton in
  Cleveland......102 D3
Carlton in Lindrick 89 F6
Carlton le
  Moorland......78 D2
Carlton Miniott......102 F1
Carlton on Trent......77 C7
Carlton Scroop......78 E2
Carluke......119 D8
Carmarthen
  =Caerfyrddin......33 B5
Carmel Anglesey......82 C3
  Carms......33 C6
  Flint......73 B5
  Guern......16
  Gwyn......82 F4
Carmont......141 F7
Carmunnock......119 D6
Carmyle......119 C6
Carmyllie......135 E5
Carnaby......97 C7
Carnach Highld......156 B3
  Highld......150 B3
  W Isles......154 H7
Carnachy......157 D10
Càrnais......154 D5
Carnbee......129 D7
Carnbo......128 D2
Carnbrea......3 B5
Carnduff......119 E6
Carnduncan......142 B3
Carne......3 C8
Carnforth......92 B4
Carn-gorm......136 B2
Carnhedryn......44 C3
Carnhell Green......2 C5
Carnkie Corn......3 C5
  Corn......3 C6
Carno......59 E6
Carnoch Highld......151 G10
  Highld......150 H6
Carnock......128 F2
Carnon Downs......3 B6
Carnousie......153 C6
Carnoustie......135 F5
Carnwath......120 E2
Carperby......101 F5
Carpley Green......100 F4
Carr......89 E6
Carradale......143 E9
Carragraich......154 H6
Carrefour
  Selous Jersey......17
Carreglefn......82 C3
Carreg-wen......45 E4
Carr Hill......111 C5
Carrick Argyll......145 E8
  Fife......129 B6
Carrick Castle......145 D10
Carrick House......159 E6
Carriden......128 F2
Carrington Gtr Man......86 E5
  Lincs......79 D6
  Midloth......121 C6
Carrog Conwy......71 C8
  Denb......72 E5
Carron Falk......127 F7
  Moray......152 D2
Carronbridge......113 E8
Carron Bridge......127 F6
Carronshore......127 F7
Carrshield......109 E8
Carrutherstown......107 B8
Carrville......111 E6
Carsaig Argyll......144 E6
  Argyll......147 J8
Carscreugh......105 D6
Carse Gray......134 D4
Carse House......144 G6
Carseriggan......105 C7
Carsethorn......107 D6
Carshalton......28 C3
Carsington......76 D2
Carskiey......143 H7
Carsluith......105 D8
Carsphairn......113 E5
Carstairs......120 E2
Carstairs
  Junction......120 E2
Carswell Marsh......38 E3
Carter's Clay......14 B4
Carterton......38 D2
Carterway Heads.110 D3
Carthew......4 D5
Cartington......117 D6
Cartland......119 E8
Cartmel......92 B3
Cartmel Fell......99 F6
Carway......33 D5
Cary Fitzpaine......12 B3
Cascob......48 C4
Cas-gwent
  =Chepstow......36 E2
Cashlie......132 E1
Cashmoor......13 C7

Casnewydd
  =Newport......35 F7
Cassey Compton......37 C7
Cassington......38 C4
Cassop......111 F6
Castell......72 C5
Castellau......34 F4
Castell-Howell......46 E3
Castell-Nedd
  =Neath......33 E8
Castell Newydd Emlyn
  =Newcastle
  Emlyn......46 E2
Castell-y-bwch......35 E6
Casterton......93 B6
Castle Acre......67 C8
Castle Ashby......53 D6
Castlebay
  =Bagh a Chaisteil......148 J1
Castle Bolton......101 E5
Castle Bromwich......62 F5
Castle Bytham......65 C6
Castlebythe......32 B1
Castle Caereinion......59 D8
Castle Camps......55 E7
Castle Carrock......108 D5
Castlecary......119 B7
Castle Cary......23 F8
Castle Combe......24 B3
Castlecraig......151 E11
Castle Donington......63 B8
Castle Douglas......106 C4
Castle Eaton......37 E8
Castle Eden......111 F7
Castlefairn......113 F7
Castle Forbes......140 C5
Castleford......88 B5
Castle Frome......49 E8
Castle Green......27 C7
Castle Gresley......63 C6
Castle Heaton......122 E5
Castle Hedingham.55 F8
Castlehill Borders......120 F5
  Highld......158 D3
  W Dunb......118 B3
Castle Hill......29 E7
Castle Huntly......128 B5
Castle Kennedy......104 D5
Castlemaddy......113 F5
Castlemartin......44 F4
Castlemilk
  Dumfries......107 B8
  Glasgow......119 D6
Castlemorris......44 B4
Castlemorton......50 F2
Castle O'er......115 E5
Castle
  Pulverbatch......60 D4
Castle Rising......67 B6
Castleside......110 E3
Castle Stuart......151 G10
Castlethorpe......53 E6
Castleton Angus......134 E3
  Argyll......145 E7
  Derbys......88 F2
  Gtr Man......87 C6
  Newport......35 F6
  N Yorks......102 D4
Castletown Ches W......73 D8
  Highld......151 G10
  Highld......158 D3
  IoM......84 F2
  T&W......111 D6
Castleweary......115 D7
Castley......95 E5
Caston......68 E2
Castor......65 E8
Catacol......143 D10
Catbrain......36 F2
Catbrook......36 D2
Catchall......2 D3
Catchems Corner......51 B7
Catchgate......110 D4
Catcleugh......116 D3
Catcliffe......88 F5
Catcott......23 F5
Caterham......28 D4
Catfield......69 B6
Catford......28 B4
Catforth......92 F4
Cathays......22 B3
Cathcart......119 C5
Cathedine......35 B5
Catherington......15 C7
Catherton......49 B8
Catlodge......138 E2
Catlowdy......108 B4
Catmore......38 F4
Caton......92 C5
Caton Green......92 C5
Catrine......113 B5
Cat's Ash......35 E7
Catsfield......18 D4
Catshill......50 B4
Cattal......95 D7
Cattawade......56 F5
Catterall......92 E4
Catterick......101 E7
Catterick Bridge......101 E7
Catterick
  Garrison......101 E6
Catterlen......108 F4
Catterline......135 B8
Catterton......95 E8
Cattistock......12 E4
Catton Northumb......109 D8
  N Yorks......95 B6
Catwick......97 E7
Catworth......53 B8
Caudlesprings......68 D2
Caulcott......39 B5
Cauldcots......135 E6
Cauldhame......126 E5
Cauldmill......115 C8
Cauldon......75 E7
Caulkerbush......107 D6
Caulside......115 F7
Caunsall......62 F2
Caunton......77 D7
Causeway End......105 C8
Causewayhead
  Cumb......107 D8
  Stirling......127 E6
Causeyend......141 C8

Causey Park
  Bridge......117 E7
Cautley......100 F1
Cavendish......56 E2
Cavendish Bridge......63 B8
Cavenham......55 C8
Caversfield......39 B5
Caversham......26 B5
Caverswall......75 E6
Cavil......96 F3
Cawdor......151 F11
Cawkwell......79 B5
Cawood......95 F8
Cawsand......6 D2
Cawston......81 E7
Cawthorne......88 D3
Cawthorpe......65 B7
Cawton......96 B2
Caxton......54 D4
Caynham......49 B7
Caythorpe Lincs......78 E2
  Notts......77 E6
Cayton......103 F8
Ceann a Bhaigh......148 B2
Ceann a Deas Loch
  Baghasdail......148 G2
Ceann Shiphoirt......155 F7
Ceann
  Tarabhaigh......154 F7
Cearsiadair......155 E8
Ceann Berain......72 C3
Cefn-brith......72 D3
Cefn Canol......73 F6
Cefn-coch......83 E8
Cefn Coch......59 B8
Cefn-coed-y-
  cymmer......34 D4
Cefn-ddwysarn......72 F3
Cefn Einion......60 F2
Cefneithin......33 C6
Cefn-gorwydd......47 E8
Cefn-mawr......73 E6
Cefn-y-bedd......73 D7
Cefn-y-pant......32 B2
Cei-bach......46 D3
Ceinewydd
  =New Quay......46 D2
Ceint......82 D4
Cellan......46 E5
Cellarhead......75 E6
Cemaes......82 B3
Cemmaes......58 D5
Cemmaes Road......58 D5
Cenarth......45 E4
Cenin......71 C5
Central......118 B2
Ceos......155 E8
Ceres......129 C6
Cerne Abbas......12 D4
Cerney Wick......37 E7
Cerrigceinwen......82 D4
Cerrigydrudion......72 E3
Cessford......116 B3
Ceunant......82 E5
Chaceley......50 F3
Chacewater......3 B6
Chackmore......52 F4
Chacombe......52 E2
Chadderton......87 D7
Chadderton Fold......87 D6
Chaddesden......76 F3
Chaddesley
  Corbett......50 B3
Chaddleworth......26 B2
Chadlington......38 B3
Chadshunt......51 D8
Chad Valley......62 F4
Chadwell......64 B4
Chadwell End......53 B8
Chadwell St Mary......29 B7
Chadwick End......51 B7
Chadwick Green......86 E3
Chaffcombe......11 C8
Chagford......10 F2
Chailey......17 C7
Chain Bridge......79 E6
Chainhurst......29 E8
Chalbury......13 D8
Chalbury Common 13 D8
Chaldon......28 D4
Chaldon Herring......13 F5
Chale......15 G5
Chale Green......15 G5
Chalfont Common......40 E3
Chalfont St Giles......40 E2
Chalfont St Peter......40 E3
Chalford......37 D5
Chalgrove......39 E6
Chalk......29 B7
Challacombe......21 E5
Challoch......105 C7
Challock......30 D4
Chalton C Beds......40 B3
  Hants......15 C8
Chalvington......18 E2
Chancery......46 B4
Chandler's Ford......14 B5
Channel Tunnel......19 B8
Channerwick......160 L6
Chantry Som......24 E2
  Suff......56 E5
Chapel......128 E4
Chapel Allerton
  Som......23 D6
  W Yorks......95 F6
Chapel Amble......4 B4
Chapel Brampton......52 C5
Chapel Chorlton......74 F5
Chapel End......63 E7
Chapel-en-le-
  Frith......87 F8
Chapel Green
  Warks......52 C2
  Warks......63 F6
Chapel Haddlesey.89 B6
Chapel Head......66 F3
Chapelhill
  Dumfries......114 E3
  Highld......151 D11
  N Ayrs......118 E2
  Perth......128 B3
  Perth......133 F7

Chapel Hill
  Aberds......153 E10
  Lincs......78 D5
  Mon......36 E2
  N Yorks......95 E6
Chapelknowe......108 B3
Chapel Lawn......48 B5
Chapel-le-Dale......93 B7
Chapel Milton......87 F8
Chapel of
  Garioch......141 B6
Chapel Row......26 C3
Chapel St
  Leonards......79 B8
Chapel Stile......99 D5
Chapelton Angus......135 E6
  Devon......9 B7
  Highld......138 C5
  S Lanark......119 E6
Chapeltown
  Blackburn......86 C5
  Moray......139 B8
  S Yorks......88 E4
Chapmanslade......24 E3
Chapmans Well......9 E5
Chapmore End......41 C6
Chappel......42 B4
Chard......11 D8
Chardstock......11 D8
Charfield......36 E4
Charford......50 C4
Charing......30 E3
Charing Cross......14 C2
Charing Heath......30 E3
Charingworth......51 F7
Charlbury......38 C3
Charlcombe......24 C2
Charlecote......51 D7
Charles......21 F5
Charlesfield......107 C8
Charleston Angus.134 E3
  Renfs......118 C4
Charlestown
  Aberdeen......141 D8
  Corn......4 D5
  Derbys......87 E8
  Dorset......12 G4
  Gtr Man......87 D6
  Highld......149 A13
  Highld......151 G9
  W Yorks......87 B7
Charlestown of
  Aberlour......152 D2
Charles Tye......56 D4
Charlesworth......87 E8
Charleton......7 E5
Charlton Hants......25 E8
  Herts......40 B4
  London......28 B5
  Northants......52 F3
  Northumb......116 F4
  Som......23 D8
  Telford......61 C5
  Wilts......13 B7
  Wilts......25 D6
  Worcs......50 E5
  W Sus......16 C2
Charlton Abbots......37 B7
Charlton Adam......12 B3
Charlton-All-
  Saints......14 B2
Charlton Down......12 E4
Charlton
  Horethorne......12 B4
Charlton Kings......37 B6
Charlton
  Mackerell......12 B3
Charlton Marshall 13 D6
Charlton
  Musgrove......12 B5
Charlton on
  Otmoor......39 C5
Charltons......102 C4
Charlwood......28 E3
Charlynch......22 F4
Charminster......12 E4
Charmouth......11 E8
Charndon......39 B6
Charney Bassett......38 E3
Charnock Richard......86 C3
Charsfield......57 D6
Chart Corner......29 D8
Charter Alley......26 D3
Charterhouse......23 D6
Charterville
  Allotments......38 C3
Chartham......30 D5
Chartham Hatch......30 D5
Chartridge......40 D2
Chart Sutton......30 E2
Charvil......27 B5
Charwelton......52 D3
Chasetown......62 D4
Chastleton......38 B2
Chasty......8 D5
Chatburn......93 E7
Chatcull......74 F4
Chatham......29 C8
Chathill......117 B7
Chattenden......29 B8
Chatteris......66 F3
Chattisham......56 E4
Chatto......116 C3
Chatton......117 B6
Chawleigh......10 C2
Chawley......38 D4
Chawston......54 D2
Chawton......26 F5
Cheadle Gtr Man......87 F6
  Staffs......75 E7
Cheadle Heath......87 F6
Cheadle Hulme......87 F6
Cheam......28 C3
Cheapside......27 C8
Chearsley......39 C7
Chebsey......62 B2
Checkendon......39 F6
Checkley Ches E......74 E4
  Hereford......49 F7
  Staffs......75 F7
Chedburgh......55 D8
Cheddar......23 D6
Cheddington......40 C2
Cheddleton......75 D6
Cheddon Fitzpaine 11 B7
Chedglow......37 E6
Chedgrave......69 E6

Chedington......12 D2
Chediston......57 B7
Chedworth......37 C7
Chedzoy......22 F5
Cheeklaw......122 D3
Cheeseman's
  Green......19 B7
Cheglinch......20 E4
Cheldon......10 C2
Chelford......74 B5
Chellaston......76 F3
Chell Heath......75 D5
Chellington......53 D7
Chelmarsh......61 F7
Chelmer Village......42 D3
Chelmondiston......57 F6
Chelmorton......75 C8
Chelmsford......42 D3
Chelsea......28 B3
Chelsfield......29 C5
Chelsworth......56 E3
Cheltenham......37 B6
Chelveston......53 C7
Chelvey......23 C6
Chelwood......23 C8
Chelwood
  Common......17 B8
Chelwood Gate......17 B8
Chelworth......37 E6
Chelworth Green......37 E7
Chemistry......74 E2
Chenies......40 E3
Cheny Longville......60 F4
Chepstow
  =Cas-gwent......36 E2
Chequerfield......89 B5
Cherhill......24 B5
Cherington Glos......37 E6
  Warks......51 F7
Cheriton Devon......21 E6
  Hants......15 B6
  Kent......19 B8
  Swansea......33 E5
Cheriton Bishop......10 E2
Cheriton Fitzpaine 10 D3
Cheriton or Stackpole
  Elidor......44 F4
Cherrington......61 B6
Cherry Burton......97 E5
Cherry Hinton......55 D5
Cherry Orchard......50 D3
Cherry Willingham 78 B3
Chertsey......27 C8
Cheselbourne......13 E5
Chesham......40 D2
Chesham Bois......40 E2
Cheshunt......41 D6
Cheslyn Hay......62 D3
Chessington......28 C2
Chester......73 C8
Chesterblade......23 E8
Chesterfield......76 B3
Chester-le-
  Street......111 D5
Chester Moor......111 E5
Chesters Borders......116 B2
  Borders......116 C2
Chesterton Cambs......55 C5
  Cambs......65 E8
  Glos......37 D7
  Oxon......39 B5
  Shrops......61 E7
  Staffs......74 E5
  Warks......51 D8
Chesterwood......109 C8
Chestfield......30 C5
Cheston......6 D4
Cheswardine......61 B7
Cheswick......123 E6
Chetnole......12 D4
Chettiscombe......10 C4
Chettisham......66 F5
Chettle......13 C7
Chetton......61 E6
Chetwode......39 B6
Chetwynd Aston......61 C7
Cheveley......55 C7
Chevening......29 D5
Chevington......55 D8
Chevithorne......10 C4
Chew Magna......23 C7
Chew Stoke......23 C7
Chewton
  Keynsham......23 C8
Chewton Mendip......23 D7
Chicheley......53 E7
Chichester......16 D2
Chickerell......12 F4
Chicklade......24 F4
Chicksgrove......24 F4
Chidden......15 C7
Chiddingfold......27 F7
Chiddingly......18 D2
Chiddingstone......29 E5
Chiddingstone
  Causeway......29 E6
Chiddingstone
  Hoath......29 E5
Chideock......12 E2
Chidham......15 D8
Chidswell......88 B3
Chieveley......26 B2
Chignall St James......42 D2
Chignall Smealy......42 C2
Chigwell......41 E7
Chigwell Row......41 E7
Chilbolton......25 F8
Chilcomb......15 B6
Chilcombe......12 E3
Chilcompton......23 D8
Chilcote......63 C6
Childer Thornton......73 B7
Child Okeford......13 C6
Childrey......38 F3
Child's Ercall......61 B6
Childswickham......51 F5
Childwall......86 F2
Childwick Green......40 C4
Chilfrome......12 E3
Chilgrove......16 C2
Chilham......30 D4
Chilhampton......25 F5
Chilla......9 D6
Chillaton......9 F6
Chillenden......31 D6

218 Chi–Cra

Chillerton 15 F5
Chillesford 57 D7
Chillingham 117 B6
Chillington Devon . . . 7 E5
  Som 11 C8
Chilmark 24 F4
Chilson 38 C3
Chilsworthy Corn. . . . 6 B2
  Devon 8 D5
Chilthorne Domer . 12 C3
Chiltington 17 C7
Chilton Bucks 39 C6
  Durham 101 B7
  Oxon 38 F4
Chilton Cantelo . . 12 B3
Chilton Foliat 25 B8
Chilton Lane 111 F6
Chilton Polden . . . 23 F5
Chilton Street . . . 55 E8
Chilton Trinity . . . 22 F4
Chilvers Coton . . . 63 E7
Chilwell 76 F2
Chilworth Hants. . . 14 C5
  Sur. 27 E8
Chimney 38 D3
Chineham 26 D4
Chingford 41 E6
Chinley 87 F8
Chinley Head. . . . 87 F8
Chinnor 39 D7
Chipnall 74 F4
Chippenhall Green 57 B6
Chippenham Cambs 55 C7
  Wilts 24 B4
Chipperfield 40 D3
Chipping Herts. . . . 54 F4
  Lancs. 93 E6
Chipping Campden 51 F6
Chipping Hill 42 C4
Chipping Norton . . 38 B3
Chipping Ongar . . 42 D1
Chipping Sodbury . 36 F4
Chipping Warden . 52 E2
Chipstable 10 B5
Chipstead Kent. . . 29 D5
  Sur. 28 D3
Chirbury 60 E2
Chirk = Y Waun . . 73 F6
Chirk Bank 73 F6
Chirmorrie 105 B6
Chirnside 122 D4
Chirnsidebridge. . 122 D4
Chirton 25 D5
Chisbury 25 C7
Chiselborough . . . 12 C2
Chiseldon 25 B6
Chiserley 87 B8
Chislehampton. . . 39 E5
Chislehurst 28 B5
Chislet. 31 C6
Chiswell Green . . . 40 D4
Chiswick 28 B3
Chiswick End 54 E4
Chisworth 87 E7
Chithurst 16 B2
Chittering 55 B5
Chitterne 24 E4
Chittlehamholt . . . 9 B8
Chittlehampton . . 9 B8
Chittoe 24 C4
Chivenor 20 F4
Chobham 27 C7
Choicelee 122 D4
Cholderton 25 E7
Cholesbury 40 D2
Chollerford 110 B2
Chollerton 110 B2
Cholmondeston . . 74 C3
Cholsey 39 F5
Cholstrey 49 D6
Chop Gate 102 E3
Choppington 117 F8
Chopwell 110 D4
Chorley Ches E . . . 74 D2
  Lancs. 86 C3
  Shrops. 61 F6
  Staffs. 62 C4
Chorleywood 40 E3
Chorlton cum
  Hardy 87 E6
Chorlton Lane . . . 73 E8
Choulton 60 F3
Chowdene 111 D5
Chowley 73 D8
Chrishall. 54 F5
Christchurch BCP . 14 E2
  Cambs 66 E4
  Glos. 36 C2
  Newport 35 F7
Christian Malford . 24 B4
Christleton. 73 C8
Christmas
  Common 39 E7
Christon 23 D5
Christon Bank . . . 117 B8
Christow. 10 F3
Chryston 119 B6
Chudleigh 7 B6
Chudleigh Knighton 7 B6
Chulmleigh 9 C8
Chunal. 87 E8
Church 86 B5
Churcham 36 C4
Church Aston . . . 61 C7
Churchbank 48 B4
Church Brampton . 52 C5
Churchbridge . . . 62 D3
Church Broughton 76 F2
Church Crookham . 27 D6
Churchdown 37 C5
Church Eaton . . . 62 C2
Churchend Essex . 42 B2
  Essex. 43 E6
  S Glos. 36 E4
Church End Cambs . 66 D3
  Cambs. 66 F2
  C Beds 40 B2
  C Beds. 53 F7
  C Beds. 54 F2
  Essex. 42 B3
  Essex. 55 E6
  E Yorks. 97 D6
  Hants. 26 D4
  Lincs 78 F5
  Warks 63 E6
  Warks 63 E6

Church End continued
  Wilts 24 B5
Church Enstone . . 38 B3
Church Fenton . . . 95 F8
Churchfield 62 E4
Churchgate Street. 41 C7
Church Green
  Devon 11 E6
  Norf. 68 E3
Church Gresley . . . 63 C6
Church
  Hanborough . . . 38 C4
Church Hill 74 C3
Church Houses . . . 102 E4
Church
  Knowle 20 E4
  N Som 23 D6
  Oxon 38 B2
  Worcs 50 B3
  Worcs 50 D4
Churchinford. . . . 11 C7
Church Knowle . . . 13 F7
Church Laneham . . 77 B8
Church Langton . . 64 E4
Church Lawford . . 52 B2
Church Lawton . . . 74 D5
Church Leigh 75 F7
Church Lench 50 D5
Church Mayfield. . 75 E7
Church Minshull . . 74 C3
Church Norton . . . 16 E2
Churchover 64 F2
Church Preen 60 E5
Church
  Pulverbatch . . . 60 D4
Churchstanton . . . 11 C6
Church Stoke 60 E2
Churchstow 6 E5
Church Stowe 52 D4
Church Street 29 B8
Church Stretton . . 60 E4
Churchtown Derbys 76 C2
  IoM 84 C4
  Lancs. 92 E4
  Mers 85 C4
Church Town
  N Lincs 89 D8
  Sur. 28 D4
Church Village. . . 34 F4
Church Warsop. . . 77 C5
Churnsike Lodge . 109 B6
Churston Ferrers . . 7 D7
Churton. 73 D8
Churwell. 88 B3
Chute Standen . . . 25 D8
Chwilog. 70 D5
Chyandour 2 C3
Cilan Uchaf 70 E3
Cilcain 73 C5
Cilcennin 46 C4
Cilfor 71 D7
Cilfrew 34 D1
Cilfynydd 34 E4
Cilgerran 45 E3
Cilgwyn Carms . . . 33 B8
  Gwyn 82 F4
  Pembs 45 F2
Ciliau Aeron. . . . 46 D3
Cill Donnain 148 F2
Cille Bhrighde. . . 148 G2
Cille Pheadair . . . 148 G2
Cilmery 48 D2
Cilsan 33 B6
Ciltalgarth 72 E2
Cilwendeg 45 F4
Cilybebyll 33 D8
Cilycwm 47 F6
Cimla 34 E1
Cinderford 36 C3
Cippyn 45 E3
Circebost 154 D6
Cirencester 37 D7
Ciribhig 154 C6
City London 41 F6
  Powys 60 F2
City Dulas 82 C4
Clachaig 145 E10
Clachan Argyll. . . 124 D3
  Argyll. 125 D7
  Argyll. 130 E2
  Argyll. 144 H6
  Highld 149 E10
  W Isles 148 D2
Clachaneasy 105 B7
Clachanmore . . . 104 E4
Clachan na Luib . . 148 B3
Clachan of
  Campsie. 119 B6
Clachan of
  Glendaruel . . . 145 E8
Clachan-Seil 124 D3
Clachan Strachur . 125 E6
Clachbreck 144 F6
Clachnabrain 134 C3
Clachtoll 156 G3
Clackmannan 127 E8
Clacton-on-Sea. . . 43 C7
Cladach
  Chireboist 148 B2
Claddach-
  knockline. 148 B2
Cladich 125 C6
Claggan Highld. . . 131 B5
  Highld 147 G9
Claigan 148 C7
Claines 50 D3
Clandown 23 D8
Clanfield Hants. . . 15 C7
  Oxon 38 D2
Clanville 25 E8
Claonaig. 145 H7
Claonel 157 J8
Clapgate Dorset. . 13 D8
  Herts. 41 B7
Clapham Bedford . 53 D8
  London. 28 B3
  N Yorks. 93 C7
  W Sus 16 D4
Clap Hill 19 B7
Clappers. 122 D5
Clappersgate . . . 99 D5
Clapton 12 D2
Clapton-in-
  Gordano. 23 B6
Clapton-on-the-
  Hill. 38 C1
Clapworthy 9 B8
Clarach 58 F3

Clara Vale 110 C4
Clarbeston 32 B1
Clarbeston Road . . 32 B1
Clarborough 89 F8
Clare 55 E8
Clarebrand 106 C4
Clarencefield 107 C7
Clarilaw 115 C8
Clark's Green 28 F2
Clarkston 119 D5
Clashandorran . . . 151 G8
Clashcoig 151 B9
Clashindarroch . . 152 E4
Clashmore
  Highld 151 C10
  Highld 156 F3
Clashnessie 156 F3
Clashnoir 139 B8
Clate 160 G7
Clathy 127 C8
Clatt 140 B4
Clatter 59 E6
Clatterford 15 F5
Clatterin Bridge . . 135 B6
Clatworthy 22 F2
Claughton Lancs . . 92 E5
  Lancs. 93 C5
  Mers 85 F4
Claverdon 51 C6
Claverham 23 C6
Clavering 55 F5
Claverley 61 E7
Claverton 24 C2
Clawdd-newydd . . 72 D4
Clawthorpe 92 B5
Clawton 9 E5
Claxby Lincs. 79 B7
  Lincs. 90 E5
Claxton Norf 69 D6
  N Yorks. 96 C2
Claybokie. 139 E6
Claybrooke Magna 63 F8
Claybrooke Parva . 63 F8
Clay Common . . . 69 F7
Clay Coton 52 B3
Clay Cross 76 C3
Claydon Oxon . . . 52 D2
  Suff 56 D5
Claygate Dumfries . 108 B3
  Kent. 29 E8
  Sur. 28 C2
Claygate Cross . . . 29 D7
Clayhanger Devon . 10 B5
  W Mid 62 D4
Clayhidon. 11 C6
Clayhill E Sus. . . . 18 C5
  Hants. 14 D4
Clay Hill 26 B3
Clay Lake 66 B2
Clayock 158 E3
Claypole 77 E8
Clayton Staffs . . . 75 E5
  S Yorks. 89 D5
  W Sus 17 C6
  W Yorks. 94 F4
Clayton Green . . . 86 B3
Clayton-le-Moors . 93 F7
Clayton-le-Woods 86 B3
Clayton West 88 C3
Clayworth. 89 F8
Cleadale 146 C7
Cleadon 111 C6
Clearbrook 6 C3
Clearwell. 36 D2
Cleasby 101 C7
Cleat 159 K5
Cleatlam. 101 C6
Cleator 98 C2
Cleator Moor. . . . 98 C2
Clebrig 157 F8
Cleckheaton 88 B2
Cleedownton 61 F5
Cleehill 49 B7
Clee St Margaret . 61 F5
Cleethorpes 91 D7
Cleeton St Mary . . 49 B8
Cleeve 23 C6
Cleeve Hill 37 B6
Cleeve Prior 51 E5
Clegyrnant 59 D6
Clehonger 49 F6
Cleish 128 E2
Cleland. 119 D8
Clench Common . . 25 C6
Clenchwarton . . . 67 B5
Clent 50 B4
Cleobury
  Mortimer 49 B8
Cleobury North. . . 61 F6
Cleongart 143 E7
Clephanton 151 F11
Clerklands 115 B8
Clestrain 159 H4
Cleuch Head 115 C8
Cleughbrae 107 B7
Clevancy 25 B5
Clevedon 23 B6
Cleveley. 38 B3
Cleveleys 92 E3
Cleverton 37 F6
Clevis 21 B7
Clewer 23 D6
Cley next the Sea . 81 C6
Cliaid 148 H1
Cliasmol 154 G5
Cliburn 99 B7
Click Mill 159 F4
Cliddesden 26 E4
Cliffburn 135 E6
Cliffe Medway . . . 29 B8
  N Yorks. 96 F2
Cliff End 19 D5
Cliffe Woods 29 B8
Clifford Hereford . 48 E4
  W Yorks. 95 E7
Clifford Chambers 51 D6
Clifford's Mesne. . 36 C4
Cliffsend. 31 C7
Clifton Bristol . . . 23 B7
  C Beds 54 F2
  Cumb. 99 B7
  Derbys. 75 E8
  Lancs. 92 F4
  Northumb 117 F8
  Nottingham . . . 77 F5
  N Yorks. 94 E4
  Oxon 52 F2
  Stirling 131 F7

Clifton continued
  S Yorks. 89 E6
  Worcs 50 E4
  York 95 D8
Clifton Campville . 63 C6
Cliftoncote. 116 B4
Clifton Green. . . . 87 D5
Clifton Hampden . 39 E5
Clifton Reynes . . . 53 D7
Clifton upon
  Dunsmore 52 B3
Clifton upon Teme . 50 D2
Cliftonville 31 B7
Climaen gwyn. . . 33 D8
Climping. 16 D4
Climpy 120 D2
Clink. 24 E2
Clint 95 D5
Clint Green 68 C3
Clintmains 122 F2
Cliobh 154 D5
Clippesby 69 C7
Clipsham 65 C6
Clipston 64 F4
Clipstone 77 C5
Clitheroe 93 E7
Cliuthar 154 H6
Clive 60 B5
Clivocast 160 C8
Clixby 90 D5
Clocaenog 72 D4
Clochan. 152 B4
Clock Face 86 E3
Clockmill 122 D3
Cloddiau 60 D2
Clodock 35 B7
Clola. 153 D10
Clophill 53 F8
Clopton Northants . 65 F7
  Suff 57 D6
Clopton Corner . . 57 D6
Clopton Green . . . 55 D8
Closeburn 113 E8
Close Clark 84 E2
Closworth 12 C3
Clothall 54 F3
Clotton 74 C2
Clough Foot 87 B7
Cloughton 103 E8
Cloughton
  Newlands. 103 E8
Clousta 160 H5
Clouston 159 G3
Clova Aberds 140 B3
  Angus 134 B3
Clovelly 8 B5
Clove Lodge 100 C4
Clovenfords 121 F7
Clovenstone 141 C6
Clovullin 130 C4
Clow Bridge. 87 B6
Clowne 76 B4
Clows Top 50 B2
Cloy 73 E7
Cluanie Inn 136 C3
Cluanie Lodge. . . 136 C3
Clun 60 F3
Clunbury. 60 F3
Clunderwen 32 C2
Clune 138 B3
Clunes 136 F5
Clungunford 49 B5
Clunie Aberds . . . 153 C6
  Perth 133 E8
Clunton 60 F3
Cluny 128 E4
Cluny Castle 138 E2
Clutton Bath 23 D8
  Ches W. 73 D8
Clwt-grugoer 72 C3
Clwt-y-bont 83 E5
Clydach Mon. . . . 35 C6
  Swansea 33 D7
Clydach Vale 34 E3
Clydebank 118 B4
Clydey 45 F4
Clyffe Pypard. . . . 25 B5
Clynder 145 E11
Clyne 34 D2
Clynelish. 157 J11
Clynnog-fawr. . . . 82 F4
Clyro 48 E4
Clyst Honiton . . . 10 E4
Clyst Hydon 10 D5
Clyst St George. . . 10 F4
Clyst St Lawrence . 10 D5
Clyst St Mary . . . 10 E4
Cnoc Amhlaigh. . . 155 D10
Cnwch-coch 47 B5
Coachford. 152 D4
Coad's Green 5 B7
Coal Aston 76 B3
Coalbrookdale . . . 61 D6
Coalbrookvale. . . 35 D5
Coalburn 119 F8
Coalburns 110 C4
Coalcleugh 109 E8
Coaley 36 D4
Coalhall 112 C4
Coalhill 42 E3
Coalpit Heath . . . 36 F3
Coalport 61 D6
Coalsnaughton . . 127 E8
Coaltown of
  Balgonie 128 E4
Coaltown of
  Wemyss 128 E5
Coalville 63 C8
Coalway 36 C2
Coat 12 B2
Coatbridge. 119 C7
Coatdyke 119 C7
Coate Swindon . . . 38 F1
  Wilts 24 C5
Coates Cambs . . . 66 E3
  Glos. 37 D6
  Lancs. 93 E8
  Notts 90 F2
  W Sus 16 C3
Coatham 102 B3
Coatham
  Mundeville . . . 101 B7
Coatsgate 114 D3
Cobbaton 9 B7
Cobbler's Green . . 69 E5
Coberley 37 C6
Cobham Kent 29 C7
  Sur. 28 C2
Cobholm Island . . 69 D8

Cobleland. 126 E4
Cobnash 49 C6
Coburty 153 B9
Cockayne 102 E4
Cock Bank 73 E7
Cock Bridge. 139 D8
Cockburnspath. . . 122 B3
Cock Clarks 42 D4
Cockenzie and Port
  Seton 121 B7
Cockerham 92 D4
Cockermouth . . . 107 F8
Cockernhoe Green 40 B4
Cockfield Durham . 101 B6
  Suff. 56 D3
Cockfosters 41 E5
Cocking 16 C2
Cockington 7 C6
Cocklake 23 E6
Cockley Beck 98 D4
Cockley Cley 67 D7
Cockshutt. 60 B4
Cockthorpe 81 C5
Cockwood 10 F4
Cockyard 49 F6
Codda 5 B6
Coddenham. 56 D5
Coddington
  Ches W. 73 D8
  Hereford 50 E2
  Notts 77 D8
Codford St Mary . . 24 F4
Codford St Peter . . 24 F4
Codicote 41 C5
Codmore Hill . . . 16 B4
Codnor 76 E4
Codrington 24 B2
Codsall 62 D2
Codsall Wood . . . 62 D2
Coed Duon
  = Blackwood. . . 35 E5
Coedely 34 F4
Coedkernew 35 F6
Coed Mawr 83 D5
Coed Morgan . . . 35 C7
Coedpoeth 73 D6
Coed-Talon 73 D6
Coedway 60 C3
Coed-y-bryn 46 E2
Coed-y-paen 35 E7
Coed-yr-ynys . . . 35 B5
Coed Ystumgwern . 71 E6
Coelbren. 34 C2
Coffinswell 7 C6
Cofton Hackett . . 50 B5
Cogan 22 B3
Cogenhoe. 53 C6
Cogges 38 D3
Coggeshall 42 B4
Coggeshall Hamlet 42 B4
Coggins Mill 18 C2
Coignafearn
  Lodge 138 C2
Coig
  Peighinnean. . . 155 A10
Coig Peighinnean
  Bhuirgh 155 B9
Coilacriech 140 E2
Coilantogle 126 D4
Coilleag 148 G2
Coillore 149 E8
Coity 34 F3
Colaboll 157 H8
Colan 4 C3
Colaton Raleigh . . 11 F5
Colbost. 148 D7
Colburn 101 E6
Colby Cumb. 100 B1
  IoM 84 E2
  Norf. 81 D8
Colchester 43 B6
Colcot 22 C3
Cold Ash 26 C3
Cold Ashby 52 B4
Cold Ashton 24 B2
Cold Aston 37 C8
Coldbackie 157 D9
Coldbeck 100 D2
Coldblow 29 B6
Cold Blow. 32 C2
Cold Brayfield . . . 53 D7
Coldean 17 D7
Coldeast 7 B6
Colden 87 B7
Colden Common . 15 B5
Coldfair Green . . . 57 C8
Coldham. 66 D4
Cold Hanworth . . 90 F4
Coldharbour Glos. 36 D2
  Kent. 29 D6
  Sur. 28 E2
Cold Harbour . . . 78 F2
Cold Hatton 61 B6
Cold Hesledon . . . 111 E7
Cold Higham 52 D4
Coldingham 122 C5
Cold Kirby 102 F3
Cold Newton 64 D4
Cold Northcott . . 8 F4
Cold Norton 42 D4
Cold Overton . . . 64 C5
Coldrain 128 D2
Coldred 31 E6
Coldridge 9 D8
Coldstream Angus. 134 F3
  Borders 122 F4
Coldwaltham. . . . 16 C4
Coldwells 153 D11
Coldwells Croft. . . 140 B4
Coldyeld 60 E3
Cole 23 F8
Colebatch. 60 F3
Colebrook 10 D5
Colebrooke 10 E2
Coleby Lincs 78 C2
  N Lincs. 90 C2
Coleford Devon . . 10 D2
  Glos. 36 C2
  Som 23 E8
Cole Green 41 C5
Cole Henley 26 D2
Colehill 13 D8
Coleman's Hatch . 29 F5
Colemere 73 F8
Colemore 26 F5
Coleorton 63 C8
Colerne 24 B3

Colesbourne 37 C6
Colesden 54 D2
Coles Green 56 E4
Cole's Green 57 C6
Coleshill Bucks. . . 40 E2
  Oxon 38 E2
  Warks 63 F6
Colestocks 11 D5
Colgate 28 F3
Colgrain 126 F2
Colinsburgh. 129 D6
Colinton 120 C5
Colintraive 145 F9
Colkirk 80 E5
Collace 134 F2
Collafirth 160 G6
Collaton St Mary . 7 D6
College Milton . . . 119 D6
Collessie 128 C4
Collier Row 41 E8
Collier's End 41 B6
Collier's Green . . . 18 B4
Collier Street. . . . 29 E8
Colliery Row 111 E6
Collieston 141 B9
Collin 107 B7
Collingbourne
  Ducis 25 D7
Collingbourne
  Kingston 25 D7
Collingham Notts . 77 C8
  W Yorks. 95 E6
Collington 49 C8
Collingtree. 53 D5
Collins Green 86 E3
Colliston 135 E6
Collycroft 63 F7
Collynie 153 E8
Collyweston. 65 D6
Colmonell 104 A5
Colmworth 54 D2
Colnabaichin. . . . 139 D8
Colnbrook 27 B8
Colne Cambs 54 B4
  Lancs. 93 E8
Colne Edge 93 E8
Colne Engaine . . . 56 F2
Colney 68 D4
Colney Heath. . . . 41 D5
Colney Street . . . 40 D4
Coln Rogers. 37 D7
Coln St Aldwyn's . 37 D8
Coln St Dennis . . . 37 C7
Colpy 153 E6
Colquhar. 121 E6
Colsterdale 101 F6
Colsterworth. . . . 65 B6
Colston Bassett . . 77 F6
Coltfield 151 E14
Colthouse. 99 E5
Coltishall 69 C5
Coltness 119 D8
Colton Cumb 99 F5
  Norf. 68 D4
  N Yorks. 95 E8
  Staffs. 62 B4
  W Yorks. 95 F6
Col Uarach 155 D9
Colva 48 D4
Colvend 107 D5
Colvister 160 D7
Colwall Green . . . 50 E2
Colwall Stone . . . 50 E2
Colwell 110 B2
Colwich 62 B4
Colwick 77 E6
Colwinston 21 B8
Colworth 16 D3
Colwyn Bay
  = Bae Colwyn . . 83 D8
Colyford 11 E7
Colyton 11 E7
Combe Hereford . . 48 C5
  Oxon 38 C4
  W Berks. 25 C8
Combe Common . 27 F7
Combe Down . . . 24 C2
Combe Florey . . . 22 F3
Combe Hay 24 D2
Combe Martin. . . 20 E4
Combe Moor 49 C5
Combe Raleigh . . 11 D6
Comberbach 74 B3
Comberton Cambs. 54 D4
  Hereford 49 C6
Combe
  St Nicholas . . . 11 C8
Combpyne 11 E7
Combridge. 75 F7
Combrook 51 D8
Combs Derbys. . . . 75 B7
  Suff. 56 D4
Combs Ford 56 D4
Combwich 22 E4
Comers 141 D5
Comins Coch. . . . 58 F3
Commercial End . . 55 C6
Commins Capel
  Betws 46 D5
Commins Coch. . . 58 D5
Commondale 102 C4
Common Edge . . . 92 F3
Commonmoor . . . 5 C7
Commonside. . . . 74 B2
Common Side . . . 76 B3
Compstall. 87 E7
Compton Devon . . 7 C6
  Hants. 15 B5
  Sur. 27 E6
  Sur. 27 E7
  W Berks. 26 B3
  Wilts 25 D6
  W Sus 15 C8
Compton Abbas . . 13 C6
Compton Abdale . 37 C7
Compton Bassett . 24 B5
Compton
  Beauchamp. . . . 38 F2
Compton Bishop . 23 D5
Compton
  Chamberlayne . 13 B8
Compton Dando . 23 C8
Compton Dundon . 23 F6
Compton Martin. . 23 D7
Compton
  Pauncefoot . . . 12 B4
Compton Valence . 12 E3

Comrie continued
  Perth 127 B6
Conaglen House. . 130 C4
Concraigie 133 E8
Conchra 145 E9
Conder Green . . . 92 D4
Conderton 50 F4
Condicote 38 B1
Condorrat 119 B7
Condover 60 D4
Coneyhurst 16 B5
Coneysthorpe . . . 96 B3
Coneythorpe 95 D6
Coney Weston . . . 56 B3
Conford 27 F6
Congash 139 B6
Congdon's Shop. . 5 B7
Congerstone 63 D7
Congham 80 E3
Congleton 75 C5
Congl-y-wal 71 C8
Congresbury 23 C6
Congreve 62 C3
Conicavel 151 F12
Coningsby 78 D5
Conington Cambs . 54 C4
  Cambs. 65 F8
Conisbrough 89 E6
Conisby 142 B3
Conisholme 91 E8
Coniston Cumb . . 99 E5
  E Yorks. 97 F7
Coniston Cold . . . 94 D2
Conistone 94 C2
Connah's Quay . . 73 C6
Connel 124 B5
Connel Park 113 C6
Connor Downs . . . 2 C4
Conon Bridge . . . 151 F8
Conon House. . . . 151 F8
Cononley 94 E2
Conordan 149 E10
Consall 75 E6
Consett 110 D4
Constable Burton 101 E6
Constantine. 3 D6
Constantine Bay . . 4 B3
Contin 150 F7
Contlaw. 141 D7
Conwy 83 D7
Conyer. 30 C3
Conyers Green . . . 56 C2
Cooden 18 E4
Cooil 84 E3
Cookbury 9 D6
Cookham. 40 F1
Cookham Dean. . . 40 F1
Cookham Rise. . . . 40 F1
Cookhill 51 D5
Cookley Suff 57 B7
  Worcs 62 F2
Cookley Green . . . 39 E6
Cookney 141 E7
Cookridge. 95 E5
Cooksbridge 17 C8
Cooksmill Green . 42 D2
Coolham. 16 B5
Cooling 29 B8
Coombe Corn . . . 4 D4
  Corn. 8 C4
  Hants. 15 C7
  Wilts 25 D6
Coombe Bissett . . 14 B2
Coombe Hill. 37 B5
Coombe Keynes . . 13 F6
Coombes 17 D5
Coopersale
  Common 41 D7
Cootham. 16 C4
Copdock 56 E5
Copford Green . . . 43 B5
Copgrove 95 C6
Copister 160 F6
Cople 54 E2
Copley 101 B5
Coplow Dale 75 B8
Copmanthorpe . . 95 E8
Coppathorne. . . . 8 D4
Coppenhall 62 C3
Coppenhall Moss . 74 D4
Copperhouse . . . 2 C4
Coppingford 65 F8
Copplestone 10 D2
Coppull 86 C3
Coppull Moor . . . 86 C3
Copsale. 17 B5
Copster Green . . . 93 F6
Copston Magna . . 63 F8
Copt Heath. 51 B6
Copt Hewick 95 B6
Copthorne Shrops. 60 C4
  Sur. 28 F4
Copt Oak 63 C8
Copy's Green 80 D5
Copythorne 14 C4
Corbets Tey 42 F1
Corbridge. 110 C2
Corby 65 F5
Corby Glen. 65 B6
Cordon 143 E11
Coreley 49 B8
Cores End 40 F2
Corfe 11 C7
Corfe Castle 13 F7
Corfe Mullen 13 E7
Corfton 60 F4
Corgarff 139 D8
Corhampton 15 B7
Corlae 113 E6
Corley 63 F7
Corley Ash 63 F6
Corley Moor 63 F6
Cornaa 84 D4
Cornabus 142 D4
Cornel 83 E7
Corner Row 92 F4
Corney 98 E3
Cornforth 111 F6
Cornhill 152 C5
Cornhill-on-
  Tweed 122 F4
Cornholme. 87 B7
Cornish Hall End . 55 F7
Cornquoy 159 J6
Cornsay 110 E4
Cornsay Colliery. . 110 E4
Corntown Highld . 151 F8
  V Glam. 21 B8
Cornwell. 38 B2

Cornwood 6 D4
Cornworthy 7 D6
Corpach 130 B4
Corpusty 81 D7
Corran Highld . . . 130 C4
  Highld 149 H13
Corranbuie 145 G7
Corrany 84 D4
Corrie 143 D11
Corrie Common . . 114 F5
Corriecravie 143 F10
Corriemoillie. . . . 150 E6
Corriemulzie
  Lodge 150 B6
Corrievarkie
  Lodge 132 B2
Corrievorrie 138 B3
Corrimony 150 H6
Corringham Lincs . 90 E2
  Thurrock 42 F3
Corris 58 D4
Corris Uchaf 58 D4
Corrour Shooting
  Lodge 131 C8
Corrow 125 E7
Corry 149 F11
Corrykinloch 156 G6
Corrymuckloch . . 133 F5
Corrynachenchy . 147 G9
Corry of
  Ardnagrask . . . 151 G8
Corsback 158 C4
Corscombe 12 D3
Corse Aberds. . . . 152 D6
  Glos. 36 B4
Corse Lawn 50 F3
Corse of Kinnoir . 152 D5
Corsewall. 104 C4
Corsham 24 B3
Corsindae. 141 D5
Corsley 24 E3
Corsley Heath . . . 24 E3
Corsock 106 B4
Corston Bath. . . . 23 C8
  Wilts 37 F6
Corstorphine. . . . 120 B4
Cors-y-Gedol . . . 71 E6
Cortachy. 134 D3
Corton Suff 69 E8
  Wilts 24 E4
Corton Denham . . 12 B4
Coruanan Lodge . 130 C4
Corunna 148 B3
Corwen 72 E4
Coryton Devon . . 9 F6
  Thurrock 42 F3
Cosby 64 E2
Coseley 62 E3
Cosgrove 53 E5
Cosham 15 D7
Cosheston 32 D1
Cossall 76 E4
Cossington Leics . 64 C3
  Som 23 E5
Costa 159 F4
Costessey 68 C4
Costock 64 B2
Coston 64 C5
Cote 38 D3
Cotebrook 74 C2
Cotehill 108 D4
Cotes Cumb 99 F6
  Leics. 64 B2
  Staffs. 74 F5
Cotesbach. 64 F2
Cotgrave 77 F6
Cothall 141 C7
Cotham 77 E7
Cothelstone 22 F3
Cotherstone. 101 C5
Cothill 38 E4
Cotleigh 11 D7
Cotmanhay 76 E4
Coton Cambs 54 D5
  Northants 52 B4
  Staffs. 62 B2
  Staffs. 75 F6
Coton Clanford . . 62 B2
Coton Hill Shrops. . 60 C4
  Staffs. 75 F6
Coton in the Elms . 63 C6
Cott 7 C5
Cottam E Yorks . . 97 C5
  Lancs. 92 F5
  Notts 77 B8
Cottartown 151 H13
Cottenham. 54 C5
Cotterdale 100 E3
Cottered 41 B6
Cotteridge 50 B5
Cotterstock 65 E7
Cottesbrooke . . . 52 B5
Cottesmore. 65 C6
Cotteylands 10 C4
Cottingham
  E Yorks. 97 F6
  Northants 64 E5
Cottingley 94 F4
Cottisford 52 F3
Cotton Staffs 75 E7
  Suff. 56 C4
Cotton End. 53 E8
Cottown Aberds . . 140 B4
  Aberds. 141 C6
  Aberds. 153 D8
Cotwalton 75 F6
Couch's Mill 5 D6
Coughton Hereford . 36 B2
  Warks 51 C5
Coulaghailtro . . . 144 G6
Coulags. 150 G2
Coulby Newham. . 102 C3
Coulderton 98 D1
Coulin 150 F3
Coull Aberds 140 D4
  Argyll. 142 B3
Coulport 145 E11
Coulsdon 28 D3
Coulston 24 D4
Coulter 120 F3
Coulton 96 B2
Cound 61 D5
Coundon Durham . 101 B7
  W Mid 63 F7
Coundon Grange. 101 B7
Countersett. 100 F4
Countess 25 E6
Countess Wear . . 10 F4

Countesthorpe . . 64 E2
Countisbury 21 E6
County Oak 28 F3
Coupar Angus . . . 134 E2
Coup Green 86 B3
Coupland 122 F5
Cour 143 D9
Courance 114 E3
Court-at-Street . . 19 B7
Courteenhall. . . . 53 D5
Courtsend 43 E6
Courtway 22 F4
Cousland 121 C6
Cousley Wood . . . 18 B3
Cove Argyll. 145 E11
  Borders 122 B3
  Devon 10 C4
  Hants. 27 D6
  Highld 155 H13
Cove Bay 141 D8
Cove Bottom 57 B8
Covehithe 69 F8
Coven 62 D3
Coveney 66 F4
Covenham
  St Bartholomew . 91 E7
Covenham St Mary 91 E7
Coventry 51 B8
Coverack 3 E6
Coverham 101 F6
Covesea 152 A1
Covington Cambs . 53 B8
  S Lanark. 120 F2
Cowan Bridge . . . 93 B6
Cow Ark 93 E6
Cowbeech 18 D3
Cowbit 66 C2
Cowbridge Lincs . . 79 E6
  Som 21 E8
Cowbridge
  = Y Bont-Faen. . 21 B8
Cowdale 75 B7
Cowden 29 E5
Cowdenbeath . . . 128 E3
Cowdenburn 120 D5
Cowers Lane 76 E3
Cowes 15 E5
Cowesby 102 F2
Cowfold 17 B6
Cowgill 100 F2
Cowie Aberds . . . 141 F7
  Stirling 127 F7
Cowley Devon . . . 10 E4
  Glos. 37 C6
  London. 40 F3
  Oxon 39 D5
Cowleymoor 10 C4
Cowling Lancs . . . 86 C3
  N Yorks. 94 E2
  N Yorks. 101 F7
Cowlinge 55 D8
Cowpe 87 B6
Cowpen 117 F8
Cowpen Bewley . . 102 B2
Cowplain 15 C7
Cowshill 109 E8
Cowslip Green . . . 23 C6
Cowstrandburn . . 128 E2
Cowthorpe 95 D7
Coxbank 74 E3
Coxbench 76 E3
Cox Common . . . 69 F6
Coxford Norf 80 E4
  Soton. 14 C4
Cox Green 27 B6
Coxheath 29 D8
Coxhill 31 E6
Coxhoe 111 F6
Coxley 23 E7
Cox Moor 76 D5
Coxwold 95 B8
Coychurch 21 B8
Coylton 112 B4
Coylumbridge. . . 138 C5
Coynach 140 D3
Coynachie 152 E4
Coytrahen 34 F2
Crabadon 7 D5
Crabbs Cross 50 C5
Crabtree 17 B6
Crackenthorpe . . 100 B1
Crackington Haven . 8 E3
Crackley 51 B7
Crackleybank . . . 61 C7
Crackpot 100 E4
Cracoe 94 C2
Craddock 11 C5
Cradhlastadh . . . 154 D5
Cradley 50 E2
Cradley Heath . . . 62 F3
Crafthole. 5 D8
Craggan 139 B6
Craggie Highld . . 151 H10
  Highld 157 H11
Cragg Vale 87 B8
Craghead. 110 D5
Crai 34 B2
Craibstone 152 C4
Craichie 135 E5
Craig Dumfries . . . 106 B3
  Dumfries 106 C3
  Highld 150 G3
Craiganor Lodge . 132 D3
Craig Castle 140 B3
Craig-cefn-parc . . 33 D7
Craigdam 153 E8
Craigdarroch
  Dumfries 113 E7
  Highld 150 F7
Craigdhu. 150 G7
Craigearn 141 C6
Craigellachie 152 D2
Craigencross 104 C4
Craigend Perth. . . 128 B3
  Stirling 127 F6
Craigendive 145 E9
Craigendoran . . . 126 F2
Craigends 118 C4
Craigens Argyll. . . 142 B3
  E Ayrs. 113 C5
Craighat 126 F3
Craighead 129 D8
Craighlaw Mains . 105 C7
Craighouse 144 G4
Craigie Aberds . . . 141 C8
  Dundee 134 F4
  Perth 128 B3
  Perth 133 E8

Craigie *continued*

S Ayrs. 118 F4
Craigiefield 159 G5
Craigielaw 121 B7
Craiglockhart 120 B5
Craigmalloch 112 E4
Craigmillar 121 B7
Craigmore 145 G10
Craignant 73 F6
Craigneuk
N Lanark 119 C7
N Lanark 119 D7
Craignure 124 B3
Craigo 135 C6
Craigow 128 D2
Craig Penllyn 21 B8
Craigrothie 129 C5
Craigroy 151 F14
Craigruie 126 B3
Craigston Castle . 153 C7
Craigton Aberdeen . 141 D7
  Angus 134 D3
  Angus 135 F5
  Highld 151 B9
Craigtown 157 D11
Craig-y-don 83 C7
Craig-y-nos 34 C2
Craik 115 D6
Crail 129 D8
Crailing 116 B2
Crailinghall 116 B2
Craiselound 89 E8
Crakehill 95 B7
Crakemarsh 75 F7
Crambe 96 C3
Cramlington 111 B5
Cramond 120 B4
Cramond Bridge . 120 B4
Cranage 74 C4
Cranberry 74 F5
Cranborne 13 C8
Cranbourne 27 B7
Cranbrook Devon. . 10 E5
  Kent 18 B4
Cranbrook
  Common 18 B4
Crane Moor 88 D4
Crane's Corner 68 C2
Cranfield 53 E7
Cranford 28 B2
Cranford
  St Andrew 53 B7
Cranford St John . 53 B7
Cranham Glos. 37 C5
  London. 42 F1
Crank 86 E3
Crank Wood 86 D4
Cranleigh 27 F8
Cranley 57 B5
Cranmer Green 56 B4
Cranmore 14 F4
Cranna 153 C6
Crannich 147 G8
Crannoch 152 C4
Cranoe 64 E4
Cransford 57 C7
Cranshaws 122 C2
Cranstal 84 B4
Crantock 4 C2
Cranwell 78 E3
Cranwich 67 E7
Cranworth 68 D2
Craobh Haven . 124 E3
Crapstone 6 C3
Crarae 125 F5
Crask Inn 157 G8
Crask of Aigas . 150 G7
Craskins 140 D4
Craster 117 C8
Craswall 48 F4
Cratfield 57 B7
Crathes Aberds . 141 E6
Crathie Aberds . 139 E8
  Highld 137 E8
Crathorne 102 D2
Craven Arms 60 F4
Crawcrook 110 C4
Crawford Lancs . 86 D2
  S Lanark 114 B2
Crawfordjohn 113 B8
Crawick 113 C7
Crawley Hants . 26 F2
  Oxon 38 C3
  W Sus 28 F3
Crawley Down 28 F4
Crawleyside 110 E2
Crawshawbooth 87 B6
Crawton 135 B8
Cray N Yorks. 94 B2
  Perth 133 C8
Crayford 29 B6
Crayke 95 B8
Crays Hill 42 E3
Cray's Pond 39 F6
Creacombe 10 C3
Creagan 130 E3
Creag Ghoraidh . 148 D2
Creaguaineach
  Lodge 131 C7
Creaksea 43 E5
Creaton 52 B5
Creca 108 B2
Credenhill 49 E6
Crediton 10 D3
Creebridge 105 C8
Creech Heathfield . 11 B7
Creech St Michael . 11 B7
Creed 3 B8
Creekmouth 41 F7
Creeting Bottoms . 56 D5
Creeting St Mary . 56 D4
Creeton 65 B7
Creetown 105 D8
Creggans 125 E6
Cregneash 84 F1
Creg-ny-Baa. . 84 D3
Cregrina 48 D3
Creich 128 B5
Creigiau 34 F4
Cremyll 6 D2
Creslow 39 C8
Cressage 61 D5
Cressbrook 75 B8
Cresselly. 32 D1
Cressing 42 B3
Cresswell
  Northumb 117 E8
  Staffs. 75 F6

Cresswell Quay. . 32 D1
Cresswell 76 B5
Cretingham 57 C6
Cretshengan 144 G6
Crewe Ches E. 74 D4
  Ches W. 73 D8
Crewgreen 60 C3
Crewkerne 12 D2
Crianlarich 126 B2
Cribyn 46 D4
Criccieth 71 D5
Crich 76 D3
Crichie 153 D9
Crichton 121 C6
Crick Mon 36 E1
  Northants 52 B3
Crickadarn 48 E2
Cricket Malherbie . 11 C8
Cricket St Thomas . 11 D8
Crickheath 60 B2
Crickhowell. 35 C6
Cricklade 37 E8
Cricklewood 41 F5
Cridling Stubbs . 89 B6
Crieff 127 B7
Criggion 60 C2
Crigglestone 88 C4
Crimond 153 C10
Crimonmogate. . 153 C10
Crimplesham 67 D6
Crinan 144 D6
Cringleford 68 D4
Cringles 94 E3
Crinow 32 C2
Cripplesease. 2 C4
Cripplestyle. 13 C8
Cripp's Corner 18 C4
Croasdale 98 C2
Crockenhill 29 C6
Crockernwell 10 E2
Crockerton 24 E3
Crocketford or
  Ninemile Bar . . . 106 B5
Crockey Hill 96 E2
Crockham Hill 28 D5
Crockleford Heath. . 43 B6
Crockness 159 J4
Crock Street 11 C8
Croeserw 34 E2
Croes-goch 44 B3
Croes-lan 46 E2
Croesor 71 C7
Croesyceiliog
  Carms 33 C5
  Torf 35 E7
Croes-y-mwyalch . 35 E7
Croesywaun. 82 F5
Croft Leics 64 E2
  Lincs 79 C8
  Pembs 45 E3
  Warr 86 E4
Croftamie 126 F3
Croftmalloch 120 C2
Crofton Wilts 25 C7
  W Yorks 88 C4
Croft-on-Tees 101 D7
Crofts of
  Benachielt. 158 G3
Crofts of Haddo . 153 E8
Crofts of
  Inverthernie. . . . 153 D7
Crofts of Meikle
  Ardo 153 D8
Crofty. 33 E6
Croggan 124 C3
Croglin 109 E5
Croich 150 B7
Crois Dughaill. . 148 F2
Cromarty 151 E10
Cromblet 153 E7
Cromdale 139 B6
Cromer Herts 41 B5
  Norf 81 C8
Cromford 76 D2
Cromhall 36 E3
Cromhall Common . 36 E3
Cromor 155 E9
Cromra 137 E8
Cromwell 77 C7
Cronberry 113 B6
Crondall 27 E5
Cronk-y-Voddy . 84 D3
Cronton 86 F2
Crook Cumb. 99 E6
  Durham 110 F4
Crookedholm 118 F4
Crookes 88 F4
Crookham
  Northumb 122 F5
  W Berks. 26 C3
Crookham Village . 27 D5
Crookhaugh. 114 B4
Crookhouse. 116 B3
Crooklands 99 F7
Crook of Devon. . 128 D2
Cropredy 52 E2
Cropston 64 C2
Cropthorne 50 E4
Cropton 103 F5
Cropwell Bishop. . 77 F6
Cropwell Butler. . 77 F6
Cros 155 A10
Crosbost 155 E8
Crosby Cumb. 107 F7
  IoM 84 E3
  N Lincs 90 C2
Crosby Garrett . 100 D2
Crosby
  Ravensworth . 100 C1
Crosby Villa. 107 F7
Croscombe 23 E7
Cross 23 D6
Crossaig 143 C9
Crossal 149 E9
Crossapol 146 G2
Cross Ash 35 C8
Cross-at-Hand. . 29 E8
Crossburn 119 B8
Crossbush 16 D4
Crosscanonby 107 F7
Crossdale Street . 81 D8
Crossens 85 C4
Crossflatts 94 E4
Crossford Fife. 128 F2
  S Lanark 119 E8
Crossgate 66 B2
Crossgatehall 121 C6
Crossgates Fife . 128 F3
  Powys. 48 C2

Crossgill 93 C5
Cross Green Devon. . 9 F5
  Suff. 56 D2
  Suff. 56 D3
  Warks 51 D8
Cross-hands 32 B2
Cross Hands Carms. . 33 C6
  Pembs 32 C1
Crosshill E Ayrs. . . . 112 B4
  Fife 128 E3
  S Ayrs. 112 D3
Cross Hill 76 E4
Crosshouse 118 F3
Cross Houses 60 D5
Crossings 108 B5
Cross in Hand
  E Sus 18 C2
  Leics 64 F2
Cross Inn Ceredig. . 46 C4
  Ceredig. 46 D2
  Rhondda 34 F4
Crosskeys 35 E6
Cross Keys 29 D6
Crosskirk 157 B13
Cross Lane Head . 61 E7
Crosslanes 60 C3
Cross Lanes Corn. . 3 D5
  N Yorks. 95 C8
  Wrex. 73 E7
Crossle 118 C4
Crosslee 115 C6
Crossmichael 106 C4
Crossmoor 92 F4
Cross Oak 35 B5
Cross of
  Jackston 153 E7
Cross o'th'hands . 76 E2
Crossroads Aberds . 141 E6
  E Ayrs. 118 F4
Cross Street. 57 B5
Crossway Hereford . 49 F8
  Mon 35 C8
  Powys 48 D2
Crossway Green. . 50 C3
Crossways 13 F5
Crosswell 45 F3
Crosswood 47 B5
Crosthwaite 99 E6
Croston 86 C2
Crostwick 69 C5
Crostwight 69 B6
Crothair 154 D6
Crouch 29 D7
Crouchend 13 B8
Crouch Hill 12 C5
Crouch House
  Green 28 E5
Croughton 52 F3
Crovie 153 B8
Crowan 2 C5
Crowborough 18 B2
Crowcombe 22 F3
Crowdecote 75 C8
Crowden 87 E8
Crow Edge 88 D2
Crowell 39 E7
Crowfield Northants . 52 E4
  Suff. 56 D5
Crow Hill 36 B3
Crowhurst E Sus. . 18 D4
  Sur. 28 E4
Crowhurst Lane
  End 28 E4
Crowland 66 C2
Crowlas 2 C4
Crowle N Lincs. . . 89 C8
  Worcs 50 D4
Crowmarsh
  Gifford 39 F6
Crown Corner 57 B6
Crownhill 6 D2
Crownland 56 C4
Crowntown 2 C5
Crows-an-wra 2 D2
Crowshill 68 D2
Crowsnest 60 D3
Crowthorne 27 C6
Crowton 74 B2
Croxall 63 C5
Croxby 91 E5
Croxdale 111 F5
Croxden 75 F7
Croxley Green 40 E3
Croxton Cambs. . 54 C3
  N Lincs 90 C4
  Norf. 67 F8
  Staffs. 74 F4
Croxtonbank 74 F4
Croxton Kerrial 64 B5
Croy Highld 151 G10
  N Lanark 119 B7
Croyde 20 F3
Croydon Cambs. . 54 E4
  London. 28 C4
Crubenmore
  Lodge 138 E2
Cruckmeole. 60 D4
Cruckton 60 C4
Cruden Bay 153 E10
Crudgington 61 C6
Crudwell. 37 E6
Crug 48 B3
Crugmeer 4 B4
Crugybar 47 F5
Crulabhig 154 D6
Crumlin = Crymlyn. . 35 E6
Crumpsall. 87 D6
Crundale Kent 30 E4
  Pembs 44 D4
Cruwys Morchard . 10 C3
Crux Easton 26 D2
Crwbin. 33 C5
Crya 159 H4
Cryers Hill 40 E1
Crymlyn 83 D6
Crymych 45 F3
Crynant 34 D1
Crynfryn 46 C4
Cuaig 149 C12
Cuan. 124 D3
Cubbington 51 C8
Cubeck 100 F4
Cubert 4 D2
Cubley 88 D3
Cubley Common. . 75 F8
Cublington Bucks . 39 B8
  Hereford 49 F6

Cuckfield 17 B7
Cucklington 13 B5
Cuckney 77 B5
Cuckoo Hill 89 E8
Cuddesdon 39 D6
Cuddington Bucks. . 39 C7
  Ches W. 74 B3
Cuddington Heath. . 73 E8
Cuddy Hill 92 F4
Cudham 28 D5
Cudworth Som. . . 11 C8
  S Yorks. 88 D4
Cuffley. 41 D6
Cuiashader 155 B10
Cuidhir 148 H1
Cuidhtinis 154 J5
Culbo. 151 E9
Culbokie. 151 F9
Culburnie. 150 G7
Culcabock 151 G9
Culcairn 151 E9
Culcharry 151 F11
Culcheth. 86 E4
Culdrain 152 E5
Culduie 149 D12
Culford 56 B2
Culgaith 99 B8
Culham 39 E5
Culkein 156 F3
Culkein Drumbeg . 156 F4
Culkerton 37 E6
Cullachie 139 B5
Cullen 152 B5
Cullercoats 111 B6
Cullicudden 151 E9
Cullingworth. 94 F3
Cullipool 124 D3
Cullivoe 160 C7
Culloch 127 C6
Culloden 151 G10
Cullompton 10 D5
Culmaily. 151 B11
Culmazie 105 D7
Culmington 60 F4
Culmstock 11 C6
Culnacraig 156 J3
Culnaknock 149 B10
Culpho. 57 E6
Culrain 151 B8
Culross 127 F8
Culroy 112 C3
Culsh Aberds. . . 140 E2
  Aberds. 153 D8
Culshabbin 105 D7
Culswick. 160 J4
Cultercullen 141 B8
Cults Aberdeen . . 141 D7
  Aberds. 152 E5
  Dumfries. 105 E8
Culverstone Green . 29 C7
Culverthorpe. 78 E3
Culworth. 52 E3
Culzie Lodge 151 D8
Cumberland
  Village 119 B7
Cumberworth 79 B8
Cuminestown 153 C8
Cumlewick 160 L6
Cummersdale 108 D3
Cummertrees 107 C8
Cummingston 152 B1
Cumnock 113 B5
Cumnor 38 D4
Cumrew 108 D5
Cumwhinton 108 D4
Cumwhitton 108 D5
Cundall. 95 B7
Cunninghamhead . 118 E3
Cunnister 160 D7
Cupar 129 C5
Cupar Muir. 129 C5
Cupernham 14 B4
Curbar 76 B2
Curbridge Hants . 15 C6
  Oxon 38 D3
Curdridge. 15 C6
Curdworth 63 E5
Curland 11 C7
Curlew Green 57 C7
Currarie 112 E1
Curridge 26 B2
Currie 120 C4
Curry Mallet. 11 B8
Curry Rivel. 11 B8
Curtisden Green. . 29 E8
Curtisknowle. 6 D5
Cury. 3 D5
Cushnie. 153 B7
Cushuish. 22 F3
Cusop. 48 E4
Cutcloy 105 F8
Cutcombe 21 F8
Cutgate. 87 C6
Cutiau 58 C3
Cutlers Green 55 F6
Cutnall Green 50 C3
Cutsdean 51 F5
Cutthorpe 76 B3
Cutts 160 K6
Cuxham 39 E6
Cuxton 29 C8
Cuxwold 91 D5
Cwm Bl Gwent . . . 35 D5
  Denb 72 B4
  Swansea 33 E7
Cwmafan 34 E1
Cwmaman 34 E4
Cwmann 46 E4
Cwmavon 35 D6
Cwmbach Carms . 32 B3
  Carms 33 D5
  Powys 48 E2
  Powys 48 F3
Cwmbâch 34 D4
Cwmbelan 59 F6
Cwmbrân
  = Cwmbran. . . 35 E6
Cwmbran
  = Cwmbrân. . . 35 E6
Cwmbrwyno 58 F4
Cwm-byr 46 F5
Cwmcarn 35 E6
Cwmcarvan 36 D1
Cwm-Cewydd 59 C5
Cwm-cou 45 E4
Cwmcych 45 F4
Cwmdare 34 D3

Cwmderwen 59 D6
Cwmdu Carms . . . 33 B6
  Powys. 35 B5
Cwmduad. 46 F2
Cwm-Dulais 33 D7
Cwmdwr 47 F6
Cwmfelin Bridgend . 34 F2
  M Tydf 34 D4
Cwmfelin Boeth. . 32 C2
Cwm-felin-fach. . 35 E5
Cwmfelin Mynach . 32 B3
Cwmffrwd 33 C5
Cwm Ffrwd-oer. . 35 D6
Cwmgiedd 34 C1
Cwmgors 33 C8
Cwmgwili 33 C6
Cwmgwrach 34 D2
Cwm-hesgen 71 E8
Cwmhiraeth. 46 F2
Cwm-hwnt. 34 D3
Cwm Irfon 47 E7
Cwmisfael 33 C5
Cwm-Llinau 58 D5
Cwmllynfell 33 C8
Cwm-mawr 33 C6
Cwmorgan 45 F4
Cwm-parc 34 E3
Cwm Penmachno . 71 C8
Cwmrhos 35 B5
Cwmsychpant. . . 46 E3
Cwmtillery 35 D6
Cwm-twrch Isaf. . 34 C1
Cwm-twrch Uchaf . 34 C1
Cwmwysg 34 B2
Cwm-y-glo Carms. . 33 C6
  Gwyn. 82 E5
Cwmyoy 35 B6
Cwmystwyth 47 B6
Cwrt. 58 D3
Cwrt-newydd 46 E3
Cwrt-y-cadno. . . 47 E5
Cwrt-y-gollen 35 C6
Cydweli
  = Kidwelly. . . 33 D5
Cyffordd Llandudno
  Junction 83 D7
Cyffylliog 72 D4
Cyfronydd 59 D8
Cymer 34 E2
Cyncoed 35 F5
Cynghordy 47 E7
Cynheidre 33 D5
Cynwyd 72 E4
Cynwyl Elfed 32 B4
Cywarch 59 C5

D

Dacre Cumb. 99 B6
  N Yorks. 94 C4
Dacre Banks 94 C4
Daddry Shield . . . 109 F8
Dadford 52 F4
Dadlington. 63 E8
Dafarn Faig 71 C5
Dafen. 33 D6
Daffy Green 68 D2
Dagenham 41 F7
Daglingworth 37 D6
Dagnall 40 C2
Dail Beag 154 C7
Dail bho Dheas . 155 A9
Dail bho Thuath . 155 A9
Daill 142 B4
Dailly. 112 D2
Dail Mor 154 C7
Dairsie or
  Osnaburgh . . . 129 C6
Daisy Hill 86 D4
Dalabrog. 148 F2
Dalavich 125 D5
Dalbeattie 106 C5
Dalblair 113 C6
Dalbog 135 B5
Dalbury 76 F2
Dalby IoM 84 E2
  N Yorks. 96 B2
Dalchalloch 132 C4
Dalchalm. 157 J12
Dalchenna 125 E6
Dalchirach. 152 E1
Dalchork 157 H8
Dalchreichart . . . 137 C5
Dalchruin 127 C6
Dalderby 78 C5
Dale 44 E3
Dale Abbey 76 F4
Dale Head. 99 C6
Daless. 151 H11
Dalfaber. 138 C5
Dalgarven 118 E2
Dalgety Bay 128 F3
Dalginross 127 B6
Dalguise 133 D6
Dalhalvaig. 157 D11
Dalham. 55 C8
Dalinlongart . . . 145 E10
Dalkeith 121 C6
Dallam. 86 E3
Dallas. 151 F14
Dalleagles 113 C5
Dallinghoo. 57 D6
Dallington E Sus. . 18 D3
  Northants 52 C5
Dallow. 94 B4
Dalmadilly. 141 C6
Dalmally 125 C7
Dalmarnock. 119 C6
Dalmary 126 E4
Dalmellington. . . 112 D4
Dalmeny 120 B4
Dalmigavie. 138 C3
Dalmigavie
  Lodge 138 B3
Dalmore 151 E9
Dalmuir 118 B4
Dalnabreck. 147 E9
Dalnacardoch
  Lodge 132 B4
Dalnacroich. 150 F6
Dalnaglar Castle . 133 C8
Dalnahaitnach . 138 B4

Dalnaspidal
  Lodge 132 B3
Dalnavaid 133 C7
Dalnavie. 151 D9
Dalnawillan
  Lodge 157 E13
Dalness. 131 D5
Dalnessie 157 H9
Dalqueich. 128 D2
Dalreavoch 157 J10
Dalry 118 E2
Dalrymple. 112 C3
Dalserf 119 D8
Dalston 108 D3
Dalswinton 114 F2
Dalton Dumfries. . 107 B8
  Lancs. 86 D2
  Northumb 110 B4
  Northumb 110 D2
  N Yorks. 95 B7
  N Yorks. 101 D6
  S Yorks. 89 E5
Dalton-in-Furness . 92 B2
Dalton-le-Dale . 111 E7
Dalton-on-Tees . 101 D7
Dalton Piercy 111 F7
Dalveich 126 B5
Dalvina Lodge . 157 E9
Dalwhinnie 138 F2
Dalwood. 11 D7
Dalwyne 112 E3
Damerham. 14 C2
Damgate. 69 D7
Dam Green. 68 F3
Damnaglaur 104 F5
Damside. 120 E4
Dam Side. 92 E4
Danaway 30 C2
Danbury 42 D3
Danby 103 D5
Danby Wiske . . . 101 E8
Dandaleith. 152 D2
Danderhall. 121 C6
Danebridge 75 C6
Dane End 41 B6
Danehill. 17 B8
Danemoor Green. . 68 D3
Danesford 61 E7
Daneshill. 26 D4
Dangerous Corner . 86 C3
Danskine 121 C8
Darcy Lever 86 D5
Darenth. 29 B6
Daresbury 86 F3
Darfield. 88 D5
Darfoulds 77 B5
Dargate. 30 C4
Darite. 5 C7
Darlaston 62 E3
Darley 94 D5
Darley Bridge 76 C2
Darley Head. 94 D4
Darlingscott 51 E7
Darlington 101 C7
Darliston 74 F2
Darlton 77 B7
Darnall. 88 F4
Darnick 121 F8
Darowen 58 D5
Darra 153 D7
Darracott 20 F3
Darras Hall. 110 B4
Darrington 89 B5
Darsham. 57 C8
Dartford 29 B6
Dartford Crossing . 29 B6
Dartington. 7 C5
Dartmeet 6 B4
Dartmouth 7 D6
Darton. 88 D4
Darvel 119 F5
Darwell Hole 18 D3
Darwen. 86 B4
Datchet. 27 B7
Datchworth 41 C5
Datchworth Green . 41 C5
Daubhill 86 D5
Daugh of
  Kinnermony . . . 152 D2
Dauntsey 37 F6
Dava. 151 H13
Davenham 74 B3
Davenport Green . 87 C6
Daventry 52 C3
Davidson's Mains . 120 B5
Davidstow 8 F3
David's Well. 48 B2
Davington 115 D5
Daviot Aberds. . . 141 B6
  Highld 151 H10
Davoch of
  Grange. 152 C4
Davyhulme 87 E5
Dawley 61 D6
Dawlish. 7 B7
Dawlish Warren. . 7 B7
Dawn 83 D8
Daws Heath. 42 F4
Daw's House Corn. . 8 F5
  Corn. 8 F5
Dawsmere 79 F7
Dayhills. 75 F6
Daylesford 38 B2
Ddôl-Cownwy. . . 59 C7
Ddrydwy 82 D3
Deadwater 116 E2
Deaf Hill 111 F6
Deal 31 D7
Deal Hall 43 E6
Dean Cumb. 98 B2
  Devon 6 C5
  Devon 20 E4
  Dorset. 13 C7
  Hants. 15 B6
  Som. 23 E8
Deanburnhaugh. . 115 C6
Deane Gtr Man . . . 86 D4
  Hants. 26 D3
Deanich Lodge . 150 C6
Deanland 13 C7
Dean Prior. 6 C5
Dean Row 87 F6
Deans 120 C3
Deanscales 98 B2
Deanshanger 53 F5
Deanston 127 D6
Dearham 107 F7
Debach 57 D6
Debden Essex. . . 41 E7
  Essex. 55 F6

Debden Cross 55 F6
Debenham. 57 C5
Dechmont 120 B3
Deddington 52 F2
Dedham. 56 F4
Dedham Heath. . 56 F4
Deebank 141 E5
Deene 65 E6
Deenethorpe. 65 E6
Deepcar 88 E3
Deepcut. 27 D7
Deepdale. 100 F2
Deeping Gate 65 D8
Deeping St James . 65 D8
Deeping
  St Nicholas . . . 66 C2
Deerhill. 152 C4
Deerhurst. 37 B5
Deerness 159 H6
Defford 50 E4
Defynnog. 34 B3
Deganwy 83 D7
Deighton N Yorks. . 102 D1
  W Yorks. 88 C2
  York 96 E2
Deiniolen 83 E5
Delabole. 8 F2
Delamere 74 C2
Delfrigs. 141 B8
Dell Lodge 139 C6
Delnabo 139 C7
Delnadamph . . . 139 D8
Delph. 87 D7
Delves 110 E4
Delvine 133 E8
Dembleby. 78 F3
Denaby Main 89 E5
Denbigh
  = Dinbych. . . 72 C4
Denbury 7 C6
Denby 76 E3
Denby Dale 88 D3
Denchworth 38 E3
Dendron. 92 B2
Denel End. 53 F8
Denford 53 B7
Dengie. 43 D5
Denham Bucks. . . 40 F3
  Suff. 55 C8
  Suff. 57 B5
Denham Street. . 57 B5
Denhead Aberds. . 153 C9
  Fife. 129 C6
Denhead of
  Arbilot 135 E5
Denhead of Gray . 134 F3
Denholm 115 C8
Denholme 94 F3
Denholme Clough. . 94 F3
Denio. 70 D4
Denmead 15 C7
Denmore 141 C8
Denmoss 153 D6
Dennington 57 C6
Denny 127 F7
Dennyloanhead . 127 F7
Denshaw. 87 C7
Denside. 141 E7
Densole 31 E6
Denston 55 D8
Denstone 75 E8
Dent 100 F2
Denton Cambs. . . 65 F8
  Darl. 101 C7
  E Sus. 17 D8
  Gtr Man 87 E7
  Kent. 31 E6
  Lincs. 77 F8
  Norf. 69 F5
  Northants 53 D6
  N Yorks. 94 E4
  Oxon. 39 D5
Denton's Green . 86 E2
Denver 67 D6
Denwick 117 C8
Deopham 68 D3
Deopham Green. . 68 E3
Depden 55 D8
Depden Green. . . 55 D8
Deptford London . . 28 B4
  Wilts. 24 F5
Derby 76 F3
Derbyhaven. 84 F2
Dereham 68 C2
Deri 35 D5
Derril. 8 D5
Derringstone. 31 E6
Derrington 62 B2
Derriton 8 D5
Derryguaig. 146 H7
Derry Hill 24 B4
Derrythorpe 90 D2
Dersingham 80 D2
Dervaig 146 F7
Derwen 72 D4
Derwenlas 58 E4
Desborough 64 F5
Desford. 63 D8
Detchant. 123 F6
Detling 29 D8
Deuddwr. 60 C2
Devauden. 36 E1
Devil's Bridge 47 B6
Devizes 24 C5
Devol 118 B3
Devonport. 6 D2
Devonside 127 E8
Devoran 3 C6
Dewar 121 E6
Dewlish 13 E5
Dewsbury. 88 B3
Dewsbury Moor. . 88 B3
Dewshall Court. . 49 F6
Dhoon 84 D4
Dhoor 84 C4
Dhowin 84 B4
Dial Post 17 C5
Dibden 14 D5
Dibden Purlieu. . 14 D5
Dickleburgh 68 F4
Didbrook. 51 F5
Didcot 39 F5
Diddington. 54 C2
Diddlebury 60 F5
Didley 49 F6
Didling. 16 C2

Cra–Dra 219

Didmarton 37 F5
Didsbury. 87 E6
Didworthy. 6 C4
Digby 78 D3
Digg 149 B9
Diggle 87 D8
Digmoor. 86 D2
Digswell Park 41 C5
Dihewyd 46 D3
Dilham. 69 B6
Dilhorne 75 E6
Dillarburn 119 E8
Dillington 54 C2
Dilston 110 C2
Dilton Marsh 24 E3
Dilwyn 49 D6
Dinas Carms 45 F4
  Gwyn. 70 D3
Dinas Cross 45 F2
Dinas Dinlle 82 F4
Dinas-Mawddwy . 59 C5
Dinas Powys 22 B3
Dinbych
  = Denbigh. . . 72 C4
Dinbych-y-Pysgod
  = Tenby. 32 D2
Dinder 23 E7
Dinedor. 49 F7
Dingestow 36 C1
Dingle 85 F4
Dingleden 18 B5
Dingley 64 F4
Dingwall 151 F8
Dinlabyre 115 E8
Dinmael 72 E4
Dinnet 140 E3
Dinnington Som. . 12 C2
  S Yorks. 89 F6
  T&W 110 B5
Dinorwic. 83 E5
Dinton Bucks. . . 39 C7
  Wilts. 24 F5
Dinwoodie Mains . 114 E4
Dinworthy 8 C5
Dippen 143 F11
Dippenhall 27 E6
Dipple Moray . . . 152 C3
  S Ayrs. 112 D2
Diptford 6 D5
Dipton 110 D4
Dirdhu 139 B6
Dirleton 129 F7
Dirt Pot 109 E8
Discoed. 48 C4
Diseworth 63 B8
Dishes 159 F7
Dishforth 95 B6
Disley 87 F7
Diss 56 B5
Disserth 48 D2
Distington 98 B2
Ditcham 15 B8
Ditcheat 23 F8
Ditchingham 69 E6
Ditchling 17 C7
Ditherington 60 C5
Dittisham 7 D6
Ditton Halton. . . 86 F2
  Kent. 29 D8
Ditton Green 55 D7
Ditton Priors 61 F6
Divach 137 B7
Divlyn 47 F6
Dixton Glos. 50 F4
  Mon. 36 C2
Dobcross 87 D7
Dobwalls 5 C7
Doccombe 10 F2
Dochfour House. . 151 H9
Dochgarroch. . . 151 G9
Docking 80 D3
Docklow. 49 D7
Dockray 99 B5
Dockroyd 94 F3
Doc Penfro
  = Pembroke Dock. . 44 E4
Dodburn. 115 D7
Doddinghurst. . . 42 E1
Doddington
  Cambs. 66 E3
  Kent. 30 D3
  Lincs 78 B2
  Northumb 123 F5
  Shrops. 49 B8
Doddiscombsleigh . 10 F3
Dodford Northants . 52 C4
  Worcs 50 B4
Dodington
  S Glos. 24 A2
  Som. 22 E3
Dodleston 73 C7
Dodworth. 88 D4
Doe Green. 86 F3
Doe Lea. 76 C4
Dogdyke. 78 D5
Dogmersfield 27 D5
Dogridge 37 F7
Dogsthorpe. 65 D8
Dog Village. 10 E4
Dolanog 59 D7
Dolau Powys 48 C3
  Rhondda 34 F3
Dolbenmaen 71 C6
Dolfach 59 D6
Dolfor 59 F8
Dol-ffôr 58 D5
Dolgarrog 83 E7
Dolgellau 58 C4
Dolgran 46 F3
Dolhendre 72 F2
Doll. 157 J11
Dollar 127 E8
Dolley Green 48 C4
Dollwen 58 F3
Dolphin. 73 B5
Dolphinholme. . . 92 D5
Dolphinton. 120 E4
Dolton 9 C7
Dolwen Conwy . . . 83 D8
  Powys 59 D6
Dolwyd 83 D8
Dolwyddelan 83 F7
Dôl-y-Bont 58 F3
Dol-y-cannau 48 E4
Dolyhir 48 D4
Dolywern 73 F6

Donibristle 128 F3
Donington 78 F5
Donington on Bain . 91 F6
Donington South
  Ing. 78 F5
Donisthorpe 63 C7
Donkey Town 27 C7
Donnington Glos. . 38 B1
  Hereford 50 F2
  Shrops. 61 D5
  Telford. 61 C7
  W Berks. 26 C2
Donnington Wood. . 61 C7
Donyatt. 11 C8
Doonfoot 112 C3
Dorback Lodge . 139 C6
Dorchester Dorset. . 12 E4
  Oxon. 39 E5
Dordon 63 D6
Dore 88 F4
Dores 151 H8
Dorking 28 E2
Dormansland 28 E5
Dormanstown . . . 102 B3
Dormington 49 E7
Dormston 50 D4
Dornal 105 B6
Dorney 27 B7
Dornie 149 F13
Dornoch 151 C10
Dornock 108 C2
Dorrery 158 E2
Dorridge. 51 B6
Dorrington Lincs. . 78 D3
  Shrops. 60 D4
Dorsington. 51 E6
Dorstone 48 E5
Dorton. 39 C6
Dorusduain 136 B2
Dosthill 63 E6
Dottery 12 E2
Doublebois 5 C6
Dougarie 143 E9
Doughton. 37 E5
Douglas IoM 84 E3
  S Lanark. 119 F8
Douglas & Angus . 134 F4
Douglastown . . . 134 E4
Douglas Water . 119 F8
Douglas West . . . 119 F8
Doulting. 23 E8
Dounby 159 F3
Doune Highld . . . 156 J7
  Stirling. 127 D6
Doune Park 153 B7
Douneside 140 D3
Dounie 151 B8
Dounreay 157 C12
Dousland 6 C3
Dovaston 60 B3
Dove Holes. 75 B7
Dovenby 107 F7
Dover. 31 E7
Dovercourt 57 F6
Doverdale. 50 C3
Doveridge 75 F8
Doversgreen 28 E3
Dowally 133 E7
Dowbridge. 92 F4
Dowdeswell. 37 C6
Dowlais. 34 D4
Dowland 9 C7
Dowlish Wake. . . 11 C8
Down Ampney. . . 37 E8
Downcraig
  Ferry. 145 H10
Downderry. 5 D8
Downe. 28 C5
Downend IoW. . . 15 F6
  S Glos. 23 B8
  W Berks. 26 B2
Downfield. 134 F3
Downgate. 5 B8
Downham Essex. . 42 E3
  Lancs. 93 E7
  Northumb 122 F4
Downham Market . 67 D6
Down Hatherley. . 37 B5
Downhead 23 E8
Downhill Perth. . . 133 F7
  T&W. 111 D6
Downholland
  Cross. 85 D4
Downholme 101 E6
Downies 141 E8
Downley. 39 E8
Down St Mary . . . 10 D2
Downside Som. . . 23 E8
  Sur. 28 D2
Down Thomas . . . 6 D3
Downton Hants. . 14 E3
  Wilts. 14 B2
Downton on the
  Rock. 49 B6
Dowsby 65 B8
Dowsdale 66 C2
Dowthwaitehead. . 99 B5
Doxey. 62 B3
Doxford 117 B7
Doxford Park . . . 111 D6
Doynton 24 B2
Draffan 119 E7
Dragonby 90 C3
Drakeland Corner . 6 D3
Drakemyre 118 D2
Drake's Broughton . 50 E4
Drakes Cross 51 B5
Drakewalls. 6 B2
Draughton
  Northants 53 B5
  N Yorks. 94 D3
Drax 89 B7
Draycote 52 B2
Draycott Derbys . 76 F4
  Glos. 51 F6
  Som. 23 D6
Draycott in the
  Clay. 63 B5
Draycott in the
  Moors. 75 E6
Drayford 10 C2
Drayton Leics. . . 64 E5
  Lincs. 78 F5
  Norf. 68 C4
  Oxon. 38 E4

Drayton continued
Oxon 52 E2
Ptsmth 15 D7
Som 12 B2
Worcs 50 B4
Drayton Bassett 63 D5
Drayton Beauchamp 40 C2
Drayton Parslow 39 B8
Drayton St Leonard 39 E5
Drebley 94 D3
Dreemskerry 84 C4
Dreenhill 44 D4
Drefach Carms 33 C6
Carms 46 F2
Dre-fach Carms 33 C7
Ceredig 46 E4
Drefelin 46 F2
Dreghorn 118 F3
Drellingore 31 E6
Drem 121 B8
Dresden 75 E6
Dreumasdal 148 E2
Drewsteignton 10 E2
Driby 79 B6
Driffield EYorks 97 D6
Glos 37 E7
Drigg 98 E2
Drighlington 88 B3
Drimnin 147 F8
Drimpton 12 D2
Drimsynie 125 E7
Drinisiadar 154 H6
Drinkstone 56 C3
Drinkstone Green 56 C3
Drishaig 125 D7
Drissaig 124 D5
Drochil 120 E4
Drointon 62 B4
Droitwich Spa 50 C3
Droman 156 D4
Dron 128 C3
Dronfield 76 B3
Dronfield Woodhouse 76 B3
Drongan 112 C4
Dronley 134 F3
Droxford 15 C7
Droylsden 87 E7
Druid 72 E4
Druidston 44 D3
Druimarbin 130 B4
Druimavuic 130 E4
Druimdrishaig 144 F6
Druimindarroch 147 C9
Druimyeon More 143 C7
Drum Argyll 145 F8
Perth 128 D2
Drumbeg 156 F4
Drumblade 152 D5
Drumblair 153 D6
Drumbuie
Dumfries 113 F5
Highld 149 E12
Drumburgh 108 D2
Drumburn 107 C6
Drumchapel 118 B5
Drumchardine 151 G8
Drumchork 155 J13
Drumclog 119 F6
Drumderfit 151 F9
Drumeldrie 129 D6
Drumelzier 120 F4
Drumfearn 149 G11
Drumgask 138 E2
Drumgley 134 D4
Drumguish 138 E3
Drumin 152 E1
Drumlasie 140 D5
Drumlemble 143 G7
Drumligair 141 C8
Drumlithie 141 F6
Drummoddie 105 E7
Drummond 151 E9
Drummore 104 F5
Drummuir 152 D3
Drummuir Castle 152 D3
Drumnadrochit 137 B8
Drumnagorrach 152 C5
Drumoak 141 E6
Drumpark 107 A5
Drumphail 105 C6
Drumrash 106 B3
Drumrunie 156 J4
Drums 141 B8
Drumsallie 130 B3
Drumstinchall 107 D5
Drumsturdy 134 F4
Drumtochty Castle 135 B6
Drumtroddan 105 E7
Drumuie 149 D9
Drumuillie 138 B5
Drumvaich 127 D5
Drumwhindle 153 E9
Drunkendub 135 E6
Drury 73 C6
Drury Square 68 C2
Drybeck 100 C1
Drybridge Moray 152 B4
N Ayrs 118 F3
Drybrook 36 C3
Dryburgh 121 F8
Dry Doddington 77 E8
Dry Drayton 54 C4
Dryhope 115 B5
Drylaw 120 B5
Drym 2 C5
Drymen 126 F3
Drymuir 153 D9
Drynoch 149 E9
Dryslwyn 33 B6
Dryton 61 D5
Dubford 153 B8
Dubton 135 D5
Duchally 156 H6
Duchlage 126 F2
Duck Corner 57 E7
Duckington 73 D8
Ducklington 38 D3
Duckmanton 76 B4
Duck's Cross 54 D2
Duddenhoe End 55 F5
Duddingston 121 B5
Duddington 65 D6
Duddleswell 17 B8
Duddo 122 E5
Duddon 74 C2
Duddon Bridge 98 F4
Dudleston 73 F7
Dudleston Heath 73 F7
Dudley T&W 111 B5
W Mid 62 E3
Dudley Port 62 E3
Duffield 76 E3
Duffryn Neath 34 E2
Newport 35 F6
Dufftown 152 E3
Duffus 152 B1
Dufton 100 B1
Duggleby 96 C4
Duirinish 149 E12
Duisdalemore 149 G12
Duisky 130 B4
Dukestown 35 C5
Dukinfield 87 E7
Dulas 82 C4
Dulcote 23 E7
Dulford 11 D5
Dull 133 E5
Dullatur 119 B7
Dullingham 55 D7
Dulnain Bridge 139 B5
Duloe Bedford 54 C2
Corn 5 D7
Dulsie 151 G12
Dulverton 10 B4
Dulwich 28 B4
Dumbarton 118 B3
Dumbleton 50 F5
Dumcrieff 114 D4
Dumfries 107 B6
Dumgoyne 126 F4
Dummer 26 E3
Dumpford 16 B2
Dumpton 31 C7
Dun 135 D6
Dunain House 151 G9
Dunalastair 132 D4
Dunan 149 F10
Dunans 145 D9
Dunball 22 E5
Dunbar 122 B2
Dunbeath 158 H3
Dunbeg 124 B4
Dunblane 127 D6
Dunbog 128 C4
Duncanston 151 F8
Duncanstone 140 B4
Dun Charlabhaigh 154 C6
Dunchurch 52 B2
Duncote 52 D4
Duncow 114 F2
Duncraggan 126 D4
Duncrievie 128 D3
Duncton 16 C3
Dundas House 159 K5
Dundee 134 F4
Dundeugh 113 F5
Dundon 23 F6
Dundonald 118 F3
Dundonnell 150 C3
Dundonnell Hotel 150 C3
Dundonnell House 150 C4
Dundraw 108 E2
Dundreggan 137 C6
Dundreggan Lodge 137 C6
Dundrennan 106 E4
Dundry 23 C7
Dunecht 141 D6
Dunfermline 128 F2
Dunfield 37 E8
Dunford Bridge 88 D2
Dungworth 88 F3
Dunham 77 B8
Dunham-on-the-Hill 73 B8
Dunhampton 50 C3
Dunham Town 86 F5
Dunholme 78 B3
Dunino 129 C7
Dunipace 127 F7
Dunira 127 B6
Dunkeld 133 E7
Dunkerton 24 D2
Dunkeswell 11 D6
Dunkeswick 95 E6
Dunkirk Kent 30 D4
Norf 81 E8
Dunk's Green 29 D7
Dunlappie 135 C5
Dunley Hants 26 D2
Worcs 50 C2
Dunlichity Lodge 151 H9
Dunlop 118 E4
Dunmaglass Lodge 137 B8
Dunmore Argyll 144 G6
Falk 127 F7
Dunnet 158 C4
Dunnichen 135 E5
Dunninald 135 D7
Dunning 128 C2
Dunnington
EYorks 97 D7
Warks 51 D5
York 96 D2
Dunnockshaw 87 B6
Dunollie 124 B4
Dunoon 145 F10
Dunragit 105 D5
Dunrostan 144 E6
Duns 122 D3
Dunsby 65 B8
Dunscore 113 F8
Dunscroft 89 D7
Dunsdale 102 C4
Dunsden Green 26 B5
Dunsfold 27 F8
Dunsford 10 F3
Dunshalt 128 C4
Dunshillock 153 D9
Dunskey House 104 D4
Dunsley 103 C6
Dunsmore 40 D1
Dunsop Bridge 93 D6
Dunstable 40 B3
Dunstall 63 B5
Dunstall Common 50 E3
Dunstall Green 55 C8
Dunstan 117 C8
Dunstan Steads 117 B8
Dunster 21 E8
Duns Tew 38 B4
Dunston Lincs 78 C3
Norf 68 D5
Staffs 62 C3
T&W 110 C5
Dunsville 89 D7
Dunswell 97 F6
Dunsyre 120 E3
Dunterton 5 B8
Duntisbourne Abbots 37 D6
Duntisbourne Leer 37 D6
Duntisbourne Rouse 37 D6
Duntish 12 D4
Duntocher 118 B4
Dunton Bucks 39 B8
C Beds 54 E3
Norf 80 D4
Dunton Bassett 64 E2
Dunton Green 29 D6
Dunton Wayletts 42 E2
Duntulm 149 A9
Dunure 112 C2
Dunvant 33 E6
Dunvegan 148 D7
Dunwich 57 B8
Dunwood 75 D6
Dupplin Castle 128 C2
Durdar 108 D4
Durgates 18 B3
Durham 111 E5
Durisdeer 113 D8
Durisdeermill 113 D8
Durkar 88 C4
Durleigh 22 F4
Durley Hants 15 C6
Wilts 25 C7
Durnamuck 150 B3
Durness 156 C7
Durno 141 B6
Duror 130 D3
Durran Argyll 125 E5
Highld 158 D3
Durrington Wilts 25 E6
W Sus 16 D5
Dursley 36 E4
Durston 11 B7
Durweston 13 D6
Dury 160 G6
Duston 52 C5
Duthil 138 B5
Dutlas 48 B4
Duton Hill 42 B2
Dutson 8 F5
Dutton 74 B2
Duxford Cambs 55 E5
Oxon 38 E3
Dwygyfylchi 83 D7
Dwyran 82 E4
Dyce 141 C7
Dye House 110 D2
Dyffryn Bridgend 34 E2
Carms 32 B4
Pembs 44 B4
Dyffryn Ardudwy 71 E6
Dyffryn Castell 58 F4
Dyffryn Ceidrych 33 B8
Dyffryn Cellwen 34 D2
Dyke Lincs 65 B8
Moray 151 F12
Dykehead Angus 134 C3
N Lanark 119 D8
Stirling 126 E4
Dykelands 135 C7
Dykends 134 D2
Dykeside 153 D7
Dykesmains 118 E2
Dylife 59 E5
Dymchurch 19 C7
Dymock 50 F2
Dyrham 24 B2
Dysart 128 E5
Dyserth 72 B4

E

Eadar Dha Fhadhail 154 D5
Eagland Hill 92 E4
Eagle 77 C8
Eagle Barnsdale 77 C8
Eagle Moor 77 C8
Eaglescliffe 102 C2
Eaglesfield Cumb 98 B2
Dumfries 108 B2
Eaglesham 119 D5
Eaglethorpe 65 E7
Eairy 84 E2
Eakley Lanes 53 D6
Eakring 77 C6
Ealand 89 C8
Ealing 40 F4
Eals 109 D6
Eamont Bridge 99 B7
Earby 94 E2
Earcroft 86 B4
Eardington 61 E7
Eardisland 49 D6
Eardisley 48 E5
Eardiston Shrops 60 B3
Worcs 49 C8
Earith 54 B4
Earle 117 B5
Earley 27 B5
Earlham 68 D5
Earlish 149 B8
Earls Barton 53 C6
Earls Colne 42 B4
Earl's Croome 50 E3
Earlsdon 51 B8
Earlsferry 129 E6
Earlsfield 78 F2
Earlsford 153 E8
Earl's Green 56 C4
Earlsheaton 88 B3
Earl Shilton 63 E8
Earlsmill 151 F12
Earl Soham 57 C6
Earl Sterndale 75 C7
Earlston Borders 121 F8
E Ayrs 118 F4
Earl Stonham 56 D5
Earlswood Mon 36 E1
Sur 28 E3
Warks 51 B6
Earnley 16 E2
Earsairidh 148 J2
Earsdon 111 B6
Earsham 69 F6
Earswick 96 D2
Eartham 16 D3
Easby N Yorks 101 D6
N Yorks 102 D3
Easdale 124 D3
Easebourne 16 B2
Easenhall 52 B2
Eashing 27 E7
Easington Bucks 39 C6
Durham 111 E7
E Yorks 91 C7
Northumb 123 F7
Oxon 39 E6
Oxon 52 F2
Redcar 103 C5
Easington Colliery 111 E7
Easington Lane 111 E6
Easingwold 95 C8
Easole Street 31 D6
Eassie 134 E3
East Aberthaw 22 C2
East Adderbury 52 F2
East Allington 7 E5
East Anstey 10 B3
East Appleton 101 E7
East Ardsley 88 B4
East Ashling 16 D2
East Auchronie 141 D7
East Ayton 103 F7
East Bank 35 D6
East Barkwith 91 F5
East Barming 29 D8
East Barnby 103 C6
East Barnet 41 E5
East Barns 122 B3
East Barsham 80 D5
East Beckham 81 D7
East Bedfont 27 B8
East Bergholt 56 F4
East Bilney 68 C2
East Blatchington 17 D8
East Boldre 14 D4
Eastbourne 18 F3
East Brent 22 D5
Eastbridge 57 C8
East Bridgford 77 E6
East Buckland 21 F5
East Budleigh 11 F5
Eastburn 94 E3
East Burrafirth 160 H5
East Burton 13 F6
Eastbury London 40 E3
W Berks 25 B8
East Butsfield 110 E4
East Butterwick 90 D2
Eastby 94 D3
East Cairnbeg 135 B7
East Calder 120 C3
East Carleton 68 D4
East Carlton
Northants 64 F5
W Yorks 94 E5
East Chaldon 13 F5
East Challow 38 F3
East Chiltington 17 C7
East Chinnock 12 C2
East Chisenbury 25 D6
Eastchurch 30 B3
East Clandon 27 D8
East Claydon 39 B7
East Clyne 157 J12
East Coker 12 C3
Eastcombe 37 D5
East Combe 22 F3
East Common 96 F2
East Compton 23 E8
Eastcote London 40 F4
Northants 52 D4
W Mid 51 B6
Eastcott Corn 8 C4
Wilts 24 D5
East Cottingwith 96 E3
Eastcourt Wilts 25 C7
Wilts 37 E6
East Cowes 15 E6
East Cowick 89 B7
East Cowton 101 D8
East Cramlington 111 B5
East Cranmore 23 E8
East Creech 13 F7
East Croachy 138 B2
East Croftmore 139 C5
East Curthwaite 108 E3
East Dean E Sus 18 F2
Hants 14 B3
W Sus 16 C3
East Down 20 E5
East Drayton 77 B7
East Ella 90 B4
East End Dorset 13 E7
E Yorks 91 B6
Hants 14 E4
Hants 15 B7
Hants 26 C2
Herts 41 B7
Kent 18 B5
N Som 23 B6
Oxon 38 C3
Easter Ardross 151 D9
Easter Balmoral 139 E8
Easter Boleskine 137 B8
Easter Compton 36 F2
Easter Cringate 127 F6
Easter Davoch 140 D3
Easter Earshaig 114 D3
Easter Fearn 151 C9
Easter Galcantray 151 G11
Eastergate 16 D3
Easterhouse 119 C6
Easter Howgate 120 C5
Easter Howlaws 122 E3
Easter Kinkell 151 F8
Easter Lednathie 134 C3
Easter Milton 151 F12
Easter Moniack 151 G8
Eastern Green 63 F6
Easter Ord 141 D7
Easter Quarff 160 K6
Easter Rhynd 128 C3
Easter Row 127 E6
Easter Silverford 153 B7
Easter Skeld 160 J5
Easterton 24 D5
Eastertown 22 D5
Eastertown of Auchleuchries 153 E10
Easter Whyntie 152 B6
East Farleigh 29 D8
East Farndon 64 F4
East Ferry 90 E2
Eastfield N Lanark 119 C8
N Yorks 103 F8
Eastfield Hall 117 D8
East Fortune 121 B8
East Garston 25 B8
Eastgate Durham 110 F2
Norf 81 E7
East Ginge 38 F4
East Goscote 64 C3
East Grafton 25 C7
East Grimstead 14 B3
East Grinstead 28 F4
East Guldeford 19 C6
East Haddon 52 C4
East Hagbourne 39 F5
East Halton 90 C5
Eastham 85 F4
East Ham 41 F7
Eastham Ferry 85 F4
Easthampstead 27 C6
East Hanney 38 E4
East Hanningfield 42 D3
East Hardwick 89 C5
East Harling 68 F2
East Harlsey 102 E2
East Harnham 14 B2
East Harptree 23 D7
East Hartford 111 B5
East Harting 15 C8
East Hatley 54 D3
East Hauxwell 101 E6
East Haven 135 F5
Eastheath 27 C6
East Heckington 78 E4
East Hedleyhope 110 E4
East Hendred 38 F4
East Herrington 111 D6
East Heslerton 96 B5
East Hoathly 18 D2
Easthope 61 E5
Easthorpe Essex 43 B5
Leics 77 F8
Notts 77 D7
East Horrington 23 E7
East Horsley 27 D8
East Horton 123 F6
Easthouses 121 C6
East Huntspill 22 E5
East Hyde 40 C4
East Ilkerton 21 E6
East Ilsley 38 F4
Eastington Devon 10 D2
Glos 36 D4
Glos 37 C8
East Keal 79 C6
East Kennett 25 C6
East Keswick 95 E6
East Kilbride 119 D6
East Kirkby 79 C6
East Knapton 96 B4
East Knighton 13 F6
East Knoyle 24 F3
East Kyloe 123 F6
East Lambrook 12 C2
East Lamington 151 D10
East Langdon 31 E7
East Langton 64 E4
East Langwell 157 J10
East Lavant 16 D2
East Lavington 16 C3
East Layton 101 D6
Eastleach Martin 38 D2
Eastleach Turville 38 D1
East Leake 64 B2
East Learmouth 122 F4
Eastleigh Devon 9 B6
Hants 14 C5
East Leigh 9 D8
East Lexham 67 C8
East Lilburn 117 B6
Eastling 30 D3
East Linton 121 B8
East Liss 15 B8
East Looe 5 D7
East Lound 89 E8
East Lulworth 13 F6
East Lutton 96 C5
East Lydford 23 F7
East Mains 141 E5
East Malling 29 D8
East March 134 F4
East Marden 16 C2
East Markham 77 B7
East Marton 94 D2
East Meon 15 B7
East Mere 10 C4
East Mersea 43 C6
East Mey 158 C5
East Molesey 28 C2
Eastmoor Derbys 76 B3
Norf 67 D7
East Morden 13 E7
East Morton 94 E3
East Ness 96 B2
East Newton 97 F8
Eastney 15 E7
Eastnor 50 F2
East Norton 64 D4
East Nynehead 11 B6
East Oakley 26 D3
Eastoft 90 C2
East Ogwell 7 B6
Eastoke 15 E8
Easton Cambs 54 B2
Cumb 108 B4
Cumb 108 D2
Devon 10 F2
Dorset 12 G4
Hants 26 F3
Lincs 65 B6
Norf 68 C4
Som 23 E7
Suff 57 D6
Wilts 24 B3
Easton Grey 37 F5
Easton-in-Gordano 23 B7
Easton Maudit 53 D6
Easton on the Hill 65 D7
Easton Royal 25 C7
East Orchard 13 C6
East Ord 123 D5
East Panson 9 E5
Eastpark 107 C7
East Peckham 29 E7
East Pennard 23 F7
East Perry 54 C2
East Portlemouth 6 F5
East Prawle 7 F5
East Preston 16 D4
East Putford 9 C5
East Quantoxhead 22 E3
East Rainton 111 E6
East Ravendale 91 E6
East Raynham 80 E4
Eastrea 66 E2
East Rhidorroch Lodge 150 B5
Eastriggs 108 C2
East Rigton 95 E6
Eastrington 89 B8
East Rounton 102 D2
East Row 103 C6
East Rudham 80 E4
East Runton 81 C7
East Ruston 69 B6
Eastry 31 D7
East Saltoun 121 C7
East Sleekburn 117 F8
East Somerton 69 C7
East Stockwith 89 E8
East Stoke Dorset 13 F6
Notts 77 E7
East Stour 13 B6
East Stourmouth 31 C6
East Stowford 9 B8
East Stratton 26 F3
East Studdal 31 E7
East Suisnish 149 E10
East Taphouse 5 C6
East-the-Water 9 B6
East Thirston 117 E7
East Tilbury 29 B7
East Tisted 26 F5
East Torrington 90 F5
East Tuddenham 68 C3
East Tytherley 14 B3
East Tytherton 24 B4
East Village 10 D3
Eastville Bristol 23 B8
Lincs 79 D7
East Wall 60 E5
East Walton 67 C7
Eastwell 64 B4
East Wellow 14 B4
East Wemyss 128 E5
East Whitburn 120 C2
Eastwick Herts 41 C7
Shetland 160 F5
East Williamston 32 D1
East Winch 67 C6
East Winterslow 25 F7
East Wittering 15 E8
East Witton 101 F6
Eastwood Notts 76 E4
Southend 42 F4
W Yorks 87 B7
East Woodburn 116 F5
East Woodhay 26 C2
East Worldham 26 F5
East Worlington 10 C2
East Worthing 17 D5
Eathorpe 51 C8
Eaton Ches E 75 C5
Ches W 74 C2
Leics 64 B4
Norf 68 D5
Notts 77 B7
Oxon 38 D4
Shrops 60 F3
Shrops 60 F5
Eaton Bishop 49 F6
Eaton Bray 40 B2
Eaton Constantine 61 D5
Eaton Green 40 B2
Eaton Hastings 38 E2
Eaton on Tern 61 B6
Eaton Socon 54 D2
Eavestone 94 C5
Ebberston 103 F6
Ebbesbourne Wake 13 B7
Ebbw Vale = *Glyn Ebwy* 35 D5
Ebchester 110 D4
Ebford 10 F4
Ebley 37 D5
Ebnal 73 E8
Ebrington 51 E6
Ecchinswell 26 D2
Ecclaw 122 C3
Ecclefechan 107 B8
Eccles Borders 122 E3
Gtr Man 87 E5
Kent 29 C8
Ecclesall 88 F4
Ecclesfield 88 E4
Ecclesgreig 135 C7
Eccleshall 62 B2
Eccleshill 94 F4
Ecclesmachan 120 B3
Eccles on Sea 69 B7
Eccles Road 68 E3
Eccleston Ches W 73 C8
Lancs 86 C3
Mers 86 E2
Eccleston Park 86 E2
Eccup 95 E5
Echt 141 D6
Eckford 116 B3
Eckington Derbys 76 B4
Worcs 50 E4
Ecton 53 C6
Edale 88 F2
Edburton 17 C6
Edderside 107 E7
Edderton 151 C10
Eddistone 8 B4
Eddleston 120 E5
Edenbridge 28 E5
Edenfield 87 C5
Edenhall 109 F5
Edenham 65 B7
Eden Park 28 C4
Edensor 76 C2
Edentaggart 126 E2
Edenthorpe 89 D7
Edentown 108 D3
Ederline 124 E4
Edern 70 D3
Edgarley 23 F7
Edgbaston 62 F4
Edgcott Bucks 39 B6
Som 21 F7
Edge 60 D3
Edgebolton 61 B5
Edge End 36 C2
Edgefield 81 D6
Edgefield Street 81 D6
Edge Green 73 D8
Edge Hill 85 F4
Edgeside 87 B6
Edgeworth 37 D6
Edgmond 61 C7
Edgmond Marsh 61 B7
Edgton 60 F3
Edgware 40 E4
Edgworth 86 C5
Edinample 126 B4
Edinbane 149 C8
Edinburgh 121 B5
Edingale 63 C6
Edingight House 152 C5
Edingley 77 D6
Edingthorpe 69 A6
Edingthorpe Green 69 A6
Edington Som 23 F5
Wilts 24 D4
Edintore 152 D4
Edithmead 22 E5
Edith Weston 65 D6
Edlesborough 40 C2
Edlingham 117 D7
Edlington 78 B5
Edmondsham 13 C8
Edmondsley 110 E5
Edmondthorpe 65 C5
Edmonstone 159 F6
Edmonton 41 E6
Edmundbyers 110 D3
Ednam 122 F3
Ednaston 76 E2
Edradynate 133 D5
Edrom 122 D4
Edstaston 74 F2
Edstone 51 C6
Edvin Loach 49 D8
Edwalton 77 F5
Edwardstone 56 E3
Edwinsford 46 F5
Edwinstowe 77 C6
Edworth 54 E3
Edwyn Ralph 49 D8
Edzell 135 C5
E Eachwick 110 B4
Efail Isaf 34 F4
Efailnewydd 70 D4
Efailwen 32 B2
Efenechtyd 72 D5
Effingham 28 D2
Effirth 160 H5
Efford 10 D3
Egdon 50 D4
Egerton Gtr Man 86 C5
Kent 30 E3
Egerton Forstal 30 E2
Eggborough 89 B6
Eggbuckland 6 D3
Eggington 40 B2
Egginton 63 B6
Egglescliffe 102 C2
Eggleston 100 B4
Egham 27 B8
Egleton 65 D5
Eglingham 117 C7
Egloshayle 4 B5
Egloskerry 8 F4
Eglwysbach 83 D8
Eglwys-Brewis 22 C2
Eglwys Cross 73 E8
Eglwys Fach 58 E3
Eglwyswen 45 F3
Eglwyswrw 45 F3
Egmanton 77 C7
Egremont Cumb 98 C2
Mers 85 E4
Egton 103 D6
Egton Bridge 103 D6
Eight Ash Green 43 B5
Eignaig 130 E1
Eil 138 C4
Eilanreach 149 G13
Eileanach Lodge 151 E8
Eilean Darach 150 C4
Einacleite 154 E6
Eisgean 155 F8
Eisingrug 71 D7
Elan Village 47 C8
Elberton 36 F3
Elburton 6 D3
Elcho 128 B3
Elcombe 37 F8
Eldernell 66 E3
Eldersfield 50 F3
Eldersli 118 C4
Eldon 101 B7
Eldrick 112 F2
Eldroth 93 C7
Eldwick 94 E4
Elfhowe 99 E6
Elford Northumb 123 F7
Staffs 63 C5
Elgin 152 B2
Elgol 149 G10
Elham 31 E5
Elie 129 D6
Elim 82 C3
Eling 14 C4
Elishader 149 B10
Elishaw 116 E4
Elkesley 77 B6
Elkstone 37 C6
Ellan 138 B4
Elland 88 B2
Ellary 144 F6
Ellastone 75 E8
Ellemford 122 C3
Ellenbrook 84 E3
Ellenhall 62 B2
Ellen's Green 27 F8
Ellerbeck 102 E2
Ellerburn 103 F6
Ellerby 103 C5
Ellerdine Heath 61 B6
Ellerhayes 10 D4
Elleric 130 E4
Ellerker 90 B3
Ellerton E Yorks 96 F3
Shrops 61 B7
Ellesborough 39 D8
Ellesmere 73 F8
Ellesmere Port 73 B8
Ellingham Norf 69 E6
Northumb 117 B7
Ellingstring 101 F6
Ellington Cambs 54 B2
Northumb 117 E8
Elliot 135 F6
Ellisfield 26 E4
Ellistown 63 C8
Ellon 153 E9
Ellonby 108 F4
Ellough 69 F7
Elloughton 90 B3
Ellwood 36 D2
Elm 66 D4
Elmbridge 50 C4
Elmdon Essex 55 F5
W Mid 63 F5
Elmdon Heath 63 F5
Elmers End 28 C4
Elmesthorpe 63 E8
Elmfield 15 E7
Elm Hill 13 B6
Elmhurst 62 C5
Elmley Castle 50 E4
Elmley Lovett 50 C3
Elmore 36 C4
Elmore Back 36 C4
Elm Park 41 F8
Elmscott 8 B4
Elmsett 56 E4
Elmstead Market 43 B6
Elmsted 30 E5
Elmstone 31 C6
Elmstone Hardwicke 37 B6
Elmswell E Yorks 97 D5
Suff 56 C3
Elmton 76 B5
Elphin 156 H5
Elphinstone 121 B6
Elrick 141 D7
Elrig 105 E7
Elsdon 117 E5
Elsecar 88 E4
Elsenham 41 B8
Elsfield 39 C5
Elsham 90 C4
Elsing 68 C3
Elslack 94 E2
Elson 73 F7
Elsrickle 120 E3
Elstead 27 E7
Elsted 16 C2
Elsthorpe 65 B7
Elstob 101 B8
Elston Notts 77 E7
Wilts 25 E5
Elstone 9 C8
Elstow 53 E8
Elstree 40 E4
Elstronwick 97 F8
Elswick 92 F4
Elsworth 54 C4
Elterwater 99 D5
Eltham 28 B5
Eltisley 54 D3
Elton Cambs 65 E7
Ches W 73 B8
Derbys 76 C2
Glos 36 C4
Hereford 49 B6
Notts 77 F7
Stockton 102 C2
Elton Green 73 B8
Elvanfoot 114 C2
Elvaston 76 F4
Elveden 56 B2
Elvingston 121 B7
Elvington Kent 31 D6
York 96 E2
Elwick Hrtlpl 111 F7
Northumb 123 F7
Elworth 74 C4
Elworthy 22 F2
Ely Cambs 66 F5
Cardiff 22 B3
Emberton 53 E6
Embleton Cumb 107 F8
Northumb 117 B8
Embo 151 B11
Emborough 23 D8
Embo Street 151 B11
Embsay 94 D3
Emersons Green 23 B8
Emery Down 14 D3
Emley 88 C3
Emmbrook 27 C5
Emmer Green 26 B5
Emmington 39 D7
Emneth 66 D4
Emneth Hungate 66 D5
Empingham 65 D6
Empshott 27 F5
Emstrey 60 C5
Emsworth 15 D8
Enborne 26 C2
Enchmarsh 60 E5
Enderby 64 E2
Endmoor 99 F7
Endon 75 D6
Endon Bank 75 D6
Enfield 41 E6
Enfield Wash 41 E6
Enford 25 D6
Engamoor 160 H4
Engine Common 36 F3
Englefield 26 B4
Englefield Green 27 B7
Englesea-brook 74 D4
English Bicknor 36 C2
Englishcombe 24 C2
English Frankton 60 B4
Enham Alamein 25 E8
Enmore 22 F4
Ennerdale Bridge 98 C2
Enoch 113 D8
Enochdhu 133 C7
Ensay 146 G6
Ensbury 13 E8
Ensdon 60 C4
Ensis 9 B7
Enstone 38 B3
Enterkinfoot 113 D8
Enterpen 102 D2
Enville 62 F2
Eolaigearraidh 148 H2
Eorabus 146 J6
Eòropaidh 155 A10
Epperstone 77 E6
Epping 41 D7
Epping Green
Essex 41 D7
Herts 41 D5
Epping Upland 41 D7
Eppleby 101 C6
Eppleworth 97 F6
Epsom 28 C3
Epwell 51 E8
Epworth 89 D8
Epworth Turbary 89 D8
Erbistock 73 E7
Erbusaig 149 F12
Erchless Castle 150 G7
Erdington 62 E5
Eredine 125 E5
Eriboll 156 D7
Ericstane 114 C3
Eridge Green 18 B2
Erines 145 F7
Eriswell 55 B8
Erith 29 B6
Erlestoke 24 D4
Ermine 78 B2
Ermington 6 D4
Erpingham 81 D7
Errogie 137 B8
Errol 128 B4
Erskin 118 B4
Erskine Bridg 118 B4
Ervie 104 C4
Erwarton 57 F6
Erwood 48 E2
Eryholme 101 D8
Eryrys 73 D6
Escomb 101 B6
Escrick 96 E2
Esgairdawe 46 E5
Esgairgeiliog 58 D4
Esh 110 E4
Esher 28 C2
Esholt 94 E4
Eshott 117 E8
Eshton 94 D2
Esh Winning 110 E4
Eskadale 150 H7
Eskbank 121 C6
Eskdale Green 98 D3
Eskdalemuir 115 E5
Eske 97 E6
Eskham 91 E7
Esk Valley 103 D6
Esprick 92 F4
Essendine 65 C7
Essendon 41 D5
Essich 151 H9
Essington 62 D3
Esslemont 141 B8
Eston 102 C3
Eswick 160 H6
Etal 122 F5
Etchilhampton 24 C5
Etchingham 18 C4
Etchinghill Kent 19 B8
Staffs 62 C4
Ethie Castle 135 E6
Ethie Mains 135 E6
Etling Green 68 C3
Eton 27 B7
Eton Wick 27 B7
Etteridge 138 E2
Ettersgill 100 B3
Ettingshall 62 E3
Ettington 51 E7
Etton E Yorks 97 E5
Pboro 65 D8
Ettrick 115 C5
Ettrickbridge 115 B6
Ettrickhill 115 C5
Etwall 76 F2
Euston 56 B2
Euximoor Drove 66 E4
Euxton 86 C3
Evanstown 34 F3
Evanton 151 E9
Evedon 78 E3
Evelix 151 B10
Evenjobb 48 C4
Evenley 52 F3
Evenlode 38 B2
Evenwood 101 B6
Evenwood Gate 101 B6
Everbay 159 F7
Evercreech 23 F8
Everdon 52 D3
Everingham 96 E4
Everleigh 25 D7
Everley 103 F7
Eversholt 53 F7
Evershot 12 D3
Eversley 27 C5
Eversley Cross 27 C5
Everthorpe 96 F5
Everton C Beds 54 D3
Hants 14 E3
Mers 85 E4
Notts 89 E7
Evertown 108 B3
Evesbatch 49 E8
Evesham 50 E5
Evington 64 D3
Ewden Village 88 E3
Ewell 28 C3
Ewell Minnis 31 E6
Ewelme 39 E6
Ewen 37 E7
Ewenny 21 B8
Ewerby 78 E4
Ewerby Thorpe 78 E4
Ewes 115 E6
Ewesley 117 E6
Ewhurst 27 E8
Ewhurst Green
E Sus 18 C4
Sur 27 F8
Ewloe 73 C7
Ewloe Green 73 C6
Ewood 86 B4
Eworthy 9 E6
Ewshot 27 E6
Ewyas Harold 35 B7
Exbourne 9 D8
Exbury 14 E5
Exebridge 10 B4
Exelby 101 F7
Exeter 10 E4

Exford . . . 21 F7
Exhall . . . 51 D6
Exley Head . . . 94 F3
Exminster . . . 10 F4
Exmouth . . . 10 F5
Exnaboe . . . 160 M5
Exning . . . 55 C7
Exton Devon . . . 10 F4
  Hants . . . 15 B7
  Rutland . . . 65 C6
  Som . . . 21 F8
Exwick . . . 10 E4
Eyam . . . 76 B2
Eydon . . . 52 D3
Eye Hereford . . . 49 C6
  Pboro . . . 66 D2
  Suff . . . 56 B5
Eye Green . . . 66 D2
Eyemouth . . . 122 C6
Eyeworth . . . 54 E3
Eyhorne Street . . . 30 D2
Eyke . . . 57 D7
Eynesbury . . . 54 D2
Eynort . . . 149 F8
Eynsford . . . 29 C6
Eynsham . . . 38 D4
Eype . . . 12 E2
Eyre Highld . . . 149 C9
  Highld . . . 149 E10
Eythorne . . . 31 E6
Eyton Hereford . . . 49 C6
  Shrops . . . 60 F3
  Wrex . . . 73 E7
Eyton upon the Weald Moors . . . 61 C6

F

Faceby . . . 102 D2
Facit . . . 87 C6
Faddiley . . . 74 D2
Fadmoor . . . 102 F4
Faerdre . . . 33 D7
Failand . . . 23 B7
Failford . . . 112 B4
Failsworth . . . 87 D6
Fain . . . 150 D4
Fairbourne . . . 58 C3
Fairburn . . . 89 B5
Fairfield Derbys . . . 75 B7
  Stockton . . . 102 C2
  Worcs . . . 50 B4
  Worcs . . . 50 E5
Fairford . . . 38 D1
Fair Green . . . 67 C6
Fairhaven . . . 85 B4
Fair Hill . . . 108 F5
Fairlie . . . 118 D2
Fairlight . . . 19 D5
Fairlight Cove . . . 19 D5
Fairmile . . . 11 E5
Fairmilehead . . . 120 C5
Fairoak . . . 74 F4
Fair Oak . . . 15 C5
Fair Oak Green . . . 26 C4
Fairseat . . . 29 C7
Fairstead Essex . . . 42 C3
  Norf . . . 67 C6
Fairwarp . . . 17 B8
Fairy Cottage . . . 84 D4
Fairy Cross . . . 9 B6
Fakenham . . . 80 E5
Fakenham Magna . . . 56 B3
Fala . . . 121 C7
Fala Dam . . . 121 C7
Falahill . . . 121 D6
Falcon . . . 49 F8
Faldingworth . . . 90 F4
Falfield . . . 36 E3
Falkenham . . . 57 F6
Falkirk . . . 119 B8
Falkland . . . 128 D4
Falla . . . 116 C3
Fallgate . . . 76 C3
Fallin . . . 127 E7
Fallowfield . . . 87 E6
Fallsidehill . . . 122 E2
Falmer . . . 17 D7
Falmouth . . . 3 C7
Falsgrave . . . 103 F8
Falstone . . . 116 F3
Fanagmore . . . 156 E4
Fangdale Beck . . . 102 E3
Fangfoss . . . 96 D3
Fankerton . . . 127 F6
Fanmore . . . 146 G7
Fannich Lodge . . . 150 E5
Fans . . . 122 E2
Far Bank . . . 89 C7
Far Bletchley . . . 53 F6
Farcet . . . 66 E2
Far Cotton . . . 52 D5
Farden . . . 49 B7
Fareham . . . 15 D6
Farewell . . . 62 C4
Far Forest . . . 50 B2
Farforth . . . 79 B6
Faringdon . . . 38 E2
Farington . . . 86 B3
Farlam . . . 109 D5
Farlary . . . 157 J10
Far Laund . . . 76 E3
Farleigh N Som . . . 23 C6
  Sur . . . 28 C4
Farleigh Hungerford . . . 24 D3
Farleigh Wallop . . . 26 E4
Farlesthorpe . . . 79 B7
Farleton Cumb . . . 99 F7
  Lancs . . . 93 C5
Farley Shrops . . . 60 D3
  Staffs . . . 75 E7
  Wilts . . . 14 B3
Farley Green . . . 27 E8
  Wokingham . . . 26 C5
Farleys End . . . 36 C4
Farlington . . . 96 C2
Farlow . . . 61 F6
Farmborough . . . 23 C8
Farmcote Glos . . . 37 B7
  Shrops . . . 61 E7
Farmington . . . 37 C8
Farmoor . . . 38 D4
Farmtown . . . 152 C5
Farnborough Hants 27 D6
  London . . . 28 C5
  Warks . . . 52 E2

Farnborough continued
  W Berks . . . 38 F4
Farnborough Green . . . 27 D6
Farncombe . . . 27 E7
Farndish . . . 53 C7
Farndon Ches W . . . 73 D8
  Notts . . . 77 D7
Farnell . . . 135 D6
Farnham Dorset . . . 13 C7
  Essex . . . 41 B7
  N Yorks . . . 95 C6
  Suff . . . 57 C7
  Sur . . . 27 E6
Farnham Common 40 F2
Farnham Green . . . 41 B7
Farnham Royal . . . 40 F2
Farnhill . . . 94 E3
Farningham . . . 29 C6
Farnley N Yorks . . . 94 E5
  W Yorks . . . 95 F5
Farnley Tyas . . . 88 C2
Farnsfield . . . 77 D6
Farnworth Gtr Man . 86 D5
  Halton . . . 86 F3
Farr Highld . . . 138 D4
  Highld . . . 151 H9
  Highld . . . 157 C10
Farr House . . . 151 H9
Farringdon . . . 10 E5
Farrington Gurney . 23 D8
Far Sawrey . . . 99 E5
Farsley . . . 94 F5
Farthinghoe . . . 52 F3
Farthingloe . . . 31 E6
Farthingstone . . . 52 D4
Farway . . . 11 E6
Fasag . . . 149 C13
Fascadale . . . 147 D8
Faslane Port . . . 145 E11
Fasnacloich . . . 130 E4
Fasnakyle Ho . . . 137 B6
Fassfern . . . 130 B4
Fatfield . . . 111 D6
Fattahead . . . 153 C6
Faugh . . . 108 D5
Fauldhouse . . . 120 C2
Faulkbourne . . . 42 C3
Faulkland . . . 24 D2
Fauls . . . 74 F2
Faversham . . . 30 C4
Favillar . . . 152 E2
Fawdington . . . 95 B7
Fawfieldhead . . . 75 C7
Fawkham Green . . . 29 C6
Fawler . . . 38 C3
Fawley Bucks . . . 39 F7
  Hants . . . 15 D5
  W Berks . . . 38 F3
Fawley Chapel . . . 36 B2
Faxfleet . . . 90 B2
Faygate . . . 28 F3
Fazakerley . . . 85 E4
Fazeley . . . 63 D6
Fearby . . . 101 F6
Fearn . . . 151 D11
Fearnan . . . 132 E4
Fearnbeg . . . 149 C12
Fearnhead . . . 86 E4
Fearn Lodge . . . 151 C9
Fearnmore . . . 149 B12
Fearn Station . . . 151 D11
Featherstone Staffs 62 D3
  W Yorks . . . 88 B5
Featherwood . . . 116 D4
Feckenham . . . 50 C5
Feering . . . 42 B4
Feetham . . . 100 E4
Feizor . . . 93 C7
Felbridge . . . 28 F4
Felbrigg . . . 81 D8
Felcourt . . . 28 E4
Felden . . . 40 D3
Felin-Crai . . . 34 B2
Felindre Carms . . . 33 B6
  Carms . . . 33 B8
  Carms . . . 46 F2
  Carms . . . 47 F5
  Ceredig . . . 46 D4
  Powys . . . 59 F8
  Swansea . . . 33 D7
Felindre Farchog . 45 F3
Felinfach Ceredig . . 46 D4
  Powys . . . 48 F2
Felinfoel . . . 33 D6
Felingwmisaf . . . 33 B6
Felingwmuchaf . . 33 B6
Felinwynt . . . 45 D4
Felixkirk . . . 102 F2
Felixstowe . . . 57 F6
Felixstowe Ferry . . 57 F7
Felkington . . . 122 E5
Felkirk . . . 88 C4
Fell Side . . . 108 F3
Felmersham . . . 53 D7
Felmingham . . . 81 E8
Felpham . . . 16 E3
Felsham . . . 56 D3
Felsted . . . 42 B2
Feltham . . . 28 B2
Felthorpe . . . 68 C4
Felton Hereford . . . 49 E7
  Northumb . . . 117 D7
  N Som . . . 23 C7
Felton Butler . . . 60 C3
Feltwell . . . 67 E7
Fenay Bridge . . . 88 C2
Fence . . . 93 F8
Fence Houses . . . 111 D6
Fen Ditton . . . 55 C5
Fen Drayton . . . 54 C4
Fen End . . . 51 B7
Fengate Norf . . . 81 E7
  Pboro . . . 66 E2
Fenham . . . 123 E6
Fenhouses . . . 79 E5
Feniscliffe . . . 86 B4
Feniscowles . . . 86 B4
Feniton . . . 11 E6
Fenlake . . . 53 E8
Fenny Bentley . . . 75 D8
Fenny Bridges . . . 11 E6
Fenny Compton . . . 52 D2
Fenny Drayton . . . 63 E7
Fenny Stratford . . . 53 F6
Fenrother . . . 117 E7
Fen Side . . . 79 D6

Fenstanton . . . 54 C4
Fenton Cambs . . . 54 B4
  Lincs . . . 77 B8
  Lincs . . . 77 D8
  Stoke . . . 75 E5
Fenton Barns . . . 129 F7
Fenton Town . . . 123 F5
Fenwick E Ayrs . . . 118 E4
  Northumb . . . 110 B3
  Northumb . . . 123 E6
  S Yorks . . . 89 C6
Feochaig . . . 143 G8
Feock . . . 3 C7
Feolin Ferry . . . 144 G3
Ferindonald . . . 149 H11
Feriniquarrie . . . 148 C6
Ferlochan . . . 130 E3
Fern . . . 134 C4
Ferndale . . . 34 E4
Ferndown . . . 13 E8
Ferness . . . 151 G12
Ferney Green . . . 99 E6
Fernham . . . 38 E2
Fernhill Heath . . . 50 D3
Fernhurst . . . 16 B2
Fernie . . . 128 C5
Ferniegair . . . 119 D7
Fernilea . . . 149 E8
Fernilee . . . 75 B7
Ferrensby . . . 95 C6
Ferring . . . 16 D4
Ferrybridge . . . 89 B5
Ferryden . . . 135 D7
Ferry Hill . . . 66 F3
Ferryhill Aberdeen . 141 D8
  Durham . . . 111 F5
Ferryhill Station . 111 F6
Ferry Point . . . 151 C10
Ferryside . . . 32 C4
Fersfield . . . 68 F3
Fersit . . . 131 B7
Ferwig . . . 45 E3
Feshiebridge . . . 138 D4
Fetcham . . . 28 D2
Fetterangus . . . 153 C9
Fettercairn . . . 135 B6
Fettes . . . 151 F8
Fewcott . . . 39 B5
Fewston . . . 94 D4
F Faccombe . . . 25 D8
Ffairfach . . . 33 B7
Ffair-Rhos . . . 47 C6
Ffaldybrenin . . . 46 E5
Ffarmers . . . 47 E5
Ffawyddog . . . 35 C6
Fforest . . . 33 D6
Fforest-fach . . . 33 E7
Ffostrasol . . . 46 E2
Ffos-y-ffin . . . 46 C3
Ffridd-Uchaf . . . 83 F5
Ffrith . . . 73 D6
Ffrwd . . . 82 F4
Ffynnon ddrain . . 33 B5
Ffynnongroyw . . . 85 F2
Ffynnon-oer . . . 46 D4
Fidden . . . 146 J6
Fiddes . . . 141 F7
Fiddleford . . . 13 C6
Fiddlers Hamlet . . 41 D7
Field . . . 75 F7
Field Broughton . . 99 F5
Field Dalling . . . 81 D6
Field Head . . . 63 D8
Fifehead Magdalen 13 B5
Fifehead Neville . . 13 C5
Fifield Oxon . . . 38 C2
  Wilts . . . 25 D6
  Windsor . . . 27 B7
Fifield Bavant . . . 13 B8
Figheldean . . . 25 E6
Filands . . . 37 F6
Filby . . . 69 C7
Filey . . . 97 A7
Filgrave . . . 53 E6
Filkins . . . 38 D2
Filleigh Devon . . . 9 B8
  Devon . . . 10 C2
Fillingham . . . 90 F3
Fillongley . . . 63 F6
Filton . . . 23 B8
Fimber . . . 96 C4
Finavon . . . 134 D4
Fincham . . . 67 D6
Finchampstead . . 27 C5
Finchdean . . . 15 C8
Finchingfield . . . 55 F7
Finchley . . . 41 E5
Findern . . . 76 F3
Findhorn . . . 151 E13
Findhorn Bridge . 138 B4
Findochty . . . 152 B4
Findo Gask . . . 128 B2
Findon Aberds . . . 141 E8
  W Sus . . . 16 D5
Findon Mains . . . 151 E9
Findrack House . . 140 D5
Finedon . . . 53 B7
Fingal Street . . . 57 C6
Fingask . . . 141 B6
Fingerpost . . . 50 B2
Fingest . . . 39 E7
Finghall . . . 101 F6
Fingland Cumb . . 108 D2
  Dumfries . . . 113 C7
Finglesham . . . 31 D7
Fingringhoe . . . 43 B6
Finlarig . . . 132 F2
Finmere . . . 52 F4
Finnart . . . 132 D2
Finningham . . . 56 C4
Finningley . . . 89 E7
Finnygaud . . . 152 C5
Finsbury . . . 41 F6
Finstall . . . 50 C4
Finsthwaite . . . 99 F5
Finstock . . . 38 C3
Finstown . . . 159 G4
Fintry Aberds . . . 153 C7
  Dundee . . . 134 F4
  Stirling . . . 126 F5
Finzean . . . 140 E5
Fionnphort . . . 146 J6
Fionnsbhagh . . . 154 J5
Firbeck . . . 89 F6
Firby N Yorks . . . 96 C3

Firby continued
  N Yorks . . . 101 F7
Firgrove . . . 87 C7
Firsby . . . 79 C7
Firsdown . . . 25 F7
First Coast . . . 150 B2
Fir Tree . . . 110 F4
Fishbourne IoW . . 15 E6
  W Sus . . . 16 D2
Fishburn . . . 111 F6
Fishcross . . . 127 E7
Fisherford . . . 153 E6
Fisher Place . . . 99 C5
Fisher's Pond . . . 15 B5
Fisherstreet . . . 27 F7
Fisherton Highld . 151 F10
  S Ayrs . . . 112 C2
Fishguard = Abergwaun . . 44 B4
Fishlake . . . 89 C7
Fishleigh Barton . . 9 B7
Fishponds . . . 23 B8
Fishpool . . . 36 B3
Fishtoft . . . 79 E6
Fishtoft Drove . . . 79 E6
Fishtown of Usan 135 D7
Fishwick . . . 122 D5
Fiskavaig . . . 149 E8
Fiskerton Lincs . . . 78 B3
  Notts . . . 77 D7
Fitling . . . 97 F8
Fittleton . . . 25 E6
Fittleworth . . . 16 C4
Fitton End . . . 66 C4
Fitz . . . 60 C4
Fitzhead . . . 11 B6
Fitzwilliam . . . 88 C5
Fiunary . . . 147 G9
Five Acres . . . 36 C2
Five Ashes . . . 18 C2
Fivecrosses . . . 74 B2
Fivehead . . . 11 B8
Five Oak Green . . 29 E7
Five Oaks Jersey . . 17
  W Sus . . . 16 B4
Five Roads . . . 33 D5
Flack's Green . . . 42 C3
Flackwell Heath . . 40 F1
Fladbury . . . 50 E4
Fladdabister . . . 160 K6
Flagg . . . 75 C8
Flamborough . . . 97 B8
Flamstead . . . 40 C3
Flamstead End . . . 41 D6
Flansham . . . 16 D3
Flanshaw . . . 88 B4
Flasby . . . 94 D2
Flash . . . 75 C7
Flashader . . . 149 C8
Flask Inn . . . 103 D7
Flaunden . . . 40 D3
Flawborough . . . 77 E7
Flawith . . . 95 C7
Flax Bourton . . . 23 C7
Flaxby . . . 95 D6
Flaxholme . . . 76 E3
Flaxley . . . 36 C3
Flaxpool . . . 22 F3
Flaxton . . . 96 C2
Fleckney . . . 64 E3
Flecknoe . . . 52 C3
Fledborough . . . 77 B8
Fleet Hants . . . 27 D6
  Hants . . . 15 D6
  Lincs . . . 66 B3
Fleetham . . . 117 B7
Fleet Hargate . . . 66 B3
Fleetlands . . . 15 D6
Fleetville . . . 40 D4
Fleetwood . . . 92 E3
Flemingston . . . 22 B2
Flemington . . . 119 D6
Flempton . . . 56 C2
Fleoideabhagh . . 154 J5
Fletchertown . . 108 E2
Fletching . . . 17 B8
Flexbury . . . 8 D4
Flexford . . . 27 D7
Flimby . . . 107 F7
Flimwell . . . 18 B4
Flint = Y Fflint . . 73 B6
Flintham . . . 77 E7
Flint Mountain . . 73 B6
Flinton . . . 97 F8
Flintsham . . . 48 D5
Flitcham . . . 80 E3
Flitwick . . . 53 F8
Flixborough . . . 90 C2
Flixborough Stather . . 90 C2
Flixton Gtr Man . . 86 E5
  N Yorks . . . 97 B6
  Suff . . . 69 F6
Flockton . . . 88 C3
Flodaigh . . . 148 C3
Flodden . . . 122 F5
Flodigarry . . . 149 A9
Flood's Ferry . . . 66 E3
Flookburgh . . . 92 B3
Florden . . . 68 E4
Flore . . . 52 C4
Flotterton . . . 117 D5
Flowton . . . 56 E4
Flush House . . . 88 D2
Flushing Aberds . 153 D10
  Corn . . . 3 C7
Flyford Flavell . . . 50 D4
Foals Green . . . 57 B6
Fobbing . . . 42 F3
Fochabers . . . 152 C3
Fochriw . . . 35 D5
Fockerby . . . 90 C2
Fodderletter . . . 139 B7
Fodderty . . . 151 F8
Foel . . . 59 D6
Foel-gastell . . . 33 C6
Foffarty . . . 134 E4
Foggathorpe . . . 96 F3
Fogo . . . 122 E3
Fogorig . . . 122 E3
Foindle . . . 156 E4
Folda . . . 134 C1
Fole . . . 75 F7
Foleshill . . . 63 F7
Folke . . . 12 C4
Folkestone . . . 31 F6
Folkingham . . . 78 F3
Folkington . . . 18 E2

Folksworth . . . 65 F8
Folkton . . . 97 B6
Folla Rule . . . 153 E7
Follifoot . . . 95 D6
Folly Gate . . . 9 E7
Fonthill Bishop . . 24 F4
Fonthill Gifford . . 24 F4
Fontmell Magna . . 13 C6
Fontwell . . . 16 D3
Foolow . . . 75 B8
Foots Cray . . . 29 B5
Forbestown . . . 140 C2
Force Mills . . . 99 E5
Forcett . . . 101 C6
Ford Argyll . . . 124 E4
  Bucks . . . 39 D7
  Devon . . . 9 B6
  Glos . . . 37 B7
  Northumb . . . 122 F5
  Shrops . . . 60 C4
  Staffs . . . 75 D7
  W Sus . . . 16 D3
Fordcombe . . . 29 E6
Fordell . . . 128 F3
Forden . . . 60 D2
Ford End . . . 42 C2
Forder Green . . . 7 C5
Fordham Cambs . . 55 B7
  Essex . . . 43 B5
  Norf . . . 67 E6
Fordhouses . . . 62 D3
Fordingbridge . . . 14 C2
Fordon . . . 97 B6
Fordoun . . . 135 B7
Ford's Green . . . 56 C4
Fordstreet . . . 43 B5
Ford Street . . . 11 C6
Fordwells . . . 38 C3
Fordwich . . . 31 D5
Fordyce . . . 152 B5
Forebridge . . . 62 B3
Forest . . . 109 F8
Forest Becks . . . 93 D7
Forestburn Gate . . 117 E6
Foresterseat . . . 152 C1
Forest Gate . . . 41 F7
Forest Green . . . 28 E2
Forest Hall . . . 99 D7
Forest Head . . . 109 D5
Forest Hill . . . 39 D5
Forest Lane Head . 95 D6
Forest Lodge Argyll . . . 131 E6
  Highld . . . 139 C6
  Perth . . . 133 B6
Forest Mill . . . 127 E8
Forest Row . . . 28 F5
Forestside . . . 15 C8
Forest Town . . . 77 C5
Forfar . . . 134 D4
Forgandenny . . . 128 C2
Forge . . . 58 E4
Forge Side . . . 35 D6
Forgewood . . . 119 D7
Forgie . . . 152 C3
Forglen House . . . 153 C6
Formby . . . 85 D4
Forncett End . . . 68 E4
Forncett St Mary . 68 E4
Forncett St Peter . 68 E4
Forneth . . . 133 E7
Fornham All Saints . . . 56 C2
Fornham St Martin . . . 56 C2
Forres . . . 151 F13
Forrestfield . . . 119 C8
Forrest Lodge . . . 113 F5
Forsbrook . . . 75 E6
Forse . . . 158 G4
Forse House . . . 158 G4
Forsinain . . . 157 E12
Forsinard . . . 157 E11
Forsinard Station . 157 E11
Forston . . . 12 E4
Fort Augustus . . 137 D6
Forteviot . . . 128 C2
Fort George Guern . 16
  Highld . . . 151 F10
Forth . . . 120 D2
Forthampton . . . 50 F3
Forth Road Bridge . . . 120 B4
Fortingall . . . 132 E4
Forton Hants . . . 26 E2
  Lancs . . . 92 D4
  Shrops . . . 60 C4
  Som . . . 11 C8
  Staffs . . . 61 B7
Forton Heath . . . 60 C4
Fortrie . . . 153 D6
Fortrose . . . 151 F10
Fortuneswell . . . 12 G4
Fort William . . . 131 B5
Forty Green . . . 40 E2
Forty Hill . . . 41 E6
Forward Green . . . 56 D4
Fosbury . . . 25 D8
Fosdyke . . . 79 F6
Foss . . . 132 D4
Foss Cross . . . 37 D7
Fossebridge . . . 37 C7
Foster Street . . . 41 D7
Foston Derbys . . . 75 F8
  Lincs . . . 77 E8
  N Yorks . . . 96 C2
Foston on the Wolds . . . 97 D7
Fotherby . . . 91 E7
Fotheringhay . . . 65 E7
Foubister . . . 159 H6
Foulby . . . 88 C4
Foulden Borders . . 122 D5
  Norf . . . 67 E7
Foulis Castle . . . 151 E8
Foul Mile . . . 18 D3
Foulridge . . . 93 E8
Foulsham . . . 81 E6
Fountainhall . . . 121 E7
Four Ashes Staffs . 62 F2
  Suff . . . 56 B4
Four Crosses Powys . . . 59 D7
  Powys . . . 60 C2
  Wrex . . . 73 D6
Four Elms . . . 29 E5

Four Forks . . . 22 F4
Four Gotes . . . 66 C4
Fourlane Ends . . . 76 D3
Four Lane Ends . . 74 C2
Four Lanes . . . 3 C5
Fourlanes End . . . 74 D5
Four Marks . . . 26 F4
Four Mile Bridge . 82 D2
Four Oaks E Sus . . 19 C5
  W Mid . . . 62 E5
  W Mid . . . 63 F6
Fourpenny . . . 151 C11
Four Roads Carms . 33 D5
  IoM . . . 84 F2
Fourstones . . . 109 C8
Four Throws . . . 18 C4
Fovant . . . 13 B8
Foveran . . . 141 B8
Fowey . . . 5 D6
Fowley Common . . 86 E4
Fowlis . . . 134 F3
Fowlis Wester . . 127 B8
Fowlmere . . . 54 E5
Fownhope . . . 49 F7
Fox Corner . . . 27 D7
Foxdale . . . 84 E2
Foxearth . . . 56 E2
Foxfield . . . 98 F4
Foxham . . . 24 B4
Foxhole Corn . . . 4 D4
  Swansea . . . 33 E7
Foxholes . . . 97 B6
Foxhunt Green . . . 18 D2
Foxley Norf . . . 81 E6
  Wilts . . . 37 F5
Fox Street . . . 43 B6
Foxt . . . 75 E7
Foxton Cambs . . . 54 E5
  Durham . . . 102 B1
  Leics . . . 64 E4
Foxup . . . 93 B8
Foxwist Green . . . 74 C3
Foxwood . . . 49 B8
Foy . . . 36 B2
Foyers . . . 137 B7
Fraddam . . . 2 C4
Fraddon . . . 4 D4
Fradley . . . 63 C5
Fradswell . . . 75 F6
Fraisthorpe . . . 97 C7
Framfield . . . 17 B8
Framingham Earl . 69 D5
Framingham Pigot 69 D5
Framlingham . . . 57 C6
Frampton Dorset . 12 E4
  Lincs . . . 79 F6
Frampton Cotterell . . . 36 F3
Frampton Mansell 37 D6
Frampton on Severn . . . 36 D4
Frampton West End . . . 79 E6
Framsden . . . 57 D5
Framwellgate Moor . . . 111 E5
Franche . . . 50 B3
Frankby . . . 85 F3
Frankley . . . 62 F3
Frank's Bridge . . . 48 D3
Frankton . . . 52 B2
Frant . . . 18 B2
Fraserburgh . . . 153 B9
Frating Green . . . 43 B6
Fratton . . . 15 E7
Freathy . . . 5 D8
Freckenham . . . 55 B7
Freckleton . . . 86 B2
Freeby . . . 64 B5
Freehay . . . 75 E7
Freeland . . . 38 C4
Freester . . . 160 H6
Freethorpe . . . 69 D7
Freiston . . . 79 E6
Fremington Devon . 20 F4
  N Yorks . . . 101 E5
Frenchay . . . 23 B8
Frenchbeer . . . 9 F8
Frenich . . . 126 D3
Frensham . . . 27 E6
Fresgoe . . . 157 C12
Freshfield . . . 85 D3
Freshford . . . 24 C2
Freshwater . . . 14 F4
Freshwater Bay . . 14 F4
Freshwater East . . 32 E1
Fressingfield . . . 57 B6
Freston . . . 57 F5
Freswick . . . 158 D5
Fretherne . . . 36 D4
Frettenham . . . 68 C5
Freuchie . . . 128 D4
Freuchies . . . 134 C2
Freystrop . . . 44 D4
Friar's Gate . . . 29 F5
Friarton . . . 128 B3
Friday Bridge . . . 66 D4
Friday Street . . . 18 E3
Fridaythorpe . . . 96 D4
Friern Barnet . . . 41 E5
Friesland . . . 146 F4
Friesthorpe . . . 90 F4
Frieston . . . 78 E2
Frieth . . . 39 E7
Frilford . . . 38 E4
Frilsham . . . 26 B3
Frimley . . . 27 D6
Frimley Green . . . 27 D6
Frindsbury . . . 29 B8
Fring . . . 80 D3
Fringford . . . 39 B6
Frinsted . . . 30 D2
Frinton-on-Sea . . 43 B8
Friockheim . . . 135 E5
Friog . . . 58 C3
Frisby on the Wreake . . . 64 C3
Friskney . . . 79 D7
Friskney Eaudike . . 79 D7
Friskney Tofts . . . 79 D7
Friston E Sus . . . 18 F2
  Suff . . . 57 C8
Fritchley . . . 76 D3
Fritham . . . 14 C3
Frith Bank . . . 79 E6
Frith Common . . . 49 C8

Frithelstock . . . 9 C6
Frithelstock Stone . 9 C6
Frithville . . . 79 D6
Frittenden . . . 30 E2
Frittiscombe . . . 7 E6
Fritton Norf . . . 68 E5
  Norf . . . 69 D7
Fritwell . . . 39 B5
Frizinghall . . . 94 F4
Frizington . . . 98 C2
Frocester . . . 36 D4
Frodesley . . . 60 D5
Frodingham . . . 90 C2
Frodsham . . . 74 B2
Frogden . . . 116 B3
Froggatt . . . 76 B2
Froghall . . . 75 E7
Frogmore Devon . . 7 E5
  Hants . . . 27 D6
Frognall . . . 65 C8
Frogshail . . . 81 D8
Frolesworth . . . 64 E2
Frome . . . 24 E2
Frome St Quintin . 12 D3
Fromes Hill . . . 49 E8
Fron Denb . . . 72 C4
  Gwyn . . . 70 D4
  Gwyn . . . 82 F5
  Powys . . . 48 C2
  Powys . . . 59 E8
  Powys . . . 60 D2
Froncysyllte . . . 73 E6
Frongoch . . . 72 F3
Frostenden . . . 69 F7
Frosterley . . . 110 F3
Frotoft . . . 159 F5
Froxfield . . . 25 C7
Froxfield Green . . 15 B8
Froyle . . . 27 E5
Fryerning . . . 42 D2
Fryton . . . 96 B2
Fulbeck . . . 78 D2
Fulbourn . . . 55 D6
Fulbrook . . . 38 C2
Fulford Som . . . 11 B7
  Staffs . . . 75 F6
  York . . . 96 E2
Fulham . . . 28 B3
Fulking . . . 17 C6
Fullarton Glasgow . 119 C6
  N Ayrs . . . 118 F3
Fuller's Moor . . . 73 D8
Fuller Street . . . 42 C3
Fullerton . . . 25 F8
Full Sutton . . . 96 D3
Fullwood . . . 118 D4
Fulmer . . . 40 F2
Fulmodeston . . . 81 D5
Fulnetby . . . 78 B3
Fulstow . . . 91 E7
Fulwell . . . 111 D6
Fulwood Lancs . . . 92 F5
  S Yorks . . . 88 F4
Fundenhall . . . 68 E4
Fundenhall Street . 68 E4
Funtington . . . 15 D8
Funtley . . . 15 D6
Funtullich . . . 127 B6
Funzie . . . 160 D8
Furley . . . 11 D7
Furnace Argyll . . . 125 E6
  Carms . . . 33 D6
Furnace End . . . 63 E6
Furneaux Pelham . 41 B7
Furzehill . . . 21 E6
Furze Platt . . . 40 F1
Fyfett . . . 11 C7
Fyfield Essex . . . 42 D1
  Glos . . . 38 D2
  Hants . . . 25 E7
  Oxon . . . 38 E4
  Wilts . . . 25 C6
Fylingthorpe . . . 103 D7
Fyvie . . . 153 E7

G

Gabhsann bho Dheas . . . 155 B9
Gabhsann bho Thuath . . . 155 B9
Gablon . . . 151 B10
Gabroc Hill . . . 118 D4
Gaddesby . . . 64 C3
Gadebridge . . . 40 D3
Gaer . . . 35 B5
Gaerllwyd . . . 35 E8
Gaerwen . . . 82 D4
Gagingwell . . . 38 B4
Gaick Lodge . . . 138 F3
Gailey . . . 62 C3
Gainford . . . 101 C6
Gainsborough Lincs 90 E2
  Suff . . . 57 E5
Gainsford End . . . 55 F8
Gairloch . . . 149 A13
Gairlochy . . . 136 F4
Gairney Bank . . . 128 E3
Gairnshiel Lodge 139 D8
Gaisgill . . . 99 D8
Gaitsgill . . . 108 E3
Galashiels . . . 121 F7
Galgate . . . 92 D4
Galhampton . . . 12 B4
Gallaberry . . . 114 F2
Gallachoille . . . 144 E6
Gallanach Argyll . . 124 C4
  Argyll . . . 146 F5
Gallantry Bank . . 74 D2
Gallatown . . . 128 E4
Galley Common . . 63 E7
Galleyend . . . 42 D3
Galleywood . . . 42 D3
Gallin . . . 132 E2
Gallowfauld . . . 134 E4
Gallows Green . . . 75 E7
Galltair . . . 149 F13
Galmisdale . . . 146 C7
Galmpton Devon . . 6 E4
  Torbay . . . 7 D6
Galphay . . . 95 B5
Galston . . . 118 F5
Galtrigill . . . 148 C6
Gamblesby . . . 109 F6
Gamesley . . . 87 E8

Gamlingay . . . 54 D3
Gammersgill . . . 101 F5
Gamston . . . 77 B7
Ganarew . . . 36 C2
Ganavan . . . 124 B4
Gang . . . 5 C8
Ganllwyd . . . 71 E8
Gannochy Angus . 135 B5
  Perth . . . 128 B3
Gansclet . . . 158 F5
Ganstead . . . 97 F7
Ganthorpe . . . 96 B2
Ganton . . . 97 B5
Garbat . . . 150 E7
Garbhallt . . . 125 F6
Garboldisham . . . 68 F3
Garden City . . . 73 C7
Gardenstown . . . 153 B7
Garden Village Wrex . . . 73 D7
  W Yorks . . . 95 F7
Garderhouse . . . 160 J5
Gardham . . . 97 E5
Gardin . . . 160 G6
Gare Hill . . . 24 E2
Garelochhead . . 145 D11
Garford . . . 38 E4
Garforth . . . 95 F7
Gargrave . . . 94 D2
Gargunnock . . . 127 E6
Garlic Street . . . 68 F5
Garlieston . . . 105 E8
Garlinge Green . . 30 D5
Garlogie . . . 141 D6
Garmond . . . 153 C8
Garmony . . . 147 G9
Garmouth . . . 152 B3
Garnant . . . 33 C7
Garndiffaith . . . 35 D6
Garndolbenmaen . 71 C5
Garnedd . . . 83 F7
Garnett Bridge . . 99 E7
Garnfadryn . . . 70 D3
Garnkirk . . . 119 C6
Garnlydan . . . 35 C5
Garnswllt . . . 33 D7
Garn-yr-erw . . . 35 C6
Garrabost . . . 155 D10
Garraron . . . 124 E4
Garras . . . 3 D6
Garreg . . . 71 C7
Garrick . . . 127 C7
Garrigill . . . 109 E7
Garriston . . . 101 E6
Garroch . . . 113 F5
Garrogie Lodge . . 137 C8
Garros . . . 149 B9
Garrow . . . 133 E5
Garryhorn . . . 113 E5
Garsdale . . . 100 F2
Garsdale Head . . 100 E2
Garsdon . . . 37 F6
Garshall Green . . 75 F6
Garsington . . . 39 D5
Garstang . . . 92 E4
Garston . . . 86 F2
Garswood . . . 86 E3
Gartcosh . . . 119 C6
Garth Bridgend . . 34 E2
  Gwyn . . . 83 D5
  Powys . . . 47 E8
  Shetland . . . 160 H4
  Wrex . . . 73 E6
Garthamlock . . . 119 C6
Garthbrengy . . . 48 F2
Garthdee . . . 141 D8
Gartheli . . . 46 D4
Garthmyl . . . 59 E8
Garthorpe Leics . . 64 B5
  N Lincs . . . 90 C2
Garth Row . . . 99 E7
Gartly . . . 152 E5
Gartmore . . . 126 E4
Gartnagrenach . . 144 H6
Gartness N Lanark . 119 C7
  Stirling . . . 126 F4
Gartocharn . . . 126 F3
Garton . . . 97 F8
Garton-on-the-Wolds . . . 97 D5
Gartsherrie . . . 119 C7
Gartymore . . . 157 H13
Garvald . . . 121 B8
Garvamore . . . 137 E8
Garvard . . . 144 D2
Garvault Hotel . . 157 F10
Garve . . . 150 E6
Garvestone . . . 68 D3
Garvock Aberds . . 135 B7
  Invclyd . . . 118 B2
Garway . . . 36 B1
Garway Hill . . . 35 B8
Gaskan . . . 130 B1
Gastard . . . 24 C3
Gasthorpe . . . 68 F2
Gatcombe . . . 15 F5
Gateacre . . . 86 F2
Gatebeck . . . 99 F7
Gate Burton . . . 90 F2
Gateford . . . 89 F6
Gateforth . . . 89 B6
Gatehead . . . 118 F3
Gate Helmsley . . 96 D2
Gatehouse . . . 116 F3
Gatehouse of Fleet . . . 106 D3
Gatelawbridge . . 114 E2
Gateley . . . 81 E5
Gatenby . . . 101 F8
Gateshead . . . 111 C5
Gatesheath . . . 73 C8
Gateside Aberds . . 140 C5
  Angus . . . 134 E4
  Fife . . . 128 C3
  N Ayrs . . . 118 D3
Gathurst . . . 86 D3
Gatley . . . 87 F6
Gattonside . . . 121 F8
Gatwick Airport . 28 E3
Gaufron . . . 47 C8
Gaulby . . . 64 D3
Gauldry . . . 129 B5
Gaunt's Common . 13 D8
Gautby . . . 78 B4
Gavinton . . . 122 D3
Gawber . . . 88 D4
Gawcott . . . 52 F4
Gawsworth . . . 75 C5

Gawthorpe . . . 88 B3
Gawthrop . . . 100 F1
Gawthwaite . . . 98 F4
Gaydon . . . 51 D8
Gayfield . . . 159 C5
Gayhurst . . . 53 E6
Gayle . . . 100 F3
Gayles . . . 101 D6
Gay Street . . . 16 B4
Gayton Mers . . . 85 F3
  Norf . . . 67 C7
  Northants . . . 52 D5
  Staffs . . . 62 B3
Gayton le Marsh . 91 F8
Gayton le Wold . . 91 F6
Gayton Thorpe . . 67 C7
Gaywood . . . 67 B6
Gazeley . . . 55 C8
Geanies House . . 151 D11
Gearraidh Bhailteas . . . 148 F2
Gearraidh Bhaird . 155 E8
Gearraidh na h-Aibhne . . . 154 D7
Gearraidh na Monadh . . . 148 G2
Geary . . . 148 B7
Geddes House . . 151 F11
Gedding . . . 56 D3
Geddington . . . 65 F5
Gedintailor . . . 149 E10
Gedling . . . 77 E6
Gedney . . . 66 B4
Gedney Broadgate . 66 B4
Gedney Drove End . 66 B4
Gedney Dyke . . . 66 B4
Gedney Hill . . . 66 C3
Gee Cross . . . 87 E7
Geilston . . . 118 B3
Geirinis . . . 148 D2
Geise . . . 158 D3
Geisiadar . . . 154 D6
Geldeston . . . 69 E6
Gell . . . 83 E8
Gelli Pembs . . . 32 C1
  Rhondda . . . 34 E3
Gellideg . . . 34 D4
Gellifor . . . 72 C5
Gelligaer . . . 35 E5
Gellilydan . . . 71 D7
Gellinudd . . . 33 D8
Gellyburn . . . 133 F7
Gellywen . . . 32 B3
Gelston Dumfries . 106 D4
  Lincs . . . 78 E2
Gembling . . . 97 D7
Gentleshaw . . . 62 C4
Geocrab . . . 154 H6
Georgefield . . . 115 E5
George Green . . 40 F3
Georgeham . . . 20 F3
George Nympton . 10 B2
Georgetown . . . 35 D5
Gerlan . . . 83 E6
Germansweek . . . 9 E6
Germoe . . . 2 D4
Gerrans . . . 3 C7
Gerrards Cross . . 40 F3
Gestingthorpe . . 56 F2
Geuffordt . . . 60 C2
Gib Hill . . . 74 B3
Gibbet Hill . . . 64 F2
Gibbshill . . . 106 B4
Gidea Park . . . 41 F8
Gidleigh . . . 9 F8
Giffnock . . . 119 D5
Gifford . . . 121 C8
Giffordland . . . 118 E2
Giffordtown . . . 128 C4
Giggleswick . . . 93 C8
Gilberdyke . . . 90 B2
Gilchriston . . . 121 C7
Gilcrux . . . 107 F8
Gildersome . . . 88 B3
Gildingwells . . . 89 F6
Gileston . . . 22 C2
Gilfach . . . 35 E5
Gilfach Goch . . . 34 F3
Gilfachrheda . . . 46 D3
Gillamoor . . . 102 F4
Gillar's Green . . . 86 E2
Gillen . . . 148 C7
Gilling East . . . 96 B2
Gillingham Dorset . 13 B6
  Medway . . . 29 C8
  Norf . . . 69 E7
Gilling West . . . 101 D6
Gillock . . . 158 E4
Gillow Heath . . . 75 D5
Gills . . . 158 C5
Gill's Green . . . 18 B4
Gilmanscleuch . . 115 B6
Gilmerton Edin . . 121 C5
  Perth . . . 127 B7
Gilmonby . . . 100 C4
Gilmorton . . . 64 F2
Gilmourton . . . 119 E6
Gilsland . . . 109 C6
Gilsland Spa . . . 109 C6
Gilston Borders . . 121 D7
  Herts . . . 41 C7
Gilwern . . . 35 C6
Gimingham . . . 81 D8
Giosla . . . 154 E6
Gipping . . . 56 C4
Gipsey Bridge . . . 79 E5
Girdle Toll . . . 118 E3
Girlsta . . . 160 H6
Girsby . . . 102 D1
Girtford . . . 54 D2
Girthon . . . 106 D3
Girton Cambs . . . 54 C5
  Notts . . . 77 C8
Girvan . . . 112 E1
Gisburn . . . 93 E8
Gisleham . . . 69 F8
Gislingham . . . 56 B4
Gissing . . . 68 F4
Gittisham . . . 11 E6
Gladestry . . . 48 D4
Gladsmuir . . . 121 B7
Glais . . . 33 D8
Glaisdale . . . 103 D5
Glame . . . 149 D10
Glamis . . . 134 E3
Glan Adda . . . 83 D5

Glanaman . . . 33 C7
Glan Conwy Conwy . 83 D8
Conwy . . . 83 F8
Glandford . . . 81 C6
Glan-Duar . . . 46 E4
Glandwr . . . 32 B2
Glan-Dwyfach . . . 71 C5
Glandy Cross . . . 32 B2
Glandyfi . . . 58 E3
Glan Gors . . . 82 D4
Glangrwyney . . . 35 C6
Glanmule . . . 59 E8
Glanrafon . . . 58 F3
Glanrhyd Gwyn . . . 70 D3
Pembs . . . 45 E3
Glan-rhyd . . . 82 F4
Glanton . . . 117 C6
Glanton Pike . . . 117 C6
Glan-traeth . . . 82 D2
Glanvilles Wootton 12 D4
Glan-y-don . . . 73 B5
Glan-y-nant . . . 59 F6
Glan-yr-afon
Anglesey . . . 83 C6
Gwyn . . . 72 E3
Gwyn . . . 72 E4
Glan-y-wern . . . 71 D7
Glapthorn . . . 65 E7
Glapwell . . . 76 C4
Glas-allt Shiel . . . 139 F8
Glasbury . . . 48 F3
Glaschoil . . . 151 H13
Glascoed Denb . . . 72 B3
Mon . . . 35 D7
Powys . . . 59 C8
Glascorrie . . . 140 E2
Glascote . . . 63 D6
Glascwm . . . 48 D3
Glasdrum . . . 130 E4
Glasfryn . . . 72 D3
Glasgow . . . 119 C5
Glashvin . . . 149 B9
Glasinfryn . . . 83 E5
Glasnacardoch . . . 147 B9
Glasnakille . . . 149 G10
Glasphein . . . 148 D6
Glaspwll . . . 58 E4
Glassburn . . . 150 H6
Glasserton . . . 105 F8
Glassford . . . 119 E7
Glasshouse Hill . . . 36 B4
Glasshouses . . . 94 C4
Glasslie . . . 128 D4
Glasson Cumb . . . 108 C2
Lancs . . . 92 D4
Glassonby . . . 109 F5
Glasterlaw . . . 135 D5
Glaston . . . 65 D5
Glastonbury . . . 23 F7
Glatton . . . 65 F8
Glazebrook . . . 86 E4
Glazebury . . . 86 E4
Glazeley . . . 61 F7
Gleadless . . . 88 F4
Gleadsmoss . . . 74 C5
Gleann
Tholàstaidh . . . 155 C10
Gleaston . . . 92 B2
Gleiniant . . . 59 E6
Glemsford . . . 56 E2
Glen Dumfries . . . 106 B5
Dumfries . . . 106 D2
Glenamachrie . . . 124 C5
Glen Auldyn . . . 84 C4
Glenbarr . . . 143 E7
Glenbeg Highld . . . 139 B6
Highld . . . 147 E8
Glen Bernisdale . . 149 D9
Glenbervie . . . 141 F6
Glenboig . . . 119 C7
Glenborrodale . . . 147 E9
Glenbranter . . . 125 F7
Glenbreck . . . 114 B3
Glenbrein Lodge . 137 C7
Glenbrittle House 149 F9
Glenbuchat
Lodge . . . 140 C2
Glenbuck . . . 113 B7
Glenburn . . . 118 C4
Glencalvie Lodge . 150 C7
Glencanisp
Lodge . . . 156 G4
Glencaple . . . 107 C6
Glencarron
Lodge . . . 150 F3
Glencarse . . . 128 B3
Glencassley
Castle . . . 156 J7
Glenceitlein . . . 131 E5
Glencoe . . . 130 D4
Glencraig . . . 128 E3
Glencripesdale . . . 147 F9
Glencrosh . . . 113 F7
Glendavan House 140 D3
Glendevon . . . 127 D8
Glendoebeg . . . 137 D7
Glendoe Lodge . . . 137 D7
Glendoick . . . 128 B4
Glendoll Lodge . . . 134 B2
Glendoune . . . 112 E1
Glenduckie . . . 128 C4
Glendye Lodge . . . 140 F5
Gleneagles Hotel . 127 C8
Gleneagles
House . . . 127 D8
Glenegedale . . . 142 C4
Glenelg . . . 149 G13
Glenernie . . . 151 G13
Glenfarg . . . 128 C3
Glenfarquhar
Lodge . . . 141 F6
Glenferness
House . . . 151 G12
Glenfeshie Lodge 138 E4
Glenfield . . . 64 D2
Glenfinnan . . . 147 C11
Glenfoot . . . 128 C3
Glenfyne Lodge . 125 D8
Glengap . . . 106 D3
Glengarnock . . . 118 D3
Glengorm Castle . 146 F7
Glengrasco . . . 149 D9
Glenhead Farm . . . 134 C2
Glen Ho . . . 121 F5
Glenhoul . . . 113 F6
Glenhurich . . . 130 C2
Glenkerry . . . 115 C5
Glenkiln . . . 106 B5
Glenkindie . . . 140 C3
Glenlatterach . . . 152 C1
Glenlee . . . 113 F6
Glenlichorn . . . 127 C6
Glenlivet . . . 139 B7
Glenlochsie . . . 133 B7
Glenloig . . . 143 E10
Glenluce . . . 105 D6
Glenmallan . . . 125 F8
Glenmarksie . . . 150 F6
Glenmassan . . . 145 E10
Glenmavis . . . 119 C7
Glenmaye . . . 84 E2
Glenmidge . . . 113 F8
Glen Mona . . . 84 D4
Glenmore Argyll . . . 124 D4
Highld . . . 149 D9
Glenmore Lodge . 139 D5
Glenmoy . . . 134 C4
Glen Nevis House . 131 B5
Glenogil . . . 134 C4
Glen Parva . . . 64 E2
Glenprosen
Lodge . . . 134 C2
Glenprosen
Village . . . 134 C3
Glenquiech . . . 134 C4
Glenreasdell
Mains . . . 145 H7
Glenree . . . 143 F10
Glenridding . . . 99 C5
Glenrossal . . . 156 J7
Glenrothes . . . 128 D4
Glensanda . . . 130 E2
Glensaugh . . . 135 B6
Glenshero Lodge . 137 E8
Glen Sluain . . . 125 F6
Glenstockadale . . 104 C4
Glenstriven . . . 145 F9
Glentaggart . . . 113 B8
Glen Tanar
House . . . 140 E3
Glentham . . . 90 E4
Glentirranmuir . . . 127 E5
Glenton . . . 140 B5
Glentress . . . 121 F5
Glentromie
Lodge . . . 138 E3
Glen Trool Lodge . 112 F4
Glentrool Village . 105 B7
Glentruan . . . 84 B4
Glentruim House . 138 E2
Glentworth . . . 90 F3
Glenuig . . . 147 D9
Glenurquhart . . . 151 E10
Glen Village . . . 119 B8
Glen Vine . . . 84 E3
Glespin . . . 113 B8
Gletness . . . 160 H6
Glewstone . . . 36 B2
Glinton . . . 65 D8
Glooston . . . 64 E4
Glororum . . . 123 F7
Glossop . . . 87 E8
Gloster Hill . . . 117 D8
Gloucester . . . 37 C5
Gloup . . . 160 C7
Glusburn . . . 94 E3
Glutt Lodge . . . 157 F12
Glutton Bridge . . . 75 C7
Glympton . . . 38 B4
Glynarthen . . . 46 E2
Glynbrochan . . . 59 F6
Glyn-Ceiriog . . . 73 F6
Glyncoch . . . 34 E4
Glyncorrwg . . . 34 E2
Glyn-cywarch . . . 71 D7
Glynde . . . 17 D8
Glyndebourne . . . 17 C8
Glyndyfrdwy . . . 72 E5
Glyn Ebwy
= Ebbw Vale . . . 35 D5
Glynedd
= Glynneath . . . 34 D2
Glyn-neath
= Glynedd . . . 34 D2
Glynogwr . . . 34 F3
Glyntaff . . . 34 F4
Glyntawe . . . 34 C2
Gnosall . . . 62 B2
Gnosall Heath . . . 62 B2
Goadby . . . 64 E4
Goadby Marwood . 64 B4
Goatacre . . . 24 B5
Goathill . . . 12 C4
Goathland . . . 103 D6
Goathurst . . . 22 F4
Goat Lees . . . 30 E4
Gobernuisgach
Lodge . . . 156 E7
Gobhaig . . . 154 G5
Gobowen . . . 73 F7
Godalming . . . 27 E7
Godley . . . 87 E7
Godmanchester . . . 54 B3
Godmanstone . . . 12 E4
Godmersham . . . 30 D4
Godney . . . 23 E6
Godolphin Cross . . . 2 C5
Godre'r-graig . . . 34 D1
Godshill Hants . . . 14 C2
IoW . . . 15 F6
Godstone . . . 28 D4
Godwinscroft . . . 14 E2
Goetre . . . 35 D7
Goferydd . . . 82 C2
Goff's Oak . . . 41 D6
Gogar . . . 120 B4
Goginan . . . 58 F3
Golan . . . 71 C6
Golant . . . 5 D6
Golberdon . . . 5 B8
Golborne . . . 86 E4
Golcar . . . 88 C2
Goldcliff . . . 35 F7
Golden Cross . . . 18 D2
Golden Green . . . 29 E7
Golden Grove . . . 33 C6
Goldenhill . . . 75 D5
Golden Hill . . . 14 E3
Golden Pot . . . 26 E5
Golden Valley . . . 37 B6
Golders Green . . . 41 F5
Goldhanger . . . 43 D5
Gold Hill . . . 66 E5
Golding . . . 60 D5
Goldington . . . 53 D8
Goldsborough
N Yorks . . . 95 D6
N Yorks . . . 103 C6
Goldsithney . . . 2 C4
Goldsworthy . . . 9 B5
Goldthorpe . . . 89 D5
Gollanfield . . . 151 F11
Golspie . . . 157 J11
Golval . . . 157 C11
Gomeldon . . . 25 F6
Gomersal . . . 88 B3
Gomshall . . . 27 E8
Gonalston . . . 77 E6
Gonfirth . . . 160 G5
Good Easter . . . 42 C2
Gooderstone . . . 67 D7
Goodleigh . . . 20 F5
Goodmanham . . . 96 E4
Goodnestone Kent . 30 C4
Kent . . . 31 D6
Goodrich . . . 36 C2
Goodrington . . . 7 D6
Goodshaw . . . 87 B6
Goodwick = Wdig . . 44 B4
Goodworth
Clatford . . . 25 E8
Goole . . . 89 B8
Goonbell . . . 3 B6
Goonhavern . . . 4 D2
Goose Eye . . . 94 E3
Goose Green
Gtr Man . . . 86 D3
Norf . . . 68 F4
W Sus . . . 16 C5
Gooseham . . . 8 C4
Goosey . . . 38 E3
Goosnargh . . . 93 F5
Goostrey . . . 74 B4
Gorcott Hill . . . 51 C5
Gord . . . 160 L6
Gordon . . . 122 E2
Gordonbush . . . 157 J11
Gordonsburgh . . . 152 B4
Gordonstoun . . . 152 B1
Gordonstown
Aberds . . . 152 C5
Aberds . . . 153 E7
Gore . . . 31 D7
Gorebridge . . . 121 C6
Gore Cross . . . 24 D5
Gorefield . . . 66 C4
Gore Pit . . . 42 C4
Gorey Jersey . . . 17
Gorgie . . . 120 B5
Goring . . . 39 F6
Goring-by-Sea . . . 16 D5
Goring Heath . . . 26 B4
Gorleston-on-Sea 69 D8
Gornalwood . . . 62 E3
Gorrachie . . . 153 C7
Gorran Churchtown . 3 B8
Gorran Haven . . . 3 B9
Gorrenberry . . . 115 E7
Gors . . . 46 B5
Gorsedd . . . 73 B5
Gorse Hill . . . 38 F1
Gorseinon . . . 33 E6
Gorseness . . . 159 G5
Gorsgoch . . . 46 D3
Gorslas . . . 33 C6
Gorsley . . . 36 B3
Gorstan . . . 150 E6
Gorstanvorran . . . 130 B2
Gorsteyhill . . . 74 D4
Gorsty Hill . . . 62 B5
Gortantaoid . . . 142 A4
Gorton . . . 87 E6
Gosbeck . . . 57 D5
Gosberton . . . 78 F5
Gosberton Clough . 65 B8
Gosfield . . . 42 B3
Gosford . . . 49 C7
Gosforth Cumb . . . 98 D2
T&W . . . 110 C5
Gosmore . . . 40 B4
Gosport . . . 15 E7
Gossabrough . . . 160 E7
Gossington . . . 36 D4
Goswick . . . 123 E6
Gotham . . . 76 F5
Gotherington . . . 37 B6
Gott . . . 160 J6
Goudhurst . . . 18 B4
Goulceby . . . 79 B5
Gourdas . . . 153 D7
Gourdon . . . 135 B8
Gourock . . . 118 B2
Govan . . . 119 C5
Govanhill . . . 119 C5
Goveton . . . 7 E5
Govilon . . . 35 C6
Gowanhill . . . 153 B10
Gowdall . . . 89 B7
Gowerton . . . 33 E6
Gowkhall . . . 128 F2
Gowthorpe . . . 96 D3
Goxhill E Yorks . . . 97 E7
N Lincs . . . 90 B5
Goxhill Haven . . . 90 B5
Goytre . . . 34 F1
Grabhair . . . 155 F8
Graby . . . 65 B7
Grade . . . 3 E6
Graffham . . . 16 C3
Grafham Cambs . . . 54 C2
Sur . . . 27 E8
Grafton Hereford . . . 49 F6
N Yorks . . . 95 C7
Oxon . . . 38 D2
Shrops . . . 60 C4
Worcs . . . 49 C7
Grafton Flyford . . . 50 D4
Grafton Regis . . . 53 E5
Grafton
Underwood . . . 65 F6
Grafty Green . . . 30 E2
Graianrhyd . . . 73 D6
Graig Conwy . . . 83 D8
Denb . . . 72 B4
Graig-fechan . . . 72 D5
Grain . . . 30 B2
Grainsby . . . 91 E6
Grainthorpe . . . 91 E7
Grampound . . . 3 B8
Grampound Road . . 4 D4
Gramsdal . . . 148 C3
Granborough . . . 39 B7
Granby . . . 77 F7
Grandborough . . . 52 C2
Grandtully . . . 133 D6
Grange Cumb . . . 98 C4
E Ayrs . . . 118 F4
Medway . . . 29 C8
Mers . . . 85 F3
Perth . . . 128 B4
Grange
Crossroads . . . 152 C4
Grange Hall . . . 151 E13
Grange Hill . . . 41 E7
Grangemill . . . 76 D2
Grange Moor . . . 88 C3
Grangemouth . . . 127 F8
Grange of
Lindores . . . 128 C4
Grange-over-
Sands . . . 92 B4
Grangepans . . . 128 F2
Grangetown Cardiff 22 B3
Redcar . . . 102 B3
Grange Villa . . . 110 D5
Granish . . . 138 C5
Gransmoor . . . 97 D7
Granston . . . 44 B3
Grantchester . . . 54 D5
Grantham . . . 78 F2
Grantley . . . 94 C5
Grantlodge . . . 141 C6
Granton Dumfries . . 114 D3
Edin . . . 120 B5
Grantown-on-
Spey . . . 139 B6
Grantshouse . . . 122 C4
Grappenhall . . . 86 F4
Grasby . . . 90 D4
Grasmere . . . 99 D5
Grasscroft . . . 87 D7
Grassendale . . . 85 F4
Grassholme . . . 100 B4
Grassington . . . 94 C3
Grassmoor . . . 76 C4
Grassthorpe . . . 77 C7
Grateley . . . 25 E7
Gratwich . . . 75 F7
Graveley Cambs . . . 54 C3
Herts . . . 41 B5
Gravelly Hill . . . 62 E5
Gravels . . . 60 D3
Graven . . . 160 F6
Graveney . . . 30 C4
Gravesend Herts . . . 41 B7
Kent . . . 29 B7
Grayingham . . . 90 E3
Grayrigg . . . 99 E7
Grays . . . 29 B7
Grayshott . . . 27 F6
Grayswood . . . 27 F7
Graythorp . . . 102 B3
Grazeley . . . 26 C4
Greasbrough . . . 88 E5
Greasby . . . 85 F3
Great Abington . . . 55 E6
Great Addington . . 53 B7
Great Alne . . . 51 D6
Great Altcar . . . 85 D4
Great Amwell . . . 41 C6
Great Asby . . . 100 C1
Great Ashfield . . . 56 C3
Great Ayton . . . 102 C3
Great Baddow . . . 42 D3
Great Bardfield . . . 55 F7
Great Barford . . . 54 D2
Great Barr . . . 62 E4
Great Barrington . . 38 C2
Great Barrow . . . 73 C8
Great Barton . . . 56 C2
Great Barugh . . . 96 B3
Great Bavington . . 117 F5
Great Bealings . . . 57 E6
Great Bedwyn . . . 25 C7
Great Bentley . . . 43 B7
Great Billing . . . 53 C6
Great Bircham . . . 80 D3
Great Blakenham . . 56 D5
Great Blencow . . . 108 F4
Great Bolas . . . 61 B6
Great Bookham . . . 28 D2
Great Bourton . . . 52 E2
Great Bowden . . . 64 F4
Great Bradley . . . 55 D7
Great Braxted . . . 42 C4
Great Bricett . . . 56 D4
Great Brickhill . . . 53 F7
Great Bridge . . . 62 E3
Great Bridgeford . . 62 B2
Great Brington . . . 52 C4
Great Bromley . . . 43 B6
Great Broughton
Cumb . . . 107 F7
N Yorks . . . 102 D3
Great Budworth . . . 74 B3
Great Burdon . . . 101 C8
Great Burgh . . . 28 D3
Great Burstead . . . 42 E2
Great Busby . . . 102 D3
Great Canfield . . . 42 C1
Great Carlton . . . 91 F8
Great Casterton . . . 65 D7
Great Chart . . . 30 E3
Great Chatwell . . . 61 C7
Great Chesterford . 55 E6
Great Cheverell . . . 24 D4
Great Chishill . . . 54 F5
Great Clacton . . . 43 C7
Great Cliff . . . 88 C4
Great Clifton . . . 98 B2
Great Coates . . . 91 D6
Great Comberton . . 50 E4
Great Corby . . . 108 D4
Great Cornard . . . 56 E2
Great Cowden . . . 97 E8
Great Coxwell . . . 38 E2
Great Crakehall . . . 101 E7
Great Cransley . . . 53 B6
Great
Cressingham . . . 67 D8
Great Crosby . . . 85 E4
Great Cubley . . . 75 F8
Great Dalby . . . 64 C4
Great Denham . . . 53 E8
Great Doddington . 53 C6
Great Dunham . . . 67 C8
Great Dunmow . . . 42 B2
Great Durnford . . . 25 F6
Great Easton Essex . 42 B2
Leics . . . 64 E5
Great Eccleston . . . 92 E4
Great Edstone . . . 103 F5
Great Ellingham . . . 68 E3
Great Elm . . . 24 E2
Greater Doward . . . 36 C2
Great Eversden . . . 54 D4
Great Fencote . . . 101 E7
Great Finborough . 56 D4
Greatford . . . 65 C7
Great Fransham . . . 67 C8
Great Gaddesden . . 40 C3
Greatgate . . . 75 E7
Great Gidding . . . 65 F8
Great Givendale . . 96 D4
Great Glemham . . . 57 C7
Great Glen . . . 64 E3
Great Gonerby . . . 77 F8
Great Gransden . . . 54 D3
Great Green Norf . . . 69 F5
Suff . . . 56 D3
Great Habton . . . 96 B3
Great Hale . . . 78 E4
Great Hallingbury . 41 C8
Greatham Hants . . . 27 F5
Hrtlpl . . . 102 B2
W Sus . . . 16 C4
Great Hampden . . . 39 D8
Great Harrowden . . 53 B6
Great Harwood . . . 93 F7
Great Haseley . . . 39 D6
Great Hatfield . . . 97 E7
Great Haywood . . . 62 B4
Great Heath . . . 63 F7
Great Heck . . . 89 B6
Great Henny . . . 56 F2
Great Hinton . . . 24 D4
Great Hockham . . . 68 E2
Great Holland . . . 43 C8
Great Horkesley . . . 56 F3
Great Hormead . . . 41 B6
Great Horton . . . 94 F4
Great Horwood . . . 53 F5
Great Houghton
Northants . . . 53 D5
S Yorks . . . 88 D5
Great Hucklow . . . 75 B8
Great Kelk . . . 97 D7
Great Kimble . . . 39 D8
Great Kingshill . . . 40 E1
Great Langton . . . 101 E7
Great Leighs . . . 42 C3
Great Lever . . . 86 D5
Great Limber . . . 90 D5
Great Linford . . . 53 E6
Great Livermere . . . 56 B2
Great Longstone . . 76 B2
Great Lumley . . . 111 E5
Great Lyth . . . 60 D4
Great Malvern . . . 50 E2
Great Maplestead . 56 F2
Great Marton . . . 92 F3
Great Massingham 80 E3
Great Melton . . . 68 D4
Great Milton . . . 39 D6
Great Missenden . . 40 D1
Great Mitton . . . 93 F7
Great Mongeham . . 31 D7
Great Moulton . . . 68 E4
Great Munden . . . 41 B6
Great Musgrave . . 100 C2
Great Ness . . . 60 C3
Great Notley . . . 42 B3
Great Oakley Essex . 43 B7
Northants . . . 65 F5
Great Offley . . . 40 B4
Great Ormside . . . 100 C2
Great Orton . . . 108 D3
Great Ouseburn . . . 95 C7
Great Oxendon . . . 64 F4
Great Oxney
Green . . . 42 D2
Great Palgrave . . . 67 C8
Great Parndon . . . 41 D7
Great Paxton . . . 54 C3
Great Plumpton . . . 92 F3
Great Plumstead . . 69 C6
Great Ponton . . . 78 F2
Great Preston . . . 88 B5
Great Raveley . . . 66 F2
Great Rissington . . 38 C1
Great Rollright . . . 51 F8
Great Ryburgh . . . 81 E5
Great Ryle . . . 117 C6
Great Ryton . . . 60 D4
Great Saling . . . 42 B3
Great Salkeld . . . 109 F5
Great Sampford . . . 55 F7
Great Sankey . . . 86 F3
Great Saxham . . . 55 C8
Great Shefford . . . 25 B8
Great Shelford . . . 55 D5
Great Smeaton . . . 101 D8
Great Snoring . . . 80 D5
Great Somerford . . 37 F6
Great Stainton . . . 101 B8
Great Stambridge . 42 E4
Great Staughton . . . 54 C2
Great Steeping . . . 79 C7
Great Stonar . . . 31 D7
Greatstone on Sea . 19 C7
Great Strickland . . . 99 B7
Great Stukeley . . . 54 B3
Great Sturton . . . 78 B5
Great Sutton
Ches W . . . 73 B7
Shrops . . . 60 F5
Great Swinburne . 110 B2
Great Tew . . . 38 B3
Great Tey . . . 42 B4
Great Thurkleby . . . 95 B7
Great Thurlow . . . 55 D7
Great Torrington . . . 9 C6
Great Tosson . . . 117 D6
Great Totham
Essex . . . 42 C4
Essex . . . 42 C4
Great Tows . . . 91 E6
Great Urswick . . . 92 B2
Great Wakering . . . 43 F5
Great Waldingfield 56 E3
Great Walsingham 80 D5
Great Waltham . . . 42 C2
Great Warley . . . 42 E1
Great Washbourne 50 F4
Great Weldon . . . 65 F6
Great Welnetham . 56 D2
Great Wenham . . . 56 F4
Great
Whittington . . . 110 B3
Great Wigborough 43 C5
Great Wilbraham . . 55 D6
Great Wishford . . . 25 F5
Great Witcombe . . . 37 C6
Great Witley . . . 50 C2
Great Wolford . . . 51 F7
Greatworth . . . 52 E3
Great Wratting . . . 55 E7
Great Wymondley . 41 B5
Great Wyrley . . . 62 D3
Great Wytheford . . 61 C5
Great Yarmouth . . . 69 D8
Great Yeldham . . . 55 F8
Greave . . . 87 B6
Greeba . . . 84 D3
Green . . . 72 C4
Greenbank . . . 160 C7
Greenburn . . . 120 C2
Greendikes . . . 117 B6
Green End . . . 54 D2
Greenfield C Beds . . 53 F8
Flint . . . 73 B5
Gtr Man . . . 87 D7
Highld . . . 136 D5
Oxon . . . 39 E7
Greenford . . . 40 F4
Greengairs . . . 119 B7
Greenham . . . 26 C2
Green Hammerton 95 D7
Greenhaugh . . . 116 F3
Greenhead . . . 109 C6
Greenhill Falk . . . 119 B8
Kent . . . 31 C5
Leics . . . 63 C8
London . . . 40 F4
Greenhills . . . 118 D3
Greenhithe . . . 29 B6
Greenholm . . . 118 F5
Greenholme . . . 99 D7
Greenhouse . . . 115 B8
Greenhow Hill . . . 94 C4
Greenigoe . . . 159 H5
Greenland . . . 158 D4
Greenlands . . . 39 F7
Green Lane . . . 59 E8
Greenlaw Aberds . . 153 C6
Borders . . . 122 E3
Greenlea . . . 107 B7
Greenloaning . . . 127 D7
Greenmount . . . 87 C5
Greenmow . . . 160 L6
Greenock . . . 118 B2
Greenock West . . . 118 B2
Greenodd . . . 99 F5
Green Ore . . . 23 D7
Greenrow . . . 107 D8
Green St Green . . . 29 C5
Greenside . . . 110 C4
Greensidehill . . . 117 C5
Greens Norton . . . 52 E4
Greenstead Green . 42 B4
Greensted . . . 41 D8
Green Street . . . 40 E4
Greenwich . . . 28 B4
Greet . . . 50 F5
Greete . . . 49 B7
Greetham Lincs . . . 79 B6
Rutland . . . 65 C6
Greetland . . . 87 B8
Gregg Hall . . . 99 E6
Gregson Lane . . . 86 B3
Greinetobht . . . 148 A3
Greinton . . . 23 F6
Gremista . . . 160 J6
Grenaby . . . 84 E2
Grendon Northants . . 53 C6
Warks . . . 63 D6
Grendon Common . 63 E6
Grendon Green . . . 49 D7
Grendon
Underwood . . . 39 B6
Grenofen . . . 6 B2
Grenoside . . . 88 E4
Greosabhagh . . . 154 H6
Gresford . . . 73 D7
Gresham . . . 81 D7
Greshornish . . . 149 C8
Gressenhall . . . 68 C2
Gressingham . . . 93 C5
Gresty Green . . . 74 D4
Greta Bridge . . . 101 C5
Gretna . . . 108 C3
Gretna Green . . . 108 C3
Gretton Glos . . . 50 F5
Northants . . . 65 E5
Shrops . . . 60 E5
Grewelthorpe . . . 94 B5
Greygarth . . . 94 B4
Grey Green . . . 89 D8
Greynor . . . 33 D6
Greysouthen . . . 98 B2
Greystoke . . . 108 F4
Greystone Angus . . 135 E5
Dumfries . . . 107 B6
Greywell . . . 26 D5
Griais . . . 155 C9
Grianan . . . 155 D9
Gribthorpe . . . 96 F3
Gridley Corner . . . 9 E5
Griff . . . 63 F7
Griffithstown . . . 35 E6
Grimbister . . . 159 G4
Grimblethorpe . . . 91 F6
Grimeford Village . 86 C4
Grimethorpe . . . 88 D5
Griminis . . . 148 C2
Grimister . . . 160 D6
Grimley . . . 50 C3
Grimness . . . 159 J5
Grimoldby . . . 91 F7
Grimpo . . . 60 B3
Grimsargh . . . 93 F5
Grimsbury . . . 52 E2
Grimsby . . . 91 C6
Grimscote . . . 52 D4
Grimscott . . . 8 D4
Grimsthorpe . . . 65 B7
Grimston E Yorks . . . 97 F8
Leics . . . 64 B3
Norf . . . 80 E3
York . . . 96 D2
Grimstone . . . 12 E4
Grinacombe Moor . . 9 E6
Grindale . . . 97 B7
Grindigar . . . 159 H6
Grindiscol . . . 160 K6
Grindle . . . 61 D7
Grindleford . . . 76 B2
Grindleton . . . 93 E7
Grindley . . . 62 B4
Grindley Brook . . . 74 E2
Grindlow . . . 75 B8
Grindon Northumb . 122 E5
Staffs . . . 75 D7
Grindonmoor Gate 75 D7
Gringley on the
Hill . . . 89 E8
Grinsdale . . . 108 D3
Grinshill . . . 60 B5
Grinton . . . 101 E5
Griomsidar . . . 155 E8
Grishipoll . . . 146 F4
Grisling Common . 17 B8
Gristhorpe . . . 103 F8
Griston . . . 68 E2
Gritley . . . 159 H6
Grittenham . . . 37 F7
Grittleton . . . 37 F5
Grizebeck . . . 98 F4
Grizedale . . . 99 E5
Grobister . . . 159 F7
Groby . . . 64 D2
Groes Conwy . . . 72 C4
Neath . . . 34 F1
Groes-faen . . . 34 F4
Groesffordd Marli . 72 B4
Groeslon Gwyn . . . 82 E5
Gwyn . . . 82 F4
Groes-lwyd . . . 60 C2
Grogport . . . 143 D9
Gromford . . . 57 D7
Gronant . . . 72 A4
Groombridge . . . 18 B2
Grosmont Mon . . . 35 B8
N Yorks . . . 103 D6
Groton . . . 56 E3
Grougfoot . . . 120 B3
Grouville Jersey . . . 17
Grove Dorset . . . 12 G5
Kent . . . 31 C6
Notts . . . 77 B7
Oxon . . . 38 E4
Grove Park . . . 28 B5
Grovesend . . . 33 D6
Grove Vale . . . 62 E4
Grudie . . . 150 E6
Gruids . . . 157 J8
Gruinard House . . 150 B2
Grula . . . 149 F8
Gruline . . . 147 G8
Grunasound . . . 160 K5
Grundisburgh . . . 57 D6
Grunsagill . . . 93 D7
Gruting . . . 160 J4
Grutness . . . 160 N6
Gualachulain . . . 131 E5
Gualin House . . . 156 D6
Guardbridge . . . 129 C6
Guarlford . . . 50 E3
Guay . . . 133 E7
Guestling Green . . . 19 D5
Guestling Thorn . . . 18 D5
Guestwick . . . 81 E6
Guestwick Green . . 81 E6
Guide . . . 86 B5
Guide Post . . . 117 F8
Guilden Morden . . . 54 E3
Guilden Sutton . . . 73 C8
Guildford . . . 27 E7
Guildtown . . . 133 F8
Guilsborough . . . 52 B4
Guilsfield . . . 60 C2
Guilton . . . 31 D6
Guineaford . . . 20 F4
Guisborough . . . 102 C4
Guiseley . . . 94 E4
Guist . . . 81 E5
Guith . . . 159 E6
Guiting Power . . . 37 B7
Gulberwick . . . 160 K6
Gullane . . . 129 F6
Gulval . . . 2 C3
Gulworthy . . . 6 B2
Gumfreston . . . 32 D2
Gumley . . . 64 E3
Gummow's Shop . . . 4 D3
Gunby E Yorks . . . 96 F3
Lincs . . . 65 B6
Gundleton . . . 26 F4
Gun Hill . . . 18 D2
Gunn . . . 20 F5
Gunnerside . . . 100 E4
Gunnerton . . . 110 B2
Gunness . . . 90 C2
Gunnislake . . . 6 B2
Gunnista . . . 160 J7
Gunthorpe Norf . . . 81 D6
Notts . . . 77 E6
Pboro . . . 65 D8
Gunville . . . 15 F5
Gunwalloe . . . 3 D5
Gurnard . . . 15 E5
Gurnett . . . 75 B6
Gurney Slade . . . 23 E8
Gurnos . . . 34 D1
Gussage All Saints . 13 C8
Gussage
St Michael . . . 13 C7
Guston . . . 31 E7
Gutcher . . . 160 D7
Guthrie . . . 135 D5
Guyhirn . . . 66 D3
Guyhirn Gull . . . 66 D3
Guy's Head . . . 66 B4
Guy's Marsh . . . 13 B6
Guyzance . . . 117 D8
Gwaenysgor . . . 72 A4
Gwalchmai . . . 82 D3
Gwaun-Cae-
Gurwen . . . 33 C8
Gwaun-Leision . . . 33 C8
Gwbert . . . 45 E3
Gweek . . . 3 D6
Gwehelog . . . 35 D7
Gwenddwr . . . 48 E2
Gwennap . . . 3 C6
Gwenter . . . 3 E6
Gwernaffield . . . 73 C6
Gwernesney . . . 35 D8
Gwernogle . . . 46 F4
Gwernymynydd . . . 73 C6
Gwersyllt . . . 73 D7
Gwespyr . . . 85 F2
Gwithian . . . 2 B4
Gwredog . . . 82 C4
Gwyddelwern . . . 72 E4
Gwyddgrug . . . 46 F3
Gwydyr Uchaf . . . 83 E7
Gwynfryn . . . 73 D6
Gwystre . . . 48 C2
Gwytherin . . . 83 E8
Gyfelia . . . 73 E7
Gyffi . . . 83 D7
Gyre . . . 159 H4
Gyrn-goch . . . 70 C5

H

Habberley . . . 60 D3
Habergham . . . 93 F8
Habrough . . . 90 C5
Haceby . . . 78 F3
Hacheston . . . 57 D7
Hackbridge . . . 28 C3
Hackenthorpe . . . 88 F5
Hackford . . . 68 D3
Hackforth . . . 101 E7
Hackland . . . 159 F4
Hackleton . . . 53 D6
Hackness N Yorks . . 103 E7
Orkney . . . 159 J4
Hackney . . . 41 F6
Hackthorn . . . 90 F3
Hackthorpe . . . 99 B7
Haconby . . . 65 B8
Hacton . . . 41 F8
Hadden . . . 122 F3
Haddenham Bucks . 39 D7
Cambs . . . 55 B5
Haddington
E Loth . . . 121 B8
Lincs . . . 78 C2
Haddiscoe . . . 69 E7
Haddon Cambs . . . 65 E8
Ches E . . . 75 C6
Hade Edge . . . 88 D2
Hademore . . . 63 D5
Hadfield . . . 87 E8
Hadham Cross . . . 41 C7
Hadham Ford . . . 41 B7
Hadleigh Essex . . . 42 F4
Suff . . . 56 E4
Hadley . . . 61 C6
Hadley End . . . 62 B5
Hadlow . . . 29 E7
Hadlow Down . . . 18 C2
Hadnall . . . 60 C5
Hadstock . . . 55 E6
Hady . . . 76 B3
Hadzor . . . 50 C4
Haffenden Quarter 30 E2
Hafod-Dinbych . . . 83 F8
Hafod-Iom . . . 83 D8
Haggate . . . 93 F8
Haggbeck . . . 108 B4
Haggerston . . . 123 E6
Haggrister . . . 160 F5
Hagley Hereford . . . 49 E7
Worcs . . . 62 F3
Hagworthingham . . 79 C6
Haigh Gtr Man . . . 86 D4
S Yorks . . . 88 C3
Haigh Moor . . . 88 B3
Haighton Green . . . 93 F5
Haile . . . 98 D2
Hailes . . . 50 F5
Hailey Herts . . . 41 C6
Oxon . . . 38 C3
Hailsham . . . 18 E2
Hail Weston . . . 54 C2
Haimer . . . 158 D3
Hainault . . . 41 E7
Hainford . . . 68 C5
Hainton . . . 91 F5
Hairmyres . . . 119 D6
Haisthorpe . . . 97 C7
Hakin . . . 44 E3
Halam . . . 77 D6
Halbeath . . . 128 F3
Halberton . . . 10 C5
Halcro . . . 158 D4
Hale Gtr Man . . . 87 F5
Halton . . . 86 F2
Hants . . . 14 C2
Hale Bank . . . 86 F2
Halebarns . . . 87 F5
Hales Norf . . . 69 E6
Staffs . . . 74 F4
Halesfield . . . 61 D7
Halesgate . . . 66 B3
Halesowen . . . 62 F3
Hales Place . . . 30 D5
Hale Street . . . 29 E7
Halesworth . . . 57 B7
Halewood . . . 86 F2
Halford Shrops . . . 60 F4
Warks . . . 51 E7
Halfpenny Furze . . . 32 C3
Halfpenny Green . . 62 E2
Halfway Carms . . . 46 F5
Carms . . . 47 F7
W Berks . . . 26 C2
Halfway Bridge . . . 16 B3
Halfway House . . . 60 C3
Halfway Houses . . . 30 B3
Halifax . . . 87 B8
Halket . . . 118 D4
Halkirk . . . 158 E3
Halkyn . . . 73 B6
Halland . . . 18 D2
Hallaton . . . 64 E4
Hallatrow . . . 23 D8
Hallbankgate . . . 109 D5
Hall Dunnerdale . . . 98 E4
Hallen . . . 36 F2
Hall Green W Mid . . . 62 F5
W Yorks . . . 88 C4
Hall Grove . . . 41 C5
Halliburton . . . 122 E2
Hallin . . . 148 C7
Halling . . . 29 C8
Hallington Lincs . . . 91 F7
Northumb . . . 110 B2
Halliwell . . . 86 C5
Hall of
Tankerness . . . 159 H6
Hall of the Forest . . 60 F2
Halloughton . . . 77 D6
Hallow . . . 50 D3
Hallrule . . . 115 C8
Halls . . . 122 B2
Hallsands . . . 7 F6
Hall's Green . . . 41 B5
Hallthwaites . . . 98 F3
Hallworthy . . . 8 F3
Hallyburton
House . . . 134 F2
Hallyne . . . 120 E4
Halmer End . . . 74 E4
Halmore . . . 36 D3
Halmyre Mains . . . 120 E4
Halnaker . . . 16 D3
Halsall . . . 85 C4
Halse Northants . . . 52 E3
Som . . . 11 B6
Halsetown . . . 2 C4
Halsham . . . 91 B6
Halsinger . . . 20 F4
Halstead Essex . . . 56 F2
Kent . . . 29 C5
Leics . . . 64 D4
Halstock . . . 12 D3
Haltham . . . 78 C5
Haltoft End . . . 79 E6
Halton Bucks . . . 40 C1
Halton . . . 86 F3
Lancs . . . 92 C5
Northumb . . . 110 C2
Wrex . . . 73 F7
W Yorks . . . 95 F6
Halton East . . . 94 D3
Halton Gill . . . 93 B8
Halton Holegate . . . 79 C7
Halton Lea Gate . . 109 D6
Halton West . . . 93 D8
Haltwhistle . . . 109 C7
Halvergate . . . 69 D7
Halwell . . . 7 D5
Halwill . . . 9 E6
Halwill Junction . . . 9 D6
Ham Devon . . . 11 D7
Glos . . . 36 E3
Highld . . . 158 C4
Kent . . . 31 D7
London . . . 28 B2
Shetland . . . 160 K1
Wilts . . . 25 C8
Hambleden . . . 39 F7
Hambledon Hants . . 15 C7
Sur . . . 27 F7
Hamble-le-Rice . . . 15 D5
Hambleton Lancs . . . 92 E3
N Yorks . . . 95 F8
Hambridge . . . 11 B8
Hambrook S Glos . . . 23 B8
W Sus . . . 15 D8
Ham Common . . . 13 B6
Hameringham . . . 79 C6
Hamerton . . . 54 B2
Hametoun . . . 160 K1
Ham Green
Hereford . . . 50 E2
Kent . . . 19 C5
Kent . . . 30 C2
N Som . . . 23 B7
Worcs . . . 50 C5
Hamilton . . . 119 D7
Hammer . . . 27 F6
Hammerpot . . . 16 D4
Hammersmith . . . 28 B3
Hammerwich . . . 62 D4
Hammerwood . . . 28 F5
Hammond Street . . 41 D6
Hammoon . . . 13 C6
Hamnavoe
Shetland . . . 160 E4
Shetland . . . 160 E6
Shetland . . . 160 F6
Shetland . . . 160 K5
Hampden Park . . . 18 E3
Hamperden End . . . 55 F6
Hampnett . . . 37 C7
Hampole . . . 89 C6
Hampreston . . . 13 E8
Hampstead . . . 41 F5
Hampstead
Norreys . . . 26 B3
Hampsthwaite . . . 95 D5
Hampton London . . . 28 C2
Shrops . . . 61 F7
Worcs . . . 50 E5
Hampton Bishop . . 49 F7
Hampton Heath . . . 73 E8
Hampton in Arden . 63 F6
Hampton Loade . . . 61 F7
Hampton Lovett . . . 50 C3
Hampton Lucy . . . 51 D7
Hampton on the
Hill . . . 51 C7
Hampton Poyle . . . 39 C5
Hamrow . . . 80 E5
Hamsey . . . 17 C8
Hamsey Green . . . 28 D4
Hamstall Ridware . 62 C5
Hamstead IoW . . . 14 E5
W Mid . . . 62 E4
Hamstead
Marshall . . . 26 C2
Hamsterley
Durham . . . 110 D4
Durham . . . 110 F4
Hamstreet . . . 19 B7
Ham Street . . . 23 F7
Hamworthy . . . 13 E7
Hanbury Staffs . . . 63 B5
Worcs . . . 50 C4
Hanbury Woodend 63 B5
Hanby . . . 78 F3
Hanchurch . . . 74 E5
Handbridge . . . 73 C8
Handcross . . . 17 B6
Handforth . . . 87 F6
Handley . . . 73 D8
Handsacre . . . 62 C4
Handsworth
S Yorks . . . 88 F5
W Mid . . . 62 E4
Handy Cross . . . 9 B6
Hanford . . . 75 E5
Hanging Langford . 24 F5
Hangleton . . . 16 D4
Hanham . . . 23 B8
Hankelow . . . 74 E3
Hankerton . . . 37 E6
Hankham . . . 18 E3
Hanley . . . 75 E5
Hanley Castle . . . 50 E3
Hanley Child . . . 49 C8
Hanley Swan . . . 50 E3
Hanley William . . . 49 C8
Hanlith . . . 94 C2
Hanmer . . . 73 F8
Hannah . . . 79 B8
Hannington Hants . . 26 D3
Northants . . . 53 B6
Swindon . . . 38 E1
Hannington Wick . . 38 E1
Hansel Village . . . 118 F3

Hanslope 53 E6
Hanthorpe 65 B7
Hanwell London . . . 40 F4
  Oxon 52 E2
Hanwood 60 D4
Hanworth London . . 28 B2
  Norf. 81 D7
Happendon 119 F8
Happisburgh 69 A6
Happisburgh
  Common 69 B6
Hapsford 73 B8
Hapton Lancs 93 F7
  Norf 68 E4
Harberton 7 D5
Harbertonford . . . 7 D5
Harbledown 30 D5
Harborne 62 F4
Harborough
  Magna 52 B2
Harbottle 117 D5
Harbury 51 D8
Harby Leics 77 F7
  Notts 77 B8
Harcombe 11 E6
Harden W Mid . . . 62 D4
  W Yorks 94 F3
Hardgate 141 D6
Hardham 16 C4
Hardingham 68 D3
Hardingstone . . . 53 D5
Hardington 24 D2
Hardington
  Mandeville . . . 12 C3
Hardington Marsh . 12 D3
Hardley 14 D5
Hardley Street . . . 69 D6
Hardmead 53 E7
Hardrow 100 E3
Hardstoft 76 C4
Hardway Hants . . . 15 D7
  Som 24 F2
Hardwick Bucks . . 39 C8
  Cambs 54 D4
  Norf 67 C6
  Norf 68 F5
  Northants 53 C6
  Notts 77 B6
  Oxon 38 D3
  Oxon 39 B5
  W Mid 62 E4
Hardwicke Glos . . 36 C4
  Glos. 37 B6
  Hereford 48 E4
Hardy's Green . . . 43 B5
Hareby 79 C6
Hareden 93 D6
Harefield 40 E3
Hare Green 43 B6
Hare Hatch 27 B6
Harehills 95 F6
Harehope 117 B6
Haresceugh 109 E6
Harescombe 37 C5
Haresfield 37 C5
Hareshaw 119 C8
Hareshaw Head . . 116 F4
Hare Street 41 B6
Harewood 95 E6
Harewood End . . . 36 B2
Harford Carms . . . 46 E5
  Devon 6 D4
Hargate 68 E4
Hargatewall 75 B8
Hargrave Ches W . 73 C8
  Northants 53 B8
  Suff 55 D8
Harker 108 C3
Harkland 160 E6
Harkstead 57 F5
Harlaston 63 D6
Harlaw House . . . 141 B6
Harlaxton 77 F8
Harlech 71 D6
Harlequin 77 F6
Harlescott 60 C5
Harlesden 41 F5
Harleston Devon . . 7 E5
  Norf 68 F5
  Suff 56 D4
Harlestone 52 C5
Harle Syke 93 F8
Harley Shrops . . . 61 D5
  S Yorks 88 E4
Harleyholm 120 F2
Harlington C Beds . 53 F8
  London. 27 B8
  S Yorks 89 D5
Harlosh 149 D7
Harlow 41 C7
Harlow Hill
  Northumb 110 C3
  N Yorks 95 D5
Harlthorpe 96 F3
Harlton 54 D4
Harman's Cross . . 13 F7
Harmby 101 F6
Harmer Green . . . 41 C5
Harmer Hill 60 B4
Harmondsworth . . 27 B8
Harmston 78 C2
Harnham 110 B3
Harnhill 37 D7
Harold Hill 41 E8
Haroldston West . . 44 D3
Haroldswick 160 B8
Harold Wood 41 E8
Harome 102 F4
Harpenden 40 C4
Harpford 11 E5
Harpham 97 C6
Harpley Norf 80 E3
  Worcs 49 C8
Harpole 52 C4
Harpsdale 158 E3
Harpsden 39 F7
Harpswell 90 F3
Harpurhey 87 D6
Harpur Hill 75 B7
Harraby 108 D4
Harrapool 149 F11
Harrier 160 J1
Harrietfield 127 B8
Harrietsham 30 D2
Harrington Cumb . . 98 B1
  Lincs 79 B6
  Northants 64 F4
Harringworth . . . 65 E6

Harris. 146 B6
Harrogate 95 D6
Harrold 53 D7
Harrow 40 F4
Harrowbarrow . . . 5 C8
Harrowden. 53 E8
Harrowgate Hill . . 101 C7
Harrow on the Hill . 40 F4
Harrow Street . . . 56 F3
Harrow Weald . . . 40 E4
Harston Cambs . . 54 D5
  Leics 77 F8
Harswell 96 E4
Hart 111 F7
Hartburn
  Northumb 117 F6
  Stockton 102 C2
Hart Common . . . 86 D4
Hartest 56 D2
Hartfield 29 F5
Hartford Cambs . . 54 B3
  Ches W. 74 B3
Hartfordbridge . . . 27 D5
Hartford End 42 C2
Harthill Ches W . . 74 D2
  N Lanark 120 C2
  S Yorks 89 F5
Hart Hill 40 B4
Hartington 75 C8
Hartland 8 B4
Hartlebury 50 B3
Hartlepool 111 F8
Hartley Cumb . . . 100 D2
Hartley Kent 18 B4
  Kent 29 C7
  Northumb 111 B6
Hartley Westpall . . 26 D4
Hartley Wintney . . 27 D5
Hartlip 30 C2
Hartoft End 103 E5
Harton N Yorks . . 96 C3
  Shrops. 60 F4
  T&W 111 C6
Hartpury 36 B4
Hartshead 88 B2
Hartshill 63 E7
Hartshorne 63 B7
Hartsop 99 C6
Hart Station 111 F7
Hartwell 53 D5
Hartwood 119 D8
Harvieston 126 F4
Harvington 51 E5
Harvington Cross . 51 E5
Harwell 38 F4
Harwich 57 F6
Harwood Durham . 109 F8
  Gtr Man. 87 C5
Harwood Dale . . 103 E7
Harworth 89 E7
Hasbury 62 F3
Hascombe 27 E7
Haselbech 52 B5
Haselbury
  Plucknett. 12 C2
Haseley 51 C7
Haselor 51 D6
Hasfield 37 B5
Hasguard 44 E3
Haskayne 85 D4
Hasketon 57 D6
Hasland 76 C3
Haslemere 27 F7
Haslingden 87 B5
Haslingfield 54 D5
Haslington 74 D4
Hassall 74 D4
Hassall Green . . . 74 D4
Hassall Street . . . 30 E4
Hassendean. . . . 115 B8
Hassingham 69 D6
Hassocks 17 C6
Hassop 76 B2
Hastigrow. 158 D4
Hastingleigh 30 E4
Hastings 18 E5
Hastingwood 41 D7
Hastoe. 40 D2
Haswell 111 E6
Haswell Plough . . 111 E6
Hatch C Beds 54 E2
  Hants 26 D4
  Wilts 13 B7
Hatch Beauchamp . 11 B8
Hatch End 40 E4
Hatchet Gate . . . 14 D4
Hatch Green 11 C8
Hatching Green . . 40 C4
Hatchmere 74 B2
Hatcliffe 91 D6
Hatfield Hereford . 49 D7
  Herts 41 D5
  S Yorks 89 D7
  Worcs 50 D3
Hatfield Broad
  Oak 41 C8
Hatfield Garden
  Village 41 D5
Hatfield Heath . . . 41 C8
Hatfield Hyde . . . 41 C5
Hatfield Peverel . . 42 C3
Hatfield
  Woodhouse. . . . 89 D7
Hatford 38 E3
Hatherden 25 D8
Hatherleigh 9 D7
Hathern 63 B8
Hatherop 38 D1
Hathersage 88 F3
Hathershaw 87 D7
Hatherton Ches E . . 74 E3
  Staffs. 62 C3
Hatley St George . 54 D3
Hatt 5 C8
Hattingley 26 F4
Hatton Aberds . . 153 E10
  Derbys. 63 B6
  Lincs 78 B4
  Shrops. 60 E4
  Warks 51 C7
  Warr 86 F3
Hatton Castle . . 153 D7
Hattoncrook . . . 141 B7
Hatton Heath. . . . 73 C8
Hatton of Fintray . 141 C7
Haugh E Ayrs . . . 112 B4
  Lincs 79 B7

Haugham 91 F7
Haugh Head. . . . 117 B6
Haughley 56 C4
Haughley Green. . 56 C4
Haugh of Glass . . 152 E4
Haugh of Urr . . . 106 C5
Haughs of
  Clinterty 141 C7
Haughton Notts . . 77 B6
  Shrops. 60 B3
  Shrops. 61 C5
  Shrops. 61 D7
  Shrops. 61 E6
  Staffs. 62 B2
Haughton Castle . 110 B2
Haughton Green. . 87 E7
Haughton Moss . . 74 D2
Haultwick 41 B6
Haunn Argyll . . . 146 G6
  W Isles 148 G2
Haunton 63 C6
Hauxley 117 D8
Hauxton 54 D5
Havant 15 D8
Haven 49 D6
Haven Bank 78 D5
Haven Side. 91 B5
Havenstreet 15 E6
Havercroft 88 C4
Haverfordwest
  =Hwlffordd. . . . 44 D4
Haverhill 55 E7
Haverigg 92 B1
Havering-atte-
  Bower. 41 E8
Haveringland . . . 81 E7
Haversham 53 E6
Haverthwaite . . . 99 F5
Haverton Hill . . . 102 B2
Hawarden
  =Penarlâg. 73 C7
Hawcoat 92 B2
Hawen 46 E2
Hawes 100 F3
Hawes' Green . . . 68 E5
Hawes Side 92 F3
Hawford 50 C3
Hawick 115 C8
Hawkchurch 11 D8
Hawkedon 55 D8
Hawkenbury Kent . 18 B2
  Kent 30 E2
Hawkeridge 24 D3
Hawkerland 11 F5
Hawkesbury S Glos . 36 F4
  Warks 63 F7
Hawkesbury Upton 36 F4
Hawkes End 63 F7
Hawk Green 87 F7
Hawkhill 117 C8
Hawkhurst 18 B4
Hawkinge 31 F6
Hawkley 15 B8
Hawkridge 21 F7
Hawkshead 99 E5
Hawkshead Hill . . 99 E5
Hawksland 119 F8
Hawkswick 94 B2
Hawksworth Notts . 77 E7
  W Yorks 94 E4
  W Yorks 95 F5
Hawkwell 42 E4
Hawley Hants . . . 27 D6
  Kent 29 B6
Hawling 37 B7
Hawnby 102 F3
Haworth 94 F3
Hawstead 56 D2
Hawthorn Durham . 111 E7
  Rhondda 35 F5
  Wilts 24 C3
Hawthorn Hill
  Brack. 27 B6
  Lincs 78 D5
Hawthorpe 65 B7
Hawton 77 D7
Haxby 96 D2
Haxey 89 D8
Haydock 86 E3
Haydon 12 C4
Haydon Bridge . . 109 C8
Haydon Wick . . . 37 F8
Haye 5 C8
Hayes London . . . 28 C5
  London. 40 F4
Hayfield Derbys . . 87 F8
  Fife 128 E4
Hay Green 66 C5
Hayhill 112 C4
Hayhillock 135 E5
Hay Street 41 B6
Hayton Aberdeen . 141 D8
  Cumb 107 E8
  Cumb 108 D5
  E Yorks 96 E4
  Notts 89 F8
Hayton's Bent . . . 60 F5
Haytor Vale. 7 B5
Haywards Heath. . 17 B7
Haywood 89 C6
Haywood Oaks . . 77 D6
Hazelbank 119 E8
Hazelbury Bryan. . 12 D5
Hazeley 26 D5
Hazel Grove 87 F7
Hazelhurst 87 D7
Hazel Street 18 B3
Hazelton 37 C7
Hazelton Walls . . 128 B5
Hazelwood 76 E3
Hazlemere 40 E1
Hazlerigg 110 B5
Hazlewood 94 D3
Hazon 117 D7
Heacham 80 D2
Headbourne
  Worthy 26 F2
Headbrook 48 D5
Headcorn 30 E2

Headingley. 95 F5
Headington 39 D5
Headlam 101 C6
Headless Cross. . . 50 C5
Headley Hants . . . 26 C3
  Hants. 27 F6
  Sur. 28 D3
Head of Muir . . . 127 F7
Headon 77 B7
Heads 119 E7
Heads Nook . . . 108 D4
Heage 76 D3
Healaugh N Yorks . 95 E7
  N Yorks. 101 E5
Heald Green 87 F6
Heale Devon 20 E5
  Som 23 E8
Healey Gtr Man . . 87 C6
  Northumb 110 D3
  N Yorks. 101 F6
Healing 91 C6
Heamoor 2 C3
Heanish 146 G3
Heanor 76 E4
Heanton
  Punchardon . . . 20 F4
Heapham 90 F2
Hearthstane . . . 114 B4
Heasley Mill. 21 F6
Heast 149 G11
Heath Cardiff. . . . 22 B3
  Derbys. 76 C4
Heath and Reach . 40 B2
Heathcote 75 C8
Heath End Hants . 26 C3
  Sur. 27 E6
  Warks 51 C7
Heather. 63 C7
Heathfield Devon . 7 B6
  E Sus 18 C2
  Som 11 B6
Heathhall 107 B6
Heath Hayes 62 C4
Heath Hill 61 C7
Heath House 23 E6
Heathrow Airport. . 27 B8
Heathstock 11 D7
Heathton 62 E2
Heath Town 62 E3
Heatley 86 F5
Heaton Lancs . . . 92 C4
  Staffs. 75 C6
  T&W 111 C5
  W Yorks 94 F4
Heaton Moor . . . 87 E6
Heaverham 29 D6
Heaviley 87 F7
Heavitree 10 E4
Hebburn 111 C6
Hebden 94 C3
Hebden Bridge . . 87 B7
Hebron Anglesey . 82 C4
  Carms 32 B2
  Northumb 117 F7
Heck 114 F3
Heckfield 26 C5
Heckfield Green . . 57 B5
Heckfordbridge . . 43 B5
Heckington 78 E4
Heckmondwike . . 88 B3
Heddington 24 C4
Heddle 159 G4
Heddon-on-the-
  Wall 110 C4
Hedenham 69 E6
Hedge End 15 C5
Hedgerley 40 F2
Hedging 11 B8
Hedley on the
  Hill. 110 D3
Hednesford 62 C4
Hedon 91 B5
Hedsor 40 F2
Hedworth. 111 C6
Hegdon Hill 49 D7
Heggerscales . . . 100 C3
Heglibister. . . . 160 H5
Heighington Darl . 101 B7
  Lincs 78 C3
Heights of Brae . . 151 E8
Heights of
  Kinlochewe . . . 150 E3
Heilam 156 C7
Heiton 122 F3
Hele Devon 10 D4
  Devon. 20 E4
Helensburgh . . . 145 E11
Helford 3 D6
Helford Passage . . 3 D6
Helhoughton. . . . 80 E4
Helions
  Bumpstead . . . 55 E7
Hellaby 89 E6
Helland 5 B5
Hellandbridge . . . 5 B5
Hellesdon 68 C5
Hellidon 52 D3
Hellifield 93 D8
Hellingly. 18 D2
Hellington 69 D6
Hellister 160 J5
Helm. 117 E7
Helmdon 52 E3
Helmingham 57 D5
Helmington Row . 110 F4
Helmsdale 157 H13
Helmshore 87 B5
Helmsley 102 F4
Helperby 95 C7
Helperthorpe . . . 97 B5
Helpringham 78 E4
Helpston 65 D8
Helsby 73 B8
Helsey 79 B8
Helston 3 D5
Helstone. 8 F2
Helton 99 B7
Helwith Bridge . . 93 C8
Hemblington . . . 69 C6
Hemel Hempstead . 40 D3
Hemingbrough . . 96 F2
Hemingby 78 B5
Hemingford
  Abbots 54 B3
Hemingford Grey . 54 B3
Hemingstone . . . 57 D5
Hemington Leics . 63 B8
  Northants 65 F7
  Som 24 D2

Hemley 57 E6
Hemlington 102 C3
Hemp Green 57 C7
Hempholme. 97 D6
Hempnall 68 E5
Hempnall Green . . 68 E5
Hempriggs
  House 158 F5
Hempstead Essex . 55 F7
  Medway. 29 C8
  Norf 69 B7
  Norf 81 D7
Hempsted. 37 C5
Hempton Norf . . . 80 E5
  Oxon 52 F2
Hemsby 69 C7
Hemswell 90 E3
Hemswell Cliff . . . 90 F3
Hemsworth 88 C5
Hemyock 11 C6
Henbury Bristol . . 23 B7
  Ches E. 75 B5
Hendon London. . . 41 F5
  T&W 111 D7
Hendre 73 C5
Hendreforgan . . . 34 F3
Hendy 33 D6
Heneglwys 82 D4
Hen-feddau fawr . . 45 F4
Henfield 17 C6
Henford 9 E5
Henghurst 19 B6
Hengoed Caerph . . 35 E5
  Powys 48 D4
  Shrops. 73 F6
Hengrave 56 C2
Henham 41 B8
Heniarth 59 D8
Henlade 11 B7
Henley Shrops . . . 49 B7
  Som 23 F6
  Suff 57 D5
  W Sus 16 B2
Henley-in-Arden . . 51 C6
Henley-on-
  Thames 39 F7
Henley's Down . . 18 D4
Henllan Ceredig . . 46 E2
  Denb 72 C4
Henllan Amgoed . 32 B2
Henllys 35 E6
Henlow 54 F2
Hennock 10 F3
Henny Street . . . 56 F2
Henryd 83 D7
Henry's Moat. . . . 32 B1
Hensall 89 B6
Henshaw. 109 C7
Hensingham 98 C1
Henstead 69 F7
Henstridge. 12 C5
Henstridge Ash. . . 12 B5
Henstridge Marsh . 12 B5
Henton Oxon. . . . 39 D7
  Som 23 E6
Henwood 5 C7
Heogan 160 J6
Heol-las 33 E7
Heol Senni 34 B3
Heol-y-Cyw 34 F3
Hepburn 117 B6
Hepple 117 D5
Hepscott 117 F8
Heptonstall 87 B7
Hepworth Suff . . . 56 B3
  W Yorks 88 D2
Herbrandston . . . 44 E3
Hereford 49 E7
Heriot 121 D6
Hermiston 120 B4
Hermitage
  Borders 115 E8
  Dorset 12 D4
  W Berks 26 B3
  W Sus 15 D8
Hermon Anglesey . 82 E3
  Carms 33 B7
  Carms 46 F2
  Pembs 45 F4
Herne 31 C5
Herne Bay 31 C5
Herner. 9 B7
Hernhill 30 C4
Herodsfoot 5 C7
Herongate 42 E2
Heronsford 104 A5
Herriard 26 E4
Herringfleet 69 E7
Herringswell 55 B8
Hersden 31 C6
Hersham Corn . . . 8 D4
  Sur. 28 C2
Herstmonceux . . 18 D3
Herston 159 J5
Hertford 41 C6
Hertford Heath . . 41 C6
Hertingfordbury . . 41 C6
Hesketh Bank . . . 86 B2
Hesketh Lane . . . 93 E6
Hesket
  Newmarket . . . 108 F3
Heskin Green . . . 86 C3
Hesleden 111 F7
Hesleyside 116 F4
Heslington 96 D2
Hessay 95 D8
Hessenford 5 D8
Hessett 56 C3
Hessle 90 B4
Hest Bank 92 C4
Heston. 28 B2
Hestwall 159 G3
Heswall 85 F3
Hethe 39 B5
Hethersett 68 D4
Hethersgill 108 C4
Hethpool 116 B4
Hett 111 F5
Hetton 94 D2
Hetton-le-Hole . . 111 E6
Hetton Steads . . 123 F6
Heugh 110 B3
Heugh-head 140 C2
Heveningham . . . 57 B7
Hever 29 E5
Heversham 99 F6
Hevingham 81 E7
Hewas Water 3 B8

Hewelsfield 36 D2
Hewish N Som . . . 23 C6
  Som 12 D3
Heworth 96 D2
Hexham. 110 C2
Hextable. 29 B6
Hexton 54 F2
Hexworthy 6 B4
Hey 93 E8
Heybridge Essex . . 42 D4
  Essex. 42 E2
Heybridge Basin . . 42 D4
Heybrook Bay . . . 6 E3
Heydon Cambs . . 54 E5
  Norf. 81 E7
Heydour 78 F3
Heylipol 146 G2
Heylor 160 E4
High Ackworth . . . 88 C5
Higham Derbys . . 76 D3
  Kent 29 B8
  Lancs 93 F8
  Suff 55 C8
  Suff 56 F4
Higham Dykes . . 110 B4
Higham Ferrers . . 53 C7
Higham Gobion . . 54 F2
Higham on the Hill 63 E7
Highampton 9 D6
Higham Wood . . . 29 E6
High Angerton . . 117 F6
High Bankhill . . . 109 E5
High Barnes . . . 111 D6
High Beach 41 E7
High Bentham . . . 93 C6
High Bickington . . 9 B8
High Birkwith . . . 93 B7
High Blantyre . . . 119 D6
High
  Bonnybridge. . . 119 B8
High Bradfield . . . 88 E3
High Bray 21 F5
Highbridge Highld . 136 F4
  Som 22 E5
Highbrook 28 F4
High Brooms 29 E6
High Bullen. 9 B7
Highburton 88 C2
Highbury. 23 E8
High Buston . . . 117 D8
High Callerton . . 110 B4
High Catton 96 D3
Highclere. 26 C2
Highcliffe 14 E3
High Cogges 38 D3
High Coniscliffe . . 101 C7
High Cross Hants . 15 B8
  Herts 41 C6
High Easter 42 C2
High Eggborough . 89 B6
High Ellington . . . 101 F6
Higher Ansty . . . 13 D5
Higher Ashton . . . 10 F3
Higher Ballam . . . 92 F3
Higher Bartle . . . 92 F5
Higher Boscaswell . 2 C2
Higher
  Burwardsley . . . 74 D2
High Ercall 61 C5
Higher Clovelly . . . 8 B5
Higher End. 86 D3
Higher Kinnerton . 73 C7
Higher
  Penwortham . . . 86 B3
Higher Town 2 E4
Higher Walreddon . 6 B2
Higher Walton
  Lancs 86 B4
  Warr 86 F3
Higher Wheelton . 86 B4
Higher Whitley . . 86 F4
Higher Wincham . 74 B3
Higher Wych . . . 73 E8
High Etherley . . . 101 B6
Highfield E Yorks . . 96 F3
  Gtr Man 86 D5
  N Ayrs 118 D3
  Oxon 39 B5
  S Yorks 88 F4
  T&W 110 D4
Highfields Cambs . 54 D4
  Northumb 123 D5
High Garrett 42 B3
Highgate. 41 F5
High Grange . . . 110 F4
High Green Norf . . 68 D4
  S Yorks 88 E4
  Worcs 50 E3
High Halden 19 B5
High Halstow . . . 29 B8
High Ham 23 F6
High Harrington . . 98 B2
High Hatton 61 B6
High Hawsker . . . 103 D7
High Hesket . . . 108 E4
High Hesleden . . 111 F7
High Hoyland . . . 88 C3
High Hunsley . . . 97 F5
High Hurstwood . . 17 B8
High Hutton 96 C3
High Ireby 108 F2
High Kelling 81 D7
High Kilburn 95 B8
High Lands 101 B6
Highlane Ches E . . 75 C5
  Derbys. 88 F5
High Lane Gtr Man . 87 F7
  Worcs 49 C8
High Laver 41 D8
Highlaws 107 E8
Highleadon 36 B4
High Legh 86 F5
Highleigh 16 E2
High Leven 102 C2

Highley 61 F7
High Littleton . . . 23 D8
High Lorton 98 B3
High Marishes . . . 96 B4
High Marnham . . 77 B8
High Melton. . . . 89 D6
High Mickley . . . 110 C3
High Mindork . . . 105 D7
Highmoor Cross . . 39 F7
Highmoor Hill . . . 36 F1
Highnam 36 C4
Highnam Green . . 36 B4
High Newton . . . 99 F6
High Newton-by-the-
  Sea. 117 B8
High Nibthwaite . . 98 F4
High Offley 61 B7
High Ongar 42 D1
High Onn 62 C2
High Roding 42 C2
High Row 108 F3
High Salvington . . 16 D5
High Sellafield . . . 98 D2
High Shaw 100 E3
High Spen 110 D4
Highsted 30 C3
High Stoop. 110 E4
High Street Corn . . 4 D4
  Kent 18 B4
  Suff 56 E2
  Suff 57 B8
  Suff 57 D8
Highstreet Green . 55 F8
High Street Green . 56 D4
Hightae 107 B7
High Throston . . . 111 F7
Hightown Ches E . 75 C5
  Mers 85 D4
Hightown Green . . 56 D3
High Toynton . . . 79 C5
High Trewhitt . . 117 D6
High Valleyfield. . 128 F2
Highway 24 B5
High Westwood . . 110 D4
High Wray 99 E5
High Wych 41 C7
High Wycombe . . 40 E1
Hilborough 67 D8
Hilcote 76 D4
Hilcott 25 D6
Hildenborough . . 29 E6
Hilden Park 29 E6
Hildersham 55 E6
Hilderstone 75 F6
Hilderthorpe . . . 97 C7
Hilfield 12 D4
Hilgay 67 E6
Hill Pembs 32 D2
  S Glos. 36 E3
  W Mid 62 E5
Hillam 89 B6
Hillbeck 100 C2
Hillborough 31 C6
Hillbrae Aberds . . 141 B6
  Aberds. 152 D6
Hill Brow 15 B8
Hillbutts 13 D7
Hillclifflane 76 E2
Hillcommon 11 B6
Hill Dale 86 C2
Hill Dyke 79 E6
Hillend 128 F3
Hill End Durham . . 110 F3
  Fife 128 E2
  N Yorks. 94 D3
Hillerton 10 E2
Hillesden 39 B6
Hillesley 36 F4
Hillfarance 11 B6
Hillhead Aberds . . 152 E5
  Devon 7 D7
  S Ayrs 112 C4
Hill Head Hants . . 15 D6
  Northumb 110 C2
Hillhead of
  Auchentumb. . . 153 C9
Hillhead of
  Cocklaw 153 D10
Hillhouse 121 D8
Hilliclay. 158 D3
Hillingdon 40 F3
Hillington Glasgow 118 C5
  Norf 80 E3
Hillmorton 52 B3
Hill Mountain . . . 44 E4
Hillockhead
  Aberds. 140 C3
  Aberds. 140 D2
Hill of Beath. . . . 128 E3
Hill of Fearn. . . . 151 D11
Hill of
  Mountblairy . . . 153 C6
Hill Ridware 62 C4
Hillside Aberds . . 141 E8
  Angus 135 C7
  Mers 85 C4
  Orkney 159 J5
  Shetland 160 G6
Hillswick. 160 F4
Hill Top Durham . . 100 B4
  Hants 14 D5
  W Mid 62 E3
  W Yorks 88 C4
Hillway 15 F7
Hillwell 160 M5
Hilmarton 24 B5
Hilperton 24 D3
Hilsea 15 D7
Hilston. 97 F8
Hilton Aberds . . . 153 E9
  Cambs 54 C3
  Cumb 100 B2
  Derbys. 76 F2
  Dorset 13 D5
  Durham 101 B6
  Highld 151 C10
  Shrops. 61 E7
  Stockton 102 C2
Himbleton 50 D4
Himley 62 E2
Hincaster 99 F7
Hinckley 63 E8
Hinderclay 56 B4
Hinderton 73 B7

Hinderwell 103 C5
Hindford 73 F7
Hindhead 27 F6
Hindley 86 D4
Hindley Green. . . 86 D4
Hindlip. 50 D3
Hindolveston . . . 81 E6
Hindon 24 F4
Hindringham . . . 81 D5
Hingham 68 D3
Hinstock 61 B6
Hintlesham 56 E4
Hinton Hants 14 E3
  Hereford 48 F5
  Northants 52 D3
  S Glos. 24 B2
  Shrops. 60 D4
Hinton Ampner . . 15 B6
Hinton Blewett . . 23 D7
Hinton
  Charterhouse . . 24 D2
Hinton-in-the-
  Hedges 52 F3
Hinton Martell . . 13 D8
Hinton on the
  Green 50 E5
Hinton Parva . . . 38 F2
Hinton St George . 12 C2
Hinton St Mary . . 13 C5
Hinton Waldrist . . 38 E3
Hints Shrops 49 B8
  Staffs. 63 D5
Hinwick 53 C7
Hinxhill 30 E4
Hinxton 55 E5
Hinxworth 54 E3
Hipperholme . . . 88 B2
Hipswell 101 E6
Hirael 83 D5
Hiraeth. 32 B2
Hirn 141 D6
Hirnant 59 B7
Hirst N Lanark . . 119 C8
  Northumb 117 F8
Hirst Courtney . . 89 B7
Hirwaen 72 C5
Hirwaun 34 D3
Hiscott 9 B7
Histon 54 C5
Hitcham 56 D3
Hitchin 40 B4
Hither Green 28 B4
Hittisleigh 10 E2
Hive 96 F4
Hixon 62 B4
Hoaden 31 D6
Hoaldalbert 35 B7
Hoar Cross 62 B5
Hoarwithy 36 B2
Hoath 31 C6
Hobarris 48 B5
Hobbister 159 H4
Hobkirk 115 C8
Hobson 110 D4
Hoby 64 C3
Hockering 68 C3
Hockerton 77 D7
Hockley 42 E4
Hockley Heath . . 51 B6
Hockliffe 40 B2
Hockwold cum
  Wilton 67 F7
Hockworthy 10 C5
Hoddesdon 41 D6
Hoddlesden 86 B5
Hoddomcross . . 107 B8
Hoddom Mains . . 107 B8
Hodgeston 32 E1
Hodley 59 E8
Hodnet 61 B6
Hodthorpe 76 B5
Hoe Hants 15 C6
  Norf 68 C2
Hoe Gate. 15 C7
Hoff 100 C1
Hoggard's Green . 56 D2
Hoggeston 39 B8
Hogha Gearraidh. 148 A2
Hoghton 86 B4
Hognaston 76 D2
Hog Patch 27 E6
Hogsthorpe 79 B8
Holbeach 66 B3
Holbeach Bank . . 66 B3
Holbeach Clough . 66 B3
Holbeach Drove . . 66 C3
Holbeach Hurn . . 66 B3
Holbeach St Johns 66 C3
Holbeach St Marks 79 F6
Holbeach
  St Matthew . . . 79 F7
Holbeck Notts . . . 76 B5
  W Yorks 95 F5
Holbeck
  Woodhouse. . . . 76 B5
Holberrow Green . 50 D5
Holbeton 6 D4
Holborn 41 F6
Holbrook Derbys . . 76 E3
  Suff 57 F5
  S Yorks 88 F5
Holburn. 123 F6
Holbury 14 D5
Holcombe Devon . 7 B7
  Som 23 E8
Holcombe Rogus . 11 C5
Holcot 53 C5
Holden 93 E7
Holdenby 52 C4
Holdenhurst 14 E2
Holdgate 61 F5
Holdingham 78 E3
Holditch 11 D8
Holefield 122 F4
Holehouses 74 B4
Hole-in-the-Wall . 36 B3
Holemoor. 9 D6
Holestane 113 E8
Holford 22 E3
Holgate 95 D8
Holker 92 B3
Holkham 80 C4
Hollacombe 9 D5
Holland Orkney . . 159 C7
  Orkney 159 F7
Holland Fen 78 E5
Holland-on-Sea . . 43 C8
Hollandstoun . . . 159 C8
Hollee 108 C2

Hollesley 57 E7
Hollicombe 7 C6
Hollingbourne . . . 30 D2
Hollington Derbys . 76 F2
  E Sus 18 D4
  Staffs. 75 F7
Hollington Grove . 76 F2
Hollingworth . . . 87 E8
Hollins 87 D6
Hollinsclough . . . 75 C7
Hollins Green . . . 86 E4
Hollins Lane 92 D4
Hollinwood
  Gtr Man 87 D7
  Shrops. 74 F2
Hollocombe. 9 C8
Holloway 76 D3
Hollowell 52 B4
Hollow Meadows . 88 F3
Hollybush Caerph . 35 D5
  E Ayrs 112 C3
  Worcs 50 F2
Holly End 66 D4
Holly Green 50 E3
Hollym. 91 B7
Hollywood 51 B5
Holmbridge. 88 D2
Holmbury St Mary . 28 E2
Holmbush. 4 D5
Holmcroft 62 B3
Holme Cambs . . . 65 F8
  Cumb. 92 B5
  Notts 77 D8
  N Yorks. 102 F1
  W Yorks 88 D2
Holme Chapel . . . 87 B6
Holme Green. . . . 95 E8
Holme Hale 67 D8
Holme Lacy 49 F7
Holme Marsh . . . 48 D5
Holme next the
  Sea. 80 C3
Holme-on-Spalding-
  Moor 96 F4
Holme on the
  Wolds 97 E5
Holme Pierrepont . 77 F6
Holmer 49 E7
Holmer Green . . . 40 E2
Holme
  St Cuthbert . . . 107 E8
Holmes Chapel . . 74 C4
Holmesfield 76 B3
Holmeswood . . . 86 C2
Holmewood 76 C4
Holme Wood . . . 94 F4
Holmfirth 88 D2
Holmhead
  Dumfries 113 F7
  E Ayrs 113 B5
Holmisdale 148 D6
Holmpton 91 B7
Holmrook 98 E2
Holmsgarth . . . 160 J6
Holmwrangle . . . 108 E5
Holne 6 C5
Holnest 12 D4
Holsworthy 8 D5
Holsworthy Beacon . 9 D5
Holt Dorset 13 D8
  Norf 81 D6
  Wilts 24 C3
  Worcs 50 C3
  Wrex 73 D8
Holtby 96 D2
Holt End Hants . . 26 F4
  Worcs 51 C5
Holt Fleet 50 C3
Holt Heath 50 C3
Holton Oxon 39 D6
  Som 12 B4
  Suff 57 B7
Holton cum
  Beckering 90 F5
Holton Heath. . . . 13 E7
Holton le Clay . . . 91 D6
Holton le Moor . . 90 E4
Holton St Mary . . 56 F4
Holt Park 95 E5
Holwell Dorset . . 12 C5
  Herts 54 F2
  Leics 64 B4
  Oxon 38 D2
Holwick 100 B4
Holworth. 13 F5
Holy Cross 50 B4
Holyhead
  =Caergybi 82 C2
Holy Island . . . 123 E7
Holymoorside . . . 76 C3
Holyport 27 B6
Holystone 117 D5
Holytown 119 C7
Holywell Cambs . . 54 B4
  Corn. 4 D2
  Dorset 12 D3
  E Sus 18 F2
  Northumb 111 B6
Holywell
  =Treffynnon . . . 73 B5
Holywell Green . . 87 C8
Holywell Lake . . . 11 B6
Holywell Row . . . 55 B8
Holywood 114 F2
Homer 61 D6
Homersfield 69 F5
Hom Green 36 B2
Homington 14 B2
Honeyborough . . 44 E4
Honeybourne . . . 51 E6
Honeychurch . . . 9 D8
Honey Hill. 30 C5
Honey Street . . . 25 C6
Honey Tye 56 F3
Honiley 51 B7
Honing 69 B6
Honingham 68 C4
Honington Lincs . . 78 E2
  Suff 56 B3
  Warks 51 E7
Honiton 11 D6
Honley 88 C2
Hood Green 88 D4
Hooe E Sus. 18 E3
  Plym 6 D3

224 Hoo–Kin

Hooe Common 18 D3
Hoo Green 86 F5
Hook E Yorks 89 B8
Hants. 26 D5
London 28 C2
Pembs 44 D4
Wilts 37 F7
Hooke 12 E3
Hookgate 74 F4
Hook Green Kent 18 B3
Kent 29 C7
Hook Norton 51 F8
Hookway 10 E3
Hookwood 28 E3
Hoole 73 C8
Hooley 28 D3
Hoop 36 D2
Hoo St Werburgh 29 B8
Hooton 73 B7
Hooton Levitt 89 E6
Hooton Pagnell 89 D5
Hooton Roberts 89 E5
Hope Derbys 88 F2
Devon 6 F4
Highld 156 B7
Powys 60 D2
Shrops 60 D3
Staffs 75 D8
Hope = Yr Hôb 73 D7
Hope Bagot 49 B7
Hope Bowdler 60 E4
Hope End Green 42 B1
Hope Green 87 F7
Hopeman 152 B1
Hope Mansell 36 C3
Hopesay 60 F3
Hope's Green 42 F3
Hope under Dinmore 49 D7
Hopley's Green 48 D5
Hopperton 95 D7
Hop Pole 65 C8
Hopstone 61 E7
Hopton Shrops 60 B3
Shrops 61 B5
Staffs 62 B3
Suff 56 B3
Hopton Cangeford 60 F5
Hopton Castle 49 B5
Hoptonheath 49 B5
Hopton on Sea 69 D8
Hopton Wafers 49 B8
Hopwas 63 D5
Hopwood Gtr Man 87 D6
Worcs 50 B5
Horam 18 D2
Horbling 78 F4
Horbury 88 C3
Horcott 38 D1
Horden 111 E7
Horderley 60 F4
Hordle 14 E3
Hordley 73 F7
Horeb Carms 33 B6
Carms 33 D5
Ceredig 46 E2
Horfield 23 B8
Horham 57 B6
Horkesley Heath 43 B5
Horkstow 90 C3
Horley Oxon 52 E2
Sur 28 E3
Hornblotton Green 23 F7
Hornby Lancs 93 C5
N Yorks 101 E7
N Yorks 102 D1
Horncastle 79 C5
Hornchurch 41 F8
Horncliffe 122 E5
Horndean Borders 122 E4
Hants 15 C8
Horndon 6 B3
Horndon on the Hill 42 F2
Horne 28 E4
Horniehaugh 134 C4
Horning 69 C6
Horninghold 64 E5
Horninglow 63 B6
Horningsea 55 C5
Horningsham 24 E3
Horningtoft 80 E5
Hornsby 108 D5
Horns Corner 18 C4
Horns Cross Devon 9 B5
E Sus 18 C5
Hornsea 97 E8
Hornsea Bridge 97 E8
Hornsey 41 F6
Hornton 51 E8
Horrabridge 6 C3
Horringer 56 C2
Horringford 15 F6
Horsebridge Devon 6 B2
Hants 25 F8
Horse Bridge 75 D6
Horsebrook 62 C2
Horsehay 61 D6
Horseheath 55 E7
Horsehouse 101 F5
Horsell 27 D7
Horseman's Green 73 E8
Horseway 66 F4
Horsey 69 B7
Horsford 68 C4
Horsforth 94 F5
Horsham Worcs 50 D2
W Sus 28 F2
Horsham St Faith 68 C5
Horsington Lincs 78 C4
Som 12 B5
Horsley Derbys 76 E3
Glos 37 E5
Northumb 110 C3
Northumb 116 E4
Horsley Cross 43 B7
Horsleycross Street 43 B7
Horsleyhill 115 C8
Horsleyhope 110 E3
Horsley Woodhouse 76 E3
Horsmonden 29 E7
Horspath 39 D5
Horstead 69 C5
Horsted Keynes 17 B7
Horton Bucks 40 C2
Dorset 13 D8
Lancs 93 D8
Northants 53 D6
S Glos 36 F4
Shrops 60 B4
Som 11 C8
Staffs 75 D6
Swansea 33 F5
Wilts 25 C5
Windsor 27 B8
Horton-cum-Studley 39 C5
Horton Green 73 E8
Horton Heath 15 C5
Horton in Ribblesdale 93 B8
Horton Kirby 29 C6
Hortonlane 60 C4
Horwich 86 C4
Horwich End 87 F8
Horwood 9 B7
Hose 64 B4
Hoselaw 122 F4
Hoses 98 E4
Hosh 127 B7
Hosta 148 A2
Hoswick 160 L6
Hotham 96 F4
Hothfield 30 E3
Hoton 64 B2
Houbie 160 D8
Houdston 112 E1
Hough Ches E 74 D4
Ches E 75 B5
Hougham 77 E8
Hough Green 86 F2
Hough-on-the-Hill 78 E2
Houghton Cambs 54 B3
Cumb 108 D4
Hants 25 F8
Pembs 44 E4
W Sus 16 C4
Houghton Conquest 53 E8
Houghton Green E Sus 19 C6
Warr 86 E4
Houghton-le-Side 101 B7
Houghton-le-Spring 111 E6
Houghton on the Hill 64 D3
Houghton Regis 40 B3
Houghton St Giles 80 D5
Houlland Shetland 160 F7
Shetland 160 H5
Houlsyke 103 D5
Hound 15 D5
Hound Green 26 D5
Houndslow 122 E2
Houndwood 122 C4
Hounslow 28 B2
Hounslow Green 42 C2
Housay 160 F8
House of Daviot 151 G10
House of Glenmuick 140 E2
Housetter 160 E5
Houss 160 K5
Houston 118 C4
Houstry 158 G3
Houton 159 H4
Hove 17 D6
Hoveringham 77 E6
Hoveton 69 C6
Hovingham 96 B2
How 108 D5
Howbrook 88 E4
How Caple 49 F8
Howden Borders 116 B2
E Yorks 89 B8
Howden-le-Wear 110 F4
Howe Highld 158 D5
Norf 69 D5
N Yorks 101 F8
Howe Bridge 86 D4
Howe Green 42 D3
Howell 78 E4
How End 53 E8
Howe of Teuchar 153 D7
Howe Street Essex 42 C2
Essex 55 F7
Howey 48 D2
Howgate 120 D5
How Green 29 E5
Howick 117 C8
Howle Durham 101 B5
Telford 61 B6
Howlett End 55 F6
Howley 11 D7
Hownam 116 C3
Hownam Mains 116 B3
Howpasley 115 D6
Howsham N Lincs 90 D4
N Yorks 96 C3
Howslack 114 D3
Howtel 122 F4
Howton 35 B8
Howtown 99 C6
Howwood 118 C3
Hoxne 57 B5
Hoy 159 H3
Hoylake 85 F3
Hoyland 88 D4
Hoylandswaine 88 D3
Hubberholme 94 B2
Hubbert's Bridge 79 E5
Huby N Yorks 95 C8
N Yorks 95 E5
Hucclecote 37 C5
Hucking 30 D2
Hucknall 76 E5
Huddersfield 88 C2
Huddington 50 D4
Hudswell 101 D6
Huggate 96 D4
Hugglescote 63 C8
Hughenden Valley 40 E1
Hughley 61 E5
Hugh Town 2 E4
Huish Devon 9 C7
Wilts 25 C6
Huish Champflower 11 B5
Huish Episcopi 12 B2
Huisinis 154 F4
Hulcott 40 C1
Hulland 76 E2
Hulland Ward 76 E2
Hullavington 37 F5
Hullbridge 42 E4
Hulme 87 E6
Hulme End 75 D8
Hulme Walfield 74 C5
Hulverstone 14 F4
Hulver Street 69 F7
Humber 49 D7
Humber Bridge 90 B4
Humberston 91 D7
Humbie 121 C7
Humbleton E Yorks 97 F8
Northumb 117 B5
Humby 78 F3
Hume 122 E3
Humshaugh 110 B2
Huna 158 C5
Huncoat 93 F7
Huncote 64 E2
Hundalee 116 C2
Hunderthwaite 100 B4
Hundleby 79 C6
Hundle Houses 79 D5
Hundleton 44 E4
Hundon 55 E8
Hundred Acres 15 C6
Hundred End 86 B2
Hundred House 48 D3
Hungarton 64 D3
Hungerford Hants 14 C2
W Berks 25 C8
Hungerford Newtown 25 B8
Hungerton 65 B5
Hungladder 149 A8
Hunmanby 97 B6
Hunmanby Moor 97 B7
Hunningham 51 C8
Hunny Hill 15 F5
Hunsdon 41 C7
Hunsingore 95 D7
Hunslet 95 F6
Hunsonby 109 F5
Hunspow 158 C4
Hunstanton 80 C2
Hunstanworth 110 E2
Hunsterson 74 E3
Hunston Suff 56 C3
W Sus 16 D2
Hunstrete 23 C8
Hunt End 50 C5
Hunter's Quay 145 F10
Hunthill Lodge 134 B4
Huntingdon 54 B3
Huntingfield 57 B7
Huntingford 24 F3
Huntington E Loth 121 B7
Hereford 48 D4
Staffs 62 C3
York 96 D2
Huntingtower 128 B2
Huntley 36 C4
Huntly 152 E5
Huntlywood 122 E2
Hunton Kent 29 E8
N Yorks 101 E6
Hunt's Corner 68 F3
Hunt's Cross 86 F2
Huntsham 10 B5
Huntspill 22 E5
Huntworth 22 F5
Hunwick 110 F4
Hunworth 81 D6
Hurdsfield 75 B6
Hurley Warks 63 E6
Windsor 39 F8
Hurlford 118 F4
Hurliness 159 K3
Hurn 14 E2
Hurn's End 79 E7
Hursley 14 B5
Hurst N Yorks 101 D5
Som 12 C2
Wokingham 27 B5
Hurstbourne Priors 26 E2
Hurstbourne Tarrant 25 D8
Hurst Green E Sus 18 C4
Lancs 93 F6
Hurstpierpoint 17 C6
Hurst Wickham 17 C6
Hurstwood 93 F8
Hurtmore 27 E7
Hurworth Place 101 D7
Hury 100 C4
Husabost 148 C7
Husbands Bosworth 64 F3
Husborne Crawley 53 F7
Husthwaite 95 B8
Hutchwns 21 B7
Huthwaite 76 D4
Huttoft 79 B8
Hutton Borders 122 D5
Cumb 99 B6
Essex 42 E2
E Yorks 97 D6
Lancs 86 B2
N Som 22 D5
Hutton Buscel 103 F7
Hutton Conyers 95 B6
Hutton Cranswick 97 D6
Hutton End 108 F4
Hutton Gate 102 C3
Hutton Henry 111 F7
Hutton-le-Hole 103 E5
Hutton Magna 101 C6
Hutton Roof Cumb 93 B5
Cumb 108 F3
Hutton Rudby 102 D2
Hutton Sessay 95 B7
Hutton Village 102 C3
Hutton Wandesley 95 D8
Huxley 74 C2
Huxter Shetland 160 G7
Shetland 160 H5
Huxton 122 C4
Huyton 86 E2
Hwlffordd = Haverfordwest 44 D4
Hycemoor 98 F2
Hyde Glos 37 D5
Gtr Man 87 E7
Hants 14 C2
Hyde Heath 40 D2
Hyde Park 89 D6
Hydestile 27 E7
Hylton Castle 111 D6
Hyndford Bridge 120 E2
Hynish 146 H2
Hyssington 60 E3
Hythe Hants 14 D5
Kent 19 B8
Hythe End 27 B8
Hythie 153 C10

I

Ibberton 13 D5
Ible 76 D2
Ibsley 14 D2
Ibstock 63 C8
Ibstone 39 E7
Ibthorpe 25 D8
Ibworth 26 D3
Ichrachan 125 B6
Ickburgh 67 E8
Ickenham 40 F3
Ickford 39 D6
Ickham 31 D6
Ickleford 54 F2
Icklesham 19 D5
Ickleton 55 E5
Icklingham 55 B8
Ickwell Green 54 E2
Icomb 38 B2
Idbury 38 C2
Iddesleigh 9 D7
Ide 10 E3
Ideford 7 B6
Ide Hill 29 D5
Iden 19 C6
Iden Green Kent 18 B4
Kent 18 B5
Idle 94 F4
Idlicote 51 E7
Idmiston 25 F6
Idole 33 C5
Idridgehay 76 E2
Idrigill 149 B8
Idstone 38 F2
Idvies 135 E5
Iffley 39 D5
Ifield 28 F3
Ifold 27 F8
Iford 17 D8
Ifton Heath 73 F7
Ightfield 74 F2
Ightham 29 D6
Iken 57 D8
Ilam 75 D8
Ilchester 12 B3
Ilderton 117 B6
Ilford 41 F7
Ilfracombe 20 E4
Ilkeston 76 E4
Ilketshall St Andrew 69 F6
Ilketshall St Lawrence 69 F6
Ilketshall St Margaret 69 F6
Ilkley 94 E4
Illey 62 F3
Illingworth 87 B8
Illogan 3 B5
Illston on the Hill 64 E4
Ilmer 39 D7
Ilmington 51 E7
Ilminster 11 C8
Ilsington 7 B5
Ilston 33 E6
Ilton N Yorks 94 B4
Som 11 C8
Imachar 143 D9
Imeraval 142 D4
Immingham 91 C5
Impington 54 C5
Ince 73 B8
Ince Blundell 85 D4
Ince in Makerfield 86 D3
Inchbare 135 C6
Inchberry 152 C3
Inchbraoch 135 D7
Incheril 150 E3
Inchgrundle 134 B4
Inchina 150 B2
Inchinnan 118 C4
Inchkinloch 157 E8
Inchlaggan 136 D4
Inchlumpie 151 D8
Inchmore 150 G6
Inchnacardoch Hotel 137 C6
Inchnadamph 156 G5
Inch of Arnhall 135 B6
Inchree 130 C4
Inchture 128 B4
Inchyra 128 B3
Indian Queens 4 D4
Inerval 142 D4
Ingatestone 42 E2
Ingbirchworth 88 D3
Ingestre 62 B3
Ingham Lincs 90 F3
Norf 69 B6
Suff 56 B2
Ingham Corner 69 B6
Ingleborough 66 C4
Ingleby Derbys 63 B7
Lincs 77 B8
Ingleby Arncliffe 102 D2
Ingleby Barwick 102 C2
Ingleby Greenhow 102 D3
Inglemire 97 F6
Inglesbatch 24 C2
Inglesham 38 E2
Ingleton Durham 101 B6
N Yorks 93 B6
Inglewhite 92 E5
Ingliston 120 B4
Ingoe 110 B3
Ingol 92 F5
Ingoldisthorpe 80 D2
Ingoldmells 79 C8
Ingoldsby 78 F3
Ingon 51 D7
Ingram 117 C6
Ingrow 94 F3
Ings 99 E6
Ingst 36 F2
Ingworth 81 E7
Inham's End 66 E2
Inkberrow 50 D5
Inkpen 25 C8
Inkstack 158 C4
Inn 99 D6
Innellan 145 F10
Innerleithen 121 F6
Innerleven 129 D5
Innermessan 104 C4
Innerwick E Loth 122 B3
Perth 132 E2
Innis Chonain 125 C7
Insch 140 B5
Insh 138 D4
Inshore 156 C6
Inskip 92 F4
Instoneville 89 C6
Instow 20 F3
Intake 89 D6
Inver Aberds 139 E8
Highld 151 C11
Perth 133 E7
Inverailort 147 C10
Inveraldie 134 F4
Inveralligin 149 C13
Inverallochy 153 B10
Inveran 151 B8
Inveraray 125 E6
Inverarish 149 E10
Inverarity 134 E4
Inverarnan 126 C2
Inverasdale 155 J13
Inverbeg 126 E2
Inverbervie 135 B8
Inverboyndie 153 B6
Inverbroom 150 C4
Invercassley 156 J7
Invercauld House 139 E7
Inverchaolain 145 F9
Invercharnan 131 E5
Inverchoran 150 F5
Invercreran 130 E4
Inverdruie 138 C5
Inverebrie 153 E9
Invereck 145 E10
Inverernan House 140 C2
Invereshie House 138 D4
Inveresk 121 B6
Inverey 139 F6
Inverfarigaig 137 B8
Invergarry 137 D6
Invergelder 139 E8
Invergeldie 127 B6
Invergordon 151 E10
Invergowrie 134 F3
Inverguseran 149 H12
Inverhadden 132 D3
Inverharroch 152 E3
Inverherive 126 B2
Inverie 147 B10
Inverinan 125 D5
Inverinate 136 B2
Inverkeilor 135 E6
Inverkeithing 128 F3
Inverkeithny 153 D6
Inverkip 118 B2
Inverkirkaig 156 H3
Inverlael 150 C4
Inverlochlarig 126 C3
Inverlochy Argyll 125 C7
Highld 131 B5
Inverlussa 144 E5
Inver Mallie 136 F4
Invermark Lodge 140 F3
Invermoidart 147 D9
Invermoriston 137 C7
Invernaver 157 C10
Inverneill 145 E7
Inverness 151 G9
Invernettie 153 D11
Invernoaden 125 F7
Inveroran Hotel 131 E6
Inverpolly Lodge 156 H3
Inverquharity 134 D4
Inverquhomery 153 D10
Inverroy 137 F5
Inversanda 130 D3
Invershiel 136 C2
Invershin 151 B8
Inversnaid Hotel 126 D2
Inverugie 153 D11
Inveruglas 126 D2
Inveruglass 138 D4
Inverurie 141 B6
Invervar 132 E3
Inverythan 153 D7
Inwardleigh 9 E7
Inworth 42 C4
Iochdar 148 D2
Iping 16 B2
Ipplepen 7 C6
Ipsden 39 F6
Ipsley 51 C5
Ipstones 75 D7
Ipswich 57 E5
Irby 85 F3
Irby in the Marsh 79 C7
Irby upon Humber 91 D5
Irchester 53 C7
Ireby Cumb 108 F2
Lancs 93 B6
Ireland Orkney 159 H4
Shetland 160 L5
Ireland's Cross 74 E4
Ireleth 92 B2
Ireshopeburn 109 F8
Irlam 86 E5
Irnham 65 B7
Iron Acton 36 F3
Ironbridge 61 D6
Iron Cross 51 D5
Irongray 107 B6
Ironmacannie 106 B3
Ironside 153 C8
Ironville 76 D4
Irstead 69 B6
Irthington 108 C4
Irthlingborough 53 B7
Irton 103 F8
Irvine 118 F3
Isauld 157 C12
Isbister Orkney 159 F3
Orkney 159 G4
Shetland 160 D5
Shetland 160 G7
Isfield 17 C8
Isham 53 B6
Isle Abbotts 11 B8
Isle Brewers 11 B8
Isleham 55 B7
Isle of Whithorn 105 F8
Isleornsay 149 G12
Islesburgh 160 G5
Islesteps 107 B6
Isleworth 28 B2
Isley Walton 63 B8
Islibhig 154 E4
Islington 41 F6
Islip Northants 53 B7
Oxon 39 C5
Istead Rise 29 C7
Isycoed 73 D8
Itchen 14 C5
Itchen Abbas 26 F3
Itchen Stoke 26 F3
Itchingfield 16 B5
Itchington 36 F3
Itteringham 81 D7
Itton 9 E8
Itton Common 36 E1
Ivegill 108 E4
Iver 40 F3
Iver Heath 40 F3
Iveston 110 D4
Ivinghoe 40 C2
Ivinghoe Aston 40 C2
Ivington 49 D6
Ivington Green 49 D6
Ivybridge 6 D4
Ivy Chimneys 41 D7
Ivychurch 19 C7
Ivy Cross 13 B6
Ivy Hatch 29 D6
Iwade 30 C3
Iwerne Courtney or Shroton 13 C6
Iwerne Minster 13 C6
Ixworth 56 B3
Ixworth Thorpe 56 B3

J

Jack Hill 94 D5
Jack in the Green 10 E5
Jacksdale 76 D4
Jackstown 153 E7
Jacobstow 8 E3
Jacobstowe 9 D7
Jameston 32 E1
Jamestown Dumfries 115 E6
Highld 150 F7
W Dunb 126 F2
Jarrow 111 C6
Jarvis Brook 18 C2
Jasper's Green 42 B3
Java 124 B3
Jawcraig 119 B8
Jaywick 43 C7
Jealott's Hill 27 B6
Jedburgh 116 B2
Jeffreyston 32 D1
Jellyhill 119 B6
Jemimaville 151 E10
Jersey Farm 40 D4
Jesmond 111 C5
Jevington 18 E2
Jockey End 40 C3
Johnby 108 F4
John o'Groats 158 C5
John's Cross 18 C4
Johnshaven 135 C7
Johnston E Renfs 118 C4
Pembs 44 D4
Johnstonebridge 114 E3
Johnstown Carms 33 C5
Wrex 73 E7
Joppa Edin 121 B6
S Ayrs 112 C4
Jordans 40 E2
Jordanthorpe 88 F4
Jump 88 D4
Jumpers Green 14 E2
Juniper Green 120 C4
Jurby East 84 C3
Jurby West 84 C3

K

Kaber 100 C2
Kaimend 120 E2
Kaimes 121 C5
Kalemouth 116 B3
Kames Argyll 124 D4
Argyll 145 F8
E Ayrs 113 B6
Kea 3 B7
Keadby 90 C2
Keal Cotes 79 C6
Kearsley 87 D5
Kearstwick 99 F8
Kearton 100 E4
Kearvaig 156 B5
Keasden 93 C7
Keckwick 86 F3
Keddington 91 F7
Kedington 55 E8
Kedleston 76 E3
Keelby 91 C5
Keele 74 E5
Keeley Green 53 E8
Keeston 44 D4
Keevil 24 D4
Kegworth 63 B8
Kehelland 2 B5
Keig 140 C5
Keighley 94 E3
Keil 130 D3
Keilarsbrae 127 E7
Keilhill 153 C7
Keillmore 144 E5
Keillor 134 E2
Keillour 127 B8
Keills 142 B5
Keils 144 G4
Keinton Mandeville 23 F7
Keir Mill 113 E8
Keisby 65 B7
Keiss 158 D5
Keith 152 C4
Keith Inch 153 D11
Keithock 135 C6
Kelbrook 94 E2
Kelby 78 E3
Keld Cumb 99 C7
N Yorks 100 D3
Keldholme 103 F5
Kelfield N Lincs 90 D2
N Yorks 95 F8
Kelham 77 D7
Kellan 147 G8
Kellas Angus 134 F4
Moray 152 C1
Kellaton 7 F6
Kelleth 100 D1
Kelleythorpe 97 D5
Kelling 81 C6
Kellingley 89 B6
Kellington 89 B6
Kelloe 111 F6
Kelloholm 113 C7
Kelly 9 F5
Kelly Bray 5 B8
Kelmarsh 52 B5
Kelmscot 38 E2
Kelsale 57 C7
Kelsall 74 C2
Kelsall Hill 74 C2
Kelshall 54 F4
Kelsick 107 D8
Kelso 122 F3
Kelstedge 76 C3
Kelstern 91 E6
Kelston 24 C2
Keltneyburn 132 E4
Kelton 107 B6
Kelty 128 E3
Kelvedon 42 C4
Kelvedon Hatch 42 E1
Kelvin 119 D6
Kelvinside 119 C5
Kelynack 2 C2
Kemback 129 C6
Kemberton 61 D7
Kemble 37 E6
Kemerton 50 F4
Kemeys Commander 35 D7
Kemnay 141 C6
Kempley 36 B3
Kempsey 50 E3
Kempsford 38 E1
Kemps Green 51 B6
Kempshott 26 D4
Kempston 53 E8
Kempston Hardwick 53 E8
Kempton 60 F3
Kemp Town 17 D7
Kemsing 29 D6
Kemsley 30 C3
Kenardington 19 B6
Kenchester 49 E6
Kencot 38 D2
Kendal 99 E7
Kendoon 113 F6
Kendray 88 D4
Kenfig 34 F2
Kenfig Hill 34 F2
Kenilworth 51 B7
Kenknock 132 F1
Kenley London 28 D4
Shrops 61 D5
Kenmore Highld 149 C12
Perth 132 E4
Kenn Devon 10 F4
N Som 23 C6
Kennacley 154 H6
Kennacraig 145 G7
Kennerleigh 10 D3
Kennet 127 E8
Kennethmont 140 B4
Kennett 55 C7
Kennford 10 F4
Kenninghall 68 F3
Kenninghall Heath 68 F3
Kennington Kent 30 E4
Oxon 39 D5
Kennoway 129 D5
Kenny Hill 55 B7
Kennythorpe 96 C3
Kenovay 146 G2
Kensaleyre 149 C9
Kensington 28 B3
Kensworth 40 C3
Kensworth Common 40 C3
Kentallen 130 D4
Kentchurch 35 B8
Kentford 55 C8
Kentisbeare 11 D5
Kentisbury 20 E5
Kentisbury Ford 20 E5
Kentmere 99 D6
Kenton Devon 10 F4
Suff 57 C5
T&W 110 C5
Kenton Bankfoot 110 C5
Kentra 147 E9
Kents Bank 92 B3
Kent's Green 36 B4
Kent's Oak 14 B4
Kent Street E Sus 18 D4
Kent 29 D7
W Sus 17 B6
Kenwick 73 F8
Kenwyn 3 B7
Keoldale 156 C6
Keppanach 130 C4
Keppoch 136 B2
Keprigan 143 G7
Kepwick 102 E2
Kerchesters 122 F3
Keresley 63 F7
Kernborough 7 E5
Kerne Bridge 36 C2
Kerris 2 D3
Kerry 59 F8
Kerrycroy 145 G10
Kerrysdale 149 A13
Kerry's Gate 49 F5
Kersall 77 C7
Kersey 56 E4
Kershopefoot 115 F7
Kersoe 50 F4
Kerswell 11 D5
Kerswell Green 50 E3
Kesgrave 57 E6
Kessingland 69 F8
Kessingland Beach 69 F8
Kessington 119 B5
Kestle 3 B8
Kestle Mill 4 D3
Keston 28 C5
Keswick Cumb 98 B4
Norf 68 D5
Norf 81 D9
Ketley 61 C6
Ketley Bank 61 C6
Ketsby 79 B6
Kettering 53 B6
Ketteringham 68 D4
Kettins 134 F2
Kettlebaston 56 D3
Kettlebridge 128 D5
Kettleburgh 57 C6
Kettlehill 128 D5
Kettleholm 107 B8
Kettleness 103 C6
Kettleshume 75 B6
Kettlesing Bottom 94 D5
Kettlesing Head 94 D5
Kettlestone 81 D5
Kettlethorpe 77 B8
Kettletoft 159 E7
Kettlewell 94 B2
Ketton 65 D6
Kew 28 B2
Kew Bridge 28 B2
Kewstoke 22 C5
Kexbrough 88 D4
Kexby Lincs 90 F2
York 96 D3
Key Green 75 C5
Keyham 64 D3
Keyhaven 14 E4
Keyingham 91 B6
Keymer 17 C7
Keynsham 23 C8
Keysoe 53 C8
Keysoe Row 53 C8
Keyston 53 B8
Keyworth 77 F6
Kibblesworth 110 D5
Kibworth Beauchamp 64 E3
Kibworth Harcourt 64 E3
Kidbrooke 28 B5
Kiddemore Green 62 D2
Kidderminster 50 B3
Kiddington 38 B4
Kidlington 38 C4
Kidmore End 26 B4
Kidsgrove 74 D5
Kidstones 100 F4
Kidwelly = Cydweli 33 D5
Kiel Crofts 124 B5
Kielder 116 E2
Kierfiold Ho 159 G3
Kilbagie 127 F8
Kilbarchan 118 C4
Kilbeg 149 H11
Kilberry 144 G6
Kilbirnie 118 D3
Kilbride Argyll 124 C4
Argyll 124 C5
Highld 149 F10
Kilburn Angus 134 C3
Derbys 76 E3
London 41 F5
N Yorks 95 B8
Kilby 64 E3
Kilchamaig 145 G7
Kilchattan 144 D2
Kilchattan Bay 145 H10
Kilchenzie 143 F7
Kilcheran 124 B4
Kilchiaran 142 B3
Kilchoan Argyll 124 D3
Highld 146 E7
Kilchoman 142 B3
Kilchrenan 125 C6
Kilconquhar 129 D6
Kilcot 36 B3
Kilcoy 151 F8
Kilcreggan 145 E11
Kildale 102 D4
Kildalloig 143 G8
Kildary 151 D10
Kildermorie Lodge 151 D8
Kildonan 143 F11
Kildonan Lodge 157 G12
Kildonnan 146 C7
Kildrummy 140 C3
Kildwick 94 E3
Kilfinan 145 F8
Kilfinnan 137 E5
Kilgetty 32 D2
Kilgwrrwg Common 36 E1
Kilham E Yorks 97 C6
Northumb 122 F4
Kilkenneth 146 G2
Kilkerran 143 G8
Kilkhampton 9 E6
Killamarsh 89 F5
Killay 33 E7
Killbeg 147 G9
Killean 143 D7
Killearn 126 F4
Killen 151 F9
Killerby 101 C6
Killichonan 132 D2
Killiechonate 136 F5
Killiechronan 147 G8
Killiecrankie 133 C6
Killiemor 146 H7
Killiemore House 146 J7
Killilan 150 H2
Killimster 158 E5
Killin 132 F2
Killinallan 142 A4
Killinghall 95 D5
Killington 99 F8
Killingworth 111 B5
Killin Lodge 137 D8
Killmahumaig 144 D6
Killochyett 121 E7
Killocraw 143 E7
Killundine 147 G8
Kilmacolm 118 C3
Kilmaha 124 E5
Kilmahog 126 D5
Kilmalieu 130 D2
Kilmaluag 149 A9
Kilmany 129 B5
Kilmarie 149 G10
Kilmarnock 118 F4
Kilmaron Castle 129 C5
Kilmartin 124 F4
Kilmaurs 118 E4
Kilmelford 124 D4
Kilmeny 142 B4
Kilmersdon 23 D8
Kilmeston 15 B6
Kilmichael 143 F7
Kilmichael Glassary 145 D7
Kilmichael of Inverlussa 144 E6
Kilmington Devon 11 E7
Wilts 24 F2
Kilmonivaig 136 F4
Kilmorack 150 G7
Kilmore Argyll 124 C4
Highld 149 H11
Kilmory Argyll 144 F6
Highld 147 D8
Highld 149 H8
N Ayrs 143 F10
Kilmuir Highld 148 D7
Highld 149 A8
Highld 151 D10
Highld 151 G9
Kilmun Argyll 124 D5
Argyll 145 E10
Kilncadzow 119 E8
Kilndown 18 B4
Kilnhurst 89 E5
Kilninian 146 G6
Kilninver 124 C4
Kiln Pit Hill 110 D3
Kilnsea 91 C8
Kilnsey 94 C2
Kilnwick 97 E5
Kilnwick Percy 96 D4
Kiloran 144 D2
Kilpatrick 143 F10
Kilpeck 49 F6
Kilphedir 157 H12
Kilpin 89 B8
Kilpin Pike 89 B8
Kilrenny 129 D7
Kilsby 52 B3
Kilspindie 128 B4
Kilsyth 119 B7
Kiltarlity 151 G8
Kilton Notts 77 B5
Som 22 E3
Kilton Thorpe 102 C4
Kilvaxter 149 B8
Kilve 22 E3
Kilvington 77 E7
Kilwinning 118 E3
Kimberley Norf 68 D3
Notts 76 E5
Kimberworth 88 E5
Kimblesworth 111 E5
Kimble Wick 39 D8
Kimbolton Cambs 53 C8
Hereford 49 C7
Kimcote 64 F2
Kimmeridge 13 G7
Kimmerston 123 F5
Kimpton Hants 25 E7
Herts 40 C4
Kinbrace 157 F11
Kinbuck 127 D6
Kincaple 129 C6
Kincardine Fife 127 F8
Highld 151 C9
Kincardine Bridge 127 F8
Kincardine O'Neil 140 E4
Kinclaven 134 F1
Kincorth 141 D8
Kincorth House 151 E13
Kincraig 138 D4
Kincraigie 133 E6
Kindallachan 133 E6
Kineton Glos 37 B7
Warks 51 D8
Kinfauns 128 B3
Kingairloch 130 D2
Kingarth 145 H9
Kingcoed 35 D8
King Edward 153 C7
Kingerby 90 E4
Kingham 38 B2
Kingholm Quay 107 B6
Kinghorn 128 F4
Kingie 136 D4
Kinglassie 128 E4
Kingoodie 128 B5
King's Acre 49 E6
Kingsand 6 D2
Kingsbarns 129 C7
Kingsbridge Devon 6 E5
Som 21 F8
King's Bromley 62 C5
Kingsburgh 149 C8
Kingsbury London 41 F5
Warks 63 E6
Kingsbury Episcopi 12 B2
King's Caple 36 B2
Kingsclere 26 D3
King's Cliffe 65 E7
Kingscote 37 E5
Kingscott 9 C7
King's Coughton 51 D5
Kingscross 143 F11
Kingsdon 12 B3
Kingsdown 31 E7
Kingseat 128 E3
Kingsey 39 D7
Kingsfold 28 F2
Kingsford E Ayrs 118 E4
Worcs 62 F2
Kingsforth 90 C4
Kingsgate 31 B7
Kingsheanton 20 F4
King's Heath 62 F4
Kings Hedges 55 C5
King's Hill 29 D7
Kingshouse Hotel 131 D6
Kingside Hill 107 D8
Kingskerswell 7 C6
Kingskettle 128 D5
Kingsland Anglesey 82 C2
Hereford 49 C6
Kings Langley 40 D3
Kingsley Ches W 74 B2
Hants 27 F5
Staffs 75 E7
Kingsley Green 27 F6
Kingsley Holt 75 E7
Kingsley Park 53 C5

King's Lynn . . . 67 B6
King's Meaburn . . . 99 B8
King's Mills . . . 73 E7
Kingsmuir Angus . 134 E4
Fife . . . 129 D7
Kings Muir . . . 121 F5
King's Newnham . . 52 B2
King's Newton . . . 63 B7
Kingsnorth . . . 19 B7
King's Norton Leics 64 C3
W Mid . . . 51 B5
King's Nympton . . 9 C8
King's Pyon . . . 49 D6
King's Ripton . . . 54 B3
King's Somborne . . 25 F8
King's Stag . . . 12 C5
King's Stanley . . . 37 D5
King's Sutton . . . 52 F2
Kingstanding . . . 62 E4
Kingsteignton . . . 7 B6
King Sterndale . . . 75 B7
King's Thorn . . . 49 F7
Kingsthorpe . . . 53 C5
Kingston Cambs . . 54 D4
Devon . . . 6 E4
Dorset . . . 13 D5
Dorset . . . 13 G7
E Loth . . . 129 F7
Hants . . . 14 D2
IoW . . . 15 F5
Kent . . . 31 D5
Moray . . . 152 B3
Kingston Bagpuize 38 E4
Kingston Blount . . 39 E7
Kingston by Sea . . 17 D6
Kingston Deverill . 24 F3
Kingstone Hereford. 49 F6
Som . . . 11 C8
Staffs . . . 62 B4
Kingston Gorse . . . 16 D4
Kingston Lisle . . . 38 F3
Kingston
Maurward . . . 12 E5
Kingston near
Lewes . . . 17 D7
Kingston on Soar . 64 B2
Kingston Russell . . 12 E3
Kingston St Mary . 11 B7
Kingston Seymour. 23 C6
Kingston upon
Hull . . . 90 B4
Kingston upon
Thames . . . 28 C2
Kingston Vale . . . 28 B3
Kingstown . . . 108 D3
King's Walden . . . 40 B4
Kingswear . . . 7 D6
Kingswells . . . 141 D7
Kingswinford . . . 62 F2
Kingswood Bucks . 39 C6
Glos . . . 36 E4
Hereford . . . 48 D4
Kent . . . 30 D2
Powys . . . 60 D2
S Glos . . . 23 B8
Sur . . . 28 D3
Warks . . . 51 B6
Kings Worthy . . . 26 F2
Kingthorpe . . . 78 B4
Kington Hereford . . 48 D4
Worcs . . . 50 D4
Kington Langley . . 24 B4
Kington Magna . . 13 B5
Kington
St Michael . . . 24 B4
Kingussie . . . 138 D3
Kingweston . . . 23 F7
Kininvie House . . 152 D3
Kinkell Bridge . . 127 C8
Kinknockie . . . 153 D10
Kinlet . . . 61 F7
Kinloch Fife . . . 128 C4
Highld . . . 146 B6
Highld . . . 149 G11
Highld . . . 156 F6
Perth . . . 133 E8
Perth . . . 134 E2
Kinlochan . . . 130 C2
Kinlochard . . . 126 D3
Kinlochbeoraid .147 C11
Kinlochbervie . . 156 D5
Kinlocheil . . . 130 B3
Kinlochewe . . . 150 E3
Kinloch Hourn . . 136 D2
Kinloch Laggan . 137 F8
Kinlochleven . . . 131 C5
Kinloch Lodge . . 157 D8
Kinlochmoidart .147 D10
Kinlochmorar . . 147 B11
Kinlochmore . . . 131 C5
Kinloch Rannoch .132 D3
Kinlochspelve . . 124 C2
Kinloid . . . 147 C9
Kinloss . . . 151 E13
Kinmel Bay . . . 72 A3
Kinmuck . . . 141 C7
Kinmundy . . . 141 C7
Kinnadie . . . 153 D9
Kinnaird . . . 128 B4
Kinnaird Castle . 135 D6
Kinneff . . . 135 B8
Kinnelhead . . . 114 D3
Kinnell . . . 135 D6
Kinnerley . . . 60 B3
Kinnersley Hereford 48 E5
Worcs . . . 50 E3
Kinnerton . . . 48 C4
Kinnesswood . . . 128 D3
Kinninvie . . . 101 B5
Kinnordy . . . 134 D3
Kinoulton . . . 77 F6
Kinross . . . 128 D3
Kinrossie . . . 134 F1
Kinsbourne Green. 40 C4
Kinsey Heath . . . 74 E3
Kinsham Hereford . 49 C5
Worcs . . . 50 F4
Kinsley . . . 88 C5
Kinson . . . 13 E8
Kintbury . . . 25 C8
Kintessack . . . 151 E12
Kintillo . . . 128 C3
Kintocher . . . 140 D4
Kinton Hereford . . 49 B6
Shrops . . . 60 C3
Kintore . . . 141 C6
Kintour . . . 142 C5
Kintra Argyll . . . 142 D4
Argyll . . . 146 J6

Kintraw . . . 124 E4
Kinuachdrachd. . 124 F3
Kinveachy . . . 138 C5
Kinver . . . 62 F2
Kippax . . . 95 F7
Kippen . . . 127 E5
Kippford or
Scaur . . . 106 D5
Kirbister Orkney . 159 F7
Orkney . . . 159 H4
Kirbuster . . . 159 F3
Kirby Bedon . . . 69 D5
Kirby Bellars . . . 64 C4
Kirby Cane . . . 69 E6
Kirby Cross . . . 43 B8
Kirby Grindalythe . 96 C5
Kirby Hill N Yorks. 95 C6
N Yorks . . . 101 D6
Kirby Knowle . . . 102 F2
Kirby-le-Soken . . 43 B8
Kirby Misperton . 96 B3
Kirby Muxloe . . . 64 D2
Kirby Row . . . 69 E6
Kirby Sigston . . . 102 E2
Kirby Underdale . . 96 D4
Kirby Wiske . . . 102 F1
Kirdford . . . 16 B4
Kirk . . . 158 E4
Kirkabister . . . 160 K6
Kirkandrews . . . 106 E3
Kirkandrews upon
Eden . . . 108 D3
Kirkbampton . . . 108 D3
Kirkbean . . . 107 D6
Kirk Bramwith . . . 89 C7
Kirkbride . . . 108 D2
Kirkbuddo . . . 135 E5
Kirkburn Borders . 121 F5
EYorks . . . 97 D5
Kirkburton . . . 88 C2
Kirkby Lincs . . . 90 E4
Mers . . . 86 E2
N Yorks . . . 102 D3
Kirkby Fleetham . 101 E7
Kirkby Green . . . 78 D3
Kirkby-in-Ashfield 76 D5
Kirkby-in-Furness 98 F4
Kirkby la Thorpe . 78 E3
Kirkby Lonsdale . 93 B6
Kirkby Malham . . 93 C8
Kirkby Mallory . . 63 D8
Kirkby Malzeard . 94 B5
Kirkbymoorside . 102 F4
Kirkby on Bain . . 78 C5
Kirkby Overflow . 95 E6
Kirkby Stephen. . 100 D2
Kirkby Thore . . . 99 B8
Kirkby Underwood 65 B7
Kirkby Wharfe . . 95 E8
Kirkcaldy . . . 128 E4
Kirkcambeck . . . 108 C5
Kirkcarswell . . . 106 E4
Kirkcolm . . . 104 C4
Kirkconnel . . . 113 C7
Kirkconnell . . . 107 C6
Kirkcowan . . . 105 C7
Kirkcudbright . . 106 D3
Kirkdale . . . 85 E4
Kirk Deighton . . . 95 D6
Kirk Ella . . . 90 B4
Kirkfieldbank . . 119 E8
Kirkgunzeon . . . 107 C5
Kirk Hallam . . . 76 E4
Kirkham Lancs . . 92 F4
N Yorks . . . 96 C3
Kirkhamgate . . . 88 B3
Kirk Hammerton . 95 D7
Kirkheaton
Northumb . . . 110 B3
W Yorks . . . 88 C2
Kirkhill Angus . . 135 C6
Highld . . . 151 G8
Midloth . . . 120 C5
Moray . . . 152 E2
Kirkhope . . . 115 B6
Kirkhouse . . . 121 F6
Kirkiboll . . . 157 D8
Kirkibost . . . 149 G10
Kirkinch . . . 134 E3
Kirkinner . . . 105 D8
Kirkintilloch . . 119 B6
Kirk Ireton . . . 76 D2
Kirkland Cumb . . 98 C2
Cumb . . . 109 F6
Dumfries . . . 113 C7
Dumfries . . . 113 B8
Kirk Langley . . . 76 F2
Kirkleatham . . . 102 B3
Kirklevington . . 102 D2
Kirkley . . . 69 E8
Kirklington Notts. . 77 D6
N Yorks . . . 101 F8
Kirklinton . . . 108 C4
Kirkliston . . . 120 B4
Kirkmaiden . . . 104 F5
Kirk Merrington . 111 F5
Kirkmichael Perth. 133 D7
S Ayrs . . . 112 D3
Kirk Michael . . . 84 C3
Kirkmuirhill . . . 119 E7
Kirknewton
Northumb . . . 122 F5
W Loth . . . 120 C4
Kirkney . . . 152 E5
Kirk of Shotts . . 119 C8
Kirkoswald Cumb. 109 E5
S Ayrs . . . 112 D2
Kirkpatrick
Durham . . . 106 B4
Kirkpatrick-
Fleming . . . 108 B2
Kirk Sandall . . . 89 C6
Kirksanton . . . 98 F3
Kirk Smeaton . . . 89 C6
Kirkstall . . . 95 F5
Kirkstead . . . 78 C4
Kirkstile . . . 152 E5
Kirkstyle . . . 158 C5
Kirkton Aberds . . 140 B5
Aberds . . . 153 D6
Angus . . . 134 E4
Borders . . . 115 C8
Dumfries . . . 114 B2
Fife . . . 129 B5
Highld . . . 149 F13
Highld . . . 150 G2

Kirkton continued
Highld . . . 151 B10
Highld . . . 151 F10
Perth . . . 127 C8
S Lanark . . . 114 B2
Stirling . . . 126 D4
Kirktonhill . . . 121 D7
Kirkton Manor . . 120 F5
Kirkton of Airlie . 134 D3
Kirkton of
Auchterhouse . 134 F3
Kirkton of
Auchterless . . 153 D7
Kirkton of
Barevan . . .151 G11
Kirkton of
Bourtie . . . 141 B7
Kirkton of
Collace . . . 134 F1
Kirkton of Craig . 135 D7
Kirkton of
Culsalmond . . 153 E6
Kirkton of Durris 141 E6
Kirkton of
Glenbuchat . . 140 C2
Kirkton of
Glenisla . . . 134 C2
Kirkton of
Kingoldrum. . 134 D3
Kirkton of Largo . 129 D6
Kirkton of
Lethendy . . . 133 E8
Kirkton of Logie
Buchan . . . 141 B8
Kirkton of
Maryculter . . 141 E7
Kirkton of
Menmuir . . . 135 C5
Kirkton of
Monikie . . . 135 F5
Kirkton of Oyne . 141 B5
Kirkton of Rayne . 153 F6
Kirkton of Skene . 141 D7
Kirkton of Tough.
Kirktown. . . .153 C10
Kirktown of
Alvah. . . .153 B6
Kirktown of
Deskford . . . 152 B5
Kirktown of
Fetteresso . . 141 F7
Kirktown of
Mortlach. . . 152 E3
Kirktown of
Slains . . . 141 B9
Kirkurd . . . 120 E4
Kirkwall . . . 159 G5
Kirkwhelpington . 117 F5
Kirk Yetholm . . . 116 B4
Kirmington . . . 90 C5
Kirmond le Mire . 91 E5
Kirn . . . 145 F10
Kirriemuir . . . 134 D3
Kirstead Green . . 69 E5
Kirtlebridge . . . 108 B2
Kirtleton . . . 115 F5
Kirtling . . . 55 D7
Kirtling Green . . 55 D7
Kirtlington . . . 38 C4
Kirtomy . . . 157 C10
Kirton Lincs . . . 79 F6
Notts . . . 77 C6
Suff . . . 57 F6
Kirton End . . . 79 E5
Kirton Holme . . . 79 E5
Kirton in Lindsey . 90 E3
Kislingbury . . . 52 D4
Kites Hardwick . . 52 C2
Kittisford . . . 11 B5
Kittle . . . 33 F6
Kitt's Green . . . 63 F5
Kitt's Moss . . . 87 F6
Kittybrewster . . . 141 D8
Kitwood . . . 26 F4
Kivernoll . . . 49 F6
Kiveton Park . . . 89 F5
Knaith . . . 90 F2
Knaith Park . . . 90 F2
Knap Corner . . . 13 B6
Knaphill . . . 27 D7
Knapp Perth . . . 134 F2
Som . . . 11 B8
Knapthorpe . . . 77 D7
Knapton Norf . . . 81 D9
York . . . 95 D8
Knapton Green . . 49 D6
Knapwell . . . 54 C4
Knaresborough . . 95 D6
Knarsdale . . . 109 D6
Knauchland . . . 152 C5
Knaven . . . 153 D8
Knayton . . . 102 F2
Knebworth . . . 41 B5
Knedlington . . . 89 B8
Kneesall . . . 77 C7
Kneesworth . . . 54 E4
Kneeton . . . 77 E7
Knelston . . . 33 F5
Knenhall . . . 75 F6
Knettishall . . . 68 F2
Knightacott . . . 21 F5
Knightcote . . . 51 D8
Knightley Dale . . 62 B2
Knighton Devon . . 6 E3
Leicester . . . 64 D2
Staffs . . . 61 B7
Staffs . . . 74 F4
= Tref-y-Clawdd . . 48 B4
Knightswood . . . 118 C5
Knightwick . . . 50 D2
Knill . . . 48 C4
Knitsley . . . 110 E4
Kniveton . . . 76 D2
Knock Argyll . . . 147 H8
Cumb . . . 100 B1
Moray . . . 152 C5
Knockally . . . 158 H3
Knockan . . . 156 H5
Knockandhu . . . 139 B8
Knockando
House . . . 152 D1
Knockbain . . . 151 F9
Knockbreck . . . 148 B7
Knockbrex . . . 106 E2
Knockdee . . . 158 D3
Knockdolian . . . 104 A5

Knockenkelly . . . 143 F11
Knockentiber . . . 118 F3
Knockespock
House . . . 140 B4
Knockfarrel . . . 151 F8
Knockglass . . . 104 D4
Knockholt . . . 29 D5
Knockholt Pound. 29 D5
Knockin . . . 60 B3
Knockinlaw . . . 118 F4
Knocklearn . . . 106 B4
Knocknaha . . . 143 G7
Knocknain . . . 104 C3
Knockrome . . . 144 F4
Knocksharry . . . 84 D2
Knodishall . . . 57 C8
Knolls Green . . . 74 B5
Knolton . . . 73 F7
Knolton Bryn . . . 73 F7
Knook . . . 24 E4
Knossington . . . 64 D5
Knott End-on-Sea. 92 E3
Knotting . . . 53 C8
Knotting Green . . 53 C8
Knottingley . . . 89 B6
Knotts Cumb . . . 99 B6
Lancs . . . 93 D7
Knotty Ash . . . 86 E2
Knotty Green . . . 40 E2
Knowbury . . . 49 B7
Knowe . . . 105 B7
Knowehead . . . 113 E6
Knowesgate . . . 117 F5
Knowes of Elrick. 152 C6
Knoweton . . . 119 D7
Knowhead . . . 153 C9
Knowle Bristol . . 23 B8
Devon . . . 10 D2
Devon . . . 11 F5
Devon . . . 20 F3
Shrops . . . 49 B7
W Mid . . . 51 B6
Knowle Green . . . 93 F6
Knowle Park . . . 94 E3
Knowl Hill . . . 27 B6
Knowlton Dorset . 13 C8
Kent . . . 31 D6
Knowsley . . . 86 E2
Knowstone . . . 10 B3
Knox Bridge . . . 29 E8
Knucklas . . . 48 B4
Knuston . . . 53 C7
Knutsford . . . 74 B4
Knutton . . . 74 E5
Knypersley . . . 75 D5
Kuggar . . . 3 E6
Kyleakin . . . 149 F12
Kyle of Lochalsh 149 F12
Kylerhea . . . 149 F12
Kylesknoydart. . 147 B11
Kylesku . . . 156 F5
Kylesmorar . . . 147 B11
Kylestrome . . . 156 F5
Kyllachy House . . 138 B3
Kynaston . . . 60 B3
Kynnersley . . . 61 C6
Kyre Magna . . . 49 C8

L
Labost . . . 155 C7
Lacasaidh . . . 155 E8
Lacasdal . . . 155 D9
Laceby . . . 91 D6
Lacey Green . . . 39 E8
Lach Dennis . . . 74 B4
Lackford . . . 55 B8
Lacock . . . 24 C4
Ladbroke . . . 52 D2
Laddingford . . . 29 E7
Lade Bank . . . 79 D6
Ladock . . . 4 D3
Lady . . . 159 D7
Ladybank . . . 128 C5
Ladykirk . . . 122 E4
Ladysford . . . 153 B9
La Fontenelle Guern. 16
Laga . . . 147 E9
Lagalochan . . . 124 D4
Lagavulin . . . 142 D5
Lagg Argyll . . . 144 F4
N Ayrs . . . 143 F10
Laggan Argyll . . 142 C3
Highld . . . 137 E5
Highld . . . 138 E2
Highld . . . 147 D10
S Ayrs . . . 112 F2
Lagganulva . . . 146 G7
Laide . . . 155 H13
Laigh Fenwick . . 118 E4
Laigh Glengall . . 112 C3
Laighmuir . . . 118 E4
Laindon . . . 42 F2
Lair . . . 150 G3
Lairg . . . 157 J8
Lairg Lodge . . . 157 J8
Lairg Muir . . . 157 J8
Laisterdyke . . . 94 F4
Laithes . . . 108 F4
Lake IoW . . . 15 F6
Wilts . . . 25 F6
Lakenham . . . 68 D5
Lakenheath . . . 67 F7
Lakesend . . . 66 E5
Lakeside . . . 99 F5
Laleham . . . 27 C8
Laleston . . . 21 B7
Lamarsh . . . 56 F2
Lamas . . . 81 E8
Lambden . . . 122 E3
Lamberhurst
Quarter. . . 18 B3
Lamberton . . . 123 D5
Lambeth . . . 28 B4
Lambhill . . . 119 C5
Lambley Northumb.109 D6
Notts . . . 77 E6
Lamborough Hill . 38 D4
Lambourn . . . 25 B8
Lambourne End . . 41 E7
Lambs Green . . . 28 F3
Lambston . . . 44 D4
Lambton . . . 111 D5
Lamerton . . . 6 B2
Lamesley . . . 111 D5

Laminess . . . 159 E7
Lamington
Highld . . . 151 D10
S Lanark . . . 120 F2
Lamlash . . . 143 E11
Lamloch . . . 112 E5
Lamonby . . . 108 F4
Lamorna . . . 2 D3
Lamorran . . . 3 B7
Lampardbrook . . 57 C6
Lampeter = Llanbedr
Pont Steffan . . 46 E4
Lampeter Velfrey . 32 C2
Lamphey . . . 32 D1
Lamplugh . . . 98 B2
Lamport . . . 53 B5
Lamyatt . . . 23 F8
Lana . . . 8 E5
Lanark . . . 119 E8
Lancaster . . . 92 C4
Lanchester . . . 110 E4
Lancing . . . 17 D5
Landbeach . . . 55 C5
Landcross . . . 9 B6
Landerberry . . . 141 D6
Landford . . . 14 C3
Landford Manor . 14 B3
Landimore . . . 33 E5
Landkey . . . 20 F4
Landore . . . 33 E7
Landrake . . . 5 C8
Landscove . . . 7 C5
Landshipping . . . 32 C1
Landshipping
Quay . . . 32 C1
Landulph . . . 6 C2
Landwade . . . 55 C7
Lane . . . 4 C3
Laneast . . . 8 F4
Lane End Bucks . . 39 E8
Cumb . . . 98 E3
Dorset . . . 13 E6
Hants . . . 15 B6
IoW . . . 15 F7
Lancs . . . 93 E8
Lane Ends Lancs . 93 D7
Lancs . . . 93 F7
N Yorks . . . 94 E2
Laneham . . . 77 B8
Lanehead Durham. 109 E8
Northumb . . . 116 F3
Lane Head Derbys. 75 B8
Durham . . . 101 C6
Gtr Man . . . 86 E4
W Yorks . . . 88 D2
Lanercost . . . 109 C5
Laneshaw Bridge . 94 E2
Lane Side . . . 87 B5
Lanfach . . . 35 E6
Langar . . . 77 F7
Langbank . . . 118 B3
Langbar . . . 94 D3
Langburnshiels . 115 D8
Langcliffe . . . 93 C8
Langdale . . . 157 E9
Langdale End . . 103 E7
Langdon . . . 8 F4
Langdon Beck . . 109 F8
Langdon Hills . . 42 F2
Langdyke . . . 128 D5
Langenhoe . . . 43 C6
Langford C Beds . 54 E2
Devon . . . 10 D5
Essex . . . 42 D4
Notts . . . 77 D8
Oxon . . . 38 D2
Langford Budville . 11 B6
Langham Essex . . 56 F4
Norf . . . 81 C6
Rutland . . . 64 C5
Suff . . . 56 C3
Langhaugh . . . 120 F5
Langho . . . 93 F7
Langholm . . . 115 F6
Langleeford . . . 117 B5
Langley Ches E . . 75 B6
Hants . . . 14 D5
Kent . . . 30 D2
Northumb . . . 109 C8
Slough . . . 27 B8
Warks . . . 51 C6
W Sus . . . 16 B2
Langley Burrell . . 24 B4
Langley Common . 76 F2
Langley Heath . . 30 D2
Langley Lower
Green . . . 54 F5
Langley Marsh . . 11 B5
Langley Park . . . 110 E5
Langley Street . . 69 D6
Langley Upper
Green . . . 54 F5
Langney . . . 18 E3
Langold . . . 89 F6
Langore . . . 8 F5
Langport . . . 12 B2
Langrick . . . 79 E5
Langridge . . . 24 C2
Langridge Ford . . 9 B7
Langrigg . . . 107 E8
Langrish . . . 15 B8
Langsett . . . 88 D3
Langshaw . . . 121 F8
Langside . . . 127 C6
Langskaill . . . 159 D5
Langstone Hants . 15 D8
Newport . . . 35 E7
Langthorne . . . 101 E7
Langthorpe . . . 95 C6
Langthwaite . . . 101 D5
Langtoft E Yorks . 97 C6
Lincs . . . 65 C8
Langton Durham . 101 C6
Lincs . . . 78 C5
Lincs . . . 79 B6
N Yorks . . . 96 C3
Langton by
Wragby . . . 78 B4
Langton Green
Kent . . . 18 B2
Suff . . . 56 B5
Langton Herring . 12 F4
Langton
Matravers . . 13 G8
Langtree . . . 9 C6
Langwathby . . . 109 F5
Langwell House . 158 H3
Langwell Lodge . 156 J4

Langwith . . . 76 C5
Langwith Junction 76 C5
Langworth . . . 78 B3
Lanivet . . . 4 C5
Lanlivery . . . 5 D5
Lanner . . . 3 C6
Lanreath . . . 5 D6
Lansallos . . . 5 D6
Lansdown . . . 37 B6
Lanteglos Highway . 5 D6
Lanton Borders . . 116 B2
Northumb . . . 122 F5
Lapford . . . 10 D2
Laphroaig . . . 142 D4
La Planque Guern. . 16
Lapley . . . 62 C2
Lapworth . . . 51 B6
Larachbeg . . . 147 G9
Larbert . . . 127 F7
Larden Green . . . 74 D2
Largie . . . 152 E6
Largiemore . . . 145 E8
Largoward . . . 129 D6
Largs . . . 118 D2
Largybeg . . . 143 F11
Largymore . . . 143 F11
Larkfield . . . 118 B2
Larkhall . . . 119 D7
Larkhill . . . 25 E6
Larling . . . 68 F2
Larriston . . . 115 E8
Lartington . . . 101 C5
Lary . . . 140 D2
Lasham . . . 26 E4
Lashenden . . . 30 E2
Lassington . . . 36 B4
Lassodie . . . 128 E3
Lastingham . . . 103 E5
Latcham . . . 23 E6
Latchford Herts . . 41 B6
Warr . . . 86 F4
Latchingdon . . . 42 D4
Latchley . . . 6 B2
Lately Common . . 86 E4
Lathbury . . . 53 E6
Latheron . . . 158 G3
Latheronwheel . . 158 G3
Latheronwheel
House . . . 158 G3
Lathones . . . 129 D6
Latimer . . . 40 E3
Latteridge . . . 36 F3
Lattiford . . . 12 B4
Latton . . . 37 E7
Latton Bush . . . 41 D7
Lauchintilly . . . 141 C6
Lauder . . . 121 E8
Laugharne . . . 32 C4
Laughterton . . . 77 B8
Laughton E Sus . . 18 D2
Leics . . . 64 F3
Lincs . . . 78 F3
Lincs . . . 90 E2
Laughton Common 89 F6
Laughton en le
Morthen. . . 89 F6
Launcells . . . 8 D4
Launceston . . . 8 F5
Launton . . . 39 B6
Laurencekirk . . 135 B7
Laurieston
Dumfries . . . 106 C3
Falk . . . 120 B2
Lavendon . . . 53 D7
Lavenham . . . 56 E3
Laverhay . . . 114 D4
Laversdale . . . 108 C4
Laverstock . . . 25 F6
Laverstoke . . . 26 E2
Laverton Glos . . . 51 F5
N Yorks . . . 94 B5
Som . . . 24 D2
Lavister . . . 73 D7
Law . . . 119 D8
Lawers Perth . . . 127 B6
Perth . . . 132 F3
Lawford . . . 56 F4
Lawhitton . . . 9 C7
Lawkland . . . 93 C7
Lawley . . . 61 D6
Lawnhead . . . 62 B2
Lawrenny . . . 32 D1
Lawshall . . . 56 D2
Lawton . . . 49 D6
Laxey . . . 84 D4
Laxfield . . . 57 B6
Laxfirth Shetland . 160 H6
Shetland . . . 160 J6
Laxford Bridge . . 156 E5
Laxo . . . 160 G6
Laxobigging . . . 160 F6
Laxton E Yorks . . 89 B8
Northants . . . 65 E6
Notts . . . 77 C7
Laycock . . . 94 E3
Layer Breton . . . 43 C5
Layer de la Haye . 43 C5
Layer Marney . . . 43 C5
Layham . . . 56 E4
Laylands Green . . 25 C8
Laytham . . . 96 F3
Layton . . . 92 F3
Lazenby . . . 102 B3
Lazonby . . . 108 F5
Lea Derbys . . . 76 D3
Hereford . . . 36 B3
Lincs . . . 90 F2
Shrops . . . 60 D4
Wilts . . . 37 F6
Leabrooks . . . 76 D4
Leac a Li . . . 154 H6
Leachkin . . . 151 G9
Leadburn . . . 120 D5
Leaden Roding . . 42 C1
Leadgate Cumb . . 109 E7
Durham . . . 110 D4
T&W . . . 110 D4
Leadhills . . . 113 C8
Leafield . . . 38 C3
Leagrave . . . 40 B3
Leake . . . 102 E2
Leake
Commonside . . 79 D6
Lealholm . . . 103 D5
Lealt Argyll . . . 144 D5
Highld . . . 149 B10
Leamington
Hastings . . . 52 C2
Leamonsley . . . 62 D5
Leamside . . . 111 E6
Leanaig . . . 151 F8
Leargybreck . . . 144 F4
Leasgill . . . 99 F6
Leasingham . . . 78 E3
Leasingthorne . . 101 B7
Leasowe . . . 85 E3
Leatherhead . . . 28 D2
Leatherhead
Common . . . 28 D2
Leathley . . . 94 E5
Leaton . . . 60 C4
Leaveland . . . 30 D4
Leavening . . . 96 C3
Leaves Green . . . 28 C5
Leazes . . . 110 D4
Lebberston . . . 103 F8
Lechlade-on-
Thames . . . 38 E2
Leck . . . 93 B6
Leckford . . . 25 F8
Leckfurin . . . 157 D10
Leckhampstead
Bucks . . . 52 F5
W Berks . . . 26 B2
Leckhampstead
Thicket . . . 26 B2
Leckhampton . . . 37 C6
Leckie . . . 150 E3
Leckmelm . . . 150 B4
Leckwith . . . 22 B3
Leconfield . . . 97 E6
Ledaig . . . 124 B5
Ledburn . . . 40 B2
Ledbury . . . 50 F2
Ledcharrie . . . 126 B4
Ledgemoor . . . 49 D6
Ledicot . . . 49 C6
Ledmore . . . 156 H5
Lednagullin . . . 157 C10
Ledsham Ches W . 73 B7
W Yorks . . . 89 B5
Ledston . . . 88 B5
Ledston Luck . . . 95 F7
Ledwell . . . 38 B4
Lee Argyll . . . 146 J7
Devon . . . 20 E3
Hants . . . 14 C4
Lancs . . . 93 D5
Shrops . . . 60 B4
Leeans . . . 160 J5
Leebotten . . . 160 L6
Leebotwood . . . 60 E4
Leece . . . 92 C2
Leechpool . . . 44 D4
Lee Clump . . . 40 D2
Leeds Kent . . . 30 D2
W Yorks . . . 95 F5
Leedstown . . . 2 C5
Leek . . . 75 D6
Leek Brookhurst . 60 B5
Leek Wootton . . . 51 C7
Lee Mill . . . 6 D4
Leeming . . . 101 F7
Leeming Bar . . . 101 E7
Lee Moor . . . 6 C3
Lee-on-the-
Solent . . . 15 D6
Lees Derbys . . . 76 F2
Gtr Man . . . 87 D7
W Yorks . . . 94 F3
Leeswood . . . 73 C6
Legbourne . . . 91 F7
Legerwood . . . 121 E8
Legsby . . . 90 F5
Leicester . . . 64 D2
Leicester Forest
East . . . 64 D2
Leigh Dorset . . . 12 D4
Glos . . . 37 B5
Gtr Man . . . 86 D4
Kent . . . 29 E6
Shrops . . . 60 D3
Sur . . . 28 E3
Wilts . . . 37 E7
Worcs . . . 50 D2
Leigh Beck . . . 42 F4
Leigh Common . . 12 B5
Leigh Delamere . . 24 B3
Leigh Green . . . 19 B6
Leigh on Sea . . . 42 F4
Leigh Park . . . 15 D8
Leigh Sinton . . . 50 D2
Leighswood . . . 62 D4
Leighterton . . . 37 E5
Leighton N Yorks . 94 B4
Powys . . . 60 D2
Shrops . . . 61 D6
Som . . . 24 E2
Leighton
Bromswold . . 54 B2
Leighton Buzzard. 40 B2
Leigh upon
Mendip . . . 23 E8
Leigh Woods . . . 23 B7
Leinthall Earls . . 49 C6
Leinthall Starkes . 49 C6
Leintwardine . . . 49 B6
Leire . . . 64 E2
Leirinmore . . . 156 C7
Leiston . . . 57 C8
Leitfie . . . 134 E2
Leith . . . 121 B5
Leitholm . . . 122 E3
Lelant . . . 2 C4
Lelley . . . 97 F8
Lem Hill . . . 50 B2
Lemmington Hall. 117 C7
Lempitlaw . . . 122 F3
Lenchwick . . . 50 E5
Lendalfoot . . . 112 F1
Lendrick Lodge . 126 D4
Lenham . . . 30 D2
Lenham Heath . . 30 E3
Lennel . . . 122 E4
Lennoxtown . . . 119 B6
Lenton Lincs . . . 78 F3
Nottingham . . . 77 F5
Lentran . . . 151 G8
Lenwade . . . 68 C3
Leny House . . . 126 D5
Lenzie . . . 119 B6
Leoch . . . 134 F3

Leochel-Cushnie . 140 C4
Leominster . . . 49 D6
Leonard Stanley . 37 D5
Leorin . . . 142 D4
Lepe . . . 15 E5
Lephin . . . 148 D6
Lephinchapel . . . 145 D8
Lephinmore . . . 145 D8
Le Planel Guern. . 16
Leppington . . . 96 C3
Lepton . . . 88 C3
Lerryn . . . 5 D6
Lerwick . . . 160 J6
Lesbury . . . 117 C8
Le Skerne
Haughton . . . 101 C8
Leslie Aberds . . . 140 B4
Fife . . . 128 D4
Lesmahagow . . . 119 F8
Lesnewth . . . 8 E3
Lessendrum . . . 152 D5
Lessingham . . . 69 B6
Lessonhall . . . 108 D2
Leswalt . . . 104 C4
Letchmore Heath . 40 E4
Letchworth . . . 54 F3
Letcombe Bassett . 38 F3
Letcombe Regis . 38 F3
Letham Angus . . 135 E5
Falk . . . 127 F7
Fife . . . 128 C5
Perth . . . 128 B2
Letham Grange . . 135 E6
Lethenty . . . 153 D8
Letheringham . . . 57 D6
Letheringsett . . . 81 D6
Lettaford . . . 10 F2
Lettan . . . 159 D8
Letterewe . . . 150 D2
Letterfearn . . . 149 F13
Letterfinlay . . . 137 E5
Lettermorar . . . 147 C10
Lettermore . . . 146 G7
Letters . . . 150 C4
Letterston . . . 44 C4
Lettoch Highld . . 139 B6
Highld . . . 151 H13
Letton Hereford . . 48 E5
Hereford . . . 49 B5
Letton Green . . . 68 D2
Letty Green . . . 41 C5
Letwell . . . 89 F6
Leuchars . . . 129 B6
Leuchars House . 152 B2
Leumrabhagh . . 155 F8
Levan . . . 118 B2
Levaneap . . . 160 G6
Levedale . . . 62 C2
Leven E Yorks . . . 97 E7
Fife . . . 129 D5
Levencorroch . . . 143 F11
Levens . . . 99 F6
Levens Green . . . 41 B6
Levenshulme . . . 87 E6
Levenwick . . . 160 L6
Leverburgh
= An t-Ob. . . 154 J5
Leverington . . . 66 C4
Leverton . . . 79 E7
Leverton Highgate 79 E7
Leverton
Lucasgate . . . 79 E7
Leverton Outgate . 79 E7
Le Villocq Guern. . 16
Levington . . . 57 F6
Levisham . . . 103 E6
Levishie . . . 137 C7
Lew . . . 38 D3
Lewannick . . . 8 F4
Lewdown . . . 9 F6
Lewes . . . 17 C8
Leweston . . . 44 C4
Lewisham . . . 28 B4
Lewiston . . . 137 B8
Lewistown . . . 34 F3
Lewknor . . . 39 E7
Leworthy Devon . 8 D5
Devon . . . 21 F5
Lewtrenchard . . . 9 F6
Lexden . . . 43 B5
Ley Aberds . . . 140 C4
Corn . . . 5 C6
Leybourne . . . 29 D7
Leyburn . . . 101 E6
Leyfields . . . 63 D6
Leyhill . . . 40 D2
Leyland . . . 86 B3
Leylodge . . . 141 C6
Leymoor . . . 88 C2
Leys Aberds . . . 153 C10
Perth . . . 134 F2
Leys Castle . . . 151 G9
Leysdown-on-Sea 30 B4
Leysmill . . . 135 E6
Leys of Cossans . 134 E3
Leysters Pole . . . 49 C7
Leyton . . . 41 F6
Leytonstone . . . 41 F6
Lezant . . . 5 B8
Leziate . . . 67 C6
Lhanbryde . . . 152 B2
Liatrie . . . 150 H5
Libanus . . . 34 B3
Libberton . . . 120 E2
Liberton . . . 121 C5
Liceasto . . . 154 H6
Lichfield . . . 62 D5
Lickey . . . 50 B4
Lickey End . . . 50 B4
Lickfold . . . 16 B3
Liddel . . . 159 K5
Liddesdale . . . 130 D1
Liddington . . . 38 F2
Lidgate . . . 55 D8
Lidget . . . 89 D7
Lidget Green . . . 94 F4
Lidgett . . . 77 C6
Lidlington . . . 53 F7
Lidstone . . . 38 B3
Lieurary . . . 158 D2
Liff . . . 134 F3
Lifton . . . 9 F5
Liftondown . . . 9 F5
Lighthorne . . . 51 D8
Lightwater . . . 27 C7
Lightwood . . . 75 E6
Lightwood Green
Ches E . . . 74 E3
Wrex . . . 73 E7

Lilbourne . . . 52 B3
Lilburn Tower . . 117 B6
Lilleshall . . . 61 C7
Lilley Herts . . . 40 B4
W Berks . . . 26 B2
Lilliesleaf . . . 115 B8
Lillingstone
Dayrell . . . 52 F5
Lillingstone Lovell. 52 E5
Lillington Dorset . 12 C4
Warks . . . 51 C8
Lilliput . . . 13 E8
Lilstock . . . 22 E3
Lilyhurst . . . 61 C7
Limbury . . . 40 B3
Limebrook . . . 49 C5
Limefield . . . 87 C6
Limekilnburn . . 119 D7
Limekilns . . . 128 F2
Limerigg . . . 119 B8
Limerstone . . . 14 F5
Limington . . . 12 B3
Limpenhoe . . . 69 D6
Limpley Stoke . . 24 C2
Limpsfield . . . 28 D5
Limpsfield Chart . 28 D5
Linby . . . 76 D5
Linchmere . . . 27 F6
Lincluden . . . 107 B6
Lincoln . . . 78 B2
Lincomb . . . 50 C3
Lincombe . . . 6 C5
Lindale . . . 99 F6
Lindal in Furness . 92 B2
Lindean . . . 121 F7
Lindfield . . . 17 B7
Lindford . . . 27 F6
Lindifferon . . . 128 C5
Lindley . . . 88 C2
Lindley Green . . . 94 E5
Lindores . . . 128 C4
Lindridge . . . 49 C8
Lindsell . . . 42 B2
Lindsey . . . 56 E3
Linford Hants . . . 14 D2
Thurrock . . . 29 B7
Lingague . . . 84 E2
Lingards Wood . . 87 C8
Lingbob . . . 94 F3
Lingdale . . . 102 C4
Lingen . . . 49 C5
Lingfield . . . 28 E4
Lingreabhagh . . 154 J5
Lingwood . . . 69 D6
Linicro . . . 149 B8
Linkenholt . . . 25 D8
Linkhill . . . 18 C5
Linkinhorne. . . 5 B8
Linklater . . . 159 K5
Linksness . . . 159 H3
Linktown . . . 128 E4
Linley . . . 60 E3
Linley Green . . . 49 D8
Linlithgow
Bridge . . . 120 B2
Linshiels . . . 116 D4
Linsiadar . . . 154 D7
Linsidemore . . . 151 B8
Linslade . . . 40 B2
Linstead Parva . . 57 B7
Linstock . . . 108 D4
Linthwaite . . . 88 C2
Lintlaw . . . 122 D4
Lintmill . . . 152 B5
Linton Borders . . 116 B3
Cambs . . . 55 E6
Derbys . . . 63 C6
Hereford . . . 36 B3
Kent . . . 29 E8
Northumb . . . 117 E8
N Yorks . . . 94 C2
W Yorks . . . 95 E6
Linton-on-Ouse . 95 C7
Linwood Hants . . 14 D2
Lincs . . . 90 F5
Renfs . . . 118 C4
Lionacleit . . . 148 D2
Lional . . . 155 A10
Liphook . . . 27 F6
Liscard . . . 85 E4
Liscombe . . . 21 F7
Liskeard . . . 5 C7
L'Islet Guern. . . 16
Liss . . . 15 B8
Lissett . . . 97 D7
Liss Forest . . . 15 B8
Lissington . . . 90 F5
Lisvane . . . 35 F5
Liswerry . . . 35 F7
Litcham . . . 67 C8
Litchborough . . . 52 D4
Litchfield . . . 26 D2
Litherland . . . 85 E4
Litlington Cambs . 54 E4
E Sus . . . 18 E2
Little Abington . . 55 E6
Little Addington . 53 B7
Little Alne . . . 51 C6
Little Altcar . . . 85 D4
Little Asby . . . 100 D1
Little Assynt . . . 156 G4
Little Aston . . . 62 D4
Little Atherfield . . 15 F5
Little Ayre . . . 159 J4
Little-ayre . . . 160 G5
Little Ayton . . . 102 C3
Little Baddow . . 42 D3
Little Badminton . 37 F5
Little Ballinluig . . 133 D6
Little Bampton . . 108 D2
Little Bardfield . . 55 F7
Little Barford . . . 54 D2
Little Barningham . 81 D7
Little Barrington . 38 C2
Little Barrow . . . 73 B8
Little Barugh . . . 96 B3
Little Bavington . 110 B2
Little Bealings . . 57 E6
Littlebeck . . . 103 D6
Little Bedwyn . . . 25 C7
Little Bentley . . . 43 B7
Little
Berkhamsted . 41 D5
Little Billing . . . 53 C6
Little Birch . . . 49 F7

Little Blakenham 56 E5
Little Blencow 108 F4
Little Bollington 86 F5
Little Bookham 28 D2
Littleborough
Gtr Man 87 C7
Notts 90 F2
Littlebourne 31 D6
Little Bowden 64 F4
Little Bradley 55 D7
Little Brampton 60 F3
Little Brechin 135 C5
Littlebredy 12 F3
Little Brickhill 53 F7
Little Brington 52 C4
Little Bromley 43 B6
Little Broughton 107 F7
Little Budworth 74 C2
Little Burstead 42 E2
Littlebury 55 F6
Littlebury Green 55 F5
Little Bytham 65 C7
Little Carlton Lincs 91 F7
Notts 77 D7
Little Casterton 65 D7
Little Cawthorpe 91 F7
Little Chalfont 40 E2
Little Chart 30 E3
Little Chesterford 55 E6
Little Cheverell 24 D4
Little Chishill 54 F5
Little Clacton 43 C7
Little Clifton 98 B2
Little Colp 153 D7
Little Comberton 50 E4
Little Common 18 E4
Little Compton 51 F7
Little Cornard 56 F2
Little Cowarne 49 D8
Little Coxwell 38 E2
Little Crakehall 101 E7
Little Cressingham 67 D8
Little Crosby 85 D4
Little Dalby 64 C4
Little Dawley 61 D6
Littledean 36 C3
Little Dens 153 D10
Little Dewchurch 49 F7
Little Downham 66 F5
Little Driffield 97 D6
Little Dunham 67 C8
Little Dunkeld 133 E7
Little Dunmow 42 B2
Little Easton 42 B2
Little Eaton 76 E3
Little Eccleston 92 E4
Little Ellingham 68 E3
Little End 41 D8
Little Eversden 54 D4
Little Faringdon 38 D2
Little Fencote 101 E7
Little Fenton 95 F8
Littleferry 151 B11
Little Finborough 56 D4
Little Fransham 68 C2
Little Gaddesden 40 C2
Little Gidding 65 F8
Little Glemham 57 D7
Little Glenshee 133 F6
Little Gransden 54 D3
Little Green 24 E2
Little Grimsby 91 E7
Little Gruinard 150 C2
Little Habton 96 B3
Little Hadham 41 B7
Little Hale 78 E4
Little Hallingbury 41 C7
Littleham Devon 9 B6
Devon 10 F5
Little Hampden 40 D1
Littlehampton 16 D4
Little Harrowden 53 B6
Little Haseley 39 D6
Little Hatfield 97 E7
Little Hautbois 81 E8
Little Haven 44 D3
Little Hay 62 D5
Little Hayfield 87 F8
Little Haywood 62 B4
Little Heath 63 F7
Littlehempston 7 C6
Little Hereford 49 C7
Little Horkesley 56 F3
Little Horsted 17 C8
Little Horton 94 F4
Little Horwood 53 F5
Littlehoughton 117 C8
Little Houghton
Northants 53 D6
S Yorks 88 D5
Little Hucklow 75 B8
Little Hulton 86 D5
Little Humber 91 B5
Little Hungerford 26 B3
Little Irchester 53 C7
Little Kimble 39 D8
Little Kineton 51 D8
Little Kingshill 40 E1
Little Langdale 99 D5
Little Langford 25 F5
Little Laver 41 D8
Little Leigh 74 B3
Little Leighs 42 C3
Little Lever 87 D5
Little London Bucks 39 C6
E Sus 18 D2
Hants 25 E8
Hants 26 D4
Lincs 66 B2
Lincs 66 B4
Norf 81 E7
Powys 59 F7
Little Longstone 75 B8
Little Lynturk 140 C4
Little Malvern 50 E2
Little Maplestead 56 F2
Little Marcle 49 F8
Little Marlow 40 F1
Little Marsden 93 F8
Little Massingham 80 E3
Little Melton 68 D4
Littlemill Aberds 140 E2
E Ayrs 112 C4
Highld 151 F12
Northumb 117 C8
Little Mill 35 D7
Little Milton 39 D6
Little Missenden 40 E2
Littlemoor 12 F4
Littlemore 39 D5
Little Musgrave 100 C2
Little Ness 60 C4
Little Neston 73 B6
Little Newcastle 44 C4
Little Newsham 101 C6
Little Oakley Essex 43 B8
Northants 65 F5
Little Orton 108 D3
Little Ouseburn 95 C7
Littleover 76 F3
Little Paxton 54 C2
Little Petherick 4 B4
Little Pitlurg 152 D4
Little Plumpton 92 F3
Little Plumstead 69 C6
Little Ponton 78 F2
Littleport 67 F5
Little Raveley 54 B3
Little Reedness 90 B2
Little Ribston 95 D6
Little Rissington 38 C1
Little Ryburgh 81 E5
Little Ryle 117 C6
Little Salkeld 109 F5
Little Sampford 55 F7
Little Sandhurst 27 C6
Little Saxham 55 C8
Little Scatwell 150 F6
Little Sessay 95 B7
Little Shelford 54 D5
Little Singleton 92 F3
Little Skillymarno 153 C9
Little Smeaton 89 C6
Little Snoring 81 D5
Little Sodbury 36 F4
Little Somborne 25 F8
Little Somerford 37 F6
Little Stainforth 93 C8
Little Stainton 101 B8
Little Stanney 73 B8
Little Staughton 54 C2
Little Steeping 79 C7
Little Stoke 75 F6
Littlestone on Sea 19 C7
Little Stonham 56 C5
Little Stretton Leics 64 D3
Shrops 60 E4
Little Strickland 99 C7
Little Stukeley 54 B3
Little Sutton 73 B7
Little Tew 38 B3
Little Thetford 55 B6
Little Thirkleby 95 B7
Littlethorpe Leics 64 E2
N Yorks 95 C6
Little Thurlow 55 D7
Little Thurrock 29 B7
Littleton Ches W 73 C8
Hants 26 F2
Perth 134 F2
Som 23 F6
Sur 27 C8
Sur 27 E7
Littleton Drew 37 F5
Littleton-on-Severn 36 F2
Littleton Pannell 24 D5
Little Torboll 151 B10
Little Torrington 9 C6
Little Totham 42 C4
Little Toux 152 C5
Littletown 111 E6
Little Town Cumb 98 C4
Lancs 93 F6
Little Urswick 92 B2
Little Wakering 43 F5
Little Walden 55 E6
Little Waldingfield 56 E3
Little Walsingham 80 D5
Little Waltham 42 C3
Little Warley 42 E2
Little Weighton 97 F5
Little Weldon 65 F6
Little Welnetham 56 C2
Little Wenlock 61 D6
Little Whittingham Green 57 B6
Littlewick Green 27 B6
Little Wilbraham 55 D6
Little Wishford 25 F5
Little Witley 50 C2
Little Wittenham 39 E5
Little Wolford 51 F7
Littleworth Bedford 53 E8
Glos 37 D5
Oxon 38 E3
Staffs 62 C4
Worcs 50 D3
Little Wratting 55 E7
Little Wymington 53 C7
Little Wymondley 41 B5
Little Wyrley 62 D4
Little Yeldham 55 F8
Litton Derbys 75 B8
N Yorks 94 B2
Som 23 D7
Litton Cheney 12 E3
Liurbost 155 E8
Liverpool 85 E4
Liverpool Airport 86 F2
Liversedge 88 B3
Liverton Devon 7 B6
Redcar 103 C5
Livingston 120 C3
Livingston Village 120 C3
Lixwm 73 B5
Lizard 3 E6
Llaingoch 82 C2
Llaithddu 59 F7
Llan 59 D5
Llanaber 58 C3
Llanaelhaearn 70 C4
Llanafan 47 B5
Llanafan-fawr 47 D8
Llanallgo 82 C4
Llanandras =Presteigne 48 C5
Llanarmon 70 D5
Llanarmon Dyffryn Ceiriog 73 F5
Llanarmon-yn-Ial 73 D5
Llanarth Ceredig 46 D3
Mon 35 C7
Llanarthne 33 B6
Llanasa 85 F2
Llanbabo 82 C3
Llanbadarn Fawr 58 F3
Llanbadarn Fynydd 48 B3
Llanbadarn-y-Garreg 48 E3
Llanbadoc 35 E7
Llanbadrig 82 B3
Llanbeder 35 E7
Llanbedr Gwyn 71 E6
Powys 35 B6
Powys 48 E3
Llanbedr-Dyffryn-Clwyd 72 D5
Llanbedrgoch 82 C5
Llanbedrog 70 D4
Llanbedr Pont Steffan =Lampeter 46 E4
Llanbedr-y-cennin 83 E7
Llanberis 83 E5
Llanbethêry 22 C2
Llanbister 48 B3
Llanblethian 21 B8
Llanboidy 32 B3
Llanbradach 35 E5
Llanbrynmair 59 D5
Llancarfan 22 B2
Llancayo 35 D7
Llancloudy 36 B1
Llancynfelyn 58 E3
Llandaff 22 B3
Llandanwg 71 E6
Llandarcy 33 E8
Llandawke 32 C3
Llanddaniel Fab 82 D4
Llanddarog 33 C6
Llanddeiniol 46 B4
Llanddeiniolen 82 E5
Llandderfel 72 F3
Llanddeusant Anglesey 82 C3
Carms 34 B1
Llanddew 48 F2
Llanddewi 33 F5
Llanddewi-Brefi 47 D5
Llanddewi'r Cwm 48 E2
Llanddewi Rhydderch 35 C7
Llanddewi Velfrey 32 C2
Llanddoged 83 E8
Llanddona 83 D5
Llanddowror 32 C3
Llanddulas 72 B3
Llanddwywe 71 E6
Llanddyfynan 82 D5
Llandefaelog Fach 48 F2
Llandefaelog-tre'rgraig 35 B5
Llandefalle 48 E3
Llandegai 83 D5
Llandegfan 83 D5
Llandegla 73 D5
Llandegley 48 C3
Llandegveth 35 E7
Llandegwning 70 D3
Llandeilo 33 B7
Llandeilo Graban 48 E2
Llandeilo'r Fan 47 F7
Llandeloy 44 C3
Llandenny 35 D8
Llandevenny 35 F8
Llandewednock 3 E6
Llandewi Ystradenny 48 C3
Llandinabo 36 B2
Llandinam 59 F7
Llandissilio 32 B2
Llandogo 36 D2
Llandough V Glam 21 B8
V Glam 22 B3
Llandovery =Llanymddyfri 47 F6
Llandow 21 B8
Llandre Carms 47 E5
Ceredig 58 F3
Llandrillo 72 F4
Llandrillo-yn-Rhos 83 C8
Llandrindod =Llandrindod Wells 48 C2
Llandrindod Wells =Llandrindod 48 C2
Llandrinio 60 C2
Llandudno 83 C7
Llandudno Junction =Cyffordd Llandudno 83 D7
Llandwrog 82 F4
Llandybie 33 C7
Llandyfaelog 33 C5
Llandyfan 33 C7
Llandyfriog 46 E2
Llandyfrydog 82 C4
Llandygwydd 45 E4
Llandynan 73 E5
Llandyrnog 72 C5
Llandysilio 60 C2
Llandyssil 59 E8
Llandysul 46 E3
Llanedeyrn 35 F6
Llanedi 33 D6
Llaneglwys 48 F2
Llanegryn 58 D2
Llanegwad 33 B6
Llaneilian 82 B4
Llanelian-yn-Rhos 83 D8
Llanelidan 72 D5
Llanelieu 48 F3
Llanellen 35 C7
Llanelli 33 E6
Llanelltyd 58 C4
Llanelly 35 C6
Llanelly Hill 35 C6
Llanelwedd 48 D2
Llanelwy =St Asaph 72 B4
Llanenddwyn 71 E6
Llanengan 70 E3
Llanerchymedd 82 C4
Llanerfyl 59 D7
Llanfachraeth 82 C3
Llanfachreth 71 E8
Llanfaelog 82 D3
Llanfaelrhys 70 E3
Llanfaenor 35 C8
Llanfaes Anglesey 83 D6
Powys 34 B4
Llanfaethlu 82 C3
Llanfaglan 82 E4
Llanfair 71 E6
Llanfair-ar-y-bryn 47 F7
Llanfair Caereinion 59 D8
Llanfair Clydogau 46 D5
Llanfair-Dyffryn-Clwyd 72 D5
Llanfairfechan 83 D6
Llanfair Kilgheddin 35 D7
Llanfair-Nant-Gwyn 45 F3
Llanfairpwllgwyngyll 82 D5
Llanfair Talhaiarn 72 B3
Llanfair Waterdine 48 B4
Llanfair-ym-Muallt =Builth Wells 48 D2
Llanfairyneubwll 82 D3
Llanfairynghornwy 82 B3
Llanfallteg 32 C2
Llanfaredd 48 D2
Llanfarian 46 B4
Llanfechain 59 B8
Llanfechan 47 D8
Llanfechell 82 B3
Llanfendigaid 58 D2
Llanferres 73 C5
Llan Ffestiniog 71 C8
Llanfflewyn 82 C3
Llanfihangel-ararth 46 F3
Llanfihangel-Crucorney 35 B7
Llanfihangel Glyn Myfyr 72 E3
Llanfihangel Nant Bran 47 F8
Llanfihangel-nant-Melan 48 D3
Llanfihangel Rhydithon 48 C3
Llanfihangel Rogiet 35 F8
Llanfihangel Tal-y-llyn 35 B5
Llanfihangel-uwch-Gwili 33 B5
Llanfihangel-y-Creuddyn 47 B5
Llanfihangel-yn-Ngwynfa 59 C7
Llanfihangel yn Nhowyn 82 D3
Llanfihangel-ypennant Gwyn 58 D3
Gwyn 71 C6
Llanfihangel-ytraethau 71 D6
Llanfilo 48 F3
Llanfoist 35 C6
Llanfor 72 F3
Llanfrechfa 35 E7
Llanfrothen 71 C7
Llanfrynach 34 B4
Llanfwrog Anglesey 82 C3
Denb 72 D5
Llanfyllin 59 C8
Llanfynydd Carms 33 B6
Flint 73 D6
Llanfyrnach 45 F4
Llangadfan 59 C7
Llangadog 33 B8
Llangadwaladr Anglesey 82 E3
Powys 73 F5
Llangaffo 82 E4
Llangain 32 C4
Llangammarch Wells 47 E8
Llangan 21 B8
Llangarron 36 B2
Llangasty Talyllyn 35 B5
Llangathen 33 B6
Llangattock 35 C6
Llangattock Lingoed 35 B7
Llangattock nigh Usk 35 D7
Llangattock-Vibon-Avel 36 C1
Llangedwyn 59 B8
Llangefni 82 D4
Llangeinor 34 F3
Llangeitho 46 D5
Llangeler 46 F2
Llangelynin 58 D2
Llangendeirne 33 C5
Llangennech 33 D6
Llangennith 33 E5
Llangenny 35 C6
Llangernyw 83 E8
Llangian 70 E3
Llanglydwen 32 B2
Llangoed 83 D6
Llangoedmor 45 E3
Llangollen 73 E6
Llangolman 32 B2
Llangors 35 B5
Llangovan 36 D1
Llangower 72 F3
Llangrannog 46 D2
Llangristiolus 82 D4
Llangrove 36 C2
Llangua 35 B7
Llangunllo 48 B4
Llangunnor 33 C5
Llangurig 47 B8
Llangwm Conwy 72 E3
Mon 35 D8
Pembs 44 E4
Llangwnnadl 70 D3
Llangwyfan 72 C5
Llangwyfan-isaf 82 E3
Llangwyllog 82 D4
Llangwyryfon 46 B4
Llangybi Ceredig 46 D5
Gwyn 70 C5
Mon 35 E7
Llangyfelach 33 E7
Llangynhafal 72 C5
Llangynidr 35 C5
Llangynin 32 C3
Llangynog Carms 32 C4
Powys 59 B7
Llangynwyd 34 F2
Llanhamlach 34 B4
Llanharan 34 F4
Llanharry 34 F4
Llanhennock 35 E7
Llanhiledd =Llanhilleth 35 D6
Llanhilleth =Llanhiledd 35 D6
Llanidloes 59 F6
Llaniestyn 70 D3
Llanifyny 59 F5
Llanigon 48 F4
Llanilar 46 B5
Llanilid 34 F3
Llanilltud Fawr =Llantwit Major 21 C8
Llanishen Cardiff 35 F5
Mon 36 D1
Llanllawddog 33 B5
Llanllechid 83 E6
Llanllowell 35 E7
Llanllugan 59 D7
Llanllwch 32 C4
Llanllwchaiarn 59 E8
Llanllwni 46 F3
Llanllyfni 82 F4
Llanmadoc 33 E5
Llanmaes 21 C8
Llanmartin 35 F7
Llanmihangel 21 B8
Llanmorlais 33 E6
Llannefydd 72 B3
Llannon 33 D6
Llannor 70 D4
Llanon 46 C4
Llanover 35 D7
Llanpumsaint 33 B5
Llanreithan 44 C3
Llanrhaeadr 72 C4
Llanrhaeadr-ym-Mochnant 59 B8
Llanrhian 44 B3
Llanrhidian 33 E5
Llanrhos 83 C7
Llanrhyddlad 82 C3
Llanrhystud 46 C4
Llanrosser 48 F4
Llanrothal 36 C1
Llanrug 82 E5
Llanrumney 35 F6
Llanrwst 83 E8
Llansadurnen 32 C3
Llansadwrn Anglesey 83 D5
Carms 47 F5
Llansaint 32 D4
Llansamlet 33 E7
Llansannan 72 C3
Llansannor 21 B8
Llansantffraed Ceredig 46 C4
Powys 35 B5
Llansantffraed Cwmdeuddwr 47 C8
Llansantffraed-in-Elvel 48 D2
Llansawel 46 F5
Llansilin 60 B2
Llansoy 35 D8
Llanspyddid 34 B4
Llanstadwell 44 E4
Llansteffan 32 C4
Llanstephan 48 E3
Llantarnam 35 E7
Llanteg 32 C2
Llanthony 35 B6
Llantilio Crossenny 35 C7
Llantilio Pertholey 35 C7
Llantood 45 E3
Llantrisant Anglesey 82 C3
Mon 35 E7
Rhondda 34 F4
Llantrithyd 22 B2
Llantwit Fardre 34 F4
Llantwit Major =Llanilltud Fawr 21 C8
Llanuwchllyn 72 F2
Llanvaches 35 E8
Llanvair Discoed 35 E8
Llanvapley 35 C7
Llanvetherine 35 C7
Llanveynoe 48 F5
Llanvihangel Gobion 35 D7
Llanvihangel-Ystern-Llewern 35 C8
Llanwarne 36 B2
Llanwddyn 59 C7
Llanwenog 46 E3
Llanwern 35 F7
Llanwinio 32 B3
Llanwnda Gwyn 82 F4
Pembs 44 B4
Llanwnnen 46 E4
Llanwnog 59 E7
Llanwrda 47 F6
Llanwrin 58 D4
Llanwrthwl 47 C8
Llanwrtud =Llanwrtyd Wells 47 E7
Llanwrtyd 47 E7
Llanwrtyd Wells =Llanwrtud 47 E7
Llanwyddelan 59 D7
Llanyblodwel 60 B2
Llanybri 32 C4
Llanybydder 46 E4
Llanycefn 32 B1
Llanychaer 44 B4
Llanycil 72 F3
Llanycrwys 46 E5
Llanymawddwy 59 C6
Llanymddyfri =Llandovery 47 F6
Llanymynech 60 B2
Llanynghenedl 82 C3
Llanynys 72 C5
Llan-y-pwll 73 D7
Llanyre 48 C2
Llanystumdwy 71 D5
Llanywern 35 B5
Llawhaden 32 C1
Llawnt 73 F6
Llawr Dref 70 E3
Llawryglyn 59 E6
Llay 73 D7
Llechcynfarwy 82 C3
Llecheiddior 71 C5
Llechfaen 34 B4
Llechryd Caerph 35 D5
Ceredig 45 E4
Llechrydau 73 F6
Lledrod 46 B5
Llenmerewig 59 E8
Llethrid 33 E6
Llidiad Nenog 46 F4
Llidiardau 72 F2
Llidiart-y-parc 72 E5
Llithfaen 70 C4
Llong 73 C6
Llowes 48 E3
Llundain-fach 46 D4
Llwydcoed 34 D3
Llwyn 60 F2
Llwyncelyn 46 D3
Llwyndafydd 46 D2
Llwynderw 60 D2
Llwyn-du 35 C6
Llwyndyrys 70 C4
Llwyngwril 58 D2
Llwyn-hendy 33 E6
Llwynmawr 73 F6
Llwyn-têg 33 D6
Llwyn-y-brain 32 C2
Llwyn-y-groes 46 D4
Llwynypia 34 E3
Llynclys 60 B2
Llynfaes 82 D4
Llysfaen 83 D8
Llyswen 48 F3
Llysworney 21 B8
Llys-y-frân 32 B1
Llywel 47 F7
Loan 120 B2
Loanend 122 D5
Loanhead 121 C5
Loans 118 F3
Loans of Tullich 151 D11
Lobb 20 F3
Loch a Charnain 148 D3
Loch a' Ghainmhich 155 E7
Lochailort 147 C10
Lochaline 147 G9
Lochanhully 138 B5
Lochans 104 D4
Locharbriggs 114 F2
Lochassynt Lodge 156 G4
Lochavich House 124 D5
Lochawe 125 C7
Loch Baghasdail =Lochboisdale 148 G2
Lochboisdale = Loch Baghasdail 148 G2
Lochbuie 124 C2
Lochcarron 149 E13
Loch Choire Lodge 157 F9
Lochdhu 157 E13
Lochdochart House 126 B3
Lochdon 124 B3
Lochdrum 150 D5
Lochead 144 F6
Lochearnhead 126 B4
Lochee 134 F3
Lochend Highld 151 H8
Highld 158 D4
Locherben 114 E2
Loch Euphoirt 148 B3
Lochfoot 107 B5
Lochgair 145 D8
Lochgarthside 137 C8
Lochgelly 128 E3
Lochgilphead 145 E7
Lochgoilhead 125 E8
Loch Head 105 E7
Lochhill 152 B2
Lochindorb Lodge 151 H12
Lochinver 156 G3
Lochlane 127 B7
Loch Loyal Lodge 157 E9
Lochluichart 150 E6
Lochmaben 114 F3
Lochmaddy =Loch nam Madadh 148 B4
Lochmore Cottage 158 F2
Lochmore Lodge 156 F5
Loch nam Madadh =Lochmaddy 148 B4
Lochore 128 E3
Lochportain 148 A4
Lochranza 143 C10
Lochs Crofts 152 B3
Loch Sgioport 148 E3
Lochside Aberds 135 C7
Highld 151 F11
Highld 156 D7
Highld 157 F11
Lochslin 151 C11
Lochstack Lodge 156 E5
Lochton 141 E6
Lochty Angus 135 C5
Fife 129 D7
Perth 128 B2
Lochuisge 130 D1
Lochurr 113 F7
Lochwinnoch 118 D3
Lochwood 114 E3
Lochyside 131 B5
Lockengate 4 C5
Lockerbie 114 F4
Lockeridge 25 C6
Lockerley 14 B3
Locking 23 D5
Lockinge 38 F4
Lockington E Yorks 97 E5
Leics 63 B8
Lockleywood 61 B6
Locks Heath 15 D6
Lockton 103 E6
Lockwood 88 C2
Loddington Leics 64 D4
Northants 53 B6
Loddiswell 6 E5
Loddon 69 E6
Lode 55 C6
Loders 12 E2
Lodsworth 16 B3
Lofthouse N Yorks 94 B4
W Yorks 88 B4
Loftus 103 C5
Logan 113 B5
Loganlea 120 C2
Logan Mains 104 E4
Loggerheads 74 F4
Logie Angus 135 C6
Fife 129 B6
Moray 151 F13
Logiealmond Lodge 133 F6
Logie Coldstone 140 D3
Logie Hill 151 D10
Logie Newton 153 E6
Logie Pert 135 C6
Logierait 133 D6
Login 32 B2
Lolworth 54 C4
Lonbain 149 C11
Londesborough 96 E4
London Colney 40 D4
Londonderry 101 F8
Londonthorpe 78 F2
Londubh 155 J13
Lonemore 151 C10
Long Ashton 23 B7
Longbar 118 D3
Long Bennington 77 E8
Longbenton 111 C5
Longborough 38 B1
Long Bredy 12 E3
Longbridge Warks 51 C7
W Mid 50 B5
Longbridge Deverill 24 E3
Long Buckby 52 C4
Longburton 12 C4
Long Clawson 64 B4
Longcliffe 76 D2
Long Common 15 C6
Long Compton Staffs 62 B2
Warks 51 F7
Longcot 38 E2
Long Crendon 39 D6
Long Crichel 13 C7
Longcroft 119 B7
Longden 60 D4
Long Ditton 28 C2
Longdon Staffs 62 C4
Worcs 50 F3
Longdon Green 62 C4
Longdon on Tern 61 C6
Longdown 10 E3
Longdowns 3 C6
Long Drax 89 B7
Long Duckmanton 76 B4
Long Eaton 76 F4
Longfield Kent 29 C7
Shetland 160 M5
Longford Derbys 76 F2
Glos 37 B5
London 27 B8
Shrops 74 F3
Telford 61 C7
W Mid 63 F7
Longfordlane 76 F2
Longforgan 128 B5
Longformacus 122 D2
Longframlington 117 D7
Long Green 50 F3
Longham Dorset 13 E8
Norf 68 C2
Long Hanborough 38 C4
Longhaven 153 E11
Longhill 153 C9
Longhirst 117 F8
Longhope Glos 36 C3
Orkney 159 J4
Longhorsley 117 E7
Longhoughton 117 C8
Long Itchington 52 C2
Longlane Derbys 76 F2
W Berks 26 B2
Long Lawford 52 B2
Longlevens 37 B5
Longley 88 D2
Longley Green 50 D2
Long Load 12 B2
Longmanhill 153 B7
Long Marston Herts 40 C1
N Yorks 95 D8
Warks 51 E6
Long Marton 100 B1
Long Melford 56 E2
Longmoor Camp 27 F5
Longmorn 152 C2
Long Newnton 37 E6
Longnewton Borders 115 B8
Stockton 102 C1
Long Newton 121 C8
Longney 36 C4
Longniddry 121 B7
Longnor Shrops 60 D4
Staffs 75 C7
Longparish 26 E2
Longport 75 E5
Long Preston 93 D8
Longridge Lancs 93 F6
Staffs 62 C3
W Loth 120 C2
Longriggend 119 B8
Long Riston 97 E7
Longrock 2 C4
Longsdon 75 D6
Longshaw 86 D3
Longside 153 D10
Long Sight 87 D7
Longstanton 54 C4
Longstock 25 F8
Longstone 32 D2
Longstowe 54 D4
Long Stratton 68 E4
Long Street 53 E5
Long Sutton Hants 26 E5
Lincs 66 B4
Som 12 B2
Longthorpe 65 E8
Long Thurlow 56 C4
Longthwaite 99 B6
Longton Lancs 86 B2
Stoke 75 E6
Longtown Cumb 108 C3
Hereford 35 B7
Longview 86 E2
Longville in the Dale 60 E5
Long Whatton 63 B8
Longwick 39 D7
Long Wittenham 39 E5
Longwitton 117 F6
Longwood 61 D6
Longworth 38 E3
Longyester 121 C8
Lonmay 153 C10
Lonmore 148 D7
Looe 5 D7
Loose 29 D8
Loosley Row 39 D8
Lopcombe Corner 25 F7
Lopen 12 C2
Loppington 60 B4
Lopwell 6 C2
Lorbottle 117 D6
Lorbottle Hall 117 D6
Lornty 134 E1
Loscoe 76 E4
Losgaintir 154 H5
Lossiemouth 152 A2
Lossit 142 C2
Lostford 74 F3
Lostock Gralam 74 B3
Lostock Green 74 B3
Lostock Hall 86 B3
Lostock Junction 86 D4
Lostwithiel 5 D6
Loth 159 E7
Lothbeg 157 H12
Lothersdale 94 E2
Lothmore 157 H12
Loudwater 40 E2
Loughborough 64 C2
Loughor 33 E6
Loughton Essex 41 E7
M Keynes 53 F6
Shrops 61 F6
Lound Lincs 65 C7
Notts 89 F7
Suff 69 E8
Lount 63 C7
Louth 91 F7
Love Clough 87 B6
Lovedean 15 C7
Lover 14 B3
Loversall 89 E6
Loves Green 42 D2
Lovesome Hill 102 E1
Loveston 32 D1
Lovington 23 F7
Low Ackworth 89 C5
Low Barlings 78 B3
Low Bentham 93 C6
Low Bradfield 88 E3
Low Bradley 94 E3
Lowbridge House 99 D7
Low Brunton 110 B2
Low Burnham 89 D8
Low Burton 101 F7
Low Buston 117 D8
Lowca 98 B1
Low Catton 96 D3
Low Clanyard 104 F5
Low Coniscliffe 101 C7
Low Crosby 108 D4
Low Dalby 103 F6
Lowdham 77 E6
Low Dinsdale 101 C8
Lowe 74 F2
Lowe Hill 75 D6
Low Ellington 101 F7
Lower Aisholt 22 F4
Lower Arncott 39 C6
Lower Ashton 10 F3
Lower Assendon 39 F7
Lower Badcall 156 E4
Lower Bartle 92 F4
Lower Basildon 26 B4
Lower Beeding 17 B6
Lower Benefield 65 F6
Lower Boddington 52 D2
Lower Brailes 51 F8
Lower Breakish 149 F11
Lower Broadheath 50 D3
Lower Bullingham 49 F7
Lower Cam 36 D4
Lower Chapel 48 F2
Lower Chute 25 D8
Lower Cragabus 142 D4
Lower Crossings 87 F8
Lower Cumberworth 88 D3
Lower Darwen 86 B4
Lower Dean 53 C8
Lower Diabaig 149 B12
Lower Dicker 18 D2
Lower Dinchope 60 F4
Lower Down 60 F3
Lower Drift 2 D3
Lower Dunsforth 95 C7
Lower Egleton 49 E8
Lower Elkstone 75 D7
Lower End 40 B2
Lower Everleigh 25 D6
Lower Farringdon 26 F5
Lower Foxdale 84 E2
Lower Frankton 73 F7
Lower Froyle 27 E5
Lower Gledfield 151 B8
Lower Green 81 D5
Lower Hacheston 57 D7
Lower Halistra 148 C7
Lower Halstow 30 C2
Lower Hardres 31 D5
Lower Hawthwaite 98 F4
Lower Heath 75 C5
Lower Hempriggs 151 E14
Lower Hergest 48 D4
Lower Heyford 38 B4
Lower Higham 29 B8
Lower Holbrook 57 F5
Lower Hordley 60 B3
Lower Horsebridge 18 D2
Lower Killeyan 142 D3
Lower Kingswood 28 D3
Lower Kinnerton 73 C7
Lower Langford 23 C6
Lower Largo 129 D6
Lower Leigh 75 F7
Lower Lemington 51 F7
Lower Lenie 137 B8
Lower Lydbrook 36 C2
Lower Lye 49 C6
Lower Machen 35 F6
Lower Maes-coed 48 F5
Lower Mayland 43 D5
Lower Midway 63 B7
Lower Milovaig 148 C6
Lower Moor 50 E4
Lower Nazeing 41 D6
Lower Netchwood 61 E6
Lower Ollach 149 E10
Lower Penarth 22 B3
Lower Penn 62 E2
Lower Pennington 14 E4
Lower Peover 74 B4
Lower Pexhill 75 B5
Lower Place 87 C7
Lower Quinton 51 E6
Lower Rochford 49 C8
Lower Seagry 37 F6
Lower Shelton 53 E7
Lower Shiplake 27 B5
Lower Shuckburgh 52 C2
Lower Slaughter 38 B1
Lower Stanton St Quintin 37 F6
Lower Stoke 30 B2
Lower Stondon 54 F2
Lower Stow Bedon 68 E2
Lower Street Norf 69 C6
Norf 81 D8
Lower Strensham 50 E4
Lower Stretton 86 F4
Lower Sundon 40 B3
Lower Swanwick 15 D5
Lower Swell 38 B1
Lower Tean 75 F7
Lower Thurlton 69 E7
Lower Tote 149 B10
Lower Town 44 B4
Lower Tysoe 51 E8
Lower Upham 15 C6
Lower Vexford 22 F3
Lower Weare 23 D6
Lower Welson 48 D4
Lower Whitley 74 B3
Lower Wield 26 E4
Lower Winchendon 39 C7
Lower Withington 74 C5
Lower Woodend 39 F8
Lower Woodford 25 F6
Lower Wyche 50 E2
Lowesby 64 D4
Lowestoft 69 E8
Loweswater 98 B3
Low Etherley 101 B6
Low Fell 111 D5
Lowford 15 C5
Low Fulney 66 B2
Low Garth 103 D5
Low Gate 110 C2
Lowgill Cumb 99 E8
Lancs 93 C6
Low Grantley 94 B5
Low Habberley 50 B3
Low Ham 12 B2
Low Hesket 108 E4
Low Hesleyhurst 117 E6
Low Hutton 96 C3
Lowick Northants 65 F6
Northumb 123 F6
Lowick Bridge 98 F4
Lowick Green 98 F4
Low Laithe 94 C4
Lowlands 35 E6
Low Leighton 87 F8
Low Lorton 98 B3
Low Marishes 96 B4
Low Marnham 77 C8
Low Mill 102 E4
Low Moor Lancs 93 E7
W Yorks 88 B2
Lowmoor Row 99 B8
Low Moorsley 111 E6
Low Newton 99 F6
Low Newton-by-the-Sea 117 B8
Lownie Moor 134 E4
Low Row Cumb 108 F3
Cumb 109 C5
N Yorks 100 E4
Low Salchrie 104 C4
Low Smerby 143 F8
Lowsonford 51 C6
Lowther 99 B7
Lowthorpe 97 C6
Lowton 86 E4
Lowton Common 86 E4
Low Torry 128 F2
Low Worsall 102 D1
Low Wray 99 D5
Loxbeare 10 C4
Loxhill 27 F8
Loxhore 20 F5
Loxley 51 D7
Loxton 23 D5
Loxwood 27 F8
Lubcroy 156 J6
Lubenham 64 F4
Luccombe 21 E8
Luccombe Village 15 G6
Lucker 123 F7
Luckett 5 B8
Luckington 37 F5
Lucklawhill 129 B6
Luckwell Bridge 21 F8
Lucton 49 C6
Ludag 148 G2
Ludborough 91 E6
Ludchurch 32 C2
Luddenden 87 B8
Luddenden Foot 87 B8
Luddesdown 29 C7
Luddington N Lincs 90 C2
Warks 51 D6
Luddington in the Brook 65 F8
Lude House 133 C5
Ludford Lincs 91 E6
Shrops 49 B7
Ludgershall Bucks 39 C6
Wilts 25 D7
Ludgvan 2 C4
Ludham 69 C6
Ludlow 49 B7
Ludwell 13 B7
Ludworth 111 E6
Luffincott 8 E5
Lugar 113 B5
Lugate Burn 122 B2
Lugg Green 49 C6
Luggiebank 119 B7

Lugton.........118 D4
Lugwardine.....49 E7
Luib.........149 F10
Lulham........49 E6
Lullenden......28 E5
Lullington Derbys..63 C6
  Som........24 D2
Lulsgate Bottom..23 C7
Lulsley.......50 D2
Lumb.........87 B8
Lumby........95 F7
Lumloch......119 C6
Lumphanan....140 D4
Lumphinnans...128 E3
Lumsdaine.....122 C4
Lumsden......140 B3
Lunan.......135 D6
Lunanhead....134 D4
Luncarty.....128 B2
Lund E Yorks....97 E5
  N Yorks......96 F2
  Shetland....160 C7
Lunderton....153 D11
Lundie Angus..134 F2
  Highld.......136 C4
Lundin Links..129 D6
Lunga.......124 E3
Lunna.......160 G6
Lunning.....160 G7
Lunnon........33 F6
Lunsford's Cross..18 D4
Lunt.........85 D4
Luntley.......49 D5
Luppitt.......11 D6
Lupset........88 C4
Lupton........99 F7
Lurgashall.....16 B3
Lusby.......126 E2
Luson..........6 E4
Luss........126 E2
Lussagiven....144 E5
Lusta........149 C7
Lustleigh.....10 F2
Luston.......49 C6
Luthermuir...135 C6
Luthrie......128 C5
Luton Devon......7 B7
  Luton.......40 B3
  Medway......29 C8
Lutterworth...64 F2
Lutton Devon.....6 D3
  Lincs........66 B4
  Northants....65 F8
Lutworthy....10 C2
Luxborough....21 F8
Luxulyan.......5 D5
Lybster.....158 G4
Lydbury North..60 F3
Lydcott......21 F5
Lydd.........19 C7
Lydden.......31 E6
Lyddington....65 E5
Lydd on Sea....19 C7
Lydeard
  St Lawrence...22 F3
Lyde Green.....26 B5
Lydford........8 F7
Lydford-on-Fosse.23 F7
Lydgate.......87 B7
Lydham.......60 E3
Lydiard Green...37 F7
Lydiard Millicent.37 F7
Lydiate.......85 D4
Lydlinch......12 C5
Lydney.......36 D3
Lydstep......32 E1
Lye..........62 F3
Lye Green Bucks..40 D2
  E Sus........18 B2
Lyford........38 E3
Lymbridge Green..30 E5
Lyme Regis....11 E8
Lyminge......31 E5
Lymington....14 E4
Lyminster.....16 D4
Lymm.........86 F4
Lymore.......14 E3
Lympne.......19 B8
Lympsham......22 D5
Lympstone....10 F4
Lynchat......138 D3
Lyndale House..149 C8
Lyndhurst....14 D4
Lyndon.......65 D6
Lyne..........27 C8
Lyneal........73 F8
Lyne Down.....49 F8
Lyneham Oxon...38 B2
  Wilts.......24 B5
Lynemore....139 B6
Lynemouth....117 E8
Lyne of
  Gorthleck...137 B8
Lyne of Skene..141 C6
Lyness.......159 J4
Lyng Norf......68 C3
  Som........11 B8
Lynmouth.....21 E6
Lynsted......30 C3
Lynton.......21 E6
Lyon's Gate...12 D4
Lyonshall.....48 D5
Lytchett Matravers..13 E7
Lytchett Minster..13 E7
Lyth.........158 D4
Lytham........85 B4
Lytham St Anne's..85 B4
Lythe.......103 C6
Lythes......159 K5

M

Mabe Burnthouse....3 C6
Mabie.......107 B6
Mablethorpe...91 F9
Macclesfield...75 B6
Macclesfield
  Forest.......75 B6
Macduff......153 B7
Mace Green....56 E5
Macharioch...143 H8
Machen.......35 F6
Machrihanish..143 F7
Machynlleth...58 D4
Machynys......33 E6
Mackerel's
  Common....16 B4
Mackworth....76 F3

Macmerry.....121 B7
Madderty....127 B8
Maddiston...120 B2
Madehurst....16 C3
Madeley Staffs..74 E4
  Telford........61 D6
Madeley Heath..74 E4
Madeley Park..74 E4
Madingley.....54 C4
Madley.......49 F6
Madresfield....50 E3
Madron........2 C3
Maenaddwyn...82 C4
Maenclochog...32 B1
Maendy........22 B2
Maentwrog....71 C7
Maen-y-groes..46 D2
Maer.........74 F4
Maerdy Conwy..72 E4
  Rhondda......34 E3
Maesbrook....60 B2
Maesbury.....60 B3
Maesbury Marsh..60 B3
Maesgwyn-Isaf..59 C8
Maesgwynne...32 B3
Maeshafn......73 C6
Maesllyn......46 E2
Maesmynis....48 E2
Maesteg......34 E2
Maestir.......46 E4
Maes-Treylow...48 C4
Maesybont....33 C6
Maesycrugiau...46 E3
Maesymeillion..46 E3
Magdalen Laver..41 D8
Maggieknockater 152 D3
Magham Down..18 D3
Maghull.......85 D4
Magor........35 F8
Magpie Green...56 B4
Maiden Bradley..24 F3
Maidencombe....7 C7
Maidenhall.....57 E5
Maidenhead....40 F1
Maiden Law...110 E4
Maiden Newton..12 E3
Maidens......112 D2
Maidensgrave...57 E6
Maiden's Green..27 B6
Maidenwell Corn...5 B6
  Lincs.......79 B6
Maiden Wells..44 F4
Maidford......52 D4
Maids Moreton..52 F5
Maidstone.....29 D8
Maidwell......52 B5
Mail........160 L6
Main.........59 C8
Maindee.......35 F7
Mainsforth...111 F6
Mains of Airies..104 C3
Mains of
  Allardice....135 B8
Mains of
  Annochie...153 D9
Mains of Ardestie 135 F5
Mains of Balhall..135 C5
Mains of
  Ballindarg..134 D4
  Kent.........29 E8
  T&W........111 B6
  Wilts........25 D5
Marden Beech..29 E8
Marden Thorn..29 E8
Mardy.........35 C7
Marefield......64 D4
Mareham le Fen..79 C5
Mareham on the
  Hill.........79 C5
Marehay.......76 E3
Marehill......16 C4
Maresfield....17 B8
Marfleet......90 B5
Marford.......73 D7
Margam........34 F1
Margaret Marsh..13 C6
Margaret Roding..42 C1
Margaretting...42 D2
Margate.......31 B7
Margnaheglish..143 E11
Margrove Park..102 C4
Marham.......67 C7
Marhamchurch...8 D4
Marholm.......65 D8
Mariandyrrs...83 C6
Marianglas....82 C5
Marian-glas....82 C5
Mariansleigh..10 B2
Marionburgh..141 D6
Marishader...149 B9
Marjoriebanks..114 F3
Mark Dumfries..104 D5
  S Ayrs......104 B4
  Som........23 E5
Markbeech....29 E5
Markby.......79 B7
Mark Causeway...23 E5
Mark Cross E Sus..17 C8
  E Sus.......18 B2
Market
  Harborough...64 F4
Markethill...134 F2
Market Lavington..24 D5
Market Overton..65 C5
Market Rasen..90 F5
Market Stainton..78 B5
Market Warsop..77 C5
Market Weighton..96 F4
Market Weston..56 B3
Markfield.....63 C8
Markham......35 D5
Markham Moor..77 B7
Markinch....128 D4
Markington....95 C5
Marksbury....23 C8
Marks Tey.....43 B5
Markyate.....40 C3
Marland.......87 C6
Marlborough...25 C6
Marlbrook Hereford 49 D7
  Worcs........50 B4
Marlcliff......51 D5
Marldon.......7 C6
Marlesford....57 D7
Marley Green..74 E2
Marley Hill..110 D5

Marley Mount..14 E3
Marlingford...68 D4
Mar Lodge....139 E6
Marloes.......44 E2
Marlow Bucks...39 F8
  Hereford......49 B6
Marlow Bottom..40 F1
Marlpit Hill...28 E5
Marlpool......76 E4
Marnhull......13 C5
Marnoch.....152 C5
Marnock.....119 C7
Marple........87 F7
Marple Bridge..87 F7
Marr..........89 D6
Marrel.......157 H13
Marrick......101 E5
Marrister....160 G7
Marros........32 D3
Marsden T&W...111 C6
  W Yorks......87 C8
Marsett......100 F4
Marsh Devon....11 C7
  W Yorks......94 F3
Marshall's Heath..40 C4
Marshalsea....11 D8
Marshalswick...40 D4
Marsham......81 E7
Marshaw......93 D5
Marsh Baldon..39 E5
Marshborough..31 D7
Marshbrook....60 F4
Marshchapel...91 E7
Marshfield Newport 35 F6
  S Glos.......24 B2
Marshgate......8 E3
Marsh Gibbon..39 B6
Marsh Green Devon 10 E5
  Kent.........28 E5
  Staffs.......75 D5
Marshland
  St James.....66 D5
Marshland
  St James.....66 D5
Marsh Lane....76 B4
Marshside.....85 C4
Marsh Street..21 E8
Marshwood....11 E8
Marske......101 D6
Marske-by-the-
  Sea........102 B4
Marston Ches W..74 B3
  Hereford......49 D5
  Lincs........77 E8
  Oxon........39 D5
  Staffs.......62 B3
  Staffs.......62 C2
  Warks........63 E6
  Wilts.......24 D4
Marston Doles..52 D2
Marston Green..63 F5
Marston Magna..12 B3
Marston Meysey..37 E8
Marston
  Montgomery...75 F8
Marston
  Moretaine....53 E7
Marston on Dove..63 B6
Marston
  St Lawrence..52 E3
Marston Stannett..49 D7
Marstow.......36 C2
Marsworth....40 C2
Marten........25 D7
Marthall......74 B5
Martham.......69 C7
Martin Hants..13 C8
  Kent.........31 E7
  Lincs........78 C5
  Lincs........78 D4
Martin Dales..78 C4
Martin Drove End..13 B8
Martinhoe.....21 E5
Martinhoe Cross..21 E5
Martin
  Hussingtree..50 C3
Martin Mill...31 E7
Martinscroft...86 F4
Martinstown...12 F4
Martlesham....57 E6
Martlesham Heath..57 E6
Martletwy......32 C1
Martley.......50 D2
Martock.......12 C2
Marton Ches E..75 C5
  E Yorks......97 F7
  Lincs........90 F2
  Mbro.......102 C3
  N Yorks......95 C7
  N Yorks.....103 F5
Marton-le-Moor..95 B6
Martyr's Green..27 D8
Martyr Worthy..26 F3
Marwick......159 F3
Marwood.......20 F4
Marybank.....150 F7
Maryburgh....151 F8
Maryhill.....119 C5
Marykirk.....135 C6
Marylebone....86 D3
Marypark.....152 E1
Maryport Cumb..107 F7
  Dumfries....104 F5
Mary Tavy......6 B3
Maryton.......135 D6
Marywell Aberds..140 E4
  Aberds......141 E8
  Angus.......135 E6
Masham.......101 F7
Mashbury......42 C2
Masongill.....93 B6
Masonhill....112 B3
Mastin Moor...76 B4
Mastrick.....141 D7
Matching......41 C8
Matching Green..41 C8
Matching Tye...41 C8
Matfen.......110 B3
Matfield......29 E7
Mathern.......36 E2
Mathon........50 E2
Mathry........44 B3
Matlaske......81 D7
Matlock.......76 C2
Matlock Bath...76 D2
Matson........37 C5
Mattersey.....89 F7

Mattersey.....89 F7
Mattersey Thorpe..89 F7
Mattingley....26 D5
Mattishall....68 C3
Mattishall Burgh..68 C3
Maud........153 D9
Maugersbury...38 B2
Maughold......84 C4
Mauld.......150 H7
Maulden......53 F8
Maulds Meaburn..99 C8
Maunby......102 F1
Maund Bryan...49 E7
Maundown......11 B5
Mautby.......69 C7
Mavis Enderby..79 C6
Mawbray.....107 E7
Mawdesley....86 C2
Mawdlam.......34 F2
Mawgan........3 D6
Maw Green.....74 D4
Mawla.........3 B6
Mawnan........3 D6
Mawnan Smith...3 D6
Mawsley.......53 B6
Maxey........65 D8
Maxstoke......63 F6
Maxton Borders..122 F3
  Kent.........31 E7
Maxwellheath..122 F3
Maxwelltown..107 B6
Maxworthy......8 E4
Mayals........33 E7
May Bank......74 E5
Maybole.....112 D3
Mayfield E Sus..18 C2
  Midloth....121 C6
  Staffs.......75 E8
  W Loth.....120 C2
Mayford.......27 D7
Mayland.......43 D5
Maynard's Green..18 D2
Maypole Mon....36 C1
  Scilly.........2 E4
Maypole Green
  Essex.......43 B5
  Norf........69 E7
  Suff........57 C6
Maywick.....160 L5
Meadle.......39 D8
Meadowtown...60 D3
Meaford......75 F5
Meal Bank.....99 E7
Mealsgate...108 E2
Meanwood.....95 F5
Mearbeck.....93 C8
Meare........23 E6
Meare Green..11 B8
Mears Ashby..53 C6
Measham.......63 C7
Meath Green..28 E3
Meathop.......99 F6
Meaux........97 F6
Meavy.........6 C3
Medbourne...64 E4
Medburn.....110 B4
Meddon........8 C4
Meden Vale....77 C5
Medlam.......79 D6
Medmenham....39 F8
Medomsley...110 D4
Medstead.....26 F4
Meerbrook.....75 C6
Meer End......51 B7
Meers Bridge..91 F8
Meesden......54 F5
Meeth.........9 D7
Meggethead..114 B4
Meidrim......32 B3
Meifod Denb...72 D4
  Powys.......59 C8
Meigle N Ayrs..118 C1
  Perth.......134 E2
Meikle Earnock 119 D7
Meikle Ferry..151 C10
Meikle Forter..134 C1
Meikle Gluich..151 C9
Meikleour.....134 F1
Meikle Pinkerton 122 B3
Meikle Strath..135 B6
Meikle Tarty..141 B8
Meikle Wartle..153 E7
Meinciau......33 C5
Meir.........75 E6
Meir Heath....75 E6
Melbourne Derbys..63 B7
  E Yorks......96 E3
  S Lanark....120 E3
Melbury Abbas..13 B6
Melbury Bubb..12 D3
Melbury Osmond..12 D3
Melbury Sampford 12 D3
Melby.......160 H3
Melchbourne..53 C8
Melcombe
  Bingham....13 D5
Melcombe Regis..12 F4
Meldon Devon....9 E7
  Northumb....117 F7
Meldreth......54 E4
Meldrum House..141 B7
Melfort......124 D4
Melgarve....137 E7
Meliden.......72 A4
Melin-y-coed..83 E8
Melin-y-grug..59 D7
Melin-y-Wig...72 E4
Melkinthorpe..99 B7
Melkridge...109 C7
Melksham.....24 C4
Melldalloch..145 F8
Melling Lancs..93 B5
  Mers........85 D4
Melling Mount..86 D2
Mellis........56 B5
Mellon Charles..155 H13
Mellon Udrigle..155 H13
Mellor Gtr Man..87 F7
  Lancs........93 F6
Mellor Brook..93 F6
Matterdale End..99 B5

Melmerby Cumb..109 F6
  N Yorks......95 B6
  N Yorks.....101 F5
Melplash......12 E2
Melrose.....121 F8
Melsetter...159 K3
Melsonby....101 D6
Meltham......88 C2
Melton.......57 D6
Meltonby......96 D3
Melton Constable..81 D6
Melton Mowbray..64 C4
Melton Ross...90 C4
Melvaig.....155 J12
Melverley.....60 C3
Melverley Green..60 C3
Membury......11 D7
Memsie......153 B9
Memus.......134 D4
Menabilly......5 D5
Menai Bridge
  = Porthaethwy..83 D5
Mendham......69 F5
Mendlesham...56 C5
Mendlesham
  Green.......56 C4
Menheniot......5 C7
Mennock.....113 D8
Menston......94 E4
Menstrie....127 E7
Menthorpe....96 F2
Mentmore......40 C2
Meoble.....147 C10
Meole Brace...60 C4
Meols.........85 E3
Meonstoke....15 C7
Meopham......29 C7
Meopham Station..29 C7
Mepal.........66 F4
Meppershall...54 F2
Merbach......48 E5
Mere Ches E...74 B4
  Wilts.......24 F3
Mere Brow.....86 C2
Mereclough....93 F8
Mere Green....62 E5
Mereside......92 F3
Mereworth....29 D7
Mergie.......141 F6
Meriden.......63 F6
Merkadale....149 E8
Merkland Dumfries 106 B4
  S Ayrs.....112 E2
Merkland Lodge..156 G7
Merley........13 E8
Merlin's Bridge..44 D4
Merrington....60 B4
Merrion.......44 F4
Merriott......12 C2
Merrivale......6 B3
Merrow........27 D7
Merrymeet......5 C7
Mersham......30 E4
Merstham.....28 D3
Merston.......16 D2
Merstone.....15 F6
Merther........3 B7
Merthyr.......32 B3
Merthyr Cynog..47 F8
Merthyr-Dyfan..22 C3
Merthyr Mawr...21 B7
Merthyr Tudful
  = Merthyr Tydfil..34 D4
Merthyr Tydfil
  = Merthyr Tudful..34 D4
Merthyr Vale...34 E4
Merton
  Devon.........9 C7
  London.......28 B3
  Norf.........68 E2
  Oxon........39 C5
Mervinslaw...116 C2
Meshaw.......10 C2
Messing......42 C4
Messingham...90 D2
Metfield......69 F5
Metheringham..78 C3
Methil......129 E5
Methlem.......70 D2
Methley.......88 B4
Methlick......153 E8
Methven.....128 B2
Methwold......67 E7
Methwold Hythe..67 E7
Mettingham...69 F6
Mevagissey.....3 B9
Mewith Head...93 C7
Mexborough...89 D5
Mey.........158 C4
Meysey Hampton..37 E8
Miabhag W Isles..154 G5
  W Isles.....154 H6
Miabhig.....154 D5
Michaelchurch..36 B2
Michaelchurch
  Escley.......48 F5
Michaelchurch on
  Arrow.......48 D4
Michaelston-le-
  Pit.........22 B3
Michaelston-y-
  Fedw........35 F6
Michaelstow....5 B5
Michaelston-super-
  Ely.........22 B3
Michaeldever...26 F3
Michelmersh...14 B4
Mickfield.....56 C5
Micklebring...89 E6
Mickleby.....103 C6
Mickleham....28 D2
Mickleover....76 F3
Micklethwaite..94 E4
Mickleton Durham..110 F4
  Glos.........51 E6
Mickletown....88 B4
Mickle Trafford..73 C8
Mickley.......95 B5
Mickley Square..110 C3
Mid Ardlaw...153 B9
Mid Auchinleck..118 B3
Midbea.......159 D5
Mid Beltie...140 D5
Mid Calder...120 C3
Mid Cloch Forbie..153 C7
Mid Clyth....158 G4
Middle Assendon..39 F7
Middle Aston..38 B4

Melmerby Cumb..109 F6
Middle Barton..38 B4
Middlebie...108 B2
Middle
  Cairncake..153 D8
Middle Claydon..39 B7
Middle Drums..135 D5
Middleforth Green 86 B3
Middleham...101 F6
Middle Handley..76 B4
Middlehope....60 F4
Middle Littleton..51 E5
Middle Maes-coed 48 F5
Middlemarsh...12 D4
Middle Mill....44 C3
Middlemuir...141 B8
Middle Rasen..90 F4
Middle Rigg..128 D2
Middlesceugh..108 E3
Middleshaw Cumb..99 F7
  Dumfries....107 B8
Middlesmoor...94 B3
Middlestone..111 F5
Middlestone
  Moor.......110 F5
Middlestown...88 C3
Middlethird..122 E2
Middleton Aberds..141 C7
  Argyll......146 G2
  Cumb........99 F8
  Derbys......75 C8
  Derbys......76 D2
  Essex........56 F2
  Gtr Man......87 D6
  Hants........26 E2
  Hereford......49 C7
  Lancs........92 D4
  Midloth.....121 D6
  Norf.........67 C6
  Northants....64 F5
  Northumb....117 F6
  Northumb....123 F7
  N Yorks......94 E4
  N Yorks.....103 F5
  Perth.......128 D3
  Perth.......133 E8
  Shrops......49 B7
  Shrops......60 B3
  Shrops......60 E2
  Suff........57 C8
  Swansea......33 F5
  Warks........63 E6
  W Yorks......88 B3
Middleton Cheney..52 E2
Middleton Green..75 F6
Middleton Hall..117 B5
Middleton-in-
  Teesdale....100 B4
Middleton Moor..57 C8
Middleton One
  Row........102 C1
Middleton-on-
  Leven.......102 D2
Middleton-on-Sea 16 D3
Middleton on the
  Hill.........49 C7
Middleton-on-the-
  Wolds.......96 E5
Middleton Priors..61 E6
Middleton
  Quernham...95 B6
Middleton St George.101 C8
Middleton Scriven..61 F6
Middleton Stoney..39 B5
Middleton Tyas..101 D7
Middletown Cumb..98 D1
  Powys........60 C3
Middle Tysoe...51 E8
Middle Wallop..25 F7
Middlewich....74 C3
Middle Winterslow..25 F7
Middle Woodford..25 F6
Middlewood
  Green.......56 C4
Middlezoy.....23 F5
Midfield....157 C8
Midge Hall....86 B3
Midgeholme..109 D6
Midgham......26 C3
Midgley W Yorks..87 B8
  W Yorks......88 C3
Midhopestones..88 E3
Midhurst......16 B2
Mid Lavant...16 D2
Midlem......115 B8
Mid Main....150 H7
Midmar......141 D5
Midsomer Norton..23 D8
Midton......118 B2
Midtown Highld..155 J13
  Highld.....157 C8
Midtown of
  Buchromb....152 D3
Mid Urchany..151 G11
  Highld.......79 D6
Mid Walls....160 H4
Midway.......87 F7
Mid Yell.....160 D7
Migdale.....151 B9
Migvie......140 D3
Milarrochy...126 E3
Milborne Port..12 C4
Milborne
  St Andrew....13 E6
Milborne Wick..12 B4
Milbourne
  Northumb....110 B4
  Wilts.......37 F6
Milburn......100 B1
Milbury Heath..36 E3
Milcombe......52 F2
Milden........56 E3
Mildenhall Suff..55 B8
  Wilts.......25 C7
Mildmay.......48 B5
Milebrook.....48 B5
Milebush......29 E8
Mile Cross....68 C5
Mile Elm......24 C4
Mile End Essex..43 B5
  Glos.........36 C2
Mileham.......68 C2
Mile Oak......17 D6
Milesmark...128 F2
Milfield.....122 F5
Milford Derbys..76 E3
  Devon.........8 B4
  Powys.......59 E7
  Staffs.......62 B3
  Sur..........27 E7
  Wilts........14 B2

Milford Haven
  = Aberdaugleddau..44 E4
Milford on Sea..14 E3
Milkwall......36 D2
Milkwell......13 B7
Millarston...118 C4
Millbank
  Aberds.....153 D11
  Highld.....158 D3
Millbeck......98 B4
Millbounds..159 E6
Millbreck....153 D10
Millbridge....27 E6
Millbrook C Beds..53 F8
  Corn..........6 D2
  Hants.........14 C4
Mill Common...69 F7
Millcorner....18 C5
Milldale......75 D8
Millden Lodge..135 B5
Milldens....135 D5
Mill End Bucks..39 F7
  Herts.......54 F4
Millerhill...121 C6
Miller's Dale..75 B8
Miller's Green..76 D2
Millgreen....61 B6
Mill Green Essex..42 D2
  Norf.........68 F4
  Suff.........56 E3
Millhalf.......48 E4
Millhayes.....11 D7
Millhead......92 B4
Millheugh...119 D7
Mill Hill.....41 E5
Millholme.....99 E7
Millhouse Argyll..145 F8
  Cumb........108 F3
Millhousebridge..114 F4
Millhouse Green..88 D3
Millhouses....88 F4
Millikenpark..118 C4
Millin Cross...44 D4
Millington....96 D4
Mill Lane.....27 D5
Millmeece.....74 F5
Mill of Kingoodie 141 B7
Mill of Muiresk..153 D6
Mill of Sterin..140 E2
Mill of Uras..141 F7
Millom........98 F3
Millook........8 E3
Mill Place....90 D3
Millpool.......5 B6
Millport....145 H10
Millquarter..113 F6
Mill Side.....99 F6
Mill Street...68 C3
Millthorpe....78 F4
Millthrop....100 E1
Milltimber...141 D7
Milltown Corn....5 D6
  Derbys.......76 C3
  Devon.......20 F4
  Dumfries...108 B3
Milltown of
  Aberdalgie..128 B2
Milltown of
  Auchindoun..152 D3
Milltown of
  Edinvillie..152 D2
Milltown of
  Kildrummy..140 C3
Milltown of
  Rothiemay..152 D5
Milltown of
  Towie.......140 C3
Milnathort..128 D3
Milner's Heath..73 C8
Milngavie...119 B5
Milnrow......87 C7
Milnshaw.....87 B5
Milnthorpe....99 F6
Milo..........33 C6
Milson........49 B8
Milstead.....30 D3
Milston......25 E6
Milton Angus..134 E3
  Cambs.......55 C5
  Cumb.......109 C5
  Derbys.......63 B7
  Dumfries...105 D6
  Dumfries...106 B5
  Dumfries...113 F8
  Highld.....150 F7
  Highld.....150 H6
  Highld.....151 D10
  Highld.....151 G8
  Highld.....158 E5
  Moray......152 B5
  N Som.......22 C5
  Notts........77 B7
  Oxon.........38 E4
  Oxon.........52 F2
  Pembs.......32 D1
  Perth.......127 C8
  Ptsmth.......15 E7
  Stirling....126 D4
  Stoke........75 D6
  W Dunb......118 B4
Milton Abbas..13 D6
Milton Abbot...6 B2
Milton Bridge..120 C5
Milton Bryan..53 F7
Milton Clevedon..23 F8
Milton Coldwells 153 E9
Milton Combe...6 C2
Milton Damerel..9 C5
Milton End....37 D8
Milton Ernest..53 D8
Milton Green..73 D8
Miltonhill...151 E13
Milton Hill....38 E4
Miltonise....105 B5
Milton Keynes..53 F6
Milton Keynes
  Village......53 F6
Milton Lilbourne..25 C6
Milton Malsor..52 D5
Milton Morenish 132 F3
Milton of
  Auchinhove..140 D4

Milton of
  Balgonie....128 D5
Milton of
  Buchanan...126 E3
Milton of
  Campfield..140 D5
Milton of
  Campsie....119 B6
Milton of
  Corsindae..141 D5
Milton of
  Cushnie....140 C4
Milton of
  Dalcapon...133 D6
Milton of
  Edradour...133 D6
Milton of
  Gollanfield..151 F10
Milton of
  Lesmore....140 B3
Milton of Logie..140 D3
Milton of Murtle..141 D7
Milton of Noth..140 B4
Milton of Tullich..140 E2
Milton on Stour..13 B5
Milton Regis..30 C3
Milton under
  Wychwood...38 C2
Milverton Som..11 B6
  Warks......51 C8
Milwich........75 F6
Minard........124 F4
Minchinhampton..37 D5
Mindrum.....122 F4
Minehead......21 E8
Minera........73 D6
Minety........37 E7
Minffordd Gwyn..58 C4
  Gwyn........71 D6
  Gwyn........83 D5
Miningsby.....79 C6
Minions........5 B7
Minishant....112 C3
Minllyn.......59 C5
Minnes......141 B8
Minngearraidh..148 F2
Minnigaff....105 C8
Minnonie....153 B7
Minskip.......95 C6
Minstead......14 C3
Minsted.......16 B2
Minster Kent..30 B3
  Kent.........31 C7
Minsterley....60 D3
Minster Lovell..38 C3
Minsterworth..36 C4
Minterne Magna..12 D4
Minting.......78 B4
Mintlaw......153 D9
Minto.......115 B8
Minton.......60 E4
Minwear......32 C1
Minworth......63 E5
Mirbister....159 F4
Mirehouse.....98 C1
Mireland....158 D5
Mirfield......88 C3
Miserden......37 D6
Miskin........34 F4
Misson........89 E7
Misterton Leics..64 F2
  Notts.......89 E8
  Som........12 D2
Mistley.......56 F5
Mitcham......28 C3
Mitcheldean...36 C3
Mitchell........4 D3
Mitchel Troy..36 C1
Mitcheltroy
  Common.....36 D1
Mitford......117 F7
Mithian........4 D2
Mitton.........62 C2
Mixbury......52 F4
Moat.........108 B4
Moats Tye....56 D4
Mobberley Ches E..74 B4
  Staffs.......75 E7
Moccas.......49 E5
Mochdre Conwy..83 D8
  Powys.......59 F7
Mochrum.....105 E7
Mockbeggar...14 D2
Mockerkin.....98 B2
Modbury........6 D4
Moddershall...75 F6
Moelfre Anglesey..82 C5
  Powys.......59 B8
Moffat......114 D3
Moggerhanger..54 E2
Moira........63 C7
Molash........30 D4
Mol-chlach..149 G9
Mold
  = Yr Wyddgrug..73 C6
Moldgreen....88 C2
Molehill Green..42 B1
Molescroft....97 E6
Molesden....117 F7
Molesworth...53 B8
Moll.........149 E10
Molland.......10 B3
Mollington Ches W..73 B7
  Oxon.........52 E2
Mollinsburn..119 B7
Monachty......46 C4
Monachylemore..126 C3
Monar Lodge..150 G5
Monaughty....48 C4
Monboddo House 135 B7
Mondynes....135 B7
Monevechadan..125 E7
Monewden.....57 D6
Moneydie....133 F7
Moniaive....113 E7
Monifieth...134 F4
Monikie......135 F4
Monimail....128 C4
Monington....45 E3
Monk Bretton..88 D4
Monken Hadley..41 E5
Monk Fryston..89 B6
Monkhopton...61 E6
Monkland.....49 D6
Monkleigh......9 B6
Monknash.....21 B8

Monkokehampton .. 9 D7
Monkseaton 111 B6
Monks Eleigh 56 E5
Monk's Gate 17 B6
Monks Heath 74 B5
Monk Sherborne .. 26 D4
Monkshill 153 D7
Monks Kirby 63 F8
Monks Soham 57 C6
Monkspath 51 B6
Monks Risborough 39 D8
Monk Street 42 B2
Monkswood 35 D7
Monkton Devon ... 11 D6
  Kent 31 C6
  Pembs 44 E4
  S Ayrs 112 B3
Monkton Combe .. 24 C2
Monkton Deverill . 24 D3
Monkton Farleigh . 24 C3
Monkton
  Heathfield 11 B7
Monkton Up
  Wimborne 13 C8
Monkwearmouth 111 D6
Monkwood 26 F4
Monmouth
  = Trefynwy 36 C2
Monmouth Cap. .. 35 B7
Monnington on
  Wye 49 E5
Monreith 105 E7
Monreith Mains. 105 E7
Montacute 12 C2
Montcoffer
  House 153 B6
Montford Argyll .145 G10
  Shrops 60 C4
Montford Bridge . 60 C4
Montgarrie 140 C4
Montgomery
  = Trefaldwyn ... 60 E2
Montrave 129 D5
Montrose 135 D7
Mont Saint Guern .. 16
Montsale 43 E6
Monxton 25 E8
Monyash 75 C8
Monymusk 141 C5
Monzie 127 B7
Monzie Castle .. 127 B7
Moodiesburn 119 B6
Moonzie 128 C5
Moor Allerton ... 95 F5
Moorby 79 C5
Moor Crichel 13 D7
Moordown 13 E8
Moore 86 F3
Moorend 36 D4
Moor End E Yorks .. 96 F4
  York 96 D2
Moorends 89 C7
Moorgate 88 E5
Moorgreen 76 E4
Moorhall 76 B3
Moorhampton ... 49 E5
Moorhead 94 F4
Moorhouse Cumb .108 D3
  Notts 77 C7
Moorlinch 23 F5
Moor Monkton ... 95 D8
Moor of Granary. 151 F13
Moor of
  Ravenstone..... 105 E7
Moor Row 98 C2
Moorsholm 102 C4
Moorside 87 D7
Moor Street 30 C2
Moorthorpe 89 C5
Moortown Hants .. 14 D2
  IoW 14 F5
  Lincs 90 E4
Morangie 151 C10
Morar 147 B9
Morborne 65 E8
Morchard Bishop . 10 D2
Morcombelake ... 12 E2
Morcott 65 D6
Morda 60 B2
Morden Dorset ... 13 E7
  London 28 C3
Mordiford 49 F7
Mordon 101 B8
More 60 E3
Morebath 10 B4
Morebattle 116 B3
Morecambe 92 C4
Morefield 150 B4
Moreleigh 7 D5
Morenish 132 F2
Moresby 98 B1
Moresby Parks ... 98 C1
Morestead 15 B6
Moreton Dorset ... 13 F6
  Essex 41 D8
  Mers 85 E3
  Oxon 39 D6
  Staffs 61 C7
Moreton Corbet .. 61 B5
Moretonhampstead
  .... 10 F2
Moreton-in-Marsh 51 F7
Moreton Jeffries . 49 E8
Moreton Morrell . 51 D8
Moreton on Lugg . 49 E7
Moreton Pinkney . 52 E3
Moreton Say 74 F3
Moreton Valence . 36 D4
Morfa Carms 33 C6
  Carms 33 E6
Morfa Bach 32 C4
Morfa Bychan ... 71 D6
Morfa Dinlle 82 F4
Morfa Glas 34 D2
Morfa Nefyn 70 C3
Morfydd 72 E5
Morgan's Vale ... 14 B2
Moriah 58 B5
Morland 99 B7
Morley Derbys .. 76 E3
  Durham 101 B6
  W Yorks 88 B3
Morley Green ... 87 F6
Morley St Botolph . 68 E3
Morningside Edin . 120 B5

Morningside continued
  N Lanark 119 D8
Morningthorpe ... 68 E5
Morpeth 117 F8
Morphie 135 C7
Morrey 62 C5
Morris Green 55 F8
Morriston 33 E7
Morston 81 C6
Mortehoe 20 E3
Mortimer 26 C4
Mortimer's Cross. 49 C6
Mortimer West
  End 26 C4
Mortlake 28 B3
Morton Cumb 108 D3
  Derbys 76 C4
  Lincs 65 B7
  Lincs 77 C8
  Lincs 90 E2
  Norf 68 C4
  Notts 77 D7
  S Glos 36 E3
  Shrops 60 B2
Morton Bagot ... 51 C6
Morton-on-
  Swale 101 E8
Morvah 2 C3
Morval 5 D7
Morvich Highld .136 B2
  Highld 157 J10
Morville 61 E6
Morville Heath ... 61 E6
Morwenstow 8 C4
Mosborough 88 F5
Moscow 118 E4
Mosedale 108 F3
Moseley W Mid .. 62 E3
  W Mid 62 F4
  Worcs 50 D3
Moss Argyll 146 G2
  Highld 147 E9
  S Yorks 89 C6
  Wrex 73 D7
Mossat 140 C3
Mossbank 160 F6
Moss Bank 86 E3
Mossbay 98 B1
Mossblown 112 B4
Mossbrow 86 F5
Mossburnford ... 116 C2
Mossdale 106 B3
Moss Edge 92 E4
Mossend 119 C7
Moss End 27 B6
Mosser 98 B3
Mossfield 151 D9
Mossgiel 112 B4
Mosside 134 D4
Mossley Ches E ... 75 C5
  Gtr Man 87 D7
Mossley Hill 85 F4
Moss of
  Barmuckity ... 152 B2
Moss Pit 62 B3
Moss-side 151 F11
  Moss Side 92 F3
Mosstodloch 152 B3
Moston Ches E ... 74 C3
  Gtr Man 87 D6
  Shrops 61 B5
Mostyn 85 F2
Mostyn Quay ... 85 F2
Motcombe 13 B6
Mothecombe 6 E4
Motherby 99 B6
Motherwell 119 D7
Mottingham 28 B5
Mottisfont 14 B4
Mottistone 14 F5
Mottram in
  Longdendale ... 87 E7
Mottram
  St Andrew 75 B5
Mouilpied Guern ... 16
Mouldsworth 74 B2
Moulin 133 D6
Moulsecoomb ... 17 D7
Moulsford 39 F5
Moulsoe 53 E7
Moulton Ches W .. 74 C3
  Lincs 66 B3
  Northants 53 C5
  N Yorks 101 D7
  Suff 55 C7
  V Glam 22 B2
Moulton Chapel ... 66 C2
Moulton Eaugate . 66 C3
Moulton St Mary . 69 D6
Moulton Seas End . 66 B3
Mounie Castle .. 141 B6
Mount Corn 4 D2
  Corn 5 C6
  Highld 151 G12
Mountain 94 F3
Mountain Ash
  = Aberpennar ... 34 E4
Mountain Cross . 120 E4
Mountain Water . 44 C4
Mountbenger ... 115 B6
Mount Bures 56 F3
Mount Canisp ... 151 D10
Mountfield 18 C4
Mountgerald ... 151 E8
Mount Hawke 3 B6
Mountjoy 4 C3
Mountnessing ... 42 E2
Mounton 36 E2
Mount Pleasant
  Ches E 74 D5
  Derbys 63 C6
  Derbys 76 E3
  Flint 73 B6
  Hants 14 E3
  W Yorks 88 B3
Mountsorrel 64 C2
Mount Sorrel 13 B8
Mount Tabor 87 B8
Mousehole 2 D3
Mousen 123 F7
Mouswald 107 B7
Mow Cop 75 D5
Mowhaugh 116 B4
Mowsley 64 F3
Moxley 62 E3
Moy Highld 137 F7

Moy continued
  Highld 151 H10
Moy Hall 151 H10
Moy House 151 E13
Moyles Court 14 D2
Moylgrove 45 E3
Moy Lodge 137 F7
Muasdale 143 D7
Much Birch 49 F7
Much Cowarne ... 49 E8
Much Dewchurch . 49 F6
Muchelney 12 B2
Much Hadham ... 41 C7
Much Hoole 86 B2
Muchlarnick 5 D7
Much Marcle 49 F8
Muchrachd 150 H5
Muckernich 151 F8
Mucking 42 F2
Muckleford 12 E4
Mucklestone 74 F4
Muckleton 61 B5
Muckley Corner .. 62 D4
Muckton 91 F7
Mudale 157 F8
Muddiford 20 F4
Mudeford 14 E2
Mudford 12 C3
Mudgley 23 E6
Mugdock 119 B5
Mugeary 149 E9
Muggington 76 E2
Muggleswick 110 E3
Muie 157 J9
Muir 139 F6
Muirden 153 C7
Muirdrum 135 F5
Muirhead Angus. 134 F3
  Fife 128 D4
  N Lanark 119 C6
  S Ayrs 118 F3
Muirhouselaw ... 116 B2
Muirhouses 128 F2
Muirkirk 113 B6
Muirmill 127 F6
Muir of Fairburn . 150 F7
Muir of Fowlis ... 140 C4
Muir of Ord 151 F8
Muir of Pert 134 F4
Muirshearlich ... 136 F4
Muirskie 141 E7
Muirtack 153 E9
Muirton Highld . 151 E10
  Perth 127 C8
  Perth 128 B3
Muirton of
  Ardblair 134 E1
Muirton of
  Ballochy 135 C6
Muiryfold 153 C7
Muker 100 E4
Mulbarton 68 D4
Mulben 152 C3
Mulindry 142 C4
Mullardoch
  House 150 H5
Mullion 3 E5
Mullion Cove 3 E5
Mumby 79 B8
Munderfield Row . 49 D8
Munderfield
  Stocks 49 D8
Mundesley 81 D9
Mundford 67 E8
Mundham 69 E6
Mundon 42 D4
Mundurno 141 C8
Munerigie 137 D5
Muness 160 C8
Mungasdale 150 B2
Mungrisdale 108 F3
Munlochy 151 F9
Munsley 49 E8
Munslow 60 F5
Murchington 9 F8
Murcott 39 C5
Murkle 158 D3
Murlaggan Highld .136 E3
  Highld 137 F6
Murra 159 H3
Murrayfield 120 B5
Murrow 66 D3
Mursley 39 B8
Murthill 134 D4
Murthly 133 F7
Murton Cumb ... 100 B2
  Durham 111 E6
  Northumb 123 E5
  York 96 D2
Musbury 11 E7
Muscoates 102 F4
Musdale 124 C5
Musselburgh ... 121 B6
Muston Leics 77 F8
  N Yorks 97 B6
Mustow Green ... 50 B3
Mutehill 106 E3
Mutford 69 F7
Muthill 127 C7
Mutterton 10 D5
Muxton 61 C7
Mybster 158 E3
Myddfai 34 B1
Myddle 60 B4
Mydroilyn 46 D3
Myerscough 92 F4
Mylor Bridge 3 C7
Mynachlog-ddu ... 45 F3
Mynydd Bach ... 47 B6
Mynydd-bach ... 36 E1
Mynydd Bodafon . 82 C4
Mynydd Isa 73 C6
Mynyddygarreg . 33 D5
Mynytho 70 D4
Myrebird 141 E6
Myrelandhorn ... 158 E4
Myreside 128 B4
Myrtle Hill 47 F6
Mytchett 27 D6
Mytholm 87 B7
Mytholmroyd 87 B8
Myton-on-Swale . 95 C7
Mytton 60 C4

N

Naast 155 J13
Naburn 95 E8
Nackington 31 D5
Nacton 57 E6
Nafferton 97 D6
Na Gearrannan ..154 C6
Nailbridge 36 C3
Nailsbourne 11 B7
Nailsea 23 B6
Nailstone 63 D8
Nailsworth 37 E5
Nairn 151 F11
Nalderswood ... 28 E3
Nancegollan 2 C5
Nancledra 2 C3
Nanhoron 70 D3
Nannau 71 E8
Nannerch 73 C5
Nanpantan 64 C2
Nanpean 4 D4
Nanstallon 4 C5
Nant-ddu 34 C4
Nanternis 46 D2
Nantgaredig 33 B5
Nantgarw 35 F5
Nant-glas 47 C8
Nantglyn 72 C4
Nantgwyn 47 B8
Nantlle 82 F5
Nantmawr 60 B2
Nantmel 48 C2
Nantmor 71 C7
Nant Peris 83 F6
Nant Uchaf 72 D4
Nantwich 74 D3
Nant-y-Bai 47 E6
Nant-y-cafn 34 D2
Nantycaws 33 C5
Nant-y-derry ... 35 D7
Nant-y-ffin 46 F4
Nant-y-pandy ... 83 D6
Naphill 39 E8
Nappa 93 D8
Napton on the Hill. 52 C2
Narberth
  = Arberth 32 C2
Narborough Leics . 64 E2
  Norf 67 C7
Nasareth 82 F4
Naseby 52 B4
Nash Bucks 53 F5
  Hereford 48 C5
  Newport 35 F7
  Shrops 49 B8
Nash Lee 39 D8
Nassington 65 E7
Nasty 41 B6
Nateby Cumb 100 D2
  Lancs 92 E4
Natland 99 F7
Naughton 56 E4
Naunton Glos ... 37 B8
  Worcs 50 F3
Naunton
  Beauchamp... 50 D4
Navenby 78 D2
Navestock Heath . 41 E8
Navestock Side ... 42 E1
Navidale 157 H13
Nawton 102 F4
Nayland 56 F3
Nazeing 41 D7
Neacroft 14 E2
Neal's Green 63 F7
Neap 160 H7
Near Sawrey 99 E5
Neasham 101 C8
Neath
  = Castell-Nedd .. 33 E8
Neath Abbey 33 E8
Neatishead 69 B6
Nebo Anglesey... 82 B4
  Ceredig 46 C4
  Conwy 83 F8
  Gwyn 82 F4
Necton 67 D8
Nedd 156 F4
Nedderton 117 F8
Nedging Tye 56 E4
Needham 68 F5
Needham Market . 56 D4
Needingworth ... 54 B4
Needwood 63 B5
Neen Savage 49 B8
Neen Sollars 49 B8
Neenton 61 F6
Nefyn 70 C4
Neilston 118 D4
Neinthirion 59 D6
Neithrop 52 E2
Nelly Andrews
  Green 60 D2
Nelson Caerph ... 35 E5
  Lancs 93 F8
Nelson Village... 111 B5
Nemphlar 119 E8
Nempnett
  Thrubwell 23 C7
Nene Terrace 66 D2
Nenthall 109 E7
Nenthead 109 E7
Nenthorn 122 F2
Nerabus 142 C3
Nercwys 73 C6
Nerston 119 D6
Nesbit 123 F5
Ness 73 B7
Nesscliffe 60 C3
Neston Ches W ... 73 B6
  Wilts 24 C3
Nether Alderley ... 74 B5
Netheravon 25 E6
Nether Blainslie . 121 E8
Nether Booth ... 88 F2
Netherbrae 153 C7
Netherbrough ... 159 G4
Netherburn 119 E8
Nether Burrow ... 93 B6
Netherbury 12 E2
Netherby Cumb .108 B3
  N Yorks 95 E6
Nether Cerne ... 12 E4

Nether Compton .. 12 C3
Nethercote 52 C3
Nethercott 20 F3
Nether Crimond . 141 B7
Nether Dalgliesh . 115 D5
Nether Dallachy . 152 B3
Netherend 36 D2
Nether Exe 10 D4
Netherfield 18 D4
Nether Glasslaw . 153 C8
Nether Handwick. 134 E3
Nether Haugh ... 88 E5
Nether Heage ... 76 D3
Nether Heyford ... 52 D4
Nether
  Hindhope 116 C3
Nether
  Howcleuch 114 C3
Nether Kellet ... 92 C5
Nether
  Kinmundy 153 D10
Nether Langwith . 76 B5
Netherlaw 106 E4
Nether Leask ... 153 E10
Nether Lenshie... 153 D6
Netherley Aberds . 141 E7
  Mers 86 F2
Nethermill 114 F3
Nether Monynut . 122 C3
Nethermuir 153 D9
Nether Padley ... 76 B2
Nether Park 153 C10
Netherplace 118 D5
Nether Poppleton . 95 D8
Netherseal 63 C6
Nether Silton ... 102 E2
Nether Stowey ... 22 F3
Netherthird 113 C5
Netherthong 88 D2
Netherthorpe ... 89 F6
Netherton Angus . 135 D5
  Devon 7 B6
  Hants 25 D8
  Mers 85 D4
  Northumb 117 D5
  Oxon 38 E4
  Perth 133 D8
  Stirling 119 B5
  W Mid 62 F3
  Worcs 50 E4
  W Yorks 88 C2
  W Yorks 88 C3
Nethertown Cumb . 98 D1
  Highld 158 C5
Nether Urquhart . 128 D3
Nether Wallop ... 25 F8
Nether Wasdale .. 98 D3
Nether Whitacre . 63 E6
Netherwitton ... 117 E7
Netherwood 113 B6
Nether Worton ... 52 F2
Nethy Bridge ... 139 B6
Netley 15 D5
Netley Marsh ... 14 C4
Netteswell 41 C7
Nettlebed 39 F7
Nettlebridge 23 E8
Nettlecombe 12 E3
Nettleden 40 C3
Nettleham 78 B3
Nettlestead 29 D7
Nettlestead Green. 29 D7
Nettlestone 15 E7
Nettleton Lincs ... 90 D5
  Wilts 24 B3
Neuadd 33 B7
Nevendon 42 E3
Nevern 45 E2
New Abbey 107 C6
New Aberdour ... 153 B8
New Addington ... 28 C4
Newall 94 E4
New Alresford ... 26 F3
New Alyth 134 E2
Newark Orkney ...159 D8
  Pboro 66 D2
Newark-on-Trent . 77 D7
New Arley 63 F6
Newarthill 119 D7
New Ash Green ... 29 C7
New Barn 29 C7
New Barnetby ... 90 C4
Newbarns 92 B2
New Barton 53 C6
New Bewick 117 B6
Newbiggin Cumb .. 92 C2
  Cumb 98 E2
  Cumb 99 B6
  Cumb 99 B8
  Cumb 109 E5
  Durham 100 B4
  N Yorks 100 E4
  N Yorks 100 F4
Newbiggin-by-the-
  Sea 117 F9
Newbigging Angus 134 E2
  Angus 134 F4
  S Lanark 120 E3
Newbigging-on-
  Lune 100 D2
New Bilton 52 B2
Newbold Derbys .. 76 B3
  Leics 63 C8
Newbold on Avon. 52 B2
Newbold on Stour. 51 E7
Newbold Pacey... 51 D7
Newbold Verdon . 63 D8
Newbolds 62 D3
Newborough
  Anglesey 82 A4
  Pboro 66 D2
  Staffs 62 B5
Newbottle
  Northants 52 F3
  T&W 111 D6
Newbourne 57 E6
New Bradwell ... 53 E6
New Brancepeth . 110 E5
Newbridge Caerph . 35 E6
  Ceredig 46 D4
  Corn 2 C3
  Corn 5 C8
  Dumfries 107 B6
  Edin 120 B4
  Hants 14 C3

Newbridge continued
  IoW 14 F5
  Pembs 44 B4
  New Bridge 73 E6
Newbridge Green . 50 F3
Newbridge-on-
  Usk 35 E7
Newbridge on
  Wye 48 D2
New Brighton Flint . 73 C6
  Mers 85 E4
New Brinsley 76 D4
New Broughton ... 73 D7
New Buckenham . 68 E3
Newbuildings ... 10 D2
Newburgh Aberds . 141 B8
  Aberds 153 C9
  Borders 115 C6
  Fife 128 C4
  Lancs 86 C2
Newburn 110 C4
Newbury 26 C2
Newbury Park ... 41 F7
Newby Cumb 99 B7
  Lancs 93 E8
  N Yorks 102 C3
  N Yorks 103 E8
Newby Bridge ... 99 F5
Newby East 108 D4
New Byth 153 C8
Newby West 108 D3
Newby Wiske ... 102 F1
Newcastle Mon .. 35 C8
  Shrops 60 F2
Newcastle Emlyn
  = Castell Newydd
  Emlyn 46 E2
Newcastleton or
  Copshaw Holm . 115 F7
Newcastle-under-
  Lyme 74 E5
Newcastle upon
  Tyne 110 C5
New Catton 68 C5
Newchapel Pembs . 45 F4
  Powys 59 F6
  Staffs 75 D5
  Sur 28 E4
New Cheriton ... 15 B6
Newchurch Carms . 32 B4
  IoW 15 F6
  Kent 19 B7
  Lancs 93 F8
  Mon 36 E1
  Powys 48 D4
  Staffs 62 B5
New Costessey ... 68 C4
New Cowper 107 E8
Newcraighall ... 121 B6
New Cross Ceredig . 46 B5
  London 28 B4
New Cumnock ... 113 C6
New Deer 153 D8
New Delaval 111 B5
Newdigate 28 E2
New Duston 52 C5
New Earswick ... 96 D2
New Edlington ... 89 E6
New Elgin 152 B2
New Ellerby 97 F7
Newell Green ... 27 B6
New Eltham 28 B5
New End 51 D5
Newenden 18 C5
Newent 36 B4
Newerne 36 D3
New Farnley 94 F5
New Ferry 85 F4
Newfield Durham . 110 F5
  Highld 151 D10
Newford 2 E4
Newfound 26 D3
New Fryston 89 B5
Newgale 44 C3
New Galloway ... 106 B3
Newgate 81 C6
Newgate Street ... 41 D6
New Gilston 129 D6
New Grimsby 2 E3
New Hainford ... 68 C5
Newhall Ches E 74 E3
  Derbys 63 B6
Newhall House ... 151 E9
Newhall Point ... 151 E10
Newham 117 B7
Newham Hall ... 117 B7
New Hartley 111 B6
Newhaven Derbys . 75 D8
  E Sus 17 D8
  Edin 121 B5
New Haw 27 C8
New Hedges 32 D2
New Herrington . 111 D6
Newhey 87 C7
New Hinksey ... 39 D5
New Holkham ... 80 D4
New Holland 90 B4
Newholm 103 C6
New Houghton
  Derbys 76 C4
  Norf 80 E3
Newhouse 119 C7
New Houses 93 B8
New Humberstone . 64 D3
New Hutton 99 E7
New Hythe 29 D8
Newick 17 B8
Newingreen 19 B8
Newington Kent .. 19 B8
  Kent 30 C2
  Kent 31 C7
  Notts 89 E7
  Oxon 39 E6
  Shrops 60 F4
New Inn Carms ... 46 F3
  Mon 36 D1
  Pembs 45 F2
  Torf 35 E7
New Invention
  Shrops 48 B4
  W Mid 62 D3
New Kelso 150 G2
New Kingston ... 64 B2
New Lanark 119 E8
Newland Glos ... 36 D2
  Hull 97 F6
  Hants 14 C3

Newland continued
  N Yorks 89 B7
  Worcs 50 E2
Newlandrig 121 C6
Newlands Borders . 115 E8
  Highld 151 G10
  Moray 152 C3
  Northumb 110 D3
Newland's Corner . 27 E8
Newlandsmuir ... 119 D6
Newlands of
  Geise 158 D2
Newlands of
  Tynet 152 B3
Newlands Park ... 82 C2
New Lane 86 C2
New Lane End ... 86 E4
New Leake 79 D7
New Leeds 153 C9
New Longton ... 86 B3
Newlot 159 G6
New Luce 105 C5
Newlyn 2 D3
Newmachar 141 C7
Newmains 119 D8
New Malden 28 C3
Newmarket Suff... 55 C7
  W Isles 155 D9
New Marske 102 B4
New Marton 73 F7
New Micklefield ... 95 F7
Newmill Borders . 115 C7
  Corn 2 C3
  Moray 152 C4
New Mill Aberds .. 141 F6
  Herts 40 C2
  Wilts 25 C6
  W Yorks 88 D2
Newmill of
  Inshewan 134 C4
New Mills Ches E .. 87 F5
  Corn 4 D3
  Derbys 87 F7
  Powys 59 D7
Newmills of
  Boyne 152 C5
Newmiln 133 F8
Newmilns 118 F5
New Milton 14 E3
New Moat 32 B1
Newnham Cambs.. 54 D5
  Glos 36 C3
  Hants 26 D5
  Herts 54 F3
  Kent 30 D3
  Northants 52 D3
Newnham Bridge . 49 C8
New Ollerton ... 77 C6
New Oscott 62 E4
Newpark 129 C6
New Park 95 D5
New Pitsligo ... 153 C8
New Polzeath 4 B4
Newport Devon ... 20 F4
  Essex 55 F6
  E Yorks 96 F4
  Highld 158 H3
  IoW 15 F6
  Norf 69 C8
  Telford 61 C7
Newport
  = Casnewydd 35 F7
Newport
  = Trefdraeth 45 F2
Newport-on-Tay . 129 B6
Newport Pagnell . 53 E6
Newpound
  Common 16 B4
Newquay 4 C3
New Quay
  = Ceinewydd 46 D2
New Rackheath ... 69 C5
New Radnor 48 C4
New Rent 108 F4
New Ridley 110 D3
New Road Side ... 94 E2
New Romney ... 19 C7
New Rossington . 89 E7
New Row Ceredig . 47 B6
  Lancs 93 F6
  N Yorks 102 C4
New Sarum 25 F6
Newsbank 74 C5
Newseat Aberds .. 153 D10
  Aberds 153 E7
Newsham
  Northum 111 B6
  N Yorks 101 C6
  N Yorks 102 F1
Newsholme
  E Yorks 89 B8
  Lancs 93 D8
New Silksworth . 111 D6
Newsome 88 C2
Newstead Borders 121 F8
  Northum 117 B7
  Notts 76 D5
New Stevenston . 119 D7
New Street 75 D8
New Street Lane . 74 F3
New Swanage ... 13 F8
Newthorpe 95 F7
Newton Argyll . 125 E6
  Borders 116 B2
  Bridgend 21 B7
  Cambs 54 E5
  Cambs 66 C4
  Cardiff 22 B4
  Ches W 73 C8
  Ches W 74 B2
  Cumb 92 B2
  Derbys 76 D4
  Dorset 13 C5
  Dumfries 108 B2
  Dumfries 114 E4
  Gtr Man 87 E7
  Hereford 48 E5
  Hereford 49 D7
  Highld 151 G10
  Highld 151 G10
  Highld 156 F5
  Lancs 92 F4
  Lancs 93 B5
  Lancs 93 D6
  Lincs 78 F3
  Moray 152 B1
  Norf 67 C8

Newton continued
  Northants 65 F5
  Northumb 110 C3
  Notts 77 E6
  Perth 133 F5
  S Lanark 119 C6
  S Lanark 120 F2
  Staffs 62 B4
  Suff 56 E3
  Swansea 33 F7
  S Yorks 89 D6
  Warks 52 B3
  Wilts 14 B3
  W Loth 120 B3
Newton Abbot 7 B6
Newtonairds ... 113 F8
Newton Arlosh ... 107 D8
Newton Aycliffe . 101 B7
Newton Bewley ... 102 B2
Newton
  Blossomville .. 53 D7
Newton
  Bromswold 53 C7
Newton Burgoland 63 D7
Newton by Toft ... 90 F4
Newton Ferrers ... 6 E3
Newton Flotman . 68 E5
Newtongrange ... 121 C6
Newton Hall 110 C3
Newton Harcourt . 64 E3
Newton Heath ... 87 D6
Newtonhill Aberds 141 E8
  Highld 151 G8
Newton House .. 141 B5
Newton Kyme ... 95 E7
Newton-le-Willows
  Mers 86 E3
  N Yorks 101 F7
Newton Longville . 53 F6
Newton Mearns . 118 D5
Newtonmill 135 C6
Newtonmore ... 138 E3
Newton Morrell . 101 D7
Newton
  Mulgrave 103 C5
Newton of
  Ardtoe 147 D9
Newton of
  Balcanquhal ... 128 C3
Newton of
  Falkland 128 D4
Newton on Ayr ... 112 B3
Newton on Ouse .. 95 D8
Newton-on-
  Rawcliffe 103 E6
Newton-on-the-
  Moor 117 D7
Newton on Trent . 77 B8
Newton Park ... 145 G10
Newton Purcell ... 52 F4
Newton Regis ... 63 D6
Newton Reigny ... 108 F4
Newton St Cyres.. 10 E3
Newton St Faith .. 68 C5
Newton St Loe ... 24 C2
Newton St Petrock . 9 C6
Newton Solney ... 63 B6
Newton Stacey ... 26 E2
Newton Stewart . 105 C8
Newton Tony ... 25 E7
Newton Tracey ... 9 B7
Newton under
  Roseberry 102 C3
Newton upon
  Derwent 96 E3
Newton Valence .. 26 F5
New Totley 76 B3
Newtown Argyll . 125 E6
  BCP 13 E8
  Ches W 74 B2
  Corn 3 D6
  Cumb 107 E7
  Cumb 108 C5
  Derbys 87 F7
  Devon 10 B2
  Glos 36 D3
  Glos 50 F4
  Hants 14 B4
  Hants 14 C3
  Hants 15 C7
  Hants 15 D5
  Hants 26 C2
  Hereford 49 E8
  Highld 137 D6
  IoM 84 E3
  IoW 14 E5
  Northumb 117 B6
  Northumb 117 C6
  Shrops 73 F8
  Staffs 75 C6
  Staffs 75 C7
  Wilts 13 B7
Newtown
  = Y Drenewydd .. 59 E8
Newton Linford ... 64 D2
New Town 14 E4
Newtown Unthank. 63 D8
Newtown
  = Y Drenewydd .. 59 E8
Newtyle 134 E2
New Ulva 144 E6
New Walsoken ... 66 D4
New Waltham ... 91 D6
New Whittington . 76 B3
New Winton 121 B7
New Yatt 38 C3
New York Lincs ... 78 D5
  N Yorks 94 C4
Neyland 44 E4
Niarbyl 84 E2
Nibley 36 F3
Nibley Green 36 E4
Nibon 160 F5
Nicholashayne ... 11 C6
Nicholaston 33 F6
Nidd 95 C6
Nigg Aberdeen ... 141 D8
  Highld 151 D11
Nigg Ferry 151 E10
Nightcott 10 B3

Nilig 72 D4
Nine Ashes 42 D1
Ninebanks 109 D7
Nine Mile Burn . 120 D4
Nine Wells 44 C2
Ninfield 18 D4
Ningwood 14 F4
Nisbet 116 B2
Nisthouse Orkney .159 G4
  Shetland 160 G7
Niton 15 G6
Nitshill 118 C5
Noak Hill 41 E8
Nobold 60 C4
Nobottle 52 C4
Nocton 78 C3
Noke 39 C5
Nolton 44 D3
Nolton Haven ... 44 D3
No Man's Heath
  Ches W 74 E2
  Warks 63 D6
Nomansland Devon . 10 C3
  Wilts 14 C3
Noneley 60 B4
Nonikiln 151 D9
Nonington 31 D6
Noonsbrough ... 160 H4
Norbreck 92 E3
Norbridge 50 E2
Norbury Ches E ... 74 E2
  Derbys 75 E8
  Shrops 60 E3
  Staffs 61 B7
Nordelph 67 D5
Norden 87 C6
Nordley 61 E6
Norham 122 E5
Norley 74 B2
Norleywood 14 E4
Normanby N Lincs .. 90 C2
  N Yorks 103 F5
  Redcar 102 C3
Normanby-by-
  Spital 90 F4
Normanby by Stow 90 F2
Normanby le Wold. 90 E5
Norman Cross ... 65 E8
Normandy 27 D7
Norman's Bay ... 18 E3
Norman's Green . 11 D5
Normanstone ... 69 E8
Normanton Derby . 76 F3
  Leics 77 E3
  Lincs 78 E2
  Notts 77 D7
  Rutland 65 D6
  W Yorks 88 B4
Normanton le
  Heath 63 C7
Normanton on
  Soar 64 B2
Normanton-on-the-
  Wolds 77 F6
Normanton on
  Trent 77 C7
Normoss 92 F3
Norney 27 E7
Norrington
  Common 24 C3
Norris Green 85 E4
Norris Hill 63 C7
Northacre 68 E2
Northallerton ... 102 E1
Northam Devon ... 9 B6
  Soton 14 C5
Northampton ... 53 C5
North Anston ... 89 F6
North Aston 38 B4
North Baddesley . 14 C4
North
  Ballachulish ..130 C4
North Barrow ... 12 B4
North Barsham ... 80 D5
Northbeck 78 E3
North Benfleet ... 42 F3
North Bersted ... 16 D3
North Berwick ... 129 F7
Northborough ... 65 D8
Northbourne ... 31 D7
North Bovey 10 F2
North Bradley ... 24 D3
North Brentor ... 9 F6
North Brewham . 24 F2
Northbridge
  Street 18 C4
North Buckland ... 20 E3
North Burlingham . 69 C6
North Cadbury ... 12 B4
North Cairn 104 B3
North Carlton ... 78 B2
North Carrine ... 143 H7
North Cave 96 F4
North Cerney ... 37 D7
Northchapel 16 B3
North Charford ... 14 C2
North Charlton . 117 B7
North Cheriton ... 12 B4
Northchurch 40 D2
North Cliff 97 E8
North Cliffe 96 F4
North Clifton ... 77 B8
North
  Cockerington . 91 E7
North Coker 12 C3
North Collafirth . 160 E5
North Common ... 17 B7
North Connel ... 124 B5
North Cotes 91 D7
Northcott 8 E5
North Cove 69 F7
North Cowton ... 101 D7
North Crawley ... 53 E7
North Cray 29 B5
North Creake ... 80 D4
North Curry 11 B8
North Dalton ... 96 D5
North Dawn 159 H5
North Deighton ... 95 D6
Northdown 31 B7
North Duffield ... 96 F2
Northdyke 159 F3
North Elkington . 91 E6
North Elmham ... 81 E5
North Elmsall ... 89 C5

Northend Bath 24 C2
Bucks 39 E7
Warks 51 D8
North End Bucks 39 B8
Essex 42 C2
E Yorks 97 F8
Hants 26 C2
Lincs 78 E5
N Som 23 C6
Ptsmth 15 D7
Som 11 B7
W Sus 16 D5
Northenden 87 E6
North Erradale 155 J12
North Fambridge 42 E4
North Fearns 149 E10
North Featherstone 88 B5
North Ferriby 90 B3
Northfield
Aberdeen 141 D8
Borders 122 C5
E Yorks 90 B4
W Mid 50 B5
Northfields 65 D7
Northfleet 29 B7
North Frodingham 97 D7
Northgate 65 B8
North Gluss 160 F5
North Gorley 14 C2
North Green Norf 68 F5
Suff 57 C7
North Greetwell 78 B3
North Grimston 96 C4
North Halley 159 H6
North Halling 29 C8
North Hayling 15 D8
North Hazelrigg 123 F6
North Heasley 21 F6
North Heath 16 B4
North Hill Cambs 55 B5
Corn 5 B7
North Hinksey 38 D4
North Holmwood 28 E2
Northhouse 115 D7
North Howden 96 F3
North Huish 6 D5
North Hykeham 78 C2
Northiam 18 C5
Northill 54 E2
Northington 26 F3
North Johnston 44 D4
North Kelsey 90 D4
North Kelsey Moor 90 D4
North Kessock 151 G9
North Killingholme 90 C5
North Kilvington 102 F2
North Kilworth 64 F3
North Kirkton 153 C11
North Kiscadale 143 F11
North Kyme 78 D4
North Lancing 17 D5
Northlands 79 D6
Northlea 111 D7
Northleach 37 C8
North Lee 39 D8
Northleigh 11 E6
North Leigh 38 C3
North Leverton with Habblesthorpe 89 F8
Northlew 9 E7
North Littleton 51 E5
North Lopham 68 F3
North Luffenham 65 D6
North Marden 16 C2
North Marston 39 B7
North Middleton
Midloth 121 D6
Northumb 117 B6
North Molton 10 B2
Northmoor 38 D4
Northmoor Green or Moorland 22 F5
North Moreton 39 F5
Northmuir 134 D3
North Mundham 16 D2
North Muskham 77 D7
North Newbald 96 F5
North Newington 52 F2
North Newnton 25 D6
North Newton 22 F4
Northney 15 D8
North Nibley 36 E4
North Oakley 26 D3
North Ockendon 42 F1
Northolt 40 F4
Northop 73 C6
Northop Hall 73 C6
North Ormesby 102 B3
North Ormsby 91 E6
Northorpe Lincs 65 C7
Lincs 78 F5
Lincs 90 E2
North Otterington 102 F1
Northover Som 12 B3
Som 23 F6
North Owersby 90 E4
Northowram 88 B2
North Perrott 12 D2
North Petherton 22 F4
North Petherwin 8 F4
North Pickenham 67 D8
North Piddle 50 D4
North Poorton 12 E3
Northport 13 F7
North Port 125 C6
Northpunds 160 L6
North Queensferry 128 F3
North Radworthy 21 F6
North Rauceby 78 E3
Northrepps 81 D8
North Reston 91 F7
North Rigton 95 E5
North Rode 75 C5
North Roe 160 E5
North Runcton 67 C6
North Sandwick 160 D7
North Scale 92 C1
North Scarle 77 C8
North Seaton 117 F8
North Shian 130 E3
North Shields 111 C6
North Shoebury 43 F5
North Shore 92 F3
North Side Cumb 98 B2
Pboro 66 E2
North Skelton 102 C4
North Somercotes 91 E8
North Stainley 95 B5
North Stainmore 100 C3
North Stifford 42 F2
North Stoke Bath 24 C2
Oxon 39 F6
W Sus 16 C4
Northstowe 54 C5
North Street Hants 26 F4
Kent 30 D4
Medway 30 B2
W Berks 26 B4
North Sunderland 123 F8
North Tamerton 8 E5
North Tawton 9 D8
North Thoresby 91 E6
North Tidworth 25 E7
North Togston 117 D8
Northtown 159 J5
North Tuddenham 68 C3
North Walbottle 110 C4
North Walsham 81 D8
North Waltham 26 E3
North Warnborough 26 D5
North Water Bridge 135 C6
North Watten 158 E4
Northway 50 F4
North Weald Bassett 41 D7
North Wheatley 89 F8
North Whilborough 7 C6
Northwich 74 B3
Northwick 36 F2
North Wick 23 C7
North Willingham 91 F5
North Wingfield 76 C4
North Witham 65 B6
Northwold 67 E7
Northwood Derbys 76 C2
IoW 15 E5
Kent 31 C7
London 40 E3
Shrops 73 F8
Northwood Green 36 C4
North Woolwich 28 B5
North Wootton
Dorset 12 C4
Norf 67 B6
Som 23 E7
North Wraxall 24 B3
North Wroughton 38 F1
Norton E Sus 17 D8
Glos 37 B5
Halton 86 F3
Herts 54 F3
IoW 14 F4
Mon 35 C8
Northants 52 C4
Notts 77 B5
Powys 48 C5
Shrops 60 F4
Shrops 61 D5
Shrops 61 D7
Stockton 102 B2
Suff 56 C3
S Yorks 89 C6
Wilts 37 F5
Worcs 50 D3
Worcs 50 E5
W Sus 16 D3
W Sus 16 E2
Norton Bavant 24 E4
Norton Bridge 75 F5
Norton Canes 62 D4
Norton Canon 49 E5
Norton Corner 81 E6
Norton Disney 77 D8
Norton East 62 D4
Norton Ferris 24 F2
Norton Fitzwarren 11 B6
Norton Green 14 F4
Norton Hawkfield 23 C7
Norton Heath 42 D2
Norton in Hales 74 F4
Norton-in-the-Moors 75 D5
Norton-Juxta-Twycross 63 D7
Norton-le-Clay 95 B7
Norton Lindsey 51 C7
Norton Malreward 23 C8
Norton Mandeville 42 D1
Norton-on-Derwent 96 B3
Norton St Philip 24 D2
Norton sub Hamdon 12 C2
Norton Woodseats 88 F4
Norwell 77 C7
Norwell Woodhouse 77 C7
Norwich 68 D5
Norwick 160 B8
Norwood 89 F5
Norwood Hill 28 E3
Norwoodside 66 E4
Noseley 64 E4
Noss 160 M5
Noss Mayo 6 E3
Nosterfield 101 F7
Nostie 149 F13
Notgrove 37 B8
Nottage 21 B7
Nottingham 77 F5
Nottington 12 F4
Notton Wilts 24 C4
W Yorks 88 C4
Nounsley 42 C3
Noutard's Green 50 C2
Novar House 151 E9
Nox 60 C4
Nuffield 39 F6
Nunburnholme 96 E4
Nuncargate 76 D5
Nuneaton 63 E7
Nuneham Courtenay 39 E5
Nun Hills 87 B6
Nun Monkton 95 D8
Nunney 24 E2
Nunnington 96 B2
Nunnykirk 117 E6
Nunsthorpe 91 D6
Nunthorpe Mbro 102 C3
York 96 D2
Nunton 14 B2
Nunwick 95 B6
Nupend 36 D4
Nursling 14 C4
Nursted 15 B8
Nutbourne W Sus 15 D8
W Sus 16 C4
Nutfield 28 D4
Nuthall 76 E5
Nuthampstead 54 F5
Nuthurst 17 B5
Nutley E Sus 17 B8
Hants 26 E4
Nutwell 89 D7
Nybster 158 D5
Nyetimber 16 E2
Nyewood 16 B2
Nymet Rowland 10 D2
Nymet Tracey 10 D2
Nympsfield 37 D5
Nynehead 11 B6
Nyton 16 D3

O

Oadby 64 D3
Oad Street 30 C2
Oakamoor 75 E7
Oakbank 120 C3
Oak Cross 9 E7
Oakdale 35 E5
Oake 11 B6
Oaken 62 D2
Oakenclough 92 E5
Oakengates 61 C7
Oakenholt 73 B6
Oakenshaw
Durham 110 F5
W Yorks 88 B2
Oakerthorpe 76 D3
Oakes 88 C2
Oakfield 35 E7
Oakford Ceredig 46 D3
Devon 10 B4
Oakfordbridge 10 B4
Oakgrove 75 C6
Oakham 65 D5
Oakhanger 27 F5
Oakhill 23 E8
Oakhurst 29 D6
Oakington 54 C5
Oaklands Herts 41 C5
Powys 48 D2
Oakle Street 36 C4
Oakley BCP 13 E8
Bedford 53 D8
Bucks 39 C6
Fife 128 F2
Hants 26 D3
Oxon 39 D7
Suff 57 B5
Oakley Green 27 B7
Oakley Park 59 F6
Oakmere 74 C2
Oakridge Glos 37 D6
Hants 26 D4
Oaks 60 D4
Oaksey 37 E6
Oaks Green 75 F8
Oakthorpe 63 C7
Oakwoodhill 28 F2
Oakworth 94 F3
Oape 156 J7
Oare Kent 30 C4
Som 21 E7
W Berks 26 B3
Wilts 25 C6
Oasby 78 F3
Oathlaw 134 D4
Oatlands 95 D6
Oban Argyll 124 C4
Highld 147 C11
Oborne 12 C4
Obthorpe 65 C7
Occlestone Green 74 C3
Occold 57 B5
Ochiltree 112 B5
Ochtermuthill 127 C7
Ochtertyre 127 B7
Ockbrook 76 F4
Ockham 27 D8
Ockle 147 D8
Ockley 28 F2
Ocle Pychard 49 E7
Octon 97 C6
Octon Cross Roads 97 C6
Odcombe 12 C3
Odd Down 24 C2
Oddendale 99 C7
Odder 78 B2
Oddingley 50 D4
Oddington Glos 38 B2
Oxon 39 C5
Odell 53 D7
Odie 159 F7
Odiham 26 D5
Odstock 14 B2
Odstone 63 D7
Offchurch 51 C8
Offenham 51 E5
Offham E Sus 17 C7
Kent 29 D7
W Sus 16 D4
Offord Cluny 54 C3
Offord Darcy 54 C3
Offton 56 E4
Offwell 11 E6
Ogbourne Maizey 25 B6
Ogbourne St Andrew 25 B6
Ogbourne St George 25 B7
Ogil 134 C4
Ogle 110 B4
Ogmore 21 B7
Ogmore-by-Sea 21 B7
Ogmore Vale 34 E3
Okeford Fitzpaine 13 C6
Okehampton 9 E7
Okehampton Camp 9 E7
Okraquoy 160 K6
Old 53 B5
Old Aberdeen 141 D8
Old Alresford 26 F3
Oldany 156 F4
Old Arley 63 E6
Old Basford 76 E5
Old Basing 26 D4
Oldberrow 51 C6
Old Bewick 117 B6
Old Bolingbroke 79 C6
Oldborough 10 D2
Old Bramhope 94 E5
Old Brampton 76 B3
Old Bridge of Tilt 133 C5
Old Bridge of Urr 106 C4
Old Buckenham 68 E3
Old Burghclere 26 D2
Oldbury Shrops 61 E7
Warks 63 E7
W Mid 62 F3
Oldbury-on-Severn 36 E3
Oldbury on the Hill 37 F5
Old Byland 102 F3
Old Cassop 111 F6
Oldcastle Bridgend 21 B8
Mon 35 B7
Old Castleton 115 E8
Old Catton 68 C5
Old Clee 91 D6
Old Cleeve 22 E2
Old Clipstone 77 C6
Old Colwyn 83 D8
Oldcotes 89 F6
Old Coulsdon 28 D4
Old Crombie 152 C5
Old Dailly 112 E2
Old Dalby 64 B3
Old Deer 153 D9
Old Denaby 89 E5
Old Edlington 89 E6
Old Eldon 101 B7
Old Ellerby 97 F7
Oldfallow 62 C3
Old Felixstowe 57 F7
Oldfield 50 C3
Old Fletton 65 E8
Oldford 24 D2
Old Glossop 87 E8
Old Goole 89 B8
Old Hall 59 F6
Oldham 87 D7
Oldhamstocks 122 B3
Old Heath 43 B6
Old Heathfield 18 C2
Old Hill 62 F3
Old Hunstanton 80 C2
Old Hurst 54 B3
Old Hutton 99 F7
Old Kea 3 B7
Old Kilpatrick 118 B4
Old Kinnernie 141 D6
Old Knebworth 41 B5
Oldland 23 B8
Old Langho 93 F7
Old Laxey 84 D4
Old Leake 79 D7
Old Malton 96 B3
Oldmeldrum 141 B7
Old Micklefield 95 F7
Old Milton 14 E3
Old Milverton 51 C7
Old Monkland 119 C7
Old Netley 15 D5
Old Philpstoun 120 B3
Old Quarrington 111 F6
Old Radnor 48 D4
Old Rattray 153 C10
Old Rayne 141 B5
Old Romney 19 C7
Oldshore Beg 156 D4
Oldshoremore 156 D5
Old Sodbury 36 F4
Old Somerby 78 F2
Oldstead 102 F3
Old Stratford 53 E5
Old Thirsk 102 F2
Oldtown 140 B4
Old Town Cumb 99 F7
Cumb 108 E4
Northumb 116 E4
Scilly 2 E4
Oldtown of Ord 152 C6
Old Trafford 87 E6
Old Tupton 76 C3
Old Warden 54 E2
Oldway 33 F6
Oldways End 10 B3
Old Weston 53 B8
Oldwhat 153 C8
Old Whittington 76 B3
Old Wick 158 E5
Old Windsor 27 B7
Old Wives Lees 30 D4
Old Woking 27 D8
Old Woodhall 78 C5
Olgrinmore 158 E2
Oliver's Battery 15 B5
Ollaberry 160 E5
Ollerton Ches E 74 B4
Notts 77 C6
Shrops 61 B6
Olmarch 46 D5
Olney 53 D6
Olrig House 158 D3
Olton 62 F5
Olveston 36 F3
Olwen 46 E4
Ombersley 50 C3
Ompton 77 C6
Onchan 84 E3
Onecote 75 D7
Onen 35 C8
Ongar Hill 67 B5
Ongar Street 49 C5
Onibury 49 B6
Onich 130 C4
Onllwyn 34 C2
Onneley 74 E4
Onslow Village 27 E7
Onthank 118 E4
Openwoodgate 76 E3
Opinan Highld 149 A12
Highld 155 H13
Orange Lane 122 E3
Orange Row 66 B5
Orasaigh 155 F8
Orbliston 152 C3
Orbost 148 D7
Orby 79 C7
Orchard Hill 9 B6
Orchard Portman 11 B7
Orcheston 25 E5
Orcop 36 B1
Orcop Hill 36 B1
Ord 149 G11
Ordhead 141 C5
Ordie 140 D3
Ordiequish 152 C3
Ordsall 89 F7
Ore 18 D5
Oreton 61 F6
Orford Suff 57 E8
Warr 86 E4
Orgreave 63 C5
Orlestone 19 B6
Orleton Hereford 49 C6
Worcs 49 C8
Orlingbury 53 B6
Ormesby 102 C3
Ormesby St Margaret 69 C7
Ormesby St Michael 69 C7
Ormiclate Castle 148 E2
Ormiscaig 155 H13
Ormiston 121 C7
Ormsaigbeg 146 E7
Ormsaigmore 146 E7
Ormsary 144 F6
Ormsgill 92 B1
Ormskirk 86 D2
Orpington 29 C5
Orrell Gtr Man 86 D3
Mers 85 E4
Orrisdale 84 C3
Orroland 106 E4
Orsett 42 F2
Orslow 62 C2
Orston 77 E7
Orthwaite 108 F2
Ortner 92 D5
Orton Cumb 99 D8
Northants 53 B6
Orton Longueville 65 E8
Orton-on-the-Hill 63 D7
Orton Waterville 65 E8
Orwell 54 D4
Osbaldeston 93 F6
Osbaldwick 96 D2
Osbaston 60 B3
Osbournby 78 F3
Oscroft 74 C2
Ose 149 D8
Osgathorpe 63 C8
Osgodby Lincs 90 E4
N Yorks 96 F2
N Yorks 103 F8
Oskaig 149 E10
Oskamull 146 G7
Osmaston Derby 76 F3
Derbys 76 E2
Osmington 12 F5
Osmington Mills 12 F5
Osmotherley 102 E2
Ospisdale 151 C10
Ospringe 30 C4
Ossett 88 B3
Ossington 77 C7
Ostend 43 E5
Oswaldkirk 96 B2
Oswaldtwistle 86 B5
Oswestry 60 B2
Otford 29 D6
Otham 29 D8
Othery 23 F5
Otley Suff 57 D6
W Yorks 94 E5
Otterbourne 15 B5
Otterburn
Northumb 116 E4
N Yorks 93 D8
Otterburn Camp 116 E4
Otter Ferry 145 E8
Otterham 8 E3
Otterhampton 22 E4
Ottershaw 27 C8
Otterswick 160 E7
Otterton 11 F5
Ottery St Mary 11 E6
Ottinge 31 E5
Ottringham 91 B6
Oughterby 108 D2
Oughtershaw 100 F3
Oughterside 107 E8
Oughtibridge 88 E4
Oughtrington 86 F4
Oulston 95 B8
Oulton Cumb 108 D2
Norf 81 E7
Staffs 75 F6
Suff 69 E8
W Yorks 88 B4
Oulton Broad 69 E8
Oulton Street 81 E7
Oundle 65 F7
Ousby 109 F6
Ousdale 158 H2
Ousden 55 D8
Ousefleet 90 B2
Ouston Durham 111 D5
Northumb 110 B3
Outertown 159 G3
Outgate 99 E5
Outhgill 100 D2
Outlane 87 C8
Out Newton 91 B7
Out Rawcliffe 92 E4
Outwell 66 D5
Outwick 14 C2
Outwood Sur 28 E4
W Yorks 88 B4
Outwoods 61 C7
Ovenden 87 B8
Ovenscloss 121 F7
Over Cambs 54 B4
Ches W 74 C3
S Glos 36 F2
Overbister 159 D7
Overbury 50 F4
Overcombe 12 F4
Over Compton 12 C3
Overgreen 76 B3
Over Green 63 E5
Over Haddon 76 C2
Over Hulton 86 D4
Over Kellet 92 B5
Over Kiddington 38 B4
Over Knutsford 74 B4
Overleigh 23 F6
Overley Green 51 D5
Over Monnow 36 C2
Over Norton 38 B3
Over Peover 74 B4
Overpool 73 B7
Overscaig Hotel 156 G7
Overseal 63 C6
Over Silton 102 E2
Oversland 30 D4
Overstone 53 C6
Over Stowey 22 F3
Overstrand 81 C8
Over Stratton 12 C2
Over Tabley 86 F5
Overthorpe 52 E2
Overton Aberdeen 141 C7
Ches W 74 B2
Dumfries 107 C6
Hants 26 E3
Lancs 92 D4
N Yorks 95 D8
Shrops 49 B7
Swansea 33 F5
W Yorks 88 C3
Overton = *Owrtyn* 73 E7
Overton Bridge 73 E7
Overtown 119 D8
Over Wallop 25 F7
Over Whitacre 63 E6
Over Worton 38 B4
Oving Bucks 39 B7
W Sus 16 D3
Ovingdean 17 D7
Ovingham 110 C3
Ovington Durham 101 C6
Essex 55 E8
Hants 26 F3
Norf 68 D2
Northumb 110 C3
Ower 14 C4
Owermoigne 13 F5
Owlbury 60 E3
Owler Bar 76 B2
Owlerton 88 F4
Owl's Green 57 C6
Owlswick 39 D7
Owmby 90 D4
Owmby-by-Spital 90 F4
Owrtyn = *Overton* 73 E7
Owslebury 15 B6
Owston Leics 64 D4
S Yorks 89 C6
Owston Ferry 90 D2
Owstwick 97 F8
Owthorne 91 B7
Owthorpe 77 F6
Oxborough 67 D7
Oxcombe 79 B6
Oxenholme 99 F7
Oxenhope 94 F3
Oxen Park 99 F5
Oxenton 50 F4
Oxenwood 25 D8
Oxford 39 D5
Oxhey 40 E4
Oxhill 51 E8
Oxley 62 D3
Oxley Green 43 C5
Oxley's Green 18 C3
Oxnam 116 C2
Oxshott 28 C2
Oxspring 88 D3
Oxted 28 D4
Oxton Borders 121 D7
Notts 77 D6
Oxwich 33 F5
Oxwick 80 E5
Oykel Bridge 156 J6
Oyne 141 B5

P

Pabail Iarach 155 D10
Pabail Uarach 155 D10
Pace Gate 94 D4
Packington 63 C7
Padanaram 134 D4
Padbury 52 F5
Paddington 41 F5
Paddlesworth 19 B8
Paddockhaugh 152 C2
Paddockhole 115 F5
Paddock Wood 29 E7
Padfield 87 E8
Padiham 93 F7
Padog 83 F8
Padside 94 D4
Padstow 4 B4
Padworth 26 C4
Page Bank 110 F5
Pagelsham Eastend 43 E5
Pagham 16 E2
Paglesham Churchend 43 E5
Paibeil 148 B2
Paible 154 H5
Paignton 7 C6
Pailton 63 F8
Painscastle 48 E3
Painshawfield 110 C3
Painsthorpe 96 D4
Painswick 37 D5
Pairc Shiaboist 154 C7
Paisley 118 C4
Pakefield 69 E8
Pakenham 56 C3
Pale 72 F3
Palestine 25 E7
Paley Street 27 B6
Palfrey 62 E4
Palgowan 112 F3
Palgrave 56 B5
Pallion 111 D6
Palmarsh 19 B8
Palnackie 106 D5
Palnure 105 C8
Palterton 76 C4
Pamber End 26 D4
Pamber Green 26 D4
Pamber Heath 26 C4
Pamphill 13 D7
Pampisford 55 E5
Pan 159 J4
Panbride 135 F5
Pancrasweek 8 D4
Pandy Gwyn 58 D3
Mon 35 B7
Powys 59 D6
Wrex 73 F5
Pandy Tudur 83 E8
Panfield 42 B3
Pangbourne 26 B4
Pannal 95 D6
Panshanger 41 C5
Pant 60 B2
Pant-glas Carms 33 B6
Gwyn 71 C5
Pant-glâs 58 E4
Pant-glas 73 F6
Pantgwyn Carms 33 B6
Ceredig 45 E4
Pant-lasau 33 E7
Pant Mawr 59 F5
Panton 78 B4
Pantperthog 58 D4
Pant-teg 33 B5
Pant-y-Caws 32 B2
Pant-y-dwr 47 B8
Pant-y-ffridd 59 D8
Pantyffynnon 33 C7
Pantymwyn 73 C5
Pant-yr-awel 34 F3
Pant-y-Wacco 72 B5
Panxworth 69 C6
Papcastle 107 F8
Papigoe 158 E5
Papil 160 K5
Papley 159 J5
Papple 121 B8
Papplewick 76 D5
Papworth Everard 54 C3
Papworth St Agnes 54 C3
Par 5 D5
Parbold 86 C2
Parbrook Som 23 F7
W Sus 16 B4
Parc 72 F2
Parcllyn 45 D4
Parc-Seymour 35 E8
Parc-y-rhôs 46 E4
Pardshaw 98 B2
Parham 57 C7
Park 114 E2
Park Corner Oxon 39 F6
Windsor 40 F1
Parkend 36 D3
Park End Mbro 102 C3
Northumb 109 B8
Parkeston 57 F6
Parkgate Ches W 73 B6
Dumfries 114 F3
Kent 19 B5
Sur 28 E3
Park Gate 15 D6
Parkham 9 B5
Parkham Ash 9 B5
Park Hill Notts 77 D6
N Yorks 95 C6
Parkhill House 141 C7
Parkhouse 36 D1
Parkhouse Green 76 C4
Parkhurst 15 E5
Parkmill 33 F6
Parkneuk 135 B7
Parkstone 13 E8
Park Street 28 F2
Parley Cross 13 E8
Parracombe 21 E5
Parrog 45 F2
Parsley Hay 75 C8
Parsonage Green 42 D3
Parsonby 107 F8
Parson Cross 88 E4
Parson Drove 66 D3
Parson's Heath 43 B6
Partick 119 C5
Partington 86 E5
Partney 79 C7
Parton Cumb 98 B1
Dumfries 106 B3
Glos 37 B5
Partridge Green 17 C5
Parwich 75 D8
Passenham 53 F5
Paston 81 D9
Patchacott 9 E6
Patcham 17 D7
Patching 16 D4
Patchole 20 E5
Pateley Bridge 94 C4
Paternoster Heath 43 C5
Pathe 23 F5
Pathhead Aberds 135 C7
E Ayrs 113 C6
Fife 128 E4
Midloth 121 C6
Path of Condie 128 C2
Pathstruie 128 C2
Patna 112 C4
Patney 25 D5
Patrick 84 D2
Patrick Brompton 101 E7
Patrington 91 B7
Patrixbourne 31 D5
Patterdale 99 C5
Pattingham 62 E2
Pattishall 52 D4
Pattiswick Green 42 B4
Patton Bridge 99 E7
Paul 2 D3
Paulerspury 52 E5
Paull 91 B5
Paulton 23 D8
Pavenham 53 D7
Pawlett 22 E5
Pawston 122 F4
Paxford 51 F6
Paxton 122 D5
Payhembury 11 D5
Paythorne 93 D8
Peacehaven 17 D8
Peak Dale 75 B7
Peak Forest 75 B8
Peakirk 65 D8
Pearsie 134 D3
Peasedown St John 24 D2
Peasemore 26 B2
Peasenhall 57 C7
Pease Pottage 28 F3
Peaslake 27 E8
Peasley Cross 86 E3
Peasmarsh 19 C5
Peaston 121 C7
Peastonbank 121 C7
Peathill 153 B9
Peat Inn 129 D6
Peatling Magna 64 E2
Peatling Parva 64 F2
Peaton 60 F5
Peats Corner 57 C5
Pebmarsh 56 F2
Pebworth 51 E6
Pecket Well 87 B7
Peckforton 74 D2
Peckham 28 B4
Peckleton 63 D8
Pedlinge 19 B8
Pedmore 62 F3
Pedwell 23 F6
Peebles 121 E5
Peel 84 D2
Peel Common 15 D6
Peel Park 119 D6
Peening Quarter 19 C5
Pegsdon 54 F2
Pegswood 117 F8
Pegwell 31 C7
Peinchorran 149 E10
Peinlich 149 C9
Pelaw 111 C5
Pelcomb Bridge 44 D4
Pelcomb Cross 44 D4
Peldon 43 C5
Pellon 87 B8
Pelsall 62 D4
Pelton 111 D5
Pelutho 107 E8
Pelynt 5 D7
Pemberton 86 D3
Pembrey 33 D5
Pembridge 49 D5
Pembroke = *Penfro* 44 E4
Pembroke Dock = *Doc Penfro* 44 E4
Pembury 29 E7
Penallt 36 C2
Penally 32 E2
Penalt 36 B2
Penare 3 B8
Penarlâg = *Hawarden* 73 C7
Penarth 22 B3
Pen-bont Rhydybeddau 58 F3
Penbryn 45 D4
Pencader 46 F3
Pencaenewydd 70 C5
Pencaitland 121 C7
Pencarnisiog 82 D3
Pencarreg 46 E4
Pencelli 34 B4
Pen-clawdd 33 E6
Pencoed 34 F3
Pencombe 49 D7
Pencoyd 36 B2
Pencraig Hereford 36 B2
Powys 59 B7
Pendeen 2 C2
Penderyn 34 D3
Pendine 32 D3
Pendlebury 87 D5
Pendleton 93 F7
Pendock 50 F2
Pendoggett 4 B5
Pendomer 12 C3
Pendoylan 22 B2
Pendre 34 F3
Penegoes 58 D4
Pen-ffordd 32 B1
Penfro = *Pembroke* 44 E4
Pengam 35 E5
Penge 28 B4
Pengenffordd 48 F3
Pengorffwysfa 82 B4
Pengover Green 5 C7
Pen-groes-oped 35 D7
Penhale Corn 3 E5
Corn 4 D4
Penhalvaen 3 C6
Penhill 38 F1
Penhow 35 E8
Penhurst 18 D3
Peniarth 58 D3
Penicuik 120 C5
Peniel Carms 33 B5
Denb 72 C4
Penifiler 149 D9
Peninver 143 F8
Penisarwaun 83 E5
Penistone 88 D3
Penjerrick 3 C6
Penketh 86 F3
Penkill 112 E2
Penkridge 62 C3
Penley 73 F8
Penllergaer 33 E7
Penllyn 21 B8
Pen-llyn 82 C3
Pen-lon 82 E4
Penmachno 83 F7
Penmaen 33 F6
Penmaenan 83 D7
Penmaenmawr 83 D7
Penmaenpool 58 C3
Penmark 22 C2
Penmarth 3 C6
Penmon 83 C6
Penmore Mill 146 F7
Penmorfa Ceredig 46 D2
Gwyn 71 C6
Penmynydd 82 D5
Penn Bucks 40 E2
W Mid 62 E2
Pennal 58 D4
Pennan 153 B8
Pennant Ceredig 46 C4
Denb 72 D4
Denb 72 F4
Powys 59 E5
Pennant Melangell 59 B7
Pennar 44 E4
Pennard 33 F6
Pennerley 60 E3
Pennington Cumb 92 B2
Gtr Man 86 E4
Hants 14 E4
Penn Street 40 E2
Penny Bridge 99 F5
Pennycross 147 J8
Pennygate 69 B6
Pennygown 147 G8
Pennymoor 10 C3
Pennywell 111 D6
Penparc Ceredig 45 E4
Penparc *continued*
Pembs 44 B3
Penparcau 58 F2
Penperlleni 35 D7
Penpillick 5 D5
Penpol 3 C7
Penpoll 5 D6
Penpont Dumfries 113 E8
Powys 34 B3
Penrherber 45 F4
Penrhiwceiber 34 E4
Penrhiw goch 33 C6
Penrhiw-llan 46 E2
Penrhiw-pâl 46 E2
Penrhos 70 D4
Penrhôs 35 C8
Penrhos 34 C1
Penrhosfeilw 82 C2
Penrhyn Bay 83 C8
Penrhyn-coch 58 F3
Penrhyndeudraeth 71 D7
Penrhynside 83 C8
Penrice 33 F5
Penrith 108 F5
Penrose 4 B3
Penruddock 99 B6
Penryn 3 C6
Pensarn Carms 33 C5
Conwy 72 B3
Pen-sarn Gwyn 70 C5
Gwyn 71 E6
Pensax 50 C2
Pensby 85 F3
Penselwood 24 F2
Pensford 23 C8
Penshaw 111 D6
Penshurst 29 E6
Pensilva 5 C7
Penston 121 B7
Pentewan 3 B9
Pentir 83 E5
Pentire 4 C2
Pentlow 56 E2
Pentney 67 C7
Penton Mewsey 25 E8
Pentraeth 82 D5
Pentre Carms 33 C6
Powys 59 F7
Powys 60 E2
Rhondda 34 E3
Shrops 60 C3
Wrex 72 F5
Wrex 73 E6
Pentrebach M Tydf 34 D4
Swansea 33 D7
Pentre-bâch 46 E4
Pentre-bach 47 F8
Pentrebeirdd 59 C8
Pentre Berw 82 D4
Pentre-bont 83 F7
Pentrecagal 46 E2
Pentre-celyn Denb 72 D5
Powys 59 D5
Pentre-chwyth 33 E7
Pentre-cwrt 46 F2
Pentre Dolau-Honddu 47 E8
Pentredwr 73 E5
Pentre-dwr 33 E7
Pentrefelin Carms 33 B6
Ceredig 46 E5
Conwy 83 D8
Gwyn 71 D6
Pentrefoelas 83 F8
Pentre-galar 45 F3
Pentregat 46 D2
Pentre-Gwenlais 33 C7
Pentre Gwynfryn 71 E6
Pentre Halkyn 73 B6
Pentreheyling 60 E2
Pentre-Isaf 83 E8
Pentre Llanrhaeadr 72 C4
Pentre-llwyn-ll yd 47 D8
Pentre-llyn 46 B5
Pentre-llyn cymmer 72 D3
Pentre Meyrick 21 B8
Pentre-poeth 35 F6
Pentre'r Felin 83 E8
Pentre'r-felin 47 F8
Pentre-rhew 47 D5
Pentre-tafarn-yfedw 83 E8
Pentre-ty-gwyn 47 F7
Pentrich 76 D3
Pentridge 13 C8
Pen-twyn 36 D2
Pentyrch 35 F5
Penuchadre 21 B7
Penuwch 46 C4
Penwithick 4 D5
Penwyllt 34 C2
Penybanc 33 C7
Pen-y-banc 33 B7
Penybont 48 C3
Pen-y-bont Carms 32 B4
Gwyn 58 D4
Gwyn 71 E7
Powys 60 B2
Pen-y-Bont Ar Ogwr = *Bridgend* 21 B8
Penybontfawr 59 B7
Pen-y-bryn Gwyn 58 C3
Pembs 45 E3
Penycae 73 E6
Pen-y-cae 34 C2
Pen-y-cae-mawr 35 E8
Pen-y-cefn 72 B5
Pen-y-clawdd 36 D1
Pen-y-coedcae 34 F4
Penycwm 44 C3
Pen-y-fai 34 F2
Penyffordd 73 C7
Penyffridd 82 F5
Pen-y-garn Carms 46 F4
Ceredig 58 F3
Penygarnedd 59 B8
Pen-y-garnedd 82 D5
Pen-y-gop 72 E3
Penygraig 34 E3
Pen-y-graig 70 D2
Penygroes Gwyn 82 F4
Pembs 45 F3
Pen-y-groes 33 C6

Pen-y-groeslon	70	D3
Pen-y-Gwryd Hotel	83	F6
Penyrheol	35	F5
Pen-yr-heol	35	C8
Pen-yr-Heolgerrig	34	D4
Penysarn	82	B4
Pen-y-stryt	73	F5
Penywaun	34	D3
Penzance	2	C3
Peopleton	50	D4
Peover Heath	74	B4
Peper Harow	27	E7
Perceton	118	E3
Percie	140	E4
Percyhorner	153	B9
Periton	21	E8
Perivale	40	F4
Perkinsville	111	D5
Perlethorpe	77	B6
Perranarworthal	3	C6
Perranporth	4	D2
Perranuthnoe	2	D4
Perranzabuloe	4	D2
Perry Barr	62	E4
Perryfoot	88	F2
Perry Green Herts.	41	C7
Wilts	37	F6
Perry Street	29	B7
Pershall	74	F5
Pershore	50	E4
Pert	135	C6
Pertenhall	53	C8
Perth	128	B3
Perthy	73	F7
Perton	62	E2
Pertwood	24	F3
Peterborough	65	E8
Peterburn	155	J12
Peterchurch	48	F5
Peterculter	141	D7
Peterhead	153	D11
Peterlee	111	E7
Petersfield	15	B8
Peter's Green	40	C4
Peters Marland	9	C6
Peterstone Wentlooge	35	F6
Peterston-super-Ely	22	B2
Peterstow	36	B2
Peter Tavy	6	B3
Petertown	159	H4
Petham	30	D5
Petrockstow	9	D7
Pett	19	D5
Pettaugh	57	D5
Petteridge	29	E7
Pettinain	120	E2
Pettistree	57	D6
Petton Devon	10	B5
Shrops.	60	B4
Petts Wood	28	C5
Petty	153	E7
Pettycur	128	F4
Pettymuick	141	B8
Petworth	16	B3
Pevensey	18	E3
Pevensey Bay	18	E3
Pewsey	25	C6
Philham	8	B4
Philiphaugh	115	B7
Phillack	2	C4
Philleigh	3	C7
Philpstoun	120	B3
Phocle Green	36	B3
Phoenix Green	27	D5
Pica	98	B2
Piccotts End	40	D3
Pickering	103	F5
Picket Piece	25	E8
Picket Post	14	D2
Pickhill	101	F8
Picklescott	60	E4
Pickletillem	129	B6
Pickmere	74	B3
Pickney	11	B6
Pickstock	61	B7
Pickwell Devon	20	E3
Leics	64	C4
Pickworth Lincs	78	F3
Rutland	65	C7
Picton ChesW	73	B8
Flint	85	F2
N Yorks	102	D2
Piddinghoe	17	D8
Piddington Northants	53	D6
Oxon	39	C6
Piddlehinton	12	E5
Piddletrenthide	12	E5
Pidley	54	B4
Piercebridge	101	C7
Pierowall	159	D5
Pigdon	117	F7
Pikehall	75	D8
Pilgrims Hatch	42	E1
Pilham	90	E2
Pill	23	B7
Pillaton	5	C8
Pillerton Hersey	51	E8
Pillerton Priors	51	E7
Pilleth	48	C4
Pilley Hants	14	E4
S Yorks	88	D4
Pilling	92	E4
Pilling Lane	92	E3
Pillowell	36	D3
Pillwell	13	C5
Pilning	36	F2
Pilsbury	75	C8
Pilsdon	11	E8
Pilsley Derbys	75	B8
Derbys	76	C4
Pilton Devon	20	F4
Northants	65	F7
Rutland	65	D7
Som	23	E7
Pilton Green	33	F5
Pimperne	13	D7
Pinchbeck	66	B2
Pinchbeck Bars	65	B8
Pinchbeck West	66	B2
Pincheon Green	89	C7
Pinehurst	38	F1
Pinfold	85	C4
Pinged	33	D5
Pinhoe	10	E4
Pinkneys Green	40	F1
Pinley	51	B8
Pin Mill	57	F6
Pinminnoch	112	E1
Pinmore	112	E2
Pinmore Mains	112	E2
Pinner	40	F4
Pinvin	50	E4
Pinwherry	112	F1
Pinxton	76	D4
Pipe and Lyde	49	E7
Pipe Gate	74	E4
Piperhill	151	F11
Piper's Pool	8	F4
Pipewell	64	F5
Pippacott	20	F4
Pipton	48	F3
Pirbright	27	D7
Pirnmill	143	D9
Pirton Herts	54	F2
Worcs	50	E3
Pisgah Ceredig	47	B5
Stirling	127	D6
Pishill	39	F7
Pistyll	70	C4
Pitagowan	133	C5
Pitblae	153	B9
Pitcairngreen	128	B2
Pitcalnie	151	D11
Pitcaple	141	B6
Pitchcombe	37	D5
Pitchcott	39	B7
Pitchford	60	D5
Pitch Green	39	D7
Pitch Place	27	D7
Pitcombe	23	F8
Pitcorthie	129	D7
Pitcox	122	B2
Pitcur	134	F2
Pitfichie	141	C5
Pitforthie	135	B8
Pitgrudy	151	B10
Pitkennedy	135	D5
Pitkevy	128	D4
Pitkierie	129	D7
Pitlessie	128	D5
Pitlochry	133	D6
Pitmachie	141	B5
Pitmain	138	D3
Pitmedden	141	B7
Pitminster	11	C7
Pitmuies	135	E5
Pitmunie	141	C5
Pitney	12	B2
Pitscottie	129	C6
Pitsea	42	F3
Pitsford	53	C5
Pitsmoor	88	F4
Pitstone	40	C2
Pitstone Green	40	C2
Pittendreich	152	B1
Pittentrail	157	J10
Pittenweem	129	D7
Pittington	111	E6
Pittodrie	141	B5
Pitton	25	F7
Pittswood	29	E7
Pittulie	153	B9
Pityme	4	B4
Pity Me	111	E5
Pityoulish	138	C5
Pixey Green	57	B6
Pixham	28	D2
Pixley	49	F8
Place Newton	96	B4
Plaidy	153	C7
Plains	119	C7
Plaish	60	E5
Plaistow	27	F8
Plaitford	14	C3
Plank Lane	86	E4
Plas-canol	58	C2
Plas Gogerddan	58	F3
Plas Llwyngwern	58	D4
Plas Nantyr	73	F5
Plastow Green	26	C3
Plas-yn-Cefn	72	B4
Platt	29	D7
Platt Bridge	86	D4
Platts Common	88	D4
Plawsworth	111	E5
Plaxtol	29	D7
Playden	19	C6
Playford	57	E6
Play Hatch	26	B5
Playing Place	3	B7
Playley Green	50	F2
Plealey	60	D4
Plean	127	F7
Pleasington	86	B4
Pleasley	76	C5
Pleckgate	93	F6
Plenmeller	109	C7
Pleshey	42	C2
Plockton	149	E13
Plocrapol	154	H6
Ploughfield	49	E5
Plowden	60	F3
Ploxgreen	60	D3
Pluckley	30	E3
Pluckley Thorne	30	E3
Plumbland	107	F8
Plumley	74	B4
Plumpton Cumb	108	F4
E Sus	17	C7
Plumpton Green	17	C7
Plumpton Head	108	F5
Plumstead London	29	B5
Norf.	81	D7
Plumtree	77	F6
Plungar	77	F7
Plush	12	D5
Plwmp	46	D2
Plymouth	6	D2
Plympton	6	D3
Plymstock	6	D3
Plymtree	11	D5
Pockley	102	F4
Pocklington	96	E4
Pode Hole	66	B2
Podimore	12	B3
Podington	53	C7
Podmore	74	F4
Point Clear	43	C6
Pointon	78	F4
Pokesdown	14	E2
Pol a Charra	148	G2
Polbae	105	B6
Polbain	156	H2
Polbathic	5	D8
Polbeth	120	C3
Polchar	138	D4
Polebrook	65	F7
Pole Elm	50	E3
Polegate	18	E2
Poles	151	B10
Polesworth	63	D6
Polgigga	2	D2
Polglass	156	J3
Polgooth	4	D4
Poling	16	D4
Polkerris	5	D5
Polla	156	D6
Pollington	89	C7
Polloch	130	C1
Pollok	118	C5
Pollokshields	119	C5
Polmassick	3	B8
Polmont	120	B2
Polnessan	112	C4
Polnish	147	C10
Polperro	5	D7
Polruan	5	D6
Polsham	23	E7
Polstead	56	F3
Poltalloch	124	F4
Poltimore	10	E4
Polton	121	C5
Polwarth	122	D3
Polyphant	8	F4
Polzeath	4	B4
Pondersbridge	66	E2
Ponders End	41	E6
Pondtail	27	D6
Ponsanooth	3	C6
Ponsworthy	6	B5
Pont Aber	33	B8
Pont Aber-Geirw	71	E8
Pontamman	33	C7
Pontantwn	33	C5
Pontardawe	33	D8
Pontarddulais	33	D6
Pont-ar-gothi	33	B6
Pont ar Hydfer	34	B2
Pont-ar-llechau	33	B8
Pontarsais	33	B5
Pontblyddyn	73	C6
Pontbren Araeth	33	B7
Pontbren Llwyd	34	D3
Pont Cwm Pydew	72	F4
Pont Cyfyng	83	F7
Pont Cysyllte	73	E6
Pont Dolydd Prysor	71	D8
Pontefract	89	B5
Ponteland	110	B4
Ponterwyd	58	F4
Pontesbury	60	D3
Pontfadog	73	F6
Pontfaen	45	F2
Pont-faen	47	F8
Pont Fronwydd	58	B5
Pont-gareg	45	E3
Pontgarreg	46	D2
Pont-Henri	33	D5
Ponthir	35	E7
Ponthirwaun	45	E4
Pontllanfraith	35	E5
Pontlliw	33	D7
Pont-Llogel	59	C7
Pontllyfni	82	F4
Pontlottyn	35	D5
Pontneddfechan	34	D3
Pontnewydd	35	E6
Pont Pen-y-benglog	83	E6
Pontrhydfendigaid	47	C6
Pont Rhyd-goch	83	E6
Pont-Rhyd-sarn	59	B5
Pont Rhyd-y-cyff	34	F2
Pontrhydyfen	34	E1
Pont-rhyd-y-groes	47	B6
Pontrilas	35	B7
Pontrobert	59	C8
Pont-rug	82	E5
Pont Senni =Sennybridge	34	B3
Ponts Green	18	D3
Pontshill	36	B3
Pont-siân	46	E3
Pontsticill	34	C4
Pontwgan	83	D7
Pontyates	33	D5
Pontyberem	33	C6
Pontyclun	34	F4
Pontycymer	34	E3
Pontyglasier	45	F3
Pont-y-gwaith	34	E4
Pont-y-pant	83	F7
Pont y Pennant	59	B6
Pontypool =Pont-y-pŵl	35	D6
Pontypridd	34	F4
Pont-y-pŵl =Pontypool	35	D6
Pont yr Afon-Gam	71	C8
Pont-yr-hafod	44	C4
Pontywaun	35	E6
Pooksgreen	14	C4
Pool Corn.	3	B5
W Yorks	94	E5
Poole	13	E8
Poole Keynes	37	E6
Poolend	75	D6
Poolewe	155	J13
Pooley Bridge	99	B6
Poolfold	75	D5
Poolhill	36	B4
Porlock Weir	21	E7
Portachoillan	144	H6
Port Ann	145	E8
Port Appin	130	E3
Port Arthur	160	K5
Port Askaig	142	B5
Portavadie	145	G8
Port Bannatyne	145	G9
Portbury	23	B7
Port Carlisle	108	C2
Port Charlotte	142	C3
Portchester	15	D7
Portclair	137	C7
Port Clarence	102	B2
Port Driseach	145	F8
Port Ellen	142	D4
Port Elphinstone	141	C6
Port Erin	84	F1
Port Erroll	153	E10
Portesham	12	F4
Portessie	152	B4
Port e Vullen	84	C4
Port-Eynon	33	F5
Portfield Gate	44	D4
Portgate	9	F6
Port Gaverne	8	F2
Port Glasgow	118	B3
Portgordon	152	B3
Portgower	157	H13
Porth Corn.	4	C3
Rhondda	34	E4
Porthaethwy =Menai Bridge	83	D5
Porthallow Corn	3	D6
Corn.	5	D7
Porthcawl	21	B7
Porthcothan	4	B3
Porthcurno	2	D2
Port Henderson	149	A12
Porthgain	44	B3
Porthill	60	C4
Porthkerry	22	C2
Porthleven	2	D5
Porthllechog	82	B4
Porthmadog	71	D6
Porthmeor	2	C3
Porth Navas	3	D6
Portholland	3	B8
Porthoustock	3	D7
Porthpean	4	D5
Porthtowan	3	B5
Porth Tywyn =Burry Port	33	D5
Porthyrhyd Carms.	33	C6
Carms.	47	F6
Porth-y-waen	60	B2
Portincaple	145	D11
Portington	96	F3
Portinnisherrich	125	D6
Portinscale	98	B4
Port Isaac	4	A4
Portishead	23	B6
Portkil	145	E11
Port Lamont	145	F9
Portlethen	141	E8
Portling	107	D5
Port Lion	44	E4
Portloe	3	C8
Port Logan	104	E4
Portmahomack	151	C12
Portmeirion	71	D6
Portmellon	3	B9
Port Mholair	155	D10
Port Mor	146	D7
Portmore	14	E4
Port Mulgrave	103	C5
Portnacroish	130	E3
Portnahaven	142	C2
Portnalong	149	E8
Portnaluchaig	147	C9
Portnancon	156	C7
Port Nan Giùran	155	D10
Port nan Long	148	A3
Portnellan	126	B3
Port Nis	155	A10
Portobello	121	B6
Port of Menteith	126	D4
Porton	25	F6
Portpatrick	104	D4
Port Quin	4	A4
Port Ramsay	130	E2
Portreath	3	B5
Portree	149	D9
Port St Mary	84	F2
Portscatho	3	C7
Portsea	15	D7
Portskerra	157	C11
Portskewett	36	F2
Portslade	17	D6
Portslade-by-Sea	17	D6
Portsmouth Ptsmth.	15	D7
W Yorks	87	B7
Portsonachan	125	C6
Portsoy	152	B5
Port Sunlight	85	F4
Portswood	14	C5
Port Talbot	34	E1
Port Tennant	33	E7
Portuairk	146	E7
Portway Hereford	49	E6
Worcs	51	B5
Port Wemyss	142	C2
Port William	105	E7
Portwrinkle	5	D8
Poslingford	55	E8
Postbridge	6	B4
Postcombe	39	E7
Postling	19	B8
Postwick	69	D5
Potterton Aberds.	141	C8
W Yorks	95	F7
Potto	102	D2
Potton	54	E3
Pott Row	80	E3
Pott Shrigley	75	B6
Poughill Corn.	8	D4
Devon	10	D3
Poulshot	24	D4
Poulton Glos.	37	D8
Mers	85	E4
Poulton-le-Fylde	92	F3
Pound Bank	50	B2
Poundbury	12	E4
Poundfield	18	B2
Pound Green E Sus	18	C2
IoW	14	F4
Worcs	50	B2
Pound Hill	28	F3
Poundland	112	F1
Poundon	39	B6
Poundsgate	6	B5
Poundstock	8	E4
Powburn	117	C6
Powderham	10	F4
Powerstock	12	E3
Powfoot	107	C8
Powick	50	D3
Powmill	128	E2
Poxwell	12	F5
Poyle	27	B8
Poynings	17	C6
Poyntington	12	C4
Poynton	87	F7
Poynton Green	61	C5
Poystreet Green	56	D3
Praa Sands	2	D4
Pratt's Bottom	29	C5
Praze	2	C4
Praze-an-Beeble	2	C5
Predannack Wollas	3	E5
Prees	74	F2
Preesall	92	E3
Prees Green	74	F2
Preesgweene	73	F6
Prees Heath	74	F2
Prees Higher Heath	74	F2
Prees Lower Heath	74	F2
Prendergurst	122	D5
Prendwick	117	C6
Prengwyn	46	E3
Prenteg	71	C6
Prenton	85	F4
Prescot	86	E2
Prescott	60	B4
Pressen	122	F4
Prestatyn	72	A4
Prestbury ChesE	75	B6
Glos.	37	B6
Presteigne =Llanandras	48	C5
Presthope	61	E5
Prestleigh	23	E8
Preston Borders	122	D3
Brighton	17	D7
Devon	7	B6
Dorset	12	F5
E Loth	121	B8
E Yorks	97	F7
Glos.	37	D7
Glos.	49	F8
Herts	40	B4
Kent	30	C4
Kent	31	C6
Lancs	86	B3
Northumb	117	B7
Rutland	65	D5
Shrops.	60	C5
Wilts	24	B5
Wilts	25	B7
Preston Bagot	51	C6
Preston Bissett	39	B6
Preston Bowyer	11	B6
Preston Brockhurst	60	B5
Preston Brook	86	F3
Preston Candover	26	E4
Preston Capes	52	D3
Preston Crowmarsh	39	E6
Preston Gubbals	60	C4
Prestonmill	107	D6
Preston on Stour	51	E7
Preston on the Hill	86	F3
Preston on Wye	49	E5
Prestonpans	121	B6
Preston Plucknett	12	C3
Preston St Mary	56	D3
Preston-under-Scar	101	E5
Preston upon the Weald Moors	61	C6
Preston Wynne	49	E7
Prestwich	87	D6
Prestwick Northumb	110	B4
S Ayrs	112	B3
Prestwood	40	D1
Price Town	34	E3
Prickwillow	67	F5
Priddy	23	D7
Priesthaugh	115	D7
Priest Hutton	92	B5
Priest Weston	60	E2
Primethorpe	64	E2
Primrose Green	68	C3
Primrosehill	40	D3
Primrose Valley	97	B7
Princes Risborough	39	D8
Princethorpe	52	B2
Princetown Caerph	35	C5
Devon	6	B3
Prion	72	C4
Prior Muir	129	C7
Prior Park	123	D5
Priors Frome	49	F7
Priors Hardwick	52	D2
Priorslee	61	C7
Priors Marston	52	D2
Priory Wood	48	E4
Priston	23	C8
Pristow Green	68	F4
Prittlewell	42	F4
Privett	15	B7
Prixford	20	F4
Probus	3	B7
Proncy	151	B10
Prospect	107	E8
Prudhoe	110	C3
Ptarmigan Lodge	126	D2
Pubil	132	E1
Puckeridge	41	B6
Puckington	11	C8
Pucklechurch	23	B8
Pucknall	14	B4
Puckrup	50	F3
Puddington Ches W.	73	B7
Devon	10	C3
Puddledock	68	E3
Puddletown	13	E5
Pudleston	49	D7
Pudsey	94	F5
Pulborough	16	C4
Puleston	61	B7
Pulford	73	D7
Pulham	12	D5
Pulham Market	68	F4
Pulham St Mary	68	F5
Pulloxhill	53	F8
Pumpherston	120	C3
Pumsaint	47	E5
Puncheston	32	B1
Puncknowle	12	F3
Punnett's Town	18	C3
Purbrook	15	D7
Purewell	14	E2
Purfleet	29	B6
Puriton	22	E5
Purleigh	42	D4
Purley London	28	C4
W Berks	26	B4
Purlogue	48	B4
Purls Bridge	66	F4
Purse Caundle	12	C4
Purslow	60	F3
Purston Jaglin	88	C5
Purton Glos.	36	D3
Glos.	36	D3
Wilts	37	F7
Purton Stoke	37	E7
Pury End	52	E5
Pusey	38	E3
Putley	49	F8
Putney	28	B3
Putsborough	20	E3
Puttenham Herts	40	C1
Sur	27	E7
Puxton	23	C6
Pwll	33	D5
Pwllcrochan	44	E4
Pwll-glas	72	D5
Pwllgloyw	48	F2
Pwllheli	70	D4
Pwllmeyric	36	E2
Pwll-trap	32	C3
Pwll-y-glaw	34	E1
Pyecombe	17	C6
Pye Corner	35	F7
Pye Green	62	C3
Pyewipe	91	C6
Pyle	15	G5
Pyle =Y Pîl	34	F2
Pylle	23	F8
Pymoor	66	F4
Pyrford	27	D8
Pyrton	39	E6
Pytchley	53	B6
Pyworthy	8	D5

Q

Quabbs	60	F2
Quadring	78	F5
Quainton	39	C7
Quarley	25	E7
Quarndon	76	E3
Quarrier's Homes	118	C3
Quarrington	78	E3
Quarrington Hill	111	F6
Quarry Bank	62	F3
Quarryford	121	C8
Quarryhill	151	C10
Quarrywood	152	B1
Quarter	119	D7
Quatford	61	E7
Quatt	61	F7
Quebec	110	E4
Quedgeley	37	C5
Queen Adelaide	67	F5
Queenborough	30	B3
Queen Camel	12	B3
Queen Charlton	23	C8
Queenhill	50	F3
Queen Oak	24	F2
Queensbury	94	F4
Queensferry Edin.	120	B4
Queensferry Flint	73	C7
Queenstown	92	F3
Queen Street Kent	29	E7
Wilts	37	F7
Queenzieburn	119	B6
Quemerford	24	C5
Quendale	160	M5
Quendon	55	F6
Queniborough	64	C3
Quenington	37	D8
Quernmore	92	D5
Quethiock	5	C8
Quholm	159	G3
Quicks Green	26	B3
Quidenham	68	F3
Quidhampton Hants.	26	D3
Wilts	25	F6
Quilquox	153	E9
Quina Brook	74	F2
Quindry	159	J5
Quinton Northants	53	D5
W Mid	62	F3
Quintrell Downs	4	C3
Quixhill	75	E8
Quoditch	9	E6
Quoig	127	B7
Quorndon	64	C2
Quothquan	120	F2
Quoyloo	159	F3
Quoyness	159	H3
Quoys Shetland	160	B8
Shetland	160	G6

R

Raasay House	149	E10
Rabbit's Cross	29	E8
Raby	73	B7
Rachan Mill	120	F4
Rachub	83	E6
Rackenford	10	C3
Rackham	16	C4
Rackheath	69	C5
Racks	107	B7
Rackwick Orkney	159	D5
Orkney	159	J3
Radbourne	76	F2
Radcliffe Gtr Man	87	D6
Northumb	117	D8
Radcliffe on Trent	77	F6
Radclive	52	F4
Radcot	38	E2
Raddery	151	F10
Radernie	129	D6
Radford Semele	51	C8
Radipole	12	F4
Radlett	40	E4
Radley	39	E5
Radmanthwaite	76	C5
Radmoor	61	B6
Radmore Green	74	D2
Radnage	39	E7
Radstock	23	D8
Radstone	52	E3
Radway	51	E8
Radway Green	74	D4
Radwell Bedford	53	D8
Herts	54	F3
Radwinter	55	F7
Radyr	35	F5
Rafford	151	F13
Ragdale	64	C3
Raglan	35	D8
Ragnall	77	B8
Rahane	145	E11
Rainford	86	D2
Rainford Junction	86	D2
Rainham London.	41	F8
Medway	30	C2
Rainhill	86	E2
Rainhill Stoops	86	E3
Rainow	75	B6
Rainton	95	B6
Rainworth	77	D5
Raisbeck	99	D8
Raise	109	E7
Rait	128	B4
Raithby Lincs.	79	C6
Lincs	91	F7
Rake	16	B2
Rakewood	87	C7
Ram	46	E4
Ramasaig	148	D6
Rame Corn.	5	D5
Corn.	6	E2
Rameldry Mill Bank	128	D5
Ram Lane	30	E3
Ramnageo	160	C8
Rampisham	12	D3
Rampside	92	C2
Rampton Cambs.	54	C5
Notts	77	B7
Ramsbottom	87	C5
Ramsbury	25	B7
Ramscraigs	158	H3
Ramsdean	15	B8
Ramsdell	26	D3
Ramsden	38	C3
Ramsden Bellhouse	42	E3
Ramsden Heath	42	E3
Ramsey Cambs	66	F2
Essex	57	F6
IoM	84	C4
Ramseycleuch	115	C5
Ramsey Forty Foot	66	F3
Ramsey Heights	66	F2
Ramsey Island	43	D5
Ramsey Mereside	66	F2
Ramsey St Mary's	66	F2
Ramsgate	31	C7
Ramsgill	94	B4
Ramshorn	75	E7
Ramsnest Common	27	F7
Ranais	155	E9
Ranby Lincs.	78	B5
Notts	89	F7
Rand	78	B4
Randwick	37	D5
Ranfurly	118	C3
Rangag	158	F3
Rangemore	63	B5
Rangeworthy	36	F3
Rankinston	112	C4
Ranmoor	88	F4
Ranmore Common	28	D2
Rannerdale	98	C3
Rannoch Station	131	D8
Ranochan	147	C11
Ranskill	89	F7
Ranton	62	B2
Ranworth	69	C6
Raploch	127	E6
Rapness	159	D6
Rascal Moor	96	F4
Rascarrel	106	E4
Rashiereive	141	B8
Raskelf	95	B7
Rassau	35	C5
Rastrick	88	B2
Ratagan	136	C2
Ratby	64	D2
Ratcliffe Culey	63	E7
Ratcliffe on Soar	63	B8
Ratcliffe on the Wreake	64	C3
Rathen	153	B10
Rathillet	129	B5
Rathmell	93	D8
Ratho	120	B4
Ratho Station	120	B4
Rathven	152	B4
Ratley	51	E8
Ratlinghope	60	E4
Rattar	158	C4
Ratten Row	92	E4
Rattery	6	C5
Rattlesden	56	D3
Rattray	134	E1
Raughton Head	108	E3
Raunds	53	B7
Ravenfield	89	E5
Ravenglass	98	E2
Raveningham	69	E6
Ravenscar	103	D7
Ravenscraig	118	B2
Ravensdale	84	C3
Ravensden	53	D8
Ravenseat	100	D3
Ravenshead	77	D5
Ravensmoor	74	D3
Ravensthorpe Northants	52	B4
W Yorks	88	B3
Ravenstone Leics.	63	C8
M Keynes	53	D6
Ravenstonedale	100	D2
Ravenstown	92	B3
Ravenstruther	120	E2
Ravensworth	101	D6
Raw	103	D7
Rawcliffe E Yorks	89	B7
York	95	D8
Rawcliffe Bridge	89	B7
Rawdon	94	F5
Rawmarsh	88	E5
Rawreth	42	E3
Rawridge	11	D7
Rawtenstall	87	B6
Raydon	56	F4
Raylees	117	E5
Rayleigh	42	E4
Rayne	42	B3
Rayners Lane	40	F4
Raynes Park	28	C3
Reach	55	C6
Read	93	F7
Reading	26	B5
Reading Street	19	B6
Reagill	99	C8
Rearquhar	151	B10
Rearsby	64	C3
Reaster	158	D4
Reawick	160	J5
Reay	157	C12
Rechullin	149	C13
Reculver	31	C6
Redberth	32	D1
Redbourn	40	C4
Redbourne	90	E3
Redbrook Mon	36	C2
Wrex	74	E2
Redburn Highld	151	E8
Highld	151	G12
Northumb	109	C7
Redcar	102	B4
Redcastle Angus	135	D6
Highld	151	G8
Redcliff Bay	23	B6
Redding	120	B2
Reddingmuirhead	120	B2
Reddish	87	E6
Redditch	50	C5
Rede	56	D2
Redenhall	69	F5
Redesdale Camp	116	E4
Redesmouth	116	F4
Redford Aberds	135	B7
Angus	135	E5
Durham	110	F3
Redfordgreen	115	C6
Redgorton	128	B2
Redgrave	56	B4
Redhill Aberds	141	D6
N Som	23	C7
Sur	28	D3
Red Hill	50	D3
Redhouse	145	G2
Redhouses	142	B4
Red Houses Jersey	17	
Redisham	69	F7
Redland Bristol	23	B7
Orkney	159	F4
Redlingfield	57	B5
Red Lodge	55	B7
Redlynch Som	23	F9
Wilts	14	B3
Redmarley D'Abitot	50	F2
Redmarshall	102	B1
Redmile	77	F7
Redmire	101	E5
Redmoor	5	C5
Rednal	60	B3
Redpath	121	F8
Redpoint	149	B12
Red Rail	36	B2
Red Rock	86	D3
Red Roses	32	C3
Red Row	117	E8
Redruth	3	B5
Red Street	74	D5
Redvales	87	D6
Red Wharf Bay	82	C5
Redwick Newport.	35	F8
S Glos.	36	F2
Redworth	101	B7
Reed	54	F4
Reedham	69	D7
Reedness	89	B8
Reeds Beck	78	C5
Reepham Lincs.	78	B3
Norf.	81	E6
Reeth	101	E5
Regaby	84	C4
Regoul	151	F11
Reiff	156	H2
Reigate	28	D3
Reighton	97	B7
Reighton Gap	97	B7
Reinigeadal	154	G7
Reiss	158	E5
Rejerrah	4	D2
Releath	3	C5
Relubbus	2	C4
Relugas	151	G12
Remenham	39	F7
Remenham Hill	39	F7
Remony	132	E4
Rempstone	64	B2
Rendcomb	37	D7
Rendham	57	C7
Rendlesham	57	D7
Renfrew	118	C5
Renhold	53	D8
Renishaw	76	B4
Rennington	117	C8
Renton	118	B3
Renwick	109	E5
Repps	69	C7
Repton	63	B7
Reraig	149	F13
Rescobie	135	D5
Resipole	147	E10
Resolis	151	E9
Resolven	34	D2
Reston	122	C4
Retew	4	D4
Retford	89	F8
Rettendon	42	E3
Rettendon Place	42	E3
Revesby	79	C5
Revesby Bridge	79	C6
Rewe	10	E4
Rew Street	15	E5
Reydon	57	B8
Reydon Smear	57	B8
Reymerston	68	D3
Reynalton	32	D1
Reynoldston	33	E5
Rezare	5	B8
Rhaeadr Gwy =Rhayader	47	C8
Rhandirmwyn	47	E6
Rhayader =Rhaeadr Gwy.	47	C8
Rhedyn	70	D3
Rhemore	147	F8
Rhencullen	84	C3
Rhes-y-cae	73	B5
Rhewl Denb.	72	C5
Denb	73	E5
Rhian	157	H8
Rhicarn	156	G3
Rhiconich	156	D5
Rhicullen	151	D9
Rhidorroch House	150	B4
Rhifail	157	E10
Rhigos	34	D3
Rhilochan	157	J10
Rhiroy	150	C4
Rhisga =Risca	35	E6
Rhiw	70	E3
Rhiwabon =Ruabon	73	E7
Rhiwbina	35	F5
Rhiwbryfdir	71	C7
Rhiwderin	35	F6
Rhiwlas Gwyn	72	F3
Gwyn	83	E5
Powys	73	F5
Rhodes	87	D6
Rhodesia	77	B5
Rhodes Minnis	31	E5
Rhodiad	44	C2
Rhondda	34	E3
Rhonehouse or Kelton Hill	106	D4
Rhoose =Y Rhws.	22	C2
Rhôs Carms	46	F2
Neath	33	D8
Rhosaman	33	C8
Rhosbeirio	82	B3
Rhoscefnhir	82	D5
Rhoscolyn	82	D2
Rhoscrowther	44	E4
Rhosesmor	73	C6
Rhos-fawr	70	D4
Rhosgadfan	82	F5
Rhosgoch	82	C4
Rhos-goch	48	E3
Rhos-hill	45	E3
Rhoshirwaun	70	E2
Rhoslan	71	C5
Rhoslefain	58	D2
Rhosllanerchrugog	73	E6
Rhosmaen	33	B7
Rhosmeirch	82	D4
Rhosneigr	82	D3
Rhosnesni	73	D7
Rhos-on-Sea	83	C8
Rhosrobin	73	D7
Rhossili	33	F5
Rhosson	44	C2
Rhostryfan	82	F4
Rhostyllen	73	E7
Rhosybol	82	C4
Rhos-y-brithdir	59	B8
Rhos-y-garth	46	B5
Rhos-y-gwaliau	72	F3
Rhos-y-llan	70	D3
Rhos-y-Madoc	73	E7
Rhos-y-meirch	48	C4
Rhu Argyll	145	E11
Argyll	145	G7
Rhuallt	72	B4
Rhuddall Heath	74	C2
Rhuddlan Ceredig	46	E3
Denb	72	B4
Rhue	150	B3
Rhulen	48	E3
Rhunahaorine	143	D8
Rhuthun =Ruthin	72	D5
Rhyd Gwyn.	71	C7
Powys	59	D6
Rhydaman =Ammanford	33	C7
Rhydargaeau	33	B5
Rhydcymerau	46	F4
Rhydd	50	E3
Rhyd-Ddu	83	F5
Rhydding	33	E8
Rhydfudr	46	C4
Rhydlewis	46	E2
Rhydlios	70	D2
Rhydlydan	83	F8
Rhyd-moel-ddu	48	B2
Rhydness	48	E3
Rhydowen	46	E3
Rhyd-Rosser	46	C4
Rhydspence	48	E4
Rhydtalog	73	D6
Rhyd-uchaf	72	F3

Rhyd-wen 58 C4
Rhydwyn 82 C3
Rhyd-y-clafdy . . . 70 D4
Rhydycroesau . . . 73 F6
Rhydyfelin Ceredig . 68 B4
  Rhondda 34 F4
Rhyd-y-foel 72 B3
Rhyd-y-fro 33 D8
Rhyd-y-gwin 33 D7
Rhydymain 58 B5
Rhyd-y-meirch . . . 35 D7
Rhyd-y-meudwy . . 72 D5
Rhydymwyn 73 C6
Rhyd-yr-onen . . . 58 D3
Rhyd-y-sarn 71 C7
Rhyl = Y Rhyl . . . 72 A4
Rhymney
  = Rhymni 35 D5
Rhymni
  = Rhymney 35 D5
Rhynd Fife 129 B6
  Perth 128 B3
Rhynie Aberds . . . 140 B3
  Highld 151 D11
Ribbesford 50 B2
Ribblehead 93 B7
Ribbleton 93 F5
Ribchester 93 F6
Ribigill 157 D8
Riby 91 D5
Riby Cross Roads . 91 D5
Riccall 96 F2
Riccarton 118 F4
Richards Castle . . 49 C6
Richings Park . . . 27 B8
Richmond London . 28 B2
  N Yorks 101 D6
Rickarton 141 F7
Rickinghall 56 B4
Rickleton 111 D5
Rickling 55 F5
Rickmansworth . . 40 E3
Riddings Cumb . . 108 C3
  Derbys 76 D4
Riddlecombe 9 C8
Riddlesden 94 E3
Riddrie 119 C6
Ridge Dorset 13 F7
  Hants 14 C4
  Wilts 24 F4
Ridgebourne 48 C2
Ridge Green 28 E4
Ridgehill 23 C7
Ridge Lane 63 E6
Ridgeway Cross . . 50 E2
Ridgewell 55 E8
Ridgewood 17 C8
Ridgmont 53 F7
Riding Mill 110 C3
Ridleywood 73 D8
Ridlington Norf . . 69 A6
  Rutland 64 D5
Ridsdale 116 F5
Riechip 133 E7
Riemore 133 E7
Rienachait 156 F3
Rievaulx 102 F3
Rift House 111 F7
Rigg 108 C2
Riggend 119 B7
Rigsby 79 B7
Rigside 119 F8
Riley Green 86 B4
Rileyhill 62 C5
Rilla Mill 5 B7
Rillington 96 B4
Rimington 93 E8
Rimpton 12 B4
Rimswell 91 B7
Rinaston 44 C4
Ringasta 160 M5
Ringford 106 D3
Ringinglow 88 F3
Ringland 68 C4
Ringles Cross . . . 17 B8
Ringmer 17 C8
Ringmore 6 E4
Ringorm 152 D2
Ring's End 66 D3
Ringsfield 69 F7
Ringsfield Corner . 69 F7
Ringshall Herts . . 40 C2
  Suff 56 D4
Ringshall Stocks . 56 D4
Ringstead Norf . . 80 C3
  Northants 53 B7
Ringwood 14 D2
Ringwould 31 E7
Rinmore 140 C3
Rinnigill 159 J4
Rinsey 2 D4
Riof 154 D6
Ripe 18 D2
Ripley Derbys . . . 76 D3
  Hants 14 E2
  N Yorks 95 C5
  Sur 27 D8
Riplingham 97 F5
Ripon 95 B6
Rippingale 65 B7
Ripple Kent 31 E7
  Worcs 50 F3
Ripponden 87 C8
Rireavach 150 B3
Risabus 142 D4
Risbury 49 D7
Risby 55 C8
Risca = Rhisga . . 35 E6
Rise 97 E7
Riseden 18 B3
Risegate 66 B2
Riseholme 78 B2
Riseley Bedford . . 53 C8
  Wokingham . . . 26 C5
Rishangles 57 C5
Rishton 93 F7
Rishworth 87 C8
Rising Bridge . . . 87 B5
Risley Derbys . . . 76 F4
  Warr 86 E4
Risplith 94 C5
Rispond 156 C7
Rivar 25 C8
Rivenhall End . . . 42 C4
River Bank 55 C6
Riverhead 29 D6
Rivington 86 C4
Roachill 10 B3

Roade 53 D5
Road Green 69 E5
Roadhead 108 B5
Roadmeetings . . . 119 E8
Roadside 158 D3
Roadside of
  Catterline 135 B8
Roadside of
  Kinneff 135 B8
Roadwater 22 F2
Roag 149 D7
Roa Island 92 C2
Roath 22 B3
Roberton Borders . 115 C7
  S Lanark 114 B2
Robertsbridge . . . 18 C4
Roberttown 88 B2
Robeston Cross . . 44 E3
Robeston Wathen . 32 C1
Robin Hood 88 B4
Robin Hood's
  Bay 103 D7
Roborough Devon . 6 C3
  Devon 9 C7
Roby 86 E2
Roby Mill 86 D3
Rocester 75 F8
Roch 44 C3
Rochdale 87 C6
Roche 4 C4
Rochester Medway 29 C8
  Northumb 116 E4
Rochford 42 E4
Roch Gate 44 C3
Rock Corn 4 B4
  Northumb 117 B8
  Worcs 50 B2
  W Sus 16 C5
Rockbeare 10 E5
Rockbourne 14 C2
Rockcliffe Cumb . 108 C3
  Dumfries 107 D5
Rockfield Highld . 151 C12
  Mon 36 C1
Rockford 14 D2
Rockhampton . . . 36 E3
Rockingham 65 E5
Rockland All
  Saints 68 E2
Rockland St Mary . 69 D6
Rockland St Peter . 68 E2
Rockley 25 B6
Rockwell End . . . 39 F7
Rockwell Green . . 11 B6
Rodborough 37 D5
Rodbourne Swindon 37 F8
  Wilts 37 F6
Rodbourne Cheney 37 F8
Rodd 48 C5
Roddam 117 B6
Rodden 12 F4
Rode 24 D3
Rodeheath 75 C5
Rode Heath 74 D5
Rodhuish 22 F2
Rodington 61 C5
Rodley Glos 36 C4
  W Yorks 94 F5
Rodmarton 37 E6
Rodmell 17 D8
Rodmersham . . . 30 C3
Rodney Stoke . . . 23 D6
Rodsley 76 E2
Rodway 22 F4
Roecliffe 95 C6
Roe Green 54 F4
Roehampton 28 B3
Roesound 160 G5
Roffey 28 F2
Rogart 157 J10
Rogart Station . . . 157 J10
Rogate 16 B2
Rogerstone 35 F6
Roghadal 154 J5
Rogiet 36 F1
Rogue's Alley . . . 66 D3
Roke 39 E6
Roker 111 D7
Rollesby 69 C7
Rolleston Leics . . 64 D4
  Notts 77 D7
Rolleston-on-
  Dove 63 B6
Rolston 97 E8
Rolvenden 18 B5
Rolvenden Layne . 19 B5
Romaldkirk 100 B4
Romanby 102 E1
Romannobridge . . 120 E4
Romansleigh 10 B2
Romford 41 F8
Romiley 87 E7
Romsey 14 B4
Romsey Town . . . 55 D5
Romsley Shrops . . 61 F7
  Worcs 50 B4
Ronague 84 E2
Rookhope 110 E2
Rookley 15 F6
Rooks Bridge . . . 23 D5
Roos 97 F8
Roosebeck 92 C2
Rootham's Green . 54 D2
Rootpark 120 D2
Ropley 26 F4
Ropley Dean 26 F4
Ropsley 78 F2
Rora 153 C10
Rorandle 141 C5
Rorrington 60 D3
Roscroggan 3 B5
Rose 4 D2
Roseacre Kent . . . 29 D8
  Lancs 92 F4
Rose Ash 10 B2
Rosebank 119 E8
Rosebrough 117 B7
Rosebush 32 B1
Rosecare 8 E3
Rosedale Abbey . . 103 E5
Roseden 117 B6
Rosefield 151 F11
Rose Green 16 E3
Rose Grove 93 F8
Rosehall 156 J7

Rosehearty 153 B9
Rosehill 74 F3
Rose Hill E Sus . . 17 C8
  Lancs 93 F8
  Suff 57 E5
Roseisle 152 B1
Roselands 18 E3
Rosemarket 44 E4
Rosemarkie 151 F10
Rosemary Lane . . 11 C6
Rosemount 134 E1
Rosenannon 4 C4
Rosewell 121 C5
Roseworth 102 B2
Roseworthy 2 C5
Rosgill 99 C7
Roshven 147 D10
Roskhill 149 D7
Roskill House . . . 151 F9
Rosley 108 E3
Roslin 121 C5
Rosliston 63 C6
Rosneath 145 E11
Ross Dumfries . . . 106 E3
  Northumb 123 F7
  Perth 127 B6
Rossett 73 D7
Rossett Green . . . 95 D6
Rossie Ochill . . . 128 C2
Rossie Priory . . . 134 F2
Rossington 89 E7
Rosskeen 151 E9
Rossland 118 B4
Ross-on-Wye . . . 36 B3
Roster 158 G4
Rostherne 86 F5
Rosthwaite 98 C4
Roston 75 E8
Rosyth 128 F3
Rothbury 117 D6
Rotherby 64 C3
Rotherfield 18 C2
Rotherfield Greys . 39 F7
Rotherfield
  Peppard 39 F7
Rotherham 88 E5
Rothersthorpe . . . 52 D5
Rotherwick 26 D5
Rothes 152 D2
Rothesay 145 G9
Rothiebrisbane . . 153 E7
Rothienorman . . . 153 E7
Rothiesholm 159 F7
Rothley Leics . . . 64 C2
  Northumb 117 F6
Rothley Shield
  East 117 E6
Rothmaise 153 E6
Rothwell Lincs . . 91 E5
  Northants 64 F5
  W Yorks 88 B4
Rothwell Haigh . . 88 B4
Rotsea 97 D6
Rottal 134 C3
Rotten End 57 C7
Rottingdean 17 D7
Rottington 98 C1
Roud 15 F6
Rougham Norf . . 80 E4
  Suff 56 C3
Rougham Green . . 56 C3
Roughburn 137 F6
Rough Close 75 F6
Rough Common . . 30 D5
Roughlee 93 E8
Roughley 62 E5
Roughsike 108 B5
Roughton Lincs . . 78 C5
  Norf 81 D8
  Shrops 61 E7
Roughton Moor . . 78 C5
Roundhay 95 F6
Roundstonefoot . . 114 D4
Roundstreet
  Common 16 B4
Roundway 24 C5
Rousdon 11 E7
Rous Lench 50 D5
Routenburn 118 C1
Routh 97 E6
Row Corn 5 B5
  Cumb 99 F6
Rowanburn 108 B4
Rowardennan . . . 126 E2
Rowde 24 C4
Rowen 83 D7
Rowfoot 109 C6
Row Heath 43 C7
Rowhedge 43 B6
Rowhook 28 F2
Rowington 51 C7
Rowland 76 B2
Rowlands Castle . 15 C8
Rowlands Gill . . . 110 D4
Rowledge 27 E6
Rowlestone 35 B7
Rowley E Yorks . . 97 F5
  Shrops 60 D3
Rowley Hill 88 C2
Rowley Regis . . . 62 F3
Rowly 27 E8
Rowney Green . . 50 B5
Rownhams 14 C4
Rowrah 98 C2
Rowsham 39 C8
Rowsley 76 C2
Rowstock 38 F4
Rowston 78 D3
Rowton Ches W . . 73 C8
  Shrops 60 C3
  Telford 61 C6
Roxby N Lincs . . 90 C3
  N Yorks 103 C5
Roxton 54 D2
Roxwell 42 D2
Royal Leamington
  Spa 51 C8
Royal Oak Darl . . 101 B7
  Lancs 86 D2
Royal Tunbridge
  Wells 29 F2
Royal Wootton
  Bassett 37 F7
Roybridge 137 F5
Roydhouse 88 C3
Roydon Essex . . . 41 D7
  Norf 68 F3
  Norf 80 E3

Roydon Hamlet . . 41 D7
Royston Herts . . . 54 E4
  S Yorks 88 C4
Royton 87 D7
Rozel Jersey 17
Ruabon
  = Rhiwabon . . . 73 E7
Ruaig 146 G3
Ruan Lanihorne . . 3 B7
Ruan Minor 3 E6
Ruarach 136 B2
Ruardean 36 C3
Ruardean
  Woodside 36 C3
Rubery 50 B4
Ruckcroft 108 E5
Ruckinge 19 B7
Ruckland 79 B6
Ruckley 60 D5
Rudbaxton 44 C4
Rudby 102 D2
Ruddington 77 F5
Rudford 36 B4
Rudge Shrops . . . 62 E2
  Som 24 D3
Rudgeway 36 F3
Rudgwick 27 F8
Rudhall 36 B3
Rudheath 74 B3
Rudley Green . . . 42 D4
Rudry 35 F5
Rudston 97 C6
Rudyard 75 D6
Rufford 86 C2
Rufforth 95 D8
Rugby 52 B3
Rugeley 62 C4
Ruglen 112 D2
Ruilick 151 G8
Ruishton 11 B7
Ruisigearraidh . . 154 J4
Ruislip 40 F3
Ruislip Common . 40 F3
Rumbling Bridge . 128 E2
Rumburgh 69 F6
Rumford 4 B3
Rumney 22 B4
Runcorn 86 F3
Runcton 16 D2
Runcton Holme . . 67 D6
Rundlestone 6 B3
Runfold 27 E6
Runhall 68 D3
Runham Norf . . . 69 C7
  Norf 69 D8
Runnington 11 B6
Runsell Green . . . 42 D3
Runswick Bay . . . 103 C6
Runwell 42 E3
Ruscombe 27 B5
Rush Green 41 F8
Rushall Hereford . 49 F8
  Norf 68 F4
  Wilts 25 D6
  W Mid 62 D4
Rushbrooke 56 C2
Rushbury 60 E5
Rushden Herts . . 54 F4
  Northants 53 C7
Rushenden 30 B3
Rushford 68 F2
Rush Green 41 F8
Rush-head 153 D8
Rushlake Green . . 18 D3
Rushmere 69 F7
Rushmere
  St Andrew . . . 57 E6
Rushmoor 27 E6
Rushock 50 B3
Rusholme 87 E6
Rushton Ches W . 74 C2
  Northants 64 F5
  Shrops 61 D6
Rushton Spencer . 75 C6
Rushwick 50 D3
Rushyford 101 B7
Ruskie 126 D5
Ruskington 78 D3
Rusland 99 F5
Rusper 28 F3
Ruspidge 36 C3
Russell's Water . . 39 F7
Russel's Green . . 57 B6
Rusthall 18 B2
Rustington 16 D4
Ruston 103 F7
Ruston Parva . . . 97 C6
Ruswarp 103 D6
Rutherford 122 F2
Rutherglen 119 C6
Ruthernbridge . . . 4 C5
Ruthin = Rhuthun . 72 D5
Ruthrieston 141 D8
Ruthven Aberds . . 152 D5
  Angus 134 E2
  Highld 138 E3
  Highld 151 H11
Ruthven House . . 134 E3
Ruthvoes 4 C4
Ruthwell 107 C7
Ruyton-XI-Towns . 60 B3
Ryal 110 B3
Ryal Fold 86 B4
Ryall 12 E2
Ryarsh 29 D7
Rydal 99 D5
Ryde 15 E6
Rye 19 C6
Ryecroft Gate . . . 75 C6
Rye Foreign 19 C5
Rye Harbour 19 D6
Ryehill 91 B6
Rye Park 41 C6
Rye Street 50 F2
Ryhall 65 C7
Ryhill 88 C4
Ryhope 111 D7
Rylstone 94 D2
Ryme Intrinseca . . 12 C3
Ryther 95 F8
Ryton Glos 50 F2
  N Yorks 96 B3
  Shrops 61 D7
  T&W 110 C4
Ryton-on-
  Dunsmore 51 B8

S

Sabden 93 F7
Sacombe 41 C6
Sacriston 110 E5
Sadberge 101 C8
Saddell 143 E8
Saddington 64 E3
Saddle Bow 67 C6
Saddlescombe . . . 17 C6
Sadgill 99 D6
Saffron Walden . . 55 F6
Sageston 32 D1
Saham Hills 68 D2
Saham Toney . . . 68 D2
Saighdinis 148 B3
Saighton 73 C8
St Abbs 122 C5
St Abb's Haven . . 122 C5
St Agnes Corn . . . 4 D2
  Scilly 2 F3
St Albans 40 D4
St Allen 4 D3
St Andrews 129 C7
St Andrew's Major 22 B3
St Anne Ald 16
St Annes 85 B4
St Ann's 114 E3
St Ann's Chapel
  Corn 6 B2
  Devon 6 E4
St Anthony-in-
  Meneage 3 D6
St Anthony's Hill . 18 E3
St Asaph
  = Llanelwy . . . 72 B4
St Athan 22 C2
St Aubin Jersey . . 17
St Austell 4 D5
St Bees 98 C1
St Blazey 5 D5
St Boswells 121 F8
St Brelade Jersey . 17
St Breock 4 B4
St Breward 5 B5
St Briavels 36 D2
St Bride's 44 D3
St Brides Major . . 21 B7
St Bride's
  Netherwent . . . 35 F8
St Brides-super-
  Ely 22 B2
St Brides
  Wentlooge . . . 35 F6
St Budeaux 6 D2
Saintbury 51 F6
St Buryan 2 D3
St Catherine 24 B2
St Catherine's . . . 125 E7
St Clears
  = Sanclêr 32 C3
St Cleer 5 C7
St Clement 3 B7
St Clements Jersey 17
St Clether 8 F4
St Colmac 145 G9
St Columb Major . 4 C4
St Columb Minor . 4 C3
St Columb Road . 4 D4
St Combs 153 B10
St Cross South
  Elmham 69 F5
St Cyrus 135 C7
St David's 127 B8
St David's
  = Tyddewi 44 C2
St Day 3 B6
St Dennis 4 D4
St Devereux 49 F6
St Dogmaels 45 E3
St Dogwells 44 C4
St Dominick 6 C2
St Donat's 21 C8
St Edith's 24 C4
St Endellion 4 B4
St Enoder 4 D3
St Erme 4 D3
St Erney 5 D8
St Erth 2 C4
St Ervan 4 B3
St Eval 4 C3
St Ewe 3 B8
St Fagans 22 B3
St Fergus 153 C10
St Fillans 127 B5
St Florence 32 D1
St Genny's 8 E3
St George 72 B3
St George's 22 B2
St Germans 5 D8
St Giles 78 B2
St Giles in the
  Wood 9 C7
St Giles on the
  Heath 9 E5
St Harmon 47 B8
St Helena 63 D6
St Helen
  Auckland 101 B6
St Helens IoW . . 15 F7
  Mers 86 E3
St Helen's 18 D5
St Helier Jersey . . 17
  London 28 C3
St Hilary Corn . . 2 C4
  V Glam 22 B2
Saint Hill 28 F4
St Illtyd 35 D6
St Ippolyytts . . . 40 B4
St Ishmael's 44 E3
St Issey 4 B4
St Ive 5 C8
St Ives Cambs . . 54 B4
  Corn 2 B4
  Dorset 14 D2
St James South
  Elmham 69 F6
St Jidey 4 C4
St John 6 D2
St John's IoM . . . 84 D2
  Jersey 17
  Sur 27 D7
  Worcs 50 D3
St John's Chapel . 109 F8
St John's Fen End . 66 C5
St John's Highway . 66 C5

St John's Town of
  Dalry 113 F6
St Judes 84 C3
St Just 2 C2
St Just in Roseland 3 C7
St Katherine's . . . 153 E7
St Keverne 3 D6
St Kew 4 B5
St Kew Highway . 4 B5
St Keyne 5 C7
St Lawrence Corn . 4 C5
  Essex 43 D5
  IoW 15 G6
St Leonards Dorset 14 D2
  E Sus 18 E4
  S Lanark 119 D6
St Leonard's 40 D2
St Levan 2 D2
St Lythans 22 B3
St Mabyn 4 B5
St Madoes 128 B3
St Margarets 41 C6
St Margaret's . . . 49 F5
St Margaret's at
  Cliffe 31 E7
St Margaret's
  Hope 159 J5
St Margaret South
  Elmham 69 F6
St Mark's 84 E2
St Martin 5 D7
St Martins Corn . . 3 D6
  Perth 134 F1
St Martin's Jersey . 17
  Shrops 73 F7
St Mary Bourne . . 26 D2
St Mary Church . . 22 B2
St Mary Cray . . . 29 C5
St Mary Hill 21 B8
St Mary Hoo . . . 30 B2
St Mary in the
  Marsh 19 C7
St Mary's Jersey . 17
  Orkney 159 H5
St Mary's Bay . . . 19 C7
St Maughans . . . 36 C1
St Mawes 3 C7
St Mawgan 4 C3
St Mellion 5 C8
St Mellons 35 F6
St Merryn 4 B3
St Mewan 4 D4
St Michael
  Caerhays 3 B8
St Michael Penkevil 3 B7
St Michaels 49 C7
St Michael's 19 B5
St Michael's on
  Wyre 92 E4
St Michael South
  Elmham 69 F6
St Minver 4 B4
St Monans 129 D7
St Neot 5 C6
St Neots 54 C2
St Newlyn East . . 4 D3
St Nicholas Pembs 44 B3
  V Glam 22 B2
St Nicholas at
  Wade 31 C6
St Ninians 127 E6
St Osyth 43 C7
St Osyth Heath . . 43 C7
St Ouens Jersey . . 17
St Owens Cross . . 36 B2
St Paul's Cray . . . 29 C5
St Paul's Walden . 40 B4
St Peter Port Guern 16
St Peter's Jersey . 17
  Kent 31 C7
St Petrox 44 F4
St Pinnock 5 C7
St Quivox 112 B3
St Ruan 3 E6
St Sampson Guern . 16
St Stephen 4 D4
St Stephens Corn . 6 D2
  Herts 40 D4
St Stephen's 8 F5
St Teath 4 B5
St Thomas 10 E4
St Tudy 5 B5
St Twynnells . . . 44 F4
St Veep 5 D6
St Vigeans 135 E6
St Wenn 4 C4
St Weonards 36 B1
Salcombe 6 F5
Salcombe Regis . . 11 F6
Salcott 43 C5
Sale 87 E5
Saleby 79 B7
Sale Green 50 D4
Salehurst 18 C4
Salem Carms . . . 33 B7
  Ceredig 58 F3
Salen Argyll 147 G8
  Highld 147 E9
Salesbury 93 F6
Salford C Beds . . 53 F7
  Gtr Man 87 E6
  Oxon 38 B2
Salford Priors . . . 51 D5
Salfords 28 E3
Salhouse 69 C6
Saline 128 E2
Salisbury 14 B2
Sallachan 130 C3
Sallachy Highld . . 150 H2
  Highld 157 J8
Salle 81 E7
Salmonby 79 B6
Salmond's Muir . . 135 F5
Salperton 37 B7
Salph End 53 D8
Salsburgh 119 C8
Salt 62 B3
Saltaire 94 F4
Saltash 6 D2
Saltburn 151 E10
Saltburn-by-the-
  Sea 102 B4
Saltby 65 B5
Saltcoats Cumb . . 98 E2
  N Ayrs 118 E2
Saltdean 17 D7
Salt End 91 B5
Salter 93 C6
Salterforth 93 E8

Salterswall 74 C3
Saltfleet 91 E8
Saltfleetby All
  Saints 91 E8
Saltfleetby
  St Clements . . . 91 E8
Saltfleetby
  St Peter 91 F8
Saltford 23 C8
Salthouse 81 C6
Saltmarshe 89 B8
Saltney 73 C7
Salton 96 B3
Saltwick 110 B4
Saltwood 19 B8
Salum 146 G3
Salvington 16 D5
Salwarpe 50 C3
Salwayash 12 E2
Sambourne 51 C5
Sambrook 61 B7
Samhla 148 B2
Samlesbury 93 F5
Samlesbury
  Bottoms 86 B4
Sampford Arundel 11 C6
Sampford Brett . . 22 E2
Sampford
  Courtenay 9 D8
Sampford Peverell 10 C5
Sampford Spiney . 6 B3
Sampool Bridge . . 99 F6
Samuelston 121 B7
Sanachan 149 D13
Sanaigmore 142 A3
Sanclêr = St Clears 32 C3
Sancreed 2 D3
Sancton 96 F5
Sand Highld 150 B2
  Shetland 160 J5
Sandaig 149 H12
Sandale 108 E2
Sandal Magna . . . 88 C4
Sandbach 74 C4
Sandbanks 13 F8
Sandend 152 B5
Sanderstead 28 C4
Sandfields 37 B6
Sandford Cumb . . 100 C2
  Devon 10 D3
  Dorset 13 F7
  IoW 15 F6
  N Som 23 D6
  Shrops 74 F2
  S Lanark 119 E7
Sandfordhill 153 D11
Sandford on
  Thames 39 D5
Sandford Orcas . . 12 B4
Sandford
  St Martin 38 B4
Sandgate 19 B8
Sandgreen 106 D2
Sandhaven 153 B9
Sandhead 104 E4
Sandhoe 110 C2
Sandholme E Yorks 96 F4
  Lincs 79 F6
Sandhurst Brack . 27 C6
  Glos 37 B5
  Kent 18 C4
Sandhurst Cross . 18 C4
Sandhutton 102 F1
Sand Hutton 96 D2
Sandiacre 76 F4
Sandilands Lincs . 91 F9
  S Lanark 119 F8
Sandiway 74 B3
Sandleheath 14 C2
Sandling 29 D8
Sandlow Green . . 74 C4
Sandness 160 H3
Sandon Essex . . . 42 D3
  Herts 54 F4
  Staffs 75 F6
Sandown 15 F6
Sandplace 5 D7
Sandridge Herts . . 40 C4
  Wilts 24 C4
Sandringham . . . 67 B6
Sandsend 103 C6
Sandside House . . 157 C12
Sandsound 160 J5
Sandtoft 89 D8
Sandway 30 D2
Sandwell 62 F4
Sandwich 31 D7
Sandwick Cumb . 99 C6
  Orkney 159 J5
  Shetland 160 L6
Sandwith 98 C1
Sandy Carms . . . 33 D5
  C Beds 54 E2
Sandy Bank 79 D5
Sandycroft 73 C7
Sandyford
  Dumfries 114 E5
  Stoke 75 D5
Sandygate 84 C3
Sandy Haven . . . 44 E3
Sandyhills 107 D5
Sandylands 92 C4
Sandy Lane Wilts . 24 C4
  Wrex 73 E7
Sandypark 10 F2
Sandysike 108 C3
Sangobeg 156 C7
Sangomore 156 C7
Sanna 146 E7
Sanndabhaig
  W Isles 148 D3
  W Isles 155 D9
Sannox 143 D11
Sanquhar 113 D7
Santon 90 C3
Santon Bridge . . 98 D3
Santon Downham . 67 F8
Sapcote 63 E8
Sapey Common . . 50 C2
Sapiston 56 B3
Sapley 54 B3
Sapperton Glos . . 37 D6
  Lincs 78 F3
Saracen's Head . . 66 B3
Sarclet 158 F5

Sardis 33 D6
Sarn Bridgend . . . 34 F3
  Powys 60 E2
Sarnau Carms . . . 32 B4
  Ceredig 46 D2
  Gwyn 72 F3
  Powys 48 F2
  Powys 60 C2
Sarn Bach 70 E4
Sarnesfield 49 D5
Sarn Meyllteyrn . . 70 D3
Saron Carms . . . 33 C7
  Carms 46 F2
  Denb 72 C4
  Gwyn 82 E5
  Gwyn 82 F4
Sarratt 40 E3
Sarre 31 C6
Sarsden 38 B2
Sarsgrum 156 C6
Satley 110 E4
Satron 100 E4
Satterleigh 9 B8
Satterthwaite . . . 99 E5
Satwell 39 F7
Sauchen 141 C5
Saucher 134 F1
Sauchie 127 E7
Sauchieburn 135 C6
Saughall 73 B7
Saughtree 115 E8
Saul 36 D4
Saundby 89 F8
Saundersfoot . . . 32 D2
Saunderton 39 D7
Saunton 20 F3
Sausthorpe 79 C6
Saval 157 J8
Savary 147 G9
Savile Park 87 B8
Sawbridge 52 C3
Sawbridgeworth . 41 C7
Sawdon 103 F7
Sawley Derbys . . 76 F4
  Lancs 93 E7
  N Yorks 94 C5
Sawston 55 E5
Sawtry 65 F8
Saxby Leics 64 C5
  Lincs 90 F4
Saxby All Saints . 90 C3
Saxelbye 64 B4
Saxham Street . . 56 C4
Saxilby 77 B8
Saxlingham 81 D6
Saxlingham Green 68 E5
Saxlingham
  Nethergate . . . 68 E5
Saxlingham
  Thorpe 68 E5
Saxmundham . . . 57 C7
Saxondale 77 F6
Saxon Street 55 D7
Saxtead 57 C6
Saxtead Green . . 57 C6
Saxthorpe 81 D7
Saxton 95 F7
Sayers Common . 17 C6
Scackleton 96 B2
Scadabhagh 154 H6
Scaftworth 89 E7
Scagglethorpe . . . 96 B4
Scaitcliffe 87 B5
Scalasaig 144 D2
Scalby E Yorks . . 90 B2
  N Yorks 103 E8
Scaldwell 53 B5
Scale Houses . . . 109 E5
Scales Cumb . . . 92 B2
  Cumb 99 B5
  Lancs 92 F4
Scalford 64 B4
Scaling 103 C5
Scallastle 124 B2
Scalloway 160 K6
Scalpay 154 H7
Scalpay House . . 149 F11
Scalpsie 145 H9
Scamadale 147 B10
Scamblesby 79 B5
Scamodale 130 B2
Scampston 96 B4
Scampton 78 B2
Scapa 159 H5
Scapegoat Hill . . 87 C8
Scar 159 D7
Scarborough 103 F8
Scarcliffe 76 C4
Scarcroft 95 E6
Scarcroft Hill . . . 95 E6
Scardroy 150 F5
Scarff 160 E4
Scarfskerry 158 C4
Scargill 101 C5
Scarinish 146 G3
Scarisbrick 85 C4
Scarning 68 C2
Scarrington 77 E7
Scartho 91 D6
Scarwell 159 F3
Scatness 160 M5
Scatraig 151 H10
Scawby 90 D3
Scawsby 89 D6
Scawton 102 F3
Scayne's Hill . . . 17 B7
Scethrog 35 B5
Scholar Green . . . 74 D5
Scholes W Yorks . 88 B2
  W Yorks 88 D2
  W Yorks 95 F6
School Green . . . 74 C3
Scleddau 44 B4
Scofton 89 F7
Scole 56 B5
Scolpaig 148 A2
Scone 128 B3
Sconser 149 E10
Scoonie 129 D5
Scoor 146 K7
Scopwick 78 D3
Scoraig 150 B3
Scorborough 97 E6
Scorrier 3 B6
Scorton Lancs . . . 92 E5
  N Yorks 101 D7
Sco Ruston 81 E8

Scotbheinn 148 C3
Scotby 108 D4
Scotch Corner . . . 101 D7
Scotforth 92 D4
Scothern 78 B3
Scotland Gate . . . 117 F8
Scotlandwell . . . 128 D3
Scotsburn 151 D10
Scotscalder
  Station 158 E2
Scotscraig 129 B6
Scots' Gap 117 F6
Scotston Aberds . 135 B7
  Perth 133 E6
Scotstoun 118 C5
Scotstown 130 C2
Scotswood 110 C4
Scottas 149 H12
Scotter 90 D2
Scotterthorpe . . . 90 D2
Scottlethorpe . . . 65 B7
Scotton Lincs . . . 90 E2
  N Yorks 95 D6
  N Yorks 101 E6
Scottow 81 E8
Scoughall 129 F8
Scoulag 145 H10
Scoulton 68 D2
Scourie 156 E4
Scourie More . . . 156 E4
Scousburgh 160 M5
Scrabster 158 C2
Scrafield 79 C6
Scrainwood 117 D5
Scrane End 79 E6
Scraptoft 64 D3
Scratby 69 C8
Scrayingham 96 C3
Scredington 78 E3
Scremby 79 C7
Scremerston 123 E6
Screveton 77 E7
Scrivelsby 79 C5
Scriven 95 D6
Scrooby 89 E7
Scropton 75 F8
Scrub Hill 78 D5
Scruton 101 E7
Sculcoates 97 F6
Sculthorpe 80 D4
Scunthorpe 90 C2
Scurlage 33 F5
Seaborough 12 D2
Seacombe 85 E4
Seacroft Lincs . . . 79 C8
  W Yorks 95 F6
Seadyke 79 F6
Seafield S Ayrs . . 112 B3
  W Loth 120 C3
Seaford 17 E8
Seaforth 85 E4
Seagrave 64 C3
Seaham 111 E7
Seahouses 123 F8
Seal 29 D6
Sealand 73 C7
Seale 27 E6
Seamer N Yorks . . 102 C2
  N Yorks 103 F8
Seamill 118 E2
Sea Palling 69 B7
Searby 90 D4
Seasalter 30 C4
Seascale 98 D2
Seathorne 79 C8
Seathwaite Cumb . 98 C4
  Cumb 98 E4
Seatoller 98 C4
Seaton Corn 5 D8
  Cumb 107 F7
  Devon 11 F7
  Durham 111 D6
  E Yorks 97 E7
  Northumb 111 B6
  Rutland 65 E6
Seaton Burn 110 B5
Seaton Carew . . . 102 B3
Seaton Delaval . . 111 B6
Seaton Ross 96 E3
Seaton Sluice . . . 111 B6
Seatown Aberds . . 152 B5
  Dorset 12 E2
Seave Green 102 D3
Seaview 15 E7
Seaville 107 D8
Seavington
  St Mary 12 C2
Seavington
  St Michael . . . 12 C2
Sebergham 108 E3
Seckington 63 D6
Second Coast . . . 150 B2
Sedbergh 100 E1
Sedbury 36 E2
Sedbusk 100 E3
Sedgeberrow . . . 50 F5
Sedgebrook 77 F8
Sedgefield 102 B1
Sedgeford 80 D3
Sedgehill 13 B6
Sedgley 62 E3
Sedgwick 99 F7
Sedlescombe . . . 18 D4
Sedlescombe
  Street 18 D4
Seend 24 C4
Seend Cleeve . . . 24 C4
Seer Green 40 E2
Seething 69 E6
Sefton 85 D4
Seghill 111 B5
Seifton 60 F4
Seilebost 154 H5
Seion 82 E5
Seisdon 62 E2
Seisiadar 155 D10
Selattyn 73 F6
Selborne 26 F5
Selby 96 F2
Selham 16 B3
Selhurst 28 C4
Selkirk 115 B7
Sellack 36 B2
Sellafirth 160 D7
Sellibister 159 D8

Sellindge 19 B7
Sellindge Lees . . . 19 B8
Selling 30 D4
Sells Green 24 C4
Selly Oak 62 F4
Selmeston 18 E2
Selsdon 28 C4
Selsey 16 E2
Selsfield Common . 28 F4
Selsted 31 E6
Selston 76 D4
Selworthy 21 E8
Semblister 160 H5
Semer 56 E3
Semington 24 C3
Semley 13 B6
Send 27 D8
Send Marsh 27 D8
Senghenydd 35 E5
Sennen 2 D2
Sennen Cove 2 D2
Sennybridge
  = Pont Senni 34 B3
Serlby 89 F7
Sessay 95 B7
Setchey 67 C6
Setley 14 D4
Setter Shetland . . . 160 E6
  Shetland 160 H5
  Shetland 160 J7
Settiscarth 159 G4
Settle 93 C8
Settrington 96 B4
Sevenhampton 37 B7
Seven Kings 41 F7
Sevenoaks 29 D6
Sevenoaks Weald . . 29 D6
Seven Sisters 34 D2
Severn Beach 36 F2
Severnhampton . . . 38 E2
Severn Stoke 50 E3
Sevington 30 E4
Sewards End 55 F6
Sewardstone 41 E6
Sewardstonebury . 41 E6
Sewerby 97 C7
Seworgan 3 C6
Sewstern 65 B5
Sezincote 51 F6
Sgarasta Mhor . . . 154 H5
Sgiogarstaigh . . . 155 A10
Shabbington 39 D6
Shackerstone 63 D7
Shackleford 27 E7
Shade 87 B7
Shadforth 111 E6
Shadingfield 69 F7
Shadoxhurst 19 B6
Shadsworth 86 B5
Shadwell Norf 68 F2
  W Yorks 95 F6
Shaftesbury 13 B6
Shafton 88 C4
Shalbourne 25 C8
Shalcombe 14 F4
Shalden 26 E4
Shaldon 7 B7
Shalfleet 14 F5
Shalford Essex 42 B3
  Sur 27 E8
Shalford Green 42 B3
Shallowford 21 E6
Shalmsford Street . 30 D4
Shalstone 52 F4
Shamley Green 27 E8
Shandon 145 E11
Shandwick 151 D11
Shangton 64 E4
Shankhouse 111 B5
Shanklin 15 F6
Shanquhar 152 E5
Shanzie 134 D2
Shap 99 C7
Shapwick Dorset . . 13 D7
  Som 23 F6
Shardlow 76 F4
Shareshill 62 D3
Sharlston 88 C4
Sharlston
  Common 88 C4
Sharnbrook 53 D7
Sharnford 63 E8
Sharoe Green 92 F5
Sharow 95 B6
Sharpenhoe 53 F8
Sharperton 117 D5
Sharpness 36 D3
Sharp Street 69 B6
Sharpthorne 28 F4
Sharrington 81 D6
Shatterford 61 F7
Shaugh Prior 6 C3
Shavington 74 D4
Shaw Gtr Man 87 D7
  W Berks 26 C2
  Wilts 24 C3
Shawbury 61 B5
Shawdon Hall 117 C6
Shawell 64 F2
Shawford 15 B5
Shawforth 87 B6
Shaw Green 86 C3
Shawhead 107 B5
Shawhill 108 C2
Shaw Mills 95 C5
Shawton 119 E6
Shawtonhill 119 E6
Shear Cross 24 E3
Shearington 107 C7
Shearsby 64 E3
Shebbear 9 D6
Shebdon 61 B7
Shebster 157 C13
Sheddens 119 D5
Shedfield 15 C6
Sheen 75 C8
Sheepscar 95 F6
Sheepscombe 37 C5
Sheepstor 6 C3
Sheepwash 9 D6
Sheepway 23 B6
Sheepy Magna 63 D7
Sheepy Parva 63 D7
Sheering 41 C8
Sheerness 30 B3
Sheet 15 B8

Sheffield 88 F4
Sheffield Bottom . . 26 C4
Sheffield Green . . . 17 B8
Shefford 54 F2
Shefford
  Woodlands 25 B8
Sheigra 156 C4
Sheinton 61 D6
Shelderton 49 B6
Sheldon Derbys . . . 75 C8
  Devon 11 D6
  W Mid 63 F5
Sheldwich 30 D4
Shelf 88 B2
Shelfanger 68 F4
Shelfield Warks . . . 51 C6
  W Mid 62 D4
Shelford 77 E6
Shellacres 122 E4
Shelley Essex 42 D1
  Suff 56 F4
  W Yorks 88 C3
Shellingford 38 E3
Shellow Bowells . . 42 D2
Shelsley
  Beauchamp 50 C2
Shelsley Walsh . . . 50 C2
Shelthorpe 64 C2
Shelton Bedford . . 53 C8
  Norf 68 E5
  Notts 77 E7
  Shrops 60 C4
Shelton Green 68 E5
Shelve 60 E3
Shelwick 49 E7
Shenfield 42 E2
Shenington 51 E8
Shenley 40 D4
Shenley Brook End . 53 F6
Shenleybury 40 D4
Shenley Church
  End 53 F6
Shenmore 49 F5
Shennanton 105 C7
Shenstone Staffs . . 62 D5
  Worcs 50 B3
Shenton 63 D7
Shenval Highld . . . 137 B7
  Moray 139 B8
Shepeau Stow 66 C3
Shephall 41 B5
Shepherd's Green . . 39 F7
Shepherd's Port . . . 80 D2
Shepherdswell 31 E6
Shepley 88 D2
Shepperdine 36 E3
Shepperton 27 C8
Shepreth 54 E4
Shepshed 63 C8
Shepton
  Beauchamp 12 C2
Shepton Mallet . . . 23 E8
Shepton Montague . 23 F8
Shepway 29 D8
Sheraton 111 F7
Sherborne Dorset . . 12 C4
  Glos 38 C1
Sherborne
  St John 26 D4
Sherbourne 51 C7
Sherburn Durham . 111 E6
  N Yorks 97 B5
Sherburn Hill 111 E6
Sherburn in Elmet . 95 F7
Shere 27 E8
Shereford 80 E4
Sherfield English . . 14 B3
Sherfield on
  Loddon 26 D4
Sherford 7 E5
Sheriffhales 61 C7
Sheriff Hutton 96 C2
Sheringham 81 C7
Sherington 53 E6
Shernal Green 50 C4
Shernborne 80 D3
Sherrington 24 F4
Sherston 37 F5
Sherwood Green . . . 9 B7
Shettleston 119 C6
Shevington 86 D3
Shevington Moor . . 86 C3
Shevington Vale . . 86 D3
Sheviock 5 D8
Shide 15 F5
Shiel Bridge 136 C2
Shieldaig Highld . 149 A13
  Highld 149 C13
Shieldhill Dumfries 114 F3
  Falk 119 B8
  S Lanark 120 F3
Shielfoot 147 E9
Shielhill Angus . . . 134 D4
  Involyd 118 B2
Shifford 38 D3
Shifnal 61 D7
Shilbottle 117 D7
Shildon 101 B7
Shillingford Devon . 10 C4
  Oxon 39 E5
Shillingford
  St George 10 F4
Shillingstone 13 C6
Shillington 54 F2
Shillmoor 116 D4
Shilton Oxon 38 D2
  Warks 63 F8
Shilvington 117 F7
Shimpling Norf . . . 68 F4
  Suff 56 D2
Shimpling Street . . 56 D2
Shincliffe 111 E5
Shiney Row 111 D6
Shinfield 26 C5
Shingham 67 D7
Shingle Street 57 E7
Shinner's Bridge . . 7 C5
Shinness 157 H8
Shipbourne 29 D6
Shipdham 68 D2
Shipham 23 D6
Shiphay 7 C6
Shiplake 27 B5
Shipley Derbys . . . 76 E4
  Northumb 117 C7
  Shrops 62 E2
  W Sus 16 B5
Shipley Shiels . . . 116 E3

Shipmeadow 69 F6
Shippea Hill
  Station 67 F6
Shippon 38 E4
Shipston-on-
  Stour 51 E7
Shipton Glos 37 C7
  N Yorks 95 D8
  Shrops 61 E5
Shipton Bellinger . 25 E7
Shipton Gorge 12 E2
Shipton Green 16 D2
Shipton Moyne . . . 37 F5
Shipton on
  Cherwell 38 C4
Shipton Solers 37 C7
Shiptonthorpe 96 E4
Shipton-under-
  Wychwood 38 C2
Shirburn 39 E6
Shirdley Hill 85 C4
Shirebrook 76 C5
Shiregreen 88 E4
Shirehampton 23 B7
Shiremoor 111 B6
Shireoaks 89 F6
Shirkoak 19 B6
Shirland 76 D3
Shirley Derbys 76 E2
  London 28 C4
  Soton 14 C5
  W Mid 51 B6
Shirl Heath 49 D6
Shirrell Heath 15 C6
Shirwell 20 F4
Shirwell Cross 20 F4
Shiskine 143 F10
Shobdon 49 C6
Shobnall 63 B6
Shobrooke 10 D3
Shoby 64 C3
Shocklach 73 E8
Shoeburyness 43 F5
Sholden 31 D7
Sholing 14 C5
Shoot Hill 60 C4
Shop Corn 4 B3
  Corn 8 C4
Shop Corner 57 F6
Shoreditch 41 F6
Shoreham 29 C6
Shoreham-by-Sea . 17 D6
Shore Mill 151 E10
Shoresdean 123 E5
Shoreswood 122 E5
Shoreton 151 E9
Shorncote 37 E7
Shorne 29 B7
Shortacombe 9 F7
Shortgate 17 C8
Short Heath 62 D3
Shortlanesend 3 B7
Shortlees 118 F4
Shortstown 53 E8
Shorwell 15 F5
Shoscombe 24 D2
Shotatton 60 B3
Shotesham 69 E5
Shotgate 42 E3
Shotley 57 F6
Shotley Bridge . . . 110 D3
Shotleyfield 110 D3
Shotley Gate 57 F6
Shottenden 30 D4
Shottermill 27 F6
Shottery 51 D6
Shotteswell 52 E2
Shottisham 57 E7
Shottle 76 E3
Shottlegate 76 E3
Shotton Durham . . 111 F7
  Flint 73 C7
  Northumb 122 F4
Shotton Colliery . . 111 E6
Shotts 119 C8
Shotwick 73 B7
Shouldham 67 D6
Shouldham
  Thorpe 67 D6
Shoulton 50 D3
Shover's Green . . . 18 B3
Shrawardine 60 C4
Shrawley 50 C3
Shrewley Common . 51 C7
Shrewsbury 60 C4
Shrewton 25 E5
Shripney 16 D3
Shrivenham 38 F2
Shropham 68 E2
Shrub End 43 B5
Shucknall 49 E7
Shudy Camps 55 E7
Shulishadermor . . 149 D9
Shurdington 37 C6
Shurlock Row 27 B6
Shurrery 157 D13
Shurrery Lodge . . 157 D13
Shurton 22 E4
Shustoke 63 E6
Shute Devon 10 D3
  Devon 11 E7
Shutford 51 E8
Shuthonger 50 F3
Shutlanger 52 D5
Shuttington 63 D6
Shuttlewood 76 B4
Siabost bho
  Dheas 154 C7
Siabost bho
  Thuath 154 C7
Siadar 155 B8
Siadar Iarach 155 B8
Siadar Uarach . . . 155 B8
Sibbaldbie 114 F4
Sibbertoft 64 F3
Sibdon Carwood . . 60 F4
Sibford Ferris 51 F8
Sibford Gower 51 F8
Sible Hedingham . . 55 F8
Sibsey 79 D6
Sibson Cambs 65 E7
  Leics 63 D7
Sibthorpe 77 E7
Sibton 57 C7
Sibton Green 57 B7
Sicklesmere 56 C2
Sicklinghall 95 E6
Sid 11 F6

Sidbury Devon . . . 11 E6
  Shrops 61 F6
Sidcot 23 D6
Sidcup 29 B5
Siddick 107 F7
Siddington Ches E . 74 B5
  Glos 37 E7
Sidemoor 50 B4
Sidestrand 81 D8
Sidford 11 E6
Sidlesham 16 E2
Sidley 18 E4
Sidlow 28 E3
Sidmouth 11 F6
Sigford 7 B5
Sigglesthorne 97 E7
Sighthill 120 B4
Sigingstone 21 B8
Signet 38 C2
Silchester 26 C4
Sildinis 155 F7
Sileby 64 C2
Silecroft 98 F3
Silfield 68 E4
Silian 46 D4
Silkstone 88 D3
Silkstone
  Common 88 D3
Silk Willoughby . . 78 E3
Silloth 107 D8
Sills 116 D4
Sillyearn 152 C5
Siloh 47 F6
Silpho 103 E7
Silsden 94 E3
Silsoe 53 F8
Silverburn 120 C5
Silverdale Lancs . . 92 B4
  Staffs 74 E5
Silver End 42 C4
Silvergate 81 E7
Silverhill 18 D4
Silverley's Green . . 57 B6
Silverstone 52 E4
Silverton 10 D4
Silvington 49 B8
Silwick 160 J4
Simmonburn 109 B8
Simonsbath 21 F6
Simonstone 93 F7
Simprim 122 E4
Simpson 53 F6
Simpson Cross . . . 44 D3
Sinclair's Hill 122 D4
Sinclairston 112 C4
Sinderby 101 F8
Sinderhope 109 D8
Sindlesham 27 C5
Singdean 115 D8
Singleborough . . . 53 F5
Singleton Lancs . . . 92 F3
  W Sus 16 C2
Singlewell 29 B7
Sinkhurst Green . . 30 E2
Sinnahard 140 C3
Sinnington 103 F5
Sinton Green 50 C3
Sipson 27 B8
Sirhowy 35 C5
Sisland 69 E6
Sissinghurst 18 B4
Sisterpath 122 E3
Siston 23 B8
Sithney 3 D5
Sittingbourne 30 C2
Six Ashes 61 F7
Sixhills 91 F5
Six Hills 64 B3
Six Mile Bottom . . 55 D6
Sixpenny Handley . 13 C7
Sizewell 57 C8
Skail 157 E10
Skaill Orkney 159 E5
  Orkney 159 G3
  Orkney 159 H6
Skares 113 C5
Skateraw 122 B3
Skaw 160 G7
Skeabost 149 D9
Skeabrae 159 F3
Skeeby 101 D7
Skeffington 64 D4
Skeffling 91 C7
Skegby 76 C4
Skegness 79 C8
Skelberry 160 M5
Skelbo 151 B10
Skelbrooke 89 C6
Skeldyke 79 F6
Skellingthorpe . . . 78 B2
Skellister 160 H6
Skellow 89 C6
Skelmanthorpe . . . 88 C3
Skelmersdale 86 D2
Skelmonae 153 E8
Skelmorlie 118 C1
Skelmuir 153 D9
Skelpick 157 D10
Skelton Cumb . . . 108 F4
  E Yorks 89 B8
  N Yorks 101 D5
  Redcar 102 C4
  York 95 D8
Skelton-on-Ure . . . 95 C6
Skelwick 159 D5
Skelwith Bridge . . 99 D5
Skendleby 79 C7
Skene House 141 D6
Skenfrith 36 B1
Skerne 97 D6
Skeroblingarry . . 143 F8
Skerray 157 C9
Skerton 92 C4
Sketchley 63 E8
Sketty 33 E7
Skewen 33 E8
Skewsby 96 B2
Skeyton 81 E8
Skiag Bridge 156 G5
Skibo Castle 151 C10
Skidbrooke 91 E8
Skidbrooke North
  End 91 E8
Skidby 97 F6
Skilgate 10 B4
Skillington 65 B5
Skinburness 107 D8
Skinflats 127 F8

Skinidin 148 D7
Skinnet 157 C8
Skinningrove 103 B5
Skipness 145 H7
Skippool 92 E3
Skipsea 97 D7
Skipsea Brough . . 97 D7
Skipton 94 D2
Skipton-on-Swale . 95 B6
Skipwith 96 F2
Skirbeck 79 E6
Skirbeck Quarter . . 79 E6
Skirlaugh 97 F7
Skirling 120 F3
Skirmett 39 F7
Skirpenbeck 96 D3
Skirwith 109 F6
Skirza 158 D5
Skulamus 149 F11
Skullomie 157 C9
Skyborry Green . . 48 B4
Skye of Curr 139 B5
Skyreholme 94 C3
Slackcotes 76 D4
Slackhall 87 F8
Slackhead 152 B4
Slad 37 D5
Slade Devon 20 E4
  Pembs 44 D4
Slade Green 29 B6
Slaggyford 109 D6
Slaidburn 93 D7
Slaithwaite 87 C8
Slaley 110 D2
Slamannan 119 B8
Slapton Bucks . . . 40 B2
  Devon 7 E6
  Northants 52 E4
Slatepit Dale 76 C3
Slattocks 87 D6
Slaugham 17 B6
Slaughterford 24 B3
Slawston 64 E4
Sleaford Hants . . . 27 F6
  Lincs 78 E3
Sleagill 99 C7
Sleapford 61 C6
Sledge Green 50 F3
Sledmere 96 C5
Sleightholme . . . 100 C4
Sleights 103 D6
Slepe 13 E7
Slickly 158 D4
Sliddery 143 F10
Sligachan Hotel . . 149 F9
Slimbridge 36 D4
Slindon Staffs 74 F5
  W Sus 16 D3
Slinfold 28 F2
Sling 36 D2
Slingsby 96 B2
Slioch 152 E5
Slip End C Beds . . 40 C3
  Herts 54 F3
Slipton 53 B7
Slitting Mill 62 C4
Slochd 138 B4
Slockavullin 124 F4
Sloley 81 E8
Sloothby 79 B7
Slough 27 B7
Slough Green 17 B6
Sluggan 138 B4
Slumbay 149 E13
Slyfield 27 D7
Slyne 92 C4
Smailholm 122 F2
Smallbridge 87 C7
Smallburgh 69 B6
Smallburn
  Aberds 153 D10
  E Ayrs 113 B6
Small Dole 17 C6
Smalley 76 E4
Smallfield 28 E4
Small Hythe 19 B5
Smallridge 11 D8
Smannell 25 E8
Smardale 100 D2
Smarden 30 E2
Smarden Bell 30 E2
Smeatharpe 11 C6
Smeeth 19 B7
Smeeton Westerby 64 E3
Smercleit 148 G2
Smerral 158 G3
Smethwick 62 F4
Smirisary 147 D9
Smisby 63 C7
Smithfield 108 C4
Smith Green 92 D4
Smithincott 11 C5
Smith's Green 42 B1
Smithstown 149 A12
Smithton 151 G10
Smithy Green 74 B4
Smockington 63 F8
Smoogro 159 H4
Smythe's Green . . 43 C5
Snaigow House . . 133 E7
Snailbeach 60 D3
Snailwell 55 C7
Snainton 103 F7
Snaith 89 B7
Snape N Yorks . . . 101 F7
  Suff 57 D7
Snape Green 85 C4
Snarestone 63 D7
Snarford 90 F4
Snargate 19 C7
Snave 19 C7
Snead 60 E3
Sneath Common . . 68 F4
Sneaton 103 D6
Sneatonthorpe . . 103 D7
Snelland 90 F4
Snellston 75 E8
Snettisham 80 D2
Sniseabhal 148 E2
Snitter 117 D6
Snitterby 90 E3
Snitterfield 51 D7
Snitton 49 B7
Snodhill 48 E5
Snodland 29 C7
Snowden Hill 88 D3
Snowdown 31 D6
Snowshill 51 F5
Snydale 88 C5
Soar Anglesey . . . 82 D3

Soar continued
  Carms 33 B7
  Devon 6 F5
Soar-y-Mynydd . . 47 D6
Soberton 15 C7
Soberton Heath . . 15 C7
Sockbridge 99 B7
Sockburn 101 D8
Soham 55 B6
Soham Cotes 55 B6
Solas 148 A3
Soldon Cross 8 C5
Soldridge 26 F4
Sole Street Kent . . 29 C7
  Kent 30 E4
Solihull 51 B6
Sollers Dilwyn . . . 49 D6
Sollers Hope 49 F8
Sollom 86 C2
Solva 44 C2
Somerby Leics . . . 64 C4
  Lincs 90 D4
Somercotes 76 D4
Somerford 14 E2
Somerford Keynes . 37 E7
Somerley 16 E2
Somerleyton 69 E7
Somersal Herbert . 75 F8
Somersby 79 B6
Somersham Cambs 54 B4
  Suff 56 E4
Somerton Oxon . . . 38 B4
  Som 12 B2
Sompting 17 D5
Sonning 27 B5
Sonning Common . 39 F7
Sonning Eye 27 B5
Sontley 73 E7
Sopley 14 E2
Sopwell 40 D4
Sopworth 37 F5
Sorbie 105 E8
Sordale 158 D3
Sorisdale 146 E5
Sorn 113 B5
Sornhill 118 F5
Sortat 158 D4
Sotby 78 B5
Sots Hole 78 C4
Sotterley 69 F7
Soudley 61 B7
Soughton 73 C6
Soulbury 40 B1
Soulby 100 C2
Souldern 52 F3
Souldrop 53 C7
Sound Ches E 74 E3
  Shetland 160 H5
  Shetland 160 J6
Sound Heath 74 E3
Soundwell 23 B8
Sourhope 116 B4
Sourin 159 E5
Sourton 9 E7
Soutergate 98 F4
South Acre 67 C8
Southall 40 F4
South Allington . . 7 F5
South Alloa 127 E7
Southam Glos 37 B6
  Warks 52 C2
South Ambersham 16 B3
Southampton 14 C5
South Anston 89 F6
South Ascot 27 C7
South
  Ballachulish . . . 130 D4
South Balloch . . . 112 E3
South Bank 102 B3
South Barrow 12 B4
South Beach 70 D4
South Benfleet . . . 42 F3
South Bersted 16 D3
South Brent 6 C4
South Brewham . . 24 F2
South Broomhill . . 117 E8
Southburgh 68 D2
South Burlingham . 69 D6
Southburn 97 D5
South Cadbury . . . 12 B4
South Cairn 104 C3
South Carlton 78 B2
South Cave 96 F5
South Cerney 37 E7
South Chard 11 D8
South Charlton . . . 117 B7
South Cheriton . . . 12 B4
Southchurch 43 F5
South Cliffe 96 F4
South Clifton 77 B8
South
  Cockerington . . . 91 F7
South Cornelly . . . 34 F2
Southcott 25 D6
Southcourt 39 C8
South Cove 69 F7
South Creagan . . 130 E3
South Creake 80 D4
South Croxton . . . 64 C3
South Croydon . . . 28 C4
South Dalton 97 E5
South Darenth . . . 29 C6
Southdean 116 D2
Southdene 86 E2
South Duffield . . . 96 F2
Southease 17 D8
South Elkington . . 91 F6
South Elmsall 89 C5
Southend Argyll . . 143 H7
  W Berks 26 B3
  Wilts 25 B6
South End Bucks . . 40 B1
  Cumb 92 C2
  N Lincs 90 B5
Southend-on-Sea . 42 F4
Southernden 30 E2
Southerndown . . . 21 B7
Southerness 107 D6
Southery 67 E6
South Erradale . . 149 A12
South Fambridge . 42 E4
South Fawley 38 F3
South Ferriby 90 B3
Southfield 111 B5
Southfleet 29 B7

Southgate Ceredig 46 B4
  London 41 E5
  Norf 81 E7
  Swansea 33 F6
South Glendale . . 148 G2
South Godstone . . 28 E4
South Gorley 14 C2
South Green Essex 42 E2
  Kent 30 C2
South Woodham
  Ferrers 42 E4
South Wootton . . . 67 B6
South Wraxall . . . 24 C3
South Zeal 9 E8
Soval Lodge 155 E8
Sowber Gate 102 F1
Sowerby N Yorks . 102 F2
  W Yorks 87 B8
Sowerby Bridge . . 87 B8
Sowerby Row . . . 108 F3
Sowood 87 C8
Sowton 10 E4
Soyal 151 B8
Spacey Houses . . . 95 D6
Spa Common 81 D8
Spadeadam Farm 109 B5
Spalding 66 B2
Spaldington 96 F3
Spaldwick 54 B2
Spalford 77 C8
Spanby 78 F3
Sparham 68 C3
Spark Bridge 99 F5
Sparkford 12 B4
Sparkhill 62 F4
Sparkwell 6 D3
Sparrow End 68 C2
Sparrowpit 87 F8
Sparsholt Hants . . 26 F2
  Oxon 38 F3
Spartylea 109 E8
Spaunton 103 F5
Spaxton 22 F4
Spean Bridge . . . 136 F5
Spear Hill 16 C5
Speen Bucks 39 E8
  W Berks 26 C2
Speeton 97 B7
Speke 86 F2
Speldhurst 29 E6
Spellbrook 41 C7
Spelsbury 38 B3
Spelter 34 E2
Spencers Wood . . . 26 C5
Spennithorne . . . 101 F6
Spennymoor 111 F5
Spetchley 50 D3
Spetisbury 13 D7
Spexhall 69 F6
Spey Bay 152 B3
Speybridge 139 B6
Speyview 152 D2
Spilsby 79 C7
Spindlestone 123 F7
Spinkhill 76 B4
Spinningdale 151 C9
Spirthill 24 B4
Spital Hill 89 E7
Spital in the Street 90 F3
Spithurst 17 C8
Spittal Dumfries . 105 D7
  E Loth 121 B7
  Highld 158 E3
  Northumb 123 D6
  Pembs 44 C4
  Stirling 126 F4
Spittalfield 133 E8
Spittal of
  Glenmuick 140 F2
Spittal of
  Glenshee 133 B8
Spixworth 68 C5
Splayne's Green . . 17 B8
Spofforth 95 D6
Spondon 76 F4
Spon End 51 B8
Spon Green 73 C6
Spooner Row 68 E3
Sporle 67 C8
Spott 122 B2
Spratton 52 B5
Spreakley 27 E6
Spreyton 9 E8
Spridlington 90 F4
Springburn 119 C6
Springfield
  Dumfries 108 C3
  Essex 42 D3
  Fife 128 C5
  Moray 151 F13
  W Mid 62 F4
Springholm 106 C5
Springkell 108 B2
Springside 118 F3
Springthorpe 90 F2
Spring Vale 88 D3
Spring Valley 84 E3
Springwell 111 D5
Sproatley 97 F7
Sproston Green . . 74 C4
Sprotbrough 89 D6
Sproughton 56 E5
Sprouston 122 F3
Sprowston 68 C5
Sproxton Leics . . . 65 B5
  N Yorks 102 F4
Spurstow 74 D2
Spynie 152 B2
Squires Gate 92 F3
Srannda 154 J5
Sronphadruig
  Lodge 132 B4
Stableford Shrops . 61 E7
  Staffs 74 F5
Stacey Bank 88 E3
Stackhouse 93 C8
Stackpole 44 F4
Staddiscombe 6 D3
Staddlethorpe . . . 90 B2
Stadhampton 39 E6
Stadhlaigearraidh
  . . . . 148 E2
Staffin 149 B9
Stafford 62 B3
Stagsden 53 E7
Stainburn Cumb . 107 F7
  N Yorks 94 E5
Stainby 65 B6

Staincross 88 C4
Staindrop 101 B6
Staines-upon-
  Thames 27 B8
Stainfield Lincs . . . 65 B7
  Lincs 78 B4
Stainforth N Yorks . 93 C8
  S Yorks 89 C7
Staining 92 F3
Stainland 87 C8
Stainsacre 103 D7
Stainsby 76 C4
Stainton Cumb . . . 99 B6
  Cumb 99 F7
  Durham 101 C5
  Mbro 102 C2
  N Yorks 101 E6
  S Yorks 89 E6
Stainton by
  Langworth 78 B3
Staintondale 103 E7
Stainton le Vale . . 91 E5
Stainton with
  Adgarley 92 B2
Stair Cumb 98 B4
  E Ayrs 112 B4
Stairhaven 105 D6
Staithes 103 C5
Stakeford 117 F8
Stake Pool 92 E4
Stalbridge 12 C5
Stalbridge Weston 12 C5
Stalham 69 B6
Stalham Green . . . 69 B6
Stalisfield Green . . 30 D3
Stallingborough . . 91 C5
Stalling Busk . . . 100 F4
Stalmine 92 E3
Stalybridge 87 E7
Stambourne 55 F8
Stambourne Green 55 F8
Stamford 65 D7
Stamford Bridge
  Ches W 73 C8
  E Yorks 96 D3
Stamfordham . . . 110 B3
Stanah 99 C5
Stanborough 41 C5
Stanbridge C Beds 40 B2
  Dorset 13 D8
Stanbrook 50 E3
Stanbury 94 F3
Stand Gtr Man . . . 87 D5
  N Lanark 119 C7
Standburn 120 B2
Standeford 62 D3
Standen 30 E2
Standford 27 F6
Standingstone . . . 107 F7
Standish 86 C3
Standlake 38 D3
Standon Hants . . . 14 B5
  Herts 41 B6
  Staffs 74 F5
Stane 119 D8
Stanfield 80 E5
Stanford C Beds . . 54 E2
  Kent 19 B8
Stanford Bishop . . 49 D8
Stanford Bridge . . 50 C2
Stanford Dingley . 26 B3
Stanford in the
  Vale 38 E3
Stanford-le-Hope . 42 F2
Stanford on Avon . 52 B3
Stanford on Soar . 64 B2
Stanford on Teme . 50 C2
Stanford Rivers . . 41 D7
Stanfree 76 B4
Stanghow 102 C4
Stanground 66 E2
Stanhoe 80 D4
Stanhope Borders 114 B4
  Durham 110 F2
Stanion 65 F6
Stanley Derbys . . . 76 E4
  Durham 110 D4
  Lancs 86 D2
  Perth 133 F8
  Staffs 75 D6
  W Yorks 88 B4
Stanley Common . 76 E4
Stanley Gate 86 D2
Stanley Hill 49 E8
Stanlow 73 B8
Stanmer 17 D7
Stanmore Hants . . 15 B5
  London 40 E4
  W Berks 26 B2
Stannergate 134 F4
Stanningfield 56 D2
Stanningley 94 F5
Stannington
  Northumb 110 B5
  S Yorks 88 F4
Stansbatch 48 C5
Stansfield 55 D8
Stanstead 56 E2
Stanstead Abbotts 41 C6
Stansted 29 C7
Stansted Airport . . 42 B1
Stansted
  Mountfitchet . . . 41 B8
Stanton Glos 51 F5
  Mon 35 B7
  Northumb 117 F7
  Staffs 75 E8
  Suff 56 B3
Stanton by Bridge 63 B7
Stanton-by-Dale . 76 F4
Stanton Drew 23 C7
Stanton
  Fitzwarren 38 E1
Stanton Harcourt . 38 D4
Stanton Hill 76 C4
Stanton in Peak . . 76 C2
Stanton Lacy 49 B6
Stanton Long 61 E5
Stanton-on-the-
  Wolds 77 F6
Stanton Prior 23 C8
Stanton
  St Bernard 25 C5
Stanton St John . . 39 D5
Stanton St Quintin 24 B4
Stanton Street . . . 56 C3
Stanton under
  Bardon 63 C8
Stanton upon Hine
  Heath 61 B5

Stanton Wick 23 C8
Stanwardine in the
 Fields 60 B4
Stanwardine in the
 Wood 60 B4
Stanway Essex 43 B5
 Glos. 51 F5
Stanway Green 57 B6
Stanwell 27 B8
Stanwell Moor 27 B8
Stanwick 53 B7
Stanwick-St-
 John 101 C6
Stanwix 108 D4
Stanydale 160 H4
Staoinebrig 148 E2
Stape 103 E5
Stapehill 13 D8
Stapeley 74 E3
Stapenhill 63 B6
Staple Kent 31 D6
 Som 22 E3
Staple Cross 18 C4
Staplefield 17 B6
Staple Fitzpaine . . . 11 C7
Stapleford Cambs . . 55 D5
 Herts 41 C6
 Leics 64 C5
 Lincs 77 D8
 Notts 76 F4
 Wilts 25 F7
Stapleford Abbotts 41 E8
Stapleford Tawney . 41 E8
Staplegrove 11 B7
Staplehay 11 B7
Staplehurst 29 E8
Staplers 15 F6
Stapleton Bristol . . . 23 B8
 Cumb 108 B5
 Hereford 48 C5
 Leics 63 E8
 N Yorks 101 C7
 Shrops 60 D4
 Som 12 B2
Stapley 11 C6
Staploe 54 C2
Staplow 49 E8
Star Fife 128 D5
 Pembs 45 F4
 Som 23 D6
Stara 159 F3
Starbeck 95 D6
Starbotton 94 B2
Starcross 10 F4
Stareton 51 B8
Starkholmes 76 D3
Starlings Green 55 F5
Starston 68 F5
Startforth 101 C5
Startley 37 F6
Stathe 11 B8
Stathern 77 F7
Station Town 111 F7
Staughton Green . . 54 C2
Staughton
 Highway 54 C2
Staunton Glos. 36 B2
 Glos. 36 C2
Staunton in the
 Vale 77 E8
Staunton on
 Arrow 49 C5
Staunton on Wye . . 49 E5
Staveley Cumb 99 E6
 Cumb 99 F5
 Derbys 76 B4
 N Yorks 95 C6
Staverton Devon . . . 7 C5
 Glos. 37 B5
 Northants 52 C3
 Wilts 24 C3
Staverton Bridge . . 37 B5
Stawell 23 F5
Staxigoe 158 E5
Staxton 97 B6
Staylittle 59 E5
Staynall 92 E3
Staythorpe 77 D7
Stean 94 B3
Stearsby 96 B2
Steart 22 E4
Stebbing 42 B2
Stebbing Green 42 B2
Stedham 16 B2
Steele Road 115 E8
Steen's Bridge 49 D7
Steep 15 B8
Steeple Dorset 13 F7
 Essex 43 D5
Steeple Ashton . . . 24 D4
Steeple Aston 38 B4
Steeple Barton 38 B4
Steeple
 Bumpstead 55 E7
Steeple Claydon . . . 39 B6
Steeple Gidding . . . 65 F8
Steeple Langford . . 24 F5
Steeple Morden . . . 54 E3
Steep Marsh 15 B8
Steeton 94 E3
Stein 148 C7
Steinmanhill 153 D7
Stelling Minnis 30 E5
Stemster 158 D3
Stemster House . . 158 D3
Stenalees 4 D5
Stenhousemuir . . . 127 F7
Stenigot 91 F6
Stenness 160 F4
Stenscholl 149 B9
Stenso 159 F4
Stenson 63 B7
Stenton E Loth. . . . 122 B2
 Fife 128 E4
Stenwith 77 F8
Stepaside 32 D2
Stepping Hill 87 F7
Steppingley 53 F8
Stepps 119 C6
Sterndale Moor . . . 75 C8
Sternfield 57 C7
Sterridge 20 E4
Stert 24 D5
Stetchworth 55 D7
Stevenage 41 B5
Stevenston 118 E2
Steventon Hants . . 26 E3
 Oxon 38 E4
Stevington 53 D7

Stewartby 53 E8
Stewarton Argyll . . 143 G7
 E Ayrs 118 E4
Stewkley 40 B1
Stewton 91 F7
Steyne Cross 15 F7
Steyning 17 C5
Stibb 8 C4
Stibbard 81 E5
Stibb Cross 9 C6
Stibb Green 25 C7
Stibbington 65 E7
Stichill 122 F3
Sticker 4 D4
Stickford 79 D6
Sticklepath 9 E8
Stickney 79 D6
Stiffkey 81 C5
Stifford's Bridge . . 50 E2
Stillingfleet 95 E8
Stillington N Yorks . 95 C8
 Stockton 102 B1
Stilton 65 F8
Stinchcombe 36 E4
Stinsford 12 E5
Stirchley 61 D7
Stirkoke House . . . 158 E5
Stirling Aberds . . . 153 D11
 Stirling 127 E6
Stisted 42 B3
Stithians 3 C6
Stittenham 151 D9
Stivichall 51 B8
Stixwould 78 C4
Stoak 73 B8
Stobieside 119 F6
Stobo 120 F4
Stoborough 13 F7
Stoborough Green . 13 F7
Stobshiel 121 C7
Stobswood 117 E8
Stock 42 E2
Stockbridge 25 F8
Stockbury 30 C2
Stockcross 26 C2
Stockdalewath . . . 108 E3
Stockerston 64 E5
Stock Green 50 D4
Stockheath 15 D8
Stockiemuir 126 F4
Stockingford 63 E7
Stocking Pelham . . 41 B7
Stockland 11 D7
Stockland Bristol . . 22 E4
Stockleigh English 10 D3
Stockleigh
 Pomeroy 10 D3
Stockley 24 C5
Stocklinch 11 C8
Stockport 87 E6
Stocksbridge 88 E3
Stocksfield 110 C3
Stockton Hereford . 49 C7
 Norf 69 E6
 Shrops 60 D2
 Shrops 61 E7
 Warks 52 C2
 Wilts 24 F4
Stockton Heath . . . 86 F4
Stockton-on-
 Tees 102 C2
Stockton on Teme . 50 C2
Stockton on the
 Forest 96 D2
Stock Wood 50 D5
Stodmarsh 31 C6
Stody 81 D6
Stoer 156 G3
Stoford Som 12 C3
 Wilts 25 F5
Stogumber 22 F2
Stogursey 22 E4
Stoke Devon 8 B4
 Hants 15 D8
 Hants 26 D2
 Medway 30 B2
 Suff 57 E5
Stoke Abbott 12 D2
Stoke Albany 64 F5
Stoke Ash 56 B5
Stoke Bardolph . . . 77 E6
Stoke Bliss 49 C8
Stoke Bruerne 52 E5
Stoke by Clare 55 E8
Stoke-by-Nayland . 56 F3
Stoke Canon 10 E4
Stoke Charity 26 F2
Stoke Climsland . . . 5 B8
Stoke D'Abernon . . 28 D2
Stoke Doyle 65 F7
Stoke Dry 65 E5
Stoke Farthing 13 B8
Stoke Ferry 67 E7
Stoke Fleming 7 E6
Stokeford 13 F6
Stoke Gabriel 7 D6
Stoke Gifford 23 B8
Stoke Golding 63 E7
Stoke Goldington . 53 E6
Stoke Green 40 F2
Stokeham 77 B7
Stoke Hammond . . 40 B1
Stoke Heath 61 B6
Stoke Holy Cross . . 68 D5
Stokeinteignhead . . 7 B7
Stoke Lacy 49 E8
Stoke Lyne 39 B5
Stoke Mandeville . . 39 C7
Stokenchurch 39 E7
Stoke Newington . . 41 F6
Stokenham 7 E6
Stoke on Tern 61 B6
Stoke-on-Trent 75 E5
Stoke Orchard 37 B6
Stoke Poges 40 F2
Stoke Prior
 Hereford 49 D7
 Worcs 50 C4
Stoke Rivers 20 F5
Stoke Rochford . . . 65 B6
Stoke Row 39 F6
Stoke St Gregory . . 11 B8
Stoke St Mary 11 B7
Stoke St Michael . . 23 E8
Stoke
 St Milborough . . 61 F5
Stokesay 60 F4
Stokesby 69 C7

Stokesley 102 D3
Stoke sub
 Hamdon 12 C2
Stoke Talmage 39 E6
Stoke Trister 12 B5
Stoke Wake 13 D5
Stolford 22 E4
Stondon Massey . . . 42 D1
Stone Bucks. 39 C7
 Glos. 36 E3
 Kent 19 C6
 Kent 29 B6
 Staffs. 75 F6
 S Yorks 89 F6
 Worcs 50 B3
Stone Allerton 23 D6
Ston Easton 23 D8
Stone Bridge
 Corner 66 D2
Stonebroom 76 D4
Stone Chair 88 B2
Stone Cross E Sus . 18 E3
 Kent 31 D7
Stone-edge Batch . 23 B6
Stoneferry 97 F7
Stonefield 119 D6
Stonegate E Sus . . . 18 C3
 N Yorks 103 D5
Stonegrave 96 B2
Stonehaugh 109 B7
Stonehaven 141 F7
Stonehouse Glos. . . 37 D5
 Northumb 109 D6
 S Lanark 119 E7
Stone House 100 F2
Stoneleigh 51 B8
Stonely 54 C2
Stoner Hill 15 B8
Stonesby 64 B5
Stonesfield 38 C3
Stone's Green 43 B7
Stone Street Kent . . 29 D6
 Suff 56 F3
 Suff 69 F6
Stonethwaite 98 C4
Stoneybreck 160 N8
Stoneyburn 120 C2
Stoney Cross 14 C3
Stoneygate
 Aberds 153 E10
 Leicester 64 D3
Stoneyhills 43 E5
Stoneykirk 104 D4
Stoney Middleton . 76 B2
Stoney Stanton . . . 63 E8
Stoney Stoke 24 F2
Stoney Stratton . . . 23 F8
Stoney Stretton . . . 60 D3
Stoneywood
 Aberdeen 141 C7
 Falk 127 F6
Stonganess 160 C7
Stonham Aspal . . . 56 D5
Stonnall 62 D4
Stonor 39 F7
Stonton Wyville . . . 64 E4
Stony Cross 50 E2
Stonyfield 151 D9
Stony Stratford . . . 53 E5
Stoodleigh 10 C4
Stopes 88 F3
Stopham 16 C4
Stopsley 40 B4
Stores Corner 57 E7
Storeton 85 F4
Stornoway 155 D9
Storridge 50 E2
Storrington 16 C4
Storrs 99 E5
Storth 99 F6
Storwood 96 E3
Stotfield 152 A2
Stotfold 54 F3
Stottesdon 61 F6
Stoughton Leics . . . 64 D3
 Sur 27 D7
 W Sus 16 C2
Stoul 147 B10
Stoulton 50 E4
Stourbridge 62 F3
Stourpaine 13 D6
Stourport on
 Severn 50 B3
Stour Provost 13 B5
Stour Row 13 B6
Stourton Staffs 62 F2
 Warks 51 F7
 Wilts 24 F2
Stourton Caundle . 12 C5
Stove Orkney 159 E7
 Shetland 160 L6
Stoven 69 F7
Stow Borders 121 E7
 Lincs 78 F3
 Lincs 90 F2
Stow Bardolph 67 D6
Stow Bedon 68 E2
Stowbridge 67 D6
Stow cum Quy 55 C6
Stowe 48 B5
Stowe-by-
 Chartley 62 B4
Stowe Green 36 D2
Stowell 12 B4
Stowford 9 F6
Stowlangtoft 56 C3
Stow Longa 54 B2
Stow Maries 42 E4
Stowmarket 56 D4
Stow-on-the-
 Wold 38 B1
Stowting 30 E5
Stowupland 56 D4
Strachan 141 E5
Stradbroke 57 B6
Stradishall 55 D8
Stradsett 67 D6
Stragglethorpe . . . 78 D2
Straid 112 E1
Straith 113 F8
Straiton Edin. 121 C5
 S Ayrs 112 D3
Straloch Aberds . . 141 B7
 Perth 133 C7
Stramshall 75 F7
Strang 84 E3
Stranraer 104 C4

Stratfield
 Mortimer 26 C4
Stratfield Saye 26 C4
Stratfield Turgis . . . 26 D4
Stratford
 St Andrew 57 C7
Stratford St Mary . 56 F4
Stratford Sub
 Castle 25 F6
Stratford Tony 13 B8
Stratford-upon-
 Avon 51 D6
Strath Highld 149 A12
 Highld 158 E4
Strathan Highld . . 136 E2
 Highld 156 G3
 Highld 157 C8
Strathaven 119 E7
Strathblane 119 B5
Strathcanaird . . . 156 J4
Strathcarron 150 G2
Strathcoil 124 B2
Strathdon 140 C2
Strathellie 153 B10
Strathkinness 129 C6
Strathmashie
 House 137 E8
Strathmiglo 128 C3
Strathmore
 Lodge 158 F3
Strathpeffer 150 F7
Strathrannoch . . . 150 D6
Strathtay 133 D6
Strathvaich
 Lodge 150 D6
Strathwhillan 143 E11
Strathy 157 C11
Strathyre 126 C4
Stratton Corn 8 D4
 Dorset 12 E4
 Glos. 37 D7
Stratton Audley . . . 39 B6
Stratton on the
 Fosse 23 D8
Stratton
 St Margaret 38 F1
Stratton
 St Michael 68 E5
Stratton Strawless 81 E8
Stravithie 129 C7
Streat 17 C7
Streatham 28 B4
Streatley C Beds . . 40 B3
 W Berks 39 F5
Street Lancs 92 D5
 N Yorks 103 D5
 Som 23 F6
Street Dinas 73 F7
Street End Kent . . . 30 D5
 W Sus 16 E2
Street Gate 110 D5
Streethay 62 C5
Streetlam 101 E8
Streetly 62 E4
Street Lydan 73 F8
Streetly End 55 E7
Strefford 60 F4
Strelley 76 E5
Strensall 96 C2
Stretcholt 22 E4
Strete 7 E6
Stretford 87 E6
Strethall 55 F5
Stretham 55 B6
Strettington 16 D2
Stretton ChesW . . . 73 D8
 Derbys 76 C3
 Rutland 65 C6
 Staffs. 62 C2
 Staffs. 63 B6
 Warr 86 F4
Stretton
 Grandison 49 E8
Stretton-on-
 Dunsmore 52 B2
Stretton-on-Fosse 51 F7
Stretton Sugwas . . 49 E6
Stretton under
 Fosse 63 F8
Stretton
 Westwood 61 E5
Strichen 153 C9
Strines 87 F7
Stringston 22 E3
Strixton 53 C7
Stroat 36 E2
Stromeferry 149 E13
Stromemore 149 E13
Stromness 159 H3
Stronaba 136 F5
Stronachlachar . . 126 C3
Stronchreggan . . . 130 B4
Stronchrubie 156 H5
Strone Argyll 145 E10
 Highld 136 F4
 Highld 137 B8
 Invclyd. 118 B2
Stronmilchan 125 C7
Strontian 130 C2
Strood 29 C8
Strood Green Sur . 28 E3
 W Sus 16 B4
 W Sus 28 F2
Stroud Glos 37 D5
 Hants 15 B8
Stroud Green 42 E4
Stroxton 78 F2
Struan Highld 149 E8
 Perth 133 C5
Strubby 91 F8
Strumpshaw 69 D6
Strutherhill 119 E7
Struy 150 H6
Stryt-issa 73 E6
Stuartfield 153 D9
Stubbington 15 D6
Stubbins 87 C5
Stubbs Cross 19 B6
Stubbs Green 69 E6
Stubb's Green 69 E5
Stubhampton 13 C7
Stub Place 98 E2
Stubton 77 E8
Stuckgowan 126 D2
Stuckton 14 C2
Stud Green 27 B6
Studham 40 C3
Studland 13 F8

Studley Warks 51 C5
 Wilts 24 B4
Studley Roger 95 B5
Stump Cross 55 E6
Stuntney 55 B6
Sturbridge 74 F5
Sturmer 55 E7
Sturminster
 Marshall 13 D7
Sturminster
 Newton 13 C5
Sturry 31 C5
Sturton 90 D3
Sturton by Stow . . 90 F2
Sturton le Steeple . 89 F8
Stuston 56 B5
Stutton N Yorks . . . 95 E7
 Suff 57 F5
Styal 87 F6
Styrrup 89 E7
Suainebost 155 A10
Suardail 155 D9
Succoth Aberds . . 152 E4
 Argyll 125 E8
Suckley 50 D2
Suckquoy 159 K5
Sudborough 65 F6
Sudbourne 57 D8
Sudbrook Lincs . . . 78 E2
 Mon 36 F2
Sudbrooke 78 B3
Sudbury Derbys . . . 75 F8
 London 40 F4
 Suff 56 E2
Suddie 151 F9
Sudgrove 37 D6
Suffield Norf 81 D8
 N Yorks 103 E7
Sugnall 74 F4
Suladale 149 C8
Sulaisiadar 155 D10
Sulby 84 C3
Sulgrave 52 E3
Sulham 26 B4
Sulhamstead 26 C4
Sulland 159 D6
Sullington 16 C4
Sullom 160 F5
Sullom Voe Oil
 Terminal 160 F5
Sully 22 C3
Sumburgh 160 N6
Summer Bridge . . . 94 C5
Summercourt 4 D3
Summerfield 80 D3
Summergangs 97 F7
Summer-house . . 101 C7
Summerleaze 35 F8
Summersdale 16 D2
Summerseat 87 C5
Summertown 39 D5
Summit 87 D7
Sunbury-on-
 Thames 28 C2
Sundaywell 113 F8
Sunderland Argyll . 142 B3
 Cumb 107 F8
 T&W 111 D6
Sunderland
 Bridge 111 F5
Sundhope 115 B6
Sundon Park 40 B3
Sundridge 29 D5
Sunipol 146 F6
Sunk Island 91 C6
Sunningdale 27 C7
Sunninghill 27 C7
Sunningwell 38 D4
Sunniside Durham . 110 F4
 T&W 110 D5
Sunnyhurst 86 B4
Sunnylaw 127 E6
Sunnyside 28 F4
Sunton 25 D7
Surbiton 28 C2
Surby 84 E2
Surfleet 66 B2
Surfleet Seas End . . 66 B2
Surlingham 69 D6
Sustead 81 D7
Susworth 90 D2
Sutcombe 8 C5
Suton 68 E3
Sutors of
 Cromarty 151 E11
Sutterby 79 B6
Sutterton 79 F5
Sutton Cambs 54 B5
 C Beds 54 E3
 Kent 31 E7
 London 28 C3
 Mers 86 E3
 Norf 69 B6
 Notts 77 F7
 Notts 89 F7
 Oxon 38 D4
 Pboro. 65 E7
 Shrops 61 F7
 Shrops 74 F3
 Som 23 G8
 Staffs. 61 B7
 Suff 57 E7
 Sur 27 E8
 S Yorks 89 D6
 W Sus 16 C3
Sutton at Hone . . . 29 B6
Sutton Bassett 64 E4
Sutton Benger 24 B4
Sutton Bonington . 64 B2
Sutton Bridge 66 B4
Sutton Cheney 63 D8
Sutton Coldfield . . 62 E5
Sutton Courtenay . 39 E5
Sutton Crosses . . . 66 B4
Sutton Grange 95 B5
Sutton Green 27 D8
Sutton Howgrave . 95 B6
Sutton In Ashfield . 76 D4
Sutton-in-Craven . 94 E3
Sutton Ings 97 F7
Sutton in the Elms . 64 E2
Sutton Lane Ends . . 75 B6
Sutton Leach 86 E3
Sutton Maddock . . 61 D7
Sutton Mallet 23 F5
Sutton Mandeville . 13 B7
Sutton Manor 86 E3
Sutton Montis 12 B4

Sutton on Hull 97 F7
Sutton on Sea 91 F9
Sutton on the-
 Forest 95 C8
Sutton on the Hill . 76 F2
Sutton on Trent . . . 77 C7
Sutton St Edmund . 66 C3
Sutton St Nicholas . 49 E7
Sutton Scarsdale . . 76 C4
Sutton Scotney . . . 26 F2
Sutton under
 Brailes 51 F8
Sutton-under-
 Whitestonecliffe
 . . . . 102 F2
Sutton upon
 Derwent 96 E3
Sutton Valence . . . 30 E2
Sutton Veny 24 E3
Sutton Waldron . . . 13 C6
Sutton Weaver 74 B2
Swaby 79 B6
Swadlincote 63 C7
Swaffham 67 D8
Swaffham Bulbeck 55 C6
Swaffham Prior . . . 55 C6
Swafield 81 D8
Swainby 102 D2
Swainshill 49 E6
Swainsthorpe 68 D5
Swainswick 24 C2
Swalcliffe 51 F8
Swalecliffe 30 C5
Swallow 91 D5
Swallowcliffe 13 B7
Swallowfield 26 C5
Swallownest 89 F5
Swallows Cross . . . 42 E2
Swanage 13 G8
Swanbister 159 H4
Swanbourne 39 B8
Swan Green
 ChesW 74 B4
 Suff 57 B6
Swanland 90 B3
Swanley 29 C6
Swanley Village . . . 29 C6
Swanmore 15 C6
Swannington Leics . 63 C8
 Norf 68 C4
Swanscombe 29 B7
Swansea
 = Abertawe 33 E7
Swanton Abbott . . 81 E8
Swanton Morley . . 68 C3
Swanton Novers . . 81 D6
Swanton Street . . . 30 D2
Swanwick Derbys . . 76 D4
 Hants 15 D6
Swarby 78 E3
Swardeston 68 D5
Swarister 160 E7
Swarkestone 63 B7
Swarland 117 D7
Swarland Estate . . 117 D7
Swarthmoor 92 B2
Swathwick 76 C3
Swaton 78 F4
Swavesey 54 C4
Sway 14 E3
Swayfield 65 B6
Swaythling 14 C5
Sweet Green 49 C8
Sweetham 10 E3
Sweethouse 5 C5
Sweffling 57 C7
Swepstone 63 C7
Swerford 51 F8
Swettenham 74 C5
Swetton 94 B4
Swffryd 35 E6
Swiftsden 18 C4
Swilland 57 D5
Swillington 95 F6
Swimbridge 9 B8
Swimbridge
 Newland 20 F5
Swinbrook 38 C2
Swinderby 77 C8
Swindon Glos 37 B6
 Staffs. 62 E2
 Swindon. 38 F1
Swine 97 F7
Swinefleet 89 B8
Swineshead
 Bedford 53 C8
 Lincs 78 E5
Swineshead
 Bridge 78 E5
Swiney 158 G4
Swinford Leics 52 B3
 Oxon 38 D4
Swingate 76 E5
Swingfield Minnis . 31 E6
Swingfield Street . . 31 E6
Swinhoe 117 B8
Swinhope 91 E6
Swining 160 G6
Swinithwaite 101 F5
Swinnow Moor . . . 94 F5
Swinscoe 75 E8
Swinside Hall 116 C3
Swinstead 65 B7
Swinton Borders . . 122 E4
 Gtr Man 87 D5
 N Yorks 94 B5
 N Yorks 96 B3
 S Yorks 88 E5
Swintonmill 122 E4
Swithland 64 C2
Swordale 151 E8
Swordland 147 B10
Swordly 157 C10
Sworton Heath . . . 86 F4
Swyddffynnon 47 C5
Swynnerton 75 F5
Swyre 12 F3
Sychdyn 73 C6
Sychnant 47 B8
Sychtyn 59 D6
Syde 37 C6
Sydenham London . 28 B4
 Oxon 39 D7
Sydenham Damerel . 6 B2
Syderstone 80 D4
Sydling
 St Nicholas 12 E4
Sydmonton 26 D2
Syerston 77 E7

Syke 87 C6
Sykehouse 89 C7
Sykes 93 D6
Syleham 57 B6
Sylen 33 D6
Symbister 160 G7
Symington S Ayrs . 118 F3
 S Lanark 120 F2
Symondsbury 12 E2
Symonds Yat 36 C2
Synod Inn 46 D3
Syre 157 E9
Syreford 37 B7
Syresham 52 E4
Syston Leics 64 C3
 Lincs 78 E2
Sytchampton 50 C3
Sywell 53 C6

T

Taagan 150 E3
Tàbost 155 A10
Tabost 155 F8
Tackley 38 B4
Tacleit 154 D6
Tacolneston 68 E4
Tadcaster 95 E7
Taddington 75 B8
Taddiport 9 C6
Tadley 26 C4
Tadlow 54 E3
Tadmarton 51 F8
Tadworth 28 D3
Tafarnau-bach 35 C5
Tafarn-y-gelyn 73 C5
Taff's Well 35 F5
Tafolwern 59 D5
Tai 83 E7
Taibach 34 F1
Tai-bach 59 B8
Taigh a
 Ghearraidh 148 A2
Tai-mawr 72 E3
Tain Highld 151 C10
 Highld 158 D4
Tainant 73 E6
Tainlon 82 F4
Tairbeart
 = Tarbert 154 G6
Tai'r-Bull 34 B3
Tairgwaith 33 C8
Tai-Ucha 72 D4
Takeley 42 B1
Takeley Street 41 B8
Talachddu 48 F2
Talacre 85 F2
Talardd 59 B5
Talaton 11 E5
Talbenny 44 D3
Talbot Green 34 F4
Talbot Village. 13 E8
Tale 11 D5
Talerddig 59 D6
Talgarreg 46 D3
Talgarth 48 F3
Talisker 149 E8
Talke 74 D5
Talkin 109 D5
Talladale 150 D2
Talla Linnfoots . . . 114 B4
Tallarn Green 73 E8
Tallentire 107 F8
Talley 46 F5
Tallington 65 D7
Talmine 157 C8
Talog 32 B4
Talsarn 34 B1
Tal-sarn 46 D4
Talsarnau 71 D7
Talskiddy 4 C4
Talwrn Anglesey . . 82 D4
 Wrex 73 E6
Tal-y-bont Ceredig . 58 F3
 Conwy 83 E7
 Gwyn 71 E6
 Gwyn 83 D6
Tal-y-cafn 83 D7
Talygarn 34 F4
Talyllyn 35 B5
Tal-y-llyn 58 D4
Talysarn 82 F4
Tal-y-wern 58 D5
Tame Bridge 102 D3
Tamerton Foliot . . . 6 C2
Tamworth 63 D6
Tandem 88 C2
Tandridge 28 D4
Tanerdy 33 B5
Tanfield 110 D4
Tanfield Lea 110 D4
Tangasdal 148 J1
Tangiers 44 D4
Tangley 25 D8
Tanglwst 46 F2
Tangmere 16 D3
Tangwick 160 F4
Tan Hinon 59 F5
Tankerness 159 H6
Tankersley 88 D4
Tan-lan Conwy . . . 83 E7
Tankerton 30 C5
Tannach 158 F5
Tannachie 141 F6
Tannadice 134 D4
Tannington 57 C6
Tansley 76 D3
Tansley Knoll 76 C3
Tansor 65 E7
Tantobie 110 D4
Tanton 102 C3
Tanworth-in-
 Arden 51 B6
Tan-y-bwlch 71 C7
Tan-y-fron 72 C3
Tan-y-graig
 Anglesey 82 D5
 Gwyn 70 D4
Tan-y-groes 45 E4
Tan-y-pistyll 59 B7
Tan-yr-allt 82 F4
Tanyrhydiau 47 C6
Taobh a Chaolais . 148 G2
Taobh a'Ghlinne . . 155 F8

Taobh a Thuath Loch
 Aineort 148 F2
Taobh a Tuath Loch
 Baghasdail 148 F2
Taobh Tuath 154 J4
Taplow 40 F2
Tapton 76 B3
Tarbat House. 151 D10
Tarbert Argyll 143 D7
 Argyll 144 E5
 Argyll 145 G7
Tarbert
 = Tairbeart 154 G6
Tarbet Argyll 126 D2
 Highld 147 B10
 Highld 156 E5
Tarbock Green 86 F2
Tarbrax 120 D3
Tardebigge 50 C5
Tarfside 134 B4
Tarland 140 D3
Tarleton 86 B2
Tarlogie 151 C10
Tarlscough 86 C2
Tarlton 37 E6
Tarnbrook 93 D5
Tarporley 74 C2
Tarr 22 F3
Tarrant Crawford . 13 D7
Tarrant Gunville . . 13 C7
Tarrant Hinton . . . 13 C7
Tarrant Keyneston . 13 D7
Tarrant
 Launceston 13 D7
Tarrant Monkton . 13 D7
Tarrant Rawston . . 13 D7
Tarrant Rushton . . 13 D7
Tarrel 151 C11
Tarring Neville 17 D8
Tarrington 49 E8
Tarsappie 128 B3
Tarskavaig 149 H10
Tarves 153 E8
Tarvie Highld 150 F7
 Perth 133 C7
Tarvin 73 C8
Tasburgh 68 E5
Tasley 61 E6
Taston 38 B3
Tatenhill 63 B6
Tathall End 53 E6
Tatham 93 C6
Tathwell 91 F7
Tatling End 40 F3
Tatsfield 28 D5
Tattenhall 73 D8
Tattenhoe 53 F6
Tatterford 80 E4
Tattersett 80 D4
Tattershall 78 D5
Tattershall Bridge . 78 D4
Tattershall Thorpe 78 D5
Tattingstone 56 F5
Tatworth 11 D8
Taunton 11 B7
Taverham 68 C4
Tavernspite 32 C2
Tavistock 6 B2
Taw Green 9 E8
Tawstock 9 B7
Taxal 75 B7
Tay Bridge 129 B6
Tayinloan 143 D7
Taymouth Castle . 132 E4
Taynish 144 E6
Taynton Glos. 36 B4
 Oxon 38 C2
Taynuilt 125 B6
Tayport 129 B6
Tayvallich 144 E6
Tealby 91 E5
Tealing 134 F4
Teangue 149 H11
Teanna Mhachair . 148 B2
Tebay 99 D8
Tebworth 40 B2
Tedburn St Mary . . 10 E3
Teddington Glos . . 50 F4
 London 28 B2
Tedstone
 Delamere 49 D8
Tedstone Wafre . . 49 D8
Teeton 52 B4
Teffont Evias 24 F4
Teffont Magna . . . 24 F4
Tegryn 45 F4
Teigh 65 C5
Teigncombe 9 F8
Teigngrace 7 B6
Teignmouth 7 B7
Telford 61 D6
Telham 18 D4
Tellisford 24 D3
Telscombe 17 D8
Telscombe Cliffs . . 17 D7
Templand 114 F3
Temple Corn 5 B6
 Glasgow 118 C5
 Midloth 121 D6
Temple Balsall 51 B7
Temple Bar Carms . 33 C6
 Ceredig 46 D4
Temple Cloud 23 D8
Temple Combe . . . 12 B5
Temple Ewell 31 E6
Temple Grafton . . . 51 D6
Temple Guiting . . . 37 B7
Templehall 128 E4
Temple
 Herdewyke 51 D8
Temple Hirst 89 B7
Temple
 Normanton 76 C4
Templeton Devon . 10 C3
 Pembs 32 C2
Templeton Bridge . 10 C3
Templetown 110 D4
Tempsford 54 D2
Tenbury Wells 49 C7
Tenby
 = Dinbych-y-Pysgod . 32 D2
Tendring 43 B7
Tendring Green . . . 43 B7
Ten Mile Bank 67 E6
Tenston 159 G3
Tenterden 19 B5

Ternhill 74 F3
Terregles Banks . . 107 B6
Terrick 39 D8
Terrington 96 B2
Terrington
 St Clement 66 C5
Terrington
 St John 66 C5
Teston 29 D8
Testwood 14 C4
Tetbury 37 E5
Tetbury Upton. . . . 37 E5
Tetchill 73 F7
Tetcott 8 E5
Tetford 79 B6
Tetney 91 D7
Tetney Lock 91 D7
Tetsworth 39 D6
Tettenhall 62 E2
Teuchan 153 E10
Teversal 76 C4
Teversham 55 D5
Teviothead 115 D7
Tewel 141 F7
Tewin 41 C5
Tewkesbury 50 F3
Teynham 30 C3
Thackthwaite 98 B3
Thainston 135 B6
Thakeham 16 C5
Thame 39 D7
Thames Ditton . . . 28 C2
Thames Haven . . . 42 F3
Thamesmead 41 F7
Thanington 30 D5
Thankerton 120 F2
Tharston 68 E4
Thatcham 26 C3
Thatto Heath 86 E3
Thaxted 55 F7
The Aird 149 C9
Theakston 101 F8
Thealby 90 C2
Theale Som 23 E6
 W Berks 26 B4
The Arms 67 E8
Thearne 97 F6
The Bage 48 E4
The Balloch 127 C2
The Barony 159 F3
The Bog 60 E3
The Bourne 27 E6
The Braes 149 E10
The Broad 49 C6
The Butts 24 E2
The Camp Glos. . . . 37 D6
 Herts 40 D4
The Chequer 73 E8
The City 39 E7
The Common 25 F7
The Craigs 150 B7
The Cronk 84 C3
Theddingworth . . . 64 F3
Theddlethorpe All
 Saints 91 F8
Theddlethorpe
 St Helen 91 F8
The Dell 69 E7
The Den 118 D3
The Eals 116 F3
The Eaves 36 D3
The Flatt 109 B5
The Four Alls 74 F3
The Garths 160 B8
The Green Cumb . . 98 E3
 Wilts 24 F3
The Grove 107 B6
The Hall 160 D8
The Haven 27 F8
The Heath Norf . . . 81 E7
 Suff 56 F5
The Hill 98 F3
The Howe Cumb . . 99 F6
 IoM 84 F1
The Hundred 49 C7
Thelbridge Barton . 10 C2
The Lee 40 D2
Thelnetham 56 B4
Thelveton 68 F4
Thelwall 86 F4
The Marsh Powys . . 60 E3
 Wilts 37 F7
Themelthorpe 81 E6
The Middles 110 D5
The Moor 18 C4
The Mumbles
 = Y Mwmbwls . . 33 F7
The Murray 119 D6
The Neuk 141 E6
Thenford 52 E3
The Oval 24 C2
The Pole of Itlaw . 153 C6
The Quarry 36 E4
Therfield 54 F4
The Rhos. 32 C1
The Rock 61 D6
The Ryde 41 D5
The Sands 27 E6
The Stocks 19 C6
Thetford Lincs . . . 65 C8
 Norf. 67 F8
The Throat 27 C6
The Vauld 49 E7
The Wyke 61 D7
Theydon Bois 41 E7
Thickwood 24 B3
Thimbleby Lincs . . 78 C5
 N Yorks 102 E2
Thingwall 85 F3
Thirdpart 118 E1
Thirlby 102 F2
Thirlestane 121 E8
Thirn 101 F7
Thirsk 102 F2
Thirtleby 97 F7
Thistleton Lancs . . 92 F4
 Rutland 65 C6
Thistley Green 55 B7
Thixendale 96 C4
Thockrington 110 B2
Tholomas Drove . . 66 D3
Tholthorpe 95 C7
Thomas Chapel . . . 32 D2
Thomas Close . . . 108 E4

Thomastown 152 E5
Thompson 68 E2
Thomshill 152 C2
Thong 29 B7
Thongsbridge 88 B2
Thoralby 101 F5
Thoresway 95 B5
Thorganby Lincs . . . 91 E6
N Yorks. 96 E2
Thorgill 103 E5
Thorington 57 B8
Thorington Street . 56 F4
Thorlby 94 D2
Thorley 41 C7
Thorley Street
Herts 41 C7
IoW 14 F4
Thormanby 95 B7
Thornaby-on-
Tees 102 C2
Thornage 81 D6
Thornborough
Bucks. 52 F5
N Yorks. 101 F7
Thornbury Devon . . 9 D6
Hereford 49 D8
S Glos. 36 E3
W Yorks. 94 F4
Thornby 52 B4
Thorncliffe 75 D7
Thorncombe
Dorset 11 D8
Dorset 13 D6
Thorncombe
Street 27 E8
Thorncote Green . . 54 E2
Thorncross 14 F5
Thorndon 56 C5
Thorndon Cross . . . 9 E7
Thorne 89 C7
Thorner 95 E6
Thorne
St Margaret . . . 11 B5
Thorney Notts. 77 B8
Pboro. 66 D2
Thorney Crofts . . . 91 B6
Thorney Green . . . 56 C4
Thorney Hill 14 E2
Thorney Toll 66 D3
Thornfalcon 11 B7
Thornford 12 C4
Thorngumbald 91 B6
Thornham 80 C3
Thornham Magna . 56 B5
Thornham Parva . . 56 B5
Thornhaugh 65 D7
Thornhill Cardiff . . 35 F5
Cumb. 98 D2
Derbys. 88 F2
Dumfries 113 E8
Soton. 15 C5
Stirling. 127 E5
W Yorks. 88 C3
Thornhill Edge . . . 88 C3
Thornhill Lees 88 C3
Thornholme 97 C7
Thornley Durham . 110 F4
Durham 110 F5
Thornliebank 118 D5
Thorns 55 D8
Thornsett 87 F8
Thorns Green 87 F5
Thornthwaite Cumb 98 B4
N Yorks. 94 D4
Thornton Angus . . 134 E3
Bucks. 53 F5
E Yorks. 96 F3
Fife 128 E4
Lancs. 92 E3
Leics 63 D8
Lincs 79 B6
Mbro 102 C2
Mers 85 D4
Northumb 123 E5
Pembs 44 E4
W Yorks. 94 F4
Thornton Curtis . . 90 C4
Thorntonhall 119 D5
Thornton Heath . . 28 C4
Thornton Hough . . 85 F4
Thornton in
Craven 94 E2
Thornton-le-
Beans 102 E1
Thornton-le-Clay . 96 C2
Thornton-le-
Dale 103 F6
Thornton le Moor . 90 E4
Thornton-le-
Moor 102 F1
Thornton-le-
Moors 73 B8
Thornton-le-
Street 102 F2
Thorntonloch 122 B3
Thorntonpark 122 E5
Thornton Rust 100 F4
Thornton
Steward 101 F6
Thornton Watlass 101 F7
Thornwood
Common 41 D7
Thornydykes 122 E2
Thoroton 77 E7
Thorp Arch. 95 E7
Thorpe Derbys 75 D8
E Yorks. 97 E5
Lincs 69 E7
Norf. 69 D7
Notts. 77 E7
N Yorks. 94 C3
Sur. 27 C8
Thorpe Abbotts . . 57 B5
Thorpe Acre 64 B2
Thorpe Arnold . . . 64 B4
Thorpe Audlin 89 C5
Thorpe Bassett . . 96 B4
Thorpe Bay 43 F5
Thorpe by Water . . 65 E5
Thorpe Common . . 57 F6
Thorpe
Constantine . . . 63 D6
Thorpe Culvert . . . 79 C7
Thorpe End 69 C5
Thorpe Fendykes . 79 C7

Thorpe Green
Essex 43 B7
Suff 56 D3
Thorpe Hesley 88 E4
Thorpe in Balne . . 89 C6
Thorpe in the
Fallows 90 F3
Thorpe Langton . . 64 E4
Thorpe-le-Soken . 43 B7
Thorpe le Street . . 96 E4
Thorpe Malsor . . . 53 B7
Thorpe Mandeville 52 E3
Thorpe Market . . . 81 D8
Thorpe Marriot . . . 68 C4
Thorpe Morieux . . 56 D3
Thorpeness 57 D8
Thorpe on the Hill 78 C2
Thorpe St Andrew 69 D5
Thorpe St Peter . . 79 C7
Thorpe Salvin 89 F6
Thorpe Satchville . 64 C4
Thorpe Thewles . . 102 B2
Thorpe Tilney 78 D4
Thorpe
Underwood 95 D7
Thorpe Waterville . 65 F7
Thorpe Willoughby 95 F8
Thorrington 43 C6
Thorverton 10 D4
Thrandeston 56 B5
Thrapston 53 B7
Thrashbush 119 C7
Threapland Cumb . 107 F8
N Yorks. 94 C3
Threapwood
Ches W. 73 E8
Staffs. 75 E7
Three Ashes 36 B2
Three Bridges . . . 28 F3
Three Burrows . . . 3 B6
Three Chimneys . . 18 B4
Three Cocks 48 F3
Three Crosses . . . 33 E6
Three Cups
Corner 18 C3
Threehammer
Common 69 C6
Three Holes 66 D5
Threekingham . . . 78 F3
Three Leg Cross . . 18 B3
Three Legged
Cross 13 D8
Threemile Cross . . 26 C5
Threemilestone . . 3 B6
Threemiletown . . 120 B3
Three Oaks 18 D5
Threlkeld 99 B5
Threshfield 94 C2
Thrigby 69 C7
Thringarth 100 B4
Thringstone 63 C8
Thrintoft 101 E8
Thriplow 54 E5
Throckenholt 66 D3
Throcking 54 F4
Throckley 110 C4
Throckmorton 50 E4
Throphill 117 F7
Thropton 117 D6
Throsk 127 E7
Throwleigh 9 E8
Throwley 30 D3
Thrumpton 76 F5
Thrumster 158 F5
Thrunton 117 C6
Thrupp Glos 37 D5
Oxon 38 C4
Thrushelton 9 F6
Thrussington 64 C3
Thruxton Hants . . 25 E7
Hereford 49 F6
Thrybergh 89 E5
Thulston 76 F4
Thundergay 143 D9
Thundersley 42 F3
Thundridge 41 C6
Thurcaston 64 C2
Thurcroft 89 F5
Thurgarton Norf . . 81 D7
Notts. 77 E6
Thurgoland 88 D3
Thurlaston Leics . . 64 E2
Warks. 52 B2
Thurlbear 11 B7
Thurlby Lincs 65 C8
Lincs 78 C2
Thurleigh 53 D8
Thurlestone 6 E4
Thurloxton 22 F4
Thurlstone 88 D3
Thurlton 69 E7
Thurlwood 74 D5
Thurmaston 64 D3
Thurnby 64 D3
Thurne 69 C7
Thurnham Kent . . 30 D2
Lancs. 92 D4
Thurning Norf 81 E6
Northants 65 F7
Thurnscoe 89 D5
Thurnscoe East . . 89 D5
Thursby 108 D3
Thursford 81 D5
Thursley 27 F7
Thurso 158 D3
Thurso East 158 D3
Thurstaston 85 F3
Thurston 56 C3
Thurstonfield 108 D3
Thurstonland 88 C2
Thurton 69 D6
Thurvaston 76 F2
Thuxton 68 D3
Thwaite N Yorks . . 100 E3
Suff 56 C5
Thwaites 94 E3
Thwaite St Mary . 69 E6
Thwaites Brow . . . 94 E3
Thwing 97 B6
Tibbermore 128 B2
Tibberton Glos . . . 36 B4
Telford. 61 B6
Worcs 50 D4
Tibenham 68 F4
Tibshelf 76 C4
Tibthorpe 97 D5
Ticehurst 18 B3
Tichborne 26 F3

Tickencote 65 D6
Tickenham 23 B6
Tickhill 89 E6
Ticklerton 60 E4
Ticknall 63 B7
Tickton 97 E6
Tidcombe 25 D7
Tiddington Oxon . . 39 D6
Warks 51 D7
Tidebrook 18 C3
Tideford 5 D8
Tideford Cross . . . 5 C8
Tidenham 36 E2
Tideswell 75 B8
Tidmarsh 26 B4
Tidmington 51 F7
Tidpit 13 C8
Tidworth 25 E7
Tiers Cross 44 D4
Tiffield 52 D4
Tifty 153 D7
Tigerton 135 C5
Tigh-na-Blair . . . 127 C6
Tighnabruaich . . 145 F8
Tighnafiline 155 J13
Tigley 7 C5
Tilbrook 53 C8
Tilbury 29 B7
Tilbury Juxta Clare 55 E8
Tile Cross 63 F5
Tile Hill 51 B7
Tilehurst 26 B4
Tilford 27 E6
Tilgate 28 F3
Tilgate Forest Row 28 F3
Tillathrowie 152 E4
Tilley 60 B5
Tillicoultry 127 E8
Tillingham 43 D5
Tillington Hereford . 49 E6
W Sus 16 B3
Tillington
Common 49 E6
Tillyarblet 135 C5
Tillybirloch 141 D5
Tillycorthie 141 B8
Tillydrine 140 E5
Tillyfour 140 C4
Tillyfourie 140 C5
Tillygarmond 140 E5
Tillygreig 141 B7
Tillykerrie 141 B7
Tilmanstone 31 D7
Tilney All Saints . . 67 C5
Tilney High End . . 67 C5
Tilney
St Lawrence . . . 66 C5
Tilshead 24 E5
Tilstock 74 F2
Tilston 73 D8
Tilstone Fearnall . 74 C2
Tilsworth 40 B2
Tilton on the Hill . 64 D4
Timberland 78 D4
Timbersbrook 75 C5
Timberscombe . . . 21 E8
Timble 94 D4
Timperley 87 F5
Timsbury Bath . . . 23 D8
Hants. 14 B4
Timsgearraidh . . 154 D5
Timworth Green . . 56 C2
Tincleton 13 E5
Tindale 109 D6
Tingewick 52 F4
Tingley 88 B3
Tingrith 53 F8
Tingwall 159 F4
Tinhay 9 F5
Tinshill 95 F5
Tinsley 88 E5
Tintagel 8 F2
Tintern Parva 36 D2
Tintinhull 12 C3
Tintwistle 87 E8
Tinwald 114 F3
Tinwell 65 D7
Tipperty 141 B8
Tipsend 66 E5
Tipton 62 E3
Tipton St John . . . 11 E5
Tiptree 42 C4
Tirabad 47 E7
Tiraghoil 146 J6
Tirley 37 B5
Tirphil 35 D5
Tir-y-dail 33 C7
Tisbury 13 B7
Tisman's Common 27 F8
Tissington 75 D8
Titchberry 8 B4
Titchfield 15 D6
Titchmarsh 53 B8
Titchwell 80 C3
Tithby 77 F6
Titley 48 C5
Titlington 117 C7
Titsey 28 D5
Tittensor 75 F5
Tittleshall 80 E4
Tiverton Ches W . . 74 C2
Devon 10 C4
Tivetshall
St Margaret . . . 68 F4
Tivetshall St Mary 68 F4
Tividale 62 E3
Tivy Dale 88 D3
Tixall 62 B3
Tixover 65 D6
Toab Orkney 159 H6
Shetland 160 M5
Toadmoor 76 D3
Tobermory 147 F8
Toberonochy 124 E3
Tobha Mor 148 E2
Tobhtarol 154 D6
Tobson 154 D6
Tocher 153 E6
Tockenham 24 B5
Tockenham Wick . 37 F7
Tockholes 86 B4
Tockington 36 F3
Tockwith 95 D7
Todber 13 B6
Todding 49 B6
Toddington C Beds . 40 B3
Glos 50 F5
Todenham 51 F7

Todhills 108 C3
Todlachie 141 C5
Todmorden 87 B7
Todrig 115 C7
Todwick 89 F5
Toft Cambs 54 D4
Lincs 65 C7
Toft Hill Durham . 101 B6
Lincs 78 C5
Toft Monks 69 E7
Toft next Newton . 90 F4
Toftrees 80 E4
Tofts 158 D5
Toftwood 68 C2
Togston 117 D8
Tokavaig 149 G11
Tokers Green 26 B5
Tolastadh a
Chaolais 154 D6
Tolastadh bho
Thuath 155 C10
Toll Bar 89 D6
Tollard Royal 13 C7
Toll Bar 89 D6
Toll End 62 E3
Toller Fratrum . . . 12 E3
Toller Porcorum . . 12 E3
Tollerton Notts . . . 77 F6
N Yorks 95 C8
Tollesbury 43 C5
Tolleshunt D'Arcy . 43 C5
Tolleshunt Major . 43 C5
Toll of Birness . . 153 E10
Tolm 155 D9
Tolpuddle 13 E5
Tolvah 138 E4
Tolworth 28 C2
Tomatin 138 B4
Tombreck 151 H9
Tomchrasky 137 C5
Tomdoun 136 D4
Tomich Highld . . . 137 B6
Highld 151 D9
Tomich House . . . 151 G8
Tomintoul Aberds . 139 E7
Moray 139 C7
Tomnaven 152 E4
Tomnavoulin . . . 139 B8
Tonbridge 29 E6
Tondu 34 F2
Tonfanau 58 D2
Tong Shrops 61 D7
W Yorks 94 F5
Tonge 63 B8
Tongham 27 E6
Tongland 106 D3
Tong Norton 61 D7
Tongue 157 D8
Tongue End 65 C8
Tongwynlais 35 F5
Tonna 34 E1
Ton-Pentre 34 E3
Tonwell 41 C6
Tonypandy 34 E3
Tonyrefail 34 F4
Toot Baldon 39 D5
Toothill 14 C4
Toot Hill 41 D8
Topcliffe 95 B7
Topcroft 69 E5
Topcroft Street . . 69 E5
Top of Hebers . . . 87 D6
Toppesfield 55 F8
Toppings 86 C5
Topsham 10 F4
Torbay 7 D7
Torbeg 143 F10
Torboll Farm . . . 151 B10
Torbrex 127 E6
Torbryan 7 C6
Torcross 7 E6
Tore 151 F9
Torinturk 145 G7
Torksey 77 B8
Torlum 148 C2
Torlundy 131 B5
Tormarton 24 B2
Tormisdale 142 C2
Tormitchell 112 E2
Tormore 143 E9
Tornagrain 151 G10
Tornahaish 139 D8
Tornaveen 140 D5
Torness 137 B8
Toronto 110 F4
Torpenhow 108 F2
Torphichen 120 B2
Torphins 140 D5
Torpoint 6 D2
Torquay 7 C7
Torquhan 121 E7
Torran Argyll 124 E4
Highld 149 D10
Highld 151 D10
Torrance 119 B6
Torrans 146 J7
Torranyard 118 E3
Torre 7 C7
Torridon 150 F2
Torridon House . . 149 C13
Torrin 149 F10
Torrisdale- 157 C9
Torrisdale-
Square 143 E8
Torrish 157 H12
Torrisholme 92 C4
Torroble 157 J8
Torry Aberdeen . . 141 D8
Aberds 152 E4
Torryburn 128 F2
Torterston 153 D10
Tortworth 107 B7
Tortington 16 D4
Tortworth 36 E4
Torvaig 149 D9
Torver 98 E4
Torwood 127 F7
Torworth 89 F7
Tosberry 8 B4
Toscaig 149 E12
Toseland 54 C3
Tosside 93 D7
Tostock 56 C3
Totaig Highld . . . 148 C2
Highld 149 F13
Tote 149 D9
Totegan 157 C11
Tothill 91 F8

Totland 14 F4
Totnes 7 C6
Toton 76 F5
Totronald 146 F4
Totscore 149 B8
Tottenham 41 E6
Tottenhill 67 C6
Tottenhill Row . . . 67 C6
Totteridge 41 E5
Totternhoe 40 B2
Tottington 87 C5
Totton 14 C4
Touchen End 27 B6
Tournaig 155 J13
Toux 153 C9
Tovil 29 D8
Toward 145 G10
Towcester 52 E4
Towednack 2 C3
Tower End 67 C6
Towersey 39 D7
Towie Aberds. . . . 140 C3
Aberds. 153 B8
Towiemore 152 D3
Tow Law 110 F4
Townend 118 B4
Town End Cambs . 66 E4
Cumb. 99 F6
Towngate 65 C8
Townhead Cumb . 108 F5
Dumfries 106 E3
S Ayrs. 112 D2
Townhead of
Greenlaw 106 C4
Townhill 128 F3
Town Row 18 B2
Townsend Bucks . 39 D7
Herts 40 D4
Townshend 2 C4
Town Yetholm . . 116 B4
Towthorpe 96 D2
Towton 95 F7
Towyn 72 B3
Toxteth 85 F4
Toynton All Saints . 79 C6
Toynton Fen Side . 79 C6
Toynton St Peter . 79 C7
Toy's Hill 29 D5
Trabboch 112 B4
Traboe 3 D6
Tradespark
Highld 151 F11
Orkney 159 H5
Trafford Park 87 E5
Trallong 34 B3
Tranent 121 B7
Tranmere 85 F4
Trantlebeg 157 D11
Trantlemore 157 D11
Tranwell 117 F7
Trapp 33 C7
Traprain 121 B8
Traquair 121 F6
Trawden 94 F2
Trawsfynydd 71 D8
Trealaw 34 E4
Treales 92 F4
Trearddur 82 D2
Treaslane 149 C8
Trebanog 34 E4
Trebanos 33 D8
Trebartha 5 B7
Trebarwith 8 F2
Trebetherick 4 B4
Treborough 22 F2
Trebudannon 4 C3
Trebullett 5 B8
Treburley 5 B8
Trebyan 5 C5
Trecastle 34 B2
Trecenydd 35 F5
Trecwn 44 B4
Trecynon 34 D3
Tredavoe 2 D3
Treddiog 44 C3
Tredegar 35 D5
Tredegar = Newydd
New Tredegar . . 35 D5
Tredington Glos. . 37 B6
Warks 51 E7
Tredinnick 4 B4
Tredomen 48 F3
Tredunnock 35 E7
Tredustan 48 F3
Treen 2 D2
Treeton 88 F5
Trefaldwyn
= Montgomery . . 60 D2
Trefasser 44 B3
Trefdraeth 82 D4
Trefdraeth
= Newport 45 F2
Trefecca 48 F3
Trefechan 58 F2
Trefeglwys 59 E6
Trefenter 46 C5
Treffgarne 44 C4
Treffynnon 44 C3
Treffynnon
= Holywell 73 B5
Trefgarn Owen . . 44 C3
Trefi 44 B3
Trefil 35 C5
Trefilan 46 D4
Treflach 60 B2
Trefnanney 60 C2
Trefnant 72 B4
Trefonen 60 B2
Trefor Anglesey . . 82 C3
Gwyn 70 C4
Treforest 34 F4
Trefriw 83 E7
Tref-y-Clawdd
= Knighton 48 B4
Trefynwy
= Monmouth . . . 36 C2
Tregadillett 8 F4
Tregaian 82 D4
Tregare 35 C8
Tregaron 47 D5
Tregarth 83 E6
Tregeare 8 F4
Tregeiriog 73 F5
Tregele 82 B3
Tre-Gibbon 34 D3
Tregidden 3 D6
Treglemais 44 C3
Tregole 8 E3

Tregonetha 4 C4
Tregony 3 B8
Tregoss 4 C4
Tregoyd 48 F4
Tregroes 46 E3
Tregurrian 4 C3
Tregynon 59 E7
Trehafod 34 E4
Treharris 34 E4
Treherbert 34 E3
Trekenner 5 B8
Treknow 8 F2
Trelan 3 E6
Trelash 8 E3
Trelassick 4 D3
Trelawnyd 72 B4
Trelech 45 F4
Treleddyd-fawr . . 44 C2
Trelewis 35 E5
Treligga 8 F2
Trelights 4 B4
Trelill 4 B5
Trelissick 3 C7
Trellech 36 D2
Trelleck Grange . . 36 D1
Trelogan 85 F2
Trelystan 60 D2
Tremadog 71 C6
Tremail 8 F3
Tremain 45 E4
Tremaine 8 F4
Tremar 5 C7
Trematon 5 D8
Tremeirchion 72 B4
Trenance 4 C3
Trenarren 3 B9
Trench 61 C6
Treneglos 8 F4
Trenewan 5 D6
Trent 12 C3
Trentham 75 E5
Trentishoe 20 E5
Trent Vale 75 E5
Treoes 21 B8
Treorchy = Treorci. 34 E3
Treorci = Treorchy . 34 E3
Tre'r-ddôl 58 E3
Trerulefoot 5 D8
Tresaith 45 D4
Tresawle 3 B7
Trescott 62 E2
Trescowe 2 C4
Tresham 36 E4
Tresillian 3 B7
Tresinwen 44 A4
Tresparrett 8 E3
Tresparrett Posts . 8 E3
Tressait 133 C5
Tresta Shetland . . 160 D8
Shetland 160 H5
Treswell 77 B7
Tret-Taliesin 58 E3
Trethosa 4 D4
Trethurgy 4 D5
Tretio 44 C2
Tretire 36 B2
Tretower 35 B5
Treuddyn 73 D6
Trevalga 8 F2
Trevalyn 73 D7
Trevanson 4 B4
Trevarren 4 C4
Trevarrian 4 C3
Trevarrick 3 B8
Trevaughan 32 C2
Tre-vaughan 32 B4
Treveighan 5 B5
Trevellas 4 D2
Treverva 3 C6
Trevethin 35 D6
Trevigro 5 C8
Treviscoe 4 D4
Trevone 4 B3
Trewarmett 8 F2
Trewassa 8 F3
Trewellard 2 C2
Trewen 8 F4
Trewennack 3 D5
Trewern 60 C2
Trewethern 4 B5
Trewidland 5 D7
Trewint Corn 8 E3
Corn. 8 F4
Trewithian 3 C7
Trewoofe 2 D3
Trewoon 4 D4
Treworga 3 B7
Treworlas 3 C7
Tre-wyn 35 B7
Treyarnon 4 B3
Treyford 16 C2
Trezaise 4 D4
Triangle 87 B8
Trickett's Cross . . 13 D8
Triffleton 44 C4
Trimdon 111 F6
Trimdon Colliery . 111 F6
Trimdon Grange . 111 F6
Trimingham 81 D8
Trimley Lower
Street 57 F6
Trimley St Martin 57 F6
Trimley St Mary . 57 F6
Trimpley 50 B2
Trimsaran 33 D5
Trimstone 20 E3
Trinafour 132 C4
Trinant 35 D6
Tring 40 C2
Tring Wharf 40 C2
Trinity Angus . . . 135 C6
Jersey 17
Trisant 47 B6
Trislaig 130 B4
Trispen 4 D3
Tritlington 117 E8
Trochry 133 E6
Trodigal 143 F7
Troed-rhiwdalar . 47 D8
Troedyraur 46 E2
Troedyrhiw 34 D4
Tromode 84 E3
Trondavoe 160 F5
Troon Corn. 3 C5
S Ayrs. 118 F3
Trosaraidh 148 G2
Trossachs Hotel . 126 D4

Troston 56 B2
Trottiscliffe 29 C7
Trotton 16 B2
Troutbeck Cumb . . 99 B5
Cumb. 99 D6
Troutbeck Bridge . 99 D6
Trowbridge 24 D3
Trowell 76 F4
Trow Green 36 D2
Trowle Common . . 24 D3
Trowley Bottom . . 40 C3
Trows 122 F2
Trowse Newton . . 68 D5
Trudoxhill 24 E2
Trull 11 B7
Trumaisgearraidh
. . . . 148 A3
Trumpan 148 B7
Trumpet 49 F8
Trumpington 54 D5
Trunch 81 D8
Trunnah 92 E3
Truro 3 B7
Trusham 10 F3
Trusley 76 F2
Trusthorpe 91 F9
Trysull 62 E2
Tubney 38 E4
Tuckenhay 7 D6
Tuckhill 61 F7
Tuckingmill 3 B5
Tuddenham 55 B8
Tuddenham
St Martin 57 E5
Tudeley 29 E7
Tudhoe 111 F5
Tudorville 36 B2
Tudweiliog 70 D3
Tuesley 27 E7
Tuffley 37 C5
Tufton Hants 26 E2
Pembs 32 B1
Tugby 64 D4
Tugford 61 F5
Tullibardine 127 C8
Tullibody 127 E7
Tullich Argyll . . . 125 D6
Highld 138 B2
Tullich Muir 151 D10
Tulliemet 133 D6
Tulloch Aberds . . 135 B7
Aberds. 153 E8
Perth 128 B2
Tulloch Castle . . 151 E8
Tullochgorm 125 F5
Tulloes 135 E5
Tullybannocher . . 127 B6
Tullybelton 133 F7
Tullyfergus 134 E2
Tullymurdoch . . . 134 D1
Tullynessle 140 C4
Tumble 33 C6
Tumby Woodside . 79 D5
Tummel Bridge . . 132 D4
Tunga 155 D9
Tunstall E Yorks . . 97 F9
Kent 30 C2
Lancs. 93 B6
Norf. 69 D7
N Yorks. 101 E7
Stoke 75 D5
Suff 57 D7
T&W 111 D6
Tunstead Derbys . 75 B8
Gtr Man 87 D8
Norf. 81 E8
Tunworth 26 E4
Tupsley 49 E7
Tupton 76 C3
Turgis Green 26 D4
Turin 135 D5
Turkdean 37 C8
Tur Langton 64 E4
Turleigh 24 C3
Turn 87 C6
Turnastone 49 F5
Turnberry 112 D2
Turnditch 76 E2
Turners Hill 28 F4
Turners Puddle . . 13 E6
Turnford 41 D6
Turnhouse 120 B4
Turnworth 13 D6
Turriff 153 C7
Turton Bottoms . . 86 C5
Turves 66 E3
Turvey 53 D7
Turville 39 E7
Turville Heath . . . 39 E7
Turweston 52 F4
Tushielaw 115 C6
Tutbury 63 B6
Tutnall 50 B4
Tutshill 36 E2
Tuttington 81 E8
Tutts Clump 26 B3
Tuxford 77 B7
Twatt Orkney . . . 159 F3
Shetland 160 H5
Twechar 119 B7
Tweedmouth 123 D5
Tweedsmuir 114 B3
Twelve Heads 3 B6
Twelvewoods 5 C7
Twemlow Green . . 74 C4
Twenty 65 B8
Twerton 24 C2
Twickenham 28 B2
Twigworth 37 B5
Twineham 17 C6
Twinhoe 24 D2
Twinstead 56 F2
Twinstead Green . 56 F2
Twiss Green 86 E4
Twiston 93 E8
Twitchen Devon . . 21 F6
Shrops. 49 B5
Two Bridges 6 B4
Two Dales 76 C2
Two Mills 73 B7
Twycross 63 D7
Twyford Bucks. . . 39 B6
Derbys. 63 B7
Hants. 15 B5
Leics 64 C4
Lincs 65 B6
Norf. 81 E5
Wokingham 27 B5
Twyford Common . 49 F7
Twyn-y-Sheriff . . 35 D8
Twynholm 106 D3

Twyning 50 F3
Twyning Green . . 50 F4
Twynllanan 34 B1
Twyn-y-Sheriff . . 35 D8
Twywell 53 B7
Tyberton 49 F5
Tyburn 62 E5
Tycroes 33 C7
Tycrwyn 59 C8
Tyddewi
= St David's . . . 44 C2
Tydd Gote 66 C4
Tydd St Giles . . . 66 C4
Tydd St Mary . . . 66 C4
Tyddyn-mawr . . . 71 C6
Ty-draw 83 F8
Tye 15 D8
Tye Green Essex . . 41 D7
Essex. 42 B3
Essex. 55 F6
Ty-hen Carms . . . 32 B4
Gwyn 70 D2
Tyldesley 86 D4
Tyler Hill 30 C5
Tylers Green 40 E2
Tylorstown 34 E4
Tylwch 59 F6
Ty-mawr 82 C4
Ty Mawr 46 E4
Ty Mawr Cwm . . . 72 E3
Ty-nant Conwy . . 72 E3
Gwyn 59 B6
Tyncelyn 46 C5
Tyndrum 131 F7
Tyneham 13 F6
Tynehead 121 D6
Tynemouth 111 C6
Tyne Tunnel 111 C6
Tynewydd 34 E3
Tyninghame 122 B2
Tynron 113 E8
Tyn-y-celyn 73 F5
Tyn-y-coed 60 B2
Tyn-y-fedwen . . . 72 F5
Tyn-y-ffridd 72 F5
Tyn-y-graig 47 C5
Ty'n-y-groes 83 D7
Tyn-y-maes 83 E6
Tyn-y-pwll 82 C4
Ty'r-felin-isaf . . . 83 E8
Tyrie 153 B9
Tyringham 53 E6
Tythecott 9 C6
Tythegston 21 B7
Tytherington
Ches E 75 B6
S Glos. 36 F3
Som. 24 E2
Wilts 24 E4
Tytherleigh 11 D8
Ty-uchaf 59 B7
Tywardreath 5 D5
Tywyn Conwy . . . 83 D7
Gwyn 58 D2

U

Uachdar 148 C2
Uags 149 E12
Ubbeston Green . 57 B7
Ubley 23 D7
Uckerby 101 D7
Uckfield 17 B8
Uckington 37 B6
Uddingston 119 C6
Uddington 119 F8
Udimore 19 D5
Udny Green 141 B7
Udny Station . . . 141 B8
Udston 119 D6
Udstonhead 119 E7
Uffcott 25 B6
Uffculme 11 C5
Uffington Lincs . . 65 D7
Oxon 38 F3
Shrops. 60 C5
Suff 57 D6
Ufton 51 C8
Ufton Nervet . . . 26 C4
Ugadale 143 F8
Ugborough 6 D4
Uggeshall 69 F7
Ugglebarnby . . . 103 D6
Ughill 88 E3
Ugley 41 B8
Ugley Green 41 B8
Ugthorpe 103 C5
Uidh 148 J1
Uig Argyll 145 E10
Highld 148 C6
Highld 149 B8
Uigen 154 D5
Uigshader 149 D9
Uisken 146 K6
Ulbster 158 F5
Ulceby Lincs 79 B7
N Lincs. 90 C5
Ulceby Skitter . . . 90 C5
Ulcombe 30 E2
Uldale 108 F2
Uley 36 E4
Ulgham 117 E8
Ullapool 150 B4
Ullenhall 51 C6
Ullenwood 37 C6
Ulleskelf 95 E8
Ullesthorpe 64 F2
Ulley 89 F5
Ullingswick 49 E7
Ullinish 149 E8
Ullock 98 B2
Ulnes Walton . . . 86 C3
Ulpha 98 E3
Ulrome 97 D7
Ulsta 160 E6
Ulva House 146 H7
Ulverston 92 B2
Ulwell 13 F8
Umberleigh 9 B8
Unapool 156 F5
Unasary 148 F2
Underbarrow 99 E6
Undercliffe 94 F4
Underhoull 160 C7

Underriver 29 D6
Underwood 76 D4
Undy 35 F8
Unifirth 160 H4
Union Cottage . . 141 E7
Union Mills 84 E3
Union Street 18 B4
Unstone 76 B3
Unstone Green . . 76 B3
Unthank Cumb . . 108 F4
Cumb. 109 E6
Unthank End . . . 108 F4
Upavon 25 D6
Up Cerne 12 D4
Upchurch 30 C2
Upcott 48 D5
Upend 55 D7
Up Exe 10 D4
Upgate 68 C4
Uphall 120 B3
Uphall Station . . 120 B3
Upham Devon . . . 10 D3
Hants. 15 B6
Uphampton 50 C3
Up Hatherley 37 B6
Uphill 22 D5
Up Holland 86 D3
Uplawmoor 118 D4
Upleadon 36 B4
Upleatham 102 C4
Uplees 30 C3
Uploders 12 E3
Uplowman 10 C5
Uplyme 11 E8
Up Marden 15 C8
Upminster 42 F1
Up Nately 26 D4
Upnor 29 B8
Upottery 11 D7
Upper Affcot 60 F4
Upper
Ardchronie . . . 151 C9
Upper Arley 61 F7
Upper Arncott . . . 39 C6
Upper Astrop . . . 52 F3
Upper Badcall . . 156 E4
Upper Basildon . . 26 B3
Upper Beeding . . 17 C5
Upper Benefield . . 65 F6
Upper Bighouse . 157 D11
Upper Boddington 52 D2
Upper Borth 58 F3
Upper Boyndlie . . 153 B9
Upper Brailes . . . 51 F8
Upper Breakish . 149 F11
Upper Breinton . . 49 E6
Upper Broadheath 50 D3
Upper Broughton . 64 B3
Upper Bucklebury 26 C3
Upper
Burnhaugh . . . 141 E7
Upperby 108 D4
Upper Caldecote . 54 E2
Upper Catesby . . 52 D3
Upper Chapel . . . 48 E2
Upper Church
Village 34 F4
Upper Chute 25 D7
Upper Clatford . . 25 E8
Upper Clynnog . . 71 C5
Upper
Cumberworth . . 88 D3
Upper Cwmbran . 35 E6
Upper Dallachy . 152 B3
Upper Dean 53 C8
Upper Denby 88 D3
Upper Denton . . 109 C6
Upper Derraid . . 151 H13
Upper Dicker . . . 18 E2
Upper Dovercourt 57 F6
Upper Druimfi. . . 147 F8
Upper Dunsforth . 95 C7
Upper Eathie . . . 151 E10
Upper Elkstone . . 75 D7
Upper End 75 B7
Upper Farringdon 26 F5
Upper Framilode . 36 C4
Upper Glenfintaig 137 F5
Upper Gornal . . . 62 E3
Upper Gravenhurst 54 F2
Upper Green Mon . 35 C7
W Berks 25 C8
Upper Grove
Common 36 B2
Upper Hackney . . 76 C2
Upper Hale 27 E6
Upper Halistra . . 148 C7
Upper Halling . . . 29 C7
Upper Hambleton 65 D6
Upper Hardres
Court. 31 D5
Upper Hartfield . . 29 F5
Upper Haugh . . . 88 E5
Upper Heath 61 F5
Upper Hellesdon . 68 C5
Upper Helmsley . 96 D2
Upper Hergest . . 48 D4
Upper Heyford
Northants 52 D4
Oxon 38 B4
Upper Hill 49 D6
Upper Hopton . . . 88 C2
Upper
Horsebridge . . 18 D2
Upper Hulme . . . 75 C7
Upper Inglesham . 38 E2
Upper
Inverbrough . . 151 H11
Upper Killay 33 E6
Upper
Knockando . . . 152 D1
Upper Lambourn . 38 F3
Upper Leigh 75 F7
Upper Lenie 137 B8
Upper Lochton . . 141 E5
Upper Longdon . . 62 C4
Upper Lybster . . 158 G4
Upper Lydbrook . 36 C3
Upper Maes-coed 48 F5
Upper Midway . . 63 B6
Uppermill 87 D7
Upper Milovaig . . 148 D6
Upper Minety . . . 37 E7
Upper Mitton . . . 50 B3
Upper North Dean 39 E8
Upper Obney . . . 133 F7
Upper Ollach . . . 149 E10
Upper Padley . . . 76 B2
Upper Pollicott . . 39 C7

Upper Poppleton . . 95 D8
Upper Quinton . . . 51 E6
Upper Ratley 14 B4
Upper Rissington . . 38 C2
Upper Rochford . . . 49 C8
Upper Sandaig . .149 G12
Upper Sanday 159 H6
Upper Sapey 49 C8
Upper Saxondale . . 77 F6
Upper Seagry 37 F6
Upper Shelton 53 E7
Upper
Sheringham 81 C7
Upper Skelmorlie 118 C2
Upper Slaughter . . 38 B1
Upper Soudley 36 C3
Uppersound 160 J6
Upper Stondon . . . 54 F2
Upper Stowe 52 D4
Upper Stratton . . . 38 F1
Upper Street Hants 14 C2
Norf 69 C6
Norf 69 C6
Suff 56 F5
Upper Strensham . . 50 F4
Upper Sundon 40 B3
Upper Swell 38 B1
Upper Tean 75 F7
Upperthong 88 D2
Upperthorpe 89 D8
Upper Tillyrie . . .128 D3
Upperton 16 B3
Upper Tooting . . .149 C10
Upper Tote 149 C10
Uppertown Derbys . 76 C3
Highld 158 C5
Orkney 159 J5
Upper Town 23 C7
Upper Treverward . 48 B4
Upper Tysoe 51 E8
Upper Upham 25 B7
Upper Wardington 52 E2
Upper Weald 53 F5
Upper Weedon . . . 52 D4
Upper Wield 26 F4
Upper
Winchendon . . . 39 C7
Upper Witton 62 E4
Upper Woodend . .141 C5
Upper Woodford . . 25 F6
Upper Wootton . . . 26 D3
Upper Wyche 50 E2
Uppingham 65 E5
Uppington 61 D6
Upsall 102 F2
Upshire 41 D7
Upstreet 31 C6
Up Sydling 12 D4
Upthorpe 56 B3
Upton Cambs 54 B2
ChesW 73 C8
Corn 5 B7
Dorset 12 F5
Dorset 13 E7
Hants 14 C4
Hants 15 B4
Leics 63 E7
Lincs 90 F2
Mers 85 F3
Norf 69 C6
Northants 52 C5
Notts 77 B7
Notts 77 D7
Oxon 39 F5
Pboro 65 D8
Slough 27 B7
Som 10 B4
WYorks 89 C5
Upton Bishop 36 B3
Upton Cheyney . . . 23 C8
Upton Cressett . . . 61 E6
Upton Cross 5 B7
Upton Grey 26 E4
Upton Hellions . . . 10 D3
Upton Lovell 24 E2
Upton Magna 61 C5
Upton Noble 24 F2
Upton Pyne 10 E4
Upton
St Leonard's . . . 37 C5
Upton Scudamore . 24 E3
Upton Snodsbury . 50 D4
Upton upon
Severn 50 E3
Upton Warren 50 C4
Upwaltham 16 C3
Upware 55 B6
Upwell 66 D4
Upwey 12 F4
Upwood 66 F2
Uradale 160 K6
Urafirth 160 F5
Urchfont 24 D5
Urdimarsh 49 E7
Ure 160 F4
Ure Bank 95 B6
Urgha 154 H6
Urishay Common . . 48 F5
Urlay Nook 102 C1
Urmston 87 E5
Urpeth 110 D5
Urquhart Highld . .151 F8
Moray 152 B2
Urra 102 D3
Urray 151 F8
Ushaw Moor 110 E5
Usk = Brynbuga . . 35 D7
Usselby 90 E4
Usworth 111 D6
Utkinton 74 C2
Utley 94 E3
Uton 10 E3
Utterby 91 E7
Uttoxeter 75 F7
Uwchmynydd 70 E2
Uxbridge 40 F3
Uyeasound 160 C7
Uzmaston 44 D4

V

Valley 82 D2
Valleyfield 106 D3
Valley Truckle 8 F3
Valsgarth 160 B8
Valtos 149 B10
Van 59 F6

Vange 42 F3
Varteg 35 D6
Vatten 149 D7
Vaul 146 G3
Vaynor 34 C4
Veensgarth 160 J6
Velindre 48 F3
Vellow 22 F2
Veness 159 F6
Venn Green 9 C5
Vennington 60 D3
Venn Ottery 11 E5
Venny Tedburn . . . 10 E3
Ventnor 15 G6
Vernham Dean . . . 25 D8
Vernham Street . . 25 D8
Vernolds Common . 60 F4
Verwood 13 D8
Veryan 3 C8
Vicarage 11 F7
Vickerstown 92 C1
Victoria Corn 4 C4
SYorks 88 D2
Vidlin 160 G6
Viewpark 119 C7
Vigo Village 29 C7
Vinehall Street . . . 18 C4
Vine's Cross 18 D2
Viney Hill 36 D3
Virginia Water . . . 27 C8
Virginstow 9 E5
Vobster 24 E2
Voe Shetland 160 E5
Shetland 160 G6
Vowchurch 49 F5
Voxter 160 F5
Voy 159 G3

W

Wackerfield 101 B6
Wacton 68 E4
Wadbister 160 J6
Wadborough 50 E4
Waddesdon 39 C7
Waddingham 90 E3
Waddington Lancs 93 E7
Lincs 78 C2
Wadebridge 4 B4
Wadenhoe 65 F7
Wadesmill 41 C6
Wadhurst 18 B3
Wadshelf 76 B3
Wadsley 88 E4
Wadsley Bridge . . 88 E4
Wadworth 89 E6
Waen Denb 72 C3
Denb 72 C5
Waen Fach 60 C2
Waen Goleugoed . 72 B4
Wag 157 G13
Wainfleet All
Saints 79 D7
Wainfleet Bank . . . 79 D7
Wainfleet St Mary . 79 D8
Wainfleet Tofts . . . 79 D7
Wainhouse Corner . . 8 E3
Wainscott 29 B8
Wainstalls 87 B8
Waitby 100 D2
Waithe 91 D6
Wakefield 88 B4
Wake Lady Green . 102 E3
Wakerley 65 E6
Wakes Colne 42 B4
Walberswick 57 B8
Walberton 16 D3
Walbottle 110 C4
Walcot Lincs 78 F3
NLincs 90 B2
Shrops 60 F3
Swindon 38 F1
Telford 61 C5
Walcote Leics 64 F2
Warks 51 D6
Walcot Green 68 F4
Walcott Lincs 78 D4
Norf 69 A6
Walden 101 F5
Walden Head 100 F4
Walden Stubbs . . . 89 C6
Waldersey 66 D4
Walderslade 29 C8
Walderton 15 C8
Walditch 12 E2
Waldley 75 F8
Waldridge 111 D5
Waldringfield 57 E6
Waldringfield
Heath 57 E6
Waldron 18 D2
Wales 89 F5
Walesby Lincs 90 E5
Notts 77 B6
Walford Hereford . 36 B2
Hereford 49 B5
Shrops 60 B4
Walford Heath . . . 60 C4
Walgherton 74 E3
Walgrave 53 B6
Walhampton 14 E4
Walkden 86 D5
Walker 111 C5
Walker Barn 75 B6
Walkerburn 121 F6
Walker Fold 93 E6
Walkeringham . . . 89 E8
Walkerith 89 E8
Walkern 41 B5
Walker's Green . . . 49 E7
Walkerville 101 E7
Walkford 14 E3
Walkhampton 6 C3
Walkington 97 F5
Walkley 88 F4
Walk Mill 93 F8
Wall Northumb . . .110 C2
Staffs 62 D5
Wallaceton 113 F8
Wallacetown
S Ayrs 112 B3
S Ayrs 112 D3
Wallands Park . . . 17 C8
Wallasey 85 E4
Wall Bank 60 E5
Wallcrouch 18 B3
Wall Heath 62 F2

Wallingford 39 F6
Wallington Hants . 15 D6
Herts 54 F3
London 28 C3
Wallis 32 B1
Walliswood 28 F2
Walls 160 J4
Wallsend 111 C5
Wallston 22 B3
Wall under
Heywood 60 E5
Wallyford 121 B6
Walmer 31 D7
Walmer Bridge . . . 86 B2
Walmersley 87 C6
Walmley 62 E5
Walpole 57 B7
Walpole Cross
Keys 66 C5
Walpole Highway . 66 C5
Walpole Marsh . . . 66 C4
Walpole
St Andrew 66 C5
Walpole St Peter . 66 C5
Walsall 62 E4
Walsall Wood 62 D4
Walsden 87 B7
Walsgrave on
Sowe 63 F7
Walsham le
Willows 56 B3
Walshaw 87 C5
Walshford 95 D7
Walsoken 66 C4
Walston 120 E3
Walsworth 54 F3
Walters Ash 39 E8
Walterston 22 B2
Walterstone 35 B7
Waltham Kent . . . 30 E5
NE Lincs 91 D6
Waltham Abbey . . 41 D6
Waltham Chase . . 15 C6
Waltham Cross . . . 41 D6
Waltham on the
Wolds 64 B5
Waltham
St Lawrence . . . 27 B6
Walthamstow 41 F6
Walton Cumb 108 C5
Derbys 76 C3
Leics 64 F2
Mers 85 E4
MKeynes 53 F6
Pboro 65 D8
Powys 48 D4
Som 23 F6
Staffs 75 F5
Suff 57 F6
Telford 61 C5
Warks 51 D7
WYorks 88 C4
Telford 61 C5
Walton Cardiff . . . 50 F4
Walton East 32 B1
Walton-in-
Gordano 23 B6
Walton-le-Dale . . 86 B3
Walton-on-
Thames 28 C2
Walton on the Hill
Staffs 62 B3
Sur 28 D3
Walton-on-the-
Naze 43 B8
Walton on the
Wolds 64 C2
Walton-on-Trent . 63 C6
Walton West 44 D3
Walwen 73 B6
Walwick 110 B2
Walworth 101 C7
Walworth Gate . . .101 B7
Walwyn's Castle . . 44 D3
Wambrook 11 D7
Wanborough Sur . . 27 E7
Swindon 38 F2
Wandsworth 28 B3
Wangford 57 B8
Wanlockhead 113 C8
Wansford EYorks . . 97 D6
Pboro 65 E7
Wanstead 41 F7
Wanstrow 24 E2
Wanswell 36 D3
Wantage 38 F3
Wapley 24 B2
Wappenbury 51 C8
Wappenham 52 E4
Warbleton 18 D3
Warblington 15 D8
Warborough 39 E5
Warboys 66 F3
Warbreck 92 F3
Warbstow 8 E4
Warburton 86 F5
Warcop 100 C2
Warden Kent 30 B4
Northumb 110 C2
Ward End 62 F5
Ward Green 56 C4
Wardhill 159 F7
Wardington 52 E2
Wardlaw 115 C5
Wardle ChesE 74 D3
Gtr Man 87 C7
Wardley 64 D5
Wardlow 75 B8
Wardy Hill 66 F4
Ware Herts 41 C6
Kent 31 C6
Wareham 13 F7
Warehorne 19 B6
Warenford 117 B7
Waren Mill 123 F7
Warenton 123 F7
Wareside 41 C6
Waresley Cambs . . 54 D3
Worcs 50 B3
Warfield 27 B6
Warfleet 7 D6
Wargrave 27 B5
Warham 80 C5
Warhill 87 E7
Wark Northumb . .109 B8
Northumb 122 F4
Warkleigh 9 B8
Warkton 53 B6

Warkworth
Northants 52 E2
Northumb 117 D8
Warlaby 101 E8
Warland 87 B7
Warleggan 5 C6
Warlingham 28 D4
Warmfield 88 B4
Warmingham 74 C4
Warmington
Northants 65 E7
Warks 52 E2
Warminster 24 E3
Warmlake 30 D2
Warmley 23 B8
Warmley Tower . . 23 B8
Warmonds Hill . . . 53 C7
Warmsworth 89 D6
Warmwell 13 F5
Warndon 50 D3
Warnford 15 B7
Warnham 28 F2
Warninglid 17 B6
Warren ChesE 75 B5
Pembs 44 F4
Warren Heath 57 E6
Warren Row 39 F8
Warren Street 30 D3
Warrington
M Keynes 53 D6
Warr 86 F4
Warsash 15 D5
Warslow 75 D7
Warsop 76 C5
Warter 96 D4
Warthermarske . . 94 B5
Warthill 96 D2
Wartling 18 E3
Wartnaby 64 B4
Warton Lancs 86 B2
Lancs 92 B4
Northumb 117 D6
Warks 63 D6
Warwick 51 C7
Warwick Bridge . .108 D4
Warwick on Eden 108 D4
Wasbister 159 E4
Wasdale Head . . . 98 D3
Washaway 4 C5
Washbourne 7 D5
Wash Common . . . 26 C2
Washfield 10 C4
Washfold 101 D5
Washford 22 E2
Washford Pyne . . . 10 C3
Washingborough . 78 B3
Washington T&W .111 D6
W Sus 16 C5
Wasing 26 C3
Waskerley 110 E3
Wasperton 51 D7
Wasps Nest 78 C3
Wass 95 B8
Watchet 22 E2
Watchfield Oxon . . 38 E2
Som 22 E5
Watchgate 99 E7
Watchhill 107 E8
Watcombe 7 C7
Watendlath 98 C4
Water Devon 10 F2
Lancs 87 B6
Waterbeach 55 C5
Waterbeck 108 B2
Waterden 80 D4
Water End EYorks . 96 F3
Herts 40 C3
Herts 41 D5
Waterfall 75 D7
Waterfoot E Renf .119 D5
Lancs 87 B6
Waterford Hants . . 14 E4
Herts 41 C6
Waterhead Cumb . 99 D5
Dumfries 114 E4
Waterheads 120 D5
Waterhouses
Durham 110 E4
Staffs 75 D7
Wateringbury 29 D7
Waterloo BCP 13 E8
Gtr Man 87 D7
Highld 149 F11
Mers 85 E4
N Lanark 119 D8
Norf 68 C5
Perth 133 F7
Shrops 74 F2
Waterloo Port 82 E4
Waterlooville 15 D7
Watermeetings . . .114 C2
Watermillock 99 B6
Water Newton . . . 65 E8
Water Orton 63 E5
Waterperry 39 D6
Waterrow 11 B5
Watersfield 16 C4
Waterside Aberds .141 B9
Blackburn 86 B5
Cumb 108 E2
E Ayrs 112 D4
E Ayrs 118 E4
E Dunb 119 B6
E Renf 118 D5
Water's Nook 86 D4
Waterstock 39 D6
Waterston 44 E4
Water Stratford . . 52 F4
Waters Upton 61 C6
Water Yeat 98 F4
Watford Herts 40 E4
Northants 52 C4
Watford Gap 62 D5
Wath N Yorks 94 C4
N Yorks 95 B6
N Yorks 96 B2
Wath Brow 98 C2
Wath upon
Dearne 88 D5
Watlington Norf . . 67 C6
Oxon 39 E6
Watnall 76 E5
Watten 158 E4
Wattisfield 56 B4
Wattisham 56 D4
Wattlesborough
Heath 60 C3
Watton EYorks . . . 97 D6
Norf 68 D2
Watton at Stone . . 41 C6

Wattston 119 B7
Wattstown 34 E4
Wauchan 136 F2
Waulkmill Lodge .159 H4
Waun 59 D5
Waunarlwydd 33 E7
Waunclunda 47 F5
Waunfawr 82 E5
Waungron 33 D6
Waunlwyd 35 D5
Waun-y-clyn 33 D5
Wavendon 53 F7
Waverbridge 108 E2
Waverton ChesW . . 73 C8
Cumb 108 E2
Wavertree 85 F4
Wawne 97 F6
Waxham 69 B7
Waxholme 91 B7
Way 31 C7
Wayfield 29 C8
Wayford 12 D2
Waymills 74 E2
Wayne Green 35 C8
Way Village 10 C3
Wdig = Goodwick . 44 B4
Weachyburn 153 C6
Weald 38 D3
Wealdstone 40 F4
Weardley 95 E5
Weare 23 D6
Weare Giffard 9 B6
Wearhead 109 F8
Weasdale 100 D1
Weasenham All
Saints 80 E4
Weasenham
St Peter 80 E4
Weatherhill 28 E4
Weaverham 74 B3
Weaverthorpe . . . 97 B5
Webheath 50 C5
Wedderlairs 153 E8
Wedderlie 122 D2
Weddington 63 E7
Wedhampton 25 D5
Wedmore 23 E6
Wednesbury 62 E3
Wednesfield 62 D3
Weedon 39 C8
Weedon Bec 52 D4
Weedon Lois 52 E4
Weeford 62 D5
Week 10 C2
Weeke 26 F2
Weekley 65 F5
Week St Mary 8 E4
Weel 97 F6
Weeley 43 B7
Weeley Heath 43 B7
Weem 133 E5
Weeping Cross . . . 62 B3
Weethley Gate . . . 51 D5
Weeting 67 F7
Weeton EYorks . . . 91 B7
Lancs 92 F3
N Yorks 95 E5
Weetwood Hall . .117 B6
Weir 87 B6
Weir Quay 6 C2
Welborne 68 D3
Welbourn 78 D2
Welburn N Yorks . . 96 C3
N Yorks 102 F4
Welbury 102 D1
Welby 78 F2
Welches Dam 66 F4
Welcombe 8 C4
Weld Bank 86 C3
Weldon 117 E7
Welford Northants 64 F3
W Berks 26 B2
Welford-on-Avon . 51 D6
Welham Leics 64 E4
Notts 89 F8
Welham Green . . . 41 D5
Well Hants 27 E5
Lincs 79 B7
N Yorks 101 F7
Welland 50 E2
Wellbank 134 F4
Welldale 107 C8
Well End 40 F1
Wellesbourne 51 D7
Well Heads 94 F3
Well Hill 29 C5
Welling 29 B5
Wellingborough . . 53 C6
Wellingham 80 E4
Wellingore 78 D2
Wellington Cumb . 98 D2
Hereford 49 E6
Som 11 B6
Telford 61 C6
Wellington Heath . 50 E2
Wellington Hill . . . 95 F6
Wellow Bath 24 D2
IoW 14 F4
Notts 77 C7
Wellpond Green . . 41 B7
Wells 23 E7
Wellsborough 63 D7
Wells Green 74 D3
Wells-next-the-
Sea 80 C5
Wellswood 7 C7
Well Town 10 D4
Wellwood 128 F2
Welney 66 E5
Welshampton 73 F8
Welsh Bicknor . . . 36 C2
Welsh End 74 F2
Welsh Frankton . . 73 F7
Welsh Hook 44 C4
Welsh Newton . . . 36 C1
Welshpool
= Y Trallwng . . 60 D2
Welsh St Donats . . 22 B2
Welton Cumb 108 E3
E Yorks 90 B3
Lincs 78 B3
Northants 52 C3
Welton Hill 90 F4
Welton le Marsh . . 79 C7
Welton le Wold . . 91 F6
Welwick 91 B7
Welwyn 41 C5
Welwyn Garden
City 41 C5

Wem 60 B5
Wembdon 22 F4
Wembley 40 F4
Wembury 6 E3
Wembworthy 9 D8
Wemyss Bay 118 C1
Wenallt Ceredig . . 47 B5
Gwyn 72 E3
Wendens Ambo . . 55 F6
Wendlebury 39 C5
Wendling 68 C2
Wendover 40 D1
Wendron 3 C5
Wendy 54 E4
Wenfordbridge 5 B5
Wenhaston 57 B8
Wennington Cambs. 54 B3
London 41 F8
Lancs 93 B6
Wensley Derbys . . 76 C2
N Yorks 101 F5
Wentbridge 89 C5
Wentnor 60 E3
Wentworth Cambs . 55 B5
SYorks 88 E4
Wenvoe 22 B3
Weobley 49 D6
Weobley Marsh . . 49 D6
Wereham 67 D6
Wergs 62 D2
Wern Powys 59 C6
Powys 60 C2
Wernffrwd 33 E6
Wernyrheolydd . . 35 C7
Werrington Corn . . 8 F5
Pboro 65 D8
Staffs 75 E6
Wervin 73 B8
Wessington 76 D3
Westacott 20 F4
West Acre 67 C7
West Adderbury . . 52 F2
West Allerdean . . .123 E5
West Alvington 6 E5
West Amesbury . . 25 E6
West Anstey 10 B3
West Ashby 79 B5
West Ashling 16 D2
West Ashton 24 D3
West Auckland . . .101 B6
West Ayton 103 F7
West Bagborough . 22 F3
West Barkwith . . . 91 F5
West Barnby 103 C6
West Barns 122 B2
West Barsham . . . 80 D5
West Bay 12 E2
West Beckham . . . 81 D7
West Bedfont 27 B8
West Benhar 119 C8
Westbere 31 C5
West Bergholt 43 B5
West Bexington . . 12 F3
West Bilney 67 C7
West Blatchington 17 D6
Westborough 77 E8
Westbourne BCP . . 13 E8
W Sus 15 D8
West Bowling 94 F4
West Bradford . . . 93 E7
West Bradley 23 F7
West Bretton 88 C3
West Bridgford . . . 77 F5
West Bromwich . . 62 E4
Westbrook 26 B2
West Buckland
Devon 21 F5
Som 11 B6
West Burrafirth . . 160 H4
West Burton
N Yorks 101 F5
W Sus 16 C3
Westbury Bucks . . 52 F4
Shrops 60 D3
Wilts 24 D3
Westbury Leigh . . 24 D3
Westbury-on-
Severn 36 C4
Westbury on Trym 23 B7
Westbury-sub-
Mendip 23 E7
West Butterwick . . 90 D2
Westby 92 F3
West Byfleet 27 C8
West Caister 69 C8
West Calder 120 C3
West Camel 12 B3
West Challow 38 F3
West Chelborough 12 D3
West Chevington .117 E8
West Chiltington . 16 C4
West Chiltington
Common 16 C4
West Chinnock . . . 12 C2
West Chisenbury . 25 D6
West Clandon 27 D8
West Cliffe 31 E7
Westcliff-on-Sea . 42 F4
West Clyne 157 J11
West Clyth 158 G4
West Coker 12 C3
Westcombe 23 F8
West Compton
Dorset 12 E3
Som 23 E7
Westcote 38 B2
Westcott Bucks . . . 39 C7
Devon 10 D5
Sur 28 D2
Westcott Barton . . 38 B4
West Cowick 89 B7
West Cranmore . . 23 E8
West Cross 33 F7
West Cullery 141 D6
West Curry 8 E4
West Curthwaite . 108 E3
West Darlochan . .143 F7
Westdean 18 F2
West Dean Wilts . . 14 B3
W Sus 16 C2
West Deeping 65 D8
Westdene 17 D6
West Derby 85 E4
West Dereham . . . 67 D6
West Didsbury . . . 87 E6
West Ditchburn . .117 B7
West Down 20 E4

West Drayton
London 27 B8
Notts 77 B7
West Ella 90 B4
West End Bedford . 53 D7
E Yorks 96 F5
E Yorks 97 F7
Hants 15 C5
Lancs 86 B5
Norf 68 D2
Norf 69 C8
N Som 23 C6
N Yorks 94 D4
Oxon 38 D4
S Lanark 120 E2
Suff 69 F7
Sur 27 C7
S Yorks 89 D7
Wilts 13 B7
Wilts 24 B4
W Sus 17 C6
West End Green . . 26 C4
Wester
Aberchalder . .137 B8
Wester
Balgedie 128 D3
Wester
Dechmont 120 C3
Wester Denoon . .134 E3
Westerdale Highld 158 E3
N Yorks 102 D4
Wester Fintray . . .141 C7
Westergate 16 D3
Wester
Gruinards 151 B8
Westerham 28 D5
Westerhope 110 C4
Wester Lealty 151 D9
Westerleigh 23 B9
Wester Milton . . .151 F12
Wester Newburn .129 D6
Wester Quarff . . .160 K6
Wester Skeld 160 J4
Westerton Angus . 135 D6
Durham 110 F5
W Sus 16 D2
Westerwick 160 J4
West Farleigh 29 D8
West Felton 60 B3
West Fenton 129 F6
West Ferry 134 F4
Westfield Cumb . . 98 B1
E Sus 18 D5
Hereford 50 E2
Highld 158 D2
N Lanark 119 B7
Norf 68 D2
N Yorks 120 B3
Westfields 12 D5
Westfields of
Rattray 134 E1
West Firle 17 D8
West Ginge 38 F4
West Grafton 25 C7
West Green 26 D5
West
Greenskares . .153 B7
West Grimstead . . 14 B3
West Grinstead . . 17 B5
West Haddlesey . . 89 B6
West Haddon 52 B4
West Hagbourne . 39 F5
West Hagley 62 F3
West Hall 109 C5
West Hallam 76 E4
West Halton 90 B3
Westham Dorset . . 12 G4
E Sus 18 E3
Som 23 E6
West Ham 41 F7
Westhampnett . . . 16 D2
West Handley 76 B3
West Hanney 38 E4
West Hanningfield 42 E3
West Hardwick . . . 88 C5
West Harnham . . . 14 B2
West Harptree . . . 23 D7
West Hatch 11 B7
Westhay 23 E6
Westhead 86 D2
West Head 67 D5
West Heath ChesE . 74 C5
Hants 26 D3
Hants 27 D6
West Helmsdale . .157 H13
West Hendred . . . 38 F4
West Heslerton . . 96 B5
Westhide 49 E7
Westhill Aberds . . 141 D7
Highld 151 G10
West Hill Devon . . 11 E5
E Yorks 97 C7
N Som 23 B6
West Hoathly 17 B7
West Holme 13 F6
Westhope Hereford 49 D6
Shrops 60 F4
West Horndon . . . 42 F2
Westhorpe Lincs . . 78 F5
Suff 56 C4
West Horrington . . 23 E7
West Horsley 27 D8
West Horton 123 F6
West Hougham . . . 31 E6
Westhoughton . . . 86 D4
West Houlland . . . 160 H4
Westhouse 93 B6
Westhouses 76 D4
West Humble 28 D2
West Huntington . 96 D2
West Hythe 19 B8
West Ilsley 38 F4
West Itchenor . . . 15 D8
West Keal 79 C6
West Kennett 25 C6
West Kilbride 118 E2
West Kingsdown . . 29 C6
West Kington 24 B3

West
Kinharrachie . .153 E9
West Kirby 85 F3
West Knapton 96 B4
West Knighton . . . 12 F5
West Knoyle 24 F3
West Kyloe 123 E6
Westlake 6 D4
West Lambrook . . 12 C2
West Langdon 31 E7
West Langwell . . .157 J9
West Lavington
Wilts 24 D5
W Sus 16 B2
West Layton 101 D6
West Lea 111 E7
West Leake 64 B2
West Learmouth . 122 F4
Westleigh Devon . 11 C5
Devon 20 F3
Gtr Man 86 D4
West Leigh 9 D8
Westleton 57 C8
West Lexham 67 C8
Westley Shrops . . . 60 D3
Suff 56 C2
Westley Waterless 55 D7
West Lilling 96 C2
Westlington 39 C7
West Linton 120 D4
West Liss 15 B8
West Littleton . . . 24 B2
West Looe 5 D7
West Luccombe . . 21 E7
West Lulworth . . . 13 F6
West Lutton 96 C5
West Lydford 23 F7
West Lyng 11 B8
West Lynn 67 B6
West Malling 29 D7
West Malvern 50 E2
West Marden 15 C8
West Marina 18 E4
West Markham . . . 77 B7
Westmarsh 31 C6
West Marsh 91 C6
West Marton 93 D8
West Meon 15 B7
West Mersea 43 C6
Westmeston 17 C7
Westmill 41 B6
West Milton 12 E3
Westminster 28 B4
West Minster 30 B3
West Molesey 28 C2
West Monkton . . . 11 B7
West Moors 13 D8
West Morriston . .122 E2
Westmuir 134 D3
West Muir 135 C5
Westness 159 F4
West Ness 96 B2
West Newham . . .110 B3
Westnewton Cumb 107 E8
Northumb 122 F5
West Newton
E Yorks 97 F7
Norf 67 B6
West Norwood . . . 28 B4
Westoe 111 C6
Weston Bath 24 C2
ChesE 74 D4
Devon 11 F6
Dorset 12 G4
Halton 86 F3
Hants 15 B8
Herts 54 F3
Lincs 66 B2
N Yorks 94 E4
Notts 77 C7
Shrops 61 B5
Shrops 61 E5
Staffs 62 B3
W Berks 25 B8
Weston Beggard . . 49 E7
Westonbirt 37 F5
Weston by
Welland 64 E4
Weston Colville . . 55 D7
Westoncommon . . 60 B4
Weston Coyney . . . 75 E6
Weston Favell 53 C5
Weston Green
Cambs 55 D7
Norf 68 C4
Weston Heath . . . 61 C7
Weston Hills 66 B2
Westoning 53 F8
Weston-in-
Gordano 23 B6
Weston Jones 61 B7
Weston Longville . 68 C4
Weston
Lullingfields . . 60 B4
Weston-on-the-
Green 39 C5
Weston-on-Trent . 63 B8
Weston Patrick . . . 26 E4
Weston Rhyn 73 F6
Weston-sub-Edge 51 E6
Weston-super-
Mare 22 C5
Weston Turville . . 40 C1
Weston under
Lizard 62 C2
Weston under
Penyard 36 B3
Weston
Underwood
Derbys 76 E2
M Keynes 53 D6
Westonzoyland . . 23 F5
West Orchard 13 C6
West Overton 25 C6
Westow 96 C3
West Park 111 F7
West Parley 13 E8
West Peckham . . . 29 D7
West Pelton 110 D5
West Pennard 23 F7
West Pentire 4 C2
West Perry 54 C2
Westport Argyll . .143 F7
Som 11 C8
West Putford 9 C5

Upp–Whe 235

West Quantoxhead 22 E3
West Rainton 111 E6
West Rasen 90 F4
West Raynham . . . 80 E4
West Retford 89 F7
Westrigg 120 C2
West Rounton . . .102 D2
West Row 55 B7
West Rudham 80 E4
West Runton 81 C7
Westruther 122 E2
Westry 66 E3
West Saltoun 121 C7
West Sandwick . .160 E6
West Scrafton . . .101 F5
West Sleekburn . .117 F8
West Somerton . . 69 C7
West Stafford 12 F5
West Stockwith . . 89 E8
West Stoke 16 D2
West Stonesdale .100 D3
West Stoughton . . 23 E6
West Stour 13 B5
West Stourmouth . 31 C6
West Stow 56 B2
West Stowell 25 C6
West Strathan . . .157 C8
West Stratton . . . 26 E3
West Street 30 D3
West Tanfield 95 B5
West Taphouse . . . 5 C6
West Tarbert 145 G7
West Thirston . . .117 E7
West Thorney 15 D8
West Thurrock . . . 29 B6
West Tilbury 29 B7
West Tisted 15 B7
West Tofts Norf . . 67 E8
Perth 133 F8
West Torrington . . 90 F5
West Town Hants . 15 E8
N Som 23 C6
West Tytherley . . . 14 B3
West Tytherton . . 24 B4
Westville 76 E5
West Walton 66 C4
West Walton
Highway 66 C4
Westward 108 E2
Westward Ho! 9 B6
Westwell Kent . . . 30 E3
Oxon 38 D2
Westwell Leacon . 30 D3
West Wellow 14 C3
West Wemyss 128 E5
Westwick Cambs . . 54 C5
Durham 101 C5
Norf 81 E8
West Wick 23 C5
West Wickham
Cambs 55 E7
London 28 C4
West Williamston . 32 D1
West Willoughby . 78 E2
West Winch 67 C6
West Winterslow . 25 F7
West Wittering . . 15 E8
West Witton 101 F5
Westwood Devon . 10 E5
Wilts 24 D3
West Woodburn . .116 F4
West Woodhay . . . 25 C8
West Woodlands . 24 E2
Westwoodside . . . 89 E8
West Worldham . . 26 F5
West Worlington . 10 C2
West Worthing . . . 16 D5
West Wratting . . . 55 D7
West Wycombe . . 39 E8
West Wylam 110 C4
West Yell 160 E6
Wetheral 108 D4
Wetherby 95 E7
Wetherden 56 C4
Wetheringsett . . . 56 C5
Wethersfield 55 F8
Wethersta 160 G5
Wetherup Street . 56 C5
Wetley Rocks 75 E6
Wettenhall 74 C3
Wetton 75 D8
Wetwang 96 D5
Wetwood 74 F4
Wexcombe 25 D7
Wexham Street . . 40 F2
Weybourne 81 C7
Weybread 68 F5
Weybridge 27 C8
Weycroft 11 E8
Weydale 158 D3
Weyhill 25 E8
Weymouth 12 G4
Whaddon Bucks . . 53 F6
Cambs 54 E4
Glos 37 C5
Wilts 14 B2
Whale 99 B7
Whaley 76 B5
Whaley Bridge . . . 87 F8
Whaley Thorns . . . 76 B5
Whaligoe 158 F5
Whalley 93 F7
Whalton 117 F7
Wham 93 C7
Whaplode 66 B3
Whaplode Drove . 66 C3
Whaplode
St Catherine . . 66 B3
Wharfe 93 C7
Wharles 92 F4
Wharncliffe Side . 88 E3
Wharram le Street 96 C4
Wharton 74 C3
Wharton Green . . 74 C3
Whashton 101 D6
Whatcombe 13 D6
Whatcote 51 E8
Whatfield 56 E4
Whatley Som 11 D8
Som 24 E2
Whatlington 18 D4
Whatstandwell . . 76 D3
Whatton 77 F7
Whauphill 105 E8
Whaw 100 D4
Wheatacre 69 E7

Wheatcroft 76 D3
Wheathampstead 40 C4
Wheathill 61 F6
Wheatley Devon 10 E4
Hants 27 E5
Oxon 39 D5
S Yorks 89 D6
W Yorks 87 B8
Wheatley Hill 111 F6
Wheaton Aston 62 C2
Wheddon Cross 21 F8
Wheedlemont 140 B3
Wheelerstreet 27 E7
Wheelock 74 D4
Wheelock Heath 74 D4
Wheelton 86 B4
Wheen 134 B3
Wheldrake 96 E2
Whelford 38 E1
Whelpley Hill 40 D2
Whempstead 41 B6
Whenby 96 C2
Whepstead 56 D2
Wherstead 57 E5
Wherwell 25 E8
Wheston 75 B8
Whetsted 29 E7
Whetstone 64 E2
Whicham 98 F3
Whichford 51 F8
Whickham 110 C5
Whiddon Down 9 E8
Whigstreet 134 E4
Whilton 52 C4
Whimble 9 D5
Whim Farm 120 D5
Whimple 10 E5
Whimpwell Green 69 B6
Whinburgh 68 D3
Whinnieliggate 106 D4
Whinnyfold 153 E10
Whippingham 15 E6
Whipsnade 40 C3
Whipton 10 E4
Whirlow 88 F4
Whisby 78 C2
Whissendine 64 C5
Whissonsett 80 E5
Whistlefield
Argyll 145 D10
Argyll 145 D11
Whistley Green 27 B5
Whiston Mers 86 E2
Northants 53 C6
Staffs 62 C2
Staffs 75 E7
S Yorks 88 F5
Whitbeck 98 F3
Whitbourne 50 D2
Whitburn T&W 111 C7
W Loth 120 C2
Whitburn
Colliery 111 C7
Whitby Ches W 73 B7
N Yorks 103 C6
Whitbyheath 73 B7
Whitchurch Bath 23 C8
Bucks 39 B7
Cardiff 35 F5
Devon 6 B2
Hants 26 E2
Hereford 36 C2
Oxon 26 B4
Pembs 44 C2
Shrops 74 E2
Whitchurch
Canonicorum 11 E8
Whitchurch Hill 26 B4
Whitcombe 12 F5
Whitcott Keysett 60 F2
Whiteacen 152 D2
Whiteacre Heath 63 E6
Whitebridge 137 C7
Whitebrook 36 D2
Whiteburn 121 E8
Whitecairn 105 D6
Whitecairns 141 C8
Whitecastle 120 E3
Whitechapel 93 E5
Whitecleat 159 H6
White Coppice 86 C4
Whitecraig 121 B6
Whitecroft 36 D3
Whitecross Corn 4 B4
Falk 120 B2
Staffs 62 B2
Whiteface 151 C10
Whitefarland 143 D9
Whitefaulds 112 D2
Whitefield Gtr Man 87 D6
Perth 134 F1
Whiteford 141 B6
Whitegate 74 C3
Whitehall Blackburn 86 B4
W Sus 16 B5
Whitehall Village 159 F7
Whitehaven 98 C1
Whitehill 27 F5
Whitehills Aberds 153 B6
S Lanark 119 D6
Whitehough 87 F8
Whitehouse
Aberds 140 C5
Argyll 145 G7
Whiteinch 118 C5
Whitekirk 129 F7
White Lackington 12 E5
White Ladies
Aston 50 D4
Whitelaw 119 E6
Whiteleas 111 C6
Whiteley Bank 15 F6
Whiteley Green 75 B6
Whiteley Village 27 C8
White Lund 92 C4
Whitemans Green 17 B7
White Mill 33 B5
Whitemire 151 F12
Whitemoor 4 D4
Whitemore 75 C5
Whitenap 14 B4
White Ness 160 J5
White Notley 42 C3
Whiteoak Green 38 C3
Whiteparish 14 B3
White Pit 79 B6
White Post 77 D6
Whiterashes 141 B7
White Rocks 35 B8
White Roding 42 C1
Whiterow 158 F5
Whiteshill 37 D5
Whiteside
Northumb 109 C7
W Loth 120 C2
Whitesmith 18 D2
Whitestaunton 11 C7
Whitestone Devon 10 E3
Devon 20 E3
Warks 63 F7
Whitestones 153 C8
Whitestreet Green 56 F3
Whitewall Corner 96 B3
White Waltham 27 B6
Whiteway Glos 37 C6
Glos 37 E5
Whitewell Aberds 153 B9
Lancs 93 E6
Whitewell Bottom 87 B6
Whiteworks 6 B4
Whitfield Kent 31 E7
Northants 52 F4
Northumb 109 D7
S Glos 36 E3
Whitford Devon 11 E7
Flint 72 B5
Whitgift 90 B2
Whitgreave 62 B2
Whithorn 105 E8
Whiting Bay 143 F11
Whitkirk 95 F6
Whitland 32 C2
Whitletts 112 B3
Whitley N Yorks 89 B6
Reading 26 B5
Wilts 24 C3
Whitley Bay 111 B6
Whitley Chapel 110 D2
Whitley Lower 88 C3
Whitley Row 29 D5
Whitlock's End 51 B6
Whitminster 36 D4
Whitmore 74 E5
Whitnage 10 C5
Whitnash 51 C8
Whitney-on-Wye 48 E4
Whitrigg Cumb 108 D2
Cumb 108 F2
Whitsbury 14 C2
Whitsome 122 D4
Whitson 35 F7
Whitstable 30 C5
Whitstone 8 E4
Whittingham 117 C6
Whittingslow 60 F4
Whittington Glos 37 B7
Lancs 93 B6
Norf 67 E7
Shrops 73 F7
Staffs 62 F2
Staffs 63 D5
Worcs 50 D3
Whittlebury 52 E4
Whittle-le-Woods 86 B3
Whittlesey 66 E2
Whittlesford 55 E5
Whittlestone Head 86 C5
Whitton Borders 116 B3
N Lincs 90 B3
Northumb 117 D6
Powys 48 C4
Shrops 49 B7
Stockton 102 B1
Suff 56 E5
Whittonditch 25 B7
Whittonstall 110 D3
Whitway 26 D2
Whitwell Derbys 76 B5
Herts 40 B4
IoW 15 G6
N Yorks 101 E7
Rutland 65 D6
Whitwell-on-the-
Hill 96 C3
Whitwell Street 81 E7
Whitwick 63 C8
Whitwood 88 B5
Whitworth 87 C6
Whixall 74 F2
Whixley 95 D7
Whoberley 51 B8
Whorlton Durham 101 C6
N Yorks 102 D2
Whygate 109 B7
Whyle 49 C7
Whyteleafe 28 D4
Wibdon 36 E2
Wibsey 88 A2
Wibtoft 63 F8
Wichenford 50 C2
Wichling 30 D3
Wick BCP 14 E2
Devon 11 D6
Highld 158 E5
S Glos 24 B2
Shetland 160 K6
V Glam 21 B8
Wilts 14 B2
Worcs 50 E4
W Sus 16 D4
Wicken Cambs 55 B6
Northants 52 F5
Wicken Bonhunt 55 F5
Wickenby 90 F4
Wicken Green
Village 80 D4
Wickersley 89 E5
Wickford 42 E3
Wickham Hants 15 C6
W Berks 25 B8
Wickham Bishops 42 C4
Wickhambreux 31 D6
Wickhambrook 55 D8
Wickhamford 51 E5
Wickham Market 57 D7
Wickhampton 69 D7
Wickham St Paul 56 F2
Wickham Skeith 56 C4
Wickham Street
Suff 55 D8
Suff 56 C4
Wick Hill 27 C5
Wicklewood 68 D3
Wickmere 81 D7
Wick St Lawrence 23 C5
Wickwar 36 F4
Widdington 55 F6
Widdrington 117 E8
Widdrington
Station 117 E8
Widecombe in the
Moor 6 B5
Widegates 5 D7
Widemouth Bay 8 D4
Wide Open 110 B5
Widewall 159 J5
Widford Essex 42 D2
Herts 41 C7
Widham 37 F7
Widmer End 40 E1
Widmerpool 64 B3
Widnes 86 F3
Wigan 86 D3
Wiggaton 11 E6
Wiggenhall
St Germans 67 C5
Wiggenhall St Mary
Magdalen 67 C5
Wiggenhall St Mary
the Virgin 67 C5
Wigginton Herts 40 C2
Oxon 51 F8
Staffs 63 D6
York 95 D8
Wigglesworth 93 D8
Wiggonby 108 D2
Wiggonholt 16 C4
Wighill 95 E7
Wighton 80 D5
Wigley 14 C4
Wigmore Hereford 49 C6
Medway 30 C2
Wigsley 77 B8
Wigsthorpe 65 F7
Wigston 64 E3
Wigthorpe 89 F6
Wigtoft 79 F5
Wigton 108 E2
Wigtown 105 D8
Wigtwizzle 88 E3
Wike 95 E6
Wike Well End 89 C7
Wilbarston 64 F5
Wilberfoss 96 D3
Wilberlee 87 C8
Wilburton 55 B5
Wilby Norf 68 F3
Northants 53 C6
Suff 57 B6
Wilcot 25 C6
Wilcott 60 C3
Wilcrick 35 F8
Wilday Green 76 B3
Wildboarclough 75 C6
Wilden Bedford 53 D8
Worcs 50 B3
Wildhern 25 D8
Wildhill 41 D5
Wildmoor 50 B4
Wildsworth 90 E2
Wilford 77 F5
Wilkesley 74 E3
Wilkhaven 151 C12
Wilkieston 120 C4
Willand 10 C5
Willaston Ches E 74 D3
Ches W 73 B7
Willen 53 E6
Willenhall W Mid 51 B8
W Mid 62 E3
Willerby E Yorks 97 F6
N Yorks 97 B6
Willersey 51 F6
Willersley 48 E5
Willesborough 30 E4
Willesborough
Lees 30 E4
Willesden 41 F5
Willett 22 F3
Willey Shrops 61 E6
Warks 63 F8
Willey Green 27 D7
Williamscott 52 E2
Willian 54 F3
Willingale 42 D1
Willingdon 18 E2
Willingham 54 B5
Willingham by
Stow 90 F2
Willington Bedford 54 E2
Derbys 63 B6
Durham 110 F4
T&W 111 C6
Warks 51 F7
Willington Corner 74 C2
Willisham Tye 56 D4
Willitoft 96 F3
Williton 22 E2
Willoughbridge 74 E4
Willoughby Lincs 79 B7
Warks 52 C3
Willoughby-on-the-
Wolds 64 B3
Willoughby
Waterleys 64 E2
Willoughton 90 E3
Willows Green 42 C3
Willsbridge 23 B8
Willsworthy 9 F7
Wilmcote 51 D6
Wilmington Devon 11 E7
E Sus 18 E2
Kent 29 B6
Wilminstone 6 B2
Wilmslow 87 F6
Wilnecote 63 D6
Wilpshire 93 F6
Wilsden 94 F3
Wilsford Lincs 78 E3
Wilts 25 D6
Wilts 25 F6
Wilsill 94 C4
Wilsley Pound 18 B4
Wilsom 26 F5
Wilson 63 B8
Wilsontown 120 D2
Wilstead 53 E8
Wilsthorpe 65 C7
Wilstone 40 C2
Wilton Borders 115 C7
Cumb 98 C2
Wilton *continued*
N Yorks 103 F6
Redcar 102 C3
Wilts 25 C7
Wilts 25 F5
Wimbish 55 F6
Wimbish Green 55 F7
Wimblebury 62 C4
Wimbledon 28 B3
Wimblington 66 E4
Wimborne Minster 13 E8
Wimborne St Giles 13 C8
Wimbotsham 67 D6
Wimpson 14 C4
Wimpstone 51 E7
Wincanton 12 B5
Wincham 74 B3
Winchburgh 120 B3
Winchcombe 37 B7
Winchelsea 19 D6
Winchelsea Beach 19 D6
Winchester 15 B5
Winchet Hill 29 E8
Winchfield 27 D5
Winchmore Hill
Bucks 40 E2
London 41 E6
Wincle 75 C6
Wincobank 88 E4
Windermere 99 E6
Winderton 51 E8
Windhill 151 G8
Windhouse 160 D6
Windlehurst 87 F7
Windlesham 27 C7
Windley 76 E3
Windmill Hill
E Sus 18 D3
Som 11 C8
Windrush 38 C1
Windsor N Lincs 89 C8
Windsor 27 B7
Windsoredge 37 D5
Windygates 128 D5
Windyknowe 120 C2
Windywalls 122 F3
Wineham 17 B6
Winestead 91 B6
Winewall 94 E2
Winfarthing 68 F4
Winford IoW 15 F6
N Som 23 C7
Winforton 48 E4
Winfrith
Newburgh 13 F6
Wing Bucks 40 B1
Rutland 65 D5
Wingate 111 F7
Wingates Gtr Man 86 D4
Northumb 117 E7
Wingerworth 76 C3
Wingfield C Beds 40 B2
Suff 57 B6
Wilts 24 D3
Wingham 31 D6
Wingmore 31 E5
Wingrave 40 C1
Winkburn 77 D7
Winkfield 27 B7
Winkfield Row 27 B6
Winkhill 75 D7
Winklebury 26 D4
Winkleigh 9 D8
Winksley 95 B5
Winkton 14 E2
Winlaton 110 C4
Winless 158 E5
Winmarleigh 92 E4
Winnal 49 F6
Winnall 15 B5
Winnersh 27 B5
Winscales 98 B2
Winscombe 23 D6
Winsford Ches W 74 C3
Som 21 F8
Winsham 11 D8
Winshill 63 B6
Winskill 109 F5
Winslade 26 E4
Winsley 24 C3
Winslow 39 B7
Winson 37 D7
Winson Green 62 F4
Winsor 14 C4
Winster Cumb 99 E6
Derbys 76 C2
Winston Durham 101 C6
Suff 57 C5
Winstone 37 D6
Winston Green 57 C5
Winswell 9 C6
Winterborne
Clenston 13 D6
Winterborne
Herringston 12 F4
Winterborne
Houghton 13 D6
Winterborne
Kingston 13 E6
Winterborne
Monkton 12 F4
Winterborne
Stickland 13 D6
Winterborne
Whitechurch 13 D6
Winterborne
Zelston 13 E6
Winterbourne
S Glos 36 F3
W Berks 26 B2
Winterbourne
Abbas 12 E4
Winterbourne
Bassett 25 B6
Winterbourne
Dauntsey 25 F6
Winterbourne
Down 23 B8
Winterbourne
Earls 25 F6
Winterbourne
Gunner 25 F6
Winterbourne
Monkton 25 B6
Winterbourne
Steepleton 12 F4
Winterbourne
Stoke 25 E5
Winter Gardens 42 F3
Winteringham 90 B3
Winterley 74 D4
Wintersett 88 C4
Wintershill 15 C6
Winterton 90 C3
Winterton-on-Sea 69 C7
Winthorpe Lincs 79 C8
Notts 77 D8
Winton BCP 13 E8
Cumb 100 C2
N Yorks 102 E2
Wintringham 96 B4
Winwick Cambs 65 F8
Northants 52 B4
Warr 86 E4
Wirksworth 76 D2
Wirksworth Moor 76 D3
Wirswall 74 E2
Wisbech 66 D4
Wisbech St Mary 66 D4
Wisborough Green 16 B4
Wiseton 89 F8
Wishaw N Lanark 119 D7
Warks 63 E5
Wisley 27 D8
Wispington 78 B5
Wissenden 30 E3
Wissett 57 B7
Wistanstow 60 F4
Wistanswick 61 B6
Wistaston 74 D3
Wistaston Green 74 D3
Wiston Pembs 32 C1
S Lanark 120 F2
W Sus 16 C5
Wistow Cambs 66 F2
N Yorks 95 F8
Wiswell 93 F7
Witcham 66 F4
Witchampton 13 D7
Witchford 55 B6
Witham 42 C4
Witham Friary 24 E2
Witham on the Hill 65 C7
Withcall 91 F6
Withdean 17 D7
Witherenden Hill 18 C3
Witheridge 10 C3
Witherley 63 E7
Withern 91 F8
Withernsea 91 B7
Withernwick 97 E7
Withersdale Street 69 F5
Withersfield 55 E7
Witherslack 99 F6
Withiel 4 C4
Withiel Florey 21 F8
Withington Glos 37 C7
Gtr Man 87 E6
Hereford 49 E7
Shrops 61 C5
Staffs 75 F7
Withington Green 74 B5
Withleigh 10 C4
Withnell 86 B4
Withybrook 63 F8
Withycombe 22 E2
Withycombe
Raleigh 10 F5
Withyham 29 F5
Withypool 21 F7
Witley 27 F7
Witnesham 57 D5
Witney 38 C3
Wittering 65 D7
Wittersham 19 C5
Witton Angus 135 B5
Worcs 50 C3
Witton Bridge 69 A6
Witton Gilbert 110 E5
Witton-le-Wear 110 F4
Witton Park 110 F4
Wiveliscombe 11 B5
Wivelrod 26 F4
Wivelsfield 17 B7
Wivelsfield Green 17 B7
Wivenhoe 43 B6
Wivenhoe Cross 43 B6
Wiveton 81 C6
Wix 43 B7
Wixford 51 D5
Wixhill 61 B5
Wixoe 55 E8
Woburn 53 F7
Woburn Sands 53 F7
Wokefield Park 26 C4
Woking 27 D8
Wokingham 27 C6
Wolborough 7 B6
Woldingham 28 D4
Wold Newton
E Yorks 97 B6
NE Lincs 91 E6
Wolfclyde 120 F3
Wolferton 67 B6
Wolfhill 134 F1
Wolf's Castle 44 C4
Wolfsdale 44 C4
Woll 115 B7
Wollaston
Northants 53 C7
Shrops 60 C3
Wollaton 76 F5
Wollerton 74 F3
Wollescote 62 F3
Wolsingham 110 F3
Wolstanton 75 E5
Wolston 52 B2
Wolvercote 38 D4
Wolverhampton 62 E3
Wolverley Shrops 73 F8
Worcs 50 B3
Wolverton Hants 26 D3
M Keynes 53 E6
Warks 51 C7
Wolverton
Common 26 D3
Wolvesnewton 36 E1
Wolvey 63 F8
Wolviston 102 B2
Wombleton 102 F4
Wombourne 62 E2
Wombwell 88 D4
Womenswold 31 D6
Womersley 89 C6
Wonastow 36 C1
Wonersh 27 E8
Wonson 9 F8
Wonston 26 F2
Wooburn 40 F2
Wooburn Green 40 F2
Woodacott 9 D5
Woodale 94 B3
Woodbank 143 G7
Woodbastwick 69 C6
Woodbeck 77 B7
Woodborough
Notts 77 E6
Wilts 25 D6
Woodbridge Dorset 12 C5
Suff 57 E6
Woodbury 10 F5
Woodbury
Salterton 10 F5
Woodchester 37 D5
Woodchurch Kent 19 B6
Mers 85 F3
Woodcombe 21 E8
Woodcote 39 F6
Woodcott 26 D2
Woodcroft 36 E2
Woodcutts 13 C7
Wood Dalling 81 E6
Woodditton 55 D7
Woodeaton 39 C5
Woodend Cumb 98 E3
Northants 52 E4
W Sus 16 D2
Wood End Herts 41 B6
Warks 51 B6
Warks 63 E6
Wood Enderby 79 C5
Woodend Green 52 E4
Woodfalls 14 B2
Woodfield Oxon 39 B5
S Ayrs 112 B3
Wood Field 28 D2
Woodford Corn 8 C4
Devon 7 D5
Glos 36 E3
Gtr Man 87 F6
London 41 E7
Northants 53 B7
Woodford Bridge 41 E7
Woodford Halse 52 D3
Woodgate Norf 68 C3
W Mid 62 F3
Worcs 50 C4
W Sus 16 D3
Woodgreen 14 C2
Wood Green 41 E6
Woodhall Herts 41 C5
Invclyd 118 B3
N Yorks 100 E4
Woodhall Spa 78 C4
Woodham 27 C8
Woodham Ferrers 42 E3
Woodham
Mortimer 42 D4
Woodham Walter 42 D4
Woodhaven 129 B6
Wood Hayes 62 D3
Woodhead 153 E7
Woodhey 87 C5
Woodhill 61 F7
Woodhorn 117 F8
Woodhouse Leics 64 C2
N Lincs 89 D8
S Yorks 88 F5
W Yorks 88 B4
W Yorks 95 F5
Woodhouse Eaves 64 C2
Woodhouselee 120 C5
Woodhouselees 108 B3
Woodhouse Park 87 F6
Woodhouses 63 C5
Woodhurst 54 B4
Woodingdean 17 D7
Woodkirk 88 B3
Woodland Devon 7 C5
Durham 101 B5
Woodlands Aberds 141 E6
Dorset 13 D8
Hants 14 C4
Highld 151 E8
N Yorks 95 D6
S Yorks 89 D6
Woodlands Park 27 B6
Woodlands
St Mary 25 B8
Woodlane 62 B5
Wood Lanes 87 F7
Woodleigh 6 E5
Woodlesford 88 B4
Woodley Gtr Man 87 E7
Wokingham 27 B5
Woodmancote Glos 36 E4
Glos 37 B6
Glos 37 D7
W Sus 15 D8
W Sus 17 C6
Woodmancott 26 E3
Woodmansey 97 F6
Woodmansterne 28 D3
Woodminton 13 B8
Woodnesborough 31 D7
Woodnewton 65 E7
Wood Norton 81 E6
Woodplumpton 92 F5
Woodrising 68 D2
Woodseaves Shrops 74 F3
Staffs 61 B7
Woodsend 25 B7
Woodsetts 89 F6
Woodsford 13 E5
Wood's Green 18 B3
Woodside
Aberdeen 141 D8
Aberds 153 D10
Brack 27 B7
Fife 129 D6
Hants 14 E4
Herts 41 D5
Perth 134 F2
Woodside of
Arbeadie 141 E6
Woodstock Oxon 38 C4
Pembs 32 B1
Wood Street Norf 69 B6
Sur 27 D7
Woodthorpe Derbys 76 B4
Leics 64 C2
Lincs 91 F8
York 95 E8
Woodton 69 E5
Woodtown Devon 9 B6
Devon 9 B6
Woodvale 85 C4
Woodville 63 C7
Wood Walton 66 F2
Woodyates 13 C8
Woofferton 49 C7
Wookey 23 E7
Wookey Hole 23 E7
Wool 13 F6
Woolacombe 20 E3
Woolage Green 31 E6
Woolaston 36 E2
Woolavington 22 E5
Woolbeding 16 B2
Wooldale 88 D2
Wooler 117 B5
Woolfardisworthy
Devon 8 B5
Devon 10 D3
Woolfords
Cottages 120 D3
Woolhampton 26 C3
Woolhope 49 F8
Woolhope
Cockshoot 49 F8
Woolland 13 D5
Woollaton 9 C6
Woolley Bath 24 C2
Cambs 54 B2
Corn 8 C4
Derbys 76 C3
W Yorks 88 C4
Woolmere Green 50 C4
Woolmer Green 41 C5
Woolpit 56 C3
Woolscott 52 C2
Woolsington 110 C4
Woolstanwood 74 D3
Woolstaston 60 E4
Woolsthorpe Lincs 65 B6
Lincs 77 F8
Woolston Devon 6 E5
Shrops 60 B3
Shrops 60 F4
Soton 14 C5
Warr 86 F4
Woolstone
M Keynes 53 F6
Oxon 38 F2
Woolton 86 F2
Woolton Hill 26 C2
Woolverstone 57 F5
Woolverton 24 D2
Woolwich 28 B5
Woolwich Ferry 28 B5
Woonton 49 D5
Wooperton 117 B6
Woore 74 E4
Wootten Green 57 B6
Wootton Bedford 53 E8
Hants 14 E3
Hereford 48 D5
Kent 31 E6
N Lincs 90 C4
Northants 53 D5
Oxon 38 C4
Oxon 38 D4
Shrops 49 B6
Shrops 60 B3
Staffs 62 B2
Staffs 75 E8
Wootton Bridge 15 E6
Wootton Common 15 E6
Wootton
Courtenay 21 E8
Wootton Fitzpaine 11 E8
Wootton Rivers 25 C6
Wootton
St Lawrence 26 D3
Wootton Wawen 51 C6
Worcester 50 D3
Worcester Park 28 C3
Wordsley 62 F2
Worfield 61 E7
Work 159 G5
Workington 98 B1
Worksop 77 B5
Worlaby 90 C4
World's End 26 B2
Worle 23 C5
Worleston 74 D3
Worlingham 69 F7
Worlington 55 B7
Worlingworth 57 C6
Wormald Green 95 C6
Wormbridge 49 F6
Wormegay 67 C6
Wormelow Tump 49 F6
Wormhill 75 B8
Wormingford 56 F3
Worminghall 39 D6
Wormington 50 F5
Worminster 23 E7
Wormit 129 B5
Wormleighton 52 D2
Wormley Herts 41 D6
Sur 27 F7
Wormley West
End 41 D6
Wormshill 30 D2
Wormsley 49 E6
Worplesdon 27 D7
Worrall 88 E4
Worsbrough 88 D4
Worsbrough
Common 88 D4
Worsley 86 D5
Worstead 69 B6
Worsthorne 93 F8
Worston 93 E7
Worswell 6 E3
Worth Kent 31 D7
W Sus 28 F4
Wortham 56 B4
Worthen 60 D3
Worthenbury 73 E8
Worthing Norf 68 C2
W Sus 16 D5
Worthington 63 B8
Worth Matravers 13 G7
Worting 26 D4
Wortley S Yorks 88 E4
W Yorks 95 F5
Worton N Yorks 100 E4
Wilts 24 D4
Wortwell 69 F5
Wotherton 60 D2
Wotter 6 C3
Wotton 28 E2
Wotton-under-
Edge 36 E4
Wotton
Underwood 39 C6
Woughton on the
Green 53 F6
Wouldham 29 C8
Wrabness 57 F5
Wrafton 20 F3
Wragby Lincs 78 B4
W Yorks 88 C5
Wragholme 91 E7
Wramplingham 68 D4
Wrangbrook 89 C5
Wrangham 153 E6
Wrangle 79 D7
Wrangle Bank 79 D7
Wrangle Lowgate 79 D7
Wrangway 11 C6
Wrantage 11 B8
Wrawby 90 D4
Wraxall Dorset 12 D3
N Som 23 B6
Som 23 F8
Wray 93 C6
Wraysbury 27 B8
Wrayton 93 B6
Wrea Green 92 F3
Wreay Cumb 99 B6
Cumb 108 E4
Wrecclesham 27 E6
Wrecsam
= Wrexham 73 D7
Wrekenton 111 D5
Wrelton 103 F5
Wrenbury 74 E2
Wrench Green 103 F7
Wreningham 68 E4
Wrentham 69 F7
Wrenthorpe 88 B4
Wrentnall 60 D4
Wressle E Yorks 96 F3
N Lincs 90 D3
Wrestlingworth 54 E3
Wretham 68 F2
Wretton 67 E6
Wrexham
= Wrecsam 73 D7
Wrexham Industrial
Estate 73 E7
Wribbenhall 50 B2
Wrightington Bar 86 C3
Wrinehill 74 E4
Wrington 23 C6
Writhlington 24 D2
Writtle 42 D2
Wrockwardine 61 C6
Wroot 89 D8
Wrotham 29 D7
Wrotham Heath 29 D7
Wroughton 37 F8
Wroxall IoW 15 G6
Warks 51 B7
Wroxeter 61 D5
Wroxham 69 C6
Wroxton 52 E2
Wyaston 75 E8
Wyberton 79 E6
Wyboston 54 D2
Wybunbury 74 E4
Wychbold 50 C4
Wych Cross 28 F5
Wyck 27 F5
Wyck Rissington 38 B1
Wycoller 94 F2
Wycomb 64 B4
Wycombe Marsh 40 E1
Wyddial 54 F4
Wye 30 E4
Wyesham 36 C2
Wyfordby 64 C4
Wyke Dorset 13 B5
Shrops 61 D6
Sur 27 D7
W Yorks 88 B2
Wykeham N Yorks 96 B4
N Yorks 103 F7
Wyken 61 E7
Wyke Regis 12 G4
Wykey 60 B3
Wylam 110 C4
Wylde Green 62 E5
Wyllie 35 E5
Wylye 24 F5
Wymering 15 D7
Wymeswold 64 B3
Wymington 53 C7
Wymondham Leics 65 C5
Norf 68 D4
Wyndham 34 E3
Wynford Eagle 12 E3
Wyng 159 J4
Wynyard Village 102 B2
Wyre Piddle 50 E4
Wysall 64 B3
Wythall 51 B5
Wytham 38 D4
Wythburn 99 C5
Wythenshawe 87 F6
Wythop Mill 98 B3
Wyton 54 B3
Wyverstone 56 C4
Wyverstone Street 56 C4
Wyville 65 B5
Wyvis Lodge 150 D7

Y

Yaddlethorpe 90 D2
Yafford 14 F5
Yafforth 101 E8
Yalding 29 D7
Yanworth 37 C7
Yapham 96 D3
Yapton 16 D3
Yarburgh 91 E7
Yarcombe 11 D7
Yard 22 F2
Yardley 62 F5
Yardley Gobion 53 E5
Yardley Hastings 53 D6
Yardro 48 D4
Yarkhill 49 E8
Yarlet 62 B3
Yarlington 12 B4
Yarlside 92 C2
Yarm 102 C2
Yarmouth 14 F4
Yarnbrook 24 D3
Yarnfield 75 F5
Yarnscombe 9 B7
Yarnton 38 C4
Yarpole 49 C6
Yarrow 115 B6
Yarrow Feus 115 B6
Yarsop 49 E6
Yarwell 65 E7
Yate 36 F4
Yateley 27 C6
Yatesbury 25 B5
Yattendon 26 B3
Yatton Hereford 49 C6
N Som 23 C6
Yatton Keynell 24 B3
Yaverland 15 F7
Yaxham 68 C3
Yaxley Cambs 65 E8
Suff 56 B5
Yazor 49 E6
Y Bala = *Bala* 72 F3
Y Barri = *Barry* 22 C3
Y Bont-Faen
= *Cowbridge* 21 B8
Y Drenewydd
= *Newtown* 59 E8
Yeading 40 F4
Yeadon 94 E5
Yealand Conyers 92 B5
Yealand
Redmayne 92 B5
Yealmpton 6 D3
Yearby 102 B4
Yearsley 95 B8
Yeaton 60 C4
Yeaveley 75 E8
Yedingham 96 B4
Yeldon 53 C8
Yelford 38 D3
Yelland 20 F3
Yelling 54 C3
Yelvertoft 52 B3
Yelverton Devon 6 C3
Norf 69 D5
Yenston 12 B5
Yeoford 10 E2
Yeolmbridge 8 F5
Yeo Mill 10 B3
Yeovil 12 C3
Yeovil Marsh 12 C3
Yeovilton 12 B3
Yerbeston 32 D1
Yesnaby 159 G3
Yetlington 117 D6
Yetminster 12 C3
Yettington 11 F5
Yetts o'Muckhart 128 D2
Y Felinheli 82 E5
Y Fenni
= *Abergavenny* 35 C6
Y Fflint = *Flint* 73 B6
Y Ffôr 70 D4
Y-Ffrith 72 A4
Y Gelli Gandryll
= *Hay-on-Wye* 48 E4
Yieldshields 119 D8
Yiewsley 40 F3
Y Mwmbwls
= *The Mumbles* 33 F7
Ynysboeth 34 E4
Ynysddu 35 E5
Ynysgyfflog 58 C3
Ynyshir 34 E4
Ynyslas 58 E3
Ynys-meudwy 33 D8
Ynystawe 33 D7
Ynysybwl 34 E4
Yockenthwaite 94 B2
Yockleton 60 C3
Yokefleet 90 B2
Yoker 118 C5
Yonder Bognie 152 D5
York 95 D8
Yorkletts 30 C4
Yorkley 36 D3
York Town 27 C6
Yorton 60 B5
Youlgreave 76 C2
Youlstone 8 C4
Youlthorpe 96 D3
Youlton 95 C7
Young's End 42 C3
Young Wood 78 B4
Yoxall 62 C5
Yoxford 57 C7
Y Pîl = *Pyle* 34 F2
Yr Hôb = *Hope* 73 D7
Y Rhws = *Rhoose* 22 C2
Y Rhyl = *Rhyl* 72 A4
Yr Wyddgrug
= *Mold* 73 C6
Ysbyty-Cynfyn 47 B6
Ysbyty Ifan 72 E2
Ysbyty Ystwyth 47 B6
Ysceifiog 73 B5
Yspitty 33 E6
Ystalyfera 34 D1
Ystrad 34 E3
Ystrad Aeron 46 D4
Ystradfellte 34 C3
Ystradffin 47 E6
Ystradgynlais 34 C1
Ystradmeurig 47 C6
Ystrad-mynach 35 E5
Ystradowen Carms 33 C8
V Glam 22 B2
Ystumtuen 47 B6
Ythanbank 153 E9
Ythanwells 153 C6
Ythsie 153 E8
Y Trallwng
= *Welshpool* 60 D2
Y Waun = *Chirk* 73 F6

Z

Zeal Monachorum 10 D2
Zeals 24 F2
Zelah 4 D3
Zennor 2 C3

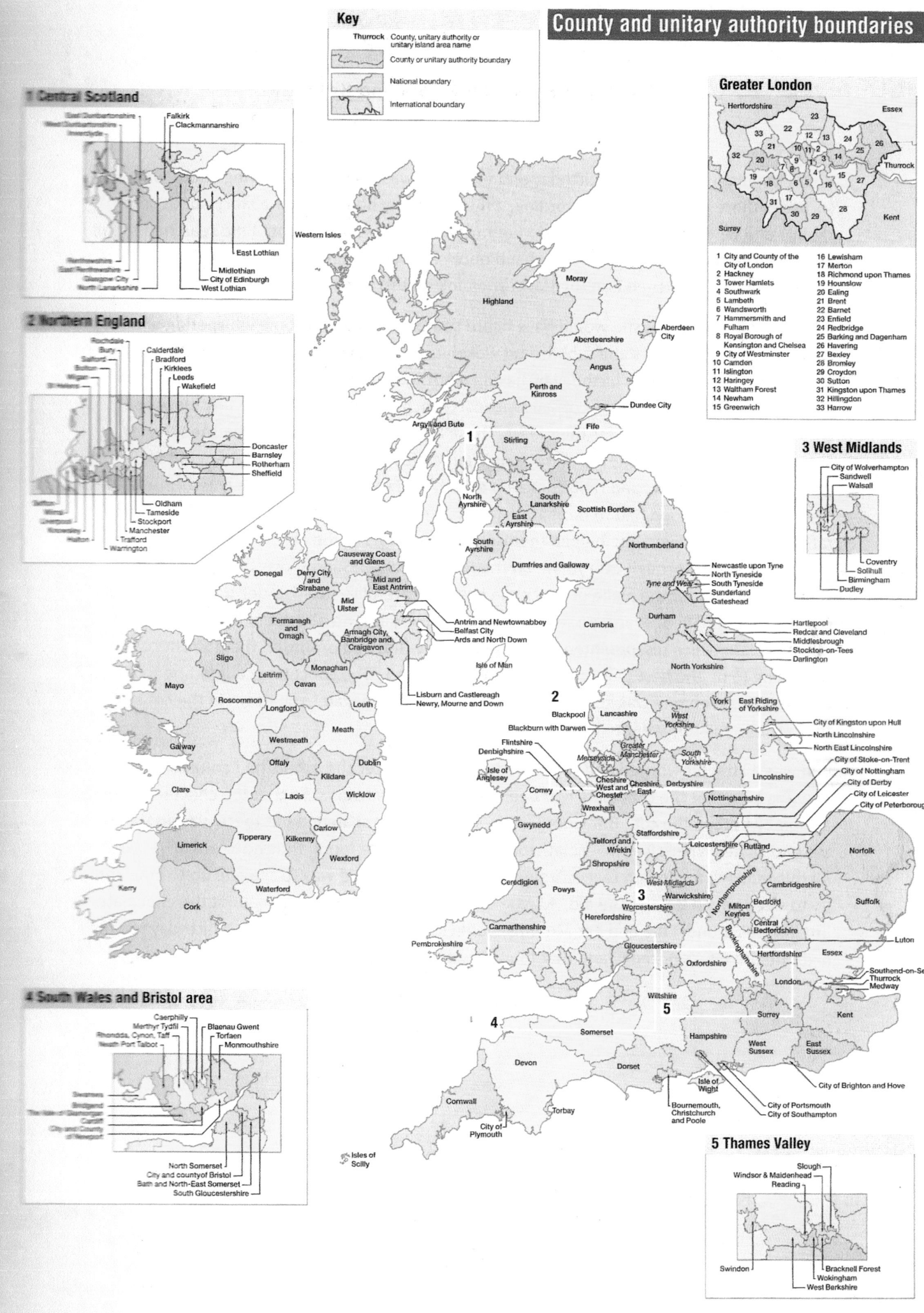

County and unitary authority boundaries

Key

Thurrock	County, unitary authority or unitary island area name
	County or unitary authority boundary
	National boundary
	International boundary

Greater London

Hertfordshire
Essex
Thurrock
Surrey
Kent

1 City and County of the City of London
2 Hackney
3 Tower Hamlets
4 Southwark
5 Lambeth
6 Wandsworth
7 Hammersmith and Fulham
8 Royal Borough of Kensington and Chelsea
9 City of Westminster
10 Camden
11 Islington
12 Haringey
13 Waltham Forest
14 Newham
15 Greenwich
16 Lewisham
17 Merton
18 Richmond upon Thames
19 Hounslow
20 Ealing
21 Brent
22 Barnet
23 Enfield
24 Redbridge
25 Barking and Dagenham
26 Havering
27 Bexley
28 Bromley
29 Croydon
30 Sutton
31 Kingston upon Thames
32 Hillingdon
33 Harrow

1 Central Scotland

East Dunbartonshire
West Dunbartonshire
Inverclyde
Falkirk
Clackmannanshire
Renfrewshire
East Renfrewshire
Glasgow City
North Lanarkshire
East Lothian
Midlothian
City of Edinburgh
West Lothian

Western Isles

2 Northern England

Rochdale
Bury
Salford
Bolton
Wigan
St Helens
Calderdale
Bradford
Kirklees
Leeds
Wakefield
Doncaster
Barnsley
Rotherham
Sheffield
Sefton
Wirral
Liverpool
Knowsley
Halton
Oldham
Tameside
Stockport
Manchester
Trafford
Warrington

3 West Midlands

City of Wolverhampton
Sandwell
Walsall
Coventry
Solihull
Birmingham
Dudley

Newcastle upon Tyne
North Tyneside
South Tyneside
Sunderland
Gateshead
Tyne and Wear

Hartlepool
Redcar and Cleveland
Middlesbrough
Stockton-on-Tees
Darlington

4 South Wales and Bristol area

Caerphilly
Merthyr Tydfil
Rhondda, Cynon, Taff
Neath Port Talbot
Blaenau Gwent
Torfaen
Monmouthshire
Swansea
Bridgend
The Vale of Glamorgan
Cardiff
City and County of Newport
North Somerset
City and county of Bristol
Bath and North-East Somerset
South Gloucestershire

5 Thames Valley

Slough
Windsor & Maidenhead
Reading
Bracknell Forest
Wokingham
West Berkshire
Swindon

Moray
Highland
Aberdeenshire
Aberdeen City
Angus
Perth and Kinross
Dundee City
Fife
Argyll and Bute
Stirling
North Ayrshire
South Lanarkshire
East Ayrshire
Scottish Borders
South Ayrshire
Dumfries and Galloway
Northumberland
Cumbria
Durham
North Yorkshire

Causeway Coast and Glens
Donegal
Derry City and Strabane
Mid and East Antrim
Mid Ulster
Fermanagh and Omagh
Antrim and Newtownabbey
Belfast City
Armagh City, Banbridge and Craigavon
Ards and North Down
Sligo
Leitrim
Cavan
Monaghan
Lisburn and Castlereagh
Newry, Mourne and Down
Isle of Man
Mayo
Roscommon
Longford
Westmeath
Meath
Louth
Galway
Offaly
Dublin
Clare
Laois
Kildare
Wicklow
Limerick
Tipperary
Kilkenny
Carlow
Wexford
Kerry
Waterford
Cork

Blackpool
Lancashire
West Yorkshire
York
East Riding of Yorkshire
Blackburn with Darwen
Flintshire
Denbighshire
Isle of Anglesey
Conwy
Greater Manchester
Merseyside
South Yorkshire
Cheshire West and Chester
Cheshire East
Derbyshire
Lincolnshire
Wrexham
Nottinghamshire
Gwynedd
Staffordshire
Telford and Wrekin
Leicestershire
Rutland
Norfolk
Shropshire
West Midlands
Northamptonshire
Cambridgeshire
Bedford
Suffolk
Ceredigion
Powys
Warwickshire
Milton Keynes
Central Bedfordshire
Worcestershire
Herefordshire
Buckinghamshire
Luton
Carmarthenshire
Gloucestershire
Oxfordshire
Hertfordshire
Essex
Pembrokeshire
Southend-on-Sea
Thurrock
Medway
London
Wiltshire
Surrey
Kent
Somerset
Hampshire
West Sussex
East Sussex
Devon
Dorset
Isle of Wight
City of Brighton and Hove
Cornwall
Torbay
City of Plymouth
Bournemouth, Christchurch and Poole
City of Portsmouth
City of Southampton
Isles of Scilly

City of Kingston upon Hull
North Lincolnshire
North East Lincolnshire
City of Stoke-on-Trent
City of Nottingham
City of Derby
City of Leicester
City of Peterborough

The Night Before Effie's Second Birthday

It was the night before Effie's birthday and everyone was excited, wondering about what surprises there would be in the morning. Effie's Mummy had read her a story about some rabbits and Effie was very tired when Mummy laid her down in her cot. Effie searched for all her favourite toys who shared her bed and once she was sure that everyone was comfortable, she clutched Bun (her favourite pink rabbit) and very quickly went to sleep.

If Effie had been awake, she would have heard some shuffling and some whispering and some giggling. The bears and rabbits had woken up. Bun had decided that everyone in the cot would celebrate Effie's birthday by having a birthday party. The bears and rabbits had secretly been collecting nibbles of sandwiches, crunches of crackers, some tiny pieces of cheese and two chocolates for their feast. These had been hidden under the sheet for several days by Bun, who now put them on a large piece of paper and set them out like birthday tea. The bears and rabbits moved quietly and sat around this lovely tea. Bun told everyone that the food had to be shared, looking sternly at brown bear who was sometimes rather greedy. So, everyone helped themselves to pawfuls of the delicious food and munched happily through everything on the pretend table. Soon it was finished and Bun searched around for the piece of chocolate she had carefully stored under the sheet, but she couldn't find it. Then, everyone searched and searched but no one could find any trace of the chocolate which disappointed everyone because Bun had promised that the chocolate was going to be the best part of the tea. It was no good. The chocolate couldn't be found and besides, everyone was getting very sleepy. Everyone began to lie down in the cot and they all immediately went to sleep.

Bun was a little bit worried and she stayed awake long after the others had gone to sleep. She was sure that the chocolate had been hidden well and was sure that the chocolate must be somewhere in the cot. But where? Bun searched and searched but there was no sign of the chocolate. Where was it? What would Effie think if she found the chocolate in her cot? All this thinking made Bun feel very sleepy and all she wanted was to snuggle up to Effie and go to sleep which is what she did. Maybe everyone had been mistaken about the chocolate but if it was found, Effie and her Mummy would know that there had been a birthday tea the night before Effie's birthday and that the bears and rabbits had magically come alive.